Growth, Maturation, and Physical Activity

Second Edition

Robert M. Malina, PhD, FACSM

Research Professor
Tarleton State University

Claude Bouchard, PhD, FACSM

Executive Director
Pennington Biomedical Research Center
Louisiana State University

Oded Bar-Or, MD, FACSM

Director
Children's Exercise and Nutrition Centre
McMaster University

Human Kinetics

Library of Congress Cataloging-in-Publication Data

Malina, Robert M.
   Growth, maturation, and physical activity / Robert M. Malina, Claude
Bouchard, Oded Bar-Or.-- 2nd ed.
      p. cm.
Includes bibliographical references and index.
   ISBN 0-88011-882-2 (hc)
   1. Human growth. 2. Exercise--Physiological aspects. I. Bouchard,
Claude. II. Bar-Or, Oded. III. Title.
   QP84.G75 2004
   612.6--dc21
                              2003001527

ISBN-10: 0-88011-882-2
ISBN-13: 978-0-88011-882-8

The Web addresses cited in this text were current as of 11/03/03, unless otherwise noted.

Acquisitions Editor: Judy Patterson Wright, PhD; **Developmental Editor:** Melissa Feld; **Assistant Editors:** Susan C. Hagan and Lee Alexander; **Copyeditor:** Ozzievelt Owens; **Proofreader**: Erin Cler; **Indexer:** Robert M. Malina; **Permission Manager:** Dalene Reeder; **Graphic Designer:** Andrew Tietz; **Graphic Artist:** Denise Lowry; **Photo Manager:** Dan Wendt; **Cover Designer:** Jack W. Davis; **Photographer (cover):** Tom Roberts; **Photographer (interior):** Randy Calvert, except where otherwise noted; **Art Manager:** Kelly Hendren; **Illustrator:** Nina Laidlaw; **Printer:** Sheridan Books

Printed in the United States of America   10   9   8   7   6   5

Human Kinetics
Web site: www.HumanKinetics.com

United States: Human Kinetics, P.O. Box 5076, Champaign, IL 61825-5076
800-747-4457
e-mail: humank@hkusa.com

Canada: Human Kinetics, 475 Devonshire Road, Unit 100, Windsor, ON N8Y 2L5
800-465-7301 (in Canada only)
e-mail: info@hkcanada.com

Europe: Human Kinetics, 107 Bradford Road, Stanningley
Leeds LS28 6AT, United Kingdom
+44 (0) 113 255 5665
e-mail: hk@hkeurope.com

Australia: Human Kinetics, 57A Price Avenue, Lower Mitcham, South Australia 5062
08 8372 0999
e-mail: info@hkaustralia.com

New Zealand: Human Kinetics, Division of Sports Distributors NZ Ltd.
P.O. Box 300 226 Albany, North Shore City, Auckland
0064 9 448 1207
e-mail: info@humankinetics.co.nz

CONTENTS

Part I Introduction

Part II Postnatal Growth

Part III   Functional Development

Part IV Biological Maturation

Part V Influencing Factors

Part VI Applications

PREFACE

The study of growth, maturation, physical activity, and performance is central to the sport sciences, physical education, human biology, and biological anthropology. A significant amount of normal biological variability in adulthood, including risk of several diseases, has its origin in the span encompassed by the prenatal period and approximately the first 2 decades of life. This revised and enlarged edition provides a comprehensive summary of biological growth and maturation, physical performance, and physical activity that spans the prenatal period, infancy, childhood, and adolescence into young adulthood. In addition to updating basic content of the first edition, specific chapters were expanded and significantly modified to accommodate recent advances in technology and science. These advances include techniques for the assessment of body composition, advances in the study of skeletal muscle and, especially, adipose tissues; progress associated with the Human Genome Project and the genetic regulation of processes underlying growth and maturation; advances in understanding the hormonal regulation of growth and maturation, including the identification of several new hormones; advances in the clarification of dietary reference intakes; and the extension of the study of risk for several adult diseases to infancy, childhood, and adolescence. The revision was also expanded to include separate discussions that are relevant to current problems in public health: the quantification of physical activity and energy expenditure, persistent undernutrition in developing countries, and the obesity epidemic in developed countries. A chapter on thermoregulation was added to highlight the unique responses of children to the environmental extremes of heat and cold, and a chapter on secular trends was also added to illustrate the plasticity of growth, maturation, and performance over time.

The revised and expanded edition has been divided into six parts. **Part I** serves to introduce basic concepts and the scope of the field encompassed by the terms growth, maturation, physical activity, and performance and to provide an overview of prenatal growth and functional development.

Part II focuses on methods of study and age-associated and sex-associated variation in body size, proportions, physique, body composition, and three specific tissues—skeletal, skeletal muscle, and adipose tissues—through approximately the first 2 decades of postnatal life. **Part III** addresses functional development in the context of physical performance and responses to exercise during childhood and adolescence. **Part IV** introduces the concept of biological maturation in terms of methods of assessment, the adolescent growth spurt, and maturity-associated variation in size, body composition, and performance. **Part V** provides an in-depth discussion of the primary factors that interact to regulate the process of growth and maturation—genes, hormones, nutrients, and energy. The potential role of physical activity as a factor affecting these processes and responses to systematic training are also considered. This section also includes specific discussions of the prevalence and consequences of chronic undernutrition and obesity and of other factors associated with variation in growth, maturation, performance, and physical activity. The final section, **part VI**, is largely applied in the context of physical activity and sport. It considers risk factors for adult diseases, many of which are related to physical inactivity and obesity; characteristics of children with several chronic clinical conditions that affect growth, maturation, performance, and activity and that are increasingly apparent in school children and adolescents; size and functional characteristics of young athletes in a variety of sports; and secular trends in growth and maturation over the past 100 to 150 years.

The first edition was designed for use in a two-course, upper-division (junior and senior) sequence in both kinesiology and human biology/biological anthropology, the first semester dealing with human growth and maturation and the second semester dealing with motor development, performance, and physical activity. The first edition was also successfully adapted by two of the authors and by many colleagues in a comprehensive, single-semester course that included lower-division students.

The text is comprehensive. Like the first edition, the revision brings together into a single volume materials essential for an understanding of the biological growth and maturation of children and adolescents and of the complexity of factors associated with the regulation of these processes and places these materials in the context of physical activity, performance, and health.

Although the first edition was aimed largely at students in the sport sciences, it is relevant to students in human biology and biological anthropology, nursing, nutrition, public health, and the pediatric exercise sciences. Students in these fields and others are increasingly expanding their interests to include childhood physical activity and inactivity in the context of health and different environmental conditions, competitive sport for children and adolescents, and motor development and performance in different cultural environments.

Each chapter begins with a comprehensive topical outline that is followed through the chapter. After reading a chapter, students can test their understanding by returning to the outline to see how well they recall the major concepts.

A detailed list of references is provided for each chapter. This list is a major change from the first edition. It facilitates the identification of specific sources and includes more general references. We have included asterisks by the references we recommend for further, more detailed reading. Where appropriate, the most recent sources available are cited. At times, however, early studies are cited. The fact that a reference is more recent does not necessarily make it more appropriate than an earlier study that first noted the specific observation. Each chapter includes tables and figures to facilitate presentation and illustration of basic concepts presented.

The revision has an international perspective. It includes data from many areas of the world. Children and adolescents are the next generation in a society, and we must appreciate and understand the process of growing and maturing. We hope the text will be useful and meet the needs of students and researchers in the sport sciences, kinesiology, human biology, biological anthropology, and related fields. We welcome comments and suggestions from both students and faculty.

ACKNOWLEDGMENTS

The authors would like to express their gratitude to the many individuals who were involved in the preparation of *Growth, Maturation, and Physical Activity, Second Edition*. The efforts of Ms. Diane Drolet and Mr. Jean-Yves Dallaire of Laval University and of Ms. Nina Laidlaw of the Pennington Biomedical Research Center in preparing the illustrations and tables are greatly appreciated. The patience of Ms. Laidlaw in understanding and tolerating the quirks of the three authors deserves special mention. We would also like to thank Mr. Randy Calvert for taking the photographs in chapter 3. Ms. Toni Finn, also of the Pennington Biomedical Research Center, facilitated arrangements for working sessions of the authors.

The efforts and suggestions of Ms. Melissa Feld and Dr. Judy Wright at Human Kinetics were invaluable. This revision had a longer gestation than expected (i.e., it is long overdue), and their patience in working with us is greatly appreciated.

Many colleagues read specific chapters and parts of chapters while the revision was in preparation or provided specific data for a chapter:

Chapter 4—Albrecht Claessens, Katholieke Universiteit Leuven; and J.E. Lindsay Carter, San Diego State University.

Chapter 7—Phil Gardiner, University of Montreal; Howie Green, University of Waterloo; and David Hood, York University.

Chapter 8—Michael Jensen, Mayo Clinic; Peter Katzmarzyk, Queen's University; Michael Goran, University of Southern California; Robert Ross, Queen's University; and Hans Hauner, University of Dusseldorf.

Chapter 10 and 11—Vern Seefeldt and John Haubenstricker, Michigan State University.

Chapters 15 and 16—Alex Roche, Shumei Sun, and W. Cameron Chumlea, Wright State University School of Medicine.

Chapters 15 and 17 and sections on scaling—Gaston Beunen, Katholieke Universiteit Leuven.

Chapter 18—Rudy Leibel, Colombia University; Molly Bray, University of Texas Health Science Center at Houston; and Slawomir Koziel, Institute of Anthropology, Wroclaw, Poland (also chapter 28).

Chapter 19—Alan Rogol, University of Virginia; and Steve Smith, Pennington Biomedical Research Center.

Chapter 20—James DeLany, Catherine Champagne, and Marlene Most, Pennington Biomedical Research Center.

Chapter 24—Mary Hediger, National Institutes of Health.

Chapter 29—Shumei Sun, Wright State University School of Medicine; and Takashi Satake, Nihon University.

Their suggestions, corrections, and guidance were invaluable, and their efforts are greatly appreciated.

The late Dorothy Eichorn of the Institute of Human Development of the University of California, Berkeley, provided the raw data from the Adolescent Growth Study in Oakland. These data were used in several figures in chapter 17.

Finally, we would like to thank the many children and adolescents we had the opportunity to teach, coach, and counsel, and with whom we conducted some of our research. They provided many insights into the dynamic processes of growth, maturation, physical activity, and performance.

CREDITS

Figure 3.1 b—Reprinted, by permission, from T.G. Lohman, A.R. Roche, and R. Martorell, 1988, Anthropometric standardization of reference manual (Champaign, IL: Human Kinetics), 6.

Figure 3.2 b—Reprinted, by permission, from T.G. Lohman, A.R. Roche, and R. Martorell, 1988, Anthropometric standardization of reference manual (Champaign, IL: Human Kinetics), 14.

Figure 12.1—Adapted, by permission, from K. Turley and J. Wilmore, 1997, "Cardiovascular responses to treadmill and cycle ergometer exercise in children and adults," Journal of Applied Physiology 83: 948-957.

Figure 12.2—Adapted, by permission, from B.S. Alpert, N.L. Flood, and W.B. Strong, "Responses to ergometer exercise in healthy biracial population of children," Journal of Pediatrics 101: 538-545.

Figure 12.3—Reprinted, by permission, from O. Bar-Or, 1983, Pediatric sports medicine for the practitioner. In Principles to clinical applications (Heidelberg, Germany: Springer-Verlag).

Figure 12.4—Reprinted, by permission, from O. Bar-Or, 1983, Pediatric sports medicine for the practitioner. In Principles to clinical applications (Heidelberg, Germany: Springer-Verlag).

Figure 12.7—Reprinted, by permission, from O. Bar-Or, 1983, Pediatric Sports Medicine for the practitioner. In Physiologic principles to clinical application (Heidelberg, Germany: Springer-Verlag).

Figure 12.8—Figure from A Primer of Molecular Biology, by G. Frost et al., copyright 1997, Elsevier Science, reproduced with permission from the publisher.

Figure 13.3—Reprinted, by permission, from D. Docherty, 1996, Measurement Techniques in pediatric exercise science (Champaign, IL: Human Kinetics), 166.

Figure 13.4—Reprinted, by permission, from D. Docherty, 1996, Measurement Techniques in pediatric exercise science (Champaign, IL: Human Kinetics), 174.

Figure 13.14—Adapted, by permission, from H. Hebestreit, K. Mimura, and O. Bar-Or, 1993, "recovery of muscle power after high-intensity short-term exercise: Comparing boys and men," Journal of Applied Physiology 74: 2875-2880.

Figure 14.1—Reprinted, by permission, from O. Bar-Or, 1983, Pediatric sports medicine for the practioner. In Physiologic principles to clinical applications (Heidelberg, Germany: Springer-Verlag).

Figure 14.3—Reprinted, by permission, from O. Bar-Or, 1989, "Temperature regulation during exercise in children and adolescents," Perspectives in Exercise Science and Sports Medicine 2: 335-367.

Figure 14.4—Reprinted, by permission, from B. Fulk, O. Bar-Or, and J.D. MacDougall, 1992, "Thermoregulatory responses of pre-, mid-, and late-, pubertal boys to exercise dry heat," Medicine and Science in Sport Exercise 24: 688-694.

Figure 18.4—Reprinted, by permission, from R. Roberts et al., 1992, A primer of molecular biology (New York: Kluwer Publishing), 22.

Figure 19.17, top panel—Reprinted, by permission, from P.E. Clayton et al., 1997, "Serum leptin through childhood and adolescence," Clinical Endocrinology 46: 727-733.

Figure 21.4—Reprinted, by permission, from H. Hebestreit et al., 1995, "Climate-related corrections for improved estimation of energy expenditure from heart rate in children," Journal of Applied Physiology 79: 47-54.

Figure 21.5—Reprinted, by permission, from R.C. Bailey et al., 1995, "The level and tempo of children's physical activities: An observational study," Medicine and Science in Sport Exercise 27: 1033-1041.

Figure 26.1—Figure from ATHEROSCLEROSIS AND ITS ORIGIN, edited by Sandler M and Bourne G. H., copyright 1963, Elsevier Science (USA), reproduced with permission from the publisher.

Figure 27.2—Adapted from The role of physical activity in the development and maintenance of eating disorders, C. Davis et al., Copyright © 1994, with permission from Elsevier.

Figure 27.4—Adapted from Anaerobic endurance and peak muscle power in children with spastic cerebral palsy, D.E. Parker et al., Copyright © 1992, with permission from Elsevier.

Figure 27.5—Reprinted, by permission, from H. Keller et al, 2000, "Anaerobic performance in 5- to 7- yr-old children of low birth weight," Medicine and Science in Sport Exercise 32: 278-283.

Table 10.4—Reprinted, by permission, from V. Seefeldt, P. Reuschlein, and P. Vogel, 1972, Sequencing motor skills within the physical education curriculum, paper presented at the annual convention of the American Association for Health, Physical Education, and Recreation, March 27, 1972, Houston, Texas.

Part I

Introduction

The biological growth and maturation of children have been systematically studied for more than 150 years. The basic concepts are built on a strong historical foundation in the medical, anthropological, and human biological sciences. Studies of physical activity, performance, and fitness of children and adolescents also have a long history. This foundation is built largely on what was traditionally called physical education and what is now called kinesiology, the physical activity sciences, or exercise and sport sciences. This text views growth, maturation, physical activity, and performance of children and adolescents as they progress from birth to young adulthood.

The first section of the book is brief. It has two chapters. The first chapter defines several basic concepts and then discusses why the study of these processes—growth, maturation, physical activity, and performance—is important to the understanding of children and adolescents and human variability. It also provides a synopsis of methods, types of studies, and data derived from each and of age ranges used to define general periods of postnatal growth. The time-honored study of Richard Scammon, an anatomist, who reported his research in 1930, is highlighted. It provides an overview of the differential nature of postnatal growth. The first chapter closes with a summary of individual studies and surveys that provide the basis for the bulk of the data included in the text. These data include longitudinal studies of growth and maturation mainly in the United States and Europe, longitudinal studies of physical performance and of risk factors for disease, and cross-sectional surveys of growth, maturation, performance, and physical activity.

Chapter 2 focuses exclusively on the prenatal period. Although the focus of the volume is the postnatal period, understanding prenatal processes is essential. The processes of growth and maturation begin shortly after conception. This chapter is not intended as a basic primer of human embryology; rather, it is designed to set the stage for the subsequent discussion of postnatal growth, maturation, physical activity, and performance. Some of the variation observed postnatally has its roots prenatally. This concept is especially important in the context of the "fetal origins hypothesis," which postulates prenatal roots for several common diseases that become manifest in adulthood. Some evidence suggests that the fetus becomes impaired or programmed metabolically in the presence of adverse fetal environmental conditions, setting the stage for metabolic or behavioral misadaptations later in postnatal life.

1 INTRODUCTORY CONCEPTS

Chapter Outline

As children progress from birth to adulthood, growth, maturation, and development are central processes. These processes are initially defined in this chapter. The relevance of these processes to physical activity and performance and to the understanding of human biological variability is then considered. Measurements and observations taken at different ages during infancy, childhood, and adolescence provide the basic information for the study of growth and maturation. The study of these processes is synonymous with measurement and observation. This chapter also considers several features of growth studies and general principles of measurement and observation. The same principles apply also to the measurement of physical activity and performance. An overview of postnatal growth and maturation and their regulation is then provided. The chapter closes with a description of the major studies of growth, maturation, performance, and physical activity, which are the primary sources of data used throughout the text.

Definitions and Context

Three terms are often used when discussing infants, children, and adolescents—they grow, mature, and develop. Growth and maturation are often used together and, at times, even synonymously, but each refers to specific biological activities. The term development is also commonly used with growth and maturation. It, however, has a broader meaning.

Growth

Growth is the dominant biological activity for about the first 2 decades of human life, including, of course, 9 months of prenatal life. Growth is an increase in the size of the body as a whole or the size attained by specific parts of the body. As children grow, they become taller and heavier, they increase in lean and fat tissues, and their organs increase in size.

Changes in size are outcomes of three underlying cellular processes: (1) an increase in cell number, or hyperplasia; (2) an increase in cell size, or hypertrophy; and (3) an increase in intercellular substances, or accretion. The increase in number is a function of cell division (mitosis), which involves the replication of DNA and the subsequent migration of the replicated chromosomes into functional and identical cells. The increase in cell size involves an increase in functional units within the cell, particularly protein and substrates, as is especially evident in the muscular hypertrophy that occurs during growth and especially with regular resistance training during adolescence. The intercellular substances are both organic and inorganic, and they often function to bind or aggregate the cells in complex networks, as collagen fibers do in providing the matrix for the adipocytes of adipose tissue.

Hyperplasia, hypertrophy, and accretion all occur during growth, but the predominance of one or another process varies with age and the tissue involved. For example, the number of neurons (brain cells) is established by midpregnancy, but the number of muscle fibers is established shortly after birth. Subsequently, both of these tissues grow primarily by hypertrophy (see figure 1.1), although in the case of brain tissue, hyperplasia of different types of nerve cells continues during the second half of pregnancy and into postnatal life. On the other hand, all three processes occur during bone growth. These cellular processes are also involved in the biological changes that underlie maturation and differentiation, which are discussed in the next two sections.

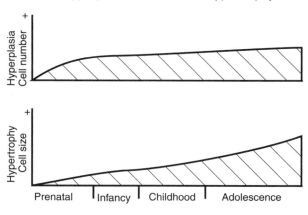

Cellular Hyperplasia and Cellular Hypertrophy

FIGURE 1.1   Schematic illustration of the growth of skeletal muscle tissue as a function of cellular hyperplasia (top) and hypertrophy (bottom).

Maturation

Maturation is more difficult to define than growth. It is often described as the process of becoming mature, or progress toward the mature state. Maturation is a process; maturity is a state. Maturation occurs in all tissues, organs, and organ systems, affecting enzymes, chemical composition, and functions. Maturity thus varies with the biological system considered. Sexual maturity is fully functional reproductive capability. Skeletal maturity is a fully ossified adult skeleton. Maturation of the nervous and endocrine systems (neuroendocrine) is a major factor in sexual, skeletal, and somatic maturation during late childhood and adolescence.

Maturation refers to the timing and tempo of progress toward the mature biological state. Timing refers to when specific maturational events occur (e.g., age at the appearance of pubic hair in boys and girls) or the age at maximum growth during the adolescent growth spurt. Tempo refers to the rate at which maturation progresses (e.g., how quickly or slowly the youngster passes from initial stages of sexual maturation to the mature state). Timing and tempo vary considerably among individuals, and variation in progress over time implies variation in rate of change.

Individuals differ considerably in the timing and tempo of maturation. For example, two children may be the same size (i.e., have the same level of attained growth), but they can be at quite different places on the path to adult size or maturity. One child may have attained 65% of adult stature, the other may have attained 75%. Individuals end up as adults with a fully ossified skeleton, but they reach this state at different times and attain different adult heights. This is the fundamental distinction between growth and maturation. The former focuses on size attained at a given point in time, whereas the latter focuses on progress (rate) in attaining adult size and maturity.

Growth and maturation are closely related. Both must be viewed as dynamic. The target is the adult state—maturity—and the processes imply movement toward this target from the moment of conception until maturity is attained. Hence, growth and maturation may also be viewed as processes that are purposive or directional.

The processes underlying growth and maturation are cellular. The study of growth and maturation involves the measurement and observation of the outcomes of these processes (e.g., size attained, level of fatness, level of maturity, or the extent to which an individual has progressed to adulthood). The measurement and observation of growth and maturation are discussed in more detail later in the book.

Development

Growth and maturation are often used in conjunction with the term development. Development denotes a broader concept that is used in two distinct contexts. The first context is biological, and here development refers to the processes of differentiation and specialization of pluripotent embryonic stem cells into different cell types, tissues, organs, and functional units. Full differentiation is attained with the onset of function in a particular tissue.

Differentiation mainly occurs early in prenatal life when tissues and organ systems are being formed, and it is highly dependent on the activation and repression of genes or sets of genes interacting with hormones and nutrients in the prenatal environment. The development of function obviously continues postnatally as different systems of the body become functionally refined.

The second context is behavioral and relates to the development of competence in a variety of interrelated domains as the child adjusts to his or her cultural milieu—the amalgam of symbols, values, and behaviors that characterize a population. Development refers to the acquisition and refinement of behaviors expected by society. One can speak of the development of social competence, intellectual or cognitive competence, and emotional competence or well being as the child's individual personality emerges within the context of the particular culture in which the child was born and reared. One can also speak of motor competence, the acquisition and refinement of skillful performance in a variety of motor activities. As children experience life at home, in the neighborhood, in school, in church, during sports and recreation, and during other community activities, they develop intellectually, socially, emotionally, morally, and motorically. In other words, they develop behavioral competence in a variety of domains.

The biological definition of development is used in the discussion of prenatal growth and functional development in chapter 2. Otherwise, the term development is used primarily in the behavioral context.

Physical Performance

The development and refinement of skillful performance in a variety of motor activities are a major developmental task of childhood and adolescence. All children, except those with serious developmental disturbances, have the potential to develop and learn a variety of fundamental and specialized movement patterns and skills. The movement patterns are eventually incorporated in specific skills that become an integral part of the developing child's behavioral repertoire.

A child's performance characteristics are related in part to the child's growth, maturation, and development. This relationship is well exemplified in the development of basic movement patterns such as walking, running, and jumping. During the first 7 or 8 years of life, the development of basic movement patterns depends largely on the individual's rate of neuromuscular maturation, the residual effects of prior movement experiences, and the current movement experiences, in addition to growth and maturity status. Once the basic movement patterns are established, learning and practice are significant factors affecting motor competence. The child's growth and maturity characteristics also become increasingly more important in performance, especially in tasks that require bursts of strength, power, and speed. Environmental conditions, which influence the opportunity to perform, and associated social interactions also contribute to the development of performance capabilities.

Physical Activity

Physical activity is a behavior that occurs in a variety of forms and contexts, including free play, house chores, exercise, school physical education, and organized sport. It refers to any body movement produced by the skeletal muscles and that results in a substantial increase over the resting energy expenditure. The measurement and quantification of physical activity and its major correlate, energy expenditure, are difficult tasks. The measurement of physical activity and energy expenditure is discussed in chapter 21.

Calls for increasing daily physical activity in all segments of the population, from those in early childhood to those in old age, are common in current discussions of public health policy. Regular physical activity is especially important in the regulation of body weight and the accretion of bone mineral during childhood and adolescence. In addition, habits of and attitudes toward physical activity developed during childhood are assumed to continue through adolescence into adulthood and may have a long-term beneficial influence on the health into adulthood. The increased energy expenditure that accompanies regular physical activity contributes to more efficient function of various systems, weight maintenance, reduced risk of several degenerative diseases, reduced risk of early mortality, and overall improvement of quality of life.

Physical activity is often confused with training for sport. Physical activity, however, is not the same as regular training. Although physical activity is integral to training, the latter refers to systematic, specialized practice for a specific sport or sport discipline for most of the year or to specific short-term experimental programs (e.g., 15 weeks of endurance training for running).

Physical Fitness

A related construct of physical activity is **physical fitness.** It is an adaptive state that varies with the individual's growth and maturity status and with habitual physical activity and lifestyle. The concept of physical fitness has evolved from a primary motor performance focus to a health-related focus. The former viewed physical fitness in the context of performance on standardized tests that measured components of fitness, whereas the latter views fitness in the context of specific functions that may offer protection against some particular degenerative diseases, such as coronary heart disease, obesity, and various musculoskeletal disorders. The measurement of specific components of physical fitness is discussed in the context of strength and motor performance in chapter 11 and in the context of cardiovascular endurance in chapter 12.

The Child and Adolescent: Biocultural Individuals

Growth and maturation are biological processes, whereas development is a broader concept that involves several behavioral domains. Physical performance, activity, and fitness include both the biological and the behavioral domains. Clearly, therefore, no set of isolated phenomena describes the growth, maturation, and development of a child or adolescent, or the level of performance, activity, and fitness. The child or adolescent must be viewed bioculturally. Biological growth and maturation do not proceed in isolation from other aspects in the personal and behavioral realms. The focus of this text is the biological aspects of growth, maturation, performance, and activity. However, both the biological and the behavioral domains interact in shaping individuals as they progress from the immature to the mature state or from infancy through childhood and adolescence into adulthood (see figure 1.2).

Growth, maturation, and development interact to mold children's self-concept, the manner in which they evaluate and perceive themselves, and their self-esteem, the value or worth that they place on themselves. Self-concept and self-esteem in turn may influence a child's perceived competence in a variety of domains, including physical activity and sport. The development of self-concept and self-esteem are often overlooked in biological discussions of childhood and adolescence, as are the influences of variation in growth and maturity often overlooked in discussions of

Interactions of Growth,
Maturation, and Development

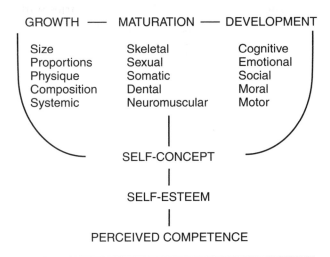

GROWTH — MATURATION — DEVELOPMENT

Size	Skeletal	Cognitive
Proportions	Sexual	Emotional
Physique	Somatic	Social
Composition	Dental	Moral
Systemic	Neuromuscular	Motor

SELF-CONCEPT

SELF-ESTEEM

PERCEIVED COMPETENCE

FIGURE 1.2 The child and adolescent as biocultural individuals—interactions of growth, maturation, and development.

behavioral development. The interactions are usually most apparent during the transition into adolescence when considerable variability exists among individuals in the timing and tempo of the adolescent growth spurt and sexual maturation. There may be a time dissociation between biological growth and maturation on one hand and social, personal, and emotional development on the other. This dislocation may affect the child's development of self-concept and self-esteem. How a child copes, or learns to cope, with sexual maturity or the adolescent growth spurt may influence the child's behavior. In this context, children and adolescents cannot be approached in an exclusively biological or in an exclusively behavioral manner. Rather, a biocultural approach that recognizes the interaction of biological and societal demands on the growing, maturing, and developing individual is essential.

Chronological Age and Age Groups

Growth, maturation, and development operate in a time framework. They are measured or observed at a single point in time or at several points over time. The point of reference is the child's chronological age. Thus, all children born on June 3, 2003, are 10 years old on June 3, 2013. However,

biological processes have their own timetables and do not celebrate birthdays. A child has only one birthday—the actual day of birth. All other birthdays are set by the calendar. Biological time does not necessarily proceed in concert with the calendar. Hence, children of the same chronological age can differ by several years in their levels of biological maturity. For example, some 12-year-old girls are already sexually mature, others are in the process of maturing sexually, and still others will not begin the process for several more years. Yet, all of the girls have the same chronological age. A similar distribution would be apparent in 14-year-old boys.

Postnatal growth is commonly, although somewhat arbitrarily, divided into three or four age periods. **Infancy** is the first year of life, up to but not including the first birthday. This definition of infancy is universally accepted, specifically in the context of worldwide public health. It is a period of rapid growth in most bodily systems and dimensions and of rapid development of the neuromuscular system. Infancy is further subdivided into the perinatal (around the time of birth, the first week), neonatal (the first month of life), and postnatal (the remainder of the first year) periods.

Childhood extends from the end of infancy (the first birthday) to the start of adolescence. It is often divided into **early childhood**, which includes the preschool years, and **middle childhood**, which generally includes the "elementary school years" into the fifth or sixth grade. In the context of public health, early childhood extends from the first birthday through 4 years of age (1.0 to 4.99 years), and middle childhood extends from 5 years of age to the beginning of adolescence. Early childhood continues the rapid growth and development of infancy, although at a decelerating rate, whereas middle childhood by comparison is a period of relatively steady progress in physical growth and maturation and in behavioral development.

The public health definition of infancy and early childhood is used for the estimation of infant and childhood mortality, both of which are accepted universally as indicators of the health and nutritional status in a community. Infant mortality refers to deaths occurring in the first year of life expressed per 1,000 live-born infants, and early childhood mortality is the number of deaths among children 1.0 to 4.99 years of year expressed per number of children in this age range in the population. High infant mortality is indicative of generally poor health conditions, which are primarily related to infectious diseases and chronic undernutrition. High early childhood mortality is generally accepted as an indication of chronic undernutrition in a population. The use of these mortality statistics in the assessment of the nutritional status of a community is discussed in more detail in chapter 23.

Adolescence is a more difficult period to define in terms of chronological age because of variation in the time of its onset and termination. The World Health Organization defines the age of adolescence as between 10 and 18 years, but the age ranges 8 to 19 years in girls and 10 to 22 years in boys are more appropriate as limits for normal variation in the onset and termination of adolescence. In this period, most bodily systems become adult both structurally and functionally (i.e., they reach maturity). Structurally, adolescence begins with acceleration in the rate of growth in stature, which marks the onset of the adolescent growth spurt. The rate of growth in height reaches a peak, then begins a slower or decelerative phase, and finally terminates with the attainment of adult stature. Functionally, adolescence is usually viewed in terms of sexual maturity, which actually begins with changes in the neuroendocrine system before overt physical changes and terminates with the attainment of mature reproductive function.

Growth curves or tables of body dimensions, performance variables, and measures of physical activity are ordinarily presented by chronological age. In the construction of curves or tables, children are grouped into age categories, but there may be variation in methods of grouping children into age categories. What range, for example, is included in a group of 6-year-old children? In earlier studies, the age labeled as 6 years included children between 5.50 and 6.49 years, so the average age for the group was about 6.0 years. In more recent studies, age groups are defined in terms of the whole year (i.e., 6.00 to 6.99 years), so the average age for the group is about 6.5 years. In some longitudinal studies, children are measured at their birthdays, plus or minus a week or two. Thus, a group of 6-year-old children in a longitudinal study would have an average age of about 6.0 years, with a very narrow range of variation about the average.

Although age is often taken for granted, care must be taken in its interpretation. Age is quite important in making comparisons among groups and in evaluating the growth of individual chil-

dren. For example, if the two groups of 6-year-old children described previously are compared, the latter (6.0 to 6.99 years) is, on the average, about 0.5 years older than the former (5.50 to 6.49 years) and would probably be taller and heavier. The method of grouping children by age thus has implications for comparisons, and the way age groups are defined in individual studies is important.

Why Study These Phenomena?

This volume presents a comprehensive overview of biological growth, maturation, physical performance, and physical activity. These aspects of human biology and development can be studied at the level of the individual and in samples of children within communities and national populations.

Understanding Human Variability

The study of these phenomena contributes to the understanding of human biological variation. A significant portion of the biological variation evident among adults in any population has its origin during the years of growth and maturation, including the prenatal period. The only way an individual can become an adult is through the processes of growth, maturation, and development. These processes are quite plastic. They can be influenced by a variety of environmental factors operating on the growing and maturing individual—nutritional intake, infant and childhood diseases, patterns of physical activity, and other environmental stresses, which interact with the individual's genetic potential for growth and maturation. The net result is a wide range of variation among individuals. An important objective is to understand the biological variability evident during the growing years in terms of its origin, distribution among different populations, and significance. Understanding the significance is quite important. Why does such variation exist, and what does it mean to the individual? What is the significance of early or late maturity for behavior and performance of the individual?

An issue of current interest is the association between growth and maturity, on one hand, and adult health on the other. This association, in turn, emphasizes the need to continue studies of "growth" into the adult years. For example, a small body of data suggests a link between low birth weight and adult hypertension, coronary heart disease, and the co-occurrence of diabetes mellitus, hypertension, and hyperlipidemia (see chapter 2). The working hypothesis for this syndrome, known as the metabolic syndrome, is that the fetal environment influences or "programs" the progression of circumstances related to these disease conditions that become manifest in adulthood. Early sexual maturity is associated with several cancers in adulthood. Overweight adolescents tend to become overweight adults. Although association does not demonstrate causality, the results emphasize the need to consider risk factors for adult diseases within a life span framework, beginning with fetal growth. The subject of overweight is considered in chapter 24 and of risk factors for adult diseases is considered in chapter 26.

In addition to a basic interest in human biological variation, the study of growth, maturation, performance, and activity provides basic information relative to several more specific issues.

Status

Status is the attained size, level of maturity, or level of performance at a given point in time. To ask about a child's growth, maturity, or performance status is to ask how the child compares with other children of the same age and sex. One can also ask about the status of a group of children in a community. This approach is used often in the context of surveys of nutritional status, physical fitness, and general health status. According to the World Health Organization, for example, the growth status of children is perhaps the best indicator of the overall health and nutritional circumstances in a community, especially in the developing areas of the world.

Progress

When taken at several points in time, measurements and observations of a child or a group of children provide an indication of progress over time. Progress implies change, which provides an estimate of rate. A child who grows 6 cm over a period of 1 year has a growth rate of 6 cm/year.

Progress also involves maturation. Is the child's level of biological maturity early (advanced), late (delayed), or average (appropriate or "on time") for the child's chronological age? Children advanced in biological maturity relative to their chronological age characteristically progress at a more rapid rate of growth than do those who are delayed in maturity relative to chronological age and who progress more slowly.

Prediction

Knowledge of growth status and rate can be used for prediction. In some instances, knowledge of how tall a child will be as an adult may be important. To this end, a child's adult height can be predicted with a reasonable degree of accuracy if the child's present height and level of skeletal maturity and the measured heights of both parents are known. The prediction of physical performance, on the other hand, is more complex because factors other than growth and maturity status (e.g., motivation and training) influence performance.

Tracking

Tracking refers to the stability of a characteristic, or the maintenance of relative rank or position within a group, over time. How stable are indicators of growth, maturity, performance, and activity from childhood through adolescence, or how stable are they from adolescence into adulthood? Tracking is related to prediction. Can adult obesity be predicted from obesity in childhood and adolescence? At least two observations of the same individual at two points in time are necessary to estimate tracking of a characteristic. Factors that influence estimates of tracking include the interval between measurements or observations, age at first observation, short-term biological variation, significant environmental change, and measurement variability. A major factor affecting tracking during adolescence is individual differences in the timing and tempo of the adolescent growth spurt and sexual maturation.

Comparison

Comparison is implicit in studies of growth, maturation, performance, and activity. A child's size, maturity, performance, and activity level can be compared with reference data for healthy children of the same age and sex. Reference data, sometimes referred to as standards or norms, are values on the growth, maturity, performance, and activity status of a large sample of healthy children free from overt disease. When a group of children are studied, they are compared either with reference data or with other groups of children of the same age and sex.

Interpretation of Physical Activity and Performance

Regular participation in physical activities is often assumed to be necessary for optimal growth and maturation. Physical activity, of course, is only one of many factors that may influence these processes. Nevertheless, understanding the normal processes of growth and maturation is important to the systematic evaluation and understanding of the potential effects of regular physical activity on these processes and outcomes.

The growth and maturity characteristics of the performer also affect performance. This relationship is especially evident in the physique characteristics of elite athletes in a variety of sports even at young ages (e.g., gymnasts, divers, figure skaters). These sports are well known for applying rather rigid selection criteria in identifying potentially talented individuals during childhood. Similarly, muscular strength is related to body size. Within a group of boys of the same age, those who are earlier in biological maturity tend to be taller, heavier, and stronger than boys who are later in maturity. Therefore, growth, maturation, and performance are related.

A related issue to physical activity and performance is the notion of trainability, or sensitivity to systematic training and practice. Is there an optimal time, or are there several optimal times, for a youngster to begin regular training to derive maximal results in the performance domain? For motor skill learning, is there an optimal period in which certain movement patterns and skills should be taught? These questions have no simple answers, but they merit serious consideration.

Types of Studies

Growth, maturation, performance, and physical activity can be studied in several ways. The type of study utilized, however, depends on the specific questions under investigation. The two basic types of studies are cross-sectional and longitudinal; a combination of the two basic types is the mixed-longitudinal study.

Cross-Sectional and Longitudinal Studies

In a cross-sectional study, individuals are usually measured or observed at a given age or at several ages, but each individual is represented only once in the sample. It is basically a cross section of a given age group, sex group, or of a given population. A longitudinal study, on the other hand, involves repeated observations on the same individuals at specific intervals over a period of time.

Both kinds of studies provide specific types of information. Results of cross-sectional studies give information on the growth, maturity, performance, or physical activity status of a sample of children and of the variability within the sample. Such studies thus provide information on size, stage of maturity, or level of performance and activity attained at the time of the survey. On the other hand, results of a longitudinal study provide information not only on status but also on change over time. Because the individuals are measured at specific intervals over time, change and rate (e.g., kg/year or cm/year) can be estimated. Cross-sectional studies do not provide accurate measures of rate or progress.

Mixed-Longitudinal Study

A mixed-longitudinal study is basically a compromise between cross-sectional and longitudinal designs. It combines data for individuals who were measured on all occasions in a study and data for individuals who were measured on only several occasions. Such a design provides information on status and rate, but special statistical treatment of the data is necessary to derive accurate estimates of rate.

Pros and Cons of Different Designs

Longitudinal studies are more difficult to conduct than cross-sectional studies. A true longitudinal study from birth to young adulthood would take approximately 20 or 25 years. Such studies are expensive and require a long-term investment of time and a well-organized logistical team. Major concerns for longitudinal studies include continued funding, recruitment and retention of subjects and staff, and using the same methodology for the duration of the study. As interests and methodologies change, new questions may arise and new methods may be incorporated. Both subjects and staff must be motivated to continue in the study, reminders need to be sent about when to come in for measurement or testing, and transportation to and from the growth center may have to be provided. New staff members require training in the techniques and protocol of the study. If a study continues across two generations, issues related to secular change must be considered. Secular change refers to changes in size and maturation between the parent and offspring generations, with children often being taller and maturing earlier than their parents. Secular changes in growth and maturation are discussed in chapter 29. Longitudinal studies have additional problems related to population mobility (a subject's family may move out of the area), mortality (some subjects may die), and normal attrition (some subjects may simply get tired of participating). Hence, the number of subjects who complete a longitudinal study tends to be small.

Several longitudinal studies have been done, primarily in North America and Europe, and these studies have provided valuable insights into the understanding of normal variability in human growth, maturation, performance, and physical activity. Several of the major longitudinal studies are briefly described later in the chapter.

Although cross-sectional studies are seemingly simpler to do than longitudinal studies, they require considerable care in sampling so that the subjects selected represent a true cross section of the population being studied. Cross-sectional studies are limited in that the only information they provide is an indication of status. Growth and performance curves derived from such studies tend to be smooth and to mask the wide range of individual variation inherent in any age group of children.

A special kind of mixed-longitudinal study design can provide a good approximation of the total growth span and include information on both growth status and rate. This type of study is the short-term, mixed-longitudinal study. Groups of children at specific ages are selected for study, for example, at 0 (birth), 4, 8, 12, and 16 years of age. Each child is then followed longitudinally at regular intervals over the next 4 years. At the termination of the study, the cohort that started at birth will be 4 years of age, the cohort that started at 4 years of age will be 8 years of age, and the cohort that started at 16 years of age will be 20 years of age. The key to such a design is the overlapping of cohorts at 4, 8, 12, and 16 years of age. For example, when subjects beginning at birth reach 4 years, how do they compare to subjects beginning the study at 4 years of age? The same applies to the other cohorts at 8, 12 and 16 years of age. Special statistical treatment of the data is required to provide the fit between cohorts and thus cover the growth period during the first 2 decades of life.

What Kind of Study?

The type of study that should be used depends on the question to be answered. If the question deals with the growth and performance status of 8-year-old children in a given community, a good cross-sectional study would suffice. On the other hand, if the question deals with the effects of a regular training program on changes in muscle tissue metabolism or on body composition during growth, a longitudinal design is necessary. To investigate performance variation during the adolescent growth spurt, a longitudinal design over several years would be necessary so that the time of initiation of the growth spurt and of the peak of the growth spurt can be identified and the magnitude of the spurt quantified. These features of the adolescent growth spurt can then be related to performance.

Generally, longitudinal studies are most useful during infancy and early childhood and again in adolescence. These are the two periods of life characterized by very rapid growth and change. Between birth and 3 years of age and during adolescence, individuals should be measured or observed every 3 months, given the rapidity of growth and maturation at this time. At other ages, measuring children at 6-month intervals, or perhaps annually, provides sufficient information.

Principles of Measurement and Observation

Measurement and observation are basic to the study of growth, maturation, performance, and physical activity. Measurements (the dimensions, performances, and levels of activity that are measured with scales, calipers, ergometers, and stopwatches) and observations (the stages of maturity or patterns or levels of activity that are observed and rated) represent the outcomes of underlying processes. The underlying processes of growth, maturation, performance, and energy expenditure are cellular, resulting from increases in cell size and number, muscular contraction, and energy metabolism, and these processes are not amenable to measurement and observation in large samples of children and adolescents. The measurements and observations are indicators of attained size, maturity, performance, or level of activity and not of the processes per se.

Specific measurements and characteristics are described where appropriate in the chapters that follow.

Meaningfulness

Measurements and observations are selected to provide specific information on size attained by the body as a whole or of its segments, about maturity status, or about performance and activity levels. This information, in turn, should be amenable to biological and behavioral interpretation. They should provide significant information that increases the understanding of growth, maturation, performance, and physical activity. In other words, measurements and observations are selected for the specific information they provide. Measurements and observations are not made for the sake of measuring and observing.

Measurement Variability

Although measurement and observation procedures are reasonably standardized and in the hands of trained observers are relatively easy to make, error or variation in the process of measuring and observing is a concern. **Random error** is a normal aspect of the measurement process and results from variation in the individuals who are making the measurements and the child being measured. Random error can be above or below the real dimension. In large-scale surveys, the pluses and minuses ordinarily cancel each other, and random error is not a major concern.

On the other hand, **systematic error** is a serious concern in growth studies. Systematic error is the tendency to consistently undermeasure or overmeasure a particular dimension or to underrate or overrate a specific stage of maturity. Such error is directional and introduces bias into the measurements and observations.

Validity and Reliability

A variety of tests and instruments are used to measure performance and physical activity, respectively. Tests and instruments should be valid and reliable. Validity means that the test measures what it is supposed to measure. Determining the true validity of any test or instrument is difficult. Most tests of performance are accepted as having face validity. The vertical jump, for example, is a valid measure of muscular power. The validity of measures of physical activity is more difficult, largely because of the lack of an adequate criterion for measuring activity. This issue is discussed in more detail in chapter 21.

Reliability is the extent to which a test or instru-

ment gives the same results on repeated trials. Several trials of performance tasks are commonly used (e.g., three for the standing long jump, two for the 50-m dash) to estimate reliability within a day, and the tests are repeated a day or two later to estimate reliability from day to day. A physical activity questionnaire may be administered over several days to estimate the reliability of responses from day to day.

Quality Control

Variability in measurement and observation is normally monitored and, if necessary, corrected by regular training sessions for technicians. Such sessions aim at quality control and try to eliminate actual and potential sources of error in gathering information on the growth, maturation, performance, and activity of children and adolescents.

Equipment must also be carefully monitored on a regular basis. Scales for measuring body weight, calipers, stopwatches, tapes, strain gauges, cycle ergometers, and gas analyzers should be regularly calibrated. A scale's readings are checked for accuracy using objects of known weight, and calipers are evaluated using objects of known width or thickness.

Types of Data

When a child's stature is measured, the result is an indication of the size attained at that point in time. Such measures are indicators of status or of distance (i.e., the size attained or the distance that the child has traversed thus far on the path to the adult state). If a child is measured at regular intervals (e.g., 6 months or every year), the differences between measurements provide estimates of growth rate (e.g., cm/year or kg/year). These estimates are indicators of the progress or velocity of growth. Increments are often quite small at most ages, which emphasizes the need for precision in measurement.

Thus, the two basic types of growth-related data are measures of status (distance) and measures of rate (velocity). The former indicates the size or the level of maturation, performance, or physical activity attained by children at one age or at successive ages, and the latter indicates the rate of growth from one age to another. These measurements are ordinarily plotted on a graph with chronological age on the horizontal axis to derive growth curves. Different types of growth curves are described in chapter 3.

Overview of Postnatal Growth: Scammon's Curves

Richard Scammon's curves of systemic growth, which were first reported in 1923 in the 11th edition of Morris' *Anatomy* (Boyd 1980) and subsequently republished in his 1930 Sigma XI lecture (Scammon 1930), provide a good starting point for a discussion of postnatal growth. Upon analysis of the weights of the body and of specific tissues and organs, Scammon proposed that the growth of different tissues and systems could be summarized in four patterns or curves of growth (see figure 1.3). The curves provide a convenient means of summarizing the differential nature of postnatal growth. The data shown in the figure are **relative**. Size attained by each type of tissue at each age is expressed as a percentage of the total increment between birth and 20 years of age (100%).

Growth of Different Body Systems

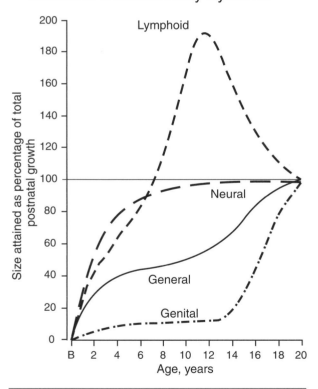

FIGURE 1.3   Scammon's curves of systemic growth.

Reprinted, by permission, from R.E. Scammon, 1930, The measurement of the body in childhood. In *The measurement of man*, edited by J.A. Harris et al. (Minneapolis, MN: University of Minnesota Press), 193.

General Curve

The general, or body, curve describes the growth of the body as a whole and the growth of most of its parts—the growth pattern of stature, weight, and most external dimensions of the body. The general curve is also characteristic of the growth pattern of most systems of the body, including muscle mass, the skeleton (with the exception of certain parts of the skull and face), the respiratory system, the heart and blood vessels, the digestive system, and the urinary system. The growth pattern is generally S-shaped (sigmoid) and has four phases: (1) rapid growth in infancy and early childhood, (2) steady but rather constant growth during middle childhood, (3) rapid growth during the adolescent spurt, and (4) slow increase and eventual cessation of growth after adolescence. The latter part of the curve continues into the third decade of life for most dimensions.

Neural Curve

The neural curve characterizes the growth of the brain, nervous system, and associated structures, such as the eyes, upper face, and parts of the skull. These tissues experience rapid growth early in postnatal life, so about 95% of the total increment in size of the central nervous system and related structures between birth and 20 years of age is already attained by about 7 years of age. Neural tissues show steady gain after 7 years of age, with a slight growth spurt during adolescence.

Genital Curve

The genital curve characterizes the growth pattern of the primary and secondary sex characteristics. Primary sex characteristics include the ovaries, fallopian tubes, uterus, and vagina in females and the testes, seminal vesicles, prostate, and penis in males. Secondary sex characteristics include breasts in females, pubic and axillary hair in both sexes, and facial hair and growth of the larynx in males. Larynx growth is related to voice changes that occur during male adolescence. Genital tissues show slight growth in infancy, followed by a latent period during most of childhood. Genital tissues then experience extremely rapid growth and maturation during the adolescent spurt.

Lymphoid Curve

The lymphoid curve describes the growth of the lymph glands, thymus gland, tonsils, appendix, and lymphoid patches of tissue in the intestine.

These tissues are involved, in general, with the child's developing immunological capacities, including resistance to infectious diseases. Lymphatic tissues show rapid growth during infancy and childhood, reaching a maximum when children are about 11 to 13 years of age. At these ages, children have, on a relative basis, about twice as much lymphoid tissue as they have as adults. The decline of the lymphoid curve during the second decade of life is related to the involution (shrinking) of the thymus and tonsils at this time.

Scammon's curves indicate the differential nature of postnatal growth. Growth occurs in different areas and tissues of the body at different times and at different rates. Although somewhat simplified and diagrammatic, the four curves give a sense of order to the structural and functional changes that occur with growth and maturation, however, with several exceptions. The craniofacial skeleton is one such exception. The upper part of the face, the orbits of the eyes, and the cranial vault follow the neural curve and complete a good portion of their growth when the child is about 7 years of age. The lower face, including the jaw, follows the general curve and has an adolescent growth spurt. Thus, the upper part of the face has a different growth pattern than the lower part.

General Regulation of Growth and Maturation

The integrated nature of growth and maturation is achieved by the interaction of genes, hormones, nutrients, and the environments in which the individual lives. This complex interaction regulates the individual's growth, neuromuscular maturation, sexual maturation, and general physical and physiological metamorphosis during the first 2 decades of life or so. Each of the regulatory factors is considered in more detail later in the book. However, the regulation of growth and maturation is complex and not fully understood.

An individual's genotype (genetic makeup) can be viewed as representing potential for growth and maturation. Whether a child attains that potential, however, depends on the environment in which the child is raised. The child's physical or physiological characteristics represent phenotypes, or observable characteristics. A phenotype is a product of the genotype and the environments in which the child is reared, as well as their interactions. The partitioning of genetic

and environmental components of variation in growth and maturation is helpful to understanding these processes.

Hormones are important regulatory agents in the processes of growth and maturation. Some growth occurs in the absence of growth-promoting hormones, which emphasizes the organism's inherent tendency to grow, but hormones are essential for the full expression of the individual's genetic potential. The hormone-producing glands and tissues are themselves influenced by genetically determined regulatory mechanisms. The nervous system is intimately involved in regulating hormone production. Because the nervous system mediates interactions with the external environments that an individual encounters, the sources for potential variation are numerous.

Perhaps the most important environmental component that is involved in the regulation of growth and maturation is nutrition. Energy and nutrient requirements are many and are highly individualized. Nutritional status in turn interacts with genotype and hormones in the regulatory processes.

A child's pattern of habitual physical activity is another important environmental component because of its influence on the balance between energy intake from the diet and energy expenditure. Daily imbalances in intake over expenditure accumulate over time and contribute to the development of excess weight and obesity, as well as to weight loss. Other environmental influences include ethnicity, socioeconomic conditions, sibship size (number of children in the family), hygiene, and the physical environment.

The regulation of growth and maturation is, therefore, complex. Many factors are involved and interact as the individual's growth and maturity are gradually expressed between conception and adulthood.

Sources of Growth, Performance, and Activity Data

Data from a number of North American and European growth studies are used throughout this volume. For a detailed account of historical aspects of growth studies in general and studies in North America and Europe in particular, see Boyd (1980), *Origins of the Study of Human Growth*, and Tanner (1981), *A History of the Study of Human Growth*. Boyd (1980) is based on the unfinished manuscript of Richard Scammon and considers early discussions of the life cycle (including description of prenatal and postnatal stages) from antiquity to 1700 and then more specific studies of growth in Europe and North America from 1700 to 1940. Tanner (1981) briefly considers the ancient world, the Middle Ages, and the Renaissance but then offers a comprehensive discussion of growth studies from the 18th century through the major North American and European longitudinal studies.

Earlier reports provide an excellent background to the relatively long history of the study of growth in Europe and the United States. Meredith (1936) reviews American research on the growth of children before 1900, and Krogman (1941) provides a comprehensive compilation of European and North American growth studies before 1940, focusing primarily on data from the 1920s and 1930s. The compilation also includes several studies of active youth and of motor performance. Krogman (1950, 1955) also presented a syllabus of concepts and techniques for the study of growth, including motor skills, which was followed by a summary of related literature published between 1950 and 1955. Meredith (1968, 1969a, 1969b, 1971, 1978, 1987) also reported summaries of data from different areas of the world dealing with specific body dimensions in specific age groups between birth and adulthood.

Roche and Malina (1983) and Malina and Roche (1983) provide detailed tabular summaries for a variety of indicators of growth, maturity, and performance in North American children since 1940 in a two-volume compendium, *Manual of Physical Status and Performance in Childhood.* Eveleth and Tanner's (1976, 1990) *Worldwide Variation in Human Growth* is a compendium of data on growth and maturation from many regions of the world and also includes a discussion of factors that influence these processes.

The subsequent discussion summarizes the major studies that form the basis for a significant portion of information used in this book. References to specific reports from many of these studies are cited in appropriate chapters throughout the text.

Longitudinal Studies of Growth and Maturation

The major longitudinal studies that provide basic information on growth and maturation were conducted in the United States and Europe.

United States Studies   Several longitudinal studies were begun in the United States in the 1920s and early 1930s: the Harvard School of Public Health in the Boston area; the Brush Foundation Study at Western Reserve University (now Case Western Reserve University) in Cleveland, Ohio; the Fels Research Institute in Yellow Springs, in south-central Ohio (now a part of the Wright State University School of Medicine); the Child Research Council in Denver, Colorado; and the Guidance Study of the University of California at Berkeley (Tanner 1948, 1981). These major United States studies include measurements of growth and maturity that span childhood and adolescence and provide the basis for many longitudinal analyses. Other growth studies, some of which included a longitudinal component, were carried out since 1917 at the Iowa Child Welfare Research Station at the University of Iowa in Iowa City. The Philadelphia Center (now the W.M. Krogman Center) for Research in Child Growth at the University of Pennsylvania carried out a mixed-longitudinal study of school-age American Black (African American) and White (European American) children from the late 1940s through the late 1960s (Krogman 1970).

Many of the subjects in the Fels study were followed into adulthood in a series of studies that continue at present (Roche 1992). Data from the Fels and Harvard studies are also being analyzed in the context of tracking of fatness and other risk factors for disease from childhood into adulthood and tracking of precursors of morbidity and mortality in adulthood (Casey et al. 1992; Must et al. 1992; Guo et al. 1994).

In addition to the Guidance Study at the University of California, a second study, the Adolescent Growth Study of children in Oakland, California, was conducted. This study included measurements of strength and motor performance of children and adolescents between 11 and 17 years of age (Espenschade 1940; Jones 1949).

Two more recent American longitudinal studies of growth have a different approach than the traditional studies. The first study is based on a longitudinal series of about 340 middle-class girls from Newton, Massachusetts, followed from 9 or 10 years of age to young adulthood. The study was begun in 1965 and included stature and weight and age at menarche. The study is unique in that the data were reported by the mothers of the girls in questionnaires sent at monthly or 6-week intervals. The reported data were supplemented by semiannual or annual height and weight measurements made by the staff of the physical education department of the local school system, beginning when the girls were 5 or 6 years of age (Zacharias and Rand 1983). The second study, the Harvard Six Cities Study, is part of an examination of the health effects of indoor and outdoor pollution on children from six regions of the United States (localities in Massachusetts, Tennessee, Ohio, Missouri, Wisconsin, and Kansas). Annual examinations included height and weight measurements, in addition to spirometry, a measure of lung function (Berkey et al. 1993).

European Studies   After the initial series of longitudinal studies in the United States, the emphasis on longitudinal growth studies shifted to Europe. The Harpenden Growth Study in the suburbs of London was begun in 1948 and included measurements of size, physique, body composition, and maturation (Tanner 1981). The setting for the study was a children's home. Before entering the home, most of the children had probably lived under socially disadvantageous conditions. However, the children were well cared for at the home and lived in relatively small cottages or family groups.

The Harpenden Growth Study was followed by a series of longitudinal studies in several European cities that were begun in the mid-1950s. The studies were coordinated by the International Children's Center in Paris and included separate longitudinal samples in Brussels, London, Paris, Stockholm, and Zurich (Tanner 1981). These studies focused primarily on growth and maturation from birth through adolescence. Another European longitudinal study, independent of those coordinated by the International Children's Center, was the Wroclaw Growth Study in southwestern Poland, which was begun in 1961. A large cohort of boys and girls was followed from 8 to 18 years of age (Bielicki and Waliszko 1975; Waliszko and Jedlinska 1976). The study also focused primarily on measures of growth and maturity.

Two other European longitudinal studies require mention. Height, weight, and secondary sex characteristics of about 700 urban school children from several centers in Sweden were monitored from 10 to 16 years of age in girls and from 10 to 18 years of age in boys between 1964 and 1971 (Lindgren 1979). In a similar study, about 1,400 school children in Newcastle upon Tyne, England, were followed from 9 to 17 years

of age beginning in 1971 (Billewicz et al. 1983). The variables included measures of growth and secondary sex characteristics. In both studies, children were examined twice a year at approximately half-yearly intervals.

Craniofacial Growth   Although growth of the head and face is not emphasized in this volume, many longitudinal studies have focused on this area of the body. For example, studies by the Fels Research Institute and the Philadelphia Center for Research in Child Growth (now the W.M. Krogman Center) routinely included measures of dental eruption and growth and craniofacial growth. More recently, the Center for the Study of Human Growth at the University of Montreal followed the craniofacial growth and dental maturation in a longitudinal sample of French Canadian children (Demirjian et al. 1973; Demirjian and Brault-Dubuc 1985). Measurements of a variety of growth and maturity variables were also taken on these children. Such studies are especially important to orthodontists because the timing of the adolescent growth spurt is important in planning the appropriate treatment.

Physical Performance and Physical Activity in Longitudinal Studies

In the mid-1950s and subsequently, a number of longitudinal studies systematically included measurements of physical performance, and a smaller number included assessment of physical activity. The Medford Boys' Growth Study of the University of Oregon, which began in 1956, developed as a result of concern for the effects of competitive sport on boys (Clarke 1971). The study included measures of growth, skeletal maturity, physique, strength, and motor performance of boys 7 through 18 years of age.

In the 1960s, several longitudinal studies focused on measurements of motor performance and aerobic power. The Prague study followed a sample of boys from about 10 to 18 years of age and included measurements of growth, skeletal maturity, body composition, and aerobic power (Parizkova 1977). The Saskatchewan Growth and Development Study of children in Saskatoon, Canada, followed a sample of boys longitudinally from 7 to 17 years of age and also included a mixed-longitudinal sample of girls in the same age range (Carron and Bailey 1974; Mirwald and Bailey 1986). In addition to measures of growth, the Saskatchewan study included measures of strength, motor performance, and aerobic power. These studies in Saskatchewan have since been followed by a mixed-longitudinal study of bone mineral accretion, the University of Saskatchewan Pediatric Bone Mineral Study.

The Motor Performance Study of Michigan State University was begun in 1967 and is almost completed (Haubenstricker et al. 1999). The study focuses on the interrelationships between growth and performance and includes semiannual measurements of a variety of growth and motor performance variables. Unfortunately, the data have not been systematically analyzed and reported in the context of its unique longitudinal focus on growth and motor performance.

The mixed-longitudinal Leuven Growth Study of Belgian Boys conducted by the Catholic University of Leuven began in 1968 and continued through 1974 (Beunen et al. 1988). The sample was national and included over 21,000 boys between 12 and 20 years of age. The longitudinal component of this national sample was large compared with other studies: 270 to 300 boys who were measured annually six times over 5 years. The study included measures of growth, skeletal maturity, motor performance, and participation in physical activity. The study continues into adulthood, and a sample of this longitudinal cohort of Belgian males has been followed at 30, 35, and 40 years of age. A cross-sectional, national survey of approximately 9,000 Flemish girls, the Leuven Growth Study of Flemish Girls, was conducted in 1979 and 1980 and includes similar data as in the boys' study (Simons et al. 1990).

Two generally similar longitudinal studies were begun in the Netherlands in the 1970s, the Nijmegen Growth Study (Prahl-Andersen et al. 1979) and the study of Growth and Health of Teenagers in Amsterdam (Kemper 1995). The Amsterdam study includes measurements of growth, maturity, motor performance, aerobic power, and habitual physical activity and also continues into adulthood with a cohort of males and females followed at about 21, 27, and 30 years of age.

Risk Factors for Disease in Longitudinal Studies

Given concern for coronary heart disease in adults, several relatively recent studies have focused on the development of risk factors for coronary heart disease (e.g., high levels of serum lipids with an abnormal lipoprotein profile, hypertension, and obesity) in children and youth. Coronary heart disease is one of the leading causes of death in North American adults, and many of the risk factors for this disease develop during childhood (Berenson 1986; Kannel et al. 1995). Several studies have attempted to track or follow the development of risk factors during childhood and adolescence; the studies thus have a longitudinal component. These studies include, for example, the Bogalusa Heart Study of Black and White children in Louisiana (Berenson et al. 1995), the Muscatine Study of primarily White Iowa school children (Lauer et al. 1993), and the Cincinnati Lipid Research Clinic's study of Black and White children in the Princeton school district (Morrison et al. 1979). The studies were begun in the 1970s and include a variety of coronary heart disease risk factors in addition to measures of growth and maturation.

Overview of Longitudinal Studies

The studies described previously all include a longitudinal component, but given the logistical problems encountered in doing such studies and the relatively large data sets involved, the studies are basically mixed-longitudinal. Results of the longitudinal and mixed-longitudinal components of these studies are used in subsequent chapters to illustrate patterns of growth, maturation, performance, physical activity, and the range of normal variation inherent in any group of children.

Cross-Sectional Surveys of Growth and Maturation

In addition to the longitudinal studies, a variety of cross-sectional studies provide important information. These studies include several national surveys. For example, nationwide surveys of stature, weight, and sexual maturation of Dutch children in the Netherlands were conducted in 1955, 1965, and 1980 (Roede and van Wieringen 1985).

Since the 1960s, the United States National Center for Health Statistics has conducted national surveys on a regular basis. Most of the surveys include height and weight, and several include a more extensive series of body measurements. The different surveys are summarized in chapter 3 (see table 3.1, page 51). These national surveys are unique in that all of them used a sampling design to permit estimates for the total United States population or for specific ethnic groups. Data from the United States national surveys provide the basis for charts of height, weight, and other dimensions or indices that are used to assess the growth status of children and adolescents.

Cross-Sectional Surveys of Performance and Physical Activity

The American Alliance for Health, Physical Education and Recreation (1976) has conducted national surveys of the motor fitness of American school-age children in 1958, 1965, and 1975, and the President's Council on Physical Fitness and Sport (Reiff et al. 1986) conducted a similar survey in 1985. National surveys of the health-related physical fitness of children 6 to 9 and 10 to 17 years of age, respectively, the first and second National Children and Youth Fitness Surveys, were conducted in 1984 and 1986 (Pate and Shephard 1989). Motor fitness focuses on performance in a variety of tasks, whereas health-related fitness focuses on indicators of cardiovascular fitness, strength, flexibility, and fatness. The National Children and Youth Fitness Surveys also included indicators of habitual physical activity.

The Canadian Association for Health, Physical Education and Recreation (1966, 1968) conducted national surveys of the motor fitness and physical working capacity (at a heart rate of 170 beats/min) of Canadian youth 7 to 17 years of age. Surveys of the motor fitness and physical working capacity of national samples of Canadian youth 7 to 17 years of age were carried out again in 1979 and 1983, respectively (Canadian Association for Health, Physical Education and Recreation 1980; Gauthier et al. 1983). The Canada Fitness Survey (1985), carried out in 1981, included measurements of physical activity, body size, fatness, physical performance, and physical activity for a nationally representative sample of children and youth. A subsample of the Canada Fitness Survey was measured again 7 years later (Stephens and Craig 1990).

The Youth Risk Behavior Surveillance System of the United States Centers for Disease Control and Prevention (Kann et al. 1998) is a questionnaire-based survey of a national sample of American high school youth in grades 9 through 12. The survey provides detailed information on reported patterns of participation in physical activity, physical education, sports, and specific exercises. The survey also includes questions dealing with dietary behaviors, perceptions of being overweight, and weight-control behaviors.

Although national surveys are cross-sectional, they are very useful because the subjects selected to participate in the surveys are chosen to be representative of the population as a whole. Such samples are called national probability samples. Results of such large-scale national surveys are the primary source for the construction of reference data used in comparing and evaluating the growth, maturity, and performance status of children.

Summary

Concepts and principles that underlie the study of growth, maturation, and physical activity performance during the first 2 decades of postnatal life are introduced. The systematic study of these features, which are characteristic of every individual, requires measurements and observations taken at different ages during infancy, childhood, and adolescence and continuing into young adulthood. The major sources of information, longitudinal and cross-sectional studies, for the understanding of growth, maturation, performance, and physical activity are also summarized. The study of growth, maturation, and performance has a long history in the disciplines of medicine, human biology, biological anthropology, and the sport sciences, whereas the systematic study of physical activity has more recent roots.

Sources and Suggested Readings

American Alliance for Health, Physical Education and Recreation (1976) AAHPER Youth Fitness Test Manual, revised 1976 edition. Washington, DC: American Alliance for Health, Physical Education and Recreation.

American Alliance for Health, Physical Education, Recreation and Dance (1980) Health-Related Physical Fitness Test Manual. Reston, VA: American Alliance for Health, Physical Education, Recreation and Dance.

Berenson GS, editor (1986) Causation of Cardiovascular Risk Factors in Children. New York: Raven Press.

Berenson GS, Wattigney WA, Bao W, Srinivasan SR, Radhakrishnamurthy B (1995) Rationale to study the early natural history of heart disease: The Bogalusa Heart Study. American Journal of the Medical Sciences 310 (suppl 1):S22-S28.

Berkey CS, Dockery DW, Wang X, Wypij D, Ferris B (1993) Longitudinal height velocity standards for U.S. adolescents. Statistics in Medicine 12:403-414.

Beunen GP, Malina RM, Van't Hof MA, Ostyn M, Renson R, Van Gerven D (1988) Adolescent Growth and Motor Performance: A Longitudinal Study of Belgian Boys. Champaign, IL: Human Kinetics.

Bielicki T, Waliszko A (1975) Wroclaw Growth Study, Part I. Females. Studies in Physical Anthropology 2:53-81.

Billewicz WZ, Thomson AM, Fellowes HM (1983) A longitudinal study of growth in Newcastle-upon-Tyne adolescents. Annals of Human Biology 10:125-133.

*Bouchard C, Shephard RJ (1994) Physical activity, fitness, and health: The model and key concepts. In C Bouchard, RJ Shephard, T Stephens (eds), Physical Activity, Fitness, and Health: International Proceedings and Consensus Statement. Champaign, IL: Human Kinetics, pp 77-88.

* Boyd E (1980) Origins of the Study of Human Growth. Eugene, OR: University of Oregon Health Sciences Foundation.

Canada Fitness Survey (1985) Physical Fitness of Canadian Youth. Ottawa: Canada Fitness Survey.

Canadian Association for Health, Physical Education and Recreation (1966) The CAHPER Fitness-Performance Test Manual for Boys and Girls 7 to 17 Years of Age. Ottawa: Canadian Association for Health, Physical Education and Recreation.

Canadian Association for Health, Physical Education and Recreation (1968) The Physical Working Capacity of Canadian Children Aged 7 to 17. Ottawa: Canadian Association for Health, Physical Education and Recreation.

Canadian Association for Health, Physical Education and Recreation (1980) CAHPER Fitness Performance II. Test Manual. Ottawa: Canadian Association for Health, Physical Education and Recreation.

Carron AV, Bailey DA (1974) Strength development in boys from 10 through 16 years. Monographs of the Society for Research in Child Development 39, serial no. 157.

Casey VA, Dwyer JT, Coleman KA, Valadian I (1992) Body mass index from childhood to middle age: A 50-year follow-up. American Journal of Clinical Nutrition 56:14-18.

Clarke HH (1971) Physical and Motor Tests in the Medford Boys' Growth Study. Englewood Cliffs, NJ: Prentice Hall.

Demirjian A, Brault-Dubuc M (1985) Croissance et developpement de l'enfant quebecois de la naissance a six ans. Montreal: La Presses de l'Universite de Montreal.

Demirjian A, Goldstein H, Tanner JM (1973) A new system of dental age assessment. Human Biology 45:211-227.

Espenschade A (1940) Motor performance in adolescence, including the study of relationships with measures of physical growth and maturity. Monographs of the Society for Research in Child Development 5, serial no. 24.

Eveleth PB, Tanner JM (1976) Worldwide Variation in Human Growth. Cambridge: Cambridge University Press.

* Eveleth PB, Tanner JM (1990) Worldwide Variation in Human Growth, 2nd edition. Cambridge: Cambridge University Press.

* Falkner F, Tanner JM, editors (1986) Human Growth, Volumes 1–3. New York: Plenum.

Gauthier R, Massicotte D, Hermiston R, Macnab R (1983) The physical work capacity of Canadian children, aged 7 to 17, in 1983: A comparison with 1968. Canadian Health, Physical Education and Recreation Journal 50:4-9 (Nov-Dec).

Guo SS, Roche AF, Chumlea WC, Gardner JD, Siervogel RM (1994) The predictive value of childhood body mass index values for overweight at 35 years. American Journal of Clinical Nutrition 59:810-819.

Haubenstricker JL, Branta CF, Seefeldt VD (1999) History of the motor performance study and related programs. In JL Haubenstricker, DL Feltz (eds), 100 Years of Kinesiology: History, Research, and Reflections. East Lansing, MI: Department of Kinesiology, Michigan State University, pp 103-125.

Jones HE (1949) Motor Performance and Growth. Berkeley: University of California Press.

Kann L, Kinchen SA, Williams BI, Ross JG, Lowry R, Hill CV, Grunbaum JA, Blumson PS, Collins JL, Kolbe LJ (1998) Youth Risk Behavior Surveillance —United States, 1997. Morbidity and Mortality Weekly Report 47(SS-3):1-89.

Kannel WB, D'Agostino RB, Belanger AJ (1995) Concept of bridging the gap from youth to adulthood. American Journal of the Medical Sciences 310 (suppl 1):S15-S21.

Kemper HCG, editor (1995) The Amsterdam Growth Study: A Longitudinal Analysis of Health, Fitness, and Lifestyle. Champaign, IL: Human Kinetics.

* Krogman WM (1941) Growth of Man. Tabulae Biologicae, Volume 20. Den Haag: Uitgeverij Dr. W. Junk (Groetschel and v. Assema Metz).

Krogman WM (1948) A handbook of the measurement and interpretation of height and weight in the growing child. Monographs of the Society for Research in Child Development 13, serial no. 48 (published in 1950).

*Krogman WM (1950) The physical growth of the child syllabus. Yearbook of Physical Anthropology 1949, 5:280-299.

Krogman WM (1955) The physical growth of children: An appraisal of studies 1950-1955. Monographs of the Society for Research in Child Development 20, serial no. 60.

Krogman WM (1970) Growth of the head, face, trunk, and limbs in Philadelphia White and Negro children of elementary and high school age. Monographs of the Society for Research in Child Development 35, serial no. 136.

Lauer RM, Clarke WR, Mahoney LT, Witt J (1993) Childhood predictors for high adult blood pressure: The Muscatine Study. Pediatric Clinics of North America 40:23-40.

Lindgren G (1979) Physical and mental development in Swedish urban schoolchildren. Studies in Education and Psychology 5. Stockholm: Department of Educational Research, Stockholm Institute of Education.

Malina RM (1978) Adolescent growth and maturation: Selected aspects of current research. Yearbook of Physical Anthropology 21:63-94.

Malina RM (1991) Fitness and performance: The interface of biology and culture. In RJ Park, HM Eckert (eds), New Possibilities/New Paradigms? Champaign, IL: Human Kinetics, pp 30-38.

Malina RM (1996) Tracking of physical activity and physical fitness across the lifespan. Research Quarterly for Exercise and Sport 67 (suppl):48-57.

*Malina RM, Roche AF (1983) Manual of Physical Status and Performance in Childhood. Volume 2. Physical Performance. New York: Plenum.

McCammon RW (1970) Human Growth and Development. Springfield, IL: Charles C Thomas.

Meredith HV (1936) Physical growth of white children: A review of American research prior to 1900. Monographs of the Society for Research in Child Development, serial no. 2.

Meredith HV (1968) Body size of contemporary groups of preschool children studied in different parts of the world. Child Development 39:335-377.

Meredith HV (1969a) Body size of contemporary groups of eight-year-old children studied in different parts of the world. Monographs of the Society for Research in Child Development 34, serial no. 125.

Meredith HV (1969b) Body size of contemporary youth in different parts of the world. Monographs of the Society for Research in Child Development 34, serial no. 131.

Meredith HV (1971) Growth in body size: A compendium of findings on contemporary children living in different parts of the world. Advances in Child Development and Behavior 6:153-238.

Meredith HV (1978) Research between 1960 and 1970 on the standing height of young children in different parts of the world. Advances in Child Development and Behavior 12:1-59.

Meredith HV (1987) Variation in body stockiness among and within ethnic groups at ages from birth to adulthood. Advances in Child Development and Behavior 20:1-60.

Mirwald RL, Bailey DA (1986) Maximal Aerobic Power. London, Ontario: Sports Dynamics.

Morrison JA, Laskarzewski PM, Rauh JL, Brookman R, Mellies M, Frazer M, Khoury P, de Groot I, Kelley K, Glueck CJ (1979) Lipids, lipoproteins, and sexual maturation during adolescence: The Princeton Maturation Study. Metabolism 28:641-649.

Must A, Jacques PF, Dallal GE, Bajema CJ, Dietz WH (1992) Long-term morbidity and mortality of overweight adolescents. New England Journal of Medicine 327:1350-1355.

Nelson S, Hans MG, Broadbent BH Jr, Dean D (2000) The Brush Inquiry: An opportunity to investigate health outcomes in a well-characterized cohort. American Journal of Human Biology 12:1-9.

Parizkova J (1977) Body Fat and Physical Fitness. The Hague: Martinus Nijhoff.

Pate RR, Shephard RJ (1989) Characteristics of physical fitness in youth. In CV Gisolfi, DR Lamb (eds), Perspectives in Exercise and Sports Medicine. Volume 2. Youth, Exercise, and Sport. Indianapolis, IN: Benchmark Press, pp 1-43.

Prahl-Andersen B, Kowalski CJ, Heydendael PHJM, editors (1979) A Mixed-Longitudinal Interdisciplinary Study of Growth and Development. New York: Academic Press.

Reiff GG, Dixon WR, Jacoby D, Guo XY, Spain CG, Hunsicker PA (1986) The President's Council on Physical Fitness and Sports 1985 National School Population Fitness Survey. Ann Arbor, MI: University of Michigan.

* Roche AF (1992) Growth, Maturation and Body Composition: The Fels Longitudinal Study 1929-1991. Cambridge: Cambridge University Press.

* Roche AF, Malina RM (1983) Manual of Physical Status and Performance in Childhood. Volume 1. Physical Status. New York: Plenum.

Roede MJ, van Wieringen JC (1985) Growth diagrams 1980: Netherlands third nation-wide survey. Tijdschrift voor Sociale Gezondheidszorg 63 (suppl), 1-34.

Simons J, Beunen GP, Renson R, Claessens ALM, Vanreusel B, Lefevre JAV (1990) Growth and Fitness of Flemish Girls: The Leuven Growth Study. Champaign, IL: Human Kinetics.

Scammon RE (1930) The measurement of the body in childhood. In JA Harris, CM Jackson, DG Paterson, RE Scammon, The Measurement of Man. Minneapolis: University of Minnesota Press, pp 173-215.

Stephens T, Craig CL (1990) The Well-Being of Canadians: Highlights of the 1988 Campbell's Survey. Ottawa: Canadian Fitness and Lifestyle Research Institute.

*Tanner JM (1948) A guide to American growth studies. Yearbook of Physical Anthropology 1947 3:28-33.

Tanner JM (1962) Growth at Adolescence, 2nd edition. Oxford: Blackwell Scientific Publications.

* Tanner JM (1981) A History of the Study of Human Growth. Cambridge: Cambridge University Press.

* Tanner JM (1989) Fetus into Man (revised and enlarged edition). Cambridge: Harvard University Press.

Waliszko A, Jedlinska W (1976) Wroclaw Growth Study, Part II. Males. Studies in Physical Anthropology 3:27-48.

Zacharias L, Rand WM (1983) Adolescent growth in height and its relation to menarche in contemporary American girls. Annals of Human Biology 10:209-222.

2 | PRENATAL GROWTH AND FUNCTIONAL DEVELOPMENT

Chapter Outline

Although this text focuses on the postnatal years, an understanding of the beginning of the processes of growth, maturation, and functional development, which start shortly after conception, is important. This chapter provides an overview of prenatal growth and the beginning of functional development and of the factors that influence these processes. The processes that characterize the prenatal period are complex and occur in a precise manner. They involve the integration of molecular, biochemical, biophysical, structural, and functional activities. The prenatal period spans, on the average, about 10 lunar months (a lunar month has 28 days), 9 calendar months, or 40 weeks.

Stages of Prenatal Growth

Prenatal growth has three distinct stages: the fertilized egg (ovum) or zygote, the embryo, and the fetus. Although specific ages are indicated for each stage, problems are involved in estimating prenatal ages. Gestational age is calculated from the first day of the mother's last normal menstrual period. The average time between the last menstrual period and ovulation and fertilization is 2 weeks. Factors that make obtaining exact gestational or prenatal ages difficult include errors and differences in maternal reporting; variation in the interval between menstruation, ovulation, and fertilization; occasional postfertilization bleeding that may be interpreted as a menstrual cycle; and perhaps intervening, unrecognized pregnancy losses.

Period of the Egg

The period of the egg is the first 2 weeks after fertilization. It is characterized by rapid cell division (mitosis) and increasing complexity. As cell division continues, the cluster of cells has a berrylike appearance and is called the morula. Eventually, a cavity develops in the morula, forming the blastocyst, which has the appearance of a cavitated disc (see figure 2.1). During the second week after fertilization, the blastocyst begins to implant itself in the wall of the uterus, and several distinct cellular layers become differentiated. Although the differentiation of each cellular layer is important in its own right, the layer of most interest is that which develops into the embryo. At the end of the second week, the embryo is clearly differentiated. The other cellular layers are vital to the early nutrition of the developing embryo and to the development of the umbilical cord and placenta. The early

embryo, however, cannot develop further unless it is successfully implanted in the uterine wall.

Period of the Embryo

The period of the embryo is the second through the eighth weeks of prenatal life. It is characterized by rapid growth (increase in cell number) and by differentiation of embryonic stem cells into specific cell types and the eventual organization of the differentiated cells into tissues, organs, and systems. Embryonic stem cells are said to be totipotent or pluripotent, which means that they have the potential to give rise to any type of differentiated cells. Differentiated cells are those that are committed to a specific cell type or tissue; for example, some embryonic stem cells are committed to become muscle cells, others become nerve cells, and still others become cartilage and bone cells. Once embryonic stem cells are committed to a specific cell type, they appear to lose their pluripotency. However, some scientists believe that the totipotency of differentiated cells can be restored in the laboratory. If proven to be true, such a restoration would

---

The Second Week of Prenatal Development: Differentiation and Implantation

7th day

Blastocyst:

    Blastodisc

    Blastula Cavity

8th day

Implantation of the Blastocyst in the Uterus, Differentiation of:

    Embryonic Plate

    Amniotic Cavity

12th-14th days

Blastocyst is Implanted in the Uterus, Differentiation of:

    Amnion Membrane

    Amniotic Cavity

    Embryo

    Yolk Sac

    Body Stalk (placenta, Umblicus)

FIGURE 2.1   Summary of major changes during the second week of prenatal development: blastocyst, differentiation of cellular layers, implantation, and the early embryo.

After Rugh and Shettles (1971).

offer major therapeutic advantages for a variety of diseases. How does an embryonic stem cell become committed to a specific cell type is not yet fully understood and represents one of the most challenging areas of research in biology. The general scenario underlying embryonic cell differentiation and morphogenesis involves the expression of specific genes, the repression of others, and the synthesis of particular proteins, transcription factors, and growth factors.

The embryonic period is thus one of organ and system formation. Changes occur in a well-defined sequence (see table 2.1). By the end of this period, the basic anatomical and physiological features are established. Subsequent changes are primarily in dimensions and proportions and in the gradual refinement of functions. These two series of changes continue for the remainder of prenatal life and postnatally until the individual attains adulthood.

Period of the Fetus

The remainder of pregnancy is the period of the fetus, the 9th through the 40th weeks. It is characterized by rapid growth in size and mass, changes in proportions, and the functional development of tissues, organs, and systems. Each of these conditions is discussed in more detail later in the chapter. In contrast to the periods of the ovum and the embryo, no new anatomic features appear during the period of the fetus.

A child is usually born at about 40 weeks of gestation, which is considered a **full-term** pregnancy. Gestational ages at term normally vary between 38 and 42 weeks.

Sex Differentiation

The generation of competent gametes through the process of meiosis results in an ovum and sperm that can enter into fertilization. Meiosis and fertilization are complex processes (see figure 2.2). The sex of a child is determined by a series of events that begin at fertilization. The first of these events is defined by the chromosome carried by the sperm that fertilizes the ovum. Because females have an XX sex chromosome constitution, each egg has a single X chromosome. Males have an XY chromosome constitution, and a sperm may carry either an X or a Y chromosome. If an X-bearing sperm fertilizes the egg, the resulting individual is a genetic female (XX); if a Y-bear-

Gamete Formation and Fertilization

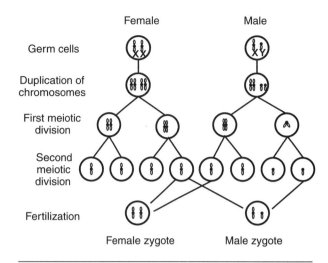

FIGURE 2.2 Gamete formation and fertilization illustrated for the XX and XY genotypes.

ing sperm fertilizes the egg, the individual is a genetic male (XY).

The primitive gonad of the mammalian embryo arises in the first 6 weeks of prenatal life and has dual potential, which means that it can develop into either a female or a male. It has two parts, an inner medulla and an outer cortex. At about week 7, the primitive gonad differentiates into the testes in genetic males (XY). This differentiation is initiated by the expression of a gene on the short arm of the Y chromosome that induces, in concert with other genes, the medulla of the primitive gonad to differentiate and develop into testes. The gene is the SRY gene, which is the acronym for the sex-determining region on the Y chromosome. The SRY gene encodes a so-called high-mobility group transcription factor, which binds to specific DNA sequences and regulates the transcription of several genes involved in determining sex. The key role played by the SRY gene is highlighted by the fact that more than 30 mutations resulting in developmental anomalies have been identified in this gene. Several other genes involved in this cascade have been identified by the analysis of rare mutations or chromosomal deletions in individuals exhibiting unique features of sex development. At present, these genes include SOX9, WT1, SF1, DAX1, SF1, DMRT1, and DMRT2. The specific role of these genes in the determination of sex is currently being elaborated (Parker et al. 1999).

The SRY gene must be active at the time of differentiation of the testes to direct male sexual

	TABLE 2.1	Timetable of Human Prenatal Development	
Age (days)	**Developmental characteristics**		**Crown-to-rump length (mm)**
1	Fertilization		
6	Implantation begins		
18	Neural plate		
20	Brain and neural groove		
21	Heart tubes begin to fuse		
22	Heart begins to beat Neural folds fusing		
23	Beginning eye and ear formation		
26	Arm buds present		
27	Leg buds present		
28			4.0
29			5.0
30	Eyes, nose, and mouth forming		
32	Hand plates present		
33			7.0
34	Cerebral vesicles distinct		
35			8.0
36	Oral and nasal cavities confluent		
37	Foot plates present		9.0
38	Upper lip formed		
39			10.0
40	Finger rays distinct Palate developing		
42			13.0
43			14.0
45	Nose distinct Toe rays appear Ossification may begin		17.0
47	Genital tubercle Urogenital membrane		
48	Trunk lengthening and straightening		
49			18.0
50	Upper limbs longer, fingers distinct		
51	Testes and ovaries distinguishable		
53	External genitalia begin to differentiate		
55	Beginnings of all essential external and internal structures present		
56			30.0
63			50.0
64	Face has human profile		
68	Genitalia have female or male characteristics, not yet fully formed		
70			61.0

Extracted from Moore (1988).

development. Subsequent differentiation and development of male morphological characteristics depends on the actions of several hormones and competent hormone receptors in the target tissues. As the developing testes begin to function, testosterone is produced, which stimulates the development of the important components of the male reproductive organs—the seminal vesicles, epididymis, and vas deferens. Subsequently, a hormone derived from testosterone (dihydrotesterone) stimulates the development of the penis, scrotum, and prostate gland. While these masculinizing activities are occurring, a third hormone produced by the fetal testis, the Mullerian suppression factor, suppresses the development of female reproductive organs in the male, the uterus and fallopian tubes.

The actions of the genes, transcription factors, and hormones are necessary for the normal development of a male (i.e., for masculinization). If they do not operate harmoniously at this early stage of development, a genetic male (XY) will develop along the female pattern and will be classified as one of many male pseudohermaphrodite types. An example of such an error in development is the individual affected with "testicular feminization." Such genetic males have only rudimentary male genitalia, often show breast development, and have a female body build.

In genetic females and in the absence of the SRY gene, the cortex of the primitive gonad initially differentiates into the ovaries around the 13th week. The gonad medulla shrinks and normal feminization occurs. Related structures (uterus, fallopian tubes, and vagina) differentiate.

The basic pattern of embryonic development in mammals, including humans, is, therefore, female, although it could be seen as neutral by some criteria. The SRY gene on the Y chromosome, in synergy with other genes, induces the differentiation of the testes. Subsequently, the hormonal action of prenatal androgens and their receptors are necessary for the development of male characteristics. Otherwise, the undifferentiated primitive gonad will develop female characteristics.

Twins and Twinning

Two types of twins exist—identical, or monozygotic (MZ), and fraternal, or dizygotic (DZ). DZ twins are formed when two female gametes (eggs, or oocytes) are fertilized by two different male gametes (sperm). The fertilized eggs or zygotes can be of the same or of different sex. DZ twins

are genetically like regular brothers and sisters who are born at different times.

MZ twins, on the other hand, are the product of a more complex phenomenon that is still not well understood. Soon after fertilization, the ovum divides into two identical zygotes under the influence of unknown factors. Genetically, MZ twins are perfect copies of each other, and they are, of course, always of the same sex.

The rate of twin births among Whites is about one in 90 births, and, among twin births, about one in three is an MZ pair. Twin births tend to cluster in families, but the familial aggregation applies only to DZ twins. Studies of twins are important in understanding the role of genetic and environmental factors in growth, maturation, and performance.

Prenatal Loss

A substantial proportion of fertilized ova aborts spontaneously. Spontaneous abortion results from a number of anomalies such as failure to undergo cell divisions, failure to implant properly in the uterine wall, or postimplantation losses. One of the important causes of spontaneous abortions is that male and female gametes that entered into fertilization carry chromosomal anomalies or some other less obvious genetic defects. As a consequence, the resulting zygotes are frequently incompetent and spontaneous abortions are often the outcome.

Several studies have been conducted with the goal of quantifying the magnitude of the spontaneous abortion phenomenon. The estimates vary from a low of 12% to a high of 62%. An attempt to reconcile the various methodologies in a single model concluded that prenatal loss caused by lack of implantation reached 12% of all fertilized eggs and early wastage was responsible for 13% of spontaneous abortions; an additional 10% of spontaneous abortions occurred in subsequently discernible pregnancies (Cunningham et al. 1997). Thus, the rate of spontaneous abortions of all fertilized eggs is about 35%.

Fetal chromosomal anomalies account for about 50% of all spontaneous pregnancy losses. Evidence indicates a significant genetic component in miscarriages: lack of a chromosome or presence of an extra chromosome (86%), structural abnormalities in a given chromosome (6%), and other genetic aberrations (8%) (Goddijn and Leschot 2000). This rate of miscarriages represents a strong selection force against inherited and other congenital anomalies in humans. Fetuses affected by chromosomal anomalies that survive the prenatal period experience some perinatal deaths. Finally, almost 1.0% of all live newborn infants have a chromosomal abnormality of some kind; these infants are generally affected by major problems such as reduced longevity, infertility, or impairment of mental functions.

Congenital Malformations

The term **congenital malformation** simply refers to an abnormal condition with which an infant is born. It does not refer to the cause of the particular defect. Birth defects can be caused by a number of factors; some are genetic, but many are environmental.

At the end of the embryonic period, all body systems are present in fundamental structure. The remainder of pregnancy is devoted to growth in size and the development of functional activity. With congenital defects, the period of the embryo is the most critical. As noted earlier, it is a period of rapid differentiation during which the basic body systems are established. The sequence of events, the timing, the direction, and the basic pattern of differentiation and development of tissues, organs, and systems are established by the developing individual's genotype. However, environmental agents or conditions are capable of altering the outcome of these processes.

Early development occurs in closely timed sequences that are very specific for the developing structures. During these sensitive periods, specific tissues are more susceptible than others to developmental insult. Interruption or interference can alter subsequent development and result in a congenital malformation.

In addition to the individual's genotype, a variety of agents are capable of affecting cellular and tissue differentiation and specialization in the embryonic period. Such agents include, for example, mechanical factors (trauma), chemicals or therapeutic drugs (thalidomide and cortisone), radiation from therapeutic treatments or other sources, infections (rubella and herpes simplex viruses), hypoxia, maternal metabolic imbalances (diabetes, alcoholism, and rheumatic disease), and maternal substance abuse (cocaine, heroin, and crack). Recently, mothers testing positive for the AIDS virus have been shown to transmit the infection to the child during pregnancy, with serious consequences for the child.

The extremely specific nature and timing of early development is well illustrated in the thalidomide tragedy in the 1960s. Thalidomide is a mild sedative that was associated with an increase in malformations in newborns. The most conspicuous malformations associated with the drug involved several defects of the limbs, which varied from minor defects of the fingers or toes to total absence of limbs. The type of defect produced by thalidomide was closely related to the stage of pregnancy at which the mother ingested the drug (see table 2.2). The sequence of development of defects corresponds closely with the sequence of short sensitive periods for different structures and organs during the first trimester. Similar data are available for other congenital defects, such as cleft palate relative to the timing and sequence of craniofacial development.

TABLE 2.2	Sensitive Periods for Thalidomide Based on Accurate Records of When the Mother Received the Drug
When the drug was taken	**Type of defect**
35th day p.m.[1]	Ear defects
40th to 42nd days p.m.	Arm defects
42nd to 44th days p.m.	Leg defects
50th day p.m.	Triphalangism (three bones) of the thumbs

[1]Day/days refer to day/days postmenstrually (p.m.), that is, since the last menstrual cycle.
Adapted from Lenz (1968).

Some of the environmental agents associated with gross structural defects during the period of the embryo may also have effects later in fetal life. The organs or structures most likely to be affected are those developing at the time the fetus is exposed to the environmental agents. These defects are usually manifest in stunted physical growth, reductions in organ size, and functional defects.

Fetal Growth

Early prenatal growth is characterized by cell division and by differentiation of cells into distinct tissues, organs, and systems. Subsequently, the rate of growth becomes more rapid, and body size increases markedly after the embryonic period.

Body Size

Sizes attained in weight and length at different prenatal ages are illustrated in figure 2.3. The fetal growth curve approximates a sigmoid, or S-shaped, curve for body weight. Approximately the first half of pregnancy is spent attaining only 10% to 12% of body weight at term. This time, of course, includes tissue differentiation, organ formation, and further development of fetal structures. In contrast, fetal length (crown-to-heel length) at about 20 weeks of gestation approaches one-half of length at term. Rate of growth in length reaches a peak of about 1 cm/4 weeks at about 20 weeks' gestation (midpregnancy) and then decreases (Tanner 1989). On the other hand, rate of growth in fetal weight increases during the second half of pregnancy, and, as term ap-

proaches, rates of growth in both dimensions are reduced considerably.

Growth curves for several fetal circumferences based on live-born infants who were born at gestational ages between 25 and 42 weeks are presented in figure 2.4. Head circumferences before 25 weeks of gestation are derived from aborted fetuses. The general similarity of prenatal growth curves for these dimensions is apparent, especially between 25 and 35 weeks. After 35 weeks of gestation, chest circumference appears to grow more rapidly, reducing the difference between head and chest circumferences. Hence, at term, head circumference is only slightly larger than chest circumference. When the circumferences are compared with fetal weight in figure 2.3, weight increases more rapidly than the circumferences after 35 weeks of gestation.

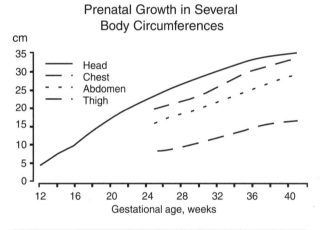

FIGURE 2.4   Prenatal growth in several body dimensions.

Data from Usher and McLean, 1969, and Kaul et al., 1986.

Proportions

Changing fetal proportions are presented in figure 2.5. The embryo has the gross anatomic features of the human form. At 2 months, the developing individual has an enormous head relative to overall size and short extremities. By midpregnancy, the fetus still has a relatively large head, but considerable growth has occurred in the trunk and extremities. Differential growth of body segments (head, trunk, and lower extremities) occurs, and as large as a child's head is at birth, it contributes proportionally less to total body length than at 2 or 5 months prenatally. In

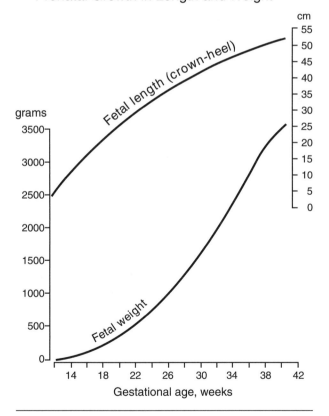

FIGURE 2.3   Prenatal growth in body weight and length.

Data from Usher and McLean, 1969, and Kaul et al., 1986.

Prenatal Changes in Body Proportions

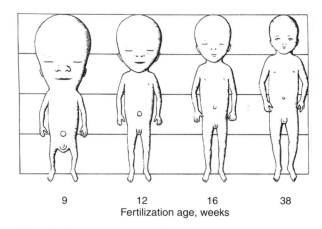

9   12   16   38
Fertilization age, weeks

FIGURE 2.5 Prenatal changes in body proportions. All stages are drawn to the same total length.

Adapted, by permission, from K.L. Moore, 1988, *The developing human*, 4th ed. (Philadelphia, PA: W.B. Saunders), 96.

contrast, the trunk and limbs contribute proportionately more to total body length at birth. The differential growth of body segments continues postnatally and influences body proportions accordingly.

Body Composition

Although weight and length are equally important as indicators of fetal growth, weight receives more attention because fetal prognosis improves with increases in fetal weight. Weight, however, is only a measure of mass, which comprises different substances and tissues, each of which contributes differentially to the total mass. Table 2.3 indicates changes in the relative contributions of water, fat, nitrogen, calcium, and phosphorus to body weight of the developing fetus. The reported values depend on fetal weight, so they are more indicative of a fetus at a specific body weight than of a fetus of a particular gestational age.

The proportion of body weight that is water decreases steadily with increasing fetal weight. The proportion of fat increases slowly at first as fetal weight increases to about 1,500 g. Above this fetal weight, the percentage of body weight that is fat increases more rapidly, especially in the time period that would approximate the last 2 months of gestation (see figure 2.3). The concentration of nitrogen increases with increasing fetal weight. Note that a slight reduction in nitrogen occurs as term approaches. The absolute amount of nitrogen actually increases at this time, but fat has an accelerated rate of growth in late gestation, which lowers the relative contribution of nitrogen and other constituents to fetal weight.

The concentrations of calcium and phosphorus are similar early in gestation. With growth, the proportion of calcium increases more rapidly than that of phosphorus. The differential increase reflects the rapid growth of the fetal skeleton compared with soft tissues. Calcium is a significant element in skeletal tissue, whereas phosphorus is distributed between hard and soft

TABLE 2.3   Relative Composition of the Developing Fetus

Approximate age (weeks)	Body weight (g)	Water (%)	Fat (%)	Nitrogen (%)	Calcium (%)	Phosphorus (%)
15	100	89.0	0.5	1.0	0.2	0.2
17	200	88.5	0.5	1.4	0.3	0.3
23	500	88.0	0.6	1.4	0.4	0.3
26	1,000	86.0	1.0	1.4	0.6	0.3
31	1,500	84.7	2.3	1.7	0.7	0.4
33	2,000	81.0	5.0	1.9	0.7	0.4
35	2,500	77.6	7.4	2.0	0.8	0.4
38	3,000	72.7	12.0	1.8	0.8	0.5
40	3,500	68.6	16.0	1.8	0.9	0.5

Values are expressed as a percentage of fetal weight.
Calculated from data presented by Widdowson (1968).

tissues. First indications of ossification of the fetal skeleton are apparent at about the eighth week of gestation.

Fetal Motor Activity

Fetal behavior arises from a definite morphological, physiological, and neuromuscular arrangement. Information on the early development of behavior comes from surgically removed fetuses, direct recording of fetal movements by means of ultrasound during normal pregnancy, and studies of infants born at varying gestational ages (see Smotherman and Robinson 1988). Heart movements can be detected by about 4 weeks after conception. As early as 5 to 6 weeks postmenstrually, simple extension-like movements of the upper part of the spine can be detected with ultrasound. Movements of the arms and legs can be detected by about 8 to 9 weeks postmenstrually, with a subsequent rapid increase in different kinds of movements.

Neuromuscular changes are quite age specific prenatally. The fetus born at 28 weeks of gestation, for example, is neurologically different from a fetus of 26 weeks or of 30 weeks, and the fetus born at 30 weeks of gestation is quite different from the fetus born at 36 weeks (Saint-Anne Dargassies 1966). Primary reflexes, muscle tone, reactivity, motility, and sensorimotor behavior tend to be specific for each gestational age.

Reflexes and reactions that are good indicators of neurological maturity during the latter part of gestation are shown in figure 2.6. The data are based on longitudinal observations of a small series of preterm infants in Bonn, Germany (Brandt 1986). The infants were born between 28 and 32 weeks of gestation, and all had body weights appropriate for their gestational ages. Their physical development was normal, except that they were born before term, or prematurely. The extrauterine progress of preterm infants is consistent with their gestational ages. That is, neurological development is a function of

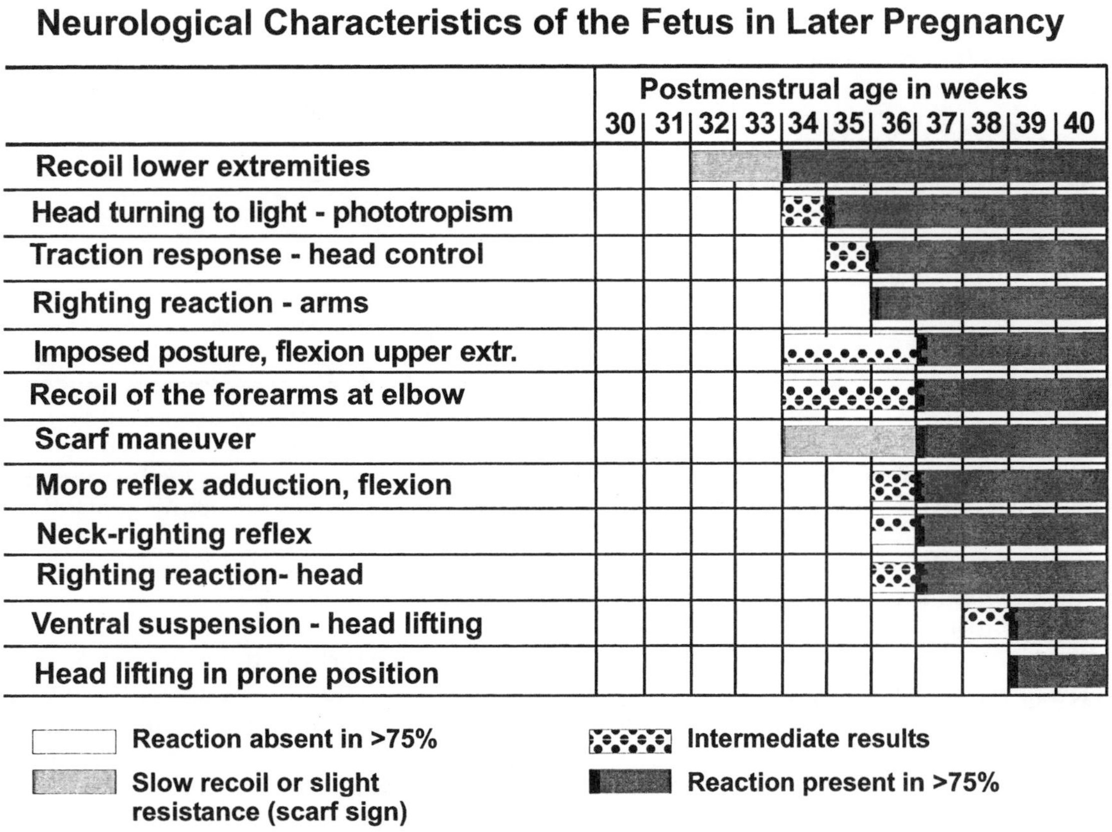

Neurological Characteristics of the Fetus in Later Pregnancy

	Postmenstrual age in weeks										
	30	31	32	33	34	35	36	37	38	39	40
Recoil lower extremities			S	S	P	P	P	P	P	P	P
Head turning to light - phototropism					I	P	P	P	P	P	P
Traction response - head control						I	P	P	P	P	P
Righting reaction - arms								P	P	P	P
Imposed posture, flexion upper extr.					I	I	I	P	P	P	P
Recoil of the forearms at elbow					I	I	I	P	P	P	P
Scarf maneuver					S	S	S	P	P	P	P
Moro reflex adduction, flexion							I	P	P	P	P
Neck-righting reflex							I	P	P	P	P
Righting reaction- head							I	P	P	P	P
Ventral suspension - head lifting									I	P	P
Head lifting in prone position										P	P

Legend: Reaction absent in >75% · Slow recoil or slight resistance (scarf sign) [S] · Intermediate results [I] · Reaction present in >75% [P]

FIGURE 2.6   Neurological characteristics of fetuses in the later stages of pregnancy.

From *Human Growth: A comprehensive treatise*, Volume 2, 1986, 510, Bone growth and maturation, A.F. Roche, Figure 22, copyright © 1986 with kind permission of Kluwer Academic Publishers.

gestational age and is also apparently independent of environmental stimuli provided by the extrauterine environment. The neurological development of preterm infants of appropriate gestational ages is thus a continuation of the prenatal pattern of functional development.

Advances in ultrasound technology and sensory transducers have permitted accurate monitoring of fetal motor activity in utero and complement maternal reports of fetal activity. Activity of the fetus is usually monitored for about 1 hour at specific times of the day. Fetal movements increase during the first half of pregnancy. On the average, motor activity is reduced from 20 weeks gestation through term, but the vigor of movement increases. Males are, on the average, more active than females. The reduction in activity with advancing gestation is related to space constraints in the uterus resulting from fetal growth and probably from changes in the fetal nervous system associated with maturation and sleep-wake cycles. Nevertheless, considerable variation in movement activity occurs among individuals during the last trimester of pregnancy (Eaton and Saudino 1992).

The motor responses of the fetus reflect in part the immediate needs of the developing fetus (Oppenheim 1981). Motor activity is a part of the developmental process. Spontaneous fetal motor activity is important in the normal prenatal development of muscles and joints. Fetal motor activity is also responsive to the uterine environment, which can be quite noisy (e.g., noises associated with the maternal digestive tract, with blood flow, and with the maternal voice). Sudden noises in the external environment can also elicit fetal motor responses. In contrast, fetal movements are reduced when mothers are smoking compared with times when they are not smoking. Fetal motor behaviors can also be viewed, to some extent, as precursors of subsequent postnatal movement behaviors and the development of locomotor and manual control in infancy (Smotherman and Robinson 1988).

Factors That Affect Birth Weight

Birth marks the transition from the uterine environment to a more variable external environment, and birth weight is perhaps the most important indicator of the status of the newborn infant. Reference values for fetal growth based on weights for a sample of approximately 3 million live-born

infants in the United States in 1991 are shown in figure 2.7. These values are not standards. A standard assumes optimal growth, which is not known. The reference values are the observed trends in birth weights in a national sample of live-born American infants in 1991. The sexes are combined, although males weigh, on the average, slightly more than females. The reference values are useful in determining fetal growth restriction (see the section on low birth weight).

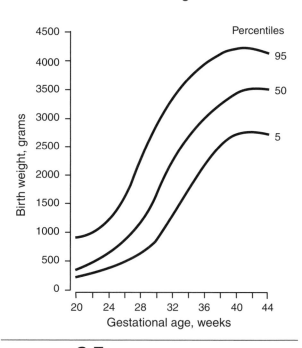

FIGURE 2.7 Smoothed percentiles of birth weight (g) for gestational age based on single live births to United States resident mothers in 1991, sexes combined (n = 3,134,879). The numbers 5, 50, and 95 refer to the 5th, 50th (median), and 95th percentiles, respectively.

Data from Alexander et al., 1996.

Weight at birth is the outcome of intrauterine growth. The major factors associated with intrauterine growth are summarized in table 2.4. Except for genotype, sex, and ethnicity, the factors affecting intrauterine growth are largely related to maternal characteristics and behaviors. The indirect effects exert their influence through one or more of the factors capable of directly influencing fetal growth. Smoking and nutritional status are major determinants of fetal growth and are discussed in more detail later in this section.

| TABLE 2.4 | Established Determinants of Intrauterine Growth and Birth Weight |

Direct

Infant sex	Gestational weight gain
Ethnicity/race	Caloric (energy) intake
Maternal height	General morbidity
Prepregnancy weight	Malaria
Paternal height and weight	Cigarette smoking
Maternal birth weight	Alcohol consumption
Parity	Tobacco chewing
Prior low-birth-weight infant	

Indirect

Maternal age	Socioeconomic status

Adapted from Kramer (1987).

Newborn boys are, on the average, slightly heavier than newborn girls. Infants of primaparous women (first pregnancy) are lighter than those of multiparous women (more than one pregnancy). Infants born to women from lower socioeconomic backgrounds are lighter than those of women from higher socioeconomic backgrounds. Many of the variables that significantly affect birth weight are themselves interrelated, for example, maternal nutritional status and socioeconomic status, or maternal weight gain during pregnancy and maternal body build. Thus, the major portion of variation in birth weight can be attributed to characteristics of the mother, either partly hereditary (e.g., size or body build) or environmental (e.g., nutritional status or socioeconomic background).

Ethnic variation in birth weight exists among American infants. Data from two studies, one from California in the 1970s and the other from New York and Chicago in 1987 to 1989, are summarized in table 2.5. The results of the studies are remarkably similar. Black and Asian infants are, on the average, lighter than White, Dominican, and Mexican infants, who differ only slightly. Although ethnic variation is affected by many of the factors mentioned previously, the variation persists even when these factors are statistically controlled in the analysis. For

| TABLE 2.5 | Ethnic Variation in Birth Weight |

Children born in Northern California in the mid-1970s

Group	n	Mean weight (g)	Differences relative to white infants — Between means (g)	Differences relative to white infants — After controlling for other variables (g)
White	20,515	3,480		
Mexican	3,051	3,420	-60	-72
Asian	2,082	3,260	-220	-167
Black	2,716	3,230	-250	-183

Children born in New York and Chicago 1987-1989

Group	n	Mean weight (g)	Differences relative to white infants — Between means (g)	Differences relative to white infants — After controlling for other variables (g)
White	215	3,503		
Dominican	153	3,484	-19	-49
Mexican	169	3,431	-72	-71
Puerto Rican	123	3,341	-162	-106
Chinese	144	3,272	-231	-215
Black	346	3,231	-272	-236

Variables that were statistically controlled in making the comparisons of ethnic/racial groups are indicated in the text.
Adapted from Shiono et al. (1986, 1997).

example, in the two series of infants summarized in table 2.5, birth weights were compared among the ethnic groups after controlling for sex of the child, parity, smoking and alcohol consumption, the time when prenatal care was initiated, maternal weight-for-stature, and gestational age. When these factors and others were controlled in the analysis, White infants were the heaviest, followed by Mexican, Asian, and Black infants in the California study and followed by Dominican, Mexican, Puerto Rican, Chinese, and Black infants in the New York and Chicago study.

Low Birth Weight

Birth weight is positively related to the survival of the newborn infant. Full-term infants with birth weights at the 10th percentile (about 2,600 g) have a relative risk of mortality that is 2.5 times greater than children with birth weights at the median. Therefore, low birth weight is a cause for much concern. Infants with birth weights below 2,500 g (5 lb and 8 oz) are classified as having low birth weight.

Two groups of infants with low birth weight must be distinguished. The first group are "preterm" infants, who are small because they are born at an early gestational age (less than 37 completed weeks), that is, before the completion of a full-term pregnancy (38 to 42 weeks). They are characterized by physiological immaturity. These infants have the size appropriate for their gestational age, or appropriate-for-date. For example, infants born at a gestational age of 28 weeks have, on the average, a birth weight of about 1,190 g, and those born at a gestational age of 32 weeks have, on the average, a birth weight of about 2,200 g. The second group of low-birth-weight infants are the "small-for-date" or "small-for-gestational-age" infants. They have birth weights that are smaller than expected for their gestational age and are commonly described as having intrauterine growth retardation or fetal growth restriction.

Although a variety of factors are involved in the restricted growth of small-for-date infants, smoking and maternal undernutrition (low energy intake or low weight gain) are the most important factors for women in developed countries. Other important factors include maternal low prepregnant weight, primiparity, sex of the infant (female), non-White ethnicity, maternal short stature, maternal low birth weight, and prior low-birth-weight history. Among rural women in developing countries, small-for-date infants are often born to women who are under-

nourished. Other factors are close birth spacing and perhaps high energy output associated with the demands of subsistence. Low energy intake or low weight gain, low prepregnant weight, a history of undernutrition during childhood and adolescence, and maternal short stature assume a more important role in women from rural areas of developing countries.

Low birth weight has significance for postnatal growth. Infants who are small for gestational age or who are born prematurely (physiologically immature) are more likely to have shorter stature during childhood and perhaps at maturity, and they also tend to be deficient in measures of neuromuscular coordination and power. They are discussed in more detail in chapter 27.

Maternal Energy and Nutrient Intake

Prenatal nutrition is related to placental, fetal, and maternal factors. Placental factors relate to circulation and the transport of nutrients from the placenta to the fetus. Problems with placental circulation may result in an inadequate supply of nutrients available to the developing fetus. Fetal factors relate to the utilization of the available nutrients. Although an adequate nutrient supply might be available to the fetus, complications in fetal metabolism may influence the proper utilization of nutrients. Maternal factors relate to the mother's overall nutritional status and especially to the adequacy of energy and nutrient intake and weight gain during the pregnancy. Inadequate maternal energy and nutrient intake can directly influence the nutritional state of the fetus and in turn fetal growth. The effects of maternal nutrition on fetal growth depend on when the energy and nutrient inadequacy occurs, how severe it is, and how long it persists. The nutritional status of the mother in the past (e.g., her own low birth weight or childhood history of chronic undernutrition) may also influence placental function and in turn the nutritional state of the fetus, even though maternal energy and nutrient intake during the pregnancy is adequate.

Maternal Smoking

Maternal use of tobacco in the form of smoking is consistently associated with intrauterine growth retardation without altering gestational length. That is, children born to mothers who smoke often have fetal growth restriction. An estimated 20% to 30% of low-birth-weight infants in the

United States can be attributed to smoking. Smoking appears to have a dosage effect: the more a mother smokes during pregnancy, the greater the prenatal growth restriction. Estimated deficits in weight and length at birth associated with smoking are, respectively, as follows:

9 cigarettes a day –	70 g; 0.7 cm
10 to 19 cigarettes a day –	160 g; 0.9 cm
≥20 cigarettes a day –	210 g; 1.0 cm (Roche 1999)

The degree of fetal growth restriction is independent of maternal dietary intake and is perhaps a result of intrauterine hypoxia associated with smoking. The effect of smoking on fetal growth is dramatically shown in cases in which mothers smoked during one pregnancy and not the other. Children born of the smoke-free pregnancies are heavier and longer at birth. The consequences of maternal smoking during pregnancy on growth of the child persist postnatally, as is evident in the small body size of these children during childhood (Roche 1999).

Maternal Alcohol Consumption

Alcohol consumption not only contributes to fetal growth restriction but also can affect the individual throughout pregnancy. It is associated with abnormal facial development occurring during the embryonic period and impaired function of the central nervous system, including microcephaly (abnormal smallness of the head and brain). Postnatal growth of these children is commonly stunted, and mental retardation and behavioral problems often occur.

The estimated frequency of "fetal alcohol syndrome" is about one in 700 births. Fully developed fetal alcohol syndrome, which includes abnormal facial development, stunted physical growth, and central nervous system dysfunction, is estimated to occur in about 33% of the children born to alcoholic mothers (Streissguth et al. 1980; Abel 1982). Partial expression of the syndrome occurs in a greater percentage of children born to alcoholic mothers. However, alcohol consumption and alcoholism are difficult to specify and define, and definitions vary among studies. Alcohol exposure is ordinarily based on maternal report, which, of course, has associated error of recall. Chronic consumption is often assumed to refer to a minimum of two drinks of alcoholic spirits a day. In a series of studies done in Seattle hospitals, level of alcohol exposure refers to the average amount of absolute alcohol consumed a day. An absolute alcohol score of 1.0 is equivalent to approximately 30 g of alcohol a day, or two drinks a day of beer, wine, or liquor (Streissguth et al. 1994).

As with smoking, alcohol consumption appears to have a dose-response effect on prenatal growth: the more alcohol a mother consumes during pregnancy, the greater the prenatal growth restriction. Estimated deficits in weight at birth associated with alcohol intake are, respectively, as follows:

≤2 drinks a day –	65 g
≥2 drinks a day –	150 g (Roche 1999)

Maternal Abuse of Other Substances

Caffeine consumption in the form of coffee is another form of substance abuse that may affect prenatal growth. Consumption of more than 4 cups of coffee a day is associated with a deficit of 220 g in birth weight (Roche 1999). Data for substance abuse associated with recreational drugs are less extensive, but suggest a seemingly greater influence on weight and length at birth:

cocaine –	500 g; 2.0 cm
heroin –	600 g; 2.4 cm
methadone –	350 g; 1.5 cm (Roche 1999)

Clearly, maternal substance abuse influences prenatal growth and ultimately size at birth. The data, however, are based on self-report and thus have limitations. Nevertheless, the sensitivity of the rapidly growing fetus to the influence of a variety of chemical substances associated with maternal behaviors is clearly apparent.

Maternal Exercise

Maternal exercise during pregnancy is an issue that is presently receiving more attention. Pregnancy places a number of physiological demands on the mother. These demands include, for example, greater energy and nutrient requirements (although the energy cost of pregnancy varies considerably). Pregnancy is also associated with an increase in blood volume to about 45%, a 20% increase in stroke volume and cardiac output, an increase in ventricular wall thickness and end-diastolic ventricular volume, an increase in minute ventilation at rest, and a decrease in functional residual pulmonary capacity (Carpenter 1994). The developing fetus, of course, needs energy, nutrients, and oxygen for metabolism and growth.

Some concern has thus been expressed about the possibility of compromising the oxygen, energy, and nutrient needs of the developing fetus through severe exercise stress on the mother. Moderate physical activity during pregnancy, particularly during the first 6 to 7 months, apparently has no effect on fetal development and is likely beneficial to the mother. The situation for strenuous exercise, and more specifically such exercise in the last 2 to 3 months of pregnancy, for fetal growth and functional development is less clear in humans. Some experimental studies with animals and limited observations on humans suggest an association between strenuous exercise and reduced birth weight (Lotgering et al. 1985; Artal 1992; Pivarnik 1998). However, no evidence proves that regular exercise in pregnant women is related to differences in gestational age at delivery or cesarean section rate (Carpenter 1994). More research is needed in this important area, especially in quantifying the energy balance during pregnancy and fetal responses in those who exercise chronically.

Overview of the Prenatal Period

In light of the preceding discussion of factors that influence birth weight and low-birth-weight infants, the sensitive or vulnerable periods of prenatal growth can be properly ended to include the entire intrauterine period. Although most of the emphasis in the study of congenital defects concentrates on the early portion of pregnancy, the significance of other factors affecting subsequent growth and functional development of different organs after the embryonic period cannot be overlooked. The major environmental factors of concern in developed countries are maternal smoking, energy intake and weight gain, and alcohol consumption. Use of drugs such as cocaine and other substances are other environmental factors of concern. Strenuous exercise during pregnancy has also been indicated as a possible additional factor that may influence birth weight.

The specific mechanisms through which these factors influence fetal growth and development are complex and beyond the scope of this text. The nutritional status of the fetus, for example, is influenced by its metabolism, the function of the placenta, and the nutritional status of the mother. Further, environmental factors such as smoking, maternal energy and nutrient intake, and alcohol consumption are themselves related. Alcohol consumption, for example, is commonly associated with diminished food intake and reduced weight gain during pregnancy.

The relationship between prenatal growth and functional development and subsequent postnatal growth, maturation, and development must be recognized. The infant with fetal growth restriction is not likely to fully make up postnatally for the reduced growth that occurred prenatally. The same probably applies for other developmental disturbances that have their roots during the prenatal period.

Such environmental factors as maternal smoking, energy and nutrient intake, and alcohol consumption may also have functional significance for brain growth and development. The relationships between these factors and subsequent conditions into which the child is born and reared are complex.

Of relevance to the importance of the prenatal and early postnatal environments for brain development is the spurt in the growth of the brain, the so-called "brain growth spurt" described by Dobbing and colleagues (Dobbing and Sands 1973; Dobbing 1990). The spurt extends from midpregnancy well into the third and fourth years postnatally. The early part of the brain growth spurt, which starts in midpregnancy and continues to about 18 months of age, is characterized by rapid multiplication of glial cells, and the later part, which lasts to 3 or 4 years of age, is largely characterized by myelinization of nerve fibers. Although multiplication of glial cells and myelinization are dominant activities in the brain growth spurt, development of several enzyme systems, development of certain reflex patterns, and changes in water and cation content are other identifiable processes that occur during the spurt. The extent and timing of the spurt varies in different regions of the brain. The cerebellum, which is important in motor development, starts its growth spurt later than the forebrain (cerebral cortex) and brain stem but completes it earlier (i.e., the cerebellum gets its growth faster and over a shorter period of time).

The proposed brain growth spurt does not include the early part of pregnancy, during which the differentiation and development of neurons, neuronal migration, and probably the early stages of differentiation and development of glial cells occur. These processes are important aspects of brain growth that may influence the overall cellular population, the formation of neuronal circuits, and basic cellular architecture of the brain (Morgane et al. 1993).

The immediate implication of such a growth spurt is that interference with fetal and early postnatal growth may influence the growth and functional development of the brain. This cause-and-effect relationship has been viewed largely in the context of chronic undernutrition in developing areas of the world (Dobbing 1990). Note, however, that undernutrition involves more than food. Chronically undernourished children also live under poor conditions economically and socially (this topic is discussed in more detail in chapter 23).

Such effects associated with the brain growth spurt late in pregnancy or early postnatally are quite different from the gross deformities associated with interference early in pregnancy. These deformities include the gross, permanent defects that occur as a result of interference during the period of the embryo. The implications of fetal growth restriction late in pregnancy on the proposed "brain growth spurt" and functional development of infants and young children need further study. Such studies should include the early part of gestation when processes contributing to the proposed spurt are established.

Fetal Origins of Adult Diseases

Events occurring prenatally may condition postnatal growth and maturation and perhaps adulthood and aging. Over the past decade, Barker and colleagues (see Barker 1992, 1998) have reported a number of studies suggesting an association between birth weight, as a marker of fetal growth, and the risk of several chronic, degenerative diseases in adulthood. This idea is called the fetal origins of adult diseases hypothesis. Some epidemiological evidence suggests a link between low birth weight and risk of adult hypertension, coronary heart disease, and diabetes mellitus, although results are contradictory. Although association does not demonstrate causality, and the studies have been challenged on statistical grounds (Lucas et al. 1999), studies providing evidence for an association between adult diseases or risk factors and birth weight are too numerous to be easily discarded. These observations have stimulated interest for adult diseases within the context of the entire human life span, including fetal growth, postnatal growth and maturation, adulthood, and aging.

The fetal origins of adult disease hypothesis stipulates that undesirable prenatal events affecting

the development, structure, and function of organs result in a biological susceptibility, which interacts with diet, environmental stresses, and other factors to cause overt disease many decades after the original insult (Goldberg and Prentice 1994). According to the hypothesis, a susceptibility acquired during prenatal life could have consequences across the life span. Much of the discussion of the fetal origins of adult diseases hypothesis has focused on nutrition of the mother and its implications for the fetus as well as birth weight. Birth weight is a surrogate for events that may have occurred during fetal growth. The complex interactions among nutrition, maternal status, and gestation relative to programming, size at birth, and adult risk are summarized in figure 2.8.

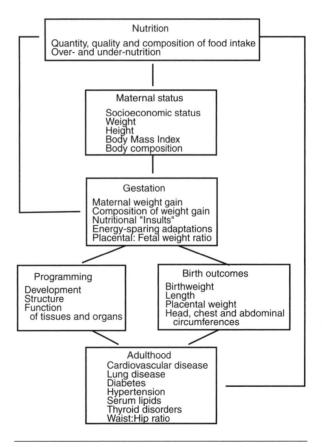

Prenatal Programming and Interactions Relative to Several Adult Diseases

FIGURE 2.8 Interactions among nutrition, maternal status, and gestation relative to the programming structure and function, size at birth, and risk for disease as an adult.

Adapted, by permission, from G.R. Goldberg and A.M. Prentice, 1994, "Maternal and fetal determinants of adult diseases," *Nutrition Reviews* 52: 191-200.

The fetal origins of adult diseases hypothesis has generated considerable interest and has stimulated a search for potential mechanisms linking low birth weight to increased susceptibility to several common diseases that are ordinarily manifested in adulthood. One of the frequently observed relationships is that between low birth weight and the risk of adult-onset (type 2) diabetes mellitus (Hales and Barker 1992). Low birth weight has been proposed to be associated with stunted growth of the pancreas with the consequence that the population of beta cells, which produce insulin, may be reduced. This reduction in insulin would, in turn, result in a diminished capacity of the pancreas to meet the body's need for insulin in the presence of insulin resistance (diminished capacity to dispose of glucose in muscle and other tissues) and hyperglycemia (elevated glucose concentration in the blood). Such a condition would increase the risk of pancreatic exhaustion and thus of diabetes. The presently available evidence, nevertheless, does not fully support this scenario. For example, a full-term infant who is very heavy at birth (high birth weight for date) is also at risk for hyperinsulinemia and thus for diabetes. The hypothesis, however, remains very interesting, and currently many studies are in progress that focus on different aspects of the problem relating fetal growth to diseases that are manifest in adulthood (see Kramer and Joseph 1996; Purdy and Metzger 1996).

Fetal growth and its outcome variables, birth weight, length, and other body dimensions are only several of many intervening variables across the life span. Associations between birth weight of full-term infants and indicators of growth and biological maturation during childhood and adolescence should also be considered. Birth weight of full-term infants is not related to skeletal maturity and to velocity of growth in stature, body mass, and the BMI in childhood (Malina et al. 1999). No relationship appears to exist between birth weight and lung function in adolescents (Matthes et al. 1994) or between birth weight and bone mineral density and content of the lumbar spine and femoral neck in young adult women (Cooper et al. 1995). The relationship between birth weight and age at menarche is not consistent among studies (Roberts et al. 1986; Cooper et al. 1996). Low birth weight among full-term infants is associated with a tendency to accumulate subcutaneous fat on the trunk in children (Malina et al. 1996) and adults (Law et al. 1992; Valdez et al. 1994), but it is apparently not related to relative weight in adults (Allison et al. 1995). Birth weight is also inversely related to systolic blood pressure in children and adults. The data for adolescents are inconsistent (Matthes et al. 1994; Law and Shiell 1996).

The contribution of early postnatal changes to outcomes in adulthood should be considered in future studies, even though an independent association may exist between birth weight and later outcomes. The hypothesis also needs to be examined in terms of the fetal environment, particularly nutritional, and of birth weight per se.

Summary

The prenatal period spans, on the average, about 10 lunar months, 9 calendar months, or 40 weeks, and the processes that characterize this period of life have major implications for postnatal growth and maturation and functional development. The prenatal period is arbitrarily divided into three periods: the egg, during which cell division and differentiation are dominant activities; the embryo, during which the differentiation of tissues, organs, and systems occurs; and the fetus, during which growth and functional development are major features. Factors that influence these processes are largely related to maternal characteristics (size and physique, social class, parity, and nutritional history) and behaviors (current nutrition, smoking, alcohol consumption, and recreational drug use). Birth weight is the primary outcome variable of prenatal growth that receives most attention. Variation in birth weight after a full-term pregnancy has been hypothesized to have implications for health later in life.

Sources and Suggested Readings

Abel EL (1982) Consumption of alcohol during pregnancy: A review of effects on growth and development of offspring. Human Biology 54:421-453.

Alexander GR, Himes JH, Kaugman RB, Mor J, Kogan M (1996) A United States national reference for fetal growth. Obstetrics and Gynecology 87:163-168.

Allison DB, Paultre F, Heymsfield SB, Pi-Sunyer FX (1995) Is the intra-uterine period really a critical period for the development of adiposity? International Journal of Obesity 19:397-402.

Artal R (1992) Exercise and pregnancy. Clinics in Sports Medicine 11:363-377.

* Barker DJP, editor (1992) Fetal and Infant Origins of Adult Disease. London: British Medical Journal.

* Barker DJP (1998) Mothers, Babies, and Health in Later Life. London: Churchill Livingstone.

Berkowitz GS, Papiernik E (1993) Epidemiology of preterm birth. Epidemiological Reviews 15:414-443.

Brandt I (1986) Patterns of early neurological development. In F Falkner, JM Tanner (eds), Human Growth. Volume 2. Postnatal Growth, Neurobiology. New York: Plenum, pp 469-518.

* Carpenter MW (1994) Physical activity, fitness, and health of the pregnant mother and fetus. In Bouchard C, Shephard RJ, Stephens T (eds), Physical Activity, Fitness, and Health. Champaign, IL: Human Kinetics, pp 967-979.

Cooper C, Cawley M, Bhalla A, Egger P, Ring F, Morton L, Barker D (1995) Childhood growth, physical activity, and peak bone mass in women. Journal of Bone and Mineral Research 10:940-947.

Cooper C, Kuh D, Egger P, Wadsworth M, Barker D (1996) Childhood growth and age at menarche. British Journal of Obstetrics and Gynecology 103:814-817.

Cunningham EG, Macdonald PC, Gant NF, Leveno KJ, Gilstrap LC, Hankins GDV, Clark SL (1997) Williams Obstetrics, 20th edition. Appleton, CT: Appleton and Lange, pp 579-605.

DiPietro JA, Hodgson DM, Costigan KA, Hilton SC (1996) Fetal neurobehavioral development. Child Development 67:2553-2567.

Dobbing J (1990) Early nutrition and later achievement. Proceedings of the Nutrition Society 49:103-118.

Dobbing J, Sands J (1973) Quantitative growth and development of the human brain. Archives of Disease in Childhood 48:757-767.

Eaton WO, Saudino KJ (1992) Prenatal activity level as a temperament dimension? Individual differences and developmental functions in fetal movement. Infant Behavior and Development 15:57-70.

Fantel AG (1978) Prenatal selection. Yearbook of Physical Anthropology 21:215-222.

Goddijn M, Leschot NJ (2000) Genetic aspects of miscarriage. Baillieres Best Practice in Research and Clinical Obstetrics and Gynaecology 14:855-865.

Goldberg GR, Prentice AM (1994) Maternal and fetal determinants of adult diseases. Nutrition Reviews 52:191-200.

Gould JB (1986) The low-birth-weight infant. In F Falkner, JM Tanner (eds), Human Growth. Volume 1. Developmental Biology, Prenatal Growth. New York: Plenum, pp 391-413.

Hales CN, Barker DJ (1992) Type 2 (non-insulin-dependent) diabetes mellitus: The thrifty phenotype hypothesis. Diabetologia 35:595-601.

Hellerstedt WL, Himes JH, Story M, Alton IR, Edwards LE (1997) The effects of cigarette smoking and gestational weight change on birth outcomes in obese and normal-weight women. American Journal of Public Health 87:591-596.

Jackson AA, Langley-Evans SC, McCarthy HD (1996) Nutritional influences in early life upon obesity and body proportions. In The Origins and Consequences of Obesity, Ciba Foundation Symposium 201. New York: Wiley, pp 118-137.

Karlberg J, Albertsson-Wikland K, Baber FM, Low LCK, Yeung CY (1996) Born small for gestational age: Consequences for growth. Acta Paediatrica 47 (suppl):8-13.

Kaul SS, Babu A, Chopra SRK (1986) Fetal growth from 12 to 26 weeks of gestation. Annals of Human Biology 13:563-570.

Kramer MS (1987) Intrauterine growth and gestational duration determinants. Pediatrics 80:502-511.

* Kramer MS, Joseph KS (1996) Enigma of fetal/infant-origins hypothesis. Lancet 348:1254-1255.

Law CM, Barker DPJ, Osmond C, Fall CHD, Simmonds SJ (1992) Early growth and abdominal fatness in adult life. Journal of Epidemiology and Community Health 46:184-186.

Law CM, Shiell AW (1996) Is blood pressure inversely related to birth weight? The strength of evidence from a systematic review of the literature. Journal of Hypertension 14:935-941.

Lenz W (1968) Timetable of human organogenesis as a tool in detecting teratogenic effects. In Memoirs of the Twelfth International Congress of Pediatrics, Mexico City, Volume 1. Mexico: Impresiones Modernas, SA, pp 294-295.

Lotgering FK, Gilbert RD, Longo LD (1985) Maternal and fetal responses to exercise during pregnancy. Physiological Reviews 65:1-36.

Lucas A (1991) Programming by early nutrition in man. In GR Bock, J Whelan (eds), The Childhood Environment and Adult Disease. New York: Wiley, pp 38-55.

* Lucas A, Fewtrell MS, Cole TJ (1999) Fetal origins of adult disease—the hypothesis revisited. British Medical Journal 319:245-249.

Malina RM, Katzmarzyk PT, Beunen G (1996) Birth weight and its relationship to size attained and relative fat distribution at 7 to 12 years of age. Obesity Research 4:385-390.

Malina RM, Katzmarzyk PT, Beunen G (1999) Relation between birth weight at term and growth rate, skeletal age and cortical bone at 6–11 years. American Journal of Human Biology 11:505-511.

Matthes JWA, Lewis PA, Davies DP, Bethel JA (1994) Relation between birth weight at term and systolic blood pressure in adolescence. British Medical Journal 308:1074-1077.

Matthes JWA, Lewis PA, Davies DP, Bethel JA (1995) Birth weight at term and lung function in adolescence: No evidence for a programmed effect. Archives of Disease in Childhood 73:231-234.

McIntire DD, Bloom SL, Casey BM, Leveno KL (1999) Birth weight in relation to morbidity and mortality among newborns. New England Journal of Medicine 340:1234-1238.

Metcoff J (1986) Association of fetal growth with maternal nutrition. In F Falkner, JM Tanner (eds), Human Growth. Volume 3. Methodology, Ecological, Genetic, and Nutritional Effects on Growth. New York: Plenum, pp 333-388.

* Moore KL (1988) The Developing Human, 4th edition. Philadelphia: Saunders.

* Morgane PJ, Austin-LaFrance R, Bronzino J, Tonkiss J, Diaz-Cintra S, Cintra L, Kemper T, Galler JR (1993) Prenatal malnutrition and development of the brain. Neuroscience and Biobehavioral Reviews 17:91-128.

Nathanielsz PW (1999) Effects of the intrauterine environment on the development of diabetes. In GA Bray, DH Ryan (eds), Nutrition, Genetics, and Obesity, Pennington Nutrition Series, Volume 9. Baton Rouge: Louisiana State University Press, pp 14-24.

Oppenheim RW (1981) Ontogenetic adaptations and retrogressive processes in the development of the nervous system and behaviour: A neuroembryological perspective. In KL Connolly, HFR Prechtl (eds), Maturation and Development: Biological and Psychological Perspectives. Philadelphia: Lippincott, pp 73-109.

Owen P, Donnet ML, Ogston SA, Christie AD, Howie PW, Patel NB (1996) Standards for ultrasound fetal growth velocity. British Journal of Obstetrics and Gynecology 103:60-69.

Parker KL, Schedl A, Schimmer BP (1999) Gene interactions in gonadal development. Annual Review of Physiology 61:417-433.

Pivarnik JM (1998) Potential effects of maternal physical activity on birth weight: Brief review. Medicine and Science in Sports and Exercise 30:400-406.

Poppitt SD, Prentice AM, Goldberg GR, Whitehead RG (1994) Energy-sparing strategies to protect human fetal growth. American Journal of Obstetrics and Gynecology 171:118-125.

Power C, Lake JK, Cole TJ (1997) Body mass index and height from childhood to adulthood in the 1958 British birth cohort. American Journal of Clinical Nutrition 66:1094-1101.

Public Health Service (1991) Healthy People 2000: National Health Promotion and Disease Prevention Objectives. Washington, DC: Department of Health and Human Services, publication PHS 91-50212.

Purdy LP, Metzger BE (1996) Influences of the intrauterine metabolic environment on adult disease: What may we infer from size at birth? Diabetelogia 39:1126-1130.

Roberts DF, Wood W, Chinn S (1986) Menarcheal age in Cumbria. Annals of Human Biology 13:161-170.

Roche AF (1994) Executive summary of workshop to consider low birthweight in relation to the revision of the NCHS growth charts for infancy (birth–3 years). Hyattsville, MD: National Center for Health Statistics (published in 1999).

Roche AF (1999) Postnatal physical growth assessment. Clinical Pediatrics and Endocrinology 8 (suppl 12):1-12.

Rugh R, Shettles LB (1971) From Conception to Birth: The Drama of Life's Beginnings. New York: Harper & Row.

Saint-Anne Dargassies S (1966) Neurological maturation of the premature infant of 28 to 41 weeks' gestational age. In F Falkner (ed), Human Development. Philadelphia: Saunders, pp 306-325.

Saul RA, Stevenson RE, Rogers RC, Skinner SA, Prouty LA, Flannery DB (1988) Growth References from Conception to Adulthood. Greenwood, SC: Greenwood Genetic Center.

Shiono PH, Klebanoff MA, Graubard BI, Berendes HW, Rhoads GG (1986) Birth weight among women of different ethnic groups. Journal of the American Medical Association 255: 48-52.

Shiono PH, Rauh VA, Park M, Lederman SA, Zuskar D (1997) Ethnic differences in birthweight: The role of lifestyle and other factors. American Journal of Public Health 87: 787-793.

Smart JL (1991) Critical periods in brain development. Ciba Foundation Symposium 156: The Childhood Environment and Adult Disease. New York: Wiley, pp 109-124.

* Smotherman WP, Robinson SR, editors (1988) Behavior of the Fetus. Caldwell, NJ: The Telford Press.

Streissguth AP, Landesman-Dwyer S, Martin JC, Smith DW (1980) Teratogenic effects of alcohol in humans and laboratory animals. Science 209:353-361.

Streissguth AP, Sampson PD, Olson HC, Bookstein FL, Barr HM, Scott M, Feldman J, Mirsky AF (1994) Maternal drinking during pregnancy: Attention and short-term memory in 14-year-old offspring—A longitudinal prospective study. Alcoholism: Clinical and Experimental Research 18:202-218.

Tanner JM (1989) Foetus into Man: Physical Growth from Conception to Maturity (revised and enlarged edition). Cambridge, MA: Harvard University Press.

Tanner JM, Thomson AM (1970) Standards for birthweight at gestation periods from 32 to 42 weeks, allowing for maternal height and weight. Archives of Disease in Childhood 45:566-569.

Uiterwaal CSPM, Anthony S, Launer LJ, Witteman JCM, Trouwborst AMW, Hofman A, Grobbee DE.(1997) Birth weight, growth, and blood pressure: An annual follow-up study of children aged 5 through 21 years. Hypertension 30 (part 1):267-271.

Usher R, McLean F (1969) Intrauterine growth of liveborn Caucasian infants at sea level: Standards obtained from measurements in 7 dimensions of infants born between 25 and 44 weeks of gestation. Journal of Pediatrics 74: 901-910.

Valdez R, Athens MA, Thompson GH, Bradshaw BS, Stern MP (1994) Birthweight and adult health outcomes in a biethnic population in the USA. Diabetologia 37:624-631.

* Vogel F, Motulsky AG (1986) Human Genetics. Berlin: Springer-Verlag.

Widdowson EM (1968) Growth and development of the fetus and newborn. In NS Assali (ed), Biology of Gestation. Volume 2. The Fetus and Neonate. New York: Academic Press, pp 1-49.

Part II

Postnatal Growth

The second section of the book is largely descriptive. It describes changes in body size, physique, body composition, and specific tissues that occur during approximately the first 2 decades of postnatal life. The focus is on age-associated and sex-associated variation.

Chapters 3 through 5 focus on somatic growth, physique, and body composition, respectively. Each chapter initially considers the basic methods used to study these features of growth and then examines variations associated with age and between sexes. Chapter 3 focuses on somatic growth. Information on a variety of body dimensions and proportions is considered. However, emphasis is primarily on height (stature) and weight, the two most commonly used measures of growth status in studies of child and adolescent health, nutrition, and performance. Chapter 4 discusses the concept of physique, or body build. Emphasis is on variation in the distribution of physiques during childhood and adolescence and then on changes that occur with growth. Chapter 5 deals with body composition. The study of body composition has expanded considerably with major changes in technology, especially for the noninvasive evaluation of bone mineral and adipose tissue. Models of body composition, methods of assessment, and changes in fat-free mass, fat mass, and relative fatness during childhood and adolescence are considered.

The first three chapters in this section deal with the body in a global sense. Chapters 6 through 8, in turn, discuss specific tissues that underlie a major portion of the variation in body size, physique, and composition—bone (skeletal), skeletal muscle, and adipose tissues, respectively. Each chapter initially approaches growth of the respective tissue from the cellular perspective, including metabolic processes, and then from a more gross perspective. Many advances in the understanding of the biology of bone, skeletal muscle, and adipose tissues have occurred during the past decade, and these developments are incorporated into the respective chapters. Bone, or skeletal tissue, makes up the skeleton, which is the framework of the body and a reservoir for minerals. Skeletal muscle is the work-producing or energy-producing tissue of the body and is thus important to the understanding of physical activity, fitness, and performance. Adipose tissue represents an energy reserve but has important metabolic functions. Moreover, excessive amounts of adipose tissue have implications for performance and physical fitness during childhood and adolescence and for health status in adulthood.

SOMATIC GROWTH

Chapter Outline

The general pattern of postnatal growth is quite similar from one individual to another, but there is considerable individual variability in size attained and rate of growth at different ages. This variability applies both to the body as a whole and to specific segments and tissues. As indicated earlier, growth processes are difficult to study directly because only the outcomes of these processes, that is, size attained by the body and specific segments and tissues, can be measured. Thus, the study of growth is synonymous to a large extent with measurement. This chapter first describes measurements commonly used in growth studies and then describes the changes in overall size, size of several body dimensions, and proportions that characterize approximately the first 2 to 3 decades of postnatal life.

Measurements Commonly Used in Growth Studies

Anthropometry (anthropos = man, metry = measure) is a set of standardized techniques for systematically taking measurements of the body and parts of the body (i.e., for quantifying dimensions of the body). It involves the use of carefully defined body landmarks for measurements, specific subject positioning for these measurements, and the use of appropriate instruments. Anthropometry is often viewed as the traditional and perhaps basic tool of biological anthropology, but it has a long tradition of use in physical education and the sport sciences, and it is once again finding increased use in the biomedical sciences.

The number of measurements that can be taken on an individual is almost limitless. An important issue is the selection of measurements. Selection depends on the purpose of a study and the specific question(s) under consideration. Each measurement should provide a specific bit of information that aids in understanding growth. To this end, several of the more commonly used anthropometric indicators of somatic growth are subsequently described and illustrated. The protocols for specific measurements are discussed in Lohman et al. (1988).

Overall Body Size

Weight and stature (height) are the two most often used measurements of growth. The terms stature and height are used interchangeably. **Body weight** is a measure of body mass and is thus more appropriately called body mass, but the term weight is entrenched in the literature. Body weight is a composite of independently varying tissues. Although a child's weight should be measured with the child nude, taking such measurements is often impractical. Therefore, weight is frequently measured with the child attired in ordinary, indoor clothing without shoes (e.g., gym shorts and a T-shirt).

Stature, or standing height, is a linear measurement of the distance from the floor or standing surface to the top (vertex) of the skull. It is measured with the subject in a standard erect posture, without shoes (see figure 3.1a). Stature is a composite of linear dimensions contributed by the lower extremities, the trunk, the neck, and the head. From birth to age 2 or 3 years, a child's stature is measured as **recumbent length**—the length while lying face up in a standardized position (see figure

3.1b). As a rule, an individual is longer when lying down than when standing erect.

Stature and weight show **diurnal variation**—variation during the course of a day. Diurnal variation can be a problem in short-term longitudinal studies, in which apparent changes might simply reflect variation in the time of the day at which the measurement was taken. For example, stature is greatest in the morning upon

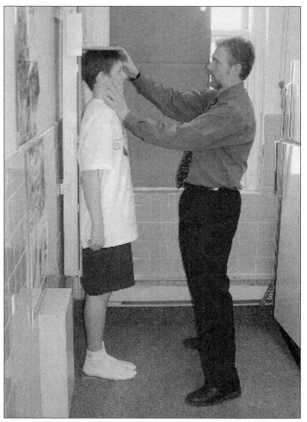

a

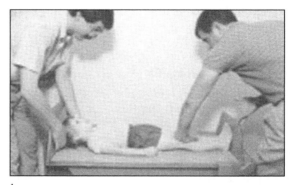

b

FIGURE 3.1   The measurement of stature (a) and recumbent length (b).

Reprinted from Lohman et al. (1988).

arising from bed and decreases as the individual assumes upright posture and walks about. The "shrinking" of stature occurs as a result of the compression of fibrous discs of cartilage that separate the vertebrae. With the force of gravity imposed by standing and walking, the discs are gradually compressed. As a result, stature diminishes by a centimeter or more. The loss of stature is limited to the vertebral column and thus to sitting height (see components of stature). Stature is regained by having the child lie still on a flat surface for about 30 minutes.

Body weight also shows diurnal variation. The individual is lightest in the morning, specifically after voiding the bladder upon arising. Body weight then increases gradually during the course of the day, and is affected by diet and physical activity. In menstruating adolescents, phase of the menstrual cycle also affects diurnal variation in body weight.

Components of Stature

Sitting height, as the name implies, is height while sitting. It is measured as the distance from the sitting surface to the top of the head with the child seated in a standard position (see figure 3.2a). This measurement is valuable when used with stature. Stature minus sitting height provides an estimate of length of the lower extremities (**subischial length,** or **leg length**). By definition, lower extremity length is the distance between the hip joint and the floor with the child standing erect. Precise location of the hip joint landmark is difficult in the living individual. Hence, lower extremity length is most often defined as the difference between stature and sitting height.

In infants and young children, sitting height is measured with the child in the same position as for recumbent length, but the measurement is taken as crown-to-rump length. With the child properly positioned, the legs are raised to a standard position, and the measurement is taken as the distance between the head and the buttocks (see figure 3.2b).

Skeletal Breadths

Breadth or width measurements are ordinarily taken across specific bone landmarks and therefore provide an indication of the robustness, or sturdiness, of the skeleton. Four of the commonly taken skeletal breadths are illustrated in figure 3.3, a through d. **Biacromial breadth** (see figure

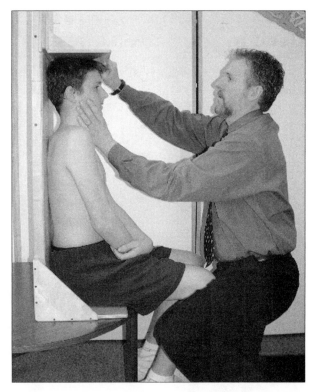

a

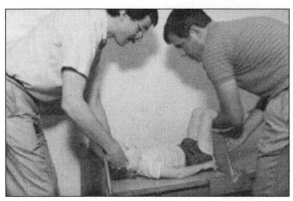

b

FIGURE 3.2 The measurement of sitting height (a) and crown-to-rump length (b).

Reprinted from Lohman et al. (1988).

3.3a) measures the distance across the right and left acromial processes of the scapulae and provides an indication of shoulder breadth. **Bicristal breadth** (see figure 3.3b) measures the distance across the most lateral parts of the iliac crests and provides an indication of hip breadth.

Breadths across the epicondyles of the femur (see figure 3.3c) and the humerus (see figure 3.3d) provide information on the robustness of the extremity skeleton. The former is a measure

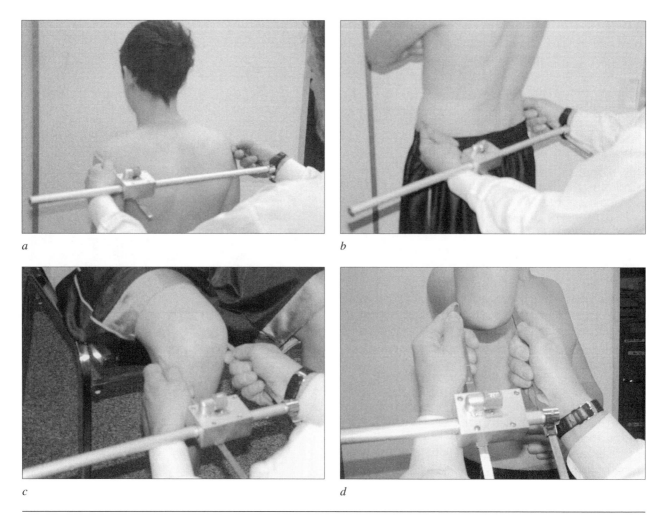

a

b

c

d

FIGURE 3.3   The measurement of skeletal breadths. Biacromial (a), bicristal (b), biepicondylar femur (c), and biepicondylar humerus (d).

of bone breadth across the knee, and the latter is a measure of bone breadth across the elbow. **Biepicondylar breadth** of the femur is often referred to as bicondylar breadth. However, the condyles of the femur and also of the humerus refer to the articular areas of the bones, whereas the epicondyles refer to the lateral and medial projections of the bones above the joint (J.E.L. Carter, personal communication).

Limb Circumferences

Limb circumferences are occasionally used as indicators of relative muscularity. Note, however, that a circumference includes bone surrounded by a mass of muscle tissue that is ringed by a layer of subcutaneous adipose tissue. Thus, a circumference does not provide a measure of muscle tissue per se; however, because muscle is the major tissue composing a circumference (except perhaps in obese individuals), limb circumferences are used to indicate relative muscular development. The two more commonly used limb measurements are the arm and calf circumferences (see figure 3.4). The arm circumference is measured with the arm hanging loosely at the side, and the measurement is taken at the point midway between the acromial process of the scapula and olecranon process of the ulna (tip of the elbow) (see figure 3.4a). The calf circumference is measured as the maximum circumference of the calf, most often with the subject in a standing position and the weight evenly distributed between both legs (see figure 3.4b).

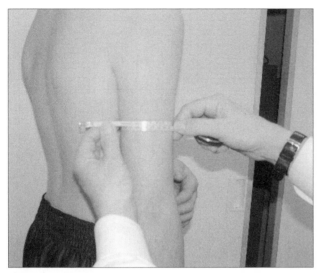
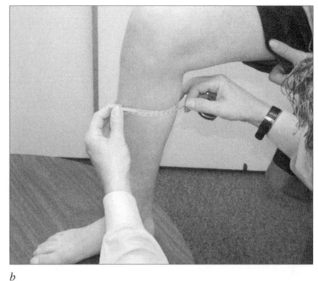

a   *b*

FIGURE 3.4   The measurement of arm (a) and calf (b) circumferences.

Skinfold Thickness

Skinfold thicknesses are indicators of subcutaneous adipose tissue, the portion of body fat located immediately beneath the skin. This thickness, in the form of a double fold of skin and underlying subcutaneous tissue, can be measured with special calipers. The resultant measurement is a skinfold thickness. Skinfolds can be measured at any number of body sites. Most often, they are measured on the extremities and on the trunk to provide information on the relative distribution of subcutaneous fat in different areas of the body. Two of the most commonly used sites in growth studies are the **triceps skinfold** (see figure 3.5a), on the back of the arm over the triceps muscle at the same level as arm circumference, and the **subscapular skinfold** (see figure 3.5b), on the back just beneath the inferior angle of the scapula. Three other skinfolds are often used in growth studies. The **medial calf skinfold** (see figure 3.5c) reflects adipose tissue on the lower extremity and is measured on the inside of the calf at the level of calf circumference. The **suprailiac skinfold** (see figure 3.5d) reflects adipose tissue on the lower part of the trunk and is measured over the iliac crest in the midaxillary line. The **abdominal skinfold** indicates subcutaneous adipose tissue on the abdominal region and is measured as a horizontal fold 3 cm lateral and 1 cm inferior to the umbilicus (see figure 3.5e).

Changes in skinfold thicknesses associated with growth and maturation are considered in more detail in the specific chapter on adipose tissue (see chapter 8).

Head Circumference

Some measurements are useful during particular phases of growth. **Head circumference** is perhaps the most important. It is routinely measured on infants and young children, usually to 3 or 4 years of age. It serves as a monitor of the growth of the brain early in life because the skull is essentially a protective case for the developing brain. Head circumference is measured from the side as the maximum circumference of the head with the tape passing above the eyebrows (supraorbital ridges) and the maximum occipital prominence. Enough pressure must be applied to compress the child's hair; if a child has braided hair, the tape must be positioned so that the braids are excluded.

Overview of Measurements

This brief set of measurements provides information on the size of the child as a whole (weight and stature) and of specific parts and tissues. Skeletal breadths describe the overall robustness of the skeleton, limb circumferences provide information on relative muscularity, and skinfold thicknesses are indicators of subcutaneous adipose

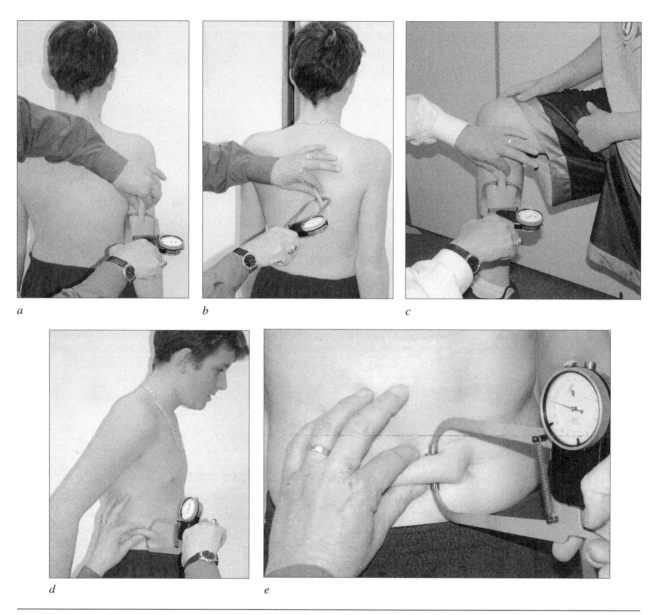

FIGURE 3.5　The measurement of skinfolds. Triceps (a), subscapular (b), medial calf (c), suprailiac (d), and abdominal (e).

tissue. The specific dimensions include both the trunk and the extremities. Individuals may be similar in overall body size and yet can vary in shape, proportions, and tissue distribution. Other dimensions can be measured, but the choice of measurements depends on the information desired in the context of a study.

The measurements described are traditional dimensions utilized in growth studies. Advances in technology now permit more direct measurements of bone, skeletal muscle, and adipose tissues. These measurements are discussed in more detail in the chapters that address growth changes in body composition and in each of these tissues (see chapters 5 through 8).

Quality Control

Implicit in studies using anthropometry is the assumption that every effort is made to ensure the accuracy and reliability of measurement and standardization of technique. Also implicit is the assumption that the measurements are taken by trained individuals. These conditions are essential to obtain accurate and reliable data and to enhance the utility of the data from a comparative perspective. Reliable and accurate data are especially critical in serial studies, in which the same child is followed longitudinally over time, either short-term or long-term, and the definition of rather small changes may be necessary and technical errors associated with measurement can mask true changes.

Error is the discrepancy between the measured value and its true quantity. Measurement error can be random or systematic. **Random measurement error** is a normal aspect of anthropometry and results from variation within and between individuals in technique of measurement, problems with measuring instruments (e.g., calibration or random variation in manufacture), and errors in recording (e.g., transposition of numbers). Random error is nondirectional—it is above or below the true dimension. In large-scale surveys, random errors tend to cancel each other and ordinarily are not a major concern. **Systematic error,** on the other hand, results from the tendency of a technician or a measuring instrument (e.g., an improperly calibrated skinfold caliper or weighing scale) to consistently undermeasure or overmeasure a particular dimension. Such error is directional and introduces bias into the data. In addition, the child under observation may be a source of measurement variability.

Replicate measurements of the same subject are used to estimate variability or error in measurement. Replicate measurements on the same individual are taken independently by the same technician after a period of time has lapsed, or they are taken on the same individual by two different technicians. If the interval between replicate measurements is too long (e.g., about 1 month) growth may be a factor that contributes to the variability within or between technicians. Replicate measurements provide an estimate of imprecision. Replicate measurements by the same individual provide an estimate of within-technician measurement variability, whereas corresponding measurements taken on the same subject by two different individuals provide an estimate of between-technician measurement variability.

The **technical error of measurement** is a widely used measure of replicability (Malina et al. 1973). It is defined as the square root of the squared differences of replicates divided by twice the number of pairs (i.e., the within-subject variance):

$$\sigma_e = \sqrt{\Sigma d^2/2N}$$

The statistic assumes that the distribution of replicate differences is normal and that errors of all pairs can be pooled. It indicates that about two-thirds of the time, the measurement in question should fall within the technical error measurement (see also Mueller and Martorell 1988).

Technical errors are reported in the units of the specific measurement. Within-technician (intraobserver) and between-technician (interobserver) technical errors of measurement for a variety of anthropometric dimensions in national surveys and several more local studies are summarized in Malina (1995).

Although the technical error of measurement provides an indicator of the replicability of a measurement over a short interval of time, it may underestimate the true measurement error. Variation within an individual child is a source of error that may not be captured in replicate measurements. This source of error may be the result of normal variation in physiology (e.g., muscle tension) and other factors specific to the child (e.g., temperament, cooperativeness, and stranger anxiety). This type of error is labeled undependability (Mueller and Martorell 1988), and an important component of undependability is the child factor or the child effect (Lampl et al. 2001).

Accuracy is another component of the measurement process. It refers to how closely measurements taken by one or several technicians approximate the "true" measurement. Accuracy is ordinarily assessed by comparing measurements taken by the technician(s) with those obtained by a well-trained or "criterion" anthropometrist (i.e., the standard of reference). However, well-trained, expert anthropometrists also make errors.

Ratios and Proportions

In addition to providing specific information in their own right, measurements can be related to each other as indices or ratios. Ratios are influenced by the relationship between the two dimensions, and the two dimensions are assumed to change in a linear manner. Ratios may yield spurious results when they are based on different types of dimensions, such as weight and stature or arm circumference and stature, or when the standard deviations of the dimensions differ considerably. Ratios based on weight and height have a long tradition in studies of growth and body build (see chapter 4), in studies of undernutrition (low weight-for-height), and in studies of the risk of overweight and obesity (excess weight-for-height). Sometimes weight is simply expressed relative to height, or either height or weight is adjusted to account for the relationship between the two measurements. The adjustment has taken several forms, for example, weight divided by height squared (the body mass index), height divided by the cube root of weight (the reciprocal ponderal index), and others.

Except for ratios of weight and height, the ratios described subsequently are based on similar measurements (e.g., two lengths or two skeletal breadths). These ratios are ordinarily calculated by dividing the larger measurement into the smaller measurement.

Ratios provide information on shape and proportions. Three ratios commonly used in growth studies are described subsequently, although in theory any two measurements can be related to each other. The use of ratios of anthropometric and various functional or performance parameters to adjust for body size differences among individuals is discussed later in the chapter.

Weight-for-Stature   The ratio of weight-for-stature or weight-for-height simply expresses a child's body weight relative to stature. It is commonly used with preadolescent children. Other things being equal, is the child's weight adequate, too heavy, or too light for the child's stature? This question is most often asked in a nutritional context. Severely undernourished children have low weight-for-stature as the soft tissues that constitute body weight (largely muscle and fat) are wasted. The same occurs in individuals with anorexia nervosa, a severe eating disorder related to a fear of becoming fat. Weight-for-stature is also used in the context of overweight. Youngsters who are overweight have high weight-for-stature; the excess weight is related to fatness. Note, however, that not all children with excess weight-for-stature are fat, because muscle mass and other nonfat tissues may contribute to the increase in weight relative to stature. This increase is related to body composition, which is discussed in detail in chapter 5.

During the adolescent growth spurt, the relationship between stature and weight is temporarily changed. The growth spurt occurs, on the average, first in stature and then in weight, so the relationship between the two measurements is altered. After growth in stature has ceased, however, weight-for-stature is once again a useful index.

At present, the relationship between weight and stature is most often expressed in the form of the **body mass index** (BMI):

$$BMI = weight/stature^2$$

where weight is in kilograms (kg) and stature is in meters (m) squared. The BMI is expressed as kg/m^2. It relates reasonably well to total-body fatness and also to the lean tissue mass of the body. The BMI is widely used at present in surveys to screen for overweight and obesity. Its usefulness stems from the fact that it is independent of stature (i.e., the correlation between the BMI and stature approaches zero). However, the utility of the BMI in infancy and childhood is questionable, and its use with adolescent males has limitations.

Sitting Height/Stature Ratio   In addition to ratios of weight-for-stature, this ratio is the next most widely used ratio in growth studies. It is calculated as:

(sitting height/stature) × 100

The ratio provides an estimate of relative trunk length and, conversely, relative leg length. It basically asks the following question: What percentage of height while standing is accounted for by height while sitting? By subtraction, the remaining percentage is accounted for by the lower extremities. Of two children with the same stature, one can have a sitting height/standing height ratio of 54% and the other can have a ratio of 51%. In the first child, sitting height accounts for 54% of stature, and by subtraction, the lower extremities account for 46%. This child is said to have relatively short legs-for-stature. In contrast, sitting height accounts for 51% of stature in the second child, and by subtraction, the legs account for 49%. The second child has relatively long legs-for-stature compared with the first child.

Shoulder–Hip Relationships   The ratio of bicristal to biacromial breadths is also used in growth studies. It relates the breadth of the hips (lower trunk) to that of the shoulders (upper trunk):

(bicristal breadth/biacromial breadth) × 100

This ratio illustrates proportional changes in shoulder and hip relationships, which become especially apparent during adolescence. Shoulder–hip relationships also vary among young athletes in several sports (e.g., gymnastics and diving). Young athletes in these sports generally have proportionally wider shoulders compared with their hips, and female athletes tend to have proportionally wider shoulders than nonathletes.

Other Ratios   Ratios of skinfold thicknesses measured on the trunk and extremities are often used to estimate relative subcutaneous adipose tissue distribution. The ratio of waist and hip circumferences is also used as an indicator of relative adipose tissue distribution, although muscle and skeletal structures also contribute to the hip girth measurement. Waist circumference by itself is primarily an indicator of adipose tissue in the abdominal area. The waist-to-hip ratio is often used with adults, but it has limited validity as an indicator of relative adipose tissue distribution in children and adolescents. The issue of relative adipose tissue distribution is discussed in detail in chapter 8.

Growth in Stature and Body Weight

Stature and weight are the most commonly used measurements in growth studies. Both dimen-

sions are often routinely measured on a regular basis (e.g., in hospitals, schools, and sports clubs to monitor growth status and progress). Hence, the pattern of growth in these two basic measurements is discussed in some detail.

Growth Status or Size Attained

The course of growth in stature and weight from birth to 18 years of age is shown in figure 3.6, a and b. The curves represent age-specific and sex-specific averages for boys and girls and do not portray the wide range of normal individual variability apparent in any group of children. The pattern of age changes is generally similar in all children, but the size attained at a given age and the timing of the adolescent growth spurt vary considerably from child to child.

From birth to early adulthood, both stature and weight follow a four-phase growth pattern: rapid gain in infancy and early childhood, rather steady gain during middle childhood, rapid gain during the adolescent spurt, and slow increase until growth ceases with the attainment of adult stature. Body weight, however, usually continues to increase into adult life.

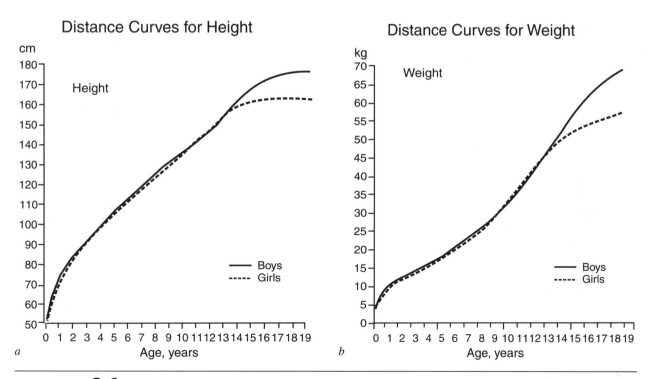

FIGURE 3.6   Distance curves for length/stature (a) and weight (b) of American children from birth to 19 years of age. Lengths are shown from birth to 2 years of age and heights are shown from 2 to 19 years of age.

Data from Kuczmarski et al., 2000.

Both sexes follow the same course of growth. Sex differences before the adolescent spurt are consistent although minor. Boys, on the average, tend to be slightly taller and heavier than girls. During the early part of the adolescent spurt, girls are temporarily taller and heavier because of their earlier growth spurt. Girls soon lose the size advantage as the adolescent spurt of boys occurs; boys catch up with and eventually surpass girls in body size, on the average. Given the normal range of individual variation, overlap exists between the sexes throughout growth and in young adulthood. Hence, some girls are taller and heavier than most boys at virtually all ages.

The type of growth curve illustrated in figure 3.6, a and b is a **distance curve.** It indicates the size attained by children at a given age, or the distance the children have traversed on the path to adult stature. Such curves are indicators of growth status. The curves presented are smooth because they are average curves representing the average statures and weights of a large number of children at each age level. The curves thus absorb the range of variation inherent in specific age groups; in other words, they absorb the individual growth pattern of each child.

Reference Data and Growth Charts

Distance or size-attained curves are commonly used for assessing the growth status of a single child or a sample of children. In making such assessments, the size attained by a child or the average size of a group of children is compared and evaluated relative to growth data derived from a large sample of healthy children free from overt disease. These data are referred to as **reference data.** They are the points of reference in assessing the growth status of a child or a group of children. The World Health Organization (1995, p. 29) defines a reference ". . . as a tool for grouping and analyzing data and provides a common basis for comparing populations." Reference values are not standards. A standard is prescriptive and suggests the way things ought to be, and as such it has an associated value judgment. Standards for the growth of children do not exist. Reference values are used.

Reference data are most often presented in the form of several curves representing different percentiles to accommodate the range of normal variability among children of the same age. A percentile is a specific point in a distribution that has a given percentage of cases above and below it. When the measurements are normally distributed, the median, or 50th percentile, approximates the average; 50% of the children in a sample are above this point and 50% are below it. If a boy has a stature that is at the 5th percentile, this means that only 5% of the boys in his age group are shorter than he is, or conversely, 95% of the boys in his age group are taller than he is. A girl with a stature at the 90th percentile for her age group is taller than 90% of the girls.

Percentiles of reference data are smooth and the ranges are quite broad. Growth charts used in the United States include the 5th, 10th, 25th, 50th, 75th, 90th, and 95th percentiles, although some include the 3rd, 5th, 10th, 25th, 50th, 75th, 90th, 95th, and 97th percentiles.

How are growth charts and the percentiles derived? First, cross-sectional data for large, representative samples of children from infancy to young adulthood are essential. Adequate numbers of boys and girls must be represented at each age level. Large numbers are needed so that the extreme percentiles (i.e., the 5th and 95th or the 3rd and 97th) can be obtained empirically rather than estimated. In small samples, the extreme percentiles are estimated and may not reflect the variation in the sample. Samples of 300 to 350 are needed at each age to derive the 5th and 95th percentiles, whereas samples of 500 are needed at each age to empirically derive the 3rd and 97th percentiles (Roche et al. 1996). A sample of 200 subjects of each sex at each age level is suggested by the World Health Organization (1995). An additional factor in countries where the population is ethnically diverse, such as the United States, is that the ethnic minorities are proportionally represented in the sample across the age range.

The growth charts for United States children are based on national surveys that have been regularly conducted since the 1960s (see table 3.1). The surveys are based on complex, multistage, stratified sampling procedures that result in the selection of a sample that is representative of the noninstitutionalized civilian population of the United States. NHES II and III (1963-1970), NHANES I (1971-1974), and NHANES II (1976-1980) included adequate numbers of children and adolescents of Black (African American) and White (European American) ancestry. NHANES III (1988 1994) oversampled African Americans and Mexican Americans compared with their numbers in the total population of the United States in 1990. Since 1999, NHANES has become a continuous survey; the first 2 years of NHANES data collection (1999-2000) have been

TABLE 3.1 Summary of National Surveys of the United States Population

National Health Examination Survey (NHES)

NHES I (1959–1962)	Adults 18 through 79 yr
NHES II (1963–1965)	Children 6 through 11 yr
NHES III (1966–1970)	Adolescents 12 through 17 yr

National Health and Nutrition Examination Survey (NHANES)

NHANES I (1971–1974)	Individuals 1 through 74 yr
NHANES II (1976–1980)	Individuals 6 mo through 74 yr
NHANES III (1988–1994)	Individuals 2 mo of age and older
NHANES (1999–2000)	Individuals birth through 74 yr

Hispanic Health and Nutrition Examination Survey (HHANES)

1982–1984	Hispanics 6 mo through 74 yr

See Kuczmarski and Johnson (1991) for details of the specific surveys, except NHANES (1999–2000). Since 1999, NHANES has become a continuous survey without a break between surveys. Data for the first 2 years (1999–2000) have been recently reported (Flegal et al. 2002; Ogden et al. 2002). Weight and stature were measured in an identical manner in each survey. The battery of other anthropometric dimensions varies among surveys.

used to evaluate changes in overweight among American children and adolescents (Ogden et al. 2002) and adults (Flegal et al. 2002).

In constructing growth charts for American children, data from the different ethnic groups were combined for two reasons. First, the differences in stature among Blacks, Whites, and Mexican Americans are rather small, and second, the sample sizes for each ethnic group are not satisfactory to meet the statistical requirements for empirically deriving the percentiles at the extremes of the distributions (Roche et al. 1996). In addition, whether the apparent growth differences among the three ethnic groups are genetic is not clear. Given the ethnic heterogeneity of the American population, ethnic-specific growth charts are not warranted. Ethnic variation in growth is discussed in more detail in chapter 25.

Methods for deriving and smoothing percentiles in the preparation of growth charts vary, and opinions differ as to which method is the best. Nevertheless, the procedure used to derive and smooth the percentiles should be simple and reproducible. It should be flexible so that one area of the curve does not determine other areas. For example, the curve representing early childhood should not determine the curve representing adolescence. The procedure should

also be robust, particularly for deriving the extreme or outlying percentiles. Major advances have occurred in the development of statistical techniques for smoothing data. If the data are not statistically smooth, the percentile lines tend to be uneven.

Reference data in the form of growth charts for weight and length/stature of American children are given in figures 3.7 through 3.10. The data are derived from national surveys conducted between 1963 and 1994, with the exception of length at birth. The data for length at birth are from surveys in two states (Roche 1999a; Kuczmarski et al. 2000).

The charts indicate the value of height or weight on the Y-axis by chronological age on the X-axis. Recumbent length is measured in children between birth and 2 or 3 years of age. Hence, two sets of reference data exist for each sex, one set for children under 3 years of age and the other set for children 2 through 20 years of age. When studying the charts, note that the absolute range of variation at birth is relatively narrow compared with that evident later on. After birth, individual variation in growth is gradually expressed, so the absolute range between the 5th and 95th percentiles gets progressively larger with age. Further, the range of variation in body weight is greater than that for stature. The skewed distribution of body weights is such that a wider range of variation occurs above the median than below the median beginning at about 4 years of age.

Reference data in the form of growth charts are simply a reference of comparison or for screening individuals or groups. They are derived from a representative sample of clinically normal children and adolescents free from overt disease at the time they were measured. The values indicated on the charts are not necessarily ideal, normal, desirable, optimal, or the standard. Reference data indicate the statures of children at different ages as they currently are rather than what they should be. In use, however, the percentiles are generally accepted as indicating the normal range of variation. They are often used to identify individuals or samples as "abnormal" if their height falls outside of a predetermined cutoff value, usually the 5th or 3rd percentile.

The situation for body weight is somewhat different, as indicated by the current concern for

CDC Growth Charts: United States

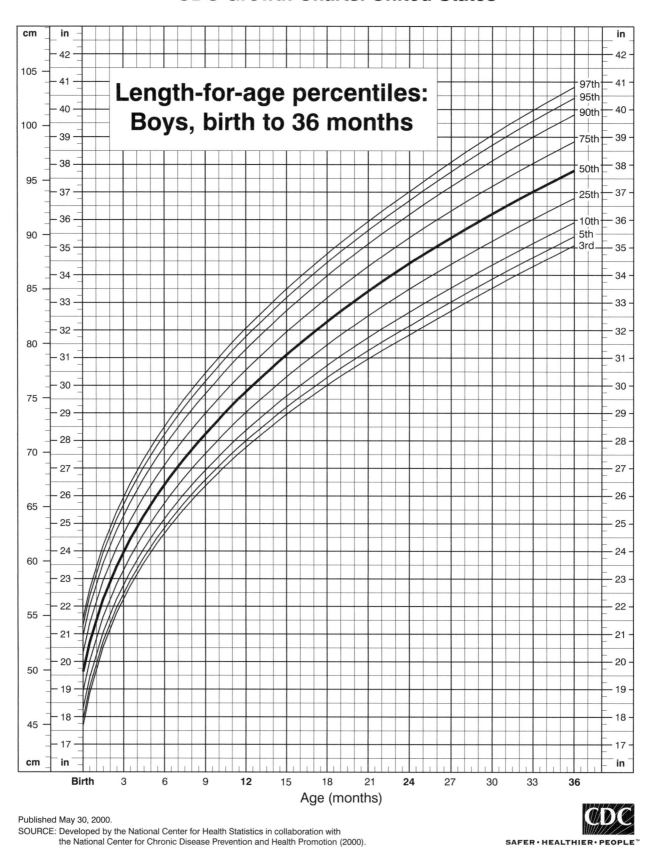

Length-for-age percentiles: Boys, birth to 36 months

Age (months)

Published May 30, 2000.
SOURCE: Developed by the National Center for Health Statistics in collaboration with
the National Center for Chronic Disease Prevention and Health Promotion (2000).

SAFER · HEALTHIER · PEOPLE™

FIGURE 3.7a Length-for-age percentiles for American boys from birth to 3 years of age. Centers for Disease Control Growth Charts (Centers for Disease Control and Prevention 2000).

Available: http://www.cdc.gov/growthcharts.htm.

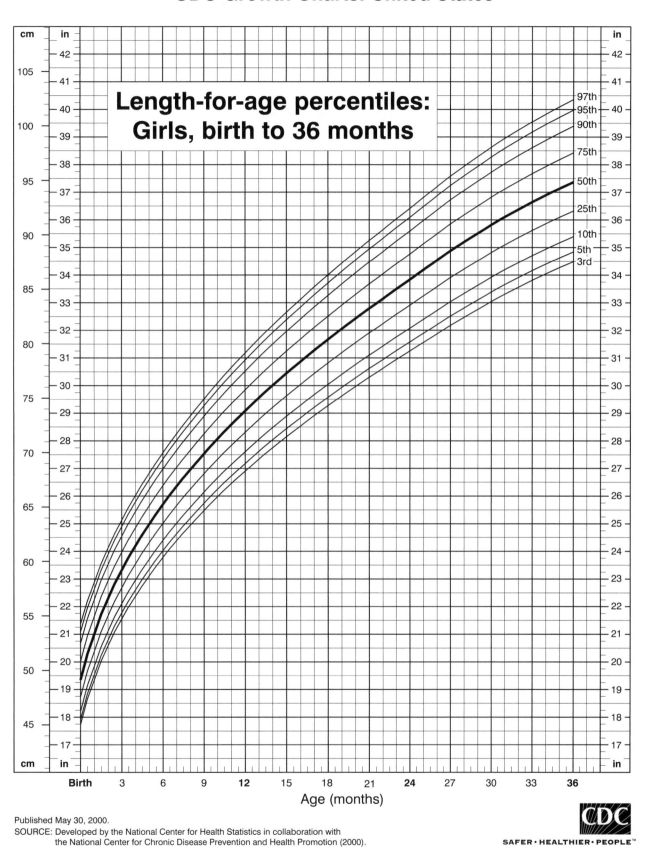

Length-for-age percentiles:
Girls, birth to 36 months

Published May 30, 2000.
SOURCE: Developed by the National Center for Health Statistics in collaboration with
    the National Center for Chronic Disease Prevention and Health Promotion (2000).

FIGURE **3.7b**   Length-for-age percentiles for American girls from birth to 3 years of age. Centers for Disease Control Growth Charts (Centers for Disease Control and Prevention 2000).

Available: http://www.cdc.gov/growthcharts.htm.

CDC Growth Charts: United States

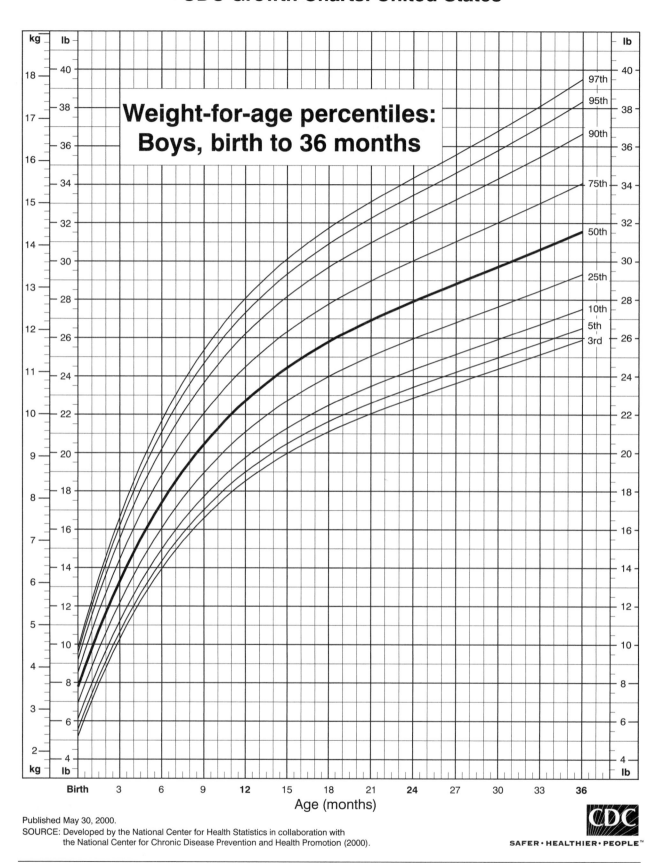

Weight-for-age percentiles:
Boys, birth to 36 months

Age (months)

Published May 30, 2000.
SOURCE: Developed by the National Center for Health Statistics in collaboration with
the National Center for Chronic Disease Prevention and Health Promotion (2000).

CDC
SAFER·HEALTHIER·PEOPLE™

FIGURE 3.8a Weight-for-age percentiles for American boys from birth to 3 years of age. Centers for Disease Control Growth Charts (Centers for Disease Control and Prevention 2000).

Available: http://www.cdc.gov/growthcharts.htm.

CDC Growth Charts: United States

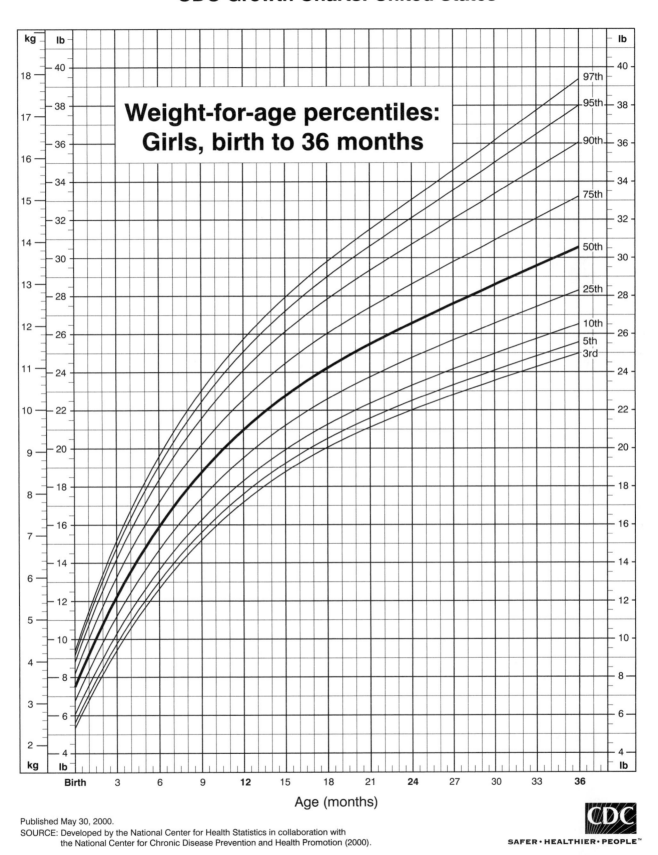

**Weight-for-age percentiles:
Girls, birth to 36 months**

Age (months)

Published May 30, 2000.
SOURCE: Developed by the National Center for Health Statistics in collaboration with
the National Center for Chronic Disease Prevention and Health Promotion (2000).

FIGURE 3.8b Weight-for-age percentiles for American girls from birth to 3 years of age. Centers for Disease Control Growth Charts (Centers for Disease Control and Prevention 2000).

Available: http://www.cdc.gov/growthcharts.htm.

CDC Growth Charts: United States

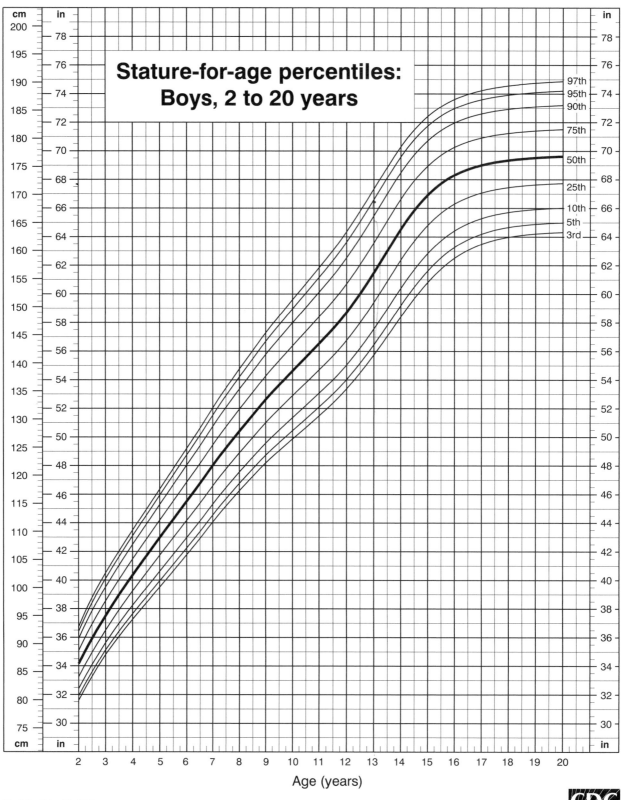

Stature-for-age percentiles:
Boys, 2 to 20 years

Published May 30, 2000.
SOURCE: Developed by the National Center for Health Statistics in collaboration with
the National Center for Chronic Disease Prevention and Health Promotion (2000).

F I G U R E 3.9a Height-for-age percentiles for American boys from 2 to 20 years of age. Centers for Disease Control Growth Charts (Centers for Disease Control and Prevention 2000).

Available: http://www.cdc.gov/growthcharts.htm.

CDC Growth Charts: United States

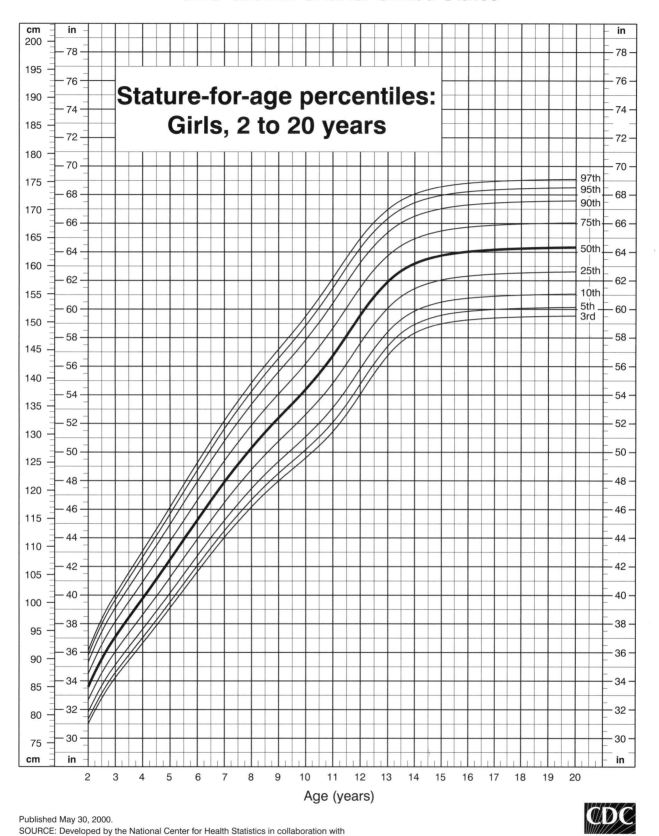

Stature-for-age percentiles: Girls, 2 to 20 years

Published May 30, 2000.
SOURCE: Developed by the National Center for Health Statistics in collaboration with
the National Center for Chronic Disease Prevention and Health Promotion (2000).

SAFER·HEALTHIER·PEOPLE™

FIGURE 3.9b Height-for-age percentiles for American girls from 2 to 20 years of age. Centers for Disease Control Growth Charts (Centers for Disease Control and Prevention 2000).

Available: http://www.cdc.gov/growthcharts.htm.

CDC Growth Charts: United States

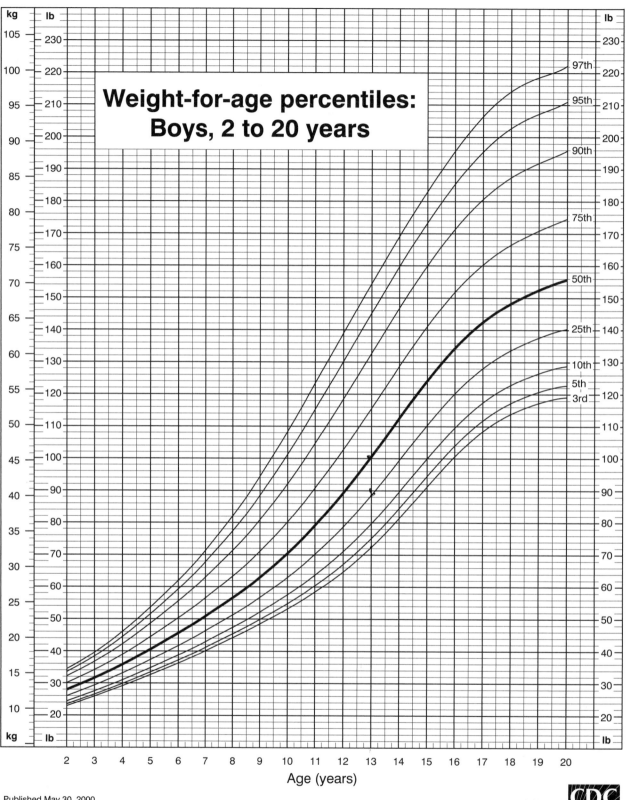

Weight-for-age percentiles: Boys, 2 to 20 years

Age (years)

Published May 30, 2000.
SOURCE: Developed by the National Center for Health Statistics in collaboration with the National Center for Chronic Disease Prevention and Health Promotion (2000).

CDC

SAFER · HEALTHIER · PEOPLE™

FIGURE 3.10a Weight-for-age percentiles for American boys from 2 to 20 years of age. Centers for Disease Control Growth Charts (Centers for Disease Control and Prevention 2000).

Available: http://www.cdc.gov/growthcharts.htm.

CDC Growth Charts: United States

Weight-for-age percentiles:
Girls, 2 to 20 years

97th
95th
90th
75th
50th
25th
10th
5th
3rd

Age (years)

Published May 30, 2000.
SOURCE: Developed by the National Center for Health Statistics in collaboration with
the National Center for Chronic Disease Prevention and Health Promotion (2000).

CDC
SAFER · HEALTHIER · PEOPLE™

FIGURE 3.10b Weight-for-age percentiles for American girls from 2 to 20 years of age. Centers for Disease Control Growth Charts (Centers for Disease Control and Prevention 2000).

Available: http://www.cdc.gov/growthcharts.htm.

the increasing prevalence of obesity in American youth, specifically in the interval between NHANES II (1976-1980) and NHANES III (1988-1994). Body weight of children and youth increased significantly from NHANES II to NHANES III, whereas height did not change significantly. As a result, body weights of children 6 years of age and older in NHANES III were not used in the derivation of the new growth charts shown in figures 3.8 and 3.10. The data were omitted because the gain in body weight from NHANES II to NHANES III was not viewed as desirable from a public health perspective (Roche 1999a; Kuczmarski et al. 2000). Excess weight tends to track from childhood into adulthood (i.e., individuals overweight as children and adolescents are more likely to be overweight when they are adults), and excess weight in adulthood has major public health implications for several diseases, especially heart disease and diabetes. In developing the new growth charts for body weight, therefore, public health authorities decided not to use the values from NHANES III. Developing percentiles for body weight using the elevated values from NHANES III would have raised the percentiles, thus giving a false sense of having satisfactory weight, specifically relative to stature. If the upper percentiles were higher (e.g., the 85th percentile), fewer individuals would have been classified as overweight, and the norm would be closer to overweight. Thus, for body weight, the charts are to some extent criterion-referenced in that public health authorities have decided on levels of weight or weight-for-stature that are presumably conducive to better health.

Use of Growth Charts

Percentiles are useful in evaluating the growth status of individual children. A girl whose stature is at the 50th percentile for her age but whose weight is at the 75th percentile has excessive weight for her stature. She is probably a stocky youngster. A boy whose stature and weight are at the 10th percentile for his age group is proportionately small. The percentile status of this boy does not indicate, however, if he is genetically small or if he has a problem in growth. This requires further clinical examination.

Percentiles are also useful for evaluating the growth status of a sample of children. For example, how might the average height and weight of a sample of 8-year-old boys from one area of the country compare with the national reference values? Where do the heights and weights of elite, young female gymnasts fall on the national growth charts? Such comparisons provide only a guide for the sample compared. Values for individual children are not considered and may range across several percentiles.

If a child is followed over time, the child's position on the growth charts can be noted. During the first 2 or 3 years of life, children tend to change positions on the growth charts (Buschang et al. 1985; Roche and Li 1998). Their heights and weights may cross several percentiles. Crossing percentiles of height and weight is common in infancy and early childhood. It reflects individual differences as each child moves to genetically determined growth percentiles. Some children who are born small may be genetically programmed to be tall, whereas others who are born large may be genetically programmed to be short.

After about 3 years of age, children tend to maintain their position on growth charts during childhood as growth becomes canalized (i.e., their heights and weights tend to remain at specific percentile positions). If a child shows a major shift in position on the charts, the shift may signal a need for clinical examination. For example, weight may continue to maintain its relative position on the chart, but growth in height might slow down. The converse is more common. Height continues to maintain its position, whereas body weight increases more than expected, suggesting the development of excess weight-for-height, which may lead to overweight or obesity.

In contrast, a child's position on growth charts often changes during adolescence because of individual differences in the timing and tempo of the growth spurt and of sexual maturation. Thus, a child may change position on growth charts at this time. A girl or boy who is advanced in maturity and enters puberty early is likely to move upward on the percentiles at this time. On the other hand, a girl or boy who is later maturing is likely to move down on the percentiles until puberty. Growth charts need to be used with care during adolescence. They do not incorporate individual differences in the timing and tempo of the growth spurt and sexual maturation. Growth charts that adjust for differential timing of the adolescent spurt have been suggested for North American (Tanner and Davies 1985) and Irish (Hoey et al. 1987) youth. They are called "tempo conditional" growth charts.

Growth Progress or Rate

The growth curve for rate or velocity of growth (cm/year or kg/year) has a different form than that for size attained in stature and weight. Growth rates are presented as a **velocity curve**. Longitudinal data are necessary to derive a velocity curve. The typical curves for stature and weight are shown in figures 3.11 and 3.12, respectively. Rates of growth differ for stature and weight during infancy and childhood. Growth in stature occurs at a constantly decelerating rate at this time. The child is getting taller but at a progressively slower rate. The rate reaches its lowest point just before the initiation of the adolescent spurt, the point at which the velocity curve begins to accelerate. Weight growth, on the other hand, occurs at a slightly but constantly accelerating rate, after a deceleration in infancy and the second year.

During the adolescent spurt, the rates of growth in both stature and weight increase or accelerate. The spurt occurs earlier in girls than

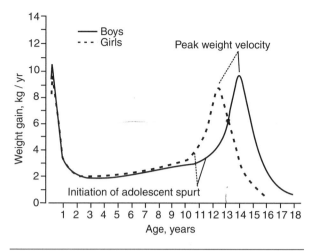

FIGURE 3.12 Typical individual velocity curves for body weight in boys and girls.

Reprinted, by permission, Tanner, Whitehouse and Takaishi, 1966, "Standards from birth to maturity for height, weight, height velocity, and weight velocity: British children, 1961-I," *Archives of Disease in Childhood* 41:454-471.

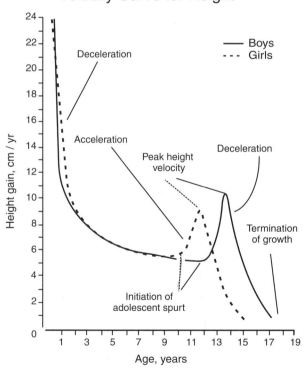

FIGURE 3.11 Typical individual velocity curves for length or stature in boys and girls.

Reprinted, by permission, Tanner, Whitehouse and Takaishi, 1966, "Standards from birth to maturity for height, weight, height velocity, and weight velocity: British children, 1961-I," *Archives of Disease in Childhood* 41:454-471.

in boys by about 2 years, on the average. Girls stop growing in stature by about 16 years of age, on the average, whereas boys continue to grow for another 2 or 3 years.

Careful examination of the typical velocity curve for stature provides an insight into explaining sex differences in adult stature. The sex difference in young adult stature is about 13 cm (see figure 3.6). How does this difference come about when the sex differences in length at birth and in stature and rate of growth during the preadolescent years are negligible? The sex difference in the magnitude of the adolescent spurt in stature is only about 2 cm. The sex difference in adult stature is caused primarily by the fact that boys, on the average, experience about 2 years more of preadolescent growth than girls. Carefully examine figure 3.11. Whereas girls are experiencing the adolescent spurt (the sharp acceleration in the velocity curve), boys are still gaining at a preadolescent rate of about 5 cm/year. Given the sex difference of about 2 years in the timing of the spurt, on average, this represents 10 cm of growth that girls do not experience. The adolescent spurt of boys then follows and is only slightly greater than that of girls. Thus, the longer period of preadolescent growth and a slightly greater spurt in boys account for the sex difference in adult stature.

Longitudinal data permit estimates of when the adolescent spurt begins and when maximum growth occurs during the spurt. The maximum rate of growth in stature during the spurt is called peak height velocity (PHV), and the age at maximum velocity of growth is called the age at PHV (see figure 3.11). The rate of growth and age at PHV provide an indication of the intensity and timing of the adolescent growth spurt, respectively. Age at PHV is an individual characteristic and is commonly used as a maturity indicator at this time. Methods of estimating the age at PHV and the relationship of the age at PHV to other maturity indicators are discussed in detail in chapters 15 and 16, which deal with biological maturation.

Midgrowth Spurt   In addition to the well-defined adolescent spurt, children may show a small growth spurt in stature and weight (an increase in velocity of growth) several years before the onset of the adolescent growth spurt. This spurt during childhood, usually between 6.5 and 8.5 years of age, is called the midgrowth spurt. Midgrowth spurts have also been identified for other body dimensions but with considerable variability in intensity of the spurts among dimensions. A sex difference in the timing of maximum velocity of the midgrowth spurt is not apparent, but the spurt occurs more frequently in boys than in girls (Tanner and Cameron 1980; Gasser et al. 1985; Sheehy et al. 1999). Note that not all children show a midgrowth spurt. This finding reflects real biological variation among individuals, but variation in the frequency of measurements in childhood is an additional factor. Children are usually measured annually during childhood, and such an interval may not be sufficiently sensitive to detect the change in velocity of growth that defines the spurt. Methods of estimating growth velocities also vary in their sensitivity to detect the midgrowth spurt.

Episodic Growth   Daily measurements of infants indicate that growth in recumbent length is episodic rather than continuous. Such short-term variation in growth rate has been labeled as pulsatile, a minigrowth spurt, and saltatory. Based on measurements made daily at the same time of day and with attention to quality control in the measurement process, considerable variation exists in growth velocity in recumbent length and standing height and in the lengths of individual bones over very short periods of time (days or weeks). During the first 2 years of life,

for example, growth in the length of infants apparently proceeds in a "saltatory" manner, with a series of stepwise increases or jumps (saltations) separated by variable periods of no growth (stasis). When weekly measurements are used in the analysis, periods of stasis during infancy vary in length from 7 to 63 days (Lampl et al. 1992). This phenomenon has also been described for a single adolescent boy. Between 12.8 and 13.9 years of age, only 12 days out of the 389 days of observation showed significant increments in stature ("saltatory episodes"). The episodes did not occur in a periodic manner; rather, the intervals between episodes were separated by 3 to 100 days of no growth. The average magnitude of a saltatory episode was 0.92 cm, and the total gain during the 389 days of observation was 11.0 cm (Lampl and Johnson 1993).

Several issues are related to the identification and interpretation of episodic or saltatory growth that need clarification. These issues include measurement error, diurnal and seasonal variation, and variation in and limitations of the mathematical models used to fit the data. Allowing for these limitations, the evidence indicates that growth in length or height is not a steady, continuous process. Growth consists of a series of intermittent episodes. These episodes probably occur in the different long bones that determine length or stature and at different times.

Percentiles for Growth Rate

Rates of growth vary considerably among children and with the season of the year. Children typically gain more in stature during the spring and summer than during the fall and winter. Growth rates are also not linear during childhood and adolescence, so interpretation may be difficult. Nevertheless, evaluation of growth rates or increments between adjacent ages over short time intervals are of interest in studies of children undergoing clinical treatment for a medical condition or undergoing intensive training in sport. Such studies based on intervals of 6 to 12 months are often labeled short-term studies, and increments calculated over the short intervals can provide an estimate of growth rate. Several percentiles (3rd, 5th, 10th, 25th, 50th, 75th, 90th, 95th, and 97th) for 6-monthly increments in stature and weight are available for American children from the Fels Longitudinal Study (Baumgartner et al. 1986). Corresponding percentiles (except the 5th and 95th) for annual velocities for stature and weight are available for Swiss children from the

Zurich Longitudinal Study (Prader et al. 1989). Reference values for height velocity are also available for a large sample of Black and White youth 7 to 18 years of age from six cities in the United States (Berkey et al. 1993) and for Belgian (Hauspie and Wachholder 1986), Polish (Chrza-stek-Spruch et al. 1989), and Japanese (Suwa et al. 1992) youth. The smoothed curves of height velocity for American youth include the 3rd, 50th, and 97th percentiles for girls having peak velocity at 9, 11, and 13 years and for boys having peak velocity at 11, 13, and 15 years. The three groups approximate early, average ("on time"), and late maturity during adolescence. Maturity-associated variation in growth during adolescence is discussed in more detail in chapter 17. Charts of size attained and velocity of growth, which include adjustments for individual differences in the timing and tempo of the adolescent spurt, are called tempo conditional.

Because the rate of growth in infancy is very rapid (see figure 3.11), reference values for growth increments over shorter intervals have been developed. Reference values for 1-month increments in length, weight, and head circumference of American and Canadian children during the first 2 years of life are available (Guo et al. 1988, 1991; Roche et al. 1989a, 1989b).

Short-term estimates of growth rate have limitations. Two measurements are needed to estimate growth increments, which causes concern for measurement variability. If possible, the same individual should make the measurements on each occasion. Such consistent use of personnel may not always be practical; therefore, measurement techniques must be consistent (Roche 1999a, 1999b). In addition, distributions of increments calculated over short intervals tend to be skewed, and short-term and long-term growth velocities are poorly correlated, so prediction of long-term growth from short-term observations is not warranted. The use and interpretation of increments over short intervals or between adjacent ages must be done with care.

Attainment of Adult Stature

The distance and velocity curves shown, respectively, in figures 3.6 and 3.11 suggest that growth in stature stops at about 16 years of age in girls and about 18 years in boys. These limits are in part a function of the criteria used to define adult stature and of the fact that most growth studies stop when children are 17 or 18 years of age, which in turn is related to schooling. Most youngsters complete high school at these ages and are no longer readily available for study as they enter college or different vocational pursuits. Yet, a good number of individuals continue to grow in stature through the college years and even into the mid-20s.

Percentiles for ages of attaining adult stature as defined by two criteria are summarized in table 3.2. The data are derived from the Fels Longitudinal Study. Median ages of attaining adult stature vary between the criteria, and the sex difference in median age of attaining adult stature also varies with the criteria. It is 2 years if the criterion is an annual increment of less than 1.0 cm, but it is only 1 year if the criterion is four successive 6-monthly increments of less than 0.5 cm. Further, median ages of attaining adult stature are later by 3 years in females and 2 years in males when the criterion of four successive 6-monthly increments of less than 0.5 cm is used. Note, however, that depending on the criterion, some girls may attain adult stature as early as about 14 years of age, whereas some children, boys more so than girls, do not attain adult stature until the early 20s.

In the series from the Fels Longitudinal Study, some individuals had their statures measured into the late 20s. Growth in stature continued for a longer time after PHV in boys (about 8 years on the average) than in girls (about 6 years on the average). Although changes were rather small, growth in stature continued for about 10 years after PHV in about 10% of the girls and boys. These observations based on longitudinal observations made into the late 20s emphasize

	Males (n = 101)			**Females (n = 91)**		
Criterion	**10th**	**50th**	**90th**	**10th**	**50th**	**90th**
Annual increment < 1.0 cm	16.5	17.5	19.0	14.3	15.5	17.0
Four successive 6 mo increments < 0.5 cm	18.3	19.5	20.0	16.0	18.5	20.0

TABLE 3.2 Percentiles for Ages at Attaining Adult Stature Defined by Two Criteria

Adapted from Roche and Davila (1972).

the need to extend growth studies into the third decade of life. A significant percentage of individuals, males more so than females, continue to grow in stature beyond 18 years of age, the age at which most growth studies cease.

Growth of the Body Mass Index

Changes in the BMI from infancy through adolescence are shown in figure 3.13 for a sample of French children followed longitudinally from birth to young adulthood. Whereas body weight increases linearly with age during childhood (see figure 3.6), the BMI declines from infancy through early childhood. It reaches its lowest point at about 5 to 6 years of age and then increases linearly with age through childhood and adolescence, into adulthood. Sex differences in the BMI are small during childhood, increase during adolescence, and persist into adulthood. Maximum rate of increase in the BMI corresponds to the adolescent growth spurt.

The rise in the BMI after it reaches a nadir at 5 to 6 years of age has been labeled the "adiposity rebound" (Rolland-Cachera et al. 1984). The authors suggest that children who have an early adiposity rebound have an increased probability of being overweight in late adolescence and young adulthood. This hypothesis is discussed later in the chapter in the context of tracking of the BMI.

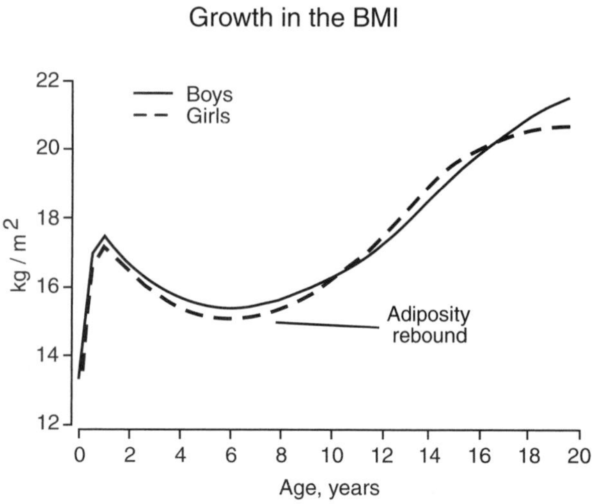

Growth in the BMI

FIGURE 3.13   Distance curves for the body mass index (BMI) in French children from birth to 21 years of age.

Data from R. Cachera et al., 1991.

The BMI is routinely used to monitor the progress of individual children in a manner similar to the use of growth charts. The new growth charts for American children and adolescents include BMI-for-age percentiles for boys and girls from 2 to 20 years of age (Centers for Disease Control and Prevention 2000). These charts are shown in figure 3.14.

The interpretation of the BMI in children, adolescents, and young adults as an indicator of fatness needs care. An elevated BMI is not necessarily indicative of excess fatness. The BMI is reasonably well correlated with total body fat and percentage body fat in heterogeneous samples but has limitations (Goran et al. 1995). For example, age-specific correlations between the BMI and components of body composition among girls 8 to 18 years of age in the Fels Longitudinal Study range from 0.37 to 0.78 for percent body fat, 0.67 to 0.90 for total-body fat, and 0.39 to 0.72 for fat-free mass. Corresponding ranges among boys are 0.64 to 0.85 for percent body fat, 0.83 to 0.94 for total-body fat, and 0.25 to 0.78 for fat-free mass (Maynard et al. 2001). Considerable overlap occurs in the correlations, so the BMI accounts for variable but significant percentages of the variance in the components of body composition. Moreover, at many ages, correlations between the BMI and fat mass and fat-free mass, respectively, are quite similar.

When chronological age is statistically controlled in heterogeneous samples of boys and girls 8 to 18 years of age, correlations are somewhat lower (see table 3.3). Partial correlations between the BMI and percent fat range from 0.28 to 0.61, between the BMI and total-body fat range from 0.46 to 0.81, and between the BMI and fat-free mass range from 0.27 to 0.64. Note that the correlations between the BMI and fat mass and fat-free mass are quite similar in four of the five samples. Correlations between the BMI and percent fat are more variable. In a more recent sample of children and adolescents 5 to 19 years of age, the BMI is highly correlated (>0.90) with percent fat and total-body fat estimated with dual-energy X-ray absorptiometry (DEXA, see chapter 5), but age is a significant covariate in the regression model (Pietrobelli et al. 1998).

The associations between the BMI and components of body composition in several samples of children and adolescents indicate a wide range of variability. Children with the same BMI will likely differ considerably in percent fat and total-body fat, which limits the use of the BMI as an indicator of fatness in individual children

CDC Growth Charts: United States

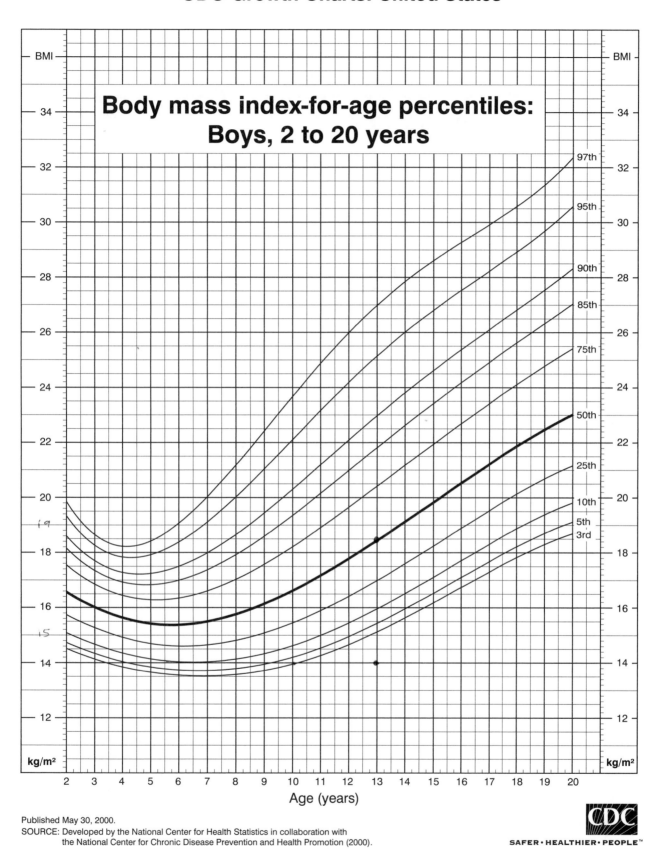

Body mass index-for-age percentiles: Boys, 2 to 20 years

BMI

kg/m²

Age (years)

97th
95th
90th
85th
75th
50th
25th
10th
5th
3rd

Published May 30, 2000.
SOURCE: Developed by the National Center for Health Statistics in collaboration with the National Center for Chronic Disease Prevention and Health Promotion (2000).

SAFER · HEALTHIER · PEOPLE™

FIGURE 3.14a BMI-for-age percentiles for American boys from 2 to 20 years of age. Centers for Disease Control Growth Charts.

Available: http://www.cdc.gov/growthcharts.htm.

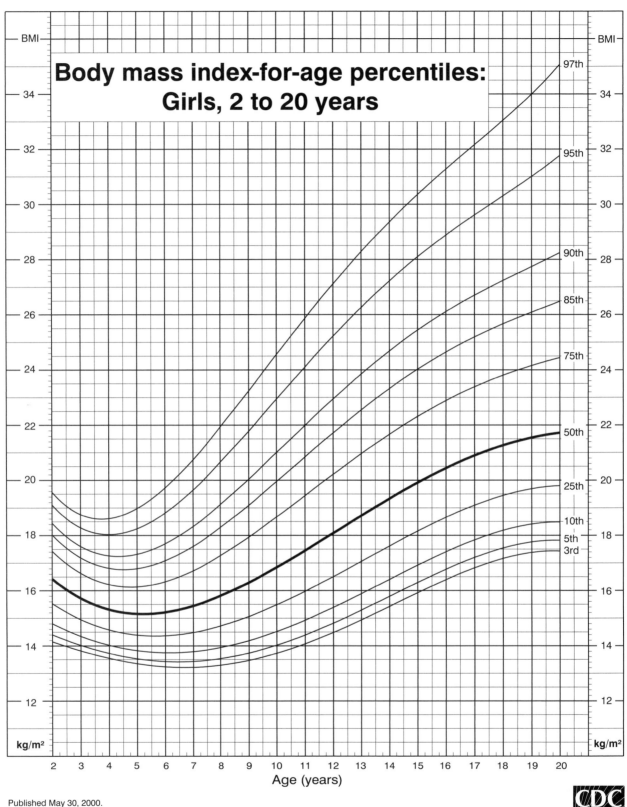

Body mass index-for-age percentiles:
Girls, 2 to 20 years

Published May 30, 2000.
SOURCE: Developed by the National Center for Health Statistics in collaboration with
the National Center for Chronic Disease Prevention and Health Promotion (2000).

SAFER · HEALTHIER · PEOPLE™

FIGURE 3.14b BMI-for-age percentiles for American girls from 2 to 20 years of age. Centers for Disease Control Growth Charts.

Available: http://www.cdc.gov/growthcharts.htm.

TABLE 3.3 Partial Correlations Between the BMI and Estimates of Body Composition in Four Samples of Children and Adolescents

Samples	Age	Correlations		
		Fat mass	Fat-free mass	Percent fat
French Canadian White	8–18 yr			
Males		0.58	0.64	0.37
Females		0.81	0.61	0.61
Mexican American	9–14 yr			
Males		0.75	0.62	0.58
American White	9–17 yr			
Females		0.46	0.53	0.28
European White	10–15 yr			
Males		0.56	0.27	0.49

The partial correlations, controlled for age, were calculated from data for the first phase of the Quebec Family Study (Bouchard, unpublished data), Mexican American boys in Austin, Texas (Zavaleta and Malina 1982), American White girls from upstate New York (Young et al. 1968), and European White boys from Vienna, Austria (Haschke 1983). See Malina and Katzmarzyk (1999) for the derivation of fat mass, fat-free mass, and percent fat.

and adolescents. The BMI is probably more of an indicator of heaviness and indirectly of body fat. Results of several correlational studies suggest that the interpretation of the BMI in children and adolescents calls for consideration of both the fat and the lean components of body composition. Nevertheless, at the extremes of heaviness, the BMI is probably a reasonable indicator of fatness in the general population.

Growth Patterns in Other Body Dimensions

Most body dimensions, with the exception of subcutaneous adipose tissue and dimensions of the head and face, follow the same general pattern of growth in size attained and rate of growth as do stature and weight. Growth is rather rapid in infancy and early childhood, slows down somewhat to a rather steady pace during middle childhood, increases sharply during the adolescent spurt, and slows down and eventually terminates as adult dimensions are attained. Many of the dimensions probably increase in size into the early or mid-20s. However, the specific body dimensions differ in the magnitude and timing of their respective adolescent growth spurts. The same procedures for estimating velocity of growth in stature and weight can be applied to other body dimensions. Peak velocities and ages at peak velocities for specific dimensions can be estimated. They are discussed in more detail in

chapter 16. In addition to the adolescent spurt, some children also show a midgrowth spurt in specific length, breadth, and circumference measurements.

In general, sex differences in the size of most dimensions are small in preadolescent children. In early adolescence, girls generally have a temporary size advantage in many dimensions because of their earlier growth spurt. Boys, however, eventually surpass girls in most dimensions as their adolescent spurts occur and, on the average, are larger in adulthood.

Examples of growth curves of attained size in several dimensions are shown in figure 3.15 for sitting height and leg length, in figure 3.16 for biacromial and bicristal breadths, and in figure 3.17 for arm and calf circumferences. Clearly, the overall shape of the size-attained curves is like those for stature and weight. The timing of the adolescent inflection varies somewhat among the measurements. The data shown are cross-sectional. Hence, the curves are rather smooth because variation among individuals in the different dimensions is masked.

Sitting Height and Leg Length

Figure 3.15 illustrates the growth of the two segments of the body that determine stature. Sex differences in estimated leg length and sitting height are negligible during childhood. Leg length of girls is, on the average, only slightly longer than that of boys for a short period early in adolescence, but sitting height of girls is greater than that of boys for a longer period. Boys surpass girls in leg length by about 12 years of age, but they do not catch up to girls in sitting height until about 14 years of age. Rapid growth of the lower extremities is characteristic of the early part of the adolescent spurt in stature; growth in the sitting height component of stature occurs later. On the other hand, growth in leg length terminates earlier than growth in sitting height, or trunk length, which continues into late adolescence and probably into the 20s. Growth in sitting height thus occurs over a longer period of time and contributes more to the adolescent gain in stature than does leg length.

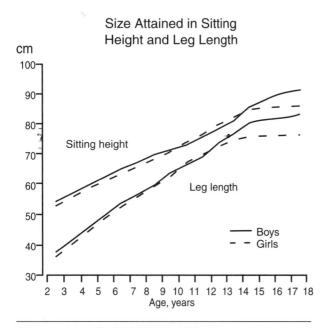

FIGURE 3.15 Distance curves for sitting height and estimated leg length in American children 2 to 18 years of age.

Data from Martorell et al., 1988.

Biacromial and Bicristal Breadths

Curves of size attained in biacromial and bicristal breadths are shown in figure 3.16. Girls are, on the average, larger than boys in bicristal breadth from middle childhood through late adolescence, but boys catch up to girls in late adolescence, and the sex difference in the width across the iliac crests in young adulthood is negligible. On the other hand, boys are larger in biacromial breadth at all ages with the exception of 10 to 12 years of age, the time of the female adolescent growth

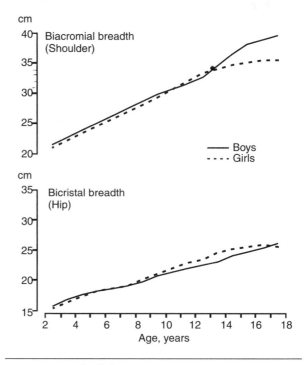

FIGURE 3.16 Distance curves for biacromial and bicristal breadths of American children 2 to 17 years of age.

Data from McCammon, 1970, and Roche and Malina, 1983.

spurt. The sex difference in the two dimensions of trunk breadth in young adulthood is related to variation in the magnitude of the adolescent gain in boys and girls (see table 3.4). During the adolescent growth spurt, boys gain more than girls in biacromial breadth (about 2.3 cm), whereas girls gain slightly more than boys in bicristal breadth (about 1.2 cm). Boys, however, gain about twice as much in biacromial breadth compared with bicristal breadth during the adolescent growth spurt, whereas the difference in the amount gained in the two trunk breadths in girls is very small. Thus, differential adolescent growth results in the sexual dimorphism evident in the two trunk measurements in young adulthood. Males have especially broad shoulders compared with females, but both sexes are similar in width across the iliac crests.

Arm and Calf Circumferences

Arm and calf circumferences (see figure 3.17) have a pattern of growth similar to that for body weight

TABLE 3.4	Mean Size at Initiation of the Adolescent Growth Spurt and in Young Adulthood, and Mean Adolescent Gains in Biacromial and Bicristal Breadths of Girls and Boys in the Harpenden Growth Study			
	Biacromial breadth		**Bicristal breadth**	
	Girls	**Boys**	**Girls**	**Boys**
Size at initiation of growth spurt (cm)	30.1	31.6	21.9	22.9
Young adult size (cm)	36.3	40.1	28.0	27.7
Adolescent gain (cm)	6.2	8.5	6.0	4.8

Standard deviations of the means range between 0.9 and 1.9 cm.

Adapted from Tanner et al. (1976).

Size Attained in Arm and Calf Circumferences

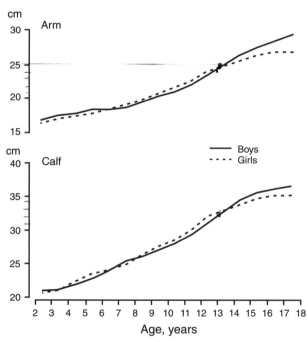

FIGURE 3.17 Distance curves for arm and calf circumferences of American children 2 through 17 years of age.

Data from Johnson et al., 1981.

(see figure 3.6). This similarity is related, of course, to the fact that limb circumferences are composed of soft tissues, muscle and fat, both of which are related to body weight. The sex difference in arm circumference in young adulthood is greater, on the average, than that for calf circumference. This difference is related to the especially greater adolescent spurt in arm muscle mass in males, which is considered in more detail in chapter 16.

Head Circumference

Growth in head circumference from birth to 18 years of age is shown in figure 3.18. A small but consistent sex difference exists at all ages. Head circumference shows rapid growth between birth and 2 years of age and then slower growth thereafter. This pattern of rapid growth early in postnatal life is characteristic of the pattern of growth in brain weight (see figure 1.3, page 13). Growth in head circumference then continues at a slower pace. A slight but clear spurt during adolescence, as expected, occurs earlier in girls than in boys. The adolescent growth spurt is difficult

Size Attained in Head Circumference

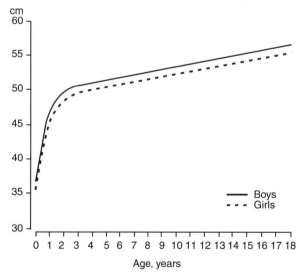

FIGURE 3.18 Distance curves for head circumference in a mixed-longitudinal sample of children from the Fels Research Institute from birth to 18 years of age.

Data from Roche et al., 1987.

to detect in the distance curves shown in figure 3.17, but it becomes apparent when growth curves are mathematically fitted to longitudinal data for individual children.

As noted earlier, head circumference is monitored closely during infancy and early childhood. Updated percentile curves for head circumference from birth to 3 years of age are included in the recent growth charts for American children (Kuczmarski et al. 2000).

Changes in Body Proportions

Although the shape of the growth curve in most dimensions is quite similar to that for stature and weight, rate of growth varies among specific dimensions. This variation among specific body parts or segments is responsible for changing body proportions during growth and is a function of **allometry,** or allometric growth, which refers to the systematic relationships between body dimensions as they grow. Expressing the size of one dimension relative to another indicates the relative proportions of the two dimensions. These ratios are ordinarily viewed as ratios or percentages, and two in particular contribute to the understanding of allometric growth and sex differences and to the impact of the adolescent growth spurt on body proportions: the ratio of sitting height to stature and the ratio of bicristal to biacromial breadths.

Sitting Height/Stature Ratio

The ratio of sitting height to stature is an index of the relative contribution of the trunk and, by subtraction, the lower extremities to stature. The growth curve for this ratio is presented in figure 3.19. The ratio is highest in infancy and declines through childhood into adolescence. It is lowest during the adolescent growth spurt, 10 to 12 years of age in girls and 12 to 14 years of age in boys, and then increases into late adolescence. The ratio should be interpreted as follows. During infancy and childhood, the lower extremities grow faster than the trunk. As a result, sitting height contributes progressively less to stature with age, and the ratio declines. Thus, the legs of a child at entry to school (about 6 years of age) are quite well proportioned relative to stature, in contrast to the newborn infant, who has especially short legs relative to overall length. The ratio continues to decline and reaches its lowest point early in the

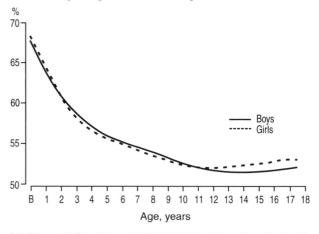

FIGURE 3.19   Sitting height/stature ratios of American children from birth through 17 years of age.
Data from Roche and Malina, 1983.

adolescent growth spurt because the legs experience their growth spurt earlier than the trunk. The growth spurt in the trunk follows that of the legs, and the ratio increases. Hence, the increase in the ratio in late adolescence indicates the late growth in trunk length at a time when growth in the length of the lower extremities has already ceased (see figure 3.15).

The sitting height/stature ratio is virtually identical for boys and girls until about 10 or 11 years of age, when it becomes slightly higher in girls and remains so through adolescence into adulthood. Before adolescence, both boys and girls are proportionately similar in terms of relative leg length or relative trunk length. However, during adolescence and into adulthood, females have, on the average, relatively shorter lower extremities than males for the same stature.

Bicristal/Biacromial Ratio

The changing relationships between the shoulders and hips are shown in figure 3.20. The obvious broadening of the shoulders relative to the hips is characteristic of male adolescence, and the broadening of the hips relative to the shoulders is characteristic of female adolescence. The importance of the term **relative** should be emphasized. Absolute breadth across the iliac crests is, on the average, quite similar in late adolescent males and females (see figure 3.16). However, the ratio of bicristal to biacromial breadths indicates the differential growth of these two trunk dimensions during childhood and adolescence. The ratio is higher in girls than in boys at virtually all ages between 6 and 17 years. Bicristal breadth constitutes a greater percentage of biacromial breadth in girls than in boys, and thus, girls have broader hips relative to their shoulders. The ratio is quite constant in both boys and girls between about 6 and 11 years of age and then declines in males but remains quite stable in females. The decline in the ratio is the result of the biacromial breadth getting larger at a faster rate than bicristal breadth during male adolescence (see table 3.4). Thus, the denominator in the ratio increases at a faster rate than the numerator, and the ratio declines. In females, on the other hand, both dimensions increase at approximately the same rate, and the ratio remains fairly stable. Differential growth during adolescence contributes to the sex difference in the proportional relationship of the shoulders and hips at this time, which continues into adulthood.

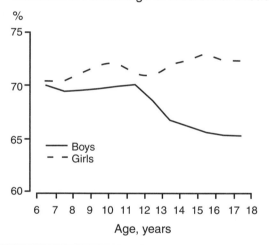

FIGURE 3.20   Ratios of bicristal to biacromial breadths of American children from 6 through 17 years of age.

Data from Roche and Malina, 1983.

Adjusting for Variation in Body Size—Scaling

The size, shape, and proportions of the body influence performance in strength, motor, aerobic, and anaerobic tasks and also influence several physiological variables that are important for performance. A relevant question is the following: "How should performance or function be compared among individuals of various sizes?" The biological principle of scaling is central to this question. Scaling can be defined as the structural and functional consequences of changes in size, or scale, among otherwise similar organisms (Schmidt-Nielsen 1984).

The concept of scaling is a fundamental principle of engineering and a basic concept in the zoological sciences, particularly among comparative mammalian physiologists. Engineers have long recognized that when the size of a structure is increased, three parameters could possibly change—the dimensions, the materials, or the design of the structure.

Ratio Standards

Traditionally, performance and physiological measurements are expressed as a ratio (e.g., strength per unit body mass [kg/kg] or stature [kg/cm] or peak oxygen uptake per unit body mass [ml/kg/min]), to adjust or "normalize" the function for body size. These ratios are labeled as ratio standards. Although the use of ratios to adjust functional measures for individual differences in body size may provide misleading information, the practice continues because ratios are simple to calculate and reasonably easy to understand (Tanner 1949; Packard and Boardman 1987). An implicit assumption in the use of ratios is that the Y intercept is zero. Ratios are influenced by the relationship between the two dimensions that are used to derive the ratio. The relationship is assumed to be linear. The latter assumption does not necessarily hold for measures of size and function. Ratios may also yield spurious results when they are based on different types of dimensions, such as weight (or stature) and measures of strength or oxygen consumption, or when the standard deviations of the parameters differ considerably. Although adjustments are made for body size in calculating a ratio, significant associations often remain between the ratio and the variable of interest (e.g., strength or peak $\dot{V}O_2$). In addition, ratios often overestimate function of small people and underestimate function of large people. This inaccuracy limits their applicability to children of various sizes and limits comparability of performance differences between children and adults.

Dimensionality Scaling

Scaling in dimensionality theory assumes that proportions among body segments remain reasonably constant during late childhood, adolescence, and adulthood (Asmussen 1973). According to dimensionality theory, changes in specific body segments, performance, and physiological functions that accompany growth and maturation can be estimated from the proportional relationships to body length (*l*). When applied to children and adolescents, the measure of body length is standing height (*h*). Thus, the length of specific body segments or the size of certain body organs will be proportional to *h*; the surface area or cross-sectional area of the segments or organs will be proportional to length squared (h^2); and the volume or mass of the segments or organs will be proportional to length cubed (h^3). These proportional relationships can also be applied to performance tasks and physiological functions. For example, because strength of a muscle is proportional to its cross-sectional area, muscle strength should be scaled to h^2. Likewise, because time (t) is proportional to *h* (Asmussen 1973), oxygen uptake (volume per unit time) is proportional to $h^3/h = h^2$.

The dimensionality approach holds only for organisms in which body proportions do not change, which, of course, is not true during growth and maturation. In addition, presently available data often indicate discrepancies between the theoretical and observed components.

Allometric Scaling

Allometry refers to differential growth—differences in proportions correlated with changes in absolute magnitude of the total organism or part of it. Allometry is used to determine the relationship between variables that are affected by proportional changes resulting from variation in size and rate of growth. Allometric scaling attempts to accommodate differential growth in function and size, assuming a nonlinear relationship between function and size.

When allometry is applied to longitudinal records for individuals, it is called ontogenetic allometry. Longitudinal data collected over a period of time in the same individuals are preferred in the calculation of ontogenetic allometry coefficients. In contrast, when allometry is applied to cross-sectional samples, it is called phylogenetic allometry. This approach has been used most often in the allometric scaling of performance to body size, which is discussed later in chapters 11, 12, and 17.

The basic allometric equation, sometimes called a power function, is that proposed by Huxley (1932),

$$y = a \cdot x^k$$

where *y* is the dependent variable (e.g., strength, peak $\dot{V}O_2$), *x* is the independent variable (body mass or height), *k* is the allometric coefficient, *a* is a constant or proportionality coefficient, and *a* and *k* are calculated from a linear regression after double logarithmic transformation of the variables of interest (e.g., body weight and peak $\dot{V}O_2$ or height and strength). The basic allometric equation is thus transformed to a logarithmic form for calculation:

$$log\ y = log\ a + k\ log\ x.$$

The mathematics of allometric scaling can be complex.

Allometric scaling has been applied most often to changes in body size and aerobic power during growth (see chapter 12). Allometric scaling has limited validity for small sample sizes, and the consistency of exponents among studies is marginal. Ontogenetic allometry of aerobic power has been used only sparingly.

Multilevel Modeling

Multilevel modeling is the most recent approach to evaluating the relationship between function and body size. It is based on the fact that biological data have a hierarchical structure involving several levels. Longitudinal growth data include at least two levels, the individual subject and the occasions on which the subject is seen, representing variation between individuals and variation within individuals, respectively. The method has been applied to estimating parameters of the growth curve (e.g., the midgrowth and adolescent growth spurts) (Goldstein 1986). The multilevel modeling method permits use of data for all individuals in a study, including those with only one or two observations, to estimate parameters of the growth curve for the sample.

Multilevel modeling has also been applied to functional measures, specifically mixed-longitudinal data for maximal aerobic power and muscular strength (Baxter-Jones et al. 1993; Nevill et al. 1998). These analyses attempt estimate changes in functional measures that are independent of changes in body size that occur with growth and maturity. The results are discussed in more detail in chapters 16 and 17.

Multilevel modeling is mathematically complex, which may limit its application. Its use is relatively recent, and the contributions of the method to understanding growth per se and functional changes associated with growth and maturity remain to be elaborated.

Overview of Scaling

The fundamental question related to scaling is the following: "How should differences in body size among children and adolescents be partitioned mathematically or statistically in attempting to explain performance or function?" The choice of scaling approach to allow for variation in body size depends on the specific question that is addressed and the level of sophistication desired.

Most current discussions focus on allometric scaling, which begs the question: "When should allometry be used?" Calder (1987, p. 112) suggests "As useful as allometry may be, we lack general consensus on principles of its application." The following points have been emphasized by Schmidt-Nielsen (1984, p. 32) to clarify the application of allometry:

1. Allometric equations are descriptive; they are not biological laws.

2. Allometric equations are useful for showing how a variable quantity is related to body size, all other things being equal.

3. Allometric equations are valuable tools because they may reveal principles and connections that otherwise remain obscure.

4. Allometric equations are useful as a basis for comparisons and can reveal deviations from a general pattern.

5. Allometric equations are useful in estimating the expected magnitude of some variable for a given body size.

6. Allometric equations cannot be used to extrapolate beyond the range of the data on which they are based.

Does scaling of strength, motor performance, peak $\dot{V}O_2$, anaerobic power, or other functions modify interpretation of the changes associated with growth and maturation? This question is considered in the specific chapters dealing with strength and motor performance (chapter 11), aerobic power (chapter 12), anaerobic power (chapter 13), and maturity-associated variation in performance (chapter 17). Nevertheless, for practical purposes and for ease of calculation and interpretation, many functions are still expressed as simple ratios during childhood and adolescence.

Tracking

Tracking attempts to establish the stability of a characteristic over time. It refers to the maintenance of relative rank or position within a group over time. Longitudinal data for at least two points in time are necessary. Interage correlations (Pearson or rank order) between the repeated measurements are used most often in estimating the tracking or stability of a characteristic. As a guide, correlations less than 0.30 are considered low, those between 0.30 and 0.60 are moderate, and those greater than 0.60 indicate reasonably good tracking. These ranges are, of course, arbitrary. In general, the closer the timespan between measurements, the higher the correlation. As the time interval increases between measurements, interage correlations generally decline. Other factors that influence interage correlations include age at first observation, short-term biological variation, significant environmental change, and measurement variability. A major factor affecting tracking during adolescence is individual differences in the timing and tempo of the adolescent growth spurt and sexual maturation.

Other approaches to tracking have used various percentiles, risk analysis, and linear models. Percentiles focus on the extent to which individuals remain at the same percentile position over time. Risk analysis emphasizes the risk or odds of maintaining a specific characteristic (e.g., overweight versus nonoverweight). Linear models permit use of data for unequally spaced intervals and can account for missing data.

Tracking of Body Dimensions

Tracking of attained body size is estimated through the use of autocorrelations or self-correlations in longitudinal samples. These values are correlations between the size of individuals as children at different ages and as adults (e.g., birth length and adult stature, length at age 1 and adult stature, and length at age 2 and adult stature). The correlations indicate the relative position of an individual within the group at different ages between birth and adulthood. Low correlations from year to year indicate change in positions within the group, or instability, whereas high correlations from year to year indicate maintenance of positions within the group, or stability.

Correlations between measurements taken near birth and at subsequent ages during childhood and adolescence and adult measurements for several body dimensions of children in the Harpenden Growth Study are shown in figure 3.21. Correlations between measurements taken near birth and adult dimensions tend to be quite low, about 0.1 to 0.3. The correlations increase considerably until 2 or 3 years of age and then tend to remain moderately high to high and stable until the years near adolescence. Thus, after 2 or 3 years of age, children tend to maintain their position within the group from year to year for stature, weight, and skeletal lengths and breadths. Young adult values for British children in the Harpenden Growth Study were taken at 19 to 21 years of age (Tanner and Whitehouse 1982). Thus, the values for young adults do not necessarily correspond to adult dimensions, especially for body weight. The sample is also somewhat dated. The children were followed a generation or two before the present generation of children, which shows a marked increase in the prevalence of overweight. Nevertheless, the pattern of correlations provides some insights into the tracking of body dimensions.

Correlations between body size measured in the years of the transition into adolescence and adult size tend to decline relative to those for the immediately preceding ages. The decline in correlations indicates some instability or changes in the position of individuals within the group. The instability at this time is the result of individual variation in the timing, tempo, duration, and magnitude of the adolescent growth spurt. Some girls may begin their adolescent growth spurts as early as 9 years of age and more or less suddenly shoot ahead of their peers in stature and weight. Their positions in the group change and in turn alter the correlations with adult dimensions. The decline in correlations at the time of adolescence occurs earlier in girls than in boys and reflects the sex difference in the timing of the adolescent growth spurt. As children pass through the adolescent growth spurt, correlations gradually increase and approximate unity in young adulthood.

Growth Curves of Individual Children

The growth status of individual children tends to remain at or near certain percentile levels on reference charts after about 2 or 3 years of age until adolescence. However, before 2 or 3 years of age, percentile levels of individual children often change. Shifts usually occur between adjacent channels or percentiles on the growth chart but may occasionally cross two or more percentile lines. The term **decanalization** is suggested when longitudinal data for a child shift across at least two percentile lines on the growth chart (Roche and Li 1998). Decanalization is relatively common in infancy and early childhood and is of no concern in the absence of disease. Such shifts commonly reflect the gradual expression of the child's genetic potential for height. For example,

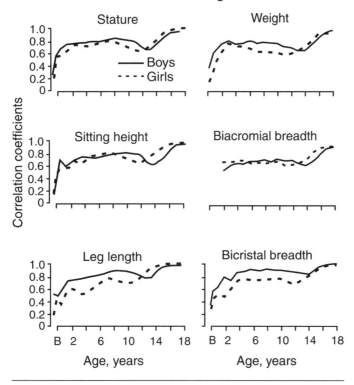

Correlations Between Size During Childhood and Size in Young Adulthood

FIGURE 3.21 Correlations between measurements taken near birth and at subsequent ages during childhood and adolescence and young adult measurements for several anthropometric dimensions of children in the Harpenden Growth Study.

Data from Tanner and Whitehouse, 1982.

children who have the genetic potential for large size as an adult, which may be estimated from parental heights, may be small, average, or large in size at birth. Children who have the genetic potential for small size as an adult may also be small, average, or large in size at birth. Between birth and 2 or 3 years of age, the positions of children on growth charts may thus change somewhat dramatically. This is illustrated in figures 3.22 and 3.23, which show the lengths of three boys and three girls, respectively, followed from birth to 3 years of age and plotted relative to selected percentiles of the new United States growth charts.

The subsequent statures of the boys and girls shown in figures 3.22 and 3.23 are plotted relative to the United States reference data in figures 3.24 and 3.25. Variation at a given chronological age is considerable as shown in the range of percentiles encompassed by the three boys. However, each boy and girl tends to remain at certain percentile levels on reference charts after about 2 or 3 years of age until adolescence (i.e., their growth tends to track well, and their position relative to the reference data is generally stable). During the adolescent growth spurt, all children change in percentile positions.

During adolescence, changes in percentile levels and occasionally decanalization are common because of the individuality of the timing and tempo of the adolescent growth spurt. Between 8 and 12 years of age in girls and between 10 and 14 years of age in boys, an increase in percentile levels is associated with rapid maturation, whereas a decrease in percentile levels is associated with slow maturation. However, after 12 years of age in girls and 14 years of age in boys, rapid maturation is associated with a decrease in percentile levels, whereas slow maturation is associated with an increase in percentile levels (Roche and Li 1998). Maturity-related issues are discussed in more detail in chapter 16.

Growth in height is thus an individual characteristic and tends to be canalized (i.e., to follow specific channels on growth charts). Growth in body weight, on the other hand, is not as canalized as growth in stature. Rather, sudden changes in percentile levels during childhood are often indicative of alterations in the environmental conditions under which the child is being reared.

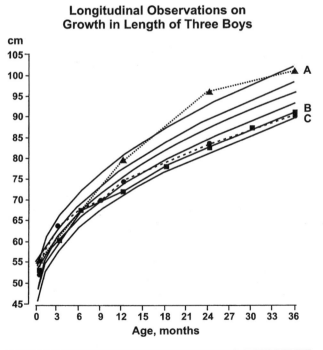

FIGURE 3.22 Lengths of three boys followed longitudinally from birth to 3 years of age. The data are plotted relative to United States reference data (see figure 3.7). Only the 5th, 25th, 50th, 75th, and 95th percentiles of the reference data are shown.

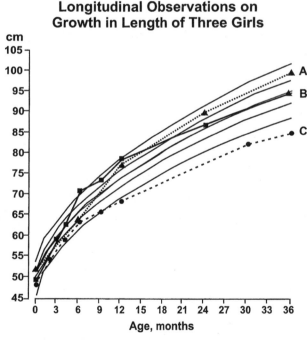

FIGURE 3.23 Lengths of three girls followed longitudinally from birth to 3 years of age. The data are plotted relative to the new United States reference data (see figure 3.7). Only the 5th, 25th, 50th, 75th, and 95th percentiles of the reference data are shown.

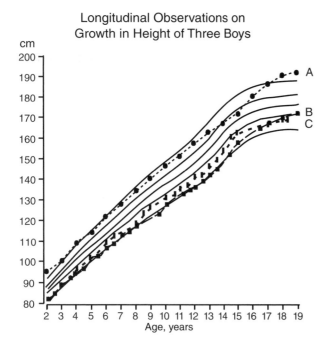

Longitudinal Observations on
Growth in Height of Three Boys

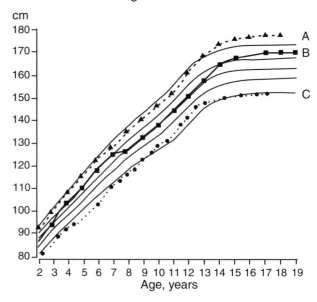

Longitudinal Observations on
Growth in Height of Three Girls

FIGURE 3.24 Heights of the boys in figure 3.22 followed from 2 to 19 years of age. The data are plotted relative to United States reference data (see figure 3.9). Only the 5th, 25th, 50th, 75th, and 95th percentiles of the reference data are shown.

FIGURE 3.25 Heights of the girls in figure 3.23 followed from 2 to 19 years of age. The data are plotted relative to United States reference date (see figure 3.9). Only the 5th, 25th, 50th, 75th, and 95th percentiles of the reference data are shown.

Factors that influence growth are considered in detail in chapters 18 through 25.

Tracking of the Body Mass Index

Correlations between the BMI during childhood and in adulthood in samples of French and United States data are shown in figure 3.26. The French data are from the Paris Longitudinal Study, and the adult values were taken between 18 and 25 years of age. The United States data are from the Fels Longitudinal Study and the adult values were taken at about 35 years of age. Correlations between childhood and adult BMI are reasonably similar in both populations of girls, whereas corresponding correlations for boys are consistently higher in the French data. The difference in males probably reflects significant changes in the BMI from late adolescence into the mid-30s in males, whereas changes in the BMI after late adolescence in young adult females are smaller. Nevertheless, the BMI tracks poorly to about 5 years of age and then at best moderately during childhood. In both sets of data, no sex

differences are present in correlations during early childhood. However, after 5 years of age, the correlations between childhood and young adult BMI in French boys are higher than in girls, whereas the corresponding correlations between childhood and adult BMI in United States girls are higher than in boys.

Other studies of tracking the BMI commonly use a single age or an age range during childhood or adolescence relative to specific ages or age ranges in adulthood, in contrast to the Paris and Fels longitudinal studies, which considered correlations from childhood through adolescence. Interage correlations for the BMI, body weight, and weight-for-height in 12 studies were recently summarized by Power et al. (1997). Correlations between childhood (<13 years of age) and adulthood (25 to 36 years of age) are generally low (~ 0.30), whereas correlations between adolescence (13 to 14 years of age) and adulthood (25 to 26 years of age) range from moderate to high (0.46 to 0.91 in males and 0.60 to 0.78 in females).

The age at the "adiposity rebound," the transition from the lowest BMI during childhood

Tracking of the BMI

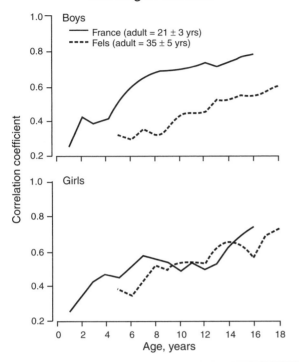

FIGURE 3.26 Correlations between the BMI at several ages during childhood and adolescence, and the BMI in adulthood.

Data from Guo et al., 1994a.

(about 5 to 6 years of age) before the increase, which continues through childhood and adolescence into adulthood, has been suggested to be predictive of later overweight. In a French longitudinal sample, children who experienced the rebound early (5.5 years of age) had, on average, a greater BMI in young adulthood (although not a BMI that classifies the individual as overweight or obese) than those who experienced the rebound later (7.0 years of age) (Rolland-Cachera et al. 1987). Data for United States children in the Fels Longitudinal Study are generally consistent with the French data. However, correlations between the age at which the adiposity rebound occurs (5.1 years in boys and 5.3 years in girls) and the BMI at 18 years of age are only in the moderate range (0.46 in boys and 0.54 in girls) (Siervogel et al. 1991). The age at the "adiposity rebound" as a risk factor for overweight/obesity in adulthood is considered in more detail in chapter 24.

As indicated earlier, the BMI is not necessarily a good indicator of fatness among children and adolescents. It is a better indicator of heaviness, which may include a major fat-free or lean component. Interpretation of the BMI as an indicator of fatness in children and adolescents thus needs caution and sensitivity.

Summary

The study of growth is largely synonymous with measurement. Measures commonly used in growth studies are initially described, and then changes in body size and specific dimensions and body proportions that occur as the individual passes from infancy through childhood and adolescence into young adulthood are summarized. Two measurements are basic to most growth studies, height and weight, and more recently, the body mass index (BMI, weight/height²) is used in many surveys. Size attained provides an indicator of growth status, and if the same individual is followed over time, an indicator of growth rate. The evaluation of growth status requires reference data or "growth charts." The new charts for United States children are described. Most body dimensions follow the same pattern of growth as height and weight, whereas body proportions show different patterns. Height and weight are rather stable (i.e., they track well across childhood and adolescence). Corresponding data for other dimensions are limited. The BMI also tracks well, but interpretation of the BMI as an indicator of fatness in children and adolescents needs caution.

Sources and Suggested Readings

Asmussen E (1973) Growth in muscular strength and power. In GL Rarick (ed), Physical Activity, Human Growth and Development. New York: Academic Press, pp 60-79.

Baumgartner RN, Roche AF, Himes JH (1986) Incremental growth tables: Supplementary to previously published charts. American Journal of Clinical Nutrition 43:711-722.

Baxter-Jones A, Goldstein H, Helms P (1993) The development of aerobic power in young athletes. Journal of Applied Physiology 75:1160-1167.

Berkey CA, Dockery DW, Wang X, Wypij D, Ferris B (1993) Longitudinal height velocity standards for US adolescents. Statistics in Medicine 12:403-414.

Berkey CS, Reed RB, Valadian I (1983) Midgrowth spurt in height of Boston children. Annals of Human Biology 10: 25-30.

Bloom BS (1964) Stability and Change in Human Characteristics. New York: Wiley.

Buschang PH, Tanguay R, Demirjian A (1985) Growth instability of French-Canadian children during the first three years of life. Canadian Journal of Public Health 76:191-194.

Butler GE, McKie M, Ratcliffe SG (1990) The cyclical nature of prepubertal growth. Annals of Human Biology 17: 177-198.

Calder WA (1987) Scaling energetics of homeothermic vertebrates: An operational allometry. Annual Review of Physiology 49:107-120.

* Cameron N (1984) The Measurement of Human Growth. London: Croon-Helm.

Centers for Disease Control and Prevention (2000) National Center for Health Statistics CDC growth charts: United States. www.cdc.gov/growthcharts.htm.

Chrzastek-Spruch H, Susanne C, Hauspie RC, Kozlowska MA (1989) Individual growth patterns and standards for height and height velocity based on the Lublin (Poland) longitudinal growth study. In JM Tanner (ed), Auxology 88: Perspectives in the Science of Growth and Development. London: Smith-Gordon, pp 161-166.

Cold S, Hansen S, Overvad K, Rose C (1998) A woman's body build and the risk of breast cancer. European Journal of Cancer 34:1163-1174.

Cole TJ (1994) Do growth chart centiles need a face lift? British Medical Journal 308:641-642.

Cole TJ, Bellizzi MC, Flegal KM, Dietz WH (2000) Establishing a standard definition for child overweight and obesity worldwide: International survey. British Medical Journal 320:1240-1243.

Cole TJ, Freeman JV, Preece MA (1998) British 1990 growth reference centiles for weight, height, body mass index and head circumference fitted by maximum penalized likelihood. Statistics in Medicine 17:407-429.

Deurenberg P, Weststrate JA, Seidell JC (1991) Body mass index as a measure of body fatness: Age- and sex-specific prediction formulas. British Journal of Nutrition 65:104-114.

Dietz WH, Robinson TN (1998) Use of the body mass index (BMI) as a measure of overweight in children and adolescents. Journal of Pediatrics 132:191-193.

Flegal KM, Carroll MD, Ogden CL, Johnson CL (2002) Prevalence and trends in obesity among US adults, 1999–2000. Journal of the American Medical Association 288:1723-1727.

Freeman JV, Cole TJ, Chinn S, Jones PRM, White EM, Preece MA (1995) Cross sectional stature and weight reference curves for the UK, 1990. Archives of Disease in Childhood 73:17-24.

Garn SM, Leonard WR, Rosenberg K (1986) Body build dependence, stature dependence and influence of lean tissue on the body mass index. Ecology of Food and Nutrition 19:163-165.

Gasser T, Muller HG, Kohler W, Prader A, Largo R, Molinari L (1985) An analysis of the mid-growth and adolescent spurts of height based on acceleration. Annals of Human Biology 12:129-148.

* Gerver WJM, de Bruin R (1996) Paediatric Morphometrics: A Reference Manual. Utrecht, The Netherlands: Wetenschappelijke Uitgeverij Bunge.

Goldstein H (1986) Efficient statistical modelling of longitudinal data. Annals of Human Biology 13:129-141.

Goran MI, Allison DB, Poehlman ET (1995) Issues relating to normalization of body fat content in men and women. International Journal of Obesity 19:638-643.

Gunther B (1975) Dimensional analysis and theory of biological similarity. Physiological Reviews 55:659-699.

Guo SS, Roche AF, Chumlea WC, Gardner JD, Siervogel RM (1994a) The predictive value of childhood body mass index values for overweight at age 35 years. American Journal of Clinical Nutrition 59:810-819.

Guo SS, Roche AF, Fomon SJ, Nelson SE, Chumlea WC, Rogers RR, Baumgartner RN, Ziegler EE, Siervogel RM (1991) Reference data on gains in weight and length during the first two years of life. Journal of Pediatrics 119:355-362.

Guo SS, Roche AF, Moore WM (1988) Reference data for head circumference and one-month increments from one to twelve months. Journal of Pediatrics 113:490-494.

Guo SS, Roche AF, Moore WM (1999) The revised U.S. national growth charts. Nutrition and the M.D. 25:1-4 (July).

Guo SS, Salisbury S, Roche AF, Chumlea WC, Siervogel RM (1994b) Cardiovascular disease risk factors and body composition: A review. Nutrition Research 14:1721-1777.

Hamill PVV, Drizd TA, Johnson CL, Reed RD, Roche AF (1977) NCHS growth curves for children, birth–18 years. United States. DHEW Publication No. (PHS) 78-1650. Washington, DC: US Government Printing Office.

Haschke F (1983) Body composition of adolescent males. Acta Paediatrica Scandinavica 307 (suppl): 1-23.

Hauspie RC, Wachholder A (1986) Clinical standards for growth velocity in height of Belgian boys and girls, aged 2 to 18 years. International Journal of Anthropology 1:339-348.

Hermanussen M (1998) The analysis of short-term growth. Hormone Research 49:53-64.

Hoey HMCV, Tanner JM, Cox LA (1987) Clinical growth standards for Irish children. Acta Paediatrica Scandinavica, 338 supplement 338:1-31.

Huxley JS (1932) Problems in Relative Growth. London: Methuen.

Johnson CL, Fulwood R, Abraham S, Bryner JD (1981) Basic data on anthropometric measurements and angular measurements of the hip and knee joints for selected age groups 1–74 years of age, United States, 1971–1975. DHHS Publication No. (PHS) 81-1669. Washington, DC: US Government Printing Office.

Johnston FE (1986) Somatic growth of the infant and preschool child. In F Falkner, JM Tanner (eds), Human Growth. Volume 2. Postnatal Growth, Neurobiology. New York: Plenum, pp 3-24.

* Krogman WM (1948) A handbook of the measurement and interpretation of height and weight in the growing child. Monographs of the Society for Research in Child Development 13, serial no. 48 (published in 1950).

* Kuczmarski RJ, Johnson C (1991) National nutritional surveys assessing anthropometric status. In JH Himes (ed), Anthropometric Assessment of Nutritional Status. New York: Wiley, pp 319-335.

* Kuczmarski RJ, Ogden CL, Grummer-Strawn LM, Flegal KM, Guo SS, Wei R, Mei Z, Curtin LR, Roche AF, Johnson CL (2000) CDC growth charts: United States. Advance Data from Vital and Health Statistics, no. 314. Hyattsville, MD: National Center for Health Statistics, (see www.cdc.gov/growthcharts.htm).

Kushner RF (1993) Body weight and mortality. Nutrition Reviews 51:127-136.

Lampl M, Birch L, Picciano MF, Johnson ML, Frongillo EA (2001) Child factor in measurement dependability. American Journal of Human Biology 13:548-557.

Lampl M, Cameron N, Veldhuis JD, Johnson ML (1995) Patterns of human growth. Science 268:442-447.

Lampl M, Johnson ML (1993) A case study of daily growth during adolescence: A single spurt or changes in the dynamics of saltatory growth? Annals of Human Biology 20:595-603.

Lampl M, Veldhuis JD, Johnson ML (1992) Saltation and stasis: A model of human growth. Science 258:801-803.

Li J, Park WJ, Roche AF (1998) Decanalization of weight and stature during childhood and adolescence. American Journal of Human Biology 10:351-359.

Lindgren G, Aurelius G, Tanner J, Healy M (1994) Standards for height, weight and head circumference from one month to six years based on Stockholm children born in 1980. Acta Paediatrica 83:360-366.

* Lohman TG, Roche AF, Martorell R, editors (1988) Anthropometric Standardization Reference Manual. Champaign, IL: Human Kinetics.

McCammon RB (1970) Human Growth and Development. Springfield, IL: Charles C Thomas.

* Malina RM (1995) Anthropometry. In PJ Maud, C Foster (eds), Physiological Assessment of Human Fitness. Champaign, IL: Human Kinetics, pp 205-219.

Malina RM (1997) Anthropometry in physical education and sport sciences. In F Spencer (ed), History of Physical Anthropology: An Encyclopedia. Volume 1. New York: Garland Publishing, pp 90-94.

Malina RM, Hamill PVV, Lemeshow S (1973) Selected body measurements of children 6–11 years, United States. DHEW Publication No (HSM) 73-1605. Washington, DC: US Government Printing Office.

Malina RM, Hamill PVV, Lemeshow S (1974) Body dimensions and proportions, White and Negro children 6–11 years, United States. DHEW Publication No. (HRA) 75-1625. Washington, DC: US Government Printing Office.

Malina RM, Katzmarzyk PT (1999) Validity of the body mass index as an indicator of the risk and presence of overweight in adolescents. American Journal of Clinical Nutrition 70 (suppl):131S-136S.

* Malina RM, Roche AF (1983) Manual of Physical Status and Performance in Childhood. Volume 2. Physical Status. New York: Plenum.

Martorell R, Malina RM, Castillo RO, Mendoza FS, Pawson IG (1988) Body proportions in three ethnic groups: Children and youths 2–17 years in NHANES II and HHANES. Human Biology 60:205-222.

Maynard LM, Wisemandle W, Roche AF, Chumlea WC, Guo SS, Siervogel RM (2001) Childhood body composition in relation to body mass index. Pediatrics 107:344-350.

Meredith HV (1978) Human Body Growth in the First Ten Years of Life. Columbia, SC: State Printing Company.

Mirwald RL, Bailey DA (1997) Seasonal height velocity variation in boys and girls 8–18 years. American Journal of Human Biology 9:709-715.

Molinari L, Largo RH, Prader A (1980) Analysis of the growth spurt at age seven (mid-growth spurt). Helvetica Paediatrica Acta 35: 325-334.

Mueller WH, Martorell R (1988) Reliability and accuracy of measurement. In TG Lohman, AF Roche, R Martorell (eds), Anthropometric Standardization Reference Manual. Champaign, IL: Human Kinetics, pp 83-86.

Najjar MF, Rowland M (1987) Anthropometric reference data and prevalence of overweight. United States. DHHS Publication No. (PHS) 87-1688. Washington, DC: US Government Printing Office.

Nevill AM, Holder RL, Baxter-Jones A, Round JM, Jones DA (1998) Modeling developmental changes in strength and aerobic power in children. Journal of Applied Physiology 84:963-970.

Norton K, Olds T, editors (1996) Anthropometrica: A Textbook of Body Measurement for Sports and Health Courses. Sydney: University of New South Wales Press.

Ogden CL, Flegal KM, Carroll MD, Johnson CL (2002) Prevalence and trends in overweight among US children and adolescents, 1999–2000. Journal of the American Medical Association 288:1728-1732.

Packard G, Boardman T (1987) The misuse of ratios to scale physiological data that vary allometrically with body size. In M Feder, A Bennet, W Burggren, R Huey (eds.), New Directions in Ecological Physiology. Cambridge: Cambridge University Press, pp 216-236.

Pietrobelli A, Faith MS, Allison DB, Gallagher D, Chiumello G, Heymsfield SB (1998) Body mass index as a measure of adiposity among children and adolescents: A validation study. Journal of Pediatrics 132:204-210.

Power C, Lake JK, Cole TJ (1997) Body mass index and height from childhood to adulthood in the 1958 British birth cohort. American Journal of Clinical Nutrition 66:1094-1101.

Prader A, Largo RH, Molinari L, Issler C (1989) Physical growth of Swiss children from birth to 20 years of age. Helvetica Paediatrica Acta 52 (suppl):1-125.

* Roche AF (1984) Anthropometric methods: New and old, what they tell us. International Journal of Obesity 8:509-523.

Roche AF (1999a) Postnatal physical growth assessment. Clinical Pediatrics and Endocrinology 8 (suppl 12):1-12.

Roche AF (1999b) Lessons from the establishment and maintenance of long-term serial growth studies. Japanese Journal of Physical Education 44:133-151.

Roche AF, Davila GH (1972) Late adolescent growth in stature. Pediatrics 50:874-880.

Roche AF, Guo SS (2001) The new growth charts. Pediatric Basics 94:2-13 (Nov).

Roche AF, Guo SS, Johnson CL, Kuczmarski RJ, Briefel RR (1996) Revision of the US National Center for Health Statistics Growth Charts. In BE Bodszar, C Susanne (eds), Studies in Human Biology. Budapest: Eotvos University Press, pp 105-112.

Roche AF, Guo SS, Moore WM (1989a) Weight and recumbent length from 1 to 12 months of age: Reference data for 1-month increments. American Journal of Clinical Nutrition 49:599-607.

Roche AF, Guo SS, Towne B (1997) Opportunities and difficulties in long-term studies of growth. International Journal of Sports Medicine 18:S151-S161.

Roche AF, Guo SS, Yeung DL (1989b) Monthly growth increments from a longitudinal study of Canadian infants. American Journal of Human Biology 1:271-280.

Roche AF, Himes JH (1980) Incremental growth charts. American Journal of Clinical Nutrition 33:2041-2052.

Roche AF, Li J (1998) Changes in percentile levels for growth. Pediatric Forum 9:30-34.

* Roche AF, Malina RM (1983) Manual of Physical Status and Performance in Childhood. Volume I. Physical Status. New York: Plenum.

Roche AF, Mukherjee D, Guo S, Moore WM (1987) Head circumference reference data: Birth to 18 years. Pediatrics 79:706-712.

Roche AF, Siervogel RM, Chumlea WC, Webb P (1981) Grading body fatness from limited anthropometric data. American Journal of Clinical Nutrition 34:2831-2838.

Rolland-Cachera MF, Bellisle F, Sempe M (1989) The prediction in boys and girls of the weight/height^2 index and various

skinfold measurements in adults: A two decade follow-up study. International Journal of Obesity 13:305-311.

Rolland-Cachera MF, Cole TJ, Sempe M, Tichet J, Rossignol C, Charraud A (1991) Body mass index variations: Centiles from birth to 87 years. European Journal of Clinical Nutrition 45:13-21.

Rolland-Cachera MF, Deheeger M, Guilloud-Bataille M, Avons P, Patois E, Sempe M (1987) Tracking the development of adiposity from one month of age to adulthood. Annals of Human Biology 14:219-229.

Rolland-Cachera MF, Deheeger M, Bellisle F, Sempe M, Guilloud-Bataille M, Patois E (1984) Adiposity rebound in children: A simple indicator for predicting obesity. American Journal of Clinical Nutrition 39:129-135.

* Saul RA, Stevenson RE, Rogers RC, Skinner SA, Prouty LA, Flannery DB (1988) Growth References from Conception to Adulthood. Greenwood, SC: Greenwood Genetic Center.

* Schmidt-Nielsen K (1984) Scaling: Why Is Animal Size So Important? Cambridge: Cambridge University Press.

Sheehy A, Gasser T, Molinari L, Largo RH (1999) An analysis of variance of the pubertal and midgrowth spurts for length and width. Annals of Human Biology 26:309-331.

Siervogel RM, Roche AF, Guo S, Mukherjee, Chumlea WC (1991) Patterns of change in weight/stature^2 from 2 to 18 years: Findings from long-term serial data for children in the Fels longitudinal growth study. International Journal of Obesity 15:479-485.

Suwa S, Tachibana K, Maesaka H, Tanaka T, Yokoya S (1992) Longitudinal standards for height and weight velocity for Japanese children from birth to maturity. Clinical Pediatrics and Endocrinology 1:5-13.

Tanner JM (1949) Fallacy of per-weight and per-surface area standards, and their relation to spurious correlation. Journal of Applied Physiology 2:1-15.

* Tanner JM (1962) Growth at Adolescence, 2nd edition. Oxford: Blackwell Scientific Publications.

Tanner JM, Cameron N (1980) Investigation of the mid-growth spurt in height, weight and limb circumferences in single year velocity data from the London 1966–67 growth survey. Annals of Human Biology 7:565-577.

Tanner JM, Davies PSW (1985) Clinical longitudinal standards for height and height velocity for North American children. Journal of Pediatrics 107:317-329.

Tanner JM, Healy MJR, Lockhart RD, MacKenzie JD, Whitehouse RH (1956) Aberdeen growth study. 1. The prediction of adult body measurements from measurements taken each year from birth to 5 years. Archives of Disease in Childhood 31:372-381.

Tanner JM, Whitehouse RH (1982) Atlas of Children's Growth. Normal Variation and Growth Disorders. New York: Academic Press.

Tanner JM, Whitehouse RH, Takaishi M (1966) Standards from birth to maturity for height, weight, height velocity, and weight velocity: British children, 1965. Archives of Disease in Childhood 41:454-471, 613-635.

Tanner JM, Whitehouse RH, Marubini E, Resele LF (1976) The adolescent growth spurt of boys and girls of the Harpenden Growth Study. Annals of Human Biology 3:109-126.

Wales JKH, Gibson AT (1994) Short-term growth: Rhythms, chaos, or noise? Archives of Disease in Childhood 71: 84-89.

* World Health Organization (1995) Physical Status: The Use and Interpretation of Anthropometry. Geneva: World Health Organization, Technical Report Series, No. 854.

Young CM, Bogan AD, Roe DA, Lutwak L (1968) Body composition of preadolescent and adolescent girls. IV. Total body water and creatinine excretion. Journal of the American Dietetic Association 53:579-587.

Zavaleta AN, Malina RM (1982) Growth and body composition of Mexican American boys 9 through 14 years of age. American Journal of Physical Anthropology 57: 261-271.

4

DEVELOPMENT OF PHYSIQUE

Chapter Outline

Physique refers to an individual's body form, the configuration of the entire body rather than its specific features. The study of physique is a single aspect of an area of study sometimes labeled **human constitution,** which involves the interrelationships and interdependency among an individual's structural, functional, and behavioral characteristics. Constitution is a rather comprehensive and general concept.

Physique, or body build, is probably the single aspect of constitution that is most amenable to systematic study because it can be readily observed. Physique has been related to a variety of behavioral, occupational, disease, and performance variables, primarily in adults. The development of physique during childhood and adolescence, and its relationships with other variables such as biological maturity, performance, and behavior, have been studied less extensively (Malina and Rarick 1973). Relationships between components of physique and risk factors for cardiovascular disease evident in adults are also apparent in children and adolescents (Katzmarzyk et al. 1998; Malina et al. 1997), and relationships between physique and performance are generally similar in youth and adults (Malina and Rarick

1973; Malina 1992). Data for young athletes in gymnastics and diving, for example, indicate that those who are successful tend to have physiques that are similar to adult athletes in these sports (Carter and Heath 1990), which suggests that physique is a significant selective factor and perhaps a contributor to success in some sports.

The study of physique during growth permits a better understanding of variation in adult physique. Like other morphological characteristics, variation evident in adults has its genesis during childhood and adolescence. When are adult patterns established? How stable is an individual's physique from childhood to adulthood? How do individual differences in rate of growth and maturation, for example, influence the development of physique?

The development of physique has central importance in the study of growth, maturation, and performance. This chapter considers physique from several perspectives. First, methods of assessing physique and their applicability to children and youth are described, with emphasis on the somatotype (soma = body) concept of William Sheldon (see concept of somatotype). Examples of somatotypes of individuals and the distribution of somatotypes in samples of children and adolescents are then considered. Finally, change and stability in somatotype during growth are discussed.

Concept of Somatotype

The rating and classification of physique or body form as a whole (as opposed to specific features) have a long history. Hippocrates offered a twofold classification of physiques centuries ago: **habitus phthisicus** (linear) and **habitus apoplecticus** (lateral). Since this early effort at classifying the human form, numerous attempts at classifying physiques have been made, some rather simple and others more elaborate (Comas 1957). Despite the many attempts at describing and classifying physiques, all efforts eventually describe body form in terms of two or three major types: lateral (round), muscular, and linear.

Anthropometric dimensions are often used to make inferences about physique. Thus, a child who is at the 50th percentile for weight and the 25th percentile for stature is often described as "short and stocky." A child at the 75th percentile for stature and the 25th percentile for weight is described as "slender" or "linear" in build. In a similar manner, the sitting height/stature and bicristal/biacromial ratios described in chapter 3 are indicators of relative proportions. Individuals are often described as having relatively "short legs" or "broad shoulders." These are general statements about an individual's physique—the configuration of the individual's body build.

Although ratios and indices derived from various combinations of anthropometric dimensions provide significant insights into physique, they have limitations. Used alone, they are neither adequate nor accurate indicators of physique. A child with a high weight-for-stature is not necessarily short and stocky; the child could simply be obese. Similarly, a child with low weight-for-stature might be chronically undernourished rather than simply linear in build. Rather than providing a complete assessment of physique, indices and ratios by themselves function primarily as a guide.

The conceptual approach of William Sheldon and colleagues (1940) to the assessment of physique is most commonly used today. Although the initial publication has three authors, Sheldon was the primary contributor and the method is generally attributed to him. The approach is based on the premise that continuous variation occurs in the distribution of physiques, and this variation is related to differential contributions of three specific components that characterize the configuration of the body—endomorphy, mesomorphy, and ectomorphy. **Endomorphy** is characterized by the predominance of the digestive organs and by softness and roundness of contours throughout the body. **Mesomorphy** is characterized by the predominance of muscle, bone, and connective tissues, so muscles are prominent with sharp definition. **Ectomorphy** is characterized by linearity and fragility of build, with limited muscular development and predominance of surface area over body mass. The contribution of the three components defines an individual's **somatotype.** By themselves, the components have limited meaning.

Methods in the Assessment of Physique

Methods for the assessment of body build have a long history. A variety of protocols have been described and almost all classify physiques into three categories corresponding to lateral, muscular, and linear types. The emphasis was on types, which did not accommodate variation in body build within and among individuals (see Tanner 1953; Comas 1957; Damon 1970). The somatotype concept of Sheldon added a different dimension to the study of physique by focusing on the variable contribution of the three components to an individual's body build and providing a means of quantifying the contribution of each.

Sheldonian Somatotypes

Sheldon's method of estimating somatotype utilizes height and weight and three standardized photographs of front, side, and rear views of the nude subject standing before a calibrated grid. Height and weight are used in the form of the reciprocal ponderal index, height divided by the cube root of weight, to estimate linearity (high index, low ponderosity) and laterality (low index, high ponderosity). The configuration of the body as a whole—its contours, relief, relative proportions, robustness, and delicateness—is based on evaluation of the photographs. Size is not a factor. In its original form, the method involved the measurement of 17 diameters on the negatives or photographs, but it soon became photoscopic (i.e., subjective evaluation of the standardized photographs).

Each component of physique is assessed individually. Ratings are based on a 7-point scale, with 1 representing the least expression, 4 representing moderate or medium expression, and 7 representing the fullest expression of the particular component being assessed. The ratings of each component determine the somatotype, which is expressed by three numerals. The first number refers to endomorphy, the second to mesomorphy, and the third to ectomorphy. This sequence is the standard way of reporting somatotypes.

The extreme somatotypes are 7-1-1 (extreme endomorphy), 1-7-1 (extreme mesomorphy), and 1-1-7 (extreme ectomorphy). If one of the components is dominant, the individual's somatotype is described by that component. Thus, a child with a somatotype of 2-6-2 is labeled a mesomorph (see figure 4.1); the child is low in endomorphy and ectomorphy but high in mesomorphy. An individual with a somatotype of 3-4-3 has a balanced physique with no clear dominance of any component (see figure 4.2). The somatotypes of the children in figures 4.1 and 4.2 were rated on the basis of Sheldon's original adult male criteria (Sheldon et al. 1954). Criteria for defining somatotype components in children or females were not published by Sheldon.

Although Sheldon's method appears rather simple, proficiency in assessment requires detailed training and practice. Because photoscopic criteria are used, the method involves a high degree of subjectivity, but in the hands of a trained observer, the method is quite reliable.

The method of somatotyping was developed on adult males. The application of the method to studying the development of physique in children and adolescents was not addressed by Sheldon and his colleagues. How does an individual's somatotype change with growth and maturation? Changes in somatotype during growth are considered later in the chapter.

Sheldon subsequently modified the original somatotype method in an attempt to eliminate some of the subjectivity and account for possible variation with age. Assumptions in the original method were that an individual's somatotype did not change with age, nutritional status, or state of physical training. These assumptions were soon questioned because somatotype varies with age and nutritional state. Somatotype may also be modified to some extent by a systematic program of weight training, but continued training is required to maintain the changes.

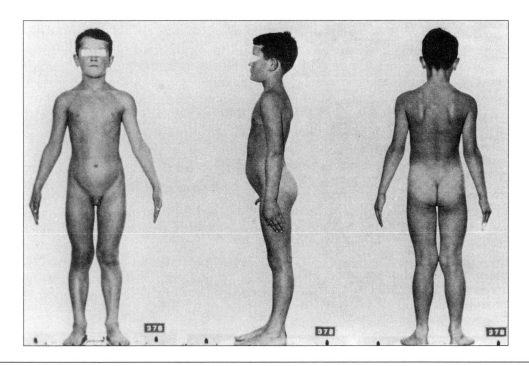

FIGURE 4.1 Somatotype photographs of a preadolescent boy with a mesomorphic physique. His somatotype is 2-6-2.

Adapted, by permission, from G. Peterson, 1967, *Atlas for somatotyping children* (Assen, The Netherlands: Koninklijke Van Gorcum & Company), 34.

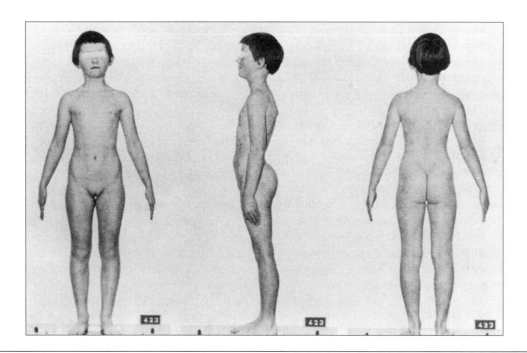

FIGURE 4.2   Somatotype photographs of a preadolescent girl with a balanced physique. Her so-matotype is 3-4-3.

Adapted, by permission, from G. Petersen, 1967, *Atlas for somototyping children* (Assen, The Netherlands: Koninklijke Van Gorcum & Company), 34.

The modified method for estimating somato-type involves the use of adult stature, a minimal stature/weight ratio derived from the reciprocal ponderal index, and a trunk index derived from the ratio of the areas of the thoracic (upper) and abdominal (lower) trunk measured on somato-type photographs. This index is assumed to be constant throughout life. Difficulties in applying the modified method to children are obvious. Adult stature must be predicted. Longitudinal data for stature and weight are necessary to es-timate the minimal stature/weight ratio during growth. Once these are determined, a series of age-adjusted and sex-specific tables must be used to arrive at an estimate of the somatotype (Sheldon et al. 1969). Thus, the modified method is not practical.

An important conceptual change was incor-porated into Sheldon's modified approach. In the original method, somatotype measured only body shape, independent of body size. In the modified method, size is introduced as a factor in the form of adult stature. Thus, the modified method indicates body shape and size.

The modified method has been applied to children but with limited success (Walker 1978; Walker and Tanner 1980). Correlations between the trunk index measured at preschool and late

adolescent ages in the same children are moder-ate (about 0.6 to 0.7). Although the correlations suggest a degree of stability of the index, the index is not constant during growth. In two series of boys, one 9 through 16 years of age and the other 5 through 18 years of age, the modified somatotyping method consistently overestimated endomorphy and mesomorphy, and results for ectomorphy were variable.

Modifications of Sheldon's Method

Sheldon's method of somatotyping was criticized on the grounds that an individual's somatotype was not fixed but could change, that the photo-scopic procedures were too subjective, and that the scale from 1 to 7 was arbitrary and limiting. Hence, several modifications of Sheldon's method were developed.

Parnell's Phenotypic Method   Parnell (1958) utilized several anthropometric dimensions to derive an estimate of physique based on stature, weight, three skinfolds, two limb circumfer-ences, and two bone breadths of the limbs. The anthropometric dimensions were used to derive estimates of three components—fat (F), muscularity (M), and linearity (L)—in place of Sheldon's endomorphy, mesomorphy, and ectomorphy, respectively. The latter terms, however, were used on Parnell's charts, thus adding some confusion. Each component was rated on a 7-point scale, and physique was essentially interpreted as a Sheldonian somatotype.

Heath-Carter Method   Heath (1963) modified Sheldon's original method by opening the component rating scales to accommodate a broader range of variation, and by establishing a linear relationship between somatotype ratings and the stature/weight ratio. The modification was still basically photoscopic, but Heath and Carter (1967) subsequently incorporated these changes with the anthropometric procedures of Parnell (1958). The resulting approach was the Heath-Carter method (Carter and Heath 1990), which combines both photoscopic and anthropometric procedures to estimate somatotype. Somatotype was defined as representing the individual's "present morphological conformation." In practice, the Heath-Carter method of somatotyping is used primarily in its anthropometric form. Anthropometry is more objective, and obtaining standardized somatotype photographs is difficult and costly.

The three components of somatotype described in the Heath-Carter method are of particular interest because they introduce specific body composition concepts. Although body composition is discussed in more detail in chapter 5, this area of study attempts to partition body weight into its lean and fat components, which are labeled fat-free mass and fat mass, respectively. Sheldon's original somatotype concept, however, refers only to body shape and not to body composition. Thus, both methods use the term **somatotype,** but it has a different meaning in each.

The somatotype components and the dimensions used in the Heath-Carter anthropometric protocol to derive each component are as follows:

1. **Endomorphy.** The first component, endomorphy, is described as relative fatness or leanness. It is derived from the sum of three skinfolds: the triceps, subscapular, and suprailiac. The suprailiac fold is measured over the anterior superior spine of the iliac crest, in contrast to the suprailiac fold often used in growth studies, which is measured over the iliac crest in the midaxillary line (see chapter 3). This component has a continuum from lowest (relative leanness) to highest (relative fatness) values.

2. **Mesomorphy.** The second component, mesomorphy, refers to relative musculoskeletal development adjusted for stature. It is described as expressing fat-free mass relative to stature. Mesomorphy is derived from biepicondylar breadths of the humerus and femur, flexed-arm circumference (in contrast to relaxed-arm circumference) corrected for the thickness of the triceps skinfold, and calf circumference corrected for the thickness of the medial calf skinfold. Correcting the circumferences is simply a matter of subtracting the skinfold thickness from the circumference. These four measurements of the upper and lower extremities are then adjusted for stature.

3. **Ectomorphy.** The third component, ectomorphy, is the relative linearity of build. It is based on the reciprocal ponderal index (height divided by the cube root of body weight).

Although the components are described separately, they are related because they are components of a single entity, the individual's somatotype. Each component contributes variably to a somatotype. Hence, it is relative fatness, relative musculoskeletal development, and relative linearity in reference to a physique, which is a composite of the three components.

The first (endomorphy) and second (mesomorphy) components in the Heath-Carter method introduce specific body composition concepts. Evidence for children and young adults, however, is not consistent with these notions. The percentage of body weight as fat correlates moderately well with endomorphy, but fat-free mass correlates rather poorly with mesomorphy (Slaughter and Lohman 1977; Slaughter et al. 1977). Further, the relationship between mesomorphy and limb muscularity based on dual-energy X-ray absorptiometry (DEXA, see chapter 5) is generally low in athletes (Arngrimsson et al. 2000). These observations call into question the validity of referring to mesomorphy as fat-free mass. It also indicates the need for careful evaluation and validation of relationships implied in the concepts used to define physique. Rather than claiming that the somatotype assesses both shape and composition, body composition estimates would be better considered as complements to the study of physique. They are related, but they also are quite different conceptually and methodologically.

The algorithms for estimating a somatotype with the Heath-Carter anthropometric protocol are as follows (Carter and Heath 1990):

A. Endomorphy = −0.7182 + 0.1451(SumSkf)
− 0.00068(SumSkf^2) + 0.0000014(SumSkf^3)

where SumSkf refers to the sum of the triceps, subscapular, and supraspinale skinfolds (mm); an adjustment for stature is made where SumSkf is multiplied by 170.18/height (cm); SumSkf^2 and SumSkf^3 refer to the sum of skinfolds (mm) squared and cubed, respectively.

B. Mesomorphy = (0.858 biepicondylar breadth of the humerus + 0.601 biepicondylar breadth of the femur + 0.188 corrected arm circumference + 0.161 corrected calf circumference) − (stature × 0.131) + 4.50

where corrected arm circumference and corrected calf circumferences are the respective limb circumferences minus the triceps and medial calf skinfolds (in cm), respectively.

C. Ectomorphy = HWR × 0.732 − 28.58

where HWR = stature (cm)/$^3\sqrt{}$weight (kg) [stature divided by the cube root of body weight]. If HWR < 40.75 but > 38.25, ectomorphy = HWR × 0.463 − 17.63. If HWR < 38.25, a rating of 0.1 is assigned.

If the calculation for any component is zero or negative, a value of 0.1 is assigned because by definition a rating cannot be zero or negative.

The principles of quality control in anthropometry described in the preceding chapter also apply to the estimate of somatotype. Intraobserver and interobserver measurement variability can influence the reproducibility of somatotype components in the Heath-Carter anthropometric protocol. Errors are less than 0.5 somatotype units when the body dimensions are measured by experienced technicians (Bouchard 1985).

Although the anthropometric protocol is widely used with children, its validity with children 6 years of age and younger has not been established. This may explain why some studies indicate high ratings of mesomorphy in young children (Carter and Heath 1990).

Differences Among Methods

The differences among the various methods of assessing physique are obvious. Sheldon's original method is basically photoscopic, and his modification results in essentially a different method. Parnell's approach is anthropometric. The Heath-Carter method in its original form combines photoscopic and anthropometric procedures, although the anthropometric protocol is most widely used at present. All methods include three basic components, and all recognize the continuous nature of variation in the distribution of the components of physique and of physiques per

se. The three methods also use a ratio of height and weight in the form of the reciprocal ponderal index to estimate ectomorphy.

The first and third components can be recognized with a reasonable degree of accuracy and might simply represent the extremes of a single continuum, extreme linearity to extreme ponderousness. The second component presents a major problem in physique assessment and may not be comparable between Sheldon's approach and the anthropometric modifications. An estimate of mesomorphy that does not include a measurement on the trunk in the anthropometric procedures to estimate somatotype does not appear to make biological sense. The trunk is a significant component of the physique, and in Sheldon's photoscopic method, the distinction between mesomorphy and endomorphy depends to a large extent on the development of the upper (thorax and chest) versus the lower (abdominal) areas of the trunk. The trunk index in Sheldon's modified method emphasizes the contribution of the trunk to the estimate of somatotype, but it requires standardized photographs and specific area measurements. Mesomorphy in the photoscopic approach possibly has an upper trunk or thoracic emphasis, whereas mesomorphy in the anthropometric protocols indicates limb musculoskeletal development (Claessens et al. 1986).

Physique assessments derived from the various methods and modifications all incorporate the terms **endomorphy, mesomorphy,** and **ectomorphy,** as well as the term **somatotype.** Hence, rather than being used in the sense originally defined by Sheldon, somatotype has become, more or less, a generic term referring to an individual's physique. Estimates of somatotype must, therefore, always indicate the method used. Indication of the method is especially important in comparisons of earlier and more recent studies.

Somatotyping Children and Adolescents

Somatotype assessment of children has met with varying degrees of success and with some problems. Assessing physique in young children is difficult because no suitable reference material exists for comparison in the photoscopic method. In addition, cultural biases may prohibit taking somatotype photographs of children and adolescents, especially girls. Sheldon's criteria for adult males have been used by some researchers to develop criteria for children, and his modified method requires longitudinal data, which thus limits its use in many studies.

The applicability of the Heath-Carter anthropometric method to young children (less than 6 years of age) is also questionable. The validity of anthropometrically derived components in young children needs to be established. Differential growth of specific dimensions and tissues (specifically skinfolds), rapidly changing body proportions, and lack of suitable somatotype reference materials are important considerations. On the other hand, the anthropometric protocol has been used quite regularly with older children and adolescents 10 to 18 years of age and in samples of child and adolescent athletes in a variety of sports (Carter and Heath 1990).

The physiques of growing individuals are subsequently considered in the context of three issues (1) sex differences in the distribution of somatotypes of individual children and in average somatotypes, (2) changes in somatotype during growth, drawing on examples of individual children and grouped data for longitudinal and several cross-sectional samples, and (3) the stability of an individual's physique during growth, which has generally received more attention in view of Sheldon's initial assertion that an individual's somatotype is fixed and does not change with age.

Examples of Somatotypes of Individuals During Growth

Somatotype photographs of several children from the Harpenden Growth Study, who were followed longitudinally from early childhood through late adolescence or young adulthood, are shown in figures 4.3 through 4.7. The young adult somatotype of each child is indicated in the figures. A boy and a girl with balanced somatotypes are shown in figures 4.3 and 4.4, respectively. Their young adult somatotypes are nearly identical, 4-3-4 and 4.5-3-4, the only exception being sexual dimorphism in the morphology of the hips. Boys with predominantly mesomorphic and ectomorphic young adult somatotypes are shown in figures 4.5 and 4.6, respectively, and a predominantly endomorphic girl is shown in figure 4.7. A longitudinal series of photographs for a predominantly ectomorphic girl were not available.

Changes in somatotype during growth are apparent in the figures 4.3 through 4.7. Change appears to take place between about 3 to 4 and 8 years of age. The changes most likely reflect the redistribution of subcutaneous adipose tissue, the

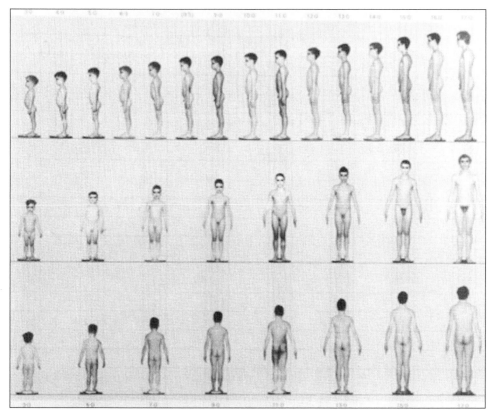

FIGURE 4.3 Somatotype photographs of a boy followed from 3 to 17 years of age. The young adult somatotype is balanced, 4-3-4.

Adapted, by permission, from Tanner and Whitehouse, 1982, *Atlas of children's growth: Normal variation and growth disorders* (London: Academic Press).

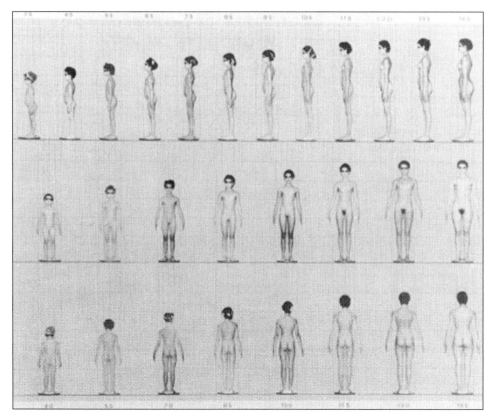

FIGURE 4.4 Somatotype photographs of a girl followed from 4 to 14.5 years of age. The somatotype at 14.5 years is balanced, 4.5-3-4.

Adapted, by permission, from Tanner and Whitehouse, 1982, *Atlas of children's growth: Normal variation and growth disorders* (London: Academic Press).

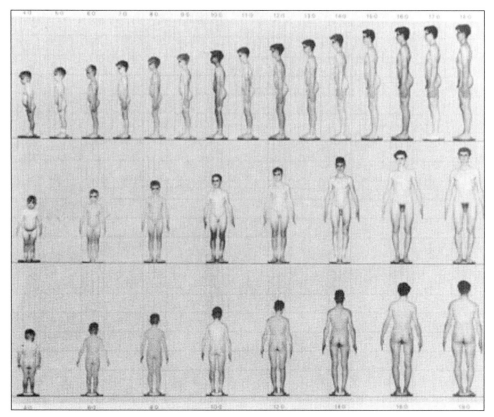

FIGURE 4.5 Somatotype photographs of a boy followed from 4 to 18 years of age. The young adult somatotype is predominantly mesomophic, 2.5-5.5-2.

Adapted, by permission, from Tanner and Whitehouse, 1982, *Atlas of children's growth: Normal variation and growth disorders* (London: Academic Press).

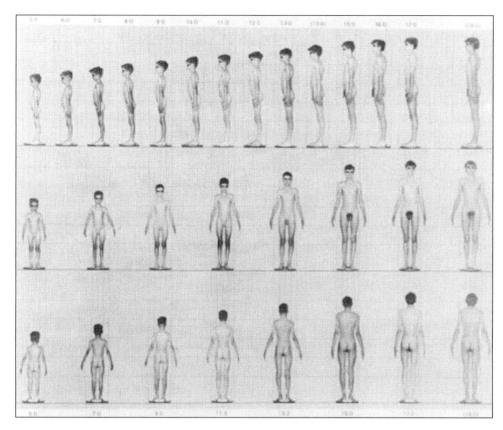

FIGURE 4.6 Somatotype photographs of a boy followed from 5 to 18 years of age. The young adult somatotype is predominantly ectomorphic, 2-3-6.

Adapted, by permission, from Tanner and Whitehouse, 1982, *Atlas of children's growth: Normal variation and growth disorders* (London: Academic Press).

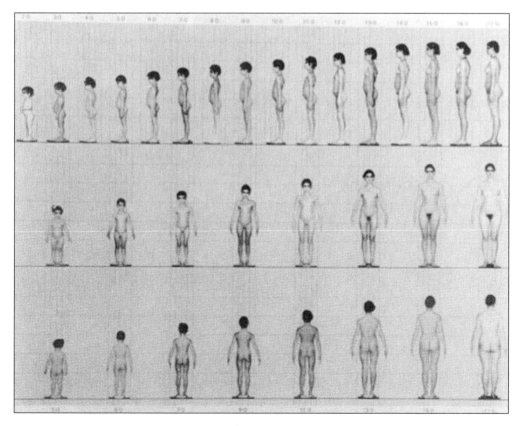

FIGURE 4.7 Somatotype photographs of a girl followed from 3 to 17.5 years of age. The young adult somatotype is predominantly endomorphic, 6-3-2.

Adapted, by permission, from Tanner and Whitehouse, 1982, *Atlas of children's growth: Normal variation and growth disorders* (London: Academic Press).

development of muscle tissue, and the lengthening of the legs relative to stature at these ages. Other changes become apparent during adolescence and revolve around shifts in the relationship between the shoulders and hips, the accumulation of subcutaneous adipose tissue in girls, and the development of muscle mass in boys. Some changes thus occur in specific components of the individual's somatotype during growth, primarily during the transition from early to middle childhood and during adolescence. Although changes in somatotype occur during growth, they are generally not dramatic in most children, and an individual's young adult physique is quite recognizable during childhood.

Distributions of Somatotypes

The difference in physique between boys and girls is especially apparent in the distribution of somatotypes in reasonably large samples of children. In a sample of 374 preschool boys and girls 2 to 5 years of age, only 25% of the boys' ratings reached or exceeded a value of 4 for endomorphy, whereas more than 50% of the girls' ratings reached or exceeded this value for the first component. In mesomorphy, on the other hand, more than 50% of the boys reached or surpassed a rating of 4, whereas only 16% of the girls reached or exceeded a rating of 4 in mesomorphy (Walker 1962). The physiques of male and female endomorphs or of male and female mesomorphs are fairly much alike, but endomorphic girls outnumber endomorphic boys and mesomorphic boys outnumber mesomorphic girls, which represents a sex difference that is perhaps genetic in origin. In other words, a large sample of children and youth will have more endomorphic girls than endomorphic boys and more mesomorphic boys than mesomorphic girls.

Petersen's *Atlas for Somatotyping Children* (1967) presents perhaps the largest published collection of somatotype photographs of children. It is based on a cross-sectional sample of Dutch children 5 to 16 years of age. Sheldon's original criteria for adult males were applied to derive the somatotypes of the children. Although these data have been criticized (Carter and Heath 1990), the series of 560 photographs provides a valuable resource for evaluating variation in somatotypes of a large sample of children. The distribution of somatotypes in this series of primarily preadolescent

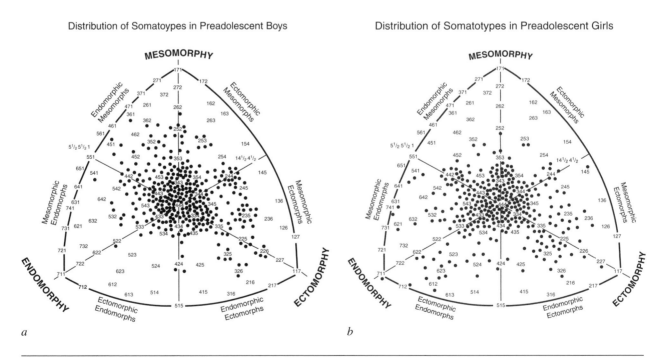

FIGURE **4.8**   Distributions of somatotypes in a sample of primarily preadolescent Dutch boys (*a*) and girls (*b*).

Adapted, by permission, from G. Petersen, 1967, *Atlas for somatotyping children* (Assen, The Netherlands: Koninklijke Van Gorcum & Company), 99.

Dutch children is illustrated in figure 4.8. Most of the children tend toward a balanced physique (central portion of the somatocharts), but the greater concentrations of girls in the endomorphic sector (see figure 4.8b) and of boys in the mesomorphic sector (see figure 4.8a) are obvious. Boys are distributed throughout the somatotype spectrum more than girls, who tend to cluster in the central and the endomorphic sectors. However, considerable overlap occurs in the distributions of somatotypes of boys and girls. Similar distributions are evident in the somatotypes of small samples of late adolescents of both sexes in the Harpenden Growth Study (see figure 4.9).

Sex differences in somatotype center primarily on endomorphy and mesomorphy. On the average, from preschool ages through young adulthood, males are more mesomorphic, slightly more ectomorphic, and less endomorphic than females. Females, on the other hand, are consistently more endomorphic than males. In contrast to the cross-sectional data for Dutch children presented by Petersen (1967), the *Atlas of Children's Growth* by Tanner and Whitehouse (1982) includes longitudinal series of somatotype photographs of British children in the Harpenden Growth Study. Both of these sources provide good guides to somatotyping children and adolescents, to variation in somatotypes among children and adolescents of the same age and sex, to sex differences in somatotype, and to individual variation in somatotypes during growth and maturation.

Change in Somatotype During Growth

Mean somatotypes for several longitudinal samples of boys and girls seen at different ages between early childhood and young adulthood are summarized in tables 4.1 and 4.2, respectively. Because longitudinal data for girls are not as extensive as for boys, two cross-sectional samples are also included in table 4.2. Standard deviations for mean components approximate 1.0 to 1.5 somatotype units and are not shown in the tables. The method of estimating somatotype in each study is indicated in the tables.

Anthropometric estimates of endomorphy are generally lower than those based on the photoscopic method, whereas estimates of ectomorphy are generally similar because both the photoscopic and anthropometric methods used the same stature/weight ratio. Mesomorphy is the component that varies most between the photoscopic and anthropometric methods. The photoscopic method appears to give a somewhat higher estimate of mesomorphy. This higher estimate is especially apparent in the Belgian boys followed from 13 to 18 years of age. Somatotypes

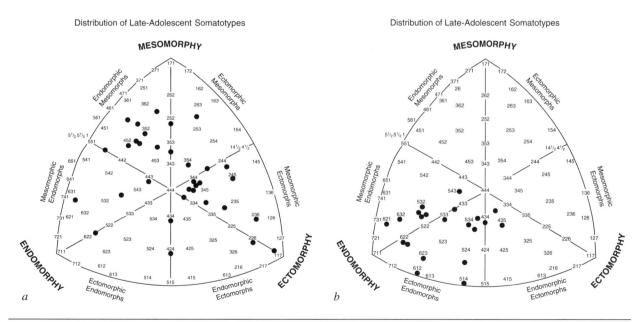

FIGURE 4.9   Distributions of young late-adolescent somatotypes in 33 boys (*a*) and 21 girls (*b*) from the Harpenden Growth Study.

Adapted, by permission, from Tanner and Whitehouse, 1982, *Atlas of children's growth: Normal variation and growth disorders* (London: Academic Press).

TABLE 4.1   Mean Somatotypes of Boys in Several North American and European Longitudinal Studies

Age (yr)	Connecticut (Walker 1978) Anthroposcopic			England (Walker and Tanner 1980) Anthroposcopic			Oregon (Clarke 1971) Anthroposcopic			California (Zuk 1958) Anthroposcopic		
	Endo	Meso	Ecto	Endo	Meso	Ecto	Endo	Meso	Ecto	Endo	Meso	Ecto
2-5	3.7	4.2	4.1									
5				3.5	3.8	3.8						
6												
7												
8				3.5	3.9	4.0						
9							3.4	4.2	2.9			
10							3.5	4.1	2.9			
11				3.5	3.8	4.0	3.4	4.2	3.2			
12							3.5	4.1	3.2	3.2	3.3	3.9
13							3.5	4.0	3.2			
14				3.5	3.8	4.2	3.3	4.1	3.3			
15							3.3	4.1	3.5			
16							3.4	4.2	3.4			
17										2.9	4.1	4.3
18	4.1	4.3	3.6[a]	3.5	4.0	3.9						

Note: Somatotypes—Endo = endomorphy, Meso = mesomorphy, Ecto = ectomorphy.

[a]Late adolescent somatotype.

of this longitudinal sample were estimated with a modification of Sheldon's original procedures and with the Heath-Carter anthropometric method. In modifying Sheldon's procedures, the Parnell scale for endomorphy (sum of the triceps, subscapular, and suprailiac skinfolds) and the Heath-Carter scale for ectomorphy (height divided by the cube root of weight) were used to derive preliminary estimates of the first and third components, respectively. These estimates were then used as guides in photoscopically rating endomorphy and ectomorphy from the somatotype photographs of each boy relative to *Atlas of Men* (Sheldon et al. 1954). Each boy's somatotype photographs were compared with those of young adult males (16 to 24 years of age) in the *Atlas* to derive a photoscopic rating of somatotype. The method used in this study is thus basically photoscopic and uses anthropometric data only as a guide in the process.

Estimates of somatotype based on modification of the photoscopic method and on the Heath-Carter anthropometric method yield different estimates in adolescent boys. Heath-Carter

anthropometric somatotypes are generally lower in endomorphy and higher in mesomorphy at most ages. A similar trend is evident in the sample of Czech boys compared with the others. This sample, however, was engaged in regular physical activity during the course of the study, which may be related to the lower endomorphy ratings.

Changes in mean components appear to be relatively small from childhood through adolescence. Allowing for variation among the samples for which data are available, several trends are suggested, particularly in the anthropometric estimates of somatotypes. Endomorphy tends to increase with age in girls and to decrease with age in boys, especially during adolescence. Ectomorphy appears to increase with age up to the time of maximum growth in height (about 12 years of age) in girls, and then declines. Ectomorphy tends to increase with age from childhood into adolescence in boys, and then declines in late adolescence. Mesomorphy appears to decline with age in girls and to increase gradually with age in males; the increase in males is especially apparent

Belgium (Claessens et al. 1986)						Belgium (Hebbelinck et al. 1995)			Czech Republic (Parizkova and Carter 1976)			Canada (Carter et al. 1997)		
Anthroposcopic			Anthropometric			Anthropometric			Anthropometric			Anthropometric		
Endo	Meso	Ecto	Endo	Meso	Ecto	Endo	Meso	Ecto	Endo	Meso	Ecto	Endo	Meso	Ecto
						2.1	4.2	2.6						
						2.0	4.1	3.0				2.9	3.6	1.6
						2.0	4.1	3.3				2.7	3.6	2.0
						2.1	4.0	3.5				2.7	3.5	2.3
						2.2	4.0	3.6				2.6	3.6	2.6
						2.3	3.9	3.7	2.1	4.1	3.4	2.7	3.7	2.9
						2.4	3.9	3.8	2.1	3.9	3.6	2.7	3.7	3.1
3.5	3.5	3.7	2.2	4.1	3.6	2.3	3.9	3.9	1.9	4.0	3.6	2.6	3.8	3.4
3.5	3.7	3.5	2.3	4.1	3.7	2.0	3.9	4.1	2.3	4.0	3.8	2.6	3.8	3.6
3.5	3.6	3.6	2.6	3.8	3.7	1.8	3.8	4.1	1.5	3.8	3.8	2.6	3.9	3.8
3.4	3.7	3.8	2.7	4.1	3.8	1.8	3.8	4.0	1.6	3.8	3.7	2.5	4.0	3.7
3.4	3.9	3.6	2.5	4.0	3.5	1.8	3.8	3.9	1.8	3.8	3.5			
3.5	4.0	3.4	2.6	3.9	3.4				2.3	4.3	3.3			

in late adolescence. The late-adolescent decline in ectomorphy in males is probably related to the late adolescent increase in mesomorphy, which is illustrated in the generally higher values for mesomorphy at 18 years of age.

Somatotypes of two samples of boys and one sample of girls were also estimated in adulthood, thus permitting comparison of late adolescent and adult somatotypes (see table 4.3). The Czech sample of males was studied at 24 years of age, and the California sample of males and females was studied at 33 years of age. The two samples of males show an increase in mesomorphy and a decline in ectomorphy between late adolescence and adulthood. In the Czech sample of males, mean endomorphy and mesomorphy increase, whereas mean ectomorphy decreases from 17 to 18 years of age. These trends continue from 18 to 24 years of age. The sample was actively training during most of adolescence, so some of the changes in late adolescence and into adulthood may reflect changes in the pattern of habitual physical activity, especially the effects of training on subcutaneous fatness. On the other hand,

mean endomorphy remains rather stable in the sample of California males. In the females, mean endomorphy and mesomorphy increase, whereas mean ectomorphy declines between 17 and 33 years of age.

Tracking

The mean values presented in tables 4.1 and 4.2 show small differences in somatotype from age to age. These values, of course, are derived from grouped data and do not represent individual children, who may in fact change in somatotype ratings from one age to another. Some children may change in one direction, and others may change in the opposite direction. When the individuals are grouped with the entire sample, individual changes are thus canceled; hence, the need to consider the evidence for tracking or stability of physique during growth. How well does an individual's somatotype track during childhood and adolescence? Is the early childhood somatotype predictive of the young adult somatotype?

TABLE 4.2 Mean Somatotypes of Girls in Several North American and European Longitudinal and Cross-Sectional Studies

	Longitudinal									Cross-sectional					
	Connecticut (Walker 1978)			California (Zuk 1958)			Belgium (Hebbelinck et al. 1995)			Belgium (Claessens, unpublished)			Quebec (Bouchard, unpublished)		
	Anthroposcopic			Anthroposcopic			Anthropometric			Anthropometric			Anthropometric		
Age (yr)	Endo	Meso	Ecto	Endo	Meso	Ecto	Endo	Meso	Ecto	Endo	Meso	Ecto	Endo	Meso	Ecto
2-5	4.4	3.5	3.8												
6							2.8	4.4	2.3	2.1	4.2	2.4			
7							2.7	4.2	2.8	2.2	4.1	2.7			
8							2.8	4.1	2.9	2.3	3.9	3.1			
9							2.9	4.0	3.2	2.6	3.7	3.3			
10							3.1	3.9	3.3	2.9	3.6	3.4	2.9	4.0	3.1
11							3.1	3.9	3.5	3.0	3.5	3.5	2.8	3.6	3.7
12				3.9	3.3	3.5	3.0	3.8	3.5	3.2	3.3	3.6	2.7	3.4	3.8
13							3.1	3.5	3.4	3.5	3.1	3.4	3.3	3.1	3.6
14							3.2	3.5	3.4	3.8	3.0	3.3	3.6	3.2	3.2
15							3.1	3.5	3.3	3.9	3.0	3.1	3.6	3.1	3.3
16							3.2	3.5	3.1	4.0	3.1	2.9	3.7	3.4	2.9
17				4.3	3.5	3.3	3.4	3.6	2.9	4.0	3.1	2.9	3.6	3.3	3.1
18	5.1	3.3	3.4[a]							4.1	3.1	2.8	3.8	3.5	2.8

Note: Somatotypes—Endo = endomorphy, Meso = mesomorphy, Ecto = ectomorphy.

[a]Late adolescent somatotype.

TABLE 4.3 Changes in Mean Somatotype From Late Adolescence Into Adulthood in Two Longitudinal Samples

| | Age (yr) | Somatotype components | | | Reference |
		Endo	Meso	Ecto	
Males	17	2.9	4.1	4.3	Zuk (1958)
	33	3.0	4.7	3.7	
Females	17	4.3	3.5	3.3	Zuk (1958)
	33	4.7	3.9	2.8	
Males	17	1.7	4.0	3.4	Carter and Parizkova (1978)
	18	2.4	4.7	3.0	
	24	2.7	5.4	2.5	

Note: Somatotypes—Endo = endomorphy, Meso = mesomorphy, Ecto = ectomorphy.

Correlations between an individual's somatotype rating at one or several ages during childhood with his or her rating at another age, usually late adolescence or young adulthood, are commonly used to estimate the stability or tracking of somatotype during growth. Note, however, that an individual's somatotype is defined by the three components together. Focusing on the correlation for a specific component at different ages independent of ratings of the other components is not appropriate.

Information on the relationship between childhood and young adult somatotype is quite limited. Relationships between photoscopic estimates of somatotype in early childhood (2 to 5 years of age) and at 18 years of age are moderate, with correlations of about 0.4 to 0.6 for both sexes (Walker 1978). Relationships improve as children get older as shown in figure 4.10 for boys in the Harpenden Growth Study. Correlations between photoscopic ratings of childhood and young adult mesomorphy and ectomorphy are moderately high, about 0.7 and 0.8, from 4 years of age on. The correlations for endomorphy improve from 5 to 8 years of age, and then remain moderate, although lower than those for mesomorphy and ectomorphy through adolescence. This trend for endomorphy suggests that some changes occur in somatotype in the transition from early to middle childhood, most likely reflecting changes in fatness. From 8 years of age, on the other hand, stability of somatotype ratings is quite good.

Interage correlations between anthropometric somatotype ratings at each age from 6 to 16 years and somatotype at 17 years in Belgian boys (n = 52) and girls (n = 30) are shown in figure 4.11. As

FIGURE 4.10 Correlations between photoscopic somatotype ratings during childhood and adolescence (5, 8, 11, and 14 years of age) and somatotype ratings at 18 years of age for boys in the Harpenden Growth Study.

Data from Walker and Tanner, 1980.

noted earlier in the chapter, the validity of the anthropometric somatotype protocol with young children has not been established, and this may explain why some interage correlations at these ages are quite low, especially for mesomorphy. The correlations for boys are consistently lower than those based on the photoscopic method shown in figure 4.10. Correlations between mesomorphy ratings at 6 to 7 and 17 years of age are very low, but then almost double at 8 years of age. Subsequently, correlations between

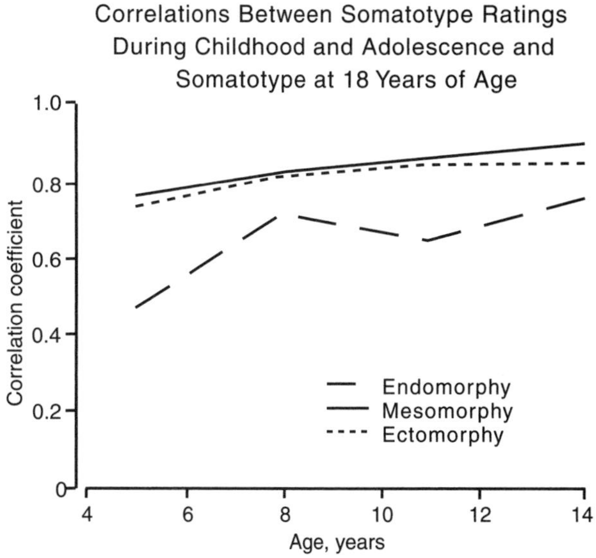

Correlations Between
Somatotype Ratings from
6 to 16 Years and Somatotype
at 17 Years of Age

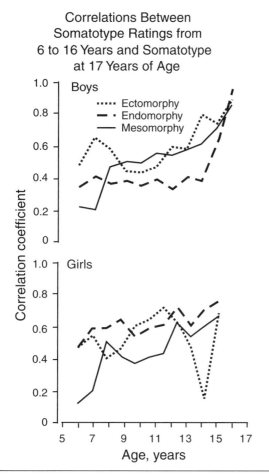

FIGURE 4.11   Correlations between anthropometric somatotype ratings at each age from 6 to 16 years of age and somatotype at 17 years of age in Belgian boys (top) and girls (bottom). The values plotted are partial correlations, controlling for the other two components while calculating the interage correlation for the component in question.

Data from Hebbelinck et al., 1995.

childhood estimates of mesomorphy and the late adolescent estimate increase gradually. Interage correlations for ectomorphy are variable between 6 and 9 years of age, and then increase gradually. On the other hand, interage correlations between childhood ratings of endomorphy and the late adolescent estimate are uniformly low from 6 to 14 years of age, and then increase considerably. These trends for boys suggest that predicting somatotype at 17 years of age from anthropometric somatotype estimates made between 6 and 14 years of age would be difficult.

The corresponding correlations for Belgian girls show a generally similar pattern for mesomorphy, but the correlations are lower. Inter-

age correlations between childhood ratings of endomorphy and the late-adolescent estimate are consistently higher in girls than in boys, especially between 6 and 14 years of age. Interage correlations for ectomorphy are variable between 6 and 8 years of age, increase to 12 years of age, but then decrease, approaching 0.00 at 15 years of age. Thus, as in boys, predicting somatotype at 17 years of age from anthropometric estimates of somatotype made between 6 and 15 years of age in girls would be difficult.

Earlier studies of the tracking of somatotype focused on adolescence given the significant changes in size, proportions, and body composition that occur at this time. Correlations between somatotype ratings made at early and late adolescent ages are ordinarily considered (see table 4.4). The lower age limit in the studies presents a problem. At 12 to 13 years of age, girls are both farther along in the adolescent growth spurt and closer to sexual maturity than boys are, and this difference may contribute to the higher correlations. On the other hand, a sample of 12-to-13-year-old boys most likely includes some who are preadolescent and others who are already in their growth spurts. Individual differences in the timing and tempo of the growth spurt and sexual maturation within a single chronological age group will influence interage correlations. With few exceptions, the correlations for boys suggest moderate tracking for ectomorphy and a bit more variation in mesomorphy and endomorphy from early to late adolescence. The variation is probably both biological and methodological. Boys experience a rather marked increase in muscle mass and a decrease in subcutaneous adipose tissue on the extremities during the adolescent growth spurt. The stature spurt occurs somewhat earlier than the spurt in muscle mass, as boys apparently first "stretch" and then "fill out." Hence, one might expect less tracking in mesomorphy and endomorphy during male adolescence.

Information on the tracking of somatotype components in girls over adolescence is limited to two studies (see table 4.4). Correlations between ratings at 12 and 17 years of age are moderately high for ectomorphy and a bit lower for endomorphy. The interage correlations for mesomorphy differ in the two studies. The interage correlation for the photoscopic estimate (0.83) is more than twice as high as that for the anthropometric estimate (0.36). The correlations for girls, although limited, overlap those for boys over the same age interval and suggest moderate tracking of somatotype.

TABLE 4.4 Correlations Between Ratings of Somatotype Components at Early- and Late-Adolescent Ages in North American and European Boys and Girls

Sex	Ages	Correlated method[b]	Components[a] Endo	Meso	Ecto	Reference
Male	12–17	SH[c]	0.66	0.73	0.71	California (Zuk 1958)
	12–17	SH	0.45	0.50	0.71	California (Hunt and Barton 1959)
	12–17	SH	0.54	0.51	0.62	California (Barton and Hunt 1962)
	12–17	SH[c]	0.50	0.60	0.67	Oregon (Clarke 1971)
	12–17[d]	HC	0.29	0.50	0.55	Belgium (Hebbelinck et al. 1995)
	13–16[d]	HC	0.66	0.59	0.66	Saskatchewan (Carter et al. 1997)
	13–18	HC	0.56	0.81	0.70	Czech Republic (Parizkova and Carter 1976)
	13–18	SH	0.78	0.57	0.79	Belgium (Claessens et al. 1986)
		HC	0.79	0.73	0.82	
Female	12–17	SH[c]	0.67	0.83	0.84	California (Zuk 1958)
	12–17[d]	HC	0.60	0.36	0.73	Belgium (Hebbelinck et al. 1995)

[a]Components—Endo = endomorphy; Meso = mesomorphy; Ecto = ectomorphy.

[b]Methods—SH = Sheldon photoscopic, HC = Heath-Carter anthropometric ratings.

[c]The somatotype photographs were rated by Barbara Heath. Although the published reports indicate that Sheldon's method was used, J. E. Lindsay Carter indicated to the authors that Heath's modification of the method was actually used.

[d]Partial correlations for each component with the other two components held constant.

Summary

Methods for the assessment of physique or body build and their applicability to children and youth are described, primarily in the context of the somatotype. Variation in somatotype among children and adolescents is considerable, and the difference between sexes is largely in the distribution of somatotypes in samples of boys and girls. Changes in somatotype from childhood through adolescence are described on the basis of observations from several cross-sectional and longitudinal studies. Somatotype is a moderately stable characteristic of the individual from late childhood on, but variation during adolescence is associated with individual differences in the timing and tempo of the adolescent growth spurt and sexual maturation.

Sources and Suggested Readings

Arngrimsson SA, Evans EM, Saunders MJ, Ogburn CL, Lewis RD, Cureton KJ (2000) Validation of body composition estimates in male and female distance runners using estimates from a four-component model. American Journal of Human Biology 12:301-314.

Barton WH, Hunt EE (1962) Somatotype and adolescence in boys: a longitudinal study. Human Biology 34:254-270.

Bouchard C (1985) Reproducibility of body composition and adipose tissue measurements in humans. In AF Roche (ed), Body Composition Assessments in Youth and Adults. Columbus, OH: Ross Laboratories, pp 9-13.

Carter JEL, Heath BH (1986) Comparison of somatotypes of young adults by two methods. In T Reilly, J Watkins, J Borms (eds), Kinanthropometry III. London: E & FN Spon, pp 63-67.

* Carter JEL, Heath BH (1990) Somatotyping—Development and Applications. Cambridge: Cambridge University Press.

Carter JEL, Mirwald RL, Heath-Roll BH, Bailey DA (1997) Somatotypes of 7- to 16-year-old boys in Saskatchewan, Canada. American Journal of Human Biology 9:257-272.

Carter JEL, Parizkova J (1978) Changes in somatotypes of European males between 17 and 24 years. American Journal of Physical Anthropology 48:251-254.

Claessens A, Beunen G, Simons J (1986) Stability of anthroposcopic and anthropometric estimates of physique in Belgian boys followed longitudinally from 13 to 18 years of age. Annals of Human Biology 13:235-244.

Claessens A, Beunen G, Simons J, Swalus P, Ostyn M, Renson R, Van Gerven D (1980) A modification of Sheldon's anthroposcopic somatotype method. Anthropologiai Kozlemenyek 24:45-54.

Clarke HH (1971) Physical and Motor Tests in the Medford Boys' Growth Study. Englewood Cliffs, NJ: Prentice-Hall.

Comas J (1957) Manual of Physical Anthropology. Springfield, IL: C C Thomas.

* Damon A (1970) Constitutional medicine. In O Von Mering, L Kasdan (eds), Anthropology and the Behavioral and Health Sciences. Pittsburgh: University of Pittsburgh Press, pp 179-205.

* Heath BH (1963) Need for modification of somatotype methodology. American Journal of Physical Anthropology 21:227-233.

Heath BH, Carter JEL (1967) A modified somatotype method. American Journal of Physical Anthropology 27:57-74.

Hebbelinck M, Duquet W, Borms J, Carter JEL (1995) Stability of somatotypes: A longitudinal study of Belgian children age 6 to 17 years. American Journal of Human Biology 7: 575-588.

Hunt EE, Barton WH (1959) The inconstancy of physique in adolescent boys and other limitations of somatotyping. American Journal of Physical Anthropology 17:27-35.

Katzmarzyk PT, Malina RM, Song TMK, Bouchard C (1998) Somatotype and indicators of metabolic fitness in youth. American Journal of Human Biology 10:341-350.

Lohman TG, Slaughter MH, Selinger A, Boileau RA (1978) Relationship of body composition to somatotype in college men. Annals of Human Biology 5:147-157.

Malina RM (1992) Physique and body composition: Effect on performance and effects of training, semistarvation, and overtraining. In KD Brownell, J Rodin, JH Wilmore (eds), Eating, Body Weight and Performance in Athletes. Philadelphia: Lea & Febiger, pp 94-111.

Malina RM, Katzmarzyk PT, Song TMK, Theriault G, Bouchard C (1997) Somatotype and cardiovascular risk factors in healthy adults. American Journal of Human Biology 9:11-19.

Malina RM, Merrett DMS, Bonci CM, Ryan RC, Wellens RE (1996) Relationship between androgyny and somatotype in female athletes and non-athletes. In LS Sidhu, SP Singh (eds), Human Biology: Global Developments. Ludhiana, India: USF Publishers, pp 27-37.

* Malina RM, Rarick GL (1973) Growth, physique, and motor performance. In GL Rarick (ed), Physical Activity: Human

Growth and Development. New York: Academic Press, pp 125-153.

Parizkova J, Carter JEL (1976) Influence of physical activity on stability of somatotypes in boys. American Journal of Physical Anthropology 44:327-340.

Parnell RW (1958) Behaviour and Physique: An Introduction to Practical and Applied Somatometry. London: Edward Arnold.

Petersen G (1967) Atlas for Somatotyping Children. Assen, The Netherlands: Royal Vangorcum Ltd.

Sheldon WH, Dupertuis CW, McDermott E (1954) Atlas of Men: A Guide for Somatotyping the Adult Male at All Ages. New York: Harper and Brothers.

Sheldon WH, Lewis NDC, Tenney AM (1969) Psychotic patterns and physical constitution. In DV Siva Sankar (ed), Schizophrenia: Current Concepts and Research. New York: PJD Publications, pp 838-912.

* Sheldon WH, Stevens SS, Tucker WB (1940) The Varieties of Human Physique. New York: Harper and Brothers.

Slaughter MH, Lohman TG (1977) Relationship of body composition to somatotype in boys ages 7 to 12 years. Research Quarterly 48:750-758.

Slaughter MH, Lohman TG, Boileau RA (1977) Relationship of Heath and Carter's second component to lean body mass and height in college women. Research Quarterly 48:759-768.

* Tanner JM (1953) Growth and constitution. In AL Kroeber (ed), Anthropology Today. Chicago: University of Chicago Press, pp 750-770.

Tanner JM (1988) Human growth and constitution. In GA Harrison, JM Tanner, DR Pilbeam, PT Baker, Human Biology: An Introduction to Human Evolution, Variation, Growth, and Adaptability, 3rd edition. New York: Oxford University Press, pp 337-435.

Tanner JM, Whitehouse RH (1982) Atlas of Children's Growth: Normal Variation and Growth Disorders. New York: Academic Press.

Walker RN (1962) Body build and behavior in young children. I. Body build and nursery school teachers' ratings. Monographs of the Society for Research in Child Development 27, serial no. 84.

Walker RN (1978) Pre-school physique and late-adolescent somatotype. Annals of Human Biology 5:113-129.

Walker RN (1979) Sheldon's trunk index and the growth of the thoracic and lumbar trunk. Annals of Human Biology 6:315-336.

Walker RN, Tanner JM (1980) Prediction of adult Sheldon somatotypes I and II from ratings and measurements at childhood ages. Annals of Human Biology 7:213-224.

Wilmore JH (1970) Validation of the first and second components of the Heath Carter modified somatotype method. American Journal of Physical Anthropology 32:369-372.

Zuk GH (1958) The plasticity of the physique from early adolescence through adulthood. Journal of Genetic Psychology 92:205-214.

Chapter

5

BODY COMPOSITION

Chapter Outline

The preceding chapters have concentrated on changes in size of the body and its parts, changes in body proportions, and changes in physique, all of which pertain to external dimensions and characteristics of the body and only indirectly reflect the chemical elements and tissues that constitute body weight. Body weight is a gross measure of the mass of the body, which can be studied at several levels from basic chemical elements and specific tissues to the entire body. The terms weight and mass are used interchangeably throughout.

The area of study that is labeled body composition attempts to partition and quantify body weight or mass into its basic components. This chapter considers models and methods used for studying body composition, the applicability of the models and methods to growing individuals, and changes in body composition during growth.

Models of Body Composition

The study of body composition has been historically driven by the availability of methods to measure, or more correctly, estimate it. In other words, the research was to some extent directed by what could be measured rather than what the researchers wanted to measure. Over the past 10 to 15 years, however, significant progress has been made in the development and refinement of techniques to estimate the composition of the body so that virtually all components of the body can now be measured. This progress has thus resulted in the modification of the models that provide the framework for studying body composition.

Five Levels of Body Composition

Wang and colleagues (1992) (see also Heymsfield et al. 1996) suggest that body composition can be approached at five levels (see table 5.1). The model provides a comprehensive framework within which the lure and difficulty inherent in the study of body composition can be appreciated.

TABLE 5.1	The Five Levels of Body Composition Research	
Level	**Components**
I	Atomic—Oxygen, carbon, hydrogen, nitrogen, and other elements
II	Molecular—Water, protein, minerals, glycogen, and lipid
III	Cellular—Cells and extracellular fluids and solids
IV	Tissue—Skeletal muscle, visceral, skeleton, adipose, and residual
V	Whole body

Adapted from Wang et al. (1992).

The **atomic level** includes the basic chemical elements. Of the 106 elements that exist in nature, about 50 elements are found in the human body. More important, with technological advances, all 50 elements can be measured in the living subject. Four elements constitute more than 95% of body mass—oxygen, carbon, hydrogen, and nitrogen. These four elements plus seven others —sodium, potassium, phosphorus, chloride, calcium, magnesium, and sulfur—account for 99.5% of body mass (Heymsfield et al. 1996).

The **molecular level** of body composition includes water, lipid (fat), protein, and minerals. A very small amount of carbohydrate in the form of glycogen, about 300 to 500 g in adults, is found largely in the liver and skeletal muscle. Thus, body weight is viewed as follows:

body weight = water + protein + mineral + fat

Most of the mineral is located in bone tissue, with a small fraction in other tissues. Historically, the percentage contribution of each of the four components to body mass was derived from chemical analyses of human cadavers. Advances in technology now permit estimation of the basic components in vivo, in other words, in the living individual.

The **cellular level** of body composition views weight as composed of cells and substances outside of the cells—extracellular fluids and extracellular solids. The body cell mass is defined by intracellular fluids and intracellular solids and is the metabolically active component of the body. At present, methods are not available to measure the solids within cells in vivo. The primary extracellular solids are bone minerals and other components of connective tissues. Adipocytes or fat cells are a component of the cell mass of the body. They store lipids and form fat mass. Thus,

body weight = body cell mass + extracellular fluids + extracellular solids + fat mass

The **tissue level** of body composition focuses on the contribution of specific tissues to body weight. The primary tissues are skeletal muscle, adipose, bone, blood, the viscera, and brain. Skeletal muscle, adipose, and bone tissues have historically been a primary focus in growth studies using traditional technology such as radiographs (X-rays) and anthropometry. New technologies permit more refined assessment of these primary tissues, for example, the mineral content of bone tissue or subcutaneous versus internal adipose tissue.

The fifth level of body composition research is the **whole body**—size, shape, and physique. Anthropometry is the basic tool for estimating the size and configuration of the body. The body mass index (BMI) and skinfold thicknesses are perhaps the most widely used anthropometric indicators at this level of body composition. The BMI is reasonably well correlated with total and percentage body fat in large and heterogeneous samples, although it has limitations, especially with children and adolescents (see page 64). Skinfolds are indicators of subcutaneous adipose tissue and also are used in prediction equations to estimate overall body fatness.

Two other whole-body properties are very important in the study of body composition—the volume and density of the body. Body weight and volume are used to estimate body density, which in turn is used to estimate relative fatness. Density is discussed in more detail later in the chapter.

Multicomponent Models of Body Composition

A variety of models have been used to partition body mass into meaningful components or compartments. These models have evolved from the traditional two-component model to models including three, four, or more compartments.

Two-Component Model   The two-component model has traditionally had the widest application in the study of body composition. The lean aspect of body weight is referred to as **fat-free mass** (FFM), and the remainder is **fat mass** (FM). The term lean body mass is occasionally used, but fat-free mass is more appropriate. Fat-free mass is a biochemical concept, whereas lean body mass is a more anatomical concept that includes some essential lipids.

The two-component model is expressed as follows:

body weight = FFM + FM

FM is the more labile of the two compartments; it is readily influenced, for example, by habits of diet and physical activity. A shortcoming of the two-component model is the heterogeneous composition of the FFM. It includes water, protein, mineral (bone and soft tissue mineral), and glycogen, which were difficult to measure with the available technology. As technology evolved, so did models for estimating body composition.

Three-Component Model   The three-component model includes FM but partitions FFM into total-body water (TBW) and fat-free dry mass (FFDM). Thus, in the three-component model,

body weight = TBW + FFDM + FM

Water is the largest component of body weight and the majority is located in lean tissues. It can also be readily measured throughout the life span (see measurement of total-body water-hydrometry). Fat-free dry mass includes protein, glycogen, bone mineral, and soft tissue mineral.

Four-Component Model   With the development of techniques to measure bone mineral, the four-component model is a logical extension of the three-component model. The fat-free dry mass is partitioned in bone mineral (BM) and the residual. Thus, in the four-component model,

body weight = TBW + BM + FM + residual

Overview of Multicomponent Models   All of the models include fat mass. Fat mass is the aspect of body composition that has lately received most attention because of concern for excessive fatness as a risk factor of disease. Fat mass also has a negative influence on physical performance and may limit physical activity.

Fat mass, however, is also heterogeneous. Fat, or more appropriately lipid, is physiologically divided into essential and nonessential lipids. The essential lipids are vital components of cells and physiological functions. About 10% of total lipids in the body are essential lipids. The remaining lipids, 90% of total-body lipids, are nonessential. They are triglycerides, which provide a storage form of available energy and perhaps thermal insulation (Heymsfield et al. 1996). The small amount of essential lipids in the body are usually not considered in estimates of body composition and are usually grouped with the residual component or with fat mass, depending on the model and method of measurement.

The partitioning of fat-free mass into its different fractions presents several problems. Error is inherent in the measurement of each component, and the more components included in a model the higher the chances of error. The techniques available for the measurement of total-body water, potassium, calcium, and sodium each have associated error. Once measured, these properties of the body must be converted to the body composition component of interest. The transformation of the measured property to the component is essentially mathematical and includes a variety of assumptions. Multicomponent models are assumed to be additive, and the separately measured properties can be summed to provide an estimate of the whole. Thus, the measurement of body composition is essentially an estimate of body composition.

The various models approach body composition in a holistic manner. Some models permit estimates of specific components (e.g., total-body fat, bone mineral, muscle tissue, and nonmuscle lean tissue). The holistic approach also does not provide information about the anatomical distribution or regional development of tissues in the body. Some techniques, however, do permit the regional study of bone and adipose tissues and, to a lesser extent, skeletal muscle tissue. This ability is important relative to specific compositional changes, sites of change, and the genesis of sex differences in body composition with growth and maturation.

The different models of body composition have been largely developed on adults. They also assume that during periods of stable body weight, the various components exist in a steady state, which means that constant or relatively constant relationships exist among the components. These constant relationships permit the development of procedures to estimate the different fractions of body weight in adults. The application of these procedures to children and adolescents requires caution. The proportions of each component and the relationships among components change during growth and maturation. This topic is discussed later in the chapter.

Methods for Estimating Body Composition

A listing of methods of estimating body composition in vivo is given in table 5.2. The methods are quite numerous, and some are quite complex. The methods of estimating body composition are sufficiently different in technique that one may question whether they provide reasonably similar estimates of body composition.

Of special importance to studies of growing individuals is the fact that the methods have been developed on adults. The formulas for estimating FFM or FM, or components of the FFM, and the assumptions underlying the procedures are based primarily on adults and in some cases only

young adult males. Their application to growing children may thus result in spuriously high or low estimates of body composition. Allowing for these limitations and others (discussed later in the chapter), five commonly used methods for estimating body composition are described subsequently. Three have been regularly used with children and adolescents for about 40 years or more—the measurement of body density, body water, and potassium concentration. Two more recent methods—dual-energy X-ray absorptiometry (DEXA) and bioelectrical impedance analysis (BIA)—are also described. The specific protocols for each of these methods and their limitations are discussed in detail in separate chapters in Roche et al. (1996).

Measurement of Body Density—Densitometry

Density is mass per unit volume. The density of specific body tissues varies considerably. The density of fat (0.9007 g/cm^3), for example, is lower than the density of water (1.0 g/cm^3) and

TABLE 5.2   Summary of Methods Used to Estimate Body Composition

Method	Use
Underwater weighing, gas displacement	Estimates body volume and density, which is converted to percent body fat
^{40}K whole-body counting	Estimates potassium content of body, which is converted to fat-free mass (FFM)
Isotope dilution	Estimates total-body water which is converted to FFM, compartments of total-body water can also be estimated
Neutron activation analysis	Uses isotopes of nitrogen and calcium to estimate lean tissue and mineral
Bioelectrical impedance	Estimates FFM because lean tissues conduct electricity better than fat
Uptake of fat-soluble gases	Estimates fat mass (FM)
24-hr urinary creatinine excretion	Estimates muscle mass
3-methylhistidine excretion	Estimates muscle mass
Dual-energy X-ray absorptiometry (DEXA)	Estimates bone mineral, also lean and fat tissues
Magnetic resonance imaging (MRI)	Estimates fat, muscle, and bone without ionizing radiation, plus chemical composition
Computerized axial tomography	Estimates bone, muscle, and fat
Ultrasound	Estimates fat, muscle, and bone
Radiography	Estimates fat, muscle, and bone
Anthropometry	Estimates subcutaneous fat and predicts FM and FFM

Compiled from Malina (1969), Heymsfield (1985), Forbes (1986), Roche et al. (1996).

lower than the density of lean tissues (1.100 g/cm³ and higher). If these figures are viewed in the context of the body as a whole, a body with a low density has more fat than a body with a high density. Thus, density is inversely related to body fat content—the greater the proportion of fat, the lower the body density. Thus, body density measurements permit an estimate of the percentage of body weight that is fat.

Densitometry refers to the measurement of body density. The most common method is underwater (hydrostatic) weighing, but air or helium displacement techniques have also been used. In the underwater weighing procedure, body mass is determined first by weighing the subject in the usual manner in air. Then body volume is determined by the Archimedean principle that the volume of a body is equal to the water it displaces when fully submerged. The subject's weight is thus measured when the subject is completely submerged in the water. The difference between the subject's weight in the air and weight while submerged in the water is the weight of the displaced volume of water, correcting for the density of the water at the time of underwater weighing. Two other volumes affect body volume—the air remaining in the lungs (residual volume) and the air in the gastrointestinal tract. Thus, the formula for deriving body density (Db) is as follows:

$$Db = \frac{M_A}{\frac{(M_A - M_W)}{DW} - (RV + VGI)}$$

where: Db is body density in grams per cubic centimeter (g/cm³),

M_A is body mass in air,

M_W is body mass when completely submerged in water,

D_W is density of the water at the specified temperature,

RV is the residual volume of air in the airways and lungs during weighing, and

VGI is the volume of gas in the gastrointestinal tract.

Residual volume is measured indirectly, but occasionally it is estimated. Residual volume varies with stature during growth and with stature, sex, and age during adulthood. Children often do not exhale sufficiently while submerged; as a result, the volume of air in the airways and

lungs will exceed the theoretical residual volume. In young adults of both sexes, residual volume usually varies between 1 and 2 liters, but variation within and among individuals can be substantial. The volume of gas in the gastrointestinal tract is also variable among individuals, and a value of 100 ml is ordinarily used.

The measurement of body density by air or helium displacement involves the same principles as those for the underwater weighing method. The air or helium displacement techniques have been used in several studies of infants.

Two formulas are used most frequently to convert body density to the percentage of body weight that is fat (relative fatness):

$$\% \, fat = \frac{4.570}{Db} - 4.142$$

(Brozek et al. 1963), and

$$\% \, fat = \frac{4.950}{Db} - 4.500 \ (Siri \ 1956)$$

The formulas and their underlying assumptions are derived from adults. The two equations give generally similar estimates of relative fatness except for the very lean and very obese (Going 1996). Their application to children ordinarily gives elevated fat estimates.

The estimate of percent fat (% fat) is based on the assumption that the densities of the fat (0.9007 g/cm³) and fat-free (1.100 g/cm³) components are known and are constant and that adults are identical in composition except for variability in the proportion of fat. The densities of the components of fat-free tissue at 36°C also vary:

water = 0.9937 g/cm³

protein = 1.34 g/cm³

bone mineral = 2.982 g/cm³

non–bone mineral = 3.317 g/cm³ (Brozek et al. 1963)

The proportions and chemical composition of the various components of fat-free tissue change with growth and maturation, and individuals also differ in the composition of fat-free tissue.

If an estimate of FM (absolute amount of fat) is desired, it is derived by multiplication:

FM = body weight × % fat.

FFM is obtained by subtraction:

FFM = body weight – FM.

Measurement of Total-Body Water (TBW)—Hydrometry

Water is the largest compositional component of the body. It varies between 55% and 65% of body weight in normally hydrated young adult males, with lower values for females. Thus, the TBW of 70-kg young adult males can vary between about 38 and 45 kg of water. The emphasis is on normal hydration. Hydration varies after strenuous exercise and on hot days. In some disease states, severe protein-energy undernutrition, and extreme obesity, hydration of the body can also vary considerably.

Most of the water in the body is in lean tissues, so the measurement of TBW provides a means for estimating FFM. Water constitutes approximately 72% to 74% of the FFM in normally hydrated adults, although the estimated water content of FFM has been reported to vary between 67% and 74%. The mean (± standard deviation) hydration of the FFM is estimated at 73.9±1.5% in nine different mammalian species ranging from the mouse to humans (Wang et al. 1999). On the other hand, adipose tissue is relatively nonaqueous and contains a small proportion of water, about 20%.

The measurement of TBW is based on two principles of isotope dilution. The first principle is that certain substances dilute or distribute themselves evenly throughout a fluid space or compartment of the body. The second principle is that the dilution of a known amount of substance, an isotope tracer, administered into an unknown volume or mass enables the calculation of the unknown volume or mass. Thus,

$$C_1 V_1 = C_2 V_2$$

where C_1 and V_1 are the known concentration and volume of the isotope tracer before dilution, and C_2 and V_2 are the concentration and volume of the tracer after mixing.

Hence, the unknown volume of dilution can be calculated as follows:

$$V_2 = \frac{C_1 V_1}{C_2}$$

where C_2 is the concentration of the isotope tracer after complete dilution.

Thus, the isotope dilution method consists of administering a known amount of a stable isotope tracer, allowing it sufficient time to dilute or mix, and then measuring its concentration after dilution and after correcting for the amount of the tracer lost from the body by excretion or exhalation.

Three isotopes are commonly used to measure TBW. Deuterated water (^2H, deuterium) and tritiated water (^3H, tritium) are isotopes of hydrogen, and ^{18}O-labeled water (^{18}O is the heavy isotope of oxygen). Tritium has a limitation in that it involves a small radiation dose for the subject.

TBW varies somewhat during the course of a day, depending on fluid intake and physical activity level. Hence, it is ordinarily measured in the morning after an overnight fast. The isotope is administered to the subject based on body weight. Time is then permitted for its equilibration with body water, usually 2 to 4 hours depending on the isotope. Finally, the concentration of the isotope in serum, urine, or saliva is measured. Thus,

$$TBW = \frac{A - E}{C}$$

where A is the amount of isotope administered, E is the amount of isotope excreted, and C is the concentration of isotope in serum water, urine, or saliva.

Then, assuming that the percentage of water in FFM is constant in adults, FFM is estimated as follows:

$$FFM = \frac{TBW}{0.732}$$

FM is estimated by subtraction:

FM = body weight − FFM.

TBW is often subdivided into the water that is within the cells (intracellular water [ICW]) and water that is outside of the cells (extracellular water [ECW]). An estimated 57% and 43% of TBW are intracellular and extracellular, respectively, in young adult males (Schoeller 1996). ECW is ordinarily measured with the same isotope dilution principles as TBW but with either chloride or bromide as the isotope. These isotopes pass through capillary walls but not through cell walls and thus provide an estimate of water outside of the cells. ECW is quite heterogeneous. It is composed mainly of water in support and transport tissues: plasma, dense connective tissue (tendon, cartilage, and bone), interstitial lymph, and transcellular fluids (cerebrospinal fluid and joint fluids). ECW transports nutrients and removes wastes from the cells. ICW corresponds closely to skeletal muscle mass, the work-producing tissue of the body, but is not exclusively limited to it. Once ECW is estimated, ICW is derived by subtraction as follows:

ICW = TBW – ECW

Measurement of Body Potassium— Whole-Body Counting

Potassium occurs mostly in cells and especially in muscle tissue. Hence, measurement of the concentration of potassium in the body can provide an estimate of FFM. This estimate is made by measuring the amount of potassium-40 (^{40}K), a naturally occurring isotope of potassium. ^{40}K accounts for 0.0118% of the naturally occurring potassium in the human body (Ellis 1996). The concentration of ^{40}K is measured with highly sensitive detection instruments called whole-body counters, which count the gamma emissions of the naturally occurring potassium.

A constant proportion of potassium is assumed to be in the FFM. However, a sex difference exists in adults. Furthermore, some data suggest a decrease in total-body potassium per unit FFM with age in adults and a possible ethnic difference between American Black and White adults (Ellis 1996). The following proportions are commonly used to estimate FFM from whole-body counting, 68.1 mEq/kg (2.66 g/kg) in males and 64.2 mEq/kg (2.51 g/kg) in young adult females (Forbes 1986, 1987). Thus, allowing for variation in potassium content, FFM is estimated as follows:

$$FFM = \frac{mEq\,K}{68.1} \text{ in males, and}$$

$$FFM = \frac{mEq\,K}{64.2} \text{ in females.}$$

FM is then derived by subtraction:

FM = body weight – FFM.

More recent studies indicate variation in the potassium content of the FFM, particularly values lower than the suggested proportions used to estimate FFM (Ellis 1996). Nevertheless, most of the available data for estimating body composition from measures of total-body potassium utilize the constants reported by Forbes (1986, 1987).

Dual-Energy X-Ray Absorptiometry (DEXA)

Dual energy X-ray absorptiometry (DEXA) is used to measure bone mineral and soft tissue composition of the body. It provides estimates of the composition of the total body and of specific regions in the form of bone mineral, fat-free soft tissues (sometimes called bone-free lean tissue) and fat. The method requires a low radiation exposure in the form of two photon beams, one of low energy and the other of high energy, which are passed through the body. Radiation exposure with DEXA is low (0.05 to 1.5 mrem), depending on the machine and how quickly the total-body scan is done (Lohman 1996). DEXA scans take about 20 minutes, but newer machines can complete a whole-body scan in about 5 minutes. The DEXA unit measures the attenuation of the low-dose X-ray beam as it passes through different tissues of the body. How much of each photon beam is absorbed by the atoms in bone mineral and soft tissues of the body is recorded during the scan and converted to estimates of bone mineral and soft tissues (Goran 1997). The DEXA instrument must be linked with appropriate computer algorithms to derive estimates of bone mineral, fat-free soft tissue, and fat tissue content of the total body. The algorithms also permit division of the body into anatomical segments—arms, legs, trunk, and head—to permit estimates of regional body composition.

The derivation of fat and fat-free soft tissue from DEXA scans is based on the ratio of soft tissue attenuation of the low-energy and high-energy photon beams as they pass through the body. The attenuation of the low-energy and high-energy soft tissues is known based on scans of pure fat and fat-free soft tissues and theoretical calculations. The attenuation of fat and fat-free soft tissues is assumed to be constant. The attenuation for fat is lower than that for fat-free soft tissues. Using these constants and the scans from the DEXA unit, the amount of fat and fat-free soft tissue is calculated.

The derivation of bone mineral requires adjustment for the soft tissue overlying bone. DEXA technology provides an estimate of total-body bone mineral content (g) and total bone area (cm^3). The ratio of total-body bone mineral to total bone area is used to estimate bone mineral density (g/cm^3). DEXA basically measures the cross-sectional area of a scan (total bone area) and not bone volume; hence, expressing bone mineral relative to bone area is only an approximation of bone mineral density.

Several types of commercially available DEXA instruments are presently in use, primarily in hospitals, clinics, and research centers for the measurement of bone mineral. Each type of unit has its own computer algorithms for deriving estimates of body composition, and therefore interinstrument differences should come as no surprise. However, these differences cause concern for the comparability of measurements, especially of soft tissue, from machines produced by different manufacturers. All of them assume that the attenuation characteristics of bone, fat-free soft tissue, and fat are known and constant (Lohman 1996). DEXA has been developed primarily on adults but is being used more frequently with children and adolescents to study the accrual of bone mineral and to a lesser extent to estimate fat and fat-free soft tissue.

Bioelectrical Impedance Analysis (BIA)

The method of estimating body composition from bioelectrical impedance analysis (BIA) is based on the fact that lean tissue has a greater electrolyte and water content than fat. This difference in electrolyte content permits an estimate of FFM from the magnitude of the body's electrical conductivity or from the body's impedance to an electrical current as it flows from the source (usually the ankle) to the sink (usually the wrist) electrodes. The FFM has low impedance and high conductivity, whereas FM, which has a relatively low water and electrolyte content, has high impedance and low conductivity.

BIA uses an imperceptible electrical current, which is introduced into the body via electrodes placed on the ankle. The injected current passes through the body, and the voltage that is produced is measured by voltage-sensing electrodes placed on the wrist (National Institutes of Health 1994; Baumgartner 1996). The ratio of voltage to the current is impedance. Impedance to the flow of the current is related to the shape, volume, and length of the body, which is the conductor of the current. Because impedance is proportional to the geometry of the conductor, variation in body shape may be a factor in the application of BIA.

BIA thus measures the voltage for the path from the ankle to the wrist. It yields a measure of resistance, which is the major component of impedance. Resistance is usually converted to

total-body water (TBW), which is then transformed into an estimate of FFM, as described earlier in this section. The equation used to convert resistance to an estimate of TBW usually includes stature.

Several types of commercially available BIA units are presently in use, and differences exist among the units. They are portable (the size of a brief case) and relatively cheap. BIA is also convenient, rapid, and noninvasive. As such, it is finding increased application for estimates of body composition in population surveys. As with other methods of estimating body composition, BIA has many underlying assumptions, which need to be verified, especially for children and adolescents (National Institutes of Health 1994; Baumgartner 1996).

Applications to Children and Adolescents

The foregoing approaches to body composition provide an estimate of FFM and FM. Body density (Db) is converted to percent fat, and TBW, ^{40}K, and BIA (resistance) yield estimates of FFM. The other half of the two-component model is derived by subtraction, as indicated previously. The three-component model involves the simultaneous measurement of Db and TBW to derive an estimate of percent fat, and the four-component model includes Db, TBW, and total-body bone mineral to estimate percent fat. The multicomponent models have been applied to children and adolescents and provide the advantage of greater accuracy of body composition estimates. However, the cost and technical constraints of the required methodology may limit their applicability outside of the clinical or laboratory setting.

Most of the available body composition data for children and adolescents are derived from the two-component model using Db, TBW, or ^{40}K. The assumptions underlying the methods are based on adults, so application of these models to children should to be done with care, recognizing the inherent limitations of the methods, constants, and resulting estimates. For example, fat estimates from densitometry are based on the assumption that the density of fat and lean tissues is constant. FFM estimates from TBW and ^{40}K are based on the assumption that the water and potassium contents, respectively, of the FFM are constant. They also assume that the density of fat and lean tissues and the water and potassium contents of the FFM are the same in children and adults, which is not the case. The important issue in growing individuals is when are adult density, water concentration, and potassium concentration of lean tissue achieved? Conversely, how does the composition of lean tissue change with growth and maturation?

In addition to these important biological issues, logistical issues are also a factor in applying these methods to growing and maturing individuals. Densitometry by underwater weighing and water displacement requires no chemical analysis, and the basic equipment is perhaps the least expensive. However, the densitometric method is somewhat slow and often requires training subjects to become comfortable with the procedure. The lower age limit for its use with children is about 7 or 8 years of age. The measurement of ^{40}K is noninvasive, but the equipment is very expensive and quite sensitive. The time required to measure ^{40}K varies with the type of counter and size of the subject. It is usually given as 5 to 30 minutes. A major problem, which may limit the utility of ^{40}K measurements, is that children have difficulty remaining still in the constrained environment of the counter. Finally, measurement of TBW requires overnight fasting and 2 to 4 hours for mixing of the isotope before chemical analysis with special equipment. If tritiated water is used, the problem of exposure to a radioactive isotope arises.

BIA is finding increased application for estimates of body composition in children and adolescents. BIA is useful for describing the body composition of groups, but estimates have large errors in individuals, which limits its application. BIA is influenced by nutritional and hydration status and is not sensitive to acute changes in electrolytes and fluids. Significant variation also exists between BIA machines produced by different manufacturers. The resistance (R) function of impedance is used most often with stature (length of the conductor) to estimate FFM, but uncertainty persists about the appropriate hydration factor to use in converting R to FFM. Other equations use R and stature in conjunction with body weight, circumferences, and skinfold thicknesses to estimate FFM (Baumgartner 1996).

DEXA is used most often to estimate bone mineral content and bone mineral density, within the limitations of the density estimate indicated previously. DEXA estimates of total-body bone mineral content are also used in the four-component model (water, fat-free soft tissue, bone mineral, and fat) to increase the accuracy of body com-

position estimates. The procedures require the measurement of Db, TBW, and bone mineral, and whether the time and expense involved markedly improves the accuracy of the body composition estimates is not clear.

Changes in total-body and regional bone mineral content during growth are discussed in more detail in chapter 6. DEXA is also being used more often to estimate fat-free mass, total-body fat, and percent fat. The accuracy of these estimates, however, is not yet verified relative to estimates derived from the more established methods of body composition assessment, specifically densitometry and hydrometry. Of relevance are how effectively DEXA deals with regions of the body that contain a large amount of bone such as the head and trunk and how the results influence estimates of fatness.

An important issue in all body composition studies is validation. How accurately does a given technique estimate the specific components of body composition? What is the appropriate criterion against which to compare estimates of body composition derived from the different methods and models? Do the different methods and models provide the same estimates of FFM, FM, and percent fat? The assessment of bone mineral content increases the accuracy of the four-component model over the three-component model. However, the instrument to measure bone mineral content is reasonably expensive. Is this expense justifiable, given the small increase in the accuracy of the body composition estimates? These and other questions need to be addressed in evaluating the application of the new technologies and multicomponent models to growing and maturing individuals. Also, as indicated earlier, most of the methods and the assumptions underlying the derivation of the estimates of FFM, FM, and percent fat are based on studies of adults.

A more basic question is the following: Why do we want to estimate the body composition of infants, children, and adolescents? Obviously, knowing how the different components of body composition vary with age, sex, and maturity status is important. Variation in body composition associated with age and sex is discussed subsequently. Maturity-associated variation is discussed in chapter 17. Considerable progress has been made in estimating the genetic contribution to body composition (see chapter 18). Estimates of body composition are also relevant to studies of performance (see chapters 11 and 12), thermoregulation (see chapter 14), physical activity (see chapter 22), risk factors for several diseases (see chapter 26), and sport (see chapter 28).

Concept of Chemical Maturity

If the principles and methods for estimating body composition are to be accurately applied to children, a determination must be made of when, during growth, adult values for the primary components of the FFM are attained. When adult values are attained, chemical maturity is reached. The concept of chemical maturity is not a new concept. It was introduced by Moulton (1923, p. 80) and was defined as follows: "The point at which the concentration of water, proteins, and salts [minerals] becomes comparatively constant in the fat-free cell is named the point of chemical maturity of the cell."

Changes in the chemical composition of the body during growth can be appreciated in a comparison of the infant and young adult reference males in table 5.3. The concept of the **reference body** has developed to provide a basis for comparison in the derivation of indirect estimations of body composition in vivo. Many of the equations for estimating body composition from Db, TBW, and ^{40}K are based on constants derived from these reference values. They are, in a sense, the standard against which many indirect methods are checked. The reference body, although useful as a general reference of comparison, is limited in that the data used to develop it are derived from biochemical analyses of a very small number of individuals who are not necessarily representative of normal young adults. As such, the information is not as precise as it might appear. Advances in the technology for assessing body composition, such as neutron activation and DEXA, now permit more direct estimates of major elements in the body and bone mineral, respectively, and thus more accurate reference values.

Comparison of the reference infant and adult values indicates some of the major changes in body composition that occur with growth. During growth, the relative contribution of water to body mass decreases, and the relative contributions of protein, mineral, and fat to body mass increase. In addition, the relative contributions of protein and mineral to FFM increase during growth, whereas the contribution of water to FFM decreases. Thus, growth is an accretive process, adding or accumulating solids at the expense of fluids.

TABLE 5.3	Body Weight, Body Density, and Relative Composition of the Reference Bodies of the Male Infant at Birth and the Young Adult Male	
	Infant at birth	**Young adult male**
Body weight (kg)	3.5	65.3
Body density (g/cm³)	1.024	1.064
Compartments as % of body weight:		
Water	75.1	62.4
Protein	11.4	16.4
Fat	11.0	15.3
Mineral	2.5	5.9
Fat-free mass	89.0	84.7
Compartments as % of fat-free mass:		
Water	84.4	73.8
Protein	12.8	19.4
Mineral	2.8	6.8

For the reference infant, mineral includes 0.8% "residue."

Adapted from Fomon (1966) and Brozek et al. (1963).

Composition of the Fat-Free Mass in Children and Adolescents

At present, chemical composition data for a young adult reference female or for the years between infancy and adulthood are not available. Several groups of researchers have used both direct and indirect estimates of body composition from a variety of sources to derive estimates of reference values for the composition of FFM in infants, children, and adolescents. These estimates of the composition of FFM are summarized in table 5.4.

The relative contribution of water to FFM declines during childhood. The FFM of newborns and infants has a high water content. In contrast, the relative contribution of protein to FFM increases. The estimated relative contribution of mineral, primarily bone mineral, to FFM is rather stable in infancy and early childhood and then increases more or less linearly with age. Thus, with growth and maturation, the relative contribution of solids (protein and mineral) to

TABLE 5.4	Estimated Composition of the Fat-Free Mass (FFM) During Growth				
	Compartments of the FFM (%)				
Age (years)	**Water**	**Protein**	**Mineral**	**Potassium (g/kg)**	**Density (g/cm³)**
Males					
Birth	80.6	15.0	3.7	1.92	1.063
1	79.0	16.6	3.7	2.21	1.068
3	77.5	17.8	4.0	2.39	1.074
5	76.6	18.5	4.3	2.49	1.078
7–9	76.8	18.1	5.1	2.40	1.081
9–11	76.2	18.4	5.4	2.45	1.084
11–13	75.4	18.9	5.7	2.52	1.087
13–15	74.7	19.1	6.2	2.56	1.094
15–17	74.2	19.3	6.5	2.61	1.096
17–20	74.0	19.4	6.6	2.63	1.099
Females					
Birth	80.6	15.0	3.7	1.92	1.064
1	78.8	16.9	3.7	2.24	1.069
3	77.9	17.7	3.7	2.38	1.071
5	77.6	18.0	3.7	2.42	1.073
7–9	77.6	17.5	4.9	2.32	1.079
9–11	77.0	17.8	5.2	2.34	1.082
11–13	76.6	17.9	5.5	2.36	1.086
13–15	75.5	18.6	5.9	2.38	1.092
15–17	75.0	18.9	6.1	2.40	1.094
17–20	74.8	19.2	6.0	2.41	1.095

The estimated relative composition of FFM in the data of Fomon et al. (1982) does not add to 100 because the small, constant percentage of carbohydrate (0.6%) is not included in the table. The protein content of the FFM in the estimates of Lohman (1986) is derived by subtraction: 100 – water – mineral = protein.

Data from birth to 5 years of age are adapted from Fomon et al. (1982), and those for the other ages are adapted from Lohman (1986).

FFM increases, and the relative contribution of water decreases.

Sex differences in the relative composition of FFM are negligible during infancy and become apparent in early childhood. After about 3 years of age, the estimated relative composition of FFM indicates less water and more protein and mineral in boys. Thus, water constitutes a slightly greater percentage of FFM in females. The sex difference is also reflected in the estimated potassium content and density of FFM. From about 3 years of age, the estimated potassium content and the density of FFM are greater in boys than in girls. The difference probably reflects the sex difference in muscle mass and bone mineral.

The values given in table 5.4 are relevant to estimates of body composition from Db, TBW, and ^{40}K. The young child is not chemically mature. The estimated water content of FFM does not approach the 72% to 74% suggested in studies of adults until late adolescence. Thus, use of the adult constant of 0.732 to estimate FFM from TBW in children results in overestimation of FFM and underestimation of FM. Similarly, the potassium content of FFM in children is not equal to the suggested adult constants of 2.66 g/kg for males and 2.51 g/kg for females.

The estimated composition of FFM in late childhood appears to be nearing adult reference values, but children are not yet chemically mature. The major difference is in mineral content, specifically bone mineral, which increases considerably in the second decade of life. The gain in skeletal mineral between 10 years of age and young adulthood reflects, to a large extent, the growth and maturation of the skeleton during the adolescent growth spurt. The relative mineral content of FFM in boys, for example, increases from 5.4% at about 10 years of age to 6.6% between 17 and 20 years of age. The gain in relative mineral content of FFM from early through late adolescence (1.2%) is about 22% of the initial value at age 10. The corresponding increase in the mineral content of FFM in girls is less, 5.2% to 6.1%, between early and late adolescence, a relative increase of about 16%. Thus, chemical maturity of FFM is apparently not attained until after the adolescent growth spurt, probably about 16 to 18 years of age in girls and 18 to 20 years of age in boys.

Note that the information summarized in table 5.4 represents estimates of the chemical composition of the FFM from infancy into young adulthood. The approximations are derived in part from available biochemical cadaver analyses and analyses of specific tissue samples and from in vivo estimates of TBW, potassium, nitrogen, calcium, and bone mineral. The estimates vary somewhat from laboratory to laboratory, as is apparent in table 5.4. Estimates should not be expected to all be identical because different data, assumptions, and methods are used in their derivations. Efforts to arrive at the more accurate estimates of the chemical composition of the FFM continue. For example, the hydration of the FFM, based on a combination of in vivo techniques, was estimated as 72.7% in 5-year-old to 10-year-old children compared with 70.8% in adults (Hewitt et al. 1993). Unfortunately, adolescents were not included in this study. Nevertheless, the important conclusion to be derived from these estimates and ongoing studies is that the chemical maturity of FFM changes during growth and maturation and is not attained until late adolescence or young adulthood. Hence, the equations and constants based on adult values and earlier studies are often adjusted for the chemical immaturity of the FFM in growing and maturing individuals.

Changes in Body Density and Total-Body Water During Growth

Body density and total-body water measured in a variety of samples of North American and European children, adolescents, and young adults were compiled from the literature to illustrate age trends and sex differences in these basic parameters used to estimate body composition. Data for Db are from 32 studies, and those for TBW are from 11 studies. The total sample for Db is 3,667 (2,110 males and 1,557 females) from 8 to 20 years of age, and that for TBW is 1,152 (675 males and 477 females) from infancy to 22 years of age. Subjects were primarily of European ancestry (White), but several samples of American Blacks were also included. Reported means for TBW and Db adjusted for varying sample sizes and the data were then consolidated to yield a composite growth curve for each (Malina et al. 1988; Malina 1989). Measurements of Db are not available for adequate numbers of children under 8 years of age. Although only TBW is considered, TBW and ^{40}K show a similar growth curve from infancy through young adulthood.

Growth curves for TBW and Db derived from in vivo measurements are shown in figure 5.1. TBW follows a growth pattern like that of stature and weight, that is, a relatively rapid rise in infancy and then a more gradual increase through childhood. The adolescent spurt follows, and the increase in TBW is greater in males than in females. TBW reaches a plateau at about 15 to 16 years of age in females and increases into the early 20s in males. Sex differences are minor in infancy and childhood, although males tend to have, on the average, slightly greater water content than females. With the onset of the female adolescent growth spurt at about 10 years of age, the sex difference in TBW is reduced, but it soon becomes quite marked when the male adolescent spurt occurs.

Body density declines in males from about 8 to 10 years of age but then increases more or less linearly to about 16 to 17 years of age. In females, on the other hand, Db decreases from about 8 to 11 years of age, then increases only slightly, and finally reaches a plateau by about 14 years of age. Both sexes also show a slight decline in body density in late adolescence and young adulthood. The body density for pooled samples of Japanese adolescents 11 to 18 years of age (777

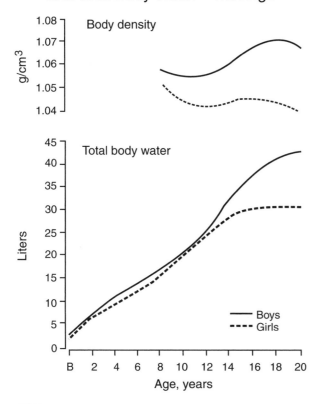

Changes in Body Density
and Total Body Water with Age

FIGURE 5.1 Growth curves for density and total-body water. Data points are based on moving averages and smoothed.

Data from Malina, 1989, and Malina et al., 1988.

males and 680 females) grouped by age and sex is consistent with that for American adolescents shown in figure 5.1 (Tahara et al. 2002).

Body density is inversely related to body fat content, although not linearly. Males have greater densities than females at all ages and thus have a correspondingly lower percentage of body fat. Although data are lacking for early childhood, estimates of density based on volume measurement with the air displacement technique indicate, on the average, slightly greater body density in newborn males than females.

Growth in Fat-Free Mass, Fat Mass, and Percent Fat

The TBW and Db values were subsequently converted to estimates of FFM and percent fat, respectively, using the age-specific and sex-specific estimates of the water content and density of FFM presented in table 5.4. This procedure thus allows for the changing chemical composition of FFM during growth. FFM and percent fat were then used in conjunction with the body weights of the composite samples to estimate FM and percent fat from TBW and to estimate FM and FFM from Db, as described earlier in the chapter. The weights and statures of the subjects in the samples from which TBW and Db were obtained compare favorably with reference data for United States children described in chapter 3. The estimates of FFM, FM, and percent fat thus provide an approximation of the growth patterns of these indicators of body composition.

Age-associated and sex-associated variation in FFM, FM, and percent fat are shown in figures 5.2 and 5.3 for estimates derived from TBW and Db, respectively. The figures are drawn to the same scale, but the age ranges differ. FFM follows a growth pattern like that of stature and weight,

Changes in Body Composition
from Birth to Young Adulthood

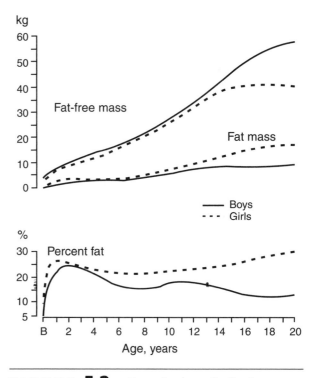

FIGURE 5.2 Growth curves for fat-free mass, fat mass, and relative fatness derived from measurements of total-body water.

Data from Malina, 1989, and Malina et al., 1988.

Changes in Body Composition from
Late Childhood to Young Adulthood

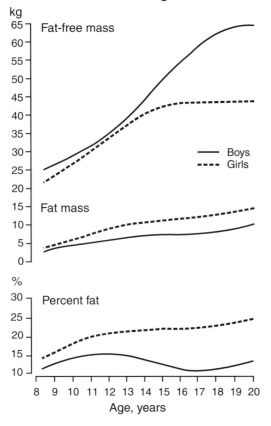

Fat-Free Mass per Unit Height from
Late Childhood to Young Adulthood

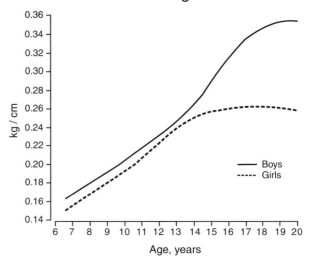

F I G U R E 5.4   Changes in fat-free mass per unit stature during growth.

Data from Malina, 1989, and Malina et al., 1988.

F I G U R E 5.3   Growth curves for fat-free mass, fat mass, and relative fatness derived from measurements of body density.

Data from Malina, 1989, and Malina et al., 1988.

and sex differences become clearly established during the adolescent growth spurt. Young adult values of FFM are reached earlier in females, at about 15 to 16 years of age compared with 19 to 20 years of age in males. In late adolescence and young adulthood, males have, on the average, an FFM that is about 1.5 times larger than that of females. The average FFM of young adult females is thus only about 70% of the mean value for young adult males. The difference reflects the male adolescent spurt in muscle mass and the sex difference in stature in young adulthood. The latter is illustrated in figure 5.4, in which FFM is expressed per unit stature. Sex differences in FFM per unit stature are small in childhood and early adolescence, but after 14 years of age, males have more FFM for the same stature as females. The sex difference increases with age. Young adult males have about 0.36 kg of FFM for

each centimeter of stature, whereas females have only about 0.26 kg of FFM for each centimeter of stature.

Estimated FM or total-body fat increases during the first 2 or 3 years of life and then shows little change through 5 or 6 years of age (see figure 5.2). The sex difference in FM is negligible at these ages. Subsequently, FM increases more rapidly in girls than in boys (see figures 5.2 and 5.3). FM increases through adolescence in girls, but it appears to reach a plateau or to change only slightly near the time of the adolescent growth spurt in boys (about 13 to 15 years). In contrast to FFM, females have, on the average, about 1.5 times the FM of males in late adolescence and young adulthood.

Changes in total-body fat expressed as a percentage of body mass are shown in the lower sections of figures 5.2 and 5.3. Relative fatness increases rapidly in both sexes during infancy and then gradually declines during early childhood. Girls have a slightly greater percentage of body weight as fat than boys during infancy and early childhood, but from 5 to 6 years of age through adolescence, girls consistently have a greater percentage of body fat than boys. The relative fatness of females increases gradually through adolescence in the same manner as FM. Relative fatness also increases gradually in males until just before the adolescent growth spurt (about

11 to 12 years) and then gradually declines. Percent fat reaches its lowest point at about 16 to 17 years of age in males and then gradually rises into young adulthood. Thus, in contrast to estimates of FM, relative fatness declines during male adolescence. The decline in percent fat is caused by the rapid growth of FFM and slower accumulation of FM at this time. Hence, fat contributes a lesser percentage to body weight in male adolescence.

The relative accuracy of FFM, FM, and percent fat derived from composite values based on Db for diverse samples in the literature can be evaluated by comparing them to corresponding estimates of FFM, FM, and percent fat based on a multicomponent model. Estimated FFM, FM, and percent fat for a mixed-longitudinal analysis of subjects from the Fels Longitudinal Study are plotted relative to the composite values in figures 5.5 and 5.6. The Fels data are derived from subjects who had at least six serial measurements of Db between 8 and 23 years of age. A multicomponent model incorporating age-specific and sex-specific estimates of the density and major components of FFM (as reported in table 5.4) was used to derive percent fat, FM, and FFM in the Fels data (Guo et al. 1997).

Estimates of FFM in the two samples of females compare closely, whereas estimates of FFM in Fels males are slightly, but consistently, lower than estimates for the composite sample. Estimates of FM are, on the other hand, consistently higher in Fels females and quite close in the two samples of males. When expressed on a relative basis, percent fat is consistently higher in the Fels males and females, although the differences in late adolescent males are small. Corresponding estimates of percent fat in a pooled sample of Japanese adolescents 11 to 18 years of age are generally similar with the two samples of American adolescents (Tahara et al. 2002). Allowing for variation in estimates of body composition and underlying assumptions, these comparisons suggest that composite estimates provide an accurate indication of the growth patterns of FFM, FM, and percent fat from childhood to young adulthood.

To illustrate the impact of adolescence on body composition, changes in densitometric estimates of body composition from early to late adolescence (10 or 11 to 18 or 19 years of age) are summarized in table 5.5. The estimates for the composite sample and the Fels mixed-longitudinal sample are quite similar in males, whereas the estimate

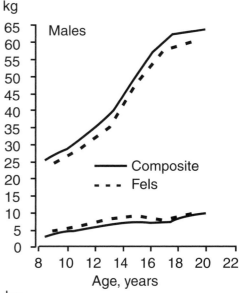

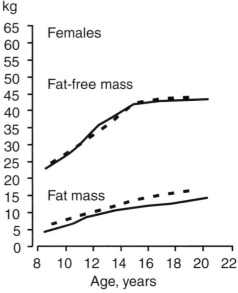

FIGURE 5.5 Growth curves for fat-free mass and fat mass derived for the composite samples in figure 5.3 compared with multicomponent estimates in the mixed-longitudinal Fels study.

Data from Guo et al., 1997.

for FFM is greater in the composite sample of females. Males gain almost twice as much FFM as females over adolescence, and females gain about twice as much FM as males. The net result is a decline in relative fatness in males and an increase in relative fatness in females.

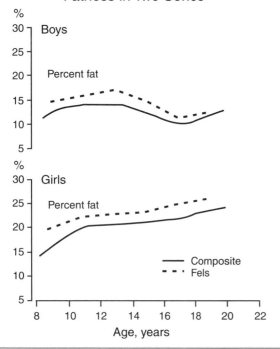

Comparison of Relative
Fatness in Two Series

FIGURE 5.6   Growth curves for relative fatness derived for the composite samples in figure 5.3 compared with multicomponent estimates in the mixed-longitudinal Fels study.

Data from Guo et al., 1997.

TABLE 5.5	Estimated Changes in Densitometric Estimates of Body Composition From Early to Late Adolescence in the Composite and the Fels Mixed-Longitudinal Samples	
	Males	**Females**
Composite sample[a]		
Fat-free mass	32.5 kg	17.3 kg
Fat mass	3.2 kg	7.1 kg
% Fat	-2.7 %	+5.0 %
Fels sample[b]		
Fat-free mass	31.3 kg	14.0 kg
Fat mass	3.4 kg	7.4 kg
% Fat	-3.5 %	+3.8 %

[a]Adapted from Malina et al. (1988) and Malina (1989).

[b]Estimated from Guo et al. (1997). The estimates are the differences between the two age groups, 10 to12 and 18 to 20 years of age. The midpoint of these 2-year age groups are, respectively, 11.0 and 19.0 years.

Tracking

Data on the stability of estimates of FFM, FM, and percent fat during infancy and childhood are not presently available. In a sample of 41 Czech boys followed from about 12 to 18 years of age, the interage correlation for FFM was 0.60, whereas those for FM and percent fat were 0.25 and 0.20, respectively (Parizkova 1977). FFM appears to track better than FM, suggesting that estimates of fatness are not as stable as estimates of lean tissue across male adolescence. The correlation for FFM reflects the dependence of FFM on body size, height perhaps more than weight. The interage correlations for height and weight between 12 and 18 years of age in the Czech boys were 0.68 and 0.50, respectively.

Tracking of FFM, FM, and percent fat in the mixed-longitudinal sample of the Fels Research Institute is shown in table 5.6. Tracking was based on the extent to which individuals remained in the upper third and in the lower two-thirds of the distributions within each age group over time (Guo et al. 1997). From 8 to 18 years of age, 83% of girls and 70% of boys remained in the upper third of the distribution for FFM, indicating moderately high tracking of FFM. FM and percent fat track moderately in boys; 60% and 72% of boys remained in the upper third from 8 to 18 years of age for FM and percent fat, respectively. In contrast, 43% and 46% of girls remained in the upper third from 8 to 18 years of age for FM and percent fat, respectively. This result suggests that FM and percent fat track less well in girls in the upper thirds of the respective distributions. For children in the middle and lower thirds of the distributions, the three indicators of body composition track at moderate to moderately high levels. FFM tracks somewhat better in girls, whereas FM and percent fat track somewhat better in boys. The sex difference may reflect the advanced maturity status of girls and individual differences in the timing and tempo of the growth spurt and puberty. Growth of FFM is completed in many girls by 18 years of age, whereas it continues into the early 20s in many boys.

In the longitudinal component of the Quebec Family Study, interage correlations over 12 years from baseline ages of 8 to 18 years, controlling for age at baseline and length of the follow-up period, were 0.59 and 0.64 for FM, 0.50 and 0.57 for percent fat, and 0.65 and 0.57 for FFM in males and females, respectively (Campbell et al. 2001).

TABLE 5.6 Tracking of Components of Body Composition in the Fels Mixed-Longitudinal Sample From 8 to 18 Years of Age

	Percentage remaining in the upper tertile		Percentage remaining in the middle and lower tertiles	
	Boys	**Girls**	**Boys**	**Girls**
Fat-free mass	70%	83%	84%	91%
Fat mass	60%	46%	80%	72%
% fat	72%	43%	86%	71%

Adapted from Guo et al. (1997).

Longitudinal studies of densitometric indicators of body composition spanning childhood though adolescence into young adulthood demonstrate moderately high and similar stability. Sex differences are not apparent in the strength of the interage tracking correlations.

Summary

Models and methods for partitioning and quantifying body weight or mass into its basic components and the limitations of applying the methods to children and adolescents are initially discussed. Data for children and adolescents are based on a blend of traditional (densitometry, hydrometry, and whole-body counting) and more recently refined (DEXA) techniques. Major changes in body composition, specifically fat-free mass (FFM) and fat mass (FM), occur during childhood and especially in adolescence when major sex differences are established. Presently available longitudinal data indicate the FFM tracks moderately well from childhood through adolescence in both sexes, whereas FM and percent fat are less stable characteristics.

Sources and Suggested Readings

* Baumgartner RN (1996) Electrical impedance and total body electrical conductivity. In AF Roche, SB Heymsfield, TG Lohman (eds), Human Body Composition. Champaign, IL: Human Kinetics, pp 79-107.

Baumgartner RN, Chumlea WC, Roche AF (1990) Bioelectric impedance for body composition. Exercise and Sport Science Reviews 18:193-224.

Behnke AR (1961) Comment on the determination of whole body density and a resumé of body composition data. In J Brozek and A Henschel (eds), Techniques for Measuring Body Composition. Washington, DC: National Academy of Sciences-National Research Council, pp 118-133.

Boileau RA (1996) Body composition assessment in children and youths. In O Bar-Or (ed), The Child and Adolescent Athletes. Oxford: Blackwell Science, pp 523-537.

Brozek J (1966) Body composition: Models and estimation equations. American Journal of Physical Anthropology 24:239-246.

Brozek J, Henschel A, editors (1961) Techniques for Measuring Body Composition. Washington, DC: National Academy of Sciences-National Research Council.

Brozek J, Grande F, Anderson JT, Keys A (1963) Densitometric analysis of body composition: Revision of some quantitative assumptions. Annals of the New York Academy of Sciences 110:113-140.

Burmeister W (1965) Body cell mass as the basis of allometric growth functions. Annales Paediatrici 204:65-72.

Campbell PT, Katzmarzyk PT, Malina, RM, Rao DC, Perusse L, Bouchard C (2001) Stability of adiposity phenotypes from childhood and adolescence into young adulthood with contribution of parental measures. Obesity Research 9: 394-400.

Cheek DB (1968) Human Growth. Philadelphia: Lea & Febiger.

Ellis KJ (1996) Whole-body counting and neutron activation analysis. In AF Roche, SB Heymsfield, TG Lohman (eds), Human Body Composition. Champaign, IL: Human Kinetics, pp 45-61.

Flynn MA, Hanna FM, Lutz RN (1967) Estimation of body water compartments of preschool children. American Journal of Clinical Nutrition 20:1125-1128.

Fomon SJ (1966) Body composition of the infant. Part I. The male "reference infant." In F Falkner (ed), Human Development. Philadelphia: Saunders, pp 239-246.

Fomon SJ, Haschke F, Ziegler EE, Nelson SE (1982) Body composition of reference children from birth to age 10 years. American Journal of Clinical Nutrition 35:1169-1175.

Forbes GB (1986) Body composition in adolescence. In F Falkner, JM Tanner (eds), Human Growth. Volume 2. Postnatal Growth, Neurobiology. New York: Plenum, pp 119-145.

* Forbes GB (1987) Human Body Composition: Growth, Aging, Nutrition, and Activity. New York: Springer-Verlag.

Friis-Hansen B (1963) The body density of newborn infants. Acta Paediatrica 52:513-521.

* Going SB (1996) Densitometry. In AF Roche, SB Heymsfield, TG Lohman (eds), Human Body Composition. Champaign, IL: Human Kinetics, pp 3-23.

Goldman RF, Buskirk ER (1961) Body volume measurement by underwater weighing: Description of a method. In J Brozek, A Henschel (eds), Techniques for Measuring Body Composition. Washington, DC: National Academy of Sciences-National Research Council, pp 78-89.

Goran MI (1997) Energy expenditure, body composition, and disease risk in children and adolescents. Proceedings of the Nutrition Society 56:195-209.

* Goran MI (1998) Measurement issues related to studies of childhood obesity: Assessment of body composition, body fat distribution, physical activity, and food intake. Pediatrics 101:505-518.

Guo SS, Chumlea WC, Roche AF, Siervogel RM (1997) Age- and maturity-related changes in body composition during adolescence into adulthood: The Fels Longitudinal Study. International Journal of Obesity 21:1167-1175.

Guo SS, Roche AF, Houtkooper L (1989) Fat-free mass in children and young adults predicted from bioelectric impedance and anthropometric variables. American Journal of Clinical Nutrition 50:534-443.

Haschke F (1983) Body composition of adolescent males. Acta Paediatrica Scandinavica 307(suppl):1-23.

Hewitt MJ, Going SB, Williams DP, Lohman TG (1993) Hydration of the fat-free body mass in children and adults: Implications for body composition assessment. American Journal of Physiology 265:E88-E95.

Heymsfield SB (1985) Clinical assessment of lean tissues: Future directions. In AF Roche (ed), Body Composition Assessments in Youth and Adults. Columbus, OH: Ross Laboratories, pp 53-58.

Heymsfield SB, Wang J, Kehayias J, Heshka S, Lichtman S, Pierson RN (1989) Chemical determination of human body density in vivo: Relevance to hydrodensitometry. American Journal of Clinical Nutrition 50:1282-1289.

* Heymsfield SB, Wang ZM, Baumgartner RN, Ross R (1997) Human body composition: Advances in models and methods. Annual Review of Nutrition 17:527-558.

* Heymsfield SB, Wang ZM, Withers RT (1996) Multicomponent molecular models of body composition analysis. In AF Roche, SB Heymsfield, TG Lohman (eds), Human Body Composition. Champaign, IL: Human Kinetics, pp 129-147.

Holt TL, Cui C, Thomas BJ, Ward LC, Quirk PC, Crawford D, Shepherd RW (1994) Clinical applicability of bioelectric impedance to measure body composition in health and disease. Nutrition 10:221-224.

Houtkooper LB, Going SB, Lohman TG, Roche AF, Van Loan M (1992) Bioelectrical impedance estimation of fat-free body mass in children and youth: A cross-validation study. Journal of Applied Physiology 72:366-373.

Jebb SA (1997) Measurement of soft tissue composition by dual energy X-ray absorptiometry. British Journal of Nutrition 77:151-163.

* Lohman TG (1986) Applicability of body composition techniques and constants for children and youths. Exercise and Sport Sciences Reviews 14:325-357.

* Lohman TG (1996) Dual energy X-ray absorptiometry. In AF Roche, SB Heymsfield, TG Lohman (eds), Human Body Composition. Champaign, IL: Human Kinetics, pp 63-78.

* Malina RM (1969) Quantification of fat, muscle and bone in man. Clinical Orthopaedics and Related Research 65: 9-38.

Malina RM (1980) The measurement of body composition. In FE Johnston, C Susanne, AF Roche (eds), Human Physical Growth and Maturation: Methodologies and Factors. New York: Plenum, pp 35-59.

Malina RM (1989) Growth and maturation: Normal variation and the effects of training. In CV Gisolfi, DR Lamb (eds), Perspectives in Exercise Science and Sports Medicine, Vol. II, Youth, Exercise, and Sport. Indianapolis, IN: Benchmark Press, pp 223-265.

Malina RM (1996) Regional body composition: Age, sex, and ethnic variation. In AF Roche, SB Heymsfield, TG Lohman (eds), Human Body Composition. Champaign, IL: Human Kinetics, pp 217-255.

Malina RM, Bouchard C, Beunen G (1988) Human growth: Selected aspects of current research on well-nourished children. Annual Review of Anthropology 17:187-219.

Moore FD, Olesen KH, McMurrey JD, Parker HV, Ball MR, Boyden CM (1963) The Body Cell Mass and Its Supporting Environment. Philadelphia: Saunders.

Moulton CR (1923) Age and chemical development in mammals. Journal of Biological Chemistry 57:79-97.

* National Institutes of Health (1994) Bioelectrical impedance analysis in body composition measurement. Bethesda, MD: NIH Technology Assessment Statement 1994, pp 1-35.

Ogle GD, Allen JR, Humphries IRJ, Lu PW, Briody JN, Morley K, Howman-Giles R, Cowell CT (1995) Body composition assessment by dual energy X-ray absorptiometry in subjects aged 4–26 years. American Journal of Clinical Nutrition 61:746-753.

Owen GM, Jensen RL, Fomon SJ (1962) Sex-related difference in total body water and exchangeable chloride during infancy. Journal of Pediatrics 60:858-868.

Parizkova J (1976) Growth and growth velocity of lean body mass and fat in adolescent boys. Pediatric Research 10: 647-650.

Parizkova J (1977) Body Fat and Physical Fitness. The Hague: Martinus Nijhoff.

Roche AF, editor (1985) Body Composition Assessments in Youth and Adults. Columbus, OH: Ross Laboratories.

* Roche AF, Heymsfield SB, Lohman TG, editors (1996) Human Body Composition. Champaign, IL: Human Kinetics.

Schoeller DA (1996) Hydrometry. In AF Roche, SB Heymsfield, TG Lohman (eds), Human Body Composition. Champaign, IL: Human Kinetics, pp 25-43.

Siri WE (1956) The gross composition of the body. Advances in Biological and Medical Physics 4:239-280.

Siri WE (1961) Body composition from fluid spaces and density: Analysis of methods. In J Brozek, A Henschel (eds), Techniques for Measuring Body Composition. Washington, DC: National Academy of Sciences-National Research Council, pp 23-244.

Tahara Y, Moji K, Aoyagi K, Nishizawa S, Yukawa K, Tsunawake N, Muraki S, Mascie-Taylor N (2002) Age-related pattern of body density and body composition in Japanese males and females, 11 to 18 years of age. American Journal of Human Biology 14: 327-337.

Wang Z, Deurenberg P, Wang W, Pietrobelli A, Baumgartner RN, Heymsfield SB (1999) Hydration of fat-free body mass: New physiological modeling approach. American Journal of Physiology 276:E995-E1003.

Wang ZM, Pierson RN, Heymsfield SB (1992) The five-level model: A new approach to organizing body composition research. American Journal of Clinical Nutrition 56:19-28.

Withers RT, LaForgia J, Heymsfield SB (1999) Critical appraisal of the estimation of body composition via two-, three-, and four-compartment models. American Journal of Human Biology 11:175-185.

Yssing M, Friis-Hansen B (1965) Body composition of newborn infants. Acta Paediatrica Scandinavica 159 (suppl): 117-118.

BONE TISSUE IN SKELETAL GROWTH AND BODY COMPOSITION

Chapter Outline

Bone Cells

Bone Formation

Growth of a Long Bone
Growth in Length
Growth in Width
Growth Remodeling
Overview of Skeletal Growth

Bone As a Component of Body Composition
Growth in Weight of the Skeleton

Bone Mineral Measurement

Changes in Bone Mineral During Growth

Regional Variation in Bone Mineral in the Body
   Radiographic Studies
   DEXA Studies

Tracking

Summary

Sources and Suggested Readings

Bone tissue constitutes most of the skeleton, which is the permanent supportive framework of the body and accounts for approximately 98% of stature. The remainder is largely cartilage, primarily in the form of the intervertebral discs that separate the vertebrae.

The skeleton also accounts for about 15% of body weight in the newborn infant and about 17% of body weight in adults younger than 50 years of age. In older adults, the skeleton accounts for a slightly lower percentage, about 14% of body weight. In addition to bone tissue, the skeleton of the living individual includes cartilage, ligamentous and tendinous attachments, blood vessels, marrow, fat tissue, and water.

Bone tissue is an important component of stature and, in turn, of growth in stature. Bone tissue is also an important component of body mass and composition. This chapter first focuses on bone tissue in terms of the growing skeleton and then considers bone tissue as a major component of body composition during growth.

Bone Cells

Osteocytes are the definitive bone cells. They are embedded in concentric layers of bone matrix around a central canal forming a Haversian system. Bone matrix is the hard substance of bone. It has organic components (primarily collagen fibers) and inorganic components (minute crystals of mineral [hydroxyapatite] derived largely from calcium and phosphorus). A cementing or ground substance binds the fibers and crystals into a compact unit. Osteocytes are embedded in the matrix and regulate the flow of minerals and nutrients between the matrix and blood.

Other types of bone cells are involved with the processes of bone deposition and bone resorption. They are, respectively, **osteoblasts** and **osteoclasts**. Osteoblasts are bone-forming cells. They are found on the surfaces of bone and in bone cavities. Osteoblasts deposit bone on a surface, most often the outer surface of a bone. Bone deposition involves the production of collagen and ground substance. In this process, an osteoblast is entrapped in the collagen and ground substance and becomes an osteocyte. The osteocyte subsequently mineralizes the collagen with crystals of calcium and phosphorus.

Osteoclasts are cells that resorb bone tissue. They are always found in areas of a bone that are undergoing resorption—removal of bone matrix and the release of minerals into the circulation. Resorption of bone matrix occurs during growth of individual bones and is essential for maintaining their shape. Enzymes and acids produced by the osteoclasts modulate the dissolution of the organic matrix and release the calcium salts into the circulation.

The three types of bone cells are variations of a single type of cell. Osteoclasts, after a period of bone resorption, are converted to osteoblasts, which begin to deposit bone matrix. When osteoblasts are entrapped in the matrix, they become osteocytes and begin the mineralization process. In the formation and remodeling of bone tissue, osteoclasts always appear first; they are then converted to osteoblasts, which deposit bone matrix.

In the growing individual, bone deposition occurs at a more rapid rate than bone resorption. In young and middle-aged adults, rates of bone deposition and resorption are ordinarily in equilibrium, whereas in old age, bone resorption occurs at a more rapid rate than bone deposition.

Bone Formation

Individual bones are formed prenatally by **intramembranous** and **endochondral** processes. The former develops between embryonic membranes; the latter develops from cartilage. Intramembranous bones include most bones of the skull, and endochondral bones include all bones of the postcranial skeleton and some cranial bones. The mandible and clavicles are unique in that they originate both endochondrally and intramembranously. Because the postcranial skeleton is the major portion of stature and a significant aspect of physique, attention is focused on the formation and growth of endochondral bones.

Steps in the formation of endochondral bones are illustrated in figure 6.1. The description of subsequent bone formation is based on Roche (1986). A bone is formed prenatally as a cartilage model, which is a miniature scale model of the bone. The **perichondrial** membrane envelops the model. As development of the cartilage model progresses, cartilage cells in the center of the model arrange themselves into columns and hypertrophy (see figure 6.1a). Hypertrophy occurs as a result of an increase in water and fluids in the cells. Collagen fibers subsequently appear between the cells and further separate them. The hypertrophied cartilage cells eventually become calcified. At the same time, osteoblasts form on the outer surface of the cartilage model near its center. As the underlying calcified cartilage is eroded, blood vessels and osteoblasts penetrate the cartilage. The osteoblasts begin to deposit bone matrix on the surfaces of the calcified cartilage cells. The site of bone deposition in the cartilage model is called a **center of ossification** (see figure 6.1b). In the long bone illustrated in figure 6.1, the center of ossification is located in the middle part of the model. It is the **primary ossification center** and eventually forms the shaft of the bone, the **diaphysis**. Some long bones may have several centers, which eventually coalesce to form the shaft.

The endochondral bone that forms the ossification center is cancellous. It has a porous structure. Cancellous bone is composed of trabeculae, spicules of bone with a calcified cartilage core separated by blood vessels (see figure 6.1c).

Continued formation of the endochondral bone of the diaphysis involves the establishment of the marrow cavity and the growth plate (see figure 6.1d). The marrow cavity is formed by the resorption of cancellous bone by osteoclasts and deposition of compact or cortical bone by osteoblasts just beneath the periosteum. The periosteum is the membrane that covers the outer surface of the diaphysis. The layer of the periosteum next to the bone surface has the capacity to produce osteoblasts. Another membrane, the **endosteum**, lines the surface of the marrow cavity. It is a rich vascular membrane. The growth plate has a thin layer of proliferating cartilage cells (chondrocytes) adjacent to the hypertrophying cartilage cells. While bone formation is occurring in the central portion of the model, cartilage cells proliferate rapidly at both ends. In this way, the entire model increases in length. The bone increases in width more at the ends of the model than at the central portion. The diaphysis, or shaft of a long bone, includes the marrow cavity and trabeculae surrounded by dense cortical or compact bone.

Ossification of the diaphyses of all long bones (humerus, radius, ulna, femur, tibia, and fibula) and short bones (phalanges, metacarpals, and metatarsals) of the body begins prenatally. These

Formation and Growth of a Long Bone

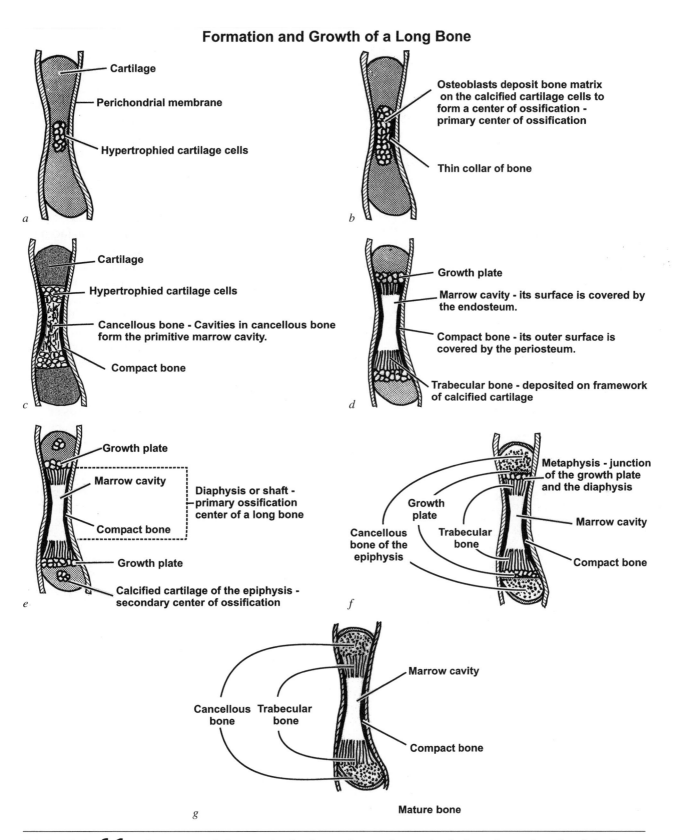

a

Cartilage

Perichondrial membrane

Hypertrophied cartilage cells

b

Osteoblasts deposit bone matrix on the calcified cartilage cells to form a center of ossification - primary center of ossification

Thin collar of bone

c

Cartilage

Hypertrophied cartilage cells

Cancellous bone - Cavities in cancellous bone form the primitive marrow cavity.

Compact bone

d

Growth plate

Marrow cavity - its surface is covered by the endosteum.

Compact bone - its outer surface is covered by the periosteum.

Trabecular bone - deposited on framework of calcified cartilage

e

Growth plate

Marrow cavity

Diaphysis or shaft - primary ossification center of a long bone

Compact bone

Growth plate

Calcified cartilage of the epiphysis - secondary center of ossification

f

Metaphysis - junction of the growth plate and the diaphysis

Growth plate

Cancellous bone of the epiphysis

Trabecular bone

Marrow cavity

Compact bone

g

Cancellous bone

Trabecular bone

Marrow cavity

Compact bone

Mature bone

FIGURE 6.1 Sequence of changes in the formation and growth of a long bone. Details of the figure are indicated in the text.

Adapted, by permission, from A.F. Roche, 1986, Bone growth and maturation. In *Human growth: A comprehensive treatise*, volume 2, edited by F. Falkner and J.M. Tanner (New York: Plenum), 26.

bones also have one or more **secondary centers of ossification**, which appear near the end of a full-term pregnancy in the humerus, femur, and tibia and after birth in other long and short bones. The secondary center of ossification forms in the cartilage at the end of the model. The secondary center gradually develops into an **epiphysis** (see figure 6.1e).

The locations of the secondary centers vary with each bone. The major long bones of the arms and legs have secondary ossification centers at both ends (as illustrated in figure 6.1e); the short bones of the hand and foot have secondary centers only at one end. The process of ossification in the secondary centers occurs in the same manner as and independently of the process in the primary center of ossification.

As the primary and secondary centers of ossification of long bones grow, the cartilage separating them is gradually reduced in thickness so that only a thin layer of cartilage remains. This layer of cartilage is the **growth plate** (see figure 6.1f), which is sometimes called the epiphyseal disc. Its primary function is linear growth (increase in length) of long and short bones. Cessation of bone growth in length occurs when the rate of proliferation of cartilage cells in the growth plate slows and ossification proceeds at a faster pace. This process eventually results in the union of the diaphysis with its corresponding epiphysis (see figure 6.1g). Activities that occur at the growth plate are described in more detail in the next section.

The process of ossification occurs in the same manner in the round and irregularly shaped bones of the body. For example, each carpal has a single center of ossification, which begins centrally in the cartilage model and gradually enlarges outwardly. The carpals all ossify postnatally. The vertebral bodies, on the other hand, have three primary centers, one for the vertebral body and two for the vertebral arches. The vertebral centers ossify early in prenatal life and fuse together postnatally.

Growth of a Long Bone

Growth of a long bone presents a unique problem: How does it grow in length and width and yet maintain its shape? The humerus of an infant, for example, has the shape of a humerus in an adult, yet the two differ considerably in length and width. In addition to growing in length and width, the bone must also be remodeled to maintain its shape.

Growth in Length

A long bone grows in length as a function of activities in the cartilaginous growth plate. The growth plate (epiphyseal disc) is a narrow band of proliferating cartilage cells and hypertrophic cartilage cells that separates the epiphysis and diaphysis. It has several distinct zones, which are schematically illustrated in figure 6.2. The first is a **reserve zone** of cartilage cells, which is next to the bony epiphysis. This layer does not apparently have a direct role in the growth function of the plate. Rather, it appears to be involved in the storage of lipid and perhaps other nutrients. The next layer is the **proliferating zone**. Two activities occur in this zone, multiplication of cartilage cells and elaboration of intercellular matrix. The combined effect of these two activities is the means by which the bone grows in length. Growth occurs in the direction of the epiphysis. Thus, a bone grows in length by the proliferation of cartilage cells, which occurs in this zone at a steady rate specific to individual bones.

Growth Plate and Metaphysis

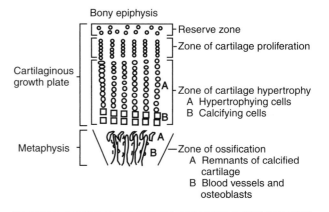

FIGURE 6.2 Schematic illustration of a growth plate and metaphysis. See the text for a more complete discussion of the activities in each zone.

Data from Siffert, 1966, and Brighton, 1978.

Rates of growth in length vary among individual bones and with age. This variation is apparent in the relative increase in lengths of bones from one age to another. Based on measurements made on standard radiographs, lengths of the femur and tibia increase by about 58% during the first year of life. The relative increases gradually decline with age to about 27% between 1 and 2 years of age, 17% between 2 and 3 years of age, to about 7% between 6 and 7 years of age. Growth of a bone in length is influenced by hormonal and nutritional factors, and the molecular mechanisms regulating these processes are gradually being elucidated.

After growth occurs as a result of activities in the proliferating layer, subsequent activities in the growth plate prepare the cartilage and matrix for eventual replacement by bone. This process occurs in the **hypertrophic zone**. The cartilage cells are arranged into columns, and collagen fibers soon appear in the intercellular matrix and separate the columns. The cells hypertrophy and then calcify, resulting in hypertrophic cartilage cells. The hypertrophy is a function of cellular swelling associated with an increase in fluid content. The hypertrophic cartilage cells are transitional because they are soon eroded and replaced with bone.

The junction of the hypertrophic zone with the diaphysis is called the **metaphysis** (see figure 6.1f). Ossification occurs in this region. Terminal branches of the diaphyseal blood vessels penetrate the hypertrophic cartilage cells and further erode them. Osteoblasts follow blood vessels in bone tissue and begin to deposit bone matrix on the surface remnants of calcified cartilage. The replacement of cartilage with bone is called **ossification**, and the newly deposited bone is called **spongiosa,** or immature bone.

The cellular basis of growth of a long bone in length is thus a function of a cycle of activities at the growth plate. The cycle includes the proliferation, hypertrophy, and degeneration of cartilage cells, which are eventually replaced by bone tissue. Cell cycle time varies among long bones and thus contributes to variation in rate of elongation among long bones of the body.

The thickness of the growth plate does not increase as a long bone grows. Simultaneous multiplication of cartilage cells in the proliferating zone and removal of calcified cartilage cells in the lowest layer of the hypertrophic zone maintain the thickness of the growth plate. Removal of calcified cartilage cells occurs as a result of vascular penetration of metaphyseal vessels. Thus, the balance between cartilage proliferation and cartilage removal maintains the thickness of the growth plate while the bone increases in length.

As the cessation of growth in length nears, the activities of the proliferating zone become slower while those in the metaphysis continue at the same rate. As a result, the growth plate is gradually narrowed. Proliferation of cartilage

cells and elaboration of intercellular matrix eventually cease, and the entire growth plate is replaced by bone. This process is called **epiphyseal union**—the union of the epiphysis with its corresponding diaphysis. Union occurs first in the central portion of the growth plate and proceeds to the periphery. When union is complete, the bone is no longer physiologically capable of growing in length.

The periphery of the growth plate is encircled by an ossification groove, which is apparently the source of new cartilage cells for the growth plate. The periphery also includes a ring of dense fibrous tissue, which provides mechanical support at the cartilage-bone junction.

Growth in Width

Growth of the diaphysis in width occurs by the simple deposition of bone on the outer or subperiosteal surface and resorption of bone on the inner or endosteal surface. Osteoblasts on the inner surface of the periosteum deposit bone matrix in successive layers until they are eventually entrapped in the matrix, become osteocytes, and regulate the formation of bone mineral. At the same time, osteoclasts resorb bone tissue on the endosteal surface so that the diaphysis gradually expands in width or diameter.

Growth Remodeling

Long bones are unique in that their widest parts are at each end. This configuration presents a special problem for a growing bone. The epiphysis, growth plate, and metaphysis are wider than the diaphysis. As the bone grows in length, the area of the bone that was once the epiphysis is now a part of the diaphysis (see figure 6.3). Thus, a need exists for constant remodeling in the metaphyseal region. The arrows in figure 6.3 indicate the direction of growth of the growth plate (A) and of the metaphysis (B). The metaphysis has an approximate V shape, and the metaphyseal region must decrease in diameter as the bone increases in length. As the growth plate proliferates in the direction of the epiphysis (C), the metaphysis grows in a linear direction (indicated by arrows adjacent to B) by depositing bone on its endosteal surface with corresponding resorption of bone from its periosteal surface. The process thus involves both internal and external remodeling in the metaphysis. Internally, the spongiosa is removed by osteoclasts and gradually replaced by lamellar bone deposited by osteoblasts.

Growth Remodeling of a Long Bone

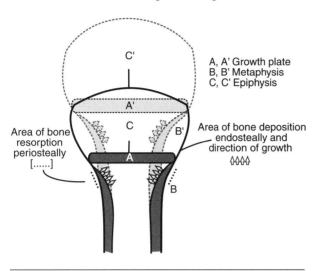

A, A' Growth plate
B, B' Metaphysis
C, C' Epiphysis

Area of bone resorption periosteally [......]

Area of bone deposition endosteally and direction of growth

F I G U R E 6.3   Growth remodeling of a long bone demonstrating Enlow's principle of the "V" in linear growth. Details of the figure are given in the text.

Data from Enlow, 1963.

Externally, osteoclasts remove bone at the junction of the metaphysis and diaphysis, causing the bone to gradually narrow.

The metaphyseal remodeling of a growing bone occurs in a manner opposite to that of diaphyseal growth in diameter. During diaphyseal growth, lamellar bone is deposited on the outer surface of the bone and resorbed on the inner surface. During metaphyseal remodeling, lamellar bone is deposited on internal surfaces and resorbed on external surfaces. The inward growth of the metaphysis gives the bone a funnel shape in this region.

Overview of Skeletal Growth

The bones of the skeleton that are the primary components of many anthropometric dimensions used in growth studies (e.g., stature, leg length, and biacromial breadth) are formed prenatally in cartilage. The cartilage model is subsequently and gradually replaced by bone tissue as each bone grows. The process begins prenatally and continues into the mid-20s for some bones. Ossification of the shafts, or diaphyses, of all long bones of the body (primary ossification centers) occurs prenatally. Secondary ossification centers develop in several long bones near the end of the prenatal period and in the remainder of long bones and the round bones during postnatal life.

Because bone tissue has a high mineral content, the appearance and progress of bone growth can be monitored with standardized radiographs. Radiographs have a long history of use in growth studies, so progress in the development of the skeleton is reasonably well documented. On the average, ossification of the secondary centers of the major long bone begins earlier and is completed earlier in girls than in boys (see table 6.1). The same is true for all other bones in the body—the short bones of the hand and foot, the epiphyses of the ilium, and the vertebrae. Note in table 6.1 that the proximal end of the humerus (shoulder) has two secondary ossification centers, one that is present at birth and another that appears by about 1 year of age. These two secondary centers eventually fuse into a single ossification center, or epiphysis, by about 4 years of age in girls and 5 years of age in boys. Epiphyseal union at the proximal end of the humerus occurs at about 16 years of age in girls and 18 years of age in boys. In contrast to the proximal end, the distal end of the humerus (elbow) has four secondary ossification centers, each of which appears at a different time postnatally. Ossification at the distal end of the humerus is completed approximately between 12 and 14 years of age in girls and between 15 and 16 years of age in boys, as the secondary centers fuse or coalesce with each other and then the diaphysis. With the exception of the femur, which has an additional center for the greater trochanter, the other major long bones have a single secondary center of ossification at each end.

Correlations between age of appearance of ossification centers and age of completion of ossification are generally negative; centers of ossification that appear earlier tend to be the last ones to complete the ossification process. In the case of long bones, this negative correlation means that those bones in which the secondary centers appear early generally experience epiphyseal union (cessation of growth in length) later.

The focus of the preceding discussion is on the growth of bones—their increase in length and width. The time of appearance of ossification centers and changes in the size and shape of the centers as they proceed from initial appearance to the completion of the ossification process as viewed on standard radiographs provide the basic information for the assessment of skeletal maturity. The concept and methods of assessing skeletal maturity are discussed in detail in chapter 15.

TABLE 6.1 Median Ages (Months) for the Onset and Completion of Ossification in the Secondary Centers of the Major Long Bones in Denver Children				
	Girls		Boys	
Area and bone	Onset	Completion	Onset	Completion
Shoulder				
Humerus, head	—	187	—	218
Humerus, greater tuberosity	9	49	14	66
Elbow				
Humerus, capitulum	7	149	10	182
Humerus, medial epicondyle	46	169	85	196
Humerus, trochlea	113	148	127	181
Humerus, lateral epicondyle	118	152	149	184
Radius, proximal epiphysis	58	162	75	194
Ulna, proximal epiphysis	104	152	135	185
Wrist				
Radius, distal epiphysis	13	191	16	216
Ulna, distal epiphysis	72	191	89	215
Hip				
Femur, head	5	170	6	195
Femur, greater trochanter	34	167	48	191
Knee				
Femur, distal epiphysis	—	177	—	199
Tibia, proximal epiphysis	—	178	—	203
Fibula, proximal epiphysis	37	182	53	206
Ankle				
Tibia, distal epiphysis	5	178	6	203
Fibula, distal epiphysis	12	179	16	203

A dash (—) indicates that ossification began in all but a few children before birth.
Adapted from Hansman (1962).

Bone As a Component of Body Composition

Historically, one of the major obstacles to estimates of body composition was the lack of a verified in vivo method for quantifying bone tissue. Earlier studies were based on analyses of the whole skeleton and bone sections, and on standard radiographs. These studies suggest variability in local bone mineralization and mass. The development of new technologies has provided noninvasive methods to assess the growth of bone and skeletal mineral status. The primary method used at present is dual-energy X-ray absorptiometry (DEXA [see chapter 5]).

Growth in Weight of the Skeleton

Early information of changes in the weight and mineralization of the skeleton during growth was derived from analyses of a limited number of skeletons of young individuals. The skeleton includes mineral, collagen, cementing substance, water, fat, and blood vessels. To obtain a measure of the weight of the skeleton (bone tissue), the skeletons must be dried and all fat must be removed. Although numbers are small, the dry, defatted skeleton weighs, on the average, about 95 g in infant boys and slightly less in infant girls. By contrast, the skeleton weighs about 4.0 kg in males and 2.8 kg in females in young adulthood. As a percentage of body weight, the dry, fat-free skeleton represents about 3% of body weight in the fetus and newborn and about 6% to 7% of body weight in adults. These estimates are for American Whites. The weight of the skeleton is, on the average, consistently heavier in American Blacks from infancy through adulthood (Trotter and Hixon 1974; see also Malina 1969, 1996).

The dry, fat-free skeletal weights for a limited number of individuals between 0.5 and 22 years of age indicate a growth curve for skeletal weight that is similar to the curves for weight and stature (Trotter and Peterson 1970). Skeletal weight increases at a more or less constant rate during early and middle childhood and then experiences a rapid rate of increase during adolescence. Skeletal weight is generally greater in boys in childhood, but the sex difference becomes especially marked during the adolescent growth spurt. Weight of the skeleton increases as calcium-rich bone tissue replaces calcium-low cartilage during growth of all bones of the skeleton, which are preformed in cartilage. Thus, bone mineral displaces water as the child grows. This process is especially apparent in the growth of long bones in length and width. Growth in width contributes significantly to the sex difference in estimated skeletal weight in late adolescence. Bones of the skull are formed within membranes and have a different pattern of growth (see the neural curve in figure 1.3, page 13). The bone mineral density (g/cm^3) of the skull is greater than that of other parts of the skeleton.

Bone Mineral Measurement

The skeleton is the mineral reservoir of the body. The mineral, which is a complex of primarily calcium and phosphate, is deposited within a soft organic matrix composed of fibers and protein polysaccharides. To determine the amount of mineral in a skeleton, the mineral and matrix must be partitioned. Partitioning is accomplished by reducing the skeleton to ash, which is composed primarily of mineral. The relative ash content of the skeleton does not differ among infants, children, adolescents, and adults. On the average, ash represents about 63% to 66% of the dry, fat-free skeletal weight, and males have a slightly higher percentage of ash weights than females at all ages. Thus, about 65% of the dry, fat-free skeletal weight is mineral. Bone mineral, estimated from ash weight (1 g of mineral equals about 1 g of ash; the actual estimate is 1.0354), represents about 2% of body weight in infants and about 4% to 5% of body weight in adults. The

differences between these percentages and those for dry, fat-free skeletal weight as a percentage of body weight given previously provide an indication of the amount of mineral in the body that is not in bone tissue. Non–bone mineral accounts for about 1% of body weight at birth and about 2% of body weight in adults. Consistent with skeletal weight, the skeleton has more mineral, on the average, in American Blacks than in American Whites from infancy through adulthood (Trotter and Hixon 1974; see Malina 1969, 1996).

DEXA technology is at present the most commonly used method to study bone mineral from early childhood into adulthood. DEXA provides an estimate of total-body bone mineral content (g) and total bone area (cm^2). The ratio of total-body bone mineral to total bone area is used to estimate bone mineral density (g/cm^2). DEXA basically measures the cross-sectional area of a scan (total bone area) and not bone volume; hence, expressing bone mineral relative to bone area is only an approximation of bone mineral density. It is not a measure of true volumetric density of bone. Neutron activation analysis (see table 5.2, page 104) can measure total-body calcium and thus estimate bone mineral. The method is complex and requires a radiation dose, so application to large samples of children is unlikely. More recently, high-resolution magnetic resonance imaging (MRI [see table 5.2 and chapter 7]) is used to visualize and quantify trabecular bone and aid in the understanding of the architecture of skeletal tissue.

Changes in Bone Mineral During Growth

Growth curves for the mineral content of the body (total-body bone mineral content) and the bone area of the body (total-body bone area) are shown in figure 6.4. Bone mineral content (figure 6.4a) increases linearly with age, with no sex difference in childhood. Girls have, on the average, a slightly greater bone mineral content than boys in early adolescence. This difference reflects their earlier adolescent growth spurt. Boys have their growth spurt later than girls and continue to increase in bone mineral content through late adolescence. The sex difference in total-body bone mineral is thus established in late adolescence. The shape of the growth curve for total-body bone mineral is similar to that for height and weight (see figure 3.6, page 49). However, whereas growth in height slows down in late adolescence, the slope of the growth curve in figure 6.4a for boys is still linear, indicating that total-body bone mineral continues

Total-Body Bone Mineral Content

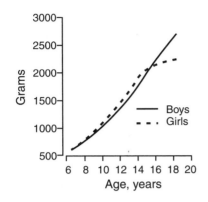

a

Total-Body Bone Area

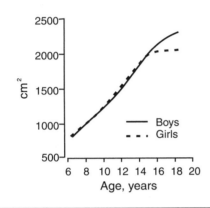

b

FIGURE 6.4 Changes in total-body bone mineral content (*a*) and in total-body bone area (*b*) from childhood through adolescence.

Data from Molgaard et al., 1997.

Bone Mineral Content Relative to Bone Area

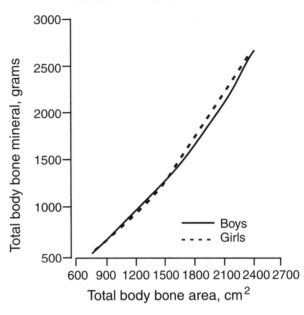

FIGURE 6.5 Total-body bone mineral content relative to total-body bone area in children and adolescents 6 to 18 years of age.

Data from Molgaard et al., 1997.

to increase into the 20s in boys. On the other hand, the growth curve for total-body bone mineral in girls appears to reach a plateau at about 15 to 16 years of age, with only a small increase in late adolescence.

Total-body bone area has a similar growth curve to total-body bone mineral content (see figure 6.4b), but the sex difference during early adolescence is negligible. The sex difference in bone area is established in late adolescence. Total-body bone mineral is plotted relative to total-body bone area in figure 6.5. No sex differences exist in total-body bone mineral up to a total-body bone area of about 1,600 cm², which is attained at about the time of the adolescent growth spurt in girls. Above this bone area, girls have slightly more total-body bone mineral per unit bone area up to a total-body bone area of about 2,400 cm², when a sex difference no longer exists. The lack of sex difference reflects the later

adolescent growth spurt of boys and accretion of bone mineral in late adolescence, indicating that the sex difference in estimated bone density has its origins in late adolescence and young adulthood, which is considered in more detail later in the chapter.

Regional Variation in Bone Mineral in the Body

Variation in bone accretion in different areas of the body was initially studied with standardized radiographs of the extremities. Although such radiographs include a radiation dose, they were routinely taken in growth studies, long before concerns about the ethical aspects of repeated exposure to radiography in healthy individuals. As a result, a considerable amount of radiographic information on bone growth is available. With the advent of the DEXA technology, radiation exposure has been reduced considerably, and data on the accretion of bone mineral in the total skeletal and in specific regions of the skeleton are more readily available.

Radiographic Studies The arm and calf were the most commonly used sites for radiographic studies because bone, muscle, and fat widths could easily be measured on standardized radiographs. A radiograph of the calf showing bone, muscle, and fat is shown in chapter 7 (see figure 7.8, page 153), which considers growth of skeletal muscle tissue. Because of the use of radiographs of the hand and wrist for skeletal maturity assessment (see chapter 15), information on changes in the bones of the hand is widely available but is usually limited to the second metacarpal.

Radiographic studies of bone focus on three aspects: the total or periosteal width, the width of the marrow or medullary cavity, and the width of cortex or compact bone. Widths are measured at the midpoint of the length of the arm, at the level of maximum width of the calf, and at the midpoint of second metacarpal length. The measurement site on the second metacarpal is illustrated in figure 6.6. Total width and width of the marrow cavity are measured, and the width of cortical bone is derived by subtraction:

$$\text{width of cortical bone} = \text{total width} - \text{marrow cavity width}$$

Measurements of width provide an indication of bone tissue only at a single level of the extremity. Because long bones are cylinders, width measurements can also be expressed as areas, using principles of circle geometry.

Changes in the widths of the second metacarpal, humerus, and tibia during growth are shown in figures 6.7 and 6.8, a and b. Total widths of each bone increase with age. Sex differences tend to be small during childhood and become clearly established in adolescence. Boys gain in total width of each bone through late adolescence, whereas girls gain in total width to about 14 to 15 years of age with little change afterward. Boys appear to gain relatively more in humerus and tibial widths than in second metacarpal width during adolescence. The late-adolescent growth in total widths in boys contributes to the increase in overall skeletal weight and total-body bone mineral noted earlier.

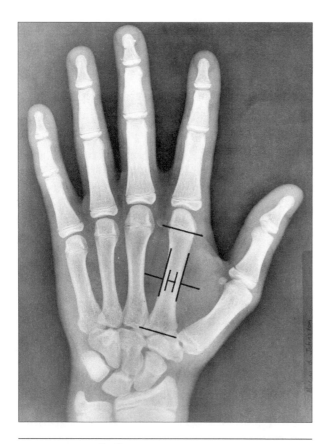

FIGURE 6.6 Radiograph of the hand and wrist showing total width and width of the marrow cavity on the second metacarpal.

Reprinted, by permission, from F.E. Johnston and E.S. Watts, 1969, "Endosteal deposition of bone at the midshaft of the second metacarpal of adolescent females," *Anatomical Record* 163: 68.

Changes in Mid-Shaft Dimensions of the Second Metacarpal

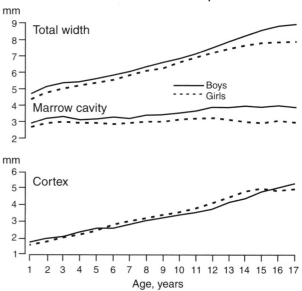

FIGURE 6.7 Changes in mean total, marrow cavity, and cortical bone widths of the second metacarpal of American children in the Ten State Nutrition Survey. Measurements of widths are made at the midshaft level.

Data from Garn et al., 1976.

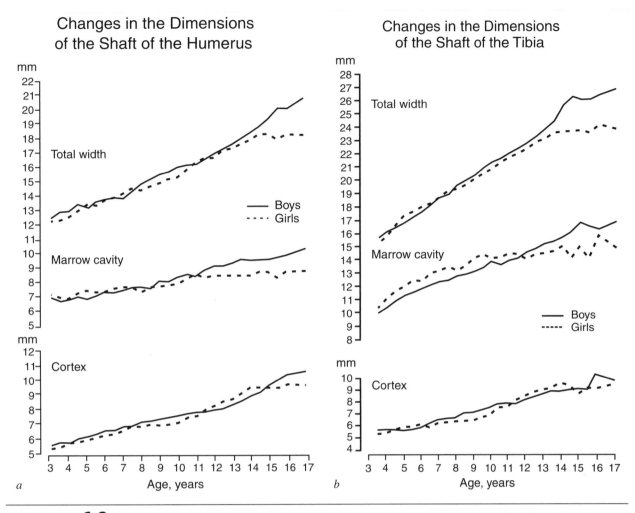

Changes in the Dimensions of the Shaft of the Humerus

a   Age, years

Changes in the Dimensions of the Shaft of the Tibia

b   Age, years

FIGURE 6.8 Changes in mean total, marrow cavity, and cortical bone widths of the humerus (*a*) and tibia (*b*) of British children in the Harpenden Growth Study. Measurements of the humerus are made at the level midway between the acromial process and head of the radius, and those of the tibia are made at the level of maximum width of the calf.

Data from Tanner et al., 1981.

In contrast to changes in total width, changes in the width of the marrow cavity during growth vary among the same three bones. The width of the marrow cavity of the second metacarpal is greater in boys than in girls at all ages. It increases only slightly with age in boys and does not change appreciably in girls. In fact, marrow cavity width appears to decrease slightly between 12 and 17 years of age in girls. This decrease suggests endosteal deposition of bone during the latter part of female adolescence.

Such a pattern, however, is not apparent in the marrow cavities of the humerus and tibia. No sex difference exists in the width of the marrow cavity of the humerus during childhood, but this dimension increases during male adolescence and does not change during female adolescence. On the other hand, the marrow cavity of the tibia is wider in girls during childhood, but during adolescence, the width of the marrow cavity in boys catches up to and surpasses the width in girls.

Thus, marrow cavity widths of the three bones do not show an adolescent widening in girls, but they widen during male adolescence. In males, adolescent gains in marrow cavity width are greatest in the tibia, followed by the humerus and then the second metacarpal.

Cortical bone widths of the three bones increase linearly with age from early childhood through adolescence in boys and from early childhood to about 14 or 15 years of age in girls. No sex differences exist in cortical bone widths during childhood. Girls have wider cortical bone widths in early adolescence, and only in late adolescence do cortical widths become larger in boys. Thus, adolescent gains in total width of the second metacarpal, humerus, and tibia in girls appear to be caused by an increase in cortical bone thickness, whereas the gains appear to be the result of increases in both cortical bone and marrow cavity widths in boys. The cessation of growth in marrow cavity widths during female adolescence is probably related to the hormonal changes at this time, and in particular, the onset of enhanced estrogen production (see chapter 19).

Changes in total, marrow cavity, and cortical bone widths of the second metacarpal, humerus, and tibia during growth show considerable variation among the three bones. The variation is especially apparent in marrow cavity and cortical bone widths. Correlations between marrow cavity and cortical width measurements tend to be low to moderate, ranging from 0.2 to 0.6 (Johnston and Malina 1970). Thus generalization from measurements of a single bone to other areas of the skeleton or to estimates of skeletal weight is difficult.

DEXA Studies   Total-body bone mineral content, estimated total-body bone mineral density, and bone mineral content and density for several regions of the body based on DEXA technology are summarized in figures 6.9, a and

b, and 6.10, a and b, respectively. Similar trends are evident in other studies, although variation may be associated with differences in delineating anatomical regions on the DEXA scans. No sex difference exists in the bone mineral content of the head and trunk from childhood through adolescence. Also no sex difference exists in total-body bone mineral and limb bone mineral content during childhood (see figure 6.9a). Girls appear to have slightly greater total-body and limb bone mineral contents at about the time of the female growth spurt (12 years of age). During the male adolescent growth spurt, total-body bone mineral and limb bone mineral are accumulated at a greater rate than in females. This greater accumulation rate contributes to the sex difference in total-body and limb bone mineral contents, which persists into late adolescence and adulthood (see figure 6.9, a and b). The late adolescent and adult sex difference in total-body bone mineral is caused by the difference in the bone mineral contents of the lower and upper limbs, which becomes established during adolescence.

Variation in estimated bone mineral density associated with age and sex is generally similar, with some exceptions. Bone mineral density of the skull does not differ in childhood but is greater in females through adolescence (see figure 6.10a). Estimated total-body, trunk, and limb bone mineral densities are greater in

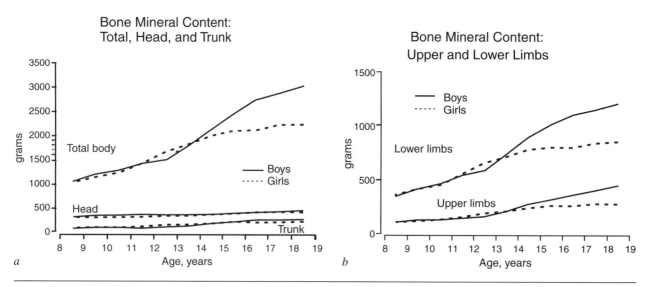

FIGURE 6.9   Changes in total-body bone mineral content and bone mineral content of the head and trunk (*a*), and the extremities (*b*) from childhood to young adulthood.

Data from Maynard et al., 1998.

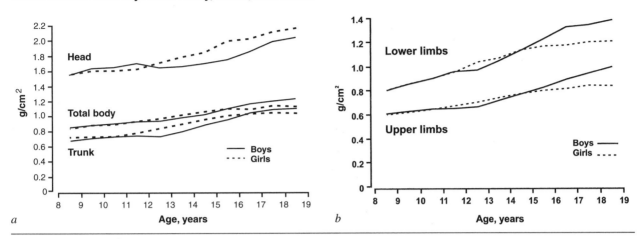

FIGURE 6.10 Changes in estimated total-body bone mineral density and bone mineral density of the head, trunk (*a*), and extremities (*b*) from childhood to young adulthood.

Data from Maynard et al., 1998.

females during the interval of the adolescent growth spurt (about 12 to 13 years of age). The greater estimated bone mineral density of the trunk in females persists into late adolescence, when males catch up to females. The sex difference in the timing of the adolescent growth spurt and in late adolescent growth of the trunk (see chapter 3) underlies this trend for bone mineral density. Not until later adolescence (16 to 18 years of age) do estimated total-body bone mineral density and the density of the upper and lower extremities and of the trunk become greater in males (see figure 6.10b). Thus, sex differences in bone mineral content and bone mineral density are established in later adolescence and continue into adulthood. Males have, on the average, a greater total-body bone mineral content and bone mineral density.

If the mean values for regional measures of bone mineral content in figure 6.9 are expressed as a percentage of total-body bone mineral content, the following trends are apparent between 8 and 18 years of age. First, the relative contribution of bone mineral content of the head to total-body bone mineral content declines from about 30% to about 15% in males and to about 20% in females. Second, the relative contribution of the trunk to total-body bone mineral is rather stable at about 9% to 10%. Third, the relative contribution of the bone mineral content of the limbs to total-body bone mineral increases from childhood through midadolescence: upper

limbs—10% to 12% in females and 10% to 15% in males; lower limbs—34% to 38% in females and 32% to 40% in males. The relative contributions of the bone mineral content of the upper and lower limbs to total-body bone mineral content are slightly greater (2% to 3%) in males, whereas the relative contribution of the bone mineral content of the trunk to total-body bone mineral content shows no sex difference.

Changes in total-body bone mineral content are most apparent later in adolescence (see figure 6.9). Total-body bone mineral content does not significantly differ in boys and girls in early puberty but is considerably greater in boys in later puberty. Studies with DEXA that focus on specific sections of a long bone or specific vertebrae indicate generally similar trends from childhood through adolescence as those in figures 6.9 and 6.10. DEXA measurements of bone mineral content and density measured at the lumbar spine and femoral neck over a 1-year interval (1-year longitudinal data) indicate substantial increments between 11 and 14 years of age in females and 13 and 17 years of age in males. These changes coincide with the adolescent growth spurt and sexual maturation. Accretion of bone mineral and increases in bone density continue after 16 years of age in girls and 17 years of age in boys, but the magnitude of the increments are only a fraction of those during the adolescent growth spurt (Theintz et al. 1992).

Tracking

Most of the information on regional accretion of bone mineral is cross-sectional, so estimates of stability across childhood and adolescence are not available. However, because bone mineral is a major component of height, the assumption that total-body bone mineral content tracks during childhood and adolescence at about the same high level as height may be reasonable (see chapters 3 and 5).

Summary

Two aspects of bone tissue are considered, first as the major component of the growing skeleton and second as a major component of body composition. Height is a composite measurement that primarily reflects the growth of individual long bones in length. As a bone grows in length, it also grows in width and remodels itself. The principles of bone growth and remodeling apply, with few exceptions, to all bones of the skeleton.

Mineral is the major component of a bone tissue and also an important feature of body composition. With advances in technology, specifically DEXA, changes in bone mineral during growth and maturation are more easily quantified. Sex differences in bone mineral are minor during childhood but become magnified during adolescence. Bone mineral accretion continues through adolescence into the mid-20s.

Sources and Suggested Readings

* Acheson RM (1966) Maturation of the skeleton. In F Falkner (ed), Human Development. Philadelphia: Saunders, pp 465-502.

Brighton CT (1978) Structure and function of the growth plate. Clinical Orthopaedics 136:22-32.

Ducy P, Schinke T, Karsenty G (2000) The osteoblast: A sophisticated fibroblast under central surveillance. Science 289: 1501-1504.

* Enlow DH (1963) Principles of Bone Remodeling. Springfield, IL: Charles C Thomas.

Faulkner RA, Bailey DA, Drinkwater DT, Wilkinson AA, Houston CS, McKay HA (1993) Regional and total body bone mineral content, bone mineral density, and total body tissue composition in children 8–16 years of age. Calcified Tissue International 53:7-12.

Frost HM (1996) Bone development during childhood: A tutorial (some insights of a new paradigm). In E Schonau (ed), Pediatric Osteology: New Developments in Diagnostics and Therapy. Amsterdam: Elsevier Science, pp 3-39.

Garn SM (1970) The Earlier Gain and the Later Loss of Cortical Bone in Nutritional Perspective. Springfield, IL: Charles C Thomas.

Garn SM, Miller RL, Larson KE (1976) Metacarpal lengths, cortical diameters and areas from the 10-State Nutrition Survey. Ann Arbor, MI: University of Michigan, Center for Human Growth and Development.

Hansman CF (1962) Appearance and fusion of ossification centers in the human skeleton. American Journal of Roentgenology 88:476-482.

Johnston FE, Malina RM (1970) Correlations of midshaft breadths and compact bone thickness among bones of the upper and lower extremities of children aged 6 to 16 years. American Journal of Physical Anthropology 32:323-327.

Johnston FE, Watts ES (1969) Endosteal deposition of bone at the midshaft of the second metacarpals of adolescent females. Anatomical Record 163:67-70.

Kibertis P, Smith O, Norman C (2000) Bone health in the balance. Science 289:1497.

Lohman TG, Slaughter MH, Boileau RA, Bunt J, Lussier L (1984) Bone mineral measurements and their relation to body density in children, youth and adults. Human Biology 56: 667-679.

Malina RM (1969) Quantification of fat, muscle and bone in man. Clinical Orthopaedics 65:9-38.

* Malina RM (1996) Regional body composition: Age, sex, and ethnic variation. In AF Roche, SB Heymsfield, TG Lohman (eds), Human Body Composition. Champaign, IL: Human Kinetics, pp 217-255.

Malina RM, Johnston FE (1970) Relations between bone, muscle and fat widths in the upper arms and calves of boys and girls studied cross-sectionally at ages 6 to 16 years. Human Biology 39:211-223.

Maresh MM (1970) Measurements from roentgenograms: Heart size, long bone lengths, bone, muscle and fat widths, skeletal maturation. In RW McCammon (ed), Human Growth and Development. Springfield, IL: Charles C Thomas, pp 155-200.

Martin AD, Bailey DA, McKay HA, Whiting S (1997) Bone mineral and calcium accretion during puberty. American Journal of Clinical Nutrition 66:611-615.

Maynard LM, Guo SS, Chumlea WC, Roche AF, Wisemandle WA, Zeller C, Town B, Siervogel RM (1998) Total body and regional bone mineral content and area bone mineral density in children aged 8–18 years: The Fels Longitudinal Study. American Journal of Clinical Nutrition 68: 1111-1117.

Molgaard C, Thomsen BL, Prentice A, Cole TJ, Michaelsen KF (1997) Whole body bone mineral content in healthy children and adolescents. Archives of Disease in Childhood 76:9-15.

Ogle GD, Allen JR, Humphries IRJ, Lu PW, Briody JN, Morley K, Howman-Giles R, Cowell CT (1995) Body-composition assessment by dual energy X-ray absorptiometry in subjects aged 4–26 years. American Journal of Clinical Nutrition 61:746-753.

Proesmans A, Goos G, Emma F, Geusens P, Nijs J, Dequeker J (1994) Total body mineral mass measured by dual photon absorptiometry in healthy children. European Journal of Pediatrics 153:807-812.

Rico H, Revilla M, Hernandez ER, Villa LF, Alvarez del Buergo M (1992) Sex differences in the acquisition of total bone mineral mass peak assessed through dual energy X-ray absorptiometry. Calcified Tissue International 51:251-254.

* Roche AF (1986) Bone growth and maturation. In F Falkner, JM Tanner (eds), Human Growth. Volume 2. Postnatal Growth, Neurobiology. New York: Plenum, pp 139-161.

Siffert RS (1966) The growth plate and its affections. Journal of Bone and Joint Surgery 48-A:546-563.

Tanner JM, Hughes PCR, Whitehouse RH (1981) Radiographically determined widths of bone, muscle and fat in the upper arm and calf from age 3–18 years. Annals of Human Biology 8:495-517.

Teitelbaum SL (2000) Bone resorption by osteoclasts. Science 289:1504-1508.

Theintz G, Buchs B, Rizzoli R, Slosman D, Clavien H, Sizonenko PC, Bonjour JPH (1992) Longitudinal monitoring of bone mass accumulation in healthy adolescents: Evidence for a marked reduction after 16 years of age at the levels of lumbar spine and femoral neck in female subjects. Journal of Clinical Endocrinology and Metabolism 75:1060-1065.

* Trotter M, Hixon BB (1974) Sequential changes in weight, density, and percentage ash weight of human skeletons from an early fetal period through old age. Anatomical Record 179:1-18.

Trotter M, Peterson RR (1970) Weight of the skeleton during postnatal development. American Journal of Physical Anthropology 33:313-323.

Zanchetta JR, Plotkin H, Alvarez-Filgueira ML (1995) Bone mass in children: Normative values for the 2–20 year old population. Bone 16:393S-399S.

SKELETAL MUSCLE TISSUE

Chapter Outline

Muscle is the largest tissue mass in the body. The three types of muscles are voluntary (or skeletal) muscles, involuntary (or smooth) muscles as in the digestive tract, and cardiac muscle. Skeletal muscle, the focus of this chapter, is generally the main energy-consuming tissue of the body and provides the propulsive force to move about and perform physical activities.

The body contains more than 500 skeletal muscles, and each consists of many smaller units, muscle fibers, which in turn are composed of myofibrils. This chapter considers skeletal muscle structure, early myogenesis, changes in the muscle fiber during growth, changes in the contractile and metabolic properties of muscle tissue, growth in muscle mass of the body, and variation in the development of muscle mass by bodily region. Like adipose tissue, skeletal muscle enjoys a high degree of malleability. This plasticity has considerable implications for

exercise biology and also for the molding of the muscle phenotypes during differentiation and subsequent growth (Pette 2001).

Muscle As a Tissue

Despite its large size relative to total-body mass, skeletal muscle in growing children has not been extensively studied, because, until recently, doing so required the use of rather invasive methods that are not ethically acceptable. However, advances in imaging techniques during the past decade have progressively changed the situation, and the investigation of the growth of skeletal muscle in children and adolescents can now be undertaken at the gross level even in longitudinal studies. Now noninvasive biochemical and metabolic studies of muscle tissue can be performed in children and adolescents with magnetic resonance techniques even though few such data are presently available.

Chemical Composition of Muscle

In the fetus, muscle fibers are small, few in number, and widely separated by extracellular material. At term, fibers are still small but are greater in number and more closely packed in the muscle. In adults, muscle fibers are larger in diameter, with little space between them. These changes reflect alterations in chemical composition, which are summarized in table 7.1. The concentrations of extracellular ions (sodium and chloride) decrease and the concentrations of intracellular constituents (potassium and phosphorus) increase with growth. The percentage of

water also declines. The size of the extracellular component of muscle tissue is first reduced by the increase in fiber number prenatally and then by the increase in fiber size postnatally.

The decrease in the relative water content of skeletal muscle tissue is accompanied by an increase in total nitrogen (see table 7.2). Both nonprotein nitrogen and cellular protein nitrogen (sarcoplasmic and fibrillar) increase with growth, prenatally to adulthood. Sarcoplasmic protein decreases during fetal growth and then increases postnatally. The relative contribution of fibrillar protein, on the other hand, does not change much prenatally but increases postnatally. The rate at which fibrillar protein accumulates postnatally may be influenced by the demands imposed on the muscle as a result of contraction

TABLE 7.1   Water and Electrolyte Composition of Human Skeletal Muscle Prenatally and Postnatally

	Fetus		Infant		
	13–14 weeks	**20–22 weeks**	**Full-term newborn**	**4–7 months**	**Adult**
Water (g/100 g)[a]	91	89	80	79	79
Na (meq/kg)	101	91	60	50	36
Cl (meq/kg)	76	66	43	35	22
K (meq/kg)	56	58	58	89	92
P (mmol/kg)	37	40	47	65	59
Na space (g/100 g)	80	71	43	35	26
Cl space (g/100 g)	67	58	35	29	18

[a] Results are expressed per g or kg of fresh muscle.

Adapted from Dickerson and Widdowson (1960).

TABLE 7.2   Concentrations of Nitrogen (N) in Various Fractions of Human Skeletal Muscle Prenatally and Postnatally (g/100 g Fresh Muscle)

	Fetus		Infant		
	13–14 weeks	**20–22 weeks**	**Full-term newborn**	**4–7 months**	**Adult**
Total N	1.1	1.5	2.1	2.9	3.1
Nonprotein N	0.1	0.2	0.2	0.3	0.3
Sarcoplasmic protein N	0.4	0.4	0.4	0.5	0.7
% total N	33.0	24.3	18.7	17.2	22.0
Fibrillar protein N	0.6	0.9	1.1	1.7	2.0
% total N	52.3	57.2	52.2	58.6	65.2
Extracellular protein N	0.1	0.2	0.4	0.5	0.1
% total N	5.5	11.8	18.2	15.9	4.6

Adapted from Dickerson and Widdowson (1960).

and activity but is also strongly influenced by key anabolic hormones. Absolute extracellular nitrogen in muscle tissue increases through infancy and then decreases to adulthood. As a percentage of total nitrogen in muscle, the extracellular fraction increases to a maximum at about birth and then decreases postnatally to a lower level in the adult. In a general way, the increase in the relative contribution of extracellular protein nitrogen appears to parallel the increase in muscle fiber number prenatally, and its decreasing relative contribution postnatally appears to parallel the increase in size.

Information about the chemical composition of muscle in children and adolescents is lacking. However, the chemical composition of muscle tissue in two boys, one 11 and the other 16 years of age, was reasonably similar to that of adults (Dickerson and Widdowson 1960), which suggests that the composition of muscle tissue may be near chemical maturity during adolescence.

Molecular Architecture of Muscle

The various components of a muscle are organized for the production of force and the execution of movement. Large numbers of molecules enter into the smooth functioning of a muscle, and these molecules can be classified in several families of compounds. The molecular architecture of muscle is subsequently described in terms of the following systems:

- Myofibrillar and contractile system
- Muscle connective tissue system
- Muscle membrane system
- Muscle tubular system
- Motor unit system
- Muscle metabolic system

These six systems are briefly defined with an emphasis on the changes taking place from birth to maturity when such data exist.

Myofibrillar and Contractile System   Skeletal muscle is composed of units known as fibers. The structural characteristics of a muscle fiber are illustrated in figure 7.1. Small muscles have typically fewer fibers than larger, stronger muscles (McComas 1996). An example of the latter type is the medial gastrocnemius, which has about 1 million fibers. A muscle fiber is a composite of about 100 to 1,000 myofibrils, which are packed together along with nuclei, mitochondria, and

other cellular sarcoplasmic constituents in a sarcolemmal membrane. The myofibril is the contractile unit of the muscle. Myofilaments, elongated structures that result from a particular arrangement of the contractile proteins, are found within a myofibril.

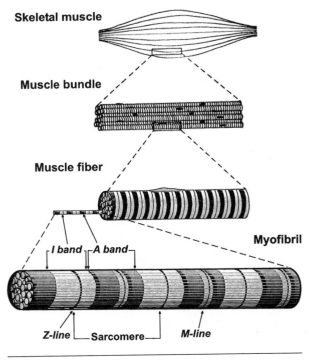

Schematic Illustration of the Skeletal Muscle Anatomical Structure

Skeletal muscle

Muscle bundle

Muscle fiber

Myofibril

I band   A band

Z-line   Sarcomere   M-line

FIGURE 7.1   Schematic representation of a skeletal muscle, muscle fiber, myofibril, and sarcomere. The most important bands and lines on the myofibril are shown.

The microscopic analysis of a muscle fiber reveals light and dark zones alternating longitudinally along the long axis of the fiber. The zones are caused by the spatial interdigitating of thin and thick filaments of contractile proteins. Narrow dark bands, known as Z lines or Z disks, can also be seen at regular intervals along the fiber. Contractile proteins are attached to structural proteins in the region of the Z line, and the unit between any two Z lines is called the sarcomere.

The myofilaments of the myofibril between two Z lines include the contractile and regulatory proteins of muscle contraction. The spatial arrangement of these proteins in the myofilament is visualized in figure 7.2. The thick portion of the myofilament is composed of myosin molecules.

Moreover, titin, the longest protein known to date, stabilizes the myosin molecules and provides elasticity to the contractile unit. Titin molecules extend from the M to the Z lines. Nebulin also provides stability to the sarcomere and is shown in figure 7.2.

Schematic Diagram of the Sarcomere

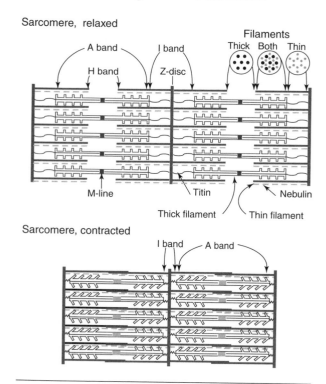

FIGURE 7.2 Schematic representation of relaxed and contracting sarcomeres, highlighting the position of the thick filaments and thin filaments.

In skeletal muscle of humans and other mammalian species, myosin is the molecule responsible for the generation of tension and movement. Myosin is a heteromeric molecule composed of two myosin heavy chains (MHCs) and four myosin light chains (MLCs) localized in the head of the rodlike structure. The mass of an MLC reaches about 15% of an MHC. Two MLC molecules are bound to each MHC polypeptide; hence, the skeletal muscle myosin is a hexamer. By convention, the MHC polypeptide is said to be made of the light meromyosin (LMM) and heavy meromyosin (HMM) subunits. LMM is the rod-shaped fragment of the molecule (carboxy terminus). HMM is at the hinge region of myosin and is defined in terms of two subfragments: sub-

fragment 1 (S1) and subfragment 2 (S2). S1 is at the amino terminus of myosin. This arrangement is schematically illustrated in figure 7.3.

Structure and Composition of the Sarcomere

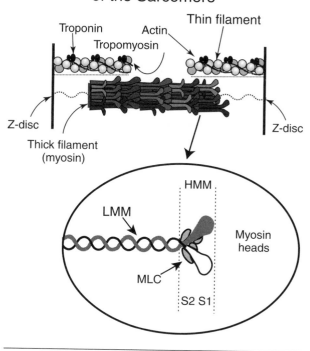

FIGURE 7.3 Thick and thin filaments of the sarcomere. The composition of the two filaments is illustrated. See text for abbreviations.

The thick filaments of the sarcomere are surrounded by thin filaments composed of three main molecules: actin, troponin, and tropomyosin. Actin and troponin are globular proteins; tropomyosin is formed from two coiled polypeptide chains. A thin filament contains about 350 actin molecules, seven times more than tropomyosin and troponin. The thin filaments are anchored to the Z lines and regulate the sarcomeric contraction. In a three-dimensional view, the MHC is surrounded by a series of thin filaments.

The distal S1 portion of myosin is required for the hydrolysis of adenosine triphosphate (ATP). It also contains the motor domain of the MHC where chemical energy is converted into mechanical energy (Lutz and Lieber 1999). The current model of force production in a skeletal muscle is defined as the actomyosin cross-bridge cycle. This cycle involves actin, myosin, and ATP in a series of events in which the energy released from the hydrolysis of ATP is converted to mechanical energy by MHC molecules in interaction with actin (Lutz and Lieber 1999).

Muscle Connective Tissue System   The connective tissue of a skeletal muscle plays a critical role in the transmission of force to the tendon and bone. The connective tissue is composed of several types of collagen and of elastin. Skeletal muscle contains three important coats of connective tissue: the endomysium surrounds each muscle fiber, the perimysium envelops the muscle fiber bundle, and the epimysium is the connective tissue wrapped around the whole muscle. All three levels of coating are interconnected. They provide passage and protection for nerves and blood vessels and harbor receptors. The changes that take place in muscle connective tissues during postnatal life are largely unknown.

Muscle Membrane System   All cells have a membrane commonly referred to as the plasma membrane. The skeletal muscle plasma membrane defines each muscle fiber and confines the contractile and cytoskeletal proteins, ions, organelles, and other cellular constituents of the cytoplasm. The membrane is composed primarily of phospholipids and is highly convoluted and fluid. The plasma membrane is also the site of transport systems, hormone receptors, and a variety of signaling molecules. The plasma membrane is, in turn, surrounded by other membrane layers that are collectively known as the sarcolemma. The sarcolemma lies under and is interwoven with the endomysium. The sarcolemma is an active cellular structure that contains acetylcholine. It provides a site for the motor nerve synaptic folds and ensures a scaffolding structure for various functions. Whether important changes take place after birth in muscle membrane composition, morphology, and function is not known.

Muscle Tubular System   A tubular subsystem (T-tubules) surrounds the myofibrils perpendicular to their longitudinal axis. The T-tubules are thought to be the main vehicle for the conduction of impulses and transport of particles from the surface to the interior of the myofibrils. A second subsystem is the sarcoplasmic reticulum, which is composed of channels that run parallel to the longitudinal axis of the myofibrils. The sarcoplasmic reticulum plays an important role in skeletal muscle contraction, as it is the site of release of

Ca^{2+}, which is a necessary event for the shortening of sarcomeres.

The following sequence of events is postulated to occur in muscle contraction. A motor nerve in the motoneuron releases acetylcholine at a terminal axon. Acetylcholine diffuses across the synaptic space and binds to acetylcholine receptors along the sarcolemma. This diffusion generates an action potential, which is transmitted along the muscle fiber. Repetitive action potentials in response to a motor command are also transmitted into the interior of the fiber via the T-tubular system, resulting in a signal to the sarcoplasmic reticulum and a release of Ca^{2+}. Increases in Ca^{2+} lead to its binding to troponin, movement of tropomyosin away from its binding on the active sites of actin, and transition from weak to strong actomyosin binding and cross-bridge cycling (Green 2000a).

With the establishment of a strong binding of the myosin head with actin (once the tropomyosin inhibition is removed through the release of large quantities of Ca^{2+}), the myosin head binds and, in the process, pulls the actin filament. Thus, the myosin and actin filaments move past each other. This postulation is the sliding filament theory of muscle contraction. The process results in sarcomere shortening and muscle contraction, which is sustained as long as Ca^{2+} levels remain high. When calcium is pumped back into the sarcoplasmic reticulum, the inhibitory effect of tropomyosin is restored and the cross-bridging cycles between myosin heads and actin stop. Muscle relaxation is thus reestablished. Whether these tubular systems are mature in skeletal muscle at birth or when they attain maturity (i.e., are fully functional) is not known.

Motor Unit System   Muscle fibers contract when they receive impulses from cells located in the spinal cord. The latter cells are referred to as the motoneurons or motor neurons. The axon from a motor neuron sends electric impulses to the muscle fibers that it innervates. The axon can send impulses to a few or to many muscle fibers. The axon also transmits other messages in the form of chemicals that are transported in the cylinder of the efferent nerve structure to distal sites. The motoneuron, the neuromuscular junction, and the muscle fibers innervated by the motoneuron constitute the motor unit. The contractile properties of the muscle fibers are related to the electrophysiological properties of the motoneuron. Some of the changes that take place in the motor unit during growth are reflected in the variation seen in muscle fiber types and other characteristics. These changes are discussed later in the chapter. However, the number of fibers within a given motor unit varies among skeletal muscles, from individual to individual, and probably with age in a given individual.

The number of motor units in a human skeletal muscle varies from approximately 100 to 3,000. The number of muscle fibers per motor unit is highly variable, with a range from about 10 for the external rectus abdominis to almost 2,000 for the medial gastrocnemius (McComas 1996). However, the number of motor units per muscle is highly variable among individuals and this phenomenon is independent of the method used to quantify motor units. For example, the adult biceps brachii contain approximately 110±40 motor units (mean ± standard deviation), and the adult vastus lateralis muscle contains 225±110 (McComas 1996). Whether this considerable heterogeneity is caused by genetic differences or by other factors is not known. Whether changes occur in the number of motor units in a given muscle or in the number of muscle fibers innervated in a motor unit from birth to maturity is also not understood.

Muscle Metabolic System   Human skeletal muscle cells (fibers), like other cells, have evolved to perform specific tasks and rely on a large number of pathways to meet the demands imposed on them. Thus, muscle cells have nuclei where chromosomes reside and where gene transcription takes place. They have transport systems to exchange molecules with the extracellular environment. They have organelles to synthesize polypeptides from gene transcripts and others to degrade molecules to be disposed of. They also have several integrated subsystems whose purpose is to generate ATP for the energy needs of the muscle cells, particularly those associated with muscle contraction and work of variable intensity and duration. Changes in several metabolic characteristics of skeletal muscle during growth are considered in a subsequent section of the chapter.

Myogenesis

The differentiation of a muscle cell is a complex process. Table 7.3 lists the major sequence of events involved in myogenesis from the early mesodermic cell to the mature skeletal muscle cell. Cell division (mitosis) does not occur in the development of skeletal muscle from the myoblast stage onward.

The appearance of muscle cells derived from pluripotent embryonic mesodermal cell populations is a phenomenon that is only partly understood. Most muscle cells are derived from embryonic somites. They evolve through the interactions of several transcription factors that act to promote or inhibit the expression of one or a series of genes that are part of the skeletal muscle differentiation program. In animal models, for example, myogenesis is totally blocked in selected body regions if the transcription factor Myf5 is not present around day 8 of embryonic life or if the MyoD factor is lacking about 36 hours later. The absence of both proteins results in an embryo without any skeletal muscle and is lethal. Similar mechanisms quite likely operate in human myogenesis and are involved in subtle but important differences in muscle mass and perhaps muscle performance capacity.

TABLE 7.3   Sequence of Events in Myogenesis

Event	Definition or feature
Mesodermic cell	One type of germ layer cells
Presumptive myoblast	A cell undergoing mitosis; mononucleated cell incapable of fusion or contractile protein synthesis
Myoblast	Mononucleated cell not undergoing mitosis; cell capable of fusion and of synthesizing myofibrillar proteins
Myotube	Multinucleated cell from fusion of myoblasts; may contain sarcomeres depending upon stage; no motor innervation; expression of several myosin heavy chains
Muscle fiber	Mature multinucleated muscle cell with myofibrils and motor innervation

An important protein in myogenesis is myostatin or growth and differentiation factor 8 (GDF-8). Myostatin is a strong negative regulator of embryonic muscle growth. For instance, a targeted knockout of the myostatin gene in mice results in a more than twofold increase in muscle mass of mice lacking myostatin (McPherron et al. 1997). The size of skeletal muscle is thought to be partly dependent on the extent of myoblast proliferation that occurs before differentiation during myogenesis (Sharma et al. 2001). Myostatin could play an important role here, as it has been shown to inhibit the proliferation of myoblasts in culture (Thomas et al. 2000). Although myostatin is known to attenuate the growth of embryonic skeletal muscle, its role in postnatal muscle growth or in skeletal muscle use and disuse is not well understood at present (Sharma et al. 2001).

Growth of muscle tissue after the embryonic period can be divided into two stages: (1) an early postembryonic stage during which myotubes (immature fibers) develop into proper muscle fibers and (2) a subsequent period of growth in girth and length. The latter stage may continue for a period of time postnatally as mature biochemical and physiological characteristics of the muscle develop. By the eighth week prenatally, the first signs of muscle contraction are observed.

The number of muscle fibers increases prenatally and perhaps for a short time postnatally. The number of fibers approximately doubles between the last trimester of gestation and 4 months of age. The extent of the postnatal increase in muscle fibers seems to be related to body size and maturity status at birth, so the postnatal increase in fiber number is generally considered as an extension of the prenatal differentiation of muscle tissue.

A muscle fiber has many nuclei. The number of nuclei varies with the length of the fiber and with age. The nuclei are located at the periphery of a fiber, just beneath the plasma cell membrane. Closely related to muscle fibers are satellite cells, which are also located at the periphery of the fibers, between the plasma membrane and the outer coating of the fiber. Some satellite cells are apparently incorporated into a muscle fiber during postnatal growth, but others remain as undifferentiated myogenic stem cells (Schiaffino and Reggiani 1996). When the muscle is challenged by injury, and perhaps other stresses, satellite cells proliferate and fuse to form new muscle fibers, which transiently go through the embryonic myogenesis program. Subsequently, they switch to adult isoforms of the contractile proteins (Schiaffino and Reggiani 1996). Both fast and slow types of myosin tend to transition toward a fast-type isoform when evolving from satellite cells to adult muscle fibers.

Muscle Fiber Types

Mature human skeletal muscle has a variety of fiber types depending on the histochemical, contractile, or metabolic criteria or combination of criteria used to classify fibers. Thus, for example, the variety includes small and large fibers, fibers with various speeds of contraction and relaxation, fibers with high or low myoglobin content, red and white fibers, and fibers with high or low glycolytic potential. One of the most useful ways to classify muscle fibers is on the basis of the rate at which they hydrolyze ATP. This rate of hydrolization is called the **myofibrillar ATPase activity** of the fibers, and it is determined by the molecular composition of the myosin molecule. Myosin ATPase activity is closely related to the contractile properties of the fiber. Thus, high ATPase activity is found in fibers that have a high speed of contraction. Conversely, a lower speed of contraction is observed in fibers exhibiting a lower capacity to split ATP in the myosin ATPase reaction.

Human muscle fibers are commonly classified into two or three categories based on histochemical characteristics related to the myosin ATPase reaction. However, at the molecular level, more families of fiber types exist, as suggested by the coexpression of myosin molecules in a given fiber type. Type I, or slow-twitch (ST), fibers are characterized by high mitochondrial oxidative enzyme activity, high-energy phosphate transfer potential, and low phosphorylase (thus, low glycogenolysis rates) and ATPase reactions. Type II, or fast-twitch (FT), fibers are characterized by high phosphorylase and ATPase reactions. Type II fibers can be divided into type IIA and type IIB or type IIX, as it is also called (Smerdu et al. 1994). Indeed, even though the convention is to refer to type IIB fibers, these fibers actually express a preponderance of MHC type IIX based on the nucleotide sequence homology with the rat IIX MHC. Type IIA fibers are often viewed as both oxidative and glycolytic, and type IIB fibers are viewed as having primarily glycolytic potential. However, an almost complete overlap of the subpopulations of type II fibers is seen when they are characterized in terms of their oxidative capacity, so it cannot be concluded that type IIA fibers are solely oxidative and type IIB fibers are not oxidative in humans. Figure 7.4 shows the three major fiber types in a cross section of the vastus lateralis muscle obtained by needle biopsy in a young adult male.

Proteins occur in different forms, which are generally coded by different genes but may also result from alternate transcription, splicing, or recombination of exons from the same genes.

The Three Common Human Skeletal Muscle Fiber Types

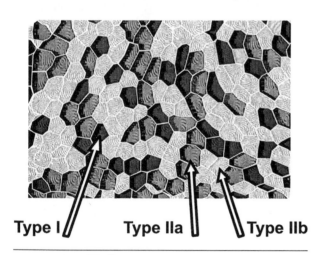

Type I   Type IIa   Type IIb

FIGURE 7.4   The three major types of fibers in the human vastus lateralis muscle. The fibers were stained following the procedures described by Mabuchi and Sreter (1980).

Data from Mabuchi and Sreter, 1980.

For instance, six MHC forms encoded by as many genes have been found to date in human skeletal muscles from the embryonic stages to adulthood (Schiaffino and Reggiani 1996). Most human muscles in postnatal life express two to three MHC isoforms in variable proportions. For most proteins (e.g., MHC, MLC, troponin, and tropomyosin), embryonic forms are observed in fetal skeletal muscle. Neonatal forms of MHC and MLC proteins are also evident in the skeletal muscle of newborn mammals. Fast and slow types of contractile proteins, and often a mixture of both, are observed in skeletal muscle with histochemically high and low ATPase activity. For example, a fast fiber includes myofibrils whose sarcomeres may include two identical or two different isoforms of MHCs and various conformations of MLCs. Coexpression of various MHCs or MLCs is the rule rather than the exception in fibers of several skeletal muscles. Table 7.4 lists the common myofibrillar protein isoforms observed in the histochemically typed skeletal muscle fibers. Other isoforms are also observed (Green 2000a).

A recent study of MHC isoforms in 100 human muscle fibers obtained from biopsy of the vastus lateralis observed that up to five combinations of MHCs were expressed in individual fibers (Bottinelli et al. 1999). Some fibers were entirely type I MHC and others were type IIA or IIB. However, some fibers coexpressed types I and IIA MHCs or types IIA and IIB. Similar results were reported in an earlier study of 65 human muscle fibers also from the vastus lateralis (Ennion et al. 1995).

Most fibers are undifferentiated before 30 weeks of gestation. Type I fibers of large size

TABLE 7.4	Myofibrillar Proteins and Protein Isoforms in Human Skeletal Muscle			
Fiber type	**MHC**	**MLC**	**Troponin (Tn)**	**Tropomyosin (TM)**
Type I	2MHC-1(β-slow)	2MLC-1s	TnC-s	TM-αs
			TnI-s	TM-αf
			TnT-s	TM-β
Type IIA	2MHC-2A	MLC-1f + MLC-1f	TnC-f	TM-αf
		MLC-3f + MLC-3f	TnI-f	TM-αs
		MLC-1f + MLC-3f	TnT-f	TM-β
Type IIB	2MHC-2B	Unknown	Unknown	Unknown

MHC = myosin heavy chain; MLC = myosin light chain; s = slow; f = fast.

Adapted from Green (2000a).

appear between 20 and 30 weeks of gestation, whereas type I fibers of normal size appear around 30 weeks. The relative distribution of the large type I fibers decreases during gestation, and their presence at birth is rare. The relative distribution of normal-size type I fibers increases from 30 weeks to term, and these fibers represent about 40% of the muscle fibers at term. Type II fibers also appear at 30 weeks and represent about 25% of the muscle fibers between 31 and 37 weeks of gestation and about 45% of the fibers at term. Thus, relative fiber type frequencies in several skeletal muscles at birth are about 40% type I and 45% type II (35% type IIA and 10% type IIB); about 15% of the fibers are undifferentiated or less clearly differentiated. Early in postnatal life, about 15% of the fibers that can be classified as type II fibers are not typical type IIA or IIB fibers and are often referred to as type IIC fibers. Type IIC fibers seem to include a mixture of types I and IIA MHCs or, in the case of immature fibers, embryonic MHCs as well. The proportion of type IIC and of less clearly defined fibers decreases during growth and attains about 5% of the skeletal muscle fibers in adults.

Type I and type II fibers gradually increase in number during the first postnatal year, whereas the relative number of undifferentiated fibers falls. Most of the increase occurs during the first month postnatally and probably is an extension of prenatal muscle differentiation. The postnatal increase occurs largely in type I fibers at the expense of the type IIB and poorly differentiated fibers. By about 1 year of age, little difference in the relative fiber distribution in the muscle tissue of children and adults is evident.

The percentage of type I fibers in three typical skeletal muscles and the diaphragm between birth and 8 years of age is shown in figure 7.5. Boys and girls are represented in the sample, and no sex difference exists in the percentage of type I fibers at these ages. Also, no clear age-associated variation is seen in percentage of type I fibers after about 1 year of age. At this age, type I fibers are more numerous than other fiber types in the quadriceps, deltoid, and rectus abdominis muscles. The opposite is observed for the diaphragm.

In contrast, some evidence indicates that the proportion of type I fibers in a muscle of mixed composition, such as the vastus lateralis, may increase slightly more in females than in males over time. A longitudinal study of 28 women and 55 men, measured initially at 16 years of age and

Proportions of Type I Fibers

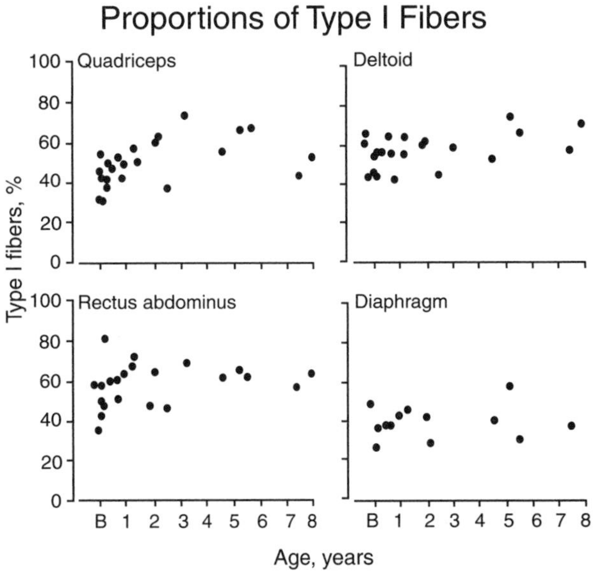

FIGURE 7.5   Proportion of type I fibers in four different muscles from birth to 8 years of age in both sexes.

Adapted from Vogler and Bove, 1985.

again at 27 years of age, indicated an increase in the proportion of type I fibers in the vastus lateralis from 51% to 55% in the women and a decrease from 55% to 48% in the men (Glenmark et al. 1992). The results are shown in table 7.5. Whether these data represent a true increase in the proportion of type I fibers with age in women and a decrease in men is not yet established with certainty. Nevertheless, cross-sectional and longitudinal observations indicate about 5% to 8% more type I fibers in vastus lateralis biopsy samples of young adult females compared with young adult males. A difference of this magnitude may have implications for metabolic adaptations to exercise, for rates of relative substrate oxidation, and perhaps for muscular strength (Simoneau and Bouchard 1989).

The distributions of the subpopulations of type II fibers may, on the average, vary during growth. For instance, infants have about 3 to 6 times more type IIA than type IIB fibers, whereas in older individuals the percentage of type IIA fibers is about 1.5 times greater than type IIB fibers (Kriketos et al. 1997). Type IIB fibers are arguably transformed more easily than other fiber types. However, because of their relatively lower number in skeletal muscle, type IIB fibers are assessed with less precision than other types of fibers. These trends must, therefore, be viewed

TABLE 7.5	Changes in Fiber Type Distribution and Relative Fiber Type Area From Adolescence to Adulthood in the Vastus Lateralis Muscle			
	Fiber type distribution (%)		Fiber type area (%)	
	I	IIA + IIB	I	IIA + IIB
Women (N = 28)				
16 years of age	51	49*	51	49
27 years of age	55	43	57	43
Men (N = 55)				
16 years of age	55*	44*	54*	46*
27 years of age	48	49	49	51

* The differences between the means at 16 and 27 years of age are significant.

Adapted from Glenmark et al. (1992).

carefully. Moreover, type II fibers are rather heterogeneous at the molecular level. About 40% of human type II fibers, for example, contain two types of myosin heavy chains.

Proportions of different types of fibers vary considerably among individuals within a given skeletal muscle. For example, a standard deviation of about 15% is observed in the percentage of type I fibers in the vastus lateralis muscle of young adult males with a mean of about 50% (Simoneau and Bouchard 1989).

Muscle Fiber Size

Diameters of muscle fibers increase gradually during gestation, with little difference in diameter among various fiber types. The marked postnatal increase in muscle girth is primarily caused by hypertrophy (continued growth of existing muscle fibers) and not by hyperplasia (increase in number of fibers). Muscle fibers increase rapidly in diameter with age and body size postnatally, but the increase in diameter varies somewhat with the muscle studied (see figure 7.6). The increase in diameter is likely related, in part, to the function or intensity of the workload to which the muscle is exposed during growth, but little is known about this phenomenon. During infancy and childhood, muscle fibers of boys and girls do not consistently differ in diameter, and adult diameters are apparently attained during adolescence. An apparent exception to this trend is the mean fiber diameter of the diaphragm muscle. After an early increase in mean fiber size between birth and 1 year of age (almost a doubling), mean fiber size remains

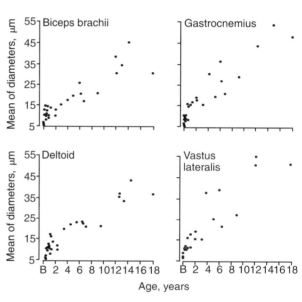

Postnatal Increase in Fiber Diameters

FIGURE 7.6   Postnatal increase in fiber diameters of selected skeletal muscles, sexes combined.

Data from Aherne et al., 1971, and Bowden and Goyer, 1960.

constant up to about 8 years of age (Vogler and Bove 1985). No data are apparently available for the fiber size of this muscle for later childhood and adolescence.

Mean fiber areas of tissue samples of the vastus lateralis muscle in untrained individuals are summarized in table 7.6. Sex differences are clear by about 16 years of age; mean muscle fiber size is larger in boys than in girls after puberty. Fiber areas increase into the mid-20s in males, which is consistent with estimates of fat-free mass and

			Mean fiber areas (μm^2)			
Age (years)	N	Sex	I	IIA	IIB	Reference
16	45	F	4,310	4,310	3,920	Hedberg and Jansson (1976)[a]
16	70	M	4,880	5,500	4,900	
20–30	25	F	3,948	3,637	2,235	Saltin et al. (1977)
20–30	10	M	5,310	6,110	5,600	
18–30	38	F	4,114	3,585	2,773	Simoneau et al. (1985)
18–30	37	M	4,518	4,718	3,901	

TABLE 7.6 Mean Fiber Areas of Different Types of Fibers of the Vastus Lateralis Muscle in Sedentary Youth and Adults

[a]These values are based on the work of Hedberg and Jansson (1976), but are reported by Saltin et al. (1977); see Malina (1986).

total muscle mass in the body. Type IIA fibers tend to be larger than type IIB fibers. However, in adolescence, type II fibers are larger than type I fibers in boys but not in girls. Fiber size does not change significantly in adulthood until middle age, at which time an age-associated decrease in fiber size occurs primarily in type II fibers (Lexell 1995). The sex difference in fiber type areas parallels those in fiber type distribution (see table 7.5). Increases in the area of type I fibers as a percentage of total fiber area are apparent in women from 16 to 27 years of age, whereas a decrease is observed in men over this age span (Glenmark et al. 1992). The converse is observed for type IIA plus IIB fiber type areas as a percentage of all fiber areas.

Early postnatal skeletal muscle growth and remodeling are associated with increases in myonuclear numbers (Allen et al. 1999). Growth in length and size of a muscle requires constant remodeling, and therefore the increase in the number of nuclei as changes take place is not surprising. The expansion of myonuclear number has even been proposed to be a necessary event for changes in myofibrillar protein and fiber length and size to occur (Allen et al. 1999).

Skeletal muscle fibers are multinucleated cells. The increase in fiber size with age occurs concomitantly with an increase in the number of nuclei in the muscle cell. The estimated number of nuclei in developing muscles has been estimated from measurements of the DNA content of samples of muscle tissue in children (Cheek 1968). Based on this method, boys show a 14-fold increase in muscle nucleus number from infancy through adolescence, whereas girls show only a 10-fold increase. Before adolescence, a sex difference in

estimated number of nuclei is not obvious, but it becomes established during adolescence. The origin of the additional nuclei is still a matter of debate, but they are apparently from satellite cells that are incorporated into muscle fibers during growth, although other mechanisms could be involved (Allen et al. 1999).

As a muscle fiber enlarges, it also grows in length. Growth in length of a muscle fiber to maturity is achieved by both an increase in the length of sarcomeres and a gain in sarcomere number. The muscle-tendon junction is apparently the primary site at which fibers grow in length.

Contractile Properties of Muscle

The maximal force that can be generated by an adult skeletal muscle is primarily a function of muscle size and neural control over force generation. Maximal force is believed to be almost independent of fiber-type composition, although the question is still a matter of debate. Some evidence suggests that the maximal voluntary force of mature human skeletal muscle reaches about 40 N/cm^2 muscle area, although the architecture of the muscle and properties of the muscle-tendon complex also have a major influence on force generation.

The contractile properties of individual motor units are defined in terms of speed of contraction (time to peak tension) and relaxation (one-half of relaxation time). In humans, mature muscles of mixed composition have slow-twitch (ST) and fast-twitch (FT) motor units. FT motor units have a contraction time more than twice as short as ST motor units (Saltin and Gollnick 1983). ST units also have a relaxation time about four times longer than FT motor units. The sarcoplasmic reticulum and Ca^{2+} release play key roles in contraction and relaxation times. Some motor units exhibit a maximal contraction time as short as 20 milliseconds, whereas others are as long as 140 milliseconds (McComas 1996). Hence, the power of a skeletal muscle is largely the reflection of the distribution of slow and fast motor units, skeletal muscle mass, and the types of MHCs and MLCs.

Currently available data, although limited, suggest that the contractile properties of skeletal muscle become mature early in infancy or in early childhood. After birth and apparently by 1 to 2 years of age, some motor units of human skeletal muscles of mixed composition acquire the properties of ST fibers as contraction times for these fibers become slower and relaxation times increase. The maturity of the contractile properties of some muscle groups is exemplified by the relative constancy in the ratio of muscle strength to muscle cross-sectional area ratio for some muscle groups (e.g., knee flexors) across age during growth. However, the ratio increases from childhood to maturity for other muscle groups (e.g., elbow flexors), suggesting that growth in contractile force proceeds at a greater rate than

the increase in muscle mass or that the ability to develop voluntary maximum force improves with age for these muscles.

Metabolic Properties of Muscle

The metabolic characteristics of human type I and type II muscle fibers that have implications for exercise and performance are summarized in table 7.7. The characteristics have been defined in mature skeletal muscle. Little information is currently available on changes that occur in most of these characteristics with growth and biological maturation.

Even though the metabolic changes that occur in different fiber types during growth cannot yet be delineated, some evidence indicates that metabolic properties change from fetal life to adulthood in intact muscle. Muscle ATP concentration is very low during fetal life, with values less than 0.5 mmol/kg of wet muscle weight. ATP concentration increases rapidly after birth and reaches about 3 mmol/kg by 1 year of age. Adult values of approximately 5 mmol/kg are reached later, but when maturity of this system is actually attained is not known.

TABLE 7.7 Summary of the Main Metabolic Characteristics of the Two Major Human Skeletal Muscle Fiber Types

Characteristic	Type I (ST)	Type II (FT)
Speed of contraction	Slow	Fast
Relaxation time	Long	Short
Myosin ATPase	Low	High
Lipid content	High	Low
Glycogen content	Low	High
ATP content	Same	Same
Creatine phosphate content	Same	Same
Mitochondrial content	High	Low
Capillary density	High	Low
Creatine kinase activity	Low	High
Phosphorylase activity (glycogenolysis)	Low	High
Phosphofructokinase (glycolysis)	Low	High
Krebs cycle enzymes	High	Low
Anaerobic capacity	Low	High
Aerobic capacity	High	Low

Creatine phosphate concentration in muscle shows a similar pattern of development. The concentration of phosphofructokinase (PFK), a regulatory enzyme of glycolysis, reaches about 3 mmol/kg of wet muscle weight late in gestation and about 8 mmol/kg at birth, a value that is still below typical adult values. However, no differences occur between adolescent girls (13 to 15 years of age) and adult women (22 to 42 years of age) for PFK and other enzymes of glycolysis assayed from samples of the vastus lateralis muscle (Haralambie 1982).

Muscle glycogen concentration varies with the skeletal muscle considered. In general, muscle glycogen concentration late in gestation is quite comparable to that seen in sedentary adults, about 75 mmol/kg of wet muscle weight. Studies of experimental animals suggest that type II fibers experience more growth of glycolytic and glycogenolytic capacities than type I fibers. However, no direct comparable data for children and adolescents exist.

Information about changes in the oxidative capacity of skeletal muscle tissue during growth is also limited. The oxidative potential of skeletal muscle can be estimated from the activity of several key enzymes, including succinate dehydrogenase (SDH). SDH activity, however, does not fully represent the changes that occur in the electron transport chain of the mitochondrion and in terminal oxidation. The concentration of the SDH enzyme is about 0.5 mmol/kg of wet muscle weight/minute from 12 to 25 weeks of gestation and then increases gradually to about 3 mmol at term. SDH concentration almost doubles early postnatally, reaching about 5 mmol by 1 month of age, a value well below the average adult value for the same human skeletal muscle. Adolescent girls have higher molecular concentrations and activity levels for several oxidative enzymes than adult women in samples of the vastus lateralis muscle (Haralambie 1982). On the other hand, considerable research on changes in the oxidative metabolism of skeletal muscle during growth has been done with small laboratory animals. These studies suggest that the oxidative capacity of skeletal muscle increases several fold early in postnatal life. The increases are evident primarily in type I and type IIA fibers, with relatively little change in type IIB fibers.

A relevant question is to what extent the oxidative capacity of the muscle fiber types during human growth is driven by the genesis of new mitochondria. The mitochondrial DNA codes for only a small fraction (probably less than 1%) of the proteins that enter into a functional organelle. All of the remaining proteins are encoded in the genomic DNA of the nucleus of the cell, and, after transcription and translation, they are exported to the mitochondria. Mitochondrial biogenesis in skeletal muscle under conditions of repeated contractile demands such as those generated by electrical stimulation or exercise training is a topic of current study (Hood et al. 1994; Hood 2001; Williams et al. 1986). Although the increase in the population of mitochondria in skeletal muscle that is likely to occur with growth (it has not been documented yet in human muscle) may have some of the characteristics of enlargement induced by contractile activity, it is also probably dependent on other mechanisms. Hormonal conditions favoring tissue accretion and a number of growth factors are also probably involved in the biogenesis of mitochondria that accompany growth in length and mass of a skeletal muscle. Further research in this area is needed. Studies are also needed on growth-related changes in the two types of skeletal muscle mitochondrial organelles, which exhibit differences in subcellular localizations in skeletal muscle (Hood et al. 1994). The precise role of age per se, changes in hormones associated with growth and maturation, activity, metabolic demands, or some combination of these factors in the biogenesis and partitioning of mitochondria in skeletal muscle needs to be clarified.

A membrane-bound pump, sarcolemma Na^+-K^+ adenosine triphosphatase (ATPase), ensures the maintenance of an inorganic Na^+ and K^+ ion membrane gradient in muscle cells. Na^+-K^+ ATPase plays an important role in the establishment and maintenance of an electrochemical gradient across the sarcolemma, which is a necessary condition for muscle contraction to occur and to be repeated. Na^+-K^+ ATPase uses ATP to drive the transport of cations against the gradient, thus allowing the processes of excitation and contraction to be maintained. The Na^+-K^+ ATPase pump is a heterodimer consisting of alpha and beta subunits. Limited data indicate that two of the three alpha genes (α_1 and α_2) are expressed in human muscle soleus, but only one of the two beta genes (β_1) is expressed (Hundal et al. 1993). Hence, human skeletal muscle appears to express two Na^+-K^+ ATPase isoforms, $\alpha_1\beta_1$ and $\alpha_2\beta_1$ (Green 2000a). Na^+-K^+ ATPase in the sarcolemma is upregulated with regular use of the muscle, and this adaptation occurs after only a few days of repeated contractile activities (Green 2000a, 2000b). However, whether the muscle Na$^+$-K$^+$ ATPase isoforms and activity change from birth to maturity is not known.

Assessing Muscle Mass of the Body

The preceding sections considered the characteristics and properties of skeletal muscle tissue. The subsequent focus is on changes in muscle mass at the gross level associated with growth. As indicated earlier, growth of muscle tissue after the first few months of postnatal life is characterized by constancy in number of fibers, an increase in fiber size and number of nuclei, and an increase in overall muscle mass. However, no exact method by which total muscle mass of the body can be measured in the living individual (in vivo) has been devised, although the new imaging techniques are thought to provide valid estimates.

Dissection Studies

Estimates of total muscle mass derived from cadaver dissection studies suggest that muscle represents about 23% to 25% of body weight at birth and about 40% of body weight in adults, although the range of reported values is considerable (Scammon 1923; Malina 1969, 1986). Many of the adult dissection specimens are older individuals, and muscle mass tends to atrophy with age, so muscle mass likely contributes an even higher percentage to body weight in young adults. Dissection data for children and adolescents are not available.

Creatinine Excretion Measurement

The amount of creatinine excreted in the urine has been often used as an indirect indicator of total muscle mass in the body (Lukaski 1997). The volume excreted is to a large extent a function of muscle mass because it is a by-product of muscle metabolism, particularly the breakdown of creatine phosphate. The relationship between the amount of creatinine excreted over 24 hours and muscle mass is reasonably constant and provides a means for estimating total muscle mass of the body. Creatinine excretion is expressed simply in g/day (24 hours) or relative to body weight as the creatinine coefficient. The former measure serves

as an index of muscle mass, whereas the latter is an estimate of the relative amount of muscle in the body. Creatinine excretion is, however, influenced by diet, particularly protein intake, and physical activity, emotional stress, the menstrual cycle, and certain disease states, in addition to normal day-to-day variation. It thus has limitations as an indicator of muscle mass. Nevertheless, urinary creatinine levels have provided useful estimates of muscle mass.

About 1 g of creatinine excreted in a 24-hour urine collection is derived from approximately 20 kg of muscle tissue. Mean 24-hour urinary creatinine excretion increases with age during growth and is greater in boys than in girls. From 10 to 18 years of age, the amount of creatinine excreted in 24 hours more than doubles in boys and almost doubles in girls, reflecting the effect of the adolescent growth spurt on muscle tissue.

Estimates of the absolute amount of muscle mass derived from creatinine excretion data are shown in figure 7.7. As expected, muscle mass increases with age, and the sex difference becomes magnified during and after puberty. When the estimates shown in figure 7.7 are expressed as a percentage of body mass (see table 7.8), relative muscle mass increases from about 42% to 54% of body weight in boys between 5 and 17 years of age. It increases from about 40% to 45% of

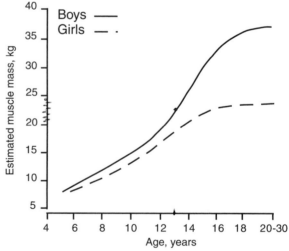

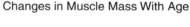

FIGURE 7.7 Age changes and sex differences in muscle mass estimated from creatinine excretion and body weight.

Data from Malina, 1969, 1986.

body weight in girls between 5 and 13 years of age and then declines somewhat after 13 years of age. Note that absolute muscle mass does not decline; rather, fat accumulation during female adolescence results in a relative increase in the percentage of body weight that is fat. Hence, the relative contribution of muscle to body weight declines somewhat at this time.

TABLE 7.8	Estimates of Muscle Mass Based on Creatinine Excretion As a Percentage of Body Weight	
	Muscle mass as a % of body weight	
Age (yr)	**Males**	**Females**
5	42.0	40.2
7	42.5	46.6
9	45.9	42.2
11	45.9	44.2
13	46.2	43.1
13.5	50.2	45.5
15	50.3	43.2
15.5	50.6	44.2
17	52.6	42.0
17.5	53.6	42.5
20-29	51.5	39.9

Cross-sectional data derived from average values for body weight and creatinine excretion.

Data are collated from several sources (Malina 1969, 1986).

Urinary excretion of 3-methylhistidine can also be used to estimate skeletal muscle mass, as it is released and not further metabolized during muscle protein degradation. Urinary creatinine and 3-methylhistidine are well correlated, supporting the concept that they are both valid indicators of total muscle mass. Data on urinary 3-methylhistidine across the years of growth are lacking.

Potassium Concentration Measurement

Muscle tissue is rich in potassium. The muscle mass of the body accounts for approximately 50% to 70% of the potassium in the body. Hence, a measure of potassium can be used as a surrogate for muscle mass. Methods of measuring potassium

concentration in the body were described in chapter 5. Potassium concentration increases with age, and a small but consistent sex difference occurs during childhood, with males having a higher concentration. The sex difference is magnified during the adolescent growth spurt, and it reflects primarily the male spurt in muscle mass.

Potassium is also contained in tissues other than muscle, so partitioning muscle mass from other lean tissues in the body is necessary. The ratio of total potassium to total nitrogen in the body is used to make this distinction. Because muscle is potassium-rich, the ratio of potassium to nitrogen indicates the proportion of muscle and nonmuscle lean tissue. Total-body nitrogen is measured by means of neutron activation techniques, whereas total-body potassium is estimated from ^{40}K measured with a whole-body counter (see chapter 5). The procedure involves two assumptions: (1) the concentrations of potassium per unit nitrogen in muscle and nonmuscle lean tissue are the same in all individuals, and (2) the concentrations do not change when tissue is gained or lost. Data are presently unavailable using this more complex approach with children and adolescents.

Imaging Methods

Two methods are particularly well suited for the assessment of muscle mass in the body as a whole and variation in muscle mass in each body region or segment. Dual-energy X-ray absorptiometry (DEXA) allows for whole-body scanning of the individual by X-rays. Attenuation of the X-rays varies with tissue composition and thickness of the area, allowing each body part to be quantified and partitioned into bone, muscle, and fat tissues. The X-ray exposure with currently available equipment is quite low for a whole-body scan, corresponding to natural radiation and radioactivity received during 5 days of normal living (Webber 1995). Magnetic resonance imaging (MRI) can also be used to assess whole-body muscle mass and the muscle content of any given body area. The technique is based on the interactions between nuclei and hydrogen atoms within the magnetic field of the magnet of the imager. MRI takes advantage of the specific proton density and relaxation times of the various tissues after the application of a pulsed radio frequency field inside the magnet. High-quality, well-contrasted images of skeletal muscle or other tissues can be obtained with this method.

Both DEXA and MRI technologies provide valid and highly reproducible estimates of lean tissues or muscle mass, particularly in adults for which the coefficient of variation for repeated measurements is less than 2%. The methods have not been used extensively in either cross-sectional or longitudinal studies of children and adolescents. Whole-body estimates of fat-free lean tissue mass (excluding bone mineral content and fat mass), based on DEXA, for 140 healthy females from late childhood to young adulthood indicate several trends (Goulding et al. 1996). The results for lean tissue mass, a surrogate for muscle mass, are summarized in table 7.9. In the youngest age group (9.6±0.8 years of age), the estimated mean lean tissue mass was 22.8 kg or about 72% of total-body mass. In early adolescent (11.3±1.2 years of age) and adolescent (12.3±0.9 years of age) girls, mean lean tissue mass accounts for about 69% of body mass, and in older adolescent girls (13.7±1.3 years of age) and young adult women (22.9±2.4 years of age), mean lean tissue mass accounts for about 66% of total body mass. Thus, whereas the absolute amount of lean tissue mass increases with age from late childhood through adolescence in girls, its relative contribution to body mass decreases gradually. Although the actual numbers are expected to be different because lean tissue mass includes more than skeletal muscle, the trends are consistent with those based on other technologies. However, the absolute amount of muscle mass varies with the method used.

Development of Muscle Tissue by Bodily Region

The preceding estimates provide an indication of total muscle mass in the body. They do not, however, indicate changes in muscle mass in different areas of the body during growth. To this end, the early radiographic approach and more recent DEXA and MRI estimates have the potential to delineate these changes with a reasonable degree of resolution, but the more recent imaging techniques have not yet been used systematically to address this issue in children and adolescents.

The width of muscle tissue can be measured on standardized radiographs of the extremities. The arm and calf are the most commonly used sites; the forearm and thigh are used to a lesser extent. An example of a soft-tissue radiograph is shown in figure 7.8. In addition to the width of muscle tissue, fat and bone widths can also be measured on radiographs. Widths of tissues in the arm are measured at the midpoint of arm length, and those of the calf are measured at the widest part of the leg. Widths provide an indication of muscle tissue only at a single level of the extremity. Because extremities are almost circular, which include bone as the central portion surrounded by muscle and fat, the width measurements can also be expressed as areas, using the principles of circle geometry.

Muscle widths of the extremities increase in size with age from infancy through adolescence (see figure 7.9). The growth curve resembles those for estimates of total muscle mass, weight, and

TABLE 7.9	Lean Tissue Mass in Four Regions of the Body From Late Childhood to Young Adulthood in Girls and Women				
Number	45	33	18	23	21
Age (yr)*	9.6 (0.8)	11.3 (1.2)	12.3 (0.9)	13.7 (1.3)	22.9 (2.4)
Height (cm)	136.1	145.8	152.7	160.9	167.5
Weight (kg)	31.7	39.7	45.0	53.4	64.0
Lean mass (kg)					
Whole body	22.8	27.5	31.2	35.9	42.5
Head	2.5	2.6	2.7	2.8	2.8
Arms	2.0	2.6	2.9	3.7	4.6
Trunk	10.5	12.6	14.2	16.6	20.4
Legs	7.6	9.8	11.0	12.9	14.7

* Mean (standard deviation). The sum of the four body segments may differ slightly from the whole-body mean because of the effects of rounding.

Adapted from Goulding et al. (1996).

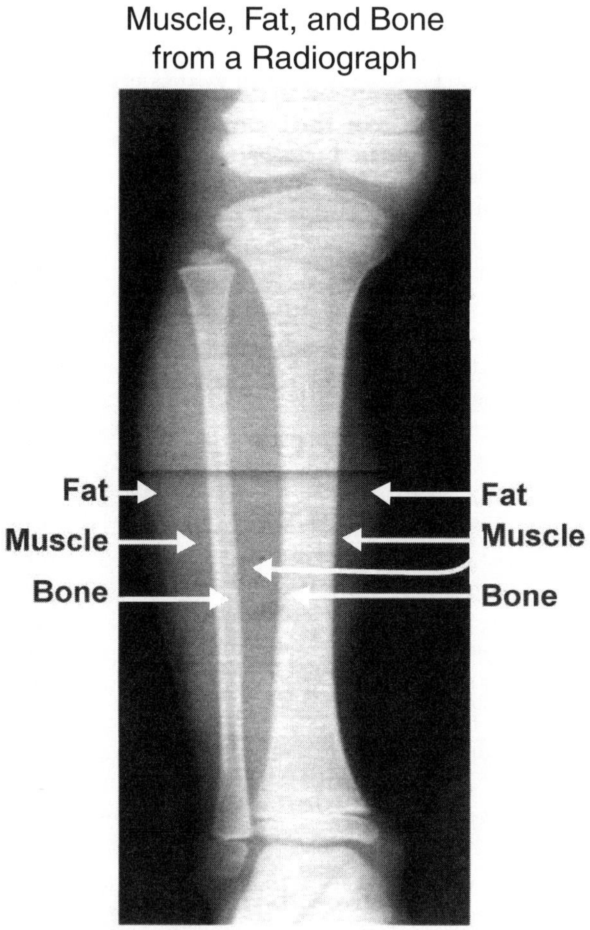

Muscle, Fat, and Bone from a Radiograph

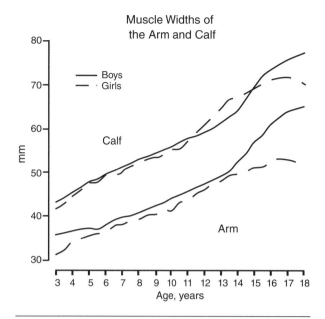

Fat → ← Fat
Muscle → ← Muscle
Bone → ← Bone

FIGURE 7.8 Soft tissue radiograph showing the definitions of fat, muscle, and bone.

Courtesy of A.F. Roche.

stature. The sex difference, although apparent, is small during childhood, boys having slightly wider muscles. By about age 11, girls begin their adolescent growth spurt and have a temporary size advantage in muscle width of the calf. No temporary size advantage occurs in girls for arm musculature; rather, the sex difference is only temporarily reduced. Boys subsequently have their adolescent growth spurt in muscle mass, thus magnifying the sex difference. The sex difference in muscle widths persists into adulthood and is more apparent for musculature of the upper extremities.

Based on earlier radiographic studies, estimated velocities of growth in muscle widths of the arm and calf are similar in boys and girls before adolescence (see figure 7.10). Males show well-defined growth spurts in both arm and calf musculature, but females show no clear evidence of such an adolescent growth spurt. Rather, the

FIGURE 7.9 Age changes and sex differences in mean widths of muscle tissue measured on radiographs of the calf and arm of British children in the Harpenden Growth Study.

Data from Tanner et al., 1981.

growth rates of muscle widths in girls show a slight increase in adolescence, followed by a plateau that lasts for 4 to 5 years. The estimated growth rate of muscle tissue in the arm during adolescence is twice as great in males as in females. On the other hand, the sex difference in rate of growth of muscle tissue in the calf is not nearly as marked as that for the arm.

Lean tissue mass has been estimated for four body segments using DEXA in females from late childhood into young adulthood (Goulding et al. 1996) (see table 7.9). The estimated lean masses, as noted earlier, are only surrogates for skeletal muscle masses. No significant changes occur in the lean tissue mass of the head (from the chin and above) between childhood and young adulthood. In contrast, the estimated lean mass of the other three body segments doubles from about 10 years of age to young adulthood. The estimated lean mass of the trunk and the legs represents about 80% of the whole-body lean tissue mass in young adult women.

From the small body of data currently available, the following trends are suggested. Imaging technologies reveal that lean tissue accounts for a greater percentage of the body mass at all ages during growth, about 70% in late childhood and slightly less at maturity. The contribution of lean

Velocity of Growth of Muscle
Widths of the Arm and Calf

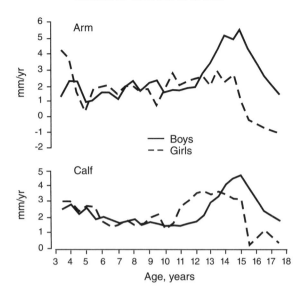

FIGURE 7.10 Age changes and sex differences in mean whole-year velocities of widths of muscle tissue measured on radiographs of the calf and arm of British children in the Harpenden Growth Study.

Data from Tanner et al., 1981.

mass in the head and neck to the total-body lean mass during growth changes only slightly, reaching about 7% to 8% in young adults. In contrast, the contribution of lean tissues of the trunk and legs increases substantially from early childhood onward. By some estimates, the leg lean mass represents about 35% of total-body musculature at maturity. On the other hand, the relative contribution of muscles of the upper extremity increases rather slightly and forms about 10% of the total lean mass in young adults. The sex difference in estimated musculature of the upper extremities is greater than the corresponding difference in estimated musculature of the lower extremities in young adults (Malina 1996). Thus, body regions contribute differentially to the total lean tissue mass and by inference to total muscle mass of the body during growth. Sex differences are established during adolescence.

The whole-body and regional measures of muscle mass are reasonably well related. Correlations between creatinine excretion data and radiographic measures of muscle widths are moderately high (about 0.7), but correlations between creatinine excretion and radiographic muscle widths with total-body potassium are higher (about 0.9).

Summary

Muscle is the largest tissue mass in the body, and skeletal muscle provides the propulsive force for physical activities. Myogenesis is a complex biological process involving a number of transcription factors that promote or inhibit the expression of genes that are part of the skeletal muscle differentiation program. Muscle fibers begin to differentiate during the second half of gestation, and the process continues into the first month of postnatal life. By about 1 year of age, little difference remains in the relative fiber distribution in the muscle tissue of children and adults. However, differences exist in the myosin heavy chains and other muscle protein isoforms between children and adults and among skeletal

muscles. Postnatal growth in girth of a muscle is primarily the result of hypertrophy and not of hyperplasia. Muscle fibers increase in diameter with age and body size postnatally. During infancy and childhood, muscle fibers of boys and girls do not consistently differ in diameter, and adult diameters are attained in late adolescence. The same trend is apparent in estimated muscle mass as a component of body composition. Sex differences are small during childhood and become established in later adolescence as boys experience major growth in muscle mass. Muscle mass continues to increase from late adolescence into the mid-20s.

Sources and Suggested Readings

Aherne W, Ayyar DR, Clarke PA, Walton, JN (1971) Muscle fibre size in normal infants, children and adolescents: An autopsy study. Journal of Neurological Science 14:171-182.

Allen DL, Roy RR, Edgerton VR (1999) Myonuclear domains in muscle adaptation and disease. Muscle and Nerve 22: 1350-1360.

* Baldwin KM (1984) Muscle development: Neonatal to adult. Exercise and Sport Sciences Reviews 12:1-19.

Bottinelli R, Pellegrino MA, Canepari M, Rossi R, Reggiani C (1999) Specific contributions of various muscle fibre types to human muscle performance: An in vitro study. Journal of Electromyography and Kinesiology 9:87-95.

Bowden DH, Goyer RA (1960) The size of muscle fibers in infants and children. Archives of Pathology 68:188-189.

Brooke MH, Engel WK (1969) The histographic analysis of human muscle biopsies with regard to fiber types: 4. Children's biopsies. Neurology 19:591-605.

Cheek DB (1968) Human Growth. Philadelphia: Lea & Febiger.

Clark LC, Thompson HL, Beck EI, Jacobson W (1951) Excretion of creatine and creatinine by children. American Journal of Diseases of Children 81:774-783.

Colling-Saltin AS (1978) Enzyme histochemistry on skeletal muscle of the human foetus. Journal of Neurological Science 39:169-185.

Colling-Saltin AS (1978) Some quantitative biochemical evaluations of developing skeletal muscles in the human fetus. Journal of Neurological Science 39:187-198.

Colling-Saltin AS (1980) Skeletal muscle development in the human fetus and during childhood. In K Berg, BO Eriksson (eds), Children and Exercise IX. Baltimore: University Park Press, pp 193-207.

Dickerson JWT, Widdowson EM (1960) Chemical changes in skeletal muscle during development. Biochemical Journal 74:247-257.

Ennion S, Pereira JS, Sargeant AJ, Young A, Goldspink G (1995) Characterization of human skeletal muscle fibres according to the myosin heavy chains they express. Journal of Muscle Research and Cell Motility 16: 35-43.

Eriksson BO (1980) Muscle metabolism in children: A review. Acta Paediatrica Scandinavica, 283 (suppl):20-28.

Firulli AB, Olson EN (1997) Modular regulation of muscle gene transcription: A mechanism for muscle cell diversity. Trends in Genetics 13:364-369.

Forbes GB (1986) Body composition in adolescence. In F Falkner, JM Tanner (eds), Human Growth. Volume 2. Postnatal Growth, Neurobiology. New York: Plenum, pp 119-145.

Fukunaga T, Kawakami Y, Kuno S, Funato K, Fukashiro S (1997) Muscle architecture and function in humans. Journal of Biomechanics 30:457-463.

Glenmark B, Hedberg G, Jansson E (1992) Changes in muscle fibre type from adolescence to adulthood in women and men. Acta Physiologica Scandinavica 146:251-259.

Goldspink G (1972) Postembryonic growth and differentiation of striated muscle. In GH Bourne (ed), The Structure and Function of Muscle. Volume 1. Structure, Part 1. New York: Academic Press, pp 179-236.

Goulding A, Taylor RW, Gold E, Lewis-Barned NJ (1996) Regional body fat distribution in relation to pubertal stage: A dual-energy X-ray absorptiometry study of New Zealand girls and young women. American Journal of Clinical Nutrition 64:546-551.

* Green HJ (2000a) Muscular Factors in Endurance. In RJ Shephard, P-O Åstrand (eds), Endurance in Sport, 2nd edition. Oxford: Blackwell Scientific Publications, pp 158-182.

Green HJ (2000b) Adaptations in the muscle cell to training: Role of the Na^+-K^+-ATPase. Canadian Journal of Applied Physiology 25:204-216.

Gros F, Buckingham M (1987) Polymorphism of contractile proteins. Biopolymers 26:S177-S192.

Haralambie G (1982) Enzyme activities in skeletal muscle of 13–15 year old adolescents. Bulletin of European Physiopathology and Respiration 18:65-74.

Hawke TJ, Garry DJ (2001) Myogenic satellite cells: Physiology to molecular biology. Journal of Applied Physiology 91:534-551.

Hedberg G, Jansson E (1976) Skelettmuskelfiber-komposition. Kapacitet och intresse for olika fisika aktiviteter bland elever i gymnasieskolan. Rapport 54, Pedagogiska Institute, Umea, Sweden.

Heymsfield SB, Arteago C, McManus C, Smith J, Moffit S (1983) Measurement of muscle mass in humans: Validity of the 24-hour urinary creatinine method. American Journal of Clinical Nutrition 37:478-494.

Hood DA (2001) Plasticity in skeletal, cardiac, and smooth muscle—Invited review: contractile activity-induced mitochondrial biogenesis in skeletal muscle. Journal of Applied Physiology 90:1137-1157.

Hood DA, Balaban A, Connor MK, Craig EE, Nishio ML, Rezvani M, Takahashi M (1994) Mitochondrial biogenesis in striated muscle. Canadian Journal of Applied Physiology 19:12-48.

Hundal HS, Marette A, Ramlal T, Liu Z, Klip A (1993) Expression of beta subunit isoforms of the Na+,K(+)-ATPase is muscle type-specific. FEBS Letters 328:253-258.

Janssen I, Heymsfield SB, Wang Z, Ross R (2000) Skeletal muscle mass and distribution in 468 men and women aged 18–88 yr. Journal of Applied Physiology 89:81-88.

Jansson E, Hedberg G (1991) Skeletal muscle fibre types in teenagers: Relationship to physical performance and activity. Scandinavian Journal of Medicine and Science in Sports 1:31-44.

Jennekens FGI, Tomlinson BE, Walton JN (1971) Data on the distribution of fibre types in five human limb muscles: An autopsy study. Journal of Neurological Science 14:245-257.

Kanehisa H, Ikegawa S, Tsunoda N, Fukunaga T (1995) Strength and cross-sectional areas of reciprocal muscle groups in the upper arm and thigh during adolescence. International Journal of Sports Medicine 16:54-60.

Kriketos AD, Baur LA, O'Connor J, Carey D, King S, Caterson ID, Storlien LH (1997) Muscle fibre type composition in infant and adult populations and relationships with obesity. International Journal of Obesity 21:796-801.

Lexell J (1995) Human aging, muscle mass, and fiber type composition. Journal of Gerontology, A Biological and Medical Sciences 50:11-16.

Lukaski H (1997) Sarcopenia: Assessment of muscle mass. Journal of Nutrition 127:S994-S997.

Lutz GJ, Lieber RL (1999) Skeletal muscle myosin II structure and function. Exercise and Sports Sciences Reviews 27: 63-77.

Mabuchi K, Sreter FA (1980) Actomyosin ATPase: II. Fiber typing by histochemical ATPase reaction. Muscle and Nerve 3:233-239.

Malina RM (1969) The quantification of fat, muscle, and bone in man. Clinical Orthopaedics 65:9-38.

Malina RM (1986) Growth of muscle tissue and muscle mass. In F Falkner, JM Tanner (eds), Human Growth. Volume 2. Postnatal Growth, Neurobiology. New York: Plenum, pp 77-99.

* Malina RM (1996) Regional body composition: Age, sex, and ethnic variation. In AF Roche, SB Heymsfield, TG Lohman (eds), Human Body Composition. Champaign, IL: Human Kinetics, pp 217-256.

Maruyama K (1997) Connectin/titin, giant elastic protein of muscle. FASEB Journal 11:341-345.

* McComas AJ (1996) Skeletal Muscle: Form and Function. Champaign, IL: Human Kinetics.

* McPherron AC, Lawler AM, Lee SJ (1997) Regulation of skeletal muscle mass in mice by a new TGF-beta superfamily member. Nature 387:83-90.

Montgomery RD (1962) Growth of human striated muscle. Nature 195:194-195.

Morkin E (1987) Chronic adaptations in contractile proteins: Genetic regulation. Annual Review of Physiology 49: 545-554.

Neubert A, Remer T (1998) The impact of dietary protein intake on urinary creatinine excretion in a healthy pediatric population. Journal of Pediatrics 133:655-659.

Oertelk G (1988) Morphometric analysis of normal skeletal muscles in infancy, childhood and adolescence: An autopsy study. Journal of Neurological Science 88:303-313.

Petersen SR, Gaul CA, Stanton MM, Hanstock CC (1999) Skeletal muscle metabolism during short-term, high-intensity exercise in prepubertal and pubertal girls. Journal of Applied Physiology 87:2151-2156.

* Pette D (2001) Plasticity in skeletal, cardiac, and smooth muscle—historical perspectives: Plasticity of mammalian skeletal muscle. Journal of Applied Physiology 90: 1119-1124.

Pons F, Damadei A, Leger JJ (1987) Expression of myosin light chains during fetal development of human skeletal muscle. Biochemical Journal 243:425-430.

Reggiani C, Bottinelli R, Stienen GJM (2000) Sarcomeric myosin isoforms: Fine tuning of a molecular motor. News in Physiology and Science 15:26-33.

Robert B (1987) La différence myogénique: Aspects moléculaires et cellulaires (Myogenic differences: Molecular and cellular aspects). Bulletin Institut Pasteur 85:37-85.

Saltin B, Henriksson J, Nygaard E, Andersen P (1977) Fiber types and metabolic potentials of skeletal muscles in sedentary men and endurance runners. Annals of the New York Academy of Science 301:3-29.

Saltin B, Gollnick PD (1983) Skeletal muscle adaptability: Significance for metabolism and performance. In LD Peachey (section ed), Handbook of Physiology. Section 10, Skeletal Muscle. Bethesda: American Physiological Society, pp 555-631.

Scammon RE (1923) A summary of the anatomy of the infant and child. In IA Abt (ed), Pediatrics. Philadelphia: Saunders, pp 257-444.

* Schiaffino S, Reggiani C (1996) Molecular diversity of myofibrillar proteins: Gene regulation and functional significance. Physiological Reviews 76:371-423.

Sharma M, Langley B, Bass J, Kambadur R (2001) Myostatin in muscle growth and repair. Exercise and Sport Science Reviews 29:155-158.

Simoneau JA, Bouchard C (1989) Human variation in skeletal muscle proportion and enzyme activities. American Journal of Physiology, Endocrinology and Metabolism 257:E567-E572.

Simoneau JA, Lortie G, Boulay MR, Thibault MC, Theriault G, Bouchard C (1985) Skeletal muscle histochemical and biochemical characteristics in sedentary male and female subjects. Canadian Journal of Physiology and Pharmacology 63:30-35.

Smerdu V, Karsch-Mizrachi I, Campione M, Leinwand L, Schiaffino S (1994) Type IIX myosin heavy chain transcripts are expressed in type IIB fibers of human skeletal muscle. American Journal of Physiology 267:C1723-C1728.

Staron RS (1997) Human skeletal muscle fiber types: Delineation, development, and distribution. Canadian Journal of Applied Physiology 22:307-327.

Stickland NC (1981) Muscle development in the human fetus as exemplified by m. sartorius: A quantitative study. Journal of Anatomy 132:557-579.

Swynghedauw B (1986) Developmental and functional adaptation of contractile proteins in cardiac and skeletal muscles. Physiological Reviews 66:710-771.

Tanner JM, Hughes PCR, Whitehouse RH (1981) Radiographically determined widths of bone, muscle and fat in the upper arm and calf from 3–18 years. Annals of Human Biology 8:495-517.

Thomas M, Langley B, Berry C, Sharma M, Kirk S, Bass J, Kambadur R (2000) Myostatin, a negative regulator of muscle growth, functions by inhibiting myoblast proliferation. Journal of Biological Chemistry 275:40235-40243.

Tskhovrebova L, Trinick J, Sleep JA, Simmons RM (1997) Elasticity and unfolding of single molecules of the giant muscle protein titin. Nature 387:308-312.

Vogler C, Bove KE (1985) Morphology of skeletal muscle in children. Archives of Pathology and Laboratory Medicine 109:238-242.

Webber CE (1995) Dual photon transmission measurements of bone mass and body composition during growth. In C Blimkie, Jr, O Bar-Or (eds), New Horizons in Pediatric Exercise Science. Champaign, IL: Human Kinetics, pp 57-76.

Welle S, Bhatt K, Thornton CA (2000) High-abundance mRNAs in human muscle: Comparison between young and old. Journal of Applied Physiology 89:297-304.

Widdowson EM (1969) Changes in the extracellular compartment of muscle and skin during normal and retarded development. Biblioteca Nutritia et Dieta 13:60-68.

Williams RS, Salmons S, Newsholme EA, Kaufman RE, Mellor J (1986) Regulation of nuclear and mitochondrial gene expression by contractile activity in skeletal muscle. Journal of Biological Chemistry 261:376-380.

8

ADIPOSE TISSUE

Chapter Outline

Changes in body composition during growth were described in chapter 5, where the focus primarily was on the two-component model that partitions body mass into fat-free mass and fat mass. In brief, absolute fat mass (in kg) increases gradually during childhood through adolescence in boys. In girls, on the other hand, fat mass appears to increase at a greater rate after about 8 years of age through adolescence. In late adolescence, the absolute fat mass of girls is, on average, about twice as large as the fat mass of boys. During the time period that encompasses adolescence, girls gain in adiposity at a rate that is almost twice as great as that in boys. In contrast to absolute fat mass, the relative contribution of adiposity to body weight shows no consistent sex difference in infancy and early childhood. However, after early childhood, girls have a higher percentage body fat than boys at all ages, that is, fat mass represents a greater percentage of body weight in girls than in boys.

The preceding considers only general trends in absolute and relative adiposity during growth.

The cellular aspects of the changes that occur in adipose tissue should also be understood. This chapter specifically focuses on the cellular components of fat mass, the adipose cells and their metabolic properties, and changes in fatness and fat topography during growth. Adipose tissue is the structural and functional component of stored lipids and adiposity. Many advances in the understanding of the biology of the adipose cells have occurred during the past decade, and these developments are summarized in this chapter. The topic of childhood and adolescent obesity is addressed in chapter 24.

The Fat Cell As a Complex Structure

The traditional view of the adipose cell was one in which the cell provided a storage structure for fatty acids in the form of triacylglycerol molecules and for the release of fatty acids when metabolic fuel was needed. Of course, fat cells are responsible for these critical functions. However, the adipose cell is now better appreciated as a more complex organ.

Fat cells are distributed throughout the body in various organs and tissues, but they are largely clustered anatomically in structures known as fat depots. A fat depot includes a large number of adipose cells, or adipocytes, held together by a scaffoldlike structure of collagen and other structural molecules. Fat depots are characterized by abundant neural connections and a rich network of blood vessels. Fat cells are also involved in a number of endocrine, autocrine, and paracrine actions (these processes are discussed in chapter 19). Thus, adipocytes not only play key roles in the flow of metabolic fuels in the body but also are involved in regulating several biological functions. A prevailing contemporary view among adipose tissue biologists is that much remains to be discovered about the biology of adipose cells.

Figure 8.1 depicts several of the newly identified features of adipocytes. The dominant feature that emerges is that of an endocrine or a secretory cell (Frühbeck et al. 2001; Ailhaud and Hauner 1998). Lipoprotein lipase (LPL) is a key enzyme in the regulation of lipid storage into adipocytes, although other pathways are also involved (Romanski et al. 2000). LPL is an adipocyte secretory product that is exported to the capillary endothelium, where it hydrolyzes fatty acids from circulating triglyceride-rich molecules such as chylomicrons and very-low-density lipoproteins. Through this process, LPL supplies fatty acids for triglyceride accumulation in adipose cells. The synthesis of the LPL enzyme by fat cells, its lipid storage action on the inner wall of capillaries, and its activity levels in the fasting or the fed state or in leanness or obesity are regulated by hormones and other factors released locally as well as distally from the fat depot.

A key peptide released by adipocytes is the recently discovered hormone leptin. Even though leptin is produced in the placenta, the stomach, and perhaps other tissues, the main site of production is the adipose cell, particularly the adipocytes in subcutaneous fat depots (Masuzaki et al. 1997). The existence of a molecule secreted by the fat cells that is involved in the regulation of energy balance had been postulated for decades, particularly as a result of landmark studies on mouse models of obesity and diabetes. However, only recently were the cloning and characterization of this factor, now known as leptin, which

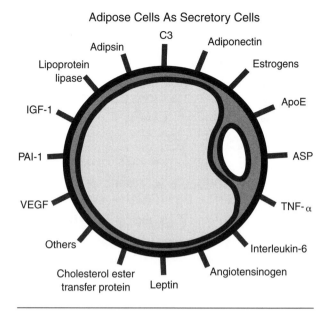

Adipose Cells As Secretory Cells

FIGURE 8.1   Overview of several molecules secreted by fat cells.

is the product of the ob or leptin gene, reported (Zhang et al. 1994). Leptin is further discussed in chapter 19 with other hormones, but for the moment, understanding that leptin secreted by adipocytes is implicated in the regulation of food intake, energy expenditure, glucose and lipid metabolism, puberty, reproductive functions, angiogenesis, and other processes is important.

Of considerable interest is the observation that adipocytes can synthesize and release an important growth-promoting molecule known as insulinlike growth factor–1 (IGF-1). Its expression by adipocytes requires the presence of growth hormone. IGF-1 is also expressed by the differentiating preadipocyte and is considered an early marker of adipogenesis (Ailhaud 1996). Human adipose tissue secretes a substance known as plasminogen activator inhibitor-1 (PAI-1). PAI-1 is a component of the fibrinolytic system, and high levels of PAI-1 are associated with a lowered fibrinolytic activity (increased blood clotting) and a higher risk of thrombosis. Obese individuals exhibit an elevated level of PAI-1 secretion, and omental fat cells (adipose cells in the omentum of the abdominal cavity) appear to produce more PAI-1 than subcutaneous adipocytes (Hauner 1999).

The renin-angiotensin system plays an important role in the regulation of blood pressure. Angiotensinogen is synthesized and secreted by adipose cells, among other tissues. Angiotensinogen is a precursor for angiotensin II, and recent studies suggest that the latter may be involved in adipogenesis (Ailhaud and Hauner 1998). Even though the hypothesis has not yet been fully confirmed, the production of angiotensinogen by adipocytes may provide the link between the expanded adipose tissue seen in obese individuals and elevated blood pressure often observed in the obese.

The adipsin-ASP (acylating stimulating protein) pathway only recently has been uncovered as a result of research on blood lipids and adipose tissue (Sniderman and Cianflone 1994). Adipose cells produce molecules that are involved in the alternative complement pathway, which is involved in immunity. Among these molecules, adipocytes secrete factors C, B, and D. Factor D is also known as adipsin. It is elevated in some but not all experimental models of obesity. ASP is a protein that results from an enzymatic modification of C3a, the end product of the alternative complement pathway. ASP stimulates triglyceride synthesis in adipose tissue. The discovery of the presence of this pathway in adipose tissue and the fact that adipsin and ASP are involved in adipose cell biology have generated interest regarding their potential contribution to adipogenesis and adipocyte size (Fried and Russell 1998; Negrel 1999).

Adipocytes secrete a cytokine known as tumor necrosis factor–alpha or TNF-α. The levels of TNF-α gene expression in adipose tissue and the blood level of the cytokine are elevated in animal models of obesity and in human obese individuals (Hotamisligil et al. 1993). Whether TNF-α is involved in a feedback loop to limit the growth of the adipocytes is not yet clear. Levels of adipose tissue TNF-α gene expression are correlated with blood levels of insulin. The adipocyte-secreted cytokine may play some role in the etiology of insulin resistance and the development of type 2 diabetes. These are only a partial listing of the substances produced and secreted by the adipocytes. Several other molecules have been identified, and others are likely to be detected in the coming years. Of those known to date, adipocytes are involved in the production of IGF-1 binding proteins, interleukin-6, adiponectin, vascular endothelial growth factor, leukemia inhibitory factor, prostaglandins E_2, I_2, and F_{2a}, cholesterol ester transfer protein, apolipoprotein E, and estrogens from adrenal steroid precursors.

Adipose cells are thus highly complex organs whose functions are not limited to storage of unneeded calories and delivery of metabolic fuel in times of fasting or starvation. Adipocytes and adipose tissue are far from being biologically passive. They are involved in complex biological systems that include the regulation of energy balance, glucose and insulin metabolism, lipid metabolism, immunity, feedback regulation of adipogenesis, production of estrogens, regulation of blood pressure, and undoubtedly other processes as well.

Stages and Mechanisms of Adipogenesis

Even though much remains to be learned about the mechanisms determining adipogenesis, the differentiation of adipose cells from precursor cells, a substantial body of knowledge has accumulated on the phenomenon based on the use of adipose cell lines and cell cultures. These in vitro studies have made possible the defining of the multiple stages of adipose cell differentiation and the main events that characterize each stage. Moreover, some of the key genes and molecules involved in the promotion or inhibition of the conversion from a precursor cell to a mature adipocyte have been identified. A thorough description and discussion of adipogenesis from in vitro studies is beyond the scope of this text. However, the interested student will find much useful material in Ailhaud (1996), Ailhaud and Hauner (1998), Negrel (1999), Spiegelman and Flier (1996), and Spiegelman et al. (1999).

If a sample of human adipose tissue is obtained, several adipose cell types are apparent under the microscope. After excluding blood cells, endothelial cells, and other nonadipose material, four types of adipose or adiposelike cells can be identified. These cells are identified in figure 8.2. Adipoblasts are formed during embryogenesis and are derived from multipotent mesenchymal cells. Whether adipoblasts can be formed during postnatal life has not been established (Ailhaud and Hauner 1998). When adipoblasts become differentiated, that is, committed to a specific path of development (see chapter 2), they progress to the stage of preadipocytes. The mechanisms by which adipoblasts initiate passage to this stage are presently unknown. Preadipocytes are characterized by the presence of a few biological markers, such as lipoprotein lipase enzyme and fatty acid transporter (FAT) protein. At the next stage, "very small fat cells" are evident; they are characterized by the presence of small lipid droplets and several markers of terminal differentiation,

Stages of Adipose Cell Differentiation

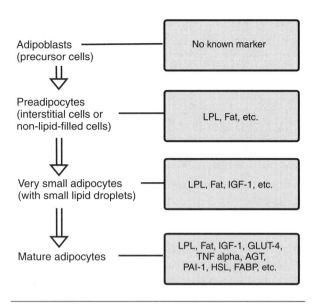

FIGURE 8.2   Stages of adipose cell differentiation and related molecular markers.

Reprinted, by permission, from G. Ailhaud and H. Hauner, 1998, Development of white adipose tissue. In *Handbook of obesity*, edited by G.A. Bray, C. Bouchard, and W.P.T. James (New York: Marcel Dekker), 359-378.

including IGF-1. Finally, the stage of "mature adipocytes" is one in which the fat cells have a diameter in the normal adult range and are characterized by the expression of several genes, including those for fatty acid binding protein, glucose

transporter 4, hormone-sensitive lipase, adipsin, TNF-α, angiotensinogen, PAI-I, and others.

Adipose tissue hyperplasia in postnatal life of human beings is thought to occur from the population of existing adipoblasts and preadipocytes. At present, no evidence exists from in vivo and in vitro studies to the effect that mature adipocytes contribute in any way to the expansion of fat cell number under physiological or even pathophysiological conditions (Negrel 1996), although cell death (apoptosis) of mature adipocytes is known to occur. Despite the fact that the in vivo molecular mechanisms involved in the differentiation process across the four stages identified in figure 8.2 are not well understood, several relevant transcription factors, coactivators, and nuclear receptors have been characterized (Spiegelman et al. 1999). Thus, the roles of peroxisome proliferator–activated receptor gamma (PPAR-γ), CCAAT/enhancer-binding protein (C/EBP) family, adipocyte determination and differentiation factor 1 (ADD-1), and sterol regulatory element–binding protein 1 (SREBP-1) have been highlighted. These molecules are known to be involved in the regulation of gene expression in adipocytes and are presumed to participate in the adipogenesis program. In addition, several antiadipogenic cytokines, growth factors, and hormones have been identified (Hauner 1996).

Endocrine abnormalities and a series of clinical investigations have been instrumental in delineating the effects of selected hormones on fat cell size and numbers. The main effects of these hormones

TABLE 8.1   Effects of Selected Hormones on Adipose Tissue Size and Cellularity Based on In Vivo and In Vitro Studies

Factor		Fat cell size	Fat cell number	Fat mass
Insulin	Excess	+	+	+
Cortisol	Excess	+	+	+
Growth hormone	Excess	–	+	–
	Deficiency	+	–	+
Testosterone	Deficiency	+	n.d.	+
Thyroid hormone	Excess	–	+	Normal
	Deficiency	Normal	–	–
TNF-α	Excess	–	n.d.	–

+ = increase; – = decrease; n.d. = not determined.

Adapted from Ailhaud and Hauner (1999).

are summarized in table 8.1 (Ailhaud and Hauner 1998). Fat cell size is generally augmented after exposure to excess insulin and glucocorticoids or deficient growth hormone and testosterone (these hormones are discussed in chapter 19). Fat cell size becomes smaller when the cell is exposed to high levels of growth hormone, thyroid hormone (triiodothyronine), or TNF-α. Fat cell number increases with high levels of insulin, cortisol, growth hormone, and thyroid hormone, but the increase is lower in the presence of growth hormone or thyroid hormone deficiencies. An important finding from the past decade of research is that exposure to a high-fat diet early in postnatal life can have consequences on adipogenesis and fat cell number (see section on white adipose tissue in postnatal life).

White and Brown Adipose Cells

The two kinds of adipose cells are **white adipose cells** and **brown adipose cells**. Even though brown adipose tissue accounts for less than 1% of the adipose mass in human adults, it has some unique features that are relevant to the study of changes in adipose tissue during growth (Cannon et al. 1999). The main features of each cell type are highlighted subsequently.

White Adipose Tissue

Some of the important differences between brown and white adipose cells are illustrated in figure 8.3. White adipose tissue is composed of fat cells (adipocytes), which generally contain a single, large droplet of lipid, primarily in the form of triglycerides. The nucleus of the adipocyte and cell organelles of the cytoplasm (i.e., mitochondria and others) are compressed to the outer edge of the cell between the lipid droplet and the cell membrane. Adipocytes are arranged in a network of lobules of different sizes and shapes that are held together by fibers of connective tissue. When a sample of adipose tissue is removed from a specific area of the body and the adipocytes are isolated after digestion of the collagen matrix, they appear round in shape. Under a light microscope, isolated adipocytes can be counted and measured. Diameters vary from about 25 μm to 150 μm. Smaller cells (i.e., those less than 25 μm) are generally defined as immature or lipid-unfilled cells, which are in transition toward a state of mature adipocytes.

Features of White and Brown Adipocytes

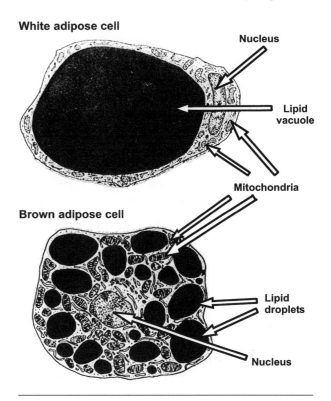

FIGURE 8.3 An illustration of morphological differences between typical white and brown adipose cells.

White adipose tissue is relatively well innervated and highly vascularized. Hence, adipocytes are interconnected with a vast network of capillaries. White adipose tissue in humans is distributed throughout the body. On average, a moderate proportion of the total adipose tissue is found internally around the viscera, kidneys, liver, and other organs, but the largest portion is distributed more superficially and serves as the reservoir of subcutaneous fat. Thus, in addition to its role as the site of the ultimate deposition of unwanted calories and other biological functions, white adipose tissue provides mechanical protection and insulation for the body and its most vital organs.

Brown Adipose Tissue

The brown adipose cell has several features that are quite different from the white adipose cell (Stock and Rothwell 1982). It contains several small lipid droplets in contrast to a single large lipid vacuole. The nucleus is not compressed to the periphery of the cell as in the white adipocyte.

The brown adipose cell also has more mitochondria, which are larger and structurally more complex than those in the white adipocyte. The main function of brown adipose tissue is not to store lipids, but to generate heat. Accordingly, brown adipose tissue is abundant in animals adapted to cold environments and in hibernating animals. In the latter, it functions to elevate body temperature during the period of arousal from hibernation.

The brown fat cell is generally smaller than the white adipocyte. Diameters range from about 15 μm to 50 μm. Their brownish appearance is caused primarily by a high concentration of cytochromes and cytochrome enzymes in the abundant mitochondria and to the rich vascular supply and, in turn, hemoglobin content of the tissue.

In contrast to white adipose tissue, brown adipose tissue in humans is present in only certain areas of the body, primarily around the kidneys, in the back of the neck, and in the interscapular region of the back in the newborn infant (Heaton 1972). After infancy, brown adipose tissue involutes and disappears in most areas of the body.

Brown adipose tissue is highly vascularized with ample contacts between cells and capillaries. In addition, it is well innervated by the sympathetic nervous system and has cell receptors that are capable of rapidly responding to hormones such as noradrenaline. Brown adipose cells store fat for their own needs and not to sustain the metabolic activities of other tissues.

The capacity of brown adipose tissue to generate heat (thermogenesis) has received considerable attention because of a possible relationship with energy balance and, in turn, obesity (Himms-Hagen and Ricquier 1998). Whether brown adipose tissue has a significant role in human obesity is doubtful, but some questions have not yet been answered. In general, thermogenesis is proportional to the consumption of oxygen, which is coupled to oxidative phosphorylation and the ensuing synthesis of ATP. The coupling between cellular respiration and ATP regeneration occurs in all cell types. In essence, the coupling between the two processes is related to a proton (H^+) gradient across the inner mitochondrial membrane. When metabolic substrates are combusted in the mitochondria, the flow of electrons creates potential differences sufficient to pump protons outside the mitochondrial membrane (Adams 2000). The resulting proton gradient favors the return of protons, which are translocated through the membrane and ATP synthase leading to ATP formation. The coupling between oxygen consumption and ATP formation is, however, not very tight. Estimates of basal mitochondrial membrane energy dissipation in the form of heat range from about 15% to 50% of the metabolic rate (Brand et al. 1999). Some of this uncoupling is caused by inefficiencies resulting in weaker proton gradients. However, in brown adipose tissue, another mechanism responsible for a proton leak has been identified. These adipocytes are characterized by the presence of a protein known to uncouple respiration from oxidative phosphorylation. The protein, known as uncoupling protein–1 (UCP-1), is located in the inner mitochondrial membrane and provides an alternative and leaking pathway for protons to reenter the mitochondria. UCP-1 allows the oxidation of metabolic substrates to proceed without the production of ATP. When the brown adipose cell is stimulated by the sympathetic nervous system or other agents, cellular respiration increases, uncoupled to the synthesis of ATP. The net result is increased dissipation of energy and augmented thermogenesis. Repeated exposure can cause growth of brown adipose tissue, an increase in mitochondrial content of brown adipocytes and UCP-1 concentration, and enhanced capacity to generate heat and maintain body temperature (Himms-Hagen and Ricquier 1998).

The biology of uncoupling proteins has experienced many exciting developments over the past several years, beginning with reports of genes coding for other uncoupling-like proteins in the human and other mammalian genomes. It began with the discovery of UCP-2, a protein found in most tissues in humans (Fleury et al. 1997), including white and brown adipose tissues. Some experimental evidence has been generated in support of the hypothesis that UCP-2 can lower the mitochondrial membrane potential and uncouple respiration, although direct demonstration is not yet available. In the same year, the cloning of a third uncoupling protein, known as UCP-3, was reported (Boss et al. 1998; Vidal-Puig et al. 1997). UCP-3 is particularly expressed in human skeletal muscle and cardiac muscle tissues. As with UCP-2, only indirect evidence supports UCP-3 as a functional uncoupler of cellular respiration and ADP phosphorylation.

The prenatal development of brown adipose tissue is not clearly established. However, the neonate has brown adipose tissue depots, particularly in the back of the neck and the interscapular region of the back, in the perirenal, periadrenal, and pericardiac areas, and in several other areas. It represents less than 1% of body weight, or about 25 g in a full-term infant weighing 3,500 g. The evidence for brown adipose tissue is primarily anatomical, but convincing evidence to support the notion of the remarkable, nonshivering, heat-generating capacity of brown adipose tissue in the neonate is still lacking. Nevertheless, brown adipose tissue is present and functional in many newborn mammals, and it can perhaps reasonably be assumed to have similar utility in the human neonate. One hypothesis is that the tissue may be useful as a protective mechanism in premature infants (i.e., those born at an early gestational age) as they face the extrauterine environment. With age, brown adipose cells accumulate lipid and become more unilocular with a single large fat droplet like white adipocytes. Fat cells at sites that contained brown adipocytes in the fetus and infant have been suggested to be inactive brown fat cells (Himms-Hagen and Ricquier 1998). The fate of these cells in adults remains unknown.

White Adipose Tissue in Prenatal Life

Studies of aborted fetuses with normal size and features for gestational age show the earliest indication of white adipose tissue in the abdominal area at about the 14th week of gestation. No sex difference exists for the presence of white adipose tissue prenatally. Early in their development, adipocytes have multiple droplets of lipid that eventually coalesce to form the typical cell with a single droplet. After the 23rd week of gestation, multiplication of adipocytes and vascularization of adipose tissue are predominant activities that contribute to the rapid gain in body weight at this time (Poissonnet et al. 1983, 1984).

The newborn infant is estimated to have approximately 5 billion adipocytes (Hager 1981). Differences in body fat content appear to be more related to the triglyceride content of adipocytes than to variation in cellularity or cell number in the tissue. In general, adipocytes of the fetus are smaller than those of adults, but late in fetal life, a population of larger, lipid-filled adipocytes becomes apparent. This stored energy is important for the infant in the transition from the protected environment of the uterus to extrauterine life. After birth, the infant must temporarily rely on endogenous metabolic fuel until feeding is initiated. Carbohydrate reserves are rapidly depleted,

and the stored triglycerides in the adipocytes become a critical source of energy under these circumstances. Accordingly, the adipocytes of the neonate must be metabolically competent to meet the demand for energy and for lipid storage as well. Little is known about the other biological properties of the adipose cells during prenatal life.

White Adipose Tissue in Postnatal Life

During postnatal life, white adipose tissue expands because of interactive changes in the size of adipocytes and cellularity of the adipose tissue organ (Bonnet 1981; Bonnet and Rocour-Brumioul 1981; Hager et al. 1977). Thus, adipocyte number increases from about 5 billion at birth to about 30 to 50 billion in the nonobese young adult. Concomitantly, the average diameter of adipocytes increases from about 30 to 40 μm at birth to about 80 to 100 μm in the young adult. The adipose organ consists of about 0.5 kg of fat at birth in both males and females and increases to approximately 10 kg in males and 14 kg in females in young normal-weight adults.

Increases in adipocyte size (hypertrophy) and number (hyperplasia) are needed to accommodate the energy storage needs of the growing organism. Adipose tissue growth-promoting factors and hormones as well as inhibitory factors are involved in the complex regulation of the growth in adipocyte size and number. The prevailing energy balance conditions can obviously have a strong impact on the unfolding of the adipogenic program during the growing years. Postnatal changes in adipose tissue not only relate to the morphological features of adipocytes but also pertain to the metabolic properties of the tissue. These topics are briefly discussed in the following paragraphs.

The reader should keep in mind that studying adipose cell properties and comparing fat depots in children and adolescents require the consent of the child and parents in addition to an approval of the procedures by an institutional review board. The review board is responsible for the protection of human subjects in human experimentation and is not generally supportive of using invasive procedures in children, unless the benefits to the individuals are much greater than the risks incurred. For these reasons, data on the topics of adipose size and cellularity as well as metabolic properties in infants, children, and adolescents are few.

Adipocyte Size

Subcutaneous adipose tissue depots can be sampled during the growing years with biopsy techniques that have been developed for this purpose. A biopsy is simply a sample of tissue or cells removed from the living individual. If the fat cells are fixed or isolated and kept in suspension, they can be individually measured. The distribution of fat cell diameters or cell weights, if a functional lipid content is assumed, can be obtained for several hundreds or thousands of adipocytes. Based on such information, the average size of adipocytes has been reported to increase twofold to threefold during the first year of postnatal life, reflecting the rapid filling of existing preadipocytes and small adipocytes. After about 1 year of age, some evidence indicates a decrease in adipocyte size, but this observation is not consistent across all studies. Subsequently, mean size of adipocytes does not increase significantly in nonobese children until the onset of puberty, and no sex difference occurs. A small increase in average adipocyte size at puberty is more obvious in girls than in boys. The overall trend of changes in average adipocyte size during growth is summarized in figure 8.4. Variability in average fat cell size increases with age through adolescence, but average fat cell size is rather stable during childhood.

The preceding considers the average sizes of adipocytes during growth. Such estimates are ideally based on the mean sizes of several fat depots of the body. However, considerable variation in size exists among adipocytes from different regions of the body, especially adipocytes derived from subcutaneous fat depots. Adipocytes of the visceral (internal) fat are, on average, smaller than those of subcutaneous fat. Among subcutaneous fat sites within the same children and adolescents, average diameters of adipocytes from the subscapular area are smaller than those from the abdominal area, which, in turn, are smaller than those from the gluteal area.

Adipocyte Number

Adipogenesis is a complex biological process that is only partially understood. For instance, increases in fat cell number are undoubtedly experienced well after the growing years, particularly in those who gain a significant amount of weight and body fat in the adult years. This expansion in the number of adipocytes is believed to occur through differentiation of adipoblasts and preadipocytes, but the exact mechanisms have not yet been described. Older adipocytes might be replaced by new ones in the life course, which suggests a slow turnover of fat cells throughout life. This hypothesis is based on cell culture and animal studies, but as of yet, no convincing data demonstrate that the phenomenon exists in humans.

To estimate the cellularity of adipose tissue in the body, accurate assessments of the total fat content of the body and of average adipocyte size in the same individual are necessary (Sjöström 1980). The latter is more difficult to derive than the former. As indicated previously, it requires multiple biopsies of several areas of the body to account for regional variation in adipocyte size. An additional problem in growth studies is the need for longitudinal observations to estimate individual variation in adipocyte number and rate of change in number with age. Not surprisingly, no study meets all of these requirements.

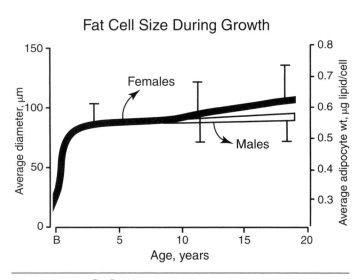

FIGURE 8.4 Schematic representation of growth changes in average adipocyte size of a typical fat depot in boys and girls. Individual differences tend to increase with age. Vertical bars indicate standard deviation. Differences among various fat depots are not shown.

Data from Bonnet and Rocour-Brumioul (1981), Knittle et al. (1979), Hager et al. (1977), Chumlea et al. (1981), and Boulton et al. (1978).

Age trends in cellularity of white adipose tissue based on several studies are summarized in figure 8.5. Cellularity of adipose tissue does not increase significantly early in postnatal life. Thus, the gain in fat mass early in life is the result of an increase in the size of existing adipocytes. However, from about 1 or 2 years of age and continuing through early and middle childhood, the number of adipocytes increases gradually twofold to threefold. With the onset of puberty, cellularity of adipose tissue practically doubles and is then followed by a plateau in late adolescence and early adulthood (Bonnet 1981; Bonnet and Rocour-Brumioul 1981). Adipocyte number is almost identical in boys and girls during childhood, but girls experience a greater increase than boys at puberty. This pattern of change in adipose cellularity is characteristic of children and adolescents of normal body weight (Chumlea et al. 1981). Cellularity of adipose tissue in obese children is greater.

Fat Cell Number During Growth

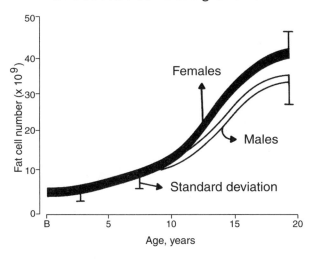

FIGURE 8.5 Schematic representation of average changes in fat cell number during growth in boys and girls. Individual differences increase considerably with age. Vertical bars indicate standard deviation.

Data from Bonnet and Rocour-Brumioul (1981), Boulton et al. (1978), Chumlea et al. (1981), Hager (1981), Hager et al. (1977), Knittle et al. (1979), Sjöström (1980), and Soriguer Escofet et al. (1996).

In the context of the general scheme depicted in figure 8.5, infancy and puberty are two periods during growth in which noticeable increases in adipocyte number occur. These periods are viewed as "critical" for the enlargement of the adipose

organ and, in turn, for the development or prevention of obesity in children and adolescents. On the other hand, the plateau in adipocyte cell number in late puberty has been occasionally interpreted as indicating that the cellularity of white adipose tissue remains relatively constant from this period through adult life. However, fat cell number can increase at any age provided that fat storage mechanisms are stimulated by chronic positive energy balance conditions. The plateau depicted in the figure represents only the average trend. In reality, a wide range of individual variability in estimated adipocyte number occurs not only during growth but also in adulthood. The increase in fat cell number from birth to the late teens may be only fivefold to sixfold in some individuals but as much as eightfold to 12-fold in others. Differences of such magnitude have implications for variation in body fat during growth and for the risk of becoming obese. Moreover, obese adults, and presumably obese children as well, with a large number of fat cells have been reported to be more resistant to weight loss than those with a predominant increase in size of the fat cells, although the evidence remains inconclusive at this time.

An important series of observations has recently been made that has implications for the topic of adipocyte cellularity during human growth. First, those who are breast-fed as babies are less likely to become obese children (von Kreis et al. 1999; Gillman et al. 2001), although the evidence is at times contradictory. Second, rodents fed a high-fat diet early in life have an increase either in fat cell size or in fat cell number (Okuno et al. 1997). Third, a diet simulating the lipid composition of maternal milk leads to an increase in fat cell size in rats (Cleary et al. 1999). In contrast, a diet deviating from the composition of rat maternal milk consumed before and after weaning caused an augmentation of fat cell numbers. Based on such studies (and a good number of them have been done) and other lines of evidence, a diet rich in polyunsaturated omega-3 fatty acids has been proposed to lead to an increase in body fat, but an increase that is less striking than when the diet is rich in omega-6 fatty acids. In the latter case, the expansion of the adipose mass is driven mainly by an increase in fat cell number. Based on these various lines of evidence, one can speculate that because maternal milk is rich in omega-3 fatty acids compared with omega-6 fatty acids, breast-feeding could represent a mechanism by which adipocyte cellularity could be kept in check in postnatal life (Ailhaud 2000).

Metabolic Properties of Fat Cells

White adipose tissue is capable of several metabolic functions, most notably the storage of lipid in the form of triglycerides and the breakdown of triglycerides in lipid mobilization (lipolysis). The major pathways of lipid storage and mobilization in the adipocyte are illustrated in figure 8.6. Free fatty acids (FFAs) are incorporated into adipocytes by two and probably more metabolic routes. The major pathway is associated with the action of the lipoprotein lipase (LPL) enzyme complex on circulating chylomicrons and very-low-density lipoproteins. In this process, LPL hydrolyzes fatty acids from the triglyceride-rich circulating lipoproteins. The liberated fatty acids subsequently enter the adipocyte. FFAs are either catabolized to meet the energy needs of the tissue or are esterified with a glycerol molecule to form triglyceride, the storage form of lipid in the adipocyte. Another pathway for the incorporation of FFAs into adipocytes is the uptake of FFAs that are transported in the bloodstream in the form of a fatty acid–albumin complex.

In the lipid mobilization process, triglycerides are broken down, liberating FFAs and glycerol. Stimulation of adipocyte membrane receptors, or reduction of the inhibitory action of other membrane receptors, triggers a cascade of cellular reactions, including activation of an enzyme, the hormone-sensitive lipase. These events are mediated by the effects of circulating hormones (e.g., catecholamines and growth hormone) on the adenylate cyclase complex, which eventually activates the hormone-sensitive lipase enzyme. The lipase causes hydrolysis of triglycerides and release of FFAs into the adipocyte pool. FFAs are thus available for release into circulation. The process of lipid mobilization resulting in the liberation of FFAs is called lipolysis.

Little is known about the metabolic processes of human adipocytes during growth and maturation. Lipolysis proceeds at a higher rate in children than in adults or aging individuals, particularly when stimulated by catecholamines, the primary lipolytic hormones. This rate increase is perhaps related to variation in the size of adipocytes, to alterations in the ratio of receptors with inhibitory and stimulatory properties, and to changes in the metabolic pathways related to the cellular response. The uptake of FFAs from LPL-induced hydrolysis of circulating triglycerides remains the predominant mechanism for lipid storage in adipocytes during growth. Metabolic differences among adipose tissue depots of the body are considered subsequently.

Metabolic Variation Among Fat Depots

Variation occurs in the metabolic activities of fat depots in different areas of the body, but it is only partly documented in adults, with little or no data for children and adolescents. The variation is related to the number and affinity of different receptors present on the surface or in the cytosol of adipocytes, to differences in sex hormones to which the adipocytes are exposed, to differential regulation of gene expression, to activities of key metabolic enzymes, and probably to other factors as well (Arner and Eckel 1998). However, the exact mechanisms for metabolic differences among different fat depots and whether they are apparent during the growing years have not been established yet.

In adult women, adipocytes in femoral adipose tissue have a high level of LPL activity compared with adipocytes in the abdominal area. In contrast, fat mobilization in femoral adipose tissue is reduced under both unstimulated and hormone-stimulated conditions. Femoral adipocytes are also more sensitive to the antilipolytic

Lipid Storage and
Mobilization in Fat Cells

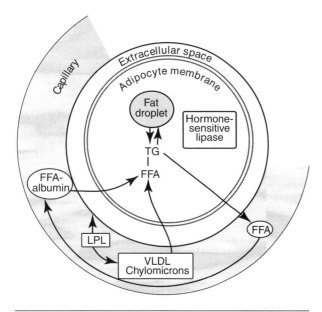

FIGURE 8.6   A simplified representation of the major lipid storage and mobilization pathways operating in adipocytes.

action of insulin. Thus, femoral adipose tissue appears to be metabolically more prone to lipid storage and somewhat resistant to lipid mobilization compared with abdominal tissue. With lactation, femoral adipose tissue increases its lipid-releasing activity and decreases its lipid storage capacity, apparently in favor of mammary adipose tissue. These differences among depots are sex-specific. In men, adipose tissue LPL activity is higher in the abdominal depot compared with lower body depots. However, abdominal versus femoral differences in lipolytic activity are considerably attenuated in men compared with women.

Small variations in adipose tissue metabolism among depots can have a major long-term impact on fat topography or distribution. Differences in metabolic properties across depots may also have clinical implications. For instance, visceral adipose tissue in the abdominal cavity is thought to be metabolically more active, as reflected by FFA flux, than adipose tissue from other areas. Such observations have led to the development of two useful concepts for the understanding of human obesity. First, obesity is not a single entity; rather, different kinds of obesities are associated with variation in absolute fat mass and in the distribution of fat. Some forms of obesity are associated with a predominance of fat storage in the abdominal area, whereas others are associated with a predominance of fat accumulation in the buttocks and upper aspects (thighs) of the lower extremities. Second, differences in fat topography are associated with individual differences in the risk of several metabolic complications that characterize obese individuals, such as type 2 diabetes, hypertension, dyslipoproteinemia, and others (see chapter 26 on risk factors). Accordingly, variation in adipose tissue metabolism among fat depots contributes to the anomalies of metabolism commonly observed in obese subjects. Even though a body of data supports this contention, several issues must be addressed. Moreover, most of the research on adipose tissue heterogeneity, metabolic properties, and types of obesity has been done with adults (Owens et al. 1998), and applications to children and adolescents should be made with care. Issues related to obesity during the growing years are the topic of chapter 24.

Little is known about variation in the metabolic characteristics of adipose tissue depots from different areas of the body during growth and maturation. However, trends in age-associated and sex-associated variations in the deposition of subcutaneous fat suggest that regional variation in fat distribution and metabolic characteristics is initiated during the adolescent growth spurt and sexual maturation. A sex difference exists in the absolute amount of subcutaneous fat during childhood but not in relative fat distribution. The sex difference in fat distribution develops at puberty. Males have a propensity to accumulate relatively more subcutaneous fat on the trunk. Females, on the other hand, have a propensity to accumulate subcutaneous fat rather equally on the trunk and extremities, although proportionally more is accumulated in the lower compared with the upper extremities. The sex difference in hormone levels at this phase of growth probably plays a role in the development of regional variation in fat distribution and in metabolic differences of adipocytes in these two regions.

Subcutaneous Fat Distribution During Growth

Fat distribution refers to the placement of fat depots on the body (i.e., fat topography). The topic is important, as variation in the distribution of fat is a risk factor in the development of several diseases in adults, such as non–insulin-dependent diabetes mellitus and cardiovascular diseases. This section deals with subcutaneous fat topography, and the next section addresses the topic of visceral fat.

Radiographic Data

Mixed-longitudinal observations for the sum of fat width measurements made on radiographs of five sites on the extremities of children in the Child Research Council Study (Denver) are shown in figure 8.7. Girls have more subcutaneous fat than boys at all ages from early infancy to 18 years of age. After a rapid rise in subcutaneous fat during the first 6 months of life, both sexes experience a reduction in subcutaneous fat through 6 or 7 years of age. Girls then show a linear increase in subcutaneous fat with age through puberty. Boys, on the other hand, show a slight increase in fat thickness between 7 and 12 or 13 years of age and then a reduction in subcutaneous fat during puberty. The increase in subcutaneous fat before male adolescence is sometimes referred to as the preadolescent fat wave.

Radiographic Subcutaneous
Fat During Growth

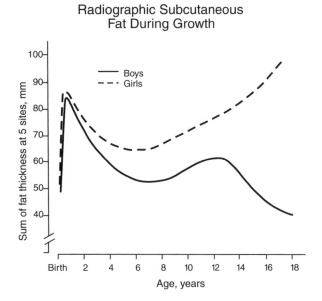

Subcutaneous Fat From
Skinfolds During Growth

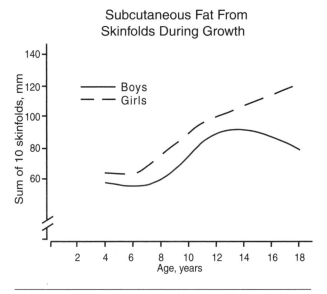

FIGURE 8.7 Age changes in subcutaneous fat based on the summed widths of radiographic fat measurements made at five sites (hip, deltoid, forearm, thigh, and calf) in a mixed-longitudinal sample of Denver children.

Data from Malina and Roche, 1983.

FIGURE 8.8 Changes in subcutaneous fat based on five trunk (pectoral, subscapular, midaxillary, paraumbilical [abdominal], and suprailiac) and five extremity (triceps, biceps, forearm, medial thigh, and medial calf) skinfolds in a mixed-longitudinal sample of Denver children.

Data from Malina and Roche, 1983.

Skinfold Thicknesses

Corresponding mixed-longitudinal observations for the sum of skinfold thicknesses measured at 10 sites, five on the trunk and five on the extremities, in the Child Research Council Study are shown in figure 8.8. Girls have, on average, more subcutaneous fat than boys at all ages between 4 and 18 years of age. Between 4 and 18 years of age, the pattern of fat accumulation in girls is virtually identical for skinfold and radiographic data. The two indicators of subcutaneous fat also correspond closely for boys between 4 and 13 years of age, but after 13 years of age, the skinfold and radiographic data differ somewhat. The latter show a sharp reduction in subcutaneous fat during male adolescence. The cause of the difference is probably the fact that radiographic fat sites are limited to the extremities, whereas skinfold sites include trunk measurements as well.

Trunk and Extremity Skinfolds

Changes in skinfolds on the trunk and extremities during growth are shown in figure 8.9. The sum of five extremity skinfolds is greater than that of five trunk skinfolds at all ages, with the exception of late adolescence in boys, and sex differences are

greater for extremity skinfolds during childhood and especially during adolescence than for trunk skinfolds. Thicknesses of both extremity and trunk skinfolds are reasonably stable between 4 and 7 years of age. After this age, extremity and trunk skinfolds increase more or less linearly to 18 years of age in girls. In boys, on the other hand, trunk skinfolds increase to about 13 years of age, decline slightly through 14 years of age, and then increase in thickness through late adolescence. Extremity skinfolds increase to about 11 or 12 years of age and then decline until about 15 or 16 years of age. The decline in the sum of extremity skinfold thicknesses is greater than that for the sum of trunk skinfolds during male adolescence. The decrease in extremity skinfolds during the adolescent spurt in males contributes to the sex difference in subcutaneous fat distribution.

The ratio of the sum of skinfold thicknesses measured on the trunk to the sum of skinfold thicknesses measured on the extremities illustrates changes in the relative distribution of subcutaneous fat during growth, that is, the proportion of subcutaneous fat on the trunk compared with that on the limbs (see figure 8.10). The ratio of trunk-to-extremity skinfolds is rather stable in both sexes during childhood.

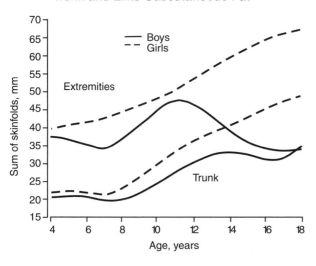

FIGURE 8.9 Age changes in trunk (sum of five) and extremity (sum of five) skinfolds in a mixed-longitudinal sample of Denver children. Specific skinfolds are indicated in the caption of figure 8.8. Based on data from the Child Research Council in Denver.

Reprinted, by permission, from Malina and Bouchard, 1988, Subcutaneous fat distribution during growth. In *Fat distribution during growth and later health outcomes*, edited by Bouchard and Johnston (New York: Liss), 63-84.

The thickness of subcutaneous fat on the trunk is approximately one-half of that on the extremities during childhood. The ratio then begins to increase with age through male adolescence but changes only slightly after 12 or 13 years of age in girls. The increasing ratio in males reflects two trends. Initially, more fat is gained on the trunk than on the extremities between about 10 and 13 years of age; as a result, the ratio increases. Subsequently, subcutaneous fat thickness continues to slowly increase on the trunk but decreases on the extremities (see figure 8.9). Males thus accumulate proportionally more subcutaneous fat on the trunk during adolescence. In females, subcutaneous trunk fat also increases more than extremity fat prepubertally (i.e., between 8 and 12 years of age), but after this age, both trunk and extremity fat appear to accumulate at a reasonably similar pace. Hence, the increase in the ratio is not as marked as in males.

The ratio of subcutaneous fat on the trunk to subcutaneous fat on the limbs indicates that the sex difference in the distribution of body fat occurs during adolescence. Before the adolescent growth spurt, no sex difference is seen in the ratio. With the onset of adolescence, which occurs on the average 2 years earlier in girls than in boys (see chapter 16), both sexes gain proportionally

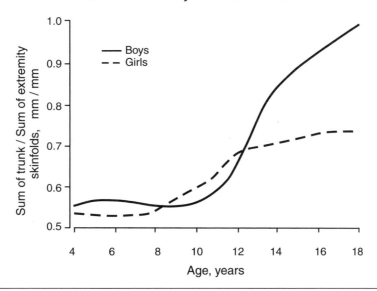

FIGURE 8.10 Age changes in the ratio of trunk-to-extremity skinfolds in a mixed-longitudinal sample of Denver children. Ratios are based on sums of five trunk and five extremity skinfolds as indicated in the caption of figure 8.8.

Reprinted, by permission, from Malina and Bouchard, 1988, Subcutaneous fat distribution during growth. In *Fat distribution during growth and later health outcomes*, edited by Bouchard and Johnston (New York: Liss), 63-84.

more fat on the trunk, but the gain is less in girls than in boys. In addition, boys experience a reduction in the thickness of subcutaneous fat on the extremities during adolescence, which accentuates the relatively greater accumulation of subcutaneous fat on the trunk at this stage of growth.

These trends are based on skinfold thicknesses, which do not take into account the changes occurring in limb sizes and areas. A better estimate of the growth changes in the adipose tissue distribution between the trunk and the extremities may be derived from whole-body DEXA. Unfortunately longitudinal data for DEXA measurements in boys and girls are not presently available. A cross-sectional study of girls ranging from late childhood into young adulthood indicates greater accumulation of trunk fat than leg or arm fat with sexual maturation (Goulding et al. 1996).

These observations need to be considered in light of the sex differences in the metabolic properties of adipose tissue. The higher adipose tissue lipoprotein lipase activity and lipid storage capacity in the buttock and femoral fat depots of females leads to adipocyte enlargement and fat accumulation in the lower body. This development sets the stage for the establishment of the female pattern of fat deposition and perhaps the gluteofemoral type of obesity that occurs in some women. On the other hand, adolescent males, and perhaps females with a weakly defined sex hormone profile, are more subject to preferential fat deposition in the trunk or abdominal region. This finding may set the stage for the establishment of the typical male pattern of abdominal obesity.

Abdominal Visceral Fat During Growth

Abdominal visceral fat is also labeled deepomental, internal, or intra-abdominal fat. It is the fat tissue that is located around the viscera, deep in the abdominal cavity. The omental and mesenteric depots have the unique characteristic of draining in the portal vein. The perirenal depots in the visceral fat compartment do not have portal drainage. Methodological advances in computerized tomography (CT) and magnetic resonance imaging have made assessment of visceral fat possible in humans. Data on this important fat depot are relatively scarce in children and adolescents, but they are expanding rapidly. Figure 8.11 illustrates abdominal visceral fat and abdominal

Cross-Sectional View of the Abdomen at the Level of L4-L5

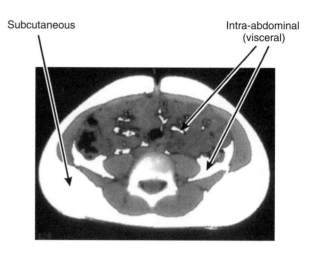

FIGURE 8.11   A CT image of abdominal fat in which visceral and subcutaneous compartments can be measured. The scan is a cross-sectional view taken at the level of the intervertebral disk between the fourth and fifth lumbar vertebrae.

subcutaneous fat. The image was obtained by CT and is a cross-sectional view at the level of the intervertebral disk between the fourth and fifth lumbar vertebrae. In this particular case, the visceral fat area is much smaller than the subcutaneous fat area.

Visceral fat can be detected as early as 4 years of age (Goran et al. 1995). The mean visceral fat area at the level of the umbilicus in 16 children, 4.4 to 8.8 years of age, is 8 cm^2. This amount of visceral fat represents about 10% of the visceral fat area commonly seen in normal-weight young adults. However, most of the visceral fat detected at these early ages is believed to be extraperitoneal or surrounds the kidneys. It does not drain into the portal vein.

Table 8.2 presents data on CT visceral fat areas for children and adolescents in comparison with adult values. On average, abdominal fat areas at the levels of the fourth and fifth lumbar vertebrae do not increase much during childhood or even adolescence. Mean areas around 30 cm^2 are typically seen during childhood. In a longitudinal study of 138 children, with a mean age of 8.1 years at the start of the study and followed for 3 years, the gain in visceral fat averaged 5.2 cm^2/ year (Huang et al. 2001). At adolescence, mean values cluster around 40 to 50 cm^2. These mean visceral fat areas are well below those observed during adulthood as shown in table 8.2 for men and women 25 to 40 years of age. However, the mean values are from studies based primarily on normal-weight children and adolescents. Significantly higher levels of visceral fat, a twofold to threefold increase at times, are observed in overweight or obese children and adolescents (Goran 1999).

In adults, the amount of abdominal visceral fat is strongly correlated with total adiposity. Thus, correlations between visceral fat areas and fat mass are in the range of 0.5 to 0.8 in several studies. The correlations imply that those with higher levels of adiposity have more visceral adipose tissue. This condition also holds true in children and adolescents, as suggested by a recent study of children 4 to 10 years of age (Goran et

al. 1997). In this sample, the correlation between visceral fat area and fat mass was 0.81. These high correlations are concordant with the observation that overweight and obese children have more abdominal visceral fat. However, considerable individual differences exist in amounts of visceral fat at any level of overall adiposity. These differences for adults are illustrated in table 8.3. Middle-aged men were selected within four BMI categories, and only those who fell within a small range for percent body fat were retained in the study (Bouchard 1994). The mean visceral fat area increased with higher BMI and percent body fat, but considerable heterogeneity was seen in visceral fat surface area. Estimates of the proportion of adipose tissue in the visceral depot vary considerably, with a range from about 10% to 60% of

TABLE 8.2 Abdominal Visceral Fat Areas From Computerized Tomography Measurements in Samples of Boys and Girls Compared With Young Adults

Age (years)	Sex	n	Abdominal visceral fat (cm²) Mean	Range	Reference
4–9	Both	16	8	2–21	Goran et al. (1995)
4–10	Both	101	31	7–102	Goran et al. (1997)
7–10	Girls	11	56	25–102	Treuth et al. (1998)
17	Girls	34	40	10–94	Unpublished *
18	Girls	27	47	15–131	Unpublished *
19	Girls	31	53	19–146	Unpublished *
25–40	Women	236	70	10–241	Unpublished *
17	Boys	28	45	9–131	Unpublished *
18	Boys	21	45	8–109	Unpublished *
19	Boys	20	56	10–147	Unpublished *
25–40	Men	186	94	16–251	Unpublished *

* Subjects from the Quebec Family Study and the Heritage Family Study cohorts. All subjects were examined using the same CT scan procedure.

TABLE 8.3 Variation in Amount of Abdominal Visceral Fat for a Given BMI and Percent Body Fat (% Fat) Classes in Males, 35 to 54 Years of Age

n	BMI (kg/m²)	% fat	Visceral fat (cm²) Mean	Minimum	Maximum
15	21–22	14–18	58	31	84
19	24–25	19–24	89	50	140
18	27–28	25–29	133	63	199
16	30–31	30–33	153	77	261

Adapted from Bouchard (1994).

total fat mass in healthy adults, the latter probably reflecting a subcutaneous lipodystrophy.

Inferences about changes in internal or deep fat as opposed to subcutaneous or superficial fat during growth can be made from the ratio of subcutaneous fat to total fat mass. Age trends in the ratio of subcutaneous fat (sum of six skinfolds) to total fat mass (based on body density, see chapter 5) are illustrated in figure 8.12. No sex difference appears in the ratio before adolescence. The ratio declines with age from 9 to 18 years of age in girls and from 9 through 13 years of age in boys. It subsequently increases with age in boys. Fat mass, the denominator, apparently increases at a faster rate than subcutaneous fat, the numerator, during childhood; hence, the ratio declines. By inference, internal fat appears to accumulate at a faster rate than subcutaneous fat during childhood in both sexes. This trend continues through adolescence in girls. In contrast, the ratio tends to increase in boys after 13 or 14 years of age. This change can be explained by the fact that boys have proportionally more subcutaneous fat on the trunk relative to fat mass and proportionally less subcutaneous fat on the extremities relative to fat mass during adolescence. The preceding trends are derived from cross-sectional data, and confirmation of the suggested trends with longitudinal data is needed. Moreover, no data are as of yet available on the changes with age in the total mass of internal fat. Thus, the trends in the ratio of subcutaneous fat to total fat mass,

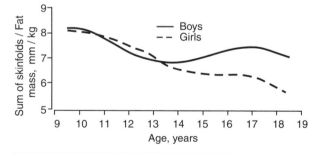

Subcutaneous Fat
Relative to Total Body Fat

FIGURE 8.12   Age changes in the ratio of subcutaneous fat (sum of six skinfolds: triceps, biceps, subscapular, suprailiac, abdominal, and medial calf) to total fat mass in French Canadian children.

Reprinted, by permission, from Malina and Bouchard, 1988, Subcutaneous fat distribution during growth. In *Fat distribution during growth and later health outcomes*, edited by Bouchard and Johnston (New York: Liss), 63-84.

which are suggestive of patterns of changes in "internal" fat deposition, cannot be verified independently with a direct measurement of the latter phenotype.

Stability of Body Fat During Growth

A central question regarding fatness during growth is its relative stability. Will the lean child grow into a lean adult? Similarly, does the fat child have a high risk of remaining fat in later life? These questions are particularly critical as the prevalence of overweight and obesity is on the rise in children and adolescents. The stability of the fat mass and percent body fat estimated with densitometry was discussed in chapter 5. Densitometric indicators of body composition, including fat-free mass, demonstrate moderately high and similar stability from childhood and adolescence into young adulthood. Apparently, no sex differences exist in the strength of the interage tracking correlations.

Tracking of subcutaneous fat has been investigated based on skinfold thicknesses and radiographic measurements of fat widths in both sexes across a broader age range. The evidence based on group data suggests two general trends. First, subcutaneous fat does not track well from birth to about 5 or 6 years of age, that is, subcutaneous fat is very labile during infancy and early childhood. Subsequently, correlations between measurements of subcutaneous fat in the same individual as a young adult and at various ages after 7 to 8 years of age are reasonably constant and moderate in magnitude. The correlations decline at the time of the adolescent growth spurt but then gradually increase. Note, however, that correlations between subcutaneous fat measurements at adjacent ages tend to be higher, ranging from 0.7 to 0.9, than those across spans of 8 or 10 years.

In the longitudinal Quebec Family Study, interage correlations over 12 years for the sum of five skinfolds were 0.66 and 0.44 in males and females, respectively, which were of similar magnitude as those for BMI, FM, and FFM (Campbell et al. 2001). In a 7-year follow-up of the 1981 Canada Fitness Survey, interage correlations for the sum of five skinfolds were generally similar to those for BMI and waist circumference in adolescence and adulthood (Katzmarzyk et al. 1999).

When individuals at specific positions within a group are considered (e.g., the fattest or the leanest at a given age), the fattest children after 6 years of age have a higher risk of remaining fat at subsequent examinations and as adults. The risk of excess fatness thus appears to be greater for those who have thicker subcutaneous fat measurements during childhood. Variation, however, is considerable and tracking excess subcutaneous fat from childhood through adolescence into adulthood is not a perfect fit. During growth, some fat individuals move away from the high fatness categories, whereas some lean children move into these categories.

Ratios of trunk and extremity skinfolds suggest that subcutaneous fat distribution is somewhat less stable during childhood. Correlations between ratios of skinfold thicknesses at each age during childhood with ratios at about 14 years of age are quite variable and moderate at best. However, in these studies, the total level of adiposity was not taken into account. The loss of subcutaneous fat on the extremities of males

during adolescence further contributes to the instability of fat distribution at this time.

Few studies have examined the stability of relative adipose tissue distribution from childhood to adulthood. Interage correlations over 7 years for the trunk-to-extremity skinfold ratio, adjusted for the sum of five skinfolds, waist circumference, and the BMI, were lower than for indicators of general adiposity, although significant (Katzmarzyk et al. 1999). Further, interage correlations over 12 years in the longitudinal component of the Quebec Family Study were 0.19 and 0.31 for the second principal component of skinfolds (a trunk-extremity contrast) and 0.41 and 0.47 for the trunk-to-extremity skinfold ratio, adjusted for the sum of five skinfolds, in males and females, respectively (Campbell et al. 2001). The results suggest an additional level of tracking for indicators of relative adipose tissue distribution beyond that for adiposity per se. As of yet, no data exist on the tracking of abdominal visceral fat with age during growth.

Summary

Adipose cells are highly complex organs that are involved in the storage of energy in the form of triglyceride and the delivery of metabolic fuel in times of fasting or starvation. Recognition that adipocytes are also endocrine and secretory cells is growing. They are involved in the regulation of energy balance, energy demands of exercise, glucose and insulin metabolism, lipid metabolism, immunity, feedback regulation of adipogenesis, production of cytokines, estrogens, and other hormones, regulation of blood pressure, and other processes. The two major types of adipose tissue are brown and white. Brown adipose tissue is a highly thermogenic organ that accounts for less than 1% of fat mass in the adult. Adipocytes in white adipose tissue increase in size (hypertrophy) and number (hyperplasia) from birth through childhood and adolescence into young adulthood. The distribution of adipose tissue in the body is currently of considerable clinical interest, and major changes occur during childhood and adolescence. Intraindividual and interindividual differences in the profile of fat deposition are associated with hormonal levels and metabolic properties of the adipocytes. Males accumulate proportionally more subcutaneous adipose tissue on the trunk during adolescence compared with females. New technologies (CT, MRI) permit differentiation of subcutaneous and visceral adipose tissue in the abdominal area, and a sex difference in visceral adiposity appears to occur during late adolescence when males accumulate proportionally more visceral adipose than females.

Sources and Suggested Readings

Adams SH (2000) Uncoupling protein homologs: Emerging views of physiological function. Journal of Nutrition 130: 711-714.

Ailhaud G (2000) Obésité, Dépistage et Prévention chez l'Enfant. Paris: INSERM, pp 203-210 (in French).

* Ailhaud G, Hauner H (1998) Development of white adipose tissue. In GA Bray, C Bouchard, WPT James (eds), Handbook of Obesity. New York: Marcel Dekker, pp 359-378.

Ailhaud G (1996) Adipose cell differentiation: A long way to Tipperary. In A Angel, H Anderson, C Bouchard, D Lau, L Leiter, R Mendelson (eds), Progress in Obesity Research: 7. London: John Libbey, pp 3-12.

Angel A, Hollenberg CH, Roncari DAK, editors (1983) The

Adipocyte and Obesity: Cellular and Molecular Mechanisms. New York: Raven.

* Arner P, Eckel RH (1998) Adipose tissue as a storage organ. In GA Bray, C Bouchard, WPT James (eds),Handbook of Obesity. New York: Marcel Dekker, pp 379-396.

Bonnet FP (1981) Introduction: White and brown adipose tissue. Main histological features and physiological role. In FP Bonnet (ed), Adipose Tissue in Childhood. Boca Raton, FL: CRC Press, pp 2-8.

Bonnet FP, Rocour-Brumioul D (1981) Normal growth of human adipose tissue. In FP Bonnet (ed), Adipose Tissue in Childhood. Boca Raton, FL: CRC Press, pp 81-107.

Boss O, Muzzin P, Giacobino JP (1998) The uncoupling proteins: A review. European Journal of Endocrinology 139:1-9.

Bouchard C (1994) Genetics of human obesities: Introductory notes. In C Bouchard (ed), The Genetics of Obesity. Boca Raton, FL: CRC Press, pp 1-15.

Boulton TJC, Dunlop M, Court JM (1978) The growth and development of fat cells in infancy. Pediatric Research 12:908-911.

Brand MD, Brindle KM, Buckingham JA, Harper HA, Rolfe DFS, Stuart JA (1999) The significance and mechanism of mitochondrial proton conductance. International Journal of Obesity 23: S4-S11.

Brook CGD (1978) Cellular growth: Adipose tissue. In F Falkner, JM Tanner (eds), Human Growth. Volume 2. Postnatal Growth. New York: Plenum, pp 21-33.

Campbell PT, Katzmarzyk PT, Malina, RM, Rao DC, Perusse L, Bouchard C (2001) Stability of adiposity phenotypes from childhood and adolescence into young adulthood with contribution of parental measures. Obesity Research 9: 394-400.

Cannon B, Matthias A, Golozoubova V, Ohlson KBE, Andersson U, Jacobsson A, Nedergaard J (1999) Unifying and distinguishing features of brown and white adipose tissues: UCP1 versus other UCPs. In B Guy-Grand, G Ailhaud (eds), Progress in Obesity Research: 8. London: John Libbey, pp 13-26.

Chumlea WC, Siervogel RM, Roche AF, Mukherjee D, Webb P (1981) Changes in adipocyte cellularity in children 10 to 18 years of age. International Journal of Obesity 6:383-389.

Cleary MP, Phillips FC, Morton RA (1999) Genotype and diet effects in lean and obese Zucker rats fed either safflower or coconut oil diets. Proceedings of the Society for Experimental Biology and Medicine 220:153-160.

Conway JM, Yanovski SZ, Avila NA, Hubbard VS (1995) Visceral adipose tissue differences in black and white women. American Journal of Clinical Nutrition 61:765-771.

Dietz WH (1999) Childhood origins of adult obesity. In B Guy-Grand, G Ailhaud (eds), Progress in Obesity Research: 8. London: John Libbey, pp 627-632.

Fleury C, Neverova M, Collins S, Raimbault S, Champigny O, Levi-Meyrueis C, Bouillaud F, Seldin MF, Surwit RS, Ricquier D, Warden CH (1997) Uncoupling protein-2: A novel gene linked to obesity and hyperinsulinemia. Nature Genetics 15:269-272.

Fried SK, Russell CD, Papaspyrou-Rao S, Ricci MR, Bunkin DA (1999) Depot differences in the regulation of adipocyte secretory products in human adipose tissue: The examples of lipoprotein lipase and leptin. In B Guy-Grand, G Ailhaud (eds), Progress in Obesity Research: 8. London: John Libbey, pp 83-88.

Fried SK, Russell CD (1998) Diverse roles of adipose tissue in the regulation of systematic metabolism and energy balance. In GA Bray, C Bouchard, WPT James (eds), Handbook of Obesity. New York: Marcel Dekker, pp 397-414.

Frühbeck G, Gomez-Ambrosi J, Muruzabal FJ, Burrell MA (2001) The adipocyte: A model for integration of endocrine and metabolic signaling in energy metabolism regulation. American Journal of Physiology: Endocrinology and Metabolism 280:E827-E847.

Gillman MW, Rifas-Shiman SL, Camargo Jr CA, Berkey CS, Frazier AL, Rockett HRH, Field AE, Colditz GA (2001) Risk of overweight among adolescents who were breastfed as infants. Journal of the American Medical Association 285:2461-2467.

* Goran MI (1999) Visceral fat in prepubertal children: Influence of obesity, anthropometry, ethnicity, gender, diet, and growth. American Journal of Human Biology 11:201-207.

Goran MI, Kaskoun M, Shuman WP (1995) Intra-abdominal adipose tissue in young children. International Journal of Obesity and Related Metabolic Disorders 19:279-283.

Goran MI, Nagy TR, Treuth MS, Trowbridge C, Dezenberg C, McGloin A, Gower BA (1997) Visceral fat in white and African American prepubertal children. American Journal of Clinical Nutrition 65:1703-1708.

Goulding A, Taylor RW, Gold E, Lewis-Barned NJ (1996) Regional body fat distribution in relation to pubertal stage: A dual-energy X-ray absorptiometry study of New Zealand girls and young women. American Journal of Clinical Nutrition 64:546-551.

Gutin B, Owens S (1999) Role of exercise intervention in improving body fat distribution and risk profile in children. American Journal of Human Biology 11:237-247.

Hager A (1981) Adipose tissue cellularity in childhood in relation to the development of obesity. British Medical Bulletin 37:287-290.

Hager A, Sjöström L, Arvidsson B, Bjorntorp P, Smith U (1977) Body fat and adipose tissue cellularity in infants: A longitudinal study. Metabolism 26:607-614.

Hauner H (1999) Human adipocytes—state of the art. In B Guy-Grand, G Ailhaud (eds), Progress in Obesity Research: 8. London: John Libbey, pp 47-54.

Hauner H (1996) Prevention of adipose tissue growth. In A Angel, H Anderson, C Bouchard, D Lau, L Leiter, R Mendelson (eds), Progress in Obesity Research: 7. London: John Libbey, pp 73-78.

Heaton JM (1972) The distribution of brown adipose tissue in the human. Journal of Anatomy 112:35-39.

* Himms-Hagen J, Ricquier D (1998) Brown adipose tissue. In GA Bray, C Bouchard, WPT James (eds), Handbook of Obesity. New York: Marcel Dekker, pp 415-442.

Hotamisligil GS, Shargill NS, Spiegelman BM (1993) Adipose expression of tumor necrosis factor-alpha: Direct role in obesity-linked insulin resistance. Science 259:87-91.

* Huang TT-K, Johnson MS, Fiugeroa-Colon R, Dwyer JH, Goran MI (2001) Growth of visceral fat, subcutaneous abdominal fat and total body fat in children. Obesity Research 9: 283-289.

Katzmarzyk PT, Perusse L, Malina RM, Bouchard C (1999) Seven year stability of indicators of obesity and adipose tissue distribution in the Canadian population. American Journal of Clinical Nutrition 69:1123-1129.

Knittle JL, Timmers K, Ginsberg-Fellner F, Brown RE, Katz DP (1979) The growth of adipose tissue in children and adolescents. Journal of Clinical Investigation 63:239-246.

Knittle JL (1978) Adipose tissue development in man. In F Falkner, JM Tanner (eds), Human Growth. Volume 2. Postnatal Growth. New York: Plenum, pp 295-315.

Kozak LP, Guerra C, Koza RA (1999) Genetic control of brown adipocyte induction. In B Guy-Grand, G Ailhaud (eds), Progress in Obesity Research: 8. London: John Libbey, pp 33-38.

Malina RM (1996) Regional body composition: Age, sex, and ethnic variation. In AF Roche, SB Heymsfield, TG Lohman (eds), Human Body Composition. Champaign, IL: Human Kinetics, pp 217-256.

Malina RM, Bouchard C (1988) Subcutaneous fat distribution during growth. In C Bouchard, FE Johnston (eds), Fat Distribution during Growth and Later Health Outcomes. New York: Alan R Liss, pp 63-84.

Malina RM, Roche AF (1983) Manual of Physical Status and Performance in Childhood. Volume 2. Physical Performance. New York: Plenum.

Martin RJ, Ramsay T, Hansman GV (1984) Adipocyte development. Pediatric Annals 13:448-453.

Masuzaki H, Ogawa Y, Sagawa N, Hosoda K, Matsumoto T, Mise H, Nishimura H, Yoshimasa Y, Tanaka I, Mori T, Nakao K (1997) Nonadipose tissue production of leptin: Leptin as a novel placenta-derived hormone in humans. Nature Medicine 3:1029-1033.

Negrel R (1999) Paracrine/autocrine signals and adipogenesis. In B Guy-Grand, G Ailhaud (eds), Progress in Obesity Research: 8. London: John Libbey, pp 55-64.

* Negrel R (1996) Fat cells cannot divide. In A Angel, H Anderson, C Bouchard, D Lau, L Leiter, R Mendelson (eds), Progress in Obesity Research: 7. London: John Libbey, pp 121-126.

Okuno M, Kajiwara K, Imai S, Kobayashi T, Honma N, Maki T, Suruga K, Goda T, Takase S, Muto Y, Moriwaki H (1997) Perilla oil prevents the excessive growth of visceral adipose tissue in rats by down-regulating adipocyte differentiation. Journal of Nutrition 127:1752-1757.

Owens S, Gutin B, Ferguson M, Allison J, Karp W, Li NA (1998) Visceral adipose tissue and cardiovascular risk factors in obese children. Journal of Pediatrics 133:41-45.

Poissonnet CM, Burdi AR, Bookstein FL (1983) Growth and development of human adipose tissue during early gestation. Early Human Development 8:1-11.

Poissonnet CM, Burdi AR, Garn SM (1984) The chronology of adipose tissue appearance and distribution in the human fetus. Early Human Development 10:1-11.

Ricquier D (1999) The family of uncoupling proteins and its role in energy expenditure and body weight control. In B Guy-Grand, G Ailhaud (eds), Progress in Obesity Research: 8. London: John Libbey, pp 381-386.

Romanski SA, Nelson RM, Jensen MD (2000) Meal fatty acid uptake in adipose tissue: Gender effects in nonobese humans. American Journal of Physiology 279:E455-E462.

Sjöström L (1980) Fat cells and body weight. In AJ Stunkard (ed), Obesity. Philadelphia: Saunders, pp 72-100.

Sniderman AD, Cianflone K (1994) The adipsin-ASP pathway and regulation of adipocyte function. Annals of Medicine 26:388-393.

Soriguer Escofet FJ, Esteva de Antoni I, Tinahone FJ, Parej A (1996) Adipose tissue fatty acids and size and number of fat cells from birth to 9 years of age—a cross-sectional study in 96 boys. Metabolism 45:1395-1401.

Spiegelman B, Castillo G, Hauser S, Puigserver P (1999) Regulation of energy balance by PPAR. In B Guy-Grand, G Ailhaud (eds), Progress in Obesity Research: 8. London: John Libbey, pp 39-46.

* Spiegelman BM, Flier JS (1996) Adipogenesis and obesity: Rounding out the big picture. Cell 87:377-389.

Stock M, Rothwell N (1982) Obesity and Leanness. Basic Aspects. London: John Libbey.

Vidal-Puig A, Solanes G, Grujic D, Flier JS, Lowell BB (1997) UCP3: An uncoupling protein homologue expressed preferentially and abundantly in skeletal muscle and brown adipose tissue. Biochemical and Biophysics Research Communications 235:79-82.

von Kries R, Loletzko B, Sauerwald T, von Mutius E, Barnert D, Grunert V, von Voss H (1999) Breast feeding and obesity: Cross sectional study. British Medical Journal 319:147-150.

Zhang Y, Proenca R, Maffei M, Barone M, Leopold L, Friedman JM (1994) Positional cloning of the mouse obese gene and its human homologue. Nature 372:425-432.

Part III

Functional Development

Part III of the text has a functional emphasis. It begins with a discussion of the heart, blood, and lungs (chapter 9). These organs and tissues constitute the system for delivering oxygen and nutrients to the tissues and for removing carbon dioxide and wastes from the tissues. Changes in the heart, blood, and lungs parallel those in body size during childhood and adolescence.

The next four chapters consider specific aspects of performance. Chapter 10 deals with the development of movement behaviors during infancy and the preschool years. Basic movements provide the substrate for the development of proficiency in more specific skills and performances in a variety of tasks. Chapter 11 focuses on changes in muscular strength and on a variety of motor performances during childhood and adolescence in the context of changes associated with age and the emergence of sex differences.

Chapters 12 and 13, respectively, consider changes in aerobic and anaerobic capacities during childhood and adolescence. The ability of the growing individual to perform under predominantly aerobic conditions and age-related and sex-related changes in adaptations to submaximal and maximal exercise are considered in chapter 12. Features of the anaerobic systems and the capacity of children and adolescents to perform under such conditions are discussed in chapter 13.

The final chapter in this section focuses on thermoregulation. Temperature of the body is maintained within relatively narrow limits under a variety of environmental conditions. This chapter presents the basic principles of temperature regulation and then discusses the effects of growth and maturation on responses to climatic heat and cold stresses.

HEART, BLOOD, AND LUNGS

Chapter Outline

An understanding of changes that occur in the circulatory and respiratory systems during growth is important for an appreciation of functional development and is essential for understanding the responses of children to exercise. Two major developmental trends are prominent in this chapter: (1) the dramatic changes that occur in the cardiorespiratory system in the transition from the fetal to the neonatal period and (2) the complex hemodynamic tuning that takes place early postnatally and continues through childhood and adolescence until these systems are fully mature. These phenomena and others related to the growth of the heart, cardiac function, blood volume and composition, and lung and respiratory functions are described in this chapter.

Features of Fetal Circulation

The heart and blood vessels are formed from cells of embryonic mesodermal origin (see chapter 2).

The main cardiogenic areas are located in the lateral portions of a horseshoe-shaped structure beneath the neural crest. They give rise to endocardial tubes that gradually move toward each other and eventually fuse to form the "primitive heart tube" at about 3 weeks after fertilization. Shortly thereafter, the primitive heart begins to beat (i.e., it contracts and relaxes). The primitive heart tube gradually grows into the pericardial cavity. It undergoes a rightward looping by cellular mechanisms that are still not understood. At about the same time as the heart is forming, angiogenic cells occur in clusters in the same horseshoe-shaped structure. These cells grow in size and migrate in various directions, giving rise to the development of blood vessels.

The structure of the heart develops its general definitive form by the end of the 6th week after fertilization, and the main blood vessels are established by the 8th week. The primitive heart tube folds and twists upon itself, and at the same time partitions into four distinct chambers. These two processes result in the proper positioning of the four heart chambers within the pericardial cavity and of the major blood vessels of the heart. Atrial and ventricular cells are from separate cell lineages that are distinguishable before cardiac looping occurs. Sets of cardiac muscle genes express distinct protein isoforms that confer the contractile and physiological properties unique to each chamber (Olson and Srivastava 1996).

Problems associated with, or interference in, these embryonic cardiac morphogenic processes can be lethal or lead to different types of congenital heart disease. Defects in cardiac looping have been described. One of them results from a mutation in the connexin 43 gene, which causes the heterotaxy syndrome in children. Defects in atrioventricular septation have also been reported. The majority of these defects are atrial septal defects for which a gene on chromosome 12 has been implicated, although its exact function remains to be identified (Olson and Srivastava 1996). In another situation, a small deletion on chromosome 22 has been shown to cause the Catch-22 syndrome in about 30% of children who exhibit it. The syndrome is characterized by aortic arch defect and other large-vessel features.

The fetal circulation is gradually established. It has several unique features that can influence functional adaptation postnatally. The main features of fetal circulation are illustrated in figure 9.1. The placenta provides the interface between the maternal and fetal circulations. The umbilical vein carries oxygen and nutrients from the placenta to the fetus, and two umbilical arteries transport venous blood from the fetus to the placenta for reoxygenation and elimination of metabolites into the maternal circulation.

Two important features of the fetal circulation must be understood. The first feature is the small amount of fetal cardiac output that passes through the fetal lungs. Two shunts shift blood from the right side of the fetal circulation to the left side, thus bypassing the lungs. This situation is, of course, temporary and is altered near or at the time of birth. The first of the two shunts is the **foramen ovale,** which is essentially a one-way opening in the septum separating the right and left atria. This opening allows for some of the blood that is returning to the right atrium to bypass the right ventricle and flow directly into the left atrium. The septal connection is closed by a one-way valve. This valve closes with the increase in pressure on the left side of the heart produced by contraction. The foramen ovale

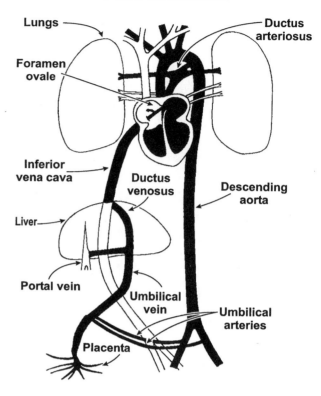

Fetal Circulation

F I G U R E 9.1   Schematic illustration of the circulatory system during fetal life.

thus allows much of the blood to bypass the fetal lungs and to be pumped into the fetal systemic circulation.

The second shunt is known as the **ductus arteriosus,** which is a small vessel that connects the main pulmonary artery with the aorta and thus serves as a right-to-left shunt. It permits a fraction of the blood that is pumped by the right ventricle of the fetal heart to be diverted into the aorta rather than entirely into the pulmonary artery.

The shunts provided by the foramen ovale and the ductus arteriosus have the effect of reducing the amount of blood, which is pumped by the right ventricle of the heart, that flows through the pulmonary circulation at a time when the lungs are not ready to assume their normal gas exchange function. Only about 10% to 15% of the blood pumped by the heart has been estimated to go through the lungs during fetal life.

The second important feature of the fetal circulatory system is the **ductus venosus,** which is a temporary vessel that allows some of the blood to pass from the umbilical vein directly to the inferior vena cava and then into the right atrium. The umbilical vein, as noted earlier, transports blood from the placenta to the fetus. The ductus venosus thus permits the oxygenated blood from the maternal circulation to pass directly into the right atrium and subsequently into fetal circulation.

Blood of the umbilical vein has an oxygen saturation of about 70%. In contrast, peripheral tissues of the fetus are exposed to fetal blood that has an oxygen saturation level of about 55% to 60%. These saturation levels are in sharp contrast to the conditions that prevail after birth, when the arterial blood has an oxygen saturation of about 97% and venous blood has an oxygen saturation of about 70%. The fetus relies on several types of hemoglobin to meet the oxygen needs of fetal tissues in the presence of the lower partial pressure of oxygen and the corresponding reduction in oxygen saturation of the fetal blood.

Human hemoglobin is composed of four globin polypeptides. Each globin chain carries a heme group bound at a specific site of the peptide. A globin peptide contains over 140 amino acids specified by the relevant gene. Children and adults carry hemoglobin composed of two α-chains and two β-chains. A small proportion of hemoglobin composed of two α-chains and two δ-chains is also seen. Other globin peptides are encoded by other genes that are expressed predominantly in fetal life. They include the ζ gene and the ε gene. Both genes are expressed in embryonic life, and their expression is greatly diminished after 10 weeks. Afterwards, the main form of hemoglobin is the fetal form that consists of two α-chains and two γ-chains. Two genes encode gamma globin peptides. They differ from one another by the presence of alanine or glycine at amino acid 136. Thus, various forms of the hemoglobin molecule enter into play to carry oxygen in the blood to tissues at various phases of fetal life and then postnatally. Seven genes have evolved to meet the demands of the drastically different environments under which tissues must be oxygenated.

Cardiopulmonary Adjustments at Birth

The transition from intrauterine life in a well-insulated aqueous environment to extrauterine life is a dramatic experience for the individual. Specific adjustments in the heart and circulatory

and respiratory systems are particularly striking. The metabolic link between the mother and fetus is severed at birth. Thus, the infant must begin breathing to guarantee oxygen delivery to the tissues and organs.

Circulatory adjustments are also initiated at the onset of breathing. The expanding lungs are accompanied by a reduction in the pulmonary vascular resistance, while systemic blood pressure increases. These adjustments permit more blood to flow through the pulmonary vessels. Secondary to these adjustments, occlusion of the umbilical cord increases pressure in the left atrium above that in the right atrium and thus pushes the interseptal valve over the foramen ovale. This action results in closure of the foramen ovale, which eventually becomes a permanent anatomical closure of this fetal shunt. The ductus arteriosus, the other fetal shunt, is also affected by the circulatory changes at this time. The higher systemic pressure is accompanied by increased aortic pressure, so blood in the ductus arteriosus can now flow in the opposite direction toward the pulmonary artery. Vasoconstriction of the ductus arteriosus and eventual complete functional closure of the temporary fetal vessel occurs shortly after birth.

The changes in the foramen ovale and ductus arteriosus of the newborn infant are especially important. If these adjustments do not proceed normally, cardiovascular consequences may result from a volume or pressure load on the heart. Several pediatric complications of the heart can be traced to these fetal structures, such as **patent ductus arteriosus,** in which the duct remains open after birth. Children with Down syndrome are at a high risk for this complication.

After the occlusion of the umbilical cord, the termination of circulation through the ductus venosus becomes important. A functional ductus venosus would allow some of the blood to bypass the hepatic circulatory network with potential hemodynamic and metabolic consequences. The ductus venosus is generally closed at birth and is fully obliterated by about 2 weeks of age. The mechanisms responsible for the closure of the ductus arteriosus and ductus venosus are still incompletely understood. Cardiac valvular abnormalities are not infrequently observed. They can cause important maladjustments in the transition from the fetal environment to the extrauterine circulatory conditions. In addition to deficiencies in several genes encoding transcription factors, growth factors, and receptors,

Postnatal Circulation

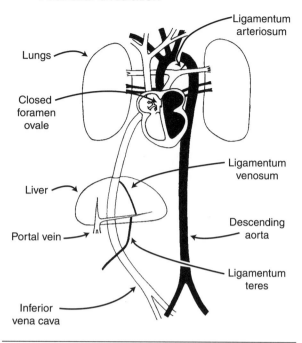

FIGURE 9.2 Schematic illustration of the circulatory system after adjustments in early postnatal life.

valvulogenesis can be disrupted by teratogens such as retinoic acid or vitamin A deficiency in the human fetus (Epstein and Buck 2000). Circulatory and vascular adjustments occurring in the infant are illustrated in figure 9.2.

Changes in Heart Size

During fetal life, the right side of the heart has about the same volume as the left side. This situation changes significantly after birth as the left side, and in particular the left ventricle, grows more rapidly than the right side of the heart. The progressive hypertrophy of the left ventricle is related to the fact that it pumps the blood against a higher pressure or resistance than the right ventricle.

The volume of the heart increases postnatally until young adulthood. The growth curve is similar to that for body weight and perhaps closer to that of the fat-free mass (see chapters 3 and 5). Heart volume is about 40 cm^3 at birth. The volume doubles by about 6 months of age, quadruples by 2 years of age, and reaches approximately 600 to 800 cm^3 in young adulthood. When calculated per body mass, heart volume is approximately 10 cm^3/kg throughout childhood and adolescence. This finding is shown in table 9.1, which is based on a study of 237 boys in whom the diameters of the heart were measured from two chest X-rays. Heart volume was calculated from the diameters assuming an elliptical shape of the heart.

When the effects of chronological age are statistically controlled with partial correlation, the relationship between heart volume and body weight (r = 0.74) is greater than that with height (r = 0.48). When age is not statistically controlled, the relationship between heart volume and body

TABLE 9.1   Heart Dimensions of Boys 8 Through 18 Years of Age

Age(years)	Body weight (kg)	Heart length (cm)	Heart width (cm)	Heart depth (cm)	Heart volume (cm³)	Heart volume/body weight (cm³/kg)
8	28.4	11.2	9.1	7.8	282	10.0
9	30.8	11.8	9.3	8.1	312	10.3
10	32.3	11.8	9.6	8.2	328	10.1
11	35.6	12.2	9.8	8.6	362	10.3
12	38.6	12.4	10.0	9.0	395	10.3
13	44.8	13.2	10.4	9.1	444	10.1
14	49.0	13.7	10.9	9.5	503	10.3
15	56.1	14.1	11.5	9.6	551	9.8
16	63.0	14.8	11.9	9.7	603	9.6
17	66.7	14.8	12.2	10.2	646	9.7
18	66.8	15.3	12.3	10.1	671	10.1

Heart dimensions are based on measurements from two chest X-rays.

Adapted from Bouchard et al. (1977).

weight is higher (r = 0.90) (Bouchard et al. 1977). Serial observations on 40 Czechoslovak boys who were followed from 11 to 18 years of age suggest an even closer relationship between heart volume and fat-free mass (Cermak and Parizkova 1975).

Heart mass, as determined from autopsy data, increases from birth until the 3rd or 4th decade of life (Seo et al. 2000). However, the ratio of heart mass to body mass declines exponentially during childhood and adolescence (see figure 9.3). Combining the data from table 9.1 and figure 9.3 clearly shows that the increase in heart volume is greater than in heart mass during the years of growth.

Left ventricular mass is an important morphological characteristic of the heart from a functional perspective. In addition to growth per se, left ventricular mass is influenced by the work performed by the myocardium (heart muscle). This influence is particularly evident during adolescence and young adulthood (De Simone et al. 1998). Left ventricular mass, as estimated by echocardiography, is linearly related to body mass and exponentially related to height (see figure 9.4). Left ventricular mass is similar in boys and girls until age 9 to 12 years, but it then grows faster in boys even when expressed per body mass (De Simone et al. 1995). Adolescent endurance athletes (e.g., swimmers and distance runners) tend to have,

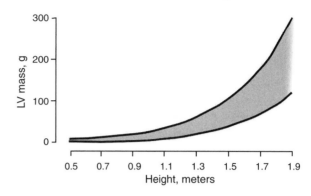

Left Ventricular Mass vs Height

FIGURE 9.4 Relationship between left ventricular (LV) mass and standing height in 373 children and adolescents. Data are based on two-dimensional (M-mode) echocardiography. The shaded area depicts the range.

Data from De Simone et al., 1998.

on average, larger estimated left ventricular mass and heart volume than nonathletes (see chapter 28). This difference probably reflects the influence of regular training.

Changes in Heart Functions

Heart rate, electrocardiographic features, stroke volume, cardiac output, and blood pressure provide a reasonable indication of changes in the functional characteristics of the cardiovascular system during growth. Many other hemodynamic functions exist, but a discussion of them is beyond the scope of this text. Cardiovascular functions during aerobic exercise are discussed in chapter 12.

Heart Rate

Average heart rate is about 140 contractions/minute in newborn infants, with a wide range of individual variation, as indicated by a standard deviation of about 20 beats/minute. Changes in heart rate during growth are shown in figure 9.5 for the mixed-longitudinal sample of children from the Child Research Council in Denver. Mean heart rates are shown for the basal state and with children at rest in a seated position. At all ages, basal heart rates (usually measured in the sleeping child) are lower than those of children at rest in the seated position. Basal heart rate decreases from about 140 beats/minute at birth to about 100 beats/minute at 1 year of age. Basal heart rate

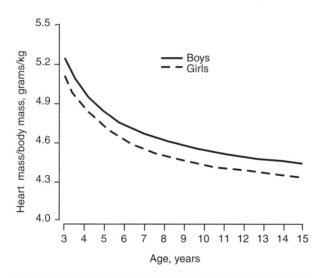

Heart Mass/Body Mass Ratio vs Age

FIGURE 9.3 Relationship between heart mass and body mass during childhood and adolescence.

Data from Rowland, 1991.

continues to decline during childhood, so that by 6 years of age it is, on average, 80 beats/minute and by 10 years of age it is about 70 beats/minute. No sex difference is seen in average heart rates during infancy and childhood. However, by 10 years of age, a slight sex difference appears. Basal heart rates are, on the average, about 3 to 5 beats/minute higher in girls than in boys. By late adolescence or young adulthood, males have average basal heart rates of approximately 57 to 60 beats/minute, whereas females have average rates of 62 to 63 beats/minute. The same trends occur in resting heart rate at the sitting position. For example, mean resting heart rates in the seated position in late adolescence are 72 and 76 beats/minute in boys and girls, respectively.

Resting Heart Rate vs Age

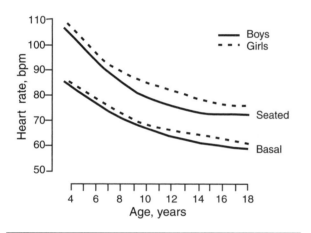

FIGURE 9.5 Changes in basal and seated heart rate in a mixed-longitudinal sample of children from Denver.

Data from Malina and Roche, 1983.

Electrocardiographic Features

The electrocardiographic activity of the newborn infant is considerably different from that of an adult. The **tachycardia** (fast heart beat) of early postnatal life translates into shorter time intervals for the various components of the electrocardiogram (ECG). The QRS interval, which is concomitant with the depolarization of the ventricular muscle, has a duration of about 0.06 second in the newborn infant but about 0.1 second in the adult. Amplitudes of the various deflections of the ECG are also higher in the adult than in the infant or the young child.

An important feature of the ECG in infants is the occasional irregularity and instability of the bioelectrical activities of the heart. The incidence of deviation from ECG norms is highest during this period of life. Anatomical changes in heart muscle, alterations in heart position within the pericardial space, progressive stabilization of the autonomic nervous system and electrical conductivity of the cardiac muscle, and developmental changes in hemodynamic properties occur simultaneously at this time and most likely underlie the episodes of apparent irregularity and instability in infancy.

Some of the ECG changes are displayed as rhythm irregularities, or **arrhythmias**. The most common of these irregularities is **sinus arrhythmia**, which is a cyclical change in rhythm, occurring in synchrony with the respiratory cycle. It is mediated by the vagus nerve and does not denote any cardiac abnormality.

Stroke Volume and Cardiac Output

The **stroke volume** of the heart refers to the volume of blood ejected from the left ventricle during one contraction. It increases considerably during childhood and adolescence. It is about 3 to 4 ml around the time of birth and increases to about 40 ml at rest just before adolescence. During the adolescent growth spurt, stroke volume increases considerably, reaching about 60 ml at rest in the young adult male.

Cardiac output represents the output of the left ventricle in 1 minute. It is the product of stroke volume and heart rate. Given the values for stroke volume and resting heart rate described earlier, cardiac output in the newborn is about 0.5 L of blood/minute. Mean values for young adult males at rest reach about 5 L/minute or about 3 L/m² of body surface area. The right side of the heart has similar stroke volume and cardiac output characteristics, although the right ventricle works against a lesser pressure gradient.

Blood Pressure

An understanding of the major features of cardiac function during growth requires a consideration of arterial blood pressure variables. Pulmonary arterial pressure and right ventricular pressure gradually decrease in the neonate and the decline appears to be closely related to the reduction in vascular resistance associated with expansion of the lungs at birth. At the same time, an increase in vascular resistance occurs in peripheral tissues that is partly associated with elevated pressure in the left ventricle and aorta. In general, systemic blood pressures in the diastolic and systolic phases of heart muscle contraction increase during growth at the same time as relative bradycardia (i.e., slowing of the heart rate) is established.

Systolic blood pressure is the highest pressure that occurs in the systemic arteries during the contraction (systole) of the left ventricle. It depends mostly on the intensity of the contraction. **Diastolic blood pressure** is the lowest pressure that occurs in the systemic arteries during the relaxation (diastole) of the left ventricle. It depends mostly on the resistance to flow in the systemic arteries.

Systolic blood pressure in the neonate varies between 40 to 75 mmHg, and it rises thereafter. Age-associated changes in blood pressure are shown in figure 9.6 for girls and boys 1 to 17 years of age. The data are based on a cross-sectional sample of more than 56,000 subjects who participated in eight nationwide studies in the United States (Rosner et al. 1993). At 1 year, median systolic blood pressure reaches about 85 to 90 mmHg, and diastolic blood pressure reaches about 45 to 50 mmHg. Sex differences in systolic blood pressure begin to appear at approximately 10 years of age. During the second decade of life, the increase in blood pressure is greater in boys than in girls, so that by 17 years, the median systolic pressure in boys is 5 to 10 mmHg higher than in girls (see figure 9.6). In contrast, diastolic blood pressure does not show a sex difference.

Blood pressure at any given age is also related to standing height, being higher in taller individuals. For example, the 90th percentile for systolic blood pressure in a 7-year-old boy, whose height is at the 5th percentile, is 106 mmHg. For a 7-year-old boy whose height is at the 50th percentile, the systolic pressure is 111 mmHg. The respective pressure for a height at the 95th percentile at 7 years of age is 115 mmHg. Likewise, in a 14-year-old girl, the 90th percentiles for systolic pressure are 119, 122, and 126 mmHg for heights at the 5th, 50th, and 95th percentiles, respectively (National High Blood Pressure Education Program Working Group 1996).

Because systolic blood pressure increases more than diastolic blood pressure during childhood and adolescence, the **pulse pressure**, that is, the

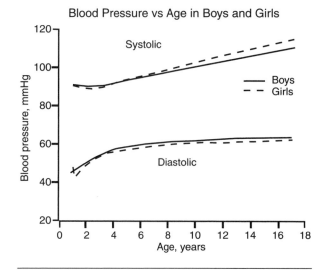

F I G U R E 9.6 Changes in median blood pressure during growth in 1-year-old to 17-year-old girls and boys. Data are based on nine studies in the United States and include 56,108 children and adolescents whose resting blood pressure was measured in the sitting position.

Data from Rosner et al., 1993.

difference between the two pressures, increases with age. In boys from the Fels Institute Longitudinal Study (Malina and Roche 1983), pulse pressure increases from 29 mmHg at 2 years of age to 43 mmHg at 18 years of age. Corresponding values for girls are less, about 32 and 36 mmHg at 2 and 18 years of age, respectively.

In summary, heart mass increases during growth but at a slower rate than the increase in total-body mass. In addition, the heart progressively adapts to performing more work, even in the resting state. Heart rate decreases by about 50% between birth and young adulthood, and cardiac output increases by about 10-fold. Systemic vascular resistance increases continuously during childhood and adolescence. Thus, a considerable increase in the power output of the heart muscle at rest occurs as the child progresses from the newborn state to maturity.

Changes in Features of Blood During Growth

The primary focus of this section is on those elements of the blood that have a relationship to exercise tolerance and health-related physical fitness.

Blood Volume

Blood volume is highly related to body mass and heart size in children with correlations generally above 0.90. Blood volume also correlates well with maximal oxygen uptake during childhood and adolescence (see chapter 12). The young adult male has, on the average, about 5 L of blood, of which about 3 L are plasma and the remainder is cells, primarily red blood cells. The newborn infant, on the other hand, has a blood volume of about 300 to 400 ml. Blood volume increases from infancy through adolescence, and the growth curve follows the general pattern of that for body mass. During adolescence, the mean blood volume of males becomes higher than that of females. The sex difference, which persists into adulthood, is a function of expansion of plasma volume and an increase in the cell content of the blood. Also at this time, sex differences in body mass and composition are established.

Hematocrit, Red Blood Cells, and Hemoglobin

An important characteristic of the blood is the **hematocrit**, which is the percentage of the blood volume occupied by blood cells. On average, the hematocrit of adult males varies between 40% and 45%, and corresponding values for adult females vary between 38% and 42%. The hematocrit is higher in the neonate because of the high level of hematopoietic activity (production of erythrocytes) during the latter part of pregnancy and the passage of blood from the umbilical vessels into the infant's circulation. The hematocrit normally reaches 50% in the newborn. Soon after birth, it decreases rapidly to about 30% by 2 to 3 months of age. Subsequently, the hematocrit increases progressively through childhood and adolescence in boys but only through childhood in girls. The sex difference is clearly established during the adolescent growth spurt and sexual maturation, reflecting changes in body mass, especially muscle mass in males, and to some extent blood loss associated with the establishment of regular menstrual cycles in females.

Both **red blood cells** and **hemoglobin** have a central role in the transport of oxygen to body tissues. The red cell count reaches, on the average, about 5.5 million/μL in adult males and 4.6 million/μL in adult females. Red blood cells are produced by the bone marrow of virtually all bones in infancy and early childhood. After about 5 years of age, however, the marrow of the long bones contributes progressively less to red cell

production. Red cells are derived from a primordial cell that differentiates into an **erythroblast**, which has the capacity to synthesize hemoglobin. Erythroblasts synthesize hemoglobin for a period of time during which they also undergo proliferation through mitotic division and progressive shrinking of the nucleus. The erythroblasts eventually become competent red blood cells, **erythrocytes**, with no nuclear material but a full complement of hemoglobin and other cytoplasmic components. Erythrocytes have a life span of about 110 to 120 days. Thus, the red blood cells are continuously replaced through closely regulated rates of production and destruction.

The red blood cell count decreases from about 4 to 4.5 million/μL at birth to about 3 million/μL at 2 months of age. The decline at this time probably reflects an inadequate genesis of erythrocytes. Subsequently, the red cell count increases to about 4 million/μL and gradually increases during childhood and adolescence in both sexes (see figure 9.7). The sex difference in red blood cell

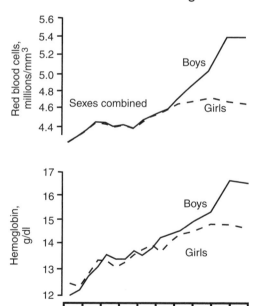

Red Blood Cells and Hemoglobin Concentration vs Age

FIGURE 9.7 Changes in red blood cells and hemoglobin concentration for boys and girls. Based on data of Mugrage and Andresen (1936, 1938).

Reprinted, by permission, from J.M. Tanner, 1962, *Growth at adolescence*, 2nd ed. (London: Blackwell Scientific Publications), 161.

count appears at about the time of puberty. The stimulation of the oxygen transporting capacity of the blood (as during regular exercise) is capable of inducing an increase in the erythrocyte content of the blood. A similar increase can be induced during a stay in the relatively hypoxic conditions of high altitude, above approximately 1.5 km.

The total hemoglobin content of the blood is related to maximal oxygen uptake, heart volume, and body mass. The correlation between total hemoglobin and body mass is about 0.90, and it increases during growth in a manner qualitatively similar to body weight. Hemoglobin concentration is relatively high in the neonate, about 20 g/100 ml, but then decreases to values as low as 10 g/100 ml between 3 and 6 months of age. Hemoglobin concentration then progressively increases with age (see figure 9.7). Typical adult hemoglobin concentrations are 16 g/100 ml in males and 14 g/100 ml in females. If this sex difference is considered relative to total blood volume, the sexual dimorphism in total hemoglobin can reach, on the average, 100 g or more. This difference may have important functional implications on oxygen transport during intense exercise.

White Blood Cells and Platelets

White blood cells, or **leucocytes**, also change during growth. At birth, the count frequently reaches above 40,000/μL, but in the adult, the total leukocyte count is about 8,000/μL. In contrast to red blood cells, which are similar to each other, white blood cells come in several varieties, which are based on their appearance under the light microscope. They are important in destroying or containing invading microorganisms (e.g., bacteria and parasites) and facilitating the body's immune response.

Platelets are important in blood clotting and repair of damage to the walls of blood vessels. The platelet count shows little change with age, remaining at about 350,000/μL.

Changes in Lungs and Respiratory Functions During Growth

The essential functions of the lungs are assumed by the placenta (fetomaternal unit) during prenatal life. At birth, however, the lungs must be sufficiently mature to rapidly assume the oxygenation and gas exchange functions, which are essential for extrauterine life.

Development and Growth of the Lungs

The genesis of the lungs begins soon after fertilization. The lungs begin as a single pouch at about 4 weeks prenatally, and the pouch soon divides. Early differentiation proceeds by branching until the bronchial tree is established by about 16 weeks. During the last 3 months of fetal life, alveoli begin to develop, but most alveoli develop postnatally.

The fetal lungs are filled with fluid, including amniotic fluid and blood constituents. During the birth process, most of the fluid is expelled when the thorax is compressed during passage through the birth canal, and the remainder is gradually drained in the lymphatic vessels. The alveoli are also compressed prenatally, but with the onset of respiration, they expand. Respiratory movements can be detected in the fetus, which suggests that the respiratory centers of the brain and the neuromuscular mechanisms essential for breathing are present before birth.

Lung tissue grows considerably postnatally, and respiratory functions progressively mature. Human lungs weigh about 60 to 70 g at birth and increase in mass by about 20-fold before maturity is attained. In contrast to the heart, which grows proportionally to body mass, the postnatal growth of the lungs is almost proportional to growth in height.

The number of alveoli increases from about 20 million at birth to about 300 million at about 8 years of age. The latter is the adult count of alveoli. When the volume of the lungs is considered relative to their mass, the former is much greater than the latter. The lungs of a newborn child can inhale about 3 ml of air/g of tissue, whereas those of an individual at maturity can inhale about 8 to 10 ml/g of tissue.

Respiratory Functions

The respiratory process has three components. The first component involves the lungs, whose primary function is the transfer of oxygen and carbon dioxide between the child and the ambient air. In this process, oxygen in the inspired air enters the lungs and subsequently diffuses from the alveoli into the circulation, binding with hemoglobin. In a similar manner, carbon dioxide in the blood diffuses into the alveoli and is subsequently removed in the expired air. The rate of alveolar gas transfer is determined by the individual's **lung diffusion capacity**. The second component involves the transport of gases in the blood to and from bodily tissues. The use of oxygen at the cellular level is the third component of the respiratory process, but consideration of cellular respiration is beyond the scope of this chapter.

Regulation of Breathing Regulatory mechanisms of breathing include the respiratory center in the brain stem; stretch receptors in the lungs that transmit proprioceptive impulses through the vagus nerve; carotid and aortic chemoreceptors in the respective blood vessels that are stimulated when the oxygen content of the blood falls; and chemoreceptors that are stimulated by increases in the carbon dioxide content of the blood or by decreases in the blood pH.

In addition, nerve impulses from the diaphragm, the intercostal muscles, the extensor muscles of the spine, the abdominal muscles, and others, as well as impulses from joints, participate in the regulation of respiratory movements, particularly during exercise. Specific details of the interactions among regulatory mechanisms that ensure a refined control of lung functions are still debated, and little is known about changes in the regulatory mechanisms that occur between birth and adulthood. However, the chemoreceptors are known to be functional in the newborn infant.

Breathing Frequency Age-associated changes in respiratory frequency in the resting state are shown in figure 9.8. Breathing frequency at birth is about 40/minute with a standard deviation of about 10. The frequency decreases rapidly to about 30/minute by the end of the first year. By 5 or 6 years of age, breathing frequency is about 22/minute and subsequently stabilizes at about 16 or 17 /minute (with a standard deviation of about 3). No consistent sex differences occur in breathing frequency.

Respiratory Rate vs Age

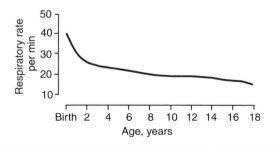

FIGURE 9.8 Changes in breathing frequency per minute during growth (sexes combined). The trend is based on data from several studies.

Pulmonary Volumes, Flows, and Capacities The measurement of several pulmonary volumes, flows, and capacities permits evaluation of the functional efficiency of the respiratory system of the growing child. Several volumes and capacities are schematically defined in figure 9.9. Four different volumes can be differentiated in total lung capacity (TLC). **Residual volume** (RV) is the volume of gas that remains in the lungs after a maximal expiration. This volume of gas cannot be expelled in a voluntary expiration. **Tidal volume** (TV) is the average volume of air expired during each cycle of normal, relaxed breathing. **Inspiratory reserve volume** (IRV) is the maximum volume of gas that can be inspired from the normal inspiratory level of TV. **Expiratory reserve volume** (ERV) is the maximum volume of gas that can be expired from the normal expiratory level of TV.

Lung Volumes and Capacities

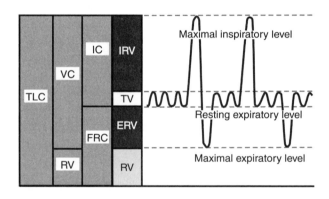

FIGURE 9.9 Schematic illustration of the major pulmonary volumes and capacities. Abbreviations and explanations are indicated in the text.

Vital capacity (VC) is the maximum volume of gas that can be expelled from the lungs after a maximal inspiration, with no time limit on the duration of the expiratory phase. In theory, VC is the sum of TV plus IRV plus ERV (see figure 9.9). **Forced vital capacity** (FVC) is the vital capacity obtained when expiration is done as hard and fast as possible. **Inspiratory capacity** (IC) is the maximal volume of gas that can be inhaled from a normal expiratory level of VT, and **functional residual capacity** (FRC) is the volume of gas remaining in the lungs after a normal expiration.

Forced-expiratory volume (FEV) and the maximal breathing capacity (**maximal voluntary ventilation** [MVV]) are also of relevance to respiratory functions. FEV and, particularly,

$FEV_{1.0}$ (the volume of gas expired in the first second of a forced vital capacity test) are important indices of the resistance of the airways to airflow (the greater the resistance, the lower the $FEV_{1.0}$). $FEV_{1.0}$ is reported in L/second. MVV is the maximal volume of expired gas with the child breathing as deeply and as rapidly as possible. It is generally measured over periods ranging from 10 to 15 seconds and reported in L/minute.

Respiratory volumes, flows, and capacities of the growing child and adolescent change more as a function of height than as a function of age (Quanjer et al. 1995). Changes in lung function related to height in children and adolescents have been documented in numerous studies. A compilation of such data was prepared by Polgar and Promadhat (1971), and reference values have been established. These reference values are used extensively in many countries (see figure 9.10). Changes in RV, FRC, $FEV_{1.0}$, VC, and TLC follow a similar growth pattern relative to standing height

in boys and girls, and all deviate only slightly from linearity. Over the same range of height from about 110 cm to 170 cm, or from about 6 years of age to young adulthood, MVV follows the same pattern of increment. It increases from about 50 L/minute to more than 100 L/minute. Although the lung volumes, flows, and capacities increase in proportion to the increase in height during growth, the relationships are not constant throughout childhood and adolescence. Noteworthy is the time of the adolescent growth spurt, during which the increase in lung functions tends to lag behind the increase in height (DeGroodt et al. 1988). This lag

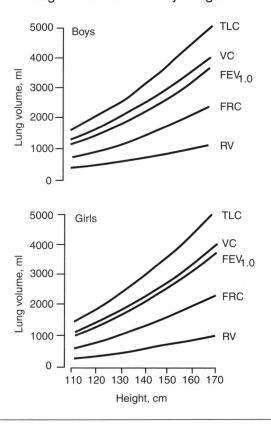

FIGURE 9.10 Changes in pulmonary volumes, flows, and capacities as a function of height in boys and girls. The units for $FEV_{1.0}$ are L/second.

Data from Polgar and Promadhat, 1971.

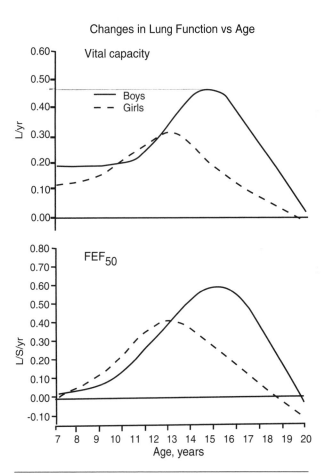

FIGURE 9.11 Changes in vital capacity (VC) and forced-expiratory flow at 50% vital capacity (FEF_{50}) as a function of age during childhood and adolescence in girls and boys. The data are from two longitudinal studies of Australian children. One cohort consisted of 281 girls and boys who were tested annually between ages 8 and 12 years of age, and the other cohort included 287 girls and boys who were tested annually between ages 12 and 18 years of age.

Data from Hibbert et al., 1995.

reflects the differential timing of growth spurts in height and lung functions (see chapter 16). As seen in figure 9.10, the general pattern of increase in lung functions as a function of height is similar in boys and girls. As a result, the peak gains in lung functions occur, on average, approximately 2 years earlier in girls, but the peak velocity itself is greater in boys (Hibbert et al. 1995) (see figure 9.11).

Gas Exchange and Transport   The exchange of gas between environmental air and the cells of body tissues is mediated through the lungs and blood. This exchange is an important aspect of normal respiratory function, but little is known of changes that occur during normal growth and maturation. In contrast, specific metabolic abnormalities of gas exchange in the child are better documented.

Changes in the partial pressures of oxygen and carbon dioxide as they are transported from inspired air to the blood and tissues and then back to the environmental air (expired air) are summarized in table 9.2. Partial pressure of oxygen falls progressively during transport from inspired air to the capillaries and cellular level where oxygen is consumed. The converse is observed for the partial pressure of carbon dioxide.

Oxygen is transported in the blood in combination with hemoglobin. One gram of hemoglobin binds about 1.3 ml O_2. At any given partial pressure of oxygen, fetal hemoglobin binds more oxygen than the adult forms of hemoglobin that appear shortly after birth (see section on hematocrit, red blood cells, and hemoglobin). The higher oxygen binding capacity of fetal hemoglobin is clearly advantageous during fetal life and perhaps in early infancy, when the transition to adult forms of hemoglobin occurs.

T A B L E 9.2	Approximate Partial Pressures of Gases at Various Levels of the O_2 Transport System When Breathing Room Air at Sea Level				
Gas	**Inspired air**	**Alveolar air**	**Arterial blood**	**Capillary blood**	**Expired air**
O_2	160	104	90	40	120
CO_2	~0.3	40	40	50	28
N_2	600	570	570	570	566
H_2O	~0	46	46	46	46

Values are expressed in mmHg.

Summary

Development of the heart, blood vessels, and lungs begins during the period of the embryo and continues through the fetal period and birth. After several critical adjustments at birth, the heart, blood, and lungs are sufficiently mature to permit efficient function outside of the protective environment of the uterus. Postnatally, heart mass and volume grow proportionally to body weight, whereas the lungs and lung volumes grow proportionally to height. The heart progressively adapts to performing more work during infancy, childhood, and adolescence, even in the resting state. Heart rate decreases by about 50% between birth and young adulthood, and cardiac output increases by about 10-fold. Power output of the heart muscle at rest increases considerably as the child progresses from the newborn state to maturity.

Sources and Suggested Readings

Bouchard C, Malina RM, Hollmann W, Leblanc C (1977) Submaximal working capacity, heart size and body size in boys 8 to 18 years. European Journal of Applied Physiology 36: 115-126.

Brotons C, Singh P, Nishio T, Labarthe DR (1989) Blood pressure by age in childhood and adolescence: A review of 129 surveys worldwide. International Journal of Epidemiology 18: 824-829.

Cermak J, Parizkova J (1975) Changes in heart volume, basic somatometric indicators and body composition during growth and adolescence. Longitudinal study in healthy boys aged 12–18 years. Review of Czechoslovak Medicine 21:134-147.

Coleman EN, Kidd BSL, Godman MJ, Walker CHM (1978) Cardiovascular disease. In JO Forfar, GC Arneil (eds.), Textbook of Paediatrics. Volume 1. Edinburgh: Churchill Livingstone, pp. 559-613.

Cornoni-Huntley J, Harlan WR, Leaverton PE (1979) Blood pressure in adolescence: The United States Health Examination Survey. Hypertension 1:566-571.

DeGroodt EG, van Pelt W, Borsboom GJ, Quanjer PH, van Zomeren BC (1988) Growth of lung and thorax dimensions during the pubertal growth spurt. European Respiratory Journal 1:102-108.

De Simone G, Devereux RB, Daniels SR, Meyer RA (1995) Gender differences in left ventricular growth. Hypertension 26:979-983.

De Simone G, Devereux RB, Kimball TR, Mureddu GF, Roman MJ, Contaldo F, Daniels SR (1998) Interaction between body size and cardiac workload: Influence on left ventricular mass during body growth and adulthood. Hypertension 31:1077-1082.

* Dickman ML, Schmidt DC, Gardner RM (1971) Spirometric standards for normal children and adolescents (ages 5 years through 18 years). American Review of Respiratory Disease 104:680-687.

* Epstein JA, Buck CA (2000) Transcriptional regulation of cardiac development: Implications form congenital heart disease and DiGeorge syndrome. Pediatric Research 48:717-724.

Harlan WR, Cornoni-Huntley J, Leaverton PE (1979) Blood pressure in childhood: The National Health Examination Survey. Hypertension 1:559-565.

Heald FP, Levy PS, Hamill PVV, Rowland M (1974) Hematocrit values of youths 12–17 years. Vital and Health Statistics, Series 11, no. 146.

* Hibbert M, Lannigan A, Raven J, Landau L, Phelan P (1995) Gender differences in lung growth. Pediatric Pulmonology 19:129-134.

Malina RM, Roche AF (1983) Manual of Physical Status and Performance in Childhood. Volume 2. Physical Performance. New York: Plenum.

Maresh MM (1948) Growth of the heart related to bodily growth during childhood and adolescence. Pediatrics 2:382-404.

Mugrage ER, Andresen MI (1936) Values for red blood cells of average infants and children. American Journal of Diseases of Children 51:775-791.

Mugrage ER, Andresen MI (1938) Red blood cell values in adolescence. American Journal of Diseases of Children 56:997-1003.

* National High Blood Pressure Education Program Working Group (1996) Update on the 1987 task force report on high blood pressure in children and adolescents: A working group report from the National High Blood Pressure Education Program. Pediatrics 98:649-658.

Olson EN, Srivastava D (1996) Molecular pathways controlling heart development. Science 272:671-676.

Polgar G, Promadhat V (1971) Pulmonary Function Testing in Children: Techniques and Standards. Philadelphia: Saunders.

Quanjer PH, Borsboom GJ, Brunekreff B, Zach M, Forche G, Cotes JE, Sanchis J, Paoletti P (1995) Spirometric reference values for white European children and adolescents: Polgar revisited. Pediatric Pulmonology 19:135-142.

Rosner B, Prineas RJ, Loggie JM, Daniels SR (1993) Blood pressure nomograms for children and adolescents, by height, sex, and age, in the United States. Journal of Pediatrics 123:871-886.

* Rowland TW (1991) "Normalizing" maximal oxygen uptake, or the search for the holy grail (per kg). Pediatric Exercise Science 3:95-102.

Seo JS, Lee SY, Won KJ, Kim DJ, Sohn DS, Yang KM, Cho SH, Park JD, Lee KH, Kim HD (2000) Relationship between normal heart size and body indices in Koreans. Journal of Korean Medical Science 15:641-646.

* Simon G, Reid L, Tanner JM, Goldstein H, Benjamin B (1972) Growth of radiologically determined heart diameter, lung width, and lung length from 5–19 years, with standards for clinical use. Archives of Disease in Childhood 47:373-381.

Tanner JM (1962) Growth at Adolescence, 2nd edition. Oxford: Blackwell.

Thurlbeck WM (1975) Postnatal growth and development of the lung. American Review of Respiratory Disease 111:803-844.

Timiras PS (1972) Developmental Physiology and Aging. New York: Macmillan.

10 MOTOR DEVELOPMENT

Chapter Outline

The acquisition of competence in motor activities is an important developmental task of childhood. All children, except some with severe disabilities, have the potential to develop and learn a variety of fundamental movement patterns and more specialized skills. Such motor activities are an integral part of children's behavioral repertoires and provide the medium through which children experience many dimensions of their environments, especially during the preschool years. This chapter focuses on the development of basic movement competencies during infancy and early childhood, although the refinement of competence in basic and more advanced movement skills continues through childhood and adolescence into adulthood. Motor performance in childhood and adolescence is discussed in detail in chapter 11.

The development of motor competence during infancy and early childhood is closely related to the morphological, physiological, and neuromuscular characteristics of the child. Motor development is dependent on and influenced by the growth and maturity characteristics of the child. The environments in which a child is reared are also important factors in motor development. These environmental experiences interact with the biological substrate of growth and maturation to determine the motor repertoire of the child. Motor activities function to meet the immediate needs of infants and young children, including establishment of the functional integrity of muscles and joints. Movement behaviors in infancy and early childhood are also to some extent precursors of subsequent motor behaviors.

This chapter provides an overview of general concepts related to motor development and performance. After a brief discussion of the reflexes of infancy and scales for evaluating motor development, the development of upright posture and independent walking is emphasized. Upright locomotion in the form of bipedal walking is perhaps the most important of human motor behaviors. This form of locomotion is evident in the hominid fossil record some 3 to 4 million years ago and has been a major force in the evolution of the human species. Other movement patterns and the development of motor competence in early childhood are then considered, followed by a brief discussion of several determinants of early motor development.

What Is Motor Development?

Motor development is the process through which a child acquires movement patterns and skills. It is a seemingly continuous process of modification that involves the interactions of several factors. These factors include neuromuscular maturation, which has a significant genetic component; the growth characteristics of the child, such as body size, proportions, and body composition; the tempo of growth and maturation; the residual effects of prior motor experiences, including prenatal experiences; and the new motor experiences per se. All of these factors occur in the context of the environments within which the child is reared—the human or social environment and the physical environment. Although the process of motor development appears to be continuous, it proceeds in the context of growth and maturation, and current data suggest that early growth proceeds in a "saltatory" manner with a series of steplike improvements separated by variable periods of no apparent growth (see chapter 3).

Motor Pattern and Skill

Movements are sometimes described in the context of patterns and skills. The concepts of pattern and skill differ in degree rather than in kind. A **pattern** is the basic movement or movements involved in the performance of a particular task. Emphasis is placed on the movements that form the pattern. Thus, many children can perform the basic movement patterns in jumping, but their levels of proficiency may vary considerably. In contrast to the movement pattern, **skill** emphasizes the accuracy, precision, and economy of performance. The motor pattern is a more general concept, whereas motor skill is a more specialized concept. The characterization of several basic motor patterns is described later in the chapter.

Classifications of Motor Activities

Movements can be viewed from a variety of perspectives. Several convenient ways of classifying motor activities are briefly described.

Fine and Gross Motor Activities

Motor activities are frequently categorized as fine and gross. **Fine motor** activities refer to movements requiring precision and dexterity as in manipulative tasks. **Gross motor** activities refer to movements of the entire body or major segments of the body, as in locomotor activities. Many motor tasks incorporate both fine and gross motor elements (e.g., the precision necessary to project a ball accurately and with sufficient speed, as in pitching a baseball, or the precision to accurately pass a soccer ball with sufficient speed to reach a teammate).

Fundamental and Specialized Motor Skills

Fundamental motor patterns are elementary forms of movement, which are often described as basic motor skills. They are often divided into locomotor, nonlocomotor, and manipulative skills. **Locomotor** skills are those in which the body is moved through space, such as in walking, running, jumping, galloping, hopping, and skipping. **Nonlocomotor** skills are those in which specific parts of the body are moved, as in pushing, pulling, bending, curling, and twisting. **Manipulative** skills are those in which objects are moved, as in throwing, catching, striking, kicking, dribbling, and related activities involving the projection and reception of objects. Locomotor, nonlocomotor, and manipulative activities can occur in various combinations. For example, skipping is a combination of hopping and walking, the hop being interspersed in the walking pattern.

Motor development involves the acquisition and refinement of basic movement patterns, which are sometimes labeled basic motor skills. These basic patterns are eventually integrated into more specialized and complex skills. For example, running and reaching to catch a thrown ball combines all three categories of fundamental movement patterns into a more specialized motor skill that is characteristic of many games and sports.

Process and Product of Movement

Motor skills can be assessed in terms of the process and the product of the respective movements. The **process** deals with the technique of performing a specific movement in terms of its components (hip rotation, arm action, and leg action) and specific mechanical elements (angle of takeoff in a jump, lengths of lever arms, and angles of inclination at specific joints). The **product,** on the other hand, concerns the result or outcome of the act—the distance that a child has jumped, the time elapsed in a dash, and other similar measures of the end products of motor performances. Outcomes of the performances of several basic motor skills are discussed in more detail in chapter 11.

The process and product of a motor performance are, in general, positively related. Good performers in terms of the product usually demonstrate proficiency in the movement process, and vice versa. Presumably, as processes are improved through normal growth and maturity and through instruction and practice, the product of performance also improves. The relationship between process and product is especially evident at the extremes of the motor performance continuum, whereas the middle range of the continuum shows considerable individuality or variability in performance. With most movement tasks, motivation is a significant factor. With a low level of motivation, a good motor process can yield a poor product, whereas under conditions of heightened motivation a poor process may yield a good motor product.

The Newborn Infant and the Reflexes of Infancy

The motor responses of the newborn infant are extensions of those established during fetal life. These patterns take the form of reflexes and reactions that are either present at birth or appear during infancy. Some of the reflexes are quite simple and are mediated at the spinal cord level; others are more complex and require the integration of brain stem centers, the labyrinths, and other developing nervous centers. The following are several of the most commonly described reflexes characteristic of the infant early in life.

Reflexes associated with feeding (e.g., sucking, rooting, and tongue retrusion reflexes) and those associated with the eyes (e.g., corneal and blinking reflexes) are well developed in the newborn infant. The **Moro reflex** is one of the most consistent reflex patterns of the infant between birth and 3 months of age. The reflex is an extensor response elicited by sudden movement of the neck region. When so stimulated, the infant reacts with extension and abduction of the extremities and a noticeable tremor in the hands and feet. The **startle reflex,** similar to the Moro reflex, is elicited by a loud noise, and the response of the extremities is more of flexion. The **palmar grasp reflex,** a flexor response elicited by placing an object such as a finger or pencil in contact with the infant's palm, is characterized by relatively strong flexion of the palm and fingers without thumb opposition.

Although the newborn infant possesses no effective means of locomotion, certain responses resemble later voluntary movements. Included among these **locomotor reflexes** are reactions similar to creeping, standing, stepping, and even swimming if the infant is placed in water.

The **tonic neck reflex,** although incompletely developed in the newborn infant, emerges during the first few months of life. When the infant's head is turned to one side, the infant responds with an increase in muscle tone and extension of both the arm and leg of the side to which the face is turned and by a flexion of the arm and leg of the opposite side.

A variety of other reflexes, the **labyrinthine** and **righting reflexes,** are not completely developed in the newborn infant but emerge later in infancy. They facilitate maintenance of the relationship between the head and other body parts (righting reflexes) or the orientation of the body relative to the force of gravity (labyrinthine reflexes). They also play an important role in the development of movements and postural control related to upright posture, independent walking, and other activities.

The reflexes related to feeding and the eyes, the Moro and startle reflexes, and the grasp reflex are often viewed as **primitive reflexes,** whereas the tonic neck, righting, and labyrinthine reflexes are viewed as **postural reflexes.** The primitive reflexes are well developed between birth and about 3 months of age, after which their intensity declines. Postural reflexes begin to emerge at about 3 months of age and increase in intensity of response throughout infancy (see figure 10.1). As cerebral control develops during infancy, specific reflex activity is gradually inhibited or incorporated into emerging voluntary movements.

Reflex Behavior and Motor
Control During Infancy

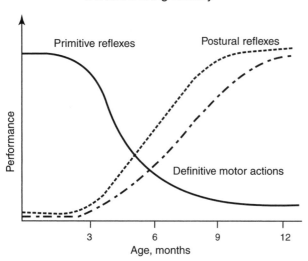

FIGURE 10.1 Schematic illustration of the declining intensity of primitive reflexes and the increasing intensity of postural reflexes in association with the development of motor control during infancy.

Reprinted, by permission, from Capute et al., 1978, *Primitive reflex profile* (Baltimore, MD: University Park Press), 10.

The motor activity of the neonate does not involve true volitional activity, and the reflexes indicate a lack of inhibition of the segmental apparatus of the nervous system by higher neural centers. As the central nervous system gradually matures in infancy and early childhood, inhibitory functions of the cerebral cortex begin to operate, and the reflex movements gradually diminish and disappear. The reflexes are not lost. They are inhibited by higher brain centers or are integrated into new movement patterns as the higher brain centers are differentiated. Their continued existence becomes apparent in cases of central nervous system pathology, during the administration of some drugs, in states of stress, and in the aged, when many reflexes can be demonstrated again. The tonic neck reflex can also be elicited in normal adults when they are placed in a variety of postural states.

The reflex responsiveness varies greatly among infants as well as within the same infant. Reflexes also vary with behavioral states. The reflexes of infancy are expressions of the immaturity of the developing nervous system and provide a means of assessing the integrity of the neuromuscular maturation processes early in life. The absence, delayed appearance or disappearance, persistence, or reappearance of certain reflexes may be indicative of neurological disorders.

Motor Development— Birth to 2 Years of Age

Development of voluntary control of movement begins in infancy and progresses through childhood. During the first 2 years of life, the child gradually attains postural, locomotor, and prehensile (reaching and grasping) control. The motor achievements of young children are often described in a variety of widely used developmental scales, which document "milestones" in early motor development. The developmental scales are used primarily to evaluate the integrity of the developing central nervous system during the first 2 or 3 years. One of the principal purposes of such scales is as a screening device to identify children with developmental problems or who might be at risk for developing such problems in the future. Developmental problems might be indicative of neurological deficits or potential learning difficulties. Emphasis is on early identification and diagnosis so that therapy or other forms of intervention can be initiated as early as necessary.

Developmental scales such as the Bayley Scales of Infant Development (Bayley 1969; 1993) and the Denver Developmental Screening Test (Frankenburg and Dodds 1967; Frankenburg et al. 1992) include a variety of gross motor, fine motor, cognitive, language, self-care, and social items and extend beyond 2 years of age. They are, to a large extent, schedules of sensory and motor achievements of children from birth to 4 years of age (Bayley) or to 6 years of age (Denver). From the perspective of early motor development, they provide normal ranges of variation for the acquisition of a variety of fine and gross motor achievements, among other behavioral competencies, during infancy and early childhood.

Ages and associated variation for the attainment of specific motor "milestones" during infancy and early childhood indicate levels of overall motor competence that infants and young children are expected to demonstrate. The wide range of variation in appearance of each item is often overlooked in motor development research. A sequential motor "unfolding" of the child is often implicit in such developmental scales, and early views of motor development considered the sequence of changes as representing genetically controlled neuromuscular maturation (McGraw 1945; Gesell 1954). Current views, on the other hand, indicate that the motor development of the infant and young child is influenced by a variety of factors, including stimulation or practice and interactions among specific movements. In an interesting example, six 3-month-old and two 7-month-old infants were "trained" daily to step on a slowly moving treadmill. The "training" resulted in improved stepping. Those infants whose stepping behavior was unstable at the start seemed to benefit more from the practice on the treadmill. The results of this experiment suggest that the developing motor system can be influenced by "training" and that infants have their own preferred stepping patterns that interacted with the "training" on the treadmill (Vereijken and Thelen 1997). The authors interpret the results as indicating that the neuromuscular pathway for stepping is in place in infancy and that stepping emerges in the context of practice on the treadmill. The results, although interesting, are limited to 8 infants, are largely descriptive, and are basically qualitative. Such "training" needs to be related to independent walking and subsequent development of other movement skills by young children. Thelen and Ulrich (1991) provide a more detailed discussion of treadmill stepping in the context of treadmill speed and coordination between the legs during the first year of life.

The range of variation in early motor development is considerable. The sequence of development is reasonably uniform but shows sequence variations and occasional omissions (an example in the progression to upright posture and walking is described in the next section). Such occurrences do not necessarily indicate developmental problems or delay; rather, they are aspects of normal variability—the individuality of motor development and perhaps of variation in rearing environments. The environments of the young child influence opportunities to move about, the frequency and type of handling by adults and siblings, types of play objects, and general stimulation.

Development of Independent Walking

Independent walking is the major motor development task during the first 2 years of life. The developmental changes leading to walking behavior are essentially a series of postural changes through which the child gains the motor control necessary to first assume upright posture, then to maintain upright posture, and finally to walk independently. The general sequence of developmental changes leading to walking behavior can be summarized as follows. The infant gradually attains control of the head, upper trunk, and upper extremities. Control of the entire trunk follows, first in the development of sitting posture with support and then sitting alone. Control of the trunk is followed by active efforts at locomotion by means of prone progression, that is, crawling on the belly or creeping on the hands and knees. Active efforts at upright posture follow, the child standing first with support and then without support. The same applies to early efforts at walking, first with support, as along a table or with the assistance of an adult. Finally, independent walking develops. Initial efforts at walking are usually characterized as "stiff-legged," "jerky," and "flat-footed," with a wide base of support and the arms outstretched for balance.

Changes in locomotion leading to independent standing and walking for a sample of Swiss infants followed longitudinally are summarized in table 10.1. The range of normal variation in ages at attaining each milestone should be noted. Sex differences are small and inconsistent. The changes from rolling over to standing and walking are reasonably uniform in neurologically unimpaired full-term and preterm infants. In this sample, 87% of the boys and girls progressed in the following sequence: rolling over, pivoting, crawling on the belly, crawling on hands and knees, crawling on hands and feet, and standing and walking. On the other hand, 13% of the sample showed a different sequence of progression: 6% of the infants progressed from crawling on the hands and knees to standing and walking, 2% progressed from crawling on the belly to standing and walking, and 2% progressed from pivoting to sitting up to shuffling and to standing and walking. The remainder showed variable sequences (e.g., bridging instead of crawling on the belly) (Largo et al. 1985). The movement experiences of infants apparently influence variability in crawling

TABLE 10.1   Percentiles for Ages (Months) at Which Healthy, Full-Term Infants Attain Developmental Milestones Leading to Independent Walking

Milestone	Boys percentiles			Girls percentiles		
	10	50	90	10	50	90
Roll to supine	3.7	5.0	6.2	3.8	5.2	6.7
Roll to prone	4.8	6.0	8.8	4.6	6.0	8.7
Pivot[a]	5.0	6.4	8.6	4.7	6.8	8.8
Crawl on stomach[b]	6.1	7.0	8.7	5.8	6.9	8.9
Creep on hands/knees	6.8	8.3	10.4	6.5	8.8	11.8
Creep on hands/feet	8.1	9.0	11.8	7.7	9.6	11.9
Sit up	7.3	9.1	11.8	6.8	8.9	11.5
Stand at rail	7.4	8.4	9.8	7.1	8.7	10.5
Pull to stand	7.5	8.5	11.3	7.3	8.9	11.5
Cruise at rail[c]	8.0	9.5	11.7	8.0	9.8	11.8
Stand momentarily	9.9	12.4	15.6	9.8	12.5	14.9
Walk, one hand held	9.2	11.5	13.0	9.5	11.8	13.5
Walk alone	10.8	13.0	15.9	11.0	13.1	15.7
Walk up and down stairs	16.2	18.9	23.7	16.0	19.7	23.8

[a]Child on stomach moves in circular manner by actions of arms and legs.
[b]Child pulls forward by coordinated action of arms and legs.
[c]Sideways walking while holding on to a table or similar stable object.
Adapted from Largo et al. (1985). Data are based on 56 boys and 55 girls from the second Zurich Longitudinal Study.

behavior. For example, infants who crawled on the belly showed more proficiency in crawling on the hands and knees than those who did not crawl on their bellies (Adolph et al. 1998). Unfortunately, this study did not relate crawling behavior to independent standing and walking.

Mean or median ages of walking for several samples of children are presented in table 10.2. The data are for boys and girls combined because evidence of sex differences in the age at walking is not consistent. The range between means or medians is about 2 to 3 months, which is relatively narrow. This narrowness is especially noteworthy because the studies summarized in the table are based on data that span about 50 years. Moreover, data on the age at walking are confounded in part by errors in maternal recall and problems of definition. Walking is variously defined as first steps, first steps alone, taking a step unassisted, walking a few steps without support, taking at least three steps without support, minimum of 10 steps without support, and walking well.

Children who do not walk independently by 17 to 18 months of age are often classified as late walkers and referred for clinical evalua-

tion. Dissociated motor development—a condition characterized by delay in the gross motor domain, no abnormal neurological signs, and normal fine motor development—is associated with late walking (Lundberg 1979). Among 65 children who could not walk at 17 months, 79% had a late pattern of learning to sit or dissociated sitting development. They sat unsupported without using the arms at the normally expected age but were very delayed in attempting to sit actively without help. In addition, 51% of the late walkers had a locomotion progression that involved shuffling (in a sitting position with or without use of the arms and hands) in contrast to crawling, and 71% had muscular hypotonia, especially of the lower trunk and lower extremities. Hypotonia refers to reduced muscle tone and definition compared with expected values for age. These observations suggest a triad of factors that may be related to late walking—dissociated development of sitting, a shuffling locomotor progression, and muscular hypotonia.

The late walking in 35 of the 65 children (54%) was idiopathic (i.e., without a known cause). Interestingly, 13 of the 35 children with idiopathic

TABLE 10.2	Mean or Median Ages at Walking (in Months) for Children in Studies Reported Since the 1930s
United States	
Iowa	13.5
California	13.0
New York	13.3
Philadelphia, White	13.3
Philadelphia, Black	13.3
Denver	12.1
Stratified U.S. sample	11.7
National sample, White	12.4
National sample, Black	11.4
American Indians	
Hopi, cradleboard used	14.3
Hopi, cradleboard not used	14.5
Tewa, cradled for daytime naps	13.7
Europe	
Brussels	12.5
London	13.2
London	12.8
London, West Indian	12.7
London, Cypriot	12.9
Newcastle (England)	12.8
Paris	13.6
Stockholm	12.4
Zurich, 1st longitudinal study	13.6
Zurich, 2nd longitudinal study	13.5

Adapted from Malina (1980), which contains the primary references for each sample. Data for the second Zurich Longitudinal Study are from Largo et al. (1985).

late walking presented a family history of shuffling, which may suggest a possible genetic influence (Lundberg 1979).

In a subsequent analysis, samples of muscle tissue of six idiopathic late walkers were studied. Compared with children who walked at the normally expected age, this small sample of idiopathic late walkers showed reduced muscle fiber size, especially type II fibers, and lower concentrations of ATP, phosphocreatinine and glycogen compared with normal children of the same age (Lundberg 1980; Lundberg et al. 1979a; see also chapter 7). These characteristics may be related to physical inactivity. Similar trends occur with muscular atrophy, whereas training can increase fiber size and concentrations of metabolic substrates. Nevertheless, reduced concentrations of stored metabolic substrates of muscle tissue or impaired substrate mobilization may have implications for motor development. For example, children with celiac disease also have reduced muscle concentrations of ATP, phosphocreatinine, and glycogen and are also delayed in motor development compared with healthy children of the same age. Celiac disease is an allergy to gluten, a protein present in wheat and other grains that influences the small intestine. It is a problem of malabsorption (inability to absorb nutrients), and it is usually discovered in infancy or early childhood. Celiac disease is characterized by diarrhea, and if it persists, it is associated with growth stunting and a protruding abdomen and thin extremities, which may suggest muscle wasting. With treatment, that is, a gluten-free diet (elimination of wheat, rye, and other grains that include gluten), levels of muscle substrates and motor development of these children are similar to normal control subjects (Lundberg et al. 1979b). These results highlight a need for study of potential physiologic and metabolic correlates of motor development.

Once walking is initiated, proficiency in this basic motor skill develops at an exponential rate. Stride length, walking speed, and cadence all increase; and movements show greater reproducibility as the walking pattern becomes more like that of an adult. Stride, or step length, is related to the physical size of the child and specifically to length of the lower extremities. Hence, a parallel increase in leg length and step length occurs as skill in walking develops during early childhood. Rotation of the hips increases gradually and contributes to the increase in stride length. Stride also includes specific actions of the foot and knee. In the mature walking pattern, foot and knee actions include knee extension before or coincident with the heel striking the surface, knee flexion during the middle portion of the support phase, and knee extension when the heel is lifted off the ground as the next stride begins.

Balance is very important in the refinement of walking and the development of other motor skills. Initial walking efforts are characterized by a wide base of support, with the feet relatively far apart and the toes pointed outward. As walking proficiency develops, the base of support gradually narrows, so the feet are placed within the lateral dimensions of the trunk and the toes point more forward. Arm movements gradually become synchronous with the walking stride, providing opposition of movement (the left arm swings forward with the step of the right leg, and the right arm swings forward with the step of the left leg).

This sequence is the general developmental sequence for walking. Independent walking does not indicate the achievement of the mature walking pattern. The mature pattern develops gradually after the onset of independent walking. By about 5 years of age, the adult walking pattern is established in the majority of children. However, stride dynamics are variable among children and vary with walking speed.

Walking requires the ability to support and balance the upright body and to execute stepping movements. The ability to walk affords the developing child a new and more rapid means of locomotion, with many possible variations. It also frees the hands from their role as supports, so a variety of manipulative experiences and skills become possible. Hence, the walking pattern is the foundation on which other movement patterns and skills develop.

Development of Fundamental Motor Skills

With the refinement of the walking pattern, the child's control of locomotor and manipulative abilities improves, so a considerable amount of independent action is possible. Thus, early childhood is a time of increasing experimentation with a variety of motor tasks. The experimentation occurs in a variety of contexts, including the home, play areas in the community, and preschool, among others. The acquisition of competence in fundamental movement patterns is one of the more important developmental tasks of early childhood. These basic patterns are the foundation on which other movements and combinations of movements are developed and refined.

Approaches to the study of the development of the fundamental motor skills commonly focus on the processes of movement by describing stages through which a child progresses, from the immature to the mature pattern, for a specific skill such as the standing long jump or the overhand ball throw. In some early studies, children were subjectively classified in terms of level of profi-

ciency in basic motor skills. On the other hand, the products or outcomes of specific skills (e.g., the distance a ball is thrown with an overhand pattern or the distance jumped), are studied less often in preschool children.

Stages of Development

A good deal of early and current motor development research has described the temporal, spatial, and sequential elements of specific movement patterns as they develop. The specific elements are generally summarized in a sequence of stages as the child progresses from an immature to a mature pattern for a specific movement. The definition and delineation of stages are to some extent arbitrary. They are superimposed on an ongoing process of development that is not necessarily continuous. Progress in motor development appears continuous when data are grouped and reported in terms of average trends. However, considerable variability exists among children. Some children may show relatively long periods of stability or minimal change followed by a burst of progress, others may regress to less mature stages before progressing to a more advanced stage, and still others may show seemingly continuous progress. A key factor in monitoring changes in stages of development is the interval between observations, which highlights a need for observations over relatively short intervals, perhaps 2 to 3 months.

Although stages are somewhat arbitrary and have limitations, they are a convenience to facilitate the observation and understanding of the motor development of young children. Stages in the developmental sequence of overarm throwing and the standing long jump, two of the more frequently studied fundamental motor skills, are summarized in tables 10.3 and 10.4.

The sequence for the overhand throw was perhaps the first to be described in a developmental context and thus has historical relevance in the study of motor development (Wild 1938). Others have described the sequence of development of the overhand throw in a bit more detail, but the sequence of changes is basically the same (Roberton 1978). More detailed quantitative analysis of the kinematic properties of the overhand throw, such as angular velocity of elbow extension, angular velocity of shoulder adduction, or angular velocities of specific joints at ball release (Yan et al. 2000), is generally consistent with the developmental model described by Wild (1938) (see also table 10.3).

TABLE 10.3	Developmental Sequence of the Overarm Throw
Stage	**Movement**
1	Arm and body movements occur in a posterior-anterior plane (back to front), with no trunk rotation and the feet are fixed in place.
2	Arm and body movements occur in a horizontal plane as a rotation component is added. The child rotates to the right in preparation to throw and then to the left in delivery. The feet still remain fixed.
3	A forward step with the leg on the same side of the body as the throwing arm is added to the pattern. Trunk rotation may decrease somewhat, but hip flexion is increased.
4	Opposition of movement as a contralateral step is added. The foot opposite the throwing arm steps forward (strides) in the preparatory phase. Weight is transferred forward from the right foot to the left foot as the hips, trunk, and shoulders rotate to the left in delivery by a right-handed child. The opposite occurs in a left-handed child.

Adapted from Wild (1938).

TABLE 10.4	Developmental Sequence of the Standing Long Jump
Stage	**Movement**
1	The vertical component of force may be greater than horizontal. The resulting jump is then upward rather than forward. Arms move backward, acting as brakes to stop the momentum of the trunk as the legs extend in front of the center of mass.
2	The arms move in an anterior-posterior direction during the preparatory phase but move sideward (winging action) during the "in-flight" phase. The knees and hips flex and extend more fully than in stage 1. The angle of takeoff is still markedly above 45 degrees. The landing is made with the center of mass above the base of support, with the thighs perpendicular to the surface rather than parallel as in the "reaching" position of stage four.
3	The arms swing backward and then forward during the preparatory phase. The knees and hips flex fully before takeoff. Upon takeoff, the arms extend and move forward but do not exceed the height of the head. The knee extension may be complete, but the takeoff angle is still greater than 45 degrees. Upon landing, the thigh is still less than parallel to the surface and the center of mass is near the base of support when viewed from the frontal plane.
4	The arms extend vigorously forward and upward upon takeoff, reaching full extension above the head at "lift-off." The hips and knees are extended fully with the takeoff angle at 45 degrees or less. In preparation for landing, the arms are brought downward and the legs are thrust forward until the thigh is parallel to the surface. The center of mass is far behind the base of support upon foot contact, but at the moment of contact, the knees are flexed and the arms are thrust forward to maintain the momentum to carry the center of gravity beyond the feet.

From V. Seefeldt, P. Reuschlein, and P. Vogel (1972). Paper presented at the national convention of the American Association for Health, Physical Education and Recreation, Houston, Texas. Reprinted by permission of the authors.

The stages for the standing long jump summarized in table 10.4 treat each stage in a global manner. The development of the jump can also be analyzed in greater detail. Specific changes for the actions of the legs, trunk, and arms, respectively, in the takeoff, flight, and landing phases of the standing long jump have been described.

Developmental sequences for a variety of fundamental motor skills are described in introductory textbooks on motor development (Wickstrom 1983; Haywood and Getchell 2001; Payne and Isaacs 1999). The descriptions include locomotor (running, jumping, hopping, galloping, and skipping), projection (throwing, kicking, and striking), and reception (catching) skills.

The stages in the sequential development of fundamental motor skills are, as noted previously, somewhat arbitrary. They are a convenience for observing and evaluating the motor development of children. Some stages consider the body as a whole (whole-body sequences), whereas others consider specific components of the movement pattern (body component sequences). This distinction is important because a child might be at an immature or intermediate stage in one component of a movement and at a more advanced stage in another component at a given age. Such variation would suggest disharmonic motor development for this basic pattern. Disharmonic motor development has not been systematically studied for the basic motor skills. On the other hand, the potential to microanalyze a movement pattern may have limited value. Focusing on elbow action in the overhand throw, for example, runs the risk of overlooking the overall pattern, which includes actions of the legs, trunk, shoulder, and hand-wrist. Components do not exist in isolation from the total movement pattern, and this interrelationship must be kept in focus.

Studies of the specific temporal, spatial, and sequential elements of basic motor skills are usually based on detailed analysis of film and video records of individual children performing specified tasks, such as a vertical jump or hopping on one foot. The studies are both cross-sectional and longitudinal, but presently available longitudinal data on the development of movement patterns have not been analyzed in a longitudinal manner. Rather, the studies are largely descriptive, focusing primarily on the patterns per se and progress through the defined stages. Little emphasis has been placed on intraindividual and interindividual variability within and between stages, and little quantitative analysis has been done.

Developmental sequences for several fundamental motor skills have been described as a part of the comprehensive Motor Performance Study at Michigan State University. The ages at which 60% of children in this mixed-longitudinal sample were able to perform a specific developmental stage for nine fundamental motor tasks are shown in figure 10.2. The numbers on each bar of the illustration denote the developmental stages, with 1 denoting to the least mature stage and 4 or 5 denoting the most mature stage for each task.

Several trends are suggested in figure 10.2. Development of the fundamental motor skills during

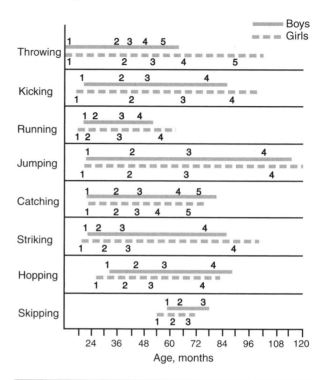

Stages of Fundamental Motor Skills

FIGURE 10.2 Ages at which 60% of boys and girls were able to perform at specific developmental levels for several fundamental motor skills. Stage 1 indicates an immature level whereas stage 4 or 5 indicates the mature level. Stages 2 and 3, and sometimes 4, are intermediate levels.

Reprinted, by permission, from Seefeldt and Haubenstricker, 1982, Patterns, phases, or stages: An analytical model for the study of developmental movement. In *The development of movement control and coordination*, edited by J.A.S. Kelso and J.E. Clark (John Wiley & Sons), 314.

early childhood progresses rapidly and continues into middle childhood for some movements. Boys tend to attain each stage of overhand throwing and kicking earlier than girls, whereas girls tend to attain each stage of hopping and skipping earlier than boys. The difference between boys and girls is most marked for overhand throwing. The attainment of specific stages, especially stages 2 and 3, of the other fundamental skills (running, jumping, catching, and striking) shows considerable similarity between boys and girls. However, more variation exists between boys and girls in the ages at which the final or mature stages are attained. For example, girls attain the final two stages of catching earlier than boys, although they do not differ in ages at attaining the earlier stages.

In contrast, the difference between boys and girls for attaining the mature form of the standing long jump is small.

The data in figure 10.2 also suggest variation in the time between the attainment of stages for a given fundamental motor skill. For example, the time between the four stages of jumping or between stages 3 and 4 for striking appears to be quite large compared with that between the earlier stages. Variation in the time between stages is, in part, a function of the relative arbitrariness of the definition of each stage for a specific skill. For example, the defined changes from one stage to the next may be too great, or the stage demands may be too difficult. An additional factor is individual variation in the time required to master each stage of a specific motor skill.

The stages of motor development during childhood should be addressed in the context of several other issues. Assuming the stages are correctly described, what is the variability in the duration of a stage within each skill? What is the relationship between the age at entry into a specific stage and subsequent progress through the stage? If a child enters stage 2 of the standing long jump later than average, does the child progress through the stage more quickly than a child who enters stage 2 earlier than average? Do differences exist (e.g., in size, physique, body composition, and prior movement experiences) among children who progress through the stages of a specific movement pattern quickly compared with those who progress through the stages slowly? What is the relationship, if any, between ages at attaining specific stages of a movement pattern, or duration of progress through the stages, and subsequent motor performance? Within a single chronological age group, say 4-year-old children, what are the characteristics, behavioral and physical, of children who show immature movement patterns compared with those who show mature movement patterns for a specific task? These questions and others have not traditionally been addressed in motor development research.

The movement patterns for most fundamental skills ordinarily develop by 6 or 7 years of age, although the mature patterns of some skills do not develop until later. As the fundamental motor skills are refined through practice, quality of performance improves, and the fundamental patterns are integrated into more complex movement sequences, such as those required for specific games and sports. However, some 6-, 7-, and 8-year-olds have not developed sufficient motor control to successfully accomplish the fundamental motor skills. Although figure 10.2 shows the ages at which 60% of children attain specific developmental levels for fundamental movement patterns, 40% of the children have not attained the specific developmental levels by these ages. Similar trends are indicated in table 10.5, which summarizes the results of an early observational study. The percentage of children rated as proficient increases with age between 2 and 7 years of age, but a significant number of 6-year-old and 7-year-old children are not yet proficient in the fundamental skills.

Assigning Scores to Stages

Some motor development research has defined the component movements of specific motor skills and assigned a score to each component,

TABLE 10.5 Percentage of Children at Each Age Rated As Proficient (Easy Coordinated Performance) in Several Fundamental Motor Skills

Motor skill	n	Age (years)	Age (months)			
			36–47	48–59	60–71	72–83
Climbing	358	2–7	50	75	72	92
Jumping	140	2–7	42	58	81	84
Hopping	160	4–7		33	76	84
Skipping	227	2–7	0	14	72	91
Galloping	139	4–7		43	78	92
Throwing	113	2–7	0	20	80	74
Catching	167	3–7	0	29	56	63

Adapted from Gutteridge (1939).

progressing from the immature to the mature pattern (as previously). Mean scores for the development of several fundamental motor skills in a mixed-longitudinal sample of children 2 through 6 years of age are presented in figure 10.3. Performances generally improve, on the average, with age on most tasks, although not necessarily in a smooth progression. Mature movement patterns (task scores 3 or higher) are attained in most skills by about 4 or 5 years of age. Catching and hitting, tasks that require eye-limb coordination, are exceptions in that the average task scores do not indicate mature patterns of movement over the age range studied. Kicking approaches the mature pattern, on the average, at 5 or 6 years of age.

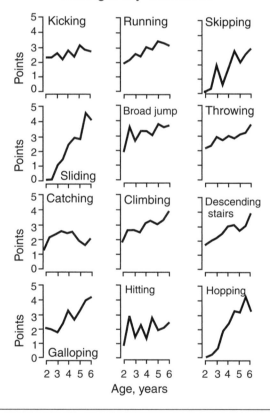

Ratings for Fundamental Motor Skills During Early Childhood

FIGURE 10.3 Means scores for several fundamental motor skills in children (sexes combined) 2 through 6 years of age. Movement skills of the children were filmed and then rated on the success of performance in each task and the number of components shown for each task. The components were rated on a 5-point scale, and a score of 3 or higher indicated the mature movement pattern for the specific task.

Data from Sinclair, 1971.

Variation in motor development within individual children, between children, and from age to age is considerable during early childhood. Preschool children often show a tendency to perform well on one occasion only to perform poorly on the next. Variation in performance between testing periods probably reflects normal variation in neuromuscular maturation, changes in body size and proportions, opportunity for practice, and motivation to perform in the test situation. Further, testing of young children requires their cooperation, which may be a factor that affects performances.

Young children may show a relatively mature pattern of movement at one age and an immature pattern at a subsequent age. This regression is suggestive of Gesell's (1954) concept of "reciprocal interweaving," in which development is characterized by alternating from mature stages to less mature stages and then back to mature stages. Such seemingly irregular developmental trends often occur without any recognizable cause and may reflect normal variability. They may be related to the fact that young children are developing and learning many new skills, so when a mature pattern is attained in one task, the child might attempt other movement pursuits that detract from the mature pattern originally demonstrated. The result may be a reversal to a less mature movement pattern. For example, a child may have mastered the overhand throw from a stationary position but may revert to an underhand pattern when trying to throw while running. A child may have mastered catching a large ball but may revert to a less mature pattern when trying to catch a smaller ball. An additional factor that must be recognized in explaining variation among children is error in observing and scoring the movement patterns of children.

Products of Performance

The preceding approaches to the development of fundamental motor skills focus on the stages leading from immature to mature patterns in the form of discrete, although somewhat arbitrary, stages. Another approach is more quantitative and focuses on the products or outcomes of specific performances of young children that are done under standardized conditions. Examples include the distance a ball is thrown, the distance the body is projected in the standing long jump, and the time elapsed in completing a 30-yard dash. The motor tasks, performed under specified conditions, are amenable to accurate measurement. An important issue is the reliability of performances of young children. Performance tests are introduced as early as 3 years of age, although considerable variation occurs within and between children, and many children may not have sufficiently mature movement patterns to perform the task as described in the test protocols. The performances of young children 3 to 5 years of age on a variety of motor tasks are included with those of older children in chapter 11.

Scales for Assessing Motor Development

The assessment of motor skills during early childhood is also important in the context of screening, prediction, and intervention. Similar to scales of infant development described earlier, these scales are designed to screen for developmental problems or the risk of such problems. The Peabody Developmental Motor Scales, for example, were developed to assess ". . . the relative developmental skill level of a child, identify skills that were not completely developed or not in the child's repertoire, and then plan an instructional program to develop those skills." (Folio and Fewell 1983, p. 1). The scale assesses fine and gross motor development in children from birth to 7 years of age and includes many of the motor milestones and fundamental motor skills described previously. A more comprehensive discussion of a variety of scales for the assessment of motor development in infancy and early childhood is provided by Burton and Miller (1998).

Early Motor Development and Growth of the Brain

Brain growth is very rapid during infancy and early childhood (see the neural curve in figure 1.3, page 13), continuing the growth pattern of the brain and associated tissues that began prenatally. Dobbing and Sands (1973) (see also Dobbing 1990) have described the rapid growth of the brain prenatally and postnatally as a "brain growth spurt." The spurt is a period of rapid growth that begins at about midpregnancy and continues through about 4 years of age. The early part of the spurt, from midpregnancy to about 18 months of age, is characterized by rapid multiplication of glial cells; the later part, which lasts until about 4 years of age, is characterized by myelinization. Glial cells are basically support cells for the primary nerve cells, the neurons, which

develop quite early in pregnancy. Myelin is a fatty sheath that covers the axons of nerve cells. During myelinization, the myelin sheath gradually thickens around the existing axon and is deposited in sheaths around new parts of the axon as it grows in length. Myelin is related to the transmission of nerve impulses—the greater the thickness, the more rapid the impulse transmission.

The proposed brain growth spurt does not include the early part of pregnancy, that is, the differentiation and development of neurons and neuronal migration and probably the early stages of differentiation and development of glial cells. Glial cells influence the overall cellular population of the brain, the formation of neuronal circuits, and basic cellular architecture of the brain (Morgane et al. 1993) and thus also have implications for functional development, including motor development in infancy and childhood.

Motor development in infancy and early childhood is related to the rapid growth of the brain and central nervous system at this time. This rapid growth reflects to a large extent neuromuscular maturation. Environmental conditions are also important and interact with these biological processes to influence the expression of motor development, so partitioning biological from environmental effects in early motor development is virtually impossible.

The association between early motor development and growth of the brain is especially apparent in infancy and may be related to the unique growth spurt of the cerebellum. Functions of the cerebellum include the development and maintenance of neuromuscular coordination, balance, and muscle tone. In contrast to the growth spurt in numbers of glial cells in other regions of the brain, the cerebellum starts its spurt later than the forebrain (cerebrum) and brain stem but completes its spurt earlier. The forebrain and brain stem begin their spurts at about midpregnancy; the cerebellum begins its spurt a month or so before term. However, by 18 months of age the estimated cell content of the cerebellum has reached adult levels, whereas the estimated cell contents of the forebrain and brain stem have attained only approximately 60% of adult numbers. Thus, the cerebellum apparently experiences the first part of the growth spurt over a shorter period of time and at a faster rate than other areas of the brain. Also during this time, the infant develops the postural control and balance necessary for independent walking, so a potentially important role for the cerebellar growth spurt can be inferred.

In addition to changes in cell number and myelinization, remodeling of the cerebral cortex and changes in electrical activity (electroencephalographic activity) also occur. Analyses of the thickness, neuronal density, and histology of the cerebral cortex of "normal" children at autopsy (usually accidental deaths) indicate that each hemisphere and lobe of the brain and each area and layer within each lobe has its own rate of development (Rabinowicz 1986). At least three or more periods of brain maturation appear to occur postnatally. The first occurs between 15 and 24 months of age, during which almost all areas of the brain reach a similar level of maturity. The second occurs between about 6 and 8 years of age and involves remodeling of the cerebral cortex (changes in thickness and neuronal density) and results in altered dendritic patterns and increased neuronal density. Although not yet clearly established, two periods of change in the maturation of the cerebral cortex may occur during adolescence. The electroencephalographic data also suggest several periods of heightened activity or spurts (Thatcher et al. 1987), but their definition, location in the brain, and timing differ somewhat from the anatomical data. More recent data based on magnetic resonance imaging of the brain also suggest structural maturation of neural pathways that support motor functions during late childhood and adolescence (Paus et al. 1999). Results of these studies have potential implications for understanding motor development and performance. However, the links between such observations and motor development and performance remain to be established.

The brain and central nervous system are obviously important in the development of motor competence. As knowledge of the developing brain and nervous system progress, more specific understanding of the neurological basis of early motor development and perhaps later motor performance will emerge.

Although the brain and central nervous system have a primary role in motor development, the environments in which an infant or young child is reared also have an influence. Rearing environments are complex and multifaceted. They include rearing style, number of children in the family, birth order, season of birth, opportunities for movement, habitual physical activity, specific practice, socioeconomic status, nutritional status, and others. Environmental effects not only interact with each other and with the child's growth and maturation but are also cumulative—influences

exerted early in life may persist as the child gets older. For example, children with fetal alcohol syndrome and with prenatal exposure to alcohol or recreational drugs such as crack cocaine may show slight but significant delays and deficits in motor development in infancy and childhood. Children who are severely malnourished in infancy may have motor deficits that persist into childhood and adolescence.

Status at Birth and Subsequent Motor Development

Early motor development is also related to a number of factors that operate before and at the time of birth. For example, fetal movements during the last 3 months of pregnancy have been related to motor development during the first year, whereas the motor status of newborn infants has been related to motor development scores later in infancy. The viability of the infant at birth and shortly afterward is ordinarily based on ratings of heart rate, breathing, muscle tone, reflex responsiveness, and color. These are called Apgar ratings. Each characteristic is rated on a scale from 0 to 2, and the five ratings are then summed into a score (which can range from 0 to 10). Apgar ratings taken at 1 and 5 minutes after birth have been related to motor development at later ages (Rosenblith 1966; Edwards 1968). Newborns who experience respiratory instability, for example, are characterized by delayed motor development later in infancy.

The significance of such associations between status at or shortly after birth as well as the specific operation of such influences in mediating or modifying motor development is not clear. An infant's status at birth, especially birth weight, is strongly related to maternal characteristics. Among full-term infants with birth weights in the normal range, weight at birth is not consistently related to early motor development (Solomons and Solomons 1964), to the age of walking alone (Pineau 1961), or to gross motor coordination at about 4 years of age (Edwards 1968). A related factor to status at birth is the mode of delivery (i.e., spontaneous, forceps, Caesarean, or breech). However, no association is apparent between mode of delivery and ages at sitting and walking and fine and gross motor coordination at 3 years of age (Silva et al. 1979).

On the other hand, extremely low birth weight (<1,000 g) associated with prematurity is related to depressed motor development, which is probably influenced by the delayed physical and neurological development of these infants. Low birth weight associated with prenatal growth restriction (i.e., small-for-date infants [see chapter 2]) is also associated with delayed motor development during infancy.

Extremely low birth weight also has implications for motor development and performance at school ages. Children with birth weights less than 1,250 g or less than 1,000 g show performance deficits on scales of fine and gross motor development and on tests of muscular performance (Marlow et al. 1989; Pohlman and Isaacs 1990; Powls et al. 1995; Small et al. 1998; Falk et al. 1997; Keller et al. 1998). The performance of low-birth-weight infants at school age (i.e., at older ages) is discussed in more detail in chapter 26, which deals with the application of principles of growth, maturation, and physical activity to children with selected clinical conditions.

Early Postnatal Growth and Motor Development

Information on the relationship of motor development to the growth characteristics of infants and young children is not extensive. Some early observational data suggest that muscular and small-boned infants and those with a linear frame walk at an earlier age (Shirley 1931). Data from the Fels Research Institute indicate that infants with a larger estimated fat-free mass attain higher scores on gross motor tests during infancy and that leg muscle mass (as measured on radiographs) at 6 months of age is predictive of walking unaided at 1 year of age (Garn 1966). Corresponding data for a longitudinal sample of French infants suggest that later walking in boys is associated with reduced estimated fat-free mass, whereas later walking in girls is associated with a higher level of estimated relative fatness (Patois et al. 1974).

More systematic analyses of the relationships between motor development and specific measures of size, body proportions, and body composition during early childhood are needed. In one of the few studies, Erbaugh (1984) considered the relationships among 29 anthropometric variables, including the Heath-Carter anthropometric somatotype and balance performance in 3-year-old and 4-year-old children. Seven variables—the leg length/tibial height ratio, foot length and breadth, estimated leg muscle area, abdominal and chest circumferences, and ectomorphy—accounted for 55% of the variance in walking on the elevated balance beam (71 cm above the floor). In contrast, five variables—height-for-age, biacromial breadth, abdominal circumference, estimated arm fat area, and ectomorphy—accounted for only 28% of the variance in performance on a stabilometer (a seesaw-type platform apparatus). The results suggest that anthropometric characteristics contribute differentially to performances on the two dynamic balance tasks. Height and weight as reflected in ectomorphy (height divided by the cube root of weight, see chapter 4) contribute significantly to performance on both balance tasks.

The results of Erbaugh (1984) emphasize the need to consider the motor development of children in the context of their growth and maturation. Early childhood, or approximately the preschool period, is characterized by changing relationships between height and weight and between the lower extremities and the trunk. For example, after an increase during the first year of life, the BMI declines to a low value at about 5 to 6 years of age and then increases (see figure 3.13, page 64). A question that needs attention is the relationship, if any, between individual differences in the age at "adiposity rebound" (see chapter 3) and subsequent motor development and performance. At the same time as the BMI declines, the ratio of sitting height to standing height declines (see figure 3.15, page 68), indicating proportionally longer legs. As a result, the position of the center of gravity is gradually lowered during early childhood. The position of the center of gravity is important in the maintenance of balance, which is important to motor development. The preschool ages are also characterized by a relatively rapid reduction in skinfold thicknesses (subcutaneous adipose tissue) between about 6 months and 3 or 4 years of age (see chapter 8). Thus, major changes are occurring in body size, proportions, and composition during this time of rapid motor development and experimentation with a variety of motor activities by children.

Overview of Motor Development

The motor development of infants and young children is often treated as a separate entity independent of the child's characteristics and the environments in which the child is reared. Motor development is the outcome of the interaction of the growing, maturing, and developing children with their environments. Child-environment interactions should be viewed in the context of changing body dimensions and proportions (body scaling) and improving levels of motor competence (action scaling). Body size, proportions, and composition change as children grow, and levels of motor proficiency change as children develop. These changes in turn influence the nature of the interactions between children and their environments. An additional factor is children's perceptions of

their environments as they relate to physical and motor characteristics.

Biological and environmental factors obviously influence motor development. Motor development is a plastic process, and variation in the sequence, timing, and tempo of development is related to a variety of biological (genotype, body size, and composition) and environmental (specific practice, rearing atmosphere, play opportunities, and objects) factors that interact in a dynamic manner. The specific contributions of such factors and their interactions to variation in motor development during infancy and early childhood need to be established.

Summary

The motor responses of the newborn infant are extensions of those established during fetal life. These patterns take the form of reflexes and reactions that are either present at birth or appear during infancy. The motor activity of the newborn is largely reflex and does not involve true volitional activity. As the central nervous system matures in infancy and early childhood, inhibitory functions of the cerebral cortex begin to operate, and the reflex movements gradually diminish as they are inhibited or integrated into movement patterns. Development of voluntary control of movement begins in infancy and progresses into childhood as the child gradually attains postural, locomotor, and prehensile control. With the refinement of walking, control of locomotor and manipulative abilities improves so that a considerable amount of independent action is possible. These basic patterns are the foundation on which other movements and combinations of movements are subsequently developed and refined. The development of motor competence during infancy and childhood is related to the morphological, physiological, and neuromuscular characteristics of the child interacting with environmental opportunities and experiences.

Sources and Suggested Readings

Adolph KE (1997) Learning in the development of infant locomotion. Monographs of the Society for Research in Child Development, serial no. 251.

Adolph KE, Vereijken B, Denny MA (1998) Learning to crawl. Child Development 69:1299-1312.

Bayley N (1935) The development of motor abilities during the first three years. Monographs of the Society for Research in Child Development, serial no. 1.

Bayley N (1965) Comparisons of mental and motor test scores for ages 1–15 months by sex, birth order, race, geographical location, and education of parents. Child Development 36:379-411.

Bayley N (1969) Manual for the Bayley Scales of Infant Development. Berkeley: Psychological Corporation.

Bayley N (1993) Bayley Scales of Infant Development, 2nd edition. San Antonio, TX: Therapy Skill Builders.

Benson JB (1993) Season of birth and onset of locomotion: Theoretical and methodological implications. Infant Behavior and Development 16:69-81.

* Brandt I (1986) Patterns of early neurological development. In F Falkner, JM Tanner (eds), Human Growth. Volume 2. Postnatal Growth, Neurobiology. New York: Plenum, pp 469-518.

* Burton AW, Miller DE (1998) Movement Skill Assessment. Champaign, IL: Human Kinetics.

Capute AJ, Accardo PJ, Vining EPG, Rubenstein JE, Harryman S (1978) Primitive Reflex Profile. Baltimore: University Park Press.

Carmichael L (1970) The onset and early development of behavior. In P Mussen (ed), Carmichael's Manual of Child Psychology, 3rd edition. New York: Wiley, pp 447-563.

* Connolly KJ (1981) Maturation and the ontogeny of motor skills. In KJ Connolly, HFR Prechtl (eds), Maturation and Development: Biological and Psychological Perspectives. Philadelphia: Lippincott, pp 216-230.

* Dobbing J (1990) Early nutrition and later achievement. Proceedings of the Nutrition Society 49:103-118.

Dobbing J, Sands J (1973) Quantitative growth and development of human brain. Archives of Disease in Childhood 48:757-767.

Edwards N (1968) The relationship between physical condition immediately after birth and mental performance at age four. Genetic Psychology Monographs 78:257-289.

Erbaugh SJ (1984) The relationship of stability performance and the physical growth characteristics of preschool children. Research Quarterly for Exercise and Sport 55:8-16.

Falk B, Eliakim A, Dotan A, Liebermann DG, Regev R, Dolphin T, Bar-Or O (1997) Birth weight and physical ability in 5- to 8-year old health children born prematurely. Medicine and Science in Sports and Exercise 29:1124-1130.

Fiorentino MR (1973) Reflex Testing Methods for Evaluating C.N.S. Development, 2nd edition. Springfield, IL: Charles C Thomas.

Folio MR, Fewell RR (1983) Peabody Developmental Motor Scales and Activity Cards. Austin, TX: PRO-ED.

Frankenburg WK, Dodds JB (1967) The Denver Developmental Screening Test. Journal of Pediatrics 71:181-191.

Frankenburg WK, Dodds JB, Archer P, Shapiro H, Bresnick B (1992) The Denver II: A major revision and restandardization of the Denver Developmental Screening Test. Pediatrics 89:91-97.

Garn SM (1966) Body size and its implications. In LW Hoffman and ML Hoffman (eds), Review of Child Development Research. New York: Russell Sage Foundation, pp 529-561.

* Gesell A (1954) The ontogenesis of infant behavior. In L Carmichael (ed), Manual of Child Psychology, 2nd edition. New York: Wiley, pp 335-373.

Gesell A, Amatruda CS (1947) Developmental Diagnosis. New York: Harper and Row.

Gomez Pellico L, Rodriquez Torres R, Dankloff Mora C (1995) Changes in walking pattern between five and six years of age. Developmental Medicine and Child Neurology 37:800-806.

Gutteridge MV (1939) A study of motor achievements of young children. Archives of Psychology 244: 1-178.

Hack M, Taylor HG, Klein N, Eiben R, Schatschneider C, Mercuri-Minich N (1994) School-age outcomes in children with birthweights under 750 g. New England Journal of Medicine 331:753-759.

Halsey CL, Collin MF, Anderson CL (1993) Extremely low birthweight children and their peers: A comparison of preschool performance. Pediatrics 91:807-811.

* Haubenstricker J, Seefeldt V (1986) Acquisition of motor skills during childhood. In V Seefeldt (ed), Physical Activity and Well-Being. Reston, VA: AAHPERD, pp 41-101.

Hausdorff JM, Zemany L, Peng C-K, Goldberger AL (1999) Maturation of gait dynamics: Stride-to-stride variability and its temporal organization in children. Journal of Applied Physiology 86:1040-1047.

Haywood KM, Getchell N (2001) Life Span Motor Development, 3rd edition. Champaign, IL: Human Kinetics.

Hempel MS (1993) Neurological development during toddling age in normal children and children at risk of developmental disorders. Early Human Development 34:47-57.

Illingworth RS (1967) The Development of the Infant and Young Child: Normal and Abnormal, 3rd edition. London: Livingstone.

Keller H, Ayub BV, Saigal S, Bar-Or O (1998) Neuromotor ability in 5- to 7-year old children with very low or extremely low birthweight. Developmental Medicine and Child Neurology 40:661-666.

* Keogh J, Sugden D (1985) Motor Skill Development. New York: Macmillan.

Largo RH, Molinari L, Weber M, Comenale Pinto L, Duc G (1985) Early development of locomotion: Significance of prematurity, cerebral palsy and sex. Developmental Medicine and Child Neurology 27:183-191.

Largo RH, Pfister D, Molinari L, Kundu S, Lipp A, Duc G (1989) Significance of prenatal, perinatal and postnatal factors in the development of AGA preterm infants at five to seven years. Developmental Medicine and Child Neurology 31: 440-456.

Lewis MC (2000) The promise of dynamic systems approaches for an integrated account of human development. Child Development 71:36-43.

Little RE, Anderson KW, Ervin CH, Worthington-Roberts B, Clarren SK (1989) Maternal alcohol use during breast-feeding and infant mental and motor development at one year. New England Journal of Medicine 321:425-430.

Lundberg AE (1979) Dissociated motor development: Developmental patterns, clinical characteristics, causal factors and outcome, with special reference to late walking children. Neuropädiatrie 10:161-182.

Lundberg AE (1980) Normal and delayed walking age: A clinical and muscle morphological and metabolic study. In K Berg, BO Eriksson (eds), Children and Exercise IX. Baltimore, MD: University Park Press, pp 23-31.

Lundberg AE, Eriksson BO, Jansson G (1979b) Muscle abnormalities in coeliac disease: Studies of gross motor development and muscle fibre composition, size and metabolic substrates. European Journal of Pediatrics 130:93-103.

Lundberg AE, Eriksson BO, Mellgren G (1979a) Metabolic substrates, muscle fibre composition and fibre size in late walking and normal children. European Journal of Pediatrics 130:79-92.

Malina RM (1980) Biosocial correlates of motor development during infancy and early childhood. In LS Greene, FE Johnston (eds), Social and Biological Predictors of Nutritional Status, Physical Growth, and Neurological Development. New York: Academic Press, pp 143-171.

Malina RM (1984) Physical activity and motor development/performance in populations nutritionally at risk. In E Pollitt, P Amante (eds), Energy Intake and Activity. New York: Alan R Liss, pp 285-302.

Marlow N, Roberts BL, Cooke RWI (1989) Motor skills in extremely low birthweight children at the age of 6 years. Archives of Disease in Childhood 64:839-847.

* McGraw MB (1945) The Neuromuscular Maturation of the Human Infant. New York: Hafner (reprinted by Columbia University Press, 1963).

Mattson SN, Riley EP (1998) A review of the neurobehavioral deficits in children with fetal alcohol syndrome or prenatal exposure to alcohol. Alcoholism: Clinical and Experimental Research 22:279-294.

* Morgane PJ, Austin-LaFrance R, Bronzino J, Tonkiss J, Diaz-Cintra S, Cintra L, Kemper T, Galler JR (1993) Prenatal malnutrition and development of the brain. Neuroscience and Biobehavioral Reviews 17:91-128.

Patois E, Roy M-P, Sempe M, Lellouch J (1974) Age de la marche et facteurs associés étudiés dans un échantillon longitudinal de 296 enfants parisiens. Archives Françaises de Pédiatrie 31:875-886 (in french).

Paus T, Zijdenbos A, Worsley K, Collins DL, Blumenthal J, Giedd JN, Rapoport JL, Evans AC (1999) Structural maturation of neural pathways in children and adolescents: In vivo study. Science 283:1908-1911.

Payne VG, Isaacs LD (1999) Human Motor Development: A Lifespan Approach, 4th edition. Mountain View, CA: Mayfield.

Pineau M (1961) Developpement de l'enfant et dimension de la familie. Biotypologie 22:25-53.

Piper MC, Byrne PJ, Darrah J, Watts MJ (1989) Gross and fine motor development of preterm infants at eight and 12 months of age. Developmental Medicine and Child Neurology 31:591-597.

Pohlman RL, Isaacs LD (1990) The previously low birth weight infant: Fundamental motor skill outcomes in the 5- to 9-year old. Pediatric Exercise Science 2:263-271.

Powls A, Botting N, Cooke RW, Marlow N (1995) Motor impairment in children 12 and 13 years old with a birthweight less than 1250 g. Archives of Disease in Childhood 73: F62-F66.

* Rabinowicz T (1986) The differentiated maturation of the cerebral cortex. In F Falkner, JM Tanner (eds), Human Growth. Volume 2. Postnatal Growth, Neurobiology. New York: Plenum, pp 385-410.

Rarick GL (1961) Motor Development during Infancy and Childhood. Madison, WI: College Printing and Typing Company.

Roberton MA (1978) Longitudinal evidence for developmental stages in the forceful overarm throw. Journal of Human Movement Studies 4:167-175.

Roberton MA (1982) Describing "stages" within and across motor tasks. In JAS Kelso, JE Clark (eds), The Development of Movement Control and Co-ordination. New York: Wiley, pp 293-307.

Roberton MA (1984) Changing motor patterns during childhood. In JR Thomas (ed), Motor Development during Childhood and Adolescence. Minneapolis: Burgess, pp 48-90.

Rosenblith (1966) Prognostic values of neonatal assessment. Child Development 37:623-631.

Saigal S, Szatmari P, Rosenbaum P, Campbell D, King S (1990) Intellectual and functional status at school entry of children who weighed 1000 grams or less at birth: A regional perspective of births in the 1980s. Journal of Pediatrics 116:409-416.

Seefeldt V, Haubenstricker J (1982) Patterns, phases, or stages: An analytical model for the study of developmental movement. In JAS Kelso, JE Clark (eds), The Development of Movement Control and Co-ordination. New York: Wiley, pp 309-319.

Shirley MM (1931) The First Two Years: A Study of Twenty-Five Babies. Volume I. Postural and Locomotor Development. Minneapolis: University of Minnesota Press.

Silva PA, Buckfield P, Spears GF (1979) Mode of delivery and developmental characteristics in a thousand Dunedin three year olds. New Zealand Medical Journal 89:79-81.

Sinclair CB (1971) Movement and Movement Patterns of Early Childhood. Richmond, VA: State Department of Education.

Small E, Bar-Or O, Van Mil E, Saigal S (1998) Muscle function of 11- to 17-year old children of extremely low birthweight. Pediatric Exercise Science 10:327-336.

Solomons G, Solomons HC (1964) Factors affecting motor performance in four month old infants. Child Development 35:1283-1295.

Thatcher RW, Walker RA, Giudice S (1987) Human cerebral hemispheres develop at different rates and ages. Science 236:1110-1113.

Thelen E (1984) Learning to walk: Ecological demands and phylogenetic constraints. In LP Lipsitt, C Rovee-Collier (eds), Advances in Infancy Research. Norwood, NJ: Ablex, pp 213-250.

Thelen E (1985) Developmental origins of motor coordination: Leg movements in human infants. Developmental Psychobiology 18:1-22.

Thelen E (1989) The (re)discovery of motor development: Learning new things from an old field. Developmental Psychology 25:946-949.

* Thelen E, Smith LB (1994) A Dynamic Systems Approach to the Development of Cognition and Action. Cambridge, MA: MIT Press.

Thelen E, Ulrich BD (1991) Hidden skills. Monographs of the Society for Research in Child Development, serial no. 223.

* Touwen BCL (1988) Motor development: Developmental dynamics and neurological examination in infancy. In E Meisami, PS Timiras (eds), Handbook of Human Growth and Developmental Biology. Volume 1: Neural, Sensory, Motor, and Integrative Development. Boca Raton, FL: CRC Press, pp 201-219.

Touwen BCL (1993) How normal is variable, or how variable is normal? Early Human Development 34:1-12.

Vereijken B, Thelen E (1997) Training infant treadmill stepping: The role of individual pattern stability. Developmental Psychobiology 30:89-102.

* Wickstrom RL (1983) Fundamental Motor Patterns, 3rd edition. Philadelphia: Lea & Febiger.

Wild M (1938) The behavior of throwing and some observations concerning its course of development in children. Research Quarterly 9:20-24.

Yan JH, Payne VG, Thomas JR (2000) Developmental kinematics of young girls' overarm throwing. Research Quarterly for Exercise and Sport 71:92-98.

Chapter

11

STRENGTH AND MOTOR PERFORMANCE

Chapter Outline

Children develop a variety of fundamental motor skills during the preschool years. The movement patterns, which underlie the basic motor skills, are reasonably well developed in most children by 6 or 7 years of age. However, the mature patterns for some basic skills are established somewhat later. As the fundamental motor skills are refined through practice and instruction (i.e., learning), the quality and quantity of performance improve, and the basic movement patterns are integrated into more complex motor skills, which are fundamental to many games and sports. This chapter considers changes in attained levels of performance in a variety of specific motor skills from early childhood through adolescence. Muscular strength is also considered because it is an essential component of many motor performances. Relationships of strength and motor performance with body size, physique and composition, scaling for body size, and tracking are also discussed. The concept of physical fitness is initially reviewed because many performance tasks are often included in fitness test batteries.

Physical Fitness

Discussions of the strength and motor performance of children and adolescents are often set in the context of physical fitness. Physical fitness is a state or a condition that permits the individual to carry out daily activities without undue fatigue and with sufficient reserve to enjoy active leisure. Fitness has historically been viewed as having three basic components: muscular strength and endurance, cardiorespiratory endurance, and motor ability (Clarke 1971). Strength is the ability to express muscular force, endurance is the ability to carry out a task over time, and motor ability includes several components that permit individuals to perform specific tasks (e.g., power, speed, agility, and flexibility).

Over the past 40 to 50 years, the physical fitness of children and adolescents focused to a large extent on performances in a variety of standardized motor tasks. This focus is best exemplified in the national physical fitness test used since the mid-1950s, the AAHPER youth fitness test (American Association for Health, Physical Education, and Recreation 1976). The AAHPER test includes the 50-yard dash (speed), standing long jump (power), shuttle run (agility), pull-ups (upper body functional strength), sit-ups (abdominal strength and endurance), softball throw for distance (power and coordination), and 600-yard run (cardiovascular endurance).

The concept of physical fitness has since evolved from a primary focus on its motor and strength components (performance-related fitness) to more emphasis on health. As a result, the concept of health-related physical fitness emerged in the late 1970s. Health-related fitness is operationally defined in three components—cardiorespiratory endurance, musculoskeletal function of the lower trunk, and body composition. Cardiovascular endurance is assessed with a 1-mile run or a 9-minute run. Musculoskeletal function of the lower trunk is viewed in terms of abdominal strength and flexibility of the lower back, which are assessed with sit-ups and the sit-and-reach, respectively. Body composition is estimated as the sum of the triceps and subscapular skinfolds (American Alliance for Health, Physical Education, Recreation and Dance 1984).

The concept of physical fitness is still evolving. More recent definitions address physical and physiological fitness, which includes morphological, muscular, motor, cardiovascular, and metabolic components (Bouchard and Shephard 1994). The term metabolic fitness is often used to include measures of serum lipids, blood pressure, blood glucose, and other risk factors for cardiovascular disease.

Physical activity is often assumed to be related to physical fitness (i.e., the more habitually active are more fit). This assumption is not necessarily true. Relationships between regular physical activity and indicators of health-related and performance-related fitness are generally low in children and adolescents. Relationships between activity and fitness are discussed in chapter 22. Other factors influence the physical fitness of youth, and growth and maturity are perhaps the most important factors. Components of fitness change with normal growth whether or not the child is physically active. They are also influenced by biological maturity. Maturity-associated variation is discussed in more detail in chapter 17.

Changes in several indicators of muscular strength and motor performance during childhood and adolescence are subsequently described. Cardiovascular performance and anaerobic power are considered in chapters 12 and 13, respectively, and risk factors or indicators of metabolic fitness are considered in chapter 26.

Measures of Strength and Motor Performance

A variety of tasks can be used to document levels of muscular strength and motor performance. Tasks that best provide an indication of the child's strength and motor performance characteristics should be used. Emphasis is placed on standardized tasks that can be used in the field or school setting, in contrast to those limited to the laboratory.

Strength is an essential component of motor performance in that a certain level of muscular strength is necessary to carry out a task. On the other hand, several motor performance tasks are commonly used as indicators of specific aspects of muscular strength. Strength is an expression of muscular force, or the individual's capacity to develop tension against an external resistance. There are several types of strength.

Static, or **isometric, strength** is the force exerted against an external resistance without any change in muscle length. It is generally measured for specific muscle groups to test such functions as grip strength, pulling or pushing strength of the shoulders, or flexion and extension strength of the elbow or knee.

Explosive strength, or **power,** is the ability of muscles to release maximal force or torque in the shortest possible time. Torque is the force exerted by a muscle times lever arm length. Outside of the laboratory, jumping tasks are commonly used as indicators of explosive strength.

Dynamic strength is the force or torque generated by repetitive contractions of muscles. Pull-ups and push-ups are commonly used to measure this component of strength.

Muscular endurance is the ability to repeat or maintain muscular contractions over time. A commonly used measure of muscular endurance is the flexed-arm hang in which the subject must maintain muscular contractions. The number of sit-ups completed in a period of time (i.e., repeated contractions) is often used as an indicator of the strength and endurance of the abdominal musculature. Muscular endurance is also discussed in chapter 13 in the context of anaerobic performance.

Tests of strength and motor performance obviously overlap. Performance tests incorporating fundamental motor skills require some combination of strength, power, and motor control.

Jumping tasks require motor coordination and muscular power to project the body horizontally forward in the standing long jump or vertically in the vertical jump (jump and reach).

Throwing tasks require coordination and power in projecting an object, most often in the form of a ball throw for distance.

Running tests are more variable. Dashes are tests of **running speed** that require power and coordination to move the body as rapidly as possible from the starting to the finishing lines. Shuttle runs are used as indicators of **agility,** the ability to rapidly change direction of movement.

Tests of balance and flexibility are also incorporated in test batteries for motor performance. Clearly, **balance** is essential to the performance of motor activities. It is measured either as **static** balance (maintenance of balance without having to move as in balancing on a beam or stick) or as **dynamic** balance (maintenance of balance while moving as in the beam walk or while standing on an unstable platform such as a seesaw or stabilometer).

Flexibility is the range of motion of different segments at various joints of the body. It is commonly viewed as the maximum range of joint motion. Flexibility is joint-specific, so no single measure is indicative of general body flexibility. Flexibility of the lower back and hip as measured by the sit-and-reach test receives most attention.

Other fundamental motor skills can also be tested (e.g., kicking for distance, catching balls tossed in a standardized manner, hopping or skipping over specified distances, and throwing for accuracy). However, data for these skills are quite often limited to the preschool and elementary school children, given the importance of fundamental motor skill development in the behavioral repertoire of children at these ages.

Performance in Early Childhood

Information on attained levels of strength and motor performance is not as extensive for early childhood as it is for middle childhood and adolescence. There is much intraindividual and interindividual variability in performance among young children, which is expressed from day to day and even from trial to trial on a given day. Changes in mean levels of performance with age should be viewed with this variability in mind.

Changes in several measures of strength and motor performance from 3 to 6 years of age are illustrated in figures 11.1 and 11.2, respectively. Except for grip strength, the other measurements of strength shown in figure 11.1 are not ordinarily used in growth studies. The data are from a study that was concerned with various measures of manual strength in young children relative to their capacities to open different types of containers (e.g., those for medications). A problem facing designers is the need to develop a container that can be opened by elderly people with diminished manual strength and perhaps arthritis but cannot be easily opened by young children. Clearly, muscular strength increases gradually during early childhood. Wrist turning strength, on average, apparently increases at a faster rate than the other three measurements. Sex differences in average strength are small and there is considerable overlap.

Performances in several fundamental motor tasks also improve during early childhood (see figure 11.2). Improvement with age is linear for all tasks except the balance test. On the average, sex differences are generally small but consistently favor boys for the running, jumping, and especially throwing. Girls perform slightly better in the balance test between 3 and 5 years of age and

Strength in Preschool Children

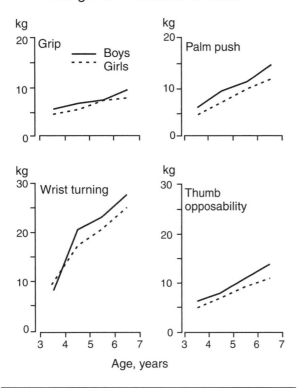

FIGURE 11.1 Mean levels of strength for several tasks in children 3 through 6 years of age.

Data from Krogman, 1971.

Motor Performances in Preschool Children

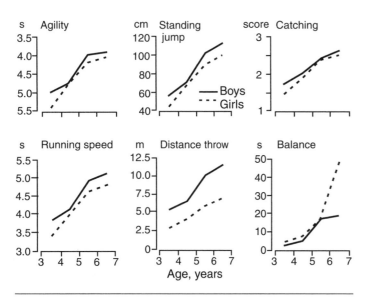

FIGURE 11.2 Mean levels of motor performance for several tasks in children 3 through 6 years of age.

Data from Morris et al., 1982.

then exceptionally better than boys at 6 years of age. Catching shows negligible differences. The trends are generally consistent with presently available knowledge about sex differences in the motor performances of young children. On the average, boys excel in tasks that require power and speed, as in jumping, throwing, and running, whereas girls excel, on the average, in tasks that require balance, such as hopping. The differences between boys and girls are relatively small, however, and there is much overlap. They probably reflect the types of activities available for preschool children, availability of suitable role models for motor skills, especially among young girls, and societal expectations for physical activity and motor skill of boys and girls at these young ages.

Performance in Middle Childhood and Adolescence

Strength and motor performance generally improve with age during middle childhood and adolescence, but the pattern of improvement is not uniform for all tasks. This section considers age trends and sex differences in several performance tasks.

Static Strength

Changes in two measures of static strength between 6 and 18 years of age are illustrated in figure 11.3. The data are derived from a mixed-longitudinal sample between 6 and 11 years of age and from a longitudinal sample from 11 to 18 years of age. Strength increases linearly with age until 13 to 14 years of age in boys, when there is acceleration in strength development, the adolescent strength spurt. In girls, strength improves linearly with age through about 16 or 17 years with no clear evidence for an adolescent spurt as in boys, which is a function of viewing the strength data cross-sectionally by age. When strength data for girls are related to the adolescent growth spurt in height, girls do, on average, show a growth spurt in strength, but it is not as intense as the spurt in boys. Adolescent spurts in measures of strength are discussed in chapter 16.

If the data from figures 11.1 and 11.3 are combined, there is a continuous increase

Static Strength, 6 to 18 years

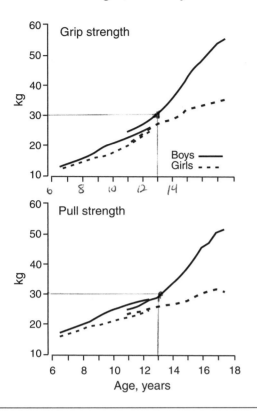

FIGURE 11.3   Mean grip strength (top) and pulling strength (bottom) between 6 and 18 years of age.

Data from Malina and Roche, 1983.

in strength from 3 years of age on. The growth curve for muscular strength is generally similar to that for body size during childhood and adolescence.

The sex difference in strength is consistent, although small, through childhood. The marked acceleration of strength development during the male adolescent growth spurt magnifies the sex difference. With increasing age during adolescence, the percentage of girls whose performance on strength tests equals or exceeds that of boys declines considerably. After 16 years of age, few girls perform as high as the average strength of boys, and, conversely, few boys perform as low as the average strength of girls.

Age trends and sex differences in other measures of static strength are similar to those for grip and pulling strength illustrated in figure 11.3. Examples are arm (biceps flexion) and leg (quadriceps extensor) strength. Although growth studies generally stop at 18 years of age, strength

continues to increase into the third decade of life, especially in males.

The physiological and neuromuscular basis of changes in muscular strength during childhood and adolescence has not received much attention. Evidence is limited to small samples of children and adolescents. For example, muscle strength and electromyographic (EMG) activity were measured in small samples of boys (n = 9) and girls (n = 7) on two occasions, 11 and 16 years of age. Torque, that is, the force exerted by a muscle times lever arm length, was measured during maximal voluntary knee extensor muscle actions (quadriceps muscles). Electrical activity of the quadriceps muscles was also recorded with surface electrodes during the measurement of torque. Torque increases significantly with age between 11 and 16 years. Sex differences are small at 11 years of age but are magnified at 16 years of age for both concentric (muscle-shortening) and eccentric (muscle-lengthening) actions. Relative increases in torque from 11 to 16 years of age are especially larger in boys, 71% to 94% compared with 52% to 53% for concentric tests in boys and girls, respectively, and 87% to 100% compared with 56% to 59% for eccentric tests in boys and girls, respectively. When adjusted for growth in body mass, however, the gains in torque for boys between 11 and 16 years of age are significant only for the eccentric tests, and those for girls are not significant. These trends suggest differential changes in the eccentric and concentric force-producing capacity of the knee extensors during adolescence in males but not in females. On the other hand, the ratio of eccentric to concentric torque per unit of EMG activity, an indicator of electromechanical efficiency, does not change with age between 11 and 16 years and does not consistently differ between boys and girls (Seger and Thorstensson 2000).

Experimental studies of isolated muscles indicate changes in relaxation times with age during childhood. Half-relaxation times of the soleus muscle of the leg decrease from about 90 milliseconds at 3 years of age to 40 milliseconds at 10 years of age in a small sample (n = 22) of boys and girls. There does not appear to be a sex difference. The estimated half-relaxation time at 10 years of age overlaps half-relaxation times in young adult males and females, 36±8 and 41±9 milliseconds, respectively (Lin et al. 1994).

Results of these two studies of small samples suggest changes in muscle dynamics with age during childhood and adolescence. They also suggest an important role for the maturation of muscle tissue per se as an integral factor in strength and performance.

Upper Body Muscular Endurance

Changes in muscular endurance of the upper body as measured by the flexed-arm hang are shown in figure 11.4. As the name of the test implies, the child grasps a horizontal bar with both hands and holds the body suspended in the air with the arms in a flexed position. The score for the test is the duration of time the child holds this position unaided until the angle at the elbows is less than 90° flexion or the child's chin rests on the bar. Muscular endurance improves linearly with age from 5 to 13 to 14 years in boys, followed by a spurt similar to that for static strength. Muscular endurance also increases with age to 16 to 17 years in girls, but there is no clear evidence of a spurt as in boys.

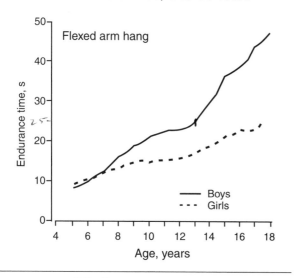

Muscular Endurance, 5 to 18 Years

FIGURE 11.4   Mean muscular endurance as measured by performance on the flexed-arm hang between 5 and 18 years of age.

Data from Motor Performance Study of Michigan State University, by permission of J.L. Haubenstricker

Abdominal Strength and Endurance

The number of sit-ups performed in 1 minute is a measure of abdominal strength and endurance. The knees are flexed so that the feet are flat on the surface and the heels are 12 to 18 inches from the buttocks. This test is included among measures of health-related fitness. Abdominal strength and endurance improves linearly with age from 6 to 13 years in boys, after which it shows somewhat accelerated development (see figure 11.5). It also increases with age to 14 years in girls, with no subsequent improvement, on the average. Sex differences are negligible in abdominal strength and endurance during childhood and become established in adolescence.

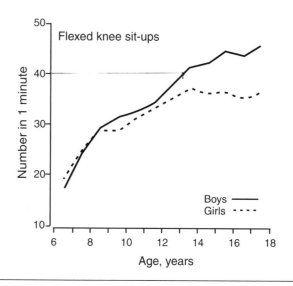

Abdominal Strength and Endurance, 6 to 18 Years

FIGURE 11.5   Mean abdominal strength and endurance as measured by the number of flexed knee sit-ups performed in 1 minute between 6 and 18 years of age.

Data from AAHPERD, 1984.

Jumping

Tests of jumping are commonly used as indicators of muscular coordination and power. Age-associated and sex-associated variation in the standing long jump and the vertical jump are shown in figure 11.6. On the average, performance in the standing long jump increases linearly with age in both sexes until 14 years in girls and 18 years in boys. After 14 years of age in girls, attained levels of performance in the standing long jump improve only slightly. Sex differences are relatively small but consistent during childhood and become magnified during adolescence. Age trends and sex differences in the vertical jump

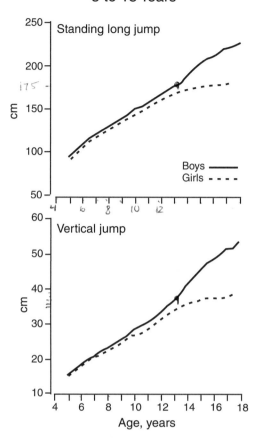

Jumping Performances, 5 to 18 Years

FIGURE 11.6 Mean performance in the standing long jump and the vertical jump between 5 and 18 years of age.

Data from Motor Performance Study of Michigan State University, by permission of J.L. Haubenstricker.

this performance task. The overhand throwing performance of girls improves only slightly between 6 and 14 years of age and then is stable. The sex difference in throwing performance during childhood is greater than for other basic skills and is magnified to a much greater extent during adolescence.

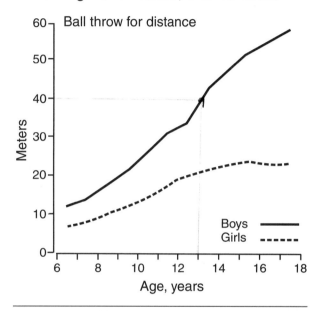

Throwing Performance, 6 to 18 Years

FIGURE 11.7 Mean performance in the softball throw for distance between 6 and 18 years of age.

Data from Haubenstricker and Seefeldt, 1986.

are similar to those for the standing long jump. The slope of the increase, however, is somewhat steeper for the vertical jump, suggesting an adolescent acceleration in males. The average vertical jumping performance of girls improves to about 14 years of age, followed by smaller gains.

Throwing

The overhand ball throw for distance is a measure of coordination and muscular power of the upper body. Mean performances of boys and girls in the softball throw for distance between 6 and 18 years of age are shown in figure 11.7. The throwing performance of boys increases markedly and linearly with age, with a change in the slope of improvement suggesting an adolescent spurt in

Running Speed

Changes in running speed during childhood and adolescence are shown in figure 11.8. The data are expressed as the time elapsed in covering 30 yards (27.4 meters). The children had a 5-yard running start, which is important to note because some tests are performed with a standing start, and some of the elapsed time is lost to individual variation in reaction time to the starting signal. This variation in reaction time is eliminated with the running start, in which children run several yards before the timing device is activated. Running speed improves in both sexes rather sharply from 5 to 8 years of age, and then the slope of improvement is less. Sex differences are small during most of childhood and are most apparent in adolescence. Speed improves from 5 to 18 years of age in boys, and the data suggest an

Running Speed, 5 to 18 Years

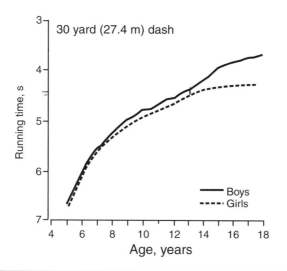

FIGURE 11.8 Mean running speed, measured as the time elapsed in covering 30 yards (27.4 meters) with a running start, between 5 and 18 years of age. The time scale is reversed because the better time is the lower time.

Data from Motor Performance Study of Michigan State University, by permission of J.L. Haubenstricker.

adolescent acceleration after 13 years of age. The running speed of girls improves up to 13 to 14 years of age, with little further improvement to 17 years of age.

Running Agility

The shuttle run is an indicator of agility. Shuttle runs require the child to run as rapidly as possible back and forth between lines set a specified distance apart, but protocols vary. Some require the child to pick up a block and return it to the starting line, whereas others involve only running back and forth. The protocol for the data shown in figure 11.9 required the child to run from the starting line to a line 30 feet (9.1 meters) away and pick up a block, to run back to the starting line and place the block there, to run back to the 30 foot line and pick up another block, and then to run back through the starting line. The score was the time elapsed in the two excursions. The pattern of age-associated and sex-associated variation in this agility shuttle run (see figure 11.9) is identical to that for the 30-yard dash (see figure 11.8). Performance improves considerably in boys and girls between 5 and 8 years of age and then continues to improve at a

somewhat lesser but more constant pace up to 13 to 14 years of age in girls and 18 years of age in boys. The data suggest an adolescent acceleration after 13 years of age in boys and little improvement after 14 years of age in girls.

Agility, 5 to 18 Years

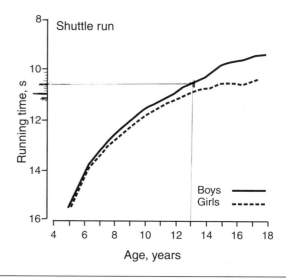

FIGURE 11.9 Mean agility as measured by performance on a shuttle run between 5 and 18 years of age. See the text for the specific protocol. The time scale is reversed because the better time is the lower time.

Data from Motor Performance Study of Michigan State University, by permission of J.L. Haubenstricker.

Flexibility

Changes in the sit-and-reach test, a measure of the flexibility of the lower back, hip, and upper thigh, are shown in figure 11.10. Girls are more flexible at all ages than boys, and the sex difference is greatest during the adolescent growth spurt and sexual maturation. Mean scores are stable from 5 to 11 years of age in girls and then increase markedly during adolescence to 15 years of age, with little subsequent improvement. Among boys, lower back flexibility declines linearly with age from 5 years, reaches a nadir at 12 years of age, and then increases through 18 years of age. The unique pattern of age-associated and sex-associated variation in this measure of flexibility is related in part to the growth of the lower extremities and the trunk during adolescence (see figure 3.19 for the ratio of sitting height to stature during growth). The

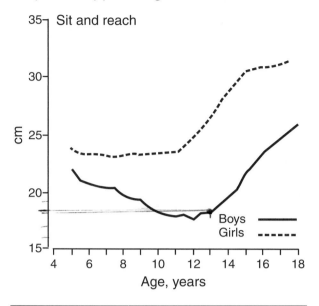

Flexibility of the Lower Back, Hip and Upper Thigh, 5 to 18 Years

FIGURE 11.10 Mean flexibility of the lower back, hip, and upper thigh as measured by the sit-and-reach test between 5 and 18 years of age.

Data from Motor Performance Study of Michigan State University, by permission of J.L. Haubenstricker.

increase in flexibility of girls after 11 years of age coincides with the adolescent growth spurt in sitting height (trunk length). In addition, adolescent growth spurts of the long bones of the upper extremity, which should influence the extent of a youngster's reach, occur close to that for sitting height. Similarly, the low point in the sit-and-reach performance of boys is generally coincident with the adolescent growth spurt in leg length, and the subsequent increase appears to coincide with the adolescent growth spurt in sitting height and upper extremity length. Anatomical and functional changes in the joints during adolescence influence their flexibility. As noted earlier, flexibility tends to be joint specific, but patterns of age changes and sex differences are generally similar.

Balance

Balance is essential to the performance of many motor tasks. The balance-beam walk is a commonly used test of balance. It requires the child to walk the length of the beam without stepping off. The test is scored as either the number of steps before stepping off the beam or the number of sec-

onds the child stays on the beam while walking, or points are given for negotiating the beam in one direction and then in return. Sometimes hopping is used as a test of balance because this basic motor skill requires that the body be supported on one leg. Results of several studies are summarized in figure 11.11. Balance improves with age, and on average, girls perform better in balance tasks during childhood. Data for adolescence are limited but indicate small differences between boys and girls and a plateau in both sexes.

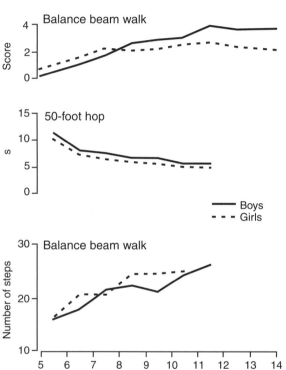

Performance in Several Balance Tasks

FIGURE 11.11 Mean performances on several tests of balance between 5 and 14 years of age.

Data from Cron and Pronko, 1957, and Keogh, 1965.

When a different balance task is used, such as a stabilometer (a movable platform on a pivot), evidence indicates better dynamic stability in girls than in boys in late childhood and adolescence. Stabilometer performances indicate less pivot displacement, both laterally and anteroposteriorly, in females than in males 9 to 14 years of age and 16 to 22 years of age. Similar results are apparent with the eyes open and closed, although pivot displacement is greater with the eyes closed in both sexes. Males of both age groups appear to be more influenced by performance conditions that require the eyes to be closed, suggesting that the dynamic balance, that is, maintenance of balance while moving or while standing on an unstable platform, of males is more dependent on vision than is the dynamic balance of females (Golomer et al. 1997).

Some literature suggests a period of "awkwardness" during the adolescent growth spurt in boys. It is generally attributed to the differential timing of growth spurts of the lower limbs and muscle mass. The awkwardness or lag in performance presumably involves problems with agility, balance, and coordination during the male growth spurt. The cross-sectional data for balance (see figure 11.11) and agility (see figure 11.9) and for pivot displacement on the stabilometer (Golomer et al. 1997) are not consistent with this notion. The concept of adolescent awkwardness is discussed in more detail in chapter 16, in which performance is related to the timing of the adolescent growth spurt.

Overview of Performance

The period between 5 and 8 years of age appears to be a transitional period in the development of strength and motor performance. Basic motor skills are reaching mature form at this time, but there is considerable variation among children. In addition, the application of these basic skills to specific test situations must be practiced or learned. Therefore, variation in the performance of specific strength and motor items at these ages is expected. Children show considerable increase in performance of some skills between 5 and 8 years of age (running speed and the shuttle run) and a steady, more gradual increase in performance in others from 5 years of age through childhood (e.g., jumping, throwing, and strength). Muscular endurance appears to show an increased pace of development in boys but not in girls. This difference may, in part, reflect a learning effect as the youngsters get adjusted to the test situation. Controlling for learning effects is a significant logistical problem in longitudinal studies of motor performance: How much of the observed improvement reflects growth-related changes and how much reflects learning to perform the tasks? The influence of specific instruction and training on strength and motor performance is considered in chapter 22.

Average performances of girls in a variety of motor tasks (dash, standing long jump, vertical jump, shuttle run, and others) improve more or less linearly from 6 to about 14 years of age, followed by a slight increase in some tasks or a plateau in others. There is much overlap between the sexes during childhood. In early adolescence, the average performances of girls fall within one standard deviation of the averages for boys; subsequently, the average performances of girls are often outside the limits defined by one standard deviation below the boys' mean performance. Overhand throwing and sit-and-reach performances are exceptions. Few girls approximate the throwing performances of boys at all ages from late childhood, but girls have greater lower back flexibility at all ages compared with boys.

Motor performance is in part related to muscular strength. Strength improves linearly with age from early childhood through about 15 years of age in girls, followed by slower improvement. This pattern is in contrast to the marked acceleration of strength development during male adolescence, so sex differences in muscular strength are considerable at this time.

A question that merits more detailed study is the relative flatness of the performance curves of girls during adolescence. Levels of performance show, on average, little improvement in many tasks after 14 to 15 years of age. Is this trend related to the biological changes associated with female adolescence (e.g., sexual maturity, fat accumulation, or changes in physique), or is it related to cultural factors (e.g., changing social interests and expectations, pressure from peers, lack of motivation, or limited opportunities to participate in performance-related physical activities)? The flatness of performance curves during adolescence probably reflects an interaction of biological and cultural factors. With recent emphasis on and opportunity for athletic competition among young girls and wider acceptability of women in the role of an athlete, the overall age-related pattern of physical performance during female adolescence may change.

Relationships of Strength and Motor Performance to Size, Physique, and Body Composition

Changes in body size, physique, and body composition associated with growth and maturation are important factors that affect strength and motor performance. The relationships, however, vary among performance measures and with age.

Relationships between body size, physique, and body composition and performance are commonly viewed as correlations that statistically express the relationship between two variables. Correlations do not indicate a cause-and-effect sequence of events. Mediating or moderating variables, as well as covariates, may be present. Correlations less than 0.30 are considered low, and those between 0.30 and 0.60 are moderate.

Body Size

Correlations between height and weight and performance on a variety of motor tasks are generally low to moderate in children and adolescents 4 to 18 years of age and are of limited predictive utility. Correlations do not differ by sex. Tasks in which the body is projected (dashes and jumps) generally show negative correlations with body weight. Tasks in which the body is raised (pull-ups) or supported (flexed-arm hang) off the ground by the arms consistently have negative correlations with body weight, and some reach into the moderate range. In contrast, correlations between stature and weight and a variety of strength tasks are higher than those for motor performance and generally fall in the moderate range. Thus, the taller and heavier individual tends to be stronger. Correlations between strength and body size also do not differ by sex.

Relationships between body size and performance are confounded in part by age. Age, height, and weight are related, so it is necessary to control for relationships among these variables when evaluating their specific contributions to variation in performance. With this procedure, the relationship between height and performance can be evaluated while statistically controlling for age and weight. The same can be done for weight, controlling for age and height, and for age, controlling for height and weight. This procedure is called partial correlation. Partial correlations for age, height, and weight and variety of motor performances do not differ between boys and girls, and several trends are apparent (Malina 1994). Age is positively related to strength and motor performance even when stature and weight are controlled. This positive relation suggests an important role of neuromuscular maturation and experience in performance on strength and motor tasks. After controlling for age and stature, body weight tends to have a negative influence on performance, especially in tasks in which the body is projected, whereas after controlling for age and body weight, correlations between stature and performance tend to be positive.

Other statistical procedures permit an estimate of the amount of variation in performance that is accounted for by age, height, and weight. In an earlier study of children and adolescents 9 to 18 years of age (Montoye et al. 1972), age, height, and weight accounted for similar percentages of variation in trunk flexibility and abdominal strength in boys and girls (5% to 18%). However, for other motor tasks, age, stature, and weight accounted for greater percentages of the variance in performances of boys (33% to 61%) than of girls (18% to 36%). These motor tasks included pull-ups in boys, flexed-arm hang in girls, standing long jump, shuttle run, 50-yard dash, softball throw for distance, and 600-yard run. The results emphasize the need to consider other anthropometric dimensions and perhaps behavioral and cultural variables in explaining variation in performance, especially in the case of girls.

Data on the relationship between other anthropometric dimensions, except skinfold thicknesses, and performance are rather limited. The trends in the available data are similar to those for height and weight. For example, correlations between leg length and performance on a variety of motor tasks range from −0.10 to +0.39 for individuals 6 years of age to young adulthood. These values are similar to those for stature. On the other hand, limb circumferences correlate with strength approximately at the same moderate magnitude as body weight, 0.40 to 0.60 (Malina 1975).

Body dimensions are related to age, height, and weight. A question of interest is the contribution of specific body dimensions to strength and motor performance after the effects of age, height, and weight are statistically controlled. Results of several such analyses in children from different health and nutritional backgrounds indicate that few variables add significantly to describing variation in strength and motor performance after age, stature, and weight are statistically controlled. Subcutaneous fatness (see section on body composition), however, tends to exert a negative influence on performance (Malina and Buschang 1985; Malina 1994; Benefice et al. 1999). Age and body size therefore appear to be primary factors influencing the strength and motor performance of children. Data for adolescents are a bit more complicated because individual differences in biological maturity associated with the adolescent growth spurt and sexual maturation must be taken into account (see chapter 17).

Physique

Studies relating physique to performance have generally focused on individual components of somatotype and do not control for variation in the other two components. This approach is thus only suggestive of relationships with performance because the three components of an individual's somatotype are related.

Correlations between somatotype components and performance tasks are variable. Those between endomorphy and performances requiring projection or movement of the body through space are consistently negative but low to moderate in magnitude in all age groups and in both sexes. These tasks include the standing long jump, vertical jump, dashes, and pull-ups. The excess fatness associated with endomorphy represents dead weight, which must be projected or moved, and thus presents a mechanical disadvantage. In contrast, endomorphy is positively related to measures of static strength, which emphasizes the importance of overall body size in static strength tests.

Mesomorphy contributes variably to motor performance. Correlations tend to be positive and low in both sexes from childhood into young adulthood. On the other hand, correlations for static strength are moderate in adolescent and young adult males. Data for adolescent females are lacking, but in young adult women, correlations between mesomorphy and strength are low.

Ectomorphy is not consistently related to motor performance during childhood but tends to be negatively related to strength and power tasks in adolescent and adult males. The low negative correlations for strength tasks emphasize the strength deficiency associated with extreme ectomorphy. Ectomorphy is apparently not a significant factor in performances of young adult women.

Overall, correlations between components of somatotype and strength and motor performance tend to be low to moderate in magnitude (Malina 1975, 1994). They rarely exceed 0.5; hence, explained variances are low and have limited predictive utility. Thus, one can infer that there is more to performance than physique. However, the situation may be somewhat different at the extremes of physique. Extreme ectomorphs tend to be deficient in muscle mass and strength, whereas extreme endomorphs have excess fat, which has negative consequences for performance. Young athletes in several sports have somatotypes that may approach the extremes. This condition is especially true for mesomorphy in sports such as gymnastics, and elite young gymnasts are indeed excellent performers of the strength and motor tasks specific to the sport.

Body Composition

A major component of fat-free mass (FFM) is skeletal muscle, the major work-performing tissue of the body. One would thus expect positive associations between FFM and performance. Absolute FFM is particularly related to static strength as might be expected from the association between strength and the cross-sectional area of a muscle. It is also important in performances that require force to be exerted against an object, such as throwing a ball, putting a shot, or weight lifting. In both strength and object-projection tasks, a large FFM is important. On the other hand, a large FFM can be a limiting factor in tasks in which the body must be projected, as in a vertical jump, or moved across space, as in a run.

Relationships between FFM and motor performance vary with age. Among 7-year-old to 12-year-old boys, for example, both absolute FFM and FFM as a percentage of body mass are moderately related to about the same extent to performances in the 50-yard dash, the standing long jump, and the vertical jump. At these preadolescent or early adolescent ages, absolute FFM is more closely related to distance throwing performance than relative FFM, indicating the role of absolute body size. Data for 7-year-old to 12-year-old girls are generally consistent with those for boys. Absolute FFM has a moderate relationship to performance in the 50-yard dash, the standing long jump, and the vertical jump, and the relationship for relative fatness is low but negative (Slaughter et al. 1977, 1980).

FFM is significantly related to strength during male adolescence. When age, stature, and weight are statistically controlled, the correlation between FFM and strength is moderate. Data relating FFM to strength of adolescent and young adult females are lacking.

In contrast to FFM, fatness generally has a negative influence on performance. From a mechanical perspective, excess fat represents an inert load (dead weight) that must be moved. Correlations between fatness, which is most often measured as skinfold thicknesses and occasionally as percent body fat and motor performance, are consistently negative and low to moderate during childhood and adolescence and in young adulthood. The negative relationship is more apparent in those events requiring the projection (jumps), rapid movement (dashes, shuttle runs), and lifting (leg lifts) of the body and the support of the body off the ground (flexed-arm hang). On the other hand, skinfold thicknesses are essentially unrelated or positively related to performance tasks involving projection or balance of an object (distance throw or stick balance), speed of arm movement (plate tapping), and flexibility of the lower back (sit-and-reach). In contrast to motor performance items, correlations between skinfold thicknesses and measures of static strength are generally positive. The positive relationship reflects the larger body size of fatter children (Beunen et al. 1983; Malina et al. 1995). Relationships between relative fat distribution and the strength and motor performances of children and adolescents have not been systematically addressed.

Overview

Although size, physique, and body composition account for a substantial portion of variation in performance, a considerable amount is not accounted for by these morphological variables. Strength and motor performance are also influenced by motivational factors, opportunity for practice, exposure to appropriate instruction, and perhaps others in the cultural environment. Habitual physical activity is an additional factor. Presently available studies tend to treat these types of factors in isolation. There is a need to include such variables in multivariate analyses of factors that influence strength and motor performance. These variables may be especially relevant in the context of examining sex differences in performance. For example, among 5-year-old children, only anthropometric variables predicted the throwing performance of boys, whereas a combination of anthropometric and family environmental variables predicted throwing performance of girls (Nelson et al. 1986).

Scaling of Strength and Motor Performance

The size, shape, and proportions of the body influence strength and motor performance.

How should performance be compared among individuals of the same age who differ in body size? The biological principle of scaling is central to this question (see chapter 3).

Dimensionality Scaling of Strength

According to dimensionality theory, the cross-sectional area of body segments will be proportional to length or height squared (h^2). Because strength of a muscle is proportional to its cross-sectional area, muscle strength should be scaled to h^2. An underlying assumption of dimensionality theory is that body proportions, or the relationships among body segments, do not change from middle childhood to adulthood. This assumption, of course, is not tenable given the major changes in, for example, the ratio of sitting height to standing height ratio during growth and the differential timing of growth spurts in specific body segments and tissues during adolescence (see chapter 15).

Nevertheless, dimensionality scaling has been applied to a cross-sectional sample of Danish children 6 to 16 years of age (Asmussen and Heeboll-Nielsen 1955; Asmussen 1973). Several measures of muscular strength were expressed relative to height. Only elbow flexor strength approximated the expected proportional increase to h^2. All other measures of strength—grip, back, abdominal, hip, and knee extension—increased with height greater than the expected h^2. These results have been confirmed in other studies (Carron and Bailey 1974; Parker et al. 1990; Kanehisa et al. 1995; Froberg and Lammert 1996). Strength increases more than predicted by dimensionality theory before adolescence, more than predicted during male adolescence, and less than predicted during female adolescence. These results suggest that improvements in muscular strength with growth and maturation are related to factors other than changes in segment length and muscle mass. Change in the central nervous system (e.g., neuromuscular maturation and enhanced recruitment and expression of motor units that control specific muscle groups) and biochemical changes in muscle tissue are such factors (see chapter 7). Hormonal changes during the adolescent growth spurt and puberty are additional factors (see chapter 19). Age per se is also a potentially confounding factor; older children are stronger than younger children of the same height.

Dimensionality Scaling of Motor Performance

Dimensionality theory was also applied to several measures of performance in the sample of Danish children described earlier in the chapter. Performance in the vertical jump (power), a dash (acceleration in the first 6 meters), and horizontal running on a treadmill (speed) was related to height. All performance items increased greater than predicted from h^2. Performances also increased with age independent of height, that is, older children performed better than younger children of the same height. The age effect may reflect neuromuscular maturation. The trend for boys, but not girls, also suggested an independent effect of the adolescent growth spurt and sexual maturation. Note, however, the data are cross-sectional, so it is difficult to infer changes associated with the adolescent growth spurt. Further, strength and power tasks tend to reach their maximal velocities of growth after maximum growth in height during the adolescent growth spurt (this is discussed in more detail in chapter 16). Other than the previously mentioned dimensionality analysis for Danish children, information on the scaling of motor performance is limited.

Tracking

Tracking refers to the tendency for an individual to maintain the same relative position within an age and sex group over a period of time. In other words, if a child is the fastest runner in the group at 7 years of age, is the child the fastest runner at 12 years of age? Tracking is ordinarily estimated by correlating attained levels of strength and motor performance for a given child at one age with levels of strength and performance of the same child at another age. Longitudinal data are thus necessary to estimate stability.

Longitudinal data for measures of strength and motor performance through childhood and ado-

TABLE 11.1	Interage Correlations for Several Measures of Muscular Strength		
Test/sample	Span (yr)	Males	Females
Grip			
U.S., Iowa	9–10/15–16	0.65	0.45
U.S., California	11–17	0.60	0.62
U.S., Oregon	7–12	0.40	
	12–17	0.34	
Poland	7–14	0.44	0.35
Arm pull			
Belgium	12–17	0.56	
	12–15	0.55	
Composite Measures			
U.S., California—4 upper body tests	9–18	0.63	0.57
U.S., Wisconsin—4 upper body tests	7–12	0.35	0.26
	7–17	0.34	0.35
	12–17	0.60	0.29
U.S., Wisconsin—4 lower body tests	7–12	0.40	0.52
	7–17	0.33	0.46
	12–17	0.61	0.57
U.S., Oregon—3 lower body tests	7–12	0.45	
	12–17	0.34	
U.S., Oregon—total body: 11 tests	7–12	0.72	
	12–17	0.43	
Canada, Saskatchewan—4 upper body tests	10–16	0.51	
Canada, Saskatchewan—2 lower body tests	10–16	0.59	
Canada, Saskatchewan—total: 6 tests	10–16	0.63	

Adapted from Malina (1996), which contains the references to the specific studies.

lescence and into young adulthood are limited. Moreover, the intervals over which measures of strength and motor performance are observed tend to vary among studies. In the subsequent discussion, only studies that report interage correlations across 3 or more years are considered. Correlations between adjacent years tend to be moderate to moderately high.

Strength

Interage correlations during childhood and adolescence for muscular strength are summarized in table 11.1. Most of the data span the adolescent years. Correlations range from low to moderately high, and sex differences are not consistent. Lower extremity strength tends to be more stable than upper extremity strength, which may be related to the weight-bearing and locomotor functions of the lower extremities. Interage correlations for indicators of functional strength—flexed-arm hang, sit-ups, and leg lifts—are generally similar to those for a variety of static strength tests (see table 11.2).

TABLE 11.2	Interage Correlations for Several Measures of Upper Body and Abdominal Muscular Strength and Endurance, and Lower Back Flexibility		
Test/sample	**Span (yr)**	**Males**	**Females**
Flexed-arm hang			
Belgium	12–17	0.57	
Canada, Saskatchewan	10–16	0.54	
U.S., Michigan	5–10	0.34	0.24
	8–14	0.52	0.44
Belgium	12–15	0.65	
Leg lifts			
Belgium	12–17	0.33	
Belgium	12–15	0.55	
Sit-ups			
Canada, Saskatchewan	10–16	0.40	
Sit-and-reach			
U.S., Michigan	5–10	0.36	0.26
	8–14	0.52	0.52
Belgium	12–15	0.72	
	12–17	0.57	

Adapted from Malina (1996), which contains the references to the specific studies.

Flexibility

Interage correlations for the sit-and-reach test are low to moderate in both sexes during childhood (see table 11.2). They are slightly higher in adolescent boys. Corresponding data for adolescent girls are not available.

Motor Performance

Interage correlations during childhood and adolescence for several measures of motor performance are summarized in table 11.3. Correlations for tests of jumping and running speed and agility are variable among studies. They vary with the interval considered and range from low to moderately high. Some of the instability in the correlations spanning ages between 5 and 10 years probably reflects variation in attainment of mature movement patterns. Similarly, instability during adolescence may reflect individuality in the timing and tempo of the adolescent growth spurt, including spurts in performance.

Adolescence to Adulthood

There is increasing interest in the tracking of strength and motor performance from adolescence into adulthood. Presently, data are limited. Results of studies of Belgian males and Dutch males and females are summarized in tables 11.4 and 11.5. Results are reasonably consistent between studies. Interage correlations for intervals spanning early adolescence (13 years of age) and adulthood tend to be lower than correlations spanning late adolescence (16 to 18 years of age) and adulthood. The correlations tend to be moderate and in some cases moderately high, and correlations for the longer interval (13 to 27 and 13 to 30 years of age) tend to be lower.

Comparisons with Measures of Growth

Interage correlations for tests of strength and motor performance are lower than those for stature, weight, physique, and fat-free mass summarized in earlier chapters but are similar to those for fat measurements. Interage correlations are influenced by a variety of factors, the most important being the interval between observations. Individual variation in the rate of growth in measures of strength and performance is another factor. The interaction and interdependence of growth and maturation with strength and performance are additional concerns. Changes in the relative positions of individuals within a group

TABLE 11.3 Interage Correlations for Several Measures of Motor Performance			
Reference	Span (yr)	Males	Females
Standing long jump			
U.S., California	6–9	0.60	0.70
	8–11	0.73	0.59
U.S., Michigan	5–10	0.46	0.38
	8–14	0.62	0.54
U.S., Wisconsin	6–12		0.74
	7–12	0.48	0.71
	7–17	0.60	0.50
	12–17	0.73	0.66
Canada, Saskatchewan	10–16	0.34	
Belgium	12–15	0.76	
U.S., California	13–16	0.72	0.68
Vertical jump			
U.S., Michigan	5–10	0.43	0.31
	8–14	0.48	0.45
Belgium	12–15	0.87	
U.S., California	13–16	0.48	
Belgium	12–17	0.61	
Dashes			
U.S., Michigan	5–10	0.52	0.16
	8–14	0.46	0.44
U.S., Wisconsin	6–12		0.70
	7–12	0.39	0.92
	7–17	0.18	0.56
	12–17	0.52	0.70
Belgium	12–15	0.58	
U.S., California	13–16	0.49	
Agility shuttle runs			
U.S., Michigan	5–10	0.24	0.46
	8–14	0.70	0.53
Belgium	12–15	0.34	
	12–17	0.43	

Adapted from Malina (1996), which contains the references to the specific studies.

TABLE 11.4 Interage Correlations for Strength and Motor Performance Between Adolescence and 30 Years of Age in Belgian Males (n = 173)	Intervals (years)	
	13–30	18–30
Arm pull	0.33	0.66
Flexed-arm hang	0.46	0.55
Leg lifts	0.44	0.53
Sit-and-reach	0.68	0.82
Vertical jump	0.52	0.69
Shuttle run	0.45	0.52

Adapted from Beunen et al. (1992).

TABLE 11.5 Interage Correlations for Strength and Motor Performance Between Adolescence and Adulthood in Dutch Males and Females	Intervals (years)			
	13–21/16–27		13–27	
	Males	Females	Males	Females
Arm pull/ weight	0.79	0.76	0.75	0.66
Flexed-arm hang	0.59	0.62	0.55	0.64
Leg lifts	0.51	0.61	0.46	0.51
Sit-and-reach	0.43	0.59	0.26	0.58
Vertical jump	0.50	0.55	0.43	0.42
Shuttle run	0.41	0.61	0.40	0.41

n = 84 males and 98 females at age 27 years; correlations between 13–21 and 16–27 years of age are averages for the two intervals.

Adapted from van Mechelen and Kemper (1995).

might, therefore, be expected, especially during adolescence. Given the moderate stability of strength and motor performance across the years spanning childhood and adolescence, predicting performance at later ages from performance at younger ages is difficult.

Although there is a significant genotypic component to strength and motor performance (see chapter 18), a variety of factors can influence strength and motor performance during childhood and adolescence, in particular opportunities for instruction and practice and systematic training. The responses of strength and motor skills to specific instruction and training are considered in chapter 22.

Summary

The period between 5 and 8 years of age appears to be one of transition in the development of strength and motor performance. Basic motor skills reach mature form at these ages, but there is considerable variation among children. Children show considerable increase in performance of some skills between 5 and 8 years of age (running speed and the shuttle run) but show a steady, more gradual increase in performance of other skills from 5 years of age through childhood (jumping, throwing, and strength). Performances of girls, on average, on a variety of tasks (dash, standing long jump, vertical jump, shuttle run, and others) improve more or less linearly from 6 to about 14 years of age, followed by a slight increase in some tasks or a plateau in others. There is much overlap between the sexes during childhood. During adolescence, in contrast, performances of boys, on average, show a marked improvement, so sex differences are magnified. Age, height, weight, physique, and body composition account for a substantial portion of variation in performance during childhood and adolescence, but a considerable amount is not accounted for by these variables. Factors not related to growth status that may contribute to the variation in performance include motivation, opportunity for practice and instruction, learning, habitual physical activity, and perhaps others in the cultural environment. The stability or tracking of indicators of strength and motor performance is less than estimates for body size, physique, and fat-free mass.

Sources and Suggested Readings

American Alliance for Health, Physical Education, Recreation and Dance (1984) Technical Manual, Health Related Physical Fitness. Reston, VA: AAHPERD.

American Association for Health, Physical Education, and Recreation (1976) Youth Fitness Test Manual, revised edition. Reston, VA: AAHPER.

Asmussen E (1973) Growth in muscular strength and power. In GL Rarick (ed), Physical Activity, Human Growth and Development. New York: Academic Press, pp 60-79.

Asmussen E, Heeboll-Nielsen K (1955) A dimensional analysis of physical performance and growth in boys. Journal of Applied Physiology 7:593-603.

Batterham AM, George KP (1997) Allometric modelling does not determine a dimensionless power function ratio for maximal muscular function. Journal of Applied Physiology 83:2158-2166.

Benefice E, Fouere R, Malina RM (1999) Early nutritional history and motor performance of Senegalese children 4–6 years of age. Annals of Human Biology 26:443-455.

* Beunen G (1996) Physical growth, maturation and performance. In R Eston, T Reilly (eds), Kinanthropometry and Exercise Physiology Laboratory Manual. London: E & FN Spon, pp 51-71.

Beunen G, Claessens A, Ostyn M, Renson R, Simons J, Van Gerven D (1985) Motor performance as related to somatotype in adolescent boys. In R Binkhorst, HCG Kemper, WHM Saris (eds), Children and Exercise IX. Champaign, IL: Human Kinetics, pp 279-284.

Beunen G, Lefevre J, Claessens AL, Lysens R, Maes H, Renson R, Simons J, Vanden Eynde B, Vanreusel B, Van Den Bossche C (1992) Age-specific correlation analysis of longitudinal physical fitness levels in men. European Journal of Applied Physiology 64:538-545.

* Beunen G, Malina RM (1988) Growth and physical performance relative to the timing of the adolescent spurt. Exercise and Sport Sciences Reviews 16:503-540.

Beunen G, Malina RM, Ostyn M, Renson R, Simons J, Van Gerven D (1983) Fatness, growth and motor fitness of Belgian boys 12 through 20 years of age. Human Biology 55:599-613.

Beunen G, Malina RM, Van't Hof M, Simons J, Ostyn M, Renson R, Van Gerven D (1988) Adolescent Growth and Motor Performance: A Longitudinal Study of Belgian Boys. Champaign, IL: Human Kinetics.

Beunen G, Ostyn M, Renson R, Simons J, Van Gerven D (1976) Skeletal maturation and physical fitness of girls aged 12 through 16. Hermes (Leuven) 10:445-457.

Beunen G, Ostyn M, Renson R, Simons J, Van Gerven D (1984) Anthropometric correlates of strength and motor performance in Belgian boys 12 through 18 years of age. In J Borms, R Hauspie, A Sand, C Susanne, M Hebbelinck (eds), Human Growth and Development. New York: Plenum, pp 503-509.

Bouchard C, Shephard RJ (1994) Physical activity, fitness, and health: The model and key concepts. In C Bouchard, RJ Shephard, T Stephens (eds), Physical Activity, Fitness, and Health. Champaign, IL: Human Kinetics, pp 77-88.

* Branta C, Haubenstricker J, Seefeldt V (1984) Age changes in motor skills during childhood and adolescence. Exercise and Sport Sciences Reviews 12:467-520.

Carron A, Bailey DA (1974) Strength development in boys from 10 through 16 years. Monographs of the Society for Research in Child Development, serial no. 157.

Clarke HH (1971) Basic understanding of physical fitness. Physical Fitness Research Digest, Series 1, No. 1.

Cron GW, Pronko NH (1957) Development of the sense of balance in school children. Journal of Educational Research 51:33-37.

Ellis JD, Carron AV, Bailey DA (1975) Physical performance in boys from 10 through 16 years. Human Biology 47:263-281.

Espenschade A (1940) Motor performance in adolescence, including the study of relationships with measures of physical growth and maturity. Monographs of the Society for Research in Child Development, serial no. 24.

Espenschade A (1960) Motor development. In WR Johnson (ed), Science and Medicine of Exercise and Sports. New York: Harper, pp 419-439.

Espenschade A, Dable RR, Schoendube R (1953) Dynamic balance in adolescent boys. Research Quarterly 24:270-275.

Froberg K, Lammert O (1996) Development of muscle strength during childhood. In O Bar-Or (ed), The Child and Adolescent Athlete. Oxford: Blackwell Science, pp 25-41.

Golomer E, Dupui P, Monod H (1997) Sex-linked differences in equilibrium reactions among adolescents performing complex sensorimotor tasks. Journal of Physiology (Paris) 91:49-55.

* Haubenstricker J, Seefeldt V (1986) Acquisition of motor skills during childhood. In V Seefeldt (ed), Physical Activity and Well-Being. Reston, VA: American Alliance for Health, Physical Education, Recreation and Dance, pp 41-102.

Jones HE (1949) Motor Performance and Growth. A Developmental Study of Static Dynamometric Strength. Berkeley: University of California Press.

Kanehisa H, Ikegawa S, Tsunoda N, Fukunaga T (1995) Strength and cross-sectional areas of reciprocal muscle groups in the upper arm and thigh during adolescence. International Journal of Sports Medicine 16:54-60.

Katzmarzyk PT, Malina RM, Song TMK, Bouchard C (1998) Physical activity and health-related fitness in youth: A multivariate analysis. Medicine and Science in Sports and Exercise 30:709-714.

Keogh J (1965) Motor Performance of Elementary School Children. Los Angeles: Department of Physical Education, University of California.

* Keogh J, Sugden D (1985) Motor Skill Development. New York: Macmillan.

Krogman WM (1971) The Manual and Oral Strengths of American White and Negro Children, Ages 3-6 Years. Philadelphia: Philadelphia Center for Research in Child Growth.

Lin J-P, Brown JK, Walsh EG (1994) Physiological maturation of muscles in childhood. Lancet 343:1386-1389.

Malina RM (1975) Anthropometric correlates of strength and motor performance. Exercise and Sport Sciences Reviews 3:249-274.

Malina RM (1991) Fitness and performance: Adult health and the culture of youth. In RJ Parks, HM Eckert (eds), New Pos-

sibilities, New Paradigms? (American Academy of Physical Education Papers No. 24), Champaign, IL: Human Kinetics, pp 30-38.

Malina RM (1992) Physique and body composition: Effects of performance and effects of training, semistarvation, and overtraining. In KD Brownell, J Rodin, JH Wilmore (eds), Eating, Body Weight and Performance in Athletes: Disorders of Modern Society. Philadelphia: Lea & Febiger, pp 94-111.

* Malina RM (1994) Anthropometry, strength and motor fitness. In SJ Ulijaszek, CGN Mascie-Taylor (eds), Anthropometry: The Individual and the Population. Cambridge: Cambridge University Press, pp 160-177.

Malina RM (1995) Physical activity and fitness of children and youth: Questions and implications. Medicine, Exercise, Nutrition, and Health 4:123-135.

* Malina RM (1996) Tracking of physical activity and physical fitness across the lifespan. Research Quarterly for Exercise and Sport 67 (suppl 3):48-57.

Malina RM, Buschang PH (1985) Growth, strength and motor performance of Zapotec children, Oaxaca, Mexico. Human Biology 57:163-181.

Malina RM, Moriyama M (1991) Growth and motor performance of Black and White children 6-10 years of age: A multivariate analysis. American Journal of Human Biology 3:599-611.

Malina RM, Roche AF (1983) Manual of Physical Status and Performance in Childhood. Volume 2. Physical Performance. New York: Plenum.

Merni F, Balboni M, Bargellini S, Menegatti G (1981) Differences in males and females in joint movement range during growth. Medicine and Sport 15:168-175.

Mizuno T, Ebashi S, Yamaji K (1973) Longitudinal study on the physique and physical performance of Japanese adolescents (12-18 years, boys and girls). Bulletin of the Faculty of Education of the University of Tokyo 13:219-235.

Montoye HJ, Frantz ME, Kozar AJ (1972) The value of age, height and weight in establishing standards of fitness for children. Journal of Sports Medicine and Physical Fitness 12:174-179.

Morris AM, Williams JM, Atwater AE, Wilmore JH (1982) Age and sex differences in motor performance of 3 through 6 year old children. Research Quarterly for Exercise and Sport 53:214-221.

Nelson JK, Thomas JR, Nelson KR, Abraham PC (1986) Gender differences in children's throwing performance: Biology and environment. Research Quarterly for Exercise and Sport 57:280-287.

Ostyn M, Simons J, Beunen G, Renson R, Van Gerven D (1980) Somatic and Motor Development of Belgian Secondary School Boys. Leuven: Catholic University of Leuven Press.

Parker DF, Round JM, Sacco P, Jones DA (1990) A cross-sectional survey of upper and lower limb strength in boys and girls during childhood and adolescence. Annals of Human Biology 17:199-211.

* Rarick GL (1973) Stability and change in motor abilities. In GL Rarick (ed), Physical Activity: Human Growth and Development. New York: Academic Press, pp 201-224.

Rarick GL, Oyster N (1964) Physical maturity, muscular strength, and motor performance of young school-age boys. Research Quarterly 35: 523-531.

Rarick GL, Smoll FL (1967) Stability of growth in strength and motor performance from childhood to adolescence. Human Biology 39:295-306.

Seger JY, Thorstensson A (2000) Muscle strength and electromyogram in boys and girls followed through puberty. European Journal of Applied Physiology 81:54-61.

Seils LG (1951) The relationship between measures of physical growth and gross motor performance of primary-grade school children. Research Quarterly 22:244-260.

Simons J, Beunen GP, Renson R, Claessens ALM, Vanreusel B, Lefevre J, editors (1990) Growth and Fitness of Flemish Girls: The Leuven Growth Study. Champaign, IL: Human Kinetics.

Slaughter MH, Lohman TG, Misner JE (1977) Relationship of somatotype and body composition to physical performance in 7- to 12-year old boys. Research Quarterly 48:159-168.

Slaughter MH, Lohman TG, Misner JE (1980) Association of somatotype and body composition to physical performance in 7–12 year-old girls. Journal of Sports Medicine and Physical Fitness 20:189-198.

Thomas JR, French KE (1985) Gender differences across age in motor performance: A meta-analysis. Psychological Bulletin 98:260-282.

van Mechelen W, Kemper HCG (1995) Habitual physical activity in longitudinal perspective. In HCG Kemper (ed), The Amsterdam Growth Study: A Longitudinal Analysis of Health, Fitness, and Lifestyle. Champaign, IL: Human Kinetics, pp 135-158.

12

AEROBIC PERFORMANCE

Chapter Outline

The two major foci of this chapter are (1) the ability of the growing individual to perform under predominantly aerobic conditions and (2) age-related and sex-related changes in adaptations to submaximal and maximal exercise. The determinants of aerobic performance during growth are considered in terms of changes in the cardiovascular and pulmonary systems and in skeletal muscle and substrate utilization. The effects of regular training on aerobic performance and on the oxygen transport system are discussed in chapter 22, and the effects of environmental temperature on aerobic performance are considered in chapter 14.

Some inconsistencies in definitions of terms used regarding maximal levels of aerobic exercise have occurred. Maximal aerobic power refers to the highest amount of chemical energy that can be transformed in the aerobic machinery of muscle mitochondria per unit time (generally per minute). Aerobic capacity denotes the total chemical energy available to perform aerobic work. Ideally, both maximal power

and capacity should be considered. However, although maximal aerobic power can be measured as maximal O_2 uptake ($\dot{V}O_2max$), no single index of aerobic capacity is accepted. Surrogate variables such as endurance performance, time to exhaustion, or biochemical indicators of the capacity for prolonged work are often used to estimate aerobic capacity. These indices are particularly hard to assess in children, mostly for ethical reasons. The focus of this chapter is maximal aerobic power.

Estimates of aerobic exercise performance that are not also influenced by anaerobic energy production are rarely possible to obtain. However, when exercise is of low to moderate intensity, or when it lasts for 8 to 10 minutes and more, the contribution of nonoxidative pathways to the energy needs of the working organism is quite small. Given these limitations, as well as others that will become apparent in the subsequent discussion, changes in the characteristics of aerobic exercise that occur during growth are reasonably well understood.

Measurement Issues

Because a test of maximal aerobic power requires an "all-out" effort, it is very important to obtain full cooperation from the young subject. Getting the child's cooperation requires explanation of the nature of the test and its objectives (using age-appropriate terms), habituation to the protocol and the equipment, and encouragement during the test itself, particularly during the last 2 to 3 minutes. With this approach, maximal effort can be elicited from most children 8 years of age and older. Obtaining an "all-out" performance from younger children is possible but more challenging, especially if the test lasts more than 6 to 8 minutes, requires the child to follow a fixed cadence of work, and uses excessive increments of work rate. The measurement of the aerobic performance of children and adolescents is central to understanding changes with growth and maturation. The subsequent sections consider several issues that must be emphasized when measuring the aerobic performance of children and adolescents.

Choice of Ergometers and Protocols

Several principles regarding the testing of aerobic performance in children and adolescents are discussed subsequently. More detailed descriptions of aerobic testing protocols are described in Bar-Or (1983) and Rowland (1996).

As a general rule, children can use the same ergometers commonly used for adolescents and adults. However, several factors related to a child's anthropometric characteristics and level of cognitive development must be considered. Although cycle ergometers are often used for children, regular adult ergometers may be unsuitable for children younger than 8 to 9 years of age and need to be modified. One modification is to allow the seat to be positioned closer to the pedals because of the child's shorter legs. In addition, the pedal shaft should be shortened so that the circumference of a pedal revolution will fit the shorter legs of a child. A musical metronome is often used with adults to obtain a constant pedaling cadence on a mechanical cycle ergometer. Young children may have difficulty following a metronome, so pacing done through visual rather than auditory cues may be easier for them.

Walking or running on a treadmill utilizes a larger muscle mass than does pedaling on a cycle ergometer. In the latter, the brunt of the effort is performed by the knee extensors. This distinc-

tion is important because the muscle mass of children's legs, when related to total-body mass, is smaller than in adults (Doré et al. 2000; Ishii et al. 1983). As a result, the highest $\dot{V}O_2$ on a cycle ergometer is, on average, about 10% lower than on a treadmill (Turley et al. 1995), where more muscle groups share the effort. The highest $\dot{V}O_2$ obtained on a cycle ergometer is, therefore, different from that obtained on a treadmill or any other exercise machine. For example, when arm cranking is used to measure maximal aerobic power, the highest $\dot{V}O_2$ is usually only 60% to 70% of that achieved through pedaling, which further shows the importance of muscle mass in eliciting the highest $\dot{V}O_2$.

Many laboratories use a treadmill for children younger than 10 years of age. Children, even those as young as 5 to 6 years of age, can master the technique of treadmill walking or running with 3 to 5 minutes of practice. Some children, however, may need several trials until they are fully habituated to treadmill walking or running (Frost et al. 1995). A disadvantage of the treadmill is the risk of tripping, whereas cycle ergometry is very safe. Treadmill testing thus requires an additional laboratory technician whose main role is to "spot" the subject. Another disadvantage of the treadmill is that some children may terminate the test prematurely because of fear of falling.

To accommodate the relatively short attention span of children and to prevent premature local muscle fatigue, tests of maximal aerobic power in children should not exceed 8 to 10 minutes. Therefore, the initial work rate and the subsequent increments in work rate must be carefully planned.

How can maximal aerobic power be measured in the absence of a metabolic cart? One alternative is to use an "all-out" incremental protocol on a cycle ergometer and to document the highest mechanical power (e.g., in Watt units) that the subject can sustain during the final stage (Bar-Or 1983). Another approach is to conduct a submaximal test and predict maximal performance, usually from submaximal heart rate. However, prediction methods based on submaximal intensities are useful for the assessment of fitness in groups of subjects, but they have a low validity in predicting performance of an individual (Åstrand and Rhyming 1954).

Another measure of aerobic performance is the anaerobic threshold (AT). According to certain testing protocols, the AT is reached when blood lactate concentration starts to accelerate during an incremental test. Other protocols define the threshold as the point at which minute ventilation ($\dot{V}O_2$) increases disproportionately to the increase in $\dot{V}O_2$ or in $\dot{V}CO_2$ (ventilatory anaerobic threshold = VAT) (Mahon et al. 1989). Although scientists still debate the actual metabolic events that are reflected by the anaerobic threshold, most agree that either AT or VAT can serve as an indicator of aerobic performance (Washington 1993). It is also a popular marker for gauging exercise intensity during aerobic training (Rotstein et al. 1986). One advantage of the AT or VAT is that they do not require an "all-out" effort. This advantage makes them attractive for use with children, particularly the VAT, which does not require blood samples. However, correlation of these thresholds with $\dot{V}O_2$max of children have ranged from very low to very high. Such inconsistency may reflect the different methods used to determine when a threshold actually occurs and intraobserver and interobserver variation.

Criteria for Achieving Maximum O_2 Uptake

Several criteria have been used to determine when a young adult subject has achieved $\dot{V}O_2$max. These criteria include a heart rate of 220 beats/min minus age in years, a respiratory exchange ratio (RER = $\dot{V}CO_2/\dot{V}O_2$) of 1.05 or higher, and a plateau (i.e., an increase of not more than 2 ml/kg·min) in $\dot{V}O_2$ despite an increase in work rate. Whereas children often achieve the HR and RER criteria, only 40% to 50% of them achieve a plateau in $\dot{V}O_2$ (Åstrand 1952). Studies have shown that children and adolescents who reach a plateau do not have a higher $\dot{V}O_2$ than those who do not (Åstrand 1952; Rivera-Brown et al. 1998). Thus, a "maximal" effort can be reasonably assumed, even without a plateau, if the child perseveres but can no longer follow the required cadence or speed, despite continuous encouragement by the investigator.

Reliability of Measurements

The reliability of measurements of maximal aerobic power in children 10 years of age or older is similar to that found in adolescents and adults but is somewhat lower in younger children. For example, coefficients of variation for repeated tests of $\dot{V}O_2$max in adolescents are about 4% to 5%. Test-retest correlation coefficients for children 10 years of age or older are usually 0.85 to 0.95. These estimates are an indication of intraindividual variation that is comparable to that seen in fully mature persons (Cunningham et al. 1977; Turley et al. 1995).

Measuring Mechanical Efficiency and Economy of Movement

The concepts of mechanical efficiency and, especially, economy of movement are important to understanding changes in aerobic performance that occur during growth. Mechanical efficiency (ME) is the ratio of mechanical work output produced by the exercising muscles and the chemical energy that is utilized to generate that work. When the activity is done during a known period of time, one can use power, rather than work units. Determination of chemical energy is based on measurement of $\dot{V}O_2$, where 1 L of oxygen reflects metabolic energy expenditure of approximately 5 kcal (21 kJ). This number varies, depending on the relative utilization of carbohydrates and fats as a source of energy. It is 4.7 for fat and 5.05 for carbohydrates. A $\dot{V}O_2$ measured during exercise not only includes the O_2 uptake required for the activity but also includes the resting metabolic rate (RMR). To obtain a valid indicator of the metabolic expenditure of the activity itself, RMR should be subtracted from the gross $\dot{V}O_2$ measured during exercise. The resulting difference has been termed net $\dot{V}O_2$.

By converting the numerator and the denominator to the same power units (e.g., Watts or kcal/min), a nondimensional ratio for ME is obtained. When multiplied by 100, ME can be presented as a percentage:

$$ME (\%) = \text{mechanical power}/(\text{metabolic power} - RMR)\ 100$$

ME of exercising humans, when measured at a steady state, is approximately 20% to 25%. It varies among individuals, mostly because of differences in RMR but also because of differences in the metabolic cost of performing specific mechanical tasks (Frost et al. 1997).

The main challenge in measuring ME is to determine the actual mechanical power produced. Whereas this determination is feasible with a well-calibrated cycle ergometer (assuming the power loss between the pedals and flywheel is known), it is much harder to make during walking or running on a treadmill, stepping up and down a step or a ladder, or during swimming. An alternative approach is, therefore, to use economy of movement instead of mechanical efficiency.

The numerator in the economy of movement equation is a quantitative value of the task performed, rather than mechanical work or power. On the treadmill or in the pool, for example, this value can be speed in meters per second.

As a result, economy of movement cannot be expressed as a ratio or as a percentage. Nevertheless, economy of movement can be compared among individuals or in the same individual over time. Changes associated with growth influence the economy of movement. This topic is considered later in the chapter.

Growth-Related Adaptations in Aerobic Performance

Several issues related to aerobic exercise in children and adolescents are considered subsequently. Recall that changes in overall body size, proportions, and composition, as well as in motor skill, occur concurrently.

Cardiovascular Responses During Aerobic Exercise

To understand the contribution of cardiovascular variables to the increase in $\dot{V}O_2$ during exercise, familiarity with the Fick principle is essential. The principle is summarized by the following equation:

$$\dot{V}O_2 = \dot{Q}\,(CaO_2 - C\bar{v}O_2)$$

where $\dot{V}O_2$ is O_2 uptake (ml O_2/min), $\dot{Q}$ is cardiac output (L blood/min), and CaO_2 and $C\bar{v}O_2$ are the content of oxygen in the arterial and mixed venous blood, respectively (ml O_2/L blood). Because cardiac output equals the product of heart rate (HR) and stroke volume (SV), the equation can be rewritten:

$$\dot{V}O_2 = HR \times SV\,(CaO_2 - C\bar{v}O_2)$$

Dimensions of the heart enlarge with age in a manner concomitant with growth in body mass (see chapter 9). The increase in size of the heart muscle is associated with an increase in stroke volume during growth when exercise is performed at the same absolute power output. Even though heart rate declines during growth, the product of heart rate and stroke volume (i.e., cardiac output) increases. At younger ages, the increase in $\dot{V}O_2$ during exercise is met by a higher arteriovenous difference in oxygen content (i.e., more oxygen is extracted from the blood at the same level of $\dot{V}O_2$) (Bar-Or et al. 1971; Turley & Wilmore 1997). This pattern is summarized in figure 12.1, where the responses of heart rate,

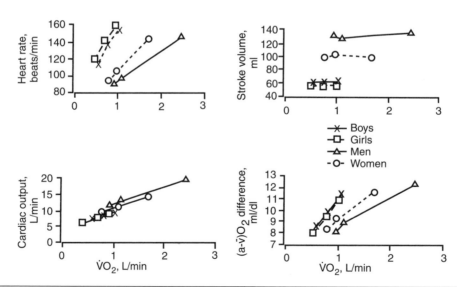

FIGURE 12.1   Cardiovascular responses of 7-year-old to 9-year-old children and young adults. Mean values for 12 girls, 12 boys, 12 women, and 12 men who performed several submaximal exercise bouts on a cycle ergometer. HR = heart rate, SV = stroke volume, $\dot{Q}$ = cardiac output, (a-$\bar{v}$)O_2 = arterio-mixed venous difference for O_2.

Adapted from Turley and Wilmore, 1997.

stroke volume, cardiac output, and arteriovenous O_2 difference at various levels of $\dot{V}O_2$ are compared between 7-year-old to 9-year-old children and young adults. The figure also demonstrates similar hemodynamic responses between girls and boys. Data are not presently available to indicate when during growth the childhood pattern of cardiovascular responses to exercise changes into an adult pattern.

Another important cardiovascular response to exercise is an increase in arterial systolic blood pressure: the higher the exercise intensity, the higher the pressure. As shown in figure 9.6 (see chapter 9, page 187), resting blood pressure increases during growth. Likewise, systolic blood pressure during exercise increases with age. This finding is summarized in figure 12.2 for maximal aerobic exercise. Little information is available on age-related changes in diastolic pressure during exercise.

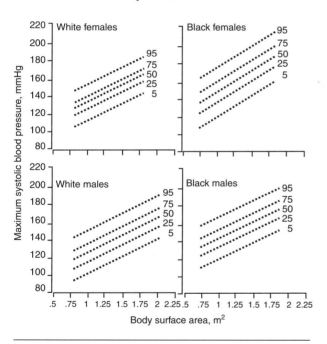

Maximal Blood Pressure
vs Body Surface Area

FIGURE 12.2 Systolic blood pressure during maximal cycle exercise in children and adolescents. American White (n = 221) and Black (n = 184) children and adolescents, 6 to 15 years of age, performed a maximal exercise test on a cycle ergometer. Blood pressure, measured by a sphygmomanometer, was determined at the last 15 seconds of the final stage. The lines denote percentiles.

Adapted from Alpert et al., 1982.

Ventilatory Responses During Aerobic Exercise

An increase in pulmonary ventilation ($\dot{V}O_E$) during exercise is a prerequisite for the ability to increase O_2 supply to, and CO_2 removal from, the working muscles. The ratio $\dot{V}_E/\dot{V}O_2$ (ventilatory equivalent) is an index of the efficiency of the pulmonary system in facilitating the enhanced O_2 supply: the higher the $\dot{V}_E/\dot{V}O_2$ ratio, the lower the ventilatory efficiency. Pulmonary ventilation is the product of respiratory frequency (breaths per minute) and the tidal volume (the volume that is ventilated with each breath).

Not all of the inspired air takes part in gas exchange. Some air, the volume of which is called dead space, remains in the airways and does not even reach the alveoli before it is expired. The volume of air that reaches the alveoli during a given time interval is called alveolar ventilation. From a functional point of view, the alveolar ventilation, rather than $\dot{V}_E$, determines the rate of gas exchange. For a given $\dot{V}O_2$, the shallower the breathing, the higher is the dead space. The ratio between tidal volume and vital capacity provides an estimate of whether breathing capacity is deep or shallow. A lower ratio indicates more shallow breathing in contrast to deep breathing.

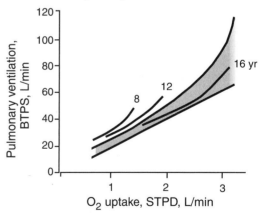

Ventilatory Response to Exercise

FIGURE 12.3 Ventilatory responses to exercise in children and adolescents. Eighty-three Norwegian boys, subdivided into three age groups, cycled at two submaximal and one maximal work rate. BTPS = body temperature, ambient pressure, saturated with water vapor; STPD = standard temperature and pressure, dry air. The gray area represents data for young adults.

Data for the children are from Andersen et al. (1974). Reproduced with permission from Bar-Or (1983).

Figures 12.3, 12.4, and 12.5 summarize changes in ventilatory functions with age during childhood and adolescence. Even though the figures are based on cross-sectional data, they suggest the following trends. First, at any given level of $\dot{V}O_2$, ventilation is higher in children than in adolescents and adults. Second, the ventilatory equivalent decreases with age. Third, respiratory rate is higher in children than in adolescents and adults during rest and at all levels of exercise. In contrast, the ratio of tidal volume to vital capacity is lower in children.

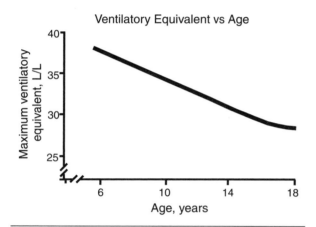

FIGURE 12.4 Ventilatory equivalent (minute ventilation divided by O_2 uptake) during maximal exercise, as related to age. A schematic presentation based on data of Andersen et al. (1974), Åstrand (1952), and Kobayashi et al. (1978).

Reproduced with permission from Bar-Or (1983).

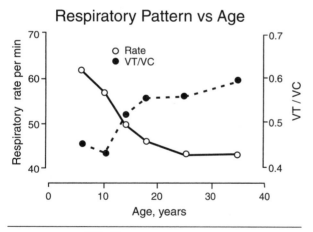

FIGURE 12.5 Respiratory rate (filled circles) and the ratio tidal volume/vital capacity (VT/VC) (open circles) in children, adolescents, and adults. Fifty-three male children, adolescents, and adults walked on a treadmill at 5.6 km/hour (3.5 miles/hour).

Data from Robinson, 1938.

This pattern suggests that the ventilatory efficiency of children is lower than in adolescents and adults, in large part because the shallow, rapid breathing of children results in a higher dead space and lower alveolar ventilation.

Changes in Economy of Movement

Economy of movement reflects the metabolic cost of performing a certain physical task. Growth-related research on the metabolic cost of specific activities has been limited to walking and running. Figure 12.6 summarizes an experiment in which girls and boys, ages 7 to 16 years of age, ran on a treadmill at several submaximal speeds. For the same running speed, the younger children have a higher O_2 cost. This difference is much greater than that expected from the relatively higher resting metabolic rate at young ages (see chapter 21) and implies a higher net O_2 cost of running in younger children.

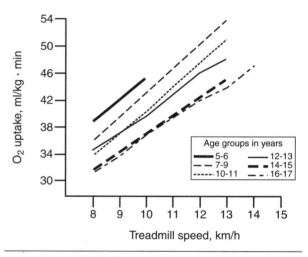

FIGURE 12.6 Oxygen cost during running, in relationship to chronological age. Sixty-seven girls, subdivided into six age groups, ran on the treadmill at several submaximal speeds. Data from Åstrand (1952).

Reprinted, by permission, from J.D. MacDougall et al., 1983, "Maximal aerobic capacity of Canadian school children: Prediction based on age-related oxygen cost of running," *International Journal of Sports Medicine* 4:194-198.

Table 12.1 shows the extent of excess $\dot{V}O_2$ per kg of body mass for locomotion in children of various ages compared with young adults. The excess cost is similar for boys and girls and is affected only slightly by the speed of locomotion (Sallis et al. 1991).

One implication of the excessive metabolic cost of locomotion in young children is that they have a lower metabolic reserve. This finding is

TABLE 12.1	Excess O₂ Cost of Locomotion per Unit Body Mass in Children and Adolescents 5 to17 Years of Age Expressed Relative to the Cost in Young Adults	
Age (years)	**Excess cost (%)**	
5	37	
7	26	
9	19	
11	13	
13	9	
15	5	
17	3	

Adapted from Sallis et al. (1991).

shown in figure 12.7, in which metabolic reserve is the difference between $\dot{V}O_2$ at maximal exercise and $\dot{V}O_2$ at a submaximal running speed of 180 m/min. Whereas a 7-year-old child needs approximately 95% of maximal aerobic power to run at that speed, the 16-year-old adolescent needs only 70% of maximum. This lower metabolic reserve is a major reason why performances of young children in an endurance run are usually inferior to those of older individuals, even in the absence of differences in $\dot{V}O_2$max. A similar pattern of circulatory reserve and, to a lesser extent,

pulmonary reserve is apparent when maximal and submaximal heart rates and pulmonary ventilation are plotted, respectively, against age.

Why is the economy of walking and running lower in young children? The intuitive answer is that the mechanical cost of locomotion may be higher in children. One reason for such a higher mechanical cost is that small persons have a shorter stride and, therefore, have to use more steps at any given speed. Indeed, a greater frequency of strides is mechanically more demanding and thus requires more chemical energy (Unnithan et al. 1990).

Recent data suggest another, possibly more important, reason for the low economy of locomotion in young children. The sequence of activation of various muscle groups in the lower limb was monitored with electromyography (recordings of the electrical signals of muscle activation) during walking and running in children and adolescents 7 to 8, 10 to 12, and 15 to 16 years of age. The test focused on the cocontraction of antagonist muscles in the thigh and the calf. During a stride cycle, when a muscle group (e.g., knee extensors) contracts, the antagonist muscle group (i.e., knee flexors) relaxes most of the time. However, a certain period of overlap occurs when both muscle groups contract simultaneously, (i.e., they cocontract). When cocontraction is excessive, the energy cost of performing the stride is high. The 7-year-old to 8-year-old children had distinctly greater cocontraction than the two older groups (see figure 12.8). The implication of these observations is that the 7-year-old to 8-year-old child does

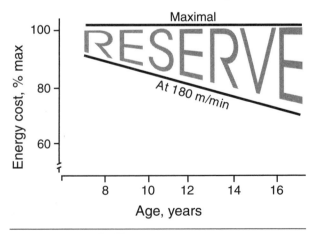

Aerobic Reserve vs Age

FIGURE 12.7 The increase of "aerobic reserve" with age. Maximal O₂ uptake and O₂ uptake during a treadmill run at 180 m/min in 134 girls and boys.

Based on data by MacDougall et al. (1983). Reproduced with permission from Bar-Or (1983).

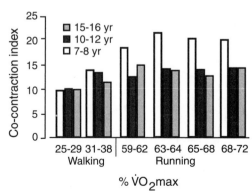

Co-contraction of Antagonist Muscles

FIGURE 12.8 Cocontraction of antagonist calf muscles in three age groups of children who walked and ran at various intensities (expressed as % $\dot{V}O_2$ max).

Reproduced with permission from Frost et al. (1997).

not yet have the optimal neuromotor control to synchronize the action between muscle groups. More research is needed to confirm changes in cocontraction during growth and maturation and whether cocontraction can be reduced through practice or training.

Changes in Submaximal Aerobic Power

Power output under predominantly aerobic conditions increases with age during growth. This increase is clearly illustrated by the changes in power output at any given heart rate. Information on the power output of children and adolescents while working at a heart rate of 170 beats/min on a cycle ergometer (physical working capacity at a heart rate of 170 bpm = PWC_{170}) is available from a variety of countries. Data from a national sample of Canadian children and youth are shown in figure 12.9. PWC_{170} (kgm/min) trebles in boys and more than doubles in girls between ages 7 and 17. In contrast, power output remains almost constant from age to age when expressed per unit body mass (i.e., PWC_{170} [kgm/kg min]). The same trends are apparent for power output at other submaximal heart rates (e.g., PWC_{130}, PWC_{150}).

Changes in Maximal Aerobic Power

Extensive observations have been made on the maximal aerobic power (represented as $\dot{V}O_2max$) of children and youth, but the majority are based on cross-sectional samples. Several longitudinal studies have been reported, but they do not generally cover a broad age range and are limited largely to males. Nevertheless, the available data are sufficient to describe major trends in age-associated, sex-associated, and maturity-associated variation in maximal aerobic power during growth.

The growth of absolute $\dot{V}O_2max$ (L/min) as indicated in four longitudinal studies is illustrated in figure 12.10. Differences in absolute values among the studies are not very important because they are neither derived from the same exercise tasks nor obtained with identical methods; however, the patterns of age-associated and sex-associated variation are quite useful. $\dot{V}O_2max$ increases continuously until about 16 years of age in boys. In girls, on the other hand, $\dot{V}O_2max$ increases until about 13 years of age and then remains at a plateau throughout adolescence. On the average, absolute $\dot{V}O_2max$ is greater in boys than in girls at all ages. Before 10 to 12 years of age, average

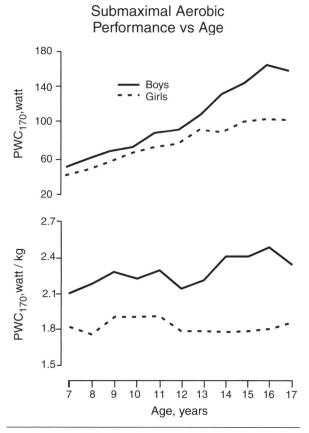

Submaximal Aerobic
Performance vs Age

FIGURE 12.9 Changes with age in power output at a heart rate of 170 beats/min (PWC_{170}) in Canadian boys and girls.

Data from Gauthier et al., 1983.

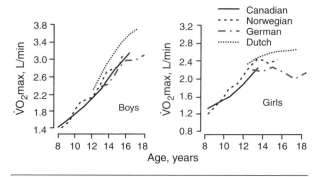

Longitudinal Changes in $\dot{V}O_2$ max

FIGURE 12.10 Changes in maximal aerobic power ($\dot{V}O_2$ max) in children from four longitudinal studies.

Reprinted, by permission, from Mirwald and Bailey, 1986, *Maximal aerobic power* (London, Ontario: Sports Dynamics), 28.

$\dot{V}O_2$max in girls reaches about 85% to 90% of the mean values of boys. After the adolescent growth spurt and sexual maturation, the mean $\dot{V}O_2$max of girls reaches only about 70% of the mean values of boys. The information on $\dot{V}O_2$max in early and middle childhood is limited in that reliable determinations of $\dot{V}O_2$max in children younger than 8 years of age are not readily available and are of doubtful validity.

The preceding discussion deals with absolute $\dot{V}O_2$max (i.e., L/min). Growth in $\dot{V}O_2$max, however, is influenced by growth in body size, so controlling for changes in body size during growth is essential. Although division by body mass is not necessarily the ideal approach of correcting for size (Welsman et al. 1996), most information to date is still based on this approach. The scaling of $\dot{V}O_2$max is considered later in this section. Changes in maximal aerobic power per unit of body mass (i.e., relative $\dot{V}O_2$max, in ml O_2/kg · min) during growth are summarized in figure 12.11. The pattern of variation with age is inconsistent across several longitudinal studies, particularly in boys. Data from the Saskatchewan Longitudinal Growth Study, which used the treadmill, show a slight decrease in average $\dot{V}O_2$max per unit body mass with age in both boys and girls. On the other hand, data from the longitudinal study of West German children, which used a cycle ergometer, show a steep decline with age. In general, body weight appears to increase at a faster rate than $\dot{V}O_2$max, particularly during and after the adolescent growth spurt and sexual maturity. The mean relative $\dot{V}O_2$max of girls is only about 90% to 95% of that for boys before 10 to 12 years of age, and by late adolescence or young adulthood, it is only about 80% of the mean value for males.

In an effort to derive a better fit between growth in maximal aerobic power and changes in body composition, $\dot{V}O_2$max has also been expressed relative to fat-free mass (FFM). Changes in $\dot{V}O_2$max during growth tend to be more closely related to FFM than to total-body mass. Nevertheless, sex differences in $\dot{V}O_2$max per unit FFM persist, and $\dot{V}O_2$max per kg FFM declines with age during and after the adolescent growth spurt and puberty. Mean $\dot{V}O_2$max/kg FFM declines by about 5 ml O_2/min in both sexes between the onset of puberty and young adulthood. On the average, preadolescent and adolescent boys have a relative $\dot{V}O_2$max/kg FFM that is about 10% higher than that of girls.

Velocity curves for $\dot{V}O_2$max (L O_2/min/year) have been reported for boys in the Saskatchewan

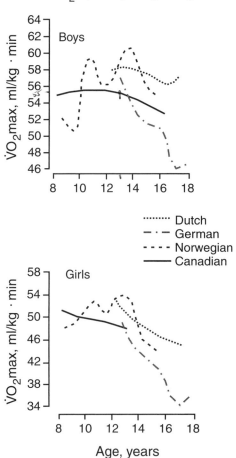

Maximal O_2 Uptake per kg vs Age

FIGURE 12.11 Changes in maximal aerobic power relative to body weight ($\dot{V}O_2$max/kg · min) in children from four longitudinal studies.

Reprinted, by permission, from Mirwald and Bailey, 1986, *Maximal aerobic power* (London, Ontario: Sports Dynamics), 28.

Longitudinal Growth Study. Growth curves for key percentiles derived from 83 boys followed from 8 to 16 years of age are shown in figure 12.12. The trends suggest slight spurts in absolute $\dot{V}O_2$max at about 9.5 and 11.5 years of age, but the adolescence spurt in $\dot{V}O_2$max begins, on average, at about 13 years of age and reaches a peak about 1 year later, near 14 years of age. The shape of the growth spurt in absolute $\dot{V}O_2$max is similar to that for stature and weight. Unfortunately, corresponding data are not available for girls, but, based on cross-sectional data, girls appear to have a less intense adolescence spurt in $\dot{V}O_2$max (see chapter 16).

Absolute maximal aerobic power and maximal aerobic power relative to body mass or fat-free mass thus show changes in mean values with age

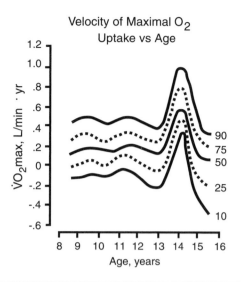

FIGURE 12.12   Velocity curves for maximal aerobic power in boys from the Saskatchewan Longitudinal Growth Study. Percentile values were derived from longitudinal yearly increments in 83 boys.

Reprinted, by permission, from Mirwald and Bailey, 1986, *Maximal aerobic power* (London, Ontario: Sports Dynamics), 28.

and differences between boys and girls. However, regardless of the manner of expressing $\dot{V}O_2$max, there is a large dispersion of individual values at all ages. Standard deviations of $\dot{V}O_2$max generally reach about 15% of mean values, which implies that some children may deviate considerably from age-specific and sex-specific means and in turn from the growth patterns illustrated previously. In addition, the $\dot{V}O_2$max scores of many individual girls are above the values of many, although a clear sex difference in favor of the boys is commonly observed in mean values.

Scaling Maximal Aerobic Power for Body Size

$\dot{V}O_2$max increases as some function of body size during growth and maturation. In an effort to derive a better fit between growth in maximal aerobic power and changes in size and individual variation in body size, $\dot{V}O_2$max has been expressed as a mathematical power function (allometry) of various body dimensions, particularly body weight and height. Mean scaling factors range from 0.47 to 1.09 in children and adolescents, but more data are available for boys than for girls. Corresponding factors for young adults range from 0.61 to 1.02 and overlap those for children and adolescents (Eisenmann and

Malina 2000). Clearly variability occurs in the scaling exponents.

Almost as many scaling factors approximate body mass to the 1.0 power (mass$^{1.0}$) as those that approximate the so-called theoretical values of 0.67 and 0.75 (see chapter 3). Thus, for practical purposes, $\dot{V}O_2$max is commonly expressed, as done in this text and others, as a simple ratio per unit body mass in children and adolescents (see also Bar-Or 1983). On the other hand, the suggestion has been made that the expression of $\dot{V}O_2$max as a ratio standard limits the understanding of changes in the oxygen transport system associated with growth and maturation (Armstrong and Welsman 1994).

Allometric scaling of $\dot{V}O_2$max has focused largely on changes occurring during puberty and on comparisons of children, adolescents, and adults. Most of the currently available allometric data are cross-sectional. Thus, implications for understanding changes in the oxygen transport system associated with growth and maturation are only suggestive. The data do not address longitudinal changes in $\dot{V}O_2$max during the adolescent growth spurt and their associations with individual differences in biological maturity, which are discussed in more detail in chapters 16 and 17.

Scaling $\dot{V}O_2$max to height in children and adolescents has received less attention. In a sample of boys followed annually from 8 to 15 years of age, $\dot{V}O_2$max increases with height to the 2.46 power (Bailey et al. 1978), and in a subsample of 25 boys followed from 8 to 16 years of age, $\dot{V}O_2$max increases with height to the 2.62 power (Ross et al. 1991). Both exponents are greater than the theoretical value of $h^{2.0}$ (see chapter 3). Intraindividual or ontogenetic allometry was not considered in these analyses.

Studies of allometric scaling do not consider variation in body composition or regional variation in muscle mass in the body that accompany growth and maturation. Larger mammals, for example, have a greater proportion of segmental muscle mass in relation to total-body mass, that is, leg muscle mass is proportional to body mass$^{1.1}$ (Nevill 1994). Thus, children and adolescents may show a disproportionate increase in muscle mass in association with growth and maturity, particularly in boys, and may, therefore, violate the assumption of geometric similarity. To account for the independent contribution of body mass and at the same time to account for the disproportionate increase in muscle mass with increasing body size, a suggestion has been made that stature should be included in the allometric equation as a covariate (Nevill 1994).

A factor that is often overlooked in discussions of allometry is measurement error. Literature dealing with allometric relationships between $\dot{V}O_2$max and body mass commonly assumes that the variable (body size) to which the other variable ($\dot{V}O_2$max) is regressed is measured without error. The implication is that no errors occur in the measurement of body mass or height. Of course, this assumption does not hold (see Beunen et al. 1997; Thomis et al. 2000).

The presently available data indicate a strong association between growth in body size and $\dot{V}O_2$max. However, how the various allometric analyses influence our understanding of the changes in $\dot{V}O_2$max that occur with growth and maturation during childhood and adolescence is not clear. More research on the theoretical foundations of these allometric relationships is clearly warranted.

Determinants of Maximal Aerobic Power

Maximal aerobic power is related to sex, body size, and maturity status of children and adolescents. However, even after controlling for these primary sources of variation in the growing individual, a substantial amount of variation in maximal aerobic power remains. It is related to structural, physiological, and biochemical factors associated with aerobic energy output.

By modifying the Fick equation for maximal values (see section on cardiovascular responses to aerobic exercise), $\dot{V}O_2$max depends on maximal heart rate, maximal stroke volume, and the maximal difference in O_2 content in the arterial and mixed-venous blood:

$$\dot{V}O_2 \, max = HRmax \times SVmax \, (CaO_2 - C\bar{v}O_2)max$$

Maximal heart rate is generally highest in children, with mean values of about 195 to 205 beats/min and standard deviations of about 10 to 15 beats/min. Maximal heart rates subsequently decline with age, beginning at prepuberty and continuing into adulthood. By late adolescence, mean maximal exercise heart rates approximate about 190 to 195 beats/min.

$\dot{V}O_2$max is also a function of maximal stroke volume (see figure 12.13), which is lower in children than in adolescents and adults. As a result, maximal cardiac output, which is the product of

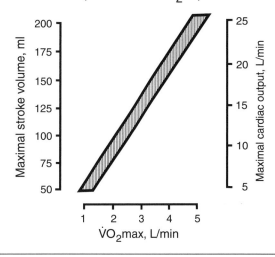

Maximal Stroke Volume and Cardiac Output vs Maximal O_2 Uptake

FIGURE 12.13 Relationship among maximal stroke volume, maximal cardiac output, and maximal O_2 uptake during growth. A schematic illustration drawn from several cross-sectional studies.

heart rate and stroke volume, is somewhat lower in children than in adults at any given level of $\dot{V}O_2$.

The size of the heart increases during growth, and the increase is generally proportional to body mass (see chapter 9). $\dot{V}O_2$max is highly correlated with the absolute size of the heart in children and adolescents (see figure 12.14). Similar relationships exist between $\dot{V}O_2$max and total hemoglobin content of the blood and between $\dot{V}O_2$max and blood volume per se (see figure 12.15).

Developmental changes in lung functions were described in chapter 9. In the context of maximal aerobic power during growth, pulmonary functions are rarely a limiting factor in determining $\dot{V}O_2$max in healthy children. Maximal pulmonary ventilation increases with age. It doubles between 8 years of age and maturity, from about 50 L/min to about 100 L/min. Children, however, have a higher breathing frequency but a more shallow breathing volume for the same pulmonary ventilation as adults.

Thus, $\dot{V}O_2$max increases during growth not only as a function of body mass but also as a function of the capacity of the oxygen transport system. These variables are, of course, highly interrelated because they grow in proportion to body mass or at the same power function of body mass (see figure 12.13).

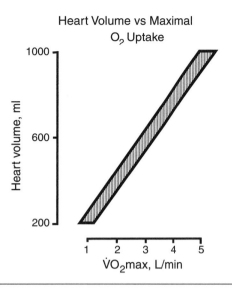

FIGURE 12.14 Relationship between volume of the heart and maximal aerobic power during growth. A schematic illustration derived from several cross-sectional studies.

Data from Åstrand, 1952.

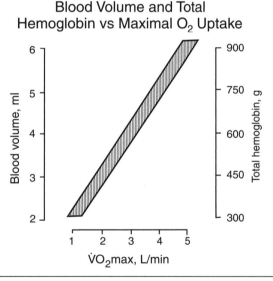

FIGURE 12.15 Relationships among blood volume, total hemoglobin, and maximal aerobic power during growth. A schematic illustration drawn from the data of Åstrand (1952).

Data from Åstrand, 1952.

Maximal aerobic power is not only determined by cardiopulmonary functions. Other potential determinants are the capacity to extract oxygen from the blood (which is reflected by the difference in the O_2 content of the arterial and mixed-venous blood), the rate of substrate utilization, and the re-

plenishment of ATP in the muscle cells. Although differences in these peripheral factors determine in part the differences in $\dot{V}O_2$max during childhood and adolescence, they are less well understood.

Limited observations suggest that the capacity to extract oxygen from the blood is slightly higher during childhood than during adolescence and in adulthood (Turley & Wilmore 1997). Thus, the arteriovenous difference in oxygen content at maximal exercise apparently decreases slightly with age and can only account for a small portion of individual differences in maximal power output. It may, however, be more significant during submaximal exercise as a mechanism that compensates for the somewhat lower cardiac output of children.

Similarly, only limited data are available for growth-related changes in substrate utilization that occur with aerobic exercise. Compared with adults, children rely more on fat utilization than on carbohydrate utilization (for details, see the section on prolonged exercise). Based on very few studies that included muscle biopsies, aerobic enzymes of the Krebs cycle seem to be as active in children as in adults (Eriksson 1980). The paucity of information reflects the ethical concerns of performing muscle biopsies and other invasive procedures in healthy children. With the advent of noninvasive methods such as magnetic resonance spectroscopy, more data should become available in the future about intramuscular substrate utilization in exercising children and adolescents. Details of anaerobic metabolism during exercise are discussed in chapter 13.

Various studies suggest that children are able to mobilize their aerobic resources more rapidly than adults (Macek & Vavra 1980). After the onset of exercise, for example, the time required to reach 50% of $\dot{V}O_2$max is shorter in children than in adults, particularly if the intensity is above the anaerobic threshold (Armon et al. 1991). This ability would imply that children incur a lower O_2 deficit at the start of exercise by relying less on the glycogen (or glucose)-to-lactate pathway. More recent data, however, suggest that this apparent difference may depend on the methodology by which $\dot{V}O_2$ transients are calculated (Hebestreit et al. 1998).

Boys recover faster than young adult men after aerobic exercise of various intensities. This difference has been shown for heart rate (Baraldi et al. 1991) as well as for $\dot{V}O_2$ (Zanconato et al. 1991). Children also recover faster than adults after anaerobic, high-intensity exercise (see chapter 13). One possible practical implication of this faster recovery is that, compared with adults, children need shorter rest periods during interval training. This hypothesis requires further research.

Stability of Maximal Aerobic Power During Growth

Few studies have considered the stability (tracking) of $\dot{V}O_2$max in individual children during growth (Malina 1996, 2001). Interage correlations for $\dot{V}O_2$max per unit body mass are generally moderate (see table 12.2). Correlations between childhood and the transition to early adolescence (0.49 to 0.56) and over short intervals in adolescence (13 to 16 years of age) are similar (0.49 to 0.61), but the correlation for a longer interval across adolescence (11 to 18 years of age) is lower (~0.30). With the exception of the moderately high correlations for $\dot{V}O_2$max between 16 and 21 years of age in Dutch youth (0.74, 0.82), correlations between $\dot{V}O_2$max in adolescence and between adolescence and young adulthood are reasonably similar and moderate (0.30 to 0.48).

Results for field tests of aerobic fitness provide generally similar results. For example, short-term tracking for the 1-mile run in children from 9 to 12 years of age is similar in magnitude, 0.56 and 0.42 for boys and girls, respectively. Among Belgian males, correlations for heart rate recovery after a step test during adolescence and at 30 years of age are of almost the same magnitude, 0.26 to 0.43 (Beunen et al. 1992). Overall, maximal aerobic power and field tests of aerobic fitness tend to track at moderate levels from childhood into adolescence and through adolescence into young adulthood.

Responses to Prolonged Exercise

Reactions to prolonged exercise (e.g., 30 minutes or more) have been studied less extensively in children and adolescents than in adults, possibly because children are less inclined habitually to perform prolonged, monotonous activities. Limited observations from the former Czechoslovakia and the Federal Republic of Germany indicate that when 13-year-old boys and 14-year-old girls exercise for 1 hour on a treadmill or a cycle ergometer, the physiological responses to such prolonged activity are quite comparable to those observed in young adults. However, blood lactate tends to be lower during prolonged exercise in children than in adults (Macek et al. 1976). As summarized in figure 12.16, children respond

TABLE 12.2 Interage Correlations for Maximal Aerobic Power ($\dot{V}O_2$max, ml/min/kg) During Childhood and Adolescence and Between Adolescence and Young Adulthood

Span (yr)	Sexes combined	Males	Females
Childhood			
6–10	0.49		
8–12	0.55		
6–12	0.56		
Adolescence			
11–18		~0.30[a]	
PHV±1.5 yr[b]		0.41	
13–16		0.49	0.61
Adolescence to adulthood			
13–21		0.36	0.46
13–21		0.35	0.42
16–21		0.74	0.82
17–25[c]		0.35	0.48
13–27		0.30	0.36

[a]Correlations were interpolated from a graph.

[b]Average interage correlations based on Fisher's z-transformations of yearly correlations before and after peak height velocity (PHV).

[c]The ages are the midpoints of the ranges reported, 15–19 and 23–27, respectively.

Adapted from Malina (1996, 2001), which contain the references to the specific studies.

Substrate Utilization during Prolonged Exercise

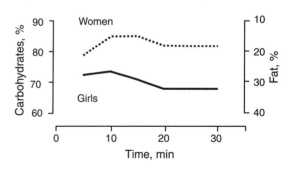

FIGURE 12.16 The relative use of carbohydrates in prepubertal girls and young adult women during 30 minutes of treadmill running at 70% $\dot{V}O_2$max. The girls consistently utilized a greater proportion of fats and a lesser proportion of carbohydrates.

Data from Martinez and Haymes, 1992.

to prolonged exercise with a lower respiratory quotient (CO_2 production divided by O_2 uptake), which suggests that they utilize relatively more lipids and less carbohydrates than do adults (Martinez and Haymes 1992).

The presently available data thus suggest that prolonged submaximal exercise is well tolerated by children and adolescents. No contraindications are apparent for participation of normal, healthy children in endurance events.

Summary

Maximal aerobic power can be measured as maximal O_2 uptake ($\dot{V}O_2$max), but no single index of aerobic capacity is accepted. Indicators commonly used to estimate aerobic capacity are not particularly suited for children and adolescents, largely for ethical reasons. $\dot{V}O_2$max increases continuously until about 16 years of age in boys, whereas in girls it increases until about 13 years of age and then remains at a plateau throughout adolescence. Absolute $\dot{V}O_2$max is, on average, greater in boys than in girls at all ages. Growth in $\dot{V}O_2$max is influenced by growth in body size. Maximal aerobic power per unit of body mass (relative $\dot{V}O_2$max, in ml O_2/kg min) is reasonably stable during childhood and adolescence in boys but declines with age in girls. In general, body weight increases at a faster rate than $\dot{V}O_2$max, especially during the adolescent growth spurt. Maximal aerobic power is related to age, sex, body size, and maturity status as well as to structural, physiological, and biochemical factors associated with aerobic energy output. Body size has received most attention, and $\dot{V}O_2$max has been expressed as a mathematical power function (allometry) of various body dimensions, particularly weight and height. However, how the various allometric analyses influence our understanding of the changes in $\dot{V}O_2$max that occur with growth and maturation during childhood and adolescence is not clear. Maximal aerobic power and other indices of aerobic fitness tend to track at moderate levels from childhood into adolescence and from adolescence into young adulthood.

Sources and Suggested Readings

Alpert BS, Flood NL, Strong WB (1982) Responses to ergometer exercise in a healthy biracial population of children. Journal of Pediatrics 101:538-545.

Andersen KL, Seliger V, Rutenfranz J, Messel S (1974) Physical performance capacity of children in Norway. Part III. Respiratory responses to graded exercise loadings—population parameters in a rural community. European Journal of Applied Physiology 33:265-274.

Armon Y, Cooper DM, Flores R, Zanconato S, Barstow TJ (1991) Oxygen uptake dynamics during high-intensity exercise in children and adults. Journal of Applied Physiology 70: 841-848.

* Armstrong N, Welsman JR (1994) Assessment and interpretation of aerobic fitness in children and adolescents. Exercise and Sport Sciences Reviews 22:435-476.

* Åstrand PO (1952) Experimental Studies of Physical Working Capacity in Relation to Sex and Age. Copenhagen: Munksgaard.

Åstrand PO, Rhyming I (1954) A nomogram for calculation of aerobic capacity (physical fitness) from pulse rate during submaximal work. Journal of Applied Physiology 7:218-221.

Bailey DA, Ross WD, Mirwald RL, Weese C (1978) Size dissociation of maximal aerobic power during growth in boys. Medicine and Sport 11:140-151.

* Bar-Or O (1983) Pediatric Sports Medicine for the Practitioner. From Physiologic Principles to Clinical Applications. New York: Springer-Verlag.

Bar-Or O, Shephard RJ, Allen CL (1971) Cardiac output of 10- to 13-year-old boys and girls during submaximal exercise. Journal of Applied Physiology 30:219-223.

Baraldi E, Cooper DM, Zanconato S, Armon Y (1991) Heart rate recovery following 1 minute exercise in children and adults. Pediatric Research 29:575-579.

Beunen GP, Malina RM, Renson R, Simons J, Lefevre J (1992) Physical activity and growth, maturation and performance: A longitudinal study. Medicine and Science in Sports and Exercise 24:576-585.

Beunen GP, Rogers DM, Woynarowska B, Malina RM (1997) Longitudinal study of ontogenetic allometry of oxygen uptake in boys and girls grouped by maturity status. Annals of Human Biology 24:33-43.

Campbell PT, Katzmarzyk PT, Malina RM, Rao DC, Perusse L, Bouchard C (2001) Prediction of physical activity and physical work capacity (PWC150) in young adulthood from childhood and adolescence with consideration of parental measures. American Journal of Human Biology 13:190-196.

Cunningham DA, MacFarlane Van Waterschoot B, Paterson DH, Lefcoe M, Sangal SP (1977) Reliability and reproducibility of maximal oxygen uptake measurement in children. Medicine and Science in Sports 9:104-108.

Doré E, Bedu M, Franca NM, Diallo O, Duché P, Van Praagh E (2000) Testing peak cycling performance: Effects of braking force during growth. Medicine and Science in Sports and Exercise 32: 493-498.

* Eisenmann JC, Malina RM (2000) Body size and endurance performance. In RJ Shephard, P-O Åstrand (eds), Endurance in Sport, 2nd edition. Oxford: Blackwell Science, pp 37-51.

Eriksson BO (1980) Muscle metabolism in children: A review. Acta Paediatrica Scandinavica 283 (suppl) 283:20-27.

Frost G, Bar-Or O, Dowling J, White C (1995) Habituation of children to treadmill walking and running: Metabolic and kinematic criteria. Pediatric Exercise Science 7: 162-175.

Frost G, Dowling J, Dyson K, Bar-Or O (1997) Cocontraction in three age groups of children during treadmill locomotion. Journal of Electromyography and Kinesiology 7:179-186.

Gauthier R, Massicotte D, Hermiston R, MacNab R (1983) The physical work capacity of Canadian children, aged 7 to 17 in 1983: A comparison with 1968. CAHPER Journal/Revue de l'ACSEPR 50:4-9 (Nov-Dec).

Hebestreit H, Kriemler S, Hughson RL, Bar-Or O (1998) Kinetics of oxygen uptake at the onset of exercise in boys and men. Journal of Applied Physiology 85:1833-1841.

Ishii K, Amano K (1983) The growth and development of leg muscle plus bone volume in Japanese young male and female, aged from 6 to 20 years. Laboratory Physiology and Biomechanics 11:50-57.

Jolicoeur P, Heusner AA (1971) The allometry equation in the analysis of the standard oxygen consumption and body weight of the white rat. Biometrics 27:841-855.

Kemper HCG, de Vente W, van Mechelen W, Twisk JWR (2001) Adolescent motor skill and performance: Is physical activity in adolescence related to adult physical fitness? American Journal of Human Biology 13:180-189.

Kobayashi K, Kitamura K, Miura M, Sodeyama H, Murase Y, Miyashita M, Matsui H (1978) Aerobic power as related to body growth and training in Japanese boys: A longitudinal study. Journal of Applied Physiology: Respiratory and Environmental Exercise Physiology 44:666-672.

* Krahenbuhl GS, Skinner JS, Kohrt WM (1985) Developmental aspects of maximal aerobic power in children. Exercise and Sport Sciences Reviews 13:503-538.

MacDougall JD, Roche PD, Bar-Or O, Moroz JR (1983) Maximal aerobic capacity of Canadian school children: Prediction based on age-related oxygen cost of running. International Journal of Sports Medicine 4:194-198.

Macek M, Vavra J (1980) The adjustment of oxygen uptake at the onset of exercise: A comparison between prepubertal boys and young adults. International Journal of Sports Medicine 1:75-77.

Macek M, Vavra J, Novosadova J (1976) Prolonged exercise in prepubertal boys. I. Cardiovascular and metabolic adjustment. European Journal of Applied Physiology 35: 291-298.

* Mahon AD, Vaccaro P (1989) Ventilatory threshold and $\dot{V}O_2$ max changes in children following endurance training. Medicine and Science in Sports and Exercise 21:425-431.

Malina RM (1996) Tracking of physical activity and physical fitness across the lifespan. Research Quarterly for Exercise and Sport 67 (suppl):48-57.

Malina RM (2001) Physical activity and fitness: Pathways from childhood to adulthood. American Journal of Human Biology 13:162-172.

Martinez LR, Haymes EM (1992) Substrate utilization during treadmill running in prepubertal girls and women. Medicine and Science in Sports and Exercise 24:975-983.

McMiken DF (1976) Maximum aerobic power and physical dimensions in children. Annals of Human Biology 3: 141-147.

* Mirwald RL, Bailey DA (1986) Maximal Aerobic Power. A Longitudinal Analysis. London: Sports Dynamics.

Nevill AM (1994) The need to scale for differences in body size and mass: An explanation of Kleiber's 0.75 mass exponent. Journal of Applied Physiology 77:2870-2873.

Nevill AM, Holder RL, Baxter-Jones A, Round JM, Jones DA (1998) Modeling developmental changes in strength and aerobic power in children. Journal of Applied Physiology 84:963-970.

Nevill AM, Ramsbottom R, Williams C (1992) Scaling physiological measurements for individuals of different body size. European Journal of Applied Physiology 65:110-117.

Rivera-Brown AM, Frontera WR (1998) Achievement of plateau and reliability of $\dot{V}O_2$ max in trained adolescents tested with different ergometers. Pediatric Exercise Science 10: 164-175.

Robinson S (1938) Experimental studies of physical fitness in relation to age. Arbeitsphysiologie: zeitschrift fur die Physiologie des Menschen Bei Arbeit und Sport 10:251-323.

Ross WD, Bailey DA, Mirwald RL, Faulkner RA, Rasmussen R, Kerr DA, Stini WA (1991) Allometric relationship of estimated muscle mass and maximal oxygen uptake in boys studied longitudinally age 8 to 16 years. In R Frenkl, I Szmodis (eds), Children and Exercise: Pediatric Work Physiology XV. Budapest, Hungary: National Institute for Health Promotion, pp 135-142.

Rotstein A, Dotan R, Tenenbaum G, Bar-Or O (1986) The effect of training on anaerobic threshold, anaerobic performance, and maximal aerobic power of preadolescent boys. International Journal of Sports Medicine 7:281-286.

* Rowland TW (1996) Developmental Exercise Physiology. Champaign, IL: Human Kinetics.

Sallis JF, Buono MJ, Freedson PS (1991) Bias in estimating caloric expenditure from physical activity in children: Implications for epidemiological studies. Sports Medicine 11:203-209.

Saris WHM, Elvers JWH, Van't Hof MA, Binkhorst RA (1986) Changes in physical activity of children aged 6 to 12 years. In J Rutenfranz, R Mocellin, F Klimt (eds), Children and Exercise XII. Champaign, IL: Human Kinetics, pp 121-130.

Sprynarova S, Parizkova J (1978) La stabilité de différences interindividuelles des paramètres morphologiques et cardiorespiratoires chez les garçons. In H Lavallée, RJ Shephard (eds), Frontiers of Physical Activity and Child Health. Quebec: Editions du Pélican, pp 131-138.

Thomis M, Rogers DM, Beunen GP, Woynarowska B, Malina RM (2000) Allometric relationship between body size and peak $\dot{V}O_2$ relative to age at menarche. Annals of Human Biology 27:623-633.

Turley KR, Rogers DM, Harper KM, Kujawa KI, Wilmore JH (1995) Maximal treadmill versus cycle ergometry testing in children: Differences, reliability, and variability of responses. Pediatric Exercise Science 7:49-60.

Turley KR, Wilmore JH (1997) Cardiovascular responses to treadmill and cycle ergometer exercise in children and adults. Journal of Applied Physiology 83:948-957.

Unnithan VB, Eston RG (1990) Stride frequency and submaximal treadmill running economy in adults and children. Pediatric Exercise Science 2:149-155.

Washington RL (1993) Anaerobic threshold. In TW Rowland (ed), Pediatric Laboratory Exercise Testing: Clinical Guidelines. Champaign, IL: Human Kinetics, pp 115-129.

Welsman JR, Armstrong N, Nevill AM, Winter EM, Kirby BJ (1996) Scaling peak $\dot{V}O_2$ for differences in body size. Medicine and Science in Sports and Exercise 28:259-265.

Winter EM (1992) Scaling: Partitioning out differences in size. Pediatric Exercise Science 4:296-301.

Zanconato S, Cooper DM, Armon Y (1991) Oxygen cost and oxygen uptake dynamics and recovery with 1 min of exercise in children and adults. Journal of Applied Physiology 71:993-998.

Chapter Outline

The yield of ATP through anaerobic energy turnover is important for growing children because many of their activities involve bursts of energy expenditure, as in sprints, rather than activities of moderate intensity over long periods of time. The energy needs of the exercising child thus cannot always be met by the O_2 transport system and the oxidative properties of the working skeletal muscles. To permit such activities, production of ATP through anaerobic mechanisms comes into play. Unlike aerobic performance, which depends primarily on the O_2 transport system, anaerobic performance is more a local characteristic of a skeletal muscle or a muscle group.

Physiologically, ATP needs of working muscle tissue are normally met through anaerobic mechanisms. Before considering changes in anaerobic performance during growth, the main features of the anaerobic energy systems—their morphological, physiological, and biochemical determinants—and relationships with exercises of various durations must be understood. This chapter provides an integrated view of anaerobic performance during growth, although much less research has been done on the anaerobic performance of children and adolescents in contrast to that for aerobic performance (chapter 12).

Anaerobic Versus Aerobic Energy Turnover

The time coordinates of aerobic and anaerobic performances are schematically illustrated in figure 13.1. They refer only to maximal exercise for the indicated duration. The energy needs of working muscles are truly met by anaerobic processes only in very short exercise bouts, such as a jump or a maximal strength test. Beyond such cases of instantaneous muscular engagements, which are characterized by an almost 100% anaerobiosis, the contribution of anaerobic energy systems decreases progressively during maximal exercises lasting from a few seconds to about 3 minutes. The anaerobic contribution is quite high in a 3-second maximal effort, reaching nearly 100% of the energy needs, but it represents only about 50% of ATP needs in a 90-second maximal exercise.

Beyond exercises of 90-second duration, the replenishment of ATP in skeletal muscle is primarily driven by the oxidation of substrates (i.e., by aerobic processes). The focus of this chapter is maximal exercise efforts, which last from about 3 to about 120 seconds.

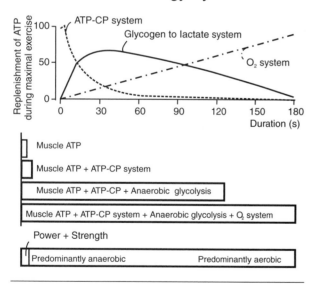

The Three Energy Systems

FIGURE 13.1 Time course of the contribution of the various systems of ATP replenishment during maximal exercise lasting from a few seconds to about 3 minutes.

Reprinted, by permission, from C. Bouchard et al., 1989, Testing anaerobic power and capacity. In *Physiological testing of the elite athlete*, 2nd ed., edited by J.D. MacDougall et al. (Champaign, IL: Human Kinetics), 1989.

To sustain the demands for ATP in working skeletal muscle tissue, the child, like the adult, relies primarily on four different energy sources: (1) ATP stored in the resting muscle, (2) rapid phosphorylation of ADP to ATP through the creatine kinase enzyme pathway and the phosphocreatine pool, (3) anaerobic glycolysis from glycogen (glucose) to lactate, and (4) aerobic energy turnover using fatty acids, glucose, and glycogen as sources, together with oxygen. These processes are schematically illustrated in figure 13.2

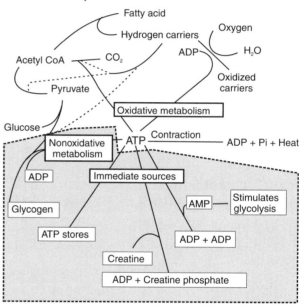

FIGURE 13.2 Schematic illustration of the most important metabolic pathways responsible for the replenishment of ATP in working skeletal muscle.

Adapted from Edington and Edgerton (1976).

Experience in the assessment of anaerobic performance over the past few decades has suggested that distinguishing performances in terms of duration is useful. Three categories of anaerobic performance are considered in this chapter: (1) short-term, which refers to a maximal effort lasting about 3 to 10 seconds, (2) intermediate, which refers to a maximal effort lasting from 20 to 50 seconds, and (3) long-term, which refers to efforts in the range of 60 to 120 seconds (see figure 13.1).

Determinants of Anaerobic Performance

The factors that limit human muscular performance under predominantly anaerobic conditions are still under debate. Nonetheless, the most probable structural and functional factors affecting anaerobic performance are described in the next section. Maximal anaerobic performance is related to body size and, in particular, to fat-free mass and muscle size. Thus, some of the age-associated and sex-associated variation in maximal anaerobic performance is most likely more related to variation in muscle mass than to any other factors.

Muscle Architecture and Fiber Type

Although the issue has not been fully investigated in human muscle tissue, the architecture of a muscle apparently plays a significant role in the power and work output that a muscle can generate. Sarcomere arrangement, muscle fiber length, muscle cross-sectional area, and total muscle mass (see chapter 7) are structural elements that contribute to the ability of a muscle to perform under anaerobic conditions, particularly in terms of absolute work output. Their contribution becomes less obvious when work output is expressed per unit body mass or fat-free mass.

The relationship between fiber type composition of a muscle and anaerobic performance is not simple. Athletes performing in anaerobic events or in sports requiring high anaerobic power and capacity tend to have a higher proportion of fast-twitch fibers than do endurance athletes and sedentary individuals. However, considerable interindividual variation occurs, even among athletes specializing in anaerobic events. Nevertheless, a high fast-twitch fiber content of the muscle appears to be advantageous for short-term anaerobic performance conditions.

Substrate Availability

ATP is present in small quantities in muscle tissue and can sustain only a few contractions when no substrates ensure its resynthesis. The regeneration of ATP in muscle is provided by the phosphagen pool and the breakdown of glycogen when mechanical work is produced under predominantly anaerobic conditions. However, variations in muscle phosphagen and glycogen concentrations per se appear unlikely to be related to individual differences in anaerobic performance.

Accumulation of Reaction Products

During maximal anaerobic exercise, muscle lactate accumulates, with a concomitant increase in hydrogen ion (H^+) concentration in muscle and body fluids. The muscle cannot buffer all of the H^+ produced, and pH thus falls from about 7.0 to as low as 6.3 after exercise, leading to exhaustion. This decline in pH, in turn, decreases the capacity to generate and sustain muscle tension. Under these conditions, the ability to buffer and resist the development of acidosis would be expected to increase anaerobic performance.

Effectiveness of Metabolic Pathways

The rate at which ATP can be regenerated during anaerobic exercise also depends on the capacities of the metabolic pathways responsible for releasing the energy stored in creatine phosphate or glycogen. The direct transfer of phosphate from creatine phosphate to ADP, which is catalyzed by the enzyme creatine kinase, allows rapid regeneration of ATP. Creatine kinase has a very high level of activity in skeletal muscle tissue, and, interestingly, muscle tissue of animals capable of high bursts of speed has the highest creatine kinase levels.

On the other hand, glycogen is converted to lactate by the process of anaerobic glycolysis. Control of glycolysis is determined largely by the catalytic and regulatory properties of two enzymes, phosphofructokinase and phosphorylase. Studies have shown that both enzymes are completely inhibited at a pH close to 6.3. Under such conditions, the rate of ATP resynthesis sustained by glycolysis is largely reduced, thus impairing the ability to continue production of work anaerobically.

Oxygen Delivery System

As shown in figure 13.1, even during "anaerobic" activities of a few seconds duration, aerobic energy turnover makes some contribution, which is facilitated by the O_2 transport system. Obviously, the longer the exercise period, the more critical the O_2 transport becomes. In a short-term anaerobic exercise bout, the O_2 delivery system does not function at maximum, and terminal oxidation contributes little to energy needs. During a 30-second task, such as the Wingate Anaerobic Test, some 20% to 25% of the energy is supplied through aerobic pathways (Inbar et al. 1996). During maximal exercise performance lasting about 60 to 120 seconds, aerobic oxidation of substrates in the mitochondria will yield an increasing proportion of the energy needs. In this case, individuals who can quickly mobilize the oxygen delivery and utilization systems and who, at the same time, have a high anaerobic power will be at an advantage for long-term anaerobic performance.

Neuromotor Control

Although anaerobic performance is determined by metabolic and other biochemical events, adequate execution of the various anaerobic tasks requires also optimal neuromotor control. For example, the height achieved in a vertical jump or the speed of sprinting depends on proficiency in motor skills and not only on the rate of production of ATP. Likewise, adequate performance of the force-velocity test or the Wingate test depends on the ability to cycle or arm crank at very fast speeds. For example, children who were of extremely low birth weight (less than 1,000 g) have been shown not only to have deficient anaerobic performance (using the Wingate test) at 5 to 8 years of age but also to have a slower reaction time, uncoordinated takeoff in the vertical jump, deficient total-body coordination, and a low maximal cycling speed (Falk et al. 1997; Keller et al. 1998). Corresponding data relating the motor characteristics of children to anaerobic performance on the Wingate test are not available.

Overview

The preceding information is derived largely from adults. Hence, its application to children and adolescents should be viewed with care. Because data for growing and maturing individuals are limited, the assumption that the determinants of anaerobic performance are somewhat similar is perhaps reasonable. A single morphological, physiological, biochemical, or neuromotor factor that determines the ability to perform under predominantly anaerobic conditions cannot be identified. The issue is further complicated by the magnitude of interindividual differences in anaerobic performance. Some of the factors re-

sponsible for these differences are considered in chapters 18 and 22.

Measurement Issues

Although the $\dot{V}O_2$max test has been accepted universally as an index of maximal aerobic power, no single laboratory or field test measures all three components (short-term, intermediate-term, and long-term) of anaerobic performance. This lack of a standardized test is one reason why research on anaerobic exercise has lagged behind research on aerobic exercise. In the past 2 decades, however, several anaerobic performance tests have been constructed and evaluated. These tests gave impetus to the better understanding of responses to anaerobic tasks as well as changes in anaerobic performance associated with growth and maturation. This section provides a brief review of performance tests that have been in use in recent years. Table 13.1 summarizes these tests and the specific components of anaerobic performance that they assess. (Bar-Or [1996] and Van Praagh [1996] provide more in-depth discussions of testing details.) Measurements of anaerobic metabolism that are not true performance tests (e.g., maximal blood lactate or accumulated oxygen deficit) are not considered.

Margaria Step-Running Test

First introduced in 1966, this test assesses peak mechanical power of a person who runs up stairs (usually two at a time) at maximal speed. The test, with some modifications, is suitable for children and adults alike. By measuring the time (t) required to make two strides, the vertical height (h) covered, and the subject's body mass (m), power (P) can be calculated:

P (kgm per second) = m (kg) 9.81 h (meter)/ t (sec)

A major advantage of the Margaria test is that it is easy to administer, as long as one has a flight of stairs and a timing system (ideally, a timer activated by photoelectric cells, but a stopwatch can also be used). The test can be administered in a school or a gymnasium, without the need for an exercise laboratory. One disadvantage is that performance is dependent on skill. Subjects need to practice the routine several times until they become proficient. In addition, step-running requires the participation of many muscle groups. This requirement is a drawback, considering that anaerobic performance is a local characteristic of a specific muscle or a muscle group.

TABLE 13.1 Laboratory-Based Anaerobic Performance Tests That Have Been Used With Children and Adolescents

Test	Anaerobic characteristic measured			Comments
	Short	Intermediate	Long	
Margaria step; running	X			Inexpensive; some skill required
Vertical jump; Sargent	X			Instantaneous power; some skill required
Vertical jump; force platform	X			Measures actual forces and power; some skill required
Isokinetic single joint	X	X	X	Useful for contractility and fatigue research
Force-velocity cycling	X			Highly reliable; elicits maximal cycling power
Quebec 10-second cycling	X			Highly reliable; better for short-term than the Wingate Test
Quebec 90-second cycling			X	Highly reliable but very demanding
Wingate	X	X		Suitable also for arm testing; highly reliable, normative data available
Isokinetic cycling	X	X		Suitable for fatigue research; expensive ergometer
Sprint; motorized treadmill	X	X(?)		Uses various muscle groups; possibly limited by fear
Sprint; nonmotorized treadmill		X	X(?)	Requires a learned skill and a harness

Short = short duration; intermediate = intermediate duration; long = long duration.

Vertical Jump—Sargent Test

Developed in 1921 by D.A. Sargent, this test is the first ever to yield reliable information on short-term maximal muscle performance. To perform the jump, the subject crouches momentarily and then, with the swing of the arms, jumps as high as possible. The measured variable is the net vertical elevation (the highest point reached by a finger with the arms extended, minus the height reached by the finger while standing), which, multiplied by body mass, is proportional to the power generated at takeoff. The test does not require equipment and can be performed at a school or gymnasium. The vertical jump is a reliable test in children and adults alike. To achieve optimal performance, subjects should practice the routine. However, some children younger than 7 to 8 years of age do not perform the test adequately, because the basic movement pattern for the vertical is not yet developed. Among children in the fourth through seventh grades (about 9 to 13 years of age), for example, about 40% do not perform the vertical jump with a mature pattern (Reuschlein and Haubenstricker 1985; see also Martin and Malina 1998). This inability may limit the utility of the vertical jump as a measure of anaerobic power.

Vertical Jump—Force Platform

In this test, the subject takes off from a platform that electronically records forces. By multiplying the vertical force exerted just before takeoff by the vertical velocity at that instant, the mechanical power can be calculated. Velocity can be calculated from the height of the jump. The power produced by this test is only 50% to 60% of the peak power generated during the first 5 to 10 seconds of all-out cycling.

Isokinetic Single Joint Test

Using an isokinetic dynamometer (e.g., Cybex or Kin Com), the subject performs repeated maximal extensions or flexions across a single joint (monoarticular tasks). Mechanical power is calculated as the product of the predetermined angular velocity and the measured highest torque in each extension or flexion. When the subject repeats the routine at a fast frequency (e.g., 30 times over a 30-second period), power diminishes gradually because of fatigue. Variables such as peak power, total work, and a fatigue index (the rate of power loss) can be calculated. Because the activity is performed by a specific muscle group (e.g., elbow flexors) and the velocity is controlled by the machine, this test is more suitable than jumping, cycling, or running tests for research on muscle contractility and fatigability. The monoarticular isokinetic test can be carried out for as little as 10 seconds and for as long as 90 to 120 seconds. It, therefore, can be used for short-duration, intermediate-duration, and long-duration testing. However, children have difficulty maintaining rapid repetitions for more than 30 seconds.

Force-Velocity Cycling Test

The test consists of several (usually five to eight) brief (5 to 7 seconds) cycling sprints on an ergometer. Each sprint is performed against a different braking force. The rationale for using several trials is that mechanical power (the product of velocity and force) will be different at different braking forces (see figure 13.3). Only one of these

forces (2.7 kg in the figure) will yield the actual peak power. This force may vary among subjects. The main asset of the force-velocity test is that it identifies the actual peak power for each subject. Peak power is less likely to occur with single cycling trials such as the Quebec 10-second cycling test and the Wingate 30-second cycling test. As further shown in figure 13.3, the fastest possible cycling speed (which would occur when the braking force is zero) and the highest possible braking force (which will occur when the velocity is zero) can also be calculated by extrapolation. The force-velocity test has been used successfully with healthy children (Bedu et al. 1991) and those with a neuromuscular disability (Van Mil et al. 1996). It can be conducted either with an isokinetic or a constant-force ergometer. The main disadvantage of this test is that it takes as much as 45 minutes to complete several sprints with adequate rest periods in between.

Quebec 10-Second and 90-Second Cycling Tests

The Quebec 10-second test requires the subject to ride on a cycle ergometer with an all-out (maximal) effort for 10 seconds. The test provides a measure of total work output in 10 seconds. It has been used with children 9 years of age and older. The braking force is set at about 0.09 kp/kg body mass but is manually adjusted during the test so that the pedaling speed reaches about 10 to 16 m/sec. The reliability of test performance repeated within 7 days is above 0.95 (Simoneau et al. 1983).

Similarly, the Quebec 90-second maximal cycling test requires a ride to exhaustion. It has been used with boys and girls 10 years of age and older. The initial braking force is set at about 0.05 kp/kg body mass, and the subject must pedal maximally for 90 seconds. Only one trial is given. The reproducibility of the test within 7 days is high, with intraclass coefficients of about 0.96.

In both Quebec anaerobic tests, the goal is to perform as much work as possible for the respective durations. The results are best measured on a Monark ergometer, with a photoelectric cell monitoring the displacement of the flywheel and the data relayed to a microprocessor. A potentiometer captures the braking force at the tension adjustment mechanism. An electric timer regulates the duration of the test and the input to the computer (Simoneau et al. 1983).

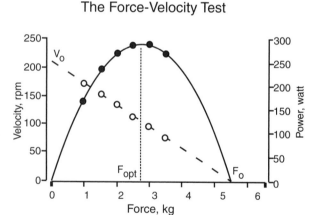

The Force-Velocity Test

FIGURE 13.3 The force-velocity test. A 10-year-old boy performed six cycling sprints, each against a different braking force. Power values (filled circles), calculated for each of the sprints, are plotted against force. The highest power was elicited in this child at a force of 2.7 kg. The velocity-force regression line (open circles) is extrapolated to determine the force at zero velocity (F_0), which is the highest possible force, and the velocity against zero force (V_0), which is the highest possible cycling velocity.
Reprinted from Docherty 1996.

Wingate Anaerobic Test

Developed in the mid-1970s at the Wingate Institute in Israel, this is now the most commonly used test for the assessment of short-term and medium-term anaerobic performance. The test consists of 30-second cycling or arm cranking at maximal speed against a predetermined braking force. The force is high enough to induce fatigue (i.e., loss of mechanical power) within several seconds (see figure 13.4). Power is calculated periodically (usually every 3 to 5 seconds) or continuously, as the product of force and velocity. The indices of performance are peak power (the highest power achieved at any 3-second period) and mean power (the average power throughout 30 seconds). The latter can also be reported as total mechanical work over 30 seconds because work equals the product of power and time. Peak power reflects short-term anaerobic performance, and mean power reflects intermediate-term performance. A fatigue index, the percentage decrease of power from peak to its lowest level, is occasionally calculated. The test, which is suitable for pedaling and for arm cranking, has been used with healthy individuals from 5 years of age to old age, as well as with individuals with nutritional, neuromuscular, and other diseases. Normative data are available for several populations. In its simplest form, the only equipment needed for the test is a mechanically braked cycle ergometer and a stopwatch. An observer counts pedal revolutions. Over the years, however, various degrees of refinements have been added, including custom-made ergometers, photoelectric counting systems, and online linkage to a computer.

The Wingate test has undergone much scientific scrutiny over the years. It is reliable and reproducible. Intraindividual coefficients of variation are 7.3% and 6.8% for peak power and mean power, respectively, among children 6 to 12 years of age (Bar-Or 1987). Performance, peak power in particular, is related to a preponderance of fast-twitch muscle fibers. The main drawback of the test is the lack of an easy way to determine the optimal braking force that would yield the highest possible power.

Isokinetic Cycling Test

Both the Quebec 10-second test and the Wingate test are done with a constant-force ergometer, in which changes in power are calculated from changes in cycling velocity. In contrast, the isokinetic cycling test requires a constant cycling velocity, in which the changes in power are derived from changes in the force exerted on the pedals. This mode of exercise offers research opportunities regarding muscle contractility and fatigability. However, isokinetic cycle ergometers may be prohibitively expensive for most laboratories.

Sprinting—Motorized Treadmill

The time that a person can keep sprinting on a motor-driven treadmill has been used as an index of intermediate-term anaerobic performance (Paterson et al. 1986). One can also calculate the mechanical power or work performed during the test, based on body mass, running velocity, and treadmill incline, but the test is based on several assumptions that have not been fully validated for the calculations. This test has been used with children and adults to estimate "total-body" anaerobic performance rather than the performance of specific muscle groups. Reported test-retest reliability with trained boys is 0.76 at age 10 and 0.84 at age 15. These values are lower than those reported for most other anaerobic performance tests. The main reason for this drawback is that some subjects, particularly untrained individuals, may terminate their run because of fear rather than as a result of having reached a real maximal effort. One way to alleviate such fear is to use a harness that would prevent falling.

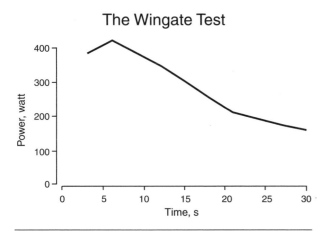

FIGURE 13.4 The Wingate anaerobic test. A typical power versus time curve for a 10-year-old boy, where power is calculated every 3 seconds. In this example, peak power is 422 W, mean power is 287 W and total work is 8,610 J.

Reproduced with permission from Bar-Or (1966).

Sprinting— Nonmotorized Treadmill

Treadmills that can be driven by the walking or running person, rather than by a motor, are currently available. To be able to perform such a task, the subject is tethered with a cable that is connected to the waist. This horizontal cable is connected to sensors that monitor horizontal traction forces and vertical displacement. Running velocity is determined at the treadmill belt. Indices of performance include maximal velocity, peak power, mean power over a predetermined time (e.g., 10 or 30 seconds), kinetic and potential energy, and the time to exhaustion. Even though nonmotorized treadmills are now available commercially, very little research is available on their suitability for children.

Growth and the Determinants of Anaerobic Performance

The morphological, physiological, and biochemical determinants of anaerobic performance change during growth. Several are summarized in table 13.2. Muscle mass, for example, increases with age, particularly during the adolescent growth spurt (see chapter 7). This increase in muscle mass has a direct consequence on the absolute anaerobic power output that can be generated. The ATP, creatine phosphate, and glycogen content of muscle tissue also increase during growth. For example, ATP and creatine phosphate concentrations in a resting muscle are about 30% less in early postnatal life than at

maturity. However, ATP concentration reaches maximal levels before the adolescent growth spurt and sexual maturity.

Children are not able to attain high blood and muscle lactate concentrations during maximal exercise compared with adults. However, maximal blood lactate concentration increases during growth, possibly as a result of hormonal maturation (see figure 13.5). Muscle lactate concentration during submaximal exercise is also lower in children and adolescents compared with adults (see figure 13.6). These observations thus suggest that growing individuals rely less on the glycogen-to-lactate metabolic pathway to

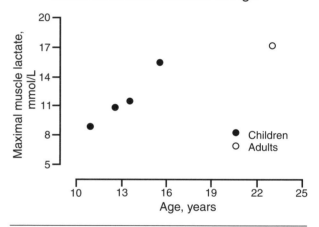

FIGURE 13.5 Muscle lactate levels during maximal exercise in children, adolescents, and young adults. Muscle biopsies were taken from boys 11 to 16 years of age and from young men at the end of a maximal O_2 uptake test.

Data from Eriksson and Saltin, 1974.

TABLE 13.2	Morphological, Physiological, Biochemical, and Neuromotor Factors That May Affect Anaerobic Performance in Children and Adolescents

Variable	Direction of change with growth
Muscle mass	Increases
Maximal oxygen debt per unit body mass	Increases or no change
Rate of anaerobic glycolysis	Increases
Muscle phosphofructokinase activity	Increases
Submaximal and maximal blood lactate levels	Increases
Submaximal and maximal muscle lactate levels	Increases
Blood pH at end of anaerobic or maximal aerobic exercise	Decreases
Neuromotor control	Improves

replenish ATP during aerobic and, in particular, anaerobic exercise. Consistent with these observations is the fact that the activity of muscle phosphofructokinase, a major regulator of anaerobic glycolysis, is lower in children and adolescents than in adults. In addition, children and adolescents are not able to generate or sustain levels of acidosis (as reflected in blood pH) as high as those reported in adults.

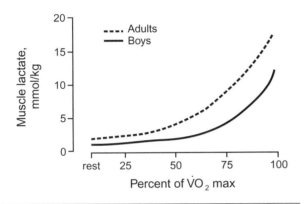

FIGURE 13.6 Muscle blood lactate at several submaximal exercise intensities in 13-year-old to 15-year-old boys and in young men.

Adapted from Eriksson (1980).

The preceding observations indicate that the biological mechanisms associated with the production of anaerobic work and tolerance of the related acidosis are not fully mature until some time after the adolescent growth spurt. However, considerable improvement occurs in anaerobic performance during childhood and adolescence and important differences appear in the growth patterns of aerobic and anaerobic performance.

Short-Duration Anaerobic Performance

Figure 13.7 illustrates changes in total work output for the Quebec 10-second cycling test in a cross-sectional sample of 220 boys and girls from 10 to 19 years of age. In boys, total work output (in joules) increases with body mass, and per kilogram of body mass, throughout the entire period. On the other hand, short-duration anaerobic performance improves only until puberty in girls and then remains rather constant. Thus,

anaerobic performance over a short duration in boys and girls is lower than that of the adults (using the observations for 19-year-old subjects as the young adult reference), even after adjustment for body mass. The same pattern of changes over age has been described for performance on the force-velocity test.

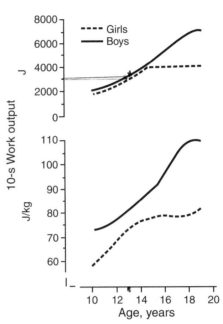

FIGURE 13.7 Changes in total work output in a 10-second maximal ergocycle test in a cross-sectional sample of 220 French-Canadian boys and girls

From Bouchard and Simoneau, 1991.

Another way of displaying age-related changes in anaerobic performance is to express the performances of children and adolescents as a percentage of values for young adults. This approach is shown in figure 13.8, which summarizes peak power data for 80 females and 85 males who performed the Wingate arm-cranking test. Children and adolescents of both sexes have a lower score than young adults, but the age-related difference is considerably greater among males. Females, even as young as 9 years of age, reach 85% of the adult values when performance is calculated per unit body mass.

Anaerobic performance of children is also lower than in adults, even when calculated per unit of muscle size. Figure 13.9 summarizes data for the maximal anaerobic performance of

Peak Power and Age: Girls vs Boys

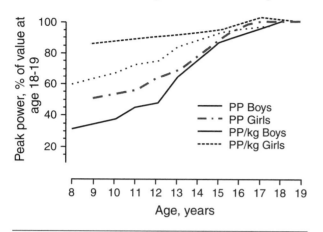

FIGURE 13.8 Short-term anaerobic performance of 80 girls and 85 boys, 9 to 19 years of age, who performed the Wingate arm-cranking test. Values for peak power (PP) and PP/kg body mass are presented as a percentage of performance at age 19.

Data are from Inbar and Bar-Or (1986), Inbar et al. (1996) and Blimkie et al. (1988).

the knee extensor muscles in a cross-sectional sample of French-Canadian children 9 to 19 years of age. Performances in short-duration, intermediate-duration, and long-duration tests of the knee extensor muscles are expressed per

unit of estimated thigh muscle cross-sectional area (based on anthropometric procedures). Thigh area and absolute values for total work output (not shown in figure 13.9) increase with age, more so in boys than in girls after 15 years of age. Total work output in the 10-second test expressed per unit of thigh muscle area improves with age until about 15 years of age in girls and 17 years of age in boys.

Intermediate-Duration Anaerobic Performance

The most commonly used measure of intermediate-duration anaerobic performance is the 30-second Wingate Anaerobic Test, which can be used with leg pedaling and arm cranking alike. Performance in this test increases with age in boys and girls. The same pattern is true when total work output (or mean power) in 30 seconds is reported per kilogram of body mass or fat-free mass. As shown in figure 13.10, absolute mean anaerobic power in 8-year-old boys is 32% of young adult values, and it increases gradually throughout childhood and adolescence. When presented per unit mass (W/kg), mean power at age 8 is still only 75% of young adult values. On the average, intermediate-duration anaerobic performance of girls per unit body mass reaches about 60% to 70% of the intermediate-duration anaerobic performance of boys.

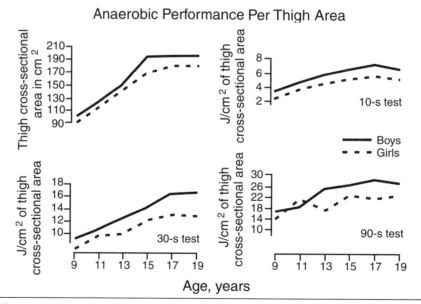

FIGURE 13.9 Changes in the estimated cross-sectional area of the thigh and in total work output per unit thigh area during 10, 30, and 90 seconds of maximal repetitive knee flexions and extensions in a cross-sectional sample of French-Canadian boys and girls.

Data from Saavedra et al., 1991.

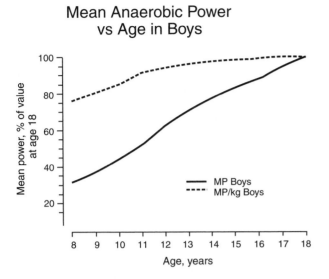

Mean Anaerobic Power vs Age in Boys

FIGURE 13.10 Age-related increase in absolute (MP) and relative (MP/kg) mean anaerobic power of the legs. 150 boys, 8 to 18 years of age, performed the Wingate leg-pedaling test. Values are presented as a percentage of adult values.

Adapted from Inbar (1996).

The same pattern of increase in age-related, intermediate-duration anaerobic performance occurs when values are corrected for the size of the exercising muscle. This pattern is shown in figure 13.9 for mechanical work output per unit of estimated muscle thigh cross-sectional area. Exercise was produced during fast repetitions of maximal knee extension over 30 seconds. Performance improves in both sexes, but the sex difference is more striking in this intermediate-duration anaerobic task than in the shorter (10-second) test.

Long-Duration Anaerobic Performance

Long-duration anaerobic performance is defined as work output during maximal exercise lasting from 1 to 2 minutes. Under such conditions, work output is supported to about the same extent by the anaerobic and aerobic energy delivery systems. The capacity to perform under long-term anaerobic conditions improves with age during growth. This improvement is indicated in the duration of running in a maximal treadmill test, by the increase in the maximal oxygen debt that can be incurred under maximal exercise conditions, and by the increase with age in maximal muscle and blood lactate values and concomitant decrease with age in blood pH.

Data on the long-duration anaerobic performance of children are not extensive, and very few valid tests exist. One cross-sectional study utilized an ice skating test in which boys skated a distance of 18.3 meters (60 feet) as quickly as possible, 12 times. Changes in performance times on this skating test for about 800 boys between 8 and 16 years of age are shown in figure 13.11. Performance improves almost linearly with age as a result of an increase in both skill and anaerobic performance.

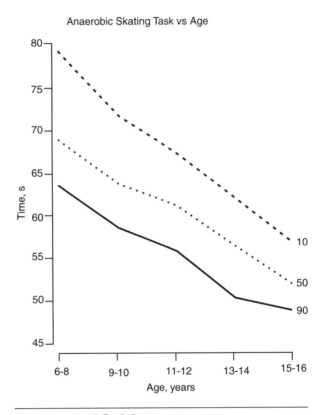

Anaerobic Skating Task vs Age

FIGURE 13.11 Changes in the time taken by boys to skate a distance of 18.3 meters 12 times. Percentiles are derived from cross-sectional data on 800 subjects.

Drawn from data reported by Larivière and Godbout (1976).

More direct data on long-duration anaerobic performance are compared with short-duration and intermediate-duration anaerobic performances in figure 13.9. Total work output in a maximal 90-second knee extension test, expressed per unit of thigh muscle cross-sectional area, improves with age more so in boys than in girls. The long-duration anaerobic performance of girls performing this task reaches a plateau at about 11 years of age, whereas the corresponding performance of boys improves until about 17 years of age. Thus, the sex difference is especially marked between 13 and 19 years of age. When total work output is expressed in an absolute manner, total joules of work during 90 seconds reach a maximum at 15 years of age in girls and 17 years of age in boys.

Longitudinal Observations and Stability of Anaerobic Performance

Longitudinal data on anaerobic performance during growth are few. The anaerobic performances of a mixed cross-sectional longitudinal sample of Canadian boys, 10.9 to 16.2 years of age at the start, were followed for 18 months (Falk and Bar-Or 1993). The boys were grouped by stage of puberty (see chapter 15) at the start of the study: 16 were prepubertal (10.9±1.0 years), 15 were pubertal (13.6±1.7 years), and five were late pubertal (16.2±0.4 years). Although some overlap occurs, age of the subjects increases with stage of puberty. The results of this short-term longitudinal study are illustrated in figure 13.12. Maximal aerobic power per unit body weight remains constant at this interval, whereas peak anaerobic power per unit body weight increases with age. Interindividual variability in aerobic performance is much

less than for anaerobic performance. A similar pattern of longitudinal change is evident among French boys (Duché et al. 1992), but longitudinal data for girls are presently not available.

Very little information is available on the stability of anaerobic performance over time. In the short-term longitudinal study of boys cited previously, correlations between measurements of anaerobic performance over the interval of 18 months are moderate to high (see table 13.3). Over this short interval, performance expressed in absolute power units tracks well, but stability is lower when performance is expressed per unit body weight.

TABLE 13.3	Short-Term Stability of Anaerobic Performance in 36 Boys 11 to 16 Years of Age Over an Interval of 18 Months	
Variable	**Rank-order correlation**
Absolute peak power (W)	0.92
Relative peak power (W/kg)	0.56
Absolute mean power (W)	0.97
Relative mean power (W/kg)	0.85

Adapted from Falk and Bar-Or (1993).

Interage correlations for the vertical jump during childhood and the transition into adolescence tend to be moderate, whereas corresponding correlations during adolescence range from moderate to high (see table 11.3). The data for adolescence are available for boys only.

Interrelationships Among Components of Anaerobic Performance

Data that consider interrelationships among different indicators of anaerobic performance are not extensive. Among boys 10 to 17 years of age, the common variance ($r^2 \times 100$) between total work over 30 seconds in the Wingate test and height of the Sargent (vertical) jump reaches 85% (Suei et al. 1998). In young adults, the common variance between performances in the Quebec 10-second and 30-second anaerobic tests reaches 96%. The common variances for performances on the Quebec 10-second and 90-second and 30-second and 90-second anaerobic tests are 77% and 90%,

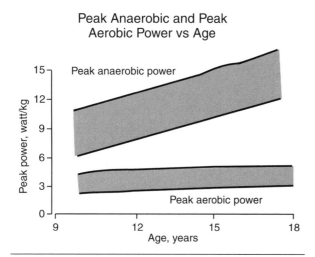

FIGURE 13.12 Short-term longitudinal changes in anaerobic and aerobic performance among boys 10.9 to 16.2 years of age at the start of the study. Each boy performed the Wingate test and an aerobic cycling test four times over 18 months. The shaded areas summarize 144 data points for each test.

Adapted from Falk and Bar-Or (1993).

respectively (Boulay et al. 1985). Although data are not extensive, they indicate that various indices of anaerobic performance are quite strongly related with each other.

Relationship Between Anaerobic and Aerobic Performances

Power output at maximal oxygen uptake remains reasonably stable at about 3 W/kg body weight in girls and 3.5 W/kg body weight in boys during growth. At the same time, short-term and intermediate-term anaerobic performances increase gradually relative to body weight. When peak anaerobic-to-aerobic power output, both measured on a cycle ergometer, is expressed as a ratio, the ratio increases from a value of 2 at about 8 years of age to about 3 during adolescence; it is then rather stable through the late teens (see figure 13.13). Thus, the ratio of peak anaerobic to aerobic power increases until about 13 to 14 years of age in girls and 14 to 15 years of age in boys and then levels off. A similar pattern is apparent in short-term longitudinal observations (Falk and Bar-Or 1993). The increase in the ratio from childhood through adolescence indicates that the anaerobic energy delivery system improves relatively more than the aerobic energy delivery system. As noted earlier, interindividual and intraindividual variability during growth is considerably greater for anaerobic performance than for aerobic performance (see figure 13.12).

Recovery After Anaerobic Exercise in Children

Individuals often need to repeat a physical task after a brief rest. Understanding the concepts of recovery after an exercise bout is thus important. Investigators have long had the impression that children recover faster than adults after a strenuous physical task. This question was addressed in boys 9 to 12 years of age and young adult men 19 to 23 years of age (Hebestreit et al. 1993, 1996). In each visit to the laboratory, subjects performed

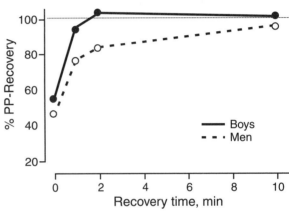
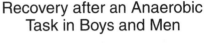
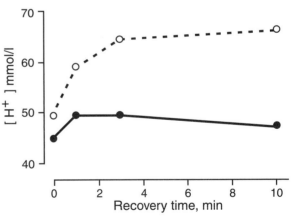

FIGURE 13.14   Rate of recovery after the Wingate anaerobic cycling test in boys (9 to 12 years of age) and young men (19 to 23 years of age) who performed pairs of Wingate tests at various rest intervals. The top graph summarizes the time needed to reproduce the performance of the first Wingate test, which is taken as 100%. This level is represented by a thin horizontal line. The bottom graph is based on measurement of hydrogen ion (H⁺) concentration in venous blood, drawn periodically after a single Wingate test.

Adapted from Hebestreit, Mimura, and Bar-Or 1993.

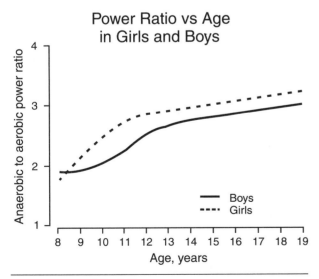

FIGURE 13.13   Changes in the anaerobic power to aerobic power ratio from cycle ergometer tests in boys and girls.

Adapted from Blimkie et al. (1986).

a pair of Wingate tests with varying rest periods in between. The study was designed to determine how much rest is needed until a subject can reproduce his performance of the initial test. Results are shown in the top part of figure 13.14. Boys have a considerably faster recovery than the men. Boys reach nearly full recovery by 2 minutes, whereas men do not recover fully even after 10 minutes. The most likely explanation for the faster recovery of boys is a lower accumulation of muscle lactate and lower acidosis in the muscles. This development is reflected in the lower H^+ levels in boys (bottom part of figure 13.14). Note also that H^+ levels start to decrease after 1 minute of recovery in boys, whereas H^+ does not decrease even after 10 minutes in men. Other physiological functions, such as heart rate, $\dot{V}O_2$, and pulmonary ventilation also recover considerably faster in boys. Corresponding data for girls and women are not available.

Summary

Performance on anaerobic tasks improves during childhood and adolescence in boys but improves until adolescence in girls and then remains rather constant. Sex differences are generally small before adolescence and are magnified during adolescence, but these trends vary to some extent with the specific anaerobic tests used. Determinants of anaerobic performance include morphological (muscle architecture and fiber type), physiological (efficiency of metabolic pathways and oxygen delivery system), biochemical (substrate availability and accumulation of reaction products), and neuromotor (motor skill and motor unit recruitment) factors, but the data are derived largely from adults. Because data for growing and maturing individuals are limited, perhaps the determinants of anaerobic performance can reasonably be assumed to be somewhat similar. Information on the tracking of anaerobic performances is limited, but available estimates indicate moderate stability during childhood and adolescence.

Sources and Suggested Readings

Bar-Or O (1983) Pediatric Sports Medicine for the Practitioner: From Physiologic Principles to Clinical Application. New York: Springer-Verlag.

* Bar-Or O (1987) The Wingate anaerobic test, an update on methodology, reliability and validity. Sports Medicine 4: 381-394.

* Bar-Or O (1996) Anaerobic performance. In D Docherty (ed), Measurement Techniques in Pediatric Exercise Science. Champaign, IL: Human Kinetics, pp 161-182.

Bedu M, Fellmann N, Spielvogel H, Falgairette G, Van Praagh E, Coudert J (1991) Force-velocity and 30s Wingate tests in boys at high and low altitudes. Journal of Applied Physiology. 70:1031-1037.

Blimkie CJR, Roche P, Bar-Or O (1986) The anaerobic-to-aerobic power ratio in adolescent boys and girls. In J Rutenfranz, R Mocellin, F Klimt (eds), Children and Exercise XII. Champaign, IL: Human Kinetics, pp 31-37.

Blimkie CJR, Roche P, Hay JT, Bar-Or O (1988). Anaerobic power of arms in teenage boys and girls: Relationship to lean tissue. European Journal of Applied Physiology 57:677-683.

* Bouchard C, Taylor AW Simoneau JA, Dulac S (1989) Testing anaerobic power and capacity. In JD MacDougall, HA Wenger, HJ Green (eds), Physiological Testing of the Elite Athlete, 2nd edition. Champaign, IL: Human Kinetics, pp 175-221.

Boulay MR, Lortie G, Simoneau JA, Hamel P, Leblanc C, Bouchard C (1985) Specificity of aerobic and anaerobic work capacities and powers. International Journal of Sports Medicine 6:325-328.

Duché P, Falgairette G, Bedu M, Fellmann N, Lac G, Coudert J (1992) Longitudinal approach of bio-energetic profile in boys before and during puberty. In J Coudert, E Van Praagh (eds), Pediatric Work Physiology: Methodological, Physiological and Pathological Aspects. Paris: Masson, pp 43-45.

Edgerton VR, Roy RR, Gregor RJ, Rugg S (1986) Morphological basis of skeletal muscle power output. In NL Jones, N. McCartney, AJ McComas (eds), Human Muscle Power. Champaign, IL: Human Kinetics, pp 43-64.

Edington DW, Edgerton VR (1976) The Biology of Physical Activity. Boston: Houghton Mifflin.

Eriksson BO (1980) Muscle metabolism in children: A review. Acta Paediatrica Scandinavica 283 (suppl):20-27.

Eriksson BO, Saltin B (1974) Muscle metabolism during exercise in boys aged 11–16 years compared to adults. Acta Paediatrica Belgica 28 (suppl):257-265.

Falk B, Bar-Or O (1993) Longitudinal changes in peak aerobic and anaerobic mechanical power of circumpubertal boys. Pediatric Exercise Science 5:318-331.

Falk B, Eliakim A, Dotan R, Liebermann DG, Regev R, Dolphin T, Bar-Or O (1997). Birth weight and physical ability in 5- to 8-year-old healthy children born prematurely. Medicine and Science in Sports and Exercise 29:1124-1130.

Grodjinovsky A, Inbar O, Dotan R, Bar-Or O (1980) Training effect on the anaerobic performance of children as measured by the Wingate anaerobic test. In K Berg, BO Eriksson (eds), Children and Exercise IX. Baltimore, MD: University Park Press, pp 139-145.

Hebestreit H, Meyer F, Htay-Htay, Heigenhauser GJF, Bar-Or O (1996). Plasma metabolites, volume and electrolytes following high-intensity exercise in boys and men. European Journal of Applied Physiology 72:563-569.

Hebestreit H, Mimura K, Bar-Or O (1993) Recovery of muscle power after high-intensity short-term exercise: Comparing boys and men. Journal of Applied Physiology 74: 2875-2880.

Hultman E, Sjoholm H (1986) Biochemical causes of fatigue. In NL Jones, N McCartney, AJ McComas (eds), Human Muscle Power. Champaign, IL: Human Kinetics, pp 215-235.

Inbar O (1996) Development of anaerobic power and local muscle endurance. In O Bar-Or (ed), The Child and Adolescent Athlete. Oxford: Blackwell Science, pp 42-53.

Inbar O, Bar-Or O (1986) Anaerobic characteristics in male children and adolescents. Medicine and Science in Sports and Exercise 18:264-269.

* Inbar O, Bar-Or O, Skinner JS (1996) The Wingate Anaerobic Test. Champaign, IL: Human Kinetics.

Jacobs I, Tesch P, Bar-Or O, Karlsson J, Dotan R (1983) Lactate in human skeletal muscle after 10 and 30s of supramaximal exercise. Journal of Applied Physiology: Respiratory, Environmental and Exercise Physiology. 55:365-367.

Keller H, Ayub BV, Saigal S, Bar-Or O (1998) Neuromotor ability in 5- to 7-year-old children with very low or extremely low birthweight. Developmental Medicine and Child Neurology. 40:661-666.

Larivière G, Godbout P (1976). Mesure de la condition physique et de l'efficacité technique de joueurs de hockey sur glâce. Normes pour différentes catégories de joueurs. Québec: Editions du Pélican.

Makrides L, Heigenhauser GJF, McCartney N, Jones NL (1985) Maximal short-term exercise capacity in healthy subjects aged 15–70 years. Clinical Science 69:197-205.

Margaria R, Aghemo P, Rovelli E (1966) Measurement of muscular power (anaerobic) in man. Journal of Applied Physiology 21:1662-1664.

* Martin JC, Malina RM (1998) Developmental variations in anaerobic performance associated with age and sex. In E Van Praagh (ed), Pediatric Anaerobic Performance. Champaign, IL: Human Kinetics, pp 45-64.

Paterson DH, Cunningham DA, Bunstead LA (1986) Recovery of O_2 and blood lactic acid: Longitudinal analysis in boys aged 11 to 15 years. European Journal of Applied Physiology 55:93-99.

Reuschlein S, Haubenstricker JL, editors (1985) 1984–1985 Physical Education Interpretive Report: Michigan Educational Assessment Program. Lansing, MI: Michigan Department of Education.

Saavedra C, LaGasse P, Bouchard C, Simoneau JA (1991) Maximal anaerobic performance of the knee extensor muscles during growth. Medicine and Science in Sports and Exercise 23:1083-1089.

Sargeant AJ, Dolan P (1986) Optimal velocity of muscle contraction for short-term (anaerobic) power output in children and adults. In J Rutenfranz, R Mocellin, F Klimt (eds): Children and Exercise XII. Champaign, IL: Human Kinetics, pp 39-42.

Simoneau JA, Lortie G, Boulay MR, Bouchard C (1983) Tests of anaerobic alactacid and lactacid capacities: Description and reliability. Canadian Journal of Applied Sport Sciences 8: 266-270.

Suei K, McGillis L, Calvert R, Bar-Or O (1998). Relationships among muscle endurance, explosiveness and strength in circumpubertal boys. Pediatric Exercise Science 10: 48-56.

Van Mil E, Schoeber N, Calvert RE, Bar-Or O (1996). Optimization of braking force in the Wingate test for children and adolescents with a neuromuscular disease. Medicine and Science in Sports and Exercise 28:1087-1092.

Van Praagh E. (1996) Testing of anaerobic performance. In O Bar-Or (ed), The Child and Adolescent Athlete. Oxford: Blackwell Science, pp 602-616.

* Van Praagh E, editor (1998) Pediatric Anaerobic Performance. Champaign, IL: Human Kinetics.

Van Praagh H, Falgairette G, Bedu M, Fellmann N, Coudert J (1989). Laboratory and field tests in 7-year-old boys. In S Oseid, K-H Carlson (eds), Children and Exercise, Volume XIII. Champaign, IL: Human Kinetics, pp 11-17.

Zanconato S, Buchtal S, Barstow TJ, Cooper DM (1993). ^{31}P-magnetic resonance spectroscopy of leg muscle metabolism during exercise in children and adults. Journal of Applied Physiology 74:2214-2218.

14 THERMOREGULATION DURING GROWTH

Chapter Outline

Any physical activity is accompanied by the production of metabolic heat. When body heat accumulates in excessive amounts, physical and mental functions may suffer. Further heat accumulation may induce heat-related illness. Likewise, exposure to a cold climate may be accompanied by excessive heat loss from the body, which also may interfere with function and good health.

In the context of thermoregulation, the body is divided into the **core** and the **periphery**. This division is mostly for functional rather than anatomical purposes. Broadly speaking, the body core includes muscles and all internal organs, and the periphery includes skin and subcutaneous fat.

The main objective of thermoregulation is to prevent core body temperature from rising or falling excessively. This objective is achieved by several physical, physiological, and behavioral mechanisms. Although the basic principles of physiological thermoregulation are similar among all humans, differences exist in the pattern in which people respond to physical activity in hot or cold climates. This chapter first presents the basic physical and physiological principles of temperature regulation and then discusses the effects of growth and maturation on responses to climatic heat and cold stresses. For more detailed reviews, see Bar-Or (1989) and Falk (1996).

The Physics of Heat Transfer

Heat is produced continuously by the body as a by-product of metabolism. During physical activity, metabolic heat increases as a function of work intensity and duration. Unless dissipated, the extra heat will induce a rise in body temperatures. An excessive rise in core body temperature (e.g., 39°C or higher) may interfere with body function, well-being, and health. Likewise, when heat loss from the body exceeds its production, body temperatures will drop. An excessive drop of core body temperature (e.g., 36°C or lower) also will interfere with function, well-being, and health.

As discussed in chapter 12, children have a higher metabolic cost per kg body mass during activities that include walking or running, compared with adolescents or adults. One implication of this difference is that the metabolic heat production per kg mass is higher in children during such activities. Whereas this condition may be beneficial in cold climates, it poses a disadvantage to the child who exercises in the heat.

The four avenues by which heat is transferred between the body and the environment are **conduction, convection, radiation,** and **evaporation.** The rates of conduction, convection, and radiation depend on the temperature gradient between the skin and the environment. When skin temperature is higher than ambient temperature, heat will flow from the skin to the environment. In contrast, when the environment is cooler than the skin, heat will flow from the body to the environment. The rate of evaporative cooling depends on the amount of fluid available for evaporation (primarily sweat in humans), on the humidity of the environment (the more humid it is, the slower the evaporation), and on wind velocity (movement of air over the skin enhances evaporation).

Whereas the rate of heat production during exercise is proportional to body mass, the rate of heat dissipation through each of the four avenues depends on the surface area of the skin. A person's **surface area–to–mass ratio,** therefore, affects the ratio of heat dissipation to heat production in both hot and cold climates. This notion is particularly important in understanding the effects of growth on thermoregulatory effectiveness, because the smaller the person, the larger the surface-to-mass ratio. An example is shown in figure 14.1. Despite his small size, the 8-year-old child has a consid-

erably larger surface-to-mass ratio (380 cm^2/kg) than does the adult (280 cm^2/kg). As a result, irrespective of physiological processes, the rates of heat conduction, convection, and radiation between the child and the environment would be faster than in the adult. Likewise, even if the sweating rate per unit of surface area is similar in children and adults, the rate of evaporation per kg body mass would be faster in the child. However, as discussed in the next section, the sweating rate of children is lower than in adults. As a result, evaporative cooling in a child is usually lower than in an adult.

Physiological Means of Thermoregulation

Two mechanisms are available to humans to prevent an excessive build-up of body heat: an increase in skin blood flow, which enhances the transfer of heat from body core to the skin, and sweating, which facilitates evaporative cooling from the wet skin. During exposure to the cold, two other mechanisms are available to prevent excessive body cooling: a reduction in skin blood flow, which reduces the transfer of heat from body core to periphery, and an increase in metabolic rate to produce additional heat. Mild increases in metabolic heat production can be achieved without shivering, but for a faster rate of heat production, shivering (i.e., rhythmic, non-intentional muscle contractions) occurs. Intense shivering can increase the metabolic rate up to fivefold and even more. All of these physiological functions are activated through centers in the brain, specifically the hypothalamus, which respond to signals such as core and skin temperatures.

Responses to Heat Associated With Growth and Maturation

The pattern of response to heat varies during childhood and adolescence. The responses relate in part to changes associated with growth and maturation.

Sweating Pattern

The sweating rate of children is lower than the rate in adolescents and adults. The difference is apparent mostly when sweating rate is calculated in volume per unit time but also when it

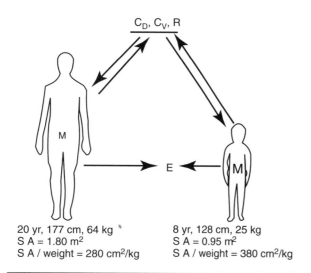

Heat Production and Transfer: Child vs Adult

C_D, C_V, R

M

E

M

20 yr, 177 cm, 64 kg
S A = 1.80 m^2
S A / weight = 280 cm^2/kg

8 yr, 128 cm, 25 kg
S A = 0.95 m^2
S A / weight = 380 cm^2/kg

FIGURE 14.1 Schematic presentation of heat production and transfer in a child and an adult. C_D = conduction, C_V = convection, R = radiation, E = Evaporation, and M = metabolic heat production. SA = body surface area. The length of arrows reflects the greater rate of heat transfer per unit mass in the child. The larger M reflects the greater heat production per unit mass in the child.

Reproduced with permission from Bar-Or (1983).

is corrected for differences in body surface area (e.g., ml/min · m² skin area). This pattern is summarized in figure 14.2, which shows that, based on cross-sectional data, sweating rate increases gradually from childhood through adolescence into adulthood. Longitudinal observations in boys have shown that the increase in sweating rate starts when the child reaches early puberty

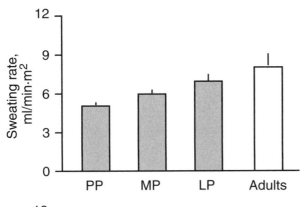

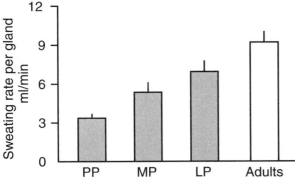

FIGURE 14.2 Sweating rate in childhood, adolescence, and young adulthood when exercising under hot, dry conditions (42°C, 20% relative humidity) at 50% maximal O₂ uptake in a climatic chamber. Boys are grouped as prepubertal (PP, n = 16, 10.9±1.0 years of age), midpubertal (MP, n = 15, 13.6±1.7 years of age), and late pubertal (LP, n = 5, 16.2±0.4 years of age). Young adult males (n = 16) ranged from 20 to 23 years of age. Values are presented in ml/min · m² (top) and per single gland (bottom). Vertical lines denote 1 SEM. Adapted from Falk et al. (1992a) and Bar-Or (1980). Stages of puberty were based on the assessment of pubic hair (see chapter 15). Because age was not statistically controlled in the analysis, the trends indicate both age and sexual maturity effects in the boys.

Adapted from Falk et al.; and Bar-Or 1990.

(Falk et al. 1992a). A similar trend occurs among girls, but, in general, the differences in sweating rates related to maturity in females are less than in males (Kawahata 1960).

Does the lower sweating rate in children result from a smaller number of heat-activated sweat glands or from a lower production of sweat by each gland? The population density of active sweat glands is inversely proportional to body surface area (see figure 14.3). The smaller individual has a larger population density of sweat glands. The lower sweating rate in children, therefore, is the result of lower production per gland. A sweat gland of an adult male produces, on average, 2.5 to 3.0 times as much sweat as in a boy who has not yet entered puberty (see figure 14.2.). The respective ratio for females is only 1.5 to 2.0 (Bar-Or 1980; Falk et al. 1992a; Kawahata 1960).

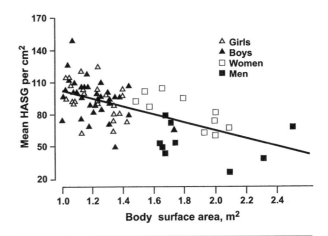

FIGURE 14.3 Population density of heat-activated sweat glands (HASG) in relation to body surface area. Each data point represents an arithmetic mean calculated from several skin sites. Subjects were American and Israeli females and males, who rested in a hot, dry environment.

Reproduced with permission from Bar-Or (1989).

The reasons for lower sweat production in children are not entirely clear. Low production may reflect smaller sweat glands but also a lower availability of energy for the production of sweat. Measurements of lactate levels in sweat suggest a lower anaerobic energy turnover in the sweat glands of prepubertal boys compared with adolescent boys (Falk et al. 1991).

Cardiovascular Responses

Research is limited on changes in cardiovascular responses to climatic heat that are associated with growth and maturation. Whereas cardiac output in children at a given O_2 uptake is slightly lower than in adults during exercise in a thermoneutral environment (Turley and Wilmore 1997), no similar data exist for exposure to the heat. As for peripheral blood flow, observations in females (Drinkwater et al. 1977) and males (Falk et al. 1992b) alike suggest that the increase in skin blood flow of children is greater than in adolescents and adults (see figure 14.4.). This increase in skin blood flow represents an important compensatory mechanism for the lower evaporative capacity of children.

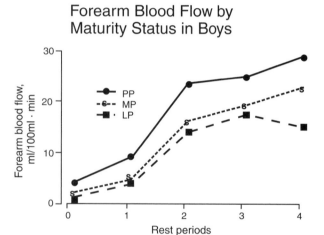

Forearm Blood Flow by Maturity Status in Boys

FIGURE 14.4 Forearm blood flow measured before and on several occasions during exercise in a climatic chamber under hot, dry conditions (42°C, 20% relative humidity) at 50% maximal O_2 uptake in boys during childhood and adolescence. Boys are grouped by stage of puberty (see figure 14.2). Measurements were taken at rest and immediately after 20-minute bouts of exercise. Vertical lines denote 1 SEM. Because age was not statistically controlled in the analysis, the trends indicate both age and sexual maturity effects in the boys (see chapter 15).

Reproduced with permission from Falk et al. (1992b).

Acclimatization and Acclimation

Upon transition from a cool or temperate climate to a warmer climate, a reduction in physical (and sometimes mental) performance occurs. This phenomenon is particularly apparent in athletes, soldiers, or other people who must perform physical tasks after an abrupt change in climatic conditions. Such a reduction in performance is temporary, and repeated exercise in the new environment gradually improves physiological functions and physical performance. **Acclimatization** denotes the gradual physiological and perceptual changes that occur when heat plus exercise exposures are performed in natural heat. The term **acclimation** is used when the exposures take place in an artificial environment, such as a climatically controlled chamber. For convenience, acclimatization is used here to represent both processes.

When first confronted with the new climate, the nonacclimatized person performs a given physical task at a high physiological strain. Specifically, heart rate, core temperature, and skin temperature are considerably higher than those obtained when the same task is performed in a cooler environment. In addition, perception of the intensity of effort is exaggerated. During the period of acclimatization, these functions gradually return to the respective levels manifested in a cooler environment, and physical performance improves. The key to such changes is a gradual increase in sweating rate, which facilitates body cooling. Fully acclimatized individuals often have twice the sweating rate of nonacclimatized peers. Ideally, an acclimatization "exposure" should consist of physical activity, rather than rest, in the hot climate. To reach full acclimatization, adults may need 7 to 10 exposures, each lasting 45 to 90 minutes. However, they can become partially acclimatized even after 4 or 5 such exposures.

Can children acclimatize to the heat? Girls and boys who live in the tropics and are naturally acclimatized show considerably higher sweating rates and lower body temperatures for a given physical task than age-matched children who live in temperate or cold climatic zones (Rivera-Brown et al. 1999). Chamber-based studies with 8-year-old to 10-year-old boys have shown that they can acclimatize but at a slower rate than young men (see figure 14.5). A boy may require twice as many exposures as needed by a young adult male to reach a certain degree of acclimatization (Inbar 1978). No similar comparative data exist for girls. Although the physiological functions of children take longer to improve, their subjective improvement, as assessed by a rating of perceived exertion, is often faster than in adults (Bar-Or and Inbar 1977). This finding is shown in

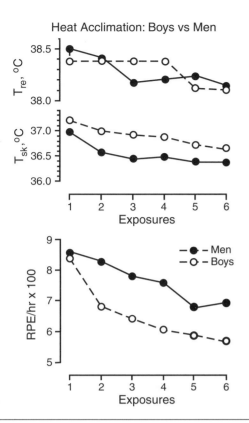

FIGURE 14.5 Acclimatization of 8-year-old to 10-year-old boys and 20-year-old to 23-year-old men to six (three times per week) acclimatization sessions (80 minutes per session) in a climatic chamber at 43°C, 21% relative humidity. T_{re} = rectal temperature, T_{sk} = mean skin temperature, RPE = rating of perceived exertion, HR = heart rate.

Adapted from Inbar (1978) and Bar-Or and Inbar (1977).

figure 14.5. Such a discrepancy between objective and subjective improvement can result in a false sense of well-being in children.

The slow acclimatization in children has practical implications, for example, for a team of athletes who travel to a warmer place (or are confronted by a climatic heat wave at home). Special attention must be given to child athletes under such conditions. They need a lighter than usual training load for a longer period of time, compared with their more mature peers.

Responses to Cold Climates

During exposure to the cold, the role of thermoregulation is to prevent excessive body cooling. When ambient temperature is lower than skin temperature, heat is transferred from the skin to the environment. The greater the temperature

gradient, the faster the heat loss. Other factors that determine the rate of heat loss are the medium that surrounds the skin (e.g., water versus air), the area of contact between the skin and the surrounding medium, and the degree of thermal insulation (e.g., clothing or subcutaneous fat). As discussed earlier, the two mechanisms by which the body can prevent excessive cooling are reduction in blood flow to the skin and an increase in metabolic heat production.

The first study that determined responses of children and adolescents to exercise in the cold was conducted among female and male club swimmers who swam in a pool at 20.3°C (Sloan and Keatinge 1973). As shown in figure 14.6, the rate of cooling is greater in younger children and decreases with age in both sexes. The ratio of surface area–to–body mass, as well as the thickness of subcutaneous fat, explained most of the variance in cooling rate. Children

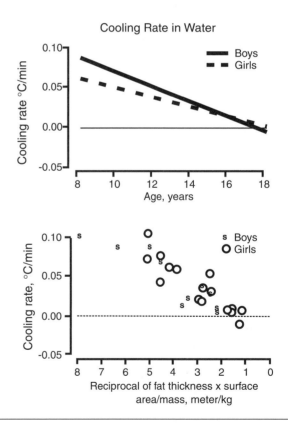

FIGURE 14.6 Cooling rate as a function of age (top) and a combined index of skinfold thickness and body surface area–to–mass ratio (bottom) in 16, 8-year-old to 19-year-old female and male swimmers. Body temperature was measured by an oral thermometer.

Adapted from Sloan and Keatinge (1973).

with a large surface-to-mass ratio and with less subcutaneous insulation had the fastest body cooling.

More recently, physiological responses were compared between 11-year-old to 12-year-old boys and young adult men who rested and then exercised (30% maximal O_2 uptake) while exposed to cold (5°C) air (Smolander et al. 1992). The boys not only managed to preserve core body temperature during the 60-minute exposure, but their temperature increased continuously during rest and exercise and became significantly higher than in the men (see figure 14.7). These responses occurred because the boys had a more effective reduction of skin blood flow (thereby reducing more effectively the flow of heat from the body core), and their cold-induced increase in metabolic rate was twice as high as in the men. Thus, despite the children's larger surface area–to–mass ratio, they managed to compensate physiologically and prevent excessive cooling. The reason for the seemingly contrasting findings in water and in air is that the thermal conductivity of water is about 30 times as high as that of air. As a result, heat flow from the skin is markedly faster in water than in air.

These findings have several practical implications. Coaches of swimming, diving, water polo, and other aquatic sports should pay special attention to young, small, lean, ambitious athletes. Such individuals may reach dangerous levels of cooling of core temperature unless their time in the water is curtailed. Because young girl swimmers are often leaner than their adolescent teammates, their cooling rate may be considerably faster. For land-based activities on a cold day, special attention should be given to the preven-

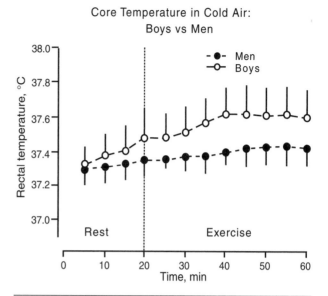

FIGURE 14.7 Core temperature during exposure to cold air in eight, 11-year-old to 12-year-old boys and 11, 19-year-old to 34-year-old men. The subjects rested for 20 minutes and then exercised at 30% maximal O_2 uptake for 40 minutes at 5°C. Subjects wore only shorts, shoes, and socks throughout the session. Vertical lines denote 1 SEM.

Adapted from Smolander et al. (1992).

tion of cold-related damage to the exposed skin. Because children's blood supply to the skin is low, their skin temperature—particularly in the fingers, toes, nose, and ears—may be very low. This condition may cause frostbite in children more frequently than in adolescents or adults. To prevent excessive cooling, make sure that young individuals wear adequate clothing.

Summary

The objective of thermoregulation is to prevent core body temperature from rising or falling excessively. The basic principles of physiological thermoregulation are similar among all humans, but data dealing with growing and maturing individuals are quite limited. Two mechanisms that prevent an excessive build-up of body heat are sweating and an increase in skin blood flow. The sweating rate of children is lower than in adolescents and adults, and this difference is the result of lower sweat production per gland. Limited data suggest that the increase in skin

blood flow of children is greater than in adolescents and adults. This difference represents a compensatory mechanism for the lower sweat production and in turn evaporative capacity in children. Two other mechanisms help to prevent excessive body cooling during cold exposure: a reduction in skin blood flow and an increase in metabolic rate to produce additional heat. Limited evidence from experimental cold exposure suggests that boys have a more effective reduction of skin blood flow and greater cold-induced increase in metabolic rate than men.

Sources and Suggested Readings

* Bar-Or O (1980) Climate and the exercising child: A review. International Journal of Sports Medicine 1:53-65.

* Bar-Or O (1983) Pediatric Sports Medicine for the Practitioner. From Physiological Principles to Clinical Applications. Springer-Verlag, New York.

Bar-Or O (1989) Temperature regulation during exercise in children and adolescents. Perspectives in Exercise Science and Sports Medicine 2:335-367.

Bar-Or O, Inbar O (1977) Relationship between perceptual and physiological changes during heat acclimatization in 8- to 10-year-old boys. In Lavallée H, Shephard RJ (eds), Frontiers of Activity and Child Health. Québec: Pélican, pp 205-214.

Drinkwater BL, Kupprat IC, Denton JE, Crist JL, Horvath SM (1977) Response of prepubertal girls and college women to work in the heat. Journal of Applied Physiology: Respiratory, Environmental and Exercise Physiology 43: 1046-1053.

Falk B (1996) Physiological and health aspects of exercise in hot and cold climates. In O Bar-Or (ed), The Child and Adolescent Athlete. Oxford: Blackwell Scientific, pp 326-349.

Falk B, Bar-Or O, Calvert R, MacDougall JD (1992a) Sweat gland response to exercise in the heat among pre-, mid-, and late-pubertal boys. Medicine and Science in Sports and Exercise 24:313-319.

Falk B, Bar-Or O, MacDougall JD (1992b) Thermoregulatory responses of pre-, mid-, and late-pubertal boys to exercise in dry heat. Medicine and Science in Sports and Exercise 24:688-694.

Falk B, Bar-Or O, MacDougall JD, Goldsmith CH, McGillis L (1992c) Longitudinal analysis of sweating response of pre-, mid-, and late-pubertal boys during exercise in the heat. American Journal of Human Biology 4: 527-535.

Falk B, Bar-Or O, MacDougall JD, McGillis L, Calvert R, Meyer F (1991) Sweat lactate in exercise in children and adolescents of varying physical maturity. Journal of Applied Physiology 71:1735-1740.

Inbar O (1978) Acclimatization to dry and hot environment in young adults and children 8–10 years old. New York: Columbia University, Doctoral Dissertation.

Kawahata A (1960) Sex differences in sweating. In H Yoshimura, K Ogata, S Itoh (eds), Essential Problems in Climatic Physiology. Kyoto: Nankodo, pp 169-184.

Rivera-Brown A, Gutierrez R, Gutierrez JC, Frontera WR, Bar-Or O (1999) Drink composition, voluntary drinking, and fluid balance in exercising, trained, heat-acclimatized boys. Journal of Applied Physiology 86:78-84.

Sloan REG, Keatinge WR (1973) Cooling rates of young people swimming in cold water. Journal of Applied Physiology 35:371-375.

Smolander J, Bar-Or O, Korhonen O, Ilmarinen J (1992) Thermoregulation during rest and exercise in the cold in pre- and early pubescent boys and young men. Journal of Applied Physiology 72:1589-1594.

Turley KR, Wilmore JH (1997) Cardiovascular responses to treadmill and cycle ergometer exercise in children and adults. Journal of Applied Physiology 83:948-957.

Part IV

Biological Maturation

The three chapters of this section deal with biological maturation. Chapter 15 discusses concepts of biological maturation and methods of assessment. It focuses on three commonly used indicators of maturity status—skeletal, sexual, and somatic. Methods used to assess each type of biological maturity are first described and then interrelationships among the maturity indicators are evaluated.

The other two chapters are somewhat more applied. Chapter 16 focuses on the timing and sequence of changes in body size, composition, and performance that occur during the adolescent growth spurt and sexual maturation. Variation among individuals in the timing of the growth spurt in height and sexual maturation is considerable. Growth spurts in other dimensions and body composition and in physical performance are also considered relative to the timing of the growth spurt in height and to the age at menarche.

Chapter 17 discusses maturity-associated variation in size, physique, body composition, and performance during childhood and adolescence. Although maturity-associated variation in growth status is apparent during childhood, it is most marked during adolescence. Maturity-associated variation in strength, motor performance, and aerobic power also occur during childhood. However, maturity-associated variation in these performances is most apparent during adolescence and in males more so than in females.

15 BIOLOGICAL MATURATION: CONCEPTS AND ASSESSMENT

Chapter Outline

Maturation is a process, whereas maturity is a state. Maturation implies progress toward maturity. Maturation occurs and maturity is eventually attained in all tissues, organs, and organ systems of the body. Thus, definitions of maturity are operational in the sense that they depend on the particular system that is studied.

When working with children and adolescents, the term maturity ordinarily refers to the level or the extent to which the individual has progressed to the mature state or adulthood. It is an operational concept because the process cannot be observed or measured directly. Individuals vary in level of maturity attained at a given point in time (maturity status at a given age), in timing (when maturational events occur), and in tempo (rate of maturation).

Each individual has an inborn biological clock that influences progress to the mature state. Matu-

ration relates biological time to calendar time. A child's tempo of biological maturation does not necessarily proceed in concert with the calendar or with the child's chronological age. Within a group of children of the same sex and chronological age, variation will occur in biological age or the level of biological maturity attained. Some children are biologically in advance of their chronological age, and others lag biologically behind their chronological age. Although two children may have the same chronological age, they may not necessarily have attained the same level of biological maturity. They vary in maturity status.

Measures of maturity vary to some extent according to the biological system that is considered. The more commonly used indicators of biological maturity in growth studies are maturation of the skeleton, sexual maturation, and somatic maturation. The three systems are reasonably well related. Eruption and calcification of the teeth are also used occasionally as maturity indicators, but the teeth tend to proceed independently of the other indicators. Developmental milestones, such as age at independent walking and nerve conduction velocity, are used as indicators of neuromuscular maturity. These two developmental milestones, however, are not related to indicators of maturity that are routinely used in growth studies.

An important issue in growth studies is the ability to measure, observe, and quantify maturity status. To be valid, an indicator must occur in all individuals as they progress to maturity. Progress from the immature to the mature state provides the basis for developing criteria that are used to assess level of maturity at a given point in time. Maturity indicators, of course, are specific to the system being used. This chapter describes indicators and methods for the assessment of skeletal, sexual, somatic, and dental maturity.

Assessing Skeletal Maturity

Skeletal maturity is perhaps the best method for the assessment of biological maturity status. All children start with a skeleton of cartilage prenatally and have a fully developed skeleton of bone in early adulthood (see chapter 6). In other words, both the beginning and end points of the process are known because the skeletal structure of all individuals progresses from cartilage to bone. The skeleton is thus an ideal indicator of maturity because its maturation spans the entire period of growth. The rate at which bones progress from the cartilage model, to initial bone formation, to the shape of the bone, and eventually to adult morphology varies among bones within an individual and among individuals.

Progress in the maturation of the skeleton can be monitored with the careful use of standardized X-rays or radiographs. The bones of the hand and wrist provide the primary basis for assessing the skeletal maturity in the growing child. Other areas of the skeleton have been and can be used (e.g., the knee, foot, and ankle), but the hand-wrist area is most widely used. Although some variation is apparent among different areas of the body, the hand-wrist area is reasonably typical of the skeleton as a whole.

Assessment of skeletal maturity from radiographs of the hand and wrist is based on changes in the developing skeleton that can be easily viewed and evaluated on the standardized radiograph. Traditionally, the left hand and wrist are used. The hand and wrist are placed flat on the X-ray plate with the fingers slightly apart; when the film is viewed, the hand-wrist skeleton is observed from the dorsal (posterior or top side) as opposed to the palmar (anterior) surface. A hand-wrist X-ray of an 8-year-old child is shown in figure 15.1, along with a schematic notation of the bones of the hand and wrist. The two categories of bones are long bones and round bones. Each long bone includes a diaphysis and an epiphysis, which are separated by the growth plate. Because the growth plate is cartilage, it does not appear on the film. All long bones, whether they are large (radius and ulna) or small (metacarpals and phalanges), grow in length by the proliferation of cartilage cells at the growth plates (see chapter 6). The carpal bones are the round bones of the hand and wrist. The term round bone is really a misnomer because carpal bones have irregular shapes. Nevertheless, the carpals and other similar bones in the skeleton all begin as an initial center of ossification, which gradually expands from the rounded center of ossification and eventually takes on the unique shape of the specific bone.

Indicators of Skeletal Maturity

The changes in each bone that occur from initial ossification to adult morphology are fairly uniform and provide the basis for assessing skeletal maturity. They are called **maturity indicators**, which are the specific features of individual bones that can be noted on a hand-wrist X-ray and that occur regularly and in a definite, irreversible order.

Maturity indicators provide three types of information for determining the level of skeletal maturity at a given point in time. The first is the initial appearance of bone centers on an X-ray, which indicates the initial replacement of cartilage by bone tissue in the specific bone involved. The second is the definition and characterization of each bone by gradual shape differentiation as the adult form gradually becomes apparent. The characterization process in the long bones involves shape changes in the epiphysis of each bone and in the epiphyseal end of its corresponding diaphysis. In the round bones, the

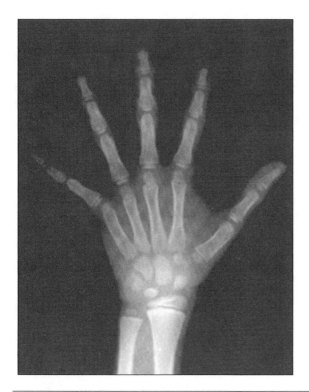
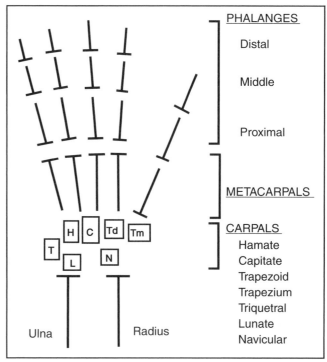

FIGURE 15.1 A hand-wrist X-ray of a boy with a chronological age of 8.0 years. Specific bones (excluding the pisiform and adductor sesamoid) are indicated in the schematic diagram. The horizontal line indicates the location of the epiphysis of each long bone (i.e., proximally or distally).

characterization process involves shape changes and enlargement unique to each carpal bone. The third type of information involves union or fusion of epiphyses with their respective diaphyses in the metacarpals, phalanges, radius, and ulna and the attainment of adult contours and shapes by the carpals. The progress of a bone from initial ossification to adult morphology can be summarized as proceeding from appearance, through characterization, to union of long bones or adult morphology of the round bones.

Methods of Assessment

The three most commonly used methods for the assessment of skeletal maturity of the hand and wrist are the Greulich-Pyle method, the Tanner-Whitehouse method, and the Fels method. The Greulich-Pyle and Tanner-Whitehouse methods are widely used in pediatric clinics and in growth studies. The more recently developed Fels method is gradually finding wider use in these settings.

Greulich-Pyle Method The Greulich-Pyle (GP) method (Greulich and Pyle 1959) is based on the

original work of Todd (1937) and is sometimes called the atlas, or inspectional, method. It was developed on participants in the Brush Foundation Study. The children were from families of high socioeconomic status in the Cleveland, Ohio, area. The method entails the matching of a hand-wrist X-ray of a specific child as closely as possible with a series of standard X-ray plates, which correspond to successive levels of skeletal maturity at specific chronological ages. A child's skeletal age (SA) is the age identified as typical of the sex-specific standard plate with which a given child's film most closely coincides. Thus, if the hand-wrist X-ray of a 7-year-old child matches the standard plate for 8-year-old children, the child's SA is 8 years.

Although the GP method is most often used in this manner, it should, more appropriately, be applied by rating the skeletal maturity of each individual bone. Each bone should be matched to the standard plates in the atlas in the same manner as described previously, and the one with which the individual bone most closely coincides is noted. The SA of the standard plate is the assigned SA of the bone in question. The process is repeated for all bones that are visible in the hand-wrist X-ray, and the child's SA is the median of the skeletal ages of each individually rated bone.

Tanner-Whitehouse Method   The Tanner-Whitehouse (TW) method is sometimes called the bone-specific approach (Tanner et al. 1962, 1975). It was developed on a cross-sectional sample of about 3,000 healthy British children. The method entails matching the features of 20 individual bones on a given film to a series of specific, written criteria for the stages through which each bone passes in its progress from initial appearance to the mature state. Variation occurs in the duration of specific stages within and between bones. Some stages may persist for a longer time (e.g., epiphyseal union), whereas others may be present for a shorter time (e.g., shape changes in the carpals). The written criteria are the basis for assessments with the TW method. Illustrations of the criteria are provided only as a guide. The 20 bones include the seven carpals (excluding the pisiform) and 13 long bones (radius, ulna, and metacarpals and phalanges of the first, third, and fifth digits). A specific point score is assigned to each stage for each bone. The scores for each bone are summed to give a skeletal maturity score, which ranges from zero (immaturity) to 1,000 (maturity). The carpal bones and the radius, ulna, and short bones each contribute 50% to the skeletal maturity score. The scores for each bone were defined so that the overall difference between different bones within each group (carpal bones and the radius, ulna, and short bones) was minimized. The summed score can be converted to a skeletal age (SA), which is referred to as the 20-bone SA.

The scoring system was changed in the revised TW method (TW2), but the maturity indicators were not changed. The TW2 method also provides for a specific carpal SA based on the seven carpal bones, and a radius, ulna, short bone (RUS) SA based on the 13 long bones, in addition to the 20-bone SA. Separate scoring systems were developed for the carpal and RUS skeletal ages (Tanner et al. 1983), but the criteria for evaluating the maturity status of each bone were not changed.

The TW method has been further modified (Tanner et al. 2001) in two ways. First, only RUS and carpal skeletal ages are considered (the 20-bone SA is no longer included). Second, the reference values are now based on samples of British, Belgian, Italian, Spanish, Argentin-

ian, American (Texas), and Japanese children and adolescents. As a result, the tables for the conversion of the skeletal maturity scores to an SA have been changed. The skeletal maturity of more recent samples (10 to 11 years of age and older) is slightly but consistently in advance of the earlier reference values. The new skeletal ages are labeled TW3 skeletal ages. Note however, the criteria for assessing the maturity status of individual bones and the assigned scores for each stage have not been changed. Only the scale for converting the skeletal maturity score to an SA has been changed.

Fels Method   The Fels method for assessing skeletal maturity of the hand-wrist was developed on children in south-central Ohio, who were participants in the Fels Longitudinal Study (Roche et al. 1988). The sample is largely middle class. Maturity indicators for each bone of the hand and wrist were initially defined and their presence then verified. The reliability of each indicator was established and then validated on a separate set of radiographs. Redundant indicators were eliminated to reduce the number that must be assessed. Criteria for specific grades of each maturity indicator are based on the shapes of each carpal bone and the epiphyses and corresponding diaphyses of the radius and ulna and of the metacarpals and phalanges of the first, third, and fifth digits. The presence or absence of the pisiform and adductor sesamoid of the first metacarpal are also used. Grades are assigned to the indicators for each bone by matching the film being assessed to the described criteria. Ratios of the linear measurements of the widths of the epiphysis and metaphysis of each of the long bones are also used.

In converting the grades and ratios to an SA at a given chronological age, the maximum likelihood method was used. This statistical approach selects the most appropriate indicators of skeletal maturity for each chronological age and in males and females. Hence, different maturity indicators are involved in assessments at different chronological ages. In this manner, redundant assessments and information are reduced. The values for the measured (epiphyseal and metaphyseal widths) and graded (assigned grades for specific bones) maturity indicators are entered into a microcomputer that calculates the SA and a standard error of estimate for the SA. The standard error provides an indication of the error inherent in the assessment. Other methods of assessing skeletal maturation do not provide an estimate of error associated with the assessment.

Comparison of Methods

The three methods of skeletal maturity assessment are actually quite similar in principle. All entail matching a hand-wrist radiograph of a child to a set of criteria that are pictorial, verbal, or both. The methods vary in criteria for making assessments and procedures used to construct a scale of skeletal maturity from which skeletal ages are assigned. In the GP method, a child's hand-wrist film is matched to standard plates in the atlas. In the TW and Fels methods, the child's film is matched to specific criteria for each bone. The criteria are based on shape differentiation of individual bones, epiphyseal union, and the attainment of adult morphology. The Fels method also utilizes ratios between linear measurements of epiphyseal and metaphyseal widths of the long bones. Criteria for long bones in the TW method include observations of the widths of the epiphyses and corresponding metaphyses; for example, the epiphysis is as wide as the metaphysis or the epiphysis is wider than the metaphysis, but ratios of linear measurements of epiphyseal and metaphyseal widths are not used.

The GP system uses all 30 bones of the hand and wrist. Note that the schematic illustration in figure 15.1 indicates only 28 bones. Two others, the adductor sesamoid of the thumb (to the left of the first metacarpophalangeal joint) and the pisiform (it is ordinarily superimposed on the triquetral), are used in the GP method. The TW method uses 20 bones—the radius, ulna, seven carpals, and the metacarpals and phalanges of the first, third, and fifth digits of the hand. The Fels method uses the same 20 bones and the pisiform and adductor sesamoid of the first metacarpal.

The methods differ in scoring. The GP method assigns an SA based either on the standard plate to which the film of a child is most closely matched or on the average of the assigned skeletal ages of each individual bone.

The scores for each of the 20 bones rated in the TW method are summed to provide a maturity score. The total score is usually converted to an SA, although the maturity score can be used by itself. The carpal bones and the long bones, by definition, each contribute 50% to the total score and, in turn, to the SA. This partition is somewhat arbitrary. The seven carpal bones ordinarily attain maturity by about 13 years of age, so their contri-

bution in later adolescence is somewhat limited. The revisions of the TW method (TW2 and TW3) provide for separate maturity scores and, in turn, separate skeletal ages for the carpal bones (carpal SA) and for the radius, ulna, and short bones (RUS SA) of the hand and wrist. This partition is useful in adolescence because the carpals attain maturity by about 13 years of age, whereas the radius, ulna, metacarpals, and phalanges continue to mature into late adolescence. However, limiting an assessment to only the 13 long bones may omit some relevant information, especially in individuals in whom the carpals may be delayed. Some individuals present disharmonic maturation, in which some centers of ossification (e.g., the carpals) are more advanced or delayed than others (e.g., the long bones). Such disharmony in maturity is commonly a genetic characteristic.

The scoring system in the Fels method statistically weights the contributions of specific indicators, depending on the sex and age of the child. For example, epiphyseal union of the radius may occur over several years, whereas the appearance of a specific shape of another bone may be present only for a short period of time. Hence, the radius is given less statistical weight and the other bone more weight in calculating the SA at this point in time. As noted earlier, the Fels method provides a standard error of the estimate for the SA.

Methods for the assessment of skeletal maturity will probably continue to evolve. The concept of skeletal age is central to the study of growth in healthy children and is also an important diagnostic tool for pediatricians and endocrinologists who work with children and adolescents with growth disorders. An important development in the assessment of skeletal maturation from hand-wrist radiographs is the use of computer-based techniques. At present, several automated computer-based protocols have been applied to the TW2 method, and the experimental results are reasonably consistent with ratings of expert assessors (Tanner and Gibbons 1994; Tanner et al. 1994; Albanese et al. 1995; Rucci et al. 1995; Van Teunenbroek et al. 1996). The potential use of DEXA to estimate the skeletal maturity of the hand-wrist has also been suggested (Braillon et al. 1998). Further refinements of the methods are necessary. For example, errors occur in interpretation associated with positioning of the hand-wrist on the radiograph and problems of misclassification of stages or grades. Nevertheless, as the computer-assisted and DEXA techniques are refined, they have the potential for more rapid and accurate assessments and elimination of interobserver variability in assessments. However, issues related to intermachine variability will need to be addressed.

Other Methods

A less commonly used method of assessing skeletal maturation of the hand-wrist is that developed by Sempé (1987) (see also Sempé and Pavia 1979) on a longitudinal sample of French children. It is based largely on the Tanner-Whitehouse method, in addition to the earlier approach of Acheson (1954, 1957). The method of Sempè has been used primarily in France and to some extent in Spain and has been used in several studies of young athletes (Jost-Relyveld and Sempè 1982; Vidalin 1988). It has not been systematically compared with the other methods in an independent sample. The GP and TW methods have been modified for Spanish children (Fernandez et al. 1991), whereas an atlas of skeletal maturity based on the TW2 method has been reported for a longitudinal sample of Japanese girls (Eto and Ashizawa 1992).

The foot and ankle and the knee have also been used in assessing skeletal maturity, but the knee has received more attention. Pyle and Hoerr (1969) applied the principles of the GP method to develop an atlas of the skeletal maturity of the knee. Roche et al. (1975a) developed a method for assessing the skeletal maturity of the knee that is based on the same principles used in developing the Fels method for the hand-wrist. Skeletal maturity of the knee is especially useful during infancy and early childhood. This anatomical region has more information than the hand and wrist early in postnatal life. Subsequently, the hand-wrist region has more information.

Acheson (1954, 1957) described a method for assessing the skeletal maturity of the knee and the hip joint and pelvis. The method described specific stages for each bone and then assigned a point score to each stage. Maturity status was based on the sum of the maturity scores. Acheson's approach, the Oxford method, was a forerunner of the TW method.

Skeletal Age

The three methods for the estimation of skeletal maturity yield a skeletal age (SA) that corresponds to the level of skeletal maturity attained by a child relative to the reference sample for each method. SA is sometimes called bone age in the clinical literature. In the Greulich-Pyle method,

the reference sample is American children in the Cleveland area of Ohio studied between 1931 and 1942. In the Tanner-Whitehouse method, the initial reference sample is British children from several areas of the country studied between 1946 and 1972. The reference sample for the Fels method is the Fels Longitudinal Study, which includes American children from southern Ohio studied between 1932 and 1986. Given the differences in the methods and in the reference samples for each, the skeletal maturity status of a child rated by all three methods may be quite different. Thus, the method used to estimate SA must be specified.

Skeletal age is expressed relative to a child's chronological age (CA). SA may simply be compared with CA. For example, a child may have a CA of 10.5 years and an SA of 12.3 years. In this instance, the child has attained the skeletal maturity equivalent to that of a child of 12.3 years and is advanced in skeletal maturity status relative to CA. A child may have a CA of 10.5 years but an SA of 9.0 years. Although chronologically 10.5 years of age, the child has only attained the skeletal maturity of a child 9.0 years of age; this child is delayed in skeletal maturity relative to CA. The terms advanced and delayed should be used carefully. In these examples, the terms simply mean that the child's SA is advanced or early, and delayed or late, respectively, relative to CA. The terms imply nothing about the factor or factors that underlie the advancement or delay in skeletal maturity.

SA may also be expressed as the difference between SA and CA (i.e., SA minus CA). Thus, in the first example given previously, $12.3 - 10.5 = +1.8$ years, and in the second example, $9.0 - 10.5 = -1.5$ years. The child in the first example is ahead in skeletal maturity status by 1.8 years over his or her CA, whereas the child in the second example is behind by 1.5 years relative to CA. At times, SA is simply divided by CA to yield a relative SA. A relative SA above 1.0 indicates advancement, and a relative SA below 1.0 indicates delay in skeletal maturity. In the previous examples, the relative SAs are 1.17 and 0.86, respectively. The use of relative SA is easier for some calculations because the negative (minus) sign is eliminated.

The assessment of SA is basically a method to estimate the level of skeletal maturity that a child has attained at a given point in time relative to reference data for healthy children. The three more commonly used methods for assessing skeletal maturity and deriving SA have their strengths and limitations. Note, however, SAs derived from the Greulich-Pyle (GP), Tanner-Whitehouse (TW1, TW2, and TW3 and carpal or RUS), and Fels methods are not equivalent. The methods differ in criteria and scoring, and the reference samples on which they are based differ considerably. For example, when the hand-wrist radiograph illustrated in figure 15.1 is assessed by each of the methods, three different skeletal ages result. The child had a chronological age of 8.0 years but an SA of 6.4 years with the GP method, 8.1 years with the TW2 20-bone method, and 6.6 years with the Fels method. Mean differences between skeletal ages with the three methods for a sample of German boys, 8 to 16 years of age, are shown in figure 15.2. Three differences are shown: GP SA – Fels SA, GP SA – TW2 20-bone SA, and Fels – TW2 20-bone SA. GP SAs are in advance of Fels SAs at 9 to 11 years of age (positive differences), but Fels SAs are then in advance of GP SAs (negative differences). The same trend is apparent for the differences between GP and TW2 20-bone SAs. On the other hand, TW2 20-bone SAs are greater than Fels SAs, especially from 10 years of age on. In adolescence, the three methods do not provide the same estimates of SA. Application of the revised TW3 reference values to independent samples for comparison with the Fels and GP methods is not presently available.

Differences in Skeletal Ages between Methods of Assessment

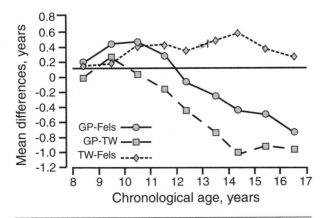

FIGURE 15.2 Mean differences between skeletal ages assessed by three methods in a sample of German boys 8 to 16 years of age. Greulich-Pyle (GP) SA – Fels SA, GP – Tanner-Whitehouse (TW) 20-bone SA, and Fels – TW2 20-bone SA.

Data from Kujawa, 1997.

As noted earlier, the skeletal maturity of more recent samples (10 to 11 years of age and older) is slightly but consistently in advance of the earlier reference values in the TW method.

Each of the methods has advantages and disadvantages. The TW2 method is more widely used at present (the TW3 revision is recent and probably limited in application at present). The Fels method is relatively new compared with GP and TW methods and, as with other new procedures, acceptance and dissemination is a slow process. The GP method is widely used clinically and is good for identifying individuals who are very advanced or very late in skeletal maturation. It is, however, not as finely tuned as the TW and Fels methods.

In summary, the changes that each bone of the hand and wrist go through from initial formation to epiphyseal union or adult morphology are the same. The three methods—GP, TW, and Fels—utilize these changes in a somewhat different manner to derive an assessment of skeletal maturity at a given point in time. The rate at which the process of skeletal maturation progresses varies among individuals and perhaps among populations.

As with anthropometry (see chapter 3), quality control in the assessment of skeletal maturity is essential. Variation within and between assessors and the reproducibility of assessments need to be considered and reported. Unfortunately, such consideration is not always the case, especially in clinical studies.

Assessing Sexual Maturity

Sexual maturation is a continuous process that extends from sexual differentiation in the period of the embryo (see chapter 2) through puberty to full sexual maturity and fertility. Puberty is a transitional period in the process. It is the transitional period between childhood and adulthood and includes the appearance of secondary sex characteristics, maturation of the reproductive system, and the adolescent growth spurt (in addition to psychological and behavioral changes, which are beyond the scope of this volume).

The assessment of sexual maturity in growth studies is based on secondary sex characteristics—breast development and menarche in girls, penis and testes (genital) development in boys, and pubic hair in both sexes. The use of secondary sex characteristics as indicators of maturity status and progress is obviously limited to the pubertal phase of growth and maturity. These indicators thus have limited applicability over the course of growth in contrast to skeletal maturation, which can be monitored from infancy into young adulthood. Menarche is treated separately because no corresponding physiological event occurs in males.

Secondary sex characteristics are outward indicators of the level of sexual maturity at a given point in time. Sexual maturity, of course, is the ability to reproduce. In females, sexual maturity involves the production of a mature ovum (egg) and the ability to carry the pregnancy through term, eventually delivering a viable offspring. In males, sexual maturity involves the production of mature sperm capable of fertilizing an ovum.

Stages of Breast, Genital, and Pubic Hair

Progress in the development of secondary sex characteristics is ordinarily summarized as five or six stages for each character. The most commonly used criteria are the stages for pubic hair, breast and genital maturation described by Tanner (1962), which are based upon the criteria of earlier studies of Reynolds and Wines (1948, 1951). Stage 1 indicates the prepubertal state—the absence of development of each characteristic. Male genitalia, for example, are approximately the same size as in early childhood, breasts show no elevation, and pubic hair is absent. Thus, stages B1, G1, and PH1 indicate the prepubertal or prepubescent state. This simply means that the overt manifestation of the specific secondary sex characteristic is not apparent. Although it is often assumed that prepubertal children are a homogeneous group that does not vary in maturity status, it should be noted that prepubertal children do vary in skeletal maturity (see Chapter 17).

Stage 2 indicates the initial, overt development of each characteristic—the initial elevation of the breasts in girls, the initial enlargement of the genitals in boys, and the initial appearance of pubic hair in both sexes. Stages 3 and 4 indicate continued maturation of each characteristic and are somewhat more difficult to evaluate. Stages B2-B4, G2-G4, and PH2-PH4 indicate the pubertal or pubescent state. These children are sexually maturing and their sexual maturity is evident in the overt development of the secondary sex characteristics. Stage 2 of a characteristic is commonly

rated as early puberty, while stages 3 and 4 of the characteristic are often rated as midpuberty.

Stage 5 indicates the adult or mature state for each characteristic. Some scales for pubic hair include a stage 6, which marks the expansion of pubic hair upwardly in the midline of the abdomen in about 80% of males, and laterally and to a lesser extent upwardly in about 10% of females (van Wieringen et al. 1971).

Each stage of breast, genital, and pubic hair development is illustrated in Figures 15.3 through 15.6. They are copies of the criteria used in nationwide surveys of Dutch children and adolescents in 1965 (van Wieringen et al. 1971) and 1980 (Roede and van Wieringen 1985). The schematic illustrations and descriptive text of the criteria for each stage were added. These were provided by Dr. Alex F. Roche of the Lifespan Health Research Center (Departments of Community Health and Pediatrics, Wright State University School of Medicine). The combination of colored plates, schematic illustrations, and descriptive text are currently used for self-assessment of sexual maturity status in the the Fels Longitudinal Study.

Ratings of the stages of sexual maturation are ordinarily made by direct observation at clinical examination. Such assessments may have limited application outside of the clinical setting because the method requires invasion of individual privacy, which is usually a matter of concern for adolescents. At times, the development of secondary sex characteristics is assessed from standardized, nude photographs of high quality. As good as the photographs may be, it is difficult to detect the initial appearance of pubic hair. For example, commonly used reference data from the Harpenden Growth Study of British youth (Marshall and Tanner 1969, 1970) have later ages for stage 2 of pubic hair. The higher values reflect the difficulty in detecting first appearance of pubic hair on photographs. Clinical observation gives a better estimate.

Given the difficulty in direct assessment of sexual maturation status in nonmedical settings, self-assessments by youth are increasingly used. Youngsters are asked to rate their stage of sexual maturity by comparison with the photographs of Tanner (1962) or van Wieringen et al. (1971), or relative to schematic drawings of the respective stages prepared after these criterion photographs. Good quality photographs of the stages with simplified descriptions and directions should be used. The stages and descriptions illustrated in

Figures 15.3 through 15.6 are currently used for self-assessments in the Fels Longitudinal Study (Roche et al. 1995).

Self-assessment of secondary sex characteristics should be done privately in a quiet room after careful explanation of the procedures and purpose of the assessment. A private cubicle with a full-length mirror is preferred. The mirror assists the adolescent in self-examination and assignment of stages (Roche et al. 1995). Self-assessments should not be done in a group setting.

There are limited data on the concordance of self-ratings of youth and those of experienced assessors. Correlations between self-ratings and physician ratings of the breasts, genitals, and pubic hair are moderate to high, ranging from 0.59 to 0.92 (Matsudo and Matsudo 1994), and some data suggest a tendency for youngsters to overestimate early stages and to underestimate later stages of sexual development (Schlossberger et al. 1992).

There is need for quality control in the assessment of secondary sex characteristics. How concordant are assessments made by two different examiners or by the same examiner on two independent occasions? The reproducibility of clinical assessments by physicians or other experienced raters is not generally reported, when in fact it should be. Results of one of the few studies are summarized in Table 15.1. Overall reproducibility is generally good, about 80%. There is, however, variability in the concordance of physician assessments among stages, ranging in one study from 40% of pubic hair stage 4 in girls to 100% for breast and pubic hair stage 1 in girls and pubic hair stage 3 in boys.

In practice, ratings of secondary sex characteristics are used as follows. A girl may be rated as in stage 2 for the breasts (B2) and stage 1 for pubic hair (PH1). Thus, breast development has begun and pubic hair has not yet appeared. This girl is just in the beginning of puberty, since the budding or initial elevation of the breasts (B2) is most often the first overt sign of sexual maturation in girls. Similarly in males, a boy may be rated in stage 2 of the genitals (G2) and stage 1 for pubic hair (PH1). He is likewise just beginning puberty, because the initial enlargement of the testes (G2) is most often the first overt sign of sexual maturation in boys.

Once the process of sexual maturation is initiated, the development of secondary sex characteristics is a continuous process that varies in tempo. The stages are superimposed on these processes. The only stage that is not arbitrary is stage 1, the lack of overt development of the respective characteristics. The definition and delineation of the other stages for each characteristic are to some extent arbitrary, as is the case for many developmental scales. It is difficult at times to delineate the beginning of a particular stage from the end of the stage. For example, a boy just entering stage 3 of the genitals (G3) and a boy nearing the end of this stage are both rated as G3, even though the latter is really more advanced in maturity than the former.

The stages are superimposed on the ongoing process of maturation, which is not necessarily continuous in its tempo. Progress in sexual maturation appears continuous when data are grouped and reported in terms of average trends. There is, however, considerable variability among adolescents. Some may show a relatively long period of minimal change followed by rapid change in a characteristic, whereas others may show seemingly continuous progress. Or, development of pubic hair and the breasts in girls, or of pubic hair and the genitalia in boys, may show uneven progress or a different tempo of maturation in some individuals. A key factor in monitoring changes in stages of development is the interval between observations. There is a need for observations over relatively short intervals during puberty, 3 to 6 months. Although stages are somewhat arbitrary and have limitations, they are a convenience to facilitate observation of the maturation of secondary sex characteristics during puberty.

TABLE 15.1	Reproducibility of Assessments of Secondary Sex Characteristics			
	Females		**Males**	
Pubertal stage	**Breasts**	**Pubic hair**	**Genitals**	**Pubic hair**
1	100	100	87	81
2	77	93	82	79
3	80	92	69	100
4	80	40	87	82
5	83	60	—	80

Concordance (%) of assessments of physicians on two separate occasions. No males were rated in genital 5.

Adapted from Matsudo and Matsudo (1994).

Stages in Breast Development—Girls

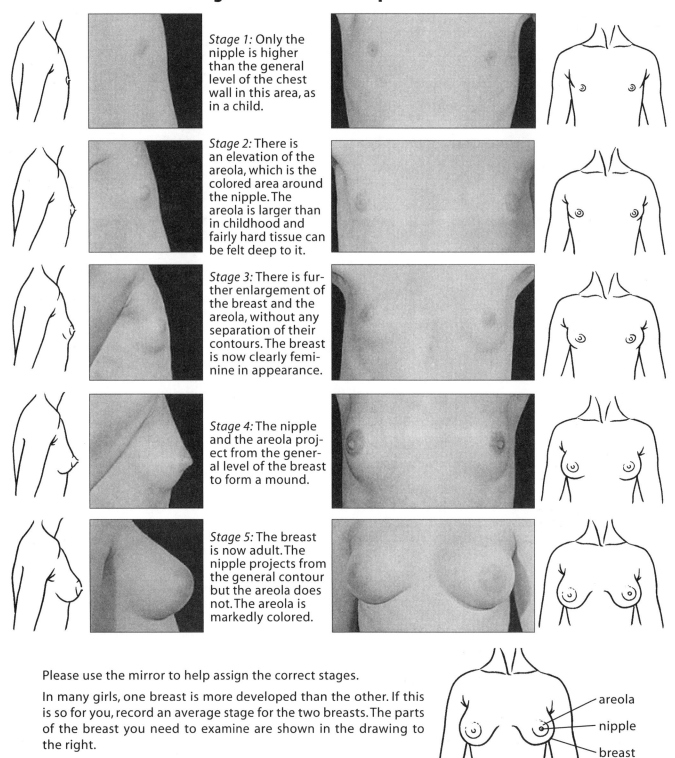

Stage 1: Only the nipple is higher than the general level of the chest wall in this area, as in a child.

Stage 2: There is an elevation of the areola, which is the colored area around the nipple. The areola is larger than in childhood and fairly hard tissue can be felt deep to it.

Stage 3: There is further enlargement of the breast and the areola, without any separation of their contours. The breast is now clearly feminine in appearance.

Stage 4: The nipple and the areola project from the general level of the breast to form a mound.

Stage 5: The breast is now adult. The nipple projects from the general contour but the areola does not. The areola is markedly colored.

Please use the mirror to help assign the correct stages.

In many girls, one breast is more developed than the other. If this is so for you, record an average stage for the two breasts. The parts of the breast you need to examine are shown in the drawing to the right.

areola

nipple

breast

FIGURE 15.3 Stages of breast development in girls. The photographs, schematic illustrations, and descriptive criteria are currently used in the Fels Longitudinal Study (see Roche et al., 1995).

The photographs of the stages are reprinted, with permission, from van Wieringen et al., 1965, *Growth diagrams* (The Netherlands: Wolters-Noordhoof). The schematic illustrations and descriptive criteria were prodived by Dr. Alex F. Roche of the Lifespan Health Research Center (Departments of Community Health and Pediatrics, Wright State University School of Medicine), and are reproduced with his permission.

Stages in Genital Development—Boys

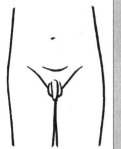 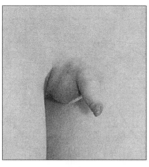

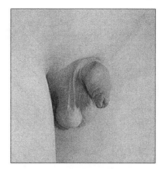 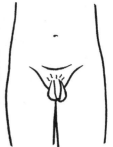

Stage 1: The penis, scrotum, and testes are of the same size and proportion as in early childhood.

Stage 2: The scrotum and testes have enlarged. The size of each testis can be judged by looking at the scrotum and also by feeling each testis through the skin of the scrotum. The skin of the scrotum becomes thinner, wrinkled and slightly red but this is difficult to see in a photograph. There is little or no change in the penis.

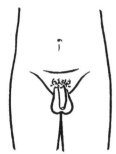 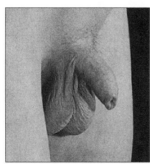

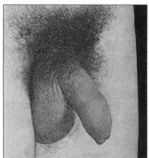 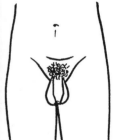

Stage 3: The penis is longer than in early childhood but there is little change in thickness. The scrotum and testes are larger than in stage 2. The scrotum now hangs down further below the base of the penis.

Stage 4: The penis is further enlarged in length and breadth. The end of the penis becomes conical and there is an enlargement where this part (the glans) joins the rest of the penis. The scrotum and testes are further enlarged and the skin of the scrotum is darker.

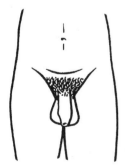 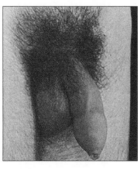

Stage 5: The penis, scrotum, and testes are adult in size and shape.

The genitalia to be graded are the penis and the scrotum and the testes, which can be felt within the scrotum. If you consider there are differences from one side of your body to the other, which is not unusual, assign a stage based on the average of the two sides.

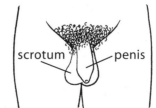 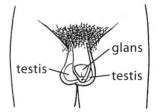

FIGURE 15.4 Stages of genital development in boys. The photographs, schematic illustrations, and descriptive criteria are currently used in the Fels Longitudinal Study (see Roche et al., 1995).

The photographs of the stages are reprinted, with permission, from van Wieringen et al., 1965, *Growth diagrams* (The Netherlands: Wolters-Noordhoof). The schematic illustrations and descriptive criteria were prodived by Dr. Alex F. Roche of the Lifespan Health Research Center (Departments of Community Health and Pediatrics, Wright State University School of Medicine), and are reproduced with his permission.

Stages in Development of Pubic Hair—Girls

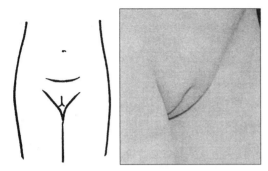

Stage 1: No pubic hair. The hair in this region does not differ from that on the front of the stomach.

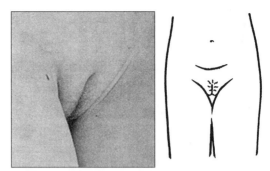

Stage 2: There is sparse, long, slightly colored hair in the pubic area that is straight or only slightly curled. It is mainly along the labia. The labia are the rounded folds of the opening of the vagina. This stage is difficult to see in a photograph, particularly if the person has fair hair. Therefore, rely more on the written description and the drawing than on the photograph.

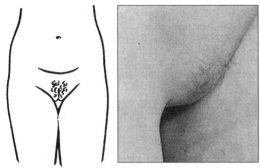

Stage 3: The pubic hair is considerably darker, coarser, and more curled than in stage 2. The pubic hair spreads sparsely over the pubic area beyond the labia.

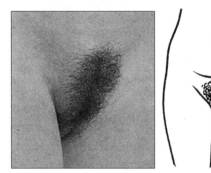

Stage 4: The pubic hair is now adult in type (colored similarly to cranial hair, coarse, curled), but the area covered is considerably smaller than in most adults. There is no spread to the inner surfaces of the thighs, that is, the pubic hair does not extend over the folds where the thighs join the stomach.

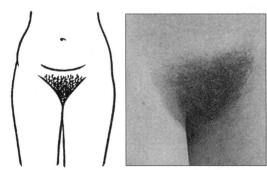

Stage 5: The pubic hair is adult in quantity and type. The area covered is an inverted triangle (▼). The pubic hair extends to the inner surfaces of the thighs. In some girls, the pubic hair extends up the front of the stomach in stage 5.

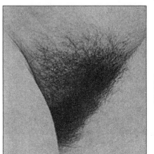

Stage 6: In about 10% of adults there is further extension of pubic hair to the sides or up onto the front of the stomach.

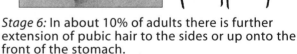

Pubic hair grows near the middle where the thighs meet the stomach.
It develops during pubescence and becomes colored and curly.

FIGURE 15.5 Stages of pubic hair development in girls. The photographs, schematic illustrations, and descriptive criteria are currently used in the Fels Longitudinal Study (see Roche et al., 1995).

The photographs of the stages are reprinted, with permission, from van Wieringen et al., 1965, *Growth diagrams* (The Netherlands: Wolters-Noordhoof). The schematic illustrations and descriptive criteria were prodived by Dr. Alex F. Roche of the Lifespan Health Research Center (Departments of Community Health and Pediatrics, Wright State University School of Medicine), and are reproduced with his permission.

Stages in Development of Pubic Hair—Boys

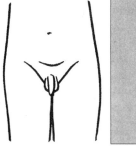 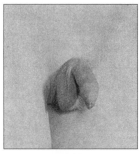

Stage 1: No pubic hair. The hair in this region does not differ from that on the front of the stomach.

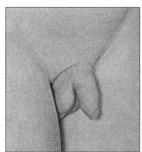 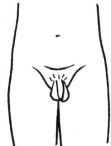

Stage 2: There is sparse, long, slightly colored hair that is straight or only slightly curled. It is at the base of the penis or on the scrotum. This stage is difficult to see in a photograph, particularly if the person has fair hair. Therefore, rely more on the written description and the drawing than on the photograph.

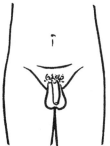 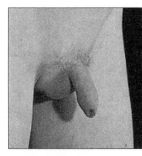

Stage 3: The pubic hair is considerably darker, coarser, and more curled. The hair is around the base of the penis.

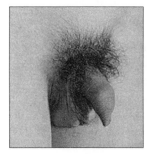 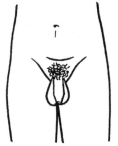

Stage 4: The pubic hair is now adult in type (colored similarly to cranial hair, coarse, curled), but the area covered is considerably smaller than in most adults. The pubic hair does not spread to the inner surface of the thighs; that is, it does not extend over the folds where the thighs join the stomach.

 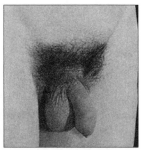

Stage 5: The pubic hair is adult in type and quantity. It covers a triangular area with a straight upper margin (▼). The pubic hair spreads to the inner surfaces of the thighs across the folds where the thighs join the stomach, but it does not extend up onto the front of the stomach beyond a straight line.

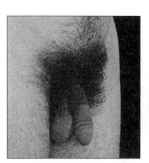 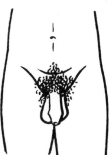

Stage 6: The pubic hair is not restricted to a triangular area but extends up to the front of the stomach so that the area covered is no longer triangular.

Pubic hair grows near the middle where the thighs meet the stomach. It develops during pubescence and becomes colored and curly.

FIGURE 15.6 Stages of pubic hair development in boys. The photographs, schematic illustrations, and descriptive criteria are currently used in the Fels Longitudinal Study (see Roche et al., 1995).

The photographs of the stages are reprinted, with permission, from van Wieringen et al., 1965, *Growth diagrams* (The Netherlands: Wolters-Noordhoof). The schematic illustrations and descriptive criteria were prodived by Dr. Alex F. Roche of the Lifespan Health Research Center (Departments of Community Health and Pediatrics, Wright State University School of Medicine), and are reproduced with his permission.

It is common in the pediatric and exercise science literature to refer to the assessment of secondary sex characteristics as "Tanner staging." This is erroneous. Secondary sex characteristics are assessed using the criteria of Tanner (1962); they are not "Tanner stages." The stages of puberty are specific to the breasts, genitals, and pubic hair, respectively. The stages are not equivalent or interchangeable, for example, G2 is not equivalent to PH2 in boys, and G3 in boys is not equivalent to B3 in girls. If a composite assessment of maturity status is needed for an individual, the average of breast and pubic hair ratings and of genital and pubic hair ratings can be used (Tanner, 1962). Taking the average of ratings, of course, has limitations. Half stages can result (e.g., what does a composite rating of 1.5 refer to, B1 and PH2, or B2 and PH1?). Or, two individuals can have the same composite rating and be assessed quite differently (e.g., one boy can be rated in G3 and PH3 with a composite rating of 3, whereas another boy can be rated as G2 and PH4 with a composite rating of 3). It is preferable to report ratings of individual characteristics and not to take the average of ratings for a composite.

Individuals should not be assessed, nor should data be reported, as "puberty stage 2" or "Tanner stage 3" without specifying the secondary sex characteristic that was used. Specific stages of each indicator should be noted (e.g., G2 or PH3).

A more direct estimate of genital maturity in males is provided by estimates of testicular volume. Volume is estimated from the size of the testes using a series of ellipsoid models of known volume, which have the shape of the testes. The models are known as the Prader orchidometer (Prader 1966; Zachman et al. 1974). The models range from 1 to 25 ml. A testicular volume ≥4 ml generally indicates the beginning of puberty. Application of the models requires direct manipulation of the testes at clinical examination as the physician attempts to match the size of each testis with the ellipsoid model that most closely matches it. Typically, both testes are assessed and the volume of each is recorded. This procedure is used most often clinically to evaluate boys with extremely late maturity or disorders of growth and sexual maturity. The orchidometer is not recommended for self-assessment.

Ages at Attaining Stages of Sexual Maturation

The ages at which individual children attain various stages of pubic hair, breast, and genital development are ordinarily derived prospectively in longitudinal studies in which children are examined at close intervals during adolescence, preferably every 3 months, but some studies do examinations every 6 months. The time of appearance of each stage and the duration of each stage of secondary sex character development (i.e., how long the individual is in a particular stage) can thus be estimated with reasonable accuracy.

The initial appearance of a specific stage cannot, in general, be observed. Age of appearance or onset of a specific stage is estimated as the midpoint of the interval between examinations when the stage was not observed and when it was first observed (Eveleth and Tanner 1990). The closer the interval between examinations, the more accurate the estimated age of appearance of a stage. Nevertheless, estimated ages at onset of a stage are generally later than the actual time of onset. Data from longitudinal studies are usually reported as mean ages at onset of a stage with associated standard deviations. The duration of a stage is estimated as the interval between the ages of appearance of consecutive stages.

Sample sizes in longitudinal studies are not usually large enough to derive population estimates and may not reflect the normal range of variation in a large sample of adolescent boys and girls. Cross-sectional surveys use a different method, the **status quo** method, to estimate ages at the attainment of specific stages of each secondary sex characteristic. The resulting estimates apply only to the population and not to individuals. A large sample of boys or girls, which spans the ages at which the particular stage normally occurs, is surveyed. Two pieces of information are needed: the exact age of the child and whether the child is in a particular stage of sexual maturity. In estimating the age of appearance of G2, for example, boys in G3, G4, and G5 are assumed to have already passed through G2. The same applies in estimating age of appearance of G3 (i.e., boys in G4 and G5 are assumed to have already passed through G3). Similar procedures and assumptions are used for estimating ages of appearance of stages of the breasts and pubic hair. Percentages at each stage of genital and pubic hair development in a sample of Mexican boys 8 to 16 years of age are shown in figure 15.7. The curves have an overall S, or sigmoid, shape. With increasing age, greater percentages of boys have attained each stage of the characteristic in question.

With the status quo method, the percentage of boys or girls in each chronological age class who

Stages of Genital Development

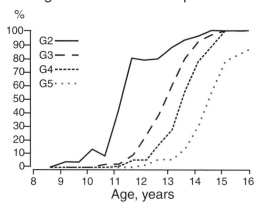

Stages of Pubic Hair Development

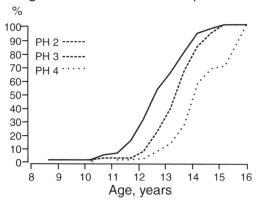

FIGURE 15.7 Percentages of boys in each stage of genital (top) and pubic hair (bottom) development by chronological age group 8 to 16 years.

Data from Guizar Vasquez et al., 1985.

have attained the particular stage is first calculated. Then, probits for each percentage are plotted for each age group and a straight line is fitted by regression to the points. Probits are derived from normal standard deviation units that correspond to a cumulative percentage. The method, which is called probit analysis, is a mathematical procedure that transforms a normal sigmoid curve into a straight line. The point at which the line intersects 50% is the estimated median age of appearance of the stage of a secondary sex characteristic in question. It also provides a standard deviation and confidence intervals, which contain 90% of the sample (5th and 95th confidence intervals). As noted earlier, the estimated median age applies only to the population and does not apply to individual boys or girls.

Some studies report mean ages for children in specific stages of sexual maturity. The mean ages are based on the ages of the children who are in each particular stage at the time of the study (i.e., the age of each child who is in a specific stage of the secondary sex characteristic under consideration). Children who are not in a particular stage are not included and the resulting estimate may be biased. As a result, mean ages based on children in a specific stage are generally later than estimated ages at onset of the stage.

Age at Menarche

Menarche refers to the first menstrual period, and the age at which menarche occurs is the most commonly reported maturity indicator of female adolescence. It is a late event in the sequence of changes associated with sexual maturation. No corresponding physiological event occurs in male adolescence. Menarche also has significant value judgments associated with its attainment in many cultures, and the psychological importance of menarche in the development of girls has no counterpart in the sexual maturation process of boys. Age at menarche is a common focus in discussions of physical activity during adolescence and of training in young female athletes.

Age at menarche can be estimated in three ways. The first two methods are identical with those used to estimate ages at onset of stages of secondary sex characteristics. In longitudinal studies, the girl or her mother is interviewed on each occasion as to whether menarche has or has not occurred, and if so, when did it occur. This method is called the prospective or longitudinal method. Girls are ordinarily examined at 3-month or 6-month intervals so that a reasonably accurate estimate of the age at onset of the first menstrual period can be determined. However, sample sizes in prospective studies are generally small.

The status quo method provides a sample or population estimate for the age at menarche. It is a statistical method, based on probits (see ages at attaining stages of sexual maturation), which requires a sample that spans approximately 9 to 17 years of age. Two pieces of information are needed, the exact age of each girl and whether or not she has attained menarche, that is, whether she is premenarcheal or postmenarcheal. Status quo data for a nationally representative sample of Belgian Flemish girls are shown in figure 15.8. The figure shows the percentage of girls in each age class who attained menarche. Probits for each percentage are then plotted for each chronological

Percentages of Girls Attaining Menarche at Each Age

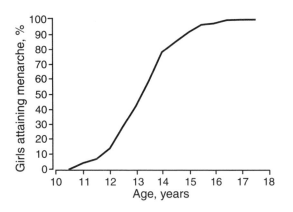

FIGURE 15.8 Percentages of girls in each chronological age group who have attained menarche in the Leuven growth study of a national sample of Flemish Belgian girls.

Data from Wellens and Malina, 1990.

age group, and a straight line is fitted to the points. The point at which the line intersects 50% is the estimated median age at menarche for the sample. As with stages of secondary sex characteristics, the probit method provides a standard deviation and confidence intervals, which contain 90% of the sample (5th and 95th confidence intervals). The estimated median age applies only to the population and does not apply to individual girls.

The retrospective method is limited to postmenarcheal adolescents, those in whom menarche has already occurred. Premenarcheal girls in the sample are excluded. With the retrospective method, girls are asked to recall as accurately as possible when menarche occurred. If the interview is done at close intervals as in longitudinal studies, the method is quite accurate. However, if it is done with older girls or with adult women, it has an error component. The method relies on the individual's memory and thus includes potential error associated with accuracy of recall. As a rule, the longer the interval between the occurrence of menarche and the age at which the individual is asked to recall the event, the lower the accuracy. Nevertheless, most teenagers and women can recall this landmark within a range of about 3 months (Damon et al. 1969; Damon and Bajema 1974; Bergsten-Brucefors 1976).

The use of prompts during the interview can assist in the recall. Prompts include such events

as season of the year, holidays, special activities, and examinations. The retrospective method should not be used to estimate the mean age at menarche in a sample of adolescents that includes girls who have not yet attained menarche. The mean will be biased toward a younger age by the inclusion of girls who have attained menarche and by the exclusion of girls who have not yet attained menarche.

The retrospective method is often used with adult women, and the majority of data for athletes are based on the retrospective method. The method is also used in clinical studies that address such issues as associations between the timing of sexual maturity and the occurrence of certain cancers (breast and uterine), reproductive health, and bone mineral content in adulthood.

Other Secondary Sex Characteristics

Under some circumstances, examination of breast, genital, and pubic hair development is impractical. Hence, other maturity indicators are occasionally used. Axillary hair, the hair in the armpits, is often rated on a three-stage scale in both sexes: 1 = none present; 2 = slight growth; and 3 = adult distribution (Billewicz et al. 1981). If axillary hair is shaved, its distribution pattern can still be noted.

Voice change in boys is another secondary sex characteristic. It is also rated on a three-stage scale: 1 = unbroken (childlike, prepubertal); 2 = signs of breaking but not fully broken (i.e., a clear change in pitch of the voice); and 3 = definitely broken voice or adult characteristics (Taranger et al. 1976; Hagg and Taranger 1980; Billewicz et al. 1981). In some instances, a two-stage scale is used: no voice change and voice change. This type of data can be analyzed with probits to estimate the age at which "breaking of the voice" and a fully broken voice occurs in boys (Prokopec and Lhotska 1994).

Facial hair in boys can also be rated. A four-stage scale is often used: 1 = none, down hair only; 2 = increase in length with pigmentation of hair at the corners of the upper lip, which spreads medially to complete the moustache; 3 = hair on the upper part of the cheeks and in the midline just below the lower lip; and 4 = hair on the sides and lower border of the chin (Billewicz et al. 1981).

The stages are somewhat arbitrary, as are those for breast, genital, and pubic hair development. Like other maturity indicators, they are continuous processes on which the stages are superimposed. Axillary and facial hair and voice change have not been used in studies of maturation during adolescence as often as the indicators of sexual maturity, perhaps because they tend to be rather late events in the sequence of changes that occur during puberty.

Circulating Levels of Hormones

The development of secondary sex characteristics reflects to a large extent the external manifestations of hormonal changes—the maturation of the ovaries in females and the testes in males and of their respective hormones. Maturation of the ovaries and testes is regulated by changes in the central nervous system, specifically, the hypothalamic-pituitary-gonadal axis (see chapter 19). Hence, circulating concentrations of the hormones that respectively stimulate the maturation of the ovaries and testes and the hormones produced by the ovaries and testes may also serve as indicators of maturity status. Such estimates are often used in the clinical setting. They require blood samples that are drawn at regular intervals under carefully controlled conditions and relatively sophisticated biochemical assays. Single serum samples have extremely limited utility because virtually all hormones are episodically secreted. Studies in which 24-hour levels of hormones are monitored or in which actual pulses of the hormones are sampled every 20 minutes or so are needed to provide a more accurate indication of a child's hormonal status. Further, the simple presence of a hormone does not necessarily imply that it is physiologically active, and variation occurs in the responsiveness of tissues to circulating hormones.

Assessing Somatic Maturity

Assessing maturity by using body measurements is not possible, because body size by itself is not an indicator of maturity. However, if longitudinal data that span adolescence are available, specifically for height, the inflection in the growth curve that marks the adolescent growth spurt can be used to derive indicators of maturity such as age at onset of the growth spurt and age at maximum rate of growth during the spurt (age at peak height velocity [PHV]). Similarly, if adult height is available, or can be estimated, the percentage of adult size attained at different ages during growth can also be used as a maturity indicator. Two children may have the same height at a given age, but one may have already attained a greater percentage of

adult size than the other and is, therefore, closer to the mature state (adult height).

Parameters of the Growth Curve

The adolescent growth spurt in height refers to the acceleration in growth at this time. In girls, it starts, on average, at about 9 or 10 years of age, peaks at about 12 years of age, and stops at about 16 years of age. In boys, the acceleration begins, on average, at about 10 or 11 years of age, peaks at about 14 years of age, and stops at about 18 years of age. Many but not all children experience an earlier midgrowth spurt in height. It is usually observed between 6.5 and 8.5 years of age. This spurt is much smaller and may not occur in some children (see chapter 3).

The growth curve for height has several parameters that provide useful information about the adolescent growth spurt and provide an indicator of somatic maturity. The two primary parameters are takeoff (TO), or initiation of the spurt, and peak height velocity (PHV), or maximum rate of growth during the spurt. The age, size, and rate of growth at TO and the age, size, and rate of growth at PHV can be derived. Age at PHV is an indicator of somatic maturity and specifically relates to timing. PHV (cm/year) provides an estimate of tempo. If adult size is available, the amount of growth during the adolescent growth spurt, the adolescent gain, can be calculated. The adolescent gain represents the difference between height at TO and adult size.

Earliest efforts at identifying parameters of the adolescent spurt were based on graphical smoothing. Size attained at a given age and estimated velocities of growth were plotted on graphs. The points were connected to provide growth curves for size attained and velocity. The velocity curve was then interpolated to provide estimates of the ages at TO and at PHV and the magnitude of PHV and adult size.

More recently, mathematically fitting curves to individual longitudinal records of height has facilitated the estimation of acceleration and velocity and in turn calculation of the timing and magnitude of the adolescent growth spurt. Curve fitting is not the only approach to the analysis of longitudinal growth data. Several other models have been described and new models are being proposed to quantify individual growth. Most mathematical models have been developed for growth in height. They are basically descriptive, that is, they characterize the growth curve for height (or other body dimensions) from birth to young adulthood or from childhood to young adulthood, depending on the completeness of the available longitudinal data.

In fitting mathematical models to growth curves, a distinction is made between structural or parametric models and polynomial or non-parametric models (Marubini 1978; Hauspie and Chrzastek-Spruch 1999). Structural models have a preselected form for the growth curve and the parameters or constants of the model have a predetermined biological meaning. Polynomial models do not have a preselected form, and their parameters may not be easy to interpret biologically. Nevertheless, regardless of the model used, curve fitting provides a convenient means of characterizing and comparing individual and group differences in parameters of the adolescent growth spurt.

Age at Peak Height Velocity

Age at peak height velocity (PHV) is an indicator of somatic maturity in longitudinal studies of adolescence. As noted earlier, it is the age at maximum rate of growth in stature during the adolescent spurt. An example of a fitted growth curve for an individual boy is shown in figure 15.9. Actual sizes attained at each age and the fitted distance curve are shown along with the derived growth velocities (smoothed velocity curve). Such

curves are a convenient means of characterizing and comparing individual and group differences in growth. For example, parameters of the adolescent growth spurts of the boys and girls illustrated in figures 3.24 (page 76) and 3.25 (page 76) are summarized in table 15.2. The parameters were derived by mathematically fitting growth curves to the height records of each child from early childhood to the attainment of adult stature.

Although age at PHV is a useful maturity indicator, it requires longitudinal data that span adolescence for its estimation. Age at PHV cannot be estimated accurately for an individual child based on only three or four annual observations during adolescence. Data should span the interval from about 9 or 10 to 16 or 17 years of age.

Age at PHV also serves as a landmark against which attained sizes and velocities of other body dimensions and physical performances or stages of sexual maturity can be expressed. Menarche, for example, occurs after PHV in girls, and peak strength development occurs after PHV in boys and girls. The relationship of growth in other body dimensions and performance to age at PHV is discussed in chapter 16.

With appropriate longitudinal data, estimates of ages at peak velocity and peak velocities for other body dimensions and some performance tasks can also be made; for example, ages at peak velocity

Distance and Velocity Curves for Growth in Height of a Child

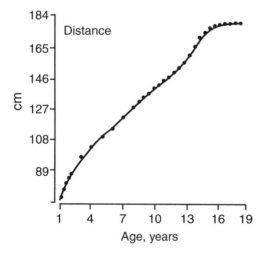
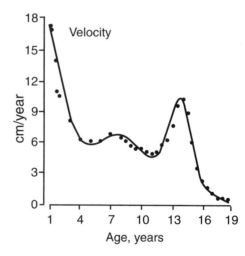

FIGURE 15.9   An example of a mathematically fitted growth curve for stature of an individual child. The circles indicate the observed statures (left) and stature velocities (right), and the continuous lines indicate distance and velocity curves fitted with a triple logistic model. The age at takeoff, or initiation of the adolescent growth spurt, for this child is 11.8 years and the age at peak height velocity is 13.8 years.

Reprinted, by permission, from M. el Lozy, 1978, "A critical analysis of the double and triple logistic growth curves," *Annals of Human Biology* 5: 389-394.

TABLE 15.2	Estimated Parameters of the Adolescent Growth Spurt of the Three Boys and Three Girls Illustrated in Figures 3.24 and 3.25.		

Boys			
Adolescent parameters	**A**	**B**	**C**
Takeoff			
Age (yr)	9.8	10.2	10.5
Height (cm)	145.7	129.0	133.8
Velocity (cm/yr)	5.4	4.5	4.5
Peak height velocity			
Age (yrs)	14.1	14.4	13.9
Height (cm)	169.9	153.4	154.5
Velocity (cm/yr)	6.1	7.7	8.9
Adult height (cm)	193.7	172.7	169.5
Girls			
Adolescent parameters	**A**	**B**	**C**
Takeoff			
Age (yr)	8.4	9.0	8.7
Height (cm)	137.2	133.8	121.2
Velocity (cm/yr)	5.6	4.9	5.3
Peak height velocity			
Age (yr)	11.8	12.4	11.4
Height (cm)	160.0	154.3	138.1
Velocity (cm/yr)	8.1	7.8	7.9
Adult height (cm)	179.0	170.2	151.5

The curve fitting was done with Preece-Baines model I adapted for the IBM PC, courtesy of R.L. Mirwald and D.A. Bailey, College of Physical Education, University of Saskatchewan, Saskatoon, Canada.

of growth in leg length, sitting height, biacromial and bicristal breadths, body weight, muscular strength, the vertical jump, and maximal oxygen uptake. Such data are available for several samples of youth followed longitudinally through adolescence but are not as extensive as data for the age at PHV. These data are discussed in chapter 16.

Percentage of Adult Stature

Another potential indicator of somatic maturity is the percentage of adult height attained at a given age. Children who are closer to their adult or mature height compared with other children of the same chronological age are more advanced in

maturity. For example, two 7-year-old boys have attained the same stature, 122 cm. For one of the boys, this stature accounts for 72% of his adult stature, whereas for the other, it accounts for only 66% of his adult stature. The first boy is closer to the mature state and is, therefore, advanced in somatic maturity compared with the second boy. The utility of percentage of adult height as a maturity indicator needs further validation, but it has been used in some longitudinal studies of interrelationships among maturity indicators. Percentage of adult height is based on values for size attained at specific ages. It is the result of variation in tempo of growth and is not an indicator of tempo per se as is PHV.

Estimates of the percentage of adult stature attained at a given age during growth require longitudinal data. As such, this maturity indicator has limited utility. However, it may have some application if a child's stature at the time of examination is expressed as a percentage of predicted adult height. Such an approach may be useful in distinguishing youngsters who are tall at a given age because they are genetically tall from those who are tall because they are advanced in maturity, that is, they have attained a greater percentage of their predicted adult stature at a given chronological age. A key issue, in this context, is the prediction of adult height.

Predicting Adult Stature

All three commonly used methods for predicting adult stature require an estimation of skeletal age (SA).

The Bayley-Pinneau method (Bayley and Pinneau 1952, see also Bayer and Bayley 1959) utilizes stature and Greulich-Pyle SA. It provides an estimate of the percentage of adult stature attained at the time of the hand-wrist radiograph.

The Roche-Wainer-Thissen method (Roche et al. 1975b, 1975c) uses CA, recumbent length (not stature), weight, midparent stature (height of the mother and father divided by 2), and Greulich-Pyle SA (based on median bone-specific SAs) to predict stature at 18 years of age.

The Tanner-Whitehouse method (Tanner et al. 1983, 2001) includes several options to predict adult stature—CA, stature, and RUS SA; CA, stature, RUS SA, and the increment in stature during the previous year; and menarcheal status and age at menarche in addition to the preceding variables.

All predictions of adult stature have an associated error, usually within the range of 3 to 5 cm. Occasionally, the error is larger, and all prediction models occasionally have outlying predictions.

Further, systematic errors may occur in prediction of adult height when the three different methods are applied to the same individual. For example, in a sample of 23 normally growing boys followed, longitudinally, serial height predictions were made from 8 to 15 years of age and compared with young adult height (18 years). Adult height was generally underpredicted by the Tanner-Whitehouse model and overpredicted by the Bayley-Pinneau and Roche-Wainer-Thissen methods (Roemmich et al. 1997). An underlying problem in the prediction of adult height is individual variation in the timing and tempo of the adolescent growth spurt and sexual maturation. An additional problem is error associated with assessments of SA.

All three methods require an estimate of SA, which limits their applicability. The Roche-Wainer-Thissen method has been modified to provide estimates of adult stature when SA is not available (Roche et al. 1983). It is based on the premise that parental statures, expressed as midparent height, provide a target range within which the adult height of the child will likely be. With this method, the child's adult height is predicted from current age, stature and weight, and midparent height. This modification of the Roche-Wainer-Thissen method has potential for application because it does not require an estimate of SA. Khamis and Roche (1994) provide age-specific equations for the prediction of adult height from a child's current height and weight and the midparent height. Standard errors with the method, which does not use SA as one of the predictor variables, are only slightly greater than those for the Roche-Wainer-Thissen, which uses SA in the prediction.

The Khamis-Roche (1994) method was applied to a sample of the Quebec Family Study who was measured at adolescent ages and again as young adults 12 years later. Adult height was predicted from age, height, and weight in adolescence (39 girls, 9.7 to 12.8 years of age; 52 boys, 9.1 to 14.7 years of age) and midparent height. Correlations between height predicted in adolescence and young adult height were 0.84 in girls and 0.74 in boys (Malina, Katzmarzyk, Bouchard, unpublished data), which suggests a reasonable degree of accuracy for the method that does not require an estimate of SA.

Beunen et al. (1997) developed a height prediction method (Beunen-Malina method) for boys 12.5 to 16.5 years of age that does not require an estimate of SA. The method uses CA, current height, sitting height, and the subscapular and triceps skinfolds to predict adult height. Standard errors with this method are 3.0 to 4.2 cm, which compare favorably with standard errors for methods incorporating SA.

The availability of methods to predict adult height with a reasonable degree of accuracy without an estimate of SA has potential application in studies where it is not possible to assess biological maturity status. Expressing current height as a percentage of predicted adult height may serve as a maturity indicator. Within an age group, individuals who have attained a greater percentage of their predicted adult height are closer to maturity than those who have attained a lesser percentage of their predicted adult height. The method was applied to youth football players (American football) who were grouped for competition by grade. Results are summarized in table 15.3. Within each

TABLE 15.3 Variation in Age and Body Size of Youth Football Players Grouped by Level of Maturity Estimated by Attained Percentage of Predicted Adult Height

Maturity tertile	n	Age (yr)		Height (cm)		Weight (kg)		BMI (kg/m²)	
		Mean	SD	Mean	SD	Mean	SD	Mean	SD
6th grade									
I Less mature	21	11.3	0.4	146.5	5.3	41.0	7.6	19.1	2.8
II Intermediate	21	11.6	0.4	149.6	5.4	44.7	7.5	19.9	2.9
III More mature	21	11.9	0.3	156.6	6.2	59.4	14.5	24.1	5.1
7th grade									
I Less mature	28	12.5	0.4	152.9	4.5	47.1	5.6	20.1	2.5
II Intermediate	30	12.7	0.3	157.6	5.5	56.7	10.8	22.9	4.4
III More mature	27	12.9	0.4	165.7	6.4	65.9	17.0	23.9	5.4

Boys are grouped into tertiles of percentage of predicted adult height within each grade.

R.M. Malina (unpublished data).

grade, players in the highest tertile of the percentage of predicted adult height (advanced) were older, taller, and heavier and had a higher BMI. On the other hand, players in the lowest tertile of the percentage of predicted adult height (delayed) were younger, shorter, and lighter and had a lower BMI. Players in the middle tertile were intermediate in age and body size between players in the highest and lowest tertiles of the percentage of predicted adult height. These results are consistent with studies using other indicators of biological maturity such as SA and stages of secondary sex characteristics (see chapter 17).

Assessing Dental Maturity

Dental maturation has been most often viewed in terms of the time or age of eruption of the deciduous (baby) and permanent teeth. The calcification of the permanent teeth is also used to estimate stage of dental maturity in a manner similar to the assessment of skeletal maturity. Criteria for assessing the calcification of seven permanent teeth in one quadrant of the mouth have been developed by Demirjian (1986) at the Center for Research in Human Growth of the University of Montreal. The procedure requires an X-ray of the seven teeth in one quadrant of the mouth (two incisors, the cuspid, two premolar or bicuspids, and the first and second molars). The criteria are based on the features that are common to a tooth; each tooth has a crown with cusps and a root. Specific stages were described for each tooth as it passes from the beginning of calcification of the cusps (the first indicators of crown formation) to the formation of the root (or roots) and eventual closure of the root (or roots) at the apex of the tooth. Point scores are assigned to each stage, and the sum of the point scores provides an indication of dental maturity, which can be converted to a dental age in a manner similar to that for skeletal age. The principle and procedures for this method of assessing dental maturity are similar to those for the assessment of skeletal maturation in the Tanner-Whitehouse method.

Interrelationships Among Maturity Indicators

Two questions are important regarding indicators of skeletal, sexual, somatic, and dental maturity in children and adolescents. The first question deals with relationships among the indicators. Do they measure the same kind of biological maturity?

The second question relates to the consistency of maturity ratings over time. Is a child who is delayed in maturity at, for example, 6 years of age also delayed at 11 years of age? The same questions can be asked of those advanced and average ("on time") in maturation.

If a youngster is rated as early, average, or late by one of the maturity indicators, will the youngster be rated as the same by the other maturity indicators? In general, indicators of skeletal, sexual, and somatic maturity are positively related to each other, but dental maturity is not strongly related to these three types of indicators. Dental maturity tends to proceed independently of skeletal, sexual, and somatic maturity.

The issue of interrelationships is complex because only skeletal maturity spans the prepubertal and pubertal years, whereas indicators of sexual maturity and age at PHV are limited to puberty and adolescence. Evidence suggests that the tempo of prepubertal growth and maturation may be somewhat independent of pubertal growth and maturation. For example, a cluster analysis of 21 indicators of maturity was carried out on data for 111 Polish boys who were followed longitudinally from 8 to 18 years of age in the Wroclaw Growth Study (Bielicki et al. 1984). The maturity indicators included the following: **sexual maturity-**ages at attaining genital and pubic hair stages 2 and 4; **skeletal maturity-**ages at attaining skeletal maturity of 11 to 15 years of age; **somatic maturity-**ages at peak velocity for height, weight, leg length, and trunk length, age at initiation of the height spurt, and ages at attaining 80%, 90%, 95%, and 99% of adult height; and **dental maturity-**ages at the eruption of 14, 20, and 26 permanent teeth. Results of the analysis indicated a general maturity factor during adolescence. This factor included the ages at peak velocities of growth and at attainment of stages of sexual maturity, skeletal ages of 14 and 15 years, ages at attaining 90%, 95%, and 99% of mature stature, and age at initiation of the adolescent growth spurt in height. Correlations among these indicators were moderate to high; none were less than 0.70 and many were greater than 0.80. The general maturity factor suggests central control of the timing of adolescent maturation, probably by the central nervous system and its hormonal correlates (see chapter 19).

The second cluster of variables, although less clearly specified, identified indicators associated with prepubertal growth and maturation. It included ages at attaining skeletal maturity equivalent to 11, 12, and 13 years and the age at attaining 80% of adult height, which are primarily indicators of prepubertal growth and maturation. The second cluster was generally independent of the maturity indicators in the first cluster.

A third cluster included the three indicators of dental maturity and was independent of the other two clusters. The indicators of dental maturity were moderately interrelated, but they were only weakly related to all other maturity indicators and were not included among those that described the general maturity factor during adolescence (Bielicki et al. 1984). Corresponding analyses of relationships among similar maturity indicators in Polish girls (Bielicki 1975) and in American boys and girls from California (Nicolson and Hanley 1953) give similar results.

Thus, a general maturity factor appears to underlie the timing of growth and maturation during adolescence. This factor discriminates among individuals who are early, average ("on time"), or late in the timing of adolescent events. However, variation occurs among maturity indicators. No one system (sexual, skeletal, or somatic) apparently provides a complete description of the timing and tempo of growth and maturation of an individual boy or girl during adolescence. An additional factor is variation in tempo of maturation. No consistent relationship exists between the age at which a stage of a secondary sex characteristic

develops (timing) and the rate of progress to the next stage (tempo). Some boys may pass from genital stages G2 to G5 in about 2 years, whereas others may take about 5 years. Similar variation in tempo occurs for breast development in girls and for pubic hair in both sexes.

Part of the variation in such analyses is related to the methods of assessing maturity. Methods of estimating ages at peak velocities and ages at attainment of specific stages of sexual and skeletal maturity differ. Secondary sex characteristics are limited to five stages and are not continuous variables, in contrast to the continuous age scale used for skeletal maturity. Intervals between observations in studies of adolescents vary among studies, which may account for some of the differences. Variation in measurement and observational procedures is an additional factor.

The independence of prepubertal indicators from the events of adolescence raises the question of maturity indicators during childhood. Skeletal maturity is the primary indicator for the prepubertal years, and if longitudinal data are available, the percentage of adult stature may be helpful. Relationships between skeletal maturity and attained percentage of adult stature are moderately high and positive during the prepubertal years. This finding is shown in figure 15.10. Children who are advanced in skeletal maturity are closer

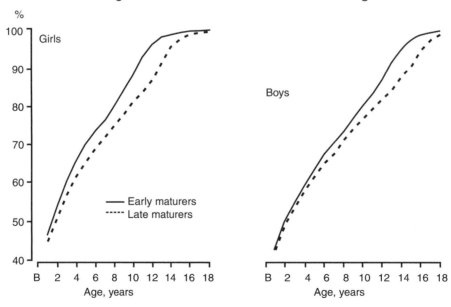

FIGURE 15.10 Percentage of adult stature attained at each age in early-maturing (advanced) and late-maturing (delayed) boys and girls.

Data from Bayley, 1962.

to adult stature at all ages during childhood and adolescence than those who are delayed in SA relative to CA. In late adolescence, catch up of those later in skeletal maturity occurs. The child who is advanced in skeletal maturity attains adult stature earlier and thus stops growing earlier, whereas the child who is later in skeletal maturity attains adult stature later and grows over a longer period of time. On the average, however, both groups attain similar adult heights, but one group attains adult height more rapidly or earlier than the other.

Indicators of sexual and somatic maturity are positively related with each other during puberty. Relationships among the timing of several indicators of sexual and somatic maturity during adolescence are shown in table 15.4. The data are limited to the ages at attaining only few maturity indicators and to the early stages of sexual maturity and are more available for girls than for boys. Correlations between ages at PHV and menarche and several less commonly used secondary sex characteristics are given in table 15.5. All of the correlations are moderate to high, which suggests that youngsters early or late in sexual maturation

are, respectively, early or late in the timing of the adolescent growth spurt in stature. Similarly, a youngster who is early or late in the appearance of one indicator of sexual maturity tends to be early or late, respectively, in the appearance of other indicators of sexual maturity. The correlations, although reasonably consistent across studies, are not perfect, which suggests variation in timing of somatic and sexual maturation.

Skeletal maturity is also related to the development of secondary sex characteristics and PHV. Relationships between CA and SA at the time of reaching certain maturational events during adolescence in the Harpenden Growth Study are summarized in table 15.6. Mean CAs and SAs at each stage of sexual and somatic maturation are quite close, but variation in SA is generally less (smaller standard deviations). Variation in SA is especially reduced at menarche and at the attainment of 95% of adult stature. Using menarche as an example, mean CA and SA at menarche are virtually identical, 13.2 and 13.3 years, respectively. However, variation in skeletal ages at menarche is reduced. The SAs of 45 of the 59

TABLE 15.4 Correlations Between Ages at Reaching Several Maturity Indicators in North American and European Adolescents

Sample	Girls						Boys		
	PHV			M		B2	PHV		G2
	B2	PH2	M	B2	PH2	PH2	G2	PH2	PH2
North American									
Massachusetts, Boston			0.71	0.86					
California, Berkeley	0.80	0.75	0.71	0.74	0.74	0.75	0.67		
Colorado, Denver	0.78		0.93					0.56	
Ohio, Yellow Springs				0.86	0.70	0.66			
Quebec, Montreal			0.81						
European									
England, Harpenden	0.82		0.91	0.64					
England, Harpenden	0.78	0.77	0.84				0.47	0.84	
England, Newcastle	0.69		0.80	0.62					
Poland, Wroclaw	0.76	0.77	0.76	0.72	0.73	0.77	0.87	0.84	0.85
Sweden, Stockholm	0.80	0.73	0.84	0.74	0.58	0.70	0.78	0.49	0.54
Sweden, Umea	0.63	0.68	0.63	0.51	0.52	0.70			
Sweden, urban			0.69						
Switzerland, Zurich	0.60	0.34	0.82	0.47	0.44	0.34	0.50	0.59	0.54

Note: PHV = peak height velocity, M = menarche, B2 = breast stage 2, PH2 = pubic hair stage 2, G2 = genital stage 2.

Adapted from Malina (1978), which contains the specific references for earlier studies. Data from Billewicz et al. (1981), Bielicki et al. (1984), Demirjian et al. (1985), and Largo and Prader (1983a, 1983b) have been added.

TABLE 15.5	Correlations Between Ages at Reaching Several Less Commonly Used Maturity Indicators in British and Swedish Adolescents					

	Newcastle, England[a]			Stockholm, Sweden[b]	
	PHV	V2	FH2		PHV
Boys					
AH2	0.66	0.68	0.65	V2	0.82
FH2	0.69	0.66		V3	0.73
V2	0.79				

	Newcastle, England[a]		
	PHV	M	B2
Girls			
AH2	0.58	0.59	0.54

PHV = peak height velocity; V2, V3 = stages 2 and 3 of voice change; AH2 = stage 2 of axillary hair development; FH2 = stage 2 of facial hair development; M = menarche; B2 = stage 2 of breast development. See text for details of the various stages.

[a] Adapted from Billewicz et al. (1981).

[b] Adapted from Hagg and Taranger (1980).

girls (76%) cluster between 12.5 and 13.5 years (40 of the 59 [68%] have SAs between 13.0 and 13.5 years). In contrast, only 25 of the 59 girls (42%) have CAs at menarche between 12.5 and 13.5 years (Marshall 1974). Thus, more variation occurs in CA at the time of menarche than in SA. The limited variability in SA at menarche reduces the correlation between SA and CA at menarche. Likewise, variability is reduced in SA at the attainment of 95% of adult stature, thus reducing the correlation between SA and CA. The same pattern is evident in the distributions of CA and SA at PHV in boys (see figure 15.11). More variation occurs in CA at the time of PHV than in SA (Hauspie et al. 1991).

Correlations between CA and SA on reaching PHV are also positive and moderate, whereas correlations between CA and SA on reaching 95% of adult height are low (see table 15.6). However, SA may vary as much as CA at the onset of sexual maturation in girls (Marshall 1974) and takeoff of the adolescent growth spurt in height in boys (Hauspie et al. 1991). As sexual maturation and the adolescent growth spurt proceed, skeletal maturity becomes more strongly related to these maturational events. This finding is shown in table 15.7 for girls and boys in the Wroclaw

TABLE 15.6	Chronological Age (CA), Skeletal Age (SA), and Correlations Between SA and CA on Reaching Selected Maturity Indicators in Girls and Boys of the Harpenden Growth Study				

	CA (yr)		SA (yr)		
Maturity indicator	Mean	SD	Mean	SD	Correlation
Girls					
Breast 2	11.0	1.1	10.9	1.0	0.69
Breast 5	14.0	0.9	14.0	0.8	0.44
Pubic hair 3	12.5	1.0	12.5	0.8	0.64
Peak height velocity	12.3	1.1	12.5	0.9	0.74
Menarche	13.2	0.8	13.3	0.4	0.35
95% Adult stature	12.8	0.8	13.0	0.3	0.18
Boys					
Genital 2	11.5	1.1	11.5	1.2	0.63
Genital 5	14.5	1.0	14.8	0.8	0.39
Pubic hair 3	13.8	0.9	13.6	1.0	0.42
Peak height velocity	13.9	1.0	14.0	0.8	0.34
95% Adult stature	14.6	0.7	15.1	0.3	0.05

Adapted from Marshall (1974).

Distributions of Chronological and Skeletal Ages at Peak Height Velocity

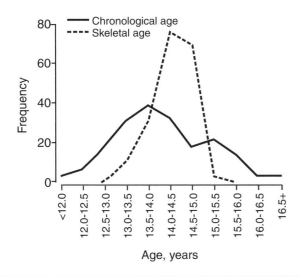

FIGURE 15.11 Frequency distribution of chronological ages and skeletal ages (TW 2 20-bone SA) at peak height velocity in boys from the Wroclaw Growth Study in Poland.

Data from Hauspie et al., 1991.

Growth Study. Correlations between SA and ages at attaining PHV; the later stages of breast, genital, and pubic hair development; menarche; and 95% of mature stature increase at successive ages. The correlations with SA are quite high near the mean ages when these maturational stages or events are attained. In boys, for example, the correlation between SA at 14 years and age at PHV (13.9 years) is 0.81. Thus, the correlations between maturational events, which occur closer in time, are higher than those separated in time. In contrast, skeletal maturity in the early pubertal years (about 9 to 10 years of age in girls and 11 to 12 years of age in boys) is not highly related to indicators of sexual and somatic maturation during adolescence. As adolescence progresses, skeletal maturity is increasingly related to these indicators of sexual and somatic maturity.

The pattern of correlation between SA and indicators of sexual and somatic maturity reflects the observation that the tempo of prepubertal growth and the events of puberty are somewhat independent. Prepubertal growth and skeletal maturation depend principally on the stimulation of growth hormone and related growth factors.

TABLE 15.7 Correlations Between Skeletal Maturity at Successive Ages and Ages at Attaining Several Indicators of Sexual and Somatic Maturity in Girls and Boys of the Wroclaw Growth Study

Skeletal maturity age (yr)	Breast 4 (13.5)	Pubic hair 4 (13.6)	PHV (11.7)	Menarche (13.1)
Girls				
10	0.49	0.51	0.58	0.51
11	0.60	0.61	0.69	0.61
12	0.65	0.64	0.73	0.68
13	0.68	0.67	0.76	0.71
14	0.70	0.68	0.79	0.73
Skeletal maturity age (yr)	**Genital 4 (14.5)**	**Pubic hair 4 (15.0)**	**PHV (13.9)**	**95% adult height (14.8)**
Boys				
11	0.25	0.29	0.26	0.29
12	0.40	0.42	0.42	0.47
13	0.62	0.61	0.68	0.71
14	0.75	0.78	0.81	0.83
15	0.83	0.82	0.89	0.93

Note: Mean ages (years) at reaching each maturity indicator are in parentheses.

Adapted from Bielicki (1975) and Bielicki et al. (1984).

Sexual maturation, the growth spurt, and the final stages of skeletal maturation (i.e., epiphyseal union), on the other hand, are primarily under the influence of both growth hormone, related growth factors, and the steroid hormones, among others. Steroid hormones are produced in larger amounts by the gonads as they mature. The tempo of prepubertal growth and the events of adolescence are thus controlled by different factors. The genetic and hormonal regulation of growth and maturation is discussed at length in chapters 18 and 19, respectively.

Summary

Maturation is a process and maturity is a state. When working with children and adolescents, the term maturity ordinarily refers to the extent to which the individual has progressed to the mature state. The three most commonly used indicators of biological maturity status in growth studies are maturation of the skeleton (skeletal age based on the bones of the hand and wrist), appearance of secondary sex characteristics (pubic hair and genitals in boys; pubic hair, breasts, and menarche in girls), and the timing of maximum growth in height during the adolescent growth spurt (age at peak height velocity). Methods of assessment, their advantages and limitations, are described. Only skeletal maturation spans infancy, childhood, and adolescence into young adulthood; sexual and somatic maturation are limited to the time of puberty and adolescence. Indicators of skeletal, sexual, and somatic maturity are well related during adolescence. The tempo of maturation before puberty (prepuberal) is somewhat independent of sexual, somatic, and skeletal maturation during puberty (pubertal). The tempo of prepubertal maturation and the events of puberty and adolescence are under different regulatory mechanisms.

Sources and Suggested Readings

Acheson RM (1954) A method of assessing skeletal maturity from radiographs: A Report from the Oxford Child Health Survey. Journal of Anatomy 88:498-508.

Acheson RM (1957) The Oxford method of assessing skeletal maturity. Clinical Orthopaedics 10:19-39.

* Acheson RM (1966) Maturation of the skeleton. In F Falkner (ed), Human Development. Philadelphia: Saunders, pp 465-502.

Albanese A, Hall C, Stanhope R (1995) The use of a computerized method of bone age assessment in clinical practice. Hormone Research 44 (suppl 3):2-7.

* Bayer LM, Bayley N (1959) Growth Diagnosis: Selected Methods for Interpreting and Predicting Development from One Year to Maturity. Chicago: University of Chicago Press.

Bayley N (1962) The accurate prediction of growth and adult height. Modern Problems in Paediatrics 7:234-255.

Bayley N, Pinneau SR (1952) Tables for predicting adult height from skeletal age: Revised for use with the Greulich-Pyle hand standards. Journal of Pediatrics 40:423-441.

Bergsten-Brucefors A (1976) A note on the accuracy of recalled age at menarche. Annals of Human Biology 3:71-73.

Beunen G (1996) Physical growth, maturation and performance. In R Eston, T Reilly (eds), Kinanthropometry and Exercise Physiology Laboratory Manual. London: E & FN Spon, pp 51-71.

Beunen G, Lefevre J, Ostyn M, Renson R, Simons J, Van Gerven D (1990) Skeletal maturity in Belgian youths assessed by the Tanner-Whitehouse method (TW2). Annals of Human Biology 17:355-376.

Beunen G, Malina RM (1988) Growth and physical performance relative to the timing of the adolescent spurt. Exercise and Sport Sciences Reviews 16:503-540.

Beunen GP, Malina RM, Lefevre J, Claessens AL, Renson R, Simons J (1997) Prediction of adult stature and noninvasive assessment of biological maturation. Medicine and Science in Sports and Exercise 29:225-230.

Bielicki T (1975) Interrelationships between various measures of maturation rate in girls during adolescence. Studies in Physical Anthropology 1:51-64.

Bielicki T, Koniarek J, Malina RM (1984) Interrelationships among certain measures of growth and maturation rate in boys during adolescence. Annals of Human Biology 11:201-210.

Billewicz WZ, Fellowes HM, Thomson AM (1981) Pubertal changes in boys and girls in Newcastle upon Tyne. Annals of Human Biology 8:211-219.

Braillon PM, Guibal AL, Pracros-Deffrenne P, Serban A, Pracros JP, Chatelain P (1998) Dual energy X-ray absorptiometry of the hand and wrist—a possible technique to assess skeletal maturation: Methodology and data in normal youths. Acta Paediatrica 87:924-929.

Brooks-Gunn J, Warren MP, Rosso J, Gargiulo J (1987) Validity of self-report measures of girls' pubertal status. Child Development 58:829-841.

Damon A, Bajema CJ (1974) Age at menarche: Accuracy of recall after thirty-nine years. Human Biology 46:381-384.

Damon A, Damon ST, Reed RB, Valadian I (1969) Age at menarche of mothers and daughters, with a note on accuracy of recall. Human Biology 41:161-175.

Deming J (1957) Application of the Gompertz curve to the observed pattern of growth in length of 48 individual boys and girls during the adolescent cycle of growth. Human Biology 29:83-122.

Demirjian A (1986) Dentition. In F Falkner, JM Tanner (eds), Human Growth. Volume 2. Postnatal Growth, Neurobiology. New York: Plenum, pp 269-298.

Demirjian A, Buschang PH, Tanguay R, Patterson DK (1985) Interrelationships among measures of somatic, skeletal, dental, and sexual maturity. American Journal of Orthodontics 88:433-438.

Duke PM, Litt IF, Gross RT (1980) Adolescents' self-assessment of sexual maturation. Pediatrics 66:918-920.

Eto M, Ashizawa K (1992) Longitudinal Observations on Physical Growth and TW2 Skeletal Maturation of Girls in Tokyo: Radiographic Atlas of Hand and Wrist. Tokyo: Therapeia.

Eveleth PB, Tanner JM (1990) Worldwide Variation in Human Growth, 2nd edition. Cambridge: Cambridge University Press.

Fernandez M, Sanchez E, Sobradillo B, Rincon JM (1991) Skeletal Maturation and Height Prediction: Atlas and Scoring Methods. Madrid: Ediciones Diaz de Santos, SA.

Filippson R, Hall K (1976) Correlation between dental maturity, height development and sexual maturation in normal girls. Annals of Human Biology 3:205-210.

Gasser T, Köhler W, Müller H-G, Kneip A, Largo R, Molinari L, Prader A (1984) Velocity and acceleration of height growth using kernel estimation. Annals of Human Biology 11:397-411.

Goldstein H (1979) The Design and Analysis of Longitudinal Studies. London: Academic Press.

Greulich WW, Pyle SI (1959) Radiographic Atlas of Skeletal Development of the Hand and Wrist, 2nd edition. Stanford, CA.: Stanford University Press.

Guizar Vazquez JJ, Rosales Lopez A, Ortiz Jalomo R, Nava Delgado SE, Salamanca Gomez F (1985) Caracteres sexuales secundarios en niños Mexicanos de 9 a 16 años. Estudio transversal. Boletin Médico del Hospital Infantil de México 42:409-414.

Hagg U, Taranger J (1980) Menarche and voice change as indicators of the pubertal growth spurt. Acta Odontologica Scandinavica 38:179-186.

Hauspie R, Bielicki T, Koniarek J (1991) Skeletal maturity at onset of the adolescent growth spurt and at peak velocity for growth in height: A threshold effect. Annals of Human Biology 18:23-29.

* Hauspie R, Chrzastek-Spruch H (1999) Growth models: Possibilities and limitations. In FE Johnston, PB Eveleth, B Zemel (eds), Human Growth in Context. London: Smith-Gordon, pp 15-24.

Jost-Relyveld A, Sempé M (1982) Analyse de la croissance et de la maturation squelettique de 80 jeunes gymnastes internationaux. Pediatrie 37:247-262.

Khamis HJ, Roche AF (1994) Predicting adult stature without using skeletal age: The Khamis-Roche method. Pediatrics 94:504-507 (see Pediatrics 95:457, 1995 for the corrected version of the tables).

Kujawa KI (1997) Skeletal maturation in boys: Comparison of methods and relationships to anthropometry and strength. Austin: University of Texas, Doctoral Dissertation.

* Largo RH, Prader A (1983a) Pubertal development in Swiss boys. Helvetica Paediatrica Acta 38:211-228.

* Largo RH, Prader A (1983b) Pubertal development in Swiss girls. Helvetica Paediatrica Acta 38:229-243.

Lindgren G (1978) Growth of school children with early, average and late ages of peak height velocity. Annals of Human Biology 5:252-267.

el Lozy M (1978) A critical analysis of the double and triple logistic growth curves. Annals of Human Biology 5:389-394.

Malina RM (1971) A consideration of factors underlying the selection of methods in the assessment of skeletal maturity. American Journal of Physical Anthropology 35:341-346.

Malina RM (1978) Adolescent growth and maturation: Selected aspects of current research. Yearbook of Physical Anthropology 21:63-94.

* Malina RM, Bouchard C, Beunen G (1988) Human growth: Selected aspects of current research on well nourished children. Annual Review of Anthropology 17:187-219.

Marshall WA (1974) Interrelationships of skeletal maturation, sexual development and somatic growth in man. Annals of Human Biology 1:29-40.

Marshall WA, Tanner JM (1969) Variation in pattern of pubertal changes in girls. Archives of Disease in Childhood 44:291-303.

Marshall WA, Tanner JM (1970) Variations in the pattern of pubertal changes in boys. Archives of Disease in Childhood 45:13-23.

* Marshall WA, Tanner JM (1986) Puberty. In F Falkner, JM Tanner (eds), Human Growth. Volume 2. Postnatal Growth, Neurobiology. New York: Plenum, pp 171-209.

* Marubini E (1978) Mathematical handling of long-term longitudinal data. In F Falkner, JM Tanner (eds), Human Growth. Volume 1. Principles and Prenatal Growth. New York: Plenum, pp 209-225.

Matsudo SMM, Matsudo VKR (1994) Self-assessment and physician assessment of sexual maturation in Brazilian boys and girls: Concordance and reproducibility. American Journal of Human Biology 6:451-455.

Nicolson AB, Hanley C (1953) Indices of physiological maturity: Deviation and interrelationships. Child Development 24: 3-38.

Normand N, Pontier J, Loevenbruck C (1989) Approche par l'analyse des données d'une méthode d'valuation de la maturation osseuse chez l'enfant. Biométrie Praximétrie 29:17-37.

Prader A (1966) Testicular size: Assessment and clinical importance. Triangle 7:240-243.

Preece MA, Baines MJ (1978) A new family of mathematical models describing the human growth curve. Annals of Human Biology 5:1-24.

Prokopec M, Lhotska L (1994) Voice breaking as indicator of adolescence in Czech boys. In K Hajnis (ed), Growth and Ontogenetic Development in Man, IV. Prague: Charles University, Department of Anthropology, pp 217-220.

Pyle SI, Hoerr NL (1969) A Radiographic Standard of Reference for the Growing Knee. Springfield, IL: Charles C Thomas.

Reynolds EL, Wines JV (1948) Individual differences in physical changes associated with adolescence in girls. American Journal of Diseases of Children 75:329-350.

Reynolds EL, Wines JV (1951) Physical changes associated with adolescence in boys. American Journal of Diseases of Children 82:529-547.

Roche AF (1980) The measurement of skeletal maturation. In FE Johnston, AF Roche, C Susanne (eds), Human Physical Growth and Maturation: Methodologies and Factors. New York: Plenum, pp 61-82.

* Roche AF (1986) Bone growth and maturation. In F Falkner, JM Tanner (eds), Human Growth. Volume 2. Postnatal Growth, Neurobiology. New York: Plenum, pp 25-60.

Roche AF, Chumlea WC, Thissen D (1988) Assessing the Skeletal Maturity of the Hand-Wrist: Fels Method. Springfield, IL: Charles C Thomas.

Roche AF, Tyleshevski F, Rogers E (1983) Non-invasive measurement of physical maturity in children. Research Quarterly for Exercise and Sport 54:364-371.

Roche AF, Wainer H, Thissen D (1975a) Skeletal Maturity. The Knee Joint As a Biological Indicator. New York: Plenum.

Roche AF, Wainer H, Thissen D (1975b) Predicting adult stature for individuals. Monographs in Paediatrics 3. Basel: Karger.

Roche AF, Wainer H, Thissen D (1975c) The RWT method for the prediction of adult stature. Pediatrics 56:1026-1033.

Roche AF, Wellens R, Attie KM, Siervogel RM (1995) The timing of sexual maturation in a group of US White youths. Journal of Pediatric Endocrinology and Metabolism 8:11-18.

Roede MJ, van Wieringen JC (1985) Growth diagrams 1980: Netherlands third nation-wide survey. Tijdschrift voor Sociale Gezondheidszorg 63 (suppl): 1-34.

Roemmich JN, Blizzard RM, Peddada SD, Malina RM, Roche AF, Tanner JM, Rogol AD (1997) Longitudinal assessment of hormonal and physical alterations during normal puberty in boys. IV: Predictions of adult height by the Bayley-Pinneau, Roche-Wainer-Thissen, and Tanner-Whitehouse methods compared. American Journal of Human Biology 9:371-380.

Rucci M, Coppini G, Nicoletti I, Cheli D, Valli G (1995) Automatic analysis of hand radiographs for the assessment of skeletal age: A subsymbolic approach. Computers and Biomedical Research 28:239-256.

Schlossberger NM, Turner RA, Irwin CE (1992) Validity of self-report of pubertal maturation in early adolescents. Journal of Adolescent Health 13:109-113.

Sempé M (1987) Analyse de la Maturation Squelettique. A Pediatrie au Quotidien. Paris: Les Editions INSERM.

Sempé M, Pavia C (1979) Atlas de la Maturation Squelettique. Lyon, France: SIMEP SA.

Shuttleworth FK (1939) The physical and mental growth of girls and boys age six to nineteen in relation to age at maximum growth. Monographs of the Society for Research in Child Development 4, serial no. 22.

Simmons K (1944) The Brush Foundation Study of child growth and development. II. Physical growth and development. Monographs of the Society for Research in Child Development 9, serial no. 37.

* Tanner JM (1962) Growth at Adolescence, 2nd edition. Oxford: Blackwell.

Tanner JM, Gibbons RD (1994) A computerized image analysis system for estimating Tanner-Whitehouse 2 bone age. Hormone Research 42:282-287.

Tanner JM, Healy MJR, Goldstein H, Cameron N (2001) Assessment of Skeletal Maturity and Prediction of Adult Height (TW3 Method), 3rd edition. London: Saunders.

Tanner JM, Oshman D, Lindgren G, Grunbaum JA, Elsouki R, Labarthe D (1994) Reliability and validity of computer-assisted estimates of Tanner-Whitehouse skeletal maturity (CASAS): Comparison with the manual method. Hormone Research 42:288-294.

Tanner JM, Whitehouse RH, Healy MJR (1962) A New System for Estimating Skeletal Maturity from the Hand and Wrist, with Standards Derived from a Study of 2,600 Healthy British Children. Paris: International Children's Centre.

Tanner JM, Whitehouse RH, Marshall WA, Healy MJR, Goldstein H (1975) Assessment of Skeletal Maturity and Prediction of Adult Height (TW2 Method). New York: Academic Press.

Tanner JM, Whitehouse RH, Cameron N, Marshall WA, Healy MJR, Goldstein H (1983) Assessment of Skeletal Maturity and Prediction of Adult Height, 2nd edition. New York: Academic Press.

Tanner JM, Whitehouse RH, Marubini E, Resele LF (1976) The adolescent growth spurt of boys and girls of the Harpenden growth study. Annals of Human Biology 3:109-126.

Taranger J, Engstrom I, Lichenstein H, Svennberg-Redegen I (1976) Somatic pubertal development. Acta Paediatrica Scandinavica 258 (suppl):121-135.

Todd TW (1937) Atlas of Skeletal Maturation. St. Louis: Mosby.

Van Teunenbroek A, De Waal W, Roks A, Chinafo P, Fokker M, Mulder P, De Muinck Keizer-Schrama S, Drop S (1996) Computer-aided skeletal age scores in healthy children, girls with Turner syndrome, and in children with constitutionally tall stature. Pediatric Research 39:360-367.

van Wieringen JC, Wafelbakker F, Verbrugge HP, De Haas JH (1971) Growth Diagrams 1965 Netherlands. Groningen: Wolters-Noordhoof Publishing.

Vidalin H (1988) Football: Traumatismes et âge osseux. Étude prospective de 11 cas. Médecine du Sport 62:195-197.

Wellens R, Malina RM (1990) The age at menarche. In J Simons, GP Beunen, R Renson, ALM Claessens, JAV Lefevre (eds), Growth and Fitness of Flemish Girls: The Leuven Growth Study. Champaign, IL: Human Kinetics, pp 119-125.

Zachman M, Prader A, Kind HP, Hafliger H, Budliger H (1974) Testicular volume during adolescence: Cross-sectional and longitudinal studies. Helvetica Paediatrica Acta 29: 61-72.

TIMING AND SEQUENCE OF CHANGES DURING ADOLESCENCE

Chapter Outline

Adolescent Growth Spurt
Parameters of the Adolescent Growth Spurt
Individual Variation

Sexual Maturity
Onset of Secondary Sex Characteristics
Menarche
Other Secondary Sex Characteristics

Sequence of Sexual and Somatic Maturity

Growth Spurts in Other Dimensions

Body Dimensions and Composition Relative to Peak Height Velocity

Body Dimensions

Body Composition
Regional Variation in Body Composition

Growth Spurts in Performance
Strength
Motor Performance
Aerobic Power

Performance Relative to Menarche

Summary

Sources and Suggested Readings

Preceding chapters have described changes in size, proportions, body composition, and performance that occur during childhood and adolescence. These are general trends associated with age and sex in a variety of morphological and functional characteristics. Variation in the timing and tempo of the adolescent growth spurt and sexual maturation alters the trends somewhat. Youngsters enter the adolescent phase of growth at varying ages (differential timing) and proceed through it at variable rates (differential tempo). Individual differences in timing and tempo during adolescence must be more closely examined in the context of how they may influence measures of growth and performance during adolescence.

Indicators of maturity status and their interrelationships were described in chapter 15. Only skeletal maturity covers the entire growth period. The other indicators are limited to adolescence and some require longitudinal data for derivation.

This chapter focuses on the timing and sequence of events that characterize the adolescent growth spurt in height and sexual maturation. Growth spurts in other body dimensions and performance are then considered, followed by a discussion of changes in body composition and performance relative to the timing of specific maturity indicators.

Adolescent Growth Spurt

The age at maximum rate of growth, or peak height velocity (PHV), during the adolescent growth spurt in height is the most commonly used indicator of somatic maturity. It is also a reference for comparison of changes in body dimensions, proportions, and composition and physical performance during the adolescent growth spurt. The question of interest is the following: How do body dimensions, body composition, and performance change relative to PHV?

An increase in the velocity of growth in height marks the initiation of the adolescent growth spurt. Velocity of growth in height eventually reaches a maximum and then gradually declines. Longitudinal data are required to identify the inflections in the growth curve and the ages at which they occur. Growth curves are fit either graphically or mathematically to individual height records to extract the change in velocity of growth and thus age at the initiation of the spurt (age at takeoff [TO]), velocity of growth when it reaches its maximum (PHV), and age at PHV.

Parameters of the Adolescent Growth Spurt

Three parameters of the adolescent growth spurt in stature—age at TO, age at PHV, and PHV (cm/year)—for samples of North American and European youth are summarized in table 16.1. Data for several samples are not included, because the curve-fitting procedure did not result in a good fit and because some of the samples included either a large number of late-maturing or early-maturing girls. Several ages and peak velocities are reported for some samples because the

parameters of the growth curve were estimated with different analytical procedures.

Allowing for variation among samples and in methods used to estimate the parameters of the adolescent growth spurt, several trends are apparent. The range among mean ages is about 2 years at TO and about 1 year at PHV in girls and boys. Mean ages at TO range from 8.2 to 10.3 years in girls and from 10.0 to 12.1 years in boys, with no clear concentration within a specific age range. With one exception (10.8 years of age for American Black girls, see chapter 25), reported mean ages at PHV in girls vary between 11.3 and 12.2 years, but about three-fourths of the mean ages (27 of 38) fall within a narrower range, 11.6 and 12.1 years. Reported mean ages at PHV in North American and European boys vary between 13.3 and 14.4 years, but three-fourths of the mean ages (28 of 37) fall within a narrower range, 13.8 and 14.1 years. Takeoff and PHV occur earlier in girls than in boys; the sex difference is, on average, about 2 years. Finally, a range of about 2 cm/year among estimated mean peak height velocities occurs in girls (7.1 to 9.1 cm/year) and boys (8.2 to 10.3 cm/year) and peak height velocity is slightly higher in boys than in girls (by about 1.0 cm/year).

As noted, some of the variation in estimated ages at TO and PHV and in peak height velocities is related to the models and procedures used to derive them. When the same models are used,

TABLE 16.1 Mean Ages at Takeoff (TO), Age at Peak Height Velocity (PHV), and PHV in European and North American Adolescents

Sample	Girls			Boys		
	Age at TO (yr)	Age at PHV (yr)	PHV (cm/yr)	Age at TO (yr)	Age at PHV (yr)	PHV (cm/yr)
Europe						
Belgium	8.5	11.6	7.4			
	9.9	11.4	7.8			
	9.9	11.7	7.8			
Belgium		11.6	7.5		14.0	9.4
Belgium					14.2	9.2
England		12.1	9.0		14.1	10.3
	10.3	11.9	8.1	12.1	13.9	8.8
	9.0	11.9	7.5	10.7	14.2	8.2
England	8.7	11.9	7.5	10.3	13.9	8.5
England		12.2			13.9	
England		12.2	8.0		14.1	9.6

Sample	Girls			Boys		
	Age at T0 (yr)	Age at PHV (yr)	PHV (cm/yr)	Age at T0 (yr)	Age at PHV (yr)	PHV (cm/yr)
Europe *(continued)*						
France	9.3	12.0	8.4	11.0	13.8	9.7
	8.8	11.9	7.7	11.2	14.0	9.5
	9.2	11.7	7.8	11.8	13.9	9.7
	8.2	11.6	7.6	10.0	13.9	8.5
Germany	9.0	12.0	7.3	10.7	14.1	9.0
Netherlands					14.0[a]	9.6[a]
Netherlands					14.4	
Poland	9.7	11.7		11.8	13.9	
				10.8	14.1	
Poland		11.8	7.8		13.8	9.1
Scotland		11.7	7.7		13.8	8.9
Sweden		11.9	8.3		14.1	9.8
Sweden	10.0	12.0	8.6	12.1	14.1	9.9
Sweden		12.0			14.0	
		12.0			14.1	
Sweden		11.7	8.0			
Switzerland	9.6	12.2	7.1	11.0	13.9	9.0
	9.0	12.1	7.1	10.6	14.0	8.7
Wales					14.1	8.5
North America						
California		11.5			13.8	
		11.7			14.1	
		11.6			13.7	
Colorado		11.4	9.1		13.4	9.6
	9.6	11.9		11.4	14.0	
Massachusetts	8.7	11.6	7.8			
Ohio		11.8	7.9		13.8	9.2
		11.8	8.3		13.8	9.8
		11.3	7.3		13.3	8.4
Harvard, six cities study						
White	9.3	11.5	8.1	10.5	13.6	9.5
Black	8.9	10.8	8.4	10.3	13.3	9.2
Quebec		12.0				
Saskatchewan	9.0	11.8	8.0	11.1	14.3	9.4

At times, several estimates of the parameters of the adolescent growth spurt are indicated for the same sample; the parameters are derived from different curve-fitting models.

[a]Medians.

Adapted from Beunen and Malina (1988), Malina et al. (1988), and Malina and Beunen (1996), which contain the primary references, sample sizes, and methods of deriving the parameters of the adolescent growth curve, with the exception of the following, which have been added to the compilation: Guo et al. (1992), Pan and Ratcliffe (1992), Wember et al. (1992), Bell (1993), Berkey et al. (1994), Malina et al. (1997), and Ledford and Cole (1998).

the estimates vary within a narrower range. The relative uniformity of the estimates of PHV is of interest, given the period over which the longitudinal studies were done. The studies in California, Colorado, and Ohio were begun in the late 1920s, a number of European studies were begun in the mid-1950s, and others were begun in the 1960s and 1970s.

The data presented in table 16.1 can be summarized as follows. First, the change in velocity that marks the initiation of the adolescent growth spurt (age at TO) occurs relatively early in the transition from childhood to adolescence. Second, timing presents a clear sex difference. On the average, girls are in advance of boys by about 2 years in age at TO and age at PHV. Third, the sex difference in the magnitude of PHV is small; girls have a slightly less intense PHV than boys. The difference is not as large compared with differences in mean ages at TO and PHV. Fourth, standard deviations around the mean ages (not shown in table 16.1) are about 1 year. Reported standard deviations for estimated ages at PHV range from 0.7 to 1.2 years in girls and 0.8 to 1.3 years in boys. Standard deviations in estimated PHV tend to be a little more than 1 cm/year. Finally, age at PHV occurs slightly earlier in American than in European samples.

Individual Variation

In contrast to variation in means and standard deviations among samples, variation among individual children in ages of TO and PHV and in PHV within a longitudinal series is considerable. This finding is shown in table 16.2 for two European studies. The studies used different methods of estimating parameters of the adolescent growth spurt in stature, and thus the estimates vary somewhat. The range of individual variation in the timing and magnitude of the adolescent growth spurt should be noted. Although the initiation of the adolescent growth spurt and PHV occurs, on the average, earlier in girls than in boys, much overlap does occur. Some children begin their adolescent growth spurt at chronological ages that place them in middle childhood, well before the age range commonly given for the transition from childhood to adolescence.

Sexual Maturity

The assessment of sexual maturity is based on the development of secondary sex characteristics—breasts and menarche in girls, genitals in boys, and pubic hair in both sexes. The criteria for pubic hair, breast, and genital maturity were described and illustrated in chapter 15.

Onset of Secondary Sex Characteristics

Median/mean ages at onset of stages of secondary sex characteristics in several longitudinal and

TABLE 16.2 Parameters of the Adolescent Growth Spurt in Swiss and British Children Illustrating Individual Differences in Age at Takeoff, Age at PHV, and PHV

	Girls			Boys		
	Mean	SD	Range	Mean	SD	Range
Age at takeoff (yr)						
Swiss	9.6	1.1	6.6–12.9	11.0	1.2	7.8–13.5
British	9.0	0.7	7.7–10.0	10.7	0.9	8.6–12.4
Age at PHV (yr)						
Swiss	12.2	1.0	9.3–15.0	13.9	0.8	12.0–15.8
British	11.9	0.7	10.3–13.2	14.2	0.9	11.9–16.2
PHV (cm/yr)						
Swiss	7.1	1.0	5.0–10.1	9.0	1.1	6.7–12.4
British	7.5	0.8	6.1–9.3	8.2	1.2	5.6–10.0

Swiss data are adapted from Largo et al. (1978) for 110 girls and 112 boys; British data are adapted from Preece and Baines (1978) for 23 girls and 35 boys.

cross-sectional samples of European and North American girls and boys are summarized in table 16.3. The data are largely based on clinical examination, although some studies used standardized physique photographs, which were enlarged, to evaluate the development of secondary sex characteristics. As indicated earlier, the initial appearance of pubic hair on photographs is difficult to detect, and the samples that used photographs have a later age of onset for PH2. Standard deviations for ages at reaching each stage of a secondary sex characteristic tend to be greater than for age at PHV, and larger standard deviations are more common for the later stages of sexual maturity. Data for the recent sample of Ohio children (Roche et al. 1995) are based on self-assessments. The earlier study of Ohio children in the Fels series in the 1940s (Reynolds and Wines 1948, 1951) was based on clinical examination. Estimated ages at onset of

specific stages of secondary sex characteristics in the earlier series do not show a consistent pattern of differences from the more recent series based on self-assessment.

Data on the development of secondary sex characteristics derived from longitudinal studies are often limited by sample sizes that are not large enough to derive estimates for a population. Moreover, the samples may not be representative of their respective populations. Population surveys that include assessments of breast, genital, and pubic hair stages are not extensive. Exceptions are the national surveys of American and Dutch children and adolescents. The Third National Health and Nutrition Examination Survey (NHANES III 1988–1994) in the United States, for example, included 4,263 children and adolescents 8.0 to 19.0 years of age (Sun et al. 2002). Selected percentiles for the age at the transition from stage 1 to stage 2 of breast and pubic hair in girls and

TABLE 16.3　Median/Mean Ages (Years) at the Onset of Stages of Sexual Maturity in European and North American Girls and Boys

	Girls breast stages				Girls pubic hair stages			
	B2	B3	B4	B5	PH2	PH3	PH4	PH5
England	11.1	12.1	13.1	15.3	11.7	12.4	12.9	14.4
Netherlands	11.0	12.1	13.4	15.2	11.3	12.2	13.3	14.9
France	11.4	12.5	13.4		11.4	12.4	13.2	
Sweden	11.0	11.8	13.1	15.6	11.5	12.0	12.9	15.2
Switzerland	10.9	12.2	13.2	14.0	10.4	12.2	13.0	14.0
Germany, East	10.8			15.7	11.1			14.6
Poland	11.3	12.4	13.4	14.5	11.8	12.6	13.5	14.7
Estonia	11.6	12.2	14.6	15.0	12.1	14.1	14.9	15.4
Turkey	10.0	11.6	12.8	15.2	10.8	11.6	12.3	13.6
Israel	10.3	11.0			10.6	11.4		
U.S., White, California	10.6	11.2		13.9	11.6	12.5	13.2	
U.S., White, Ohio	10.8	11.4	12.2	13.7	11.0	11.9	12.5	13.9
U.S., White, Ohio[a]	11.2	12.0	12.4		11.0	11.8	12.4	13.1
U.S., Mexican American	10.9	12.2	13.9	15.1	11.2	12.4	14.1	15.5
U.S., Black[b]	8.9	10.2			8.8	10.3		
U.S., White[b]	10.0	11.3			10.5	11.5		
U.S., NHANES III[c]								
White	10.4	11.7	13.3	15.5	10.6	11.8	13.0	16.3
Black	9.5	10.8	12.2	13.9	9.5	10.6	11.9	14.7
Mexican American	9.8	11.4	13.1	14.7	10.4	11.7	13.2	16.3

(continued)

T A B L E
16.3   *(continued)*

	Boys genital stages				Boys pubic hair stages			
	G2	G3	G4	G5	PH2	PH3	PH4	PH5
England	11.6	12.9	13.8	14.9	13.4	13.9	14.4	16.0
Netherlands	11.0	13.2	14.1	15.9	11.7	13.5	14.4	16.0
France	12.0	13.1	14.3		12.4	13.4	14.3	
Sweden	12.2	13.1	13.9	15.1	12.5	13.4	14.1	15.5
Switzerland	11.2	12.9	13.8	14.7	12.2	13.5	14.2	14.9
Germany, East	10.8			15.9	11.5			15.7
Poland	12.4	13.7	14.5	15.5	13.0	13.9	15.0	15.5
Poland	11.0	13.4	14.7	16.1				
Estonia	12.2	13.6	14.1	15.1	12.9	13.6	14.9	15.2
U.S., White, California	11.8	13.1	13.8	15.2				
U.S., White, Ohio	11.5	12.7	13.4	17.3	12.2	13.3	13.9	16.1
U.S., White, Ohio[a]	11.2	12.1	13.5	14.3	11.2	12.1	13.4	14.3
U.S., Mexican American	12.4	13.5	14.6	16.3	12.8	13.6	14.6	16.1
U.S., NHANES III[c]								
White	10.0	12.3	13.5	16.0	12.0	12.6	13.6	15.7
Black	9.2	11.8	13.4	15.0	11.2	12.5	13.7	15.3
Mexican American	10.3	12.5	13.8	15.8	12.3	13.1	14.1	15.7
Mexico	11.5	13.0	13.6	14.7	12.7	13.4	14.3	

[a]Based on self-assessed maturity status (Roche et al. 1995).

[b]These data are from a pediatric practice–based research network across the United States and are limited to girls 3 through 12 years of age (Herman-Giddens et al. 1997). The estimates, especially for stage 3, may be influenced by the lack of older girls in the sample.

[c]The data are from Sun et al. (2002). The values are similar to those reported for NHANES III by Herman-Giddens et al. (2001), although there is some variation in the statistical techniques used.

Adapted from Malina (1978), which contains the primary references for earlier studies. Data from Largo and Prader (1983a, 1983b), Belmaker (1982), Roche et al. (1995), Villarreal et al. (1989), Herman-Giddens et al. (1997, 2001), Grünberg and Thetloff (1997), Engelhardt et al. (1995), Willers et al. (1996), and Sun et al. (2002) were added. Note that Black and Mexican American children and adolescents were oversampled in NHANES III, which probably influences the estimates for the total sample. Ages for Mexican boys were calculated from data reported in Rosales Lopez (1984).

genitals and pubic hair in boys are shown for the national sample of American youth in table 16.4. These data provide an estimate of age at the onset of puberty. The range between the 25th and 75th percentiles tends to be about 1 year for each characteristic in each ethnic group.

The 10th and 90th percentiles for ages at attaining stages of the secondary sex characteristics in the national sample of Dutch children are given in table 16.5. These percentiles accommodate a wider range of variation, and this variation in ages at which specific stages of a secondary sex characteristic are attained within a population of adolescents should be noted.

Menarche

Age at menarche is the most commonly reported secondary sex characteristic for girls. Median ages at menarche from surveys of European and North American populations carried out in the mid-1970s through the mid-1990s are summarized in table 16.6. The estimates are based on the status quo method utilizing probit analysis. American girls attain menarche somewhat earlier than girls in most European countries, and American Black girls attain menarche earlier than American White girls (racial variation is discussed in chapter 25). Within Europe, a north-south gradient in median

TABLE 16.4
Estimated Median Ages for the Transition From Stage 1 to Stage 2 of Secondary Sex Characteristics (Onset of Puberty) and Selected Percentiles in American Girls and Boys in the Third National Health and Nutrition Examination Survey (NHANES III, 1988–1994)

	25th percentile	50th percentile	75th percentile	25th percentile	50th percentile	75th percentile
	Breasts			**Pubic hair**		
Girls						
White	9.5	10.4	11.2	9.7	10.6	11.5
Black	8.5	9.5	10.5	8.3	9.5	10.6
Mexican American	8.6	9.8	11.0	9.4	10.4	11.5
	Genitals			**Pubic hair**		
Boys						
White	8.6	10.0	11.4	11.0	12.0	12.9
Black	7.5	9.2	10.9	10.0	11.2	12.4
Mexican American	8.9	10.3	11.7	11.4	12.3	13.3

Adapted from Sun et al. (2002).

TABLE 16.5
Selected Percentiles for Ages (Years) at Onset of Stages of Secondary Sex Characteristics in a National Sample of Dutch Youth

	Percentiles		
	10th	**50th**	**90th**
Girls breast			
B2	9.1	10.5	12.3
B3	10.2	11.7	13.1
B4	11.4	12.9	14.5
B5	12.5	14.2	–
Girls pubic hair			
PH2	9.0	10.8	12.6
PH3	10.2	11.7	13.1
PH4	11.3	12.6	14.0
PH5	12.2	14.0	16.4
Boys genital			
G2	9.3	11.3	13.3
G3	11.6	13.1	14.5
G4	12.7	14.0	15.6
G5	13.5	15.3	18.6
Boys pubic hair			
PH2	9.0	11.7	13.5
PH3	11.7	13.1	14.5
PH4	12.9	14.0	15.5
PH5	13.5	15.0	18.4

Adapted from Roede and van Wieringen (1985).

ages at menarche is evident. Girls in northern regions attain menarche slightly later than girls in southern regions. This trend probably reflects genetic variation among European populations. Variation within European countries is also considerable, and some countries from the former Eastern European Socialist Bloc (e.g., Poland and Croatia) show an urban-rural gradient (see chapter 25).

The earlier summaries of Danker-Hopfe (1986) and Eveleth and Tanner (1990) include data for the 1960s and 1970s. Median ages at menarche in some European countries have not changed from the 1970s into the 1990s, whereas in other countries median ages have continued to decline. The decline in the age at menarche over time is a component of the secular trend toward earlier maturation. The trend has stopped in some countries but continues in others. On the other hand, median ages at menarche have increased slightly in the countries that formerly constituted Yugoslavia, probably reflecting the rigors and conditions associated with the war conditions that have dominated the region in the late 1980s and 1990s. This development would suggest a reversal of secular trends. Secular changes in growth and maturation are discussed in more detail in chapter 29.

Other Secondary Sex Characteristics

Variation in testicular volume with age during adolescence in mixed-longitudinal samples of

Region/country	Sample	Year(s) of survey	Median age
Europe			
Belgium	National Flemish	~1980	13.2
	Brussels	~1980	13.1
Croatia	Several cities	1991–1995	12.8–13.3
Czech Republic	National	1991	13.0
Denmark	North Zealand	1983	13.0
England	Northwest	1976	13.3
	Newcastle	1975	13.4
France	National	1974	12.8
	Paris	1979	12.8
Germany	Bremerhaven	1980	13.3
	Jena	1985	13.0
	East	1984–1986	13.5
Greece	National	1981	12.6
	Athens	1996	12.3
Hungary	Kormend	1988	12.9
	Fejér County	1992	12.7
Irish Republic	National	1985	13.5
Italy	North	1980s–1990s	12.8
	Central	1980s–1990s	12.7
	South	1980s–1990s	12.7
	Rome	1980s–1990s	12.4
	Sardinia	1987–1991	12.7
Netherlands	National	1980	13.3
	Rotterdam	1991	13.1
Poland	National		
	Cities	1988	13.0
	Towns	1988	13.4
	Villages	1988	13.5
	Warsaw	1988	12.7
Estonia	Southern part	1993–1995	13.2
Spain	Basque	1980s–1990s	12.7
	Galicia	1994	12.5
Sweden	National	1980s	12.7-13.0
Russia	Moscow	1981–1984	13.0

TABLE 16.6 Median Ages at Menarche (Years) in Samples of European and North American Girls in the Mid-1970s Through the Mid-1990s

Region/country	Sample	Year(s) of survey	Median age
North America			
United States	National[a]	1988–1994	12.4
	White		12.6
	Black		12.1
	Mexican American		12.5
	National		
	White[b]	1992–1993	12.9
	Black	1992–1993	12.2
Canada	Quebec	1978–1980	12.9
Mexico	Federal District	1976	12.3
	Federal District	1998	12.4

[a]The 1988 to 1994 data for the United States are from the Third National Health and Nutrition Examination Survey (NHANES III). The sample includes American Whites (non-Hispanic Whites), American Blacks (non-Hispanic Blacks), and Mexican Americans. American Blacks and Mexican Americans were oversampled in NHANES III, which may influence the estimate for the total sample (Chumlea et al. 2003).

[b]These data are from a pediatric practice–based research network across the United States and are limited to girls 3 through 12 years of age (Herman-Giddens et al. 1997). The estimates are probably influenced by the lack of older girls in the sample.

Ages are based on probit analysis. The data are from individual papers in Bodzsar and Susanne (1998), with the exception of the data for the Belgian national Flemish sample (Wellens et al. 1990), Estonia (Grünberg and Thetloff 1997), the United States (Herman-Giddens et al.1997; Chumlea et al. 2003), Quebec (Malina and Bouchard, unpublished), East Germany (Engelhardt et al. 1995), and Mexico (Ramos Rodriguez 1986; Siegel 1999). For more comprehensive discussions of variation in ages at menarche see Danker-Hopfe (1986) and Eveleth and Tanner (1990).

Swedish and Swiss boys are shown, respectively, by age and by stage of pubic hair in table 16.7. As expected, volume of the testis increases with age, but the distributions of the volumes tend to be skewed during puberty. The range of testicular volumes within each age group should be noted. Mean testicular volume also increases with stage of pubic hair. The difference between mean volumes is small between PH1 and PH2 (i.e., the transition into puberty) but increases, on average, by 2.5 ml between PH2 to PH3 and by 3.3 ml between PH3 to PH4. Testis volume continues to increase with further maturation of the distribution of pubic hair (Zachman et al. 1974).

Information on less commonly used indicators of secondary sex characteristics (axillary hair, facial hair, and voice change) is less extensive. Appearance and development of these characteristics occur rather late in the sequence of maturational events during adolescence. On the average, axillary hair in girls appears after PHV but before menarche, whereas in boys axillary hair appears close to or just after PHV. Facial hair and breaking of the voice in boys appear after PHV, but the timing of initial voice change varies, which probably reflects methodological differences among studies (Taranger et al. 1976; Hagg and Taranger 1980; Billewicz et al. 1981). A short-term longitudinal study of 26 boys (none of whom were singers, five observations over a 1-year period) indicates rather abrupt changes in the acoustic characteristics of the voice in the transition from G3 to G4 (Harries et al. 1997).

Sequence of Sexual and Somatic Maturity

Allowing for individual variation in timing and tempo, a clear sequence of events for sexual and somatic maturity is difficult to specify. Nevertheless, several trends are apparent in the available data. First, in most samples, budding of the breasts in girls (B2) and initial enlargement of the genitalia in boys (G2) are, on average, the first overt signs of sexual maturity. However, in some boys and girls, appearance of pubic hair coincides with or preceeds, initial breast or genital changes. Second, girls mature, on the average, in advance of boys. Stages of the breasts and genitals are not equivalent and therefore not directly comparable; hence, the comparison of ages is only suggestive. Third, PHV tends to occur earlier in the sequence of pubertal changes in girls than in boys. Fourth, menarche is a late event in the pubertal sequence, which occurs, on average, about 1 year or slightly

TABLE 16.7	Selected Percentiles and Ranges for the Volume of the Testis by Age During Adolescence in Urban Swedish Boys and by Stage of Pubic Hair Development in Urban Swiss Boys

Age (yr)	Percentiles (ml)			Range (ml)
	10	50	90	
Swedish boys				
10	1.0	1.8	2.9	1–6
11	1.1	2.2	4.4	1–15
12	1.7	3.3	9.5	1–20
13	2.6	6.0	12.4	1–20
14	5.1	10.5	19.6	2–25
15	9.6	15.0	24.9	6–25
16	14.7	20.3	25.0	12–25
17	19.8	24.8	25.0	15–25
Pubic hair	**Mean**	**SD**		
Swiss boys				
PH1	6.0	2.6		
PH2	6.8	3.6		
PH3	9.3	3.8		
PH4	12.6	4.2		
PH5	16.3	4.6		
PH6	18.9	4.0		

PH6 refers to the further extension of pubic hair along the midline of the abdomen in late adolescence.

The Swedish data are adapted from Taranger et al. (1976) and the Swiss data are adapted from Zachman et al. (1974).

more after PHV and when most girls are in stages B4 and PH4.

Variation in the sequence of events during puberty is partly genuine and partly methodological. One of the major sources of variation is the interval between observations in longitudinal studies. For example, if the interval between observations is 6 or 12 months, a girl might possibly be near the end of B2 at the first examination and might be in B4 at the next observation. Hence, B3 is not recorded for her. Also ratings of characteristics vary among studies and within and between observers in each study. As noted earlier, a later age for PH2 is often recorded in studies that used photographic data. Also, more variation occurs among ages at the terminal stages of a secondary sex characteristic. This condition may reflect real variation in attaining the final stages, difficulties in rating the adult stage, or differences in applying the criteria.

An additional factor is the tempo of transition from one stage to the next. Data for the duration of stages of sexual maturity, or intervals between stages, are not extensive but indicate considerable interindividual variability. For example, the mean interval (± standard deviation) between B2 and B3 in Swiss girls is 1.4±0.8 years, whereas the mean interval between G2 and G3 in Swiss boys is 1.7±1.0 years. Corresponding intervals between PH2 and PH3 in girls and boys are 1.8±1.0 and 1.3±0.9 years, respectively (Largo and Prader 1983a, 1983b).

The duration of the pubertal transition from initial appearance (B2, G2, and PH2) to the mature state (B5, G5, and PH5) is likewise variable. Among Swiss girls, the mean duration of maturation of the breasts is 2.2±1.1 years and of pubic hair is 2.7±1.1 years (Largo and Prader 1983b). Corresponding data for Swiss boys indicate a mean duration for genital maturation of 3.5±1.1 years and for pubic hair of 2.7±1.0 years (Largo and Prader 1983a).

The sequences described for maturation of secondary sex characteristics in girls and boys are based on average ages of attaining stages in several samples and do not necessarily apply to individual adolescents. Not all children follow the average sequence. Individual variation on reaching different stages of puberty implies variation in sequence. Tables 16.8 and 16.9 show this variation in the form of distributions of breast and pubic hair stages in girls and of genital and pubic hair stages in boys from the Zurich (Switzerland) longitudinal growth study. The concentration of girls and boys along the diagonal from left to right in the tables illustrates the overall relatedness of the maturation of these secondary sex characteristics, but variation is also considerable. Among girls in PH3 or PH4, for example, stages B2 through B5 are represented (see upper part of table 16.8). The same variation is apparent in the distribution of stages of pubic hair at B3 (see lower part of table 16.8). Similar trends are evident among boys (see table 16.9). At PH2, for example, boys are distributed across G1 through G4. At G4, PH2 through PH5 are represented in Swiss boys.

Similar variation among individuals is evident when the distributions of stages of secondary sex

TABLE 16.8 Percentages of Swiss Girls in Each Stage of Breast Development When They Reached Each Stage of Pubic Hair Development (Top), and in Each Stage of Pubic Hair Development When They Reached Each Stage of Breast Development (Bottom)

Pubic hair stage	n	Percentages in each breast stage				
		B1	B2	B3	B4	B5
PH2	103	49	46	5	0	0
PH3	114	0	36	51	12	1
PH4	106	0	4	47	33	16
PH5	99	0	1	6	34	59

Breast stage	n	Percentages in each pubic hair stage				
		PH1	PH2	PH3	PH4	PH5
B2	110	16	67	16	1	0
B3	115	2	26	50	20	2
B4	80	0	4	28	43	25
B5	102	0	0	7	29	64

Adapted from Largo and Prader (1983a).

TABLE 16.9 Percentages of Swiss Boys in Each Stage of Genital Development When They Reached Each Stage of Pubic Hair Development (Top), and in Each Stage of Pubic Hair Development When They Reached Each Stage of Genital Development (Bottom)

Pubic hair stage	n	Percentages in each genital stage				
		G1	G2	G3	G4	G5
PH2	104	9	54	33	4	0
PH3	100	0	9	49	37	5
PH4	110	0	0	6	64	30
PH5	113	0	0	0	20	80

Genital stage	n	Percentages in each pubic hair stage				
		PH1	PH2	PH3	PH4	PH5
G2	118	63	36	1	0	0
G3	116	15	50	32	3	0
G4	108	0	9	42	44	5
G5	108	0	1	10	34	55

Adapted from Largo and Prader (1983b).

characteristics are expressed relative to the timing of PHV and menarche in girls (see table 16.10). Most girls are in B2 and B3 and in PH2 and PH3 at the time of PHV, but B1, B4, and B5 and PH1 and PH4 are also represented at PHV. In other words, at the time of PHV in Zurich girls, all five stages of breast development are represented. Similarly, most girls are in B4 and PH4 at the time of menarche, but some girls are in breast and pubic hair stages 2, 3, and 5 at the time of menarche.

Corresponding trends for boys indicate that most boys are in PH3 and G4 at the time of PHV (see table 16.11). However, all five pubic hair stages and G2 through G5 are represented at PHV in Zurich boys.

The information presented in tables 16.8 through 16.11 indicates the range of variation among individuals in the timing and sequence of sexual and somatic maturation during adolescence. Hence, average values need to be accepted as such, and the normal range of variation needs to be recognized.

PHV and menarche are major events of adolescence. Menarche is a late pubertal event that occurs, on the average, about 1 year or more after PHV. Both landmarks

TABLE 16.10 Percentages of Swiss Girls at Each Stage of Breast and Pubic Hair Development at the Time of Peak Height Velocity (PHV) and Menarche

Breast stage	PHV[a]	Menarche[b]
B1	5	0
B2	43	5
B3	47	31
B4	2	40
B5	3	24
Pubic hair stage	PHV	Menarche
PH1	4	0
PH2	37	3
PH3	49	20
PH4	10	46
PH5	0	31

[a]n = 107 girls.
[b]n = 125 girls.

Adapted from Largo and Prader (1983a).

TABLE 16.11 Percentages of Swiss Boys at Each Stage of Genital and Pubic Hair Development at the Time of Peak Height Velocity (PHV)

Genital stage	%	Pubic hair stage	%
G1	0	PH1	2
G2	4	PH2	11
G3	34	PH3	61
G4	55	PH4	25
G5	7	PH5	1

Note: n = 105 boys.

Adapted from Largo and Prader (1983b).

of adolescence occur when a major percentage of adult height has already been attained. The growth in height that remains after these events have occurred is called the final phase of growth (Roche 1989). Attainment of adult height is variable among individuals in the Fels longitudinal series, and median ages are 17.3 years and 21.2 years in girls and boys, respectively (see table 3.2, page 63). The sex difference in age at attaining adult height is greater than that for the age at PHV. Growth in height after PHV and menarche in girls and boys of the Fels longitudinal series is summarized in table 16.12. The median gain in height after PHV is 15.8 cm in girls and 17.8 cm in boys, whereas the median gain in height after menarche is less than one-half of the gain after PHV in girls, 7.4 cm. However, variation about the medians is considerable. The 10th and 90th percentiles for growth in height after PHV are, respectively, 11.6 and 23.7 cm in males and 10.8

and 22.3 cm in females. The corresponding percentiles for growth in height after menarche are 4.3 and 10.6 cm, respectively. Most of the growth in height after PHV (about 70%) occurs during the first 2 years after PHV in both sexes. The trend is similar for growth in height after menarche. The relationship between growth in height after these maturational events and when these events occur is negative. Thus, later ages at PHV and menarche are associated with lesser growth in height after these indicators of maturity are reached.

Growth Spurts in Other Dimensions

Discussions of the adolescent growth spurt focus primarily on stature, in part because of the relative wealth of data on this dimension between early childhood and young adulthood and in part because most other body dimensions follow a growth curve like that for stature. However, variation occurs in the timing of growth spurts in other body dimensions relative to the growth spurt in height. The models used to estimate adolescent parameters for stature have been used to derive ages at peak velocity and peak velocities for several body dimensions. Ages at peak velocity for body dimensions are most often related to the age at PHV to illustrate the sequence of changes during the adolescent growth spurt.

Estimated age at peak weight velocity (PWV) and PWV (kg/year) are compared with age at PHV in several longitudinal samples in table 16.13. PWV occurs after PHV, and standard deviations are about 1 year. PWV is, on average, greater in boys than in girls. Although data are

TABLE 16.12 Percentiles for Growth in Height (cm) After Menarche and PHV in Girls and After PHV in Boys From the Fels Longitudinal Study

Age intervals	Menarche percentiles			PHV (girls) percentiles			PHV (boys) percentiles		
	10	50	90	10	50	90	10	50	90
0–1.0 yr	1.9	3.9	6.0	5.0	6.9	8.5	5.5	8.0	9.9
1.0–2.0 yr	0.6	1.5	3.1	2.0	4.3	6.1	2.9	4.7	6.8
2.0–3.0 yr	0.2	0.9	1.7	0.7	1.6	3.5	1.1	2.2	3.5
3.0–4.0 yr	0.0	0.5	1.1	0.3	0.9	1.9	0.4	1.0	2.0
4.0–5.0 yr	−0.3	0.3	0.8	0.0	0.6	1.1	−0.1	0.6	1.5
Total growth	4.3	7.4	10.6	10.8	15.8	22.3	11.6	17.8	23.7

Total growth refers to the amount of growth in height between the age at each maturity indicator and the cessation of growth in height, which in some individuals did not occur until the early-20s or mid-20s.

Adapted from Roche (1989).

TABLE 16.13

Means and Standard Deviations for Estimated Ages (Years) at Peak Weight Velocity (PWV) and Peak Weight Velocity (kg/yr) for Several Samples of North American and European Adolescents

| | Girls | | | | | Boys | | | | |
| | Age at PWV | | PWV (kg/yr) | | Age at PHV | Age at PWV | | PWV(kg/yr) | | Age at PHV |
Sample	Mean	SD	Mean	SD	Mean	Mean	SD	Mean	SD	Mean
North American										
California	12.3	1.3			11.7	14.5	1.3			14.1
Massachusetts	12.5	1.2	6.6	2.0	11.6					
Saskatchewan	12.1	0.7	6.8	1.2	11.8	14.5	1.1	8.7	2.3	14.3
Sasketchewan	12.3	1.2	8.7	1.4	11.8	13.8	1.1	10.3	1.9	13.4
European										
Belgium, national						14.6	1.2	8.8	2.3	14.2
England, Harpenden	12.9	1.0	8.8	1.5	12.1	14.3	0.9	9.8	2.0	14.1
Poland, Wroclaw	12.4	1.1			11.7	14.2	1.1			13.9
Poland, Warsaw	12.6	1.6	7.9	2.4	11.8	14.2	1.5	8.8	2.0	13.8
Sweden, urban	12.5	1.1	7.3	1.8	11.9	14.3	1.1	9.1	2.0	14.1

Mean ages at peak height velocity (PHV) are included for comparison.

Adapted from Malina et al. (1988), which includes the primary references, sample sizes and methods of deriving the parameters of the growth curves, with the exception of data for Warsaw adolescents (Geithner and Malina, unpublished) and the second set of data for Saskatchewan adolescents (Iuliano-Burns et al. 2001). The latter data are from the Saskatchewan Pediatric Bone Mineral Accrual Study, which was begun in 1991.

not as extensively reported for body weight as for stature, age at PWV appears to occur somewhat closer to age at PHV in boys than in girls. Among boys, the differences between mean ages at PHV and PWV range from 0.2 to 0.4 years, whereas among girls, the differences vary between 0.3 and 0.9 years. The differences in timing are related, in part, to sex differences in body composition. The adolescent weight spurt in boys includes principally gains in stature, skeletal tissue, and muscle mass, whereas the adolescent weight spurt in girls is of slightly lesser magnitude with smaller increases in skeletal and muscle mass and a larger increase in fat mass.

The timing of growth spurts in components of body composition estimated with DEXA among adolescents in the Saskatchewan Pediatric Bone Mineral Accrual Study is shown in table 16.14. Ages at peak velocities for body weight and components of body composition occur after PHV in both sexes. Estimated peak velocities of growth in body weight, lean tissue mass, and bone mineral content are greater in boys than in girls. On the other hand, estimated peak velocity of growth in fat mass is negative in both sexes, although the value for girls approaches zero. Variation in peak velocity for fat mass accumulation is considerable and is also relatively greater than for lean tissue mass and bone mineral content.

Data for ages at peak velocity and peak velocities for two segment lengths and two skeletal breadths are summarized in table 16.15. With few exceptions, standard deviations are of the same magnitude as those for height, and as expected, sex differences occur in timing and magnitude of the spurts. Differential timing of the growth spurts in segment lengths and skeletal breadths relative to PHV is also apparent. Peak velocity for estimated leg length occurs earlier than that for height, whereas peak velocity for sitting height or trunk length occurs after that for height. Variability among estimated ages at peak velocity is a result of the use of different dimensions to derive measures of trunk and leg length. For example, leg length in the two Polish studies is measured as symphyseal height (the distance from the top of the pubic symphysis to the standing surface). This dimension is difficult to measure. Indicators of trunk length in the two Polish studies are also different from the more commonly used measure of sitting height. In the Wroclaw study, trunk length is measured as the distance from the spine of the seventh cervical vertebra (cervicale) to the sitting surface (Bielicki et al. 1984), whereas in the Warsaw study, trunk length is estimated as standing height minus symphyseal height (Geithner et al. 1999). Allowing for variation in dimensions and methods of estimating ages at peak velocity, rapid growth of the lower extremities is characteristic of the early part of the adolescent growth spurt. Estimated mean ages at initiation of the growth spurts in leg length and sitting height differ by only 0.1 and 0.2 years in the British boys and girls, respectively, indicating that both growth spurts begin at about the same time. On the other hand, mean age at peak velocity in leg length is earlier than mean age at peak velocity in sitting height by 0.7 and 0.6 years in boys and girls, respectively (Tanner et al. 1976). Thus, the time from takeoff to peak velocity is shorter for leg length than for sitting height, which suggests that adolescent growth in sitting height extends over a longer period of time than adolescent growth in leg length. As a result, growth in sitting height contributes more to the adolescent gain in stature than does growth in leg length.

TABLE 16.14 Estimated Ages at Peak Velocity and Peak Velocities for Height, Weight, and Components of Body Composition in Canadian Adolescents

Measurement	Girls (n = 53)		Boys (n = 60)	
	Mean	SD	Mean	SD
Ages at peak velocity (yr)				
Stature	11.8	0.9	13.4	1.0
Lean mass	12.1	1.0	13.7	0.9
Weight	12.3	1.2	13.8	1.1
Fat mass	12.6	2.0	14.0	1.3
Bone mineral content	12.5	0.9	14.0	1.0
Peak velocities				
Stature (cm/yr)	8.6	1.1	10.4	1.2
Lean mass (kg/yr)	5.2	1.2	8.8	1.6
Weight (kg/yr)	8.7	1.4	10.3	1.9
Fat mass (kg/yr)	−0.4	1.8	−1.9	2.2
Bone mineral content (g/yr)	325	67	407	93

Estimates of body composition in the Saskatchewan Pediatric Bone Mineral Accrual Study are based on DEXA.

Adapted from Iuliano-Burns et al. (2001).

TABLE 16.15 Means and Standard Deviations for Estimated Ages (Years) at Peak Velocity (PV) and Peak Velocities (cm/yr) for Linear and Breadth Measurements in Samples of North American and European Adolescents

	Age at PHV	Leg length				Sitting height				Biacromial breadth				Biacristal breadth			
		Age at PV		PV		Age at PV		PV		Age at PV		PV		Age at PV		PV	
	Mean	Mean	SD	Mean	SD	Mean	SD	Mean	SD	Mean	SD	Mean	SD	Mean	SD	Mean	SD
Girls																	
California	11.7	11.0	1.2			11.8	1.3			11.3	1.6			12.2	1.3		
England, Harpenden	11.9	11.6	0.9	4.3	0.6	12.2	1.0	4.0	0.5	12.2	1.1	1.7	0.3	12.3	1.0	1.5	0.3
Poland, Wroclaw	11.7	11.2	1.0			12.2	1.1			11.6	0.9			11.4	0.9		
Poland, Warsaw	11.8	11.8	0.9	5.2	1.9	12.1	0.7	4.6	1.2	11.9	0.7	2.2	0.6	12.6	1.3	2.3	0.7
Sweden, Stockholm	12.0	11.6	0.9			12.2	1.0										
Boys																	
California	14.1	13.6	1.3			14.5	0.9			14.2	1.5			13.8	1.5		
Belgium, national	14.2	14.0	0.9	5.0	1.4	14.3	1.0	5.3	1.2								
England, Harpenden	13.9	13.6	0.8	4.3	0.7	14.3	0.9	4.5	0.7	14.2	0.9	2.2	0.3	14.0	1.0	1.4	0.3
Poland, Wroclaw	14.0	13.6	1.1			14.4	1.1			14.3	1.1			14.1	1.1		
Poland, Warsaw	13.8	13.0	1.0	5.3	0.9	13.8	1.6	4.8	1.1	13.6	1.3	2.3	0.6	13.1	1.6	1.9	0.4
Sweden, Stockholm	14.1	13.6	1.1			14.3	1.1										

Mean ages at PHV are included for comparison.

Adapted from Malina et al. (1988), which includes the primary references, sample sizes, and methods of deriving the parameters of the growth curves, with the exception of data for Warsaw adolescents (Geithner and Malina, unpublished).

In contrast, mean ages at peak velocity for biacromial and bicristal breadths are quite variable relative to age at PHV in several samples of adolescents. Peak velocities of growth in the two skeletal breadths on the trunk do not differ in girls, but peak velocity of growth in biacromial breadth in boys is considerably greater than that for bicristal breadth. This variation in growth velocity during the adolescent growth spurt contributes to the sexual dimorphism in the breadth of the shoulders relative to the hips that occurs at this time.

Growth of the major long bones of the upper and lower extremities also illustrates the variation in the timing of growth of different body parts and gradients in growth. Mean ages at maximum annual increments for long bones of the extremities, stature, and sitting height of children from the Child Research Council longitudinal study in Denver are shown in figure 16.1. The bone lengths were measured on standardized radiographs. As expected, maximum growth in each bone occurs earlier in girls than in boys, but greater overlap occurs between girls and boys in the bones of the lower extremity than in the bones of the upper extremity. Maximum growth is attained first by the tibia and then by the femur, followed by the fibula and the bones of the upper extremity. Maximum growth in stature occurs, on the average, more or less at the same time as maximum growth in length of the humerus and radius.

Thus, relatively long legs are characteristic of early adolescence because the bones of the lower extremity experience their growth spurts earlier than those of the upper extremity (see table 16.15, which shows earlier ages at peak velocity for estimated leg length compared with sitting height). As growth in sitting height continues into later adolescence, the appearance of having relatively long legs disappears.

Gradients in the growth of different body segments contribute to variation in body proportions. They are especially apparent during adolescence. The lower extremity experiences its growth spurt before the trunk and the upper extremity. Within the extremity, growth spurts of the more distal segments precede the spurts of the more proximal segments. This difference is illustrated in figure 16.2, which shows the lengths of upper limb segments as a percentage of size attained at about 16 years of age in girls and 18 years of age in boys. Clearly, the forearm is closer to its young adult length than is the upper arm. In boys, hand length is advanced relative to forearm length, but in this series of girls, hand and forearm length are not clearly differentiated. The age at peak velocity for a particular dimension and percentage of adult size attained at a given age are indicators of maturity. Thus, the forearm attains maximal growth velocity earlier and is thus closer to adult size; the upper arm attains

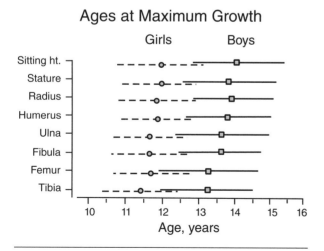

Ages at Maximum Growth

FIGURE 16.1 Mean ages at maximum growth, plus and minus 1 standard deviation, for long bones, sitting height, and stature in Denver children.

Data from Roche, 1974.

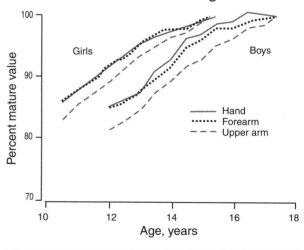

Percentage of Young Adult Size Attained at Each Age

FIGURE 16.2 Gradients in the attainment of mature (adult) lengths of segments of the upper limb in British children.

Reprinted, by permission, from Cameron et al., 1982, "A longitudinal analysis of the growth of limb segments in adolescence," *Annals of Human Biology* 9: 211-220.

maximal growth velocity later and is thus farther from adult size.

The discussion of the timing and sequence of growth spurts in body dimensions is based on mean ages at peak velocities. The group data indicate a general sequence of growth spurts, and two trends are apparent. On average, peak velocity of growth in leg length occurs before PHV, whereas peak velocities of growth in sitting height and body weight occur after PHV. Mean ages at peak velocity in other dimensions are less extensively studied and are more variable.

The suggested sequence is based on mean ages and not on the sequence of growth spurts in body dimensions within individual adolescents. The most frequently observed sequence of peak velocities in individuals is called the modal sequence (Stolz and Stolz 1951). The modal sequence often differs from the sequence of spurts based on mean ages because of individual differences in timing of growth spurts in specific body dimensions (Satake et al. 1994; Geithner et al. 1999). Variation in the timing of growth spurts of different body dimensions within individual children must be recognized. The timing of peak velocities apparently does not occur in a common order for all boys and girls, which emphasizes the individuality of the adolescent growth spurt.

Body Dimensions and Composition Relative to Peak Height Velocity

To reduce the time spread across the chronological age axis in studies of adolescent growth (i.e., to reduce the variation among individuals at this time), longitudinal data are occasionally viewed relative to a biological parameter other than chronological age. PHV is used most often as the point of reference, and changes in other dimensions and tissues are viewed in terms of time before and after PHV. Years before and after PHV are used as the time axis. In this procedure, individual children are classified by years before and after their own PHV, regardless of the age at which PHV occurs. Growth curves of individual children are plotted relative to PHV, independent of chronological age, and are then averaged. Plotting can be done for either size attained or for growth velocity of a particular dimension at each time point before or after PHV.

The concept of using a biological parameter rather than chronological age to reduce variation

along the chronological age axis was apparently first developed by Boas (1892) more than 100 years ago. However, Shuttleworth (1939) was the first to apply the method of plotting growth curves against a biological parameter rather than chronological age. Expressing attained growth and velocities of various body dimensions on a time axis relative to PHV is now common.

Body Dimensions

In the Leuven Growth Study of Belgian Boys, distance and velocity curves for 12 anthropometric dimensions that showed an adolescent growth spurt were aligned on PHV and PWV (see table 16.16). Maximum velocities for lower limb dimensions precede PHV, whereas maximum velocities for body weight, sitting height, and skeletal breadths and circumferences of the trunk and upper extremities occur after PHV. In contrast, no dimensions show a growth spurt after PWV; rather, all dimensions experience their growth spurts before or coincident with PWV. The two skeletal breadths of the trunk have growth spurts that are coincident with PWV. The timing of adolescent growth spurts in limb circumferences is to some extent confounded by loss of subcutaneous adipose tissue on the extremities during male adolescence and specifically close to PHV.

Body Composition

Serial changes in body weight, fat-free mass (FFM), and fat mass (FM) for 40 Czechoslovak boys from Prague followed from about 11 through 18 years of age relative to PHV are shown in figure 16.3. Maximum annual increments in FFM and FM appear to coincide with PHV. The boys were measured annually, and the annual increments were used to derive the velocity curve. The trends may not be as precise as those based on semiannual measurements and half-yearly velocities. Annual gains in FM are rather stable during the adolescent growth spurt, showing a slight rise at and just after PHV and becoming negative 2 and 3 years after PHV.

Near the time of PHV, the Czechoslovak boys are gaining about 7.5 kg FFM/year and about 0.8 kg FM/year, but they are declining in relative fatness by about 0.4% per year. The decline in relative fatness is a function of the marked increase in FFM during the adolescent growth spurt, so FM, although increasing slightly, constitutes a smaller percentage of body weight at this time. The estimated maximum velocity of growth in FFM in the Fels mixed-longitudinal series of boys

TABLE 16.16 Timing of Maximum Observed Velocities of Anthropometric Dimensions Relative to Peak Height Velocity and Peak Weight Velocity in Belgian Boys

Dimension	Peak height velocity			Peak weight velocity		
	Before	At	After	Before	At	After
Height				X		
Weight			X			
Sitting height			X	X		
Leg length	X			X		
Biacromial breadth			X		X	
Chest breadth			X		X	
Biepicondylar breadth			X	X		
Bicondylar breadth	X			X		
Chest circumference, inspiration			X	X		
Flexed arm circumference			X		X	
Thigh circumference	X				X	
Calf circumference	X			X		

Adapted from Beunen et al. (1988).

Gains in Body Weight and Composition Relative to Peak Height Velocity in Boys

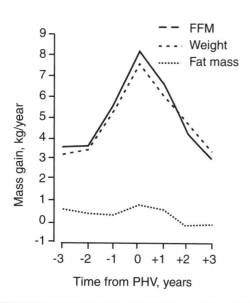

FIGURE 16.3 Annual gains in body weight, fat-free mass (FFM), and fat mass (FM) aligned on peak height velocity (PHV) in Czechoslovak boys from Prague. The study was conducted before Czechoslovakia was divided into two independent countries, the Czech Republic and Slovakia.

Reprinted, by permission, from Parizkova, 1976, "Growth and growth velocity of lean body mass and fat in adolescent boys," *Pediatric Research* 10: 647-650.

is 7.0 kg FFM/year, but it occurs about 1 year after PHV. The estimated change in relative fatness in Fels boys becomes negative about 13 years of age and reaches a maximum decline of about 0.9% per year at 15 years of age. In contrast, no clear spurt is apparent in the velocity of growth of FFM in the mixed-longitudinal series of Fels girls, whereas relative fatness increases through adolescence and reaches its smallest increase of about 0.6% per year at 15 years of age, which is well after PHV (Guo et al. 1997).

Given the lack of longitudinal data on the body composition of girls, the estimates of FFM and FM utilized to describe age and sex differences in body composition during childhood and adolescence in chapter 5 were more closely examined for the years just before and just after PHV, 11 to 13 years of age in girls and 13 to 15 years of age in boys (see table 16.17). Although the annual increments are derived from cross-sectional data from many samples, the estimates are consistent with those for the longitudinal series of Czechoslovak boys (see figure 16.3) and of Fels boys and girls (Guo et al. 1997). Changes in body composition during the interval of maximum growth in height constitute a major proportion of the changes that occur during the adolescent years. This relationship is readily apparent in a comparison of the estimates in table 16.16 for the interval of maximum growth with those in table 5.5 (page 116) for the age span 10 to 18 years.

TABLE 16.17	Changes in Densitometric Estimates of Body Composition During the Interval of Maximal Growth During Adolescence			
	Females (11–13 years of age)		**Males (13–15 years of age)**	
	Total gain	**Annual gain**	**Total gain**	**Annual gain**
FFM	7.1 kg	3.5 kg/yr	14.3 kg	7.2 kg/yr
FM	2.8 kg	1.4 kg/yr	1.5 kg	0.7 kg/yr
% Fat	1.7 %	0.9 %/yr	−1.1 %	−0.5 %/yr

Adapted from Malina et al. (1988).

Total-body bone mineral content has a growth spurt that occurs, on the average, after PHV in boys and girls. Estimated ages at peak velocity of growth in total-body bone mineral in Canadian girls and boys are, respectively, 12.5 and 14.0 years, which compare with estimated ages at PHV of 11.8 and 13.4 years in this sample (see table 16.14). Estimated velocity of bone mineral accretion during the adolescent growth spurt is consistently greater in boys than in girls, and the sex difference appears to be largest at peak velocity, 407 g/year in boys compared with 325 g/year in girls. A time lag appears to occur between peak linear growth in height and peak accrual of total-body bone mineral. Age at peak velocity of bone mineral accretion and age at menarche do not differ in this

sample of the Canadian girls, 12.5 and 12.7 years of age, respectively (Iuliano-Burns et al. 2001), which suggests that adolescent growth in bone mineral is closely related to sexual maturation.

Regional Variation in Body Composition

Regional variation in growth of fat and lean tissues on the extremities occurs during the adolescent growth spurt. Velocity curves for bone, muscle, and subcutaneous fat widths measured on standardized radiographs of children in the Harpenden Growth Study are aligned on PHV in figure 16.4. Maximum gains in humerus and tibia widths occur coincidentally with PHV in

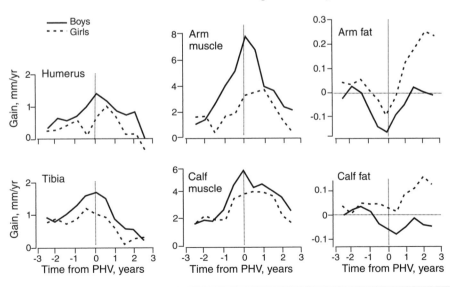

Gains in Tissue Widths of the Arm and Leg
Relative to Peak Height Velocity

FIGURE 16.4 Half-yearly gains in widths of bone, muscle, and fat on the arm and calf aligned on PHV in children of the Harpenden Growth Study.

Reprinted, by permission, from Tanner et al., 1981, "Radiographically determined widths of bone, muscle and fat in the upper arm and calf from age 3-18 years," *Annals of Human Biology* 8: 495-517.

boys. In girls, on the other hand, maximum gains in humerus width appear to occur after PHV and maximum gains in tibia width appear to occur just before PHV. Maximum gains in both bone widths are greater in boys than in girls. Peak velocities of arm and calf muscle widths occur after PHV in both sexes. Boys have a growth spurt in arm muscle that is approximately twice the magnitude of that for girls, whereas the peak in calf muscle is only slightly greater in males.

Changes in subcutaneous adipose tissue on the arm and calf show a different pattern relative to PHV. Both boys and girls show negative velocities (a fat loss) on the arm coincident with PHV, but the loss in boys is greater than the loss in girls. In the calf, on the other hand, girls show no loss of subcutaneous fat; rather, the rate of fat accumulation slows down at PHV. Boys, on the other hand, begin to lose fat on the calf during the year before PHV, and the loss (negative velocities) continues to about 6 months after PHV.

Subcutaneous adipose tissue measured as skinfold thicknesses on the trunk and extremities also changes differentially during the adolescent growth spurt. Changes in trunk and extremity skinfolds of Polish boys and girls from the Wroclaw Growth Study before and after PHV are shown in figures 16.5 and 16.6. In boys (see figure 16.5a), the three skinfolds show small changes before and after PHV. The two trunk skinfolds tend to increase in thickness just before or at PHV, whereas the triceps skinfold tends to decrease

in thickness at this time. The triceps skinfold (extremity) is, on the average, thicker than the two trunk skinfolds before PHV. After PHV, the differences among the three skinfolds are small, but the two trunk skinfolds are slightly thicker than the extremity skinfold. The pattern in girls (see figure 16.5b) is somewhat different. Changes in the three skinfolds are small before PHV, but all three increase in thickness linearly with the time interval after PHV. Girls gain more in the abdominal skinfold than in the triceps and subscapular skinfolds after PHV.

The pattern of change in the three skinfolds relative to PHV is reflected in their estimated velocities (see figure 16.6). The velocities of the three skinfolds in boys (see figure 16.6a) show a tendency to decline before PHV, to reach negative values just before or at PHV, and then to increase after PHV. The two trunk skinfolds have positive velocities (with two exceptions) before, at, and after PHV, whereas the triceps skinfold has a negative velocity from 1.5 years before to 1 year after PHV. Among girls (see figure 16.6b), on the other hand, estimated velocities of the three skinfolds change only slightly before PHV but then increase for about 2 years after PHV. The estimated velocities of the three skinfolds tend to be greater in girls than in boys, which contributes to the sex difference in subcutaneous fatness.

Thus, changes in subcutaneous adipose tissue depots in different areas of the body vary relative to PHV. This variation indicates the significant

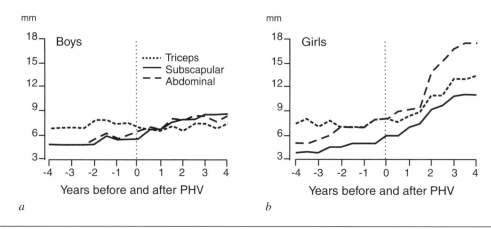

Skinfold Thicknesses Relative to Peak Height Velocity

FIGURE 16.5   Median skinfold thicknesses relative to PHV in boys (*a*) and girls (*b*) from the Wroclaw Growth Study. Drawn after Malina et al. (1999). Scales for skinfold thicknesses are the same for boys and girls to facilitate comparison.

Adapted, by permission, from R.M. Malina, S. Koziel, and T. Bielicki, 1999,"Variation in subcutaneous adipose tissue distribution associated with age, sex, and maturation," *American Journal of Human Biology* 11:189-200.

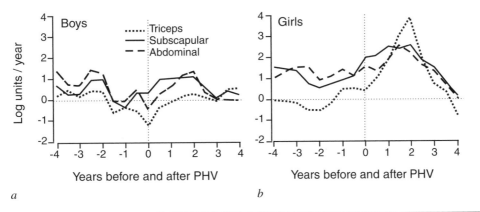

FIGURE 16.6   Median half-yearly velocities for the triceps, subscapular, and abdominal skinfolds relative to PHV in boys (*a*) and girls (*b*) from the Wroclaw Growth Study. Scales for the velocities are the same for boys and girls to facilitate comparison.

Adapted, by permission, from R.M. Malina, S. Koziel, and T. Bielicki, 1999, "Variation in subcutaneous adipose tissue distribution associated with age, sex, and maturation," *American Journal of Human Biology* 11: 189-200.

changes that occur in the relative distribution of subcutaneous fat during adolescence. Males gain proportionally more subcutaneous fat on the trunk compared with the extremities, whereas girls gain proportionally equal amounts of subcutaneous fat on the trunk and on the extremities during the adolescent growth spurt (see chapter 8). The data for subcutaneous adipose tissue should be complemented with longitudinal data for visceral adipose tissue during puberty.

Growth Spurts in Performance

Age-related trends in strength, motor performance, and aerobic power suggest acceleration in growth during adolescence in males but not consistently in females. Most boys show a clear adolescent growth spurt in performance tasks. Corresponding longitudinal data on the performances of girls that span the adolescent years are limited, so establishing the presence or absence of growth spurts is difficult.

Strength

Mean ages at peak velocity for stature, weight, and static strength for children in the Adolescent Growth Study in Oakland, California, are summarized in table 16.18. Muscular strength is a composite score based on the sum of right and left grip strength and pushing and pulling strength of the arms. Boys reach peak gains in strength, on the average, about 1.2 years after PHV and 0.8 years after PWV. When the serial records for individual adolescent boys are examined, peak strength development occurs after PHV in more than 77% of the boys, coincident with PHV in about 11%, and before PHV in about 12% (Stolz and Stolz 1951). In contrast to boys, peak strength development in this longitudinal sample of girls occurs, on the average, near PHV and 0.6 years before PWV. However, considerable variation occurs among individual girls. Peak strength development precedes PHV in about 40% of the girls, coincides with PHV in about 11%, and follows PHV in about 49% (Faust 1977).

Data for Canadian, Belgian, and Dutch boys are reasonably consistent with those for American boys from California in showing a well-defined growth spurt in muscular strength after PHV, but data for Dutch girls differ from American girls. Increments in composite scores for several upper body and several lower body strength tests in Canadian boys are consistent with the data for California boys in showing, on the average, peak gains after PHV (see figure 16.7). Data for Dutch and Belgian adolescents, based on a single test of shoulder strength (the arm pull), show velocities that reach a peak about 0.5 year after PHV in both males and females (see figure 16.8). The timing of the peak in strength development of Dutch girls occurs at about the time as the peak for Dutch and Belgian boys. The

TABLE 16.18	Means and Standard Deviations for Ages (Years) at Peak Velocity of Growth in Stature, Weight, and Muscular Strength in California Adolescents			
	Girls (n = 94)		Boys (n = 64)	
	Mean	SD	Mean	SD
Stature	11.7	1.1	14.1	0.9
Weight	12.2	1.3	14.5	1.3
Strength	11.6	2.0	15.3	1.2

Strength is a composite of right and left grip and pushing and pulling tests.

Data for boys are from Stolz and Stolz (1951) and data for girls are from Faust (1977).

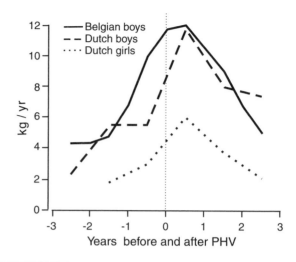

Arm Pull Strength Increments Relative to Age at Peak Height Velocity

FIGURE 16.8 Velocities of arm pull strength aligned on PHV in adolescent Belgian boys (means) and in adolescent Dutch boys and girls (medians).

Data from Kemper and Verschuur, 1985.

difference between Dutch and California adolescent girls may be a function of the use of a composite score of four strength tests in contrast to a single test in the respective analyses. Performance variability among individual tests may influence the composite score. Although the timing of the peak in strength development of Dutch girls occurs at about the same time as that for boys, peak strength gain in boys, about 12 kg/year, is about twice as great as that in girls, about 6 kg/year.

Data applying scaling procedures to changes in muscular strength during adolescence are

limited. A question of interest is the following: At the time of maximum rate of growth in height (PHV), does strength increase at a rate that is proportional to growth in body size or at a rate greater than expected for growth in body size? Quadriceps (thigh) and biceps (arm) strength around the interval of PHV were analyzed with multilevel modeling procedures in a mixed-longitudinal sample of boys and girls 8 to 17 years of age (Nevill et al. 1998). Both sexes tend to gain in strength proportionally to body size, but around the time of PHV, a sex difference appears. Boys tend to gain proportionally more in quadriceps and biceps strength than predicted by growth in body size, whereas girls gain in quadriceps strength proportionally to growth in body size but not in biceps strength. Results of the modeling analysis, which statistically controls for the contribution of body size to muscular strength, suggest a decline in biceps strength around the time of PHV in girls after change in body size is accounted for. Girls do in fact gain in biceps strength during the adolescent growth spurt; however, they gain proportionally more in body size.

The observations based on multilevel modeling analysis and the results obtained in longitudinal studies, which align gains in muscular strength on PHV, highlight the major gains in muscular strength of boys during the adolescent growth spurt. Boys show significant improve-

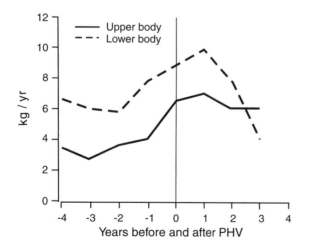

Strength Increments Relative to Age at Peak Height Velocity in Boys

FIGURE 16.7 Mean velocities of upper and lower body strength aligned on PHV in Canadian adolescent boys from the Saskatchewan Growth Study.

Data from Carron and Bailey, 1974.

ment in measurements of upper and lower body strength during the growth spurt. In contrast, the trends for girls appear to vary with the muscle group that is tested.

Motor Performance

Median velocities for six performance tasks in a longitudinal sample of approximately 220 Belgian boys are summarized in figure 16.9. Peak gains in the arm pull (static shoulder strength), vertical jump (explosive strength), and the bent arm hang (muscular endurance) occur, on the average, after PHV. The adolescent spurts in strength and muscular endurance appear to begin about 1.5 years before PHV and reach a peak about 0.5 to 1.0 year after PHV. In contrast, speed tasks (running speed and agility in the shuttle run and speed of upper limb movement in plate tapping) and flexibility of the lower back (sit-and-reach) appear to have their maximum velocities before PHV. However, the lower age limit in the study of Belgian boys, 12 years, may not permit an accurate estimate of the onset of the spurts in speed and flexibility.

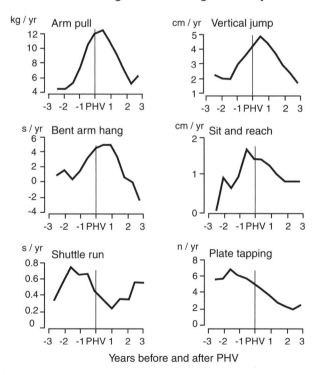

Velocities of Performance
Relative to Age at Peak Height Velocity

FIGURE 16.9 Median velocities of several tests of strength and motor performance aligned on PHV in the Leuven Growth Study of Belgian Boys.

Data from Beunen et al., 1988.

The median velocities for the six motor items in Belgian boys (see figure 16.9) are positive during the adolescent growth spurt in stature, which indicates that performance does not decline during the growth spurt. A temporary slow down in the development of muscular strength or a period of clumsiness in motor coordination of some adolescent boys has often been described in the motor performance (Espenschade 1947; Espenschade et al. 1953; Bates 1977; Newell 1984) and growth literature (Tanner 1978), suggesting a temporary period of "adolescent awkwardness" or a boy "outgrowing his strength." In one of the earliest studies, for example, Dimock (1935, 1937) noted differences in the Brace Test of Motor Ability (a series of 20 stunts requiring balance, coordination, and agility) among cross-sectional samples of adolescent boys of the same chronological age but who differed in pubertal status. Although the differences were not large, Dimock (1937, p. 246) interpreted the data in the context of a popular assumption that ". . . awkwardness in the adolescent boy is primarily the result of his rapid growth." However, he noted that ". . . this period of reduced improvement in motor ability is not the time, but precedes the period, of the most rapid growth in height and weight," that is, not during the interval of peak height velocity but during the transition from the prepubertal into the pubertal state. Dimock used stage of pubic hair as the maturity indicator and did not have an estimate of the age at PHV. Dimock correctly looked at variation in pubertal status within a chronological age group. As noted in the preceding chapter, many reports in the clinical and exercise and sport science literature still group youth by stage of pubertal development without considering the potentially independent effect of chronological age.

Available longitudinal data relating motor performances of boys to the adolescent growth spurt in the context of the concept of adolescent awkwardness or a lag in performance are not extensive. The data shown in figure 16.9 are based on group medians, and individual boys probably show temporary variations in performance during the adolescent growth spurt. In this longitudinal sample of Belgian boys, those who experienced a negative velocity in performance (i.e., their performance declined) during the year of PHV were identified. Although some boys declined in performance during the adolescent growth spurt, the decline did not occur in all tasks for the same individual. Boys who declined in motor performance during the interval of PHV were generally good performers at the beginning of the interval, and boys who declined in performance did not differ from those who improved in performance in the timing and magnitude of the height spurt (Beunen and Malina 1988).

The results suggest that maturity-associated variation in size and strength in adolescent boys, or a temporary disproportion of leg and trunk lengths relative to overall body size, are not significant factors distinguishing boys who decline from those who gain in motor performance at the time of PHV. The tasks used in the study of Belgian boys were largely dependent on strength, power, and speed and are quite different from the stunts required by the Brace Test of Motor Ability. Other performance variables, especially balance and co-ordination tests, must be considered in a similar longitudinal manner to more thoroughly evaluate the concept of adolescent awkwardness.

Mixed-longitudinal data for small samples of Portuguese boys (n = 18 to 27) and girls (n = 25 to 35) permit comparison of estimated changes in performance from about 1.5 years before to 1.0 year after PHV in both sexes (Heras Yague and de la Fuente 1998) (see figure 16.10). Allowing

for different performance tests used, the trends for Portuguese boys are generally consistent with those observed in Belgian boys. The data for girls are consistent for the power and strength tasks, but the flexibility and speed tasks show peak gains after PHV, which contrasts with the trends for Belgian boys.

Aerobic Power

Submaximal power output (W) at a heart rate of 170 beats/min (PWC_{170}) and maximal aerobic power (L/min) show adolescent growth spurts in both sexes (see table 16.19). Peak velocity of submaximal power output appears close in time to PHV in Polish boys but more than a year after PHV in Polish girls. On the other hand, peak velocity of growth in maximal aerobic power occurs close to PHV in Canadian boys and girls. Estimated velocities for PWC_{170} and $\dot{V}O_2$max at PHV are greater in boys (37.7 W/year; 0.412 L/min/year) than in girls (23.3 W/year; 0.284 L/min/year). Corresponding data for Dutch, German, and Norwegian adolescents, although not analyzed in the same manner, suggest a trend similar to that shown in Canadian adolescents. When viewed relative to PHV, absolute $\dot{V}O_2$max begins to increase several years before PHV and continues to increase through the adolescent growth spurt. Relative $\dot{V}O_2$max (ml/kg/min), on the other hand, generally begins to decline a

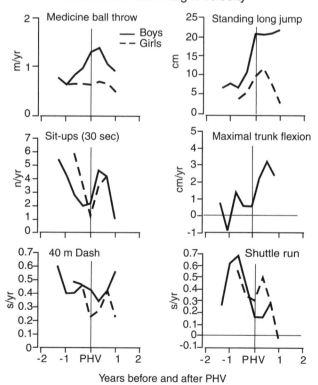

Velocities of Performance Relative to Peak Height Velocity

FIGURE 16.10 Median velocities of several tests of motor performance aligned on PHV in mixed-longitudinal data for Portuguese youth.

Data from Heras Yague and de la Fuente, 1998.

	Girls		Boys	
Sample	**Mean**	**SD**	**Mean**	**SD**
Saskatchewan, Canada[a]	(n = 22)		(n = 75)	
Stature	11.9	0.7	14.3	1.0
Weight	12.1	0.7	14.5	1.1
$\dot{V}O_2$max	12.0	0.8	14.3	1.1
Warsaw, Poland[b]	(n = 26)		(n = 31)	
Stature	11.8	0.7	13.8	1.3
Weight	12.6	1.6	14.2	1.5
PWC_{170}	13.2	0.7	13.4	0.8

TABLE 16.19 Means and Standard Deviations for Ages at Peak Velocity of Stature, Weight, and $\dot{V}O_2$max and PWC_{170} in Two Samples of Adolescents

[a]Adapted from Mirwald and Bailey (1986).
[b]Adapted from Malina et al. (1997).

year or so before PHV and continues to decline for several years after PHV.

The decline in relative maximal aerobic power reflects the rapid growth in body weight during adolescence, so oxygen uptake declines per unit body mass. It not only reflects the differential growth of body mass and $\dot{V}O_2$max at this time but also the limitations of ratio scaling (i.e., expressing $\dot{V}O_2$ per unit body mass). Some data have addressed these issues using intraindividual, or ontogenetic, scaling and multilevel modeling of $\dot{V}O_2$max during the interval of PHV. The mean ontogenetic exponent (see chapter 3) for body weight relative to $\dot{V}O_2$max in 18 active boys who were tested annually from 11 to 15 years of age is 1.19 (Paterson et al. 1987). On the other hand, corresponding exponents for body mass relative to $\dot{V}O_2$max at the time of PHV in four untrained and eight trained boys are lower, 0.78 and 1.01, respectively (Sjödin and Svedenhag 1992).

Multilevel modeling of $\dot{V}O_2$max was used in a mixed-longitudinal sample of boys and girls, 8 to 19 years of age, actively training in several sports. During the estimated interval spanning PHV, exponents for body mass relative to $\dot{V}O_2$max are 0.70 and 0.67 in boys and girls, respectively, which are similar to the theoretically expected values of body mass to the 2/3 power (see chapter 3). The exponents for body mass in these three studies are similar to those reported in cross-sectional analyses of adolescent boys and girls (see chapter 12). Exponents for height relative to $\dot{V}O_2$max during the estimated interval of PHV are also available in the multilevel analysis. The height exponents are 0.73 and 0.48, respectively, in boys and girls (Nevill et al. 1998).

The results of scaling and multilevel analyses indicate that growth of the oxygen delivery system does not proceed in concert with growth in body weight and height during the adolescent growth spurt. This finding may be reflected in differential timing of growth spurts in components of the oxygen delivery system. For example, growth spurts in the transverse diameters of the heart and lungs, as measured on standardized chest radiographs, are generally consistent with PHV, but peak growth in lung length occurs about 6 months later (Simon et al. 1972). Growth spurts in lung functions also occur, on average, after PHV (DeGroodt et al. 1988; Sherrill et al. 1989; Wang et al. 1993; Hibbert et al. 1995). Further longitudinal studies are needed to more specifically elaborate the dynamics of growth of maximal aerobic power and related functions during the adolescent growth spurt.

The development of anaerobic power has been suggested to be related to the timing of the adolescent growth spurt. Because muscle mass experiences its growth spurt after PHV, anaerobic power might be assumed to show a spurt after PHV. Presently available data are not adequate to document this speculation.

Performance Relative to Menarche

Menarche is a late event in the sequence of adolescent changes in growth and maturation. When motor performances of girls are related to the time before or after menarche, they show no tendency for peak performances before, at, or after menarche. This finding is shown in figure 16.11 for girls in the Adolescent Growth Study in Oakland, California. Most girls in the Oakland study were near menarche or beyond it when the

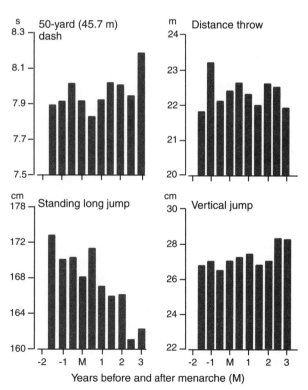

FIGURE 16.11 Mean motor performances relative to menarche in the mixed-longitudinal sample of girls in the Adolescent Growth Study in Oakland, California.

Data from Espenschade, 1940.

study started, so numbers tested 1 year before menarche are small (Espenschade 1940). Nevertheless, the mixed-longitudinal data suggest that changes in motor performance are relatively small over the interval from just before menarche to 3 years after menarche.

Absolute $\dot{V}O_2$max (L/min) increases from 2 years before to 2 years after menarche, whereas relative $\dot{V}O_2$max (ml/kg/min) declines linearly from 2 years before menarche to 2 years after menarche (see figure 16.12, a and b, respectively). To allow for differential growth in body size and maximal oxygen uptake during puberty, allometric exponents were calculated for each period before, at, and after menarche (five menarcheal groups) based on logarithmic transformations of $\dot{V}O_2$max and body weight and $\dot{V}O_2$max and height. The exponents provide an indication of the dimensional relationship between $\dot{V}O_2$max and mass or stature at a given time relative to menarche. The allometric exponents are shown

in figure 16.12, c and d for mass and stature, respectively. The lowest exponents for both mass and height occur for observations made within ± 6 months of menarche. Thus, the relationship between body mass or height and $\dot{V}O_2$max at menarche is lower compared with the relationships before and after menarche. This difference suggests two trends. First, the low exponents at menarche indicate that $\dot{V}O_2$max increases at a lower rate than expected from the increase in body weight or height. Second, the low associations between $\dot{V}O_2$max and weight or height indicate increased variation in $\dot{V}O_2$max at the time of menarche.

The preceding discussion has focused on changes in performance during the adolescent growth spurt and sexual maturation. Associated behavioral changes have not been considered. These changes may have implications for performance during adolescence, especially in girls. Variation in motivation and changing attitudes

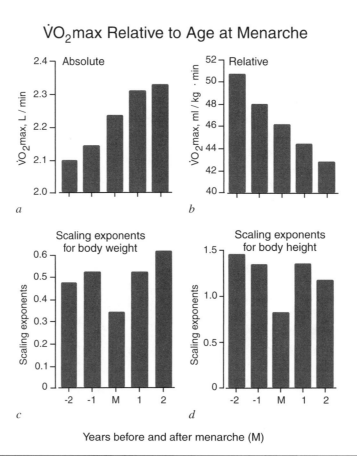

FIGURE 16.12 Mean absolute (L/min) (*a*) and relative (ml/kg/min) (*b*) $\dot{V}O_2$max at menarche in active Polish girls. Allometric exponents for body mass (*c*) and stature (*d*) are also shown for each menarcheal group.

Data from Thomis et al., 2000.

toward performance may be important factors, but they are difficult to specify. Changes in body image during this period of rapid growth and maturation may influence the motivation to perform and the performance per se. Social interests and expectations also change during the adolescent growth spurt and sexual maturation, so the significance of performance in the behavioral demands of adolescence may be altered. Study of the behavioral correlates of performance during adolescence is needed in both sexes.

Summary

From a biological perspective, the period of adolescence includes two major events, the adolescent growth spurt (somatic maturation) and sexual maturation. Youth enter this phase of growth at varying ages (differential timing) and proceed through it at variable rates (differential tempo). Timing and tempo are highly individual characteristics and are unrelated. Girls are, on average, in advance of boys in the timing of maturation, but tempo overlaps considerably. Other body dimensions, muscular strength, motor performance, and aerobic power also show well-defined adolescent spurts, but the time of the respective spurts varies relative to peak height velocity in both sexes and relative to menarche in girls.

Sources and Suggested Readings

Bates BT (1977) Scientific basis of human movement. Journal of Physical Education and Recreation 48:68-74 (Oct).

Bell W (1993) Body size and shape: A longitudinal investigation of active and sedentary boys during adolescence. Journal of Sport Sciences 11:127-138.

Belmaker E (1982) Sexual maturation of Jerusalem school girls and its association with socioeconomic factors and ethnic group. Annals of Human Biology 9:321-328.

Berkey CA, Wang X, Dockery DW, Ferris BG (1994) Adolescent height growth of U.S. children. Annals of Human Biology 21:435-442.

Beunen G (1996) Physical growth, maturation and performance. In R Eston, T Reilly (eds), Kinanthropometry and Exercise Physiology Laboratory Manual. London: E & FN Spon, pp 51-71.

* Beunen G, Malina RM (1988) Growth and physical performance relative to the timing of the adolescent spurt. Exercise and Sports Sciences Reviews 16:503-540.

Beunen G, Malina RM, Van't Hof MA, Simons J, Ostyn M, Renson R, Van Gerven D (1988) Adolescent Growth and Motor Performance: A Longitudinal Study of Belgian Boys. Champaign, IL: Human Kinetics.

Bielicki T, Koniarek J, Malina RM (1984) Interrelationships among certain measures of growth and maturation rate in boys during adolescence. Annals of Human Biology 11:201-210.

Bielicki T, Welon Z (1973) The sequence of growth velocity peaks of principal body dimensions in girls. Materialy i Prace Antropologiczne 86:3-10.

Billewicz WZ, Fellowes HM, Thomson AM (1981) Pubertal changes in boys and girls in Newcastle upon Tyne. Annals of Human Biology 8:211-219.

Boas F (1892) The growth of children. Science 19:256-257, 281-282, 20:351-352.

* Bodzsar EB, Susanne C, editors (1998) Secular Growth Changes in Europe. Budapest: Eotvos Lorand University Press.

Buckler JMH, Greene M (1999) Growth variability in normal adolescence. Acta Medica Auxologica 31:109-123.

Cameron N, Tanner JM, Whitehouse RH (1982) A longitudinal analysis of the growth of limb segments in adolescence. Annals of Human Biology 9:211-220.

Carron AV, Bailey DA (1974) Strength development in boys from 10 through 16 years. Monographs of the Society for Research in Child Development 39, serial no. 157.

* Chumlea WC, Schubert CM, Roche AF, Kulin H, Lee PA, Himes JH, Sun SS (2003) Age at menarche and racial comparisons in U.S. girls. Pediatrics 111:110-113.

Cunningham DA, Paterson DH, Blimkie CJR, Donner P (1984) Development of cardiorespiratory function in circumpubertal boys: A longitudinal study. Journal of Applied Physiology 56:302-307.

Danker-Hopfe H (1986) Menarcheal age in Europe. Yearbook of Physical Anthropology 29:81-112.

DeGroodt EG, van Pelt W, Borsboom GJ, Quanjer PH, van Zomeren BC (1988) Growth of lung and thorax dimensions during the pubertal growth spurt. European Respiratory Journal 1:102-108.

Dimock HS (1935) A research in adolescence. I. Pubescence and physical growth. Child Development 6:177-195.

Dimock HS (1937) Rediscovering the Adolescent. New York: Association Press.

Ellis JD, Carron AV, Bailey DA (1975) Physical performance in boys from 10 through 16 years. Human Biology 47:263-281.

Engelhardt L, Willers B, Pelz L (1995) Sexual maturation in East German girls. Acta Paediatrica 84:1362-1365.

Espenschade A (1940) Motor performance in adolescence, including the study of relationships with measures of physical growth and maturity. Monographs of the Society for Research in Child Development 5, serial no. 24.

Espenschade A (1947) Development of motor coordination in boys and girls. Research Quarterly 18:30-44.

Espenschade A, Dable RR, Schoendube R (1953) Dynamic balance in adolescent boys. Research Quarterly 24:270-275.

* Eveleth PB, Tanner JM (1990) Worldwide Variation in Human Growth, 2nd edition. Cambridge: Cambridge University Press.

Faust MS (1977) Somatic development of adolescent girls. Monographs of the Society for Research in Child Development 42, serial no.169.

Geithner CA, Satake T, Woynarowska B, Malina RM (1999) Adolescent spurts in body dimensions: Average and modal sequences. American Journal of Human Biology 11:287-295.

Grünberg H, Thetloff M (1997) Pubertal stages of Estonia children. Papers on Anthropology VII. Tartu, Estonia: University of Tartu, Centre of Physical Anthropology, pp 84-89.

Guizar-Vazques JJ, Rosales-Lopez A, Ortiz-Jalomo R, Nava-Delgado SE, Salamanca-Gomez F (1985) Caracteres sexuales secundarios en niños Mexicanos de 9 a 16 años. Estudio transversal. Boletin Medico del Hospital Infantil de Mexico 42:409-414.

Guo SS, Siervogel RM, Roche AF, Chumlea WC (1992) Mathematical modelling of human growth: A comparative study. American Journal of Human Biology 4:93-104.

* Guo SS, Chumlea WC, Roche AF, Siervogel RM (1997) Age- and maturity-related changes in body composition during adolescence into adulthood: The Fels Longitudinal Study. International Journal of Obesity 21:1167-1175.

Hagg U, Taranger J (1980) Menarche and voice change as indicators of the pubertal growth spurt. Acta Odontologica Scandinavica 38:179-186.

Harries MLL, Walker JM, Williams DM, Hawkins S, Hughes IA (1997) Changes in the male voice at puberty. Archives of Disease in Childhood 77:445-447.

Heras Yague P, de la Fuente JM (1998) Changes in height and motor performance relative to peak height velocity: A mixed-longitudinal study of Spanish boys and girls. American Journal of Human Biology 10:647-660.

Herman-Giddens ME, Slora EJ, Wasserman RC, Bourdony CJ, Bhapkar MV, Koch GG, Hasemeier CM (1997) Secondary sexual characteristics and menses in young girls seen in office practice: A study from the pediatric research in office settings network. Pediatrics 99:505-512.

Herman-Giddens ME, Wang L, Koch G (2001) Secondary sexual characteristics in boys: Estimates from the National Health and Nutrition Examination Survey III, 1988–1994. Archives of Pediatrics and Adolescent Medicine 155: 1022-1028.

Hibbert M, Lannigan A, Raven J, Landau L, Phelan P (1995) Gender differences in lung growth. Pediatric Pulmonology 19:129-134.

Iuliano-Burns S, Mirwald RL, Bailey DA (2001) The timing and magnitude of peak height velocity and peak tissue velocities for early, average and late maturing boys and girls. American Journal of Human Biology 13:1-8.

* Jones HE (1949) Motor Performance and Growth. Berkeley: University of California Press.

Kemper HCG, editor (1985) Growth, Health and Fitness of Teenagers. Basel: Karger.

Kemper HCG, Verschuur R (1985) Motor performance fitness tests. In HCG Kemper (ed), Growth, Health and Fitness of Teenagers. Basel: Karger, pp 96-106.

Largo RH, Gasser T, Prader A, Stuetzle W, Huber PJ (1978) Analysis of the adolescent growth spurt using smoothing spline functions. Annals of Human Biology 5:421-434.

Largo RH, Prader A (1983a) Pubertal development in Swiss boys. Helvetica Paediatrica Acta 38:211-228.

Largo RH, Prader A (1983b) Pubertal development in Swiss girls. Helvetica Paediatrica Acta 38:229-243.

Ledford AW, Cole TJ (1998) Mathematical models of growth in stature throughout childhood. Annals of Human Biology 25:101-115.

Lee PA, Guo SS, Kulin HE (2001) Age of puberty: Data from the United States of America. Acta Pathologica, Microbiologica et Immunologica Scandinavica 109:S156-S163.

Malina RM (1978) Adolescent growth and maturation: Selected aspects of current research. Yearbook of Physical Anthropology 21:63-94.

Malina RM (1989) Growth and maturation: Normal variation and the effects of training. In CV Gisolfi, DR Lamb (eds), Perspectives in Exercise Science and Sports Medicine, Volume 2. Youth, Exercise, and Sport. Indianapolis, IN: Benchmark, pp 223-265.

Malina RM (1996) Regional variation in body composition: Age, sex, and ethnic variation. In AF Roche, SB Heymsfield, TG Lohman (eds), Human Body Composition. Champaign, IL: Human Kinetics, pp 217-255.

* Malina RM, Beunen G (1996) Monitoring growth and maturation. In O Bar-Or (ed), The Child and Adolescent Athlete. Oxford: Blackwell Science, pp 647-672.

Malina RM, Bouchard C, Beunen G (1988) Human growth: Selected aspects of current research on well-nourished children. Annual Review of Anthropology 17:187-219.

Malina RM, Koziel S, Bielicki T (1999) Variation in subcutaneous adipose tissue distribution associated with age, sex, and maturation. American Journal of Human Biology 11: 189-200.

Malina RM, Woynarowska B, Bielicki T, Beunen G, Eweld D, Geithner CA, Huang YC, Rogers DM (1997) Prospective and retrospective longitudinal studies of the growth, maturation, and fitness of Polish youth active in sport. International Journal of Sports Medicine 18 (suppl 3): S179-S185.

Marshall WA, Tanner JM (1969) Variations in pattern of pubertal changes in girls. Archives of Disease in Childhood 44:291-303.

Marshall WA, Tanner JM (1970) Variations in the pattern of pubertal changes in boys. Archives of Disease in Childhood 45:13-23.

* Marshall WA, Tanner JM (1986) Puberty. In F Falkner, JM Tanner (eds), Human Growth. Volume 2. Postnatal Growth, Neurobiology. New York: Plenum, pp 171-209.

Matsudo SMM, Matsudo VKR (1994) Self-assessment and physician assessment of sexual maturation in Brazilian boys and girls: Concordance and reproducibility. American Journal of Human Biology 6:451-455.

McKay HA, Bailey DA, Mirwald DL, Davison S, Faulkner RA (1998) Peak bone mineral accrual and age at menarche in adolescent girls: A 6 year longitudinal study. Journal of Pediatrics 133:682-687.

* Mirwald RL, Bailey DA (1986) Maximal Aerobic Power. London, Ontario: Sports Dynamics.

Nevill AM, Holder RL, Baxter-Jones A, Round JM, Jones DA (1998) Modeling developmental changes in strength and aerobic power in children. Journal of Applied Physiology 84:963-970.

Newell KM (1984) Physical constraints to development of movement skills. In JR Thomas (ed), Motor Development during Childhood and Adolescence. Minneapolis, MN: Burgess, pp 105-120.

Pan H, Ratcliffe SG (1992) A new method of deriving velocity and acceleration curves for height from kernel estimation of distance. Annals of Human Biology 19:303-316.

Parizkova J (1976) Growth and growth velocity of lean body mass and fat in adolescent boys. Pediatric Research 10: 647-650.

Parizkova J (1977) Body Fat and Physical Fitness. The Hague: Martinus Nijhoff.

Paterson DH, McLellan TM, Stella RS, Cunningham DA (1987) Longitudinal study of ventilation threshold and maximal O_2 uptake in athletic boys. Journal of Applied Physiology 62:2051-2057.

Preece MA, Baines MJ (1978) A new family of mathematical models describing the human growth curve. Annals of Human Biology 5:1-24.

Prokopec M, Lhotska L (1994) Voice breaking as indicator of adolescence in Czech boys. In K Hajnis (ed), Growth and Ontogenetic Development in Man, IV. Prague: Charles University, Department of Anthropology, pp 217-220.

Ramos Rodriguez RM (1986) Crecimiento y Proporcionalidad Corporal en Adolescentes Mexicanas. Mexico, DF: Universidad Nacional Autonoma de Mexico.

Reynolds EL, Wines JV (1948) Individual differences in physical changes associated with adolescence in girls. American Journal of Diseases of Children 75:329-350.

Reynolds EL, Wines JV (1951) Physical changes associated with adolescence in boys. American Journal of Diseases of Children 82:529-547.

Roche AF (1974) Differential timing of maximum length increments among bones within individuals. Human Biology 46:145-157.

* Roche AF (1986) Progress in the analysis of serial data during the century since Bowditch and future expectations. Human Biology 58:831-850.

Roche AF (1989) The final phase of growth in stature. Growth, Genetics and Hormones 5:4-6 (Dec).

Roche AF, Wellens R, Attie KM, Siervogel RM (1995) The timing of sexual maturation in a group of US white youths. Journal of Pediatric Endocrinology and Metabolism 8:11-18.

Roede MJ, van Wieringen JC (1985) Growth diagrams 1980: Netherlands third nation-wide survey. Tijdschrift voor Sociale Gezondheidszorg 63 (suppl): 1-34.

Rosales Lopez A (1984) Masa critica y aparicion de la espermaturia en una muestra de niños de la poblacion Mexicana. Thesis, Escuela Nacional de Antropologia e Historia, Mexico, DF.

Rutenfranz J, Lange Andersen K, Seliger V, Ilmarinen J, Klimmer F, Kylian H, Rutenfranz M, Ruppel M (1982) Maximal aerobic power affected by maturation and body growth during childhood and adolescence. European Journal of Pediatrics 139:106-112.

Satake T, Kukuta F, Ozaki T (1993) Ages at peak velocity and peak velocities for seven body dimensions in Japanese children. Annals of Human Biology 20:67-70.

Satake T, Malina RM, Tanaka S, Kukuta F (1994) Individual variation in the sequence of ages at peak velocity in seven body dimensions. American Journal of Human Biology 6:359-367.

Sherrill DL, Morgan WJ, Taussig LM, Landau LI, Burrows B (1989) A mathematical procedure for estimating the spatial relationships between lung function, somatic growth, and maturation. Pediatric Research 25:316-321.

Shuttleworth FK (1937) Sexual maturation and the physical growth of girls aged six to nineteen. Monographs of the Society for Research in Child Development 2, serial no. 12.

Shuttleworth FK (1939) The physical and mental growth of girls and boys age six to nineteen in relation to age at maximum growth. Monographs of the Society for Research in Child Development 4, serial no. 22.

Siegel SR (1999) Patterns of sport participation and physical activity in urban Mexican youth. East Lansing, MI: Michigan State University, Doctoral Dissertation.

Simon G, Reid L, Tanner JM, Goldstein H, Benjamin B (1972) Growth of radiologically determined heart diameter, lung width, and lung length from 5–19 years, with standards for clinical use. Archives of Disease in Childhood 47: 373-381.

Sjödin B, Svedenhag J (1992) Oxygen uptake during running as related to body mass in circumpubertal boys: A longitudinal study. European Journal of Applied Physiology 65:150-157.

Stolz HR, Stolz LM (1951) Somatic Development of Adolescent Boys. New York: Macmillan.

* Sun SS, Schubert CM, Chumlea WC, Roche AF, Kulin HE, Lee PA, Himes JH, Ryan AS (2002) National estimates of the timing of sexual maturation and racial differences among U.S. children. Pediatrics 110: 911-919.

* Tanner JM (1962) Growth at Adolescence, 2nd edition. Oxford: Blackwell Scientific Publications.

Tanner JM (1978) Foetus into Man: Physical Growth from Conception to Maturity. London: Open Books.

Tanner JM, Hughes PCR, Whitehouse RH (1981) Radiographically determined widths of bone, muscle and fat in the upper arm and calf from 3–18 years. Annals of Human Biology 8:495-517.

Tanner JM, Whitehouse RH, Marubini E, Resele LF (1976) The adolescent growth spurt of boys and girls of the Harpenden Growth Study. Annals of Human Biology 3:109-126.

Taranger J, Engstrom I, Lichenstein H, Svennberg-Redegen I (1976) Somatic pubertal development. Acta Paediatrica Scandinavica 258 (suppl):121-135.

Thomis M, Rogers DM, Beunen GP, Woynarowska B, Malina RM (2000) Allometric relationship between body size and peak $\dot{V}O_2$ relative to age at menarche. Annals of Human Biology 27:623-633.

Villarreal SF, Martorell R, Mendoza F (1989) Sexual maturation of Mexican American adolescents. American Journal of Human Biology 1:87-95.

Wang X, Dockery DW, Wypij D, Fay ME, Ferris BG (1993) Pulmonary function between 6 and 18 years of age. Pediatric Pulmonology 15:75-88.

Wellens R, Malina RM, Beunen G, Lefevre J (1990) Age at menarche in Flemish girls: Current status and secular change in the 20th century. Annals of Human Biology 17:145-152.

Welon Z, Bielicki T (1979) The timing of the adolescent growth spurts in eight body dimensions in boys and girls of the Wroclaw Growth Study. Studies in Physical Anthropology (Wroclaw) 5:75-79.

Wember T, Goddemeier R, Manz F (1992) Height growth of German boys and girls. Annals of Human Biology 19: 361-369.

Willers B, Englehardt L, Pelz L (1996) Sexual maturation in East German boys. Acta Paediatrica 85:785-788.

Zachman M, Prader A, Kind HP, Hafliger H, Budliger H (1974) Testicular volume during adolescence: Cross-sectional and longitudinal studies. Helvetica Paediatrica Acta 29: 61-72.

MATURITY-ASSOCIATED VARIATION IN GROWTH AND PERFORMANCE

Chapter Outline

Children of the same chronological age can vary considerably in biological maturity status. Calendar time and biological time do not necessarily proceed in concert. More specifically, a child's biological age does not necessarily proceed in concert with the child's chronological age.

Variation among individuals in maturity status at a given point in time and in progress over time influences measures of growth and performance. Variation in growth and performance associated with differences in maturity status is often centered on adolescence, when individual differences in the timing and tempo of the adolescent growth spurt and sexual maturation are especially obvious. Maturity-associated variation in growth and performance is also apparent during childhood.

This chapter focuses on maturity-associated variation in growth and performance during childhood and adolescence. The approach is based largely on comparisons of children of the same chronological age but who differ in maturity status. For example, in a group of 8-year-old children, how do those late or delayed in biological maturity compare with those who are early or advanced in biological maturity?

In a related matter, children live in a society that groups them by chronological age, most notably for school and youth sports. Specific cutoff dates determine whether or not a child can enter school and determine age classifications for many organized youth sports. In other words, the calendar determines a child's age classification. Within a single-year age group (e.g., 8 years of age), the child who is 8.9 years of age is more likely taller, heavier, and stronger than the child who is 8.0 years of age, even though both are classified as 8 years of age. Thus, when children are grouped by age, variation is associated with chronological age per se and also with individual differences in biological maturity.

The impact of variation in maturity status on measures of growth and performance is usually approached in two ways. First, children of the same chronological age but who differ in maturity status are compared. Second, the statistical relationship between a maturity indicator and a growth or performance variable is estimated. This approach has traditionally been used to find the correlation between corresponding measures of maturity and performance. Multivariate statistical procedures are being increasingly used to examine the complex relationships among growth, maturity, and performance.

Classifying Children by Maturity Status

Children are commonly grouped into categories of early (advanced), average ("on time"), and late (delayed) on the basis of a maturity indicator. Methods of classification vary with the maturity indicator used.

Skeletal Age

If skeletal age (SA) is the criterion, a child whose SA is within ± 1 year of chronological age (CA) is generally classified as average or "on time." If a child's SA is in advance of CA by more than 1 year, the child is classified as early maturing. If a child's SA lags behind CA by more than 1 year, the child is classified late maturing. The important point is how the child's SA compares with CA. For example, four children may have an identical CA,

10.5 years, but each has a different SA, 12.3 years, 11.0 years, 9.8 years, and 9.0 years. In the first child, SA = 12.3 and CA = 10.5 years, giving a difference of +1.8 years. SA is in advance of CA by 1.8 years, and the child is classified as early maturing. In the second child, SA = 11.0 and CA = 10.5, giving a difference of +0.5 years. In the third child, SA = 9.8 years and CA = 10.5 years, giving a difference of –0.7 years. Because the second and third children have an SA within ± 1 year of CA, they are classified as average maturing. In the fourth child, SA = 9.0 and CA = 10.5 years, giving a difference of –1.5 years. SA lags behind CA by 1.5 years, and the child is classified as late maturing.

A reasonably broad range of variation (i.e., within ± 1 year of CA) is used to define average or "on time" maturity status. This range of variation is used because methods of assessing skeletal maturity are not perfect, and each has some associated error. The Greulich-Pyle and Tanner-Whitehouse methods do not provide an estimate of error associated with the assessments, whereas the Fels method provides a standard error (see chapter 15). Standard errors associated with the Fels method usually range between 0.25 and 0.30 years (about 3 to 4 months). Some studies of growth and performance have used a band of 3 months to define early and late maturity (Kemper et al. 1986). If SA was in advance of CA by more than 3 months, the child was classified as early maturing, and if SA was behind CA by more than 3 months, the child was classified as late maturing. This narrow band is within the error range of the methods of assessment and may mask some of the differences associated with variation in maturity status.

Secondary Sex Characteristics

During puberty, youth of the same CA can be grouped by stage of sexual maturity—stages of breast, genital, or pubic hair development or, in the case of girls, as premenarcheal and postmenarcheal. Among a sample of 12-year-old children, for example, girls can be classified by breast stage and boys can be classified by genital stage. However, such comparisons are valid only among youth of the same CA, and even within a CA group variation in age occurs. CA groups are usually defined in terms of a single year (e.g., 12.0 to 12.99 defines 12 years of age). Older children within a single age group likely differ in body size and performance from younger children within the same age group. This variation is often overlooked.

Grouping youth by stage of a secondary sex characteristic or as premenarcheal and postmenarcheal to the exclusion of CA is of limited utility. This procedure may reduce the variation within the sample to some extent, but variation independently associated with CA is overlooked. Another way to emphasize this point is that a 14-year-old girl in B2 is very different from an 11-year-old girl in B2, or an 11-year-old postmenarcheal girl is very different from a 14-year-old postmenarcheal girl. The same applies to boys. Variation in CA within a sample of boys 10.0 to 14.9 years of age classified by genital stages is shown in table 17.1. Variation in CA within each stage is minimally 2 years and is greatest in G3 where CA varies from 11.7 to 14.6 years. Nevertheless, many studies, especially of body composition and physiological function, group children and adolescents by stage of puberty without considering age variation in the analysis. In some studies, a range of up to 6 or more years may occur within a stage of puberty (Juul et al. 1994).

TABLE 17.1	Range of Chronological Ages Within Each Stage of Genital Maturation in a Sample of Boys
Genital stage	**Chronological age (years)**
G1	10.00–12.08
G2	10.75–13.17
G3	11.75–14.58
G4	12.83–14.83
G5	13.75–14.92

Adapted from Haschke (1983).

Studies of performance and training often emphasize that a sample is prepubertal. Some studies, however, assume prepubertal status on the basis of CA (usually among children under 9 or 10 years of age) and do not directly assess it. Prepubertal simply means that the children show no overt manifestations of secondary sex characteristics (i.e., they are in G1, B1, or PH1). However, prepubertal children do in fact vary in biological maturity, and the only indicator that is applicable is skeletal maturity. Table 17.2 shows the distributions of CA and SA in small samples of boys and girls 6 to 8 years of age. Within each CA group, the range of SA is seven to nine times as great as the range of CA. Although the children are reasonably homogeneous in CA, they vary considerably in biological maturity.

In longitudinal studies, growth and performance of girls who attained menarche at different ages can be compared. Girls are divided into

TABLE 17.2	Variation in Chronological Age (CA) and Skeletal Age (SA) in a Sample of Children Observed Annually From 6 to 8 Years of Age		
	Chronological and skeletal ages (years)		
	Mean	**SD**	**Range**
Girls (n = 22)			
CA (years)	6.2	0.2	6.00–6.62
SA (years)	6.6	1.1	4.22–9.24
CA	7.2	0.2	7.01–7.63
SA	7.5	1.1	4.93–10.08
CA	8.2	0.2	8.00–8.59
SA	8.6	1.1	5.71–10.61
Boys (n = 18)			
CA (years)	6.2	0.1	6.00–6.41
SA (years)	6.0	0.8	4.03–7.76
CA	7.2	0.1	7.02–7.45
SA	7.1	0.9	5.09–8.94
CA	8.2	0.1	8.01–8.46
SA	8.1	0.8	6.35–9.28

SA was assessed with the Fels method (see chapter 15). The radiographs were provided by Dr. Don Morgan.

contrasting maturity categories on the basis of age at menarche. The median age at menarche for many samples of North American and European girls approximates 13.0 years, with a standard deviation of about 1.0 year (see table 16.6 page 314). Girls with ages at menarche within ± 1 year of 13.0 years (i.e., between 12.0 and 14.0 years) are classified as average maturing or "on time." "On time" implies that menarche occurs within the expected CA range for the sample. Girls whose ages at menarche are less than 12.0 years are classified as early maturing, whereas girls whose ages at menarche are greater than 14.0 years are classified as late maturing. Similar procedures can be used for other secondary sex characteristics.

Age at Peak Height Velocity

Age at peak height velocity (PHV) can be used in a similar manner as age at menarche. Longitudinal data are required to estimate age at PHV, and boys and girls can be classified as early, average, or late based on when PHV occurred. PHV occurs, on the average, close to 12.0 years of age in girls and 14.0 years of age in boys (see table 16.1 page 308), with a standard deviation of about 1.0 year. Thus, girls and boys who attain PHV before 11.0 and 13.0 years of age, respectively, would be classified as early maturing, whereas girls and boys who attain PHV after 13.0 and 15.0 years of age, respectively, would be classified as late maturing.

Overview

The procedures for classifying children and adolescents into contrasting maturity categories have limitations. The age cutoff for determining groups is arbitrary, and some degree of error is associated with each method for assessing maturity status. Nevertheless, they are useful for illustrating maturity-associated variation in growth and performance during childhood and adolescence.

Maturity-Associated Variation in Body Size

Heights and weights of children grouped into categories of early, average, and late maturity are shown in figure 17.1. The data are from an early longitudinal study in which the children were grouped by age at PHV. Early-maturing children of both sexes are taller and heavier than average-maturing and late-maturing age and sex peers from 6 years of age and onward. If statures at each age are expressed as percentages of adult stature, early-maturing children attain a greater percentage of adult height at each age than the average-maturing and late-maturing children (see figure 15.10 page 298). Thus, they are closer to adult stature at all ages. Early-maturing children also have more weight-for-height at each age. If these values are converted to the BMI, early-maturing children have, on the average, a higher BMI than average-maturing and late-maturing children at each age during childhood and adolescence.

The size differences among children of contrasting maturity status are most apparent during adolescence, reflecting additional variation among individuals in the timing and magnitude of the adolescent growth spurt. The timing of the adolescent growth spurt (age at PHV), however, is only moderately and negatively correlated with the magnitude (PHV). Correlations range from –0.3 to –0.5 in several longitudinal studies (Beunen et al. 1988; Beunen and Malina 1988). This lack of positive correlation suggests that children who experience their growth spurts earlier tend to have a somewhat greater PHV, and children who experience their growth spurts on time or late tend to have a PHV of somewhat lesser magnitude (see table 17.3). The data shown

Body Size of Early, Average, and Late Maturing Boys

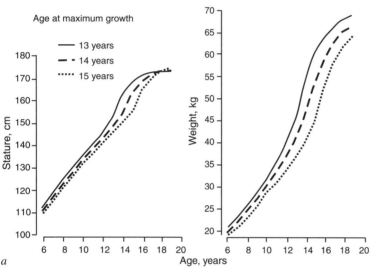

Age at maximum growth
— 13 years
- - 14 years
⋯⋯ 15 years

a

Body Size of Early, Average, and Late Maturing Girls

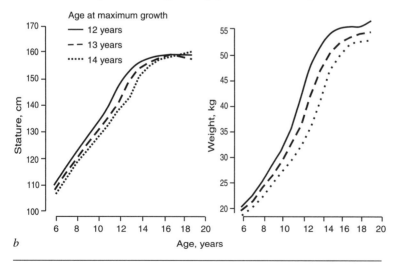

Age at maximum growth
— 12 years
- - 13 years
⋯⋯ 14 years

b

FIGURE 17.1 Mean statures and weights of early-maturing, average-maturing, and late-maturing boys (*a*) and girls (*b*). The children are grouped according to their age at maximum growth or PHV.

Data from Shuttleworth, 1939.

in table 17.3 for Swedish adolescents also indicate that children of contrasting maturity status attain, on average, similar young adult heights, although children in the respective groups differ in size at each age, in age at PHV, and in PHV. There is no apparent relationship between age at PHV and adult stature. Early-maturing children stop growing in stature first, and children in the other two maturity categories continue to grow for a longer period of time. Among Swedish adolescents, for example, late-maturing boys gain, on average, almost eight times more in stature than earlymaturing boys between 17.0 and 18.0 years of age (3.1 cm/year compared with 0.4 cm/year, table 17.3). Thus, late-maturing boys and girls, on average, eventually reach or often surpass the stature of their earlier maturing peers.

On the other hand, children in the three contrasting maturity groups in figure 17.1 do not reach similar body weights in young adulthood. Early-maturing children have, on the average, greater body weights as young adults and have greater weight-for-height (and in turn a higher BMI) than average-maturing and late-maturing children. The differences in body weight and the BMI persist into adulthood. The trends suggest physique and body composition differences among children who vary in maturity status.

Early-maturing and late-maturing children also differ in relative body proportions during growth. Early-maturing boys and girls tend to have relatively broad hips (wide hips relative to their shoulders) and, conversely, relatively narrow shoulders (relative to their hips). In contrast, late-maturing children have relatively narrow hips and relatively broad shoulders. Early and late maturers also differ in relative leg length. Leg length accounts for a greater percentage of stature in late maturers. Late-maturing youngsters tend to have relatively longer legs (lower sitting height/standing height ratio) for their stature than the early-maturing youngsters (higher sitting height/standing height ratio).

Maturity-Associated Variation in Physique

Comparisons of body size and proportions suggest that linearity of physique is associated with late maturation (i.e., less weight-for-height and relatively long legs). This association is true of both sexes and in a variety of studies looking at the relationship between somatotype components and biological maturity. Ectomorphy is related to late maturation in males and females, but associations between endomorphy and mesomorphy and maturity status are not as clear and are not consistent across studies. In part, this inconsistency reflects difficulties with the somatotype concept, that is, it is a composite of the three components. When components are treated independently, they lose some of their significance because individuals show varying combinations of the three somatotype components. In addition, most of the available data are

TABLE 17.3 Timing and Magnitude of PHV and Late Adolescent Growth in Stature in Early-Maturing, Average-Maturing (On Time), and Late-Maturing Swedish Girls and Boys

	Maturity status					
	Early		Average		Late	
	Mean	SD	Mean	SD	Mean	SD
Girls						
Age at PHV (yr)	10.7	0.4	12.0	0.4	13.5	0.6
PHV (cm/yr)	8.7	1.2	8.2	1.1	7.9	1.4
Stature gain 16 to 17 yr (cm/yr)	0.8	0.8	1.1	0.8	1.9	1.3
Boys						
Age at PHV (yr)	12.5	0.5	14.2	0.5	15.7	0.3
PHV (cm/yr)	10.7	1.5	9.7	1.1	9.2	1.8
Stature gain 17 to 18 yr (cm/yr)	0.4	0.4	1.4	1.2	3.1	1.6

The criterion of maturity status is age at PHV.

Adapted from Lindgren (1978).

based on preadolescent or early-adolescent and late-adolescent somatotypes and do not include somatotype information for the intervening years.

Correlations

Limited correlation data indicate positive relationships between skeletal maturity and endomorphy and mesomorphy and a negative relationship between skeletal maturity and ectomorphy. Among boys 9 to 17 years of age, those advanced in skeletal maturity tend to have higher ratings for endomorphy and mesomorphy, whereas those delayed in skeletal maturity have higher ratings on ectomorphy (Clarke 1971). The data further suggest that a mixture of endomorphy and mesomorphy might be predictive of early maturation, whereas mesomorphy or endomorphy by itself is not highly predictive. Extreme ectomorphy with little development of endomorphy and mesomorphy is apparently more related to late maturation than ectomorphy in varying combinations with the other two somatotype components (Barton and Hunt 1962; Hunt et al. 1958).

Early and Late Maturers

Mean somatotypes of early-maturing and late-maturing males and females seen at ages 12 and 17 years are given in table 17.4. Among boys, no clear difference is apparent in mean somatotypes of early and late maturers at 12 years, although early maturers are a bit more mesomorphic. At 17 years of age, however, early maturers are more mesomorphic and late maturers are more ectomorphic, but the two groups do not differ in endomorphy. Among girls, on the other hand, mean endomorphy and mesomorphy are higher in early maturers, and mean ectomorphy is higher in late maturers at both 12 and 17 years of age. The mean somatotypes of early-maturing and late-maturing males and females are consistent with correlational data suggesting that endomorphy and mesomorphy are associated with early maturation, and ectomorphy is associated with late maturation.

Although the data suggest a relationship between physique and maturity status, they do not provide information on the relationship between physique and the timing and tempo of the adolescent growth spurt and sexual maturation. Do individuals with different physiques go through the adolescent growth spurt and sexual maturity

TABLE 17.4	Mean Somatotypes of Early-Maturing, Average-Maturing, and Late-Maturing Boys and Girls in Early and Late Adolescence			
Age	Maturity status	Endomorphy	Mesomorphy	Ectomorphy
Boys				
12	Early	3.3	3.3	3.9
	Late	3.2	3.1	3.9
17	Early	2.8	4.3	4.0
	Late	2.9	3.9	4.4
Girls				
12	Early	4.5	3.6	2.7
	Late	3.8	3.3	3.6
17	Early	4.7	3.7	2.4
	Late	4.3	3.4	3.6

The same children are represented at 12 and 17 years of age. The criterion for maturity is skeletal age.

Adapted from Zuk (1958).

at different times and rates? Such information is available only for small samples of boys (Hunt et al. 1958). The trends suggest two reasonably consistent observations: an association between extreme ectomorphy and a later adolescent growth spurt and sexual maturity and an association between mesomorphy and earlier sexual maturity in males. Corresponding data for girls are not available. Specific details of the association between physique and maturation, which are probably reflected in body composition, need to be elaborated.

Maturity-Associated Variation in Body Composition

The discussion of the relationship between physique and maturation can be extended to body composition. The three tissues—skeletal muscle, bone, and adipose—which help define the components of somatotype, are also major components of body composition.

Correlations

Correlations between SA and tissue components of the arm and calf during childhood and adolescence are summarized in table 17.5. Bone, muscle, and fat refer to measurements of the respective tissue widths made on standardized radiographs. All correlations are positive but low to moderate. They suggest that the more mature child in a given age group has larger measurements of bone, muscle, and fat on the extremities than the less mature child. Correlations between SA and muscle widths in the arm and calf increase from childhood to adolescence in boys but change to a lesser extent in girls. Correlations between fat thickness in the calf and SA increase with age from early childhood into adolescence in both sexes, whereas corresponding correlations for fat thickness in the arm decline slightly in adolescence. The correlations between SA and bone widths are highest among the three tissues during childhood in both sexes. In adolescence, correlations between SA and muscle widths are higher than corresponding values for SA and bone widths in boys, whereas those between SA and bone and muscle widths are generally similar in girls.

The changes in correlations between tissue widths and SA across CA groups suggest that differences between children of contrasting skeletal maturity status become more pronounced with age. This finding is especially apparent for muscle

tissue during male adolescence, which reflects the male adolescent growth spurt in muscle mass and FFM and the overall larger body size of early-maturing boys compared with late-maturing boys. The same is generally true during female adolescence, but correlations between SA and bone and muscle widths are reasonably similar. Girls have a smaller adolescent growth spurt in muscle mass and FFM, and the moderate correlations for bone and muscle reflect, as in boys, the overall larger size of early-maturing girls compared with late-maturing girls.

Children of Contrasting Maturity Status

Comparisons of the tissue composition of the arm in early-maturing boys and late-maturing boys and of the calf in early-maturing girls and late-maturing girls are shown in figure 17.2. The boys are classified on the basis of the difference between

TABLE 17.5	Correlations Between Skeletal Age and Widths of Bone, Muscle, and Fat Tissue in the Arm and Calf			
Region	Age (yr)	Bone	Muscle	Fat
Boys				
Calf	0.5–5	0.27	0.19	0.05
	7–10	0.54	0.16	0.13
	11–16	0.40	0.51	0.30
Arm	7–10	0.45	0.18	0.30
	11–16	0.38	0.61	0.25
Girls				
Calf	0.5–5	0.28	0.07	0.04
	7–8	0.51	0.41	0.12
	9–14	0.38	0.39	0.28
Arm	7–8	0.29	0.27	0.33
	9–14	0.36	0.45	0.24

The age ranges for boys and girls are different because of the sex difference in the timing of the adolescent growth spurt. All correlations are averages derived from z-transformations of age-specific and sex-specific correlations weighted for sample size.

Correlations for 0.5 to 5 years of age are adapted from Hewitt (1958). All others are from Malina and Johnston (1967 and unpublished data).

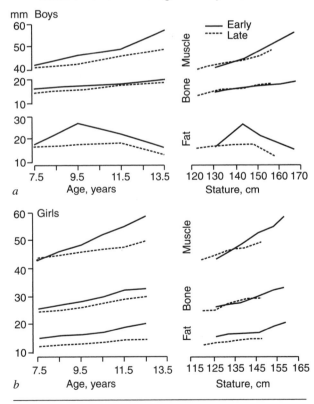

FIGURE 17.2 Tissue composition of the arm in early-maturing boys and late-maturing boys (*a*) and of the leg in early-maturing and late-maturing girls (*b*). Data are plotted by chronological age (left) and relative to stature (right).

Data from Reynolds, 1946.

SA and CA (Johnston and Malina 1966). SA was in advance of CA by an average of 1.4 years in the early-maturing boys and behind CA by an average of 1.1 years in the late-maturing boys. The girls were grouped on the basis of the initial stage of breast development; early-maturing girls showed B2 by 10.5 years, whereas late-maturing girls were still in B1 at this age (Reynolds 1946).

Early-maturing youngsters of both sexes have, on the average, larger measurements of muscle, bone, and fat in the arm and the calf (left side of figure 17.2). The differences between children of contrasting maturity groups are caused in part by overall size differences because early maturers are taller and heavier than late maturers of the same CA. When tissue widths are expressed relative to height to control for the size differences between early-maturing children and late-maturing children (right side of figure 17.2), the differences in muscle and bone widths are virtually eliminated. In other words, early-maturing boys and girls have larger muscle and bone measurements primarily as a function of their overall larger body size. However, in the case of muscle, at the upper age and size limits of the samples, early maturers appear to have larger muscle widths than late maturers even after height differences are controlled. On the other hand, early-maturing boys and girls have thicker fat widths on the arm and calf than late maturers of the same age even after adjusting for differences in height.

The relationship between maturity status and fatness of boys and girls between 6 and 17 years of age is also shown in figure 17.3. The indicator of fatness is the sum of fat widths measured at six body sites on standardized radiographs (Reynolds 1950). Early-maturing children of both sexes have more subcutaneous adipose tissue at all ages from 7 to 17 years, but the differences are most marked during adolescence. Average-maturing and late-maturing girls have similar thickness of subcutaneous adipose tissue throughout, but the differences among the three maturity groups are not very large during the preadolescent years. On the other hand, subcutaneous adipose tissue shows clear maturity-associated differences among the three groups of boys through 13 years of age, after which the average-maturing and late-maturing boys do not differ. The growth curve for early-maturing boys increases considerably to about 13 years of age and then declines sharply. The growth curves for percentage body fat and skinfold thicknesses described in chapters 5 and 8, respectively, indicate a decline in fatness during male adolescence. The growth curves for boys of contrasting maturity

status in figure 17.3 suggest that early-maturing boys and, to a lesser extent, average-maturing boys account for the decline in subcutaneous fatness typically observed during male adolescence. This issue requires further study.

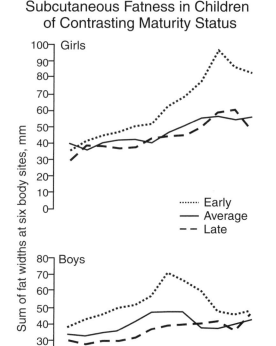

FIGURE 17.3   Sum of six subcutaneous fat widths measured on X-rays in early-, average-, and late-maturing boys and girls.

Data from Reynolds, 1950.

Maturity-associated variation in fatness during childhood and adolescence persists into adulthood. Among male and female participants in the study of Growth and Health of Teenagers in Amsterdam, those classified as early maturing during adolescence (SA, age at PHV, age at menarche) had more subcutaneous fatness (sum of four skinfolds) and an elevated BMI compared with those classified as late maturing not only during adolescence but also at 21 and 27 years of age (Van Lenthe et al. 1996a).

Estimated ages at peak velocities for components of body composition in early-maturing, average-maturing and late-maturing Canadian adolescents are summarized in table 17.6. The

TABLE 17.6 Estimated Ages at Peak Velocity and Peak Velocities for Stature, Weight, and Components of Body Composition in Canadian Adolescents of Contrasting Maturity Status

| | Girls | | | | | | Boys | | | | | |
| | Early (n = 13) | | Average (n = 27) | | Late (n = 13) | | Early (n = 15) | | Average (n = 30) | | Late (n = 15) | |
	Mean	SD	Mean	SD	Mean	SD	Mean	SD	Mean	SD	Mean	SD
Ages at peak velocity (years)												
Stature	10.5	0.4	11.8	0.4	13.0	0.4	12.2	0.5	13.4	0.3	14.7	0.5
Weight	11.2	0.9	12.3	0.9	13.4	0.9	12.9	1.0	13.8	0.9	14.9	0.7
LM	11.0	0.9	12.1	0.6	13.1	0.6	12.7	0.6	13.6	0.5	14.8	0.6
FM	11.6	2.0	12.7	1.7	13.5	2.0	12.9	1.1	14.0	0.9	15.0	1.1
BMC	11.7	0.6	12.5	0.6	13.5	0.6	13.2	0.7	13.9	0.7	15.1	0.6
Peak velocities												
Stature (cm/yr)	9.2	1.2	8.6	0.9	7.9	0.9	10.8	1.6	10.6	1.1	9.7	0.8
Weight (kg/yr)	8.4	1.6	9.1	1.3	8.1	1.5	10.7	1.7	9.9	1.9	10.7	2.0
LM (kg/yr)	5.2	1.3	5.6	1.1	4.2	0.9	9.0	1.5	9.0	1.7	8.2	1.6
FM (kg/yr)	0.2	1.0	-0.4	1.5	-0.8	2.2	-1.7	1.4	-2.4	2.7	-1.2	1.3
BMC (g/yr)	335	71	342	63	278	51	526	68	406	98	389	104

Estimates of body composition in the Saskatchewan Pediatric Bone Mineral Accrual Study are based on DEXA; LM = lean tissue mass; FM = fat mass; BMC = bone mineral content. Adolescents were classifed as early-, average- (on time), or late-maturing on the basis of age at peak height velocity.

Adapted from Iuliano-Burns et al. (2001).

participants in the Saskatchewan Paediatric Bone Mineral Accrual Study were divided into maturity groups on the basis of age at PHV. Components of body composition were estimated with DEXA. Ages at peak velocities of growth in lean tissue mass, fat mass, and bone mineral content occur, on average, earliest in early-maturing youth of both sexes, later in average-maturing youth, and latest in late-maturing youth. Variation in mean velocities for the tissue components is not large among adolescents of contrasting maturity status, but the data suggest somewhat less intense peak velocities for lean tissue mass and bone mineral content among late-maturing boys and girls compared with their respective average-maturing and early-maturing peers. The trend for fat mass is inconsistent in boys of contrasting maturity status; all three groups show a negative velocity during the adolescent growth spurt. Among girls, early maturers show a positive velocity, albeit small, during the adolescent growth spurt, whereas average-maturing and late-maturing girls show a negative velocity.

Variation in Body Composition During Sexual Maturation

Estimates of body composition based on total-body water in the framework of the two-component model (see chapter 5) in boys grouped

by stage of genital maturation within specific CA groups from 11 to 14 years are shown in figure 17.4. At 12 years of age, boys in G2 are compared with those in G3, at 13 years of age boys in G3 are compared with those in G4, and so on. Within each age group, boys advanced in maturity status are, on average, taller and heavier and have a larger FFM. In contrast, differences in percent fat and estimated fat mass are small. The larger FFM of boys advanced in maturity status is in part a function of their larger body size. When FFM is expressed per unit stature, the differences between maturity groups are reduced but not eliminated. Thus, boys advanced in maturity within an age group tend to have more FFM per unit body size than those who are later in maturation (lower right portion of figure 17.4). This trend is consistent with that observed in muscle tissue of the arm in figure 17.2.

Maturity-associated differences in body composition tend to become more marked as sexual maturation progresses, that is, differences between boys in stages G2 and G3 are small compared with those between G3 and G4 and between G4 and G5 (figure 17.4). These differences in body composition are most likely related to changes in circulating levels of the male sex hormones, which have a specific effect on the growth of muscle tissue, the major component of FFM. The level of free and biologically active testoster-

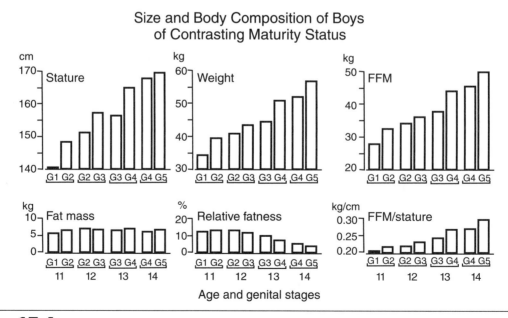

FIGURE 17.4 Body size and estimated body composition of boys within single chronological age groups who differ in stage of genital maturation.

Data from Haschke, 1983.

one increases markedly between stages G3 and G4 and continues to rise into G5 (this is discussed in chapter 19).

In contrast to FFM, percent body fat declines gradually from G2 through G5 (see figure 17.4). This decline is a function of the increase in FFM that accompanies sexual maturity in boys. FFM increases quite rapidly, whereas fat mass shows virtually no change. Hence, fat constitutes a smaller percentage of body weight as the relative contribution of FFM to body weight increases.

Corresponding data comparing girls of the same CA but at different stages of puberty are not available. Nevertheless, one would expect that the trends are probably similar to those for boys, with the exception that, within each CA group, girls more advanced in puberty are absolutely and relatively fatter than less mature girls.

Comparisons of children of contrasting maturity status utilizing the two-, three-, or four-component models of body composition (see chapter 5) are limited. Available data ordinarily are based on small samples of children who are grouped by stage of pubertal development without considering variation in CA (Rico et al. 1993; Goulding et al. 1996; Roemmich et al. 1997). Although this method is valid, variation in CA within each stage of puberty, which is not considered in the analyses, may influence interpretations. For example, is there an effect of age on body composition that is independent of stage of sexual maturity? Allowing for this limitation, the data provide insights into changes in body composition during puberty.

Differences in body composition based on estimates using the four-component model in small samples of boys and girls classified by pubertal status are summarized in table 17.7. Note the variation in CA within each of the samples, and CA per se is a factor that influences body composition at this time. As expected, adolescents in midpuberty (G3 and G4 in boys, B3 and B4 in girls) are older, taller, and heavier; have a higher body density; have greater total-body water; and have a larger estimated FFM

TABLE 17.7 Estimated Body Composition by Stage of Pubertal Development in Boys and Girls

| | Stages of puberty | | | |
| | B1 and B2 (n = 8) 8.5–13.0 yr | | B3 and B4 (n = 15) 11.0–14.3 yr | |
	Mean	SE	Mean	SE
Girls				
Age (yr)	10.4	0.4	13.3	0.3
Height (cm)	141.1	3.0	160.3	2.3
Weight (kg)	39.4	3.1	52.0	2.4
Body density (g/ml)	1.0303	0.004	1.0337	0.003
Fat-free mass (kg)	28.8	2.2	39.6	1.7
Fat mass (kg)	10.6	1.4	12.9	1.1
% Body fat	26.3	2.0	24.2	1.5
Fat-free mass				
% Water	75.5	0.7	74.4	0.5
% Mineral	5.1	0.2	5.7	0.1
% Protein	19.4	0.6	19.9	0.5
Density (g/ml)	1.086	0.003	1.091	0.002
	G1 and G2 (n = 17) 9.2–14.2 yr		**G3 and G4 (n = 7) 11.1–15.4 yr**	
	Mean	SE	Mean	SE
Boys				
Age (yr)	10.9	0.3	13.4	0.5
Height (cm)	144.7	2.1	165.8	3.7
Weight (kg)	37.4	2.3	53.5	3.8
Body density (g/ml)	1.0397	0.003	1.0515	0.005
Fat-free mass (kg)	29.7	1.6	46.2	2.7
Fat mass (kg)	7.8	1.0	7.3	1.7
% Body fat	19.9	1.4	13.7	2.4
Fat-free mass				
% Water	75.7	0.5	74.8	0.8
% Mineral	4.9	0.1	5.0	0.2
% Protein	19.4	0.5	20.2	0.8
Density (g/ml)	1.084	0.002	1.087	0.003

Adapted from Roemmich et al. (1997).

than preadolescents (G1 and B1) and early adolescents (G2 and B2). As youngsters pass from the early pubertal to midpubertal stages, estimated fat mass and percent body fat decline in boys, whereas fat mass increases in girls and percent body fat changes only slightly. The decline in fat mass in boys is small, but the decline in relative fatness is greater. This difference reflects the rapid growth of the FFM during male puberty, so fat mass contributes proportionally less to body weight. The small change in relative fatness from early puberty to midpuberty in girls also reflects the rapid growth of FFM during their adolescent growth spurt (but growth in FFM is not as marked as in boys).

Changes in the estimated composition of FFM during puberty are also indicated in table 17.7. The transition from prepuberty or early puberty to midpuberty in boys and girls is associated with a decline in the relative contribution of water to FFM, an increase in the relative contributions of protein and mineral to FFM, and an increase in the density of FFM.

Changes in total-body bone mineral content (TBMC) and total-body bone mineral density (TBMD) associated with puberty are consistent with the preceding trends. TBMC and TBMD increase with stage of puberty. Within each stage, sex differences are small until B5 and PH5 (maturity), when males have greater TBMC and TBMD than females (Molgaard et al. 1998). Other studies limited to measurements of bone mineral at specific sections of a long bone or specific vertebrae indicate similar maturity-associated gradients (Malina 1996).

Maturity-Associated Variation in Adipose Tissue Distribution

The regional distribution of adipose, skeletal, and muscle tissue changes considerably during adolescence. The extent of change is, however, masked by the individuality of timing and tempo of the adolescent growth spurt and sexual maturation. Changes in adipose, skeletal, and muscle tissues relative to PHV were discussed in chapter 16. This section compares adipose tissue distribution of individuals of contrasting maturity status. Corresponding data on regional development of bone mineral and muscle tissue are presently not available.

Among 12-year-old girls from the U.S. Health Examination Survey (1966–1970), early-maturing and late-maturing girls (defined by either SA or secondary sex characteristics) differ only in overall subcutaneous fatness (the former are fatter in five skinfolds) but not in relative subcutaneous adipose tissue distribution. The same trend is apparent in 17-year-old girls classified as early or late maturing on the basis of recalled ages at menarche. Thus, advanced maturity in girls appears to be associated with greater levels of fatness and not with a distinctive distribution of subcutaneous adipose tissue. In contrast, among 14-year-old boys, early maturers (also defined by either SA or secondary sex characteristics) have proportionally more subcutaneous adipose tissue on the trunk than late maturers. Sexual and skeletal maturity status accounted for 20% of the variance in the trunk-extremity contrast of subcutaneous adipose tissue in 14-year-old boys, but skeletal maturity accounted for only 5% of the variance in 17-year-old boys (they were already sexually mature). In contrast, none of the variance in the trunk-extremity contrast of subcutaneous adipose tissue in 12-year-old and 17-year-old girls was explained by the indicators of maturity status (Deutsch et al. 1985). In a similar analysis, skeletal age (SA) accounted for about 4%, 18%, and 8% of the variance in the trunk-extremity contrast of subcutaneous adipose tissue in 12-year-old, 14-year-old, and 17-year-old Belgian boys, respectively. On the other hand, SA accounted for only 2% to 3% of the corresponding variance in 9-year-old and 10-year-old girls and none of the variance in 12-year-old and 17-year-old girls (Beunen et al. 1992).

A sample of Belgian males was followed longitudinally from 13 to 18 years of age and then observed at 30 years of age. Early maturers (age at PHV <13.4 years, n = 35) had thicker subscapular and suprailiac skinfolds at all ages during adolescence and at 30 years of age than average (age at PHV 13.9 to 14.8 years, n = 56) and late (age at PHV >15.3 years, n = 24) maturers. The three maturity groups, on the other hand, did not consistently differ in the triceps and medial calf skinfolds (Beunen et al. 1994). At each age during adolescence and at 30 years of age, the three contrasting maturity groups differed in the ratio of subcutaneous adipose tissue on the trunk to the extremities: early > average > late (see figure 17.5). Early-maturing males had relatively more subcutaneous adipose tissue on the trunk compared with average-maturing and late-maturing males not only during adolescence but also in adulthood, which indicates persistence of maturity-associated variation in adipose tissue distribution into adulthood. The central pattern of relative subcutaneous adipose tissue distribution associated with early maturity in males is of additional interest because

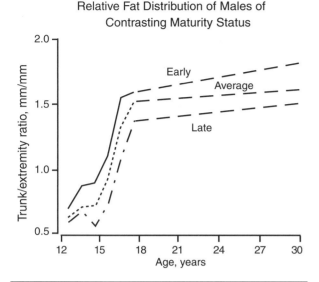

Relative Fat Distribution of Males of
Contrasting Maturity Status

FIGURE 17.5 Trunk/extremity skinfold ratios (subscapular + suprailiac/triceps + calf) in a longitudinal sample of early-maturing, average-maturing, and late-maturing Belgian boys during adolescence and at 30 years of age. Maturity status is based on age at PHV.

Data from Beunen et al., 1994.

the three contrasting maturity groups did not significantly differ in stature, weight, and the BMI at 30 years of age. Thus, for the same size and mass, early-maturing males have proportionally more subcutaneous adipose tissue on the trunk as adults than average-maturing and late-maturing males.

Results from the study of Growth and Health of Teenagers in Amsterdam are not consistent with the preceding data for Belgian males (Van Lenthe et al. 1996b). Early-maturing and late-maturing males (SA and age at PHV) in the Amsterdam did not differ in relative subcutaneous adipose tissue distribution based on ratios of skinfolds on the trunk and extremities from 13 through 16 years of age and at 21 and 27 years of age. The reason for the difference may relate to the skinfolds used in the ratios (the Dutch study did not include a lower extremity skinfold). In addition, the cutoff point for early and late maturity was narrow. An SA-CA difference of only 3 months was used to establish the early-maturing and late-maturing groups, and such a difference is probably within the range of error associated with estimates of SA. Age at PHV was also used as a criterion in the Dutch sample, but the range of variation was somewhat limited.

Corresponding results for Amsterdam girls varied with the criterion for maturity (Van Lenthe et al. 1996b). With SA as the criterion, early-maturing and late-maturing girls did not differ in relative adipose tissue distribution in adolescence and young adulthood, whereas with age at menarche as the criterion, they differed. Early-maturing girls had proportionally more subcutaneous adipose tissue on the trunk in adolescence and young adulthood. These results contrast those for the cross-sectional sample of American adolescent girls in whom SA and secondary sex characteristics were not related to relative subcutaneous adipose tissue distribution at 12 and 17 years of age. Advanced maturity in girls appeared to be associated with greater levels of fatness and not with a distinctive distribution of subcutaneous adipose tissue (Deutsch et al. 1985). Different methods of estimating skeletal maturity and relative subcutaneous fat distribution were used in both studies, and it probably influenced the results.

Data using more advanced technology to estimate subcutaneous and visceral adipose tissue in children and adolescents are limited. With magnetic resonance imaging, early (B2, 11.5 years of age) and late (B4, 14.0 years of age) pubertal girls do not differ in visceral adipose tissue area at the level of minimal waist. The late pubertal girls are especially fatter in subcutaneous adipose tissue at the waist and greater trochanter levels (de Ridder et al. 1992). Only about one-half of the late pubertal girls had reached menarche.

The relationship between menarcheal status and relative fat distribution was estimated in a cross-sectional sample of French Canadian girls. Girls were grouped as premenarcheal and postmenarcheal, and within each group, they were subdivided as younger and older. The older premenarcheal girls (12.3 years of age) and younger postmenarcheal girls (13.6 years of age; age at menarche 12.2 years) were assumed to be closer to menarche than the younger premenarcheal girls (10.2 years of age) and older postmenarcheal girls (16.4 years of age; age at menarche 13.1 years). Body density was determined from underwater weighing and converted to percent body fat. Although the data are cross-sectional, several trends are suggested (see table 17.8). First, the decline in the ratio of subcutaneous adipose tissue (sum of six skinfolds) to fat mass from younger to older premenarcheal girls suggests a relatively greater accumulation of visceral adipose tissue as menarche approaches. Subcutaneous adipose

	Fat mass (kg)	Sum of 6 skinfolds (mm)	Sum 6/fat mass (mm/kg)	Sum 3 trunk (mm)	Sum 3 extremity (mm)	T/E ratio (mm/mm)
Premenarcheal						
Younger (n = 50, 10.2 yr)	4.8	48.9	10.9	21.9	26.9	0.77
Older (n = 32, 12.3 yr)	5.5	46.3	8.8	20.7	25.5	0.83
Postmenarcheal						
Younger (n = 36, 13.6 yr)	7.7	61.5	8.0	29.6	30.8	0.94
Older (n = 96, 16.4 yr)	10.0	66.6	6.8	32.7	34.9	0.96

TABLE 17.8 Estimated Changes in Fatness and Adipose Tissue Distribution Relative to Menarche in Girls From the Quebec Family Study

Fat mass was estimated via densitometry. Sum of 6 skinfolds: triceps, biceps, medial calf (extremity), subscapular, suprailiac, abdominal (trunk). Sum6/fat mass: ratio of the sum of 6 skinfolds to fat mass. Sum 3 trunk: sum of the 3 trunk skinfolds. Sum 3 extremity: sum of the 3 extremity skinfolds. T/E ratio: Sum 3 trunk/sum 3 extremity.

Adapted from Malina (1996).

tissue does not differ between the two groups, whereas fat mass increases, which implies a gain in visceral adipose tissue at this time. Second, comparison of older premenarcheal and younger postmenarcheal girls indicates little difference in the ratio of subcutaneous adipose tissue to fat mass but greater fat mass and subcutaneous adipose tissue in the latter. Thus, a gain in overall fatness and subcutaneous adipose tissue appears to occur during the transition from the premenarcheal to the postmenarcheal state. However, proportionally more of the subcutaneous adipose tissue is accumulated on the trunk than on extremities at this time. Third, after menarche is attained, the ratio of subcutaneous adipose tissue to fat mass decreases, whereas the ratio of trunk to extremity skinfolds is similar in younger and older postmenarcheal girls. After menarche is attained, proportionally more visceral adipose tissue is apparently accumulated (a lower ratio of subcutaneous adipose tissue to fat mass), but the relative distribution of subcutaneous adipose tissue is unchanged (similar ratio of trunk to extremity skinfolds). The trends are based on cross-sectional data and should be interpreted with caution. They highlight the need for longitudinal study of changes in body composition and in the regional distribution of tissue components during puberty, especially using newer technology to assess maturity-associated variation in visceral adipose tissue.

Maturity-Associated Variation in Strength and Motor Performance

The relationship between maturity status and performance is also considered from two perspectives. First, the statistical association between indicators of biological maturity and performance are considered. Second, the performance characteristics of children of the same CA but of contrasting maturity status are compared.

Correlations During Childhood

Correlations between skeletal maturity and several strength and motor tests are summarized in table 17.9 for two samples of children between 6 and 9 years of age. Correlations between CA and performance are also included for comparison. All correlations between CA and performance are positive, and the correlations between SA and performance in the two studies compare favorably, especially in the performance items common to the two studies—running, jumping, and throwing. Correlations between SA and strength are moderate (0.35 to 0.63) and are higher than those for motor performance (0.02 to 0.56). Thus, the child who is advanced in maturity tends to be stronger and to perform better than the child of the same CA who is later in maturity.

	Boys		Girls	
	SA	CA	SA	CA
Strength				
Ankle extension	0.60	0.52		
Knee extension	0.51	0.63		
Hip flexion	0.56	0.58		
Hip extension	0.57	0.64		
Wrist flexion	0.54	0.61		
Elbow flexion	0.63	0.65		
Shoulder medial rotation	0.35	0.21		
Shoulder adduction	0.43	0.57		
Motor performance				
30-Yard dash	0.32	0.28		
40-Yard dash	0.51	0.37	0.46	0.04
Standing long jump	0.25	0.25		
Standing long jump	0.27	0.28	0.56	-0.03
Throw for distance	0.42	0.21	0.38	0.13
Throwing velocity	0.48	0.53		
Balance (stick test lengthwise)	0.07	0.13	0.03	0.09
Agility (sidestepping)	0.55	0.21	0.43	0.10
Ball striking	0.26	0.10	0.02	-0.13
Ball catching	0.45	0.21	0.49	0.02

TABLE 17.9 Correlations Between Skeletal Age (SA) and Chronological Age (CA) and Strength and Motor Performance in Primary Grade Children (About 6 to 9 Years of Age)

In the data of Seils (1951), SA was assessed on only 63 children. The corresponding correlations for CA and performance are based on second grade children only.

Compiled from Seils (1951) for children of both sexes in grades 1 to 3 and from Rarick and Oyster (1964) for second grade boys.

Note that the correlations between CA and performance in table 17.9 are generally about the same magnitude as those for SA and performance. The magnitude of the correlations is similar to those between performance and height and weight described in chapter 11. This similarity reflects the relationship among CA, SA, height, and weight during growth, so each variable by itself may not be of major consequence in understanding variability in strength and motor performance. These variables probably exert their influence on performance through their interrelationships or interactions with each other.

An important question follows from the preceding discussion: How much of the variation in strength and motor performance during childhood can be attributed to biological maturity independent of CA and body size? This question was addressed in a sample of boys and girls 7 to 12 years of age. Indicators of performance included four measures of static strength, the 35-yard dash, the standing long jump, and the ball throw for distance. The difference between SA and CA was used as the estimate of skeletal maturity independent of CA in the analysis, and the interactions among maturity, height, and weight were statistically considered. Skeletal maturity influenced the strength and motor performance of 7-year-old to 12-year-old boys and girls mainly through its interaction with height and weight. The data also suggested that skeletal maturity by itself influenced motor performance at these ages somewhat more than it influenced muscular strength (Katzmarzyk et al. 1997). Corresponding data for girls, 6 to 11 years of age, using different performance tasks did not identify a specific role for SA. However, SA and CA were treated separately in the analysis, and SA by itself appeared only sporadically among the significant predictors of motor performance (Beunen et al. 1997a). Although the results of the two studies are somewhat different, they suggest an important role for neuromuscular maturation in motor performance during childhood. Skeletal maturity viewed as the difference between SA and CA (and not as SA independent of CA) possibly reflects overall bodily maturity, perhaps including neuromuscular maturation.

Correlations During Adolescence

Correlations between maturity status and performance during adolescence in boys and girls are summarized in table 17.10. The strength and motor performance of adolescent boys is, in general, positively and significantly related to skeletal maturity. Thus, boys advanced in maturity status tend to be stronger and to perform better on motor tasks. However, correlations between

| **TABLE 17.10** | Correlations Between Chronological Age (CA), Skeletal Age (SA), and Age Deviation From Menarche (ADM) and Performance in Adolescents From the Adolescent Growth Study of the University of California |

	Boys			**Girls**			
	CA	**SA**	**SA[a]**	**CA**	**SA**	**SA[a]**	**ADM**
50-Yard dash	0.52	0.37	0.10	−0.19	−0.12	−0.02	−0.13
Standing long jump	0.71	0.56	0.25	−0.22	−0.11	−0.00	0.17
Vertical jump	0.53	0.48	0.25	0.11	0.14	0.10	0.03
Throw for distance	0.34	0.51	0.40	0.07	−0.19	−0.26	−0.07
Strength	0.39	0.50		0.19	0.42		

Age deviation from menarche refers to the number of months before or after menarche. Correlations between strength and age deviation from menarche and partial correlations for strength were not reported.

[a]Partial correlations between SA and performance controlling for CA.

Adapted from Espenschade (1940) and Jones (1949).

CA and performance are reasonably similar to those for SA and performance among boys, which reflects the interrelationships among CA, SA, and body size. When CA is statistically controlled, partial correlations between performance and SA are reduced, but the relationship between SA and power tasks (standing long jump, vertical jump, and throw for distance) persists, suggesting a maturity influence independent of CA. However, body size was not controlled in the analysis, and SA is positively related to body size in adolescent males.

The motor performance of adolescent girls, on the other hand, is not significantly related to indicators of skeletal and sexual maturity. Most correlations are low and several are negative for some motor tasks. This lack of positive correlation would suggest that late maturation in girls is associated with somewhat better performances, or conversely, early maturation in girls is associated with somewhat poorer performances. In contrast to motor performance, static strength is positively related to maturity status in girls during adolescence.

The correlational data for strength and motor performance and maturity status during adolescence are confounded, as during childhood, by interrelationships among CA, maturity status, and body size. An additional confounding factor is individual variation in the tempo of maturation during adolescence. When the effects of CA, SA, stature, and weight are statistically controlled, correlations between SA and performance are reduced. This finding was shown in the Leuven Growth Study of Belgian Boys. CA and SA by themselves, or in combination with stature and weight, explained only a small percentage of variation (0% to 17%) in several motor performance tasks but a greater percentage of the variation (up to 58%) in static strength in boys 12 to 19 years of age (Beunen et al. 1981). The largest percentage of variation in performance accounted for by CA, SA, and body size generally occurred at 14 and 15 years of age in boys. At these ages, CA, SA, stature, and weight are all highly interrelated, so it is difficult to partition specific effects of maturation by itself on strength and performance. These ages also include the interval during which growth spurts occur in stature, weight, muscle mass, strength, and performance in the majority of boys (see chapter 16). Results of a corresponding study of Belgian adolescent girls indicate a significant effect of SA in interaction with body size on static strength (up to 33% of the variance) but little influence on motor performances (with few exceptions, less than 10% of the variance) (Beunen et al. 1997a).

Overview of Correlational Studies

Results of correlational studies indicate the complexities involved in attempting to partition the contribution of biological maturity per se to variation in strength and motor performance during childhood and adolescence. Although CA, SA, height, and weight account for considerable proportions of the variance in strength and motor performance during childhood and adolescence, significant proportions of the variation are not accounted for. This, in turn, indicates that other variables, including more direct estimates of body composition and factors in the social environment, need to be considered in future studies to understand variation in strength and performance.

Children and Adolescents of Contrasting Maturity Status

The association between maturity status and performance is more apparent when adolescents within a given CA group are divided into early, average, and late maturity groups. Though somewhat arbitrary, this approach is relevant because, as indicated earlier, children function in a society, which is largely based on CA, especially for school and youth sports. When children are grouped into contrasting maturity categories, the data illustrate clear maturity gradients in the strength and motor performance of adolescent boys but variable trends in adolescent girls.

Strength   The muscular strength of the mixed-longitudinal sample of the Adolescent Growth Study in Oakland, California, was compared among groups of contrasting maturity status–based SA. On the average, SA was in advance of CA by more than 1 year in the early maturers and behind CA by more than 1 year in the late maturers. Mean CA and SA were the same in the average maturers. Early-maturing boys are stronger at all ages than average-maturing and late-maturing boys, but differences between average-maturing and late-maturing boys are small compared with those between these two maturity categories and early maturers (see figure 17.6). The maturity-associated variation in pushing strength appears to increase with age as boys progress through adolescence.

Early-maturing girls tend to be slightly stronger only early in adolescence (11 to 13 years of age), but as adolescence continues, the differences among maturity groups are reduced (see figure 17.7 top). Grip strength increases linearly with age from 11 through 17 years, whereas pushing strength reaches a plateau at about 13 to 14 years of age in girls from the three maturity categories. When the sample is grouped by menarcheal status, postmenarcheal girls are stronger than premenarcheal girls within each age from 12 to 14 years (see figure 17.7 bottom). The strength advantage of girls advanced in maturity early in adolescence reflects their larger body size. For example, mean weights and heights of early-maturing and late-maturing girls at 12 years of age differ by about 12 kg and 10 cm, respectively. With age, the size difference between early-maturing and late-maturing girls is reduced, especially

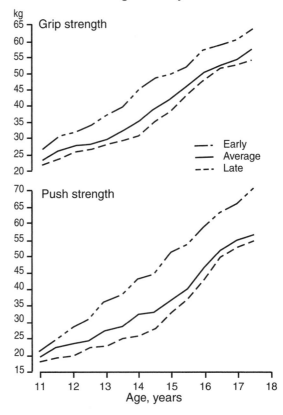

FIGURE 17.6   Mean grip strength and push strength of early-, average-, and late-maturing boys in the Adolescent Growth Study, Oakland, California. Maturity status is based on skeletal age. Means were calculated from the data of Jones (1949) which were provided by Dr. Dorothy Eichorn of the Institute of Human Development of the University of California, Berkeley.

for height. As noted in chapter 16, menarche is a late event of puberty, occurring after PHV, and strength reaches its peak rate of growth after PHV (see figure 16.8, page 328). Thus, postmenarcheal girls in any age group are probably further advanced in progress toward maturity than implied when SA is the criterion.

Ratio Scaling of Strength   Strength is related to body size, so differences between adolescents of contrasting maturity status are in part a function of differences in body size. The relationship between strength and body size is commonly expressed as a ratio in an attempt to "normalize" or reduce the size differences among children and adolescents. Although useful and simple, such

Strength of Girls of Contrasting Maturity Status

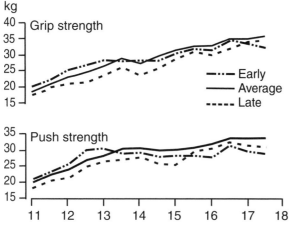

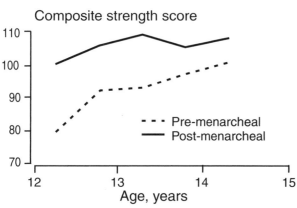

FIGURE 17.7   Mean grip strength and push strength of early-, average-, and late-maturing girls (based on skeletal age) in the Adolescent Growth Study, Oakland, California (top), and mean composite strength of premenarcheal and postmenarcheal girls of the same chronological age (bottom). Means for grip and push strength were calculated from the data of Jones (1949) which were provided by Dr. Dorothy Eichorn of the Institute of Human Development of the University of California, Berkeley. The composite strength score is based on the sum of right and left grip and push and pull strength. The data were drawn from values reported by Jones (1949).

ratios have limitations (see chapter 3). When strength is expressed per unit body weight or stature, strength differences between children of contrasting maturity status are reduced. However, the trends differ between sexes and with the denominator. Strength per unit body weight and per unit stature in boys is shown in figure 17.8. Differences between strength tests are immediately apparent

for boys. When expressed relative to body weight, the differences in grip strength among the three maturity categories are reduced dramatically, and at many ages, late-maturing boys have greater grip strength per unit body mass. This advantage does not apply, however, to pushing strength, where early-maturing boys have more strength per unit body mass from 13 to 17 years of age. Differences between average-maturing and late-maturing boys in pushing strength per unit body weight are negligible, especially after 15 years of age.

When strength is expressed per unit stature, differences among the three maturity groups of boys persist across adolescence. Early-maturing boys have more strength per unit stature at all ages except 11 years, and the difference between the early maturers and boys in the other two maturity groups increases with age for pushing strength. In contrast, the average-maturing and late-maturing boys differ only slightly in strength per unit stature.

The strength advantage for early-maturing boys when expressed relative to height probably reflects their rapid growth in stature and their larger muscle mass. During male adolescence, strength increases more than that expected for age or growth in stature, especially strength of the upper extremities. This increase is related to the larger muscle mass of the arms in early-maturing boys, even after controlling for stature variation between early-maturing and late-maturing boys (see figure 17.2). The data shown in figure 17.8 do not include boys older than 17.5 years, so whether the average and late maturers catch up in strength to the early maturers in the early or mid-20s cannot be determined. The persistence of maturity-associated differences in strength and motor performance into adulthood is addressed later in this section.

When strength is expressed per unit body weight in girls, the positions of girls in the three maturity groups are reversed (see figure 17.9). Early-maturing girls have, age for age, less strength per unit body weight than average-maturing and late-maturing girls, whereas the latter two groups do not differ. Strength per unit stature does not differ among girls in the three maturity groups.

Motor Performance   Maturity-associated variation in the motor performance of Belgian adolescent boys followed longitudinally from 12 through 17 years of age is shown in figure 17.10. Age at PHV was used to classify the boys as early

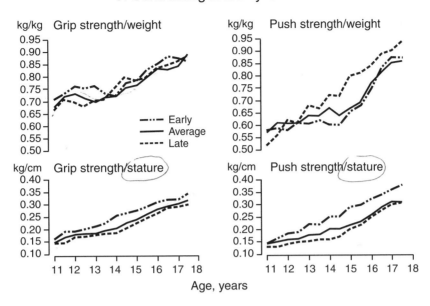

Strength per Unit Body Size in Boys
of Contrasting Maturity Status

FIGURE 17.8 Grip and push strength per unit body weight and per unit stature in early-maturing, average-maturing, and late-maturing boys in the Adolescent Growth Study, Oakland, California. Maturity status is based on skeletal age. Means were calculated from the data of Jones (1949) which were provided by Dr. Dorothy Eichorn of the Institute of Human Develoment of the University of California, Berkeley.

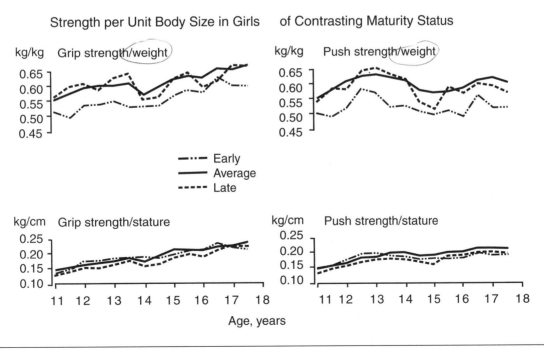

Strength per Unit Body Size in Girls   of Contrasting Maturity Status

FIGURE 17.9 Grip and push strength per unit body weight and per unit stature in early-maturing, average-maturing, and late-maturing girls in the Adolescent Growth Study, Oakland, California. Maturity status is based on skeletal age. Means were calculated from the data of Jones (1949) which were provided by Dr. Dorothy Eichorn of the Institute of Human Develoment of the University of California, Berkeley.

(13.1 years of age), average (14.1 years of age), and late (15.4 years of age) maturing (Lefevre et al. 1988). The motor tasks include static strength (arm pull), explosive strength (vertical jump), flexibility (sit-and-reach), running speed and agility (shuttle run), speed of upper limb movement (plate tapping), and muscular endurance of the trunk and upper extremities (leg lifts and flexed-arm hang, respectively). With the exception of the flexed-arm hang, the motor performances of early-maturing boys are, on the average, better than those of average-maturing and late-maturing boys, and at most ages the performances of average-maturing boys are greater than those of late-maturing boys.

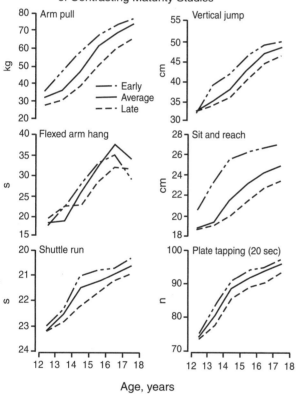

FIGURE 17.10 Mean motor performances of early-maturing, average-maturing, and late-maturing Belgian boys followed longitudinally during adolescence. Maturity status is based on age at PHV.

Data from Lefevre et al., 1988.

In an earlier study of Belgian adolescent boys using SA as the maturity indicator, height and weight were statistically controlled in making comparisons among groups of contrasting maturity status (Beunen et al. 1980). After controlling for variation in body size, early-maturing boys performed better than average-maturing and late-maturing boys at most ages after 13 years; the largest differences among maturity groups occurred at 14 and 15 years of age in most tasks. Measures of muscular strength, power, and endurance (arm strength, vertical jump, leg lifts, and flexed-arm hang) showed similar age trends. After controlling for body size, the performances of late-maturing boys consistently lagged behind those of early-maturing boys from 14 to 18 years of age. In contrast, performance differences among the maturity groups in two speed tasks, a shuttle run and plate tapping, were small compared with those for the strength and power tasks.

The motor performance of a subsample of the longitudinal series of Belgian boys was measured again at 30 years of age to evaluate the persistence of maturity-associated variation during adolescence into adulthood (Lefevre et al. 1990). At 30 years of age, early-maturing, average-maturing, and late-maturing boys do not differ in height and weight. Between 18 and 30 years of age, a crossover of performances occurs among boys of contrasting maturity status during adolescence in all tasks except speed of upper limb movement (plate tapping), in which the performance advantage of early-maturing boys persisted. At 30 years of age, late-maturing boys perform, on average, better in flexibility (sit-and-reach), explosive power (vertical jump), upper body muscular endurance (flexed-arm hang), and speed and agility (shuttle run). No differences occur among early-maturing, average-maturing, and late-maturing boys in static strength (arm pull) and abdominal muscular endurance (leg lifts) at 30 years of age. What is especially of interest is the trends in the performance data. Performances of late-maturing boys improve from 18 to 30 years of age in all tasks, whereas those of early-maturing and average-maturing boys show little change or decline. These results emphasize the continued growth of late-maturing boys beyond the age limits normally associated with the study of adolescence. They also emphasize the transient nature of maturity-associated variation in performance during adolescence. Nevertheless, in the world of boys, maturity variation in performance is real and often contributes to success in many sport activities at these ages and may contribute to reduced sport participation in late-maturing boys during adolescence.

Maturity-associated variation in the motor performance of Canadian adolescent girls followed longitudinally from 10 to 14 years of age is shown in figure 17.11. Age at menarche was used to classify the girls as early (11.3 years of age), average (12.6 years of age), and late (14.2 years of age) maturing (Little et al. 1997). The results contrast the trends apparent for boys. Late-maturing girls perform, on the average, better than average-maturing and early-maturing girls from 10 to 14 years of age in the shuttle run (speed and agility) and flexed-arm hang (upper body muscular endurance). Late-maturing girls also perform better than the other maturity groups in flexibility (sit-and-reach) at 12 to 14 years of age. In contrast, girls of contrasting maturity status do not consistently differ in static strength (arm and

back strength), running speed (20-m dash), and explosive strength (vertical jump and medicine ball throw). Generally similar results have been reported for a cross-sectional sample of Belgian girls 12 to 15 years of age grouped as early, average, and late maturing on the basis of SA (see figure 17.12). Maturity-associated variation in motor performance is not consistent from task to task and across age. Rather, considerable variation exists among the three contrasting maturity groups in the other tasks.

Overview Relationships between biological maturity and performance during adolescence vary between boys and girls. Maturity-associated variation in performance is more apparent in boys. Early-maturing boys exceed average-maturing and late-maturing boys in performance tasks that place a premium on strength, power, and speed during adolescence. The maturity criteria for most studies of boys are SA and age at PHV. Less extensive data using indicators of sexual maturity provide similar results. Boys who are advanced in sexual maturity are stronger and perform better than those who are late. Male adolescence brings about marked improvements in strength and motor performance such that considerable differences exist in the strength and motor performances of boys of contrasting maturity status at this time. The differences, which are so evident during adolescence, are not generally apparent in young adulthood, highlighting the transient nature of maturity-associated differences in performance during male adolescence.

Female adolescence brings about smaller improvements in strength and motor performance. As such, individual variation in rate of maturation has less influence on the strength and motor performance of girls and suggests that girls of contrasting maturity status do not differ greatly in motor performance. Early-maturing girls tend to be slightly stronger than late-maturing girls of the same CA in early adolescence, about 11 to 13 years of age. The differences do not persist and are no longer evident in later adolescence. Further, differences in muscular strength between girls of contrasting maturity status are not as marked as those between early-maturing and late-maturing boys.

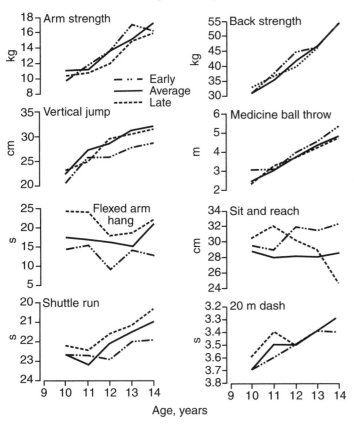

FIGURE 17.11 Mean motor performances of early-maturing, average-maturing, and late-maturing Canadian girls followed longitudinally from 10 to 14 years of age. Maturity status is based on age at menarche.

Data from Little et al., 1997.

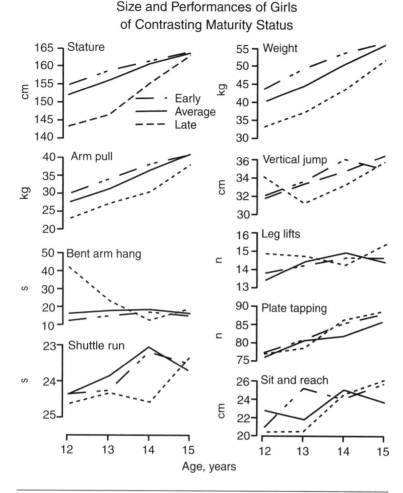

Size and Performances of Girls
of Contrasting Maturity Status

F I G U R E 17.12   Mean body size and motor performances of early-maturing, average-maturing, and late-maturing Belgian girls. Maturity status is based on skeletal age.

Drawn from data provided by Dr. Gaston Beunen, Faculty of Kinesiology and Physiotherapy, Katholieke Universiteit Leuven, Belgium.

Maturity-Associated Variation in the Adaptation to Exercise and $\dot{V}O_2$max

Data on maturity-associated variation in adaptation to submaximal exercise and maximal aerobic power ($\dot{V}O_2$max) are not as extensive as for strength and motor performance, especially during childhood. Further, the data are generally more available for boys than girls.

Correlations

Between 8 and 11 years of age, relationships among CA, SA, stature, and weight are such

that a significant contribution of SA to submaximal and maximal exercise is difficult to estimate. Correlations between various physiological indices of adaptation to submaximal exercise, such as power output and $\dot{V}O_2$ at a heart rate of 130 beats per minute, and SA tend to be generally low in boys between 9 and 11 years of age. However, between 12 and 16 years of age, the period during which most boys experience their adolescent growth spurts, correlations between power output and $\dot{V}O_2$ at a heart rate of 130 beats per minute and SA tend to reach moderate levels, 0.30 to 0.77 (Bouchard et al. 1976, 1978). These trends, which are based on cross-sectional data, suggest a stronger relationship between skeletal maturity and submaximal working capacity during male adolescence but not in the immediate preadolescent years. The interactions among CA, height, weight, and SA probably mask the influence of SA by itself, as indicated earlier in the discussion of strength and motor performance. The relationship between adaptation to submaximal exercise and SA is also mediated through the relationship between SA and heart volume. In addition to being larger in body size, boys advanced in skeletal maturity have larger absolute heart volumes and maximal aerobic power (see figure 17.13). Heart volume is a significant determinant of stroke volume and cardiac output and, in turn, aerobic power.

Heart volume is also related to body size. In a cross-sectional sample of German boys 8 to 18 years of age, the correlation between power output on a cycle ergometer and heart volume is 0.82. When CA is controlled, the correlation between power output and heart volume decreases to 0.51 (Hollmann et al. 1967). Thus, boys with a larger heart volume tend to have a greater power output. However, heart volume is related to body size (see chapter 9), and larger boys tend to have a larger heart volume. When heart volume is adjusted for body size, the correlation between heart volume per kilogram of body weight and power output on the cycle ergometer falls to 0.04. Thus, the influence of maturity status on submaximal exercise capacity or cardiopulmonary adaptation to exercise appears

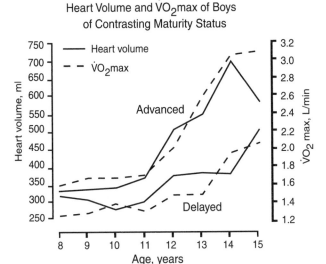

FIGURE 17.13 Absolute heart volume and maximal aerobic power in early-maturing and late-maturing 8-year-old to 15-year-old German boys. Maturity status is based on skeletal age.

Reprinted, by permission, from W. Hollmann, C. Bouchard, and G. Herkenrath, 1967, "Die Leistungsentwicklung des kindes and jugenlichen unter besonderer berucksichtigung des biologischen alters," *Arztiliche Jugendkunde* 58: 198-203.

to be mediated to a large extent by the effects of maturity status on body weight, which, in turn, is closely related to the size of the heart and skeletal muscle mass. Generally, similar results occur when CA and SA are related to physiological indices of adaptation to submaximal exercise and submaximal power output in this sample of boys (see table 17.11). Correlations between SA and the indices are virtually identical with those for CA.

TABLE 17.11	Correlations of Chronological Age (CA) and Skeletal Age (SA) With Several Indicators of Adaptation to Submaximal Exercise in German Boys 8 to 18 Years of Age		
		CA	SA
Power output at a heart rate of			
130 beats/min		0.74	0.76
Heart rate at 30 W		−0.63	−0.65
$\dot{V}O_2$/heart rate at 30 W		0.65	0.69
Systolic blood pressure at 30 W		0.50	0.53

Adapted from Bouchard et al. (1976).

Adolescents of Contrasting Maturity Status

Maturity-associated variation in $\dot{V}O_2$max in a longitudinal sample of Polish adolescents 11 to 14 years of age is illustrated in figure 17.14. Boys were divided into maturity groups based on estimated growth velocities, and girls were divided on the basis of age at menarche. Early-maturing boys have, on the average, a higher absolute $\dot{V}O_2$max (L/min) than average-maturing and late-maturing boys. The differences among maturity groups are reduced when $\dot{V}O_2$max is expressed per unit body mass (ml/min/kg), but average values tend to be higher in late-maturing boys from 11 to 13 years of age. Among girls, $\dot{V}O_2$max (L/min) is less in late-maturing girls than in early-maturing and average-maturing girls, who do not differ, but when $\dot{V}O_2$max is expressed per unit body mass, adolescent girls of contrasting maturity status do not differ. The maturity-associated trends in $\dot{V}O_2$max in adolescent boys and girls 11 to 14 years of age are consistent with those for a longitudinal sample of early-maturing and late-maturing Dutch adolescents, 12 to 17 years of age (Kemper et al. 1986). This study used a narrow band of SA (3 months) to define two maturity groups: early = SA in advance of CA by 3 or more months, and late = SA behind CA by 3 or more months. The study did not include a sample of average-maturing adolescents.

The observations for relative $\dot{V}O_2$max in both studies emphasize the interaction among maturity status, body mass, and maximal aerobic power during adolescence in both sexes. Although the size advantage of early maturers is reflected in greater absolute $\dot{V}O_2$max, more so in males than in females, functional or metabolic differences may possibly exist between adolescents of contrasting maturity status. This difference is suggested in the results of statistical analyses controlling for the effects of body size variation. When body size is accounted for, puberty itself has an independent additional effect on aerobic power across stages of puberty in males but not in females (Baxter-Jones et al. 1993). Similarly, for the Polish adolescents (see figure 17.14), after statistical correction for body mass, maturity-associated variation in $\dot{V}O_2$max persists in boys but not in girls (Malina et al. 1997). The results suggest differences, perhaps metabolic, among boys of contrasting maturity status but not among girls. Boys of contrasting maturity status and of the same CA differ not

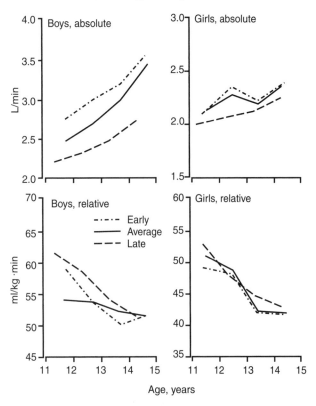

FIGURE 17.14   Mean absolute and relative $\dot{V}O_2$max in early-maturing, average-maturing, and late-maturing Polish adolescents 11 to 14 years of age. Maturity status of boys is based on estimated growth velocities, and maturity status of girls is based on age at menarche.

Data from Malina et al., 1997.

only in body size but also in FFM, muscle mass, heart volume, muscular strength, strength per unit body mass, and basal oxygen consumption. Corresponding data for girls indicate differences in fatness and basal oxygen consumption but only small differences in muscular strength.

Scaling $\dot{V}O_2$max in Individuals of Contrasting Maturity Status

Comparisons of cross-sectional samples of prepubertal (B1 and G1), circumpubertal (probably B3, B4, G3, and G4), and adult (mature) males and females are often used to evaluate age-related and maturity-related differences in $\dot{V}O_2$max adjusted for body size. Cross-sectional studies only indicate differences among the respective groups;

changes are inferred. Only longitudinal studies permit an estimate of changes in $\dot{V}O_2$max associated with the transition from childhood through adolescence into adulthood.

$\dot{V}O_2$max increases significantly across cross-sectional samples of prepubertal, circumpubertal, and adult males and between prepubertal and circumpubertal girls when the data are fitted by allometric models, which adjust for body mass (see chapter 3). Adjusted means are similar between circumpubertal and adult females (Welsman et al. 1996). Although the allometric exponents (k) do not differ among the six groups, the constants in the equation (a) are different among the three groups of males and between prepubertal and circumpubertal and adult females (the constant is not different between the latter two groups). The data thus suggest that $\dot{V}O_2$max increases with age in males from prepuberty through puberty into adulthood independent of body weight, and $\dot{V}O_2$max increases in females only from prepuberty to puberty with no change from puberty into adulthood. In other words, when body mass is taken into account (i.e., statistically adjusted), $\dot{V}O_2$max still increases in boys from prepuberty to puberty to adulthood and in girls only from prepuberty to puberty. These trends contrast those suggested by the use of ratios, that is, $\dot{V}O_2$max expressed per unit body mass remains relatively stable during childhood and adolescence in boys and decreases with age in girls, particularly during adolescence (see chapter 12).

Data specifically addressing the influence of variation in pubertal development on $\dot{V}O_2$max are limited. Among 12-year-old boys and girls, allometrically adjusted mean $\dot{V}O_2$max increases from 2.01 to 2.30 L/min in boys and 1.78 to 1.99 L/min in girls as stage of pubic hair increases (Armstrong et al. 1998).

Multilevel modeling of $\dot{V}O_2$max in a longitudinal sample of boys followed from 8 to 16 years of age shows significant effects of maturity (time before and after PHV), body mass, and estimated level of physical activity (Beunen et al. 2002). The effect of maturity is negative, which indicates that boys with an early age at PHV generally have a higher $\dot{V}O_2$max than those who have average or late ages at PHV after body mass and level of physical activity are statistically held constant.

On the other hand, intraindividual ontogenetic scaling (which is sometimes referred to as ontogenetic scaling, see chapter 3) of $\dot{V}O_2$max by body weight and stature suggests variation in scaling factors by maturity status. Results of two studies of boys are summarized in table 17.12. Intraindividual allometric exponents are greater in a combined sample of early-maturing and average-maturing boys than in late-maturing boys tested annually on a cycle ergometer from 11 to 14 years of age. Similar results are apparent in boys tested annually on a treadmill from 8 to 16 years of age. Intraindividual allometric exponents for $\dot{V}O_2$max are highest for body weight and height in early-maturing boys, intermediate in average-maturing boys, and lowest in late-maturing boys. The exponents in the two studies of boys indicate that $\dot{V}O_2$max increases at a higher rate than expected from the increase in weight or height in early-maturing boys than in late-maturing boys. Among late-maturing boys, $\dot{V}O_2$max increases at a lesser rate than expected from the increase in weight or height.

The results indicate maturity-associated variation in growth of the oxygen transport system in boys. They also emphasize the need for analyses using longitudinal data for individual subjects as they pass from childhood through adolescence to provide a better understanding of changes in the oxygen transport system associated with variation in the timing and tempo of adolescent growth and maturation.

A corresponding study of girls indicates that the increase of $\dot{V}O_2$max in girls from 11 to 14 years of age is unrelated to the increase in body mass or stature (Beunen et al. 1997b). This re-

sult may be related to the common observation that $\dot{V}O_2$max reaches a plateau or declines in some girls as they pass through the adolescent growth spurt. The study of girls was limited to 11 to 14 years of age, and most girls were probably well into their adolescent growth spurts during the interval of the study. Mean ages at takeoff of the adolescent growth spurt and PHV are about 9 and 12 years of age, respectively (see chapter 16), so longitudinal data beginning at about 8 to 9 years of age are necessary to appropriately address the issue of intraindividual allometry of $\dot{V}O_2$max and weight or height in girls.

Maturity-Associated Variation in Anaerobic Performance

Relatively little is known about the effects of maturity-associated variation on anaerobic performance. Upper body peak anaerobic power and mean anaerobic power do not consistently differ among early-maturing, average-maturing, and late-maturing girls followed from 11 to 14 years of age. However, when expressed per unit body weight, peak power and mean power tended to be slightly greater in late-maturing than in average-maturing and early-maturing girls from 11 to 13 years of age (Little et al. 1997). Corresponding data for boys are lacking. Absolute peak power and mean power (W) increased from prepubertal (PH1) to pubertal (PH2, PH3, and PH4) to postpubertal (PH5) boys, but when expressed per unit body mass (W/kg), the differences between pubertal groups were reduced considerably. Nevertheless, the trend from prepubertal to pubertal to postpubertal persisted, suggesting greater relative peak and mean anaerobic power in more mature boys (Falk and Bar-Or 1993). Age varied among the three groups and was not controlled in the analysis. Age independent of body size may be a factor affecting anaerobic performance (see chapter 13). Given the importance of body size and muscle mass in anaerobic performance, the maturity effects are probably mediated through the influence of maturity status on body size and muscle mass in boys. More recently, results of multilevel modeling of anaerobic power (Wingate Anaerobic Test, see chapter 13) in a 1-year longitudinal

TABLE 17.12 Intraindividual Allometry Exponents for $\dot{V}O_2$max by Body Mass and Height in Boys Grouped by Maturity Status and Followed Longitudinally During Adolescence

Study and maturity category	Ontogenetic allometric exponents	
	$\dot{V}O_2$max by body mass	$\dot{V}O_2$max by height
Beunen et al. (1997b) 11–14 yrs		
Early + average	0.799	2.085
Late	0.536	1.824
Beunen et al. (2002) 8–16 yrs[a]		
Early	0.948	2.768
Average	0.847	2.343
Late	0.800	2.117

[a]Calculated from data reported in Beunen et al. (2002).

study spanning 12 to 13 years of age suggested that body weight was the major contributor to peak power and mean power, although skinfold thicknesses had a slight negative effect (Armstrong et al. 2000). A specific maturity effect, over and above that associated with age and body size, on mean anaerobic power was apparent only in the later stages of pubic hair development (PH4 and PH5).

Results of the multivariate studies illustrate the complexities involved in trying to partition the specific contributions of age, growth, and maturity to aerobic and anaerobic power during adolescence. The different multivariate models do not always give similar results. Part of the problem relates to the use of stages of puberty as the maturity indicator. As noted in chapter 15, the process of sexual maturation is continuous and only five discrete pubertal stages are identified. When a youngster is evaluated at the time of study, only the stage of puberty is recorded and used in the analysis. Several potentially important bits of information are lacking: where in the stage is the youngster located (early PH3 or later PH3), how long is the youngster in the stage, and what is the rate of the youngster's progress through a stage. These are some of the limitations of using discrete stages. A more continuously distributed maturity indicator such as SA or time before and after PHV may provide additional maturity-related insights, but such data are limited.

Summary

Children of the same chronological age vary considerably in biological maturity status, and individual differences in maturity status influence measures of growth and performance during childhood and especially during adolescence. These observations are derived from correlational and multivariate studies and particularly from comparisons of youngsters of the same age who are at the extremes of the maturity continuum. Within an age group, youngsters who are advanced in maturity for their chronological age (early) are, on average, taller and heavier and have a larger fat-free mass (especially boys) and fat mass (especially girls) than youngsters delayed in maturity for their chronological age (late) during childhood. Corresponding comparisons of strength, motor, and aerobic performance between individuals of contrasting maturity status during childhood are not available. The maturity-associated differences in body size and body composition are especially marked during adolescence and are also apparent in performance. Early-maturing adolescents of both sexes are, on average, stronger and have greater absolute aerobic power than those who are late maturing. Data for motor performance during adolescence are more variable. Early-maturing boys perform better than late-maturing boys, but differences between early-maturing and late-maturing girls in many motor performance tasks are quite small. Information on maturity-associated variation in anaerobic performance is limited.

Sources and Suggested Readings

Acheson RM, Dupertuis CW (1957) The relationship between physique and rate of skeletal maturation in boys. Human Biology 29:167-193.

* Armstrong N, Welsman JR (1994) Assessment and interpretation of aerobic fitness in children and adolescents. Exercise and Sport Sciences Reviews 22:435-476.

Armstrong N, Welsman JR, Kirby B (1998) Peak oxygen uptake and maturation in 12-yr olds. Medicine and Science in Sports and Exercise 30:165-169.

Armstrong N, Welsman JR, Williams CA, Kirby BJ (2000) Longitudinal changes in young people's short-term power output. Medicine and Science in Sports and Exercise 32:1140-1145.

Barton WH, Hunt EE (1962) Somatotype and adolescence in boys: A longitudinal study. Human Biology 34:254-270.

Baxter-Jones A, Goldstein H, Helms P (1993) The development of aerobic power in young athletes. Journal of Applied Physiology 75:1160-1167.

Bayley N, Tuddenham RD (1944) Adolescent changes in body build. In NB Henry (ed), The Forty-Third Yearbook of the National Society for the Study of Education, Part 1. Adolescence. Chicago: University of Chicago, pp. 33-55.

Beunen G (1989) Biological age in pediatric exercise research. In O Bar-Or (ed), Advances in Pediatric Sport Sciences, Volume 3. Biological Issues. Champaign, IL: Human Kinetics, pp. 1-39.

Beunen G, Baxter-Jones ADG, Mirwald RL, Thomis M, Lefevre J, Malina RM, Bailey DA (2002) Intraindividual allometric development of aerobic power in 8- to 16-year-old boys. Medicine and Science in Sports and Exercise 33:503-510.

Beunen G, de Beul G, Ostyn M, Renson R, Simons J, Van Gerven D (1978a) Age of menarche and motor performance in girls aged 11 through 18. Medicine and Sport 11:118-123.

Beunen G, Lefevre J, Claessens AL, Ostyn M, Renson R, Simons J, Van Gerven D, Vanreusel B (1992) Association between skeletal maturity and adipose tissue distribution during growth. Poster presented at the annual meeting of the American Association of Physical Anthropologists, Las Vegas, NV.

* Beunen G, Malina RM (1988) Growth and physical performance relative to the timing of the adolescent spurt. Exercise and Sports Sciences Reviews 16:503-540.

Beunen GP, Malina RM, Lefevre J, Claessens AL, Renson R, Vanden Eynde B, Vanreusel B, Simons J (1997a) Skeletal maturation, somatic growth and physical fitness in girls 6–16 years of age. International Journal of Sports Medicine 18:413-419.

Beunen GP, Malina RM, Lefevre J, Claessens AL, Renson R, Simons J, Maes H, Vanreusel B, Lysens R (1994) Size, fatness and relative fat distribution of males of contrasting maturity status during adolescence and as adults. International Journal of Obesity 18:670-678.

* Beunen G, Malina RM, Van't Hof MA, Simons J, Ostyn M, Renson R, Van Gerven D (1988) Adolescent Growth and Motor Performance: A Longitudinal Study of Belgian Boys. Champaign, IL: Human Kinetics.

Beunen G, Ostyn M, Renson R, Simons J, Van Gerven D (1976) Skeletal maturation and physical fitness of girls aged 12 through 16. Hermes (Leuven) 10:445-457.

Beunen G, Ostyn M, Simons J, Renson R, Van Gerven D (1980) Motorische vaardigheid somatische ontwikkeling en biologische maturiteit. Geneeskunde en Sport 13:36-42.

Beunen G, Ostyn M, Simons J, Renson R, Van Gerven D (1981) Chronological and biological age as related to physical fitness in boys 12 to 19 years. Annals of Human Biology 8:321-331.

Beunen G, Ostyn M, Simons J, Van Gerven D, Swalus P, de Beul G (1978b) A correlational analysis of skeletal maturity, anthropometric measures and motor fitness of boys 12 through 16 years. In F Landry and WAR Orban (eds), Biomechanics of Sports and Kinanthropometry. Miami, FL: Symposia Specialists, pp. 343-349.

Beunen GP, Rogers DM, Woynarowska B, Malina RM (1997b) Longitudinal study of ontogenetic allometry of oxygen uptake in boys and girls grouped by maturity status. Annals of Human Biology 24:33-43.

Bouchard C, Hollman W, Herkenrath G (1968) Relations entre le niveau de maturite biologique, la participation a l'activite physique et certaines structures morphologiques et organiques chez des garcons de huit a dix-huit ans. Biometrie Humaine 3:101-139.

Bouchard C, Leblanc C, Malina RM, Hollmann W (1978) Skeletal age and submaximal working capacity in boys. Annals of Human Biology 5:75-78.

Bouchard C, Malina RM, Hollman W, Leblanc C (1976) Relationships between skeletal maturity and submaximal working capacity in boys 8 to 18 years. Medicine and Science in Sports 8:186-190.

Bouchard C, Malina RM, Hollman W, Leblanc C (1977) Submaximal working capacity, heart size and body size in boys 8–18 years. European Journal of Applied Physiology 36:115-126.

* Carron AV, Bailey DA (1974) Strength development in boys from 10 through 16 years. Monographs of the Society for Research in Child Development 39, serial no. 157.

Clarke HH (1971) Physical and Motor Tests in the Medford Boys' Growth Study. Englewood Cliffs, NJ: Prentice Hall.

Cunningham DA, Paterson DH, Blimkie CJR, Donner AP (1984) Development of cardiorespiratory function in circumpubertal boys: A longitudinal study. Journal of Applied Physiology 56:302-307.

de Ridder CM, de Boer RW, Seidell JC, Nieuwenhoff CM, Jeneson JAL, Bakker CJG, Zonderland ML, Erich WBM (1992) Body fat distribution in pubertal girls quantified by magnetic resonance imaging. International Journal of Obesity 16:443-449.

Deutsch MI, Mueller WH, Malina RM (1985) Androgyny of fat patterning is associated with obesity in adolescents and young adults. Annals of Human Biology 12:275-286.

Dupertuis CW, Michael NB (1953) Comparison of growth in height and weight between ectomorphic and mesomorphic boys. Child Development 24:203-214.

Espenschade A (1940) Motor performance in adolescence, including the study of relationships with measures of physical growth and maturity. Monographs of the Society for Research in Child Development 5, serial no. 24.

Falk B, Bar-Or O (1993) Longitudinal changes in peak aerobic and anaerobic mechanical power of circumpubertal boys. Pediatric Exercise Science 5:318-331.

Goulding A, Taylor RW, Gold E, Lewis-Barned MJ (1996) Regional body fat distribution in relation to pubertal stage: A dual energy X-ray absorptiometry study of New Zealand girls and young women. American Journal of Clinical Nutrition 64:546-551.

Haschke F (1983) Body composition of adolescent males. Acta Paediatrica Scandinavica 307 (suppl): 1-23.

Hewitt D (1958) Sib resemblance in bone, muscle and fat measurements of the human calf. Annals of Human Genetics 22:213-221.

Hollmann W, Bouchard C, Herkenrath G (1967) Die Leistungsentwicklung des Kindes und Jugendlichen unter besonderer Berucksichtigung des biologischen Alters. Arztliche Jugendkunde 58:198-203.

Hunt EE, Barton WH (1959) The inconstancy of physique in adolescent boys and other limitations of somatotyping. American Journal of Physical Anthropology 17:27-35.

Hunt EE, Cocke G, Gallagher JR (1958) Somatotype and sexual maturation in boys: A method of developmental analysis. Human Biology 30:73-91.

Iuliano-Burns S, Mirwald RL, Bailey DA (2001) The timing and magnitude of peak height velocity and peak tissue velocities for early, average and late maturing boys and girls. American Journal of Human Biology 13:1-8.

Johnston FE, Malina RM (1966) Age changes in the composition of the upper arm in Philadelphia children. Human Biology 38:1-21.

Jones HE (1949) Motor Performance and Growth. Berkeley: University of California Press.

Jones MA, Hitchen PL, Stratton G (2000) The importance of considering biological maturity when assessing physical fitness measured in girls and boys aged 10 to 16 years. Annals of Human Biology 27:57-65.

Juul A, Bang P, Hertel NT, Main K, Dalgaard P, Jorgensen K, Müller J, Hall K, Skakkebaek NE (1994) Serum insulin-like growth factor-I in 1030 healthy children, adolescents, and adults: Relation to age, sex, stage of puberty, testicular size, and body mass index. Journal of Clinical Endocrinology and Metabolism 78:744-752.

Katzmarzyk PT, Malina RM, Beunen GP (1997) The contribution of biological maturation to the strength and motor fitness of children. Annals of Human Biology 24:493-505.

Kemper HCG, Verschuur R (1981) Maximal aerobic power in 13- and 14-year old teenagers in relation to biologic age. International Journal of Sports Medicine 2:97-100.

Kemper HCG, Verschuur R, Ritmeester JW (1986) Maximal aerobic power in early and late maturing teenagers. In J Rutenfranz, R Mocellin, F Klimt (eds), Children and Exercise XII. Champaign, IL: Human Kinetics, pp. 213-225.

* Krahenbuhl GS, Skinner JS, Kohrt WM (1985) Developmental aspects of maximal aerobic power in children. Exercise and Sport Sciences Reviews 13:503-538.

Lefevre J, Beunen G, Simons J, Renson R, Ostyn M, Van Gerven D (1988) Motor performance as related to age at peak height velocity. Paper presented at the Fifth International Auxology Congress, Exeter University, Exeter, United Kingdom.

Lefevre J, Beunen G, Steens G, Claessens A, Renson R (1990) Motor performance during adolescence and age thirty as related to age at peak height velocity. Annals of Human Biology 17:423-435.

Lindgren G (1978) Growth of schoolchildren with early, average and late ages of peak height velocity. Annals of Human Biology 5:253-267.

Little NG, Day JAP, Steinke L (1997) Relationship of physical performance to maturation in perimenarcheal girls. American Journal of Human Biology 9:163-171.

Livson N, McNeill D (1962) Physique and maturation rate in male adolescents. Child Development 33:145-152.

* Malina RM (1996) Regional variation in body composition: Age, sex, and ethnic variation. In AF Roche, SB Heymsfield, TG Lohman (eds), Human Body Composition. Champaign, IL: Human Kinetics, pp 217-255.

Malina RM, Beunen G, Lefevre J, Woynarowska B (1997) Maturity-associated variation in peak oxygen uptake in active adolescent boys and girls. Annals of Human Biology 24:19-31.

Malina RM, Johnston FE (1967) Significance of age, sex, and maturity differences in upper arm composition. Research Quarterly 38:219-230.

McNeill D, Livson N (1963) Maturation rate and body build of women. Child Development 34:25-32.

* Mirwald RL, Bailey DA (1986) Maximal Aerobic Power. London, Ontario: Sports Dynamics.

Molgaard C, Thomsen BL, Michaelsen KF (1998) Influence of weight, age and puberty on bone size and bone mineral content in healthy children and adolescents. Acta Paediatrica 87:494-499.

Paterson DH, Cunningham DA (1985) Development of anaerobic capacity in early and late maturing boys. In RA Binkhorst, HCG Kemper, WHM Saris (eds), Children and Exercise XI. Champaign, IL: Human Kinetics, pp 119-128.

Rarick GL, Oyster N (1964) Physical maturity, muscular strength and motor performance of young school-age boys. Research Quarterly 35:523-531.

Reynolds EL (1946) Sexual maturation and the growth of fat, muscle and bone in girls. Child Development 17: 121-144.

Reynolds EL (1950) The distribution of subcutaneous fat in childhood and adolescence. Monographs of the Society for Research in Child Development 15, serial no. 50.

Rico H, Revilla M, Villa LF, Hernandez ER, Alvarez de Buergo M, Villa M (1993) Body composition in children and Tanner's stages: A study with dual-energy X-ray absorptiometry. Metabolism 42:967-970.

* Roemmich JN, Clark PA, Weltman A, Rogol AD (1997) Alterations in growth and body composition during puberty. I. Comparing multicomponent body composition models. Journal of Applied Physiology 83:927-935.

Rutenfranz J, Lange Andersen K, Seliger V, Ilmarinen J, Klimmer F, Kylian H, Rutenfranz M, Ruppel M (1982) Maximal aerobic power affected by maturation and body growth during childhood and adolescence. European Journal of Pediatrics 139:106-112.

Seils LG (1951) The relationship between measures of physical growth and gross motor performance of primary-grade school children. Research Quarterly 22:244-260.

* Shuttleworth FK (1939) The physical and mental growth of girls and boys age six to nineteen in relation to age at maximum growth. Monographs of the Society for Research in Child Development 4, serial no. 22.

* Tanner JM (1962) Growth at Adolescence, 2nd edition. Oxford: Blackwell Scientific Publications.

Tanner JM, Whitehouse RH (1982) Atlas of Children's Growth. Normal Variation and Growth Disorders. New York: Academic Press.

Thomis M, Rogers DM, Beunen GP, Woynarowska B, Malina RM (2000) Allometric relationship between body size and peak $\dot{V}O_2$ relative to age at menarche. Annals of Human Biology 27:623-633.

Van Lenthe FJ, Kemper HCG, Van Mechelen W (1996a) Rapid maturation in adolescence results in greater obesity in adulthood: The Amsterdam Growth and Health Study. American Journal of Clinical Nutrition 64:18-24.

Van Lenthe FJ, Kemper HCG, Van Mechelen W, Post GB, Twisk JWR, Welten DC, Snel J (1996b) Biological maturation and the distribution of subcutaneous fat from adolescence into adulthood: The Amsterdam Growth and Health Study. International Journal of Obesity 20:121-129.

Welsman JR, Armstrong N, Nevill AM, Winer EM, Kirby BJ (1996) Scaling peak $\dot{V}O_2$ for differences in body size. Medicine and Science in Sports and Exercise 28:259-265.

Wirth A, Trager E, Scheele K, Mayer D, Diehm K, Reischle K,

Weicker H (1978) Cardiopulmonary adjustment and metabolic response to maximal and submaximal physical exercise of boys and girls at different stages of maturity. European Journal of Applied Physiology 39:229-240.

Young CM, Bogan AD, Roe DA, Lutwak L (1968) Body composition of pre-adolescent and adolescent girls. IV. Total body water and creatinine excretion. Journal of the American Dietetic Association 53:579-587.

Zuk GH (1958) The plasticity of the physique from early adolescence through adulthood. Journal of Genetic Psychology 92:205-214.

Part V

Influencing Factors

The preceding sections of the book were largely concerned with understanding changes in size, physique, body composition, specific tissues, motor performance, strength, and aerobic and anaerobic capacities that occur during childhood and adolescence and the specific influences of individual differences in biological maturation on these processes. The chapters of this section focus on factors that influence these processes. Genes, hormones, nutrients, and energy are largely regulatory, whereas factors such as physical activity, social conditions, ethnic variation, and others can interact and influence the regulatory mechanisms.

The integrated nature of growth and maturation is largely maintained by the constant interactions of genes, hormones, nutrients, and energy. Considerable advances have been made over the past decade or so in our understanding of genes, hormones, and nutrition. Chapter 18 considers genetic regulation. It initially describes basic genetic concepts and mechanisms and then applies them to presently available data on genotypic influences on growth, maturation, and performance phenotypes.

Chapter 19 deals with hormonal regulation of growth and maturation. The endocrine, paracrine, autocrine, and intracrine systems and their modes of actions are initially considered. Then, the role of growth-promoting hormones and hormone-like molecules and the hormonal regulation of the adolescent growth spurt, sexual maturation, and the menstrual cycle are discussed.

Chapter 20 focuses on nutritional requirements for normal growth and maturation and the energetics of growth. Habitual physical activity is a major factor affecting energy requirements in children and adolescents. Physical activity, a major theme in this book, is considered in the next two chapters. Methods for the measurement of physical activity and energy expenditure, changes in levels of physical activity and energy expenditure during childhood and adolescence, and the factors that underlie these changes are considered in chapter 21. Potential influences of regular physical activity on indicators of growth, maturation, and performance, including the concept of trainability, are discussed in chapter 22.

Chronic undernutrition and obesity are two conditions that are related to nutrition and physical activity, and both have significant implications for the growth, maturation, performance, and physical activity of children and adolescents. Chronic undernutrition plagues young children in many developing countries

of the world, whereas obesity has reached epidemic proportions among children and adolescents in many developed countries. Chapter 23 first discusses basic concepts, criteria, and prevalence of chronic undernutrition and then the implications for growth, maturation, performance, and physical activity. Chapter 24 discusses the corresponding concepts related to obesity and then the associated functional consequences and long-term health implications.

This section closes with chapter 25, which highlights a variety of additional factors associated with growth, maturation, physical activity, and performance. These factors include, among others, social circumstances, racial and ethnic background, and climate. Although the factors are considered separately, their influences are complex and they undoubtedly interact with each other.

GENETIC REGULATION OF GROWTH, MATURATION, AND PERFORMANCE

Chapter Outline

Growth, maturation, and physical performance are commonly assumed to be affected by heredity, that is, they are subject to the influences of both biological and cultural inheritance. Cultural heredity, or cultural inheritance, refers to shared environmental and social conditions. Lifestyle characteristics that are transmitted from parents to their children through education, modeling, and economic status can have effects on the child's phenotypic characteristics. Cultural inheritance is generally not related to the parental genes and is not considered in this chapter.

Biological inheritance represents the influences of the parental generation on the offspring generation that are mediated by biological causes or genes. A genetic influence or effect is associated with a gene or set of genes encoded in the DNA of the chromosomes in the nucleus of the cells. The small, circular DNA in the mitochondria of the cellular cytoplasm is transmitted from the cytoplasm of the ovum to the zygote and thus exhibits a pattern of nonnuclear maternal inheritance. This chapter presents basic concepts of genetics and then focuses on the genetics of selected growth, maturation, and performance phenotypes. A more comprehensive discussion of these topics is presented in a recent text by Bouchard and colleagues (1997).

The Human Genome

The biology of the gene and the characteristics of the human genome are very complex topics about which more is learned every day. The term "genome" refers to the set of chromosomes and their DNA bases. Given that genes play a critical role in development, the student of human growth and maturation must have some understanding of genetic concepts and genetic mechanisms.

During active reproductive life, females produce sex cells called oocytes and males produce spermatocytes. In both sexes, gametogenesis, the production of gametes from these sex cells, occurs through the process of meiosis. Spermatogenesis is continuously ongoing during the years of normal sexual reproductive capability in males, and each meiotic cycle generates four competent sperm cells. In females, the process of oogenesis also yields four eggs (ova), but only one is competent for fertilization with ample cytoplasm; the other three (known as polar bodies) are lost (see figure 18.1). Male and female gametes each contain a nucleus in which 23 chromosomes are normally present. These cells are called haploid, which means they contain a single set of chromosomes. The female gamete has a single copy of each of 22 autosomes (non–sex-specific chromosomes) and of an X chromosome (a sex chromosome). The male gamete has a similar complement of autosomes, and either an X or a Y chromosome. At fertilization, the nuclear content of the female and male gametes fuse, and the diploid number of chromosomes (23 pairs) is restored. Diploid means having two sets of chromosomes. At the moment of fertilization, the chromosome complement is established as 22 pairs of autosomes, and a set of sex chromosomes consisting of either two X chromosomes (XX, a female zygote) or an X and a Y chromosome (XY, a male zygote).

As cells multiply and divide during normal development, the cell-division cycle typical of all somatic (i.e., all nongametic) cells includes the replication of the full complement of chromosomes before cell division. Members of each pair of chromosomes migrate in opposite directions as two daughter cells are formed. Each daughter cell thus has the normal diploid number of chromosomes when division is complete.

Human chromosomes can be isolated from blood lymphocytes or any other nucleated cells. Each chromosome contains a constricted region

Schematic Representation of Meiosis

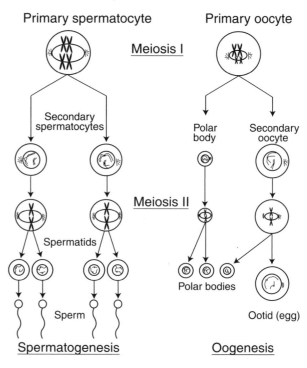

FIGURE 18.1 Meiosis in the genesis of sperm and egg cells. Only two pairs of chromosomes are shown.

called the centromere, which establishes the general appearance of the chromosome. When stained with specific dyes, a reproducible pattern of light and dark bands can be seen on each chromosome. The chromosome banding pattern results from a mixture of nucleoproteins (histones and nonhistones) that are bound to the DNA. Differences in size, location of the centromere, and banding patterns allow the chromosomes to be distinguished from each other, and, in turn, are represented as a karyotype (see figure 18.2). In a karyotype, the chromosomes are arranged by size and position of the centromere; autosomes are numbered from 1 to 22, and the sex chromosomes are noted as X and Y. The short arm of a chromosome is denoted as p and the long arm is denoted as q. Each arm is subdivided into regions numbered consecutively from the centromere to the telomere (tip of the chromosome), and each band within a given region is identified by a number. With this nomenclature, any chromosomal region can be specified by a "cytological address"; for example, 2p25 refers to chromosome 2, p arm, region 2, band 5 (see figure 18.3).

The Human Chromosomes

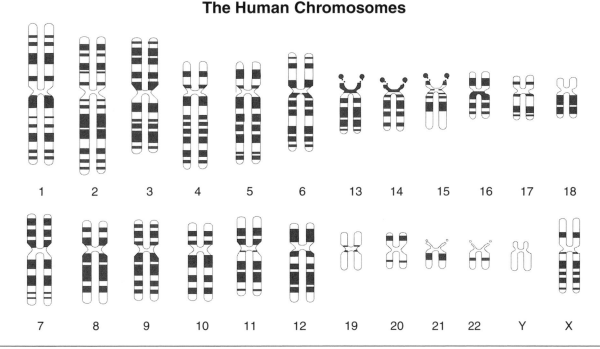

FIGURE 18.2 The normal human male (XY) karyotype. The chromosomes are ordered by size and position of the centromere.

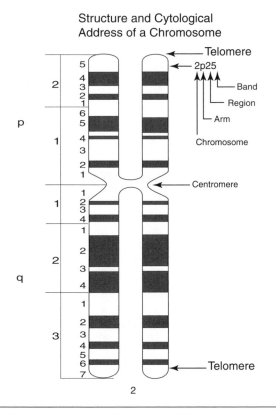

Structure and Cytological
Address of a Chromosome

FIGURE 18.3 Illustration of the numbering system used to specify a cytological address on a chromosome.

Chromosomes are composed of long chains of primary molecules, the deoxyribonucleic acids (DNA), and basic and acidic proteins packed with the DNA. Nuclear DNA is the carrier of information for biological inheritance related to differentiation and growth. The genetic material in each chromosome is a long string of the four DNA bases: adenine (A), cytosine (C), guanine (G), and thymine (T), joined together via phosphate bonds. The order and number of each nucleotide determines the "instructions" for cellular development and function. The two complementary strands are precisely folded and twisted around one another to form a double helix, with the informative base on the inside. The strands of paired complementary sequences of nucleotides are held together with relatively weak hydrogen bonds (see figure 18.4). C pairs with G, and A pairs with T. The 23 chromosomes contain about 2 meters of linear DNA, or about 3 billion pairs of nucleotides (bases). Early in 2001, a draft sequence of the DNA bases of the entire human genome became available on public websites. It was the result of a collaborative effort among several laboratories in the United States, the United Kingdom, and other countries, as well as contributions from private companies. However, gaps still exist in the genomic sequences and only

Complementary DNA Base Pairing

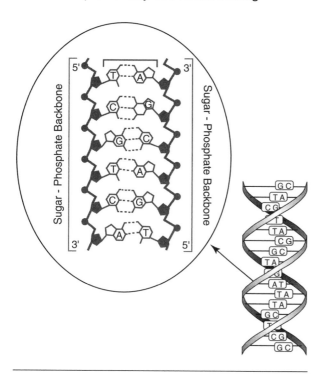

FIGURE 18.4 Schematic representation of the basic DNA structure of a chromosome. Two poly-nucleotide chains running in opposite directions with sugar-phosphate backbones on the outside and the nitrogenous bases inside paired to each other by hydrogen bonds. Adenine (A) pairs with thymine (T), and cytosine (C) pairs with guanine (G).

Reprinted with permission from Roberts et al. (1992).

about one-half of the whole genome sequence has been verified and checked for errors. The task of sequencing the whole human genome, with the exception of some sequences that pose extreme difficulties for unknown reasons at this time, has largely been completed well ahead of the target date of 2004. The availability of various lengths of DNA sequence for each chromosome allows the possibility of going beyond the crude cytological address to specify an actual physical position on a chromosome, with the goal of formulating a true physical map of the human genome. When the sequence for a chromosomal region has been resolved, the address can be precisely specified in terms of DNA sequence or distance in number of bases from landmarks. This designation is now possible for most chromosomes.

Two important events of meiosis contribute to the extraordinary amount of genetic diver-

sity characteristic of humans and other sexually reproducing species. The first event is the independent assortment of chromosome pairs during their migration to daughter cells. With 23 pairs of chromosomes in humans, there are 2^{23}, or 8,388,608, different combinations of paternal and maternal chromosomes that can occur in a gamete. The second event that enhances genetic variation is recombination. Before the migration of chromosomes to daughter cells, when homologous chromosomes are paired, crossing-over occurs. Crossing-over refers to the exchange of chromosomal segments between homologous chromosomes and results in the recombination of alleles (alternative forms of genes) between the homologous chromosomes of maternal and paternal origins. This process is illustrated in figure 18.5. For example, if a pair of chromosomes carries three genes, each existing in two different forms in the population (e.g., A and a, B and b, C and c), a crossing-over taking place between loci B and C will result in two recombinant chromosomes with new gene combinations and two nonrecombinant chromosomes carrying the parental gene combination. About two to three recombination events take place between each pair of homologous chromosomes (i.e., between pairs of chromosomes of maternal and paternal descent) during meiosis. The existing genetic variability in a population is thus amplified by "independent assortment" and "recombination" during meiosis to yield an

Recombination Between
Homologous Chromosomes

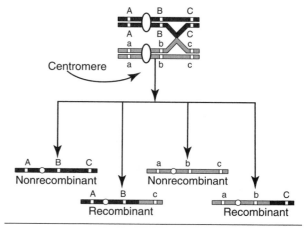

FIGURE 18.5 Consequences of one crossing-over event between two homologous chromosomes of maternal and paternal origin during meiosis. Two nonrecombinant and two recombinant chromosomes are produced.

almost infinite number of different gametes, ensuring the genetic uniqueness of each individual (except monozygotic twins).

The Human Gene

The role of genetic information is to specify the sequence of amino acids that ultimately form all proteins synthesized by the cellular machinery. Amino acids are determined by triplets of DNA bases. The set of all possible DNA triplets and the corresponding amino acids that they form is called the genetic code. The triplet ATG, for example, specifies the incorporation of the amino acid methionine, which also signals the initiation of a sequence of DNA encoding a gene. The triplets TAA, TAG, and TGA, on the other hand, signify the end of a genetic message or gene. The other 60 possible triplets of nucleotides encode for the remaining 19 amino acids with a large degree of redundancy in the number of triplets that encode each amino acid. The genetic information stored in DNA must first undergo transcription, a process by which a "working copy" of the gene is produced, before protein synthesis. The copy is made of ribonucleic acid (RNA), and the resulting copy is commonly known as messenger RNA (mRNA). A strand of mRNA is made by attaching a complementary RNA base to the strand for each DNA base during the transcription process. Thus, RNA C is added when G is specified in the DNA, and vice versa. However, for DNA A, uracil (U) is the complementary RNA base. The DNA and RNA triplets that describe the genetic code and specify the amino acids to be inserted into proteins are given in table 18.1.

The number of amino acids in proteins varies from very few to 1,000 and more, with an average of about 100. Thus, the average protein requires the coding information from about 300 DNA base pairs. With at least 3 billion pairs of nucleotides in the haploid human genome, about 20 million genes could be encoded. In contrast, geneticists at this time estimate a much lower number of genes. The current estimates range from a low of about 30,000 to a high of about 45,000 genes. Thus, much of the human genome likely consists of DNA sequence that does not encode proteins. With the progress made recently in the sequencing of the human genome and the advances in technologies for the study of the expression of thousands of genes in single experiments, the true number of genes in the human genome should be identified in the near future.

When the entire complement of human chromosomes is considered, several classes of DNA are revealed. One major class contains unique sequences of DNA that specify proteins. They are unique genes or genes with very few copies. A second class of DNA contains a moderate number of copies of given sequences. These repetitive sequences of intermediate frequency are thought to include the "housekeeping" genes that are constantly required by almost all cells for protein synthesis. A third class of DNA contains highly repetitive sequences with many copies, sometimes millions, of short sequences. Some of the highly repetitive sequences are found near the centromere region of the autosomes. The role of the repetitive sequences is currently the subject of active research. Because these repetitive sequences are quite variable between individuals and family lineages, geneticists use them as markers in efforts to understand the genetic basis of common diseases.

Studies of gene structure have increased the understanding of the nature of human genes. Such studies have shown that genes can be

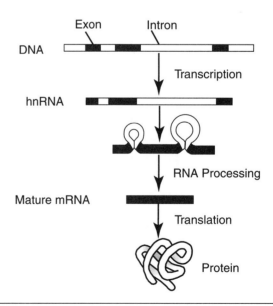

Schematic Representation of the Processing of Genetic Information

FIGURE 18.6   The entire gene includes introns and exons that are all transcribed into mRNA. The introns are spliced out as the transcript is processed into heterogeneous RNA (hnRNA) and then into mature mRNA that is subsequently translated into a polypeptide/protein.

Adapted from Francomano and Kazazian (1986).

T A B L E 18.1 DNA Codon Triplets and Corresponding Amino Acids in the Genetic Code

Condon	Amino acid	Condon	Amino acid	Condon	Amino acid	Condon	Amino acid
TTT	Phenylalanine	TCT	Serine	TAT	Tyrosine	TGT	Cysteine
TTC	Phenylalanine	TCC	Serine	TAC	Tyrosine	TGC	Cysteine
TTA	Leucine	TCA	Serine	TAA	STOP codon	TGA	STOP codon
TTG	Leucine	TCG	Serine	TAG	STOP codon	TGG	Tryptophan
CTT	Leucine	CCT	Proline	CAT	Histidine	CGT	Arginine
CTC	Leucine	CCC	Proline	CAC	Histidine	CGC	Arginine
CTA	Leucine	CCA	Proline	CAA	Glutamine	CGA	Arginine
CTG	Leucine	CCG	Proline	CAG	Glutamine	CGG	Arginine
ATT	Isoleucine	ACT	Threonine	ATT	Asparagine	AGT	Serine
ATC	Isoleucine	ACC	Threonine	AAC	Asparagine	AGC	Serine
ATA	Isoleucine	ACA	Threonine	AAA	Lysine	AGA	Arginine
ATG	Methionine START codon	ACG	Threonine	AAG	Lysine	AGG	Arginine
GTT	Valine	GCT	Alanine	GAT	Aspartate	GGT	Glycine
GTC	Valine	GCC	Alanine	GAC	Aspartate	GGC	Glycine
GTA	Valine	GCA	Alanine	GAA	Glutamate	GGA	Glycine
GTG	Valine	GCG	Alanine	GAG	Glutamate	GGG	Glycine

composed of both coding (i.e., protein-forming) and noncoding sequences. Coding sequences are known as exons, and noncoding sequences are known as introns. Within a given gene, many exons can be interspaced by introns. In addition, specific DNA sequences are required on both sides of the gene to ensure normal expression of the gene and normal processing of the transcription product. Introns and some of the flanking segments are removed or spliced out in the normal processing of the mRNA transcript so that the mature mRNA contains only the exons, or coding sequences. These events are schematically illustrated in figure 18.6. The human gene is thus a very complex macromolecule that undergoes major transformations in the course of its processing. This complexity provides fertile ground for the generation of phenotypic heterogeneity.

From Genes to Proteins to Phenotypes

The role of genes is to specify the sequence of proteins. This role is assumed through the processes of transcription and translation (see figure 18.7).

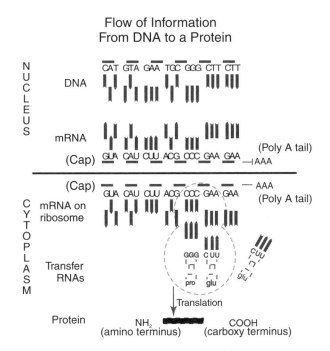

Flow of Information
From DNA to a Protein

FIGURE 18.7   Overview of the flow of information from nuclear DNA to mRNA to a polypeptide chain.

Adapted from Fraser and Nova (1986) and Roberts et al. (1992).

During transcription, a long, complementary RNA strand is synthesized based on the template provided by the sequence of DNA. Intervening and some flanking sequences are spliced out of heterogeneous RNA (hnRNA) and then further processed to a mature mRNA. The mature mRNA then migrates from the nucleus of the cell to the cytoplasm, where it binds to protein-synthesizing structures called ribosomes found in the endoplasmic reticulum. Translation of the mRNA into a specific sequence of amino acids determined by the RNA triplets takes place on the polyribosomes.

The product of translation is a polypeptide chain that will most likely undergo further posttranslational alterations and either become a simple protein or be incorporated with other polypeptides into a more complex protein. Posttranslational events are also commonly controlled by other proteins, such as enzymes, that were themselves specified by still other genes. Thus, the effects of a gene on any phenotype are mediated by the proteins specified by all the genes involved in the related pathway. Proteins are, therefore, central in the relationship between genes and phenotypes. One class of RNA, the transfer RNA (tRNA), is, however, not translated into proteins.

Proteins are ubiquitous throughout the body and constitute over 50% of the dry weight of a typical cell. Proteins are best understood in the context of their functions, which are summarized in table 18.2. Nine types of proteins are indicated in the classification. Several subdivisions could be added, but this classification is sufficient to demonstrate the central role of proteins in mediating the chain of events between genetic specifications and the expression of phenotypic characteristics. For example, enzyme proteins, although very diverse, have in common the capacity to increase the rate of biochemical reactions in cells. An enzyme typically has the property of accelerating a specific chemical reaction, however, with several exceptions. Thousands of enzymes have been identified to date.

As an example of the concepts presented previously, consider an enzyme relevant to growth and physical activity, glycogen synthase, which is a regulatory enzyme involved in the glycogen synthesis pathway of the liver and skeletal muscle. The enzyme exists in cells of both tissues in two forms—a less active, phosphorylated form and a more active, nonphosphorylated form. Phosphorylation is the process by which a phosphate molecule is added to a protein to

TABLE 18.2	A Classification of Proteins by Function
Protein	**Example**
Structural	Collagen, the human body's most abundant protein, is found in various kinds of connective tissues.
Storage	Ovalbumin is a major source of material and energy during embryonic development.
Transport	Hemoglobin transports oxygen from areas of high concentration in the lungs to areas of lower concentration in the tissues.
Receptor	Insulin receptors are proteins found embedded in the cell membrane and exposed on the surface of the cell. When insulin and the receptor combine, glucose molecules enter the cell.
Hormone	Growth hormone, released by the pituitary gland, stimulates growth of most body tissues and has widespread metabolic effects.
Protective	Antibodies are produced in response to the presence of foreign substances, organisms, or tissues in the body.
Contractile	Actin and myosin arranged in orderly arrays in muscle fibers produce shortening by sliding past each other in a controlled manner.
Regulatory	Regulatory proteins influence which genes are expressed and when they are expressed. Transcription factors are proteins that bind to DNA sequence and control the expression of specific genes.
Enzymes	Enzymes are the largest and most diverse class of proteins. Creatine kinase, which allows the phosphorylation of ADP into ATP using creatine phosphate as the substrate, is an example.

Adapted from Singer (1985).

alter its activation state. The phosphorylation of the enzyme is achieved by several enzymes from the kinase family; dephosphorylation is brought about by the action of a phosphatase enzyme. This example shows that the effectiveness of a gene product (e.g., glycogen synthase in one tissue) is modulated in part by molecules that are themselves products of other genes. The resulting phenotype (i.e., measurable liver or muscle glycogen concentrations) is thus dependent on genes involved in the enzymatic machinery. However, it is also dependent on other mechanisms, such as those related to the availability of glucose precursors and their entry into the glycolytic or glycogenic pathway, which may or may not be dependent on immediate genetic influences as well.

Another example of the relationship between genes and proteins is evident in human hemoglobin, a transport protein. Adult hemoglobin is a protein composed of four polypeptide chains, two α chains of 142 amino acids each and two β chains of 146 amino acids each, and four heme groups, which are capable of binding oxygen. Hemoglobin is the most abundant protein in red blood cells and serves to transport oxygen from the lungs to the tissues. The α chain is coded by two identical, duplicated genes located on chromosome 16. Thus, an individual normally has four genes for the α chain, two of maternal and two of paternal origin. On the other hand, the β chain is coded by the β globin gene located on chromosome 11. At the molecular level, the β globin gene has three exons and two introns; the primary transcript thus requires extensive processing before the mature mRNA stage is achieved. After translation in the protein synthesis system of the red blood cell, two α chains and two β chains fold together, binding the heme groups in a characteristic manner to produce mature hemoglobin. Thus, the expression of genes at different locations in the genome must be coordinated so that all components are present to form a functional hemoglobin molecule.

The final shape of hemoglobin is dictated by the physical and chemical properties of the polypeptide chains that enter into its composition. The chains of amino acids, with the support of chaperone molecules, fold to assume a spatial configuration that is reproduced every time such polypeptides are generated. This process is true for all gene products, including enzymes. Under such conditions, two individuals with the same genes for the α and β globin chains will have exactly the same hemoglobin product. They may show differences in the amount of protein produced, but if the structural genes are identical, they will have the same exact molecular product.

Gene Expression

Gene expression can be simply defined as the process by which genes are activated or repressed in response to biological signals from the internal or external milieu. The mechanisms of gene expression are complex. Gene expression and the underlying mechanisms are currently areas of active research because of their potential significance for the understanding of the processes of normal growth, maturation, and aging as well as of abnormal cellular growth, as in cancer.

All cells of the body have the same 23 pairs of chromosomes with the same repertoire of genes. After the zygote stage, some cells become differentiated into bone cells, muscle cells, nerve cells, and others. Such specific differentiation into distinct types of cells from the same genomic information occurs because some genes are repressed and others activated as specific cell lines and eventually develop into specific tissues. Some genes (housekeeping genes) are obviously expressed in almost all tissues because they are essential for the normal metabolic maintenance of all cells (e.g., the genes coding for the enzymes of glycolysis).

An illustration of variability in gene expression is provided by the myosin molecules. The cell lines that evolve into bone tissue do not need to maintain the heavy-chain myosin genes in an active state at any stage of this developmental path. On the other hand, the precursor cells of myogenesis and future muscle cells must be able to rely on the genes for the several forms of myosin heavy chains, which include embryonic, neonatal, slow muscle type, and fast muscle types IIA and B (see chapter 8). Thus, the myogenic cell line abundantly expresses genes that may not be visibly expressed in bone and other tissues and does so in a regulated developmental manner. However, the details of this process are still largely unknown.

A distinction must be made between gene expression during cellular differentiation early in prenatal life and subsequent gene regulation necessary to meet the demands of growth and maturation and environmental stresses on tissues and systems. During early cellular differentiation, genes are selectively repressed in certain cell lines, and the repression appears to be permanent. In contrast, in a given tissue later in life, some genes can be in an "on" or an "off" state, depending on the needs of the cells. In this case, activation and repression of the genes involved are dynamic states modulated by neural, physiological, temporal, and hormonal events associated with demands (or lack of them) imposed on the cells. The membrane and nuclear receptors characterizing a given type of cell determine the cellular response to a particular stimulus and trigger the activation of a gene or a coordinated set of genes as needed. Thus, gene regulation to meet a particular demand on the cells or tissue is largely a function of the regulation of transcription of the genes concerned. Nevertheless, some regulation can and does occur at the level of the protein via translation, the life span of the protein product, sequestration and release of protein products, and other modulators of protein actions.

The Special Case of Mitochondrial DNA

Each mitochondrion of a cell contains several copies of circular, double-stranded DNA molecules composed of 16,569 base pairs. This is a small number of base pairs compared with nuclear DNA. Mitochondrial DNA is able to replicate itself independently of nuclear DNA and has its own system of transcription and translation. Mitochondrial DNA is maternally inherited through the cytoplasm of the ovum. This small DNA codes for 13 polypeptides associated with the regeneration of ATP in the mitochondrion and for two ribosomal and 22 transfer RNA molecules. The remaining genetic information required for the synthesis of the proteins of the mitochondrion originates from nuclear DNA.

Genetic Variation in Human Genes

A question of concern to geneticists is the extent of variation in the DNA base pair sequences of the human chromosomes and particularly in the exons of structural genes. The presence of DNA sequence variation has functional implications. Gametogenesis is characterized by a rather high frequency of chromosomal and other major genetic anomalies, such that about 50% of the fertilized zygotes abort spontaneously early in pregnancy (see chapter 2). This process reflects a strong selection against embryos that have major and debilitating genetic anomalies. Despite such a strong selective pressure, however, almost 1% of live births have a chromosomal anomaly or an overt genetic defect. Such variations are rather obvious because they ordinarily have unique clinical manifestations.

Existing variation at the DNA level either produced during gametogenesis or introduced into the cells via mutation is central to understanding human genetic variation. Because gametes transmit genetic information from one generation to the next, a genetic variant in a gamete that enters into fertilization has a defined probability of being passed on to the next generation. Genetic variants present in gametes that are not successful in fertilization (are not transmitted to an offspring) go unnoticed or are lost. Likewise, genetic variation that results from mutation in somatic, or nongermline cells, affects only the individual in which the mutation occurred and cannot be passed to subsequent generations. Studies of human genetic variation are typically based on chromosomes, DNA sequence, or proteins.

The concept of polymorphism is important when considering genetic variation. A polymorphism is defined as an alteration in DNA sequence that is present in the population at a frequency of at least 1%. Genetic polymorphisms have been extensively studied for genes associated with red blood cell antigens, tissue antigens, serum proteins, red blood cell enzymes and a large series of candidate genes in humans. About 30% of gene products are polymorphic in humans, that is, three out of 10 genes show variation that can be detected by studying proteins, antigens, and other encoded products. Table 18.3 summarizes the extent of genetic individuality for only 15 sets of genes coding for red blood cell antigens and enzymes and for serum proteins. The most frequently occurring phenotype for each of the 15 genetic systems (e.g., blood group A_1 in the ABO system) was selected, and its population frequency in Whites (individuals of European ancestry) was used to compute the probability that an individual will carry the most frequently occurring phenotype for all 15 genetic systems. With this approach, about 9 individuals in 100,000 are estimated to inherit the combination of all 15 most commonly occurring phenotypes. This example considers only 15 phenotypes and does

| TABLE 18.3 | Approximate Frequency of the Most Common Phenotypes for Several Red Blood Cell and Serum Protein Systems in White (Caucasoid) Males |||

	Phenotype	Approximate frequency (%)
Blood groups	A_1	35
	MN	55
	P	80
	CCDee	35
	Se	75
	Jk (a+b+)	50
	Fy (a+b+)	45
	Xg (a+)	65
Serum proteins and erythrocyte enzymes	Hp 2-1	45
	Gc 2-1	35
	Gm (−1+2+3+5)	50
	Km (−1)	85
	acP BA	40
	PGM_1 1	60
	AK 1	90

Data from Vogel and Motulsky (1979). Adapted from Bouchard and Malina (1983).

not even include the most polymorphic genes, such as those of the HLA (human leukocyte antigen) system.

Genetic variation is quite extensive at the DNA sequence level. A base variation is estimated to occur in about every 1,000 base pairs. A single change in a nucleotide base is known as a single nucleotide polymorphism (SNP). In one detailed study of 106 genes, the number of SNPs in coding regions of the genes ranged from none for 13 genes to 29 in one gene (Cargill et al. 1999). On average, a person is estimated to be heterozygous at about 20,000 genes, resulting in changes in amino acid sequence of the gene products. Other types of polymorphic sequences are ubiquitous in introns, flanking regions of genes, and throughout the genome. Variable numbers of nucleotide sequences (e.g., CAG repeats) are found throughout the genome and are highly polymorphic in populations. It is not uncommon to find 10 or more alleles of a given length polymorph in such repeats. They have become very useful markers of human diversity. In addition, insertions and deletions of from one to many hundreds of nucleotides are also found throughout the genome.

The issue of the proportion of genetic variation common to all humans and that specific to a particular population has been the object of discussion for several decades. Most genetic variants are now generally known to be shared by the human species, and less than 10% of the variants are unique to specific populations. Genetic differences between populations or racial groups are thus relatively small compared with overall genetic diversity in the human species, Homo sapiens.

The Multifactorial Phenotype

The preceding discussion has focused on the genetic basis of heredity when differences at the protein or DNA level can be recognized. In such cases, the pattern of transmission of the genetic information can be followed across generations, and the mode of inheritance can be determined. Such determinations were made, for instance, in the early study of the genetics of the ABO blood group system. Such traits or phenotypes are discontinuous in the sense that they are not measured on a quantitative scale, and individual phenotypes (AB, A, B, or O) can be easily identified. At present, the genetics of discontinuous traits is of limited utility in the study of growth and maturation. As more is learned about DNA sequence variation in relation to the processes of growth and maturation, the genetic understanding of discontinuous traits will have more value.

The phenotypes used in the study of growth and maturation are more often measured on a continuous scale (e.g., height and weight). Such phenotypes likely result from the contribution of several to many genes, each with small to moderate effects, such that the discrete effect of a gene or a set of genes cannot be easily distinguished. These phenotypes are also affected by environmental conditions, which magnify the difficulty of establishing specific genetic effects. Moreover, the sensitivity of an individual to different environmental conditions may vary as a function of some undetermined genetic characteristics. Hence, a given set of environmental circumstances may have a strong impact on the growth

and maturation of some children but less impact on others as a result of genetic differences among individuals. Genetically determined sensitivity to environmental conditions creates difficulty in predicting just how much the growth and maturity characteristics of a child were or will be affected by factors in the environment.

Measurements used in studies of growth and maturation (e.g., body weight, stature, skeletal age, and stage of puberty) are complex traits that are known as quantitative or multifactorial phenotypes. To study such complex traits, geneticists have developed several methods. An underlying assumption is that the genes that influence multifactorial phenotypes are similar to and behave like those involved in the simpler, discontinuous traits. The methods can be divided into two broad classes: the unmeasured genotype approach and measured genotype techniques (see figure 18.8). The genetic study of multifactorial phenotypes based on the unmeasured genotype approach utilizes phenotype data gathered from families to infer transmission of genetic variation. These studies are undertaken with subjects having different kinds of biological and cultural relationships based on existing family structures. All kinds of second-generation and third-generation relatives can be considered, including grandparents, parents, children, spouses, brothers and sisters, monozygotic (MZ) and dizygotic (DZ) twins, half siblings, siblings by adoption, foster parents and adopted children, uncles and aunts, nephews and nieces, and cousins. The effects of age, sex, measurement error, and rearing conditions (relatives raised together or in separate households) must be accounted for in such analyses. Such naturally occurring situations are difficult to obtain in practice, particularly at several points during the lengthy period of human growth and maturation. Investigators thus have to compromise to estimate the influences of genes on various measures of growth and maturation. With this approach, inference about the role of genes is made from the phenotypic data.

In practice, the genetics of growth and maturation has been examined primarily through studies of the several different kinds of relatives listed in table 18.4, specifically, spouses, parents and natural offspring, full siblings (biological brothers and sisters), and MZ and DZ twins. These relatives share from 0% to 100% of their genome by immediate descent. However, unless specified otherwise, all live together as pairs of relatives and thus share a common familial environment.

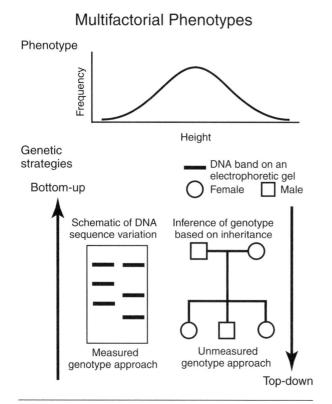

FIGURE 18.8 Bottom-up (measured) and top-down (unmeasured) approaches in the study of multifactorial phenotypes.

Adapted from Sing and Boerwinkle (1987).

From such data alone, therefore, a full clarification of the respective role of genes and of common environmental conditions in growth and maturation is not possible, let alone the significance of the genotype as a factor in the regulation of growth. Nevertheless, several generalizations about the genetics of growth and maturation

can be made on the basis of such data. These generalizations are discussed in subsequent sections of this chapter.

In contrast to the unmeasured genotype approach, the measured genotype approach is based on the direct measurement of genetic variation and attempts to relate the measured indicators of DNA sequence variation to the complex phenotype under study. The markers of DNA sequence variation can be in specific candidate genes, or they may simply be used to index a given genomic position or site on a chromosome. At present, the genetic dissection of complex human multifactorial phenotypes, such as those of interest in the study of growth and maturation of children, relies heavily on both research strategies (the quantitative genetics and the molecular genetics) being used simultaneously.

Genetics of Fetal Development

The genetics of fetal development is obviously difficult to study directly. Considerable indirect evidence, however, suggests that fetal development is influenced largely by both the genotype of the developing individual and the maternal placental environment. The first line of indirect evidence for a role of genetic factors is that about 50% of zygotes (fertilized eggs) abort spontaneously and a high proportion of these abortuses have chromosomal anomalies and major genetic defects. A second line of evidence is based on the observation that live newborns who have a chromosomal abnormality or a gene deficiency (about 1% of all newborns), generally have retarded development and developmental mal-

TABLE 18.4 Kinds of Relatives Most Frequently Used in the Study of the Genetics of Growth and Maturation

	Genes shared by descent (approximate)	Age difference (approximate)	Living together	Duration of cohabitations
Spouses	None	Small	Yes	Recent
Parent-child	50%	Large	Yes	Age of child
Full siblings	50%	Small	Yes	Growing years
DZ twins	50%	None	Yes	Growing years
MZ twins	100%	None	Yes	Growing years

Note: DZ = dizygotic; MZ = monozygotic.

formations. For instance, several mutant genes cause heart defects, sometimes fatal heart malformations or fatal disturbances in heart rhythms (Barinaga 1998).

A third line of reasoning is based on current understanding of changes in gene activation and repression over time. Successful fetal growth is highly dependent on the right genes being transcribed at the right time or being switched off or repressed in the appropriate tissue. Many genes are subject to such tight control in fetal life. An example is the set of genes associated with the production of hemoglobin specifically adapted to early and later fetal life. Several genes that enter into the production of these hemoglobins are eventually repressed at some point during fetal development and are completely silent postnatally. Another example is the developmental transition of creatine kinase in skeletal muscle (see figure 18.9). Creatine kinase (CK) is the enzyme that is involved in the rapid rephosphorylation of ADP into ATP from creatine phosphate. It is an important enzyme in the energy metabolism of muscle contraction. Early in fetal life (about 2 months), the skeletal muscle CK is determined by the CK B (B for brain) gene, and the enzyme has the form BB. Later in fetal life, the M (M for muscle) gene is transcribed in skeletal muscle along with the B gene, and a progressive switch to MB and MM forms of the enzyme occurs. Finally, in adult skeletal muscle, CK is determined entirely by the M gene. Several other gene products exhibit a similar developmental transition during fetal life.

Genetic Influences on the Newborn

In addition to developmental anomalies related to gene or chromosomal deficiencies, weight at birth is the only physical characteristic that has been studied to any extent in terms of genetic and nongenetic determinants of fetal development. None of the studies, however, has adequately controlled for the difference in maturity status of infants at birth. Nevertheless, birth weight is the first postnatal multifactorial phenotype that has been systematically studied. The contributions of fetal genotype, fetal sex, maternal genotype, maternal placental environment, and other factors to variation in birth weight have been estimated. The evidence suggests that maternal factors are responsible for much (about two-thirds) of individual differences in birth weight.

In contrast to the contribution of maternal factors, present estimates suggest that the fetal genotype accounts for only about 15% to 20% of the variation in birth weight. This genetic effect may increase in multiparous women but may decrease in those who smoke and consume alcohol during pregnancy. Smoking and alcohol consumption by the mother during pregnancy constitute environmental insults imposed on the fetus (see chapter 2). These environmental factors, in turn, have significant consequences on fetal genes associated with weight at birth.

Recently, an association has been reported between a polymorphic tandem repeat marker of the insulin gene and size at birth (Dunger et al. 1998). In a cohort of 758 single-born infants followed from birth to 2 years of age, a strong association existed between the insulin gene marker and head circumference. Babies who were homozygotes for the class III allele had larger head circumference than the homozygotes for the class I allele. Moreover, in the babies who did not experience growth catch-up or growth realignment from birth to 2 years of age (see chapter 3), the class III homozygotes had larger head circumference, body length, and body weight at birth than the other genotypes. In those who experienced catch-up growth, no association was observed with the insulin gene marker, reflecting the possibility that size at birth is strongly dependent on maternal uterine factors in these babies who are stable in weight-for-height from birth to 2 years of age. In another study published the same year, mutations in the glucokinase gene of the

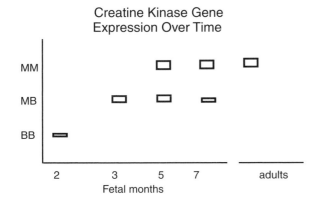

Creatine Kinase Gene Expression Over Time

FIGURE 18.9 Creatine kinase isoenzymes of human skeletal muscle during fetal life and in the adult. The enzyme evolves from the BB form early in fetal life to the MM form in mature muscle.

Adapted from Tzvetanova (1971).

fetus were shown to result in a mean reduction of birth weight of 533 g (Hattersley et al. 1998). These are the first studies showing the eventual possibility of defining the genetic component of birth size at term in the context of specific genes and mutations.

Genetics of Selected Growth Phenotypes

The study of growth is based largely on anthropometric indicators of body size and proportions and physique. Advances in technology have permitted more accurate measures of specific dimensions and tissues. The subsequent discussion summarizes currently available information on the genetic contribution to variation in these phenotypes.

Stature and Weight

Three generalizations summarize reasonably well the current knowledge on the genetic regulation of stature and weight. First, genes associated with length and weight of the newborn have only a small effect compared with genes that are responsible for adult stature and weight. Second, a set of genes is associated with adult stature and weight. Third, another independent set of genes appears to regulate the rate of growth in body size.

Parent-child, sibling, and twin studies have been used quite often to document familial and, in turn, genetic effects on growth in stature and weight. Parent-child correlations between length or weight of the child at birth and stature or weight of the parents are quite low. The correlations, however, increase progressively with age of the child and reach about 0.3 to 0.4 after the adolescent growth spurt and sexual maturation. Similarities between members of twin pairs (within twin pair correlations) for stature and weight also change with age (see table 18.5). Resemblance between DZ twins decreases with age, whereas resemblance between MZ twins increases from birth onward. The adult pattern of twin resemblance appears to be established by about 2 years of age.

The genetic control of adult stature is greater than the genetic control of adult body weight. The size of these genetic effects, however, is still debated. The genetic contribution to adult stature tends to be higher, for example, in well-nourished populations and in Whites. The contribution of the genotype to stature at any age during child-

TABLE 18.5 Twin Correlations for Stature and Body Weight				
	Stature		**Body weight**	
Age	**MZ**	**DZ**	**MZ**	**DZ**
Birth	.66	.77	.64	.71
3 months	.77	.74	.78	.66
6	.81	.70	.82	.62
12	.86	.69	.89	.58
2 years	.88	.59	.88	.55
3	.93	.59	.89	.52
4	.94	.59	.85	.50
5	.94	.57	.86	.54
6	.94	.56	.87	.57
7	.94	.51	.88	.54
8	.95	.49	.88	.54
9	.93	.68	.88	.66
10	.93	.65	.90	.60
11	.93	.62	.92	.58
12	.94	.64	.91	.66
13	.94	.63	.93	.71
14	.94	.65	.91	.68
15	.97	.70	.95	.70
16	.96	.75	.91	.65
17	.98	.79	.94	.72
18	.98	.78	.94	.71
19	.98	.88	.92	.57

Data from birth to 9 years of age are from the Louisville Twin Study, adapted from Wilson (1986). Data from 10 to 18 years of age are from the Wroclaw Twin Study, adapted from Bergmann (1988).

hood and adolescence and to adult stature is estimated at about 60% or slightly higher, that is, about 60% of the individual differences in the stature phenotype are accounted for by the genotype. Environmental factors associated with growth in stature are discussed in subsequent chapters. Similar genetic estimates for body weight adjusted for height are about 40% or slightly higher. These estimates are approximately consistent with the notion that tall parents tend to have tall children and that heavy parents tend to have heavy children. Trends for stature of children grouped by parental statures are shown in figure 18.10. Children of tall parents (TxT) are, on average, taller than children of short parents (SxS), but considerable overlap occurs, as indi-

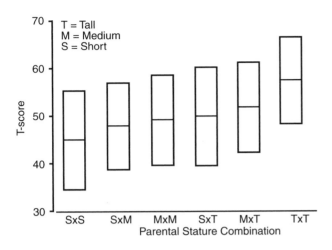

Statures of Children
by Parental Stature

T = Tall
M = Medium
S = Short

FIGURE 18.10 Statures of children (mean + one standard deviation) grouped by parental stature-mating combinations.

Drawn from data reported by Malina et al. (1970).

cated in the large standard deviations either side of the means. Thus, although the generalizations that tall parents tend to have tall children and that heavy parents tend to have heavy children are, on average, reasonable, many exceptions to these trends are seen.

The major fraction of variance in stature has been suggested to be determined by autosomal genes, and the contribution of sex-linked genes, if any, is small (Garn and Rohmann 1966). However, a study of the heights of patients with sex chromosome abnormalities suggests the presence of a gene or genes on the Y chromosome that contribute to variation in stature in males. Patients with an extra Y chromosome tend to be taller than normal, whereas those without a Y chromosome tend to be considerably shorter than normal (see table 18.6). This finding suggests a dosage effect of Y-specific growth genes. More recently, molecular markers on the Y chromosome were related to measured statures in 15 patients with Y chromosome deletions (Salo et al. 1995). The correlations between stature and the deletion

TABLE 18.6 Adult Statures of Patients With Sex Chromosome Aberrations and Reference Values for Normal Individuals

Karyotype	n	Population	Mean	SD	Difference[a] (cm)
47, XYY	14	American	188.6	7.6	+12.1
47, XYY	20	British	181.5	5.7	+6.8
47, XXY	17	Dutch	182.3	4.6	+4.3
47, XXY	52	British	177.7	7.0	+3.0
46, XY-reference		Dutch	178.0	6.4	
46, XY-reference		American	176.5	7.0	
46, XY-reference		British	174.7	6.7	
47, XXX	14	British	167.5	8.6	+5.3
46, XX-reference		Swiss	164.6	5.9	
46, XX-reference		American	163.6	7.0	
46, XX-reference		British	162.2	6.0	
45, X	54	American	143.5	6.1	−20.1
45, X	18	Swiss	143.3	4.8	−21.3
45, X	18	British	140.1	6.5	−22.1
46, X del(X)(p22–32)	13	American	154.1	4.9	−9.5
46, X, del(X)(q13–21)	6	American	153.7	8.5	−9.9
46, X, i(Xq)	8	American	140.4	5.1	−23.2
46, X, t(X; autosome)	7	American	164.1	7.9	+0.5
46, X, Xp+ = Y(+)XX male	11	British	167.2	5.8	−7.5

[a]Difference between the mean of the patients and population-specific reference data.

Adapted from Ogata and Matsuo (1993).

breakpoints on the chromosome suggested the presence of a growth control (GCY) gene that was tentatively assigned to the proximal arm of the Y chromosome close to the centromere.

Few genes have been specifically related to variation in body height. However, a few studies have revealed a likely association between sequence variation in the dopamine D2 receptor gene and stature (Comings et al. 1993, Arinami et al. 1999). The justification for considering the dopamine D2 receptor gene as a candidate gene for stature is that children exposed chronically to D2 receptor blocking drugs were taller. Arinami et al. (1999) investigated an insertion/deletion polymorphism in this gene in 79 pairs of siblings, 8 to 17 years of age, and in 125 unrelated adults. The evidence indicated linkage between stature and the marker and an association among the adults. This evidence thus led to the conclusion that variation in the dopamine D2 receptor gene may influence growth hormone production and ultimately stature.

Bone Dimensions

The lengths of individual long bones and of body segments (e.g., sitting height and leg length) are apparently under a significant degree of genetic control. Skeletal breadths also have a substantial genetic variance, although a more stringent genetic regulation of linear dimensions occurs. Estimated heritabilities of segment lengths are similar to those for stature, but heritabilities for specific bone lengths are slightly lower. Corresponding estimates for skeletal breadths are more variable. Little is presently known about the contribution of genetic mechanisms to the determination of bone size at various stages of growth and maturation (Bouchard et al. 1997).

Recently, interest has developed in the effects of mutations in specific candidate genes of bone mineral density. Markers in the vitamin D receptor and the estrogen receptor genes have been related in some studies, but not all, to bone density or osteoporosis. A genomic scan performed with 367 polymorphic markers from 218 individuals of Chinese descent constituting 153 pairs of siblings was reported for bone mineral density of the proximal and distal forearm (Niu et al. 1999). Suggestive evidence of linkage was found with markers on chromosome 2 with both proximal and distal bone mineral density and on chromosome 13 with the distal measurement only. Genes encoded in the two regions could become candidate genes for further study.

Physique

Studies of twins, siblings, and parents and their offspring indicate a significant genetic effect on somatotype. Sibling and parent-offspring correlations suggest a stronger familial aggregation for mesomorphy than for endomorphy and ectomorphy. The latter results are consistent with a study of the transmissibility of somatotype components in a nationally representative sample from Canada. Familial transmissibility was 45% for mesomorphy, 42% for ectomorphy, and 36% for endomorphy (Perusse et al. 1988). The transmissible component (including genetic and nongenetic transmission) did not exceed 50% of the phenotypic variance, suggesting that nontransmissible factors may be more important than biological and cultural inheritance. For a given phenotype, the contribution of environmental factors may be quite different by age and sex and between populations. Clearly, the roles of age, maturation, and genetic and nongenetic factors in the development of physique need further study, preferably with longitudinal data.

Skeletal Muscle

Skeletal muscle tissue is the major component of fat-free mass (FFM), and both twin and family studies indicate a significant genetic contribution to FFM. In a cohort of 706 postmenopausal women, including 227 pairs of MZ twins and 126 pairs of DZ twins, FFM was estimated by DEXA (see chapter 5). The results yielded a heritability estimate of 0.52 for FFM (Arden and Spector 1997). Two other studies, one based on data from 56 MZ and 56 DZ female twin pairs 24 to 67 years of age (Seeman et al. 1996) and the other using data from 57 MZ and 55 DZ female twin pairs 20 to 83 years of age (Nguyen et al. 1998), reported that genetic factors explained 87% and 83%, respectively, of the variance in FFM derived from DEXA measurements. In the Quebec Family Study, path analysis of familial correlations computed among various pairs of relatives by descent or adoption indicated a total transmissible variance of 40% to 50% for FFM, with a genetic effect accounting for about 30% of the variance (Bouchard et al. 1988). In a study of 65 pairs of Finnish male MZ twins, 35 to 65 years of age, familial aggregation explained 69%, 73%, and 66% of the variance in the age-adjusted cross-sectional area of the erector spinae, psoas major, and quadratus lumborum muscles, respectively (Gibbons et al. 1998). In 25 pairs of MZ twins and 16 pairs of DZ twins, 17 to 30 years of age (all males), the contribution of genetic factors to the variation in midarm muscle cross-sectional area was 92% and unique environmental factors explained the remaining 8% (Thomis et al. 1997). Therefore, based on these diverse sources of data, contribution by some undetermined genetic characteristics to individuality in FFM and estimated muscle mass may be inferred. Unfortunately, genetic data based on children and adolescents are quite limited.

The molecular structure of fast-twitch and slow-twitch fibers differs in terms of myosin heavy-chain, myosin light-chain, tropomyosin, and troponin isoforms. The isoforms of these proteins are generated by the activation and repression of sets of genes coding for these various polypeptides. For example, when muscle fibers develop from early through late fetal life into early childhood, various forms of the myosin molecule appear sequentially. In the case of myosin heavy-chain protein, embryonic, neonatal, and fast and slow forms, all encoded by different genes, are transcribed differentially depending on the age of the individual.

The molecular composition of skeletal muscle fiber types is mediated partly by genes and factors influencing transcription and translation. A central question, however, is whether innate differences influence the expression of the relevant genes and hence the fiber type composition of a given skeletal muscle. Research with MZ and DZ twins, biological brothers, and unrelated individuals suggest that the fiber type composition of a mixed muscle (vastus lateralis), although mediated by the genes, is not completely regulated by genetic mechanisms and may also be influenced by exercise training (Bouchard et al. 1986b).

Allowing for sampling and technical variation, examination of the variability in the percentage of type I fibers within specific pairs of twins suggests that genetic factors predispose some individuals to a high or low prevalence of type I or type II fibers in the vastus lateralis muscle. The mean difference in percentage of type I fibers between a member of an MZ pair and a twin control subject (n = 40 pairs) reached 9.5±6.9%, however, with considerable variation. The mean difference in percentage of type I fibers was less than 6% in 16 pairs, between 6% and 12% in 11 pairs, between 12% and 18% in five pairs, and between 18% and 23% in the remaining eight pairs. The largest difference between members of an MZ twin pair was 23%, which was observed in three pairs and was

of the same magnitude as the largest differences when samples were taken from the right and left vastus lateralis of the same individual (Simoneau and Bouchard 1995; Bouchard et al. 1997).

These and other observations have led to the suggestion that a genetic component accounts for about 45% of the variation in the proportion of type I muscle fibers in humans (Simoneau and Bouchard 1995). A summary of the genetic, environmental, and methodological sources of variation in the proportion of type I fibers in human skeletal muscle is illustrated in figure 18.11. An interesting question relates to the sources of environmental variation in the proportion of muscle fibers in MZ twins. The prenatal environment of MZ twins may be variable. For example, more than 20% of MZ twins share one chorion. The chorionic status of MZ twins, or some form of gametic or embryonic imprinting, possibly accounts for some of the intrapair variation in the muscle fiber proportions observed in MZ twins. Of course, the MZ intrapair differences may also be caused by postnatal biological events or behavioral differences.

The genotype also plays a role in the quantity of key enzymes in skeletal muscle. For example,

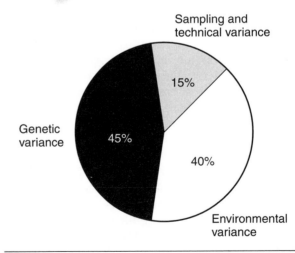

FIGURE 18.11 Estimates of the sampling and technical, environmental, and genetic variances for the proportion of type I fibers in human skeletal muscle.

Reprinted, by permission, from J.E. Simoneau and C. Bouchard, 1995, "Genetic determinism of fiber type proportion in human skeletal muscle," *Journal of the Federation of American Societies for Experimental Biology* 11: 1091-1095.

phosphofructokinase and oxoglutarate dehydrogenase are often considered regulatory enzymes of the glycolytic and citric acid cycle pathways, respectively. The quantity of these two enzymes in muscle fibers is critical for their activities and also central to the flow of substrates through the glycolytic and citric acid pathways and, in turn, to the replenishment of ATP for the energy needs of the fiber. A study of young adult DZ and MZ twins as well as nontwin brothers suggests that at least 25% and perhaps more of the variation in the muscle content of these two key enzymes is associated with a genetic effect (Bouchard et al. 1986b).

Adipose Tissue

Despite the fact that research on the morphological and metabolic properties of adipose tissue has increased considerably during the past decade, whether family lines exist for high fat cell number during growth or in adulthood is still not known. Comparison of rodent strains, however, reveals inbred strains with large or with small fat cell sizes in specific fat depots, but the evidence is stronger for fat cell numbers. The data thus suggest that these morphological features of the adipose tissue are depot specific, and that genetic differences play a role in the modulation of adipocyte size and particularly number under standardized conditions. Data on children and adolescents are lacking.

A limited number of studies in humans indicate that key metabolic properties of adipose tissue are characterized by a significant genetic component. Thus, fat mobilization through the lipolytic cascade in fat cells in vitro is more variable among DZ twin brothers than MZ twins. The same is true for the activity of lipoprotein lipase, the key enzyme of lipid storage in fat cells. Although much remains to be learned concerning the genetic determinants of the key metabolic properties of adipose tissue as a storage and endocrine organ, DNA sequence variations in genes encoding molecules involved in fat mobilization or fat storage have been identified and have been correlated with the biology of the adipose tissue.

Evidence from a variety of genetic studies performed with family members, twins, and adopted offspring with their foster and biological parents indicates that a significant genetic component to heterogeneity in body fat content exists. The heritability estimates for fat mass and other indicators of adiposity range from about 25% to 40% of the age-adjusted and sex-adjusted phenotypic variance (Bouchard et al. 1998b). Data on the BMI of MZ twins reared apart suggest that the heritability may be even higher.

The profile of subcutaneous fat distribution is also influenced by genetic determinants. For instance, in some family lines, upper body fat or abdominal fat is highly prevalent, but in other family lines, a lower body fat profile predominates. The heritability of the subcutaneous fat profile of distribution attains about 50% with proper statistical control over the influences of age, sex, and the total amount of body fat (Bouchard et al. 1998b).

An important adipose tissue phenotype is the amount of abdominal visceral fat. The visceral fat phenotype has been investigated in two family studies and several intervention studies (Katzmarzyk et al. 1999). The studies indicate a strong genetic component for the amount of abdominal visceral fat even after adjusting the phenotype for age, sex, and total amount of body fat. Heritability coefficients are on the order of 50%. A few candidate genes have been associated with individual differences in the amount of visceral fat, including the glucocorticoid receptor gene (Buemann et al. 1997).

A very active area of research at the moment is aimed at identifying the chromosomal sites and genes responsible for the individual differences in body fat content and the predisposition to obesity. Based on a recent review of the human obesity gene map, dozens of genes can play a role in modulating human heterogeneity in body fat (Perusse et al. 2001). Knockout experiments of specific candidate genes in mice and overexpression of the same and other genes also provide strong support for the hypothesis that many genes contribute to heterogeneity in body fat content.

Genetics of Maturation

Less information is available on the role of genes in the regulation of somatic, skeletal, sexual, and dental maturation. The available data indicate a major role for the genotype in the timing, tempo, and sequence of maturational events. Studies of Swedish twins, for example, indicate that the timing of the adolescent growth spurt in stature and weight and their peak growth velocities are more similar in MZ than in DZ twins (see table 18.7). The Wroclaw Longitudinal Twin Study of Polish twins reveals that the mean intrapair dif-

TABLE 18.7 Twin Correlations for Ages at Peak Height Velocity (PHV) and Peak Weight Velocity (PWV) and for Peak Height and Weight Velocities

	Age at PHV	PHV	Age at PWV	PWV
Boys				
DZ twins	0.42	0.43	0.38	0.48
MZ twins	0.85	0.75	0.68	0.76
Girls				
DZ twins	0.39	0.48	0.50	−0.07
MZ twins	0.78	0.48	0.83	0.57

Sample sizes are about 40 pairs of DZ twins of each sex and 60 pairs of MZ twins of each sex.

Adapted from Fischbein (1977).

ference in the age at peak height velocity (PHV) is larger in DZ twins compared with MZ pairs in both sexes (see table 18.8). The correlation for age at PHV and the magnitude of the stature increment at that age are also higher in MZ than in DZ twins in both girls and boys. A similar trend is observed for the weight increment at peak velocity (Bergman 1988).

Sexual maturation is also under genetic control. This finding comes largely from studies of concordance in the ages at onset of development of secondary sex characteristics among MZ and DZ twins, sibling pairs, and mother-daughter pairs. Correlations for the age at menarche are shown in table 18.9, along with mean age differences in the at-

tainment of menarche between members of the same pair. The correlation is highest in MZ twins, followed in order by DZ twins, biological sisters, and mother-daughter pairs. These data thus suggest a significant genetic effect in the regulation of the timing of menarche. Similar trends are apparent for other secondary sex characteristics (breast and pubic hair development in girls and genital and pubic hair development in boys), but the data are not as extensive as for menarche. In the Wroclaw Longitudinal Twin Study, male MZ twins followed from 8 to 18 years of age are more concordant than male DZ twins for genital developmental stages (G2 to G5) and pubic hair developmental stages (PH2 to PH5), as shown in figure 18.12 (Koniarek 1988a). The degree of concordance among brothers who are identical twins is remarkably high. Although not shown, MZ girls are also more concordant than DZ girls for stages of breast and pubic hair development in the Wroclaw twin study (Orczykowska-Swiatkowska 1988).

Skeletal age was assessed with the revised Tanner-Whitehouse (TW2) method (see chapter

TABLE 18.9 Correlations Between Female Relatives for Age at Menarche

Pairs of relatives	Mean difference in years	Correlation for age at menarche
MZ twins	0.4	0.90
DZ twins	0.8	0.60
Sisters	1.0	0.40
Mother-daughter	1.1	0.30

Trends in the correlations are based on several sources.

TABLE 18.8 Mean Intrapair Differences and Twin Correlations for Age at Peak Height Velocity (PHV) and Maximal Increments in Height (PHV) and Weight (PWV) in the Wroclaw Longitudinal Twin Study

	Age at PHV		PHV correlation	PWV correlation
	Difference (yr)	Correlation		
Boys				
DZ Twins	0.72	0.57	0.38	0.42
MZ Twins	0.25	0.93	0.81	0.64
Girls				
DZ Twins	0.75	0.59	0.23	0.36
MZ Twins	0.40	0.87	0.81	0.65

Sample sizes are about 50 pairs of DZ and MZ male twins in boys and about 40 pairs of female twins of each twin type.

Adapted from Bergman (1988).

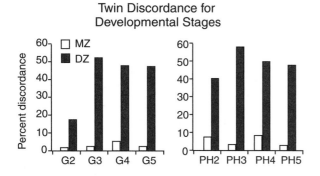

FIGURE 18.12 Percentage of discordance among members of MZ and DZ male twin pairs for genital (G2 to G5) and pubic hair (PH2 to PH5) developmental stages in the Wroclaw Longitudinal Twin Study.

Data from Koniarek, 1988a.

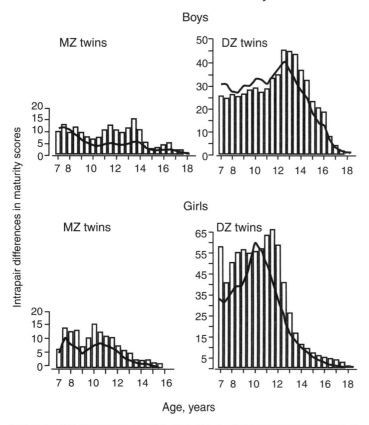

FIGURE 18.13 Mean and standard deviations for the intrapair differences in skeletal maturity scores as assessed by the Tanner-Whitehouse (TW2) method in male (upper panels) and female (lower panels) MZ and DZ twin pairs from the Wroclaw Longitudinal Twin Study.

Data from Koniarek, 1988b.

15) in 55 pairs of male MZ and 55 pairs of male DZ twins and 47 pairs of female MZ and 43 pairs of female DZ twins followed longitudinally in the Wroclaw twin study (Koniarek 1988b). As illustrated in figure 18.13, the mean intrapair difference in skeletal maturity scores is considerably less in MZ twins of both sexes than in DZ twins across the ages at which skeletal age was assessed. The standard deviation of the intrapair difference is also much smaller in the identical twins compared with the fraternal twins in boys and girls. A recent analysis of the Polish Longitudinal Twin Study indicated that the largest genetic contribution to the variance in skeletal maturity corresponded with the age at peak height velocity and peak growth in skeletal maturity (Loesch et al. 1995). The sex differences were suggested to be consistent with a predominant role of estrogen in accelerating skeletal maturation in girls, but the data for boys were supportive of a contribution of other mechanisms. Other twin and familial studies also suggest that the timing of ossification is strongly dependent on the genotype. Some studies even suggest that some of the genes involved are located on the X chromosome. As noted earlier (see chapter 15), dental maturation is generally independent of somatic, skeletal, and sexual maturation. The evidence is consistent with this notion and indicates that the formation of teeth, the sequence of dental eruption, and the age at eruption of a given tooth are significantly influenced by inherited factors. Genetic effects for various dental maturity indicators are estimated to be in the range of 80% or higher of the total variation in children and adolescents.

Genetics of Selected Performance Phenotypes

Performance phenotypes include a spectrum ranging from maximal aerobic power, anaerobic performances, and muscular strength, to specific motor skills, including motor development and learning. The subsequent discussion provides a summary of currently available information on the genetic contribution to variation in several performance phenotypes.

Aerobic Performance

The role of genetic factors in aerobic performance or cardiorespiratory endurance as assessed by maximal oxygen uptake ($\dot{V}O_2$max) has been an area of controversy for some time. The heritability of $\dot{V}O_2$max has been estimated from several twin and family studies, but no study has considered the fluctuations, if any, in the magnitude of the genetic effect with age during the growing years. The most comprehensive of the studies on this topic is the HERITAGE Family Study, which is a multicenter study designed to investigate the role of the genotype in cardiovascular, metabolic, and hormonal responses to aerobic exercise training (Bouchard et al. 1995). In 429 healthy, sedentary White adults from 86 nuclear families, two maximal ergometer exercise tests were performed on separate days, with at least 48 hours between the tests (Bouchard et al. 1998a). The variance for $\dot{V}O_2$max (adjusted for age, sex, body mass, and body composition) was 2.72 times greater between families than within families. Maximum-

likelihood estimation of familial correlations (spouse, four parent-offspring, and three sibling correlations) revealed a maximal heritability (i.e., combined effect of genetic factors and nongenetic transmission) of about 50% for $\dot{V}O_2$max. However, the significant spouse correlation indicated that the genetic heritability was less than 50%. The concept of family lines with low and high $\dot{V}O_2$max phenotypes in the sedentary state is illustrated in figure 18.14. A few candidate genes have been associated with the level of maximal aerobic power in sedentary individuals (see Bouchard et al. 2000a). Moreover, a genomic scan has revealed that four chromosomal regions were likely to harbor genes influencing human variation in $\dot{V}O_2$max (Bouchard et al. 2000a).

High values of $\dot{V}O_2$max are seen in people with larger hearts and larger stroke volumes and cardiac outputs during maximal exercise. These individuals also show resting bradycardia and slower heart rate at a given submaximal work rate. No genetic study of submaximal or maximal stroke volume and cardiac output has yet been reported.

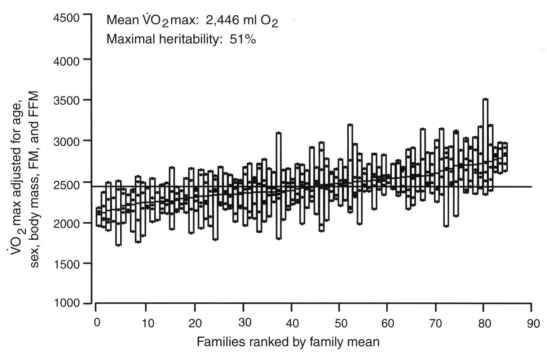

Familial Aggregation of $\dot{V}O_2$max

Mean $\dot{V}O_2$max: 2,446 ml O_2
Maximal heritability: 51%

(y-axis: $\dot{V}O_2$max adjusted for age, sex, body mass, FM, and FFM)

(x-axis: Families ranked by family mean)

FIGURE 18.14 $\dot{V}O_2$max adjusted for age, sex, body weight, fat mass, and fat-free mass plotted by family rank. Each family is enclosed in a box, with individual data points plotted as dots and each family mean as a dash. The horizontal reference line is the group mean.

However, echographic measurements of cardiac dimensions in members of nuclear families suggest a familial resemblance in several ventricular dimensions. Familial correlations among various kinds of relatives by descent and adoption were assessed for echocardiographically derived heart dimensions in the Quebec Family Study. For most cardiac dimensions, correlations were significant in both biological relatives and relatives by adoption, suggesting that both genetic and environmental factors contribute to the phenotypic variance. In 32 MZ and 21 DZ pairs of healthy male twins (Bielen et al. 1991), a path analysis model was used to partition the phenotypic variance of left ventricular structure into genetic, shared environmental, and nonshared environmental components. The data were adjusted for the effects of age and body mass. All heart structures, except left ventricular internal diameter, were significantly influenced by genetic factors, with heritability estimates ranging from 29% to 68%. The strong relationship between body size and cardiac dimensions raises the question of how much of the covariation between these two variables is explained by common genetic factors. This question was addressed in a bivariate genetic analysis of left ventricular mass and body mass in 147 MZ and 107 DZ pubertal twin pairs of both sexes (Verhaaren et al. 1991). Heritabilities of left ventricular mass reached 60% in males and 73% in females. After adjustment of left ventricular mass for body mass and sexual maturity, the genetic effect was reduced but remained significant, with heritabilities of 39% and 59% in males and females, respectively. Bivariate genetic analyses showed that the correlation between left ventricular mass and body mass was almost entirely of genetic origin, 90% of the covariation being attributed to common genes (Verhaaren et al. 1991).

Anaerobic Performance

Data on the role of heredity in anaerobic performance are very limited. Results of a study of short-term anaerobic performance (a 10-second maximal work output on a cycle ergometer) are summarized in table 18.10. Siblings by adoption were not correlated for 10-second performance per kg of body weight or FFM, whereas biological siblings and DZ twins were correlated to about the same extent (about 0.45). On the other hand, MZ twins showed a much higher degree of resemblance in this test of anaerobic performance.

TABLE 18.10	Correlations Between Pairs of Relatives for Work Output in a 10-Second Maximal Test on an Ergocycle	
	10-Second work output per kg weight	10-Second work output per kg fat-free mass
Siblings by adoption	-0.01	0.06
Brothers and sisters	0.46	0.38
DZ twins	0.58	0.44
MZ twins	0.80	0.77

Fat-free mass was estimated from underwater weighing.

Adapted from Simoneau et al. (1986).

On the basis of the data summarized in the table, the estimated genetic effect for anaerobic performance per unit of body mass reaches about 50% or perhaps more of the variation.

Muscular Strength

Several genetic studies of isometric and isotonic measures of muscular strength have been reported, but the results are not consistent. Even when the influences of age, sex, and body weight are controlled, estimates of the genotypic contribution to strength differ for the same muscle groups. The evidence clearly suggests a role for inherited characteristics in muscular strength, but the magnitude of the effect is difficult to quantify. Sampling and population variation, methodological differences, and variation in level of habitual activity of the subjects most likely contribute to difficulties in estimating the genetic effect in muscular strength. No specific gene or mutation has yet been related to human variation in muscle strength.

Early Motor Development

Most of the available research that deals with the role of inherited characteristics in motor development during infancy and early childhood has been done on twins with the motor scale of the Bayley Scales of Infant Development. MZ and DZ twins do not differ significantly from each other in motor achievements on the developmental scales. Concordance in early motor development is higher in MZ than in DZ twins. Longitudinal observations also indicate higher concordance for the overall profile of motor development in MZ twins during the first year; however, between 12 and 18 months of age, MZ twins are no more concordant than DZ twins in the rate of gain in motor development. This finding suggests the presence of shared environmental influences such as environmental pressure for similarity or mutual imitation. Additionally, difficulties in testing young children at these ages must be considered (e.g., stranger anxiety and crying).

Data dealing with specific movements are less extensive. Early observations indicate greater concordance between MZ than DZ twins for first efforts at walking. The development of other movement patterns during early childhood, such as crawling, running, and stair climbing, generally shows greater concordance among MZ twins, but the data are based largely on descriptive comparisons of single pairs of twins.

Genotypic influences on motor development may be inferred from clinical phenotypes of individuals with inherited anomalies. The behavior of infants and young children born with inherited anomalies is routinely screened, and the screening tests characteristically include developmental scales such as those described earlier. Quite often, developmental delays (e.g., delay in attaining motor development milestones such as head control or sitting alone) bring the child to a clinic for more detailed examination.

Delayed motor development is characteristic of individuals with changes in chromosome number—trisomy 21, Down syndrome; 47,XXY and 47,XYY males; and 45,X and 47,XXX females. The degree of delay varies among conditions and individuals and in some instances is seemingly mild. Late walking is an especially common characteristic, often occurring after 15 months of age. Down syndrome infants show a reduction in complex movement sequences related to kicking, which is associated with their later ages at independent walking.

The impaired motor development of children with changes in chromosome number often persists through childhood and adolescence. It is commonly reflected in poor muscle tone, clumsiness, and fine and gross motor dysfunction. For example, 45,X and 46,XXX girls and 47,XXY and 47,XYY boys show generally poorer gross and fine motor performance and mild-to-moderate impairment of sensory-motor integration (Salbenblatt et al. 1987, 1989). Children with Down syndrome also perform significantly below control subjects on tests of strength and motor performance (Francis and Rarick 1960). These findings provide evidence for both neural and structural genetic defects associated with these gross chromosomal abnormalities.

Motor Performance

This topic has been reviewed in depth by Bouchard, Malina, and Perusse (1997), where the appropriate references can be found. Estimated heritabilities for tests of sprinting, jumping, and throwing based on studies of twins and siblings are variable and range from 14% to 91%. Sex differences in heritabilities are not apparent. Heritabilities for the dashes vary somewhat with the distance but do not support the conclusion that heritability is highest for shorter dashes. A recent Japanese longitudinal study of MZ twins of both sexes and paired control subjects indicated that the intrapair difference in identical twin brothers or sisters, from about 12 to 18 years of age, was low and remained low throughout the follow-up period for both a 50-meter dash and an endurance run (Watanabe et al. 2000). An interesting study of parent-offspring similarity in motor performance compared the performances of 24 college-age men with the performances of their fathers when the latter were of college age 34 years earlier (Cratty 1960). Father-son correlations were 0.86 for the running long jump and 0.59 for the 100-yard dash. Hence, fathers and sons attained reasonably similar performances in these speed and power tasks when they were about the same age in young adulthood. These results could be caused by both inherited factors and modeling of exercise behavior from parent to child.

Balance is a skill that requires a combination of gross and fine motor control in the maintenance of equilibrium in static and dynamic tasks. Heritability estimates for various balance tests in samples of twins 8 to 18 years of age range from 0.27 to 0.86. The estimates for a ladder climb and stabilometer (dynamic balance) are lower than those for a rail balance (static balance).

Flexibility data for biological relatives are not extensive. Estimated heritability for lower back flexibility in a sample of male twins 11 to 15 years of age is 69%, whereas heritabilities in a combined sample of male and female twins 12 to 17 years of age are 84%, 70%, and 91% for flexibility of the trunk, hip, and shoulder, respectively. Familial correlations for lower back flexibility in biological siblings and parent-offspring pairs are low to moderate, ranging from 0.26 to 0.43. Although the data are limited, the preceding may suggest somewhat more genetic influence in flexibility than in strength and motor tasks.

Little is known about similarities or dissimilarities in movement patterns between twins and siblings. Systematic analysis of specific aspects of running style during the performance of a dash (stride length, tempo, and various limb and trunk angles) indicates smaller intrapair differences in MZ twin pairs than in DZ twin pairs. In a study of Polish twins (Sklad 1972), within-pair variances were consistently smaller in male than in female twins. The results suggest a significant genotypic contribution to variation in the kinematic structure of the dash. However, the smaller differences between female MZ and DZ twins also suggest that the running performance of girls may be more amenable to environmental influences, including social and motivational factors for an all-out performance. In contrast to the dash, intrapair differences for the kinetic structure of a throw for distance and the crawl stroke in swimming were similar in MZ and DZ twins (Goya et al. 1993). The results for the throw and swimming crawl thus indicate a more important role of environmental influences.

Responses to Training

The response of maximal oxygen uptake and of other phenotypes to training (i.e., their trainability) is not the same at all ages during childhood and adolescence. Thus, trainability is suggested to improve, on average, at the time of the adolescent growth spurt. The role of the genotype in the response to training has not, however, been systematically studied in children and adolescents. On the other hand, it has been considered in young adults of both sexes. Results of one such experiment are summarized in figure 18.15. Ten pairs of male MZ twins were subjected to a 20-week endurance-training program in which the exercise prescription was standardized and identical for all 20 subjects (Prud'homme et al. 1984). $\dot{V}O_2$max improved by 16% after 20 weeks. However, considerable interindividual variation in the gains was associated with training and ranged from 0% to 41%. Differences in the response to the training program were not, however, distributed randomly among the twin pairs. The within-pair correlation for training gains expressed as the percentage of improvement in $\dot{V}O_2$max was 0.82, which indicates a high degree of resemblance in trainability for individuals with the same genotype. The results thus suggest that trainability of maximal oxygen uptake

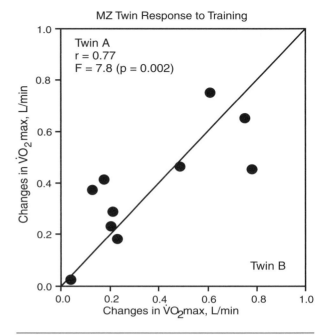

FIGURE 18.15 Within-pair MZ resemblance in the response of $\dot{V}O_2$max to 20 weeks of endurance training. The intrapair correlation for absolute changes in $\dot{V}O_2$max was 0.77.

Adapted from Prud'homme et al. (1984) and Bouchard et al. (1992).

(i.e., responsiveness to the training stimulus) is dependent on the genotype of individuals.

Substantial evidence for the presence of family lines in the trainability of $\dot{V}O_2$max comes from the HERITAGE Family Study. The adjusted (age, sex, and baseline $\dot{V}O_2$max) response in $\dot{V}O_2$max showed 2.6 times more variance between families than within families, and the model-fitting analytical procedure yielded a maximal heritability estimate of 47% (Bouchard et al. 1999). The familial aggregation of the $\dot{V}O_2$max response phenotype is illustrated in figure 18.16. These observations presumably also apply to children and adolescents. One would, therefore, expect high and low responders to regular exercise during childhood and adolescence.

Similar conclusions are apparent for the responses of endurance performance phenotypes, long-term anaerobic performance (90 seconds maximal work output), adipose tissue lipolysis and lipoprotein lipase activity, and activities of important regulatory enzymes of the ATP replenishment pathways in skeletal muscle to systematic training (Bouchard et al. 1997). Thus, many biological properties relevant to the understanding of the complex role of physical activity in growth

Familial Aggregation of the Response to Training

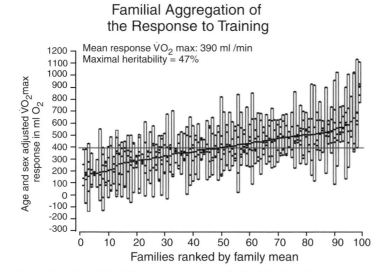

FIGURE 18.16 $\dot{V}O_2$max response to a 20-week endurance-training program. Data are adjusted for age, sex, and pretraining $\dot{V}O_2$max plotted by family rank. Each family is enclosed in a box, with individual data points plotted as dots and each family mean as a dash. The horizontal reference line is the group mean.

Reprinted, by permission, from C. Bouchard, et al., 1999, "Familial aggregation of $\dot{V}O_2$max response to exercise training: Results from the HERITAGE family study," *Journal of Applied Physiology* 87(3): 1003-1008.

and maturation most likely exhibit adaptive responses to training that are determined in part by unknown genes. A few genes have recently been shown to be associated with the responsiveness to training, particularly for $\dot{V}O_2$max response (Bouchard et al. 2000b). However, replication studies are needed before conclusions on their involvement can be reached.

Motor Learning

Motor learning implies improvement in performance with practice or instruction over time. Children and adolescents learn new motor skills or sequences of skills as they grow, with instruction as in physical education or youth sports and with practice associated with every day activities. Planned instructional programs can enhance the development of basic skills in preschool children and more complex skills in school-age children. Guided instruction by specialists or trained parents, appropriate motor task sequences, and adequate time for practice are essential components of successful instructional programs. The contribution of the genotype to the learning of motor skills is not well documented. Results of five experimental studies conducted with twins during

childhood and adolescence indicate that the rate of learning is more similar in MZ than in DZ twins (Bouchard et al. 1997). However, estimates of the genetic contribution to the learning of motor skills vary from task to task, emphasizing the specificity of motor learning. Estimates of the genetic contribution also vary over a series of practice trials or training sessions. Factors that are potentially capable of influencing the predisposition to motor learning are not considered in any of the studies (e.g., age, experience, and current level of skill).

Examples of Growth-Related Genes

Many genes can be defined as candidates for the growth and maturation processes based on human and rodent studies as well as other model species. Table 18.11 lists some of these genes along with indications of their functions and some of the consequences of deficiencies. These genes constitute only examples and should not be taken as a complete listing of the most critical genes for normal growth and biological maturation because currently there is only scant information on the latter and only in animal models.

The evidence for a role of heredity, specific genes, and mutations to normal variation in biological growth, maturity, and performance of children and adolescents reveals that relatively little is known at this time. However, the advances of the past decade in human genomics and the availability of high-throughput technologies allowing the study of DNA sequence variation in large numbers of individuals in reasonable periods of time and at low costs should make major progress possible in this field in the years ahead. The same favorable conditions should lead to advances in our understanding of the genetic and molecular basis of trainability and motor learning. Once the genes are identified, questions will become possible that have enormous significance regarding the effects of the environments and gene-environment interactions, extent of children and adolescents heterogeneity for given genotypes, responsiveness to interventions, and pediatric risks for adult-onset diseases, among others (Plomin and Rutter 1998).

TABLE 18.11 Examples of Genes Involved in Processes Related to Human Growth

Code name	Full gene name	Chromosome	Comment on function and deficiency
AR	Androgen receptor	Xq	Required for normal development of male genitalia; mutations associated with androgen insensitivity syndromes and elevated risks for some androgen sensitive cancers.
ESR1	Estrogen receptor 1	6q	Required for normal development of female reproductive organs; mutations associated with earlier menopause, risk of osteoporotic fractures, and shorter stature; mutations associated with hormone-dependent cancers.
GH1	Growth hormone	17q	Stimulates growth in many tissues, including bones and skeletal muscles; growth hormone deficiency results in short stature, delayed bone maturation, delayed puberty, obesity, and impaired cardiac performance; mutations in GH1 can cause either dwarfism or acromegalia, visceral obesity, and other anomalies.
GCCR	Glucocorticoid receptor	5q	GCCR is essential in a number of metabolic, endocrine, immune, and nervous system responses to stress and other stimuli; complete GCCR deficiency is lethal; low expression levels of the gene affect behavior; mutations in GCCR may cause glucocorticoid resistance and hypercortisolism
GDF8	Growth-differentia-tion factor–8 (also known as myostatin)	2q	GDF8 is a member of the transforming growth factor-beta superfamily; level of expression of GDF8 is inversely correlated with muscle mass in animal models and with fat-free mass in human; deletion in GDF8 is associated with skeletal muscle hypertrophy in cattle and mice; no data yet on humans.
HMGIC	High mobility group protein isoform I-C	12q	HMGIC is involved in the transcription complex predominantly during embryogenesis; it is involved in adipogenesis, with high levels of gene product leading to increased adiposity; mutations associated with lipomas in animal models.
IGF1	Insulinlike growth factor–I	12q	IGF-1 is a member of the growth hormone axis; IGF-1 gene product stimulates bone and skeletal muscle development and growth of other tissues as well; IGF-1 deficiency leads to severe growth failure, sensory deafness, and mental retardation.
LEP	Leptin	7q	LEP is predominantly expressed in adipose tissue; the LEP gene product has multiple effects; it contributes to the regulation of energy balance, glucose and lipid metabolism, puberty, and reproductive functions; LEP deficiency results in overfeeding, severe obesity, type 2 diabetes, and hypogonadism.
LEPR	Leptin receptor	1p	LEPR yields several forms of the leptin receptor; the long form is expressed in the hypothalamus and it is essential for the role of leptin on energy balance; LEPR deficiency causes overfeeding, obesity, hypothyroidism, hypogonadism, and behavioral anomalies.
PPARG2	Peroxisome proliferator-activated receptor–γ 2	3p	PPARs are members of the nuclear hormone receptor family of transcription factors; PPARG2 is expressed at high levels in adipocytes; the transcription factor is involved in adipogenesis; PPARG2 deficiency is lethal in mice; mutations are associated with diabetes, obesity, and colon cancer in humans.

More about these genes can be found at http://www.ncbi.nlm.nih.gov in the OMIN repertory; search by gene code names.

Summary

Indicators of growth, maturation, and performance are affected by biological inheritance. Biological inheritance represents the influences of the parental generation on the offspring generation that are mediated by genes. The role of specific genes and mutations in normal variation in growth, maturation, and performance of children and adolescents remains to be elucidated, in part because of the measures of growth, maturation, and performance that are complex, multifactorial phenotypes. The genetics of growth, maturation, and performance has been examined primarily through studies of different kinds of relatives, most often twins, siblings, parents and offspring, and spouses. The available data indicate a major role for the genotype in body size and body composition and in the timing, tempo, and sequence of maturational events. The genotype also has a role in indicators of performance and responses to training, but genetic effects are not as strong as those for measures of growth and maturation. Much can be learned from the study of children who have a specific genetic deficiency. Such studies reveal that a partial or complete invalidation of a single gene can result in early death, failure to thrive, or a predisposition to several diseases. Advances in genomics and other technologies will make possible the investigation of the genetic and molecular basis of normal growth and maturation in the coming decades.

Sources and Suggested Readings

Arden NK, Spector TD (1997) Genetic influences on muscle strength, lean body mass, and bone mineral density: A twin study. Journal of Bone and Mineral Research 12: 2076-2081.

Arinami T, Iijima Y, Yamakawa-Kobayashi K, Ishiguro H, Ohtsuki T, Yanagi H, Shimakura Y, Ishikawa H, Hamaguchi H (1999) Supportive evidence for contribution of the dopamine D_2 receptor gene to heritability of stature: Linkage and association studies. Annals of Human Genetics 63:147-151.

* Bailey SM, Garn SM (1986) The genetics of maturation. In F Falkner, JM Tanner (eds), Human Growth. Volume 3. Methodology; Ecological, Genetic and Nutritional Effects on Growth. New York: Plenum, pp 169-195.

Barinaga M (1998) Tracking down mutations that can stop the heart. Science 281:32-34.

Bergman P (1988) The problem of genetic determination of growth at adolescence (in Polish). Materialy i Prace Antropologiczne 108:165-216.

Bielen E, Fagard R, Amery A (1991) The inheritance of left ventricular structure and function assessed by imaging and Doppler echocardiography. American Heart Journal Heart 121:1743-1749.

Bouchard C, An P, Rice T, Skinner JS, Wilmore JH, Gagnon J, Perusse L, Leon AS, Rao DC (1999) Familial aggregation of $\dot{V}O_2$max response to exercise training: Results from the HERITAGE Family Study. Journal of Applied Physiology 87:1003-1008.

Bouchard C, Daw EW, Rice T, Perusse L, Gagnon J, Province MA, Leon AS, Rao DC, Skinner JS, Wilmore JH (1998a) Familial resemblance for $\dot{V}O_2$max in the sedentary state: The HERITAGE family study. Medicine and Science in Sports and Exercise 30:252-258.

Bouchard C, Dionne FT, Simoneau J-A, Boulay MR (1992) Genetics of aerobic and anaerobic performances. Exercise and Sport Sciences Reviews 20:27-58.

Bouchard C, Leon AS, Rao DC, Skinner JS, Wilmore JH, Gagnon J (1995) The Heritage Family Study. Aims, design, and measurement protocol. Medicine and Science in Sports and Exercise 27:721-729.

Bouchard C, Malina RM (1983) Genetics of physiological fitness and motor performance. Exercise and Sports Science Reviews 11:306-339.

* Bouchard C, Malina RM, Perusse L (1997) Genetics of Fitness and Physical Performance. Champaign, IL: Human Kinetics.

Bouchard C, Perusse L, Leblanc C, Tremblay A, Theriault G (1988) Inheritance of the amount and distribution of human body fat. International Journal of Obesity 12:205-215.

* Bouchard C, Perusse L, Rice T, Rao D (1998b) The genetics of human obesity. In GA Bray, C Bouchard, WPT James (eds), Handbook of Obesity. New York: Dekker, pp 157-190.

Bouchard C, Rankinen T, Chagnon YC, Rice T, Perusse L, Gagnon J, Borecki I, An P, Leon AS, Skinner JS, Wilmore JH, Province M, Rao DC (2000a) Genomic scan for maximal oxygen uptake and its response to training in the HERITAGE Family Study. Journal of Applied Physiology 88:551-559.

Bouchard C, Simoneau JA, Lortie G, Boulay MR, Marcotte M, Thibault MC (1986b) Genetic effects in human skeletal muscle fiber type distribution and enzyme activities. Canadian Journal of Physiology and Pharmacology 64: 1245-1251.

Bouchard C, Wolfarth B, Rivera MA, Gagnon J, Simoneau JA (2000b) Genetic determinants of endurance performance. In RJ Shephard, P-O Astrand (eds), Endurance in Sport. London: Blackwell Science, pp 223-242.

Buemann B, Vohl MC, Chagnon M, Chagnon YC, Gagnon J, Perusse L, Dionne F, Despres JP, Tremblay A, Nadeau A, Bouchard C (1997) Abdominal visceral fat is associated with a BclI restriction fragment length polymorphism at the glucocorticoid receptor gene locus. Obesity Research 5:186-192.

Cargill M, Altshuler D, Ireland J, Sklar P, Ardlie K, Patil N, Shaw N, Lane CR, Lim EP, Kalyanaraman N, Nemesh J, Ziaugra L, Friedland L, Rolfe A, Warrington J, Lipshutz R, Daley GQ, Lander ES (1999) Characterization of single-nucleotide polymorphisms in coding regions of human genes. Nature Genetics 22:231-238.

Comings DE, Flanagan SD, Dietz G, Muhleman D, Knell E, Gysin R (1993) The dopamine D_2 receptor (DRD2) as a major gene in obesity and height. Biochemical Medicine: Metabolism and Biology 50:176-185.

Cratty BJ (1960) A comparison of fathers and sons in physical ability. Research Quarterly 31:12-15.

Dunger DB, Ong KKL, Huxtable SJ, Sherriff A, Woods KA, Ahmed ML, Golding J, Pembrey ME, Ring S, the ALSPAC Study Team, Bennett ST, Todd JA (1998) Association of the INS VNTR with size at birth. Nature Genetics 19: 98-100.

Fischbein S (1977) Onset of puberty in MZ and DZ twins. Acta Geneticae Medicae et Gemellologiae (Roma) 26: 151-158.

Francis RJ, Rarick GL (1960) Motor characteristics of the mentally retarded. Cooperative Research Monograph No 1. Washington, DC: United States Department of Health, Education and Welfare.

Francomano CA, Kazazian HH (1986) DNA analysis in genetic disorders. Annual Review of Medicine 37:377-395.

Fraser FC, Nora JJ (1986) Genetics of Man. Philadelphia: Lea & Febiger.

Garn SM, Rohmann C (1966) Interaction of nutrition and genetics in the timing of growth and development. Pediatric Clinics of North America 13:353-379.

Gibbons LE, Videman T, Battie MC, Kaprio J (1998) Determinants of paraspinal muscle cross-sectional area in male monozygotic twins. Physical Therapy 78:602-610.

Goya T, Amano Y, Hoshikawa T, Matsui H (1993) Longitudinal study on the variation and development of selected sports performance in twins: Case study for one pair of female monozygous (MZ) and dizygous (DZ) twins. Sport Science 14:151-168.

* Hattersley AT, Beards F, Ballantyne E, Appleton M, Harvey R, Ellard S (1998) Mutations in the glucokinase gene of the fetus result in reduced birth weight. Nature Genetics 19: 268-270.

* Katzmarzyk PT, Perusse L, Bouchard C (1999) Genetics of abdominal visceral fat levels. American Journal of Human Biology 11:225-235.

Koniarek J (1988a) The development of secondary sex characters in male twins (in Polish). Materialy i Prace Antropologiczne 108:239-251.

Koniarek J (1988b) The skeletal development in twins (in Polish). Materialy i Prace Antropologiczne 108:273-285.

Little RE, Sing CF (1987) Genetic and environmental influences on human birth weight. American Journal of Human Genetics 40:512-526.

Loesch DZ, Hopper JL, Rogucka E, Huggins RN (1995) Timing and genetic rapport between growth in skeletal maturity and height around puberty: Similarities and differences between girls and boys. American Journal of Human Genetics 56:753-759.

Malina RM (1986) Genetics of motor development and performance. In RM Malina, C Bouchard (eds), Sport and Human Genetics. Champaign, IL: Human Kinetics, pp 23-58.

Malina RM, Holman JD, Harper AB (1970) Parent size and growth status of offspring. Social Biology 17:120-123.

Mueller WH (1986) The genetics of size and shape in children and adults. In F Falkner, JM Tanner (eds) Human Growth. Volume 3. Methodology; Ecological, Genetic and Nutritional Effects on Growth. New York: Plenum, pp 145-168.

* Nguyen TV, Howard GM, Kelly PJ, Eisman JA (1998) Bone mass, lean mass, and fat mass: Same genes or same environments? American Journal of Epidemiology 147:3-16.

Niu T, Chen C, Cordell H, Yang J, Wang B, Wang Z, Fang Z, Schork NJ, Rosen CJ, Xu X (1999) A genome-wide scan for loci linked to forearm bone mineral density. Human Genetics 104:226-233.

Ogata T, Matsuo N (1993) Sex chromosome aberrations and stature: Deduction of the principal factors involved in the determination of adult height. Human Genetics 91: 551-562.

Orczykowska-Swiatkowska Z (1988) Development of secondary sex characters in female twins (in Polish). Materialy i Prace Antropologiczne 108:253-261.

Perusse L, Leblanc C, Bouchard C (1988) Inter-generation transmission of physical fitness in the Canadian population. Canadian Journal of Sports Science 13:8-14.

Perusse L, Chagnon YC, Weisnagel SJ, Rankinen T, Snyder E, Sands J, Bouchard C (2001) The human obesity gene map: The 2000 update. Obesity Research 9:135-165.

* Plomin R, Rutter M (1998) Child development, molecular genetics, and what to do with the genes once they are found. Child Development 69:1223-1242.

Prud'homme D, Bouchard C, Leblanc C, Landry F, Fontaine E (1984) Sensitivity of maximal aerobic power to training is genotype dependent. Medicine and Science in Sports and Exercise 16:489-493.

* Roberts DF (1986) The genetics of human fetal growth. In F Falkner, JM Tanner (eds), Human Growth. Volume 3. Methodology; Ecological, Genetic and Nutritional Effects on Growth. New York: Plenum, pp 113-143.

Roberts R, Towbin J, Parker T, Bies R (1992) A Primer of Molecular Biology. New York: Chapman and Hall.

Salo P, Kaariainen H, Page DC, de la Chaoelle A (1995) Deletion mapping of stature determinants on the long arm of the Y chromosome. Human Genetics 67:727-738.

Salbenblatt JA, Meyers DC, Bender BG, Linden MG, Robinson A (1987) Gross and fine motor development in 47,XXY and 47,XYY males. Pediatrics 80:240-244.

Salbenblatt JA, Meyers DC, Bender BG, Linden MG, Robinson A (1989) Gross and fine motor development in 45,X and 47,XXX girls. Pediatrics 84:678-682.

Seeman E, Hopper JL, Young NR, Formica C, Goss P, Tsalamandris C (1996) Do genetic factors explain associations between muscle strength, lean mass, and bone density? A twin study. American Journal of Physiology 270:320-327.

Simoneau JA, Bouchard C (1995) Genetic determinism of fiber type proportion in human skeletal muscle. FASEB Journal 9:1091-1095.

Simoneau JA, Lortie G, Boulay MR, Marcotte M, Thibault MC, Bouchard C (1986) Inheritance of human skeletal muscle and anaerobic capacity adaptation to high-intensity intermittent training. International Journal of Sports Medicine 7:167-171.

Sing CF, Boerwinkle EA (1987) Genetic architecture of interindividual variation in apolipoprotein, lipoprotein and lipid phenotypes. In G Bock, GM Collins (eds), Molecular Approaches to Human Polygenic Diseases. New York: Wiley, pp 99-127.

Singer S (1985) Human Genetics: An Introduction to the Principles of Heredity, Second Edition. New York: WH Freeman.

Sklad M (1972) Similarity of movement in twins. Wychowanie Fizycznie i Sport (Warsaw) 16:119-141.

Swynghedauw B (1986) Development and functional adaptation of contractile proteins in cardiac and skeletal muscles. Physiological Reviews 66:710-771.

Thomis MA, Van Leemputte M, Maes HH, Blimkie CJ, Claessens AL, Marchal G, Willems E, Vlietinck RF, Beunen GP (1997) Multivariate genetic analysis of maximal isometric muscle force at different elbow angles. Journal of Applied Physiology 82:959-967.

Tzvetanova E (1971) Creatine kinase isoenzymes in muscle tissue of patients with neuromuscular diseases and human fetuses. Enzyme 12:279-288.

Verhaaren HA, Schieken RM, Mosteller M, Hewitt JK, Eaves LJ, Nance WE (1991) Bivariate genetic analysis of left ventricular mass and weight in pubertal twins (the Medical College of Virginia twin study). American Journal of Cardiology 68:661-668.

Vogel F, Motulsky AG (1979) Human Genetics. Berlin: Springer Verlag.

Watanabe T, Mutoh Y, Yamamoto Y (2000) Similar age-related changes in running performance and growth in adolescent monozygotic twins. American Journal of Human Biology 12:623-632.

Wilson RS (1986) Twins: Genetic influence on growth. In RM Malina, C Bouchard (eds), Sport and Human Genetics. Champaign, IL: Human Kinetics, pp 1-21.

Zacharias L, Wurtman RJ (1969) Age at menarche: Genetic and environmental influences. New England Journal of Medicine 280:868-875.

Chapter

19

HORMONAL REGULATION OF GROWTH AND MATURATION

Chapter Outline

The integrated nature of growth and maturation is maintained by a constant interaction of genes, hormones, nutrients, and factors in the environment. Growth and maturation are unified processes, and factors that influence these processes are interrelated and interdependent. This chapter considers the hormonal regulation of growth and maturation. Many advances have occurred in the past two decades concerning an understanding of the biology of hormones and their mechanisms of actions. Even though the endocrine glands produce key hormones that play critical roles in growth and maturation processes, hormonelike molecules are synthesized in other tissues and organs, and these substances contribute to growth and maturation as well. This chapter initially considers the endocrine, paracrine, autocrine, and intracrine systems and their modes of actions. Then, the role of growth-promoting hormones and hormonelike molecules is summarized, followed by a discussion of the hormonal regulation of the adolescent growth spurt, sexual maturation, and the menstrual cycle.

Endocrine, Paracrine, Autocrine, and Intracrine Systems

The traditional view of the hormonal regulation of growth is that of the endocrine pathway in which a gland secretes a hormone that is carried in the bloodstream to its site(s) of biological action. Because these endocrine products are transported in the blood, all tissues and organs of the body may be exposed to them. The response to endocrine secretions is determined primarily not by the hormones themselves but by specific receptors and other characteristics of the cells of target tissues and organs. Other pathways also exist by which hormones and hormonelike molecules exert their growth-promoting or -inhibiting effects. Figure 19.1 depicts four of the most commonly recognized systems.

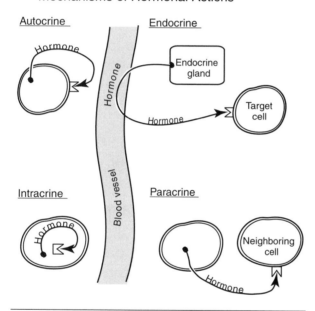

Mechanisms of Hormonal Actions

FIGURE 19.1 Comparison among endocrine, paracrine, intracrine, and autocrine mechanisms for the action of hormones and growth-promoting factors.

The paracrine hormonal system is one in which a molecule secreted by a cell has a detectable biological effect on a neighboring cell in the same or a different tissue. Numerous examples of such paths of action for growth-promoting hormones acting locally are seen. The autocrine pathway is one in which the secreted molecule affects the producing cells themselves. In the intracrine pathway, a hormonelike molecule synthesized or altered to become biologically active in a given cell type exerts its hormonal effects within these cells without, or before, being secreted. Examples of these modes of action are given throughout

this chapter. The endocrine system is the primary focus of this chapter.

Endocrine Hormones

Scientific advances of the past two decades have made expansion of the definition of hormones, endocrine glands, and tissues necessary. Traditionally, the pituitary, thyroid, parathyroids, pineal body, thymus, adrenals, pancreas, ovaries, and testes were viewed as classical endocrine glands. However, the discovery that the heart (atrial natriuretic factor), stomach (ghrelin), liver (insulinlike growth factor–I, or IGF-I), kidneys (erythropoietin), gastrointestinal tract (cholecystokinin and gastrin), adipose tissue (leptin, resistin, angiotensinogen, and tumor necrosis factor–α), and other tissues also produce hormones or growth factors with clear biological effects calls for reconsideration of the traditional view of the hormonal regulation of growth and maturation.

Endocrine hormones usually act at body sites distant from their cellular origin. As a hormone circulates via the bloodstream, virtually all body cells are exposed to it, but only those tissues that have the proper hormonal receptor respond to it. Specific effects of individual hormones and specific sensitivity of body cells to individual hormones are considered subsequently.

The chemical structure of endocrine hormones is heterogeneous. For example, hormones produced by the pituitary, parathyroid, and pancreas are proteins or derivatives of proteins. Such hormones need to interact with cell surface receptors to induce a cellular response. They do not enter the cells. A second class of endocrine hormones includes those elaborated in the testes, ovaries, and adrenal cortex. They are steroids, derivatives of cholesterol, and are subdivided into the sex steroids and the adrenal steroids. Steroid hormones bind to receptors within the cell cytoplasm. The hormone-receptor complexes are then translocated into the cell nucleus where they elicit a response mediated by the expression of genes. The nature of the genes is defined by the hormone-receptor complex and called nuclear receptor–mediated gene expression. This process is the most common mechanism of action for steroid hormones. However, evidence exists that estrogens may also elicit a cellular response independent of the nuclear receptor–mediated expression of genes. Finally, hormones produced by the adrenal medulla and thyroid are amines derived from amino acid precursors. Their mechanisms of action vary and include cell surface receptors for some (e.g., epinephrine) and nuclear receptors for others (e.g., thyroxine).

Figure 19.2 depicts two categories of mechanisms commonly observed when the action of endocrine hormones is defined at the cellular level. The illustrations constitute a simplified version of the complex chain of events taking place when a hormone elicits a cellular response. In reality, the mode of action of endocrine hormones and the pathways of biological responses are diverse.

Hormones that do not enter the cell (e.g., insulin, catecholamines, and prostaglandins) bind to receptors on the cell membrane (Wilson 1998; Carr 1998). The hormone-receptor complex on the cell surface influences the activity of membrane enzyme systems, specific membrane channels involved in ion movement, or other systems. Thus, the binding of the hormone and the cell membrane receptor triggers a series of events in the cytoplasm (rapid response) and may also influence subsequent gene expression (slow response). The membrane-bound adenylyl cyclase system is a classic example of a system responsive to circulating hormones that do not cross the cell membrane. A given hormone-receptor complex triggers one of the G protein pathways leading to activation or inhibition of the adenylyl cyclase system. For instance, catecholamines bound to the β-2 adrenergic receptor activate G protein "s," which leads to an increase in the activity of the adenylyl cyclase complex, resulting in the increased production of cyclic AMP (also known as the second messenger). Levels of cyclic AMP are involved in the regulation of a cascade of cytoplasmic enzymatic reactions associated with a variety of cellular responses.

Another example of a cell surface–mediated hormonal response occurs with insulin. The insulin receptor is a member of the protein tyrosine kinase family. When insulin binds to the external component of the receptor molecule at specific sites, the intramembrane domain of the receptor becomes activated and undergoes autophosphorylation. Phosphorylation of a number of cytosolic proteins ensues. These and other events are associated with the translocation of glucose transporters to the plasma membrane, where they facilitate insulin-mediated glucose uptake, alterations in enzyme activities, and activation of specific glucose-related metabolic pathways, to name a few.

Steroid and thyroid hormones, in contrast, exert their effects through different kinds of cellular mechanisms. Thyroid hormones bind to cell surface molecules and are internalized. They enter the cell, translocate to the nucleus, and bind to thyroid hormone–specific nuclear receptors on chromosomes in the nucleus, where they influence the transcription of defined genes. On the other hand, steroid hormones readily penetrate the cell membrane. Inside the cell, they bind to translocator molecules and migrate

Two Mechanisms of Hormonal Actions

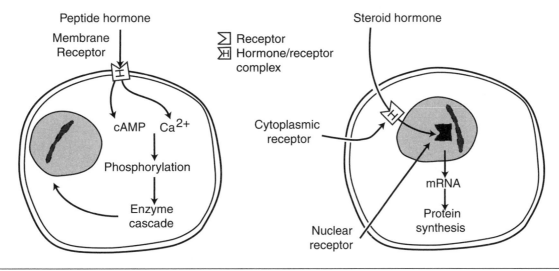

FIGURE 19.2   Schematic illustration of two mechanisms of action of hormones. Left panel: peptides or catecholamines; right panel: steroid hormones.

to the nucleus. Receptor-steroid complexes are then formed and bind to specific chromosomal sites, thereby influencing the transcription of the related genes.

The number of receptors per cell varies considerably among tissues and changes throughout life. Receptor concentration per cell for selected hormones increases (i.e., up-regulates) during growth and puberty, and decreases (i.e., down-regulates) during aging. Receptor concentration is also influenced by circulating hormones. For example, receptors for the development of the beard during male adolescence are not present during the surge of testosterone production. Testosterone apparently induces the later development of the hormonal receptors that are necessary for the development of the beard, which occurs rather late in the sequence of events characterizing male puberty (see chapter 15). The number of receptors for a particular hormone may also decrease (i.e., they are down-regulated), as a result of sustained hormonal stimulation or elevated hormone concentration.

Receptors are also specific for the hormones that will bind with them. Once the hormone binds with the appropriate receptor on the cell membrane or in the cell, forming a hormone-receptor complex, the physiological responses of the target tissue or organ are initiated. Thus, considerable potential exists for modulation of responses and, in turn, for variation in growth and maturation. This potential reflects not only variation in circulating hormone levels but also variation in receptor numbers, receptor affinity for the circulating hormones, and responsiveness of target cells. In some inherited diseases, a receptor is locked in the "on" position even in the absence of the appropriate hormone. Some of these diseases influence growth and maturation.

The actions of hormones are basically regulatory, and they can be included in one or another of three broad categories:

1. *Morphogenesis.* Hormones regulate the physical growth and maturation of the individual, that is, the rate of growth of the body and its parts and the maturation of the gonads and secondary sex characteristics. Some growth occurs in the absence of growth-promoting hormones; however, these hormones are necessary for the full expression of the intrinsic growth pattern of body tissues.

2. *Integration.* Through circulation in virtually all parts of the body, hormones are a part of complex mechanisms that integrate the activities of the body as a whole in response to internal or external stimuli, such as adaptive reactions in response to stressful situations.

3. *Maintenance.* Hormones act to maintain the internal environment of the body, for example, calcium, salt, and water balance and the disposition of available nutrients or substrates such as blood glucose.

Several endocrine hormones play key roles in growth and maturation, particularly growth hormone, thyroid hormones, insulin, and sex steroid hormones. The biology of these hormones and their influences on growth and maturation are reviewed later in the chapter.

Other Growth-Promoting Factors and Hormones

In recent decades, other growth-promoting molecules have been isolated and studied. The biology of these growth factors is one of the most dynamic fields of research. It has implications for growth and aging and recovery from injury, burn, surgery, atherosclerosis, cancer, and several other disease conditions and therapeutic modalities as well. Growth-promoting factors are secreted by many tissues of the body or by only one or a few types of cells, and they have systemic or highly localized effects. In general, growth factors are highly potent molecules that act through complex cascades of molecular events. They can also be potentiated by other growth-promoting molecules or inhibited by counterregulatory factors.

The most important growth factors include fibroblast growth factor, epidermal growth factor, nerve growth factor, platelet-derived growth factor, transforming growth factor, osteoclast growth factor, vascular endothelial growth factor, tumor necrosis factor, and insulinlike growth factors, among others. Of particular importance for growth and maturation are the insulinlike growth factors (IGF-I and IGF-II) and their binding proteins. They are considered later in the chapter. These growth-promoting molecules are highly potent, can act in a paracrine or an autocrine fashion, and may serve as second messengers for some of the endocrine hormones.

Most of the hormones secreted by the endocrine glands have likely been identified. The human genes for these hormones have been cloned, and the encoded hormones can be produced in large enough quantities for detailed studies. Some of these hormones, including growth hormone and insulin, are even commercially manufactured and made available for veterinary and human treatment purposes.

Hypothalamic and Pituitary Hormones

The hypothalamus modulates the release of several anterior pituitary hormones by secreting a series of releasing hormones into the hypothalamic-pituitary venous portal system, which drains directly into the anterior pituitary venous plexus. These releasing hormones include growth hormone–releasing hormone (GHRH), somatotropin releasing–inhibiting factor (SRIF), thyrotropin-releasing hormone (TRH), corticotropin-releasing hormone (CRH), and gonadotropin-releasing hormones (GnRH). The latter includes luteinizing hormone–releasing hormone (LHRH) and perhaps a follicle stimulating hormone–releasing hormone (FSHRH), which has been identified in several animal species but thus far not in humans. These hypothalamic releasing hormones or factors are secreted from specific hypothalamic neurons into the vascular network of the pituitary portal system. SRIF, or somatostatin, is a 14 amino acid peptide that inhibits the release of growth hormone from the anterior pituitary. Other releasing factors for other pituitary hormones exist, but those indicated previously are specifically involved in the neuroendocrine regulation of growth and maturation.

The hypothalamic hormones are released in episodic secretory bursts whose frequencies and amplitudes vary from hormone to hormone. Factors regulating the secretion of the hypothalamic hormones are not yet fully understood, but they appear to include intrinsic properties of specialized hypothalamic neurons, influences of other neural pathways, feedback inhibition from circulating hormones, circadian factors, and undoubtedly other ambient and environmental conditions. Because the nervous system is involved in the regulation of the release of these hormones, the term neuroendocrine is commonly used.

The pituitary gland or hypophysis is considered a key gland in the regulation of growth and maturation. It is located at the base of the brain in the sella turcica of the sphenoid bone. The pituitary is connected to the hypothalamus by a stalk, the pituitary stalk (see figure 19.3). The

pituitary gland has two distinct lobes, the anterior pituitary and the posterior pituitary, which are two different glands. The anterior pituitary is especially important in the regulation of growth and maturation. Six of the hormones identified as arising from the anterior pituitary are important in the context of growth and maturation: somatotropin (growth hormone), corticotropin (adrenocorticotropic hormone), thyrotropin (thyroid-stimulating hormone), two gonadotropins (follicle-stimulating hormone and luteinizing hormone), and prolactin.

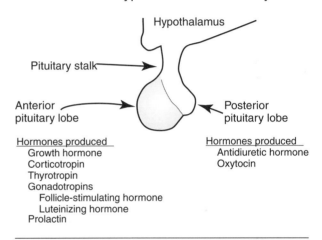

Relation of Hypothalamus to Pituitary

Hypothalamus

Pituitary stalk

Anterior pituitary lobe

Posterior pituitary lobe

Hormones produced
Growth hormone
Corticotropin
Thyrotropin
Gonadotropins
Follicle-stimulating hormone
Luteinizing hormone
Prolactin

Hormones produced
Antidiuretic hormone
Oxytocin

FIGURE 19.3 Schematic illustration of the relationship between the hypothalamus and pituitary gland.

With the exception of growth hormone (and its inhibitor somatostatin), which has general effects throughout the body, the hormones of the anterior pituitary stimulate and maintain the functional activity of other endocrine glands. Thus, thyrotropin controls the secretion of the thyroid gland, corticotropin controls the secretion of several hormones of the adrenal cortex, and the gonadotropins control the hormone production of ovaries and testes in females and males, respectively. The trophic hormones from the anterior pituitary are essential for the adequate expression of the hormones produced by the target glands (i.e., the specific gland influenced by a given trophic hormone). In the absence of the trophic hormone, a gland is completely inactive or it produces such small amounts of a particular hormone that it is ineffective in bringing about the expected physiological effect on the body. Each of the hormones produced by the anterior pituitary is considered in more detail in the next paragraph.

The posterior lobe of the pituitary is not directly related to growth and maturation, but it influences various body functions. It produces several hormones, and two are of special interest. Antidiuretic hormone (vasopressin) is involved in the regulation of water balance by controlling the rate of water excretion in the urine. Oxytocin is related to reproduction. It acts to increase the motility of the uterus, especially in the terminal aspects of gestation, and to enhance the milk letdown reflex of the breast after delivery of a newborn.

A general outline of the relationships among the hypothalamus, the anterior pituitary gland, and other endocrine glands is schematically illustrated in figure 19.4. Pituitary hormones are under hypothalamic control, mediated by releasing hormones. The hypothalamic releasing hormones flow down the pituitary stalk, through a portal venous system, to reach the anterior pituitary, where they rapidly stimulate the release of specific trophic hormones. The released hormones enter the systemic circulation and directly stimulate the appropriate target gland or organ. In turn, the target gland produces and secretes its respective hormone into circulation. The circulating hormone is usually in low concentration. It is generally bound to proteins, but a fraction also circulates in a free, unbound state. Testosterone, for example, is more active in the free state than in the protein-bound state, as is also true for other hormones. An exception to this general principle is IGF-I. In some instances, the bound IGF-I is actually more potent. The hormone released by the target gland is thus transported via the circulation to target organs or tissues to carry out its metabolic activities. The circulating hormone also feeds back to the hypothalamus and anterior pituitary, where it generally inhibits the output of releasing factors by the hypothalamus and trophic hormones by the anterior pituitary.

This type of feedback control of hormone secretion is called negative feedback. It is negative in the sense that glands tend to oversecrete. However, when the physiological effect of the specific hormone is attained, information is fed back in some way to the gland producing the hormone, that is, via the lack of trophic hormone from the anterior pituitary or some other mechanisms (e.g., counterregulatory hormones), and further secretion of the hormone is checked. On the other hand, when the gland undersecretes its hormone, the quantities of the hormone in circulation are insufficient to maintain its physiological effects. As a result, feedback decreases (e.g., diminished feedback to the hypothalamus). Then increased output of the specific releasing factor from the hypothalamus and corresponding trophic hormone from the anterior pituitary follows. The gland is thus stimulated to secrete more of its hormone into circulation.

Growth Hormone and Related Growth Factors

The synthesis and secretion of growth hormone (GH) by the anterior pituitary is regulated primarily by the hormones produced within the hypothalamus: growth hormone–releasing hormone (GHRH), which stimulates its production, and somatotropin release-inhibiting factor (SRIF, or somatostatin), which inhibits its production. These two modulators of GH synthesis and secretion bind to specific cell surface receptors in the anterior pituitary somatotropic cells, activate the adenylate cyclase cascade, and increase cyclic AMP levels leading to a stimulation or an inhibition of GH synthesis. Growth hormone is a peptide hormone of 191 amino acids. It circulates in the blood after its secretion by the anterior pituitary in a free form or bound to a GH binding protein. In adults, about 50% of GH is in the unbound form. The levels of the binding protein are low at birth but increase rapidly throughout

Schematic Relations Between Hypothalamus, Anterior Pituitary, and Other Endocrine Glands

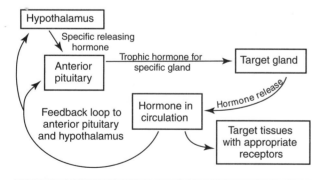

FIGURE 19.4 Schematic illustration of the relationships among the hypothalamus, the anterior pituitary, and target glands and tissues, with feedback loops.

childhood. The values of the binding protein are generally stable during adolescence. The levels are low in undernourished children, high in overweight and obese children, and decline with weight reduction (Root 1994). Target tissues for GH harbor a specific cell surface GH receptor that binds the hormone to initiate a cellular response.

Growth hormone influences protein, carbohydrate, and fat metabolism. It decreases the rate of carbohydrate uptake and utilization by tissues and enhances the mobilization of lipids from adipose tissue depots in the body to meet energy needs. These actions of GH can be seen as predominantly antagonistic to those of insulin. They are obviously important during growth but are also essential throughout life, especially for normal body composition and distribution of body fat.

The growth-promoting effects of GH result from direct biological effects of the hormone on specific tissues and also from effects that are mediated by the insulinlike growth factors. Insulinlike growth factors are strong growth-promoting molecules. Two such molecules are IGF-I and IGF-II. IGF-II plays a role especially during fetal life. It is involved in muscle differentiation and organogenesis. The role of IGF-II during postnatal life is not yet fully understood.

IGF-I is of particular interest in the regulation of linear growth. It is produced primarily in the liver but also in other tissues in response to stimulation by GH. The interactions between GH and IGF-I are complex. Some of the relationships are depicted in figure 19.5. Briefly, GH has direct effects on tissues (endocrine functions) but also stimulates the production of IGF-I in the liver and other cells. IGF-I, in turn, enters the circulation leading to growth-promoting effects at a distance from the site of production. IGF-I also has paracrine and autocrine effects near or at the site of synthesis. IGF-I stimulates protein synthesis and increases cell proliferation (mitosis) in many tissues of the body. It is thus a potent mitogen. As a result, nitrogen retention, cell division, and build-up of tissue (i.e., anabolism) occur.

IGF-I has at least six binding proteins. Less than 5% of circulating IGF-I is free; the rest is bound to IGF binding proteins and the majority to IGF binding protein–3. The binding proteins prolong the life of IGF-I in the blood and also enhance its activity. Circulating levels of IGF-I reflect levels of GH, that is, the more GH in cir-

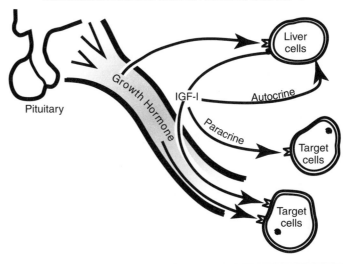

Interactions Between Growth Hormone and IGF-I

FIGURE 19.5 Interactions between growth hormone and IGF-I and autocrine, paracrine, and endocrine effects of IGF-I. The binding proteins for GH and IGF-I are not shown.

culation, the greater the amount of IGF-I. On the target cell surface is an IGF-I receptor to which the free and bound IGF-I can dock. The biology of this GH-dependent growth enhancer is complex and only partially understood at present.

The growth factor IGF-I is most active in cartilage. The growth-stimulating effect of IGF-I involves the proliferation of cartilage cells at the growth plates of long bones, resulting in linear growth (see chapter 7). The growth-stimulating effect of IGF-I at the growth plates of long bones occurs without accelerating skeletal maturation or fusion of the epiphyses. The net result is growth in length of individual bones and, in turn, stature, without accelerating skeletal maturation.

Small amounts of GH are present in the fetal pituitary gland by midgestation (about 1 to 3 milliunits per mg of pituitary tissue). The amount increases considerably by the last 2 months of a full-term pregnancy (about fivefold per mg of pituitary). Although GH is present in the fetal pituitary gland, it is apparently not essential in fetal growth. However, GH is essential for postnatal growth, which becomes quite evident early in life. The GH content of the pituitary increases progressively postnatally, reaching a maximum between 12 and 18 years of age. This level is maintained during adult life but decreases with aging.

The GH content of the anterior pituitary is not necessarily related to GH concentration in circulation. GH is released in a pulsatile manner, that is, in a series of intermittent bursts during the course of a day. Children have slightly more bursts during 24 hours than adults, so the circulating level of GH during a day is greater in children than in adults. The mean level of GH/L of blood during 24 hours is shown for boys in figure 19.6. Mean concentrations increase from childhood to adolescence and reach a peak that is almost coincident with the time of peak height velocity. Subsequently, mean 24-hour blood concentrations of GH decline.

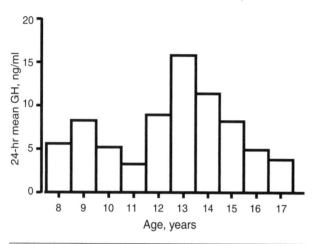

Blood Levels of Growth Hormone in Boys

FIGURE 19.6   Mean 24-hour plasma concentrations of growth hormone in boys.

Reprinted, by permission, from P.M. Martha et al., 1989, "Alterations in the pulsatile properties of circulating growth hormone concentrations during puberty in boys," *Journal of Clinical Endocrinology and Metabolism* 69: 563-570.

The frequency and amplitude of GH pulses both vary with age, and the frequency and amplitude of bursts increase as an individual passes from childhood through adolescence. Trends during puberty in males are illustrated in figure 19.7. The increase in 24-hour concentrations of GH near the time of peak height velocity (see figure 19.7a) is largely a function of an increase in the magnitude of GH pulses at this time (see figure 19.7b), rather than an increase in the number of pulses (see figure 19.7c). This increase in the magnitude suggests that the magnitude of GH pulses during the adolescent growth spurt is related to much of the growth occurring at this time. After the growth spurt, the magnitude of GH pulses declines to preadolescent levels.

The pulsatile release of GH from the anterior pituitary occurs throughout the day, but the largest bursts usually occur at night with the onset of

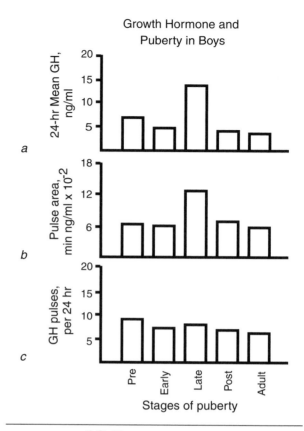

Growth Hormone and Puberty in Boys

FIGURE 19.7   Growth hormone pulses in prepubertal boys, in three groups at various stages of puberty, and in young adult males. (*a*) Mean 24-hour blood concentrations. (*b*) Mean area under the blood GH concentration curve, as identified by the cluster pulse detection algorithm. (*c*) Mean number of GH pulses as detected by the cluster algorithm. The data are for 60 males, 7 to 27 years of age. Early=PH2; Late=PH 3-5, hand-wrist epiphyses open; Post=less than 18 years, hand-wrist epiphyses fused.

Reprinted, by permission, from P.M. Martha et al., 1989, "Alterations in the pulsatile properties of circulating growth hormone concentrations during puberty in boys," *Journal of Clinical Endocrinology and Metabolism* 69: 563-570.

sleep. They occur in the early part of deep sleep, and children have a greater percentage of deep sleep than adults do. The number and intensity of nocturnal bursts of GH also increase considerably during the adolescent growth spurt and sexual maturation. However, after this phase of rapid growth, the pattern of pulsatile release of GH in adults is lower than in prepubertal children.

GH is produced throughout the 24-hour day. Single determinations of circulating levels, as in many earlier studies, simply provide a measure of GH concentration at the time the blood was sampled and are not necessarily indicative of the actual amount of GH produced during the course of a day. Thus, the continuous monitoring of circulating GH is essential. Continuous monitoring is not an easy task, and data on daily levels of GH in children and adolescents are actually relatively limited. Although the largest pulses of GH ordinarily occur during sleep, other factors can influence circulating levels, including, for example, physical activity, nutritional status, and psychological and social stresses.

Because GH is produced intermittently during the day, circulating levels vary. Circulating levels of IGF-I, on the other hand, tend to be reasonably stable during the day. Mean circulating concentrations of IGF-I reach about 50 ng/ml at birth but with considerable individual differences. They remain quite stable during infancy but rise gradually during childhood, attaining mean values of about 140 ng/ml in boys and 170 ng/ml in girls by 6 years of age. IGF-I levels increase considerably during the adolescent growth spurt, reaching an average of 415 ng/ml in girls 13 to 14 years of age and 430 ng/ml in boys 15 to 16 years of age. The surge in IGF-I during the adolescent growth spurt appears to parallel the increase in the number of bursts of GH at this time. Concentrations of IGF-I increase as statural growth accelerates (see figure 19.8). Peak levels of IGF-I tend to occur about a year or so after peak height velocity and then decline slowly in late adolescence. Given the sex difference in the timing of adolescent events, the increase in circulating concentrations of IGF-I occurs earlier in girls than in boys.

In summary, GH is necessary to support normal somatic growth after birth. The effects of GH on growth are mediated through IGF-I, which is produced primarily in the liver. In this manner, GH affects the linear growth of bones and, in turn, stature and the accretion of various tissues.

Thyroid Hormones

The thyroid gland is located in front and on either side of the trachea below the larynx. The gland consists of two lobes connected by an isthmus. Weight of the gland increases gradually through infancy and childhood, followed by considerable enlargement during adolescence. It attains about 15 g in women and 20 g in men.

Thyrotropin, or thyroid-stimulating hormone (TSH), from the anterior pituitary stimulates the production of the thyroid hormone, thyroxine (T_4). Triiodothyronine (T_3), the other thyroid hormone, is mainly produced in the target peripheral tissues by enzymatic conversion of thyroxine. Thyroxine, however, is the principal thyroid hormone in circulation. The metabolic effects of the two thyroid hormones are the same, although triiodothyronine is more potent and produces its effects more rapidly. The thyroid also secretes another hormone, calcitonin, which affects the amount of calcium in the circulation.

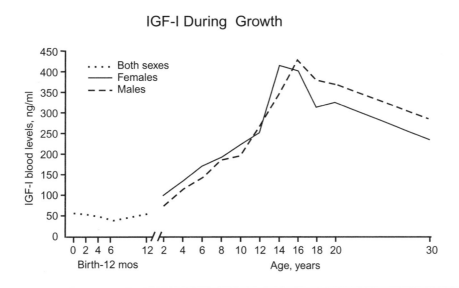

IGF-I During Growth

FIGURE 19.8 Mean plasma concentrations of IGF-I during infancy, childhood, and adolescence in boys and girls.

Drawn from the data of Esoterix Inc.

Calcitonin is considered in the discussion of the parathyroid hormones in the next section.

Differences in blood levels of thyrotropin and free thyroxine with age are shown in figure 19.9. The data are expected values reported by a clinical laboratory organization (Esoterix Inc, Endocrinology), but the trends are similar to those observed in a large cohort of males and females 1 day to 45 years of age (Nelson et al. 1993). Levels of thyrotropin and free thyroxine fall between birth and 1 month postnatally. Subsequently, blood levels of TSH remain rather stable until maturity. In contrast, free thyroxine declines slightly through puberty and reaches a plateau at maturity. About 99% of thyroxine and triiodothyronine are bound to several serum proteins, and the physiological action of thyroid hormones is mediated by nuclear receptors localized in the nucleus of cells of most tissues. These receptors are members of a superfamily of nuclear receptors, and they bind more readily to triiodothyronine than to thyroxine. The hormones enter the nucleus, bind to the chromosome-linked receptors, and activate or suppress gene expression at specific genes.

Thyroid hormones are calorigenic, that is, they stimulate oxygen uptake and energy expenditure. Hence, the major metabolic effect of thyroid hormones is a general increase in oxygen consumption in most tissues, especially those that compose the bulk of body weight (skeletal muscle, heart, liver, and kidneys). They increase mitochondrial oxidative metabolism, which is partly explained by the augmented activity of Na/K ATPase. In contrast, no acute effect of the thyroid hormones is apparently produced in several tissues, including the brain and smooth muscles of the gastrointestinal tract.

A normally functioning thyroid gland is essential for normal physiologic growth and maturation. Interestingly, the effects of GH are insignificant in the absence of thyroxine, that is, thyroxine is essential for GH to produce its full effects. Thyroid hormones apparently influence many parameters of growth and maturation, including growth of the body as a whole, skeletal growth and maturation, muscle development, sexual maturation, and mental development. Although specific growth and maturation effects are difficult to assign, the thyroid hormones accelerate most biological processes, including growth and maturation.

Levels of TSH are highest in infancy and early childhood. Adult values are attained at the end of puberty (see figure 19.9). However, free hormone concentrations remain quite constant throughout childhood and adolescence, with the exception of acutely higher levels soon after birth. No clear sex differences in blood TSH levels and thyroid hormone concentrations exist during childhood and adolescence and in adulthood. Like other pituitary hormones, thyrotropin secretion is pulsatile. Limited data in children show that the bursts of thyrotropin release are more frequent during the night hours with no difference in amplitude between the daytime and nighttime periods (Loche et al. 1994).

Much of the knowledge of specific growth and maturation effects of the thyroid gland is derived from clinical observations of individuals with abnormal thyroid function. Hypothyroid children, those with thyroid hormone deficiency, typically present growth failure. The rate of growth is reduced, linear growth of bones is impaired, infantile body proportions persist, skeletal and sexual maturation are delayed, and muscular development is deficient. If thyroid deficiency is severe and persists, somatic, sexual, and mental retardation may result. Hyperthyroid children, those with an excess of thyroid hormones, often show excessive growth initially, but loss of weight eventually occurs because of increased metabolic demands and resulting inadequacy of energy intake to meet the increased metabolic demand.

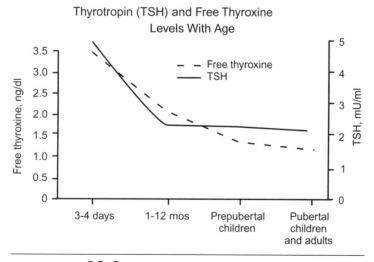

FIGURE 19.9   Age-related changes in mean blood concentrations of free thyroxine (free T$_4$) and thyrotropin (TSH, or thyroid-stimulating hormone).

Drawn from Esoterix Inc.

The single most frequent cause of hypothyroidism worldwide is iodine deficiency. However, iodine deficiency is very rare in the United States, Canada, and other Western nations where iodine is routinely added to food products. Other causes of hypothyroidism include chronic autoimmune thyroiditis, congenital defects, and others. Hypothyroidism is occasionally inherited as an autosomal recessive trait. The clinical manifestations of hypothyroidism are quite heterogenous. If present in the first months of life, it leads to irreversible mental retardation and stunted physical growth. The prevalence of hypothyroidism in newborn babies ranges from about 1 in 3,000 to 4,000 in the United States and Canada. If treated immediately after neonatal detection, infants grow and develop normally.

Parathyroid and Calcitonin Hormones

The parathyroid glands are small bodies, usually four, located on the dorsal portion of the thyroid gland. On average, each parathyroid gland weighs about 40 g. However, a small percentage of the population has only three glands, whereas as much as 15% of the population has five or six. The parathyroid glands do not seem to be under the influence of a trophic hormone from the anterior pituitary. Parathyroid hormone (PTH) secreted by the parathyroids is an essential element in the regulation of calcium and phosphate metabolism. Thus, it is needed throughout life and is especially vital for normal bone and dental growth and maturation. Because 99% of the body calcium is in bone, PTH is intimately involved in skeletal growth.

Parathyroid hormone functions to maintain a reasonably stable plasma calcium concentration. This level, which is found within narrow limits, must be maintained despite variable calcium intake and excretion and calcium requirements for bone growth and maturation. The primary action of PTH is to stimulate an increase in circulating calcium through direct action of the hormone on bone and the kidneys. PTH acts via cell surface receptors in bone and kidneys. It triggers a dissolution of bone mineral, thus increasing the flow of calcium from bone to blood and extracellular fluids. PTH stimulates osteoclastic activity and thus bone resorption in the short term. However, long-term exposure to high levels of PTH causes a decrease in osteoclastic activity

and a compensatory increase in osteoblasts. PTH also reduces renal clearance rates of calcium and increases intestinal absorption of calcium. All of these mechanisms result in higher levels of blood and extracellular fluid calcium, which feed back to the parathyroid glands to decrease the secretion of PTH.

Parathyroid hormone, therefore, contributes to the rapid regulation of calcium availability in body fluids. Differences also exist between high-pulsatile and nonpulsatile PTH levels on bone biology, which are the topics of intense research. For instance, high levels of pulsatile PTH increase bone formation and provide a foundation for the treatment of osteoporosis.

Calcitonin from the thyroid gland has effects opposite to those of PTH. Thyroid cells that produce calcitonin have a different embryonic origin than other thyroid cells. Calcitonin causes a decrease in circulating calcium and is secreted by the thyroid in response to a high plasma calcium concentration to either inhibit bone resorption or increase the rate of calcium deposition in bone.

Calcitonin and PTH function as a dual hormonal feedback system in the maintenance of plasma calcium concentrations. As calcium levels in body fluids become too high, calcitonin is secreted and calcium is thus lowered. When calcium levels are too low, PTH is secreted, and blood and extracellular fluid calcium are elevated. Because the two hormones function to regulate the amount of circulating calcium and the exchange of circulating calcium with calcium in bone, both PTH and calcitonin can be reasonably assumed to be essential to normal skeletal growth and maturation.

An important component of the pathway regulating calcium levels is vitamin D. Vitamin D is synthesized in the skin by the action of sunlight from a sterol precursor or is consumed in the diet. The product is vitamin D_3 (cholecalciferol), which is then metabolized into $25(OH)D$ in the liver and subsequently into $1\alpha, 25(OH)_2 D_3$ and $24R, 25(OH)_2 D_3$ in the kidney. The latter two compounds are considered steroid hormones, and both are necessary to observe the full spectrum of the biological effects of vitamin D. However, $1\alpha, 25(OH)_2 D_3$ plays a particularly important role in the regulation of calcium levels. It increases the absorption of calcium in the small intestine and the rate of release of calcium and phosphate from bone. The rate of production of $1\alpha, 25(OH)_2 D_3$ by the kidney is influenced by several hormones, but PTH and calcitonin are the most important, particularly in the long-term regulation of plasma calcium concentration. Short-term control is driven primarily by PTH and normal levels of 1 α, 25 (OH)$_2$ D$_3$ (1, 25-dihydroxycholecalciferol).

Hormones From the Adrenal Medulla and Cortex

The adrenal glands are small glands located over the upper pole of each kidney. Each weighs about 4 g and is composed of two distinct glands: an outer gland, the adrenal cortex (about 90% of the size of the adrenals), and an inner gland, the adrenal medulla. The growth pattern of the adrenals is characterized by a marked decrease in weight shortly after birth and a further gradual reduction during the first 3 to 6 months of life. Weight of the glands then rises through childhood and shows a growth spurt during adolescence. The size of the gland at birth is thus regained during the second decade. This growth pattern is one of the exceptions to Scammon's curves of systemic growth described in chapter 1.

The adrenal medulla is innervated by the sympathetic nervous system and secretes epinephrine (adrenaline) in response to nervous stimulation. Norepinephrine (noradrenaline) is mainly released from sympathetic nerve endings and converted enzymatically to epinephrine primarily in the adrenal medulla. The catecholamines, epinephrine and norepinephrine, act as hormones in the periphery. Their actions in various tissues and organs are mediated via cell surface receptors known as adrenergic receptors, of which there are several types (α 1 and 2 and β 1, 2, and 3). Epinephrine and norepinephrine are agonists with variable affinity and specificity for these receptor molecules. One hormone may have a stimulatory effect (coupled to a G$_s$ protein) in one tissue but an inhibitory effect (coupled to a G$_i$ protein) in another tissue. Thus, catecholamines exert a myriad of biological influences on tissues and organs and regulate levels of a number of molecules. For instance, catecholamines influence the force and rate of contraction of the cardiac muscle, systolic and diastolic blood pressure, gastrointestinal motility, bronchodilation, insulin secretion, adipose tissue lipolysis, glucose metabolism, fatty acid metabolism, and thermogenesis. Adequate regulation of catecholamine production and degradation and of epinephrine and norepinephrine metabolism is important for normal growth and maturation. An example of the consequences of a major derangement is the condition known as pheochromocytoma, a disease caused by catecholamine-producing tumors. These tumors occur most commonly in the adrenal medulla and are generally nonmalignant.

Hormones of the adrenal cortex, on the other hand, are directly involved in the regulation of growth and maturation, in addition to being essential to many other body functions. The adrenal cortex produces and secretes steroid hormones. The term steroid refers to a general class of chemically related hormones, including primarily those of the adrenal cortex and the gonads. Cholesterol derived from the diet and from endogenous cellular synthesis is the main precursor of steroid hormones. Three major categories of adrenal steroids are the mineralocorticoids, mainly aldosterone; the glucocorticoids, mainly cortisol; and the adrenal androgens, mainly dehydroepiandrosterone. The adrenal cortex also secretes, or produces by enzymatic conversion, small amounts of androstenedione, testosterone, progesterone, and other steroids.

Adrenocorticotropic hormone (ACTH) from the anterior pituitary regulates the secretion of glucocorticoids and other steroids from the adrenal cortex. The primary effect of ACTH is on glucocorticoid secretion. The secretion of aldosterone, a mineralocorticoid, is independently controlled. Figure 19.10 illustrates the

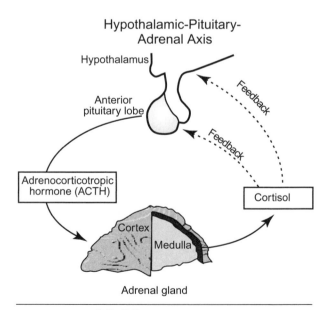

Hypothalamic-Pituitary-Adrenal Axis

Hypothalamus

Anterior pituitary lobe

Feedback

Feedback

Adrenocorticotropic hormone (ACTH)

Cortisol

Cortex

Medulla

Adrenal gland

FIGURE 19.10 Schematic representation of the hypothalamic-pituitary-adrenal axis with an emphasis on the feedback loop of cortisol to the hypothalamus and the pituitary.

hypothalamic-pituitary-adrenal axis and the feedback loop from cortisol to the pituitary and hypothalamus.

The mineralocorticoids regulate sodium and potassium homeostasis and extracellular fluid volume of the body, and the glucocorticoids are involved in enhancing carbohydrate and fat metabolism and in coping with stress, including severe stress such as infections and hemorrhage. The actions of the adrenal androgens are physiologically similar to those produced by the testes, that is, they stimulate the development of masculine characteristics and nitrogen retention (see next section). Small amounts of estrogens are also produced by the adrenal cortex. Androgens in females are derived only from the adrenal cortex, whereas those in males are derived from both the adrenal cortex and the testes. The quantities of sex hormones produced by the adrenal cortex, however, are generally not as biologically significant as those secreted by the gonads, except for the androgens in females.

Adrenal cortical steroids influence a variety of body functions and are thus essential to growth and maturation. Because the gonads and the adrenal cortex have a common embryonic origin, one might expect an interaction between the two glands. Indeed, a normally functioning adrenal cortex is necessary for complete sexual and reproductive maturity. Excess secretion of adrenal cortex hormones, or pharmacologic doses of glucocorticoids for systemic inflammation during childhood, can result in stunted growth in stature as the proliferation of cartilage cells at the growth plates is decreased. This condition is apparently caused by increased protein catabolism in bone and elsewhere in the body. The net result is the stunting of linear growth (height) and also growth in weight.

Adrenarche, the increase in adrenal androgen and estrogen production, occurs about 2 years before gonadarche, the onset of gonadal functions marked by increases in size of external genitalia and breasts. However, adrenarche is not essential for gonadarche to take place, and they are independent events (Cutler et al. 1990). The role of adrenal androgens and estrogens in pubertal events is not yet clear, but gonadal steroids play the predominant role.

Secretion of the main glucocorticoid, cortisol, increases gradually with age during growth, and the increase is proportional to the age-associated increase in body size, except perhaps in infancy. However, the relationships between serum cortisol levels or circadian cortisol ranges and body mass, body composition, or growth rate in healthy children and adolescents are thought to be secondary to other factors and do not appear to be causal (Knutsson et al. 1997). Nonetheless, when cortisol production rates are related to maturity status in adolescent boys, the rates increase, on the average, with advancing sexual maturity. However, when cortisol production is adjusted for body weight in adolescents of contrasting maturity status (see chapter 17), the differences in cortisol production across maturity categories are reduced considerably.

Gonadal Glands and Hormones

The testes and ovaries are, respectively, the male and female gonadal glands. Changes in the weights of the testes and ovaries during growth are shown in figure 19.11. Testicular weight increases slightly early in life and then

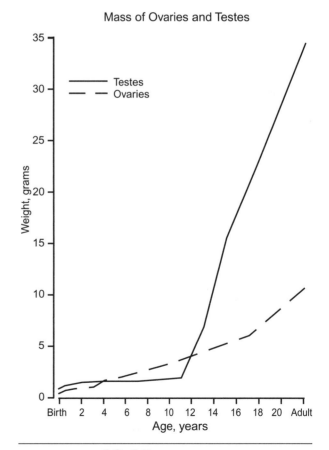

FIGURE 19.11 Changes in the mean weights of the testes and ovaries during growth.
Data from Boyd, 1952.

shows little change until puberty, when weight dramatically increases until adult values are reached. The ovaries, on the other hand, show a more gradual increase in weight during childhood, and the adolescent gain is not as dramatic as that for the testes.

The testes and ovaries each have two functional aspects, a hormone-secreting component and a gamete-producing component. The interstitial cells of Leydig produce testosterone in males. In females, the ovarian follicles produce estrogens and progesterone in quantities that vary with the phase of the menstrual cycle in mature females.

Gonadotropins

The hormone-producing and gamete-producing functions of the gonads are regulated by two gonadotropic hormones from the anterior pituitary: follicle-stimulating hormone (FSH) and luteinizing hormone (LH). In females, FSH stimulates the growth of ovarian follicles but not their complete maturation and estrogen secretion. LH promotes maturation of an ovarian follicle, ovulation, development of the corpus luteum, and stimulation of further production of estrogens by the ovary. The secretion of FSH and LH becomes cyclical in females late in puberty.

In males, FSH promotes growth of the seminiferous tubules and stimulates the production of sperm, and LH stimulates the interstitial cells of Leydig to enlarge and produce testosterone. In contrast to the cyclic secretion of FSH and LH with the attainment of sexual maturity in females, FSH and LH production remains relatively constant in males with the attainment of sexual maturity. However, gonadotropin release is pulsatile in adult men and women.

A schematic diagram of the hypothalamic-pituitary-ovarian or -testicular axis is provided in figure 19.12. Gonadotropin-releasing hormones are released into the anterior pituitary, where the production and secretion of FSH and LH are augmented. In the presence of increased production of testosterone by the testes in males, gonadotropin secretion is attenuated. A similar process occurs in females with increased levels of estrogens. In addition, low abundance molecular regulators such as inhibin (–) and activin (+) are also involved in feedback loops to the pituitary.

Changes in serum concentrations of FSH and LH with chronological age and maturity status are shown in figures 19.13 and 19.14, respectively. Blood levels of FSH are much higher in infant girls (mean of about 7.2 mIU/ml) than in infant

Hypothalamic-Pituitary-Gonadal Axis

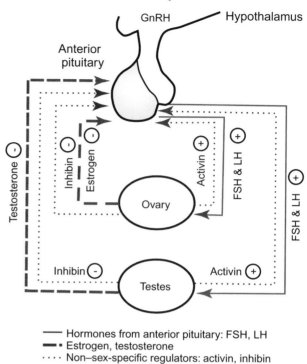

— Hormones from anterior pituitary: FSH, LH
—· Estrogen, testosterone
···· Non–sex-specific regulators: activin, inhibin

FIGURE 19.12   Schematic illustration of the hypothalamic-pituitary-ovarian/testes axis with the positive and negative regulatory pathways.

boys (1.0 mIU/ml). During childhood, values stabilize at about 2 mIU/ml in girls and 1 mIU/ml in boys. Blood levels of the gonadotropins increase with puberty in both sexes, with girls experiencing, on average, a threefold increase by stage 4 of breast and pubic hair and boys experiencing a sixfold increment with a peak at sexual maturity (stage 5 of genital and pubic hair). Stages of breast, genital, and pubic hair development are illustrated in figures 15.3 through 15.6, pages 286 to 289. Blood FSH values remain high in both men and women, with men having a slightly lower level than women. Note that a dramatic rise in FSH level occurs with menopause (a 10-fold increase, on average).

Blood levels of LH are quite variable between birth and 1 year of age with no consistent difference between boys and girls (see figure 19.14). From about 1 year of age to the onset of puberty, levels of LH are about 0.07 mIU/ml in both sexes. With the onset of puberty (stage 2 breasts and pubic hair in girls and stage 2 of genitals and pubic hair in boys), blood values of LH increase about 10-fold in girls and 20-fold in boys. LH

FSH Levels in Boys and Girls

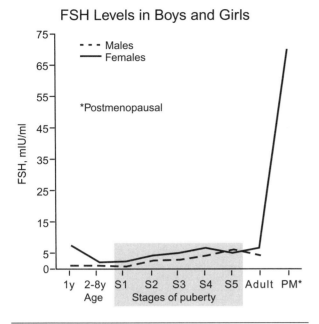

FIGURE 19.13 Changes in serum concentrations of FSH with chronological age and maturity status in boys and girls. Stages of puberty are based on secondary sex characteristics (see figures 15.3 to 15.6, pages 286 to 289).

Data from Esoterix Inc.

LH Levels in Boys and Girls

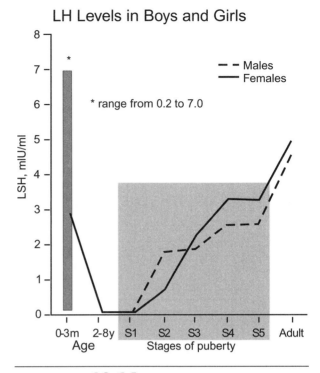

FIGURE 19.14 Changes in serum concentrations of LH with chronological age and maturity status in boys and girls. Stages of puberty are based on secondary sex characteristics (see figures 15.3 to 15.6, pages 286 to 289).

Data from Esoterix Inc.

levels then continue to rise in girls such that by early adulthood, they reach about 4 to 5 mIU/ml. In boys, the rise is more gradual, but adult levels are also, on average, about 4 to 5 mIU/ml.

Thus, gonadotropic hormones are detectable in the blood of prepubertal children before overt signs of sexual maturation become apparent. Childhood concentrations are rather stable, with much overlap between boys and girls. From about 9 or 10 years of age, blood levels of gonadotropins rise in both sexes. Blood concentrations are slightly more related to stage of sexual maturity than to chronological age. Late in puberty in girls and just before menarche, the gonadotropic hormones develop a cyclical pattern related to the menstrual cycle (described later in the chapter). The mean values shown in figures 19.13 and 19.14 do not reflect the pulsatile nature of gonadotropin release.

Sex Steroids

The numerous androgens and estrogens each have their related active or excretory metabolites. These steroid hormones are synthesized in the testes, ovaries, and adrenal cortex or are produced

by enzymatic conversion of steroid precursors in peripheral tissues, especially adipose tissue. The biosynthesis of androgens and estrogens, enzymatic conversion, transport in the blood, and metabolic clearance from the producing and target tissues are complex biological processes that have considerable implication for the regulation of growth and maturation. However, detailed consideration of these processes is beyond the scope of this text.

In males, testosterone is synthesized in the testes (and adrenal cortex) from cholesterol precursors. Although testosterone is the major and most abundant androgen in males, the most potent androgen is dihydrotestosterone, which is derived from an enzymatic conversion of testosterone. Dihydrotestosterone has about three times more androgenic activities than testosterone. Dihydrotestosterone appears to be formed from the testosterone precursor mainly in tissues that are sensitive to circulating androgens (i.e., the target tissues). Dihydrotestosterone is thought to be the major growth-promoting androgen necessary for the maturation of male secondary sex characteristics. The rate of enzymatic conversion of testosterone to dihydrotestosterone is related to body size and probably to muscle and adipose tissue masses.

Testosterone and other circulating androgens can also be converted to estrogens, including estradiol, in the peripheral tissues of males. Dihydrotestosterone and estradiol are also synthesized from the adrenal precursor androstenedione. About 25% of total daily production of the two hormones comes from secretion in the testes. Thus, the bulk of daily production of the two hormones in males comes from the enzymatic conversion of precursors in the peripheral tissues.

In females, estradiol is the most potent estrogen, and it is produced by the ovaries. Small amounts originate from the peripheral conversion of precursors secreted by the adrenal cortex. In addition to estradiol, other estrogenic hormones are produced. These hormones are biologically less potent but, nonetheless, contribute to the sexual maturation of girls. Most of the other estrogenic hormones result from the peripheral conversion of ovarian and adrenal estrogenic precursors. Testosterone and other androgens are also present in females. Androgen precursors are secreted in small amounts by both the ovaries and the adrenal cortex. Both testosterone and dihydrotestosterone are found in the blood and peripheral tissues of females but in small quantities compared with males. Testosterone is derived primarily (about 75%) from enzymatic conversion of androstenedione of adrenal origin. The remainder (25%) is produced by the ovaries.

Most studies that consider steroid hormones in growing children use testosterone and estradiol as the markers of androgenic and estrogenic activity, respectively. Ideally they should be measured repeatedly over several days under standardized conditions because blood concentrations of the hormones can be influenced by several factors. However, such data are not available from birth to maturity. Changes in blood concentrations of testosterone and estradiol with age are shown in figure 19.15. Boys have a higher level of testosterone during infancy than girls. Levels of testosterone and estradiol are quite low during childhood and amounts show no sex difference. Estradiol rises gradually in the prepubertal years in girls and then more markedly with the onset of sexual maturation. Circulating testosterone increases steadily throughout puberty in boys. The

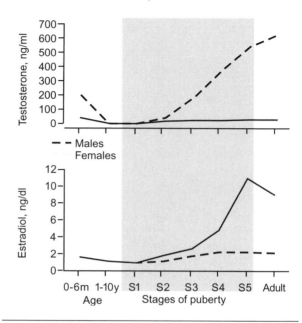

Levels of Testosterone and Estradiol in Boys and Girls

FIGURE 19.15 Changes in blood concentrations of testosterone (upper) and estradiol (lower) in boys and girls with chronological age. Stages of puberty are based on secondary sex characteristics (see figures 15.3 to 15.6, pages 286 to 289).

Data from Esoterix Inc.

sex difference in the timing of sexual maturation is clearly reflected in the time at which estradiol rises in girls and testosterone rises in boys. Estradiol levels in boys increase slightly with age.

The data shown in figure 19.5 suggest that blood concentrations of estradiol and testosterone are more related to stage of sexual maturity as expressed in secondary sex characteristics than to chronological age (Winter 1978). Estradiol increases gradually from breast stages B1 to B3, and testosterone increases from genital stages G1 to G3. Between B3 and B4 in girls and between G3 and G4 in boys, blood concentrations of estradiol and testosterone, respectively, rise dramatically. Levels of testosterone continue to increase with the maturity in males, but the production of estradiol becomes cyclical in females.

A variety of steroids are produced or converted in the adrenal cortex, and only the two principal ones are considered. Steroids of the adrenal cortex also have a pattern of age-associated and sex-associated variation, but the timing and magnitude of increases during puberty are variable. Circulating levels of dehydroepiandrosterone (and the clinically important dehydroepiandrosterone sulfate, or DHEA-S) begin to rise at about 7 years of age in boys and girls. Concentrations thus begin to rise long before any outward signs of puberty are evident. In girls, levels rise through 12 to 14 years of age and then level off. The increase in dehydroepiandrosterone in males is also gradual through the early phases of puberty. Levels then rise considerably after 16 years of age or so, thus causing a major sex difference in concentrations of this adrenal steroid hormone. Concentrations of androstenedione, another important adrenal steroid, show a later rise compared with dehydroepiandrosterone, about 10 years of age in girls and 12 to 14 years of age in boys, but overlap between the sexes is considerable.

Recent studies have shown that testosterone administration increases whole-body protein metabolism in prepubertal boys in in vivo isotopic experiments (Mauras et al. 1994). The anabolic activity was accompanied by elevated blood GH, IGF-I, and testosterone levels. In contrast, chronic exposure to estrogens in hypogonadal girls did not affect whole-body protein metabolism despite an increase in plasma IGF-I concentrations (Mauras 1995). The absence of an anabolic effect of estrogens may contribute to the sex differences in body size that arise during puberty and the adolescent growth spurt.

Effects of Gonadal and Adrenal Steroids

The effects of androgens and estrogens on growth and maturation are many. The principal sites of action for testosterone and dihydrotestosterone are the primary and secondary sex characteristics of males. These characteristics include the testes, penis, scrotum, seminal vesicles, the prostate gland, and pubic, axillary, and facial hair during male sexual maturation. Additional effects of testosterone include the thickening of the laryngeal cartilage with subsequent changes in voice pitch in adolescent males. The estrogens act to bring about corresponding changes in females, including the growth and maturation of the primary and secondary sex characteristics, that is, ovaries, fallopian tubes, uterus, vagina, external features of the female genitalia, breasts, pubic and axillary hair, and a gynoid profile of adipose tissue distribution.

Both androgens and estrogens promote generalized nitrogen retention and thus increased anabolism. Androgens are more potent in this regard than estrogens. The effects of testosterone, for example, specifically underlie the dramatic adolescent growth spurt in muscle and fat-free mass in males. The protein anabolic actions of estrogens are less than those of androgens, so the female gain in muscle mass during adolescence is primarily an effect of adrenal androgens.

Androgens also promote bone growth and skeletal maturation. They stimulate some longitudinal growth of long bones in interaction with GH and IGF-I and also promote considerable growth in bone thickness. The greater skeletal growth of boys than girls is related to testosterone secretion. Protein retention enhanced by androgens promotes the formation of cartilage and bone matrix and the deposition of calcium and phosphorus. The effects of estrogens on bone are generally similar to those of androgens, except for their influence on linear growth. Estrogens increase bone matrix formation, maintain positive calcium balance, and accelerate skeletal maturation. Moreover, estrogens are the main steroids involved in the final phase of skeletal maturation in the sense that they initiate and complete epiphyseal closure (Smith and Korach 1996). Thus, estrogens can be viewed as a primary determinant of the final stature of a child. Androgens also contribute to this process as they are aromatized to estrogens in tissues.

Estrogens promote the accumulation of fat throughout the body in females and specifically enhance the accumulation of fat about the hips, buttocks, breasts, and medial aspects of the calf. The rise in concentrations of dehydroepiandrosterone, an adrenal steroid, in boys and girls between 7 and 12 years of age, is perhaps related to the accumulation of fat in both sexes at this time (the so-called preadolescent fat wave). As the processes of sexual maturation and the adolescent growth spurt continue, males experience a fat loss on the extremities. This loss may be related to increasing androgen output, especially testosterone, which has a fat-mobilizing effect. Growth hormone also has a fat-mobilizing effect, and the hormones probably act in concert during male adolescence.

The increasing concentrations of the sex steroids during puberty influence the production of other hormones related to growth, specifically GH and IGF-I. The rise in sex steroids at this time leads to an increase in the secretion of GH, which in turn stimulates the production of IGF-I. This effect is especially pronounced in boys compared with the corresponding effect in girls. The interactions between the gonadal steroids and growth hormones become especially apparent at puberty (Kerrigan and Rogol 1992). Thus, some of the sex differences in growth and body composition during adolescence are related to the increased secretion of GH and IGF-I in males consequent to the increased production of sex steroids at this time.

Insulin and Glucagon

The pancreas is an organ with a primarily digestive function. It is located in close proximity to the duodenum of the small intestine. It provides essential digestive enzymes to the intestinal contents. In addition, 2% of the pancreatic mass, the Islets of Langerhans, is a complex endocrine gland. The hormonal secretions of the Islets of Langerhans are insulin (secreted by the β cells), glucagon (secreted by the α cells), somatostatin (produced by the δ cells), and the pancreatic polypeptide (produced by the PP cells). Insulin and glucagon are of primary interest. The actions of the two hormones are mutually antagonistic. Insulin is a blood sugar–lowering hormone, whereas glucagon is a blood sugar–raising hormone.

Insulin is essential in carbohydrate metabolism. It enhances the rate of glucose uptake in skeletal muscle, adipose cells, and other tissues by stimulating the transport of glucose and amino acids through cell membranes. The action of insulin decreases the concentration of blood glucose and increases glycogen stores (glycogenesis) in skeletal muscle and liver and the reliance on glucose as a substrate to meet the cellular energy needs. If blood glucose is excessive and glycogen stores are high, insulin may stimulate the transformation of glucose into fatty acids, which are in turn converted to triglycerides (lipogenesis). The latter is, however, a minor pathway in humans under common dietary circumstances. Insulin can inhibit glucose production by the liver and block fatty acid mobilization through inhibition of adipose tissue lipolysis. The insulin-mediated disposal of blood glucose is thus particularly important in the maintenance of glucose homeostasis and overall substrate balance.

Glucagon has the opposite effect of insulin. Its secretion increases when blood glucose levels are low. Glucagon mobilizes glucose by increasing the rate of glycogen breakdown (glycogenolysis) in the liver. Glucose is thus released into circula-

tion, and as blood glucose levels rise, glucagon secretion is inhibited. In contrast to insulin, glucagon stimulates the breakdown of triglycerides in fat stores (lipolysis) and thus increases levels of fatty acids.

Because insulin acts primarily on carbohydrate metabolism, it is important to normal growth and maturation. Insulin and GH interact in a complex manner, and insulin is essential for full expression of the effects of GH. Although insulin is capable of promoting protein synthesis in the absence of GH, GH has only a slight effect on protein synthesis in the absence of insulin. The effects of GH, IGF-I, and IGF-II on protein synthesis and, in turn, on growth are considerably greater in the presence of insulin. In contrast, insulin and GH have opposite effects on fat. The former stimulates the conversion of carbohydrates into fat and depresses lipolysis, whereas the latter stimulates the mobilization of fat.

The δ cells of the pancreas produce somatostatin. As discussed earlier, somatostatin is also secreted by hypothalamic nuclei and is a potent inhibitor of GH-releasing hormone and, in turn, of GH from the anterior pituitary. Somatostatin is also produced in other areas of the brain, in the stomach, and in the gastrointestinal tract. Many issues concerning the various physiological roles of somatostatin are still unresolved, but it is a potent inhibitor of insulin and glucagon secretion from the islet cells. Thus, pancreatic somatostatin has paracrine effects on pancreatic α and β cells.

As is the case for the parathyroid glands, the endocrine function of the pancreas is not mediated by a trophic hormone from the anterior pituitary. The control of insulin and glucagon secretion is regulated primarily through fluctuations in blood sugar concentrations and the sensitivity of insulin-sensitive target tissues to the hormones. Innervation of the pancreatic β cells by the autonomic nervous system also plays an important role in the control of insulin secretion. An increase in blood glucose stimulates the production and release of insulin, which acts to reduce blood sugar to normal levels, whereas a decrease in blood glucose stimulates the production of glucagon, which mobilizes glucose from hepatic glycogen stores. The breakdown of the hormones and their rates of disposal from the circulation and target tissues are also important regulators of concentrations of these hormones.

Insulin is also a growth-promoting hormone. It is a potent mitogenic factor associated with cellular hyperplasia and cell hypertrophy. At least 100 genes are now known to be regulated by insulin. Insulin, in some instances, increases the expression of specific genes and, in other cases, decreases the expression of genes. This role of insulin can be tissue specific and may be enhanced or diminished in the presence of other hormones or growth factors. Many cellular processes and substances are affected by insulin, such as transcription of genes encoding metabolic enzymes, hormones, transcription factors, and others. In a typical case, the insulin-sensitive genomic sequence for a gene has an insulin response element in the promoter region. An insulin-stimulated change in the phosphorylation state of a receptor or other molecules or the presence of transcription and other factors may be required for the insulin effect. Figure 19.16 displays some of the hormones and transcription factors whose gene expression is known to be enhanced or suppressed by insulin (O'Brien and Granner 1996).

Leptin

The reporting of the discovery of leptin in 1994 has resulted in the development of a new chapter in the biological sciences (Zhang et al. 1994). This discovery was the culmination of decades of research to identify a factor that could account for the obese state in ob (obese) and db (diabetic) mice. However, leptin turns out to exert a wider range of biological effects that are only partly understood at present.

Leptin, the product of the ob (mouse) or leptin (human) gene, is a hormone produced mainly by adipocytes. It is also expressed at much lower levels in the stomach and placenta. Leptin is a cytokinelike molecule that is synthesized and secreted by the adipocytes in proportion to fat mass in most people. However, for reasons that are not yet well understood, some individuals produce less leptin than expected, and others secrete more leptin than expected on the basis of their adipose mass. The former are thought to have a partial leptin production defect, whereas the latter appear to have a diminished sensitivity to circulating leptin or a leptin resistant state. Figure 19.17 depicts the relationship between blood levels of leptin, age, and body fat across a wide range of values.

During prenatal life, leptin is produced by placental and fetal tissues, presumably adipose tissue. The function of leptin in utero is still unknown. A dramatic increase in cord blood leptin is seen at about 34 weeks of gestation. Leptin concentrations rise before puberty in boys and then revert to prepubertal values about 3 years later (Roemmich and Rogol 1999). In girls, leptin

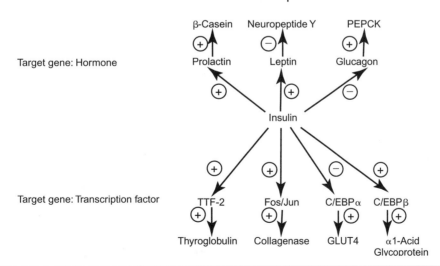

FIGURE 19.16 Indirect effects of insulin on gene expression. Insulin regulates the expression of several genes for hormones and for transcription factors. + indicates an increase in level of expression; – indicates suppression of the expression level.

Adapted, by permission, from R.M. O'Brien and D.K. Granner, 1996, "Regulation of gene expression by insulin," *Physiological Reviews* 76(4): 1109-1161.

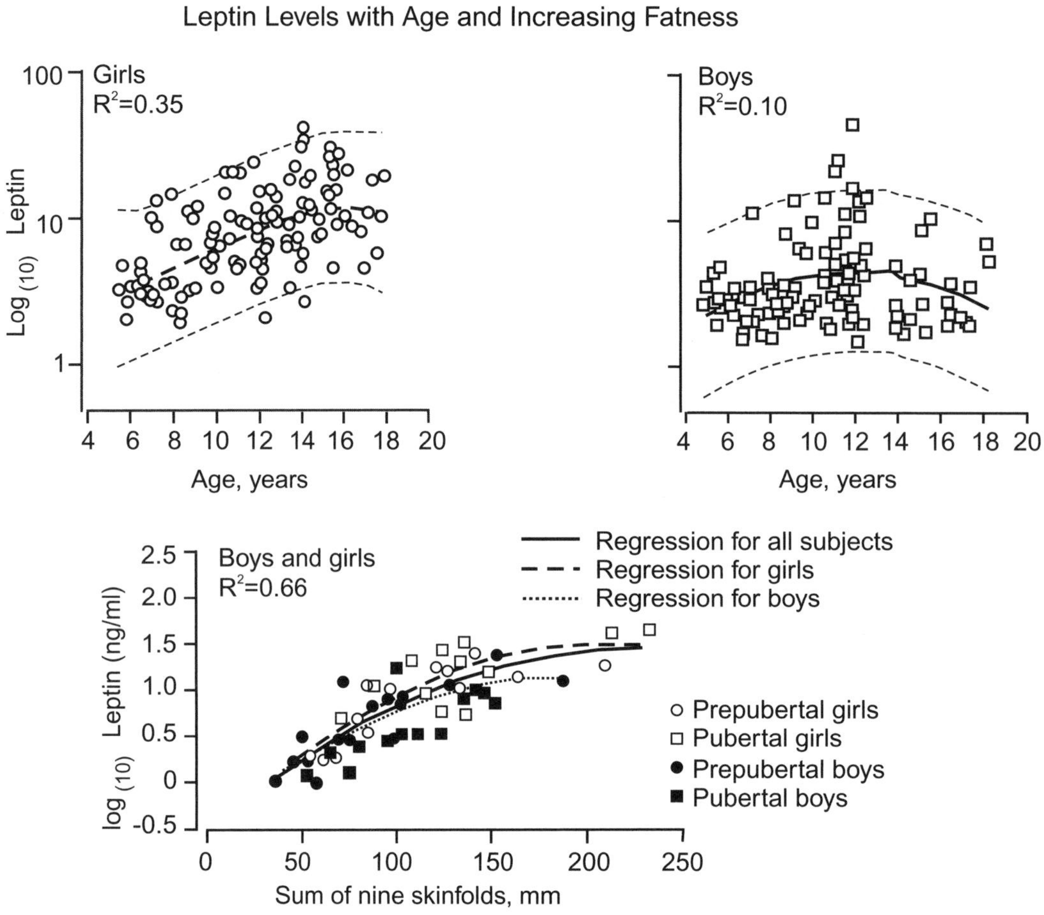

Leptin Levels with Age and Increasing Fatness

FIGURE 19.17   Relationship between blood leptin levels and age in boys and girls (Clayton et al. 1997) and with adiposity in both sexes (Roemmich et al. 1998).

Reprinted, by permission, from J.N. Roemmich et al., 1998, "Gender differences in leptin levels during puberty are related to subcutaneous fat depot and sex steroids," *American Journal of Physiology* 275: E543-551.

concentrations increase with the onset of puberty and continue to increase throughout puberty (Clayton et al. 1997; Roemmich and Rogol 1999). Girls have higher levels of leptin than boys before puberty and throughout puberty. The sex difference is particularly evident when sexual maturity is attained (see figure 19.18). This sexual dimorphism may be explained, in part, by differences in subcutaneous fat and in sex steroids between boys and girls. Subcutaneous fat is a strong correlate of leptin concentration, more so than abdominal adiposity or abdominal visceral fat (Roemmich et al. 1998). Androgens are inversely correlated with leptin levels in boys, whereas estrogens are generally positively correlated with leptin concentrations in girls (Roemmich and Rogol 1999).

Once secreted by adipocytes, the circulating leptin is bound to binding proteins in the blood.

The adipocyte secretion of leptin is pulsatile with about 30 pulses per 24-hour period (Licinio et al. 1997). The amplitude of the secretory bursts is, however, more variable than their periodicity. Thus, secretory bursts of leptin by adipocytes appear to be regulated like other glands. Peak leptin concentrations are reached around midnight, whereas the nadir is observed at about midafternoon (Roemmich and Rogol 1999).

Initially, leptin was thought to be the missing factor that predisposed some people to be in positive energy balance. Indeed, leptin is an important regulator of long-term food consumption, and leptin appears not to play an important role in the short-term regulation of appetite and satiety. For instance, leptin levels are not altered by a single meal. Leptin exerts its effects on energy balance through the hypothalamic leptin receptor. This process is schematically illustrated in figure

Mean Circulating Leptin Levels by Stage of Puberty

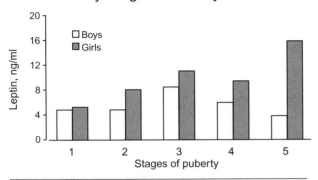

FIGURE 19.18 Blood leptin levels in boys and girls from Spain at different stages of puberty (see figures 15.3 to 15.6, pages 286 to 289). Note there is considerable variation in chronological ages of children within each stage of puberty.

Reprinted, by permission, from J. Argente et al., 1997, "Leptin plasma levels in healthy Spanish children and adolescents, children with obesity, and adolescents with anorexia nervosa and bulimia nervosa," *Turkish Journal of Pediatrics* 131(6): 833-838.

The Emerging Leptin Biology

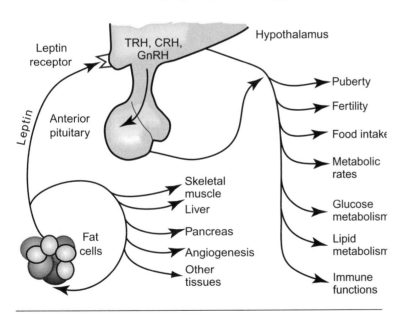

FIGURE 19.19 The leptin-leptin receptor pathway and some of the metabolic pathways in which leptin is thought to play a role. Most of the effects of leptin seem to be mediated centrally via the hypothalamic leptin receptor. Some evidence indicates that leptin has paracrine effects on adipose cells and other peripheral effects that are not centrally mediated.

19.19. Leptin reaches the central nervous system after having crossed the blood-brain barrier by a mechanism that remains to be elucidated. Leptin binds to the leptin receptor that is present at high levels in several hypothalamic neurons. Activated leptin receptors generate a response cascade whose long-term net effects are a reduction in food intake and an increase in metabolic rates.

Leptin does not act in isolation to modulate energy balance. It interacts with key molecules involved in other regulatory loops that are components of a highly redundant system. For instance, hypothalamic neuropeptide Y is a strong stimulant of appetite. A series of animal experiments have established that some of the actions of leptin on food intake are the result of its inhibitory effect on neuropeptide Y activity in the hypothalamus. α melanocyte–stimulating hormone has the potential to decrease appetite as a result of its binding to the melanocortin receptor 4 in the brain. Leptin increases the expression of proopiomelanocortin (POMC), the gene transcript that encodes several peptides, including α melanocyte–stimulating hormone. In other words, leptin potentiates the action of a number of anorexigenic (food-intake decreasing) factors and antagonizes the action of orexigenic (food-intake stimulating) agents (Friedman 1999).

Leptin is also thought to be involved in the regulation of metabolic rate even though the mechanisms are still unknown. Administration of leptin to animals undergoing caloric restriction attenuates the fall in metabolic rate commonly observed with negative energy balance (Campfield 1999). Leptin also favorably influences glucose and lipid metabolism. Overall, leptin is a potent molecule that influences many functions and is thus necessary for normal growth and maturation.

The critical role of leptin in growth is well illustrated by the clinical picture of the few patients who have been found to have inactivating mutations in the leptin (LEP) or the leptin receptor (LEPR) gene. Two kindreds with patients homozygous for LEP deficiency resulting in a complete absence of leptin have been described (Montague et al. 1997; Strobel et al. 1998). The patients exhibit severe obesity, increased food intake, and hypogonadotropic hypogonadism. A mutation in the LEPR gene leads not only to the same features as in the LEP deficient patients but also to growth retardation and hypothyroidism (Clement et al. 1998). Normal LEP and LEPR genes and normal leptin levels are, therefore, necessary for somatic growth.

After the discovery of leptin, researchers soon realized that a main function of leptin could be to protect body fat stores against severe depletion. During caloric restriction or times of undernutrition, the adipose mass progressively decreases, which leads to a diminution of leptin production and leptin release from the adipose organ. Low leptin levels tend to reset food intake at a higher level and keep the metabolic rate in check to protect energy stores. Such a system confers clear evolutionary advantages (Rosenbaum and Leibel 1999) and has implications for growth and maturation in children living under impoverished conditions.

Leptin is also required for the normal development of reproductive function and probably also for the onset of pubertal events. The mice characterized by the absence of leptin because of an autosomal recessive mutation in the ob gene are infertile. When treated with recombinant leptin, these mice become fertile. Moreover, treating normal young mice with repeated injections of recombinant leptin hastens the first signs of puberty. These observations together with the clinical profile of the adult patients with LEP or LEPR deficiencies strongly suggest that normal leptin levels play an important role in the onset of puberty. Figure 19.20 depicts the pathways that are thought to be involved in the relation between leptin levels and puberty (Issad et al. 1998). This topic is addressed later in the next section.

Leptin is also involved in the regulation of the hypothalamic-pituitary-adrenal axis. It is inversely related to levels of ACTH and cortisol. For instance, leptin deficiency is associated with high blood glucocorticoid levels and increased risk of type 2 diabetes. Leptin enhances hematopoiesis and immune functions and undoubtedly impacts other pathways and functions as well.

Regulation of Puberty

The prepubertal years are characterized as a time of relatively slow, steady growth. Anabolism dominates and a general accretion of body tissues occurs. Growth hormone, IGF-I, and the thyroid hormones have growth-stimulating properties and are involved in the maintenance of normal growth during this time. In addition, adrenal cortical hormones, insulin, parathyroid hormone, and vitamin D participate in the regulation of tissue metabolism and the growth processes. The hypothalamic-pituitary-gonadal axis is functional and has been so since early infancy. However, it is kept in check, and secretion of gonadotropins and sex steroids is low (Grumbach and Kaplan 1990).

Puberty has been defined as a "transitional period between the juvenile state and adulthood" (Grumbach 1975). From a biological point of view, the pubertal years are characterized by the maturation of the secondary sex characteristics, the attainment of the capacity for procreation, and a physical growth spurt. These events are dominated by the stimulation of the testes or ovaries by gonadotropins secreted by the anterior pituitary and the markedly elevated production of sex steroids by the gonads. Production of GH also increases, that is, the amplitude of GH secretory bursts increases, with a concomitant rise in IGF-I production as a consequence of the rise in sex steroid production during midpuberty.

Because the onset of puberty does not appear to be limited by the functional-

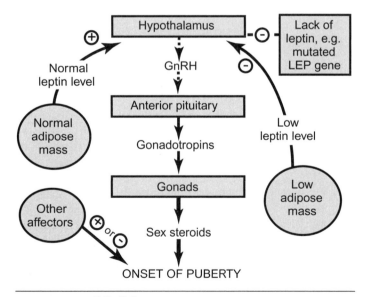

Leptin and the Onset of Puberty

FIGURE 19.20 Potential role of leptin in the onset of puberty. Leptin is not sufficient to trigger the advent of puberty. However, the absence of leptin prevents sexual maturation.

ity of the hypothalamic-pituitary-gonadal axis, its initiation is thought to reside in the central nervous system. Some evidence indicates that hypothalamic neurons from the arcuate nucleus producing gonadotropin-releasing hormone (GnRH) play a key role in this regard. Investigators have suggested that, after early infancy and throughout childhood, these neurons are inhibited by some unknown mechanisms that may involve low levels of sex hormones and secrete very little GnRH (Grumbach and Styne 1998). Late in the prepubertal period, the effectiveness of this inhibition decreases progressively, and the hypothalamic neurons begin to secrete increasing amounts of GnRH. Exposure to increasing levels of GnRH causes the anterior pituitary gonadotropic cells to increase the output of LH and FSH. In the presence of higher levels of LH and FSH, maturation of the gonads is promoted. The progressive rather than sudden maturation of the gonads brings about augmented secretion of sex steroids.

One of the first detectable signs that the sequence of events leading to sexual maturity has begun to unfold is an increase in LH secretion during sleep, late in childhood. The pulsatile release of LH gradually extends into the waking part of the day as puberty progresses. With sexual maturity, LH secretion occurs equally during the day and night in males and develops a cyclical pattern in females.

The biological events of puberty, accelerated body growth, rapid growth of the gonads, increased production of gonadotrophic and gonadal hormones, external genital development in boys, breast development and menarche in girls, and pubic hair development in both sexes have already been described (chapters 15 and 16). Puberty is not a single discrete event. It is a process fundamentally regulated by the central nervous system and presumably by specific hypothalamic neurons. Genetic factors are involved in the timing, sequence, and tempo of events associated with sexual maturation (chapter 18).

Genetic variation cannot account for all individual differences in the timing of these events. For instance, the age at menarche has decreased steadily in the Western nations during the past century but has stabilized in developed countries in recent decades (chapter 29). Environmental factors such as nutrition, energy expenditure associated with physical work, and socioeconomic conditions can also influence the age at onset of the pubertal events (chapters 23 and 25). One of the mechanisms through which these environmental factors may influence the early manifestations of puberty could

be energy balance regulation. Several early studies related low levels of body weight and adiposity to late-onset puberty (Frisch 1980). In contrast, obesity is often associated with accelerated sexual maturation in boys and girls (chapter 24). Elevated adiposity also hastens the maturation of reproductive functions in rodents (Kiess et al. 1998).

Until recently, a molecular hypothesis linking variation in energy balance to the age of onset of puberty was lacking. The discovery of leptin and the characterization of some of its central and peripheral effects have provided partial insights into the issue of the effect of some environmental factors on the timing of sexual maturation. Leptin levels are reasonable surrogates for the levels of adiposity. Leptin is also the ligand for the hypothalamic leptin receptor. Thus, leptin may serve as a messenger to signal the hypothalamus that the organism is ready to undergo sexual maturation (Kiess et al. 1998). However, leptin by itself does not appear to be the triggering factor of pubertal events. It appears to have a permissive role signaling the hypothalamus that adipocytes have enough energy stores to support sexual maturation and the energy de-

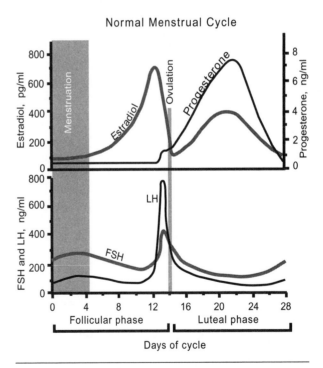

FIGURE 19.21   Cyclical profile and approximate plasma concentrations of gonadotropins and ovarian hormones during the normal menstrual cycle.

Reprinted, by permission, from A.C. Guyton, 1986, *Textbook of medical physiology*, 7th ed. (Saunders: Philadelphia), 969.

mands of reproduction (Grumbach and Styne 1998; Kiess et al. 1998). However, leptin levels do not exhibit a dramatic rise during the period that coincides with the onset of puberty in either sex, and a leptin surge does not appear necessary to trigger puberty (Roemmich and Rogol 1999). Nonetheless, a minimum level of leptin seems to be a necessary condition for sexual maturation to occur. Patients who have a total leptin deficiency because of a defective leptin gene never experience puberty (see previous section). See figure 19.20 for a summary of several of the pathways discussed in the preceding paragraphs.

Menstrual Cycle

Menstruation is the periodic shedding of the endometrium (uterine lining) that occurs with the attainment of sexual maturity. It occurs, on the average, every 28 days, with considerable variation among women. The key hormonal event in the ovarian cycle is the gonadotropin surge that precedes ovulation by 1 or 2 days. Solid evidence indicates that the GnRH neurons of the arcuate nucleus of the hypothalamus serve as the generator of a synchronized pulse signal, with a frequency of about 1 pulse/hour (Hotchkiss and Knobil 1994). The pulsatile secretion of GnRH into the anterior pituitary leads to pulsatile secretion of the gonadotropins LH and FSH, which, in turn, direct the production of ovarian hormones.

Phases of the Menstrual Cycle

By convention, the first day of menstrual bleeding is designated as the first day of the cycle. The menstrual cycle is also by convention divided into two phases, which are illustrated in figure 19.21. These two phases are referred to as the "follicular" phase and the "luteal" phase. The follicular phase of the cycle begins with menstruation, the cyclical uterine bleeding that includes blood and tissues from the uterine lining (endometrium). Menstrual bleeding lasts 3 to 7 days. Circulating levels of estrogen (estradiol) reach low levels at this time, and the hypothalamus and anterior pituitary respond by increasing production of GnRH and gonadotropic hormones, respectively. With the cessation of menstrual bleeding, the rebuilding of the endometrium lining, which was shed during the last menstruation, begins. As the uterine lining is being reconstructed under the influence of estrogens produced by the ovaries, a single dominant ovarian follicle matures

under the influence of FSH. Circulating levels of estrogens and FSH and LH gradually rise during the preovulatory period of the cycle. When the ovarian follicle is mature, it eventually ruptures and releases an egg into the fallopian tubes (ovulation). The important hormone at this time is LH, which triggers ovulation.

Ovulation occurs about 14 days after the start of menstruation. Concentrations of LH rise sharply near the end of the preovulatory period, reaching a peak called the midcycle LH peak. Concentrations of FSH show a similar pattern but attain a lower peak coincident with that of LH. Levels of estradiol rise more gradually during the preovulatory period and reach a peak coincident with the midcycle LH peak. The elevated levels of estrogens during the preovulatory period apparently enhance gonadotropin production (positive feedback) rather than decrease it (negative feedback). Levels of LH, FSH, and estrogens decline sharply just before ovulation.

After ovulation, the luteal phase of the cycle is dominated by the high levels of progesterone produced by the corpus luteum and by increasing concentrations of estrogens. Both are secreted in response to the action of LH, which is released at a progressively slowing rate. Assuming that fertilization of the released egg does not occur, the increasing levels of estrogens exert, at this phase of the cycle, a negative feedback to the hypothalamus and anterior pituitary so that production of FSH and LH is checked. Both estradiol and progesterone stimulate the reconstruction of the endometrium so that it increases in thickness during the postovulatory phase. At the end of the postovulatory phase, levels of estradiol and progesterone decline sharply. In the absence of pregnancy, the corpus luteum involutes about 2 weeks after its formation, and menstruation occurs (Hotchkiss and Knobil 1994). A new menstrual cycle is initiated.

Early Menstrual Cycles

The cyclical switching of estrogen effects from positive feedback in the preovulatory phase to negative feedback in the postovulatory phase matures sometime during midpuberty. The first menstrual bleeding is called menarche. It is a rather late event of puberty, occurring, on average, when most girls are in stage B4 for breasts and PH4 for pubic hair and about a year or so after peak height velocity (see chapter 16).

The first menstrual period and subsequent early periods are ordinarily anovulatory (i.e., no egg matures). Early menstrual cycles are also quite irregular. The development of more or less regular menstrual cycles takes place gradually over several years after menarche. This menstrual cycle length is shown in table 19.1 for a large series of girls followed over the course of the first 36 menstrual periods immediately after menarche. On the average, the first menstrual cycle after men-

arche is the longest. Cycle length then declines somewhat rapidly over the first three cycles and then more gradually over the remaining cycles. Variation around mean cycle length also declines systematically in a similar manner. In contrast, mean duration of menstrual flow in this series of adolescent girls is 5.5 days and does not vary with age at menarche and cycle number.

To recapitulate, the menstrual cycle is governed by neuroendocrine mechanisms with the major components being the hypothalamic arcuate nucleus GnRH neurons, the anterior pituitary gonadotropins, and the ovarian steroids. Undoubtedly innate trends are encoded in the hypothalamic neurons that play an important role in the periodicity and amplitude of the GnRH secretions and other inherited characteristics affecting the pituitary secretions and ovarian and uterine responses. However, other factors affect regulation of the cycle. Documented evidence exists that stress, fasting, overfeeding, demanding physical activity regimens, and other behaviors and factors have roles in influencing energy balance.

Overview of Hormones and Their Actions

By way of a summary, table 19.2 provides a list of the major hormones involved in the regulation of the processes underlying growth and maturation. The table also includes the main tissue(s) of origin of each hormone and its major activities related to growth and maturation. The list is by no means exhaustive, as large numbers of cytokines and growth factors are involved in the regulation of growth that were not reviewed in this chapter.

TABLE 19.1 Length of Menstrual Cycles Immediately After Menarche in British Girls From Newcastle Upon Tyne

Cycle number	Cycle length (days)	
	M	SD
1	49.5	30.8
2	39.8	21.7
3	35.4	17.6
4	34.8	16.0
5	32.5	13.1
6	32.6	11.8
7–9	33.5	14.2
10–12	32.4	11.5
13–18	31.4	8.9
19–24	30.8	8.5
25–30	30.4	7.9
31–36	29.5	6.1

Note: Cycle length was calculated in days, counting from and including the first day of menstrual flow up to the day preceding the next period of bleeding.

Adapted from Billewicz et al. (1980).

TABLE 19.2 A Partial List of Hormones Involved in the Regulation of Growth and Maturation

Hormone	Tissue of origin	Main growth-related effects
Adrenocorticotropic hormone (ACTH)	Anterior pituitary	Regulates secretion of glucocorticoids and androgens from adrenal cortex; increases lipolysis and glucose and amino acids uptake
Aldosterone	Adrenal cortex	Regulates sodium and potassium homeostasis and extracellular fluid volume
Androstenedione	Adrenal cortex	In males, converted into estrogens in peripheral tissues
Calcitonin	Thyroid gland	Decreases circulating calcium by either inhibiting bone resorption or increasing the rate of calcium deposition in bone
Corticotropin-releasing hormone (CRH)	Hypothalamus	Stimulates the secretion of adrenocorticotropic hormone by the anterior pituitary
Cortisol	Adrenal cortex	Increases blood glucose and fat mobilization; anti-inflammatory action

(continued)

TABLE
19.2 *(continued)*

Hormone	Tissue of origin	Main growth-related effects
Dehydroepiandrosterone	Adrenal cortex	In females, converted into testosterone in peripheral tissues
Estradiol and progesterone	Primarily ovarian follicles, also adrenal cortex	Acts on the primary and secondary sex characteristics of females; promotes nitrogen retention, tissue buildup, and skeletal maturation; promotes accumulation of fat in females
Follicle-stimulating hormone (FSH)	Anterior pituitary	Stimulation of ovarian follicles and estrogen synthesis in females; growth of seminiferous tubules and production of sperm in males
Glucagon	Pancreas (α-cells of Islets of Langerhans)	Increases the concentration of blood glucose; promotes hepatic glucose release
Gonadotropin-releasing hormone (GnRH)	Hypothalamus	Stimulates the secretion of follicle-stimulating hormone (FSH) and luteinizing hormone (LH) by the anterior pituitary
Growth hormone (GH, or somatotropin)	Anterior pituitary	Decreases the rate of carbohydrate uptake; enhances the mobilization of lipids from adipose tissue; stimulates the production of insulinlike growth factors by the liver to enhance growth of muscle and bone
Growth hormone–releasing hormone (GHRH)	Hypothalamus	Stimulates the release of growth hormone by anterior pituitary
Insulin	Pancreas (β-cells of Islets of Langerhans)	Enhances the rate of glucose uptake from blood and increases glycogen and lipid stores; stimulates transport of glucose and amino acids through cell membranes; essential for the full expression of effects of growth hormone; promotes protein synthesis
Insulinlike growth factors–I and –II	Liver and many others	Stimulate protein synthesis, cell proliferation, and nitrogen retention; stimulate the proliferation of cartilage cells at the growth plates of long bones resulting in the linear growth of bones
Leptin	Adipose tissue	Reduces appetite and increases satiety; increases energy expenditure; influences glucose and lipid metabolism; essential for puberty to occur
Luteinizing hormone (LH)	Anterior pituitary	Promotes maturation of an ovarian follicle and ovulation; stimulates estrogen and progesterone secretion from ovary; in males, stimulates testosterone production by the Leydig cells
Parathormone (PTH)	Parathyroid glands	Increases circulating calcium by stimulating bone resorption and decreasing calcium excretion in the urine
Somatotropin releasing–inhibiting factor (SRIF) or somatostatin	Hypothalamus	Inhibits the release of growth hormone
Testosterone	Primarily testes, also adrenal cortex	Acts on the primary and secondary sex characteristics of males; promotes adolescent growth spurt in muscle and fat-free mass in males; also promotes bone growth and skeletal maturation
Thyrotropin (TSH, or thyroid-stimulating hormone)	Anterior pituitary	Controls secretions of the thyroid gland
Thyrotropin-releasing hormone (TRH)	Hypothalamus	Stimulates the release of thyrotropin by the anterior pituitary
Thyroxine (T_4) and triiodothyronine (T_3)	Thyroid gland	Thyroxine is essential for growth hormone to produce its full effects; both stimulate metabolic rate and activity in most tissues

Summary

The list of the hormones involved in the regulation of the processes underlying growth and maturation is lengthy, and recent advances in understanding the biology of hormones and mechanisms of their actions highlight the complexity of these processes. In recent years, several new growth-promoting factors secreted by the liver, adipose tissue, and other organs have been identified. However, their roles in growth and maturation are poorly defined at this time. Growth hormone, IGF-I, and the thyroid hormones have growth-stimulating properties and are primarily involved in the maintenance of normal growth during childhood. The events of puberty and the adolescent growth spurt are dominated by the stimulation of the testes or ovaries by gonadotropins secreted by the anterior pituitary and the markedly elevated production of sex steroids by the gonads. Production of growth hormone increases at this time as a consequence of the rise in sex steroid production during midpuberty. The onset of puberty is mediated by changes in the central nervous system, specifically the hypothalamus. Recent evidence suggests a role for leptin in sexual maturation. Leptin is necessary for sexual maturation to occur, but it is not by itself the triggering factor of puberty.

Sources and Suggested Readings

Argente J, Barrios V, Chowen JA, Sinha MK, Considine RV (1997) Leptin plasma levels in healthy Spanish children and adolescents, children with obesity, and adolescents with anorexia nervosa and bulimia nervosa. Journal of Pediatrics 131:833-838.

Baxter JD, Frohman LA, Felig P (1995) Introduction to the endocrine system. In P Felig, JD Baxter, LA Frohman (eds), Endocrinology and Metabolism, 3rd edition. New York: McGraw-Hill, pp 3-10.

Billewicz WZ, Fellowes HM, Thomson AM (1980) Post-menarcheal menstrual cycles in British (Newcastle upon Tyne) girls. Annals of Human Biology 7:177-180.

Boyar RM (1978) Control of the onset of puberty. Annual Review of Medicine 29:509-520.

Boyd E (1952) An Introduction to Human Biology and Anatomy for First Year Medical Students. Denver: Child Research Council.

Bronson FH, Rissman EF (1986) The biology of puberty. Biological Reviews 61:157-195.

Campfield LA (1999) Multiple facets of OB protein (leptin) physiology: Integration of central and peripheral mechanisms in the regulation of energy balance. In B Guy-Grand, G Ailhaud (eds), Progress in Obesity Research: 8. London: John Libbey, pp 327-335.

Carr BR (1998) Disorders of the ovaries and female reproductive tract. In JD Wilson, DW Foster, HM Kronenberg, PR Larsen (eds), Williams Textbook of Endocrinology, 9th edition. Philadelphia: Saunders, pp 751-818.

Catt KJ (1995) Molecular mechanisms of hormone action: Control of target cell function by peptide and catecholamine hormones. In P Felig, JD Baxter, LA Frohman (eds), Endocrinology and Metabolism, 3rd edition. New York: McGraw-Hill, pp 91-168.

Clayton PE, Gill MS, Hall CM, Tillmann V, Whatmore AJ, Price DA (1997) Serum leptin through childhood and adolescence. Clinical Endocrinology 46:727-733.

Clement K, Vaisse C, Lahlou N, Cabrol S, Pelloux V, Cassuto D, Gourmelen M, Dina C, Chambaz J, Lacorte JM, Basdevant A, Bougneres P, Lebouc Y, Froguel P, Guy-Grand B (1998) A mutation in the human leptin receptor gene causes obesity and pituitary dysfunction. Nature 392: 398-401.

*Clemmons DR, Underwood LE (1991) Nutritional regulation of IGF-I and IGF binding proteins. Annual Review of Nutrition 11:393-412.

Cryer PE (1995) Diseases of the sympathocromaffin system. In P Felig, JD Baxter, LA Frohman (eds) Endocrinology and Metabolism, 3rd edition. New York: McGraw-Hill, pp 713-748.

Cutler GB Jr, Schiebinger RJ, Albertson BD, Cassorla FG, Chrousos GP, Comite F, Booth JD, Levine J, Hobson WC, Loriaux DL (1990) The adrenarche (human and animal). In MM Grumbach, PC Sizonenko, Aubert ML (eds), Control of the Onset of Puberty. Baltimore: Williams and Wilkins, pp 506-533.

Erickson GF (1995) The ovary: Basic principles and concepts. In P Felig, JD Baxter, LA Frohman (eds), Endocrinology and Metabolism, 3rd edition. New York: McGraw-Hill, pp 973-1015.

Esoterix, Inc. (2000) Endocrinology: Expected Values and S.I. Unit Conversion Tables, 5th edition. Calabasas Hills, CA: Esoteric, Inc.

Fauci AS, Braunwald E, Isselbacher KJ, Wilson JD, Martin JB, Kasper DL, Houser SL, Longo DL (1998) Harrison's Principles of Internal Medicine. New York: McGraw-Hill.

Felig P, Bergman M (1995) The endocrine pancreas: Diabetes mellitus. In P Felig, JD Baxter, LA Frohman (eds), Endocrinology and Metabolism, 3rd edition. New York: McGraw-Hill, pp 1107-1250.

* Felig P, Baxter JD, Frohman LA, editors (1995) Endocrinology and Metabolism, 3rd edition. New York: McGraw-Hill.

Friedman, JM (1999) Leptin, leptin receptors and the pathogenesis of obesity. In B Guy-Grand, G Ailhaud (eds), Progress in Obesity Research: 8. London: John Libbey, pp 307-326.

Frisch RE (1980) Pubertal adipose tissue: Is it necessary for normal sexual maturation? Evidence from the rat and human female. Federal Proceedings 39: 2395-2400.

Frohman LA (1995) Diseases of the anterior pituitary. In P Felig, JD Baxter, LA Frohman (eds), Endocrinology and Metabolism, 3rd edition. New York: McGraw-Hill, pp 289-384.

Griffin JE, Wilson JD (1998) Disorders of the testes and the male reproductive tract. In JD Wilson, DW Foster, HM Kronenberg, PR Larsen (eds), Williams Textbook of Endocrinology, 9th edition. Philadelphia: Saunders, pp 819-876.

Grumbach MM (1975) The onset of puberty. In SR Berenberg (ed), Puberty, Biologic and Psychosocial Components. Leiden: Stenfert Kroese, pp 1-21.

Grumbach MM (1980) The neuroendocrinology of puberty. In DT Krieger, JC Hughes (eds), Neuroendocrinology. Sunderland, MA: Sinauer Associates, pp 249-258.

* Grumbach MM, Kaplan SL (1990) The neuroendocrinology of human puberty: An ontogenetic perspective. In MM Grumbach, PC Sizonenko, ML Aubert (eds), Control of the Onset of Puberty. Baltimore: Williams & Wilkins, pp 1-68.

* Grumbach MM, Styne DM (1998) Puberty: Ontogeny, neuro-endocrinology, physiology, and disorders. In JD Wilson, DW Foster, HM Kronenberg, PR Larsen (eds), Williams Textbook of Endocrinology, 9th edition. Philadelphia: Saunders, pp 1509-1626.

Guyton AC (1986) Textbook of Medical Physiology, 7th edition. Philadelphia: Saunders.

* Hotchkiss J, Knobil E (1994) The menstrual cycle and its neuroendocrine control. In E Knobil, JD Neill (eds), The Physiology of Reproduction, 2nd edition. New York: Raven Press, pp 711-749.

Isaksson OGP, Lindahl A, Nilsson A, Isgaard J (1987) Mechanism of the stimulatory effect of growth hormone on longitudinal bone growth. Endocrine Reviews 8: 426-438.

* Issad T, Strobel A, Camoin L, Ozata M, Strosberg AD (1998) Leptin and puberty in humans: Hypothesis of the critical adipose mass revisited. Diabete et Metabolisme 23: 376-378.

Kahn CR, Smith RJ, Chin WW (1998) Mechanism of action of hormones that act at the cell surface. In JD Wilson, DW Foster, HM Kronenberg, PR Larsen (eds), Williams Textbook of Endocrinology, 9th edition. Philadelphia: Saunders, pp 95-144.

Kerrigan JR, Rogol AD (1992) The impact of gonadal steroid hormone action on growth hormone secretion during childhood and adolescence. Endocrine Reviews 13: 281-298.

* Kiess W, Blum WF, Aubert ML (1998) Leptin, puberty and reproductive function: Lessons from animal studies and observations in humans. European Journal of Endocrinology 138: 26-29.

Knutsson U, Dahlgren J, Marcus C, Rosberg S, Bronnegard M, Stierna P, Albertsson-Wikland K (1997) Circadian cortisol rhythms in healthy boys and girls: Relationship with age, growth, body composition, and pubertal development. Journal of Clinical Endocrinology and Metabolism 82: 536-540.

Licinio J, Mantzoros C, Negrao AB, Cizza G, Wong ML, Bongioro PB, Chrousos GP, Karp B, Allen C, Flier J, Gold PW (1997) Human leptin levels are pulsatile and inversely related to pituitary-adrenal function. Nature Medicine 3: 575-579.

Loche S, Cherubini V, Bartolotta E, Lampis A, Carta D, Tomasi P, Pintor C (1994) Pulsatile secretion of thyrotropin in children. Journal of Endocrinological Investigation 17: 189-193.

* MacGillivray MH (1995) Disorders of growth and development. In P Felig, JD Baxter, LA Frohman (eds), Endocrinology and Metabolism, 3rd edition. New York: McGraw-Hill, pp 1619-1675.

* Martha PM, Rogol AD, Veldius JD, Kerrigan JR, Goodman DW, Blizzard RM (1989) Alterations in the pulsatile properties of circulating growth hormone concentrations during puberty in boys. Journal of Clinical Endocrinology and Metabolism 69: 563-570.

Mauras N, Haymond MW, Darmaun D, Vieira NE, Abrams SA, Yergey AL (1994) Calcium and protein kinetics in prepubertal boys: Positive effects of testosterone. Journal of Clinical Investigation 93: 1014-1019.

Mauras N (1995) Estrogens do not affect whole-body protein metabolism in the prepubertal female. Journal of Clinical Endocrinology and Metabolism 80: 2842-2845.

Miller WL, Tyrrell JB (1995) The adrenal cortex. In P Felig, JD Baxter, LA Frohman (eds), Endocrinology and Metabolism, 3rd edition. New York: McGraw-Hill, pp 555-712.

Molitch ME (1995) Neuroendocrinology. In P Felig, JD Baxter, LA Frohman (eds), Endocrinology and Metabolism, 3rd edition. New York: McGraw-Hill, pp 221-288.

Montague Farooqi IS, Whitehead JP, Soos MA, Rau H, Wareham NJ, Sewter CP, Digby JE, Mohammed SN, Hurst JA, Cheetham CH, Earley AR, Barnett AH, Prins JB, O'Rahilly S (1997) Congenital leptin deficiency is associated with severe early-onset obesity in humans. Nature 387: 903-908.

Nelson JC, Clark SJ, Borut DL, Tomei RT, Carlton EI (1993) Age-related changes in serum free thyroxine during childhood and adolescence. Journal of Pediatrics 123: 899-905.

O'Brien RM, Granner DK (1996) Regulation of gene expression by insulin. Physiological Reviews 76: 1109-1161.

Preece MA (1986) Prepubertal and pubertal endocrinology. In F Falkner, JM Tanner (eds), Human Growth. Volume 2. Postnatal Growth, Neurobiology. New York: Plenum, pp 211-224.

Reichlin S (1998) Neuroendocrinology. In JD Wilson, DW Foster, HM Kronenberg, PR Larsen (eds), Williams Textbook of Endocrinology, 9th edition. Philadelphia: Saunders, pp 165-248.

Reiter EO, Grumbach MM (1982) Neuroendocrine control mechanisms and the onset of puberty. Annual Review of Physiology 44:595-613.

Roemmich JN, Clark PA, Berr SS, Mai V, Mantzoros CS, Flier JS, Weltman A, Rogol AD (1998) Gender differences in leptin levels during puberty are related to the subcutaneous fat depot and sex steroids. American Journal of Physiology 275:E543-E551.

* Roemmich JN, Rogol AD (1999). Role of leptin during childhood growth and development. Endocrinology and Metabolism Clinics of North America 28:749-764.

Root AW (1994) Serum polypeptide hormone-binding proteins. Part 1: Growth hormone–binding proteins. Growth, Genetics and Hormones 10:5-7.

Rosenbaum M, Leibel RL (1999) The role of leptin in human physiology. New England Journal of Medicine 341:913-915.

Santen RJ (1995) Gonadal disease. In P Felig, JD Baxter, LA Frohman (eds), Endocrinology and Metabolism, 3rd edition. New York: McGraw-Hill, pp 885-972.

Smith EP, Korach KS (1996) Oestrogen receptor deficiency: Consequences for growth. Acta Paediatrica 417 (suppl): 39-44.

Strewler GJ, Rosenblatt M (1995) Mineral metabolism. In P Felig, JD Baxter, LA Frohman (eds), Endocrinology and Metabolism, 3rd edition. New York: McGraw-Hill, pp 1407-1516.

Strobel A, Issad T, Camoin L, Ozata M, Strosberg AD (1998) A leptin missense mutation associated with hypogonadism and morbid obesity. Nature Genetics 18: 213-215.

Tanner JM (1962) Growth at Adolescence, 2nd edition. Oxford: Blackwell.

Tanner JM, Preece MA (eds) (1989) The Physiology of Human Growth. Cambridge, UK: Cambridge University Press.

Thorner MO, Vance ML, Laws ER Jr., Horvath E, Kovacs K (1998) The anterior pituitary. In JD Wilson, DW Foster, HM Kronenberg, PR Larsen (eds), Williams Textbook of Endocrinology, 9th edition. Philadelphia: Saunders, pp 249-340.

Tsai MJ, Clark JH, Schrader WT, O'Malley BW (1998) Mechanisms of action of hormones that act as transcription-regulatory factors. In JD Wilson, DW Foster, HM Kronenberg, PR Larsen (eds), Williams Textbook of Endocrinology, 9th edition. Philadelphia: Saunders, pp 55-94.

Underwood LE, Van Wyk JJ (1985) Normal and aberrant growth. In JD Wilson, DM Foster (eds), Williams Textbook of Endocrinology, 9th edition. Philadelphia: Saunders, pp 155-205.

Utiger RD (1995) The thyroid: Physiology, thyrotoxicosis, hypothyroidism, and the painful thyroid. In P Felig, JD Baxter, LA Frohman (eds), Endocrinology and Metabolism, 3rd edition. New York: McGraw-Hill, pp 435-520.

Van Wyk JJ, Underwood LE (1980) Growth hormone, somatomedins, and growth failure. In DT Krieger, JC Hughes (eds), Neuroendocrinology. Sunderland, MA: Sinauer Associates, pp 299-309.

Wierman ME, Crowley WF (1986) Neuroendocrine control of the onset of puberty. In F Falkner, JM Tanner (eds), Human Growth. Volume 2. Postnatal Growth, Neurobiology. New York: Plenum, pp 225-241.

Wilson JD (1998) Approach to the patient with endocrine and metabolic disorders. In AS Fauci, JB Martin, E Braunwald, DL Kasper, KJ Isselbacher, SL Hauser, JD Wilson, DL Longo (eds), Harrison's Principles of Internal Medicine, 14th edition. New York: McGraw-Hill.

Wilson JD, Foster DW, Kronenberg HM, Larsen PR, editors (1998) Williams Textbook of Endocrinology, 9th edition. Philadelphia: Saunders, pp 1965-1971.

Winter JSD (1978) Prepubertal and pubertal endocrinology. In F Falkner, JM Tanner (eds), Human Growth. Volume 2. Postnatal Growth. New York: Plenum, pp 183-213.

Young JB, Landsberg L (1998) Catecholamines and the adrenal medulla. In JD Wilson, DW Foster, HM Kronenberg, PR Larsen (eds), Williams Textbook of Endocrinology, 9th edition. Philadelphia: Saunders, pp 665-728.

Zhang Y, Proenca R, Maffei M, Barone M, Leopold L, Friedman JM (1994) Positional cloning of the mouse obese gene and its human homologue. Nature 372: 425-432.

ENERGY AND NUTRITIONAL REQUIREMENTS

Chapter Outline

Successful growth is dependent on a variety of inherited and environmental factors. Among environmental factors, nutrition is paramount. Nutritional needs and influences vary during the growing years. The nutritional requirements of rapid growth in the first 2 years of life differ, for example, from the nutritional requirements in the years of slower growth in middle childhood.

Nutrition is a process that concerns the relationship of food intake to the functioning of the organism. Physiological aspects of the process include intake of food; digestion, absorption, and transport of nutrients; transformation and storage of substrates; utilization of nutrients for the synthesis and maintenance of tissues; and mobilization of energy. Other aspects of the nutritional process relate to social and cultural conditions, which include socioeconomic background, food production and preparation, attitudes and beliefs about food, and habits of physical activity. The nutritional process has important biological consequences, which, among others, can permanently alter the functioning of the organism. Nutrition is thus broad in scope

and is of primary concern throughout the life cycle.

Eating is a social behavior, and the food that is eaten is regulated by the cultural context within which an individual lives. What is considered food in one culture may not be considered food in another culture. Cultural influences on nutrition are thus important, especially for young individuals whose intake is regulated to a large extent by the family. The dependency of the child on parents, especially the mother, and in some cases on social institutions, indicates that the nutritional environment of the developing child is not under the child's control. In adolescence, the role of peers adds another dimension to cultural influences affecting nutritional intake. In addition, the electronic media, especially television, are significant influences on the food preferences and habits of children and adolescents.

This chapter focuses on the nutritional requirements for normal growth and maturation and the energetics of growth. Consequences of chronic undernutrition or chronic overnutrition, specifically overweight and obesity, are considered in chapters 23 and 24, respectively.

Nutrients

Nutrients are components of food. Individuals eat food; they do not eat nutrients. However, the science of nutrition is best approached in terms of macronutrients and micronutrients. The six classes of nutrients are water, carbohydrates, fats, proteins, vitamins, and minerals. Water, although often taken for granted, functions primarily as a solvent and in body temperature regulation, and it is perhaps the most important nutrient. The relative water content of the body decreases from early in prenatal life through the growing years. Water constitutes about 75% of body weight at birth but only about 62% of body weight in young adulthood (see chapter 5). From birth to 1 year of age, fluid intake of about 150 ml/kg/day is recommended. The absolute requirement is probably only about 50% of this fluid intake level, but, because of abundant water losses, including those from vomiting and diarrhea, the recommended level is safer (Heird 2001).

Carbohydrates function as the main energy sources for the body. Carbohydrate stores in the body are quite small, only about 0.4% to 0.5% of body weight during childhood and young adulthood. Fats or lipids also provide energy, but much of it is stored as triacylglycerols in adipose tissue. Fat content of the body varies during growth, with considerable variation between the sexes and among individuals. Proteins are also a source of energy, but their primary functions are in the growth, maintenance, and repair of body tissues, providing the precursors for the synthesis of enzymes, hormones, antibodies, carrier molecules, contractile units, and structural elements and others.

Vitamins are primarily regulatory in function, acting as cofactors in chemical reactions in cells. They are typically required in small amounts. Minerals are also required in small amounts. The precise role of many minerals in the processes of growth and maturation, transport functions, and critical chemical reactions of metabolism, among other important physiological processes, is only gradually being understood.

Although nutrients are generally treated individually, they do not function in isolation. Rather, nutrients are dependent on other nutrients, on enzymes and hormones, and on the functional integrity of tissues and organs. The availability and utilization of carbohydrates, for example, are dependent on insulin, glucagon, and other hormones; vitamins of the B complex; the func-

tional state of the gastrointestinal tract, especially the mucous membrane; and enzyme-dependent metabolic pathways primarily in muscles, liver, and kidneys. An example of nutrient dependency is the function of zinc. It is found in high concentrations in male sex organs, and testicular zinc metabolism is partly regulated by androgens. In addition, the form of a nutrient in food can affect its absorption and utilization. Iron of vegetable origin, for example, has a low efficiency of absorption, whereas iron of animal origin is better absorbed.

Individual macronutrients (proteins, lipids, and carbohydrates) and micronutrients (vitamins and minerals) are subsequently discussed in the context of growth and maturation. Their other functions are mentioned in passing. Water requirements are discussed in the context of temperature regulation in chapter 14.

Breast-Feeding and the Infant

Feeding the newborn represents a series of unique challenges. This issue is complex and beyond the scope of the present chapter. Health authorities around the world are almost unanimous in recommending that the newborn be exclusively breast-fed for the first 4 to 6 months of life if the mother can do so adequately. However, a substantial proportion of mothers in developed countries use infant formulas or rely on breast-feeding for only a few weeks or months. Evidence indicates that feeding an infant with cow's milk may increase the risk of nutritional deficiencies. The ingestion of cow's milk by young infants results in the consumption of about three times more protein and about 50% more sodium than the recommended intakes but only about 60% of the iron and 50% of linoleic acid thought to be necessary for normal growth during infancy (Heird 2001).

Even though infant formulas commonly used in the developed countries are thought to be nutritionally adequate for infants, breast milk contains some unique constituents. Breast milk is a source of docosahexanoic acid, taurine, choline, lactoferrin, inositol, and macrophages (Bhatia et al. 2002). Differences between breast milk, cow's milk, and modern infant formulas have led to the conviction that breast-feeding the infant can result in better resistance to infection and perhaps more optimal intestinal development. Little is known about the impact of breast-feeding or infant formula–feeding on subsequent growth and functional development during childhood and adolescence, and on adulthood health outcomes.

Energy Needs

Energy requirements of the growing organism are met by the breakdown of ingested macronutrients and body energy stores. The catabolism or breakdown of energy-rich foods (primarily carbohydrates and lipids) and stored energy (primarily glycogen and triglycerides [triacylglycerides]) generates energy that is entrapped in adenosine triphosphate (ATP). The hydrolysis of ATP to adenosine diphosphate (ADP) releases free energy that is used to drive all kinds of cellular processes, including protein synthesis or skeletal muscle contraction. Only about 40 g of ATP are available in the body of an adult at a given point in time, and much less is available in the infant and the growing child. Therefore, ingested or stored metabolic fuels must be constantly broken down for the high-energy bonds to be captured for the regeneration of ATP. The term energy metabolism is used to represent all of the processes associated with the catabolism of metabolic fuels to meet the energy needs of the body. In this context, energy expenditure represents the amount of ATP hydrolyzed to ADP over a given period of time. Because molecular oxygen is required in the mitochondrion for the oxidative phosphorylation of ADP to ATP, the oxygen consumption of the body is a valid surrogate for the amount of energy expended.

The energy available as metabolic fuel after the losses in urine and feces is called the metabolizable energy. In healthy children, adolescents, and adults, energy losses in the urine and feces amount to only about 1% and 3% of ingested energy. Metabolizable energy varies among macronutrients or body energy stores (Livesey and Elia 1988). The oxidation of 1 g of carbohydrate yields approximately 4.2 kcal of metabolizable energy. The yields are about 9.4 kcal for 1 g of lipids, 4.7 kcal for 1 g of protein, and 7.1 kcal for 1 g of ethanol (alcohol). In practice, values of 4 kcal (17 kJ/g) for carbohydrate and protein, 7 kcal (29 kJ/g) for ethanol, and 9 kcal (38 kJ/g) for lipid are commonly used. Only about 40% of the energy contained in the macronutrients or metabolic fuels is conserved in the high-energy bonds of ATP. The remainder of the energy is dissipated as heat and results primarily from the imperfect coupling between oxygen uptake and ATP resynthesis in the mitochondrial respiratory chain. Assuming a mixed diet, 1 L of oxygen uptake generates approximately 5 kcal (21 kJ) of energy expenditure.

Protein is a source of both calories and essential amino acids. If energy intake is inadequate, dietary protein will be used for energy and will not be available for tissue growth and maintenance and for the synthesis of other proteins. Proteins, lipids, and carbohydrates are intimately related through various metabolic pathways that can be used for the regeneration of ATP, as some of their intermediate products can enter the tricarboxylic acid (Krebs) cycle to sustain the phosphorylation of ADP. In addition, each of the three energy nutrients provides intermediate molecules that can, under certain conditions, be used to support the conversion of one class of nutrient to another. For instance, glucose can be converted into lipids or amino acids. Fatty acids cannot be transformed into glucose, but the glycerol molecule that acts as the backbone of triglycerides can be involved in the synthesis of glucose. Moreover, some amino acids are used after deamination in lipogenesis and gluconeogenesis. In other words, metabolic regulation of energy is a complex, highly integrated process. The liver, kidneys, skeletal muscles, and adipose tissue are primarily involved in this metabolic traffic.

The relationships among the catabolic pathways for macronutrients are schematically illustrated in figure 20.1. The importance of acetyl-CoA as an intermediary molecule in the enzymatic degradation of metabolic fuels is evident. The degradation pathways lead ultimately to the oxidation of the substrates with the concomitant synthesis of ATP and the production of carbon dioxide and water. Also shown in the figure are the pathways for the biosynthesis of the stored or metabolic forms of the three macronutrients. The biosynthesis pathways are not simply the reverse of the catabolic pathways. They begin with different precursors and proceed along paths that require energy rather than generate ATP.

Calories can be regarded in terms of those ingested and those expended and in terms of energy balance. Energy balance refers to the sum total of energy intake minus energy expenditure over a given period of time. A positive energy balance (i.e., excess input over expenditure) is necessary for growth to occur over long periods of time. With a positive energy balance during growth,

Macronutrients' Catabolic and Anabolic Pathways

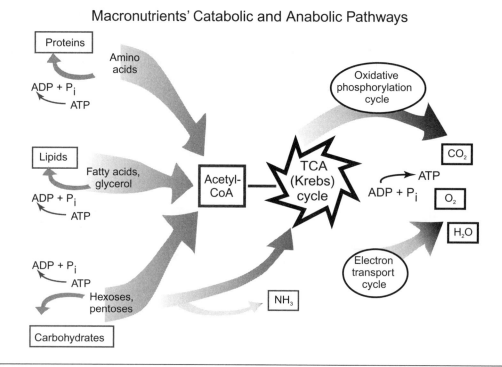

FIGURE 20.1 Catabolic and anabolic pathways for each of the three macronutrients and their interactions at the level of acetyl-CoA and the biosynthesis of larger molecules from precursors for storage in organs and tissues or for metabolic needs. (TCA = tricarboxylic acid).

energy is transformed into tissue components and results in accretion of protoplasm and protein and in cell division in some tissues, all of which are important mechanisms of growth.

When energy intake exceeds output, chemical energy in the form of triglycerides is stored in adipose tissue. Mobilization of chemical energy from adipose tissue occurs when the output of energy exceeds transiently (e.g., overnight fasting) the immediately available metabolic fuel or when energy intake is consistently below energy expenditure (negative energy balance). Energy intake and energy output influence each other. For example, chronic overfeeding results in an increase in metabolism (oxygen consumption), but a long-term increase in physical activity is followed by a corresponding increase in food intake.

Energy Requirements for Growth

Energy requirements can be viewed in terms of those necessary for the maintenance of basal and resting metabolic states; for the support of normal growth and maturation of the young organism;

for the maintenance, repair, and replacement of tissues; for the conduct of physical activities; and for unexpected or unusual stresses on the organism, such as severe illnesses or chronic diarrhea. Requirements also vary with age, sex, body mass (particularly fat-free mass), and physiological states. They are also influenced by a number of environmental factors, either directly or indirectly, such as temperature (exposure to ambient cold or heat), high altitude, infectious and parasitic disease agents, and culturally mediated dietary habits such as various forms of vegetarianism or exotic diets.

Individual variation in nutritional requirements is considerable and probably reflects variation in genes related to the processing of nutrients in the body. Thus, genotype-nutrient interactions impact individual differences in nutrient and energy needs. For example, given similar food intakes, individual variation in the efficiency of converting food energy to metabolic fuels may account for a small fraction of the obesity cases in a population of children and adolescents.

The processes of growth and maturation are obviously important for understanding energy and nutrient requirements. Growth and maturation are accompanied by significant changes in overall body mass and composition. Growth of body mass, body composition, and specific organs and tissues have been described in previous chapters. In brief, the relative water content of the body decreases during growth as solids are added (i.e., the relative contents of protein, mineral, and fat increase). For instance, the daily increment in the protein content of the body between 10 and 20 years of age is about 2 g for males and 1 g for females. However, during the period of maximum growth during adolescence, the estimated daily increment in protein content of the body is much greater, about 4 g in males and 2 g in females. Thus, the adolescent growth spurt contributes significantly to energy and nutrient requirements at this time.

The physiological processes that underlie growth and maturation have, therefore, unique nutrient and energy requirements. Much is known about the nutrient and energy needs of infants and young children and of children with clinical problems, whereas corresponding data on the nutrient and energy requirements of healthy school-age children and adolescents are less extensive. Hence, some uncertainty may exist about the nutrient and energy needs of developing individuals in a variety of circumstances.

The main components of habitual energy expenditure are listed in table 20.1 They include basal and resting energy expenditure, the thermic response to food consumption, energy expenditure associated with movement and physical activity, the energy requirements to adjust to hot or cold environments in some circumstances, and the energy expenditure of growth per se. Metabolic chamber measurements over 24-hour periods allow for the quantification of the energy expanded during the sleeping hours, the so-called sleeping metabolic rate (SMR). SMR provides the lowest metabolic rate compatible with life. In

practice, SMR is only slightly lower than basal metabolic rate (BMR), which is assessed in the awake state but lying in bed after sleep and in a fasting state. Both SMR and BMR are slightly lower than resting metabolic rate (RMR), which is typically measured by indirect calorimetry with a ventilated hood for periods ranging from 20 to 60 minutes in the morning and with the subject in the fasted resting state.

BMR of the young adult reference man (1,680 kcal/day) and woman (1,340 kcal/day), both with a BMI of 22.5 kg/m^2, accounts for most of the daily energy expenditure in the young sedentary adult (i.e., about 60% to 75%). The brain (about 20%), liver (about 20%), heart (about 10%), and kidneys (about 10%) account for large fractions of the energy expended at rest in the reference man and woman (Holliday 1978; Elia 1992). Skeletal muscle mass accounts for about 25% of the remaining energy expended under basal or resting conditions. Hence, about 85% of the energy expended at rest by the young sedentary adult is associated with the basic metabolic needs of these organs and tissues. Estimated metabolic rates of specific tissues in a 6-month-old infant and in the young adult reference man are summarized in table 20.2. The 24-hour metabolic rate for the infant is estimated at 390 kcal or 52 kcal/kg body mass. In contrast, the adult male or female has a 24-hour RMR of about 24 kcal/kg of body mass. The partitioning of the metabolic rate of the 6-month-old infant is as follows: brain, 44%; liver, 14%; heart, 4%; kidneys, 6%; skeletal muscle, 6%, and other tissues and organs, 26%. The brain contributes proportionally more to the BMR in the infant, whereas the liver and muscle mass contribute proportionally more to the BMR in the adult.

SMR, BMR, and RMR increase as a function of body mass and are closely related to the size of the fat-free mass in adults (Ravussin and Bogardus 1989). Changes in BMR during growth are illustrated in figure 20.2. BMR increases with body weight, but the increase in the BMR is smaller as adult body mass is approached. However, when BMR is expressed on per kg body mass, it declines during growth. A small difference exists between boys and girls, which becomes more apparent as boys gain more lean tissue mass during adolescence.

On the average, 6% to 8% of the energy content of ingested food is expended in thermogenesis (thermic effect of food) over the 5 to 6 hours after the consumption of a meal. The thermic response

TABLE 20.1 Components of Energy Expenditure During Childhood and Adolescence

Basal metabolic rate
Resting metabolic rate
Thermic effect of food consumption
Adjustments to hot or cold environments
Energy expenditure of physical activity
Energy requirements for growth

TABLE 20.2   Organ Size and Estimated Metabolic Rates in an Average Young Adult Male and a 6-Month-Old Infant

	Organ weight (kg)		Organ metabolic rate (kcal/kg/day)	Contribution to BMR (%)	
	Adult	Infant		Adult	Infant
Liver	1.8	0.26	200	21	14
Brain	1.4	0.71	240	20	44
Heart	0.33	0.04	440	9	4
Kidneys	0.31	0.05	440	8	6
Muscle	28.0	1.88	13	22	6
Other tissues	23.16	4.56	9	20	26
Total	70.0	7.5		100	100

The BMR in a 70 kg reference male is about 1,680 kcal/day and the BMR in a 6-month-old infant is 390 kcal/day. To convert kcal to kJ, multiply by 4.18.

Adapted from Elia (1992).

is influenced by the macronutrient composition of the food ingested. It is slightly higher with meals rich in proteins or carbohydrates than with meals of high lipid content. Variation in the thermogenic

Changes in BMR During Growth

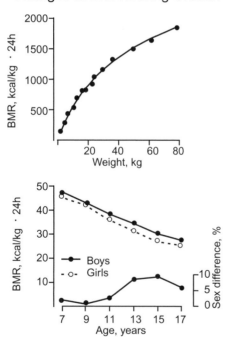

FIGURE 20.2   Changes in BMR during growth. The upper panel illustrates the relationship between BMR and body weight from infancy to maturity, and the lower panel illustrates BMR per kg body weight with age in both sexes.

Adapted from Garn and Clark, 1953.

effect of macronutrients is caused by differences in the costs of digestion, absorption, and storage of the respective macronutrients as metabolic fuels. In particular, the cost of storing lipids as triglycerides is much less than the cost of storing other nutrients and reaches about 2% to 3% of the energy content of ingested lipids (Schutz and Jequier 1998). In contrast, the thermic effects of carbohydrates, protein, and ethanol are about 8%, 20%, and 22%, respectively.

Energy expenditure associated with movement and physical activity is generally the most variable component of human energy expenditure. The energy expenditure of activity increases steadily throughout infancy (see figure 20.3). The physical activity level (PAL), which refers to total energy expenditure from doubly labeled water divided by SMR, BMR, or RMR, increased from 1.18 at 3 months of age to 1.40 at 2 years of age in a sample of 76 infants who were repeatedly measured during the first 2 years of life (Butte et al. 2000). PAL increases slightly with age during childhood and adolescence in boys and girls in industrialized countries but more so in children and adolescents in rural areas and in cities of developing countries (Torun et al. 1996). This topic is discussed in greater detail in chapter 21.

The energy needed for thermoregulatory purposes in hot or cold climatic conditions is also important. It is, however, small and generally negligible under the insulated and buffered conditions characteristic of life in industrialized societies.

The energy cost of growth is the specific component of energy expenditure of interest. Energy requirements are generally given for populations defined by age, sex, body weight, and physical activity level. The energy requirements defined by a group of experts convened by the Food and Agriculture Organization (FAO), the World Health Organization (WHO), and the United Nations University (UNU)—the FAO/WHO/UNU recommendations—are used in this chapter to quantify the average energy needs of healthy infants, children, and adolescents (World Health Organization 1985). Estimated daily energy requirements per kg body weight and as total kcal for boys and girls from birth to 1 year of age are summarized in table 20.3. The estimates are based on about 4,000 data points for normally growing infants in developed countries. The data indicate a progressive decrease in energy requirements per kg body weight from 1 month to about 6 months of age. From 6 to 9 months of age, energy needs are rather stable at about 95 kcal/kg body weight, which is apparently related to the fact that the decline in the rate of growth of the early postnatal months is not yet compensated by increased physical activity. Estimated daily energy requirements then increase again from 9 to 12 months of age.

Table 20.4 summarizes the FAO/WHO/UNU (World Health Organization 1985) data for children and adolescents 1 to 18 years of age. The methodology employed to derive the energy requirements differs for children and adolescents. From 1 to 10 years of age (childhood),

Energy Expenditure During Infancy

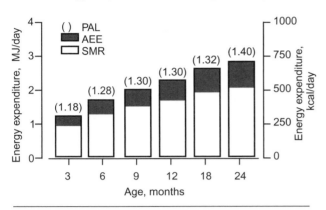

FIGURE 20.3   Sleeping metabolic rate (SMR), activity energy expenditure (AEE), and physical activity level (PAL) of children 3 to 24 months of age. The numbers of infants are 67, 60, 56, 57, 59, and 52 for ages 3, 6, 9, 12, 18, and 24 months, respectively.

Data from Butte et al., 2000.

TABLE 20.3	Average Daily Energy Requirements of Infants From Birth to 1 Year of Age				
	Median body weight[a]		**Energy requirements**[b]		
Age (mo)	**Boys (kg)**	**Girls (kg)**	**Boys and girls (kcal/kg)**	**Boys (kcal)**	**Girls (kcal)**
0.5	3.8	3.6	124	470	445
1–2	4.75	4.35	116	550	505
2–3	5.6	5.05	109	610	545
3–4	6.35	5.7	103	655	590
4–5	7.0	6.35	99	695	630
5–6	7.55	6.95	96	730	670
6–7	8.05	7.55	95	765	720
7–8	8.55	7.95	95	810	750
8–9	9.0	8.4	95	855	800
9–10	9.35	8.75	99	925	865
10–11	9.7	9.05	100	970	905
11–12	10.05	9.35	105	1,050	975

[a]National Center for Health Statistics median weights at the midpoint of the months (Hamill et al. 1977).

[b]Energy requirements are calculated from a prediction equation derived from data for observed intakes (Whitehead et al. 1981), augmented by 5% (see report for justification). To convert kcal to kJ, multiply by 4.18.

Modified from Table 21 of the FAO/WHO/UNU report (World Health Organization, 1985).

the estimates of average energy requirements are based on energy intake augmented by a fixed amount of 5%. The estimates reported for children are based on data points for 6,500 girls and 6,000 boys. During adolescence (10 to 18 years of age), estimated energy requirements are based on predicted BMR augmented by an allowance for growth (5 kcal/g of tissue gained divided by the number of days over which the gain occurred) and physical activity. BMR was predicted at median weight-for-height at each age interval. The increment for physical activity was derived from partitioning the 24-hour day into hours devoted to sleep, school, and low-intensity, moderate-intensity, and high-intensity activities. The physical activity data used to estimate the energy requirements of adolescents in table 20.4 are summarized in table 20.5. The 24-hour day was divided into time spent for sleep (8 to 9 hours/day), for school averaged over a whole year (4 to 6 hours/day), and for physical activity divided into three categories of intensity. The factorial method was used to quantify the energy expended over a typical day above BMR. The activity factor thus derived was used to multiply BMR to obtain the average energy requirements. The energy requirements were then compared with existing energy intake data, and the two data sets were generally in close agreement.

Several trends are readily apparent in the data of table 20.4. Absolute (kcal) and relative (kcal/kg) energy requirements are higher in boys than in girls. Absolute energy requirements attain a plateau at about 2,100 kcal in girls around 14 years of age, whereas they increase until maturity in boys. On the other hand, energy requirements per kg of body mass decrease in both sexes from early childhood to maturity. The decrease is rapid and more dramatic in girls than in boys. Estimates for girls are above 100 kcal/kg in early childhood but decrease gradually to 40 kcal/kg by 15 years of age. The same trend is evident in boys. Estimates decline from values above 100 kcal/kg in early childhood and then gradually decline until they reach a value of 45 kcal/kg in late adolescence (see table 20.4). The data are only estimates and have limitations because they are not based on direct measurements of energy expenditure. However, they have merit in that the data are derived from studies involving thousands of healthy children and adolescents. In the near future, more direct assessments of the actual energy requirements during the growing years may be possible as RMR measured by indirect calorimetry, activity level measured by a variety

TABLE 20.4	Average Daily Energy Requirements of Children and Adolescents			
	Energy requirements for girls		Energy requirements for boys	
Age (yr)	kcal/kg	kcal	kcal/kg	kcal
1–2	108	1,140	104	1,200
2–3	102	1,310	104	1,410
3–4	95	1,440	99	1,560
4–5	92	1,540	95	1,690
5–6	88	1,630	92	1,810
6–7	83	1,700	88	1,900
7–8	76	1,770	83	1,990
8–9	69	1,830	77	2,070
9–10	62	1,880	72	2,150
10–11	57	1,910	66	2,140
11–12	51	1,980	61	2,240
12–13	47	2,050	56	2,310
13–14	43	2,120	52	2,440
14–15	42	2,160	49	2,590
15–16	40	2,140	47	2,700
16–17	39	2,130	45	2,800
17–18	39	2,140	44	2,870

National Center for Health Statistics median weights at mid-year of the age interval (Hamill et al. 1977). Energy requirements from 1 to 2 years of age to 9 to 10 years of age were calculated from unpublished intake data of Ferro-Luzzi and Durnin plus 5% (see table 23 of the FAO/WHO/UNU report). Energy requirements from 10 to 11 years of age to 17 to 18 years of age were calculated from predicted BMR augmented by an activity factor ranging from 1.76 to 1.60 in boys and ranging from 1.65 to 1.52 in girls (see tables 24 and 28 of the FAO/WHO/UNU report). To convert kcal to kJ, multiply by 4.18.

Modified from Tables 23, 24, and 28 of the FAO/WHO/UNU report (World Health Organization 1985).

of technologies, and total energy expenditure from doubly labeled water are increasingly used in pediatric research. Methods for measuring physical activity and energy expenditure are described in chapter 21.

The energy needs for growth are of special relevance to the present discussion. What percentage of the daily energy requirement is needed to support growth, that is, the physiological process of gaining weight during infancy, childhood, and

TABLE 20.5 Time Allocation Used in the WHO Calculation of Energy Requirements of Adolescents and Activity-Adjusted BMR

Age (yr)	Sleep hours	School hours[a]	Physical activity hours			X BMR[b]	
			Light	Moderate	High	Girls	Boys
10–11	9	4	4	6.5	0.5	1.65	1.76
11–12	9	5	4	5.5	0.5	1.63	1.73
12–13	9	5	5	4.5	0.5	1.60	1.69
13–14	9	5	6	3.5	0.5	1.58	1.67
14–15	8	6	7	2.5	0.5	1.57	1.65
15–16	8	6	7	2.5	0.5	1.54	1.62
16–17	8	6	7	2.5	0.5	1.53	1.60
17–18	8	6	7	2.5	0.5	1.52	1.60

[a]Average over whole year (see table 2.5 of the FAO/WHO/UNU report [World Health Organization 1985]).

[b]Multiples of BMR. BMR was predicted from equations as illustrated in tables 26 and 27 of the FAO/WHO/UNU report.

adolescence? Two estimates of the energy cost of growth during infancy and early childhood are summarized in figure 20.4 and table 20.6. The estimates differ somewhat because they consider the energy cost of growth over different periods of time. The energy cost of growth in the first month of life is about 24% of the energy intake at this time. The first month of life, of course, is a transition period from fetal to postnatal life, and during this time, food intake is relatively low and body weight often declines. The energy cost of growth increases during the second month of life to about 30% of energy intake. It then declines systematically during the remainder of the first year and more slowly in the second year (see figure 20.4). The data summarized in table 20.6 suggest that the estimated energy cost of growth between birth and 4 months of age, approximately the period during which birth weight doubles, represents about 33% of the energy intake. This proportion declines subsequently, representing about 7% of the energy intake between 4 and 12 months of age, 1.5% of the energy intake between 12 and 24 months of age, and about 1% of the intake between 24 and 36 months of age. From such data and others summarized by the World Health Organization (1985), a value of 5 kcal/g is commonly used as the best estimate of the energy cost of weight gain in infants and children,

although lower values are possible (Millward et al. 1976). The energy cost of growth is primarily driven by the energy cost of synthesizing proteins and protein turnover. If the body mass increase is strongly influenced by a gain in adiposity, as seen today in affluent countries, the energy cost of weight gain will be less because fat deposition requires only a very small fraction of the energy contained in dietary lipids.

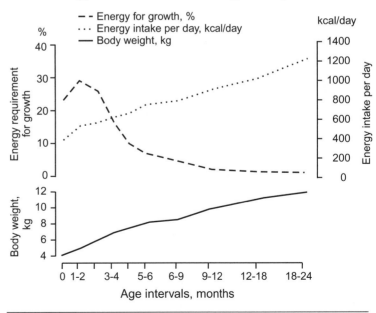

FIGURE 20.4 Energy requirements for growth during the first 2 years of life in relation to energy intake and body weight.

Data from Bergmann and Bergmann, 1986.

TABLE 20.6	Estimated Energy Requirements for Growth During Infancy and Early Childhood		
Age interval	Weight gain (kg)	Energy intake during the age interval (kcal)	Energy intake for growth (%)
0–4 mo	3.5	61,000	32.8
4–12 mo	3.5	180,000	7.4
12–24 mo	2.5	365,000	1.6
24–36 mo	2.0	400,000	1.0

Energy intake represents the estimated energy intake during the age interval considered. For example, between birth (0) and 4 months of age, the hypothetical infant consumed 61,000 kcal, and about 33% of this energy is used to support growth (increase in mass) over this age interval.

Adapted from Fomon (1974).

The relative energy needs for growth are thus greatest early in infancy and then decline rapidly during early childhood so that only a small percentage of daily energy intake is necessary to support the gain in body mass during childhood and adolescence. The decline in the proportion of daily energy intake needed to support growth reflects, in part, the rapid decline in the rate of growth during this period. Children are getting bigger but are doing so at a much slower rate. In turn, a significantly larger proportion of the daily energy intake is necessary to maintain the tissues that have accumulated with growth.

Although energy requirements per kilogram of body weight decrease with age from infancy through childhood and adolescence, the absolute amount of energy required on a daily basis increases (see table 20.4). The energy is needed primarily to maintain the body's metabolism in basal and resting states and for physical activity. Only a small percentage is needed for growth. The estimated energy requirement for growth in childhood and adolescence is only about 1% to 2% of the daily energy requirement. The majority of energy intake is thus used to meet the needs of the other components of total energy expenditure.

Dietary Reference Intake (DRI) for Energy Intake

Recommendations for energy intake during growth vary from one country to another, among

health agencies, and over time. The most recently available recommendations for energy from the Food and Nutrition Board of the Institute of Medicine of the National Academy of Sciences of the United States are used here (Food and Nutrition Board 1989, see also Baxter 2002). The recommendations were developed for applications in both the United States and Canada. More information about the dietary recommendations of the Food and Nutrition Board is available on the Web site of the National Academy of Sciences: www.nap.edu. More recent recommendations for the DRI for energy and macronutrients are currently under discussion by the Food and Nutrition Board and are expected to be available in 2003.

Recommended intake levels have changed considerably over the past 50 years or so. For instance, recommended energy intake has been lowered, reflecting in part a shift toward a less physically active lifestyle and a better understanding of nutritional requirements for health. Recommendations for specific macronutrients and micronutrients have also changed as a result of a growing understanding of the role that they play in normal growth and maturation. The definition of what is an adequate, optimal, or safe intake for the individual and at the population level has been modified. As a result, several new concepts are now in use to define the Dietary Reference Intake (DRI), although they are not all fully applicable to growth and maturation at this time because of a lack of specific data. However the concepts are important, and they are subsequently summarized.

The Recommended Dietary Allowance (RDA) in the United States and the Recommended Nutrient Intake (RNI) in Canada were used in the past to define recommended intakes. In the context of the DRIs, several new concepts provide quantitative estimates of nutrient intakes for planning and assessing diets in apparently healthy people (Food and Nutrition Board 2000). A nutrient is or will be granted an RDI if it is found in the human diet, if it has been measured in foods commonly consumed, and if it has known beneficial effects in humans. The determination of the RDI for a nutrient involves several factors: the RDA, Adequate Intake (AI), Estimated Average Requirement (EAR), and Tolerable Upper Intake Level (UL). The EAR is the level of intake of a nutrient that meets the requirements of 50% of the individuals in a particular age and sex group. By this definition, 50% of the individuals would not meet their nutrient needs at this level of intake. The RDA for a nutrient is the daily intake level sufficient to meet the requirement of almost all (97% to 98%) healthy individuals in a particular age and sex group. To set an RDA, it is necessary to have the EAR. If the EAR of a nutrient and its standard deviation are known, the RDA is set as equal to the EAR plus 2 standard deviations. If insufficient evidence is available to estimate the EAR, the AI is proposed as a reference intake level. AI is the observed mean nutrient intake for healthy individuals. Finally, the UL is the highest nutrient intake likely to pose no risk of adverse health effects for all individuals in a population. Because of the increasing popularity of fortified foods and food supplements, the UL is an important parameter that will be used more often in the future.

RDA, AI, EAR, and UL have not yet been defined for all nutrients for adults, and corresponding data are often scanty in children and adolescents. However, a collaborative effort of the United States and Canada has recently led to the development of RDIs for several, but not all, nutrients (Food and Nutrition Board 2000). These RDI figures are used whenever available in the subsequent discussion.

Figure 20.5 schematically depicts the concepts of EAR, RDA, and UL in relation to the risk of inadequate intake and the risk of adverse effects. EAR is the level of intake at which the level of inadequate intake is 50% for an individual in a given age and sex group. RDA is the level that presents a risk of inadequacy for only 2% or 3% of the people in this age and sex group. At intakes between the RDA and UL, the risk of inadequacy and the risk of excessive intake are both close to zero. However, at levels of intake above the UL, the risk of adverse effects increases.

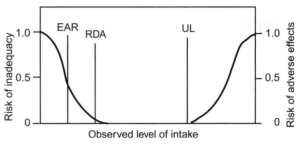

Dietary Reference Intakes

FIGURE 20.5 Risks of inadequacy and of excess in relation to observed levels of intake. Positions of EAR, RDA, and UL are depicted in relation to risk levels.

Data from Food and Nutrition Board, Institute of Medicine, and National Academy of Sciences, 1998. Available: www.nas.edu.

The energy intake of infants, children, and adolescents in the United States based on the first half of the Third National Health and Nutrition Examination Surveys (NHANES III 1988–1991) is depicted in table 20.7 (The sampling strategy used in NHANES III is described in chapter 3). The dietary intake data in NHANES III are based on 24-hour recall interviews using appropriate models of food sizes and portions. The energy intake data for United States children and adolescents of both sexes are remarkably close to the estimated energy requirements for healthy, normally growing children and adolescents proposed by the FAO/WHO/UNU (World Health Organization 1985), which are summarized in table 20.4. Mean intakes in table 20.7 are consistently lower than the medians in each age group

TABLE 20.7 Average Daily Energy Intakes (kcal) of Infants, Children, and Adolescents in the United States, Based on Data From the First Part of NHANES III, 1988–1991

Age (yr)	Girls			Boys		
	N	Mean	Median	N	Mean	Median
2–11(mo)	432	850	810	439	903	858
1–2	630	1,236	1,191	601	1,339	1,291
3–5	803	1,516	1,451	744	1,663	1,568
6–11	877	1,753	1,685	868	2,036	1,913
12–15	373	1,838	1,799	338	2,578	2,486
16–19	397	1,958	1,795	368	3,097	2,918
20–29	838	1,957	1,838	844	3,025	2,799

Data are for all ethnic groups combined. To convert kcal to kJ, multiply by 4.18.

Adapted from McDowell et al. (1994).

of boys and girls. The distribution of energy intake values is skewed to the right, and a subgroup of boys or girls in each age group has very high intakes. The latter point can be appreciated by using selected percentiles of the energy intake distribution, which are illustrated in figure 20.6. Values of the 5th percentile are about 50% of the values at the 50th percentile of energy intakes, whereas values at the 95th percentile intake are typically 100% higher than median intakes across age groups within each sex.

Very little evidence indicates that mean energy intake of children and adolescents in the United States has increased in recent times, despite the fact that the prevalence of obesity is on the rise. For example, mean energy intakes of boys and girls from infancy to maturity have been rather stable from NHANES I (1971–1974) to NHANES II (1976–1980) to NHANES III (1988–1991). This stability is illustrated in table 20.8. However, the possibility that energy intake could have increased in 16-year-old to 19-year-old girls cannot be ruled out. A larger proportion of children and adolescents in recent surveys are possibly hyperphagic compared with children in earlier surveys, despite the fact that average intakes remained stable.

The DRI for energy intake has been defined in terms of RDA by the Food and Nutrition Board. Table 20.9 lists the RDA for energy intake for boys and girls from infancy to young adulthood. The energy intake recommendations are thought to be adequate for healthy children and adolescents and should not lead to overweight or obesity if the individuals have physically active lifestyles.

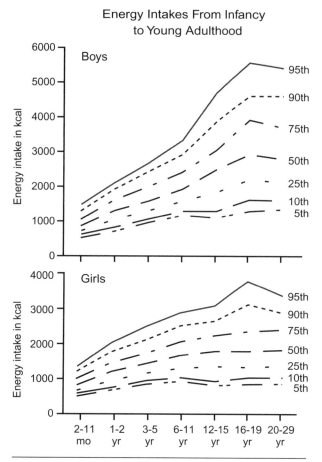

FIGURE 20.6 Estimates of daily energy intake of American boys and girls during growth: medians and the 5th, 10th, 25th, 75th, 90th, and 95th percentiles are shown.

Data from Briefel et al., 1995.

DRI for Protein Intake

Protein constitutes about 11% of body weight at birth. Protein accretion increases during growth and reaches about 16% of body weight in young adulthood. Upon hydrolysis or digestion, proteins yield amino acids. Twenty amino acids are

TABLE 20.8 Comparison of Mean Energy Intakes (kcal) of Children and Adolescents Across Three National Surveys in the United States (NHANES I, NHANES II, and NHANES III)

Age (yr)	NHANES I (1971-1974) Girls	NHANES I (1971-1974) Boys	NHANES II (1976–1980) Girls	NHANES II (1976–1980) Boys	NHANES III (1988–1991) Girls	NHANES III (1988–1991) Boys
1–2 (girls and boys)	1,350		1,287		1,289	
3–5 (girls and boys)	1,676		1,569		1,591	
6–11	2,045	2,045	1,960	1,960	1,753	2,036
12–15	1,910	2,625	1,821	2,490	1,838	2,578
16–19	1,735	3,010	1,687	3,048	1,958	3,097

To convert kcal to kJ, multiply by 4.18.

Adapted from Kennedy and Goldberg (1995).

TABLE 20.9	Recommended Dietary Allowances (RDA) for Energy intake (kcal/day)		
Age (yr)	Boys and girls	Girls	Boys
0–0.5	650		
0.5–1	850		
1–3	1,300		
4–6	1,800		
7–10	2,000		
11–14		2,200	2,500
15–18		2,200	3,000
19–24		2,200	2,900

To convert kcal to kJ, multiply by 4.18.

Adapted from the Food and Nutrition Board (1989).

commonly found in proteins. Although other amino acids exist, they are not typically found in proteins. Some amino acids are modified before incorporation into polypeptides or are altered after translation, but they are of lesser interest here.

Failure to ingest a sufficient amount of protein (i.e., amino acids), even when no growth is taking place, causes a negative nitrogen balance. Negative nitrogen balance occurs because the organism continuously breaks down tissue proteins leading to losses of nitrogen in urine (about 85%), feces (about 10%), and sweat (a fraction). In the healthy adult, about 300 g of proteins are estimated to be broken down in the body each day (Waterlow 1995). This catabolic process provides a large fraction of the amino acids needed for the synthesis of proteins over a 24-hour period, perhaps as much as 70%. The remainder comes from the digestion and absorption of dietary proteins. Nitrogen balance is achieved when protein intake is sufficient to meet the demands of protein replacement and of growth, if applicable.

Dietary proteins and their nutritional values are of primary interest in the present discussion. The nutritional value of proteins is variable and depends on their amino acid composition. If a protein is deficient in one or several amino acids, it is likely to only partially meet the needs of the organism. If the protein mixture ingested is strongly imbalanced in favor of one or a few amino acids, it may lead to an increase in nitrogen losses because these amino acids cannot readily be used for the synthesis of proteins. The body cannot store dietary protein for long periods.

The dietary protein that is not immediately used for synthesis of other proteins or tissues is used to help in meeting the energy needs of the individual. On average, about 60% of total dietary protein is converted to glucose in various tissues and organs and is used for energy or stored as glycogen and triglycerides.

Over the past 50 years amino acids have been commonly classified as essential and nonessential. In this view, essential amino acids could not be synthesized by the body and thus had to be included in the diet, whereas nonessential amino acids could be synthesized by the body and thus did not have to be in the diet (see table 20.10). This classification is not as strict as originally proposed and has limitations (Young 2001). However, the notion that some amino acids are indispensable (essential) in the sense that they are an absolute dietary requirement remains valid. Histidine, isoleucine, leucine, lysine, methionine, phenylalanine, threonine, tryptophan, and valine are nine amino acids that are indispensable. They are essential in the sense that the body cannot produce them at all or produce them at a rate necessary to support protein synthesis. Hence, they must be provided in an individual's diet. In contrast, the nonessential amino acids can be synthesized by the body and generally at an adequate rate to meet the needs of protein synthesis. However, some of the so-called nonessential or dispensable amino acids cannot be synthesized at a rate sufficient to meet cellular needs under some physiological conditions (Young 2001). For instance, low-birth-weight

TABLE 20.10	Essential and Nonessential Amino Acids	
Essential	Nonessential
Histidine	Alanine
Isoleucine	Arginine
Leucine	Aspartic acid
Lysine	Asparagine
Methionine	Cysteine
Phenylalanine	Glutamic acid
Threonine	Glutamine
Tryptophan	Glycine
Valine	Proline
	Serine
	Tyrosine

infants cannot synthesize cysteine and proline in sufficient quantities even though they are considered nonessential amino acids. Thus, nonessential amino acids should be considered conditionally and not absolutely dispensable.

A fraction of ingested amino acids is retained in the splanchnic area after digestion and absorption, which reduces the amount of amino acids that reaches the peripheral tissues. The gut and the liver extract large fractions of some amino acids (e.g., threonine), whereas the extraction level is almost zero for others (e.g., tyrosine) (Young 2001; Reeds et al. 2000). The gut and the liver thus play an important role in regulating the availability of amino acids for protein synthesis in organs and peripheral tissues.

Protein requirements recommended by the FAO/WHO/UNU (World Health Organization 1985) for different ages during growth are summarized in table 20.11. These recommendations are indicated as "safe levels of protein intake" that are considered necessary to meet the physiological needs and maintain the health of nearly all persons in a specified age group. The recommendations are based on a complex series of considerations. First, evidence from short-term and long-term nitrogen-balance studies was reviewed. Several studies, particularly those conducted in the late 1970s (Garza et al. 1977a, 1977b, 1978), had shown that the initial recommendations by the FAO/WHO/UNU in the early 1970s did in fact lead to negative nitrogen balance in many individuals. Second, the mean protein intakes for people in nitrogen balance in these and other studies were averaged. Third, the coefficient of variation of the protein requirements was estimated to be about 12.5%. Fourth, the average protein intake value was increased by 25% (2 standard deviations) so that the recommendations would meet the physiological requirements of 97% to 98% of the population. Because most of the studies were conducted with adults, the panel of experts used a factorial method to define the requirements for maintenance and the protein needs for growth. This area admittedly needs considerably more research.

Dietary protein requirements per kg body weight are highest in early infancy and decline with age, so the protein requirement at 17 years of age is, on average, only approximately 40% of that of the young infant (see table 20.11). No sex difference in the estimated dietary protein requirement occurs until adolescence, when males require more protein per kg body weight than females. The sex difference appears to be greatest at the time of the male adolescent growth spurt, about 13 to 15 years of age. The decline in dietary protein requirement per kilogram of body weight with age parallels the decline in the rate of whole-body protein synthesis and rate of growth with age.

The estimated increment in the protein content of the body of a 3-week-old infant weighing 4 kg and gaining weight at a rate of 40 g/day accounts for about 60% of the total protein requirement at this age. Increments in body protein content relative to the total protein requirement then decrease during infancy. They account for about 40% of the total protein requirement at 4 months of age and 25% of the requirement at 12 months of age. By 2.5 years of age, the increment in body protein accounts for only a small percentage of the total protein requirement, about 12%.

Thus the requirement for protein to support normal growth during the first 2 years of life is large. As the rate of growth decelerates with increasing age, so does the amount of dietary protein needed to support growth. In older children and adolescents, a major portion of the protein requirement is related to the normal turnover of protein in the body (i.e., for tissue maintenance or replacement), and only a relatively small proportion is used for growth.

Higher rates of protein synthesis and deposition can be inferred in infancy than at any other time during growth. The estimated energy requirement of protein synthesis is of the order of 1 kcal/g of protein synthesized (Waterlow 1995). This estimate takes into account the energy cost of proteolysis associated with the breakdown of cellular proteins, the cost of amino acid transport, the cost of the formation of the peptide bonds, and the costs of turnover rates of cellular constituents needed for protein synthesis such as mRNA, tRNA, and rRNA. In adults, a protein turnover rate of about 300 g/day would account for about 20% of BMR. This rate does not take into account the energy costs related to the gluconeogenesis and lipogenesis associated with the recycling of amino acid precursors. Even though direct estimates are not available, the energy cost of the high rate of protein synthesis and deposition in the first few years of life may represent a large fraction, if not all, of the elevated metabolic rate observed during this phase of growth.

RDAs for protein intakes applicable to infants, children, adolescents, and adults in the United States and Canada have been made public by the

TABLE 20.11 Recommended Safe Protein Intakes by Age and Sex From Infancy Through Adolescence

Age (yr)	Boys and girls			Girls			Boys		
	Grams of protein per kg per day	Approximate mean body weight (kg)	Mean intake (g)	Grams of protein per kg per day	Approximate mean body weight (kg)	Mean intake (g)	Grams of protein per kg per day	Approximate mean body weight (kg)	Mean intake (g)
0.25–0.5	1.86	7.0	13.0						
0.5–0.75	1.65	8.5	14.0						
0.75–1.0	1.48	9.7	14.4						
1.0–1.5	1.26	10.5	13.2						
1.5–2.0	1.17	11.5	13.5						
2–3	1.13	13.2	14.9						
3–4	1.09	15.5	16.9						
4–5	1.06	17.3	18.3						
5–6	1.02	19.1	19.5						
6–7	1.01	22.0	22.2						
7–8	1.01	23.6	23.8						
8–9	1.01	26.7	27.0						
9–10	0.99	30.1	29.8						
10–11				1.0	34	34.0	0.99	32	31.7
11–12				0.98	39	38.2	0.98	37	36.3
12–13				0.96	44	42.2	1.00	41	41.0
13–14				0.94	49	46.1	0.97	47	45.6
14–15				0.90	51	45.9	0.96	53	50.9
15–16				0.87	53	46.1	0.92	58	53.4
16–17				0.83	54	44.8	0.90	63	56.7
17–18				0.80	55	44.0	0.86	65	55.9
Adults				0.75			0.75		

Levels are from proteins such as egg white, milk, meat, and fish. Approximate mean body weights are estimated from tables 21, 23, and 24 of the report.

Adapted from the FAO/WHO/UNU (World Health Organization 1985).

Food and Nutrition Board (1998). They are summarized in table 20.12. The RDAs are generally close to the recommendations of the World Health Organization (1985) when they are converted to total intake based on approximate mean body weights used in the earlier report. Observed mean protein intakes in grams from the first part of NHANES III (1988–1991) are also shown in table 20.12. Protein intakes increase with age in both sexes in NHANES III. Mean intakes are consistently higher in boys than in girls. In boys, the percentage of calories from proteins accounts for 12% in infancy to 15% at later ages. In girls, proteins contribute 11% of calories in infancy but about 14% subsequently (McDowell et al. 1994).

When the safe protein intakes recommended by the FAO/WHO/UNU (World Health Organization 1985) are compared with the RDAs of the Food and Nutrition Board (1998), they are rather concordant. Small differences exist, such as a

| TABLE 20.12 | Recommended Dietary Allowances (RDA) for Protein Intake Compared With Actual Protein Intakes Observed in NHANES III, 1988–1991 |

RDA for protein intake (g)				NHANES III protein intake (g)		
Age (yr)	Mean girls	Mean boys	Mean both sexes	Age (yr)	Mean girls	Mean boys
0–0.5			13	2–11(mo)	25	27
0.5–1			14			
1–3			16	1–2	45	50
4–6			24	3–5	54	59
7–10			28	6–11	63	71
11–14	46	45		12–15	62	89
15–18	44	59		16–19	67	111
19–24	46	58		20–29	69	110

RDAs are from the Food and Nutrition Board (1998), and NHANES III data are from McDowell et al. (1994).

higher RDA for proteins in adolescent boys, but the magnitude of the differences is not striking. However, when the population intake data from NHANES III are compared with either the RDAs or the safe protein intake recommendations of the FAO/WHO/UNU, discrepancies are quite substantial. Mean protein intakes in grams by American children and adolescents are markedly higher than the recommended levels. In fact, infants consume about twice as much protein as the current RDA. Children consume slightly more than twice the recommended levels, and adolescents of both sexes have mean protein intakes well above the RDAs and the FAO/WHO/UNU recommended safe intakes by almost 100% in boys and by almost 50% in girls (see table 20.11). The consequences of such high protein intake levels are not known.

DRI for Lipid Intake

Dietary lipids not only represent an important concentrated source of energy but also provide essential fatty acids and serve as carriers for lipid-soluble nutrients such as vitamins A, D, E, and K. After ingestion and absorption, dietary fats deliver about 9 kcal of energy per gram. Because of the high energy density, dietary lipids are frequently targeted as one of many potential causes of the current overweight and obesity epidemic in children and adolescents. The American Academy of Pediatrics (1998) has made the following recommendations regarding lipid intake by infants, children, and adolescents: (1) total fat intake should be equivalent to at least 20%

but no more than 30% of daily caloric intake; (2) consumption of saturated fat should be less than 10% of total caloric intake; and (3) dietary cholesterol intake should be less than 300 mg/day. The recommendations can be met by a diet based on a wide variety of foods. Experts are also of the view that these levels of fat intake are compatible with normal healthy growth.

Several fatty acids are deemed essential or indispensable and need to be provided by the diet for normal growth. The evidence is strongest for linoleic acid. Infants fed a diet deficient in linoleic acid had large stools, perianal irritation, and dryness, thickening, and later desquamation of the skin (Hansen et al. 1958). Addition of linoleic acid to the diet quickly alleviated these conditions.

Linoleic acid is defined as essential because humans do not have enzymes to synthesize double bonds at the n-6 position of the carbon chain of a fatty acid (Jones and Papamandjaris 2001). In this regard, humans are also deficient for an enzyme able to synthesize double bonds at the n-3 position, which has led to the notion that linolenic acid is also likely to be an essential fatty acid that must be supplied by the diet. Some evidence indicates that dietary deficiency of linolenic acid resulted in neuropathy in children and retinopathy in animal models (Jones and Papamandjaris 2001).

Other potentially indispensable fatty acids in infants, children, and adolescents include arachidonic acid, docosahexaenoic acid (DHA), and eicosapentaenoic acid (EPA) (Jones and Papamandjaris 2001). Evidence suggests that dietary deficiency in arachidonic acid and DHA may affect brain development and visual function. In rhesus monkeys, absence of dietary DHA and EPA causes major neural tissue disturbances and pronounced behavioral changes. RDIs for these fatty acids cannot be defined at this time, but they are a focus of active research.

Table 20.13 shows age-adjusted means for total fat intake and saturated fat intake as a percentage of daily energy intake and cholesterol intake across NHANES I, NHANES II, and NHANES III (Troiano et al. 2000). Total fat intake as a percentage of energy intake has decreased over the 20-year interval covered by the three national surveys. The same is true for saturated fat as a percentage of energy intake. Similarly, cholesterol intake has consistently decreased across the three surveys.

On average, the cholesterol intake is below the recommended level of 300 mg/day, with the exception of intake by adolescent boys. In contrast, both total fat intake and saturated fat intake as percentages of total energy intake are consistently above the recommended levels of 30% and 10% of daily energy intake in girls and boys.

Relative intake as a percentage of total caloric intake, however, may not tell the entire story. Absolute consumption of various types of fats estimated from the 24-hour dietary recall in the first part of NHANES III (1988–1991) is shown in table 20.14. The increase in grams of fat intake with age is quite dramatic, particularly in boys. Adolescent boys consume daily much more than the recommended 80 g/day of fat. Adolescent

TABLE 20.13 Age-Adjusted Mean Total Fat, Saturated Fat, and Cholesterol Intake in Children and Adolescents in NHANES I, NHANES II, and NHANES III

Age (yr)	Total fat as % energy NHANES I (1971–74)	NHANES II (1976–80)	NHANES III (1988–94)	Saturated fat as % energy NHANES I (1971–74)	NHANES II (1976–80)	NHANES III (1988–94)	Cholesterol (mg/dl) NHANES I (1971–74)	NHANES II (1976–80)	NHANES III (1988–94)
Boys 2–5	36.0	34.9	32.7	13.6	12.8	12.3	264	219	200
Boys 6–11	36.7	35.7	33.8	14.0	13.3	12.6	314	272	241
Boys 12–19	37.0	36.4	33.6	13.9	13.7	11.9	411	389	341
Girls 2–5	36.5	35.7	32.9	13.9	13.3	12.4	250	218	185
Girls 6–11	35.9	35.8	33.6	13.8	13.1	12.3	249	226	220
Girls 12–9	36.7	36.4	33.8	13.6	13.1	11.7	270	230	211

The data are based on a 24-hour dietary recall and ethnic groups combined. Standard errors range from 0.21 to 0.42 for total fat, 0.14 to 0.20 for saturated fat, and 6 to 13 for cholesterol.

Adapted from Troiano et al. (2000).

TABLE 20.14 Fat Intakes in Infants, Children, Adolescents, and Young Adults in NHANES III, 1988–1991

Age (yr)	Total fat (g) Girls	Boys	Saturated fat (g) Girls	Boys	Monounsaturated fat (g) Girls	Boys	Polyunsaturated fat (g) Girls	Boys
2–11 (mo)	35	37	15	16	9	9	8	8
1–2	47	51	19	21	17	18	8	8
3–5	57	62	22	24	21	23	10	11
6–11	68	78	25	29	25	29	13	14
12–15	72	97	26	36	27	37	14	18
16–19	77	120	27	44	28	45	16	22
20–29	75	116	26	41	28	44	16	23

Adapted from McDowell et al. (1994).

boys also consume strikingly more saturated and monounsaturated fats than girls. Adult males exhibit the same pattern of intake.

A controversial topic concerning RDIs for lipids in children is that of the effects of low-fat diets on growth and functional development. The concern arises because low-fat diets increase the risk that the consumption of essential fatty acids will be suboptimal, that the absorption of fat-soluble vitamins could be compromised, and that immune functions could be impaired (Bier et al. 2000). Evidence indicates that some, but not all, children consuming less than 22% of their calories as fat exhibit impaired growth as summarized in a recent special issue of the *American Journal of Clinical Nutrition* (2000). Well-controlled clinical trials have shown that growth and functional development are not compromised in infants and young children consuming between 27% and 30% of their calories as fats (Obarzanek et al. 1997; Lagstrom et al. 1999). In the aggregate, the studies suggest that a safe level of total fat intake as a percentage of calories is on the order of 23% to 25% (Bier et al. 2000).

Carbohydrate Requirements

In contrast to lipids, carbohydrate stores in the body are small, about 0.4% to 0.5% of body weight during childhood and young adulthood. Carbohydrates are stored as glycogen primarily in skeletal muscles and the liver and are also readily available as glucose molecules in the blood. Worldwide, the main source of dietary carbohydrates is cereals (wheat, rice, maize [corn], barley, rye, oats, millet, and sorghum), followed by sugar cane, root crops, vegetables, and fruits (Mann 2001). Carbohydrate-rich foods are not only an important source of energy and fibers but also serve as a vehicle for vitamins, minerals, and other molecules such as phytochemicals and antioxidants. An expert of the FAO/WHO (1973) recommended that carbohydrate intake should be about 55% of energy intake. Most dietary carbohydrates should be from complex carbohydrate sources (e.g., breads, cereals, pasta, rice, and legumes), with only little from simple sugars (10% or less). This level is slightly above the intakes in the United States as estimated in NHANES III (McDowell et al. 1994). This difference is illustrated in table 20.15, which was constructed from single-day recall data from NHANES III.

The percentage of calories from carbohydrates is consistently below 55% in both sexes from infancy to adulthood. However, a survey of the United States Department of Agriculture suggests that carbohydrate intake may in fact be closer to 55% (Baxter 2002).

TABLE 20.15 Percentage of Calories From Carbohydrates in Infants, Children, Adolescents, and Young Adults in NHANES III, 1988–1991

Age (yr)	Girls	Boys
2–11 (mo)	52.4	52.7
1–2	53.0	53.2
3–5	54.4	54.8
6–11	52.9	53.5
12–15	54.4	54.0
16–19	52.4	49.6
20–29	50.0	47.6

Adapted from McDowell et al. (1994).

The brain, red blood cells, and a few other tissues have an almost exclusive requirement for glucose. Their estimated daily needs are of the order of 180 g/day. Gluconeogenesis from noncarbohydrate precursors (lactate, glucogenic amino acids, particularly alanine, and glycerol from lypolysis of triglycerides) generates about 130 g/day (Mann 2001). The remainder should come from ingested carbohydrates (about 50 g). In practice, however, dietary carbohydrate needs can be substantially higher as a result of differences in lifestyle, particularly in physical activity level. Population surveys indicate that children and adolescents consume significantly more than 50 g/day of carbohydrates. The average daily intake is closer to 200 g in children and 300 g in adolescents.

Vitamin Requirements

In addition to the requirements for protein, lipids, and carbohydrates are the dietary requirements for micronutrients, which need to be consumed in trace or relatively small amounts. These micronutrients include vitamins and mineral elements. A balanced diet with sufficient energy and reasonable protein, grain, vegetable, fruit, and dairy content is generally assumed to adequately meet the vitamin and mineral needs of the growing individual. This assumption is largely correct. However, because of the serious pediatric consequences to deficiencies in micronutrients, the Food and Nutrition Board of the United States and the FAO/WHO have defined recommended levels of intake of vitamins and minerals for normal growth and functional development. In response to governmental pressure and consumer demands, the food industry has developed fortified foods to help alleviate some of the most common and devastating micronutrient deficiencies. This action is one of the most striking success stories of translating scientific advances into efficacious public health measures in a free market economy.

Vitamins are primarily regulatory in function, often acting as cofactors in chemical reactions taking place within cells. They are required in very small amounts and constitute a negligible proportion of body weight. Vitamins must be provided in the diet on a daily basis because they cannot be synthesized in the body or they cannot be synthesized in large enough quantities to meet the biological needs of growth. Vitamins are divided into fat-soluble and water-soluble compounds. This division reflects, in part, the food items containing these compounds in significant amounts but also indicates their pathways of digestion, absorption, and transport in the organism.

The role of vitamins in growth and maturation, although not immediately apparent in the well-nourished child, is especially evident in stunted growth, which characterizes some severe vitamin deficiency states. Vitamins A and D, for example, are essential to the growth of skeletal tissue, and severe deficiencies of each are associated with stunted growth in stature. Vitamins are also involved in the maintenance of tissues, metabolism of other nutrients, formation of red blood cells, and normal brain development. Hence, they are essential to normal growth and maturation in a variety of ways. A discussion of each of the vitamins and the impact of vitamin deficiencies on growth and development is beyond the scope of this chapter. However, the interested student should refer to two recent detailed discussions of these topics (Bowman and Russell 2001; Berdanier 2002).

A deficiency in any one of the vitamins translates into metabolic disorders that may have serious detrimental effects on growth and maturation. A list of the fat-soluble and water-soluble vitamins, the main food sources for each, and some of the consequences of deficiencies are provided in table 20.16. Research on the biological and behavioral implications of vitamin deficiencies relies heavily on animal experimental models. Research on vitamin deprivation in humans, primarily young adults, although short-term for obvious ethical reasons, has produced a substantial body of evidence. Observations in infants, children, and adolescents are quite limited. These observations were typically made in regions of the world where a specific vitamin deficiency was endemic for a period of time.

Estimating how much of each vitamin should be consumed for normal growth is complicated by several factors. The intestinal flora play an important role not only because of their importance in the absorption of vitamins but also because they are involved in the biosynthesis of some vitamins and vitamin precursors. Cooking methods can modify the fate of the vitamin content of some foods. Consumption of alcohol, particularly when it is more than moderate, can greatly diminish the intestinal absorption of vitamins in foods. Insufficient exposure to sunlight can also interfere with nutritional status, specifically in the context of vitamin D. Moreover, a good deal of uncertainty exists regarding the true amount of each vitamin that should be available at the tissue and organ levels for normal cellular functions. For these reasons, recommended vitamin intake levels err on the high side, provided that the safe upper limit for each compound is known. Unfortunately, UL values are often not yet known for vitamins, particularly in infants. The latest recommendations from the Food and Nutrition Board are summarized in table 20.17 for fat-soluble vitamins and in table 20.18 for water-soluble vitamins. The recommendations are defined in terms of RDAs when available; otherwise AI values are indicated. UL values are also given whenever they could be defined for the age ranges of interest in this book.

Food should be the only source of vitamins when the UL value cannot be determined because of possible concerns about the ability of the growing organism to handle large amounts of vitamins as typically contained in vitamin supplements. The Food and Nutrition Board has summarized the evidence for adverse effects of vitamin consumption exceeding the UL values. The salient features are as follows. Thus far, no

TABLE 20.16   Fat-Soluble and Water-Soluble Vitamins With Indications of Consequences of Nutritional Deficiencies

	Sources	Deficiencies
Fat-soluble vitamins		
A	Fish oil, butter, liver, leafy vegetables, carrots	Night blindness, dryness of the eye, thickening of hair follicles
D	Meat, fish, cod liver oils, fortified milk	Rickets (in children), osteomalacia (in adults), worsened by lack of sunlight exposure
E	Vegetable oils, nuts, wheat germ	Abetalipoproteinemia, neurological abnormalities
K	Leafy vegetables, dairy products, vegetable oils	Impaired blood coagulation in severe cases, osteoporosis
Water-soluble vitamins		
Biotin	Meat, cereals, egg yolk, liver, vegetables	Dermatitis, skin dryness, depression, anorexia, nausea, seizures
Choline	Meats, eggs, vegetables, legumes, peanut oil	In animals: fatty liver, hepatocellular carcinoma, impaired brain development; no evidence yet in humans
Folate	Oranges, leafy vegetables, peanuts, beans, fortified grain foods	Megaloblastic anemia (accumulation of large, abnormal erythrocytes in bone marrow), reduced white blood cells and platelets, risk of neural tube defects during the first month of pregnancy
Niacin (nicotinic acid)	Meat, cereals, fish, leafy vegetables	Fatigue, digestive disturbances, pellagra with skin lesions
Pantothenic acid	Chicken, beef, liver, whole grains, potatoes, vegetables	Numbness of feet and hands, insomnia, headaches, gastric disturbances, cramps
B_1 (thiamin)	Wheat germ, ham, green vegetables, whole-grain foods	Beriberi, neurological form of beriberi
B_2 (riboflavin)	Poultry, fish, dairy products, eggs, green vegetables	Fatigue, skin lesions, corneal vascularization, brain dysfunction
B_6 (pyridoxine)	Meat, whole-grain products, vegetables, nuts	Fatigue, irritability, insomnia, convulsions, seizures
B_{12} (cobalamin)	Meat, fish, dairy products, eggs, fortified foods	Pernicious anemia, megaloblastic anemia, demyelination of SNS and neurologic disorders
C (ascorbic acid)	Fruits and vegetables	Scurvy

adverse consequences for high levels of intake of biotin, folate, pantothenic acid, riboflavin, thiamin, vitamin B_6, vitamin B_{12}, and vitamin K have been identified. Excessive intakes of choline cause a fishy body odor, sweating, hypotension, and hepatotoxicity. High intakes of niacin may cause flushing and gastrointestinal distress. Excess intake of vitamin A has teratological effects (i.e., can potentially induce malformations in the embryo, see chapter 2) and liver toxicity. Vitamin C consumption beyond the UL may result in gastrointestinal disturbances, kidney stones, and excess iron absorption. High levels of intake of vitamin D may cause hypercalcemia. Excessive consumption of vitamin E supplements may increase the risk of hemorrhagic toxicity.

Mineral Requirements

Minerals are required in small amounts for normal growth and bodily functions. Minerals constitute about 2% of body weight at birth and about 6% in young adulthood, so the relative contribution of mineral to body weight increases during growth. Much remains to be learned about the specific role of each mineral in normal adult physiology

TABLE 20.17 Dietary Reference Intakes for Fat-Soluble Vitamins: RDA (AI in Parentheses)									
	Prepubertal				**Boys**			**Girls**		
Fat-soluble vitamins	0–6 mo	7–12 mo	1–3 yr	4–8 yr	9–13 yr	14–18 yr	19–30 yr	9–13 yr	14–18 yr	19–30 yr
Vitamin A										
RDA (AI) (µg/day)	(400)	(500)	300	400	600	900	900	600	700	700
UL (µg/day)	600	600	600	900	1,700	2,800	3,000	1,700	2,800	3,000
Vitamin D (calciferol)										
RDA (AI) (µg/day)	(5)	(5)	(5)	(5)	(5)	(5)	(5)	(5)	(5)	(5)
UL (µg/day)	25	25	50	50	50	50	50	50	50	50
Vitamin E (α-tocopherol)										
RDA (AI) (mg/day)	(4)	(5)	6	7	11	15	15	11	15	15
UL (mg/day)	ND	ND	200	300	600	800	1,000	600	800	1,000
Vitamin K										
RDA (AI) (µg/day)	(2.0)	(2.5)	(30)	(55)	60	75	120	60	75	90
UL	ND	ND	ND	ND	ND	ND	ND	ND	ND	ND

ND: Not determinable because lack of data on adverse effects in the indicated age groups and concern with regard to inability to handle excess amounts. Source of intake should be from food only to prevent high levels of intake.

Adapted from the Food and Nutrition Board (1997, 1998, 2000, 2001).

and metabolism. Considerably less is known at present about the effects of each mineral in the course of embryogenesis and postnatal growth and maturation. For a comprehensive treatment of these issues, the interested student is referred to a series of chapters dealing with the dietary minerals (Bowman and Russell 2001).

Table 20.19 lists the minerals for which a reasonable body of relevant dietary and biological data have been accumulated, along with the food sources for these minerals and the main consequences of deficiencies in humans. Food supplements as a source for these minerals are not taken into account. The mineral content of foods may vary considerably depending on agriculture technologies used, type of soil, and water quality. For many of the minerals, data on the consequences of deficiencies are quite limited. Studies in which only one mineral was experimentally controlled under deprivation and refeeding conditions are difficult to perform. Minerals typically occur together with other micronutrients in foodstuffs, making targeting only one mineral without affecting anything else in the diet almost impossible. In addition to the minerals listed in table 20.19, others may be nutritionally important. However,

they are not included because no clear indications have been established about recommended intake levels, particularly in children and adolescents. These other minerals include aluminum, arsenic, boron, bromine, cadmium, germanium, lead, lithium, nickel, rubidium, silicon, tin, and vanadium (Nielsen 2001).

The role of trace minerals in growth and maturation is gradually being elaborated. Zinc deficiency, for example, is associated with growth depression and sexual immaturity, and copper deficiency is associated with anomalies of ossification. Experimental studies of animals indicate growth depression or stunting in association with specific deficiency of silicon, vanadium, manganese, iron, cobalt, nickel, zinc, and arsenic. Hence, many minerals can be reasonably assumed to have a significant role in the processes of growth and maturation.

DRIs have been developed for many minerals. The RDA or AI and UL levels for these minerals are defined in table 20.20 for the age groups of interest. The DRIs are based on intake derived from foods. Of the major minerals, calcium and phosphorus are essential to bone growth and metabolism and, in turn, to statural growth. Indeed, most

TABLE 20.18 Dietary Reference Intakes for Water-Soluble Vitamins: RDA (AI in Parentheses)

	Boys and girls				Boys			Girls		
Water-soluble vitamins	0–6 mo	7–12 mo	1–3 yr	4–8 yr	9–13 yr	14–18 yr	19–30 yr	9–13 yr	14–18 yr	19–30 yr
Biotin										
RDA (AI) (µg/day)	(5)	(6)	(8)	(12)	(20)	(25)	(30)	(20)	(25)	(30)
UL	ND	ND	ND	ND	ND	ND	ND	ND	ND	ND
Choline										
RDA (AI) (mg/day)	(125)	(150)	(200)	(250)	(375)	(550)	(550)	(375)	(400)	(425)
UL (mg/day)	ND	ND	1,000	1,000	2,000	3,000	3,500	2,000	3,000	3,500
Folate										
RDA (AI) (µg/day)	(65)	(80)	150	200	300	400	400	300	400	400
UL (µg/day)	ND	ND	300	400	600	800	1,000	600	800	1,000
Niacin										
RDA (AI) (mg/day)	(2)	(4)	6	8	12	16	16	12	14	14
UL (mg/day)	ND	ND	10	15	20	30	35	20	30	35
Pantothenic acid										
RDA (AI) (mg/day)	(1.7)	(1.8)	(2)	(3)	(4)	(5)	(5)	(4)	(5)	(5)
UL	ND	ND	ND	ND	ND	ND	ND	ND	ND	ND
Vitamin B_1 (thiamin)										
RDA (AI) (mg/day)	(0.2)	(0.3)	0.5	0.6	0.9	1.2	0.2	0.9	1.0	1.1
UL	ND	ND	ND	ND	ND	ND	ND	ND	ND	ND
Vitamin B_2 (riboflavin)										
RDA (AI) (mg/day)	(0.3)	(0.4)	0.5	0.6	0.9	1.3	1.3	0.9	1.0	1.1
UL	ND	ND	ND	ND	ND	ND	ND	ND	ND	ND
Vitamin B_6 (pyridoxine)										
RDA (AI) (mg/day)	(0.1)	(0.3)	0.5	0.6	1.0	1.3	1.3	1.0	1.2	1.3
UL (mg/day)	ND	ND	30	40	60	80	100	60	80	100
Vitamin B_{12} (cobalamin)										
RDA (AI) (µg/day)	(0.4)	(0.5)	0.9	1.2	1.8	2.4	2.4	1.8	2.4	2.4
UL	ND	ND	ND	ND	ND	ND	ND	ND	ND	ND
Vitamin C (ascorbic acid)										
RDA (AI) (mg/day)	(40)	(50)	15	25	45	75	90	45	65	75
UL (mg/day)	ND	ND	400	650	1,200	1,800	2,000	1,200	1,800	2,000

ND: Not determinable because of lack of data on adverse effects in the indicated age groups and concern with regard to inability to handle excess amounts. Source of intake should be from food only to prevent high levels of intake.

Adapted from the Food and Nutrition Board (1997, 1998, 2000, 2001).

TABLE 20.19	Minerals, Their Food Sources, and Consequences of Deficiencies	
Minerals	**Sources**	**Deficiencies**
Calcium	Milk and dairy products, corn tortillas, broccoli	Osteoporosis, poor skeletal growth
Chromium	Whole grains, meat, poultry, fish, beer	Glucose intolerance, hyperinsulinemia, weight loss, peripheral neuropathy
Copper	Shellfish, nuts, wheat bran cereals, whole grains, organ meats, chocolates	Anemia, hypopigmentation, disorders of nervous system, abnormalities of cardiovascular, immune, and skeletal systems
Fluoride	Fluoridated water, marine fish, tea	Dental caries, demineralization of bones
Iodine	Iodized salt, marine food products, fortified foods	Goiter, mental retardation, cretinism, neuromuscular impairment
Iron	Meat, poultry, fruits, vegetables, grains, fortified foods	Anemia, impaired work capacity, impaired cognitive development and immune function, impaired body temperature regulation
Magnesium	Grains, legumes, leafy vegetables, tofu, meat, fruits, dairy products	Tetany, tremors, convulsions, soft tissue calcification
Manganese	Cereals, nuts, leafy vegetables, tea, whole grains	Depressed growth, osteoporosis, glucose intolerance, impaired wound healing
Molybdenum	Milk and dairy products, legumes, grains, nuts, liver	Hypouricemia, mental disturbances, coma
Phosphorus	Milk and dairy products, meat, poultry, fish, grains	None described
Potassium	Meat, vegetables, fruits	Disorders of neurological, cardiac, and skeletal muscle function
Selenium	Meat, cereals, grains, fruits, vegetables, seafood	Cardiomyopathy, muscle pain, virulence of viral infections
Zinc	Red meat, shellfish, wheat germ, fortified cereals	Growth retardation, hypogonadism, impaired immunity, poor wound healing, mental lethargy

Adapted from the Food and Nutrition Board (1997, 1998, 2000, 2001).

of the calcium in the body is contained in bone. The estimated daily increment in the calcium content of the body between 10 and 20 years of age is approximately 210 mg in males and 110 mg in females, whereas the estimated daily increment during the peak of the adolescent growth spurt is about two times that estimated for the 10-year period (i.e., about 400 mg in males and 240 mg in females). Other minerals are involved in cellular metabolism (magnesium), in the maintenance of fluid and electrolyte balance (sodium, potassium, and chlorine), and in the synthesis, storage, and maintenance of protein (potassium). All of these processes, needless to say, are essential to normal growth and maturation.

Much higher levels of intake can be achieved with the consumption of mineral supplements. However, such high levels beyond the UL can have serious metabolic and behavioral consequences. For instance, arsenic intakes could be extremely toxic. The Food and Nutrition Board has advised that intakes above UL levels for boron can increase the risk of reproductive and developmental defects. Excessive calcium intake can cause kidney stones, hypercalcemia, and renal insufficiency. Chronic renal failure has been associated with abnormally high consumption of chromium. Copper intake beyond the UL causes gastrointestinal distress and liver damage. Enamel and skeletal fluorosis result from

TABLE 20.20 Dietary Reference Intakes for Minerals: RDA (AI in Parentheses)

Minerals	Boys and girls				Boys			Girls		
	0–6 mo	7–12 mo	1–3 yr	4–8 yr	9–13 yr	14–18 yr	19–30 yr	9–13 yr	14–18 yr	19–30 yr
Calcium										
RDA (AI) (mg/day)	(210)	(270)	(500)	(800)	(1,300)	(1,300)	(1,000)	(1,300)	(1,300)	(1,000)
UL (mg/day)	ND	ND	2,500	2,500	2,500	2,500	2,500	2,500	2,500	2,500
Chromium										
RDA (AI) (mg/day)	(0.2)	(5.5)	(11)	(15)	(25)	(35)	(35)	(21)	(24)	(25)
UL (µg/day)	ND	ND	ND	ND	ND	ND	ND	ND	ND	ND
Copper										
RDA (AI) (µg/day)	(200)	(220)	340	440	700	890	900	700	890	900
UL (µg/day)	ND	ND	1,000	3,000	5,000	8,000	10,000	5,000	8,000	10,000
Fluoride										
RDA (AI) (mg/day)	(0.01)	(0.5)	(0.7)	(1)	(2)	(3)	(4)	(2)	(3)	(3)
UL (mg/day)	0.7	0.9	1.3	2.2	10	10	10	10	10	10
Iodine										
RDA (AI) (µg/day)	(110)	(130)	90	90	120	150	150	120	150	150
UL (µg/day)	ND	ND	200	300	600	900	1,100	600	900	1,100
Iron										
RDA (AI) (mg/day)	(0.27)	11	7	10	8	11	8	8	15	18
UL (mg/day)	40	40	40	40	40	45	45	40	45	45
Magnesium										
RDA (AI) (mg/day)	(30)	(75)	80	130	240	410	400	240	360	310
UL (mg/day)	ND	ND	65	110	350	350	350	350	350	350
Manganese										
RDA (AI) (mg/day)	0.003	0.6	(1.2)	(1.5)	(1.9)	(2.2)	(2.3)	(1.6)	(1.6)	(1.8)
UL (mg/day)	ND	ND	2	3	6	9	11	6	9	11
Molybdenum										
RDA (AI) (µg/day)	(2)	(3)	17	22	34	43	45	34	43	45
UL (µg/day)	ND	ND	300	600	1,100	1,700	2,000	1,100	1,700	2,000
Phosphorus										
RDA (AI) (mg/day)	(100)	(275)	460	500	1,250	1,250	700	1,250	1,250	700
UL (mg/day)	ND	ND	3,000	3,000	4,000	4,000	4,000	4,000	4,000	4,000
Selenium										
RDA (AI) (µg/day)	(15)	(20)	20	30	40	55	55	40	55	55
UL (µg/day)	45	60	90	150	280	400	400	280	400	400
Zinc										
RDA (AI) (mg/day)	(2)	3	3	5	8	11	11	8	9	8
UL (mg/day)	4	5	7	12	23	34	40	23	34	40

ND: Not determinable because of lack of data on adverse effects in the indicated age groups and concern with regard to inability to handle excess amounts. Source of intake should be from food only to prevent high levels of intake.

Adapted from the Food and Nutrition Board (1997, 1998, 2000, 2001).

consuming too much fluoride. Excessive iodine intake is associated with elevated thyroid-stimulating hormone concentration. Gastrointestinal distress is commonly seen with high levels of iron intake. Excessive intake of magnesium as seen in the consumption of supplements is a risk for diarrhea. Neurotoxicity is seen with excessive manganese intakes. Consuming too much molybdenum can cause reproductive disturbances. Excessive intakes of nickel can cause unwarranted weight losses. Excessive consumption of phosphorus is associated with skeletal porosity, metastatic calcification, and interference with calcium absorption. Too much selenium in the diet is known to induce hair and nail brittleness and loss, and excess zinc reduces copper levels.

Summary

The study of nutrition deals with the relationship of food intake to the functioning of the organism and is of primary concern throughout the life cycle, prenatally through old age. This chapter highlights the nutritional requirements for normal growth and maturation and the energetics of growth. The requirements of infants, children, and adolescents are complex. These needs can be met with a variety of foods and in many combinations of foods, which are composed of nutrients. The six classes of nutrients are water, carbohydrates, fats, proteins, vitamins, and minerals. Nutrients are dependent on each other, on enzymes and hormones, and on the functional integrity of tissues and organs. Three nutrients, carbohydrates, fats, and proteins, are sources of energy. Individual differences in nutritional requirements are considerable, and Dietary Recommended Intakes (DRIs) are designed to accommodate this variability. Energy needs are discussed in relation to basal and resting metabolic rates, thermic effect of food, energy expenditures associated with physical activity level, and energy cost of growth. At rest, the infant expends about 52 kcal per kg of body mass, and the young adult uses about 24 kcal. During infancy, the energy cost of growth may be as high as 33% of the energy intake. In contrast, the energy requirements for growth during childhood and adolescence attain about 1% to 2% of the daily energy intake. Nutrition is a process that is influenced by the social and cultural context within which infants, children, and adolescents live.

Sources and Suggested Readings

Allen LH (2001) Pregnancy and lactation. In BA Bowman, TM Russell (eds), Present Knowledge in Nutrition. Washington, DC: ILSI Press, pp 403-415.

American Academy of Pediatrics, Committee on Nutrition (1998) Cholesterol in childhood. Pediatrics 101:141-147.

Anderson JJB, Sell ML, Garner SC, Calvo MS (2001) Phosphorus. In BA Bowman, RM Russell (eds), Present Knowledge in Nutrition. Washington, DC: ILSI Press, pp 281-291.

Bailey LB, Moyers S, Gregory JF III (2001) Folate. In BA Bowman, RM Russell (eds), Present Knowledge in Nutrition. Washington, DC: ILSI Press, pp 214-229.

Bates CJ (2001) Thiamin. In BA Bowman, RM Russell (eds), Present Knowledge in Nutrition. Washington, DC: ILSI Press, pp 184-190.

Baxter SD (2002) Nutrition for healthy children and adolescents ages 2 to 18 years. In Berdanier CD (ed), Handbook of Nutrition and Food. Boca Raton, FL: CRC Press, pp 241-297.

* Berdanier CD, editor (2002) Handbook of Nutrition and Food. Boca Raton, FL: CRC Press.

Bergman RL, Bergman KE (1986) Nutrition and growth in infancy. In F Falkner, JM Tanner (eds), Human Growth. Volume 3. Methodology; Ecological, Genetic, and Nutritional Effects on Growth. New York: Plenum, pp 389-413.

Bhatia J, Bucher C, Bunyapen C (2002) Feeding the term infant. In Berdanier CD (ed), Handbook of Nutrition and Food. Boca Raton, FL: CRC Press, pp 219-239.

Bier DM, Lauer RM, Simell O (2000) Fat intake during childhood. American Journal of Clinical Nutrition 72:1410S-1413S.

* Bowman BA, Russell RM, editors (2001) Present Knowledge in Nutrition. Washington, DC: ILSI Press.

Briefel RR, McDowell MA, Alaimo K, Caughman CR, Bischof AL, Carroll MD, Johnson CL (1995) Total energy intake of the US population: The Third National Health and Nutrition Examination Survey, 1988–1991. American Journal of Clinical Nutrition 62:1072S-1080S.

* Butte NF, Wong WW, Hopkinson JM, Heinz CJ, Mehta NR, Smith EO (2000) Energy requirements derived from total energy expenditure and energy deposition during the first 2 years of life. American Journal of Clinical Nutrition 72:1558-1564.

Das SK, Roberts SB (2001) Energy metabolism. In BA Bowman, RM Russell (eds), Present Knowledge in Nutrition. Washington, DC: ILSI Press, pp 3-12.

Dewey KG, Beaton G, Fjeld C, Lonnerdal B, Reeds P (1996) Protein requirements of infants and children. European Journal of Clinical Nutrition 50:S119-S147.

Dibley MJ (2001) Zinc. In BA Bowman, RM Russell RM (eds), Present Knowledge in Nutrition. Washington, DC: ILSI Press, pp 329-343.

Dwyer J (1981) Nutritional requirements of adolescence. Nutrition Reviews 39:56-72.

Elia M (1992) Organ and tissue contribution to metabolic rate. In JM Kinney, HN Tucker (eds), Energy Metabolism: Tissue Determinants and Cellular Corollaries. New York: Raven Press, pp 61-79.

Failla ML, Johnson MA, Prohaska JR (2001) Copper. In BA Bowman, RM Russell (eds), Present Knowledge in Nutrition. Washington, DC: ILSI Press, pp 373–383.

FAO/WHO (1973) Energy and Protein Requirements. Report of a Joint FAO/WHO ad hoc Expert Committee. World Health Organization, Technical Report Series, No. 522. Geneva: World Health Organization.

Ferland G (2001) Vitamin K. In BA Bowman, RM Russell RM (eds), Present Knowledge in Nutrition. Washington, DC: ILSI Press, pp 164-172.

Fleet JC, Cashman KD (2001) Magnesium. In BA Bowman, RM Russell (eds), Present Knowledge in Nutrition. Washington, DC: ILSI Press, pp 292-301.

Fomon SF (1974) Infant Nutrition, 2nd edition. Philadelphia: Saunders.

Food and Nutrition Board, Institute of Medicine, National Academy of Sciences (1997) Dietary reference intakes for calcium, phosphorus, magnesium, vitamin D, and fluoride. www.nap.edu.

Food and Nutrition Board, Institute of Medicine, National Academy of Sciences (1998) Dietary reference intakes for thiamin, riboflavin, niacin, vitamin B-6, folate, vitamin B-12, pantothenic acid, biotin and choline. www.nap.edu.

Food and Nutrition Board, Institute of Medicine, National Academy of Sciences (2000) Dietary reference intakes for vitamin C, vitamin E, selenium, and carotenoids. www.nap.edu.

Food and Nutrition Board, Institute of Medicine, National Academy of Sciences (2001) Dietary reference intakes for vitamin A, vitamin K, arsenic, boron, chromium, copper, iodine, iron, manganese, molybdenum, nickel, silicon, vanadium, and zinc. www.nap.edu.

Food and Nutrition Board, Subcommittee on the Tenth Edition of the RDAs (1989) Recommended Dietary Allowances, 10th edition. Washington, DC: National Academy Press.

Garn SM, Clark LC (1953) The sex difference in the basal metabolic rate. Child Development 24: 215-224.

Garrow JS, Halliday D, editors (1985) Substrate and Energy Metabolism in Man. London: John Libbey.

Garrow TA (2001) Choline and carnitine. In BA Bowman, RM Russell (eds), Present Knowledge in Nutrition. Washington, DC: ILSI Press, pp 261-270.

Garza C, Scrimshaw NS, Young VR (1977a) Human protein requirements: Evaluation of the 1973 FAO/WHO safe level of protein intake for young men at high energy intakes. British Journal of Nutrition 37:403-420.

Garza C, Scrimshaw NS, Young VR (1977b) Human protein requirements: A long-term metabolic nitrogen balance study in young men to evaluate the 1973 FAO/WHO safe level of egg protein intake. Journal of Nutrition 107: 335-352.

Garza C, Scrimshaw NS, Young VR (1978) Human protein requirements: Interrelationships between energy intake and nitrogen balance in young men consuming the 1973 FAO/WHO safe level of egg protein, with added non-essential amino acids. Journal of Nutrition 108:90-96.

Hamill PVV, Drizd TA, Johnson CL, Reed RD, Roche AF (1977) NCHS growth curves for children, birth-18 years. United States. DHEW Publication No. (PHS) 78-1650. Washington, DC: US Government Printing Office.

Hansen AE, Haggard ME, Boelsche AN, Adam DJD, Wiese HF (1958) Essential fatty acids in infant nutrition. III. Clinical manifestations of linoleic acid deficiency. Journal of Nutrition 66:565-576.

Harper AE (1985) Origin of recommended dietary allowances—an historic overview. American Journal of Clinical Nutrition 41: 140-148.

Heird WC (2001) Nutritional Requirements during Infancy. In BA Bowman, RM Russell (eds), Present Knowledge in Nutrition. Washington, DC: ILSI Press, pp 416-425.

Holliday MA (1978) Body composition and energy needs during growth. In F Falkner, JM Tanner (eds), Human Growth. Volume 2. Postnatal Growth. New York: Plenum, pp 117-139.

Jacob RA (2001) Niacin. In BA Bowman, RM Russell (eds), Present Knowledge in Nutrition. Washington, DC: ILSI Press, pp 199-206.

Johnston CS (2001) Vitamin C. In BA Bowman, RM Russell (eds), Present Knowledge in Nutrition. Washington, DC: ILSI Press, pp 175-183.

Jones PJH, Papamandjaris PAA (2001) Lipids: Cellular metabolism. In BA Bowman, RM Russell (eds), Present Knowledge in Nutrition. Washington, DC: ILSI Press, pp 104-114.

* Kennedy E, Goldberg J (1995) What are American children eating? Implications for public policy. Nutrition Reviews 53:111-126.

Lagstrom H, Seppanen R, Jokinen E, Niinikoski H, Ronnemaa T, Viikari J, Simell O (1999) Influence of dietary fat on the nutrient intake and growth of children from 1 to 5 years of age: The Special Turku Coronary Risk Factor Intervention Project. American Journal of Clinical Nutrition 69: 516-523.

Linder MC, editor (1985) Nutritional Biochemistry and Metabolism with Clinical Implications. New York: Elsevier.

Livesey G, Elia M (1988) Estimation of energy expenditure, net carbohydrate utilization, and net fat oxidation and synthesis by indirect calorimetry: Evaluation of errors with special reference to the detailed composition of fuels. American Journal of Clinical Nutrition 47:608-628.

Mann J (2001) Carbohydrates. In BA Bowman, RM Russell (eds), Present Knowledge in Nutrition. Washington, DC: ILSI Press, pp 59-71.

Mascarenhas MR, Zemel BS, Tershakovec AM, Stallings VA (2001) Adolescence. In BA Bowman, RM Russell (eds), Present Knowledge in Nutrition. Washington, DC: ILSI Press, pp 426-438.

McCormick DB (2001) Vitamin B-6. In BA Bowman, RM Russell (eds), Present Knowledge in Nutrition. Washington, DC: ILSI Press, pp 207-213.

McDowell MA, Briefel RR, Alaimo K, Bischof AM, Caughman CR, Carroll MD, Loria CM, Johnson CL (1994) Energy and macronutrient intakes of persons ages 2 months and over in the United States: Third National Health and Nutrition Examination Survey, Phase 1, 1988–91. Advanced Data 255:1-24.

Mertz W (1981) The essential trace elements. Science 213: 1332-1338.

Miller JW, Rogers LM, Rucker RB (2001) Pantothenic acid. In BA Bowman, RM Russell (eds), Present Knowledge in Nutrition. Washington, DC: ILSI Press, pp 253-260.

Millward DJ, Garlick PJ, Reeds PJ (1976) The energy cost of growth. Proceedings of the Nutrition Society 35: 339-349.

National Research Council (1989) Diet and Health: Implications for Reducing Chronic Disease Risk. Washington, DC: National Academy Press.

Newsholme EA, Leech AR (1983) Biochemistry for the Medical Sciences. London: Wiley.

Nielsen FH (2001) Boron, manganese, molybdenum, and other trace elements. In BA Bowman, RM Russell (eds), Present Knowledge in Nutrition. Washington, DC: ILSI Press, pp 384-400.

Norman AW (2001) Vitamin D. In BA Bowman, RM Russell (eds), Present Knowledge in Nutrition. Washington, DC: ILSI Press, pp 146-155.

Obarzanek E, Hunsberger SA, Van Horn L, Hartmuller VV, Barton BA, Stevens VJ, Kwiterovich PO, Franklin FA, Kimm SY, Lasser NL, Simons-Morton DG, Lauer RM. (1997) Safety of a fat-reduced diet: The Dietary Intervention Study in Children (DISC). Pediatrics 100:51-59.

Obarzanek E, Kimm SYS, Barton BA, Van Horn L, Kwiterovich PO, Simons-Morton DG, Hunsberger SA, Lasser NL, Robson AM, Franklin FA, Lauer RM, Stevens VJ, Friedman LA, Dorgan JF, Greenlick MR (2001) Long-term safety and efficacy of a cholesterol-lowering diet in children with elevated low-density lipoprotein cholesterol: Seven-year results of the Dietary Intervention Study in Children (DISC). Pediatrics 107:256-264.

Pencharz PB, Parsons H, Motil K, Duffy B (1981) Total body

protein turnover and growth in children: Is it a futile cycle? Medical Hypotheses 7: 155-160.

Preuss HG (2001) Sodium, chloride, and potassium. In BA Bowman, RM Russell (eds), Present Knowledge in Nutrition. Washington, DC: ILSI Press, pp 302-310.

Pryor WA (2001) Vitamin E. In BA Bowman, RM Russell (eds), Present Knowledge in Nutrition. Washington, DC: ILSI Press, pp 156-163.

Ravussin E, Bogardus C (1989) Relationship of genetics, age, and physical fitness to daily energy expenditure and fuel utilization. American Journal of Clinical Nutrition 49: 968-975.

Reeds PJ, Burrin DG, Stoll B, van Goudoever JB. (2000) Role of the gut in the amino acid economy of the host. In P Fürst, V Young (eds), Proteins, Peptides and Amino Acids in Enteral Nutrition. Basel: Nestec Ltd/Vevey, Karger, pp 25-46.

Reeds PJ, Fuller MF, Nicholson BA (1985) Metabolic basis of energy expenditure with particular reference to protein. In JS Garrow, D Halliday (eds), Substrate and Energy Metabolism in Man. London: Libbey, pp 46-57.

Rivlin RS (2001) Riboflavin. In BA Bowman, RM Russell (eds), Present Knowledge in Nutrition. Washington, DC: ILSI Press, pp 191-198.

Schutz Y, Jequier E (1998) Resting energy expenditure, thermic effect of food, and total energy expenditure. In GA Bray, C Bouchard, WPT James (eds), Handbook of Obesity. New York: Marcel Dekker, pp 443-455.

Scrimshaw NS, Young VR (1976) The requirements of human nutrition. Scientific American 235: 50-64.

* Scrimshaw NS, Waterlow JC, Young VR, editors (1996) Energy and protein requirements. European Journal of Clinical Nutrition 50 (suppl 1):S1-S197.

Solomons NW (2001) Vitamin A and carotenoids. In BA Bowman, RM Russell (eds), Present Knowledge in Nutrition. Washington, DC: ILSI Press, pp 127-145.

Stabler SP (2001) Vitamin B-12. In BA Bowman, RM Russell (eds), Present Knowledge in Nutrition. Washington, DC: ILSI Press, pp 230-240.

Stanbury JB, Dunn JT (2001) Iodine and the iodine deficiency disorders. In BA Bowman, RM Russell (eds), Present Knowledge in Nutrition. Washington, DC: ILSI Press, pp 344-351.

Stoecker BJ (2001) Chromium. In BA Bowman, RM Russell (eds), Present Knowledge in Nutrition. Washington, DC: ILSI Press, pp 366-372.

Sunde RA (2001) Selenium. In BA Bowman, RM Russell (eds), Present Knowledge in Nutrition. Washington, DC: ILSI Press, pp 352-365.

* Torun B, Davies PSW, Livingstone MBE, Paolisso M, Sackett R, Spurr GB (1996) Energy requirements and dietary recommendations for children and adolescents 1 to 18 years old. European Journal of Clinical Nutrition 50 (suppl 1): S37-S81.

Troiano RP, Briefel RR, Carroll MD, Bialostosky K (2000) Energy and fat intakes of children and adolescents in the United States: Data from the National Health and Nutrition Examination Surveys. American Journal of Clinical Nutrition 72:1343S-1353S.

* Waterlow JC (1995) Whole-body protein turnover in humans—past, present, and future. Annual Reviews in Nutrition 15:57-92.

Weaver CM (2001) Calcium. In BA Bowman, RM Russell (eds), Present Knowledge in Nutrition. Washington, DC: ILSI Press, pp 273-280.

Whitehead RG, Paul AA, Cole TJ (1981) A critical analysis of measured food energy intakes during infancy and early childhood in comparison with current international recommendations. Journal of Human Nutrition 35:339-348.

Widdowson EM (1962) Nutritional individuality. Proceedings of the Nutrition Society 21:121-128.

World Health Organization (1985) Energy and Protein Requirements: Report of a Joint FAO/WHO/UNU Expert Consultation. World Health Organization, Technical Report Series No. 724. Geneva: World Health Organization.

Yip R (2001) Iron. In BA Bowman, RM Russell (eds), Present Knowledge in Nutrition. Washington, DC: ILSI Press, pp 311-328.

Young VR, Scrimshaw NS (1979) Genetic and biological variability in human nutrient requirements. American Journal of Clinical Nutrition 32: 486-500.

* Young VR (2001) Protein and amino acids. In BA Bowman, RM Russell (eds), Present Knowledge in Nutrition. Washington, DC: ILSI Press, pp 43-58.

Zempleni J (2001) Biotin. In BA Bowman, RM Russell (eds), Present Knowledge in Nutrition. Washington, DC: ILSI Press, pp 241-252.

PHYSICAL ACTIVITY AND ENERGY EXPENDITURE: ASSESSMENT, TRENDS, AND TRACKING

Chapter Outline

Relationships and interactions between levels of physical activity and energy expenditure with growth and maturation are a major focus of this book. Although several earlier chapters have mentioned physical activity and energy expenditure, this chapter explores the two concepts in more detail. Methods of assessment are initially reviewed and then developmental trends, stability of activity levels, and correlates of physical activity are considered.

In recent years, associations between health and habitual physical activity have been explored in many different populations. A sedentary lifestyle is one of the major risk factors for several chronic diseases among adults (risk factors are considered in more detail in chapter 26). Under-

standing changes in activity patterns that accompany growth and maturation is, therefore, not only of theoretical value but also of paramount public health importance. In this chapter, patterns and levels of physical activity and energy expenditure are first defined. Then, the various methods available for their estimation or measurement are explored. Finally, the changes in levels of physical activity and energy expenditure during growth and maturation and the factors that underlie these changes are considered. The influence of regular physical activity on indicators of growth, maturation, and performance is discussed in chapter 22, and the influence of intensive training for sport on the growth and maturation of young athletes is discussed in chapter 28.

What Is Physical Activity?

Physical activity can be defined as: "Any bodily movement produced by skeletal muscles and resulting in energy expenditure," (Bouchard et al. 1990, p. 6). Physical activity has mechanical, physiological, and behavioral components. From a biomechanical point of view, physical activity is measured in terms of force, velocity, acceleration, mechanical power, or mechanical work produced by the body. A physiologist describes physical activity in terms of energy expenditure, using measures such as O_2 uptake, metabolic energy (e.g., in kilocalories or kilojoules), metabolic power (kcal/min or kJ/min), or the multiple of resting energy expenditure (MET). A behaviorist addresses the type of the activity (e.g., running versus calisthenics versus baseball) and the context of the activity—the environment in which the child functions (e.g., playground, school), the use of toys or apparatus, and interactions with others (e.g., friends or family members). Physical activity is a behavior that occurs within the context of the specific culture within which children and adolescents are reared. However, it is a behavior with important biological implications.

What Is Energy Expenditure?

Energy expenditure is an expression of total-body metabolism during specific time periods. Expressions such as "resting metabolic rate" and "resting energy expenditure" or "total metabolism" and "total energy expenditure" are often used. Total energy expenditure (TEE) comprises several components, only one of which reflects the individual's habitual physical activity. The three main components of TEE are: **resting energy expenditure** (REE), **diet-induced energy expenditure** (DEE, also called diet-induced thermogenesis), and **physical activity-induced and exercise-induced energy expenditure** (EEE). Thus,

$$TEE = REE + DEE + EEE$$

Another component of TEE is **adaptive energy expenditure**, which reflects increases in metabolism related to ambient conditions such as climatic heat and cold stresses, but it is commonly minor in most circumstances. Adaptive energy expenditure is considered infrequently.

Resting energy expenditure is measured in the morning in a subject who is fully rested and who has fasted overnight. The measurement is taken in the supine position, although resting metabolism can be measured in a sitting or standing person. To obtain a valid REE, climatic conditions should be thermoneutral (approximately 23°C to 25°C with 40% to 50% relative humidity) and the subject comfortably dressed. The child should be encouraged to remain still throughout the measurement, which may last 20 to 30 minutes. Remaining still for such a length of time is often difficult for young children. One way to keep the child from moving about during the measurement is to project a video.

Diet-induced energy expenditure is the increment in energy expenditure above REE, which is observed up to 3 to 4 hours after a standardized meal. This increase, which can reach as much as 10% to 15% of the REE, reflects the energy expended for the mechanical and chemical processes of digestion, as well as the absorption from the intestine and the storage of the nutrients, and is particularly influenced by the macronutrient composition of a meal.

Exercise energy expenditure is the most variable component of TEE. In a fully sedentary person (e.g., a bedridden patient) it is close to zero. In contrast, it can reach 10 to 20 times REE during intense exercise. Over 24 hours, EEE of an endurance athlete can exceed 50% of TEE.

Several methods may be used to quantify the energy that is actually expended during physical activity. The most commonly used method to express energy expenditure of a specific physical task is the ratio of exercise to resting energy expenditure (EEE/REE), which is called a metabolic equivalent (MET). Physical activity or exercise energy expenditure must be measured during the performance of a task to estimate metabolic equivalents. Tables have been collated that assign MET values to a variety of tasks, but these are based largely on measurements in adults. These estimates have limitations when applied to children and adolescents because exercise energy expenditure per unit body mass during various activities is higher in children than in adults (see chapter 12), and resting metabolic rate of children per unit body mass or per unit body surface area is higher than in adults. As a result, MET values constructed for adults may differ from those calculated for children. Table 21.1 summarizes MET values for a variety of activities calculated for children 9 to 12 years of age.

To estimate the contribution of activity-related energy expenditure over 24 hours, the ratio TEE/

TABLE 21.1	MET Values for Selected Activities in Children 9 to 12 Years of Age	
Activity	**Met value**	
Sitting quietly	1.1	
Reading while sitting	1.2	
Watching television while sitting	1.3	
Doing puzzles while sitting	1.5	
Standing quietly	1.5	
Singing while standing	1.8	
Dressing	2.6	
Eating	1.4	
Walking at a slow pace	2.8	
Walking at a firm pace	3.5	
Cycling slowly	2.5	
Cycling at a firm pace	5.0	
Spontaneous playing outdoors	4.5	
Ballet	4.4	
Gymnastics	5.0	
Judo	6.3	
Soccer game	6.0	

Adapted with permission from Saris (1986).

REE can be used. This ratio is called the "physical activity level" (PAL, also called "activity factor," or AF). The PAL can range from 1.0 (no activity at all) to 3.5 to 4.5 (extremely active individuals). Active children normally have a TEE/REE or PAL of about 1.7 to 2.0. The PAL is particularly low in sedentary children and in children who have a physical disability or a debilitating chronic disease. Sedentary children with cerebral palsy, for example, have a PAL as low as 1.5 (Van Den Berg-Emons et al. 1995).

Methods of Assessing Patterns or Levels of Physical Activity and Energy Expenditure

Over 20 different methods have been used for the assessment of physical activity and energy expenditure. This variety suggests that no single method can fully reflect a person's activity behavior and the energy cost—mechanical or physiological—of such activity. In the follow-ing sections, some of the more commonly used methods, including advantages and drawbacks, are described. Special attention is given to the suitability of the methods for use with children. A summary of methods commonly used to assess physical activity and energy expenditure is given in table 21.2.

One of the concerns regarding any method that assesses spontaneous behaviors is that the very act of measuring may induce changes in these behaviors. This phenomenon is called **reactivity**. It may occur when the subject becomes aware of the presence of an observer or the subject must wear an instrument to monitor the activity. When designing a method for assessing habitual physical activity in children and adolescents, reactivity should be kept to a minimum.

Questionnaires

Questionnaires are the most commonly used method to estimate physical activity and energy expenditure. Because of their relative simplicity and low cost, questionnaires are often used in large-scale surveys, as well as in a clinical context and in small-group studies. Answering a questionnaire is based on a subject's reading and comprehension skills and ability to recall past activities, which depends on memory and interpretation. In the case of children, response to a questionnaire may require input by a parent, teacher, or other adults who are familiar with the child's activity behavior. These requirements may limit the utility and validity of recall questionnaires, especially when used with young children. Both the reliability and the validity of recall questionnaires increase with the age of the child (Sallis 1991).

Many recall questionnaires have been developed (Sallis et al. 1993; Longmuir & Bar-Or 1994; Matkin et al. 1998). They ask the subject to recall physical activity over the span of a single day to a span of several years. In general, the shorter the time interval, the higher the validity and accuracy of recall. Questionnaires vary also in the specific questions used to describe activities. Some yield merely a description of activities, whereas others also address factors that enhance or impede the activity behaviors of children and adolescents. Very few questionnaires address the attitudes of the youngster and other family members toward physical activity.

Attempts have been made to quantify energy expenditure from questionnaires using tables that convert each activity into a metabolic

TABLE 21.2 Methods Commonly Used for the Assessment of Pattern or Level of Physical Activity (PA) and Energy Expenditure (EE)

Method	Function assessed	Advantages	Drawbacks	Comments
Questionnaire	PA	Simple, low cost; suitable for large-scale studies	Relies on memory; hard to quantify; low validity	The shorter the recall period, the higher the validity
Interview	PA	More valid than a questionnaire	Relies on memory	Interviewer can corroborate information
Diary	PA	Short recall time	Interactive	Depends on child's interpretation
Direct observation	PA (EE?)	No need for recall; context documented	Expensive; depends on observer's skill	"Gold standard" for specific behavioral aspects of activity
Time-lapse (or video) photography	PA (EE?)	Objective, hard record available	Child is limited to pre-determined area	Less expensive than direct observation
Movement counters	PA (EE?)	Objective, little interaction; low cost	Does not detect specific movements	
Accelerometry	PA, EE(?)	Same as counters, plus acceleration	Does not detect specific activities	Some validity versus measurements of EE
HR monitoring	EE	Little interaction; inexpensive	HR affected not only by metabolism	Needs individual "calibration" versus $\dot{V}O_2$
$\dot{V}O_2$				
Metabolic cart	EE	Measures metabolism	Limited activities; need for mouthpiece or face mask	Useful for ergometry and VO_2-HR "calibration"
Portable equipment	EE	Measures metabolism away from the lab	Highly interactive; expensive	Limited pediatric use in prolonged observations
Canopy	EE	Measures metabolism	RMR only	Used in conjunction with HR monitoring
Respiration chamber	EE	Precise measurement of EE	Very limited quarters; expensive	Validating other tests; ideal for BMR
Doubly labeled water	EE	Best measure of EE; not interactive	Very high cost; requires at least 1 week	"Gold standard" for average EE, but not for profile of EE

RMR = resting metabolic rate, BMR = basal metabolic rate. A question mark denotes uncertain validity.

energy value (e.g., walking a mile is equivalent to a certain number of kilojoules). This approach has a low to fair validity, particularly when used with children (Sallis et al. 1991). One reason is that such tables are based on the steady-state energy cost of an activity. However, a child's typical activity pattern (short bursts of activity that last for several seconds) seldom results in a steady state (Bailey et al. 1995). Another reason is that most data for the energy equivalents of

activities are based on adult-related studies and do not take into account the variability in body mass of children and adolescents. They also do not account for the higher energy cost of activities among children (see chapter 12). Ideally, a conversion table for use with children and adolescents should be divided into several body mass categories and, as far as possible, should use energy equivalents generated for the respective age groups. Several examples of estimated

TABLE 21.3	Metabolic Energy Equivalents of Selected Physical Activities for Several Body Mass Categories				
	Body weight category (kg)				
Activity	**20**	**30**	**40**	**50**	**60**
Basketball (game)	145	215	285	355	430
Cross-country ski (leisure)	100	150	200	250	300
Cycling					
10 km/hr	65	85	110	140	165
15 km/hr	90	130	170	210	250
Figure skating	170	250	335	420	505
Ice hockey (on-ice time)	220	330	435	545	655
Running					
8 km/hr	155	220	275	330	380
10 km/hr	200	270	330	385	450
12 km/hr	—	320	380	450	515
14 km/hr	—	—	—	510	590
Sitting					
Complete rest	35	40	40	45	50
Quiet play	45	60	65	70	80
Soccer (game)	150	225	300	380	455
Squash	—	270	355	445	535
Swimming 30 m/min					
Breast	80	120	160	200	245
Front crawl	105	155	205	260	310
Back	70	25	35	40	50
Tennis	90	140	185	230	275
Volleyball (game)	85	125	170	210	250
Walking					
4 km/hr	70	90	110	125	145
6 km/hr	100	120	135	155	180

Values are in kJ/10 min.

Adapted from Bar-Or (1983).

metabolic energy equivalents for several physical activities by body weight categories are summarized in table 21.3.

Interviews

Interviewer-administered questionnaires have a higher reliability and validity than self-administered questionnaires. An experienced interviewer can elicit much more information than the subject, teacher, or family member might volunteer. Children below the age of 10 to 12 years experience particular difficulty in describing the time spent on an activity. An interviewer can refresh the child's memory by first creating "anchors" for a day's events (for example, by establishing the time that the child got up, went to school, had lunch, returned from school, had dinner, and went to bed). Once established, such context-specific anchors or prompts can help quantify the time spent on a given activity.

A major drawback of interviews is the high cost in terms of observer time. As a result, interviews are seldom used in large-scale surveys. The use of telephone-based interviews rather than face-to-face interviews reduces such costs.

A self-administered questionnaire can be combined with a subsequent interview, as is often done in a clinical context and in small-scale studies. During the interview, one can expand on and clarify some of the written responses, as well as corroborate information through additional questions. Performing the interview after the subject has responded to the written questionnaire is another means of reducing the observer's time.

Diaries

Instead of depending on memory, subjects can record their activities as they occur or at predetermined intervals throughout the day (Bouchard et al. 1983). Information logged in the diary can include the nature of the activity and its duration. In some cases, people are asked to enter the intensity of the activity. The collated information can be quantified to estimate the level of activity. Estimates of energy expenditure can also be derived from the data by using conversion tables (Eisenmann et al. 1999), as described in the section on questionnaires. Diaries have been used successfully with children as young as 10 years of age, but their validity with younger children is not clear.

A major disadvantage of the diary method is its high degree of reactivity. The need to repeatedly record activities, in itself, may induce a change in a person's spontaneous activities and thus affect the performance of other tasks, particularly if the required frequency of logging information is high.

Direct Observation

In this method, an investigator observes the subject continuously and records the activities at a high frequency (e.g., each minute) using a coding system. This technique, which has been used successfully for time-and-motion analysis of industrial tasks, has an important value for analyzing the activity behavior of people of all ages. The main difference from questionnaires, interviews, and diaries is that the information does not depend on the subject's interpretation or memory. It is, therefore, a better indicator of the actual activities. The success of this method depends on the skill of the observer, rather than on the subject's recall ability. Two methods that have been tried with children are the Behaviors of Eating and Activity for Children's Health Evaluation System (BEACHES) (McKenzie et al. 1991) and the Fargo Activity Time Sampling (FATS)

Survey (Klesges et al. 1984). Some direct observation protocols include entries such as the following questions: Who initiated the child's current activity (e.g., parent, teacher, another child, or the subject)? Where was it performed (e.g., playground, sand pit, or in front of a television)? Did the child interact with others? Did the child play with toys? Such information offers valuable data on the behavioral aspects of physical activity.

The main drawback of this method is the very high cost of the observer's time. Furthermore, considerable amounts of time and effort are required to train a team of observers to become skilful in coding several variables each minute. Intraobserver and interobserver reliability needs to be checked periodically (see chapter 3). Another potential drawback is reactivity caused by the presence of the observer. Some individuals are likely to modify their activity pattern merely because of the observer's presence. Interestingly, the younger the child who is observed, the less the reactivity. Experience with preschoolers has shown that after only a few minutes, they ignore the presence of the observer.

Despite the above limitations, direct observation is considered a valuable method against which other methods are validated for documenting specific contexts of physical activity.

Time-Lapse Photography or Video Photography

By the use of well-positioned cameras, one can document a person's activity in a manner similar to direct observation. The main advantage of this method is that a record is kept and can be analyzed offline (Bullen et al. 1964; Ellis & Schotts 1978). The same record can be analyzed by several investigators, which increases objectivity. Photography induces less reactivity than does direct observation but has a disadvantage because the subject is limited to certain areas within view of the camera (e.g., schoolyard or gymnasium). Photography also has associated expenses for equipment.

Movement Counters

Whereas the previous methods focus on the behavioral aspects of physical activity (with some derivation of energy expenditure), movement counters document objectively some mechanical aspects of an activity. Counters have a mechanical or electronic mechanism that is sensitive to motion, usually in a single plane, and when activated, they can count and register the number of movements. By attaching the device to a body part (e.g., waist, wrist, or ankle), an objective measurement is obtained of the number of movements performed over time by that body part.

The best-known movement counters are **pedometers**. These small devices are usually attached to the waist, and, by registering vertical motion, they can count strides. Assuming a certain stride length, the distance covered over the duration of the measurement can be calculated. Studies have shown that certain pedometers provide a valid measurement of distance covered (Saris & Binkhorst 1977; Eston et al. 1998). The major disadvantage of pedometers is that they are not sensitive to the intensity of the strides and, therefore, cannot distinguish between slow and fast walking or between walking and running. They also cannot detect whether the walk (or run) is performed on the level, uphill, or downhill. Another limitation is that pedometers do not sense movements of body parts other than the waist. For example, they may not register movement during cycling. Therefore, whereas they may be useful for adults, whose main leisure activity may be walking or jogging, they are less suitable for children, who have a larger activity repertoire. Attempts have been made to estimate the EE of body movements sensed by pedometers or other movement counters. These estimates usually have a low validity.

Accelerometry

An important addition to movement counters has been developed in recent years. This improvement is the ability to sense and register **acceleration** within a movement and not merely the number of movements. Most rhythmic movements require repeated cycles of acceleration and deceleration of body segments. By sensing these changes, an accelerometer can yield important information about mechanical events that are not registered by counters such as the pedometer.

One of the first commercially available accelerometers was the Caltrac. In this instrument, movements cause a twist of a ceramic transducer that emits a current proportional to the mechanical force acting on it. Various studies have been performed over the years, validating the Caltrac against direct observation, heart rate monitoring, doubly labeled water, and respiration chambers (Bray et al. 1992; Simons-Morton & Huang 1997). Whereas correlation coefficients for adults range from 0.50 to 0.90, they are generally lower for children (Klesges et al. 1985). The lower coefficients may reflect the larger variability of body movements in children than in adults, many of which

may not have been sensed by the Caltrac. Another shortcoming of this device is that it provides a single value over the total time of observation and thus ignores changes in intensity and number of motions at any point during the observation.

A more recent commercial development is the Tritrac accelerometer, which can sense movements in three planes, compared with a single plane sensed by the Caltrac (Eston et al. 1997; Jakicic et al. 1999). Sensing in three planes captures movements that would have been ignored by the Caltrac. The Tritrac stores the counts sequentially over time, which provides a profile of the amount and intensity of body movements at various points in time (see figure 21.1). Such a profile can then be superimposed on the profile achieved by other methods, such as direct observation or heart rate monitoring. Attempts have been made

Activity Profile Using Tritrac Accelerometry

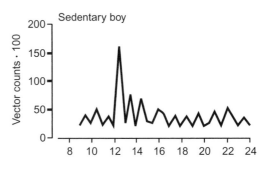

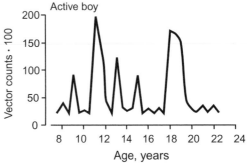

FIGURE 21.1 A profile of the output generated by a Tritrac accelerometer over a period of 16 hours. The top graph is typical of a sedentary child, whose activities are limited to a physical education class. The bottom graph summarizes body movements of a child who walked to and from school, took part in a physical education class, was active during recess, and took part in a training session after school.

Data from the Children's Exercise and Nutrition Centre, McMaster University.

to derive energy expenditure levels from Tritrac data (Jakicic et al. 1999). More research is needed, however, to validate this approach. The Tritrac accelerometer is much more expensive than the Caltrac, which makes the latter more suitable for large-scale studies.

Another accelerometer that has been used with children is the CSA (Computer Science and Applications). The device is lightweight (70 g) and small (6.6 × 4.3 × 1.5 cm), and like the Tritrac, it can store information sequentially. An advantage over the Tritrac is that the CSA can be programmed to turn itself on and off at predetermined intervals. Its disadvantage, compared with the Tritrac, is that the CSA senses movement in one plane only. When validated against heart rate monitoring, correlations range between 0.50 and 0.74 for each monitored day in 7- to 15-year-old girls and boys (Janz 1994).

Heart Rate Monitoring

Heart rate (HR) monitoring is the most popular method for estimating energy expenditure over long periods of time (e.g., 24 to 72 hours). In this method, a person's HR is monitored continuously using a lightweight monitor. HR monitoring has been used extensively in adult and pediatric research, yielding important information about energy expenditure in various populations (Torun 1984; Freedson 1991; Armstrong and Bray 1991; Atkins et al. 1997). The method is based on the linear relationship between oxygen uptake and HR at a wide range of exercise intensities. $\dot{V}O_2$, in turn, is an excellent indicator of the metabolic energy expended aerobically during a given time period.

Because the $\dot{V}O_2$–HR regression varies among individuals (and in the same individual, with changes in aerobic fitness), it has to be measured directly in each subject. Such "calibration" requires a visit to an exercise laboratory, in which $\dot{V}O_2$ and HR can be measured simultaneously at rest and at several exercise intensities.

Whereas the $\dot{V}O_2$–HR relationship is linear during submaximal exercise, a different regression line reflects the relationship at rest. Many investigators, therefore, draw two regression lines, one for rest (measured in conditions such as lying down, sitting, and standing still) and one for exercise (see figure 21.2). This refinement is important because, during a 24-hour monitoring, many of the HR values are taken at rest, and using only the exercise regression line will not reflect the real $\dot{V}O_2$ in the resting individual. Research-

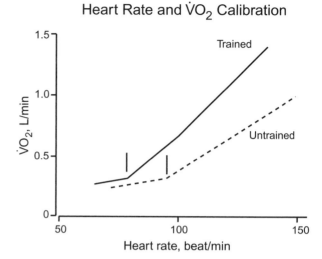

Heart Rate and $\dot{V}O_2$ Calibration

FIGURE 21.2 "Calibration" lines for the $\dot{V}O_2$–HR relationship in two 12-year-old boys. One child was untrained and the other child was an endurance athlete. Steady-state values were taken at rest (lying supine, sitting, and standing still) and during four submaximal exercise tasks. The regression lines were drawn separately for rest and for exercise. The vertical line was drawn at the flex point. It denotes transition from the use of the resting regression line to the use of the exercise line.

ers have debated how to determine the transition point below which one should use the resting regression line, and beyond which, plot the exercise regression line. A commonly used approach is to take the standing value as the transition point, which is called the **flex point** (Spurr et al. 1988; Livingstone et al. 1992). Once the regression lines and the 24-hour HR profile have been drawn, a profile of energy expenditure over the whole period of monitoring, or segments thereof, can be constructed (see figure 21.3).

The HR method, particularly with the availability of small monitors, is socially acceptable by children and causes minimal reactivity. The child loses interest in the monitor within a few minutes after its installation and resumes her or his spontaneous activity pattern. The commonly used telemetric HR monitors (e.g., Sport Tester, Polar Vantage XL) are highly valid tools for measuring HR in children as young as 4 years of age, compared with direct electrocardiographic monitoring (Bar-Or et al. 1996).

The major drawback of HR monitoring is that factors other than metabolic rate can influence heart rate. These factors include climatic conditions, core body temperature, aerobic fitness,

Energy Expenditure Profile
Using Heart Rate Monitoring

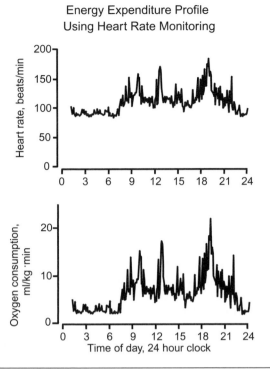

Nomogram Correcting Heart
Rate for Climatic Heat

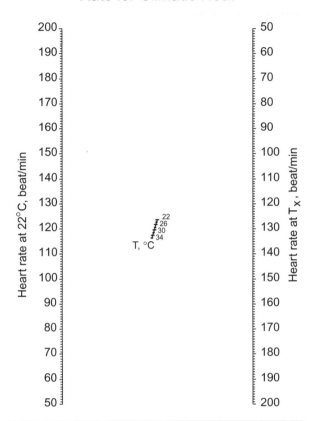

FIGURE 21.3   A profile of heart rate and the equivalent V̇O₂ over 24 hours in a 10-year-old girl. Heart rate was monitored by a Sport Tester, Polar Vantage XL.

Data from the Children's Exercise and Nutrition Centre, McMaster University.

FIGURE 21.4   Nomogram for the correction of heart rate as observed at ambient temperature T_x, to heart rate at 22°C, assuming an equal V̇O₂. Based on data for 8-year-old to 11-year-old girls and boys.

Reprinted from Hebestreit et al. 1995.

resting (or basal) HR, size of the contracting muscles, nature of muscle contraction (e.g., dynamic versus static), time since the last meal, level of body hydration, and emotional state. These effects are apparent mostly at rest or during low-intensity activities. The effect of climate on HR is important. For example, when children perform an activity at 35°C, their HR is higher by as much as 15 to 25 beat/min than when the same energy is expended at 22°C (Hebestreit et. al. 1995)

Because of the above, HR monitoring often overestimates actual metabolic energy expenditure, particularly if outdoor activities are performed in a hot or cold environment. A recently developed nomogram (Hebestreit et al. 1995) is available that can be used to correct for the effect of climatic heat stress on HR (see figure 21.4).

In the absence of an exercise laboratory, one can use an alternative approach to describe a person's physical activity level even without a V̇O₂–HR calibration line. In this method, one does not convert the number of heartbeats into units of metabolic work or power, but simply presents the

data as raw HR values. One can assume that certain HR ranges reflect a specific degree of effort. For example, in an 8-year-old child, an HR of 170 beat/min or more reflects a very intense effort, an HR of 150 to 169 beat/min reflects an intense effort, and an HR of 130 to 149 beat/min reflects a moderate effort.

Another refinement of the HR monitoring method is to subtract the basal HR, obtained while the child is asleep (or lying comfortably in a thermoneutral environment), from the HR monitored during waking hours. The resulting **net HR** is assumed to better reflect the individual's activity level. A variation of the above approach, when basal HR is not available, is to subtract the lowest values of the 24-hour HR from each of the other values (Mimura et al. 1991).

Measuring O$_2$ Uptake

$\dot{V}O_2$ is an excellent surrogate for determining energy expenditure. One can assume that 1 L of O$_2$ consumed is equivalent to 5 kcal expended, and the estimate can be refined by correcting for the observed respiratory exchange ratio (the ratio between CO$_2$ production in unit time and O$_2$ consumed at that time). Historically, methods for collecting expired air evolved from the use of a Tissot spirometer or Douglas bags, flow meters, and gas analyzers. In this section, four different methods are discussed: metabolic cart, a portable device, the canopy method, and the respiration chamber.

Metabolic Cart   At present, the most commonly used system is the computerized metabolic cart. This apparatus synchronizes and integrates the measurements of minute ventilation and concentrations of expired gases to calculate $\dot{V}O_2$ and related metabolic and respiratory variables. Mass spectrometry is the most sophisticated method for analyzing the expired gases, but it is prohibitively expensive for most exercise laboratories.

The subject must remain close to the metabolic cart during the measurement. This restriction limits the activity repertoire to, for example, cycle ergometry, step climbing, and treadmill running or walking and does not allow for monitoring energy expenditure under free-living conditions. Determining energy expenditure in the laboratory is useful, however, for the construction of conversion tables, as used, for example, with questionnaires, and for $\dot{V}O_2$–HR "calibration."

Using a Portable Device   Portable devices allow for direct measurement of $\dot{V}O_2$ while the subject is moving freely, away from the laboratory. In the original approach developed in the 19th century, the subject carried a bag on the back and breathed all the expired air into it. Because of limited capacity, bags had to be replaced every few minutes, which was cumbersome and caused frequent interruptions of the subject's activity. Developed in the 1940s, the Kofrany-Michaelis device solved the above problem by collecting only samples of the expired air, rather than the whole air volume, from a container carried on a subject's back. This device allowed for longer collection periods than the Douglas bag. The main disadvantage of the Kofrany-Michaelis system was its heavy weight and large size. It proved useful for analyzing energy expenditure of some industrial and military tasks, but it was unsuitable for pediatric research or for use in sports activities.

Portable $\dot{V}O_2$ analyzers have been miniaturized in recent years. These lightweight devices collect samples of expired air and also analyze gas concentrations (Novitsky et al. 1995). To use a portable analyzer, the subject must exhale into the apparatus through a face mask. For children, this requirement is rather limiting, and they can seldom tolerate it for more than 15 to 20 minutes. Although the miniaturized portable analyzers have markedly increased the scope of monitoring energy expenditure in adults, they are still of limited use for children.

Canopy Method   This approach is also called the "ventilated hood" method. It has been used for measuring resting metabolic rate and the thermic effect of food while the subject is lying down (Blaak et al. 1992). The transparent canopy is placed over the subject's head. Room air is pumped through the canopy at a predetermined, measured rate. The outgoing air is directed to gas analyzers, which determine the O$_2$ and CO$_2$ concentration. Knowing the airflow and the difference between the concentration of the inspired gases and those leaving the canopy allows the $\dot{V}O_2$ and $\dot{V}CO_2$ to be calculated but not the minute ventilation or other ventilatory variables.

The main advantage of the canopy method is that there is no need for a mouthpiece, nose clip, or face mask, which makes the method easier for a subject who has to lie still for prolonged periods. This method is particularly useful for infants and young children, but measurements are limited to resting metabolism.

Using a Respiration Chamber   Special chambers have been constructed that are large enough for human beings to remain in for prolonged periods of time while their metabolic rate is determined continuously. These rooms are hermetically sealed, with one exception: a pipe system provides a continuous, measurable flow of outside air into the chamber and a similar system evacuates the same volume of air into gas analyzers placed outside the chamber. By knowing the flow rate and the difference in gas concentration between the incoming and the outgoing air, one can calculate $\dot{V}O_2$ and $\dot{V}CO_2$ but not minute ventilation or other ventilatory variables. This principle is similar to that used with the canopy described above.

The main advantage of respiratory chambers over other methods used for determining O_2 uptake is that observations can last as long as several weeks and need neither mouthpiece nor face mask. Chambers can be furnished and equipped with amenities such as toilet, telephone, and television so that subjects can conduct normal life routines, albeit in very limited quarters. This method has been used successfully with children (Blaak et al. 1992; Emons et al. 1992).

Respiration chambers have been used to determine sleeping metabolic rate overnight or the metabolic rate of daily indoor-living routines. In addition, they have been used to validate other methods for estimating energy expenditure, such as accelerometry, HR-monitoring, and doubly labeled water analysis (see next section). Subjects can exercise and train in the chamber using an ergometer or other exercise machines.

The obvious limitation of this method is that the subject is restricted to a small space, and the daily routine seldom reflects spontaneous activity behavior. Construction and operation of a respiration chamber system are rather expensive.

Doubly Labeled Water Analysis

The doubly labeled water (DLW) technique was originally developed for research with animals but has emerged as the "gold standard" method to date for the measurement of energy expenditure under free-living conditions in humans during early infancy (Davies et al. 1991) and childhood (Livingstone et al. 1992) and through adolescence into adulthood. In this method, the subject drinks water that contains an accurately measured amount of two stable isotopes: ^2H and ^{18}O. Within 4 to 8 hours, the isotopes become fully diluted in the total-body water compartment (see chapter 5). Periodic measurements of isotope concentrations in a body fluid (e.g., urine or saliva) are taken for 10 to 14 days. Based on these values, the elimination rate from the body of each of the isotopes is calculated. Whereas the ^{18}O isotope is eliminated both through H_2O and CO_2, the ^2H isotope is eliminated only through H_2O. Therefore, the difference in elimination rate of the two isotopes reflects the elimination rate of CO_2, which is proportional to energy expenditure. The DLW method is also the least reactive method because it does not interfere with spontaneous activity.

The main limitation of the DLW method is the very high cost of the ^{18}O isotope (several hundred dollars per dose) and the need for a very-high-

precision isotope-ratio mass spectrometer. As a result, only a handful of laboratories worldwide use the DLW technique routinely. Another limitation is that the measurement yields a single value of energy expenditure over the whole observation period without any indication about changes in EE over that period.

The Need to Combine Methods

As apparent in the preceding discussion, numerous approaches address the behavioral, mechanical, and physiological aspects of the level of physical activity as well as components of energy expenditure. However, none of these approaches alone can cover all aspects of physical activity and energy expenditure. To obtain a comprehensive picture of the habitual level of physical activity and energy expenditure of an individual, a combination of methods may be needed. The choice of such combinations depends on the specific objectives of the study and on the availability of equipment and personnel.

Developmental Trends in Physical Activity and Energy Expenditure

Studies in various countries have noted age-related and sex-related changes in the pattern and, particularly, in the amount of daily physical activity and energy expenditure. The pattern of activity in children and adolescents, including favorite active pursuits during leisure time, is subsequently discussed, followed by consideration of age-related and sex-related changes in the amount of physical activity and energy expenditure.

Patterns of Participation in Physical Activity

Among children 3 to about 10 years of age, physical activity is often spontaneous and non-organized and is of intermittent brief bouts. For example, based on direct observations, 6-year-old to 10-year-old girls and boys performed mostly intermittent activities of short duration (Bailey et al. 1995). As shown in figure 21.5, the median duration for light-to-moderate activity bouts was 6 seconds. Most of the high-intensity bouts did not exceed 3 seconds and 95% of them lasted less than 15 seconds. In contrast, activities of older children

Duration of Spontaneous Activities Performed by Children

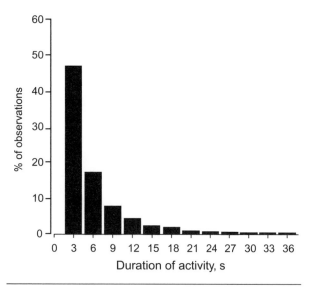

FIGURE 21.5 Distribution of high-intensity activities in children by the duration of each activity bout. The median duration of these activities was 3 seconds, and 95% lasted fewer than 15 seconds.

Reprinted from Bailey et al. 1995.

and adolescents tend to be more organized and of a more regular, prolonged nature.

Only a handful of studies document the type of activities and sports that children and adolescents pursue. An example is a study done among Canadian attendees of day care centers (Russell et al. 1992). The most common spontaneous activities were as follows: climbing, running races, jumping, cycling, swinging, and sliding. In the second National Children and Youth Fitness Survey in the United States (Ross and Pate 1987a), parents of children 10 years of age and younger reported that they engaged mostly in swimming, racing/

sprinting, baseball, softball, cycling, and soccer (Ross et al. 1987b).

Among adolescents, a major part of physical activity occurs after school hours (Katzmarzyk et al. 1998; Sallis et al. 1996). A study of 6th through 8th grade students in Michigan suggests that organized sport activities contribute about 20% of total daily energy expenditure in boys and approximately 16% in girls. In this sample, organized sports accounted for 55% of all moderate-to-vigorous activities in the boys and 65% in the girls (Katzmarzyk et al. 1998). Based on the first National Children and Youth Fitness Survey, cycling was the most popular leisure-time activity among boys in grades 5 through 9 and among girls in grades 5 and 6. Basketball was the most popular activity for boys in grades 10 to 12, and for girls swimming was most popular in grades 7 to 12 (Ross et al. 1985b). Table 21.4 presents a summary of findings from a nationwide survey of Canadian children and adolescents 10 years of age and older (Stephens & Craig 1990). In response to a question about activities "that are not related to work," the most popular activity at ages 10 to 14 years was cycling for boys and swimming for girls. Cycling was the most popular at ages 15 to 19 in both sexes. In the second decade of life, cycling seems to be the most popular recreational physical activity in the United States and Canada. Obviously, the above choices vary among societies, climatic regions, season, and weather conditions, but at present no data provide systematic comparisons under these conditions.

Age-Related and Sex-Related Decline in Activity and Energy Expenditure

Both the level of physical activity and the 24-hour energy expenditure decline with age, particularly in the second decade of life. Investigators have

TABLE 21.4	Reported Recreational Physical Activities Among Canadian Adolescents 10 to 19 Years of Age				
Group	**Walking**	**Gardening**	**Swimming**	**Bicycling**	**Dancing**
Boys 10–14	57	34	77	90	25
Girls 10–14	62	26	87	86	46
Boys 15–19	51	40	58	74	38
Girls 15–19	75	30	70	67	59

Values are the percentage (%) of adolescents reporting the specific activity in each sex and age group.

Based on data from the 1988 Campbell Survey (Stephens and Craig 1990).

also suggested that the decline begins as early as 6 years of age (Saris et al. 1986) or even earlier (Torun et al. 1996). The reduction in physical activity and energy expenditure among girls starts earlier, and is often more rapid, than among boys. Figures 21.6 and 21.7 summarize this pattern using cross-sectional and longitudinal data, respectively. The data of figure 21.6 are of particular importance because they are based on the doubly labeled water method, which is considered the "gold standard" for the measurement of total energy expenditure. About 50% to 60% of the decline in total energy expenditure is caused by the age-related decrease in basal metabolic rate (see chapter 20 and figure 20.2, page 434). Longitudinal observations of Dutch adolescents show that the decline in energy expenditure, as assessed by HR monitoring, is apparent at 11 years of age in females, but only at 14 years of age in males (Verschuur & Kemper 1985).

The decline in activity among a large sample of United States adolescents is documented in table 21.5. The prevalence of 9th grade girls who perform vigorous activities at least three times per week is only 60% of that for boys in the same grade. This percentage drops consistently with age, falling to 40% in the 12th grade. Further, minority youth, American Blacks in particular, are less active than American Whites (Centers for Disease Control 1992). Ethnic variation in physical activity is discussed in more detail in chapter 23.

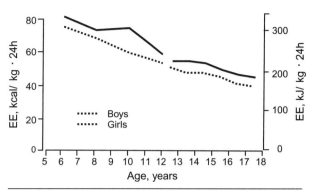

FIGURE 21.7   Longitudinal changes in energy expenditure, assessed by heart rate monitoring, among Dutch girls and boys.

Data from Saris et al., 1986, and Verschuur and Kemper, 1985.

TABLE 21.5	Percentages of High School Students in the United States Who Participated in Vigorous Physical Activity for 3 or More Days a Week		
Category	**Females**	**Males**	**Total**
Grade			
9	30.6	51.1	40.1
10	27.1	54.6	40.1
11	23.4	50.2	40.7
12	17.3	43.8	36.0
Race/ethnicity			
White	27.5	51.4	39.3
Black	17.4	42.7	29.2
Hispanic	20.9	49.9	34.5
Total	24.8	49.6	37.0

Based on 11,631 students sampled for the United States Youth Risk Behavior Survey 1990 (Centers for Disease Control 1992).

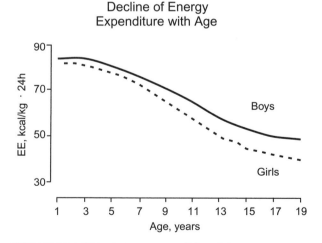

FIGURE 21.6   Decline in daily energy expenditure per kg body weight in healthy children and adolescents. Data are based on several studies from various countries, in which energy expenditure was estimated with the doubly labeled water method.

Adapted from Torun et al. (1996).

In addition to a decline in spontaneous activities, attendance in school physical education declines as well. In the first National Children and Youth Fitness Survey conducted in the 1980s (Ross et al. 1985), 97% of 1st through 6th graders participated in physical education classes. However, by the 11th and 12th grades, attendance decreased to 49%. Attendance in physical education classes in the United States has declined further during the 1990s. Daily participation in physical education among high school students was 42% in 1991 and only 25% in 1995 (Centers for Disease Control and Prevention 1997).

Tracking of Physical Activity Levels

The potential relationship between childhood and adolescent activity behavior and that of adults assumes that physical activity tracks from childhood through adolescence into adulthood. The subsequent discussion is based on several comprehensive reviews of the topic, which contain references to the primary sources (Malina 1996a, 2001a, 2001b, 2001c). The measures of levels of physical activity vary among studies. Short-term studies (2 to 3 years) indicate that physical activity tracks at low to moderate levels in the transition from early to middle childhood. Beginning at about 4 years of age, interage correlations range from 0.16 to 0.57. Level of physical activity tracks moderately during childhood and during the transition into adolescence. Over a span of 3 years during adolescence, interage correlations for activity are also moderate, but over spans of 5 and 6 years, correlations are lower. Allowing for differences in methods used to assess habitual physical activity, the results of the studies are generally consistent in indicating low-to-moderate tracking of levels of physical activity during childhood and adolescence. This pattern is consistent with observations on attitudes and involvement in activity during adolescence.

The transition from high school into the work force or the university is an interval that has not been studied often. Available data indicate moderate interage correlations (males, 0.54; females, 0.30) for level of physical activity between 18 and 21 years of age. Tracking studies that span intervals of 5 to 17 years of age from adolescence into adulthood are summarized in table 21.6. Interage correlations are lower, and, as the interval increases, the correlations decrease even further. For example, the correlation between measures of physical activity at 13 and 30 years of age in Belgian males is 0.09, whereas corresponding correlations for Dutch males and females between 13 and 27 years of age are 0.05 and 0.17, respectively (see table 21.6). Studies on the probability of remaining active or inactive in adolescence and in adulthood also suggest moderate track-

TABLE 21.6	Interage Correlations for Level of Physical Activity From Adolescence Into Young Adulthood in Several European Samples		
Sample	**Span (yr)**	**Males**	**Females**
Finnish	15–21	0.27	0.27
	18–24	0.43	0.37
Swedish	17–25[a]	0.31	0.30
Belgian	13–30	0.09	
	13–35	0.20	
	18–30	0.31	
	18–35	0.18	
Dutch	13–21	0.20/0.19[b]	0.18/0.33[b]
	13–27	0.05/0.09[b]	0.17/0.11[b]
	16–21	0.37/0.54[b]	0.25/0.25[b]
	16–27	0.09/0.16[b]	0.16/0.13[b]

[a]These ages are the midpoints of the ranges for 15–19 and 23–27 years, respectively.

[b]The first correlation refers to weekly habitual physical activity and the second refers to estimated energy expenditure in organized sports.

Adapted from Malina (1996a, 2001a, 2001b, 2001c) which contains references for the specific studies. These reviews also include a more detailed discussion of tracking of activity level from adolescence into adulthood.

ing, which, in turn, suggests a need to evaluate individuals at the extremes of the activity-inactivity continuum.

Data relating levels of physical activity during childhood and adolescence to levels of activity at older ages are relatively sparse. Correlations between several indicators of childhood and adolescent experiences in physical activity as recalled by adults 40 years of age and older and their current exercise habits are low. However, they suggest a potentially important role for proficiency in motor skills during childhood and adolescence and emphasize a need to give youth a voice or choice in their physical activity and sport participation.

The low interage correlations for indicators of physical activity during childhood, adolescence, and young adulthood also reflect to some extent errors associated with most methods used to estimate physical activity. For example, low-intensity physical activities are more difficult to recall, especially walking and household chores. Different indicators of physical activity are often used at different ages, raising the question of whether activity assessments in childhood measure the same attributes and contexts of activity as assessments in adolescence or in adulthood. Also, commonly used descriptors of physical activity—mild, moderate, or heavy (intense)—likely have different meanings among individuals and at different ages.

Changes in activity level and other components of lifestyle associated with normal growth and maturation are an additional source of variation. Studies of the stability of levels of physical activity do not consider factors that may influence activity. Many factors exert an influence on the physical activity habits of children and adolescents and merit more systematic study in the context of tracking.

Correlates of Physical Activity Levels in Childhood and Adolescence

Numerous biological, familial, psychological, societal, and cultural factors may influence activity behavior in children and adolescents. Levels of physical activity and energy expenditure also depend on variation in the physical environment, such as climate, weather, and seasonal changes. A comprehensive review (Sallis et al. 2000) of correlates of physical activity in children (3 to 12 years

of age) and adolescents (13 to 18 years of age) has identified a number of significant variables, both positive and negative, that influence level of physical activity. The majority of factors that were identified are aspects of the social environments of children and adolescents and highlight a potentially important role for interactions among the correlates of physical activity.

Although many factors can exert an influence on the level of physical activity of children and adolescents, notably lacking in the review are indicators of growth and maturity. These data are omitted because biological factors are not ordinarily included in large-scale surveys and more detailed observational studies of activity habits. The BMI is the only growth-related variable included in several studies, and it is used as a proxy for fatness. Results for the BMI are equivocal. Of the studies including the BMI, about one-half indicate a negative association, whereas the remainder indicate no relationship with level of physical activity (Sallis et al. 2000). Indicators of physical fitness are also not included among the correlates of level of physical activity, which is surprising because activity and fitness are related, albeit at generally low levels (see chapter 22).

A more comprehensive list of factors actually or potentially associated with levels of physical activity and energy expenditure in children and adolescence is presented in table 21.7. Only some of the factors have received reasonably thorough study. The studies are usually based on correlational analyses and as such indicate only

T A B L E 21.7	Factors Associated With Physical Activity and Energy Expenditure in Children and Adolescents			
Biological	**Psychological**	**Social**	**Physical environment**
Heredity	Self-efficacy	Parental attitudes and behaviors	Area of residence
Sex	Self-concept for activity	Peer attitudes and behaviors	Availability of facilities
Adiposity and nutritional status	Perception of barriers to activity	Socioeconomic status	Safety considerations
Health status	Perception of physical competence	Time spent on viewing television	Day of the week and holidays
Sexual maturity	Attitudes about activity	Time spent on computer games	Season of the year
Proficiency in motor skills	Beliefs about activity	Cultural values	Climate
Physical fitness			

Some of the associations are established whereas others are suggested.

associations and nothing about cause and effect. Some of the factors in the table have been suggested as correlates of physical activity but have not been systematically studied. The following discussion briefly considers some of these factors that may affect levels of physical activity and energy expenditure during childhood and adolescence. Several of the factors are also discussed in more detail in other chapters.

Biological Factors

Results of several studies of family members and twins are compatible with the notion that genetic and cultural factors transmitted across generations may predispose an individual to be more or less active. In addition, some of the variation in components of energy expenditure has a genetic basis (Bouchard et al. 1997; see also chapter 18), suggesting that the predisposition to activity or inactivity, and to greater or lesser levels of energy expenditure, is in part genetic. However, the extent of the genetic contribution to habitual physical activity and the nature of the genes involved remain to be further investigated. The sex of a child is genetically determined (see chapter 2), and evidence from a variety of studies indicates greater levels of energy expenditure in males than in females, beginning prenatally (Eaton and Enns 1983; Eaton & Yu 1988).

Both obesity and undernutrition are associated with reduced levels of physical activity in children and adolescents. Some studies, but not all, show a reduction in 24-hour energy expenditure per kg body mass among obese infants, children, and adolescents (see chapter 24). Chronic protein-energy undernutrition often results in reduced resting metabolism and 24-hour energy expenditure, which may reflect the body's attempt to conserve energy in physical activity to meet the needs of growth (see chapter 23).

Health status is a major determinant of levels of physical activity. As a group, children with a chronic disease or a physical or mental disability are less active than healthy peers (see chapter 27). The pathological condition in itself may limit a patient's activity, but psychological factors and parental and social expectations are often more important in keeping children with a chronic disease or disability sedentary.

Changes associated with sexual maturity in females are often accompanied by a reduction in physical activity. This association can be explained, in part, by psychosocial factors associated with the transition into puberty and with sexual maturation, including a decline in self-esteem, changing interests in pursuits other than physical activities and sports, and perhaps a prevailing public perception that success in sports requires "masculinity." However, the reduction in activity may also be related to biological changes associated with puberty. These changes include an increase in fatness, relative broadening of the pelvis and an increase in the angle between the femur and the tibia (which may affect the mechanics of some activities), discomfort before and during the menstrual period, and a reduction in blood hemoglobin.

Finally, proficiency in motor skills is an obvious determinant of physically active pursuits. Success in sports reflects to a large extent training and practice, and, as a general rule, individuals tend to pursue activities in which they are skilled and successful. Are the more skilled more likely to be active? Similarly, are the more physically fit more likely to be active? Does physical fitness influence level of physical activity? Intuitively, one would assume that the answer is yes, but research has yielded equivocal findings (see chapter 22).

Psychological Factors

Several psychological factors are associated with level of physical activity. Self-efficacy refers to confidence in one's physical abilities. Self-efficacy is highly correlated to present activity behavior as well as to activity behavior in the future. Self-concept in the context of physical activity is likewise an important predictor of activity level. Perception of barriers to activity (e.g., lack of sports facilities, limited access to facilities, or having a "disease") also correlates with level of activity.

Attitudes about activity among adolescents appear to have only a weak to moderate association with activity behavior. No links between physical activity and personality characteristics, self-confidence, or social adequacy have been proved. Knowledge about possible relationships between the risk of a chronic disease in adulthood and a sedentary lifestyle in early years seldom induces adolescents and, in particular, children to increase their activity levels. Most research on potential psychological and behavioral factors believed to be associated with physical activity has been conducted with adolescents. Whether the same findings apply to children has yet to be demonstrated.

Social Factors

During the first decade of life, but less so during adolescence, a child's activity pattern is related, in part, to parental activity and attitudes. Parents serve as role models for activity and also can directly influence the activity of their child (Malina 1996b). For example, participation in a sports program often depends on the parent's willingness and ability to take the child to the venue and to provide equipment and other resources. However, correlations between activity levels and estimated energy expenditure of parents and their offspring are generally low, less than 0.3 (Perusse et al. 1988; Sallis et al. 1988, 1992), suggesting that other factors are involved and perhaps limitations of the physical activity assessment protocols. When examined in more detail among young children and their parents, children with active parents are more likely to be active (Freedson and Evenson 1991; Moore et al. 1991). In a study of children 4 to 7 years of age, active fathers or mothers were more likely to have active children compared with inactive fathers or mothers, with odds ratios of 3.5 and 2.0, respectively. However, when both parents were active, their children were 5.8 times more likely to be active as children of two inactive parents (Moore et al. 1991).

As children move into school, they display greater independence from the family, and the influence of peers becomes more important in the context of physical activity and perhaps interacts with parental influences. During adolescence, the influence of peers is stronger, and parental influence is reduced.

Socioeconomic status of the family is an important factor that can influence physical activity. Socioeconomic status is variably defined within and among different cultures, so generalizations are difficult. Within developed countries, variation in socioeconomic status probably operates through providing or limiting access to facilities and programs. A related factor is a relatively safer home environment in better-off families (e.g., suburban versus inner city). In the United States, low socioeconomic status is frequently associated with minority ethnic or racial status. Ethnic and racial variation in growth, performance, and physical activity is discussed in chapter 25.

In many areas of the developing world, low socioeconomic status is compounded with chronic undernutrition, which affects growth, motor development, and physical activity (see chapter 23).

Television viewing and computer games are sedentary pursuits, which, for many children and adolescents, occupy a major portion of after-school time. In North America, a child or adolescent may spend 3 to 4 hours per day on these pursuits (Gortmaker et al. 1996). Some evidence suggests that energy expenditure decreases below "resting" values when a child watches television (Klesges et al. 1993). Other observations, however, suggest that when children are given incentives to decrease time spent on watching television, overall activity level and time spent outdoors is increased (Epstein et al. 1997). This finding is important because the time spent outdoors is a major determinant of a child's overall activity behavior (Sallis et al. 2000)

Physical Environment

Availability of activity facilities close to home may be an important determinant of a child's level of physical activity (Sallis et al. 1990). Safety concerns have become increasingly dominant in the decision of parents as to whether a child should be allowed to spend time outdoors or to walk to and from school. This issue has become important primarily in urban areas because time spent outdoors is positively associated with higher levels of physical activity.

Seasonal variation often affects activity behavior, mostly because of associated climatic changes (Blanchard 1987; Ross et al. 1985a; Shephard et al. 1980). The influence of more extreme climates on levels of physical activity is discussed in more detail in chapter 25. In temperate and cold climatic regions, level of physical activity often increases in the summer months, although this is not necessarily the case in warm and hot regions. Based on a national survey in the United States, 5th to 12th grade boys and girls spend more time in physical activities during the summer than in the winter, and the seasonal trend does not vary with age (Ross et al. 1985a). The greater activity level during the summer reflects observations that children are more active when outdoors (Klesges et al. 1990; Mimura et al. 1991). Seasonal variation in physical activity also occurs in relation to summer vacations and prolonged holidays. Whereas most children are more active during vacation time, others, whose main activity is school-based, show a reduction in activity.

In Canada and Finland, where winters are often harsh and days during winter are short, activity levels during the summer are twice as high as during the winter (Shephard 1986; Telama et al. 1985). For example, among 3-year-old and 6-year-old Finnish girls, parents reported 6.7 hours of outdoor activities per day in the summer in contrast to only 3.3 hours of outdoor play per day in the winter. Corresponding values for boys were 7.0 and 3.7 hours of outdoor activities per day, respectively (Telama et al. 1985).

Spontaneous physical activity during weekends also appears to be greater than during weekdays (Shephard et al. 1980; Huang and Malina 1996). Therefore, studies of the level of physical activity and energy expenditure in children and adolescents should include both weekdays and weekends.

Summary

Energy expenditure in physical activity is a major component of overall energy expenditure that has important biological implications not only during childhood and adolescence but also throughout adult life. The assessment of physical activity and energy expenditure is complex, and many methods have been used with varying degrees of success. Energy expenditure per kilogram of body mass declines from childhood through adolescence. Estimated levels of physical activity and energy expenditure in physical activity are reasonably stable during childhood but decline during adolescence. Many factors can influence patterns and levels of physical activity and energy expenditure in children and adolescents. These factors include biological, social, and psychological factors as well as aspects of the physical environment. Each factor by itself, and in combination with others, needs more detailed study, especially in the context of the multiple demands on children and adolescents as they grow, mature, and develop.

Sources and Suggested Readings

Armstrong N, Bray S (1991) Physical activity patterns defined by heart rate monitoring. Archives of Diseases of Children 66:245-247.

Atkins S, Stratton G, Dugdill, Reilly T (1997) The free-living physical activity of schoolchildren: A longitudinal study. In N Armstrong, B Kirby, J Welsman (eds), Children and Exercise XIX. London: E & FN Spon, pp 145-150.

Bailey RC, Olson J, Pepper SL, Porszasz J, Barstow TJ, Cooper DM (1995) The level and tempo of children's physical activities: An observational study. Medicine and Science in Sports and Exercise 27:1033-1041.

* Bar-Or O (1983) Pediatric Sports Medicine for the Practitioner. From Physiologic Principles to Clinical Applications. New York: Springer Verlag.

Bar-Or T, Bar-Or O, Waters H, Hirji A, Russell S (1996) Validity and social acceptability of the Polar Vantage XL for measuring heart rate in preschoolers. Pediatric Exercise Science 8:115-121.

Beunen GP, Philippaerts RM, Delvaux K, Thomis M, Claessens AL, Vanreusel B, Vanden Eynde B, Lysens R, Renson R, Lefevre J (2001) Adolescent physical performance and adult physical activity in Flemish males. American Journal of Human Biology 13:173-179.

Blaak EE, Westerterp KR, Bar-Or O, Wouters LJM, Saris WHM (1992) Total energy expenditure and spontaneous activity in relation to training in obese boys. American Journal of Clinical Nutrition 55:777-782.

Blanchard S (1987) Effects of ambient temperature and relative humidity on 8- and 10-year-old children involved in endurance activities working at 60% of maximal oxygen consumption. College Park, MD: University of Maryland, Unpublished Master's Thesis. .

Bouchard C, Malina RM, Perusse L (1997) Genetics of Fitness and Physical Performance. Champaign, IL: Human Kinetics.

Bouchard C, Shephard RJ, Stephens T, Sutton JR, McPherson BDE, editors (1990) Exercise, Fitness and Health: A Concensus of Current Knowedge. Champaign, IL: Human Kinetics.

Bouchard C, Tremblay A, Lebanc C, Lortie G, Savard R, Thériault G (1983) A method to assess energy expenditure in children and adults. American Journal of Clinical Nutrition 37:461-467.

Bray MS, Morrow JR, Pivarnik JM, Bricker JT (1992) Caltrac validity for estimating caloric expenditure with children. Pediatric Exercise Science 4:166-179.

Bullen BA, Reed RB, Mayer J (1964) Physical activity of obese and nonobese adolescent girls appraised by motion picture sampling. American Journal of Clinical Nutrition 14:211-223.

Campbell PT, Katzmarzyk PT, Malina RM, Rao DC, Lerusse L, Bouchard C (2001) Prediction of physical activity and physical work capacity (PWC150) in young adulthood from childhood and adolescence with consideration of parental measures. American Journal of Human Biology 13:190-196.

Centers for Disease Control (1992) Vigorous physical activity among high school students— United States, 1990. Morbidity and Mortality Weekly Reports 41:91-94.

Centers for Disease Control and Prevention (1997) Guidelines for School and Community Programs to Promote Lifelong Physical Activity among Young People. Morbidity and Mortality Weekly Reports 46:1-24.

Davies PSW, Day JME, Lucas A (1991) Energy expenditure in early infancy and later body fatness. International Journal of Obesity 15:727-731.

Eaton WO, Enns LR (1983) Sex differences in human motor activity. Psychological Bulletin 100:19-29.

Eaton WO, Yu AP (1988) Are sex differences in child motor activity level a function of sex differences in maturational status? Child Development 60:1005-1011.

Eisenmann JC, Katzmarzyk PT, Thériault G, Song TMK, Malina RM, Bouchard C (1999) Physical activity and pulmonary function in youth: The Quebec Family Study. Pediatric Exercise Science 11:208-217.

Ellis MJ, Scholtz GJL (1978) Activity and Play of Children. Englewood Cliffs, NJ: Prentice Hall.

Emons HJG, Groenenboom DC, Westerterp KR, Saris WHM (1992) Comparison of heart rate monitoring combined with indirect calorimetry and the doubly labeled water ($^2H_2{}^{18}O$) method for the measurement of energy expenditure in children. European Journal of Applied Physiology 65:99-103.

Epstein LH, Saelens BE, Myers MD, Vito D (1997) Effects of decreasing sedentary behaviors on activity choice in obese children. Health Psychology 16:107-113.

Eston RG, Rowlands AV, Ingledew DK (1997) Validation of the Tritrac-R3D (TM) activity monitor during typical children's activities. In N Armstrong, B Kirby, J Welsman (eds), Children and Exercise XIX. London: E & FN Spon, pp 132-138.

Eston RG, Rowlands AV, Ingledew DK (1998) Validity of heart rate, pedometry, and accelerometry for predicting the energy cost of children's activities. Journal of Applied Physiology 84:362-371.

Freedson PS (1991) Electronic motion sensors and heart rate as measures of physical activity in children. Journal of School Health 61:220-223.

Freedson PS, Evenson S (1991) Familial aggregation in physical activity. Research Quarterly in Exercise and Sport 62: 384-389.

* French SA, Story M, Jeffery RW (2001) Environmental influences on eating and physical activity. Annual Reviews of Public Health 22:309-335.

* Gortmaker SL, Must A, Sobol AM, Peterson K, Colditz GA, Dietz WH (1996) Television viewing as a cause of increasing obesity among children in the United States, 1986–1990. Archives of Pediatrics and Adolescent Medicine 105: 356-362.

Hebestreit H, Bar-Or O, McKinty C, Riddell M, Zehr P (1995) Climate-related corrections for improved estimation of energy expenditure from heart rate in children. Journal of Applied Physiology 79:47-54.

Huang Y-C, Malina RM (1996) Physical activity and correlates of estimated energy expenditure in Taiwanese adolescents 12–14 years of age. Amercan Journal of Human Biology 8:225-236.

Jakicic JM, Winters C, Lagally K, Ho J, Robertson RJ, Wing RR (1999) The accuracy of the TriTrac-R3D accelerometer to estimate energy expenditure. Medicine and Science in Sports and Exercise 31:747-754.

Janz KF (1994) Validation of the CSA accelerometer for assessing children's physical activity. Medicine and Science in Sports and Exercise 26:369-375.

Katzmarzyk PT, Malina RM (1998) Contribution of organized sports participation to estimated daily energy expenditure in youth. Pediatric Exercise Science 10:378-386.

Katzmarzyk PT, Malina RM, Song TMK, Bouchard C (1998) Television viewing, physical activity, and health-related fitness of youth in the Quebec Family Study. Journal of Adolescence Health 23:318-325.

Kemper HCG, de Vente W, van Mechelen W, Twisk JWR (2001) Adolescent motor skill and performance: Is physical activity in adolescence related to adult physical fitness? American Journal of Human Biology 13:180-189.

Klesges RC, Coates TJ, Klesges LM, Holzer B, Gustavson J, Barnes J (1984) The FATS: An observational system for assessing physical activity in children and associated parent behavior. Behavioral Assessment 6:333-345.

Klesges RC, Eck LH, Hanson CL, Haddock CK, Klesges LM (1990) Effects of obesity, social interactions, and physical environment on physical activity in preschoolers. Health Psychology 9:435-449.

Klesges RC, Klesges LM, Swenson AM, Pheley AM. (1985) A validation of two motion sensors in the prediction of child and adult physical activity level. American Journal of Epidemiology 122:400-410.

Klesges RC, Shelton ML, Klesges LM (1993) Effects of television on metabolic rate: Potential implications for childhood obesity. Pediatrics 91:281-286.

Livingstone MBE, Coward WA, Prentice AM, Davies PSW, Strain JA, McKenna PG, Mahoney CA, White JA, Stewart CM, Kerr MJ (1992) Daily energy expenditure in free-living children: Comparison of heart-rate monitoring with the doubly labeled water ($^2H_2{}^{18}O$) method 1-3. American Journal of Clinical Nutrition 56:343-352.

Longmuir PE, Bar-Or O (1994) Physical activity of children and adolescents with a disability: methodology and effects of age and gender. Pediatric Exercise Science 6:168-177.

Malina RM (1996a) Tracking of physical activity and physical fitness across the lifespan. Research Quarterly in Exercise and Sport 67: 48-57.

* Malina RM (1996b) Familial factors in physical activity and performance of children and youth. Journal of Human Ecology, Special Issue No. 4: 131-143.

Malina RM (2001a) Physical activity and fitness: Pathways from childhood to adulthood. American Journal of Human Biology 13:162-172.

* Malina RM (2001b) Adherence to physical activity from childhood to adulthood: A perspective from tracking studies. Quest 53:346-355.

* Malina RM (2001c) Tracking of physical activity across the lifespan. President's Council on Physical Fitness and Sports Research Digest, Series 3, No. 14.

Matkin CC, Bachrach L, Wang MC, Kelsey J (1998) Two measures of physical activity as predictors of bone mass in young cohort. Clinical Journal of Sports Medicine 8:201-208.

McKenzie TL, Sallis JF, Patterson TL, Elder JP, Berry CC, Rupp JW, Atkins CJ, Buono MJ, Nader PR (1991) BEACHES: An observational system for assessing children's eating and physical activity behaviors and associated events. Journal of Applied Behavior Analysis 24:141-151.

Mimura K, Hebestreit H, Bar-Or O (1991) Activity and heart rate in preschool children of low and high motor ability: 24-hour profiles. Medicine and Science in Sports and Exercise 23:S12 (abstract).

Moore LL, Lombardi E, White MJ, Campbell JL, Oliveira SA, Ellison RC (1991) Influence of parents' physical activity levels on activity levels of young children. Journal of Pediatrics 118:215-219.

Novitsky S, Segal KR, Chatr-Aryamontri B, Guvakov D, Katch VL (1995) Validity of a new portable indirect calorimeter: The AeroSport TEEM 100. European Journal of Applied Physiology 70:462-467.

Perusse L, Leblanc C, Bouchard C (1988) Familial resemblance in lifestyle components: Results from the Canada Fitness Survey. Canadian Journal of Public Health 79:201-205.

Ross JG, Dotson CO, Gilbert GG (1985a) Are kids getting appropriate activity? The National Children and Youth Fitness Study. Journal of Physical Education, Recreation and Dance 82:40-43.

Ross JG, Dotson CO, Gilbert GG, Katz SJ (1985b) After physical education...physical activity outside of school physical education programs. The National Children and Youth Fitness Study. Journal of Physical Education, Recreation and Dance 56:35-39.

Ross JG, Dotson CO, Gilbert GG, Katz SJ (1985c) What are kids doing in school physical education? Journal of Physical Education, Recreation and Dance 56:73-90.

Ross JG, Pate RR (1987a) The National Children and Youth Fitness Study II: A summary of findings. Journal of Physical Education, Recreation and Dance 58:51-56.

Ross JG, Pate RR, Casperson CJ, Damberg CL, Svilar M (1987b) Home and community in children's exercise habits. Journal of Physical Education, Recreation and Dance 58: 5-92.

Russell SJ, Hyndford C, Beaulieu A (1992) Active living for Canadian Children and Youth: A Statistical Profile. Ottawa: Canadian Fitness and Lifestyle Research Institute.

Sallis JF (1991) Self-report measures of children's physical activity. Journal of School Health 61:215-219.

Sallis JF, Alcaraz JE, McKenzie TL, Hovell MF, Koltai ZSM, Nader PR (1992) Parental behavior in relation to physical activity and fitness in 9-year-old children. American Journal of Diseases of Children 146:1383-1388.

Sallis JF, Buono MJ, Freedson PS (1991) Bias in estimating caloric expenditure from physical activity in children: Implications for epidemiological studies. Sports Medicine 11:203-209.

Sallis JF, Buono MJ, Roby JJ, Micale FG, Nelson JA (1993) Seven-day recall and other physical activity self-reports in children and adolescents. Medicine and Science in Sports and Exercise 25:99-108.

Sallis JF, Hovell MF, Hofstetter CR, Elder JP, Caspersen CJ, Hackley M, Powell KE (1990) Distance between homes and exercise facilities related to the frequency of exercise among San Diego residents. Public Health Reports 105:179-185.

Sallis JG, Patterson TL, Buono MJ, Atkins CJ, Nader PR (1988) Aggregation of physical activity habits in Mexican American and Anglo families. Journal of Behavioral Medicine 11:31-41.

* Sallis JF, Prochaska JJ, Taylor WC (2000) A review of correlates of physical activity of children and adolescents. Medicine and Science in Sports and Exercise 32:963-975.

Sallis JF, Zakarian JM, Hovell MF, Hofstetter CR (1996) Ethnic, socioeconomic, and sex differences in physical activity among adolescents. Journal of Clinical Epidemiology 49:125-134.

Saris WH (1986) Habitual physical activity in children: Methodology and findings in health and disease. Medicine and Science in Sports and Exercise 18:253-263.

Saris WHM, Binkhorst RA (1977) The use of pedometer and actometer in studying daily physical activity in man. Part II: Validity of pedometer and actometer measuring the daily physical activity. European Journal of Applied Physiology 37:229-235.

Saris WHM, Elvers JWH, Van't Hof MA, Binkhorst RA (1986) Changes in physical activity of children aged 6 to 12 years. In J Rutenfranz, R Mocellin, F Klimt (eds), Children and Exercise XII. Champaign, IL: Human Kinetics, pp 121-130.

* Shephard RJ (1986) Fitness of a Nation: Lessons from the Canada Fitness Survey. Basel: Karger.

Shephard RJ, Jequier JC, Lavallée H, La Barre R, Rajic M (1980) Habitual physical activity: Effects of sex, milieu, season, and required activity. Journal of Sports Medicine and Physical Fitness 20:55-66.

Simons-Morton BG, Huang IW (1997) Heart rate monitor and Caltrac assessment of moderate-to-vigorous physical activity among preadolescent children. Medicine and Science in Sports and Exercise 23:S60 (abstract)

Spurr GB, Prentice AM, Murgatroyd PR, Goldberg GR, Reina JC, Christman NT (1988) Energy expenditure from minute-by-minute heart-rate recording: Comparison with indirect calorimetry. American Journal of Clinical Nutrition 48:552-559.

Stephens T, Craig CL (1990). The well-being of Canadians: Highlights of the 1988 Campbell's Survey. Ottawa, Canadian Fitness and Lifestyle Research Institute.

Taylor WC, Blair SN, Cummings SS, Wun CC, Malina RM (1999) Childhood and adolescent physical activity patterns and adult physical activity. Medicine and Science in Sports and Exercise 31: 118-123.

Telama R, Viikari J, Valimaki I, Siren-Tiusanen H, Akerblom HK, Uhart M, Dahl M, Pesonen E, Lahde PL, Pietikainen M, Suoninen P (1985) Atherosclerosis precursors in Finnish children and adolescents. X. Leisure-time physical activity. Acta Paediatrica Scandinavica 318:169-180.

* Torun B (1984) Physiological measurements of physical activity among children under free-living conditions. In E Pollitt, P Amante (eds), Energy Intake and Activity. New York: Alan R Liss, pp 159-184

* Torun B, Davies PSW, Livingstone MBE, Paolisso M, Sackett R, Spurr GB (1996) Energy requirements and dietary energy recommendations for children and adolescents 1 to 18 years old. European Journal of Clinical Nutrition 50:S37-S81

Van Den Berg-Emons HJG, Saris WHM, de Barbanson DC, Westerterp KR, Huson A, van Baak MA (1995) Daily physical activity of school children with spastic diplegia and of healthy controls. Journal of Pediatrics 127:578-584.

Verschuur R, Kemper HCG (1985) Habitual physical activity in Dutch teenagers measured by heart rate. In RA Binkhorst, HCG Kemper, WHM Saris (eds), Children and Exercise XI. Champaign, IL: Human Kinetics, pp 194-202.

Chapter 22 PHYSICAL ACTIVITY AS A FACTOR IN GROWTH, MATURATION, AND PERFORMANCE

Chapter Outline

Physical Activity

Approaches to the Study of Physical Activity

Activity and Stature

Activity, Body Weight, and Body Composition

Activity and Physique

Activity and Specific Tissues
- Skeletal Tissue
- Skeletal Muscle Tissue
- Adipose Tissue

Activity and Biological Maturity
- Skeletal Maturity
- Somatic Maturity
- Sexual Maturity

Overview of Activity, Growth, and Maturation

Activity, Fitness, and Performance
- Correlational Studies
- Comparison of the Habitually Active and Inactive
- Comparison of the Fit and Unfit
- Activity, Fitness and Performance: An Overview

The Concept of Trainability
- Motor Skills
- Muscular Strength
- Anaerobic Power
- Aerobic Power
- Variable Training Modes
- Trainability: An Overview

Summary

Sources and Suggested Readings

Growth and maturation are maintained by the interactions of genes, hormones, and nutrients. Genes, hormones, and nutrients interact among themselves and also with the environments in which the child lives. Physical activity is an environmental factor that is often viewed as exerting a favorable influence on growth and maturation. Additional environmental factors include socioeconomic status of the family, illness history, nutritional status, family size, climate, and others. The present chapter focuses on physical activity as a factor that may influence growth, maturation, and performance. Physical activity should be recognized as only one of many environmental factors that may affect these processes. Current concern for the increasing prevalence of inactivity or sedentarism in children and adolescents (see chapter 21) makes a discussion of the potential role of physical activity highly relevant.

Regular physical activity is often assumed to be important to normal growth and maturation. Studies spanning nearly a century have suggested that regular physical activity, including training for sport, has a stimulatory influence on growth and maturity. In one of the first comprehensive reviews of "exercise and growth," the following was suggested:

"There seems to be little question that certain minima of muscular activity are essential for supporting normal growth and for maintaining the protoplasmic integrity of the tissues. What these minima mean in terms of intensity and duration of activity has not been ascertained" (Rarick 1960, p. 460).

At the same time, concern was also expressed and is still currently expressed about potentially negative influences of physical activity, specifically of intensive training for sport during childhood and adolescence. This issue is addressed in chapter 28, which focuses on young athletes and critically evaluates training for sport as a factor that may influence growth and maturation. For the present, note that regular physical activity is not equivalent to intensive training for sport.

This chapter considers habitual physical activity as a factor that may influence the growth and maturation of children and adolescents. Are the physical and physiological demands of habitual physical activity during childhood and adolescence capable of altering individual patterns of growth and maturation? The chapter also considers the role of physical activity in performance and physical fitness. Finally, the concept of trainability, the responses of children and adolescents to systematic training programs, is considered.

Physical Activity

Physical activity and energy expenditure and methods of assessment were defined in chapter 21. The mechanical and energetic aspects of activity are potentially important in the context of growth and maturity. Most discussions of physical activity refer to a child's estimated level of habitual physical activity, that is, the level of physical activity that characterizes the lifestyle of the individual. It is usually quantified in terms of amount of time in activity (hours/week), an activity score, or energy expended in light or moderate-to-vigorous activities. Estimates are ordinarily derived from questionnaires, interviews, diaries, and heart rate integrators or a combination of methods. Presently available techniques for estimating physical activity have measurement limitations.

Qualification and quantification of physical activity programs for children and adolescents are necessary. Describing a program as mild, moderate, or vigorous physical activity or describing children as active or inactive is insufficient. Physi-

cal activity needs to be defined in more specific terms if the effects of activity on growth, maturity, and performance are to be identified and partitioned from other factors known to affect these outcomes. Partitioning requires more details about number of sessions per week, duration of activity sessions or distance covered in each session, intensity of the activity, type of activity (e.g., sprint, speed, endurance, or strength), and perhaps estimated energy expenditure.

Approaches to the Study of Physical Activity

Three approaches have been used to evaluate the potential influence of physical activity on growth, maturity, and performance. The first approach is correlational. It considers the relationship between an estimate of habitual physical activity and an indicator of growth, maturity, and performance (e.g., the correlation with level of physical activity and subcutaneous fatness).

The second approach compares the characteristics of children and adolescents who are habitually physically active to those who are not active. Criteria for habitual activity and inactivity vary among studies. "Inactive" youth in many studies participate in regular physical education and other normal physical activities of childhood and adolescence. Thus, they are not really inactive; they are inactive relative to youth who engage in physical activities on a more regular basis. As an example, samples of Belgian boys classified as active and nonactive were followed longitudinally from 13 to 18 years of age. The former participated in physical activities (largely sport activities, but they were not athletes) for more than 5 hours/week/year for each of the first 3 years of the study; the latter participated in no more than 1.5 hours/week/year for each of the first 3 years of the study. The first three years of the study, 13-16 years, corresponds to the interval of the adolescent growth spurt. However, depending on the school system in which the boys were enrolled, compulsory physical education varied between 1 and 3 hours per week (Beunen et al. 1992).

Comparisons of athletes and nonathletes during childhood and adolescence are occasionally used to make inferences about the influence of physical activity. Athletes are assumed to have been training regularly, and differences relative to nonathletes are attributed to the physical activity involved in the training program. The problem with this approach is subject selectivity. Successful young athletes are different from nonathletes, quite often in size and maturity status. In addition, some sports (e.g., gymnastics and figure skating) have fairly rigid selection criteria. These issues and others are discussed in more detail in chapter 28.

The third approach is experimental. It involves comparison of individuals exposed to a specific physical activity program (treatment group) and those not exposed to the activity program (control group). The physical activity stimulus varies among studies in type, intensity, and duration, and subjects often vary in age at time of initiation of the program. Problems are encountered in defining and quantifying the physical activity stimulus within and across studies. Selection of subjects, variation in growth and maturity status among subjects, motivation to be active, regularity of the activity program, control of outside activity, and other factors make comparison of experimental studies difficult.

In studies of physical activity in children and adolescents, the physical activity stimulus is rarely monitored over several years. Most experimental programs are specific and short term (e.g., 15 or 20 weeks of endurance training in running or swimming or 8 or 12 weeks of resistance training). Rarely is a specific activity program monitored over several years. Occasionally, a systematic program of sport skill practice is the physical activity stimulus. Nevertheless, physical activity is not the same as regular training for sport. Physical activity is integral to training for sport, but training for sport refers to systematic, specialized practice for a specific sport or sport discipline for most of the year and usually over several years.

Extreme unilateral activity involving specialized use of the arm is occasionally used to illustrate the effects of physical activity on limb muscle, skeletal, and adipose tissues. The individual is the control subject, as the dominant limb (experimental or active limb) is compared with the nondominant limb (control or less active limb). Presently available studies tend to focus on athletes in racket sports such as tennis and squash, and these sports are considered in chapter 28.

Activity and Stature

Regular physical activity has no apparent effect on attained height and rate of growth in height. Longitudinal data on active and inactive boys followed from childhood through adolescence

and girls followed during childhood are shown in figure 22.1. The means indicate either no differences or only small differences in height between the active and inactive during childhood and adolescence and in young adulthood. The issue of subject selection, probably self-selection, in the active and inactive groups is a factor to consider in making comparisons. Although few early studies suggest an increase in stature with regular activity, the observed changes are usually quite small, and selection of subjects and maturity status at the time of training or at the time of making the comparisons were not controlled.

Heights of Active and Inactive Youth

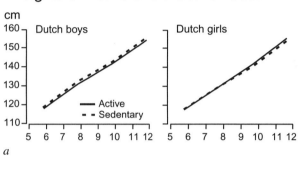

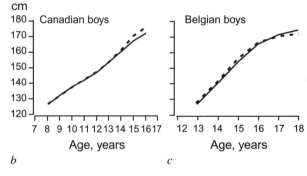

FIGURE 22.1   Mean heights of active and inactive children and adolescents: Dutch boys and girls from 6 to 12 years of age *(a)*, Canadian boys from 8 to 16 years of age *(b)*, and Belgian boys from 13 to 18 years of age *(c)*.

Data from Saris et al., 1986, Mirwald and Bailey, 1986, and Beunen et al., 1992.

On the other hand, regular activity does not have a negative effect on growth in height. This finding is relevant because the short stature and a slower rate of growth of young athletes in some sports are accepted as evidence that training may stunt growth (see chapter 28). In addition to completeness of the available data, several important factors are not considered drawing such a conclusion—small size as a selection criterion in some sports, interindividual variation in biological maturity, and parental size (a proxy for genetic potential), among others.

Activity, Body Weight, and Body Composition

Differences in body weights of active and inactive boys and girls are generally small and not significant (see figure 22.2). The data vary among studies; for example, inactive boys in the Canadian sample tend to be heavier than active boys, especially during adolescence.

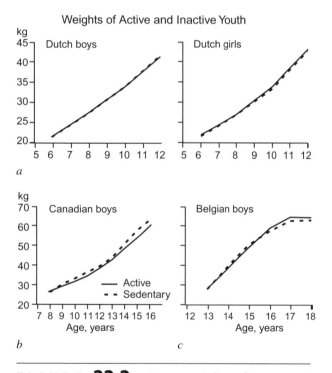

a

b

c

F I G U R E 22.2   Mean weights of active and inactive children and adolescents: Dutch boys and girls from 6 to 12 years of age (a), Canadian boys from 8 to 16 years of age (b), and Belgian boys from 13 to 18 years of age (c).

Data from Saris et al., 1986, Mirwald and Bailey, 1986, and Beunen et al., 1992.

Components of body weight can be potentially influenced by regular activity. Presently available data are derived primarily from the two-compartment model, body weight = FFM + FM. Some data suggest that regular physical activity is associated with a decrease in fatness and an

increase in FFM. Partitioning effects of training on FFM from expected changes associated with growth and maturation is difficult, specifically during adolescence. Both sexes have a significant adolescent growth spurt in FFM, males more so than females (see chapters 5 and 16).

In the frequently cited study of Parizkova (1970, 1977), 40 Czechoslovak boys were divided into three groups with different physical activity and training programs and were followed longitudinally from 11 to 18 years of age. The active boys (n = 8, >6 hours/week) were selected primarily for basketball (6) and athletics (2). The other two groups had less regular physical activity: moderate activity (n = 18, 4 hours/week in sport activity but not on a regular basis) and limited activity (n = 13, <2 hours/week in unsystematic sport activity, including physical education). The activity levels of the three groups are described a bit differently by Sprynarova (1974): active is 4 hours/week, 11 to 15 years of age, 6 hours/week 15 to 18 years of age; moderate activity is 2 hours/week, 11 to 15 years of age or 3 hour/wk 15 to 18 years of age; limited activity is 1 hour/week 11 to 15 years of age or no regular activity 15 to 18 years of age. The active boys were especially taller than boys in the other two groups throughout the study and heavier from 13 to 18 years of age (see figure 22.3).

The groups differed only slightly in body composition at the beginning of the study, but during the course of the study and at its end, the most active boys had significantly more FFM and less fat than the moderately and least active boys (see figure 22.4). The latter two groups differed only slightly in FFM, but the boys with limited physical activity had greater relative fatness. Given the negligible differences in FFM between the boys with moderate and limited activity, the need for a more intense activity stimulus to produce changes in FFM during growth is apparent. The active group was also advanced in skeletal maturity and attained PHV at an earlier age, showing a growth pattern characteristic of early maturing boys. Their greater heights and larger gains in FFM compared with the other groups are probably related in part to their advanced maturity status, which was not controlled in the comparison.

Von Dobeln and Eriksson (1972) (see also Eriksson 1972) conducted a short-term study of nine boys, 11 to 13 years of age. The program included 5 months of endurance activities that were designed to increase maximal aerobic power. Significant gains were noted in potassium concentration measured by whole-body counting of potassium

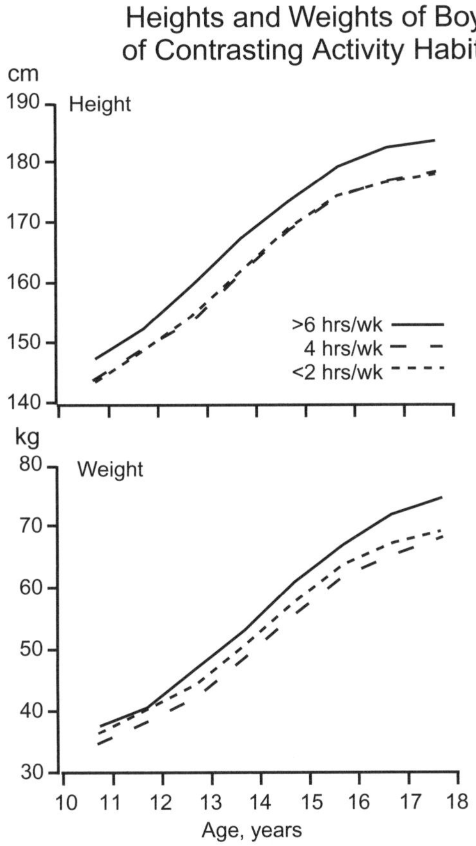

Heights and Weights of Boys of Contrasting Activity Habits

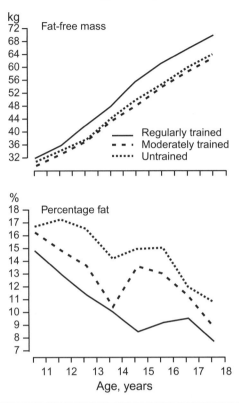

FIGURE 22.3 Mean heights and weights of Czechoslovak boys grouped by level of physical activity and followed longitudinally for 8 years.

Data from Parizkova, 1970, 1977.

Body Composition of Boys of Contrasting Activity Habits

FIGURE 22.4 Estimated fat-free mass (FFM) and percentage fat in Czechoslovak boys grouped by level of physical activity and followed longitudinally for 8 years.

Data from Parizkova, 1970, 1977.

40 (^{40}K) (see chapter 5). The boys gained, on the average, 0.5 kg in weight and 12 g of potassium. A 12-g increase in potassium corresponds to a gain of about 4 kg of muscle mass, which would indicate that the 0.5-kg gain in body weight was accompanied by a loss of about 3 kg of fat during the endurance training program. Relative to growth in height during the experiment, the gain in potassium, an index of FFM and in particular muscle mass, after the training program was 6% greater than expected, whereas the gain in weight was 5% less than expected. The boys gained an average of 3.5 cm in height over the duration of the program, suggesting that the adolescent growth spurt may have occurred in some boys during the course of the study. The observed changes in body composition could probably reflect, in part, those that accompany the adolescent growth spurt in boys and not necessarily the effect of the training program. Moreover, endurance programs are not ordinarily associated with large gains in FFM.

Individual data for the nine boys (see table 22.1) may help to clarify these issues. Three of the boys had body weights above one standard deviation of Swedish reference data and five boys lost weight during the training program. With one exception, the largest gains in height and potassium were observed in boys who were in midpuberty to late puberty. A testicular volume (see chapter 15) less than 4 ml indicates the prepubertal state. Among Swedish boys, the 90th percentiles for the volume of the testes are 4.4 and 9.5 ml at 11 and 12 years of age, respectively (Taranger et al. 1976). The oldest prepubertal boy (13.0 years of age) had a large gain in potassium. The results thus suggest that the gains in potassium and, in turn, estimated FFM and height are more likely associated with age and sexual maturity rather than with the training program.

The studies of Parizkova (1970, 1977) and Von Dobeln and Eriksson (1972) illustrate the

	Testicular volume (ml)	Body weight (kg)	Height (cm)	Potassium (g)
Age (yr)				
11.3	< 4.8	−1.9	3.4	7.1
11.5	< 4.8	−1.1	2.9	7.4
11.6	< 4.8	2.0	2.7	8.3
13.0	< 4.8	−0.7	1.9	17.4
11.3	4.8–9.0	−0.4	1.7	8.3
11.6	4.8–9.0	1.7	3.9	10.1
11.8	> 9.0	−2.3	4.1	10.8
12.2	> 9.0	3.1	5.4	15.6
13.2	> 9.0	4.4	5.6	18.1

TABLE 22.1 Changes in Body Weight, Height, and Potassium Content in 9 Boys Over 0.6 Year, Including 0.5 Year of Regular Training

Age is the midpoint of the 0.6 year interval. Testicular volume was estimated after the training program.

Calculated after Von Dobeln and Eriksson (1972).

difficulties in attempting to partition changes associated with regular physical activity or short-term training programs from changes that accompany normal growth and maturation during male adolescence. Nevertheless, the results of these two studies summarize the information on the potential influence of regular physical activity on body composition during growth. Boys regularly engaged in physical activity programs may have more FFM and less fat than those who are not regularly active. However, are the changes in body composition associated with regular activity greater than those associated with normal growth and maturation? The increase in FFM observed in youth regularly active over a period of several years would seem to suggest an increase greater than that expected with normal growth and maturity. On the other hand, a good deal of the variation in body composition associated with regular physical activity or inactivity is associated with fatness, which fluctuates inversely with the activity stimulus. Fatness tends to decrease during periods of regular activity and to increase during periods of inactivity. Thus, changes in response to short-term training programs often reflect fluctuating levels of fatness with minimal or no changes in FFM.

The influence of regular physical activity on fatness is especially apparent in several studies

of obese children. For example, a daily program of aerobic activity for 2 years resulted in marked decreases in skinfold thicknesses of obese children (Sasaki et al. 1987). Two short-term training programs, one for 10 weeks and the other for 4 months, show a significant decrease in estimated percentage body fat in obese children 7 to 11 years of age (Gutin et al. 1996, 1997).

Data comparing the body composition of active and nonactive girls during childhood and adolescence, or comparing changes in body composition associated with a program of regular physical activity are limited. Morris et al. (1997) compared the body composition of two groups of 9-year-old and 10-year-old girls, one that followed a 10-month training program and another that followed a normal pattern of physical activity. Girls in the two groups were similar in age, height, weight, body composition, and stage of sexual maturity at the start of the study. The training program included 30 minutes of high-impact aerobic and strength training activities three times per week. After 10 months, the trained girls had a greater gain in estimated lean mass (2.2±1.1 kg) and a smaller increase in fat mass (0.5±0.8 kg) than the girls who followed their normal pattern of physical activity (1.4±1.4 kg lean mass and 1.0±0.8 kg fat mass). Note that both groups gained in lean and fat masses over 10 months; on the average, fatness did not decrease. Also, considerable overlap existed between the trained and control groups, but individual differences among the girls after 10 months were, unfortunately, not reported. Although the results are suggestive, they indicate difficulties inherent in attempting to partition growth-related from training-related changes in estimated body composition.

The question of sex differences in the responses of FFM and FM to regular programs of physical activity during growth needs further study. Evidence for young adults indicates a significant decline in percentage fat and subcutaneous fat and an increase in FFM in males but not in females after 15 weeks of high-intensity training on a cycle ergometer (Tremblay et al. 1988).

Activity and Physique

Methodological variation and individual differences in the stability of somatotype during adolescence confound the evaluation of the effects of regular activity on physique. In the three groups of boys with different activity programs from 11 to 18 years of age (see figure 22.4), distributions of somatotypes did not differ among the groups, suggesting no effect of the programs on somatotype. The boys did change in somatotype over adolescence, but the changes occurred in a random manner and were not associated with the respective physical activity programs. Regular physical activity does not appear to have a significant effect on somatotype during growth.

Some forms of high-intensity resistance training may result in muscular hypertrophy of the body parts specifically exercised (e.g., arm and shoulder musculature in response to weight or resistance training programs). Such changes may, at times, be rather extreme, and give the impression of altered physique. However, the changes are rather localized and are not sufficient to alter an individual's somatotype. Moreover, several months after the cessation of resistance programs, measures of muscular development commonly revert to pretraining values, indicating the transient nature of soft tissue responses to training and the need for regular activity to maintain the changes (Malina and Rarick 1973). These data are derived from young adults. Corresponding resistance training data for growing and maturing individuals are not available.

Activity and Specific Tissues

Skeletal tissue, skeletal muscle, and adipose tissues are primary components of body mass. The skeleton is the framework of the body and the main reservoir of mineral. Skeletal muscle is the major work-producing and oxygen-consuming tissue and is the producer of physical activity. Adipose tissue represents energy in stored form.

Skeletal Tissue

Tensile and compressive forces associated with muscular contraction and weight bearing are generally viewed as essential stimuli for skeletal tissue or bone formation and growth. Thus, the intermittent compression of growth plates with weight bearing and physical activity and the localized effects of muscular contraction at the insertions of muscles on bones are apparently essential for bone growth. Regular physical activity during childhood and adolescence is associated with increased bone mineral content, but the osteogenic influence of activity is generally specific to the skeletal sites at which the mechanical strains occur (Kannus et al. 1996).

Correlational studies indicate a positive relationship between habitual physical activity and bone mineralization. Active children and adolescents have greater bone mineral content than those who are less active or inactive. The differences are especially apparent between children and adolescents in the highest and lowest quartiles of estimated physical activity, which is shown in table 22.2 for girls 8 to 13 years of age. More recently, data from a 6-year longitudinal study indicate a significant influence of habitual physical activity on bone mineral accrual during the adolescent growth spurt (see table 22.3). Boys and girls with high activity levels have a greater peak velocity of accrual of bone mineral (g/year) and a greater amount of bone mineral accumulated during the interval of the adolescent growth spurt than do normally active boys and girls. The latter, in turn, have greater corresponding bone mineral values than the least active boys and girls. After peak velocity of bone mineral accrual, active boys and girls have 9% and 17% greater total-body bone mineral, respectively, than their inactive peers (Bailey et al. 1999).

TABLE 22.2 Total-Body Bone Mineral Content (BMC) and Bone Mineral Density (BMD) in Girls 7 to 13 Years of Age Grouped by Quartile of Physical Activity

Quartile of physical activity	BMC (g)		BMD (g/cm^2)	
	M	SD	M	SD
I (lowest activity)	1212	223	0.884	0.06
II	1286	208	0.883	0.06
III	1374	231	0.899	0.06
IV (highest activity)	1441	227	0.914	0.05

Estimates of physical activity are based on total energy expenditure adjusted for the body mass index.

Adapted from Ilich et al. (1998).

Differences in bone mineralization are more pronounced for weight-bearing activities compared with non–weight-bearing activities, and similar trends are apparent in boys and girls (Slemenda et al. 1991, 1994; Morris et al. 1997; Nordstrom et al. 1998). Among prepubertal boys and girls, those in the highest quartile of weight-bearing physical activity (most active) have an increase in bone mineral 4% to 7% greater than

TABLE 22.3	Total-Body Bone Mineral Content (BMC) Accrual in Boys and Girls Grouped by Level of Habitual Physical Activity					
	Peak BMC accrual (g/yr)		BMC accrued 1 year ± peak (g)		BMC 1 year after peak (g)	
Activity status	M	SD	M	SD	M	SD
Girls						
Inactive	280	50	503	88	1571	199
Average	325	60	577	96	1815	211
Active	367	72	618	112	2003	449
Boys						
Inactive	367	78	640	137	2104	395
Average	395	84	712	140	2198	341
Active	476	81	816	137	2511	355

Inactive subjects are in the lowest quartile of physical activity; average subjects are in the middle two quartiles of activity; active subjects are in the highest quartile of physical activity.

Adapted from Bailey et al. (1999).

those in the lowest quartile of weight-bearing activity (least active) (Slemenda et al. 1994).

Of particular importance in the context of the beneficial effects of physical activity on skeletal tissue during childhood and adolescence is the observation that bone mineral established during childhood and adolescence is a determinant of bone mineral status in adulthood. Near-adult values of bone mineral are attained in late adolescence, particularly in girls. More active young adults of both sexes generally have more highly mineralized skeletons than nonactive adults. The greater skeletal mineral content in young adulthood presumably represents the cumulative beneficial effects of regular physical activity on bone mineralization during childhood and adolescence.

In contrast to bone mineralization, regular physical activity does not influence bone growth in length. The pressure effects of weight bearing and physical activity are apparently required for normal growth of a bone in length. On the other hand, excessive pressure may inhibit linear growth, although no evidence has yet been submitted to this effect in healthy, adequately nourished children and adolescents. The delineation of excessive pressure, of course, is problematic.

Skeletal Muscle Tissue

Postnatal growth of skeletal muscle tissue is characterized by a generally constant number of fibers and an increase in fiber size and number of nuclei. Some forms of physical activity may result in some hypertrophy of skeletal muscle and increases in contractile proteins and enzyme concentrations. However, the concept of the specificity of physical activity must be emphasized in the responses of muscle tissue to habitual activity programs. Muscular hypertrophy is associated primarily with high-resistance activities (e.g., weight training) and may not occur with endurance training. Hypertrophy occurs in the existing muscle fibers and not as a result of an increase in the number of fibers. Progressive strength training results in an increase in the size of muscle composed of type II (fast-twitch) fibers, which suggests a specific hypertrophy of type II fibers. In contrast, endurance training is associated with an increase in the relative area of type I (slow-twitch) fibers and an increase in activities of enzymes associated with the use of fatty acids as a substrate and of oxidative phosphorylation in the mitochondria. Prolonged, intensive strength and endurance programs may have important effects on the proportions of type I and type II fibers in the active muscle (Saltin and Gollnick 1983).

The preceding observations are based on responses of young adult muscle tissue to specific training programs. Corresponding data for growing and maturing children and adolescents are not extensive, but available results are generally similar in direction as those of adults. Resistance training in prepubertal boys and girls results in gains in strength without hypertrophy of muscle tissue. Pubertal boys, on the other hand, experience hypertrophy in conjunction with an increase in strength in response to resistance training (Sale 1989). A question of interest relates to the partitioning of training-related changes from those associated with normal growth and maturity, particularly in adolescent boys. Similarly, do training-related changes in muscle mass in adolescents persist after the training program has stopped? How much activity is needed to maintain the training-induced changes? Studies of adults indicate that gains in muscularity associated with resistance training revert to pretraining values when the resistance program is stopped.

No strong evidence suggests that fiber type distribution in youth can be changed as a result of specific training protocols. A 5-month endurance-training program was associated with increases in succinate dehydrogenase and phosphofructokinase activities in 11-year-old boys (Eriksson 1972). Results of a comparison of the effects of 3-month sprint and endurance training programs on 16-year-old boys are summarized in figures 22.5 and 22.6. Neither program affected fiber distribution. The endurance-trained group showed an increase in the surface area of both type I and type II fibers, whereas the sprint-trained group did not (see figure 22.5). The endurance-trained group showed an increase in succinate dehydrogenase activity but no change in phosphofructokinase activity, whereas the sprint-trained group showed an increase in phosphofructokinase and no change in succinate dehydrogenase activity (see figure 22.6). Corresponding data for young females are not available. The limited data suggest that regular training has the potential to modify the metabolic capacity of muscle in adolescents.

A unique feature of the study of 16-year-old boys is that the responses of muscle tissue enzymes to 6 months of no supervised training were also monitored. After 6 months of no regular training, enzyme activities returned to levels that did not differ from the pretraining values (see figure 22.6). This observation indicates an important feature of training studies. Monitoring changes associated with training after the training program ceases permits a more accurate evaluation of the effects of training on growth. Changes in response to short-term training programs are generally not permanent and depend on regular activity for their maintenance.

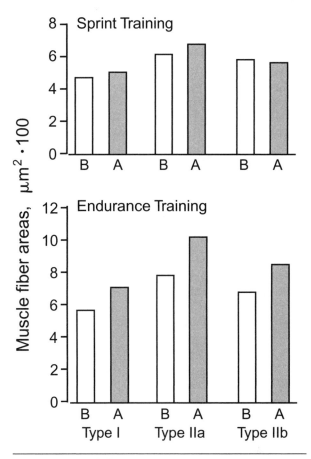

FIGURE 22.5   Changes in muscle fiber areas in 16-year-old boys after 3 months of sprint or endurance training. B = before training; A = after training.

Data from Fournier et al., 1982.

Adipose Tissue

In studies of children and youth, adipose tissue is often measured subcutaneously in the form of skinfold thicknesses. Although cross-sectional comparisons of active and less active children and adolescents indicate thinner skinfolds in the former, longitudinal data for active and nonactive boys and girls followed from 6 to 12 years of age (Saris et al. 1986) and adolescent boys followed from 13 to 18 years of age (Beunen et al. 1992) indicate small differences between activity groups (see figure 22.7). The differences in skinfold thicknesses are well within the range of technical error associated with the measurement of skinfolds (Malina 1995a). Intensive physical

Changes in Skeletal Muscle Enzyme Activities After Three Months of Exercise Training and Six Months of Detraining

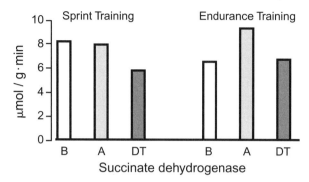

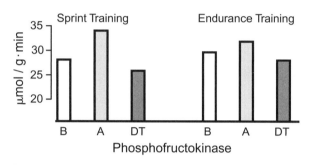

FIGURE 22.6 Changes in skeletal muscle enzyme activities in 16-year-old boys after 3 months of sprint or endurance training and 6 months of detraining. B = before training; A = after training; DT = after detraining.

Data from Fournier et al., 1982.

Skinfold Thicknesses in Active and Inactive Youth

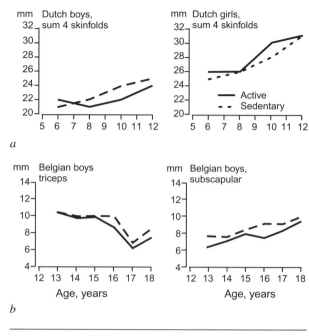

FIGURE 22.7 Mean skinfold thicknesses of active and inactive children and adolescents: Dutch boys and girls 6 to 12 years of age, sum of four skinfolds *(a)*; and Belgian boys 13 to 18 years of age, triceps and subscapular skinfolds *(b)*.

Data from Saris et al., 1986, and Beunen et al., 1992.

activity is most likely essential to modify skinfold thicknesses in children and adolescents.

Data dealing with potential effects of training on subcutaneous fat distribution during growth are limited. Cross-sectional data for male adolescents suggests an association between time spent in vigorous physical activity and proportionally less subcutaneous adipose tissue on the trunk (Dionne et al. 2000). In young adult males, intensive aerobic training for 15 and 20 weeks is associated with a greater reduction in trunk than in extremity skinfolds, whereas corresponding changes in young adult females are evenly distributed between trunk and extremity sites (Despres et al. 1985; Tremblay et al. 1988). In obese children 7 to 11 years of age, a 4-month physical activity program resulted in minimal change in abdominal visceral adipose tissue but a loss of abdominal subcutaneous adipose tissue (Gutin and Owens 1999; Gutin and Humphries

1998). The results suggest a differential influence on adipose tissue in the abdominal region.

Although changes in overall fatness and subcutaneous adipose tissue associated with habitual physical activity are reasonably well documented, information on the effects of regular activity on adipose tissue cellularity and metabolism in children and adolescents is lacking. Evidence from adults indicates that the decrease in fatness with training is attributable solely to a reduction in fat cell size and not to changes in fat cell number. Similar changes in fat cell size, and not number, also occur with caloric restriction.

Information on the effects of regular activity on adipose tissue cellularity during childhood and adolescence is lacking. Adipose tissue cellularity increases gradually during childhood and then more rapidly with the onset of puberty (see chapter 8). The possible effect of regular physical activity programs on adipose tissue cellularity during growth merits consideration.

In all likelihood, such programs would have to be initiated early in life, perhaps during the preschool years. Aerobic activity programs have been implemented with 3-year-old to 5-year-old children (Alpert et al. 1990; Mo-suwan et al. 1998).

Regular physical activity also affects adipose tissue metabolism. Trained individuals have an increased ability to mobilize and oxidize fat, which is associated with increased levels of lipolysis (Despres et al. 1984). Corresponding observations on adipose tissue metabolism in children and adolescents are not presently available.

Activity and Biological Maturity

The effects of regular physical activity on maturity indicators used in growth studies, especially during adolescence, are difficult to quantify. The same hormones regulate somatic, skeletal, and sexual maturation during adolescence, so regular activity, if it has an effect, should influence the different indicators of maturity in a generally similar manner.

Skeletal Maturity

Although regular physical activity functions to enhance the accrual of bone mineral, it does not influence skeletal maturity of the hand and wrist as these bone are radiographically assessed. Active and nonactive boys followed longitudi-

nally from 13 to 18 years of age do not differ in SA (Beunen et al. 1992).

Somatic Maturity

Age at PHV is not affected by level of habitual physical activity, and presently available data are limited to boys. Small samples of boys classified as physically active and inactive for the years before and during the adolescent growth spurt do not differ in estimated ages at PHV (see table 22.4). The magnitude of PHV in active and inactive boys also does not differ and is well within the range of variation observed during the adolescence growth spurt (see table 16.1, page 308). By inference, peak velocity of growth in height during the adolescent growth spurt is not affected by regular activity. Corresponding data are not available for girls (although some data are available for girls active in sport [see chapter 28]).

Sexual Maturity

Information is quite limited on the effects of regular physical activity on sexual maturation. Discussions most often focus on females rather than on both sexes, and specific emphasis is on age at menarche, which is a late pubertal event (see chapter 16).

Some epidemiological data suggest an association with habitual physical activity and later menarche (Merzenich et al. 1993), but contradictory findings are also evident (Moisan et al. 1990,

TABLE 22.4 Estimated Mean Ages at Peak Height Velocity and Peak Height Velocity in Active and Nonactive Adolescent Boys

Activity status	n	Age at PHV (yr)		PHV (cm/yr)		Reference
		M	SD	M	SD	
Active	14	14.3	1.2	8.7	1.1	Mirwald and Bailey (1986)
Inactive	11	14.1	0.7	9.9	1.4	Mirwald and Bailey (1986)
Active	32	14.2	0.8	9.4	1.5	Beunen et al. (1992)
Inactive	32	14.1	0.8	8.9	2.1	Beunen et al. (1992)
Moderate active	19	14.5	1.0	9.7	1.5	Sprynarova (1987)
Limited active	12	14.6	1.2	9.8	1.5	Sprynarova (1987)
Active	7	13.3[a]				Kobayashi et al. (1978)
Average active	43	13.3[a]				Kobayashi et al. (1978)

The ranges of mean ages at PHV and peak velocities, based on a variety of methods, reported in European and North American longitudinal studies are, respectively, 13.3 to 14.4 years and 8.2 to 10.3 cm/yr (see table 16.1).

[a]These are samples of Japanese boys. Age at PHV occurs earlier, on average, in Japanese than in European and North American adolescents.

1991). The association between habitual physical activity and later menarche is not strong and is confounded by other factors. Much of the discussion on the association between physical activity and age at menarche, however, focuses on later mean ages at menarche, which are commonly reported in athletes in many but not in all sports (Malina 1983, 1998; chapter 28). Later mean ages at menarche are commonly inferred to be a consequence of regular training for sport before menarche (i.e., training "delays" menarche). Use of the term "delay" in the context of physical activity or training is misleading because it implies that regular physical activity or training "causes" menarche to be later than normal. The data dealing with the inferred relationship between training and later menarche are based on association and are retrospective and do not permit such a conclusion. Two comprehensive discussions of physical activity and female reproductive health indicate the complexity of issues involved and have concluded as follows:

> "although menarche occurs later in athletes than in nonathletes, it has yet to be shown that exercise delays menarche in anyone" (Loucks et al. 1992, p. S288), and, "the general consensus is that while menarche occurs later in athletes than in nonathletes, the relationship is not causal and is confounded by other factors" (Clapp and Little 1995, pp. 2–3).

Longitudinal data on the sexual maturation of habitually active and nonactive boys and girls are not available.

Overview of Activity, Growth, and Maturation

The developing organism clearly adapts to the stresses imposed by physical activity. The responses are, to a large extent, not sufficient to significantly alter the processes of growth and maturation as they are ordinarily monitored. Physical activity can be an important factor in the regulation of body weight and specifically fatness. Regular physical activity also functions to enhance skeletal mineral. It is a significant factor in the structural and functional integrity of skeletal muscle tissue, but effects of activity programs on muscle tissue are reversible and are specific to the type of training program.

Physical activity is presumably important in normal growth and maturation but how much

activity is necessary is not known. Apparently, the day-to-day activities of childhood and adolescence are adequate to maintain the integrity of growth and maturation processes, with the possible exception of adipose tissue. Physical inactivity in combination with a chronically excessive energy intake is associated with greater levels of fatness. Both are the primary contributors to the current epidemic of obesity in children and adolescents (see chapter 24).

Activity, Fitness, and Performance

Individuals who are more habitually physical active are generally assumed to be more physically fit, and that the relationship between activity and fitness is assumed to be causal. The available data, however, do not support such a generalization. Physical activity and fitness are related, but the relationship is moderate at best.

Correlational Studies

Data from the Second National Children and Youth Fitness Survey in the United States in 1986 indicate generally low relationships between estimated activity and fitness of 6-year-old to 9-year-old children. Correlations between 28 indicators of physical activity and cardiorespiratory endurance were low, ranging from −0.22 to +0.24. Subsequent multivariate analyses indicated that physical activity, age, and sex accounted for only 21% of the variation in the run-walk, the measure of cardiorespiratory endurance used in the survey (Pate et al. 1990). Thus, about 80% of the variation in endurance is not accounted for by physical activity, age, and sex, suggesting that other factors are involved. A similar analysis relating habitual physical activity to components of health-related fitness of 528 fourth grade children also resulted in low correlations. The estimated percentage of variance in the physical fitness items accounted for by physical activity, after controlling for sex, was also low, 3% to 11% (Sallis et al. 1993).

Studies of adolescents provide similar results. Correlations between hours of physical activity per week and indicators of motor and health-related physical fitness in a small sample (n = 25) of 12-year-old boys and girls reach moderate levels: motor coordination, 0.48; basic motor skills, 0.51; static strength, 0.42; and $\dot{V}O_{2}max$, 0.67 (Schmucker et al. 1984). Among boys and girls 12 to 15 years of age, correlations between indicators of physical activity and the 1-mile walk-run are 0.37 and 0.39 (Aaron et al. 1993). In large samples of Belgian adolescents of both sexes 13 to 18 years of age, age-specific correlations between physical activity (hours of active sport practice) and 11 tests of motor- and health-related physical fitness are uniformly low, –0.03 to +0.29 (Renson et al. 1990). Results of a multivariate analysis of several measures of physical activity and health-related physical fitness in Canadian youth 9 to 18 years of age (Katzmarzyk et al. 1998a) provide consistent results. Physical activity (total daily energy expenditure and energy expenditure in moderate-to-vigorous physical activity) and inactivity (time viewing television) account for 11% to 21% of the variance in measures of health-related fitness (sit-ups, static leg strength, PWC_{150}, and the sum of six skinfolds). Thus, significant relationships exist between indicators of activity and fitness, but a large part of the variability, about 80% to 90%, in health-related fitness is not accounted for by physical activity or inactivity.

Comparison of the Habitually Active and Inactive

The relationship between physical activity and fitness is possibly masked, in part, by the normal range of variability in heterogeneous samples of children and adolescents. The relationship may be more apparent in comparisons of groups at the extremes of the physical activity continuum, but criteria for classifying individuals as active or inactive are variable. In the First National Children and Youth Fitness Survey in the United States in 1984, active and inactive 10-year-old to 12-year-old youth do not differ in the 1-mile run (cardiorespiratory endurance), whereas at 13 to 15 years of age, active youth perform better in the mile run than inactive youth. Among youth 16 years of age and older, active boys perform better than inactive boys in the mile run, whereas active and inactive girls do not differ (Blair et al. 1989). Results for a comparison of active and inactive Taiwanese adolescents 12 to 14 years of age are summarized on table 22.5, those in the highest quartile for estimated daily energy expenditure (active) perform better in the 1-mile run and sit-and-reach (lower back flexibility) than those in the lowest quartile (inactive). On the other hand, the activity groups do not differ in sit-ups (abdominal strength and endurance) and the sum of four skinfolds (Huang and Malina 2002).

TABLE 22.5	Comparison of the Health-Related Physical Fitness of Active and Inactive Taiwanese Boys and Girls 12 to 14 Years of Age			
	Active		Inactive	
	Mean	SD	Mean	SD
Boys				
1-mile run (sec)	504.7	87.3	580.1	95.1
Sit-ups (n/1 min)	35.7	9.9	33.4	8.7
Sit-and-reach (cm)	29.6	7.5	23.8	6.9
Sum skinfolds (mm)	50.7	25.0	49.2	29.9
Girls				
1-mile run (sec)	625.6	97.6	682.2	95.4
Sit-ups (n/1 min)	22.9	6.9	23.9	8.0
Sit-and-reach (cm)	28.4	6.5	25.7	5.9
Sum skinfolds (mm)	71.3	17.7	72.2	23.3

Note: For boys, n = 34 per group; for girls, n = 36 per group.

Adapted from Huang and Malina (2002).

These cross-sectional observations are reasonably consistent with several longitudinal studies of active and inactive adolescents. In the Saskatchewan Growth Study (Mirwald et al. 1981; Mirwald and Bailey 1986), boys classified as inactive have lower absolute (see figure 22.8a) and relative (see figure 22.8b) maximal aerobic power ($\dot{V}O_2$max) than active boys and those with average levels of physical activity during childhood and adolescence. The inactive boys also have an adolescent spurt in maximal aerobic power that is less than that observed in the active and average boys (see figure 22.8c). Although active boys have a higher absolute $\dot{V}O_2$max than boys with average activity levels before the adolescent growth spurt, the two groups do not differ during the adolescent growth spurt (see figure 22.8a–b). However, before, during, and after the adolescent growth spurt, active boys have a higher relative $\dot{V}O_2$max than boys with average levels of physical activity (see figure 22.8c).

Among Belgian boys followed longitudinally from 13 to 18 years of age, those classified as active perform better than inactive boys only in the pulse rate recovery after a step test and the flexed-arm hang. On the other hand, active and inactive boys do not differ in leg lifts, sit-and-reach, static arm pull strength, the vertical

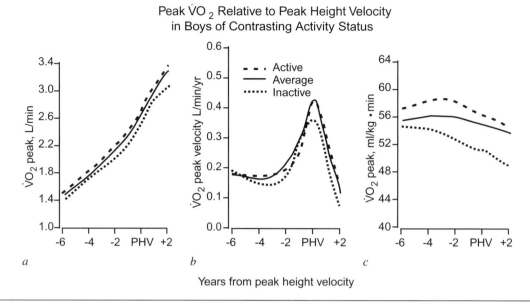

FIGURE 22.8   Absolute maximal aerobic power *(a)*, velocity of change in absolute maximal aerobic power *(b)*, and relative maximal aerobic power *(c)* plotted in terms of years before and after peak height velocity (PHV) for boys classified as active, average in activity, and inactive.

Reprinted, by permission, from Mirwald and Bailey, 1986, *Maximal aerobic power* (London, Ontario: Sports Dynamics), 28.

jump, a shuttle run, and speed of upper limb movement (Beunen et al. 1992). Among Dutch adolescents followed from 13 to 16 years of age, active boys perform better than inactive boys in the 12-minute run (cardiorespiratory endurance), the flexed-arm hang and shuttle run, whereas active girls perform better than inactive girls only in $\dot{V}O_2$max and the 12-minute run. In contrast, active and inactive boys and girls, respectively, do not differ in static arm strength, the sit-and-reach, vertical jump, and speed of upper limb movement (Verschuur 1987).

Although methods of classifying youth as active and inactive vary among studies, and although data are more available for boys than for girls, one observation is seemingly consistent in both cross-sectional and longitudinal studies. More active youth are more fit in cardiorespiratory endurance tasks, measured primarily in the form of endurance runs and $\dot{V}O_2$max. On the other hand, results of comparisons for other components of physical fitness are inconsistent, suggesting that habitual physical activity is only one of several factors that influence physical fitness.

Comparison of the Fit and Unfit

Comparisons of the habitual physical activity of fit and unfit children and adolescents may help to clarify the situation, but data are not presently extensive. Are the more fit in fact more active? This question was addressed in Taiwanese youth 12 to 14 years of age. The youth were classified as fit (highest quartile) or unfit (lower quartile) for the four components of health-related physical fitness. Boys and girls classified as fit in the 1-mile run and the sit-and-reach have a significantly greater estimated daily energy expenditures (kcal/kg/day) than those classified as unfit (see table 22.6). In contrast, boys and girls classified as fit and unfit in sit-ups and sum of skinfolds do not differ in estimated energy expenditure (Huang and Malina 2002).

The activity status of fit and unfit youth in each health-related fitness item is heterogeneous. For example, among 34 boys classified as physically fit based on performance in the 1-mile run, 15 are in the highest quartile for estimated energy expenditure (active) and seven are in the lowest quartile for estimated energy expenditure (inactive). In contrast, among the 34 boys classified as unfit in the 1-mile run, three are active and 16 are inactive. Results are similar for girls. Among the 36 girls classified as fit in the 1-mile run, 16 are active and eight are inactive, whereas among the 36 girls classified as unfit in the 1-mile run, five are active and 13 are inactive. The activity status of youth classified as fit and unfit in the other health-related fitness tests show similar overlap

Fitness Variable	Energy Expenditure (kcal/kg/day)			
	Unfit		Fit	
	Mean	SE	Mean	SE
Boys				
One-mile run	39.7	1.1	43.8	1.1
Timed sit-ups	41.0	1.0	42.3	1.0
Sit-and-reach	38.9	0.8	42.9	0.8
Sum of skinfolds	41.6	0.9	41.2	1.0
Girls				
One-mile run	38.3	0.7	40.8	0.7
Timed sit-ups	38.8	0.7	38.2	0.7
Sit-and-reach	37.7	0.8	40.1	0.8
Sum of skinfolds	39.5	0.6	37.7	0.6

TABLE 22.6 Estimated Energy Expenditure per Unit Body Mass per Day of Taiwanese Boys and Girls, 12-14 Years of Age, Classified as Unfit and Fit on Each of Four Health-Related Physical Fitness Items (n=34 per Group in Each Sex)

Adapted from Huang and Malina (2002). Subjects in the lowest and highest quartiles of each fitness variable were classified, respectively, as unfit and fit. The quartiles were inverted for the one-mile run and sum of skinfolds because a lower value indicates a better level of fitness and a higher value indicates a poorer level of fitness.

(Huang and Malina 2002). Thus, although youth classified as fit in some health-related fitness items are, on the average, more active, variability is high . These results echo earlier observations from a study relating habitual physical activity to maximal aerobic power in 14-year-old to 18-year-old boys and girls:

"A among those with the poorest fitness, there are sedentary, moderately active, and very active children. Similarly, there are sedentary, moderately active, and very active children among those who are in excellent physical condition." (Lange Anderson et al. 1984, p. 435)

Activity, Fitness, and Performance: An Overview

Although physical activity and health-related physical fitness are significantly correlated, the relationship is not strong, and indicators of activity account for a relatively small percentage of the variation in several indicators of fitness. Several factors probably contribute to these observations in children and adolescents. First, measures of activity are imperfect at best and tests of fitness vary in validity and reliability. Second, children's levels of habitual physical activity do not regularly reach elevated aerobic levels for sustained periods of time. Hence, why should a strong relationship between aerobic fitness and physical activity be expected? Also, is $\dot{V}O_2$max the best measure of fitness, or is it a laboratory measure that is a reference for comparison? The field measures of fitness reflect the operational definition of health-related fitness, which may need modification (Malina 1995).

Growth and maturation per se also affect relationships between activity and fitness. Components of fitness change with growth and maturation independent of physical activity, and partitioning effects of activity from expected changes is difficult. For example, a late-maturing boy might not do well on fitness tests requiring muscular strength simply because he is smaller than average and has less muscle mass. Similarly, an early-maturing boy might have an advantage on some fitness tests because he is taller, heavier, and stronger than average-maturing boys. Among girls, early maturers might not do well on fitness tests requiring support or projection of the body because they tend to be fatter than average-maturing and late-maturing girls (see chapter 17).

Time spent in inactive pursuits such as television viewing, video games, and other sedentary activities is another factor that may influence physical fitness. However, the relationship between time spent viewing television and indicators of health-related fitness is not strong (Katzmarzyk et al. 1998b).

The Concept of Trainability

Although the relationship between physical activity and physical fitness is not strong, systematic programs of physical activity, largely in the context of specific instructional and training programs, have beneficial effects on several indicators of fitness. Evidence from experimental physical education programs and specific training programs for motor skill, aerobic power, muscular strength, and muscular endurance indicate that various components of motor- and health-related fitness improve with practice and training. Results of these studies are often discussed in the context of trainability.

Trainability refers to the responsiveness of children and adolescents at different stages of growth and maturity to a training stimulus. It is related to the concepts of readiness and critical periods. Youth are often suggested, for example, to be more susceptible to the beneficial effects of training during periods of rapid growth and maturation. This issue has been related primarily to the effects of systematic training on the development of muscular strength and aerobic and anaerobic power, but it also applies to the effects of instruction and practice on the development of proficiency in motor skills.

Factors that may influence trainability include age, sex, variation in growth and maturity status, prior experiences (such as early opportunities to practice motor skills or levels of habitual physical activity), preinstruction or pretraining levels of skill, strength and aerobic and anaerobic power (current phenotype), genotype, and genotype and environment interactions. With the exception of studies of responses of sedentary young adults to aerobic or strength training, these factors are not ordinarily controlled in studies of the responsiveness of children and adolescents to training.

In the context of trainability presented here, only interventional studies and longitudinal studies are considered to explore the trainability of children and adolescents. The term training also includes instruction and practice. Cross-sectional studies are often used to make inferences about the trainability of children and adolescents. Such studies compare groups that are variously labeled as trained and untrained, active and inactive, or athletes and nonathletes. This approach includes a selection bias. In addition to possible genetic predisposition of active, trained, or athletic youth, some of the variation in a biological variable of interest may also be explained by environmental factors (i.e., exercise training) and genetic-environment interactions.

Discussions of trainability deal with two related, but different, questions: (1) What are the responses of children and adolescents to systematic training programs? (2) How responsive are children and adolescents to specific training programs? The first question deals with the effects of training programs, whereas the second question deals with the trainability of children and adolescents.

Motor Skills

Most neural structures are near adult form and most fundamental movement patterns are reasonably well established by 6 to 8 years of age. Therefore, these ages might be expected to be ideal for specific instruction and practice in the basic motor skills. This assumption is in fact common, but systematic data are not extensive. Children refine motor patterns and learn new skills and sequences of skills as they grow and mature, with instruction (as in physical education or organized youth sports) and with practice associated with everyday activities. Planned instructional programs can enhance the development of basic motor skills in preschool children and more complex skills in school-age children. Guided instruction by specialists, trained parents or qualified coaches, appropriate motor task sequences, and adequate time for practice are essential components of successful instructional programs at young ages (Haubenstricker and Seefeldt 1986). Because the skills utilized in most sports are combinations and modifications of the fundamental movement patterns, a beneficial role for early instruction and practice for the transition into organized sport during middle childhood is suggested. More data are necessary in this area, and other issues need to be addressed. For example, the role of parental, sibling, and peer modeling in the motor development of children merits consideration, given the amount of time that these individuals spend with each other in a variety of activities. Several factors in the social or cultural domain that influence motor development and performance are considered in chapter 25.

Instruction and practice in basic movement skills per se and in combinations or modifications of these skills, as in the requirements for specific sports, are beneficial during middle childhood and adolescence. However, partitioning learning effects from those expected with growth and maturation may be difficult.

A question that needs study in the learning and refinement of motor skills is the potential role of the genotype. Are improvements in motor skill associated with practice and learning dependent on genetic characteristics? Several experimental studies have considered the pattern of learning of motor skills in adolescent twins (Bouchard et al. 1997). Except for the stabilometer task, which places a premium on dynamic balance and coordination, the tasks used in these experimental studies tend to be fine motor skills that stress manual dexterity and precision of movement. The results suggest the rate of learning is more similar in monozygotic (MZ) than in dizygotic (DZ) twins. However, estimates of the genetic contribution to learning vary from task to task, emphasizing the specificity of motor learning. Estimates of the genetic contribution also vary over a series of practice trials or training sessions.

A study of Polish twins 9 to 13 years of age considered three parameters of the learning curves associated with practice of four tasks: plate tapping with the hand, tapping with one foot, mirror tracing, and a ball toss for accuracy (Sklad 1975). The level of learning and rate of learning are more similar in MZ than in DZ twins, and intrapair correlations tend to be higher in male than in female MZ twins. The final level of skill attained, the third parameter of the learning curve, is, however, quite variable between twin types and sexes and among the four tasks.

Factors that are potentially capable of influencing the trainability of motor skills are not considered in the available studies. The data suggest that the genotype is an important determinant of the ease or difficulty with which new motor skills are learned or of the improvement in performance that occurs with practice. More detailed study of the individuality of responses to specific training programs or to regular practice of motor tasks during childhood and adolescence is needed.

Muscular Strength

Historically, resistance training for the development of strength was not recommended for prepubertal children. Resistance programs typically involve the use of weights or specially designed machines to provide the resistance against which a particular muscle group must work. Circulating androgenic hormones in sufficient quantities in prepubertal boys were generally believed to preclude strength improvement with such specific training. Secondary factors included risk of injury in unsupervised resistance training programs and potential for premature closure of epiphyses caused by excessive loads. This conservative view has since been altered. Resistance training is now recommended as a safe and effective means of developing strength in children and adolescents, providing the activity is performed in a supervised setting with proper techniques and safety precautions (American Academy of Pediatrics 2001).

Results of two studies of resistance training in prepubertal boys are summarized in figures 22.9 and 22.10, a through c. In the first study of boys 6 to 11 years of age, 19 boys trained on a supervised circuit of exercises on eight hydraulic resistive units plus sit-ups and stationary cycling, three times a week for 14 weeks, while 10 control subjects did no formal training (Weltman et al. 1986). In the second study of boys 9 to 11 years of age, 27 boys trained with eight different exercises on an apparatus, three times a week for 10 weeks, while 12 control subjects did no formal training (Blimkie et al. 1989). As expected, the trained boys made greater gains in strength than the control subjects in each study. However, the control subjects also improved to some extent on several of the strength measurements. This finding reflects, in part, a learning effect (how to perform the tests), the effects of normal day-to-day physical activities, and probably normal growth-associated changes in strength over the duration of the experiments.

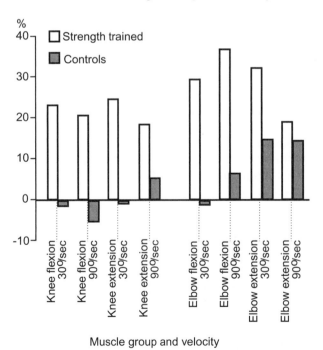

Changes in Strength After 14 Weeks of Resistance Training in Prepubertal Boys

FIGURE 22.9 Relative changes in muscular strength after 14 weeks of resistance training in prepubertal boys 6 to 11 years of age.

Data from Weltman et al., 1986.

Changes in Strength After 10 Weeks of Resistance Training in Prepubertal Boys

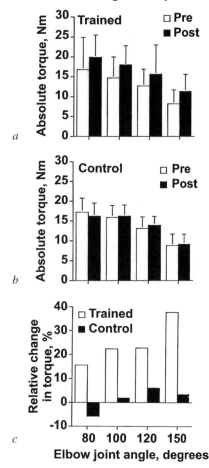

FIGURE 22.10 Absolute and relative changes in muscular strength after 10 weeks of resistance training in prepubertal boys 9 to 11 years of age. (*a*) Absolute changes in the trained group, (*b*) absolute changes in the control group, and (*c*) relative changes in the trained and control groups.

Data from Blimkie et al, 1989.

Prepubertal children respond to resistance training programs with gains in muscular strength but show minimal muscular hypertrophy. The data on hypertrophy are variable for several reasons. First, the training program may not have been sufficiently long or intense. Gains in strength after training programs less than 6 weeks are generally associated with neuromuscular factors. Second, estimates of muscle size are often limited to limb circumferences or limb circumferences corrected for the thickness of skinfolds. Both estimates are only indirect indicators of muscle size. Third, ages of subjects in the experimental studies span several years, such as 6 to 11 years (Weltman et al. 1986) or 5 to 11 years (Faigenbaum et al., 1999). Studies that are based on more narrowly defined age groups, such as 9 to 11 (Blimkie et al. 1989), or 9.0±0.3 and 11.0±0.3 years (Fukunaga et al. 1992), show small but significant gains in estimated arm muscle area in the older trained and control subjects.

A potentially confounding factor is variation in biological maturity. In the study of Fukunaga et al. (1992), skeletal age is significantly related to the gains in estimated muscle area associated with resistance training (r = 0.36). Thus, variation in maturity status may have an important role in mediating the response to training. Studies of the responses of children to resistance training simply classify them as prepubertal, which is not sufficiently sensitive to individual differences in biological maturity. Skeletal age varies by as much as 5 years within samples of 6-year-old, 7-year-old, and 8-year-old children (see table 17.2, page 339). Thus controlling for biological maturity in studies of the responses of young children to strength training is important, and at these ages, skeletal maturity is the only indicator that is available.

Other characteristics of children enrolled in resistance training studies may also need to be considered more carefully. In the recent study of Faigenbaum et al. (1999) on children 5.2 to 11.8 years of age, combined samples boys and girls who comprised two training groups were, on average, significantly heavier than the control group by 7.7 kg and 12.1 kg. The training groups were also taller, on average, by 3.2 cm and 5.6 cm. If the mean values for height and weight were used to estimate the body mass index, the two experimental groups would be classified as obese at the start of the training program. Unfortunately, the body size differences among the groups were not controlled in the analysis.

As a group, prepubertal children respond positively to systematic resistance training programs. Intraindividual differences in responses to the training programs are not considered or reported. Do all children respond in a similar manner? Are specific age-related and maturity-related effects on the response to training evident? As noted previously, some studies are based on samples that span a broad age range (e.g., 6 to 11 years or 5 to 11 years), and the analyses do not control for the age variation. Do younger and older children make similar gains with training? The data of Fukunaga et al. (1992) suggest smaller absolute gains in younger children.

Several studies of prepubertal children include small numbers of girls. Little or no sex difference in responses to resistance training among prepubertal children is apparent (Sale 1989; Fukunaga et al. 1992; Blimkie and Sale 1998), but data on strength training in girls are not extensive as for boys. In one of the few studies that focused exclusively on girls, three groups of 7-year-old to 19-year-old girls trained three times per week for 5 weeks in isometric knee extension, vertical jumping, or sprint running, while a fourth group served as a control (Nielsen et al. 1980). The responses were specific to the type of training program, particularly for isometric knee extension and vertical jumping, whereas responses to the sprint running protocol were small (see figure 22.11). The maturity status of the girls was not controlled in the analysis. Of interest, nevertheless, younger girls (<13.5 years of age) appeared to experience greater relative gains than older girls.

Variation in response to training by pubertal status has received somewhat more consideration. Relative changes in strength in small samples (the total sample was 33) of prepubertal (G1, PH1), pubertal (G2–G4, PH2–PH4), and postpubertal (G5, PH5) boys after a 9-week resistive exercise program are summarized in figure 22.12. Prepubertal boys made the largest relative gains, followed by the pubertal and then by the postpubertal boys. Relative gains were greater in the upper extremity (Pfeiffer and Francis 1986). Mean ages varied among the three groups, 10.3±1.2, 13.1±1.0, and 19.7±1.2 years. The range of variation in maturity status of the pubertal boys is another factor. The pubertal sample included those just beginning puberty (G2, PH2) and those in late puberty (G4, PH4). Age and variation in maturity were not considered in the analysis of gains associated with training in the three groups, and both are confounding factors in the interpretation of the results. The focus in this study was on relative gains. Absolute strength is probably less trainable in prepubertal than in pubertal and postpubertal youth (Sale 1989; Blimkie and Sale 1998).

The relatively small increases in muscle size compared with gains in strength suggest that the response to the resistance-training stimulus in prepubertal children is largely neural. The nature of the responses is not known with certainty, but probably includes enhanced motor unit recruitment and frequency of motor unit firing. The pattern of motor unit recruitment may also be altered, and changes in muscle activation and

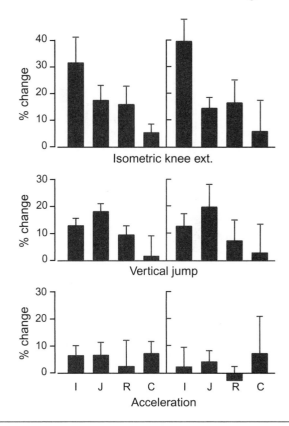

Changes in Strength, Power and Speed of Girls After Five Weeks of Training

FIGURE 22.11 Relative changes in isometric strength (I, knee extension) and two measures of functional strength (J, vertical jump and R, acceleration in sprint running) of girls after 5 weeks of specific training in the respective tasks. C refers to a control group. The left panel includes all girls in the study, and the right panel includes only smaller (<155 cm) and younger (<13.5 yr) girls.

Reprinted, by permission, from B. Nielsen et al., 1980, Training of 'functional muscular strength' in girls 7-19 years old. In *Children and exercise IX*, edited by K. Berg and B.O. Eriksson (Baltimore, MD: University Park Press), 69-78.

intrinsic contractile characteristics with strength training are also possibilities (Ramsey et al. 1990; Ozmun et al. 1994). Strength gains associated with resistance training among pubertal subjects are likely related to neuromotor changes, but among boys advanced in puberty (G3–G4, PH3–PH4) increased circulating levels of gonadal hormones are additional factors that contribute to muscular hypertrophy and strength (see chapter 19).

The preceding studies focus on resistance training. Programs designed to improve muscular

Changes in Strength of Boys of Contrasting
Maturity Status After Nine Weeks of Training

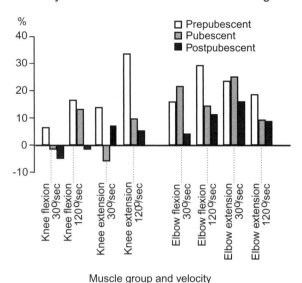

FIGURE 22.12 Relative changes in muscular strength after 9 weeks of strength training in prepubertal, pubertal, and postpubertal boys.

Data from Pfeiffer and Francis, 1986.

endurance also result in strength increments. This finding is shown in table 22.7, which indicates relative changes in muscular strength and endurance after a 5-week endurance-training program on an upper body ergometer in small samples of boys 8 to 14 years of age. The boys exercised on the ergometer to exhaustion at one-third of maximum strength 6 days per week (except Sunday). As expected, boys in the trained group made significant gains, whereas control subjects, who did not train, had more variable responses.

	Relative Changes in Muscular Strength and Endurance After 5 Weeks of Training on an Arm Ergometer in Japanese Boys			
TABLE 22.7				
	Maximal strength		**Muscular endurance**	
Age	**Trained**	**Control**	**Trained**	**Control**
8	34.2%	0%	34.3%	2.6%
10	29.6	13.5	45.6	3.5
12	23.3	−3.9	44.8	−3.9
14	6.5	−4.0	60.0	6.1

Adapted from Ikai (1966).

Among the trained subjects, younger boys made greater relative gains in maximal arm strength, and the older boys made greater relative gains in muscular endurance. The results thus suggest possible differential responses to the type of training stimulus, depending on age.

A question of interest to resistance training is the transfer of gains in strength to other performance tasks. The observations on girls (see figure 22.11) have implications for the transfer of gains with one mode of training to other aspects of performance. The girls who did isometric strength training also improved in the vertical jump and acceleration in sprint running, and girls who did vertical jump training also improved in isometric strength and acceleration in sprint running. Gains were relatively greater in the domain that was specifically trained, that is, girls who did isometric training made greater relative gains in isometric strength, and girls who did vertical jump training made greater relative gains in the vertical jump. On the other hand, girls who did sprint training did not improve in acceleration in sprint running but did make small relative gains in isometric strength and the vertical jump.

Other data dealing with transfer of strength training to other aspects of performance are limited. In a study of boys 6 to 11 years of age, 14 weeks of resistance training was associated with improvements in the vertical jump and the sit-and-reach (Weltman et al. 1986). Among boys and girls 7 to 12 years of age, 8 weeks of strength training was associated with negligible changes in the vertical jump and the sit-and-reach (Faigenbaum et al. 1996). The results are variable and also highlight the difficulty in partitioning the effects of a training program from expected changes associated with normal growth. They also indicate the need to consider the body size characteristics of the subjects in the analysis of changes in performance associated with training.

The transfer of strength gains associated with resistance training to endurance performance in children and adolescents has not been considered. The endurance community has generally advised against resistance exercises. This view has changed somewhat recently but is still not widely accepted. Data for adults indicate that 5-km performance time can be improved by replacing one-third of the total training volume with an explosive-type strength-training program (jump training) and lower body resistance exercise (squats). The improvement was related to a change in running economy and measures of anaerobic capacity (maximal anaerobic treadmill speed, vertical jump, and 20-meter sprint speed), and $\dot{V}O_2$ max was maintained throughout the period of resistance exercise training (Paavolainen et al. 1999).

Two other questions dealing with strength training in children and adolescents need further study. The first question is the persistence of strength gains after the cessation of resistance training, and the second question is the amount of training needed to maintain strength gains associated with training. Limited data for prepubertal children indicate that gains in strength associated with resistance training tend to revert to control values several weeks after the cessation of training, and information on the training requirements for the maintenance of strength gains is inconclusive (Blimkie and Sale 1998). Corresponding data for adolescents are lacking.

The role of genetic factors in the response to strength training of children and adolescents has not been investigated. Among five pairs of young adult MZ twins who did isokinetic strength training for 10 weeks, as many interindividual differences in the response to training occurred within members of any given pair of twins as between pairs (Thibault et al. 1986). In a similar study, a 10-week resistance-training program for the elbow flexors was used with young adult male twins (25 MZ and 16 DZ pairs). Twin resemblances for gains in strength with training within MZ twin pairs were significant only for 1 RM (maximal resistance that can be moved a single time through the full range of motion) and isometric strength, but the within-pair correlations were at best moderate (0.46 and 0.30, respectively). Intrapair correlations for MZ twins for other measures of strength were low or negative, and corresponding intrapair correlations for DZ twins were generally similar to those for MZ twins (Thomis et al. 1998). The limited results thus far suggest that the response to strength training in young adult males is independent of the genotype.

Anaerobic Power

Anaerobic power and capacity have been ordinarily assessed using various whole-body tasks performed over a short period of time at high intensities—the vertical jump, 40-yard dash, 30-second all-out cycling, and treadmill time to exhaustion at high workloads. Maximal blood lactate level after short-term, high-intensity work has also been used to assess anaerobic capacity.

Methodological concerns as well as variation in the frequency, duration, intensity, and methods of training make comparisons among studies difficult.

Data on the trainability of anaerobic capacity in children and adolescents are limited, and whether anaerobic power and capacity are trainable is unclear. Two experimental studies suggest that anaerobic power is increased after a period of high-intensity training in youth. Peak power and mean power, measured by the Wingate test, increased by 14% and 10%, respectively, in 10-year-old to 11-year-old boys engaged in a 9-week interval training program (Rothstein, et al. 1986) and by 3% to 4% in 11-year-old to13-year-old boys after a 6-week, high-intensity cycling or sprint program (Grodjinovsky et al. 1980). The small training effect in the latter study may be the result of the length of the study and the relative duration of each training session—only 10 to 15 minutes per session as part of a physical education class. The lack of data emphasizes the need for study of the trainability of anaerobic power in children and adolescents.

Definitive mechanisms have not been established for growth-related changes in adaptive responses to short-term, high-intensity exercise programs (Inbar and Bar-Or 1986). Puberty appears to be an important period in the development of anaerobic power, which probably reflects changes in body size, muscle mass, and glycolytic capacity. Neural factors may also contribute to training-induced changes in anaerobic tasks.

Moderately strong relationships exist between laboratory measures of anaerobic power and field performance in children and adolescents (Rowland 1996), which suggests a transfer of training-related improvements in anaerobic power and short-burst activities during sports participation. However, association is not firm evidence for casual inference. For example, a 20% improvement in treadmill time to exhaustion (7 mph at 18% grade) after a 12-week program of high-speed activities did not result in a significant change in 40-yard dash time in 10-year-old to 11-year-old elite soccer players (Mosher et al. 1985). Although sprint speed did not improve, changes probably occurred in the ability to resist fatigue during short-term, high-intensity intermittent bouts of sprints (i.e., repeated bouts of sprints).

Data on the contribution of the genotype to the response to anaerobic training are quite limited. Among adults, the genotype is implicated in the response of short-term anaerobic performance (10-second all-out cycling) to a 15-week program of intermittent high-intensity exercise only when results are expressed per unit thigh muscle volume (Simoneau and Bouchard 1998). Interindividual differences in response to the high-intensity training program were considerable and suggest "high" and "low" responders to anaerobic training.

The anaerobic threshold (AT), which corresponds to the exercise capacity at which lactic acid begins to accumulate in the blood, is related to anaerobic performance. Other terms have been used to represent the AT, such as lactate threshold and ventilatory threshold. Although each is assessed differently, the terms are related and generally represent the same concept. The anaerobic threshold is expressed as either $\dot{V}O_2$ at AT (L/min or ml/kg/min) or as a percentage of $\dot{V}O_2$max (i.e., 85% of peak $\dot{V}O_2$). AT can be useful as an index of either anaerobic or aerobic fitness (Rowland 1996). Training-induced changes in AT are summarized in table 22.8. The available data indicate that AT is trainable in boys 8 to 14 years of age either as increases in $\dot{V}O_2$ at AT or as a percentage of $\dot{V}O_2$max. The limited number of studies includes only males and small sample sizes, and they vary in specific training protocols.

Potential mechanisms involved in training-induced changes of AT in youth have not been examined. Blood lactate depends on rates of production and clearance; hence, skeletal muscle morphology and function influence these processes. Hormones (catecholamines) and pubertal status also influence skeletal muscle metabolism in youth. The development of the sensitivity of

respiratory control may be an additional factor. Moderately strong relationships exist between AT and endurance performance in children and adolescents (Rowland 1996), but no training study has specifically examined the transfer of AT to improvements in endurance performance.

Aerobic Power

Relative changes in $\dot{V}O_2$max per unit body weight (ml/kg/min) associated with training in children and adolescents are summarized in table 22.9. The data include boys and girls. The samples are arbitrarily grouped into three age categories: ≤ 10 years, 10 to 13 years, and ≥ 14 years, and studies in which subjects were grouped across a broad age range (e.g., 8 to 13 or 10 to 15 years) were excluded. Sample sizes vary among studies, as do the frequency, intensity, and duration of the aerobic training programs.

The data indicate relatively little trainability of maximal aerobic power in children younger than 10 years of age. Changes in $\dot{V}O_2$max per unit body weight (ml/kg/min) in children younger than 10 years of age are generally less than 5%, and in several studies, negative changes are apparent. Whether these results are the consequences of low trainability (i.e., a low adaptive potential to aerobic training), of inadequacies in the training programs, or of expression of $\dot{V}O_2$ per unit body mass (see chapter 12) is not certain. If young children can be assumed to be habitually more physically active than adolescents and adults, a more intensive aerobic training program may be required to induce significant changes in maximal aerobic

TABLE 22.8   Studies of the Effects of Training on the Anaerobic Threshold in Boys

Study	n	Age (yr)	Training protocol[a]	Main findings[a]
Mahon and Vaccaro (1989)	8	10–14	8 wk run training	Increase by 19% in VT (ml/kg/min); increase in VT (%$\dot{V}O_2$peak) from 67% to 74%
Haffor et al. (1990)	5	11	Interval training 5 days/wk for 6 wk	Increase in VT (%$\dot{V}O_2$peak) from 59% to 72%
Becker and Vaccaro (1983)	11	9–11	8 wk cycle training at HR midway between VT and HR max for 40 min, 3 days/wk	Increase in VT (ml/kg/min and %$\dot{V}O_2$peak) in both training and control groups
Rothstein et al. (1986)	28	10–11	9 wk interval training	Increase in running velocity and %$\dot{V}O_2$ peak at blood lactate threshold

[a]VT = ventilatory threshold; HR = heart rate.

		Relative changes in peak $\dot{V}O_2$ (ml/kg/min) in specific studies				
Age (yr)	N	≤ 0%	+1 to +5%	+6 to +10%	+11 to +15%	>15%
≤10	13	4	8			1
10–13	12	1	2	3	2	4
14+	3			1		2

TABLE 22.9 Relative Changes in Peak $\dot{V}O_2$ Associated With Training in Children and Adolescents

N refers to the number of training studies in the indicated age range.

Based on reviews of Mocellin (1975), Rowland (1985), and Pate and Ward (1990).

power. Anticipated changes should be less than in a sedentary individual because young children are closer to maximal training status at the onset. When young subjects are rather sedentary at the start of a program, short-term training studies (several weeks to a few months) generally yield improvements in maximal aerobic power similar to those observed in young adults, and sex differences are small.

Most activities of young children proceed at submaximal work rates, so maximal aerobic power may not be the appropriate measure. Changes in submaximal work efficiency in response to training may be more appropriate to consider. The effects of instruction and practice on the development of proficiency in running have been previously investigated to a limited extent. For example, submaximal running economy did not improve after an 11-week running training program in 10-year-old children (Petray and Krahenbuhl 1985).

Several training studies report only absolute changes in peak oxygen uptake associated with training in young girls, and results are equivocal (McManus et al. 1997; Welsman et al. 1997). The results may be confounded, in part, by failure to control for changes in body mass during the training program.

Payne and Morrow (1993) used meta-analysis to summarize information on trainability of $\dot{V}O_2$max in children and early adolescents. A total of 69 studies were screened, but only 28 met the criteria for inclusion in the analysis: healthy, ≤13 years of age, data for training and control groups, measurements of $\dot{V}O_2$max before and after a systematic training program, and descriptive statistics (sample sizes, means, and standard deviations) for $\dot{V}O_2$max per unit body weight. The results indicate a gain of about 2 ml/kg/min with training or <5% in children and early adolescents ≤13 years of age and

no differences by sex, mode of exercise testing (treadmill versus cycle), or quality of the training program (frequency, duration, and intensity).

Among older children and adolescents, responses of aerobic power to training improve, but the results vary among studies. This inconsistency may be expected because training programs vary, outside activity is difficult to control, and changes in body size and composition are not ordinarily considered. The variability may relate, in part, to individual variation in the timing and tempo of the adolescent growth spurt and sexual maturation, and maximal aerobic power (L/min) shows a clear adolescent spurt that occurs close in time to that for height (see chapter 16). The variability also reflects sampling and methodological differences among studies.

In an attempt to identify independent effects of an aerobic training program on "prepubertal" children, Tolfrey et al. (1998) controlled for preintervention and postintervention values of habitual physical activity and percentage body fat by including these values in the analyses to identify independent effects of an exercise training program on prepubertal children. Age-matched and sexual maturity–matched control subjects were used. Subjects were in either pubertal stages 1 and 2 of breast and pubic hair (girls) or genital and pubic hair (boys). The results indicated that 12 weeks of stationary cycling exercise at 80% of maximum heart rate for 30 minutes, 3 times per week did not have a significant effect on $\dot{V}O_2$max. Although sexual maturity status of the subjects did not change during the study, combining prepubertal (stage 1) and early pubertal (stage 2) subjects may influence the results. Nevertheless, the approach of Tolfrey et al. (1998) is a good model for exercise training studies in children.

Improvements in $\dot{V}O_2$max associated with aerobic training involve structural and functional adaptations in the oxygen transport system—

lungs, heart, blood, vascular system, and oxidative capacity of skeletal muscle. Based on the Fick equation, improvements reflect increases in heart rate, stroke volume or arteriovenous O_2 difference, or their respective determinants. Maximal heart rate does not change after exercise training. Several early studies indicate that maximal stroke volume, blood volume, and oxidative enzymes increase after exercise training of youth (Rowland 1996). Capillary density after exercise training of youth remains unchanged. Training-induced changes in other components of the oxygen transport system (pulmonary diffusing capacity, cardiac contractility, hemoglobin and myoglobin content, and mitochondrial volume density) remain to be determined. However, ethical limitations are apparent in applying these techniques to children and adolescents.

As in studies of strength training, individual differences in response to the aerobic training programs are not ordinarily reported. Do all children respond in a similar manner? Results from a study of 35 boys and girls, 10.9 to 12.8 years of age, who participated in a 12-week aerobic training program are shown in figure 22.13. Although the mean change in $\dot{V}O_2$max per unit body weight was 6.5%, the range was from –2.4% to 19.7% (Rowland and Boyajian 1995). Individual differences in response to the aerobic training program are thus clearly evident. The results also indicate that mean values may be somewhat misleading. Unfortunately, age-related and maturity-related effects on the response to the aerobic training program were not considered.

A question of interest is the transfer of aerobic training to performance in endurance events. Endurance performance (e.g., 1-mile run time, distance covered in a 12-minute run) improves with age regardless of training. Relative $\dot{V}O_2$max (ml/kg/min) remains stable, and running economy improves with age. Thus, when an exercise training intervention is introduced, what portion of change can be attributed to training? This question is difficult to answer.

How changes in specific physiological parameters associated with exercise training influence endurance performance has received little attention. Age-related changes in $\dot{V}O_2$max and running economy suggest that improvement in running economy leads to an improvement in endurance performance. A 7-year follow-up study of 10-year-old boys indicates no change in $\dot{V}O_2$max per unit body mass, a decline in the submaximal oxygen cost of locomotion (234 to 203 ml/kg/km), and an increase in the distance covered on a 9-minute

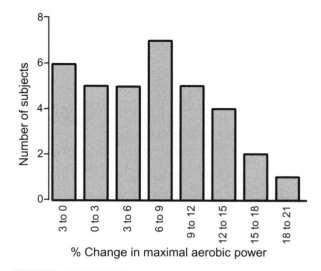

FIGURE 22.13 Distribution of relative gains in $\dot{V}O_2$max per unit body weight (ml/min/kg) in a combined sample of boys and girls 10.9 to 12.8 years of age after a 12-week aerobic training program.

Data from Rowland and Boyajian, 1995.

run (1,637 to 2,115 meters) (Krahenbuhl et al. 1989). Similar results are apparent in a mixed-longitudinal sample of young male distance runners followed for 2 to 5 years (Daniels et al. 1978). The results are influenced, to some extent, by the manner of expressing $\dot{V}O_2$max. When $\dot{V}O_2$max is expressed per unit $kg^{0.75}$, the opposite conclusion is suggested: $\dot{V}O_2$max increases, and running economy remains stable through childhood and adolescence. The endurance performance paradigm thus remains unclear.

Experimental studies of the effects of systematic training on aerobic power are short term and ordinarily do not include a follow-up component. Thus, as in the case of strength training, information is lacking on the persistence of improvements in aerobic power after the cessation of training and on the amount of regular physical activity needed to maintain the improvements associated with training. Some data indicate a reversion to pretraining levels when the training programs cease (Eriksson et al. 1971).

The present evidence suggests that maximal aerobic power (ml/kg/min) has limited trainability in children younger than 10 years of age; on the other hand, maximal aerobic power is trainable in older children, adolescents, and young adults. The evidence also indicates considerable individual differences in the response to aerobic training. Among early adolescents (see figure 22.13) and young adults (see chapter 18), some individuals exhibit a pattern of high response to the training program, whereas others present a pattern of no or minimal response, with a wide range of variation between the extremes. The variation in response among individuals suggests a potentially important role for the genotype in mediating responses to aerobic training.

This issue was addressed in several studies of MZ twins. Individuals of the same genotype (within twin pairs) were more similar in the response of $\dot{V}O_2$max to a standard training program than those with different genotypes (between twin pairs). Gains in $\dot{V}O_2$max consistently showed more variation within DZ twin pairs than within MZ twin pairs, which is consistent with the view that the genotype conditions, in part, the response to aerobic training. Specific genetic characteristics that contribute to individual differences in responses to training are as yet undetermined but are the focus of many studies at present (Bouchard et al. 1997).

Variable Training Modes

The data considered in the discussion of the trainability of motor skills, strength, anaerobic power, and aerobic power are largely based on studies in which a single training emphasis was utilized. Data combining several different modes of training that persist over several years during childhood and adolescence are less extensive. One such experiment compared two training protocols in Polish boys who were 12 years of age at the start of the study (Prus and Szopa 1997). One group (A) placed primary emphasis on endurance, followed by emphasis on speed and then strength, whereas the other group (B) placed primary emphasis on speed, followed by strength and then endurance. Heart rate monitoring during the endurance sessions and the relationship between actual effort and maximal effort in strength and speed sessions were used to estimate training intensity. The estimated load was equivalent to about one-half of the intensity of training of young competitive athletes in specialized sport programs. The boys trained with the respective protocols three times per week during the first year of the study, did no formal training for the second year, and then trained with the respective protocols three times per week during the third year. A control group (C) had 2 hours per week of physical education. The two experimental groups (n = 20 per group) and the control group (n = 50) were tested several times each year using a variety of tests requiring strength, speed, power, and endurance. Several trends are apparent in the results (see figure 22.14).

First, the two experimental groups made greater improvements than the control group in all performance tasks during the first year. The control subjects made gains in almost all of the tests during the first year but at a much lower level. Second, during the year of no training, the performances of the two experimental groups declined to the levels of control group in the speed and endurance tasks (60 m, 300 m, and 1,000 m runs and the Cooper test). In contrast, performances in the strength and power tasks (standing long jump, medicine ball throw, pull-ups, and static strength) remained rather stable and above the control group. Third, with the resumption of training in the third year, the performances of the boys in the experimental groups improved again and the slope of the gains appeared to be somewhat greater than during the first year. Fourth, the training group that placed emphasis first on endurance and then on speed and strength (group A) showed better performances on the Cooper test (distance covered in a 12-minute run) than the training group that placed emphasis first on speed and then on strength and endurance (group B). Fifth, group B showed better performances than group A on the 60-m dash, the standing long jump, medicine ball throw, pull-ups, and static strength. Sixth, the two training groups did not consistently differ in the 300-m and 1,000-m runs.

The growth and maturity characteristics of the boys were not incorporated into the analysis, although the performance curves of the control group tended to improve with age. Hence, partitioning training effects from those associated with normal growth and maturation is difficult. The study spanned ages 12 to 15 years, the interval during which most boys experience their adolescent growth spurts and pass through puberty. Individual differences in the timing and tempo of the spurts in growth and performance may, therefore, influence the trends from 12 to 15 years of age. Nevertheless, the results of this study highlight to some extent the specificity of training and suggest transfer to other tasks. They also illustrate the effects of removing the training stimulus or detraining, but they do not address the training requirements for the maintenance of improvements associated with the training programs.

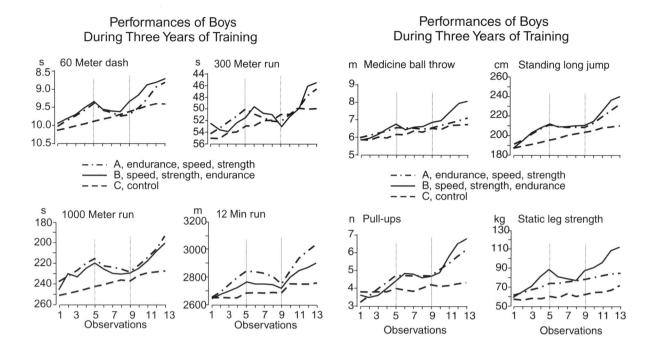

FIGURE 22.14   Mean performances of three groups of boys, two trained groups and a control group. The boys were 12 years of age at the start of the study, which lasted for 3 years. The trained groups differed in training emphasis: group A placed primary emphasis on endurance, followed by emphasis on speed and then strength activities, and group B placed primary emphasis on speed, followed by strength and then endurance activities. Group C, the control group, participated in school physical education for 2 hours per week. The vertical lines on each panel indicate when the training emphasis changed.

Data from Prus and Szopa, 1997.

Trainability: An Overview

The majority of information on the trainability of children and adolescents are derived from studies of boys. Although sex differences in the available data are small, especially during childhood, further information on girls is needed, especially during the transition into and during adolescence.

The growth and maturity characteristics of subjects are generally not incorporated into the analysis of gains or changes associated with a training program. As a result, partitioning training effects from those associated with normal growth and maturation is difficult at times.

Results of trainability studies highlight the specificity of training but suggest transfer to other tasks. More studies need to examine the transfer of gains in functional capacity to field-related performances. Requirements for the maintenance of improvements associated with specific training protocols also need further study.

Many presently available technologies are invasive and thus have limitations in applicability to youth, but some current technology (e.g., magnetic resonance imagining and spectroscopy) may facilitate understanding of this area. Appropriate animal models, therefore, may help understand structural and functional adaptations to training in young subjects.

Summary

The growing and maturing child and adolescent adapt to the stresses imposed by physical activity, especially systematic activity. Regular physical activity does not alter the processes of growth and maturation as they are ordinarily monitored but is an important factor in the regulation of body weight and specifically fatness. Regular physical activity functions to enhance skeletal mineral and is a significant factor in the structural and functional integrity of skeletal muscle tissue. Physical inactivity in combination with a chronically excessive energy intake is associated with greater levels of fatness. Although regular physical activity is related to health-related physical fitness, the relationship is not strong, and indicators of activity account for a relatively small percentage of the variation in several indicators of fitness. Results of trainability studies highlight the specificity of training.

Sources and Suggested Readings

Aaron DJ, Kriska AM, Dearwater SR, Anderson RL, Olsen TL, Cauley JA, Laporte RE (1993) The epidemiology of leisure physical activity in an adolescent population. Medicine and Science in Sports and Exercise 25:847-853.

Alpert B, Field T, Goldstein S, Perry S (1990) Aerobics enhances cardiovascular fitness and agility in preschoolers. Health Psychology 9:48-56.

American Academy of Pediatrics (2001) Strength training by children and adolescents. Pediatrics 107:1470-1472.

Armstrong N, Van Mechelen W (1998) Are young people fit and active? In S Biddle, J Sallis, N Cavill (eds), Young and Active? Young People and Health-Enhancing Physical Activity - Evidence and Implications. London: Health Education Authority, pp 69-97.

Bailey DA (1997) The Saskatchewan Pediatric Bone Mineral Accrual Study: Bone mineral acquisition during the growing years. International Journal of Sports Medicine 19 (suppl): S191-S194.

Bailey DA, Malina RM, Mirwald RL (1986) Physical activity and growth of the child. In F Falkner, JM Tanner (eds), Human Growth. Volume 2. Postnatal Growth, Neurobiology. New York: Plenum, pp 147-170.

Bailey DA, McKay HA, Mirwald RL, Crocker PRE, Faulkner RA (1999) A six year longitudinal study of the relationship of physical activity to bone mineral accrual in growing children: The University of Saskatchewan Bone Mineral Accrual Study. Journal of Bone and Mineral Research 14: 1672-1679.

Bar-Or O (1983) Pediatric Sports Medicine for the Practitioner. New York: Springer-Verlag.

Bar-Or O, Baranowski T (1994) Physical activity, adiposity, and obesity among adolescents. Pediatric Exercise Science 6: 348-360.

Becker DM, Vaccaro P (1983) Anaerobic threshold alterations caused by endurance training in young children. Journal of Sports Medicine 23:445-449.

Beunen GP, Malina RM, Renson R, Simons J, Ostyn M, Lefevre J (1992) Physical activity and growth, maturation and performance: A longitudinal study. Medicine and Science in Sports and Exercise 24:576-585.

Beunen GP, Philippaerts RM, Delvaux K, Thomis M, Claessens AL, Vanreusel B, Vanden Eynde B, Lysens R, Renson R, Lefevre J (2001) Adolescent physical performance and adult physical activity in Flemish males. American Journal of Human Biology 13:173-179.

Blair SN, Clark DG, Cureton KJ, Powell KE (1989) Exercise and fitness in childhood: Implications for a lifetime of health. In CV Gisolfi, DR Lamb (eds), Perspectives in Exercise Science and Sports Medicine. Volume II. Youth, Exercise, and Sport. Indianapolis, IN: Benchmark Press, pp 401-430.

Blimkie CJR, Ramsay J, Sale D, MacDougall D, Smith K, Garner S (1989) Effects of 10 weeks of resistance training on strength development in prepubertal boys. In S Oseid, H-K Carlsen (eds), Children and Exercise XIII. Champaign, IL: Human Kinetics, pp 183-197.

* Blimkie CJR, Sale DG (1998) Strength development and trainability during childhood. In E Van Praagh (ed), Pediatric Anaerobic Performance. Champaign, IL: Human Kinetics, pp 193-224.

Boileau RA, Lohman TG, Slaughter MH (1985) Exercise and body composition of children and youth. Scandinavian Journal of Sports Science 7:17-27.

Booth MA, Booth MJ, Taylor AW (1974) Rat fat cell size and number with exercise training, detraining and weight loss. Federation Proceedings 33:1959-1963.

Bouchard C, Malina RM, Perusse L (1997) Genetics of Fitness and Physical Performance. Champaign, IL: Human Kinetics.

Bouchard C, Thibault M-C, Jobin J (1981) Advances in selected areas of human work physiology. Yearbook of Physical Anthropology 24:1-36.

Campbell PT, Katzmarzyk PT, Malina RM, Rao DC, Lerusse L, Bouchard C (2001) Prediction of physical activity and physical work capacity (PWC150) in young adulthood from childhood and adolescence with consideration of parental measures. American Journal of Human Biology 13:190-196.

Clapp JF, Little KD (1995) The interaction between regular exercise and selected aspects of women's health. American Journal of Obstetrics and Gynecology 173:2-9.

Daniels J, Oldridge N, Nagle F, White B (1978) Differences and changes in $\dot{V}O_2$ among young runners 10 to 18 years of age. Medicine and Science in Sports 10:200-203.

Despres J-P, Bouchard C, Savard R, Tremblay A, Marcotte M, Theriault G (1984) The effect of a 20-week endurance training program on adipose-tissue morphology and lipolysis in men and women. Metabolism 33:235-239.

Despres JP, Bouchard C, Tremblay A, Savard R, Marcotte M (1985) Effects of aerobic training on fat distribution in male subjects. Medicine and Science in Sports and Exercise 17:113-118.

Dionne I, Almeras N, Bouchard C, Tremblay A (2000) The association between vigorous physical activities and fat deposition in male adolescents. Medicine and Science in Sports and Exercise 32:392-395.

Eriksson BO (1972) Physical training, oxygen supply and muscle metabolism in 11–13 year old boys. Acta Physiological Scandinavica, 384 (suppl):1-48.

Eriksson BO, Engstrom I, Karlberg P, Saltin B, Thoren C (1971) A physiological analysis of former girl swimmers. Acta Paediatrica Scandinavica 217 (suppl):68-72.

Faigenbaum AD, Westcott WL, Micheli LJ, Outerbridge AR, Long CJ, LaRosa-Loud R, Zaichkowsky LD (1996) The effects of strength training and detraining on children. Journal of Strength and Conditioning Research 10:109-114.

Faigenbaum AD, Westcott WL, LaRosa Loud R, Long C (1999) The effects of different resistance training protocols on muscular strength and endurance development in children. Pediatrics 104:1-7.

Fournier M, Ricci J, Taylor AW, Ferguson RJ, Montpetit RR, Chairman BR (1982) Skeletal muscle adaptation in adolescent boys: Sprint and endurance training and detraining. Medicine and Science in Sports and Exercise 14:453-456.

Fukunaga T, Funato K, Ikegawa S (1992) The effects of resistance training on muscle area and strength in prepubescent age. Annals of Physiological Anthropology 11:357-364.

Grodjinovosky A, Inbar O, Dotan R, Bar-Or O (1980) Training effect on the anaerobic performance of children as measured by the Wingate anaerobic test. In K Berg, BO Erisson (eds), Children and Exercise IX. Baltimore: University Park Press, pp 139-145.

Gutin B, Cucuzzo N, Islam S, Smith C, Stachura ME (1996) Physical training, lifestyle education, and coronary risk factors in obese girls. Medicine and Science in Sports and Exercise 28:19-23.

* Gutin B, Humphries M (1998) Exercise, body composition, and health in children. In D Lamb, R Murray (eds), Perspectives in Exercise Science and Sports Medicine. Vol 11. Exercise, Nutrition, and Weight Control. Carmel, IN: Cooper, pp 295-347.

Gutin B, Owens S (1999) Role of exercise intervention in improving body fat distribution and risk profile in children. American Journal of Human Biology 11:237-247.

Gutin B, Owens S, Slavens G, Riggs S, Treiber F (1997) Effects of physical training on heart period variability in obese children. Journal of Pediatrics 130:938-943.

Haffor AA, Harrison AC, Catledge Kirk, PA (1990) Anaerobic threshold alterations caused by interval training in 11 year olds. Journal of Sports Medicine and Physical Fitness 30:53-56.

Haubenstricker J, Seefeldt V (1986) Acquisition of motor skills during childhood. In V Seefeldt (ed), Physical Activity and Well-Being. Reston, VA: American Alliance for Health, Physical Education, Recreation and Dance, pp 41-101.

Huang YC, Malina RM (2002) Physical activity and health-related fitness in Taiwanese adolescents. Journal of Physiological Anthropology 21:11-19.

Ikai M (1966) The effects of training on muscular endurance. In K Kato (ed), Proceedings of the International Congress of Sports Sciences, 1964. Tokyo: University of Tokyo Press, pp. 145-158.

Ilich JZ, Skugor M, Hangartner T, Baoshe A, Matkovic V (1998) Relation of nutrition, body composition and physical activity to skeletal development: A cross-sectional study in preadolescent females. Journal of the American College of Nutrition 17:136-147.

Inbar O, Bar-Or O (1986) Anaerobic characteristics in male children and adolescents. Medicine and Science in Sports and Exercise 18:264-269.

Kannus P, Sievanen H, Vuori I (1996). Physical loading, exercise, and bone. Bone 18:1S-3S.

Katzmarzyk PT, Malina RM, Song TMK, Bouchard C (1998a) Physical activity and health-related fitness in youth: A multivariate analysis. Medicine and Science in Sports and Exercise 30:709-714.

Katzmarzyk PT, Malina RM, Song TMK, Bouchard C (1998b) Television viewing, physical activity, and health-related fitness of youth in the Quebec Family Study. Journal of Adolescent Health 23:318-325.

Kemper HCG, de Vente W, van Mechelen W, Twisk JWR (2001) Adolescent motor skill and performance: Is physical activity in adolescence related to adult physical fitness? American Journal of Human Biology 13:180-189.

Kobayashi K, Kitamura K, Miura M, Sodeyama H, Murase Y, Miyashita M, Matsui H (1978) Aerobic power as related to body growth and training in Japanese boys: A longitudinal study. Journal of Applied Physiology 44:666-672.

Krahenbuhl GS, Morgan DW, Pangrazi RP (1989) Longitudinal changes in distance running performance in young males. International Journal of Sports Medicine 10:92-96.

Krahenbuhl GS, Skinner JS, Kohrt WM (1985) Developmental aspects of aerobic power in children. Exercise and Sport Sciences Reviews 13:503-538.

Lange Andersen K, Ilmarinen J, Rutenfranz J, Ottman W, Berndt I, Kylian H, Ruppel M (1984) Leisure time sport activities and maximal aerobic power during late adolescence. European Journal of Applied Physiology 52:431-436.

* Loucks AB, Vaitukaitis J, Cameron JL, Rogol AD, Skrinar G, Warren MP, Kendrick J, Limacher MC (1992) The reproductive system and exercise in women. Medicine and Science in Sports and Exercise 24:S288-S293.

Mahon AD, Vaccaro P (1989) Ventilatory threshold and $\dot{V}O_2$ max changes in children following endurance training. Medicine and Science in Sports and Exercise 21:425-431.

Malina RM (1979) The effects of exercise on specific tissues, dimensions and functions during growth. Studies in Physical Anthropology 5:21-52.

Malina RM (1983) Menarche in athletes: A synthesis and hypothesis. Annals of Human Biology 10:1-24.

Malina RM (1989) Growth and maturation: Normal variation and the effects of training. In CV Gisolfi, DR Lamb (eds), Perspectives in Exercise Science and Sports Medicine. Volume II. Youth, Exercise, and Sport. Indianapolis, IN: Benchmark Press, pp 223-265.

* Malina RM (1990) Growth, exercise, fitness, and later outcomes. In C Bouchard, RJ Shephard, T Stephens, JR Sutton, BD McPherson (eds), Exercise, Fitness, and Health: A Consensus of Current Knowledge. Champaign, IL: Human Kinetics, pp 637-653.

* Malina RM (1994) Physical activity: Relationship to growth, maturation, and physical fitness. In C Bouchard, RJ Shephard, T Stephens (eds), Physical Activity, Fitness, and Health. Champaign, IL: Human Kinetics, pp 918-930.

Malina RM (1995) Physical activity and fitness of children and youth: Questions and implications. Medicine, Exercise, Nutrition, and Health 4:123-135.

Malina RM (1998) Physical activity, sport, social status and Darwinian fitness. In SS Strickland, PS Shetty (eds), Human Biology and Social Inequality. Cambridge, UK: Cambridge University Press, pp 165-192.

Malina RM, Rarick GL (1973) Growth, physique, and motor performance. In GL Rarick (ed), Physical Activity, Human Growth and Development. New York: Academic Press, pp 125-153.

McManus AM, Armstrong N, Williams CA (1997) Effect of training on the aerobic power and anaerobic performance of prepubertal girls. Acta Paediatrica 86:456-459.

Merzenich H, Boeing H, Wahrendorf J (1993) Dietary fat and sports activity as determinants for age at menarche. American Journal of Epidemiology 138:217-224.

Mirwald RL, Bailey DA (1986) Maximal Aerobic Power. London, Ontario: Sport Dynamics.

Mirwald RL, Bailey DA, Cameron N, Rasmussen RL (1981) Longitudinal comparison of aerobic power in active and inactive boys aged 7.0 to 17.0 years. Annals of Human Biology 8:405-414.

Mocellin R (1975) Jugend und sport. Medizinische Klinik 70: 1443-1457.

Moisan J, Meyer F, Gingras S (1990) A nested case-control study of the correlates of early menarche. American Journal of Epidemiology 132:953-961.

Moisan J, Meyer F, Gingras S (1991) Leisure physical activity and age at menarche. Medicine and Science in Sports and Exercise 23:1170-1175.

Morris FL, Naughton GA, Gibbs, JL, Carlson JS, Wark JD (1997) Prospective ten-month exercise intervention in premenarcheal girls: Positive effects on bone and lean mass. Journal of Bone and Mineral Research 12:1453-1462.

Mosher RE, Rhodes EC, Wenger HA, Filsinger B (1985) Interval training: the effects of a 12 week programme on elite prepubertal male soccer players. Journal of Sports Medicine 25:5-9.

Mo-suwan L, Pongprapai S, Junjana C, Puetpaiboon A (1998) Effects of a controlled trial of a school-based exercise program on the obesity indexes of preschool children. American Journal of Clinical Nutrition 68:1006-1011.

Nielsen B, Nielsen K, Behrendt Hansen M, Asmussen E (1980) Training of "functional muscular strength" in girls 7-19 years old. In K Berg, BO Eriksson (eds), Children and Exercise IX. Baltimore: University Park Press, pp 69-78.

Nordstrom P, Pettersson U, Lorentzon R (1998) Type of physical activity, muscle strength, and pubertal stage as determinants of bone mineral density and bone area in adolescent boys. Journal of Bone and Mineral Research 13:1141-1148.

Ozmun JC, Mikesky AE, Surburg PR (1994) Neuromuscular adaptations following prepubescent strength training. Medicine and Science in Sports and Exercise 26:510-514.

Paavolainen L, Hakkinen K, Hamalainen I, Nummela A, Rusko H (1999) Explosive-strength training improves 5-km running time by improving running economy and muscle power. Journal of Applied Physiology 86:1527-1533.

Parizkova J (1970) Longitudinal study of the relationship between body composition and anthropometric characteristics in boys during growth and development. Glasnik Antropoloskog Drustva Jugoslavije 7:33-38.

Parizkova J (1977) Body Fat and Physical Fitness. The Hague: Martinus Nijhoff.

Pate RR, Dowda M, Ross JG (1990) Associations between physical activity and physical fitness in American children. American Journal of Diseases of Children 144: 1123-1129.

* Pate RR, Ward DS (1990) Endurance exercise trainability in children and youth. Advances in Sports Medicine and Fitness 3:37-55.

* Payne VG, Morrow JR (1993) Exercise and $\dot{V}O_2$ max in children: A meta-analysis. Research Quarterly for Exercise and Sport 64:305-313.

Petray CK, Krahenbuhl GS (1985) Running training, instruction on running technique, and running economy in 10-year old males. Research Quarterly of Exercise and Sport 56: 251-255.

Pfeiffer RD, Francis RS (1986) Effects of strength training on muscle development in prepubescent, pubescent, and postpubescent males. Physician and Sports Medicine 14: 134-143 (Sep).

Prus G, Szopa J (1997) Adaptabilnosc wybranych zdolnosci motorycznych u chlopcow miedzy 12 a 15 rokiem zycia: Rezultaty eksperymentu "trening-detrening-retrening." Antropomotoryka 16:27-42.

Rabinowicz R (1986) The differentiated maturation of the cerebral cortex. In F Falkner, JM Tanner (eds), Human Growth. Volume 2. Postnatal Growth, Neurobiology. New York: Plenum, pp 385-410.

Ramsay JA, Blimkie CJR, Smith K, Garner S, MacDougall JD, Sale DG (1990) Strength training effects in pre-pubescent boys. Medicine and Science in Sports and Exercise 22:605-614.

* Rarick GL (1960) Exercise and growth. In WR Johnson (ed), Science and Medicine of Exercise and Sports. New York: Harper and Brothers, pp 440-465.

Renson R, Beunen G, Claessens AL, Colla R, Lefevre J, Ostyn M, Schueremans C, Simons J, Taks M, Van Gerven D (1990) Physical fitness variation among 13 to 18 year old boys and girls according to sport participation. In G Beunen, J Ghesquiere, T Reybrouck, AL Claessens (eds), Children and Exercise. Stuttgart: Ferdinand Enke Verlag, pp 136-144.

Riddoch C (1998) Relationships between physical activity and physical health in young people. In S Biddle, J Sallis, N Cavill (eds), Young and Active? Young People and Health-Enhancing Physical Activity — Evidence and Implications. London: Health Education Authority, pp 17-48.

Rothstein A, Dotan R, Bar-Or O, Tenenbaum G (1986) Effect of training on anaerobic threshold, maximal aerobic power and anaerobic performance of preadolescent boys. International Journal of Sports Medicine 7:281-286.

* Rowland TW (1985) Aerobic response to endurance training in prepubescent children: A critical analysis. Medicine and Science in Sports and Exercise 17:493-497.

Rowland TW (1996) Developmental Exercise Physiology. Champaign, IL: Human Kinetics.

Rowland TW, Boyajian A (1995) Aerobic response to endurance exercise training in children. Pediatrics 96:654-658.

* Sale D (1989) Strength and power training during youth. In CV Gisolfi, DR Lamb (eds), Perspectives in Exercise Science and Sports Medicine. Volume II. Youth, Exercise, and Sport. Indianapolis, IN: Benchmark Press, pp 165-216.

Sallis JF, McKenzie TL, Alcaraz JE (1993) Habitual physical activity and health-related physical fitness in fourth grade children. American Journal of Diseases of Children 147: 890-896.

Saltin B, Gollnick PD (1983) Skeletal muscle adaptability: Significance for metabolism and performance. In LD Peachey (ed), Handbook of Physiology, Section 10, Skeletal Muscle. Bethesda, MD: American Physiological Society, pp 555-631.

Saris WHM, Elvers JWH, van't Hof MA, Binkhorst RA (1986) Changes in physical activity of children aged 6 to 12 years. In J Rutenfranz, R Mocellin, F Klimt (eds), Children and Exercise XII. Champaign, IL: Human Kinetics, pp 121-130.

Sasaki J, Shindo M, Tanaka H, Ando M, Arakawa K (1987) A long-term aerobic exercise program decreases the obesity index and increases the high density lipoprotein cholesterol concentration in obese children. International Journal of Obesity 11:339-345.

Schmucker B, Rigauer B, Hinrichs W, Trawinski J (1984) Motor abilities and habitual physical activity in children. In J Ilmarinen, I Valimaki (eds), Children and Sport. Berlin: Springer Verlag, pp 46-52.

Scott JP (1986) Critical periods in organizational processes. In F Falkner, JM Tanner (eds), Human Growth. Volume 1. Developmental Biology, Prenatal Growth. New York: Plenum, pp 181-196.

Simoneau JA, Bouchard C (1998) The effects of genetic variation on anaerobic performance. In E Van Praagh (ed), Pediatric Anaerobic Performance. Champaign, IL: Human Kinetics, pp 5-21.

Sklad M (1975) The genetic determination of the rate of learning of motor skills. Studies in Physical Anthropology 1:3-19.

Slemenda CW, Miller JZ, Hui SL, Reister TK, Johnston CC (1991) Role of physical activity in the development of skeletal mass in children. Journal of Bone and Mineral Research 6:1227-1233.

Slemenda CW, Reister TK, Hui SL, Miller JA, Christian JC, Johnston CC (1994) Influences on skeletal mineralization in children and adolescents: Evidence for varying effects of sexual maturation and physical activity. Journal of Pediatrics 125:201-207.

Sprynarova S (1987) The influence of training on physical and functional growth before, during and after puberty. European Journal of Applied Physiology 56:719-724.

* Steinhaus AH (1933) Chronic effects of exercise. Physiological Reviews 13:103-147.

Taranger J, Engstrom I, Lichenstein H, Svennberg-Redegen I (1976) Somatic pubertal development. Acta Paediatrica Scandinavica 258 (suppl):121-135.

Thatcher RW, Walker RA, Giudice S (1987) Human cerebral hemispheres develop at different rates and ages. Science 236:1110-1113.

Thibault MC, Simoneau JA, Cote C, Boulay MR, Lagasse P, Marcotte M, Bouchard C (1986) Inheritance of human muscle enzyme adaptation to isokinetic strength training. Human Heredity 36:341-347.

Thomis MA, Beunen GP, Maes HH, Blimkie CJ, Van Leemputte M, Claessens AL, Marchal G, Willems E, Vlietinck RF (1998) Strength training: Importance of genetic factors. Medicine and Science in Sports and Exercise 30:724-731.

Tolfrey K, Campbell I, Batterham A (1998) Aerobic trainability of prepubertal boys and girls. Pediatric Exercise Science 10:248-263.

Tremblay A, Despres J-P, Bouchard C (1985) The effects of exercise-training on energy balance and adipose tissue morphology and metabolism. Sports Medicine 2:223-233.

Tremblay A, Despres JP, Bouchard C (1988) Alteration in body fat and fat distribution with exercise. In C Bouchard, FE Johnston (eds), Fat Distribution during Growth and Later Health Outcomes. New York: Alan R Liss, pp 297-312.

Verschuur R (1987) Daily physical activity: Longitudinal changes during the teenage period. Haarlem, The Netherlands: Uitgeverrij de Vrieseborch.

Von Dobeln W, Eriksson BO (1972) Physical training, maximal oxygen uptake and dimensions of the oxygen transporting and metabolizing organs in boys 11-13 years of age. Acta Paediatrica Scandinavica 61:653-660.

Welsman JR, Armstrong N, Withers S (1997) Responses of young girls to two modes of aerobic training. British Journal of Sports Medicine 31:139-142.

Weltman A, Janney C, Rians CB, Strand K, Berg B, Tippitt S, Wise J, Cahill BR, Katch FI (1986) The effects of hydraulic resistance strength training in pre-pubertal males. Medicine and Science in Sports and Exercise 18:629-638.

23 UNDERNUTRITION IN CHILDHOOD AND ADOLESCENCE

Chapter Outline

Criteria

Prevalence

Forms of Undernutrition

Undernutrition in Preschool Children
Low Birth Weight
Growth
Infections and Parasites
Cultural Practices and Undernutrition
Motor Development
Physical Activity

Undernutrition in School-Age Children
Growth and Maturity
Performance
Physical Activity

Long-Term Consequences of Undernutrition

Summary

Sources and Suggested Readings

The nutritional status of individuals and populations spans a broad range, from the extremes of deficiency to excess. Undernutrition varies from starvation, to severe protein-energy malnutrition, to specific deficiency states, and to the more common mild-to-moderate form. Undernutrition is a heterogeneous term that may have different meanings among specialists who work in the respective areas. The "normal" state of nutrition is quite variable. The energy and nutrient needs associated with normal growth, maturation, and function are considered in chapter 20, and issues related to physical activity and energy expenditure are considered in chapters 21 and 22. This chapter focuses on chronic undernutrition. First, basic concepts, criteria, and prevalence are specified and then implications for growth, maturation, performance, and physical activity are discussed.

The term undernutrition, which is often referred to as malnutrition, implies a lack of energy and nutrients in the diet over time (i.e., it is a chronic condition). Undernutrition refers to an absolute or relative deficiency of energy or nutrients that make those available to the child inadequate for the needs of growth. Undernutrition is difficult to quantify, but its presence is ordinarily established in public health and clinical contexts with the use of anthropometry, specifically weight and length/height (see Criteria). Undernutrition during infancy and early childhood receives most emphasis because of its association with morbidity and mortality early in life and its long-term consequences; however, undernutrition can occur at any time during the life cycle.

Criteria

Weight and length/height are used to define the criteria for undernutrition. Methods of measuring weight, length, and height and reference data for evaluating body size are discussed in chapter 3.

Chronic undernutrition is a major problem of infants and young children (birth to 5 years of age) in many developing or poorly developed countries of the world. Three different forms of undernutrition among children younger than 5 years of age are defined by the World Health Organization (de Onis and Blossner 1997). The definitions are based on age, weight, and length/height:

1. Underweight—weight-for-age more than two standard deviations below the international reference median

2. Stunting—length/height-for-age more than two standard deviations below the international reference median

3. Wasting—weight-for-length/height more than two standard deviations below the international reference median

The international reference is age-specific and sex-specific for boys and girls. The currently used reference is that for United States children (World Health Organization 1995; Hamill et al. 1977; de Onis and Blossner 1997). These classifications can be used with school-age children, especially stunting, but are of limited utility during adolescence because of individual differences in the timing and tempo of the adolescent growth spurt and sexual maturation.

Each of the designations has a specific meaning in the context of undernutrition. Underweight or lightness refers to a deficiency in body weight compared with better-nourished children of the same age and sex. It may reflect either inadequate weight gain or weight loss, which may occur over time (i.e., chronic) or over a short period of time (i.e., acute). Stunting refers to inadequate length/height (i.e., linear growth) compared with that expected for a child of the same age and sex. It is ordinarily accepted as an indicator of long-term, or chronic, nutritional deficiency or inadequate health conditions. Some genetically short children may be labeled as stunted, but in lesser developed areas of the world, the majority of short children are stunted in growth, reflecting the generally impoverished nutritional and health circumstances under which they live. Wasting refers to a deficiency of weight relative to that expected for a given length/height. It is an indicator of either current severe weight loss or long-term gradual weight loss.

Prevalence

The estimated prevalence and numbers (in millions) of underweight, stunted, and wasted children under 5 years of age in different regions of the world in 1995, based on the World Health Organization global data base on child growth and malnutrition, are summarized in table 23.1. The data do not include the United States, Canada, Australia, New Zealand, and countries of Europe. No consistent differences are evident in estimated prevalence rates for boys and girls, but variation by geographic region is seen. The prevalence and numbers of nutritionally compromised young children are generally highest in the Southeast Asian and African regions and lowest in the Americas (Latin America and the Caribbean). When areas of the world are classified economically, the least-developed countries

TABLE 23.1 Estimated Prevalences (%) and Numbers in Millions (n) of Children Under 5 Years of Age in Different Regions of the World Classified As Underweight, Stunted, and Wasted in 1995

Region	Underweight %	Underweight n	Stunted %	Stunted n	Wasted %	Wasted n
Africa	30.4	31.2	40.2	41.3	8.3	8.5
Americas	7.6	5.8	13.5	10.3	2.8	2.1
Eastern Mediterranean	24.9	17.3	34.3	23.9	7.5	5.2
Southeast Asia	50.1	82.7	50.2	82.9	15.9	26.3
Western Pacific	20.6	28.9	32.8	46.0	4.4	6.2
Overall	27.8	169.5	34.9	213.1	8.4	50.2

Regions are as defined by the World Health Organization. The Americas includes Latin America and the Caribbean and does not include the United States and Canada. Criteria for underweight, stunting, and wasting are defined in the text.

Adapted from the de Onis and Blossner (1997).

have the highest prevalence of underweight (40%), stunted (48%), and wasted (11%) children under 5 years of age. Corresponding prevalences in other developing countries are underweight (29%), stunted (36%), and wasted (9%). These percentages translate into about 421 million children under 5 years of age in developing countries (de Onis and Blossner 1997), which emphasizes the burden of undernutrition among young children in most of the world. Estimated prevalences and numbers of children suffering from undernutrition vary among specific countries within each geographic region; country-specific estimates are reported in de Onis and Blossner (1997).

Forms of Undernutrition

Undernutrition has several forms, some of which are well defined clinically. Starvation refers to the lack of food (i.e., energy and nutrients). Specific nutrient deficiencies, as the name implies, refer to a lack of a specific nutrient or nutrients in the diet (e.g., vitamin A deficiency, zinc deficiency, or folic acid deficiency). Protein-energy malnutrition is the most common form of undernutrition. It is somewhat of a misnomer because a diet deficient in protein and energy is also deficient in other nutrients essential to support normal growth. Protein-energy malnutrition includes two classic forms, marasmus and kwashiorkor.

Marasmus is a severe deficiency in energy, protein, and other nutrients that occurs most often during the first year of life, although it can occur at all ages. It is associated with starvation or a grossly inadequate diet and is characterized by extreme underweight, severe wasting of muscle and adipose tissues, and behavioral apathy (Jelliffe 1966; Coward and Lunn 1981; Monckeberg 1985).

Kwashiorkor is also a severe deficiency in energy, protein, and other nutrients. It occurs most often during the second year of life but can also occur later in childhood. Kwashiorkor is associated with changes in diet and behavioral treatment that are associated with weaning. In many developing areas of the world, weaning occurs during the second year of life. Kwashiorkor is characterized by underweight, although not as severe as in marasmus, apathy, and especially edema, the accumulation of fluid outside of the vascular bed. The edema is caused by a deficiency in serum albumin (hypoalbuminemia) and probably other proteins associated with a poor diet (Jackson and Golden 1986; Pereira 1986).

The edema may give the child the appearance of pudginess, but this appearance is misleading, given the underlying nutritional deficiencies.

Severe protein-energy malnutrition also occurs in undifferentiated form, which includes less distinct clinical features compared with those that characterize marasmus and kwashiorkor. Undifferentiated protein-energy malnutrition is associated with growth stunting and variable degrees of wasting.

In contrast to these more severe forms, mild-to-moderate protein-energy malnutrition is the most common form of undernutrition. It is often referred to as chronic undernutrition because it is associated with a deficiency of energy and nutrients over a period of several years and is often characteristic of a community or population. This form of undernutrition is difficult to quantify and is established with the use of anthropometry, specifically weight and length/height as described previously. In this context, mild-to-moderate undernutrition refers to absolute or relative deficiencies of energy and nutrients that make those available to the child inadequate to meet the needs of growth. Although undernutrition can occur at any time in the life cycle, undernutrition during infancy and early childhood receives most emphasis in public health because of its immediate and long-term consequences.

Chronic undernutrition in a population is associated with three factors that interact in a complex manner: inadequate diet, an environment characterized by a high prevalence of infectious and parasitic diseases, and sociocultural practices associated with feeding children and the provision of an adequate diet. An additional factor in some developing or less-developed countries is the diversion of national resources for political or military activities with the net result being severe undernutrition in a major segment of the population.

Undernutrition in Preschool Children

Undernutrition refers to a deficiency of energy or nutrients in the diet. It can refer to a single nutrient or to multiple nutrients. The deficiency or deficiencies can be short term or can persist over time.

Chronic undernutrition persists over several years. In many developing countries, it begins with compromised maternal nutrition during pregnancy and continues in the life of the infant and young child. Chronic undernutrition has well-documented effects. These include stunted growth, reduced muscle mass, delayed or impaired neuromuscular and motor development during childhood, and reduced physical activity, among others, in young children.

The effects of chronic undernutrition are mediated, in part, by factors other than nutritional state. Undernourished children are more likely to be exposed at the same time to other risks that may negatively influence or compromise growth, motor development, performance, and physical activity. These risks include biological factors such as greater exposure to infectious and parasitic diseases and perhaps exposure to pollutants such as lead; poorly educated parents who may not be competent in child rearing and caregiving practices; occasional parental neglect; poor home and school environments; and socioeconomic factors such as parental unemployment, limited access to health care facilities, and child labor (Pollitt 1987, 1996; Dobbing 1990). Such biological, psychosocial, and socioeconomic risk factors are themselves interrelated. Nevertheless, they contribute to an overall environmental impoverishment that influences growth and functional development of infants and children.

Low Birth Weight

Chronic maternal undernutrition during pregnancy often results in reduced birth weight. The infants are often "small for date" and have experienced intrauterine growth stunting (see chapter 3). Reduced birth weight, in turn, is a risk factor for infant mortality, as is illustrated in table 23.2 for an indigenous community in rural Guatemala that was characterized by chronic undernutrition. Mean birth weight during the interval of the study was 2,549 g. Only 7.5% of the infants were born preterm (before 37 weeks of gestation), and about 35% of the full-term infants had low birth weights (2500 g or less). The high prevalence of "small for date" infants reflects, to a large extent, poor maternal nutritional status. The low-birth-weight children, in turn, account for about 71% of infant deaths. Further, children whose growth is stunted prenatally generally remain, on average, smaller postnatally than children who experienced a good nutritional environment in utero. The growth and functional characteristics of extremely low-birth-weight infants in developed countries, which is caused by prematurity, are discussed in chapter 27.

TABLE 23.2 Infant Mortality by Birth Weight Category in a Rural Guatemalan Community Between 1964 and 1973

Birth weight (g)	Number of live births	Infant mortality[a]	Deaths as % of all live births
<1,501	5	4	0.9
1,501–2,000	28	15	3.5
2,000–2,500	146	10	2.3
2,501–3,000	207	11	2.6
3,001–3,500	43	1	0.2
>3,500	1	0	0.0
Total	430	41	9.5

[a]Deaths during the first year of life. The estimated infant mortality for the community during this period was about 98/1,000 live births.

Adapted from Mata (1978).

Growth

As noted earlier, undernutrition can occur at any age postnatally, but it has its most serious consequences during the preschool years. The effects of undernutrition on growth depend on the timing (when it occurs), severity (how serious it is), and duration (how long it persists) of the nutritional stress. Typical growth curves for length and weight of preschool children from areas with chronic mild-to-moderate undernutrition are shown in figure 23.1. Size at birth does not differ that markedly between children from areas with mild-to-moderate undernutrition and reference values for well-nourished children. Growth progresses reasonably well for 3 to 6 months. This condition reflects the nutritional value of breast milk, which is adequate by itself to meet the needs of the infant at this time. However, between 3 and 6 months of age, breast milk by itself may not be adequate to meet the nutrient and energy needs of the rapidly growing infant. If the infant's diet is not supplemented at these ages, which often occurs in developing areas of the world, growth stunting may occur. The growth curve of children from areas with chronic mild-to-moderate undernutrition thus begins to move away from or falter relative to that expected for well-nourished children. After 6 months of age, mean values for length and weight continue to move toward the lower percentiles, quite often stabilizing at the 5th percentiles in the second and third years of

Growth of Undernourished Preschool Children

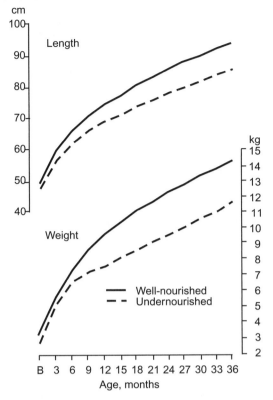

FIGURE 23.1 Mean lengths and weights of well-nourished and undernourished preschool Mexican children.

Data from Ramos Galvan, 1975, and Scholl, 1975.

life. Thus, considerable growth stunting occurs during early childhood and persists into middle childhood and adolescence (see Undernutrition in School Age Children).

Infections and Parasites

Infectious and parasitic diseases of childhood are contributing factors to the growth stunting associated with chronic undernutrition. The more common conditions include measles, respiratory infections such as pneumonia and strep throat, and intestinal parasites such as protozoans (amoebas), nematode roundworms, hookworms, and helminths (wormlike parasites). Chronic undernutrition and infectious/parasitic diseases are believed to interact in a synergistic manner (i.e., one condition enhances the effects of the other). Thus, an undernourished child is more susceptible to infectious disease, and a child with an infectious or parasitic disease is more prone to undernutrition. For example, many parasites

that lodge in the intestinal tract are responsible for diarrhea and dysentery, which contribute to the deterioration of the nutritional status of the chronically undernourished child. The role of climatic conditions (temperature, humidity, and rainfall), habits of personal hygiene, and lack of adequate sanitation facilities, especially for drinking water and waste disposal, are important factors in the maintenance and spread of infectious and parasitic diseases in many areas of the world.

The specific effects of infectious/parasitic diseases on growth are difficult to partition. In an attempt to estimate the contribution of such diseases on growth, rural Guatemalan children were followed longitudinally from the first month of life to 7 years of age and classified as having high and low frequencies of bouts of diarrhea during this interval (Martorell et al. 1975). The children lived in four communities in which chronic mild-to-moderate undernutrition was endemic, and chronic diarrhea was a relatively common occurrence. The gain in weight and length between birth and 7 years of age for the total sample of children in the communities was less than corresponding gains in well-nourished children by an average of 4.9 kg and 12.8 cm, respectively. However, children with a high frequency of diarrhea gained significantly less weight (1.5 kg) and length (3.5 cm) than those with a low frequency of diarrhea during the interval of the study. The poor growth performance of the rural Guatemalan children thus reflects the combined effects of chronically poor or marginal nutritional status and a significant infectious/parasitic disease load.

How infections influence the growth of children is not known, although two potential mechanisms are suspected. Infections may either have a direct impact on nutritional status, or they may have a direct effect on growth processes. For example, diarrhea and fever are generally accompanied with reduced food intake and thus directly impact nutritional status of the child. Infections may also have more direct nutritional effects. Some intestinal parasites, for example, influence nutrient absorption and contribute to nutrient loss. Ascaris (an intestinal roundworm) infection is associated with impaired lactose absorption (Hlaing 1993). Schistosomiasis and hookworm are associated with iron loss, and the intensity of the infection is proportional to blood loss and severity of anemia (Stephenson 1993). Finally, some infections such as HIV contribute to elevated resting energy expenditure and increase nutritional requirements. Thus, infectious and parasitic diseases may interfere with micronutrient metabolism, which may, in turn, influence growth processes. Because linear growth is compromised by chronic undernutrition, a question of interest is the influence of micronutrient metabolism during infection on activities of the growth plates, the sites of linear growth of the skeleton and, in turn, height (see chapter 6).

Intestinal parasite infestation is significant among preschool children in developing areas of the world. For example, among 102 preschool children in a rural Guatemalan community, about 54% had ascaris (helminth), 27% had giardia (protozoan), and 8% had amoeba. Many of the children had multiple intestinal parasites (Gupta and Urrutia 1982). The growth progress of children in this community who were treated with drugs to reduce the parasite load gained more in weight and height than those who were not treated. Over a 1-year period, treated children gained about 0.3 kg more in weight and 1.0 cm more in height than untreated children. The cumulative growth deficits associated with intestinal parasite infestation in early childhood, and of course, the beneficial effects of controlling parasite load on growth are suggested in these results.

Cultural Practices and Undernutrition

Cultural practices and limited education have an important role in affecting the nutritional status of preschool children. Food distribution within the family follows local cultural patterns, and quite often children are among the last to be fed. Many cultures have specific views as to what a sick child or a child with chronic diarrhea should or should not be fed. For example, in some parts of the developing world, whole milk is believed to be not good for diarrhea, and as a result, milk is withdrawn from the diet of the child or diluted with water, quite often with water that is not properly purified. Why is milk withdrawn? Vomiting often accompanies diarrhea and curdled milk appears in the vomit. The mother believes the milk "turned bad" in the stomach and therefore does not give it to the sick child. A related factor is the withdrawal of "cold foods" such as fruits during illness and replacement with warm liquids such as warm rice water or warm water and noodles.

In general, a common view in rural areas is that a child with fever or diarrhea should not eat solid foods because they would upset the stomach more so. Loss of appetite (anorexia) accompanies high fever and severe diarrhea. Hence, because the child does not request food (no appetite), many mothers simply do not provide any. The net result, quite often, is less nutrients and energy available to the child, who is already undernourished, at a time when the child needs them. Hence, a three-way interaction among chronic undernutrition, infectious/parasitic diseases, and cultural practices/lack of education contributes to the poor growth of chronically mild-to-moderately undernourished children.

Motor Development

A reasonable amount of cross-cultural literature considers the early motor development of children, especially during the first 2 years of life (Leiderman et al. 1977; Nugent et al. 1989). The data are largely derived from infant developmental scales (see chapter 10). Results are reported as global motor development scores or as ages of attaining specific motor milestones as sitting alone and independent walking. Unfortunately, researchers in the cross-cultural and nutritional areas of study do not consider fundamental movement skills such as running, jumping, and throwing.

Motor development progresses in a satisfactory manner during the first year of life in samples of infants from different areas of the world. However, a developmental lag toward the end of the first year, which continues into the second and third years, is commonly observed in children living under chronic mild-to-moderate nutritional and economically impoverished conditions. The lag in motor development reflects the combined effects of compromised nutritional status, the break in continuity of rearing at weaning, and reduced physical activity. Stunting of growth in size and muscle mass also becomes especially apparent during the second half of the first year and during the second year of life. The consequences of the lag in motor development for the child are several. First, delay in locomotion may slow the acquisition of other motor skills and social behaviors. Second, reduced physical activity associated with undernutrition may slow the refinement of independent locomotion and limit exploratory behaviors, which, in turn, influences other motor and social skills and physical activity. Third, children who are delayed or compromised in the development of motor proficiency may induce caretaking or rearing behaviors and other social behaviors that further limit physical activity and motor development (Pollitt 1987, 1995, 1996).

In contrast to mild-to-moderate undernutrition, preschool children suffering from severe undernutrition (marasmus, kwashiorkor, or some combination) are especially compromised in early motor development. Recovery of motor development after nutritional rehabilitation is variable and depends, in part, on the treatment program. Long-term complications of severe early nutritional problems affect motor development and performance during early childhood. One of the more comprehensive studies of motor development under conditions of severe protein-energy malnutrition is that of Cravioto (1980), who carried out an ecological study of all live births in a single year in a rural community in Mexico. Of the 334 live-born children, 22 experienced severe protein-energy malnutrition between 1 and 4 years of age (17 between the first and third birthdays; kwashiorkor developed in 15 children and marasmus developed in 7). All were treated and nutritionally rehabilitated. The motor scores of the severely undernourished children declined linearly during the first 3 years. Over the course of the observational period, three children died and one family moved from the community after the child's nutritional recovery. The remaining 18 children were subsequently tested on several motor tasks at the age of 75 months (about 6 years), 22 to 69 months after nutritional rehabilitation and recovery from severe undernutrition. The motor tasks included gross and fine coordination; arm, leg, and abdominal strength; shoulder, leg, and back flexibility; agility and speed; and static and dynamic balance. The children who recovered from severe undernutrition were compared with several groups of children of the same birth cohort: a randomly selected control group, a group matched for socioeconomic status within the community, and a group matched for home stimulation scores. Overall, about 2 to 5 years after nutritional rehabilitation and recovery, children who were severely undernourished in infancy and early childhood had lower motor proficiency scores in tests of coordination, agility, balance, and strength compared with other children living under similar conditions in the community. The flexibility measure did not differ among the groups of children.

Physical Activity

Clinical observations of severely undernourished children indicate reduced levels and lack of interest in physical activity. More specific data on levels of physical activity associated with undernutrition are not extensive. This lack of data is related, in part, to difficulties in quantifying physical activity in field situations.

Under quasiexperimental conditions of reduced energy intake (from 120 to 150 kcal/kg/day to 70 to 90 kcal/kg/day), six preschool Guatemalan children showed markedly reduced levels of activity (walking, running, tricycling, and games) as assessed by time-and-motion studies. An energy intake of 70 to 90 kcal/kg/day was equivalent to that observed in dietary surveys of Guatemalan preschool children, with other dietary components and feeding conditions being the same (Viteri and Torun 1981). Of particular note, energy expenditure in the form of physical activity was reduced, apparently to maintain weight gain. A subsequent observational study of Guatemalan children 2 to 4 years of age who were recovering from protein-energy undernutrition in the hospital suggested that a 6-week program of mild physical activity facilitated the recovery process. The "active" children participated in games and other activities that raised the heart rate by approximately 26 beats/min above resting and required an estimated energy expenditure of 50 kcal/hour. The other children, who were also recovering from protein-energy undernutrition, participated in activities requiring an average heart rate of about 17 beats/min above resting and an energy expenditure of about 38 kcal/hour (Viteri and Torun 1981). Circumstantial evidence from daycare nutrition centers in Guatemala is consistent with these hospital observations. Mean time to discharge from the centers varied inversely with opportunity for physical activity. Hence, reduction in physical activity is associated with chronic undernutrition, whereas a program of light activity may facilitate recovery from bouts of severe undernutrition (Torun and Viteri 1994).

A comprehensive field study of physical activity and related behaviors in infants and children 4 to 24 months of age from a rural community in Mexico highlights the association of nutritional status and physical activity (Chavez and Martinez 1984). The frequency of foot contacts with a supporting surface in nonambulatory children and the number of steps in mobile children were used as an index of physical activity. In addition, some of the children received a nutritional supplementation, whereas others did not. Note, however, the children were "not clearly malnourished." Significantly reduced levels of physical activity were recorded for children who were unsupplemented compared with supplemented children. The activity difference between the groups was already apparent at 4 months of age and increased with age so that the supplemented group was about six times more active at 24 months of age.

More detailed observations of the children indicated an important role for mother-child interactions in addition to nutritional status and body size differences between the two samples of rural children in Mexico. The more active children made more demands on their mothers, thus increasing the frequency and quality of caretaking behaviors and in turn stimulation for further activity and presumably practice of motor skills. The supplemented group also scored consistently higher on gross and fine motor items of the Gesell scale. In contrast, mothers of the unsupplemented children had more limited interactions with their children, which involved three primary maternal activities: placing the youngsters in a cradle or rocking them, carrying the youngsters on their backs in a shawl, and holding the youngsters in their arms for feeding (Chavez and Martinez 1975; Chavez et al. 1975). These observations thus emphasize the important role of factors other than nutritional status in the physical activity and motor development of preschool children. Information relating reduced physical activity to the development of specific movement patterns in undernourished preschool children is apparently not available.

Undernutrition in School-Age Children

School-age children represent the next generation of economically active members of a community. In developing areas of the world, they represent to a large extent the survivors of a selection process involving chronic undernutrition, infectious and parasitic diseases, and socially and economically impoverished circumstances. An understanding of the growth, maturation, performance, and physical activity characteristics of school-age children in communities with a high prevalence of mild-to-moderate undernutrition is important. Chronic mild-to-moderate undernutrition in school-age children and adolescents is associated with smaller body size and reduced muscle mass, reduced levels of physical performance (strength, motor, and aerobic), and reduced levels of physical activity.

Growth and Maturity

The growth status of school children from rural areas in southern Mexico characterized by conditions of chronic mild-to-moderate undernutrition is shown relative to values for well-nourished Mexican children in figure 23.2. Chronically undernourished children remain, on average, small. Their adolescent growth spurt is also delayed, on average, by more than 1 year compared with well-nourished children, and age at menarche is later in girls from the rural Mexican communities, about 14.5 years, which is almost 2 years later than median ages for better-nourished middle-class girls in several cities of Mexico, 12.5 to 12.7

Growth of Undernourished School Children

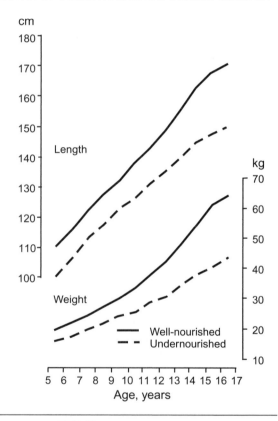

FIGURE 23.2 Mean heights and weights of well-nourished and mild-to-moderately undernourished Mexican school children. Data for well-nourished children in Mexico City are from Ramos Galvan (1975), and data for chronically undernourished school children from several communities in the Valley of Oaxaca surveyed in the 1970s are from Malina (1983). The graphs are drawn from data in the original reports.

Data from Ramos Galvan, 1975, and Malina, 1983.

years (Malina et al. 1977, 1980). Similar results are reported for rural areas in Africa with a pattern of chronic undernutrition (Benefice and Malina 1996; Simondon et al. 1997).

Longitudinal observations of undernourished school children over a 1-year period indicate growth rates in height that are only slightly less than well-nourished children, but the reduced growth rate is associated with a slower rate of growth in estimated leg length (height minus sitting height) and not in sitting height (Buschang and Malina 1983; Buschang et al. 1986). The small difference in growth rate suggests that the growth status of mild-to-moderately undernourished school age children is largely reflective of environmental insults associated with undernutrition during the preschool years. However, further growth stunting occurs during childhood and perhaps continues into adolescence, and this stunting is accounted for by diminished growth rates in leg length.

Stunted growth is associated with reduced muscle mass. In field studies of nutritional status, muscle mass is often estimated from measures of relaxed-arm circumference and the triceps skinfold (see chapter 3 for the measurement protocols). Both measurements are taken at the same level midway between the acromial and olecranon processes and are used to derive an estimate of midarm muscle circumference as follows:

$$C_m = C_a - \pi S_t$$

where C_m is the estimated midarm muscle circumference (cm), C_a is relaxed-arm circumference (cm), and S_t is the triceps skinfold (cm).

This procedure assumes that the arm is a circle and that subcutaneous adipose tissue is evenly distributed. It does not take into account the size of the humerus (see Malina 1995). Although the procedure has limitations, it is based on two readily accessible and relatively reliable measurements that are quite suitable for field surveys and are culturally acceptable in most communities.

The growth curve of estimated midarm muscle circumference in well-nourished and chronically undernourished Mexican children is shown in figure 23.3. The data are for the same children whose height and weight are illustrated in figure 23.2. Clearly, estimated muscle mass is reduced in undernourished children, and the reduction in muscle mass is proportional to their smaller body size.

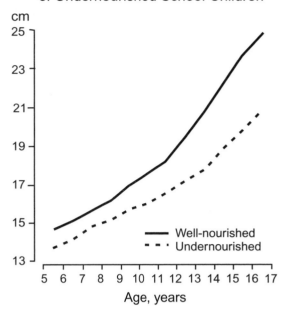

FIGURE 23.3 Mean estimated midarm muscle circumference of well-nourished and undernourished school children. Drawn from the data of Frisancho (1981) for well-nourished American children and of Malina (1983) for chronically undernourished Mexican school children (see figure 23.2).

Data from Frisancho, 1981, and Malina, 1983.

Performance

The small body size and reduced muscle mass associated with chronic, mild-to-moderate undernutrition are related to reduced levels of strength, motor performance, and maximal aerobic power in samples of school-age children in developing areas of the world. Lower absolute levels of performance are generally proportional to the reduced stature and body weight of children living under conditions of chronic, mild-to-moderate undernutrition. This finding is illustrated in table 23.3 for a sample of 9-year-old children resident in an agricultural community in southern Mexico. Compared with well-nourished children, the body size and performance of the rural children are considerably reduced (top part of the table). However, when performances are expressed per unit weight or height, the performances of the mild-to-moderately undernourished children are quite similar to those of the better-nourished children (lower part of the table). The undernourished children

TABLE 23.3   Mean Strength and Motor Performances of Chronically Mild-to-Moderately Undernourished and Well-Nourished 9-Year-Old Children

	Boys		Girls	
	Well-nourished	Undernourished	Well-nourished	Undernourished
Body size				
Height (cm)	135.3	120.3	133.8	120.4
Weight (kg)	31.4	23.2	30.7	22.5
Absolute levels of performance				
Grip strength (kg)	19.8	12.4	16.8	11.7
35-yard dash (s)	6.2	7.0	6.5	7.8
Standing long jump (cm)	139.4	112.9	124.0	97.5
Performances per unit body weight				
Grip (kg/kg)	0.6	0.5	0.5	0.5
Dash (s/kg)	0.2	0.3	0.2	0.3
Jump (cm/kg)	4.4	5.0	4.0	4.3
Performances per unit height				
Grip (kg/cm)	0.15	0.10	0.13	0.10
Dash (s/cm)	0.05	0.06	0.05	0.06
Jump (cm/cm)	1.03	0.94	0.93	0.81

The undernourished children are from rural Mexico and the well-nourished children are from Philadelphia. Data are based on data reported in Malina and Buschang (1985) and Malina and Roche (1983).

perform commensurately with their reduced body size.

Similar trends are apparent in maximal aerobic power. They are illustrated in figure 23.4 for undernourished urban boys from low socioeconomic background in Cali, Colombia (Spurr et al. 1983). Absolute $\dot{V}O_2$max (L/min) is reduced in undernourished compared with nutritionally normal boys from the same socioeconomic background and well-nourished boys of upper socioeconomic background (upper part of the figure). However, when $\dot{V}O_2$max is expressed per unit body weight (ml/kg/min), undernourished boys do not differ from the nutritionally normal and well-nourished boys (lower part of the figure). At most ages, maximal aerobic power per kilogram of body weight is higher in the undernourished boys.

Because the performances of school children living under conditions of mild-to-moderate undernutrition are often proportional to their reduced body size, they are sometimes described as "small but efficient." Note, however, their performances are, on average, absolutely less than those of well-nourished children. Moreover, the effect of small body size on performances of

school children varies among motor tasks and between populations (Malina et al. 1987). The same applies to adults who were raised under such impoverished health and nutritional conditions, leading an economist to propose the "small but healthy" hypothesis (Seckler 1980, see also Pelto and Pelto 1989). Under this hypothesis, the smallness (growth stunting) and reduced muscle mass are the primary adaptations to conditions of chronic undernutrition, and capacity for physical work is not impaired. This hypothesis is misleading because the conditions that produce chronic undernutrition (i.e., inadequate diet, poor home environments, and infectious and parasitic diseases) are themselves unhealthy (Martorell 1989). Stunted growth and reduced capacity for performance in a variety of tasks are the results of these impoverished and unhealthy conditions. Further, in the real world of children, adolescents, and adults, physical tasks and corresponding performances are not scaled for individual differences in body size.

A question of interest is the influence of variation in nutritional history on subsequent performance at school ages. This question was addressed in a sample of Senegalese children,

Aerobic Power of Undernourished and Well-Nourished Boys

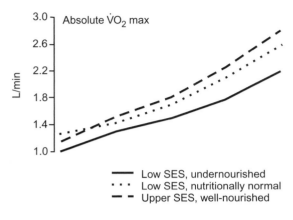

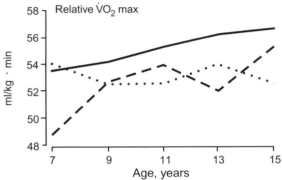

FIGURE 23.4   Absolute (L/min) and relative (ml/kg/min) aerobic power ($\dot{V}O_2$max) in undernourished and nutritionally normal Colombian boys from a low socioeconomic background and in well-nourished Colombian boys from a high socioeconomic background.

Data from Spurr et al., 1983.

on average, 5 and 6 years of age (Benefice and Malina 1996; Benefice et al. 1999). The children were divided into three groups on the basis of their nutritional history during early childhood: chronic mild-to-moderate undernutrition, hospitalized for severe undernutrition, and nutritionally normal from well-off circumstances. In general, the nutritionally normal group performed better on a variety of performance tasks than the two undernourished groups, who did not consistently differ from each other. When body size and arm circumference were statistically controlled, the differences among groups disappeared with the exception of several items related to balance and coordination. Reduced body size thus appears to be the primary determinant of reduced performances in primary school children with different nutritional histories. However, children with compromised nutritional histories during infancy and early childhood may have persistent difficulties with some tasks requiring balance and coordination.

A history of undernutrition during early childhood also influences aerobic performance in adolescence. This finding is shown in table 23.4 for a sample of male adolescents in India who were grouped on the basis of their nutritional status at 5 years of age (Satyanarayana et al. 1979). Height at 5 years of age expressed as deviations from the reference (degree of growth stunting) was used as the indicator of early nutritional status. Adolescent boys with a history of growth stunting had reduced PWC_{170} measured in absolute terms (kpm/min). PWC_{170} was especially reduced in severely stunted boys. However, when expressed relative to body size (kpm/kg/min), PWC_{170} did

TABLE 23.4   Early Nutritional Status, Body Size, and Aerobic Performance of Adolescent Boys 14 to 17 Years of Age in India

Nutritional status (height) at 5 years of age	Height (cm)	Weight (kg)	PWC_{170} (kpm/min)	PWC_{170} (kpm/kg/min)	Heart rate at 300 (kpm/min)
Normal nutrition (> –2 SD)	160.0	41.2	632	15.1	137
Undernutrition					
Mild (–2 SD to –3 SD)	150.4	35.3	555	15.5	146
Moderate (–3 to –4 SD)	147.4	34.3	533	15.4	148
Severe (> –4 SD)	138.3	27.7	357	12.7	163

PWC_{170} refers to power output at a heart rate of 170 beats per minute (see chapter 12). The boys were classified on the basis of their height at 5 years of age. Boys classified as nutritionally normal had a height that was within two SDs (standard deviations) of the reference for well-nourished Indian children. Boys classified as undernourished had heights more than two SDs below the reference and the greater the deviation from the reference, the greater the level of undernutrition or growth stunting.

Adapted from Satyanarayana et al. (1979).

not differ among adolescent boys with normal height and mild and moderate stunting at 5 years of age, whereas boys with severe growth stunting at 5 years of age had a markedly reduced PWC_{170} per unit body weight. The severely stunted boys also had a higher heart rate for the same work rate. Given the association between severe stunting and reduced muscle mass, the results suggest long-term consequences of compromised childhood nutritional status on aerobic fitness during adolescence, which probably persists into adulthood. This condition is of significance in areas of the world that depend on regular physical activity for economic subsistence. Physically smaller individuals produce less absolute work, which may influence income and, in turn, economic conditions of the family.

A related issue is the potential role of improved nutrition during infancy and early childhood in populations nutritionally at risk on later physical working capacity. This circumstance was addressed in adolescents in four rural Guatemalan communities (Haas et al. 1995). A nutritional supplement containing protein and energy (called **atole**) was made available in two of the communities, and a supplement containing only energy (called **fresco**) was made available in the other two communities. Participation in the supplementation program was voluntary. Records of the precise amount of the supplements consumed between birth and 7 years of age (1969–1977) were kept. Samples of the children followed during infancy and childhood were subsequently studied in adolescence at 14 to 18 years of age. The maximum aerobic power of the Guatemalan adolescents grouped by supplementation status during infancy and childhood is summarized in table 23.5. Boys who received the atole had absolutely and relatively greater $\dot{V}O_2max$ than boys who received fresco. Corresponding comparisons of adolescent girls who received the different supplements during infancy and childhood indicated smaller differences in absolute and relative $\dot{V}O_2max$ that were in the same direction as those observed in boys.

The data summarized in the preceding section indicate reduced absolute levels of strength, motor performance, physical working capacity, and maximal oxygen uptake in chronically undernourished children of school age compared with better-nourished children. The absolute differences emphasize the deficit in body size and specifically muscle mass associated with chronic undernutrition. The amount of muscle mass available to perform or do work is a significant factor affecting performances of undernourished children in a variety of tasks. On the other hand, improved nutritional conditions early in life in communities with a poor nutritional history may favorably impact performance in adolescence.

Physical Activity

School-age children of marginal-to-poor nutritional status show decreased total daily energy expenditure and energy expended in physical activity because of their smaller body size. Reduced activity may limit practice of motor skills in play and games and, in turn, contribute to performance deficiencies. In addition, quasiexperimental observations in Colombia suggest that mild-to-moderately undernourished boys differ

TABLE 23.5 Maximal Aerobic Power ($\dot{V}O_2max$) of Guatemalan Adolescents 14 to 18 Years of Age by Supplementation Status During Infancy and Childhood

| Supplement | Maximal aerobic power ($\dot{V}O_2max$) | | | | | |
| | L/min | | ml/kg/min (weight) | | ml/kg/min (FFM) | |
	Mean	SD	Mean	SD	Mean	SD
Males						
Atole	2.62	0.54	54.4	6.4	65.5	7.1
Fresco	2.24	0.54	48.6	6.5	59.2	7.2
Females						
Atole	1.74	0.26	36.6	4.0	47.3	4.7
Fresco	1.65	0.31	34.5	4.5	45.3	5.8

FFM refers to fat-free mass.

Adapted from Haas et al. (1995).

from nutritionally normal boys in their capacity to increase energy expenditure in physical activity when given the opportunity to participate in a sport program (Spurr 1990). The undernourished boys simply could not keep up with the better-nourished boys during sport activities.

In addition to nutritional status, infectious load associated with intestinal parasites may influence physical activity and fitness of children. Treatment of undernourished school-age Kenyan children for hookworm, whipworm (trichuris), and roundworm (ascaris), for example, was associated with increased levels of spontaneous physical activity, improved cardiovascular fitness (step test), and improved growth and appetite (Stephenson et al. 1994; Adams et al. 1994). Similarly, treatment of undernourished school-age children for schistosomiasis was also associated with improved step-test performance (Stephenson et al. 1985). A related factor is illness, and during periods of illness, children tend to be less active. What is the potential effect of chronic illness on activity? Among mild-to-moderately undernourished school-age Kenyan children, moderate physical activity on the playground was negatively correlated with the frequency of mild illness, especially respiratory and gastrointestinal illness. On the other hand, light activity on the playground was positively correlated with the frequency of illness (Neumann et al. 1992).

Available evidence indicates a reduction in total energy expenditure and energy expenditure in physical activity associated with a history of chronic mild-to-moderate undernutrition in school-age children. To date, however, more interest has been shown in the quantification of energy expenditure of school children living under marginal nutritional circumstances than on the quality of physical activity and movement experiences relevant to the development of proficiency of motor skills.

Long-Term Consequences of Undernutrition

The preceding discussions of childhood and adolescent undernutrition focused on consequences for growth, maturation, performance, and physical activity. A history of chronic undernutrition in the early years of life also has implications or, more specifically, consequences for adult health.

Individuals who survive an infancy and childhood characterized by chronic undernutrition and associated environmental conditions attain shorter heights as adults (i.e., they are also stunted). Short stature in women is associated with poor reproductive health and outcomes. Short maternal height is a risk factor for increased infant mortality. Studies in Guatemala, for example, indicate an inverse relationship between maternal height and infant mortality. Short maternal height (126.3 to 140.2 cm) was associated with the highest infant mortality (205 per 1,000 live born). Corresponding infant mortalities for Guatemalan women of medium (140.3 to 144.7 cm) and tall (144.8 to 158.6 cm) heights were 150 and 101 per 1,000 live born, respectively (Martorell et al. 1981). Short maternal height is also a risk factor for low birth weight, which is related to infant mortality (see table 23.5). Consequence of low birth weight for adult health should also be considered in the context of the fetal origins of adult disease hypothesis (see chapter 2).

Small body size in adults is also associated with reduced physical working capacity. Among adults with a history of chronic undernutrition during childhood, productivity under conditions of moderate and hard work is related to body size, and the evidence clearly indicates that bigger is better (Spurr 1988, 1990; Martorell and Arroyave 1988). In many areas of the developing world, the small body size of adults has a negative impact on the productivity of workers and the economic well-being of their families and, in turn, on the nutritional status of their children.

Some evidence suggests that adults with a history of growth stunting tend to accumulate proportionally more subcutaneous adipose tissue on the trunk compared with the extremities (Schroeder et al. 1999). A central pattern of fat distribution, or abdominal fatness, is an independent risk factor for cardiovascular disease and adult onset diabetes (see chapter 24). Further, increasing numbers of adults in developing areas of the world show an elevated BMI, suggesting an increased prevalence of overweight and obesity (Martorell et al. 1998; World Health Organization 1998).

The results thus indicate a striking contrast—the concurrent occurrence of chronic undernutrition in preschool children and increased prevalence of overweight, obesity, and chronic diseases in adults. Current estimates of overweight in school children in developing countries suggest that the problem may become apparent at these ages. The prevalence of overweight and wasting among preschool children in specific countries within Africa, Asia, and Latin America and the Caribbean is summarized in chapter 24. Overweight and wasting represent the extremes of weight-for-height relationships, and both are common among preschool children in many developing countries. This finding suggests an epidemiological paradox—persistent undernutrition (wasting) in the presence of increasing overweight as countries go through an economic and nutrition transition (Popkin et al. 1996). Issues related to overweight and obesity are discussed in more detail in chapter 24.

Summary

Undernutrition is a heterogeneous state that is routinely defined in terms of weight-for-age, length/height-for-age, and weight-for-height relative to an international reference for healthy, adequately nourished children. Chronic undernutrition during infancy and early childhood is associated with compromised growth, delayed motor development, and reduced physical activity. These insults early in life have long-term consequences that may persist into adulthood. Children and adolescents who were undernourished early in life are smaller, have reduced fat-free and muscle mass, and are deficient in strength, motor performance, and aerobic power compared with healthy, adequately nourished age and sex peers. Some evidence also indicates a reduction in total energy expenditure and energy expenditure in physical activity associated with a history of chronic mild-to-moderate undernutrition in school-age children.

Sources and Suggested Readings

Adams EL, Stephenson LS, Latham MC, Kinoti SN (1994) Physical activity and growth of Kenyan school children with hookworm, *Trichuris trichiura* and *Ascaris lumbricoides* infections are improved after treatment with albendazole. Journal of Nutrition 124:1199-1206.

Akesode EA, Ahbode HA (1983) Prevalence of obesity among Nigerian school children. Social Science in Medicine 17: 107-111.

Benefice E, Cames C (1999) Physical activity patterns of rural Senegalese adolescent girls during the dry and rainy seasons measured by movement registration and direct observation methods. European Journal of Clinical Nutrition 53:636-643.

Benefice E, Fouere R, Malina RM (1999) Early nutritional history and motor performance of Senegalese children 4–6 years of age. Annals of Human Biology 26:443-455.

Benefice E, Garnier D, Ndiaye G (2001) High levels of habitual physical activity in West African adolescent girls and relationship to maturation, growth and nutritional status: Results from a 3-year prospective study. American Journal of Human Biology 13:808-820.

Benefice E, Malina RM (1996) Body size, body composition and motor performances of mild-to-moderately undernourished Senegalese. Annals of Human Biology 23:307-321.

Buschang PH, Malina RM (1983) Growth in height and weight of mild-to-moderately undernourished Zapotec school children. Human Biology 55:587-597.

Buschang PH, Malina RM, Little BB (1986) Linear growth of Zapotec schoolchildren: Growth status and yearly velocity for leg length and sitting height. Annals of Human Biology 13:225-234.

Chavez A, Martinez C (1975) Nutrition and development of children from poor rural areas. V. Nutrition and behavioral development. Nutrition Reports International 11: 477-489.

Chavez A, Martinez C (1984) Behavioral measurements of activity in children and their relation to food intake in a poor community. In E Pollitt, P Amante (eds), Energy Intake and Activity. New York: Alan R Liss, pp 303-321.

Chavez A, Martinez C, Yaschine T (1975) Nurtition, behavioral development, and mother-child interaction in young rural children. Federation Proceedings 34:1574-1582.

Coward WA, Lunn PG (1981) The biochemistry and physiology of kwashiorkor and marasmus. British Medical Bulletin 37: 19-24.

* Cravioto J (1980) Severe malnutrition and development of motor skills in children. Annales Nestle 44:22-41.

Cravioto J, Arrieta R (1986) Nutrition, mental development, and learning. In F Falkner, JM Tanner (eds), Human Growth: A Comprehensive Treatise, Volume 3: Methodology; Ecological, Genetic, and Nutritional Effects on Growth, 2nd edition. New York: Plenum, pp 501-536.

* Dobbing J (1990) Early nutrition and later achievement. Proceedings of the Nutrition Society 49:103-118.

Eveleth PB, Tanner JM (1990) Worldwide Variation in Human Growth, 2nd edition. Cambridge: Cambridge University Press.

Fellmann N, Coudert J (1998) Malnutrition and anaerobic performance in children. In E Van Praagh (ed), Pediatric Anaerobic Performance. Champaign, IL: Human Kinetics, pp 319-335.

Frisancho AR (1981) New norms of upper limb fat and muscle areas for assessment of nutritional status. American Journal of Clinical Nutrition 34:2540-2545.

Gupta MC, Urrutia JJ (1982) Efecto del tratamiento quimioterapeutico periodico de parasitos intestinales en el crecimiento de ninos preescolares. Archivos Latinoamericanos de Nutricion 32:825-849.

* Haas JD, Martinez EJ, Murdoch S, Conslik E, Rivera JA, Martorell R (1995) Nutritional supplementation during the preschool years and physical work capacity in adolescent and young adult Guatemalans. Journal of Nutrition 125 (suppl):1078S-1089S.

Habicht J-P, Martorell R, Yarbrough C, Malina RM, Klein RE (1974) Height and weight standards for preschool children: How relevant are ethnic differences in growth potential? Lancet 1:611-615.

Hamill PVV, Drizd TA, Johnson CL, Reed RD, Roche AF (1977) NCHS growth curves for children, birth–18 years. United States. DHEW Publication No. (PHS) 78-1650. Washington, DC: US Government Printing Office.

Hernandez-Beltran M, Butte N, Villalpando S, Flores-Huerta S, Smith OE (1996) Early growth faltering of rural Meso-amerindian breast-fed infants. Annals of Human Biology 3:223-235.

Hlaing T (1993) Ascariasis and childhood malnutrition. Parasitology 107:S125-S136.

Jackson AA, Golden MHN (1986) Protein energy malnutrition: Kwashiorkor and marasmic kwashiorkor. Part I. Physiopathology. In O Brunser, F Carrazza, M Gracey, B Nichols, J Senterre (eds), Clinical Nutrition of the Young Child. New York: Raven Press, pp 133-142.

Jelliffe DB (1966) The Assessment of the Nutritional Status of the Community. Geneva: World Health Organization, Monograph Series No. 53.

Liederman PH, Tulkin SR, Rosenfield A, editors (1977) Culture and Infancy: Variations in the Human Experience. New York: Academic Press.

Malina RM (1983) Growth and maturity profile of primary school children in the Valley of Oaxaca, Mexico. Garcia de Orta, Series Antropobiologia (Lisbon) 2:153-158.

* Malina RM (1984) Physical activity and motor development/ performance in populations nutritionally at risk. In E Pollitt, P Amante (eds), Energy Intake and Activity. New York: Alan R. Liss, pp 285-302.

Malina RM (1985) Growth and physical performance of Latin American children and youth: Socioeconomic and nutritional contrasts. Collegium Antropologicum 9:9-31.

Malina RM (1994) Anthropometry, strength and motor fitness. In SJ Ulijaszek, CGN Mascie-Taylor (eds), Anthropometry: The Individual and the Population. Cambridge, UK: Cambridge University Press, pp 160-177.

Malina RM (1995) Anthropometry. In PJ Maud, C Foster (eds), Physiological Assessment of Human Fitness. Champaign, IL: Human Kinetics, pp 205-219.

Malina RM, Buschang PH (1985) Growth, strength and motor performance of Zapotec children, Oaxaca, Mexico. Human Biology 57:163-181.

Malina RM, Chumlea WC, Stepick CD, Gutierez Lopez F (1977) Age at menarche in Oaxaca, Mexico, schoolgirls, with comparative data for other areas of Mexico. Annals of Human Biology 4:551-558.

Malina RM, Himes JM, Stepick CD, Gutierez Lopez F, Buschang PH (1980) Growth of rural and urban children in the Valley of Oaxaca, Mexico. American Journal of Physical Anthropology 55:269-280.

Malina RM, Katzmarzyk PT, Siegel SR (1998) Overnutrition, undernutrition and the body mass index: Implications for strength and motor fitness. In J Parizkova, AP Hills (eds), Physical Fitness and Nutrition during Growth. Basel: S Karger, pp 13-26.

Malina RM, Little BB, Shoup RF, Buschang PH (1987) Adaptive significance of small body size: Strength and motor performance of school children in Mexico and Papua New Guinea. American Journal of Physical Anthropology 73:489-499.

Malina RM, Roche AF (1983) Manual of Physical Status and Performance in Childhood. Volume 2. Physical Performance. New York: Plenum.

Malina RM, Selby HA, Aronson WL, Buschang PH, Chumlea WC (1980) Re-examination of the age at menarche in Oaxaca, Mexico. Annals of Human Biology 7:281-282.

Martorell R (1989) Body size, adaptation and function. Human Organization 48:15-20.

Martorell R, Arroyave G (1988) Malnutrition, work output and energy needs. In KJ Collins, DF Roberts (eds), Capacity for Work in the Tropics. Cambridge, UK: Cambridge University Press, pp 57-75.

Martorell R, Delgado HL, Valverde V, Klein RE (1981) Maternal stature, fertility, and infant mortality. Human Biology 53: 303-312.

Martorell R, Gonzalez-Cossio T (1987) Maternal nutrition and birth weight. Yearbook of Physical Anthropology 30: 195-220.

Martorell R, Khan LK, Hughes ML, Grummer-Strawn LM (1998) Obesity in Latin American women and children. Journal of Nutrition 128:1464-1473.

Martorell R, Yarbrough C, Lechtig A, Habicht J-P, Klein RE (1975) Diarrheal disease and growth retardation in preschool Guatemalan children. American Journal of Physical Anthropology 43:341-346.

* Mata LJ (1978) The Children of Santa Maria Cauque: A Prospective Field Study of Health and Growth. Cambridge, MA: MIT Press.

Monckeberg F (1985) Protein energy malnutrition: Marasmus. In O Brunser, F Carrazza, M Gracey, B Nichols, J Senterre (eds), Clinical Nutrition of the Young Child. New York: Raven Press, pp 121-132.

Neumann C, McDonald MA, Sigman, M, Bwibo N (1992) Medical illness in school age Kenyans in relation to nutrition, cognition, and playground behaviors. Developmental and Behavioral Pediatrics 13:392-398.

Nugent JK, Lester BM, Brazelton TB, editors (1989) The Cultural Context of Infancy. Volume 1. Biology, Culture, and Infant Development. Norwood, NJ: Ablex Publishing Corporation.

* de Onis M, Blossner M (1997) WHO Global Database on Child Growth and Malnutrition. Geneva: World Health Organization, WHO/NUT/77.4.

Pelto GH, Pelto PJ (1989) Small but healthy? An anthropological perspective. Human Organization 48:11-15.

Pereira SM (1986) Protein energy malnutrition: Kwashiorkor and marasmic kwashiorkor. Part II. Clinical aspects and treatment. In O Brunser, F Carrazza, M Gracey, B Nichols, J Senterre (eds), Clinical Nutrition of the Young Child. New York: Raven Press, pp 143-149.

Pollitt E (1987) A critical review of three decades of research on the effects of chronic energy malnutrition on behavioral development. In B Schurch, NS Scrimshaw (eds), Chronic Energy Deficiency: Consequences and Related Issues. Lausanne, Switzerland: International Dietary Energy Consultancy Group/Nestles Foundation, pp. 77-93.

* Pollitt E, (ed) (1995) Undernutrition and behavioral development in children. Journal of Nutrition 125 (suppl): 2211S-2284S.

* Pollitt E (1996) A reconceptualization of the effects of undernutrition on children's biological, psychosocial, and behavioral development. Social Policy Report, Society for Research in Child Development 10, no. 5.

Popkin BM, Richards MK, Monteiro CA (1996) Stunting is associated with overweight in children of four nations that are undergoing the nutrition transition. Journal of Nutrition 126:3009-3016.

Ramos Galvan R (1975) Somatometria pediatrica estudio semilongitudinal en ninos de la ciudad de Mexico. Archivos de Investigacion Medica 6 (suppl 1) pp 1-396.

Rivera J, Martorell R (1988) Nutrition, infection, and growth. Part I: Effects of infection on growth. Clinical Nutrition 7: 156-162.

Rivera J, Martorell R (1988) Nutrition, infection, and growth. Part II: Effects of malnutrition on infection and general conclusions. Clinical Nutrition 7:163-167.

Roche AF, Malina RM (1983) Manual of Physical Status and Performance in Childhood. Volume 1. Physical Status. New York: Plenum.

Rona RJ, Wainwright AH, Altman DG, Irwig LM, Florey C du V (1979) Surveillance of growth as a measurement of health in the community. In WW Holland, J Ipsen, J Kostrzewski (eds), Measurment of Levels of Health. Copenhagen: World Health Organization, Regional Office for Europe, pp 397-404.

Sachs JD, Mellinger AD, Gallup JL (2001) Geography of poverty and wealth. Scientific American 285:70-75 (Mar).

Satyanarayana K, Naidu AN, Rao BSN (1979) Nutritional deprivation in childhood and the body size, activity, and physical work capacity of young boys. American Journal of Clinical Nutrition 32:1769-1775.

Scholl TO (1975) Body size in developing nations: Is bigger really better? Philadelphia: Temple University, Doctoral Dissertation.

SchroederDG, Martorell R, Flores R (1999) Infant and child growth and fatness and fat distribution in Guatemalan adults. American Journal of Epidemiology 149:177-185.

Seckler D (1980) "Malnutrition": An intellectual odyssey. Western Journal of Agricultural Economics 5:219-227.

Shephard RJ (1978) Human Physiological Work Capacity. Cambridge, UK: Cambridge University Press.

Simondon KB, Simon I, Simondon F (1997) Nutritional status and age at menarche of Senegalese adolescents. Annals of Human Biology 24:521-532.

* Spurr GB (1983) Nutritional status and physical work capacity. Yearbook of Physical Anthropology 26:1-35.

* Spurr GB (1988) Body size, physical work capacity, and productivity in hard work: Is bigger better? In JC Waterlow (ed), Linear Growth Retardation in Less Developed Countries. New York: Raven Press, pp 215-239.

Spurr GB (1990) Physical activity and energy expenditure in undernutrition. Progress in Food and Nutrition Science 14:139-192.

Spurr GB, Reina JC, Dahners HW, Barac-Nieto M (1983) Marginal malnutrition in school-aged Colombian boys: Functional consequences in maximum exercise. American Journal of Clinical Nutrition 37:834-847.

Stephenson L (1993) The impact of schistosomiasis on human nutrition. Parasitology 107:S107-S123.

Stephenson LS, Latham MC, Adams EJ, Kinoti SN, Perter A (1994) Physical fitness, growth and appetite of Kenyan school boys with hookworm, Trichuris trichiura and Ascaris lumbricoides infections are improved four months after a single does of albendazole. Journal of Nutrition 123: 1036-1046.

Stephenson LS, Latham MC, Kurz KM, Miller D, Kinoti SN, Odouri ML (1985) Urinary iron loss and physical fitness of Kenyan children with urinary schistosomiasis. American Journal of Tropical Medicine and Hygiene 34:322-330.

Torun B, Viteri FE (1994) Influence of exercise on linear growth. European Journal of Clinical Nutrition 48 (suppl): S186-S189.

Viteri FE, Torun B (1981) Nutrition, physical activity and growth. In M Ritzen, A Aperia, K Hall, A Larsson, A Zetterberg, R Zetterstrom (eds), The Biology of Normal Human Growth. New York: Raven, pp 265-273.

Waterlow JS (1993) Reflections on stunting. In C Gopalan (ed), Recent Trends in Nutrition. Delhi: Oxford University Press, pp 18-34.

Waterlow JC, Buzina R, Keller W, Lanes JM, Nichaman MZ,

Tanner JM (1977) The presentation and use of height and weight data for comparing the nutritional status of children under the age of 10 years. Bulletin of the World Health Organization 55:489-498.

World Health Organization (1995) Physical Status: The Use and Interpretation of Anthropometry. Geneva: World Health Organization Technical Report Series No. 854.

World Health Organization (1998) Obesity: Preventing and Managing the Global Epidemic. Report of a WHO Consultation on Obesity. Geneva: World Health Organization.

OBESITY IN CHILDHOOD AND ADOLESCENCE

Chapter Outline

The nutritional status of individuals and populations spans a broad range from the extremes of undernutrition to overnutrition. The energy and nutrient needs associated with normal growth, maturation, and function were considered in chapter 20, and issues related to physical activity and energy expenditure were considered in chapters 21 and 22. This chapter focuses on obesity. First, basic concepts, correlates, criteria, and prevalence of overweight and obesity are specified, and then implications for growth, maturation, performance, physical activity, and self-concept are discussed.

The terms overweight and obesity are often used interchangeably, but they are not synonymous. Overweight is characterized by a moderate degree of excess weight-for-height, whereas obesity is a more severe state. The subsequent discussion of prevalence indicates the specific criteria used and the terminology of the authors of the individual studies cited.

Overweight and obesity are occasionally referred to as a state of overnutrition, but the term overnutrition is misleading. Overweight and obesity occur as a result of an imbalance between energy intake and energy expenditure in which intake exceeds expenditure; physical inactivity is an essential component of the equation. In general, overweight is more likely to result from behavioral factors such as dietary practices and lack of physical activity, whereas obesity typically has a stronger behavioral and metabolic and possibly genetic etiology (Bouchard 2000b). Overweight and obesity may occur in early childhood, but their prevalence is more common during childhood, adolescence, and adulthood. They have associated functional consequences and long-term health implications.

Indicators

Weight and length/height are used to define criteria for overweight and obesity. Methods for measuring weight, length, and height and reference data for evaluating body size were discussed in chapter 3. Weight and height are used in the form of weight-for-height, particularly during infancy and early childhood and as the body mass index (BMI [wt/ht²]), in older children, adolescents, and adults.

Criteria and Prevalence

During infancy and early childhood, weight-for-height (length in children between birth and 2 or 3 years of age) is used to define overweight. Children younger than 5 years of age (i.e., birth to 4.99 years) who have a weight-for-length or weight-for-height more than two standard deviations above international reference medians (Hamill et al. 1977) are classified as overweight (World Health Organization 1995; de Onis and Blossner 1997, 2000). No consistent differences are present in estimated prevalence rates for boys and girls. Overweight among children younger than five years of age is not a significant problem in developing countries of the world, with estimated prevalences of 2% and 3% in the least-developed and other developing countries, respectively. Prevalences of overweight among children younger than 5 years of age vary among geographic areas (see table 24.1) and range from about 5% in Latin America and the Caribbean to 3% in Africa and 2% in Southeast Asia.

Although the estimated prevalences of overweight by World Health Organization geo-graphic regions are low, variation exists among and within countries. Better-developed countries within a geographic region and more affluent sectors of society within a country have a higher prevalence of overweight. The prevalence of overweight among preschool children (birth to 5 years of age) in specific countries within Africa, Asia, and Latin America and the Caribbean are illustrated in figure 24.1. The prevalence of wasting (weight-for-height more than two standard deviations below the international reference, see chapter 23) within each country is also indicated for comparison because both represent the extremes of weight-for-height relationships. In general, as the prevalence of overweight increases, the prevalence of wasting within a country decreases. However, both overweight and wasting of preschool children are common in many countries. This dichotomy suggests an epidemiological paradox—persistent undernutrition (wasting) in the presence of increasing overweight as countries go through an economic and nutrition transition (Popkin et al. 1996).

National survey data that span several years are available for 36 countries (Africa, 16 countries; Latin America and the Caribbean, 13 countries, and Asia, 7 countries) in the World Health Organization global data base on child growth and nutrition. Comparisons across time are possible, from approximately the 1980s through the mid-1990s. A trend towards an increasing prevalence of overweight (defined as an increase ≥ 0.1 percentage points per year) is evident in 14 countries. Countries showing an increasing trend are located in Latin America and the Caribbean and Africa. No trend exists (< 0.1 to > -0.1 percentage points per year) in 14 countries and a declining trend (≤ -0.1 percentage points per year) in eight countries. Countries in the three geographic regions (Africa, Asia, and Latin America and the Caribbean) are included among those with no trend or a declining trend in the prevalence of overweight (de Onis and Blossner 2000).

Weight-for-height has also been used as the indicator for overweight in United States surveys of preschool children, who are defined as children younger than 6 years of age (Ogden et al. 1997, 2002). The age span is thus birth through 71 months (in contrast to the World Health Organization data, which refer to children from birth through 59 months). A weight-for-height above the 95th percentile of the United States growth reference in the 1970s (Hamill et al. 1977) is defined as overweight. These are the reference values for American children that are also used by the

	Overweight	
Region	**%**	**n**
Africa	2.8	2.9
Americas	4.8	3.6
Eastern Mediterranean	4.2	2.9
Southeast Asia	1.7	2.8
Western Pacific	3.8	5.3

TABLE 24.1 Estimated Prevalence (%) and Numbers in Millions (n) of Children Under 5 Years of Age in Different Regions of the World Classified As Overweight in 1995

Regions are as defined by the World Health Organization. Overweight is defined as weight-for-height more than two standard deviations above age-specific and sex-specific reference values (Hamill et al. 1977; see text for details).

Adapted from the World Health Organization (1997).

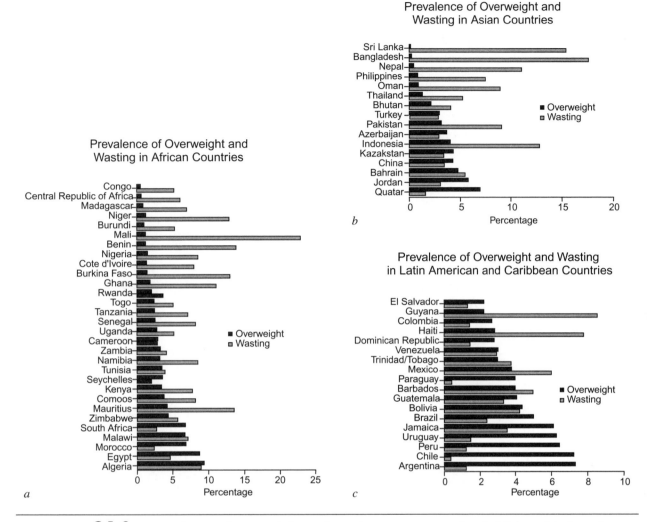

FIGURE 24.1   Prevalence of overweight and wasting among preschool children (birth to 5 years of age) in three geographic regions of the world in 1995: (*a*) Africa, (*b*) Asia, and (*c*) Latin America and the Caribbean. Geographic regions are as defined by the United Nations. See text for the criteria of overweight and wasting.

Data from de Onis and Blossner, 1997.

World Health Organization. As noted earlier, the growth charts from the 1970s have been updated (Kuczmarski et al. 2000; see chapter 3). The earlier reference values provide a baseline for estimating changes in the prevalence of overweight in American preschool children. The prevalence of overweight in nationally representative samples of American preschool children in 1988 to 1994, using weight-for-height above the 95th percentile as the criterion, is 2.1% and 4.8% in 2-year-old and 3-year-old boys and girls, respectively, and 5.0% and 10.8% in 4-year-old and 5-year-old boys and girls, respectively (Ogden et al. 1997). The fact that the prevalence of overweight is twice as prevalent among 4-year-old and 5-year-old chil-

dren compared with 2-year-old and 3-year-old children indicates the early origins of the problem in the American population.

More recently, the BMI has been used to define overweight and obesity in American children 2 years of age and older. In the recent national survey of American children and adolescents 2 to 19 years of age (NHANES 1999–2000), a BMI between the 85th and 95th percentiles was defined as "at risk of overweight" and a BMI at or above the 95th percentile was defined as "overweight" (Ogden et al. 2002). The prevalence of overweight in this nationally representative sample of American children and adolescents in 1999 to 2000 is summarized in table 24.2. Statistically, 5% of the population is expected to be at or above the 95th percentile. However, about 10% of 2-year-old to 5-year-old children and 15% of 6-year-old to 19-year-old children and adolescents have BMIs at or above the 95th percentiles of the United States growth charts. Ethnic variation in the prevalence of overweight exists among American children and adolescents, which is discussed in chapter 25. The prevalence of the risk of overweight and overweight is also increasing in children and adolescents in many developing countries (Akesode and Ahbode 1983; Malina 1995; Cameron and Getz 1997; Martorell et al. 1998; Peña Reyes et al. 2002).

TABLE 24.2 Estimated Prevalence (%) and Standard Errors (SE) of Overweight Among American Children and Adolescents 2 to 19 Years of Age in 1999 to 2000

Age group (yr)	Males %	SE	Females %	SE
2–5	9.9	2.2	11.0	2.5
6–11	16.0	2.3	14.5	2.5
12–19	15.5	1.6	15.5	1.6

Overweight is defined as a BMI-for-age and sex at or above the 95th percentile of the 2000 Centers for Disease Control and Prevention growth charts (see chapter 3).
Adapted from Ogden et al. (2002).

Although the BMI has limitations as an indicator of fatness (see chapter 3), it is regularly used in public health and nutritional surveys to monitor the prevalence of overweight/obesity in children, adolescents, and adults throughout the world. However, cutoff points of the BMI and reference data used to define individuals as overweight and obese often vary among studies. Therefore, consensus about criteria or cutoff points to estimate prevalences across populations is necessary. The World Health Organization (1998) developed a classification for utilizing the BMI in international surveys of adults. The recommended criteria for overweight and obesity and for degrees of obesity in adults are summarized in table 24.3. The range of the BMI for normal weight and underweight are also indicated.

The prevalence of excess weight, or elevated BMIs, among adults has increased dramatically in developed countries of the world and also in

TABLE 24.3 Criteria for the Classification of Overweight and Obesity in Adults Based on the Body Mass Index (BMI)

Classification	BMI (kg/m²)	Obesity class
Underweight	<18.5	
Normal weight	18.5–24.9	
Overweight	25.0–29.9	
Obese	30.0–34.9	I
	35.0–39.9	II
	≥40.0	III

Adapted from the World Health Organization (1998).

the upper classes of developing countries. The increasing prevalence of overweight and obesity among adults in the face of persistent chronic undernutrition in many developing countries (see chapter 23) presents an epidemiological paradox (World Health Organization 1998; British Nutrition Foundation 1999).

The striking trend for the increased prevalence of obesity among adults is shown in figure 24.2, which illustrates the prevalence of obesity (using the recommendation of the World Health Organization, BMI ≥ 30.0 kg/m²) among American adults of both sexes in each state for 2 years, 1991 and 2000. Whereas no state had a prevalence of obesity of more than 20% in 1991, 10 years later, 23 states had a prevalence of obesity among adults of 20% and more (Mokdad et al. 2001). These data are derived from the Behavioral Risk Factor Surveillance System (BRFSS), which is a cross-sectional survey conducted by the Centers for Disease Control and Prevention with the support of the state health departments. Similar temporal trends are evident in the Canadian adults (Katzmarzyk 2002a, 2002b). Such data have major implications for children and adolescents because the prevalence of obesity is also increasing at these young ages.

More recently, an international reference for the definition of overweight and obesity during childhood and adolescence has been developed as an extension of the criteria indicated for adults. Age-specific and sex-specific cutoff points for overweight and obesity were developed from pooled data from six nationally representative cross-sectional growth surveys—Brazil, Great Britain, Hong Kong, the Netherlands, Singapore, and the United States (excluding the more

Prevalence of Obesity Among U.S. Adults, 1991

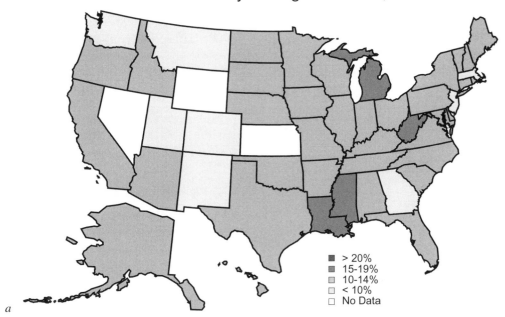

a

Prevalence of Obesity Among U.S. Adults, 2000

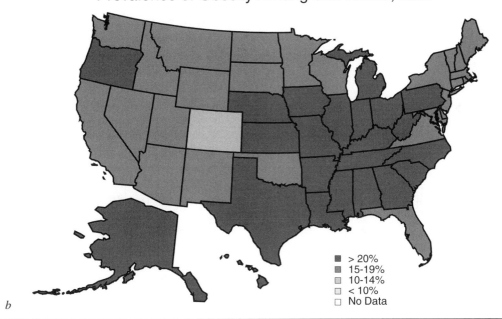

b

FIGURE 24.2   Prevalence of obesity among adults from the 50 states of the United States in 1991 (*a*) and 2000 (*b*) based on data from the Behavioral Risk Factor Surveillance System. Obesity is defined as a BMI ≥ 30 kg/m².

Adapted from A.H. Mokdad et al., 2001, "The continuing epidemics of obesity and diabetes in the United States," *Journal of the American Medical Association* 286(10):1195-1200.

recent health survey between 1988 and 1994, NHANES III). Based on the criteria for adults, a BMI of 25 kg/m² at 18 years of age was considered overweight and a BMI of 30 kg/m² at 18 years of age was considered obese (see table 24.3). In

establishing the cutoff points for overweight and obesity in children and adolescents, curves were mathematically fit to the pooled BMI data from 2 years of age on, so that they passed through a BMI of 25 kg/m² and 30 kg/m² at 18 years of age

TABLE 24.4	Recommended Cutoff Points for the Body Mass Index (BMI) As an Indicator of Overweight and Obesity in Males and Females 2 to 18 Years of Age			
	Overweight		**Obese**	
Age (yr)	**Males**	**Females**	**Males**	**Females**
2	18.41	18.02	20.09	19.81
2.5	18.13	17.76	19.80	19.55
3	17.89	17.56	19.57	19.36
3.5	17.69	17.40	19.39	19.23
4	17.55	17.28	19.29	19.15
4.5	17.47	17.19	19.26	19.12
5	17.42	17.15	19.30	19.17
5.5	17.45	17.20	19.47	19.34
6	17.55	17.34	19.78	19.65
6.5	17.71	17.53	20.23	20.08
7	17.92	17.75	20.63	20.51
7.5	18.16	18.03	21.09	21.01
8	18.44	18.35	21.60	21.57
8.5	18.76	18.69	22.17	22.18
9	19.10	19.07	22.77	22.81
9.5	19.46	19.45	23.39	23.46
10	19.84	19.86	24.00	24.11
10.5	20.20	20.29	24.57	24.77
11	20.55	20.74	25.10	25.42
11.5	20.89	21.20	25.58	26.05
12	21.22	21.68	26.02	26.67
12.5	21.56	22.14	26.43	27.24
13	21.91	22.58	26.84	27.76
13.5	22.27	22.98	27.25	28.20
14	22.62	23.34	27.63	28.57
14.5	22.96	23.66	27.98	28.87
15	23.29	23.94	28.30	29.11
15.5	23.60	24.17	28.60	29.29
16	23.90	24.37	28.88	29.43
16.5	24.19	24.54	29.14	29.56
17	24.46	24.70	29.41	29.69
17.5	24.73	24.85	29.70	29.84
18	25.00	25.00	30.00	30.00

Adapted from Cole et al. (2000). The data are based on six nationally representative cross-sectional samples from Brazil, Great Britain, Hong Kong, the Netherlands, Singapore, and the United States.

(retrofitting). The values at each half year from 2 to 18 years of age are the respective cutoff points for overweight and obesity (Cole et al. 2000). These internationally recommended age-specific and sex-specific cutoff points of the BMI between 2 and 18 years of age are shown in table 24.4. Estimates of the prevalence of overweight and obesity using these criteria with different populations of children and adolescents are not yet available, but the criteria promise to be useful for international comparisons.

Correlates of Overweight and Obesity

The etiology of overweight and obesity includes a variety of correlates associated with the individual (age, sex), family, behavior, and metabolism, including endocrine and neuroendocrine variability (Bouchard 2000b; York and Bouchard 2000). Correlates of overweight and obesity in each of these categories are summarized in table 24.5. Complex interactions among the correlates are important and add to the difficulty in specifying causes of overweight/obesity. Genotype is an additional factor. The involvement of a specific gene in the etiology of obesity, that is, a deficiency in a single gene (DNA sequence variation), is rare. On the other hand, genes that may predispose an individual to obesity have been identified (Perusse et al. 2001; Bouchard 2002; Leibel 2002). These genes probably operate through interactions with specific factors in the environment (i.e., genotype-environment interactions [see chapter 18]). Evidence from genetic epidemiology, for example, indicates a significant familial risk for obesity, but the risk of obesity is not entirely caused by genetic factors (Katzmarzyk et al. 1999). In other words, both familial genetic and nongenetic factors are involved in the etiology of overweight/obesity.

The complexity of factors summarized in table 24.5 makes establishing a distinct etiology for overweight/obesity during childhood and adolescence and its association with overweight/obesity in adulthood difficult. The issue is more complicated when considering infants, children, and adolescents, who are growing and maturing. Three periods during the years of growth and maturation have been suggested as sensitive or at risk for the development of overweight/obesity in adulthood—the prenatal period, "adiposity rebound," and adolescence (Dietz 1997). In contrast,

TABLE 24.5   Factors Associated With Overweight and Obesity

Factor	Trends and comments
Individual	
Age	1. Childhood obesity is a risk factor for adult obesity
	2. Body fat content increases during adulthood
	3. Maximal prevalence of overweight/obesity occurs between 55 and 65 years
Sex	1. Girls and women have more body fat than boys and men
	2. Sex difference in the prevalence of overweight/obesity varies among populations and among ethnic groups within a population
Familial	
Parental overweight/obesity	1. Parental overweight/obesity increases the likelihood of overweight/obesity in the child
Socioeconomic status (SES)	1. There are more obese in the high SES in developing countries
	2. There are more obese in the low SES in developed countries
Behavioral	
Energy intake	1. Overfeeding causes weight gain and leads to obesity
Dietary fat intake	1. Dietary fat is related to the prevalence of overweight in ecological studies
	2. High-fat diets cause weight gain
	3. Low-fat diets reduce body weight
Physical activity (PA) level	1. A low level of PA is a risk factor for weight gain
	2. Sedentary behavior is higher in obese individuals
	3. Regular PA may alter body composition by reducing fatness
	4. Regular PA contributes to weight loss and weight maintenance
	5. High levels of PA increase sympathetic nervous activity and resting metabolic rate
Television viewing	1. The more hours spent viewing television daily or weekly, the greater the likelihood of becoming obese
Smoking	1. Smoking is associated with a lower body weight
	2. Cessation of smoking is associated with increase in body weight in most individuals
Metabolic/endocrine	
Resting metabolic rate (RMR)	1. A low body mass and composition-adjusted RMR is a risk factor for weight gain, but contradictory data have been reported
	2. Overweight and obese individuals have a higher absolute RMR
Thermic response to food	1. Obese individuals have a depressed response in some studies, but contradictory results are common
Sympathetic nervous system (SNS)	1. Low SNS activity may be a risk factor for weight gain
	2. SNS activity is increased with overfeeding and weight gain
Lipid oxidation rate	1. Gain in body fat decreases the respiratory quotient (RQ)
	2. A high RQ is a risk factor for weight gain, but contradictory results have been reported
	3. The formerly obese have a higher RQ than the never obese

(continued)

TABLE 24.5 *(continued)*

Factor	Trends and comments
Metabolic/endocrine (continued)	
Blood leptin level	1. Low leptin levels are weakly related to weight gain, but contradictory results have been reported 2. Most obese individuals have high leptin levels
Growth hormone (GH) level	1. Low GH level is a risk factor for weight gain 2. Most obese individuals have low GH levels
Insulin sensitivity	1. Obese individuals are often insulin resistant and hyperinsulinemic 2. Insulin resistance protects against weight gain, but contradictory results have been reported
Hypothalamic-pituitary-adrenal (HPA) axis and cortisol levels	1. Obese individuals generally have a hyper-responsive adrenal and hyperactive HPA axis 2. Obese individuals have elevated rates of cortisol production but also accelerated degradation
Sex steroid levels	1. Obese men often have low androgen levels 2. Obese women often have high androgen levels with further elevation of adrenocorticotropic hormone
Adipose tissue metabolism	1. Catecholamine-induced lipolysis is reduced in obesity 2. Lipogenesis from glucose is increased in adipose cells of obese individuals 3. Adipose tissue lipoprotein lipase (LPL) is increased in obesity 4. Elevated adipose LPL activity remains high in those with a reduced level of obesity 5. High adipose tissue LPL is a risk factor for weight gain
Skeletal muscle metabolism	1. Proportion of type I skeletal muscle (SM) fibers is not affected by obesity 2. Proportion of type IIb SM fibers is often elevated in obesity 3. Oxidative enzyme markers in SM are inversely related to obesity 4. LPL activity in SM is low in obesity
Energy and nutrient partitioning	1. Under conditions of positive energy balance, some individuals channel more food carbons into proteins 2. High rates of lipid accretion could be a risk factor for further weight gain

Adapted from Bouchard (2000b).

breastfeeding during infancy has been suggested to have a protective effect on the later development of overweight/obesity (Butte 2001).

Birth Weight

The link between prenatal conditions and overweight/obesity in adulthood is based on associations between birth weight and adult BMI, which suggest either a U-shaped or J-shaped pattern of association in some studies (Martorell et al. 2001). According to the U-shaped pattern, low and high birth weights, which are indicative of fetal undernutrition and overnutrition, respec-

tively, are associated with a greater likelihood of being overweight/obese in adulthood. According to the J-shaped pattern, low birth weight is associated with a slight increase in adult overweight, whereas high birth weight is associated with a greater increase in adult overweight. Data supporting both hypotheses are limited. Some data appear to be consistent with the J-shaped pattern (Curhan et al. 1996a), but other data do not indicate an increased risk for overweight/obesity associated with low birth weights (Curhan et al. 1996b; Whitaker and Dietz 1998). Adult age at follow-up varies among studies, and potential confounders, such as reported birth weights and adult heights and weights, other risk factors for obesity, and statistical adjustment for age, also vary among studies. On the other hand, many studies indicate birth weights in the normal range among most overweight/obese adults such that neither the U-shaped nor the J-shaped hypotheses is consistently supported (Serdula et al. 1993).

"Adiposity Rebound"

The rise in the BMI after it reaches its low point at about 5 to 6 years of age has been labeled the "adiposity rebound" (Rolland-Cachera et al. 1984). Note, however, that the age at which the low point in the growth curve of the BMI is reached varies among individuals. After the nadir is reached, the BMI continues to increase through childhood and adolescence into adulthood (see chapter 3 for a discussion of the growth curve for the BMI). An early age at rebound, that is, an earlier age at the nadir of the growth curve for the BMI and subsequent increase, may be predictive of or a risk factor for overweight/obesity in childhood, adolescence, and adulthood. In a French longitudinal series (see table 24.6), children with an early (≤ 5.5 years of age) rebound of the BMI had a greater BMI in young adulthood (21.2 ± 2.5 years of age) than those who had a later rebound (≥ 7.0 years of age). The young adult BMI in boys with an early adiposity rebound (23.2 ± 2.8 kg/m^2) was almost equivalent to the 75th percentile for French men (23.7 kg/m^2) but was below a BMI of 25.0 kg/m^2, the accepted cutoff for overweight in adults. Given the standard deviation about the mean BMI of those with an early "adiposity rebound," not all are at risk for overweight. The corresponding value for girls with an early "adiposity rebound" (21.3 ± 2.6 kg/m^2) was between the median (20.6 kg/m^2) and

75th (22.4 kg/m^2) percentiles for French women (Rolland-Cachera et al. 1991) but was well below 25.0 kg/m^2. Although the trends suggest that an early rebound in the BMI is associated, on average, with a larger BMI in young adulthood, the early rebound groups did not have a BMI that approached the cutoff for overweight, and clearly most individuals did not have a BMI that would classify them as overweight (BMI ≥ 25.0 kg/m^2), let alone obese (BMI ≥ 30.0 kg/m^2).

In a similar study, the age at "adiposity rebound" was estimated from insurance records for a sample of 390 adults 21 to 29 years of age (Whitaker et al. 1998). All individuals had at least two clinical visits with measured height and weight in each of three age intervals: 1.5 to 4, 4 to 8, and 8 to16 years. All had measured adult height and weight between 21 and 29 years of age. The BMI at "adiposity rebound" was statistically estimated, with mean ages of 5.4 ± 1.7 years and 5.8 ± 1.9 years in females and males, respectively. Individuals were then classified as having early (< 4.8 years), middle ($4.8 < 6.2$ years), and late (≥ 6.2 years) ages at rebound and also as having a lean, medium, and heavy BMI at rebound. Note, the criteria for defining early, middle, and late ages at "adiposity rebound" and the ages at which adult BMI were calculated are different from those used by Rolland-Cachera et al. (1987). The occurrence of obesity in young adults (BMI ≥ 27.8 kg/m^2 in males and ≥ 27.3 kg/m^2 in females) grouped by tertile of age and BMI at "adiposity rebound" are shown in table 24.7. A trend for greater probability of overweight/obesity is seen in those with an earlier rebound and a heavier BMI at rebound, but the small numbers of subjects in each cell is a limiting factor.

Data from the Fels Longitudinal Study followed a large series of males (n = 180) and females (n = 158) from infancy to 35 to 45 years of age (Guo et al. 2000). An earlier adiposity rebound was a predictor of overweight (BMI ≥ 25.0 kg/m^2) at 35 to 45 years of age in females but not in males.

A question of potential interest in discussions of the "adiposity rebound" concerns maturity-associated variation. As early as 6 or 7 years of age, children advanced in biological maturation are, on average, taller, heavier, and fatter than children who are delayed, and this difference in weight and fatness persists through childhood and adolescence. This trend is consistent when indicators of current maturity status (i.e., skeletal age at 6 to 7 years or pubertal status at 9 to 10 years of age) or when indicators of maturity

TABLE 24.6 The Body Mass Index (kg/m^2) in Young Adulthood by Age at "Adiposity Rebound"

Age at "rebound"	Males Mean	SD	Females Mean	SD
Early ($\leq$5.5 yr)	23.2	2.8	21.3	2.6
Average (6–6.5 yr)	21.5	2.3	20.8	2.8
Late ($\geq$7 yr)	20.3	2.0	19.6	2.2

Adapted from Rolland-Cachera et al. (1987). Young adulthood is 21±2.5 years.

TABLE 24.7	Frequency of Obesity (OB) in Young Adults Grouped by Tertile of Estimated Age and BMI at "Adiposity Rebound" (AR)					
	Lean		**Medium**		**Heavy**	
Age at AR	**n**	**OB**	**n**	**OB**	**n**	**OB**
Females						
Early	18	2	30	5	32	7
Middle	20	0	32	3	27	5
Late	33	0	25	1	11	1
Males						
Early	10	1	11	3	16	7
Middle	14	1	17	2	23	8
Late	30	1	13	1	17	2

Obesity in adulthood was defined as a BMI ≥ 27.8 kg/m² in males and ≥ 27.3 kg/m² in females.

Adapted from Whitaker et al. (1998).

variation during adolescence (i.e., age at peak height velocity) are used (see chapter 17). Hence, a question of interest is the maturity status of children who vary in age at "adiposity rebound"—Is an early rebound associated and thus confounded with advanced biological maturity at this age? In the study of French children, no differences in skeletal age (Greulich-Pyle method) among the three "adiposity rebound" groups (early, average, and late) at 4, 6, and 8 years of age were present. Between 10 and 16 years of age, those with a late rebound tended to be slightly late in skeletal maturity compared with those with an early rebound (Rolland-Cachera et al. 1984). The differences in skeletal age between the early and late groups, however, are rather small and well within the range of variation associated with assessments of skeletal age with the Greulich-Pyle method (see chapter 15). Hence no firm conclusion can be reached at this stage on this particular issue.

In summary, the "adiposity rebound" refers to accelerated growth in the BMI after it reaches its nadir sometime between 5 and 8 years of age. The presently available data indicate a relationship between age at the increase in the BMI in childhood and the BMI in young adulthood. Individuals in whom the increase in the BMI occurs earlier tend to have, on average, a higher BMI in young adulthood, although not all have a young adult BMI that would classify them as overweight/obese by accepted criteria (see tables 24.6 and 24.7).

The "adiposity rebound" is an estimated point in time, and changes in the BMI after this event are not ordinarily considered. The pattern of change in the BMI from childhood through adolescence into adulthood is an additional factor that influences the risk of overweight/obesity in adulthood (Guo et al. 2000).

Although the relationship between the rebound of the BMI and adult BMI is suggestive, little consideration is given to other factors that occur around the time of the rebound and subsequently. In addition to growth in the BMI per se, other changes that occur about the time of the "adiposity rebound" include the midgrowth spurt in stature (see chapter 3), changes in individual skinfolds and perhaps subcutaneous fat distribution (see chapter 8), the establishment of movement patterns associated with fundamental skills (see chapter 10), and behavioral changes associated with regular attendance at school. How these factors may influence changes in the BMI at this time or perhaps interact with the BMI to influence levels of habitual physical activity and energy intake is not known.

Adolescence

The accumulation of body fat and changes in the relative distribution of fat, both subcutaneous and visceral, associated with differential timing of sexual maturation are implicated as risk factors for overweight/obesity. Age-associated and sex-associated changes in fatness and fat distribution were described in chapter 8, and maturity-associated variation in fatness and fat distribution were described in chapter 17. Among girls more so than boys, earlier onset of puberty (initial development of breasts and pubic hair) and early menarche are associated with higher levels of fatness and higher risk for overweight and obesity. Note, however, that early-maturing girls also differ in the weight-for-height relationship and thus have an elevated BMI compared with late-maturing girls, and this trend is already apparent in childhood (see chapter 17). Although data are limited, sexual maturation is also associated with proportionally greater accumulation of visceral fat.

In contrast, males ordinarily decline in relative fatness (% fat) during puberty because of the rapid growth of the fat-free mass. However, the absolute amount of fatness increases from childhood through adolescence. Individual differences in the timing of sexual maturation and the adolescent growth spurt are an additional factor. Like girls, early maturing boys tend to have, on average, more weight-for-height and, in turn, a higher BMI during childhood, which persists through adolescence. The elevated BMI is associated with both increased fat-free mass and fat mass. Sexual maturation in males is also associated with a proportionally greater accumulation of subcutaneous fatness on the trunk (central adiposity), and boys advanced in maturity status have more central adiposity not only during adolescence but also in young adulthood (see chapter 17).

The velocity (rate) of growth in the BMI during the adolescent growth spurt is associated with increased risk of overweight in adulthood. In the Fels Longitudinal Study, the maximum rate of growth of the BMI and the BMI at maximum velocity during adolescence were associated with overweight (BMI $\geq$ 25.0 kg/m^2) at 35 to 45 years of age in both sexes, whereas the age at maximum rate of growth of the BMI was not related to adult overweight (Guo et al. 2000). The rate of increase in the BMI was more strongly related to later overweight in males than in females, but the BMI at maximum velocity was a better predictor of adult overweight in females than in males.

If the observations of the Fels Longitudinal Study on the age at "adiposity rebound" and growth of the BMI during adolescence are placed in context, the following quotation summarizes the situation reasonably well:

> "...the earlier a child is 'fat', the 'fatter' the child. The earlier a child is 'fat', the earlier the child will be fat at a later age. The fatter a child is at one age, the fatter that child will be at a later age." (Guo et al. 2000, p. 1633)

An additional factor that may be potentially associated with increased risk of overweight during adolescence may be related to physical activity. Estimated levels of physical activity and energy expenditure decline, on average, from early adolescence into young adulthood (see chapter 21). Reduced energy expenditure in the face of constant or elevated energy intake may result in a positive energy balance and contribute to the accumulation of weight, specifically fatness.

Although specific factors associated with the onset of overweight/obesity during adolescence remain to be specified, a large fraction of the adolescent overweight/obesity cases persist into adulthood. The risk of retaining a high BMI from adolescence into adulthood increases with age as boys and girls pass through adolescence (Guo et al. 1994a).

Breast-Feeding

Breast-feeding during infancy has been suggested to have a potentially preventive role in the development of overweight/obesity in childhood and adolescence and even adulthood. At present, however, the evidence is equivocal. Several examples will serve to illustrate some of the complexities in trying to establish a causal link between breast-feeding and protection from subsequent overweight/obesity.

Part of the difficulty in studying the role of breast-feeding is in accurately establishing infant feeding practices, which are ordinarily reported by mothers. Allowing for potential errors in maternal reports (often provided via questionnaires), categories used in studies are variably defined as follows: "ever breast-fed," given breast milk some time during infancy; "fully breast-fed" or "exclusively breast-fed," given breast milk only and water; "partially breast-fed," given breast milk supplemented by formula or milk; and "never breast-fed," given exclusively cow's milk or formula. Duration of breast-feeding is a related issue, and establishing groups on the basis of duration also varies among studies. The age at which formula or milk or solid foods are introduced into the infant's diet is an additional factor. Maternal characteristics such as ethnicity, BMI, state of nutrition, feeding practices, education, and socioeconomic status are also potentially confounding factors, and when these (and others) are statistically controlled in some analyses, the effect of breast-feeding is reduced.

Examples of several recent studies of the potential protective effect of breast-feeding and later overweight/obesity are subsequently considered. In a national sample of United States children, relationships between breast-feeding and the risk of overweight (BMI $\geq$ 85th < 95th percentiles of age-specific and sex-specific reference values) at 3 to 5 years of age were inconsistent (Hediger et al. 2001). In a large sample of German children 5 to 6 years of age, on the other hand, the prevalence of obesity (BMI > 97th percentile of children enrolled in the sample) was 4.5% in those who were never breast-fed compared with 2.8% in those who were breast-fed (von Kries et al. 1999). The data for German children also suggested a dose-response effect—the longer the duration of breast-feeding, the lower the risk of obesity at 5 to 6 years of age. A study of a longitudinal cohort of British children who were born in 1946 used a comparable analysis as the preceding study of German children, but the results indicated no association between breast-feeding and overweight or obesity at 6 years of age (Wadsworth et al. 1999).

Among German children 9 to 10 years of age (Liese et al. 2001), longer duration of breast-feeding and exclusive breast-feeding were associated with a reduced risk of overweight (BMI ≥ 90th percentiles of German reference values). Data for United States adolescents 9 to 14 years of age also suggest a protective effect for breast-feeding (Gillman et al. 2001). Adolescents who received more breast milk than infant formula or who were breast-fed for a longer duration had a reduced risk of overweight (BMI > 95th percentile of age-specific and sex-specific reference values). Data relating breast-feeding to the risk of overweight in adulthood are limited and the results of two studies are inconclusive (Butte 2001).

The role of breast-feeding as a preventive factor in reducing the risk of overweight/obesity in childhood, adolescence, and adulthood, although interesting, is not firmly established. Nevertheless, the results beg the issue of how breast-feeding may exert a protective effect. For example, breast-fed infants regulate the amount of breast milk they consume, whereas the intake of formula-fed infants is regulated by the person feeding the infant. As was discussed in chapter 8, breast milk is rich in omega 3 fatty acids, which seem to prevent an increase in fat cell number as compared with infant formulas. Although the evidence derived from human studies is quite limited, more data are available from rodent models. Breast milk and infant formulas might also elicit different hormonal and growth factor responses that influence the proliferation of adipocytes and subsequently fatness. An additional factor is the influence of mode of infant feeding on subsequent food preferences and eating behaviors (Dietz 2001).

The growth and body composition of breast-fed and formula-fed infants are related issues. Evidence from several well-controlled studies in which feeding groups were clearly specified indicate that breast-fed infants have a lower rate of weight gain and consume less energy and protein compared with formula-fed infants (Butte 2001). Breast-fed and formula-fed infants also differ in body composition during infancy. Data derived from the multicomponent model of body composition using total-body water, total-body potassium, and bone mineral measurement (see chapter 5) indicate lower estimated fat-free mass and higher fat mass and percent fat in breast-fed than in formula-fed groups during the first 6 months of life. However, the differences in estimated body composition early in life do not persist into the second year (Butte et al. 2000). A similar approach using weight and arm circumference indicated no differences during the second year of life and also at 5 years of age among groups of children classified as exclusively breast-fed for 4 months, breast-fed for more than 4 months, partially breast-fed, and never breast-fed (Hediger et al. 2000).

Consequences of Obesity for Children and Adolescents

Even though the concepts of overweight and obesity have been more specifically defined internationally, they are often used synonymously in the literature. Thus, for convenience, the term obesity is used in the subsequent discussion. The presence of obesity, defined by a high weight-for-height, is not marked in children 2 to 3 years of age, but it is already established in significant numbers of 4-year-old and 5-year-old children, especially girls (see table 24.2). During middle childhood and continuing through childhood and adolescence, obesity as defined by a high BMI is a major public health problem in the United States (see table 24.2) and worldwide (World Health Organization 1998; British Nutrition Foundation 1999). Given the increased prevalence of obesity in children and adolescents, questions of interest relate to the growth, maturity, performance, and physical activity characteristics of obese individuals. Obese children and adolescents also present a profile of risk factors that characterize several diseases that ordinarily become manifest in adults. However, some of the metabolic complications are becoming increasingly more apparent during adolescence (e.g., adult-onset diabetes mellitus [type 2 diabetes]).

The subsequent discussion focuses on issues related to growth, performance, and physical activity of obese children and adolescents. How do obese children compare with nonobese children? How do obese children perform on tests of strength, motor proficiency, and physical fitness? How active are obese children?

Growth and Maturation

Several early studies of clinical samples of obese children indicate an overall larger body size, including height and fat-free mass, and advanced skeletal maturity compared with nonobese children (Forbes 1964; Cheek et al. 1970). Similar trends are evident in a survey of children 6 to 12 years of age, who were classified obese on the basis of either a skinfold thickness (triceps skinfold) or the BMI (Malina et al. 1989). Obese children were taller than average and advanced in skeletal maturity compared with nonobese children. Children classified as obese by the BMI were also taller and more advanced in skeletal maturity than children classified as obese by the triceps skinfold.

The size and maturity characteristics of obese children and adolescents are especially evident in comparisons with lean children of the same age and sex. In a national sample of Belgian (Flemish) girls, the body size and skeletal maturity of the fattest 5% and leanest 5% within each age group from 6 to 17 years of age were compared. Fatness was estimated by the sum of five skinfolds and the fattest girls were assumed to be obese (Beunen et al. 1994; Malina et al. 1995). This assumption is reasonable because their mean heights approximated the reference median for United States children (Kuczmarski et al. 2000) during childhood but were slightly below the median in adolescence; in contrast, their mean weights approximated the 90th percentile of the reference at most ages. The obese (fattest) girls were taller than the nonobese (leanest) girls age for age from 6 to 15 years; subsequently, the differences between groups were small. Obese girls were also taller compared with the Belgian reference from 6 to 13 years of age. Skeletal age was in advance of chronological age, and percentage of predicted adult height attained at each age was also advanced in obese girls. Both skeletal age and percentage of predicted adult height indicate advanced biological maturity status in obese girls compared with nonobese girls during childhood and most of adolescence. The later-maturing nonobese girls catch up in height but not weight in later adolescence, 16 to 17 years of age (Beunen et al. 1994). The same trends are also apparent in comparisons of obese and nonobese Belgian boys 12 to 17 years of age using the same protocol and criteria (Beunen et al. 1982). Obese boys are taller and advanced in skeletal maturity compared with nonobese boys.

The trends for girls and boys suggest that the tallness of obese children results in part from their advanced skeletal maturity. As late-maturing children approach maturity in later adolescence, the height differences between the obese and nonobese are reduced to insignificant levels. The exact mechanism for the more rapid growth and advanced maturity of obese children and adolescents is not clear. The high concentra-

tion of plasma insulin, which is often found in obese individuals, has been suggested as a potentially important factor (Horswill et al. 1997).

Physical Performance and Fitness

Fatness generally has a negative influence on performance of a variety of motor and cardiovascular fitness tests (see chapter 11). From a mechanical perspective, excess fat represents an inert load (dead weight) that must be moved. The effects of obesity (i.e., excessive fatness) on performance are especially apparent in comparisons of the obese and nonobese. Comparisons of the performances of obese and nonobese Belgian girls, defined as the fattest 5% and leanest 5%, respectively, in each age group from 7 to 17 years of age, illustrate the negative influence of obesity on most measures of physical performance (Malina et al. 1995). Comparisons of the obese and nonobese on tests of strength, flexibility, and motor proficiency are illustrated in figures 24.3 and 24.4. With the exception of speed of arm movement

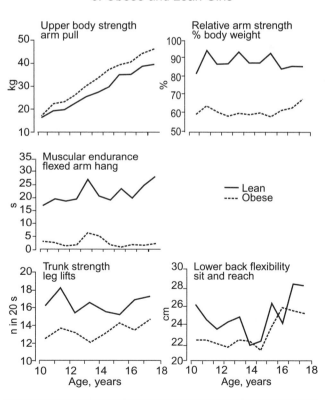

FIGURE 24.3 Strength and flexibility of obese and lean Belgian girls.

Data from Malina et al., 1995.

(plate tapping) and the sit-and-reach (flexibility), obese girls attain, on average, significantly poorer results than nonobese girls in the shuttle run (speed and agility), standing long jump and vertical jump (power), flexed-arm hang (functional strength), sit-ups and leg lifts (abdominal strength), and flamingo stand (balance). On the other hand, obese girls are absolutely stronger (static-arm pull strength), but per unit body size, obese girls are not as strong as nonobese girls. Similar comparisons of the performances of obese and nonobese Belgian boys 12 to18 years of age show identical results (Beunen et al. 1983). Obese boys exceed nonobese boys only in absolute arm strength. Nonobese boys perform better, on average, than obese boys on all other tests of motor performance at all ages. The obese and nonobese do not differ on the sit-and-reach, a measure of lower back flexibility.

A more detailed study of muscular strength in

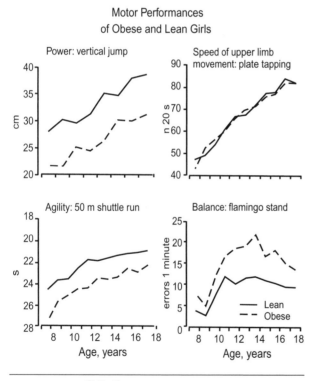

Motor Performances
of Obese and Lean Girls

FIGURE 24.4   Motor performances of obese and lean Belgian girls.

Data from Malina et al., 1995.

boys 9 to 13 years of age indicates higher absolute values for isometric and isokinetic strength in the obese. However, no differences between the obese and nonobese are apparent when strength

is calculated per unit body weight or per unit estimated cross-sectional area of the muscle groups involved. In addition, the obese and nonobese do not differ in muscle contractile characteristics or in the rate of motor unit recruitment (Blimkie et al. 1989, 1990). The results suggest that the poorer motor performances of obese children and adolescents are not caused by a deficiency in muscular strength.

The poorer motor performances of obese girls and boys on tasks that require the movement or projection of the body mass is probably caused by the inert, noncontributory load imposed by excessive adipose tissue. The performance success of nonobese girls and boys on many motor tasks is related in part to their low fatness levels. In contrast, the absolute strength and power output of the obese children reflect their larger body size, including muscle mass, but nonobese girls and boys demonstrate greater strength and power per unit body size. Lean, nonobese children are smaller than obese children but have proportionally more lean tissue for their body size, so they are "as strong as they appear" despite their small body size. In contrast, obese children are not as strong as their overall body size might suggest. Appearance may be a factor in some sports and physical activities in which youngsters may be assigned or excluded based exclusively on the basis of body size without considering strength and proficiency in motor skills.

Proficiency in motor skills has been generally overlooked in studies of obese children. Little is known about the motor development of children who are either obese during early childhood or who become obese at this time. Are children with an early "adiposity rebound" (previously discussed in chapter) delayed or less proficient in the development of fundamental motor skills? What are the characteristics of obese children and adolescents in a broader array of motor skills and activities? What is the role of proficiency in motor skills, or lack thereof, in establishing patterns of habitual activity during childhood and adolescence?

Proficiency in motor skills may facilitate or place constraints on physical activity and other components of lifestyle, access to physical activities, the frequency, duration, or intensity of activities, and the experience of success in activities important to children and adolescents. Interactions among obesity, motor fitness, and physical inactivity may include the following scenario. Obese children are less proficient in motor skills and components of health-related physical fitness. This lack of ability reduces the likelihood of experiencing success in the performance of activities important to children and adolescents (e.g., youth sports). As a result, they are less likely to engage in such physical activities, which may contribute to a sedentary lifestyle and a lower level of physical fitness.

The physical fitness of obese children and adolescents has received more attention, specifically in the context of aerobic power. Overall, obese children and adolescents are less physically fit than their nonobese age and sex peers. Comparisons of submaximal power output at a heart rate of 170 beats per minute during childhood, early adolescence, and late adolescence in obese and lean Belgian girls are summarized in table 24.8. Obese girls have greater absolute power output than nonobese girls, but per unit body size, obese girls have a considerably lower power output. The observations for PWC_{170} are consistent with reduced cardiovascular fitness as measured by the heart rate response to a step test (Bar-Or 1983; Malina et al. 1995) and lower aerobic power determined through maximal O_2 uptake per unit body mass (Bar-Or 1983; Cooper et al. 1990; DeMeersman et al. 1985), submaximal ergometry (Mocellin and Rutenfranz 1971), or the ventilatory anaerobic threshold (Reybrouck et al. 1987; Zanconato et al. 1989). Endurance time during a maximal treadmill test is also shorter (Rowland 1991).

The difference in the aerobic fitness of obese and nonobese children and adolescents needs to be considered in the context of several factors. Do the differences reflect abnormal physiological function, variation in the energy costs of movement, a lower level of habitual physical activity, or perhaps measurement bias? Are they affected by degree of obesity?

In this context, obese subjects are often classified on the basis of their body weight compared with a reference value (relative weight) and not by the BMI. The weight of the obese subject is expressed as a percentage of the reference value for the appropriate age and sex (100% is called ideal weight in the clinical literature). Thus, a child with a relative weight of 150% has a body weight that is 50% greater than that expected for the child's age and sex, and a child with a relative weight of 300% has a body weight that is 200% greater than the reference value (100%) for age and sex.

Extremely obese children and adolescents (147% to 300% of ideal body weight) have lower than expected pulmonary functions at rest—lung diffusion capacity, forced expiratory volume in 1 second (an index of airway narrowing), and respiratory muscle endurance (Inselman et al. 1993). On the other hand, subjects with a milder degree of obesity (135% to 140% of ideal body weight) show no abnormality in pulmonary functions at rest (Bosisio et al. 1984). Other functions that are deficient in some obese children and adolescents include a slower response time of ventilation and release of CO_2 from the body to an increase in metabolic demands (Cooper et al. 1990).

The trends in the pulmonary function data emphasize an important point in discussions of obesity. Obesity is often taken as a single entity without attention to the degree of overweight or excess body fat. This inaccuracy may influence conclusions because the children or adolescents with extreme obesity will likely respond differently to exercise tests than youngsters with a milder degree of obesity. Indeed, when a continuum of adiposity levels is used as the independent variable, the reduction in aerobic performance and pulmonary functions occurs primarily in

TABLE 24.8	Submaximal Power Output at a Heart Rate of 170 Beats Per Minute (PWC_{170}) in Obese and Lean Belgian Girls 7 to 17 Years of Age							
	Absolute PWC_{170} (W)				Relative PWC_{170} (W/kg)			
	Obese		Lean		Obese		Lean	
Age group (yr)	Mean	SE	Mean	SE	Mean	SE	Mean	SE
7–9	52.1	13.2	35.4	4.7	1.4	0.2	1.7	0.2
10–12	74.3	24.0	48.1	9.7	1.5	0.2	1.7	0.3
13–15	106.8	22.5	66.9	17.1	1.6	0.2	1.7	0.3
16–17	113.5	16.2	83.6	9.5	1.6	0.2	1.8	0.1

Adapted from Malina et al. (1995).

individuals with a marked degree of obesity (Bar-Or 1983; Rowland 1991).

A related question is the energy cost of physical activity in the obese. The energy cost of movement differs between obese and lean children and adolescents. The obese have high metabolic costs (O_2 uptake) during a submaximal treadmill walk or run (Maffeis et al. 1993) and cycle ergometry (Zanconato et al. 1989) compared with those with normal weight. However, when adjusted for body mass or fat-free mass, the obese and nonobese have similar O_2 uptakes (Katch et al. 1988; Maffeis et al. 1993). Limited kinematic data suggest that the walking style of the obese is normal, even though their self-selected walking pace is slow (Hills and Parker 1992). The synchronization between muscle groups while walking (measured via electromyography) also shows no aberrations in the obese and is presumably similar in the obese and nonobese (Hills and Parker 1993). This finding would suggest that the higher metabolic cost of locomotion in the obese child and adolescent is caused by their overall higher body mass.

Physical Activity

Is obesity a function of reduced habitual physical activity, or is reduced physical activity a function of obesity? The literature on physical activity and energy expenditure in childhood and adolescent obesity is equivocal. Data that indicate a reduction in habitual energy expenditure as a primary causative factor in obesity in children are relatively scant. On the other hand, more data suggest that excessive energy intake in relation to energy expenditure is a strong risk factor in childhood obesity (Davies 1993).

Interest in the role of physical activity, or inactivity, in the lifestyle of obese children and adolescents is considerable. From a negative perspective, a study of 35 obese and 28 nonobese adolescents 12 to 18 years of age indicated that the maintenance of obesity in adolescents is not related to reduced energy expenditure (Bandini et al. 1990), and a comparison of 12 overweight and 12 nonoverweight prepubertal girls 7 to 10 years of age indicated no differences in energy expenditure per unit of fat-free mass and in physical activity level (Treuth et al. 1998). In contrast, physical activity has been suggested to vary with degree of obesity with the highly obese showing lower levels of activity than the mildly obese, who show normal levels of activity (Shah and Jeffery 1991). Are the obese less active than the nonobese? In a study of eight obese and five nonobese girls 7 to 10 years of age, physical activity expressed as energy expenditure per unit body weight (kcal/kg) was less in the obese girls (Manos et al. 1993). When habitual physical activity is assessed by questionnaires or observed by time and motion analysis, obese children and adolescents appear less active than their lean peers (Bar-Or et al. 1998; Dionne et al. 2000).

Whether obesity is also accompanied by a lower 24-hour energy expenditure is a subject of disagreement (see table 24.9). Some studies suggest that basal and resting metabolic rates are lower in obese than in nonobese children (Kaplan et al. 1996), but others find no such difference (Salbe et al. 1997; Treuth et al. 2000). Stud-

TABLE 24.9 Summary of Current Knowledge of Total Daily Energy Expenditure (EE) and Childhood Obesity Based on Studies Using Doubly Labeled Water As the Criterion

Variable	Major finding	Comment
Absolute EE (mJ/24 hr)	Obese > nonobese	
EE per unit weight (mJ/kg/24hr)	Obese ≤ nonobese	
EE per unit FFM (mJ/kg FFM/24 hr)	Obese = nonobese	
Ethnic variation	American Indian = American White; American Black = American White	Prevalence of obesity is higher in Indian and Black children
Obese versus nonobese parents	Parental obesity is not a factor	
EE as a predictor of future childhood obesity	Infant EE does not predict future obesity	When mothers are obese, infants with lower EE may be at higher risk for obesity

Adapted from Goran (1997).

ies using doubly labeled water indicate greater absolute energy expenditure (kcal/24 hours) in the obese than nonobese, but after adjustment or "normalization" for differences in body composition, energy expenditure is the same in the obese and nonobese (Goran 1997).

Time spent viewing television is commonly implicated in the increased prevalence of obesity in children and adolescents. Surveys of children and adolescents in the United States indicate an association between the likelihood of becoming obese and the number of hours per week of watching television (Dietz and Gortmaker 1985; Gortmaker et al. 1996). In a nationally representative sample of children and adolescents 8 to 16 years of age, time spent viewing television is associated with obesity, more so in girls than in boys (Crespo et al. 2001). After adjusting for ethnicity, prior level of overweight (4 years earlier), maternal overweight, socioeconomic status, and scores on aptitude tests in a nationally representative sample of 746 American adolescents 10 to 15 years of age, the odds ratio for becoming overweight (BMI > 85th percentile) is 5.3 for those who watch more than 5 hours of television per day compared with those who watch television for zero to 2 hours per day (see table 24.10). Moreover, the likelihood of recovering from overweight over a 4-year period is inversely related to the extent of television viewing (Gortmaker et al. 1996). Based on epidemiological and statistical reasoning, the authors suggest a cause-and-effect relationship between the extent of television viewing and

obesity during adolescence, even though the data are cross sectional.

The majority of studies dealing with the relationship between television viewing and obesity indicate a positive association. However, not all studies report a relationship between television viewing among children and adolescents and obesity (Robinson et al. 1993; Wolf et al. 1993). The reasons for the discrepancy are not clear and probably reflect sampling variation (i.e., more local or regional compared with national samples), variation in indicators of fatness or obesity, self-reporting of television viewing time, and associated familial factors, among others.

If television viewing is a causal factor in the genesis of childhood obesity, is the effect caused by the low energy expenditure of sitting (the same may be inferred for computer games and the Internet)? No data confirm a relationship between total energy expenditure and the extent of television viewing. On the other hand, snacking and the exposure to food-related commercials may possibly be primary factors in the association between television viewing and obesity, that is, excess energy intake in association with reduced energy expenditure (Story and Faulkner 1990).

In the aggregate, the studies on physical activity levels and metabolic rates in obese and normal weight children are equivocal, which should not be surprising, because these studies have focused on obese children once they are obese. Obesity is the mechanism by which energy balance is restored in people who are in positive energy balance for extended periods of time. To define the specific contribution of the level of physical activity or the degree of sedentariness to the risk of becoming obese in children and adolescents will require that longitudinal studies of initially normal-weight boys and girls be undertaken. In this manner, the role of physical activity level, degree of sedentariness, and metabolic rates in the progression to an obese state can be defined. Moreover, such studies are strongly dependent on the procedures used to scale indicators of activity and, even more important, metabolic rates. Simply reporting metabolic rate per unit of body mass in the comparison of obese and normal-weight children is not sufficient to adequately control for size and composition differences.

TABLE 24.10	Relationship Between the Prevalence of Overweight (BMI >85th Percentile) and Reported Time Spent Viewing Television		
Television viewing (hr/day)	n	Prevalence (%)	Adjusted odds ratio
0–2	69	11.6	1.00
2–3	114	22.6	1.72
3–4	129	27.7	2.84
4–5	134	29.5	3.01
>5	300	32.8	5.26

The odds ratios were adjusted for ethnicity, maternal overweight, the individual's overweight status 4 years earlier, socioeconomic status, family size, and aptitude test scores.

Adapted from Gortmaker et al. (1996). Data are based on a representative sample of United States adolescents of both sexes, 10 to 15 years of age.

Self-Esteem

Self-concept refers to perception of self, whereas self-esteem or self-worth refers to the value placed on one's self-concept, although the terms are often used interchangeably. Changes in self-concept/self-esteem occur during childhood and adolescence. The specific domains or competencies of self-esteem/self-worth have implications for obesity and physical activity. Among children and adolescents 8 to 15 years of age, first physical appearance and then social acceptance have an important impact on self-worth, whereas more specific competencies (i.e., scholastic and athletic), although important, contribute relatively less to self-worth at these ages (Harter 1989). Most studies of self-concept or self-worth do not include actual measures of physical or athletic competence and do not include measures of size, physique, and maturity status. Nevertheless, physical appearance and social acceptability have more impact on a child's sense of self-worth than other more specific competencies late in childhood and especially in the transition into adolescence. This time is a period of change in size, physique, and body composition and in sexual maturity as youth make the transition from childhood to adolescence.

Self-esteem declines in girls during the transition into puberty, and early-maturing girls do not fare well compared with girls average ("on time") and late in maturation (Brooks-Gunn and Peterson 1983; Simmons and Blyth 1987). Ethnic variation also exists. Longitudinal data from the National Heart, Lung and Blood Institute Growth and Health Study indicate that the developmental pattern for self-esteem differs for American Black girls compared with American White girls (Brown et al. 1998). Global self-worth declines in White girls but is stable in Black girls from 9 to 14 years of age, and adjusting for stage of sexual maturation, BMI and household income does not alter the trends. Further, as the BMI increases, scores for global self-worth, physical appearance, and social acceptance decrease, but the decrease in scores for physical appearance and social acceptance with an increase in the BMI are less in Black than in White girls.

A comprehensive review of self-esteem and obesity in children and adolescents suggests several trends and indicates areas that need further research (French et al. 1995). In 13 of 25 cross-sectional studies, self-esteem is lower in the obese, but the associations are modest and self-esteem scores are within the range of normal variability. Self-esteem scores in the obese show age-related differences. The association between self-esteem and obesity is stronger in adolescents (13 to 18 years of age) than in children (7 to 12 years of age). Ethnic variation in the association is possible, specifically among girls. Obesity apparently has a more negative impact on the self-esteem of White adolescent girls compared with Black and other non-White girls, which emphasizes the need to consider ethnic variation in perceptions or social acceptance of obesity (Allan et al. 1993; Kumanyika 1993a, 1993b; Neumark-Sztainer et al. 1997).

The age range 7 to 12 years, labeled as childhood, includes the transition into puberty, and the impact of individual differences in the timing of puberty needs consideration (see chapter 16). Unfortunately, studies of self-esteem do not ordinarily include an indicator of biological maturity and do not consider variation in maturity timing. As noted previously, obesity is associated with advanced biological maturity in childhood and adolescence.

Five of six cross-sectional studies reviewed by French et al. (1995) included a measure of "body esteem," the value an individual places on the body or physical appearance. Obese children and adolescents have lower "body esteem" scores compared with children and adolescents who are normal weight. Two prospective studies considered initial self-esteem and later obesity, but the results are inconsistent. Six of eight treatment studies of obese children and adolescents indicate improved self-esteem associated with weight loss.

Long-Term Consequences of Obesity

The preceding discussion of obesity focused on associations with and consequences for growth, maturation, performance, physical activity, and self-esteem. A history of obesity during childhood and adolescence also has implications, or more specifically, consequences for adult health. The increased prevalence of obesity among children and adolescents is accompanied by an increased prevalence of obesity in adults in many countries throughout the world (World Health Organization 1998, British Nutrition Foundation 1999; Flegal and Troiano 2000; Flegal et al. 2002; Katzmarzyk 2002a, 2002b).

Data from the Fels and Harvard longitudinal growth studies indicate significant tracking of fatness and other risk factors for disease from childhood through adolescence into adulthood and of precursors of morbidity and mortality in adulthood (Casey et al. 1992; Must et al. 1992; Guo et al. 1994a). For example, a high BMI (> 85th percentile) during childhood is predictive of a high BMI in adulthood, and a high BMI during adolescence is more predictive of adult obesity (Guo et al. 1994a). These predictions of overweight and obesity in adulthood from the BMI in childhood and adolescence have recently been extended using the new BMI-for-age growth charts (see chapter 3). For example, the probability of obesity defined as a BMI $\geq$ 30 kg/m^2 at 35 years of age for a boy with a BMI at the 85th percentile of the BMI-for-age growth charts is 17%; the corresponding probability for a 10-year-old girl with a BMI at the 85th percentile of the BMI-for-age growth charts is 23%. The probability of adult obesity increases with age during adolescence (Guo et al. 2002).

During adulthood, the BMI tracks at moderate and strong levels with correlations ranging from about 0.5 to 0.8 (Fabsitz et al. 1992; Casey et al. 1992). Obesity in adulthood, defined by a high BMI (> 28.0 kg/m^2) is associated with several diseases per se, risk factors for several diseases, and mortality (Bray 2000). These associations include elevated blood pressures and serum lipids (Guo et al. 1994b; Rocchini 1998), heart disease (Saltzman and Benotti 1998), diabetes (Albu and Pi-Sunyer 1998), some cancers (Cold et al. 1998), and mortality from all causes and specifically heart disease (Blair and Lee 1998; Katzmarzyk et al. 2002).

Obesity during childhood and adolescence is associated with elevated lipids, hypertension, hyperinsulemia, and other risk factors for cardiovascular disease and adult onset diabetes (Guo et al. 1994b; Gutin and Barbeau 2000). Risk factors for several degenerative diseases in adulthood are discussed in more detail in chapter 26. In the present context, note that a profile of risk factors associated with several adult diseases is associated with obesity in children and adolescents. Moreover, risk factors associated with childhood and adolescent obesity tend to persist into adulthood (Malina 1990; Guo et al. 1994b).

Obesity in adulthood and related health complications have major economic implications in the health care delivering system. The estimated health care costs associated with obesity in the United States in 1995 reached approximately 70 billion dollars (Colditz 1999; Colditz and Mariani 2000). If the costs of a sedentary lifestyle are added to those for obesity (Katzmarzyk et al. 2000), the economic implications for health care delivery systems in developed countries are staggering.

Treatment

Long-term studies of obese children and adolescents indicate a high rate of relapse after treatment (Lloyd 1977; Epstein et al. 1998). More successful treatment programs with long-term effects are family-based and include a combination of behavior modification, nutrition education and dietary change, and enhanced physical activity for both children and their parents (Epstein et al. 1990, 1998).

What is the role of systematic programs of physical activity in the treatment of childhood and adolescent obesity? Such data are very limited. A comprehensive review of the available controlled studies of physical activity in the treatment of childhood and adolescent obesity indicates several trends (Epstein and Goldfield 1999). Regular physical activity in conjunction with diet is more effective in reducing obesity than is diet alone. This finding suggests that exercise adds to the effect of dietary regulation in short-term treatment of obesity in children and adolescents. Controlled data dealing with the effect of exercise alone in the treatment of childhood and adolescent obesity are inadequate. Changes in the physical fitness of obese children and adolescents treated with a program of activity and diet, or with only a program of activity, are greater compared with those treated with only dietary regulation and control patients receiving no exercise.

A related question deals with the role of systematic programs of exercise on energy expenditure and overall pattern of physical activity in obese children and adolescents. This question has implications for a potential carry-over effect from the specific program to the general pattern of physical activity that characterizes the individual. Among obese boys, however, a systematic exercise program was associated with an increase in total energy expenditure but with relatively little change in level of spontaneous physical activity (Blaak et al. 1992).

More novel approaches are needed for the treatment of childhood and adolescent obesity. Saelens and Epstein (1998), for example, used "behavioral engineering" to increase the level of physical activity among obese youth. Activities valued by youth (video games and watching videos) were made contingent on physical activity. To achieve this effect, the television was activated only when pedal speed on a stationary bicycle reached 60 rpm. Thus, valued sedentary activities (i.e., television viewing) can be used to reinforce physical activities. These results have implications for research into the modification of activity choices in treatment programs for obese youth. They likewise have implications for the prevention of obesity, such as riding a stationary bicycle while watching television or videos and other means of encouraging physical activity in the context of valued sedentary activities.

The limited success of treatment programs for childhood and adolescent obesity emphasizes a primary role for prevention rather than for cure in childhood and adolescent obesity. Prevention needs to begin in early childhood and continue through adolescence into adulthood and needs to include the individual, the family, the community, and perhaps national organizations (see Gill 1997). Given the importance of reducing sedentary behavior in the prevention of obesity, further understanding is needed of how and why individuals make choices for sedentary and physically active pursuits (Epstein and Roemmich 2001).

The role of the school is especially important for children and adolescents. Because school attendance is mandatory, programs that can be carried out within the school setting are a logical focus of efforts to reduce obesity. Incorporating dietary and physical activity components into the curriculum is associated with a reduction in the prevalence of obesity, more so among females than males (Gortmaker et al. 1999a, 1999b). Evidence indicates that a school-based intervention aimed at reducing time viewing television is associated with a reduction in fatness (Robinson 1999). Thus, the prevention of obesity should be targeted as an outcome in schools.

Many schools potentially have a pool of experts, notably health and physical education teachers, nurses, counselors, and dietitians, who can provide instruction and guidance and who can monitor the progress of individual children and adolescents. Given the close ties between schools and their respective communities, the lines of communication between teachers (including nurses and counselors) and parents are reasonably well established. Most schools also have indoor and outdoor facilities, as well as the necessary equipment for physical activity. Because school attendance is mandatory, children and adolescents are in a sense a "captive" population for 5 days per week throughout most of the year.

The potential for the school setting in the prevention of childhood and adolescent overweight/ obesity is obvious. In-service education of teachers and related personnel on prevention per se and specific educational and physical activity programs would be needed. However, research is needed to identify the best and most cost-effective designs for programs aimed at preventing obesity, increasing habitual physical activity, and improving dietary behaviors.

Summary

Overweight is characterized by a moderate degree of excess weight-for-height, most often expressed as a BMI ≥ 85th < 95th percentile, whereas obese is a more severe state, a BMI ≥ 95th percentile. The terms overweight and obesity are used variably in studies. In the United States national surveys, the terms "risk of overweight" (BMI ≥ 85th < 95th percentile [i.e., overweight]) and "overweight" (BMI ≥ 95th percentile [i.e., obese]) are used. Overweight and obesity occur as a result of an imbalance between energy intake and energy expenditure in which intake exceeds expenditure, and physical inactivity is an essential component of the equation. Three sensitive periods for the development of obesity have been suggested, prenatal, adiposity rebound, and adolescence, and breast-feeding during infancy has been postulated as having a protective influence on the later development of obesity. Obese children and adolescents tend to be, on average, taller and advanced in skeletal maturity compared with nonobese children. Excess fatness associated with obesity has a negative influence on performance of a variety of motor and cardiovascular fitness tests and also on self-esteem. Although physical inactivity is an essential factor in the etiology of obesity, the literature on physical activity and energy expenditure in childhood and adolescent obesity is equivocal. Overweight and obesity during childhood and adolescence often persist into adulthood and has major consequences for adult health.

Sources and Suggested Readings

Akesode EA, Ahbode HA (1983) Prevalence of obesity among Nigerian school children. Social Science in Medicine 17: 107-111.

Albu J, Pi-Sunyer FX (1998) Obesity and diabetes. In GA Bray, C Bouchard, WPT James (eds), Handbook of Obesity. New York: Marcel Dekker, pp 697-707.

Allan JD, Mayo K, Michel Y (1993) Body size values of white and black women. Research in Nursing and Health 16: 323-333.

Bandini LG, Schoeller DA, Dietz WH (1990) Energy expenditure in obese and nonobese adolescents. Pediatric Research 27:198-203.

Bar-Or O (1983) Pediatric Sports Medicine for the Practitioner: From Physiologic Principles to Clinical Applications. New York: Springer Verlag.

* Bar-Or O, Foreyt J, Bouchard C, Brownell KD, Dietz WH, Ravussin E, Salbe AD, Schwenger S, St. Jeor S, Torun B (1998) Physical activity, genetic and nutritional considerations in childhood weight management. Medicine and Science in Sports and Exercise 30:2-10.

Beunen G, Malina RM, Lefevre JA, Claessens AL, Renson R, Vanreusel B (1994a) Adiposity and biological maturation in girls 6–16 years of age. International Journal of Obesity 18:542-546.

Beunen G, Malina RM, Ostyn M, Renson R, Simons J, Van Gerven D (1982) Fatness and skeletal maturity of Belgian boys 12 through 17 years of age. American Journal of Physical Anthropology 59:387-392.

Beunen G, Malina RM, Ostyn M, Renson R, Simons J, Van Gerven D (1983) Fatness, growth and motor fitness of Belgian boys 12 through 20 years of age. Human Biology 55:599-613.

Blaak EE, Westerterp KR, Bar-Or O, Wouters LJM, Satis WHM (1992) Total energy expenditure and spontaneous activity in relation to training in obese boys. American Journal of Clinical Nutrition 55:777-782.

Blair SN, Bouchard C, editors (1999) Physical activity in the prevention and treatment of obesity and its comorbidities: American College of Sports Medicine roundtable. Medicine and Science in Sports and Exercise 31 (suppl): S497-S667.

* Blair SN, Lee I-M (1998) Weight loss and risk of mortality. In GA Bray, C Bouchard, WPT James (eds), Handbook of Obesity. New York: Marcel Dekker, pp 805-818.

Blimkie CJR, Ebbesen B, MacDougall D, Bar-Or O (1989) Voluntary and electrically evoked strength characteristics of obese and nonobese preadolescent boys. Human Biology 61:515-532.

Blimkie CJR, Sale DG, Bar-Or O (1990) Voluntary strength, evoked twitch contractile properties and motor unit activitation of knee extensors in obese and non-obese adolescent males. European Journal of Applied Physiology 61:313-318.

Boisisio E, Sergi M, Di Natale B, Chiumello G (1984) Ventilatory volumes, flow rates, transfer factor and its components in obese adults and children. Respiration 45:321-326.

* Bouchard C, editor (2000a) Physical Activity and Obesity. Champaign, IL: Human Kinetics.

Bouchard C (2000b) Introduction. In C Bouchard (ed), Physical Activity and Obesity, Champaign, IL: Human Kinetics, pp 3-19.

Bouchard C (2002) Genetic influences on body weight. In CG Fairburn, KD Brownell (eds), Eating Disorders and Obesity: A Comprehensive Handbook, 2nd edition. New York: Guilford Press, pp 16-21.

Bray GA (2000) Overweight, mortality, and morbidity. In C Bouchard (ed), Physical Activity and Obesity. Champaign, IL: Human Kinetics, pp 31-53.

* British Nutrition Foundation (1999) Obesity: The Report of the British Nutrition Foundation Task Force. Oxford, UK: Blackwell Science.

Brooks-Gunn J, Peterson A (1983) Girls at Puberty: Biological and Psychosocial Perspectives. New York: Plenum.

Brown KM, McMahon RP, Biro FM, Crawford P, Schreiber GB, Similo SL, Waclawiw M, Striegel-Moore R (1998) Changes in self-esteem in black and white girls between the ages of 9 and 14 years: The NHLBI Growth and Health Study. Journal of Adolescent Health 23:7-19.

* Butte NF (2001) The role of breast-feeding in obesity. Pediatric Clinics of North America 48:189-198.

Butte NF, Wong WW, Hopkinson JM, Smith EO, Ellis KJ (2000) Infant feeding mode affects early growth and body composition. Pediatrics 106:1355-1366.

Cameron N, Getz B (1997) Sex differences in the prevalence of obesity in rural African adolescents. International Journal of Obesity 21:775-782.

Casey VA, Dwyer JT, Coleman KA, Valadian I (1992) Body mass index from childhood to middle age: A 50-year follow-up. American Journal of Clinical Nutrition 56:14-18.

Cheek DB, Schultz RB, Parra A, Reba RC (1970) Overgrowth of lean and adipose tissues in adolescent obesity. Pediatric Research 4:268-279.

Cold S, Hansen S, Overvad K, Rose C (1998) A woman's body build and the risk of breast cancer. European Journal of Cancer 34:1163-1174.

Colditz GA (1999) Economic costs of obesity and inactivity. Medicine and Science in Sports and Exercise 31(suppl): S663-S667.

Colditz GA, Mariani A (2000) The cost of obesity and sedentarism in the United States. In C Bouchard (ed), Physical Activity and Obesity. Champaign, IL: Human Kinetics, pp 55-65.

Cole TJ, Bellizzi MC, Flegal KM, Dietz WH (2000) Establishing a standard definition for child overweight and obesity worldwide: International survey. British Medical Journal 320:1240-1243.

Cooper DM, Poage J, Barstow TJ, Springer C (1990) Are obese children truly unfit? Minimizing the confounding effect of body size on the exercise response. Journal of Pediatrics 116:223-230.

Crespo CJ, Smit E, Troiano RP, Bartlett SJ, Macera CA, Andersen RE (2001) Television watching, energy intake, and obesity in US children: Results from the third National Health and Nutrition Examination Survey, 1988–1994. Archives of Pediatric and Adolescent Medicine 155:360-365.

Curhan GC, Chertow GM, Willett WC, Spiegelman D, Colditz GA, Manson JE, Speizer FE, Stampfer MJ (1996a) Birth weight and adult hypertension and obesity in women. Circulation 94:1310-1315.

Curhan GC, Willett WC, Rimm EB, Spiegelman D, Ascherio AL, Stampfer MJ (1996b) Birth weight and adult hypertension, diabetes mellitus, and obesity in U.S. men. Circulation 94: 3246-3250.

Davies PSW (1993) Energy metabolism and obesity in childhood. Hormone Research 39 (suppl 3): 77-80.

Davies PSW, Gregory J, White A (1995) Physical activity and body fatness in preschool children. International Journal of Obesity 19:6-10.

Delany JP (1998) Role of energy expenditure in the development of pediatric obesity. American Journal of Clinical Nutrition 68(suppl):950S-955S.

DeMeersman RE, Stone S, Schaefer DC, Miller WW (1985) Maximal work capacity in prepubescent obese and non-obese females. Clinical Pediatrics 24:199-200.

* de Onis M, Blossner M (1997) WHO Global Database on Child Growth and Malnutrition. Geneva: World Health Organization, WHO/NUT/77.4.

* de Onis M, Blossner M (2000) Prevalence and trends of overweight among preschool children in developing countries. American Journal of Clinical Nutrition 72:1032-1039.

Dietz WH (1998) Health consequences of obesity in youth: Childhood predictors of adult disease. Pediatrics 101 (suppl):518-525.

Dietz WH (1997) Periods of risk in childhood for the development of adult obesity: What do we need to learn? Journal of Nutrition 127:1884S-1886S.

Dietz WH (2001) Breastfeeding may help prevent childhood overweight. Journal of the American Medical Association 285:2506-2507.

Dietz WH, Gortmaker SL (1985) Do we fatten our children at the television set? Obesity and television viewing in children and adolescents. Pediatrics 75:807-812.

Dionne IN, Almeras C, Bouchard C, Tremblay A (2000) The association between vigorous physical activities and fat deposition in male adolescents. Medicine and Science in Sports and Exercise 32:392-395.

Epstein LH, Goldfield GS (1999) Physical activity in the treatment of childhood overweight and obesity: Current evidence and research issues. Medicine and Science in Sports and Exercise 31(suppl):S553-S559.

Epstein LH, Myers MD, Raynor HA, Saelens BE (1998) Treatment of pediatric obesity. Pediatrics 101 (suppl):554-570.

Epstein LH, Roemmich JN (2001) Reducing sedentary behavior: Role of modifying physical activity. Exercise and Sport Sciences Reviews 29:103-108.

* Epstein LH, Valoski A, Wing RR, McCurley J (1990) Ten-year follow-up of behavioral, family-based treatment of obese children. Journal of the American Medical Association 264: 2519-2523.

Fabsitz RR, Carmelli D, Hewitt JK (1992) Evidence for independent genetic influences on obesity in middle age. International Journal of Obesity 16:657-666.

Flegal KM, Carroll MD, Ogden CL, Johnson CL (2002) Prevalence and trends in obesity among US adults, 1999–2000. Journal of the American Medical Association 288:1723-1727.

Flegal KM, Troiano RP (2000) Changes in the distribution of body mass index of adults and children in the US population. International Journal of Obesity 24:807-818.

Forbes GB (1964) Lean body mass and fat in obese children. Pediatrics 34:308-314.

* French SA, Story M, Jeffery RW (2001) Environmental influences on eating and physical activity. Annual Reviews of Public Health 22:309-335.

* French SA, Story M, Perry CL (1995) Self-esteem and obesity in children and adolescents: A literature review. Obesity Research 3:479-490.

Gill TP (1997) Key issues in the prevention of obesity. British Medical Bulletin 53:359-388.

Gillman MW, Rifas-Shiman SL, Camargo CA, Berkey CS, Frazier AL, Rockett HRH, Field AE, Colditz GA (2001) Risk of overweight among adolescents who were breastfed as infants. Journal of the American Medical Association 285: 2461-2467.

Goran MI (1997) Energy expenditure, body composition, and disease risk in children and adolescents. Proceedings of the Nutrition Society 56:195-209.

Gortmaker SL, Cheung LWY, Peterson KE, Chomitz G, Cradle JH, Dart H, Fox MK, Bullock RB, Sobol AM, Colditz G, Field AE, Laird N (1999a) Impact of a school-based interdisciplinary intervention on diet and physical activity among urban primary school children: Eat well and keep moving. Archives of Pediatric and Adolescent Medicine 153:975-983.

Gortmaker SL, Must A, Sobol AM, Peterson K, Colditz GA, Dietz WH (1996) Television viewing as a cause of increasing obesity among children in the United States, 1986–1990. Archives of Pediatric and Adolescent Medicine 105:356-362.

Gortmaker SL, Peterson K, Wiecha J, Sobol AM, Dixit S, Fox MK, Laird N (1999b) Reducing obesity via a school-based interdisciplinary intervention among youth: Planet Health. Archives of Pediatric and Adolescent Medicine 153:409-418.

Guo SS, Huang C, Maynard LM, Demerath E, Towne B, Chumlea WC, Siervogel RM (2000) Body mass index during childhood, adolescence and young adulthood in relation to adult overweight and adiposity: The Fels Longitudinal Study. International Journal of Obesity 24: 1628-1635.

Guo SS, Roche AF, Chumlea WC, Gardner JD, Siervogel RM (1994a) The predictive value of childhood body mass index values for overweight at age 35 years. American Journal of Clinical Nutrition 59:810-819.

Guo SS, Salisbury S, Roche AF, Chumlea WC, Siervogel RM (1994b) Cardiovascular disease risk factors and body composition: A review. Nutrition Research 14:1721-1777.

Guo SS, Wu W, Chumlea WC, Roche AF (2002) Predicting overweight and obesity in adulthood from body mass index values in childhood and adolescence. American Journal of Clinical Nutrition 76:653-658.

Gutin B, Barbeau P (2000) Physical activity and body composition in children and adolescents. In C Bouchard (ed), Physical Activity and Obesity. Champaign, IL: Human Kinetics, pp 213-245.

Hamill PVV, Drizd TA, Johnson CL, Reed RD, Roche AF (1977) NCHS growth curves for children, birth – 18 years. United States. DHEW Publication No. (PHS) 78-1650. Washington, DC: US Government Printing Office.

Harter S (1989) Causes, correlates, and the functional role of global self-worth: A life-span perspective. In J Kolligian and R Sternberg (eds), Perceptions of Competence and Incompetence across the Life-Span. New Haven, CT: Yale University Press, pp 67-97.

Hediger ML, Overpeck MD, Kuczmarski RJ, Ruan WJ (2001) Association between infant breastfeeding and overweight in young children. Journal of the American Medical Association 285:2453-2460.

Hediger ML, Overpeck MD, Ruan WJ, Troendle JF (2000) Early infant feeding and growth status of US-born infants and children aged 4–71 mo: Analyses from the Third National Health and Nutrition Examination Survey, 1988–1994. American Journal of Clinical Nutrition 72:159-167.

Hills AP, Parker AW (1992) Locomotor characteristics of obese children. Child: Care, Health and Development 18:29-34.

Hills AP, Parker AW (1993) Electromyography of walking in obese children. Electromyography and Clinical Neurophysiology 33:225-233.

Himes JH, Dietz WH (1994) Guidelines for overweight in adolescent preventive services: Recommendations from an expert committee. American Journal of Clinical Nutrition 59:307-317.

Horswill CA, Zipf WB, Kien CL, Kahle EB (1997) Insulin's contribution to growth in children and the potential for exercise to mediate insulin action. Pediatric Exercise Science 9:18-32.

Inselman LA, Milanese A, Deurloo A (1993) Effect of obesity on pulmonary function in children. Pediatric Pulmonology 16:130-137.

Kaplan AS, Zemel BS, Stallings VA (1996) Differences in resting energy expenditure in prepubertal black children and white children. Journal of Pediatrics 129:643-647.

Katch V, Becque MD, Marks C, Moorehead C, Rocchini A (1988) Oxygen uptake and energy output during walking of obese male and female adolescents. American Journal of Clinical Nutrition 47:26-32.

Katzmarzyk PT (2002a) The Canadian obesity epidemic, 1985–1998. Canadian Medical Association Journal 166: 1039-1040.

Katzmarzyk PT (2002b) The Canadian obesity epidemic: An historical perspective. Obesity Research 10:666-674.

Katzmarzyk PT, Craig Cl, Bouchard C (2002) Adiposity, adipose tissue distribution and mortality rates in the Canada Fitness Survey follow-up study. International Journal of Obesity 26:1054-1059.

Katzmarzyk PT, Gledhill N, Shephard RJ (2000) The economic burden of physical inactivity in Canada. Canadian Medical Association Journal 163:1435-1440.

Katzmarzyk PT, Perusse L, Rao DC, Bouchard C (1999) Familial risk of obesity and central adipose tissue distribution in the general Canadian population. American Journal of Epidemiology 149:933-942.

Kuczmarski RJ, Ogden CL, Grummer-Strawn LM, Flegal KM, Guo SS, Wei R, Mei Z, Curtin LR, Roche AF, Johnson CL (2000) CDC growth charts: United States. Advance Data from Vital and Health Statistics, no. 314. Hyattsville, MD: National Center for Health Statistics.

Kumanyika S (1993a) Ethnicity and obesity development in children. Annals of the New York Academy of Sciences 699:81-92.

Kumanyika S (1993b) Special issues regarding obesity in minority populations. Annals of Internal Medicine 119: 650-654.

Leibel RL (2002) The molecular genetics of body weight regulation. In CG Fairburn, KD Brownell (eds), Eating Disorders and Obesity: A Comprehensive Handbook, 2nd edition. New York: Guilford Press, pp 26-31.

Liese AD, Hirsch T, von Mutius E, Keil U, Leupold W, Weiland SK (2001) Inverse association of overweight and breast feeding in 9 to 10-year-old children in Germany. International Journal of Obesity 25:1644-1650.

Lloyd JK (1977) Prognosis of obesity in infancy and childhood. Postgraduate Medical Journal 53 (suppl):111-114.

Maffeis C, Schutz Y, Schena F, Zaffanello M, Pinelli L (1993) Energy expenditure during walking and running in obese and nonobese prepubertal children. Journal of Pediatrics 123:193-199.

Malina RM (1975) Anthropometric correlates of strength and motor performance. Exercise and Sport Sciences Reviews 3:249-274.

Malina RM (1990) Growth, exercise, fitness, and later outcomes. In C Bouchard, RJ Shephard, T Stephens, JR Sutton, BD McPherson (eds), Exercise, Fitness, and Health:

A Consensus of Current Knowledge. Champaign, IL: Human Kinetics, pp 637-653.

Malina RM (1994) Anthropometry, strength and motor fitness. In SJ Ulijaszek, CGN Mascie-Taylor (eds), Anthropometry: The Individual and the Population. Cambridge: Cambridge University Press, pp 160-177.

Malina RM (1995) Cardiovascular health status of Latin American children and youth. In CJR Blimkie, O Bar-Or (eds), New Horizons in Pediatric Exercise Science. Champaign, IL: Human Kinetics, pp 195-220.

Malina RM, Beunen GP, Claessens AL, Lefevre J, Vanden Eynde B, Renson R, Vanreusel B, Simons J (1995) Fatness and fitness of girls 7 to 17 years. Obesity Research 3:221-231.

Malina RM, Katzmarzyk PT, Siegel SR (1998) Overnutrition, undernutrition and the body mass index: Implications for strength and motor fitness. In J Parizkova, AP Hills (eds), Physical Fitness and Nutrition during Growth. Basel: S Karger, pp 13-26.

Malina RM, Skrabanek MF, Little BB (1989) Growth and maturity status of black and white children classified as obese by different criteria. American Journal of Human Biology 1:193-199.

Manos TM, Gutin B, Rhodes T, Spandorfer PR, Jackson LW, Litaker MS (1993) Energy expenditure and intake in obese and nonobese African American girls. Annals of the New York Academy of Sciences 699:275-277.

Martorell R, Khan LK, Hughes ML, Grummer-Strawn LM (1998) Obesity in Latin American women and children. Journal of Nutrition 128:1464-1473.

Martorell R, Stein AD, Schroeder DG (2001) Early nutrition and later adiposity. Journal of Nutrition 131:847S-880S.

Mocellin R, Rutenfranz J (1971) Investigations of the physical working capacity of obese children. Acta Paediatrica Belgica 217 (suppl):77-79.

Mokdad AH, Bowman BA, Ford ES, Vinicor F, Marks JS, Koplan JP (2001) The continuing epidemics of obesity and diabetes in the United States. Journal of the American Medical Association 286:1195-1200.

Must A, Jacques PF, Dallal GE, Bajema CJ, Dietz WH (1992) Long-term morbidity and mortality of overweight adolescents. New England Journal of Medicine 327:1350-1355.

Neumark-Sztainer D, Story M, French SA, Hannan PJ, Resnick MD, Blum RW (1997) Psychosocial concerns and health-compromising behaviors among overweight and non-overweight adolescents. Obesity Research 5:237-249.

Ogden CL, Flegal KM, Carroll MD, Johnson CL (2002) Prevalence and trends in overweight among US children and adolescents, 1999–2000. Journal of the American Medical Association 288:1728-1732.

Ogden CL, Troiano RP, Briefel RR, Kuczmarski RJ, Flegal KM, Johnson CL (1997) Prevalence of overweight among pre-school children in the United States, 1971 through 1994. Pediatrics 99. http://www.pediatrics.org/cgi/content/full/99/4/e1.

Pena Reyes ME, Cardenas Barahona EE, Cahuich MB, Barragan A, Malina RM (2002) Growth status of children 6–12 years from two different geographic regions of Mexico. Annals of Human Biology 28:11-25.

Perusse L, Chagnon YC, Weisnagel JS, Rankinen T, Snyder E, Sands J, Bouchard C (2001) The human obesity gene map: The 2000 update. Obesity Research 9:135-168.

Popkin BM, Richards MK, Monteiro CA (1996) Stunting is associated with overweight in children of four nations that are undergoing the nutrition transition. Journal of Nutrition 126:3009-3016.

Reybrouck T, Weymans M, Vinckx J, Stijns H, Vanderschueren-Lodeweyckx M (1987) Cardiorespiratory function during exercise in obese children. Acta Paediatrica Scandinavica 76:342-348.

Robinson TN (1999) Reducing children's television viewing to prevent obesity: A randomized control trial. Journal of the American Medical Association 282:1561-1567.

Robinson TN, Hammer LD, Killen JD, Kraemer HC, Wilson DM, Harward C, Taylor CB (1993) Does television viewing increase obesity and reduce physical activity? Cross-sectional and longitudinal analysis among adolescent girls. Pediatrics 91:273-280.

Rocchini AP (1998) Obesity and blood pressure regulation. In GA Bray, C Bouchard, WPT James (eds), Handbook of Obesity. New York: Marcel Dekker, pp 677-695.

Rolland-Cachera MF, Cole TJ, Sempe M, Tichet J, Rossignol C, Charraud A (1991) Body mass index variations: Centiles from birth to 87 years. European Journal of Clincal Nutrition 45:13-21.

Rolland-Cachera MF, Deheeger M, Guilloud-Bataille M, Avons P, Patois E, Sempe M (1987) Tracking the development of adiposity from one month of age to adulthood. Annals of Human Biology 14:219-229.

Rolland-Cachera MF, Deheeger M, Bellisle F, Sempe M, Guilloud-Bataille M, Patois E (1984) Adiposity rebound in children: A simple indicator for predicting obesity. American Journal of Clinical Nutrition 39:129-135.

Rowland TW (1990) Exercise and Children's Health. Champaign, IL: Human Kinetics.

Rowland TW (1991) Effects of obesity on aerobic fitness in adolescent females. American Journal of Diseases of Children 145:764-768.

Saelens BE, Epstein LH (1998) Behavioral engineering of activity choice in obese children. International Journal of Obesity 22:275-277.

Salbe AD, Fontville AM, Harper IT, Ravussin E (1997) Low levels of physical activity in 5 year old children. Journal of Pediatrics 131:423-429.

Salbe AD, Ravussin E (2000) The determinants of obesity. In C Bouchard (ed), Physical Activity and Obesity. Champaign, IL: Human Kinetics, pp 69-102.

Saltzman E, Benotti PN (1998) The effects of obesity on the cardiovascular system. In GA Bray, C Bouchard, WPT James (eds), Handbook of Obesity. New York: Marcel Dekker, pp 637-649.

* Serdula MK, Ivery D, Coates RJ, Freedman DZ, Williamson DF, Byers T (1993) Do obese children become obese adults? A review of the literature. Preventive Medicine 22:167-177.

Shah M, Jeffery RW (1991) Is obesity due to overeating and inactivity, or to a defective metabolic rate? A review. Annals of Behavioral Medicine 13:73-81.

Simmons RG, Blyth DA (1987) Moving into Adolescence: The Impact of Pubertal Change and Social Context. New York: Aldine de Gruyter.

Stevens J (1995) Obesity, fat patterning and cardiovascular risk. Advances in Experimental Medicine and Biology 369:21-27.

Story M, Faulkner P (1990) The prime-time diet: A content analysis of eating behavior in television program content and commercials. American Journal of Public Health 80:738-740.

Treuth MS, Butte NF, Wong WW (2000) Contribution of energy expenditure to obesity. American Journal of Clinical Nutrition 71:893-900.

Treuth MS, Figueroa-Colon R, Hunter GR, Weinsier RL, Butte NF, Goran MI (1998) Energy expenditure and physical fitness in overweight vs non-overweight prepubertal girls. International Journal of Obesity Research 22:440-447.

* Troiano RP, Flegal KM (1998) Overweight children and adolescents: Description, epidemiology, and demographics. Pediatrics 101:497-504.

von Kries R, Koletzko B, Sauerwald T, von Mutius E, Barnert D, Grunert V, von Voss H (1999) Breast-feeding and obesity: Cross-sectional study. British Medical Journal 319: 147-150.

Wadsworth M, Marshall S, Hardy R, Paul A (1999) Breast-feeding and obesity: Relation may be accounted for by social factors. British Medical Journal 319:1576.

Whitaker RC, Dietz WH (1998) Role of the prenatal environment in the development of obesity. Journal of Pediatrics 132:768-776.

Whitaker RC, Pepe MS, Wright JA, Seidel KD, Dietz WH (1998) Early adiposity rebound and the risk of adult obesity. Pediatrics 101:E51-E56.

Wolf AM, Gortmaker SL, Cheung L, Gray HM, Herzog DB, Colditz GA (1993) Activity, inactivity, and obesity: Differences related to race, ethnicity, and age among girls. American Journal of Public Health 83:1625-1627.

World Health Organization (1995) Physical Status: The Use and Interpretation of Anthropometry. Geneva: World Health Organization Technical Report Series No. 854.

World Health Organization (1998) Obesity: Preventing and Managing the Global Epidemic. Report of a WHO Consultation on Obesity. Geneva: World Health Organization.

York D, Bouchard C (2000) How obesity develops: Insights from the new biology. Endocrine 13:143-154.

Zanconato S, Baraldi E, Santuz P, Rigon F, Vido L, Da Dalt L, Zacchello F (1989) Gas exchange during exercise in obese children. European Journal of Pediatrics 148: 614-617.

Chapter 25

OTHER FACTORS AFFECTING GROWTH, MATURATION, PERFORMANCE, AND ACTIVITY

Chapter Outline

The preceding chapters in this section considered the primary factors that influence growth and maturation—genes, hormones, energy, and nutrients. Regular programs of physical activity may influence body weight and composition but have little effect on growth in height and maturity. Chronic undernutrition and obesity have well-described affects on growth, maturity, and performance and may also influence physical activity. Other factors may influence these processes and outcomes, but the extent and exact manner of their influence are difficult to specify. Several such factors are considered in this chapter, including social circumstances, racial and ethnic background, and climate. Although the factors are considered separately, they are complex and undoubtedly interact with each other.

Social Conditions, Growth, and Maturation

The conditions into which children are born and subsequently reared can influence growth and maturation. These conditions include quality of living conditions, family size or number of siblings, place of residence (urban or rural), and overall socioeconomic circumstances. All are related, and accounting for the effects of specific social factors is difficult.

Socioeconomic Status

General living conditions associated with socioeconomic status (SES) include variation in educational background of parents, purchasing power for food and, in turn, nutritional status, access to and use of health-care facilities and programs, and overall regularity of lifestyle. The SES of a child's family is a significant factor that can affect growth and maturation. Criteria of SES vary considerably among studies and among different countries, so comparisons are difficult. Criteria relevant to one area, cultural group, or country are not necessarily relevant to others. Commonly used indicators of SES in developed, western countries include annual family income, per capita income, occupation and education of the head of the household, and place of residence. Children from better-off socioeconomic circumstances within a country tend to be, on average, taller and heavier than those from poorer socioeconomic conditions.

Growth status of 8-year-old children from the extremes of the socioeconomic spectrum within several developing countries is shown in figure 25.1. Differences in size attained by children from contrasting socioeconomic backgrounds vary among countries. However, overall health and nutritional circumstances associated with low SES and inequitable distribution of resources in many developing countries magnify differences between the upper and lower social strata.

During adolescence and especially in later adolescence, however, girls from lower SES in developed countries tend to be, on average, fatter than those in the upper SES. An inverse relationship between social class and fatness, which becomes evident during the transition into adolescence, persists into adulthood. Factors related to this trend are discussed in the section dealing with psychological and emotional factors affecting growth and maturity.

In contrast to measures of body size, SES variation in age at PHV and age at menarche is generally smaller. Data for three European countries are summarized in table 25.1. The indicator of SES is based on the occupation and education of the fathers in each study. Among British and Polish adolescents, those from better-off socioeconomic circumstances attain PHV and menarche,

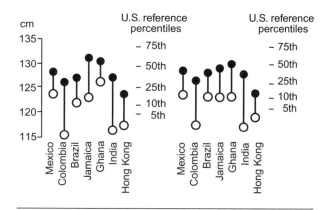

Socioeconomic Contrasts
in Growth Studies

FIGURE 25.1   Mean statures of 8-year-old urban upper (filled circles) and lower (open circles) SES children in several developing countries relative to United States reference data: left panel—girls, right panel—boys.

Sources of data are: Mexico (Villanueva,1979), Colombia (Rueda-Williamson et al. 1969; Macias et al. 1978), Brazil (Marques et al. 1974), Jamaica (Ashcroft and Lovell 1964), Ghana (Kpedekpo 1970), India (Vijaya Raghavan et al. 1971), and Hong Kong (Chang et al. 1963).

on average, slightly earlier than those in lesser socioeconomic conditions. In contrast, SES differences in PHV and menarche are not evident among Swedish adolescents.

SES variation in growth and maturity is generally specific to a given country. Generalization from one country to another is difficult because criteria of socioeconomic circumstances vary and do not necessarily have the same meaning. Social welfare programs also vary among countries and may function to balance economic or income differentials among families and in turn SES differentials in growth and maturity status of children.

Family Size

Family size, the number of siblings or children in a family, may be a confounding factor in evaluating the effects of SES on growth and maturity because larger family sizes occur more often among those of lower SES. The effects of variation in the number of siblings on the stature of British children 5 to 11 years of age are shown in figure 25.2. Among better-off children whose fathers worked in nonmanual occupations (higher SES), number of siblings does not affect height except in large families (five or more siblings). On the other

| TABLE 25.1 | Variation in Mean Ages at Peak Height Velocity (PHV) and Menarche With Socioeconomic Status (SES) in Adolescents From Developed Countries |||

	Father's occupation		
	Nonmanual	**Skilled manual**	**Unskilled manual**
England, Newcastle upon Tyne[a]			
PHV (females)	12.0	12.2	12.2
Menarche	13.2	13.4	13.4
PHV (males)	14.1	14.0	14.3
	Father's education		
	Academic	**Secondary**	**Primary/vocational**
Poland, Wroclaw[b]			
PHV (females)	11.4	11.9	11.9
Menarche	12.7	13.3	13.3
PHV (males)	13.8	13.9	14.1
	Father's occupation		
	Employers	**Salaried employees**	**Manual workers**
Sweden, urban[c]			
PHV (females)	12.0	12.0	11.8
Menarche	13.1	13.1	13.1
PHV (males)	14.0	14.0	14.1

	Annual family income			
	1 (high)	**2**	**3**	**4 (low)**
PHV (females)	11.9	11.9	12.1	11.8
Menarche	13.0	13.2	13.2	13.1
PHV (males)	14.2	14.1	14.1	14.0

Note the different criteria of SES.
[a]Adapted from Billewicz et al. (1981).
[b]Adapted from Bielicki (1986).
[c]Adapted from Lindgren (1976).

hand, among children whose fathers worked in manual occupations (lower SES), there is seen a gradient for a reduction in the height of children from families with one or two children through families with five or more children (Rona et al. 1979). Similar trends are also apparent for the heights of adolescents (Billewicz et al. 1983). After taking into account differences in birth weight, maternal height, and age at PHV, adolescents from large families (five or more children) of unskilled manual workers are significantly shorter than average.

Age at menarche also shows variation with family size. Girls from larger families tend to attain menarche, on average, later than girls from smaller families (see table 25.2). Not all studies control for both SES and number of children in the family. Among British girls from Newcastle upon Tyne, for example, the difference in mean age at menarche is caused entirely by a later age at menarche among girls from larger families whose fathers worked in manual occupations.

The estimated effects of variation in the number of siblings on the age at menarche in several samples of American and European girls are shown in table 25.3. Estimated effects vary from 0.1 to 0.2 years per additional sibling in the family. For example, if the mean age at menarche for the population is 13.0 years, the estimated age at menarche for girls from a family with four

Variation in Height by Family Size

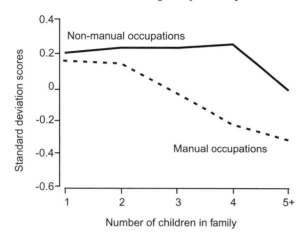

FIGURE 25.2 Statures of English children 5 to 11 years of age expressed as mean standard deviation units according to their father's occupational status (indicator of SES) and number of children in the family. Standard deviation scores above zero indicate statures above British reference averages, and those below zero indicate statures below the reference averages.

Data from Rona et al., 1979.

children might be expected to vary between 13.4 and 13.8 years. In contrast to the number of siblings in the family, birth order or position among the siblings does not appear to have a significant effect on size attained or age at menarche.

The effect of family size on growth and menarche is often related to SES, that is, larger families in many countries tend to be from poorer economic circumstances. Mechanisms that link the number of children in the family to growth and maturation are not known at present. Nevertheless, how can the sibling number effect be explained? The number of children in the family is possibly an indirect estimate of birth spacing or birth crowding. As birth intervals decline, that is, the interval between the termination of one pregnancy and the beginning of the next pregnancy declines, mortality in infancy and early childhood increases (Wray 1971). Birth interval has a small effect on growth in height—shorter intervals are associated with shorter heights (Grant 1964) and on menarche—the shorter the interval, the later the menarche of the next child (Douglas 1966). These observations, although limited, would seem to suggest that the time interval between the births of children might be

TABLE 25.2   Mean Ages at Menarche According to Family Size in Samples of European Girls

| Family size | England | | Belgium[a] |
	South Shields[b]	Newcastle[c]	Flemish (national)
1	13.04	13.06	12.94
2	13.14	13.13	13.14
3	13.45	13.47	13.19
4	13.68	13.37	13.27
5+	13.66	13.62	13.47

| | Poland | | | |
| | Wroclaw[d] | | | |
Family size	White collar	Laborer	Warsaw[e]	Rural[e]
1	12.93	12.81	12.72	13.09
2	12.91	13.19	12.94	13.43
3	13.23	13.28	13.04	13.51
4	13.29	13.50		13.55
5+				13.68

[a]Adapted from Wellens (1984).

[b]Adapted from Roberts et al. (1971).

[c]Adapted from Roberts et al. (1975).

[d]Adapted from Piasecki and Waliszko (1975). A family size of 4 indicates four or more children in the family.

[e]Adapted from Laska-Mierzejewska et al. (1982). In Warsaw, a family size of 3 indicates three or more children in the family.

TABLE 25.3	Estimated Effects of Family Size (Number of Children in the Family) on the Age at Menarche in Several American and European Samples

Samples	Estimated years per additional sibling in the family
United States	
High school students	0.12*
University students	0.08*
University students	0.19*
Belgium	
School girls	0.11
Romania	
School girls	0.17
United Kingdom	
School girls	0.18
School girls	0.15
University students	0.15*
University students	0.12*

The reported values are regression coefficients. Those with an asterisk (*) are partial regression coefficients controlling for birth order.

Adapted from Malina et al. (1997), which contains the references to specific studies.

a factor mediating the effects of family size on growth and maturation.

Psychological/Emotional Factors

Many case studies of children and adolescents clearly indicate the influence of adverse living conditions, particularly psychosocial or emotional circumstances, on growth and maturation (Patton 1963; Money 1977). This condition is sometimes labeled "psychosocial dwarfism" or "deprivation dwarfism" in the clinical literature. Size attained is stunted and maturity is severely delayed, often by as much as 2 to 3 years. Children reared under such psychological and emotional circumstances ordinarily do not have specific endocrine or metabolic disorders or a familial history of growth retardation, and their diets are often adequate. The mechanisms through which a stressful home environment influences growth and maturation are not known, but most likely include maternal deprivation, isolation of

the child from others, a disorganized family life, and, occasionally, physical abuse. Nevertheless, the matrix of environmental circumstances associated with "deprivation dwarfism" can lead to impaired or suppressed growth hormone production and inadequate dietary intake or impaired nutrient utilization.

More specific aspects of the home environment also need consideration. Several recent studies, for example, suggest a potential influence of household composition (e.g., presence or absence of the father) and familial distress (e.g., death of a parent, divorce, or parental alcoholism) on indicators of growth and maturity. For example, girls in father-absent homes tend to attain menarche at an earlier age (Surbey 1990; Graber et al. 1995; Ge et al. 1996; Ellis et al. 1999; Ellis and Garber 2000), and familial distress is associated with an earlier age at menarche and shorter adult height (Hulanicka 1999; Hulanicka et al. 2001). Although the associations are not strong, they suggest a role for family relationships and quality of life within the household as potential factors, among others, that may influence growth and maturity.

The influence of the psychological or emotional conditions under which food is distributed and eaten can also have an effect on the growth of children. This finding was apparent, for example, after World War II in the weights and statures of children in two, small municipal orphanages in West Germany in 1948 (Widdowson 1951). Children in both orphanages had the same diet for 6 months. During the next 6 months, however, one of the orphanages received unlimited amounts of bread in addition to extra jam and orange juice, but the other orphanage did not. The statures and weights of the children were measured every 2 weeks for 1 year. During the first 6 months of observation, children in the two orphanages gained weight at different rates. Over the course of the next 6 months, however, children in the orphanage that received extra rations of bread gained only about the same amount of weight as they did over the first 6 months of observation, whereas those in the other orphanage, which received the same rations as in the first 6 months, gained considerably more weight. The differential growth of children in the two orphanages was apparently related to emotional stresses associated with the manner in which they were treated by the adults in charge of each orphanage. The housemother in the orphanage that received more rations was very strict and often publicly reprimanded and criticized the children during mealtimes.

The psychological or emotional environment under which food is eaten may influence the amount eaten and perhaps the utilization of energy and nutrients by the growing individual. Even though adequate nutrition was available in the orphanages, the housemothers were apparently significant factors affecting the nutritional process and, in turn, growth. Thus, nutrition is more than food and nutrients. Eating is a social activity, and the context of the activity can influence the outcomes.

From another perspective, many adolescent girls, and to a much lesser extent adolescent boys, have concerns about their body weight. The emphasis on and preference for slenderness in United States, Canada, and many European countries and in upper social strata of many Latin American countries impacts girls at relatively young ages so that many feel pressures to be slender beginning at 9 and 10 years of age. As girls progress through adolescence, concerns for body weight and the desire to be thin increase. Approximately two-thirds of adolescent girls are not satisfied with their weight (Moore 1993). Many girls begin self-imposed dieting and in some cases major restriction of energy intake arising from a fear of becoming fat or in an obsessive pursuit of thinness. This condition may result in severe malnutrition associated with growth failure and delayed maturation (Pugliese et al. 1983; Lifshitz and Moses 1988).

Uncontrolled dieting may contribute to the development of eating disorders during adolescence, such as anorexia nervosa and bulimia. They occur primarily in girls who are or who perceive themselves as being overweight or who have a fear of becoming fat, a weight phobia, or an obsession with thinness. Anorexia nervosa refers to an almost total lack of food intake caused by a morbid fear of becoming fat or obese, whereas bulimia refers to episodes of binge eating followed by vomiting and use of laxatives or diuretics. Anorexics are characterized by extreme weight loss (they appear emaciated), delayed sexual maturity, and if maturity has occurred, secondary amenorrhea. Bulimics, on the other hand, typically have a mild to moderate weight loss and menstrual irregularities. Both conditions typically occur in adolescence, anorexia in early adolescence and bulimia in late adolescence. Anorexia often occurs during the transition from childhood into adolescence as girls attempt to deal with changes in size and body composition associated with the onset of puberty. The peak age of occurrence of anorexia is about 14 years, but it can also occur earlier or later, and the peak age of occurrence of bulimia is about 19 years (Steinhausen 1994). Clinical consequences of anorexia and implications for physical activity and fitness are discussed in more detail in chapter 27.

In summary, many factors in the social environment of the child are apparently capable of influencing growth and maturation. The specific operation of these factors is, however, difficult to specify. Nevertheless, the processes of growth and maturation are quite plastic, and psychosocial conditions and pressures are capable of exerting a powerful influence.

Area of Residence

SES variation in growth and maturity may be influenced by area of residence, which has been viewed most often in an urban or rural context. In the late 19th century and in the early 20th century, children resident in rural areas in the United States and western European countries were generally taller and heavier than those in urban areas. However, by about the 1930s, conditions improved in the urban centers, especially related to access to health services and housing, so that rural-urban differences were reduced or reversed (Meredith 1979, 1982). At present, differences in living conditions between urban and rural areas are quite negligible, so virtually no differences exist in size attained and maturity status between children in urban and rural areas in the United States, Canada, and most western European countries (Hamill et al. 1972; van Wieringen et al. 1971; Eveleth and Tanner 1976, 1990).

In contrast, some European countries, especially in Eastern Europe (e.g., Poland and Romania) and the Mediterranean area (e.g., Greece) continue to show an urban-rural gradient in growth and maturity (Bielicki 1986). Studies of 19-year-old Polish conscripts best illustrate urban-rural differences because they account for factors that potentially confound the comparisons. Among young adult males surveyed in 1986, conscripts from rural areas whose fathers were peasants and who were from large families (five or more children) were about 4 cm shorter than conscripts from large cities whose fathers were college educated and involved in nonmanual work and were from small families (one or two children), about 173 cm compared with 177 cm, respectively (Bielicki et al. 1992). Corresponding heights in 1995 were about 174 cm for conscripts from rural areas with fathers who were peasants and with parents who had only an elementary school education, compared with about 179 cm for conscripts from large cities with parents who had a college education (Bielicki et al. 1997). The trends for Polish conscripts suggest that the urban-rural contrast in young adult height has not changed over time from 1965 to 1995. Similar trends are also apparent in Polish children 6 to 18 years of age (Hulanicka et al. 1990). Rural Polish girls also attain menarche later than urban girls, although the difference between mean ages has declined from about 1 year to 0.6 year from surveys in 1955 to 1988 (Bielicki et al. 1981; Hulanicka and Waliszko 1991).

Similar urban-rural contrasts are evident among Han children and adolescents in China (Han are the dominant ethnic group in China). Differences between mean heights of urban and rural Chinese boys 7 to 18 years of age range between 2.9 and 5.7 cm; corresponding differences between mean heights of urban and rural girls range between 2.1 and 5.6 cm (Lin et al. 1992a). The urban-rural difference contrast is also reflected in later ages at menarche in rural girls (Lin et al. 1992b; Ohsawa et al. 1997). Similar urban-rural contrasts are evident in the growth and maturity status of children and adolescents in parts of Africa (Spurgeon et al. 1984; Cameron et al. 1992).

Urban-rural differences in growth and maturation reflect to a large extent the distribution of and access to resources within a country. These resources include economic, educational, nutritional and health-related resources. Such resources are often concentrated in urban centers and are limited in the extent to which they filter into the rural areas of some countries.

Urban-rural contrasts in many developing countries of Africa, Asia, and Latin America are magnified by chronic nutritional problems in the rural areas (see chapter 23), in addition to marked economic inequities. In the more developed countries of these regions, the urban-rural contrast in growth and maturity reflects SES variation, that is, the larger size and earlier maturity of urban children reflects the better-off economic circumstances and access to resources of city residents (Eveleth and Tanner 1990).

Cities in many developing areas of the world are rapidly expanding as a result of rural-to-urban migration. Quite commonly, migrants from rural areas form irregular settlements on a city's edge. Such neighborhoods are variously labeled in the literature, but a common term appears to be "shanty towns." Health and nutritional conditions associated with migration are generally poor. A comparison of the growth status of rural children and children resident in urban shantytowns (**colonias populares**) in southern Mexico in the early 1970s indicated relatively small differences. Boys in the colonias were slightly, but consistently, taller and heavier than boys in rural indigenous communities, but girls in both communities did not differ in height and weight (Malina et al. 1981). Urban colonia and rural girls also did not differ in age at menarche (Malina et al. 1980). One of the colonias and one of the rural communities were surveyed again in 2000. Urban-rural differences in height and weight declined over time in boys 6 to 9 years of age but decreased in height and increased in weight in boys 10 to 12 years of age. In contrast, urban-rural differences in height among girls 6 to 9 years of age were the same in both surveys but were larger for weight in the recent survey, and urban-rural differences in height and weight increased over time in girls 10 to 12 years of age (Malina and Peña-Reyes 2002). Given the relatively high rate of migration from rural to urban areas in Latin American cities (as well as in other parts of the developing world), the need for ongoing studies of the growth status of children who migrate with their families is highlighted. With a longer duration of residence in urban areas, growth status may improve compared with children in rural areas.

Smoking

Infants born to mothers who smoked regularly during pregnancy have lower birth weights and lengths, the effect being greater on weight than on length (see chapter 2). Maternal smoking during pregnancy also has an influence on postnatal growth. The estimated deficits of growth in length and weight, respectively, associated with maternal smoking during pregnancy is 0.5 cm and 10 g between 6 months and 2 years of age, 0.8 cm and 400 g between 2 and 6 years of age, and 1.2 cm and 1,400 g between 6 and 12 years of age (Roche 1999). The deficits in growth perhaps reflect the effects of smoking during pregnancy per se and exposure to secondary smoke in the home during childhood. The effects of maternal substance abuse (cocaine, heroin, and methadone) during pregnancy on postnatal growth during the first 2 to 3 years are somewhat smaller than those associated with smoking. Estimated deficits of growth in length and weight at 2 years of age associated with maternal cocaine use are 1.8 cm and 537 g. Corresponding deficits in length and weight at 3 years of age associated with maternal methadone use are 1.6 cm and 300 g. Maternal use of heroin is associated with a small deficit in length at 3 years, 0.3 cm, and with an increase in weight, 200 g (Roche 1999). Potential effects of combined smoking and substance abuse are not available. The preceding estimates need to be viewed with a degree of caution. They are based on self-reports, so specific dosages are not generally known and multiple substances may be used.

Estimated effects of parental smoking on the heights of 6-year-old to 11-year-old children suggest a dose-response effect—the greater the number of cigarettes smoked, the greater the effect on growth (see table 25.4). Children from homes where parents smoke tend to be, on average, shorter than those from homes where parents do not smoke, and maternal smoking has a greater influence on growth in height than paternal smoking (Berkey et al. 1984). Although the differences in attained height during childhood are small, about 1 cm between means, results are reasonably consistent across studies. In addition, children from homes where parents smoke also experience an increased number of days sick per year, especially with respiratory ailments.

These results indicate a significant influence of smoking, perhaps combined effects of smoking during pregnancy and subsequent parental smoking in the home, on growth in stature. Because children tend to spend more time with their

mothers, one might expect maternal smoking to have a more important effect than paternal smoking. Nevertheless, passive smoking (i.e., breathing in smoke exhaled by parents and smoke emitted from cigarettes) is related to size attained by children. On the other hand, currently available information indicates no significant effect of parental smoking on the rate of growth in stature. This apparently incongruous finding suggests, perhaps, an important role for long-term effects of prenatal exposure to smoke on size attained during childhood, but the results are not conclusive.

An effect of passive smoking on growth and maturation during adolescence is not established. Active smoking may also become a significant factor at this time, but carefully controlled studies of active smoking by the child on growth and maturation are not available.

Social Conditions, Motor Development, Performance, and Activity

Motor development, performance, and physical activity occur in a social context (e.g., home, play, and school). Each of these contexts places specific demands on the motor competencies and physical activity of infants, children, and adolescents. The specific influences of social conditions have not been systematically evaluated in the context of motor development, performance, and activity. Social conditions interact with the child's rate of neuromuscular maturation, physical characteristics and rate of growth, prior and current experiences in motor activities, and habitual physical activity. A biosocial or biocultural framework is essential for discussions of social conditions on motor development and performance. The child carries out motor acts in a social context.

As in the case of growth and maturation, the specific influences of social conditions on motor development, performance, and activity are difficult to indicate. Quality of living conditions, family size or number of siblings, interactions among siblings, area of residence (urban-rural or inner city–suburban), and overall socioeconomic circumstances, all of which are related, are potentially important factors to consider.

Socioeconomic Status

As noted earlier, variation in lifestyle associated with social class is often viewed in the context of socioeconomic status (SES). Commonly used in-

TABLE 25.4	Estimated Deficits in Height in 6-Year-Old to 11-Year-Old Children Associated With Parental Cigarette Smoking	
	Estimated deficits in height (cm)	
	Maternal smoking	**Paternal smoking**
Cigarettes/day	**Mean**	**Mean**
Nonsmoker	0	0
Light smoker (1–9/day)	−0.45	−0.04
Heavy smoker (10+/day)	−0.65	−0.10

Data are adjusted for age, sex, SES, use of cooking fuel, city of residence, and maternal or paternal smoking.
Adapted from Berkey et al. (1984).

dicators of SES include income, educational level and occupation of parents, and neighborhood of residence. These indicators per se do not directly influence motor competence and physical activity. Rather, SES more likely influences motor competence and activity through effects on lifestyle, such as rearing practices, opportunity for activity, and access to special instruction, equipment, and facilities. A confounding factor with SES is its association with ethnicity and race in many parts of the world. In the United States, for example, many children of African American (Black) and Mexican American (Hispanic) ancestry are reared under low SES conditions and, in many instances, poverty.

Rearing practices and parental supervision are often said to vary with SES. Accordingly, lower SES is said to be characterized by a more permissive rearing atmosphere, which provides greater freedom for physical activity and, in turn, enhances motor competence during early childhood. At school ages, lower SES children are often described as having greater freedom to move about a neighborhood than children of higher SES. Such an atmosphere is assumed to be conducive to greater freedom of activity and opportunity for practice of motor skills and, in turn, greater proficiency (Malina 1973b, 1980).

Systematic analyses of the relationship between SES and motor development are not entirely consistent with the socioeconomic hypothesis. In a national sample of American Black and White infants, for example, no differences were seen in the motor scores of infants grouped either by educational level of the mother or father (Bayley 1965), both of which are often used as a proxy for SES. Variation in motor development among ethnic groups in the United States and Europe is also often attributed to class differences in rearing, but class differences are not always consistent across studies (Hindley et al. 1966; Malina 1980). Information on social class and motor achievements at ages beyond 2 years are not extensive, and several studies indicate no relationship between SES and motor performance of school-age American children. Results of studies in the United States that relate motor development to SES during early childhood, however, are inconclusive both within and between ethnic groups (ethnic variation is considered later in the chapter), and data for school-age children indicate that SES does not consistently influence motor performance (Malina 1973b, 1980, 1988). In a large sample of Polish youth, parental education and family living conditions (income, family size, and living area), commonly used proxies for SES, had only a weak influence on a variety of motor performances (Wolanski 1993).

The role of variation in SES of the family on habitual physical activity of children and adolescence has received some attention. Among Taiwanese adolescents 12 to 14 years of age, no SES differences were seen in estimated total energy expenditure and energy expenditure in moderate-to-vigorous activities in boys for either weekdays or weekend days. Corresponding data for Taiwanese girls indicated no differences in estimated total energy expenditure by SES on either weekdays or weekend days but greater expenditure energy in low SES girls in moderate-to-vigorous activities on weekend days. Although these trends are suggestive, SES accounted for relatively little of the explained variance in estimated total energy expenditure and energy expenditure in moderate-to-vigorous physical activity in Taiwanese adolescents (Huang and Malina 1996). In contrast, SES was related to physical activities of other samples of adolescents. For example, in a sample of Canadian adolescents, high SES was related to the student's intention to exercise (Godin and Shephard 1986). Paternal occupation was significantly related to the overall frequency of exercise in 7th and 8th grade American boys and girls (Gottlieb and Chen 1985), whereas educational level of the father affected the sport involvement and diversity of Belgian adolescent boys—the higher the educational level, the greater the amount of sport practiced per week over 1 year and the greater diversity of sport participation (Renson et al. 1980).

Specific aspects of the socioeconomic environment may affect motor competence and physical activity, but these are not detected by the commonly used indices of SES. More important, the translation of specific SES or familial characteristics into variation in motor performance and physical activity is not ordinarily done. What is unique about a high or low SES familial environment that may affect the activity and performance of individuals in these households? SES, for example, is a factor that influences access to many organized sports and club programs, often at relatively young ages, in which children receive specialized instruction and practice under the guidance of trained coaches.

Rearing Style

Variation in rearing atmosphere is frequently indicated as a significant factor influencing motor development during infancy and childhood. Rearing style is a multifactorial construct that has changed through time. These changes have been described for child care practices in the United States from the 1930s through the 1970s (Bronfenbrenner 1958; Waters and Crandall 1964). From 1940 to 1960, for example, mothers, regardless of social class, showed a tendency to be less coercive and more permissive. Rearing practices also vary with social class and ethnicity/race, but much overlap occurs (Hess 1970; Jackson 1973). The structure of the family and the trend to more single parent families and more widespread availability of day care have changed more rapidly from the 1970s into the 1990s. Additional factors in the United States that affect rearing conditions and lifestyle are changes in the composition of the population associated with recent immigrations and in the distribution of resources in the United States (Hernandez 1994).

The issue of interest is the predictive and explanatory power of observed rearing differences on the child's motor development and performance. This issue has not been systematically investigated. Part of the problem is methodological; the nature of parent–child relationships and their situational context are not stable. As such, the translation of observed differences in rearing practices to motor development and performance is difficult. For example, cultural conditioning for specific sex-associated roles begins early in life, and sex differences exist in how boys and girls are reared. Yet, sex differences in motor development, as measured by developmental scales such as the Bayley Scales of Infant Development, Gesell Scales, or the Denver Developmental Screening Test, during the first year or two of life are not systematically apparent, and evidence for sex differences in the age at independent walking is not consistent. However, by about 2 to 3 years of age, sex differences are apparent in some motor tasks, and they persist into the school ages. Similar trends are also suggested in ages at which the majority of children attain specific stages of specific movement patterns (see figure 10.2, page 204). Although considerable overlap exists between boys and girls in early childhood, the fact that sex differences appear at relatively young ages would seem to beg an explanation. Sex differences in early motor competence need to be examined in the context of opportunity for and frequency of practice, appropriateness of models (e.g., how often do girls throw with their fathers?), and guided instruction. These are specific components of rearing style that may more directly relate to the development of competence in motor skills. The potential interactions between growth, maturity, and motor characteristics of the child with rearing conditions need consideration. For example, how do the motor characteristics of a child, or level of motor proficiency, influence the rearing environment? Mothers of infants who were rated as competent on the Bayley Scales of development interacted more with their infants in a manner that focused on the child's abilities and interests (Moore 1977). The characteristics of the child, including motor characteristics, are thus important factors in eliciting specific behaviors from the parents, which may serve to reinforce infant behaviors. These observations need to be extended to older ages.

Data relating rearing to motor proficiency at older ages are scanty and at times unclear. One study suggests a positive relationship between a high disciplinarian attitude of the mother and the development of the standing long jump, but a positive relationship between a low disciplinarian attitude of the mother and the development of overhand throwing (Schnabl-Dickey 1977). Among children in primary grades (kindergarten through grade 3), social variables that influenced throwing performance vary with age, but generally reflected parental influences, parent–child interactions, and play experiences in both sexes (East and Hensley 1985). Interestingly, the influence of social variables on throwing performance decreases with age, suggesting that the influence of social factors decreases with increased proficiency. In another study of children in primary grades, mothers of small samples of low SES 7-year-old to 9-year-old children were classified at exerting authoritarian or nonauthoritarian control. The former referred to active maternal efforts to shape, control, and evaluate the behavior of their children to meet a set standard of conduct, whereas the latter referred to the lack of such maternal control efforts. Boys and girls whose mothers were classified as exerting nonauthoritarian control performed significantly better in a 30-yard dash and the standing long jump than those whose mothers were classified as authoritarian (Lee 1980). Results of such studies, of course, are only associational and do not imply a cause-and-effect sequence between rearing style and motor development. Specific motor patterns might differ in degree of environmental sensitivity, which may, in turn, be related to differential rates of neuromuscular maturation of motor patterns. More specific research is essential to understanding the translation of rearing styles and attitudes into variation in motor competence. The research needs to be extended to older ages and to habits of physical activity. Virtually all studies indicate that girls, on average, are less active than boys (Pratt et al. 1999).

Sibling Interactions

The influence of SES and rearing on motor development and performance may be mediated in part by the presence of siblings in the household. Thus, a child's position in the family and sibling sex status may be potentially important influencing factors. Studies of birth order and sibling interaction ordinarily do not include motor proficiency as the primary focus. Nevertheless, several questions merit investigation. Does the motor development of an only child differ from that of a child with siblings? Does the sex of siblings have an influence on motor development? Do sibling interactions differ by age and sex? Are motor development and performance affected by number of siblings in the family as is statural growth and sexual maturation? These questions and others concerning family structure, sibling interactions, and parent–child interactions as influences on motor development and performance need more detailed study.

Firstborn infants generally show advanced motor behavior compared with later-born infants. This observation is generally related to greater maternal indulgence and therefore stimulation of the firstborn compared with later-born children (Malina 1980, 1983). Whether the accelerated motor development persists beyond infancy or after a second child is born is not known.

Some evidence indicates age-associated and perhaps sex-associated variation in movement and observational behaviors of 3-year-old to 5-year-old siblings during participation in gross motor activities (Erbaugh and Clifton 1984). Under experimental conditions involving body-oriented and object-oriented motor activities, older siblings initiated performance of body-oriented activities such as climbing and jumping and repeated and practiced object-oriented tasks such as striking and throwing more than younger siblings. In contrast, younger siblings imitated the movements of older siblings under conditions of both body-oriented and object-oriented play conditions more often than older siblings imitated activities of younger siblings. These observations

suggest an important role for modeling interactions among siblings, that is, older siblings more often serve as a model for the younger sibling. Further, younger boys in this experimental study generally imitated older siblings more often than did younger girls, and younger boys in mixed-sex sibling pairs imitated their older sisters more often than boys in other sibling pairs. Younger boys possibly imitate gross motor activities more than girls, or older sisters may be more nurturing of younger brothers than are older brothers or older sisters of younger sisters.

Sibling interactions between opposite-sex siblings are of particular interest to motor performance. Do girls with an older brother differ from girls with an older sister in strength, motor, and aerobic performance tasks? Similarly, do boys with an older sister differ in performance compared with boys with an older brother? The potential role for sibling interactions as a factor that influences the performance and activity pursuits of children and adolescents merits further study.

Data relating birth order to specific performances are limited. Among 12-year-old Hungarian children, differences between firstborn and later-born boys and girls in several performance tasks (grip strength, 60-m sprint, 12-minute run, standing long jump, and several tests of balance and coordination) were negligible (Farmosi et al. 1986). Generally similar trends were observed in the Azores Growth Study of boys and girls 10 to 15 years of age (Sobral 1989). No consistent birth-order effects were found in several measures of performance-related and health-related physical fitness (medicine ball throw, softball throw, standing long jump, sit-ups, 25-m dash, and heart rate response to a 1-minute run) in boys. On the other hand, several birth-order effects were seen among Azores girls, but no consistent pattern was apparent. For example, performance tended to improve with birth order in the softball throw for distance, the standing long jump, and the dash, whereas in grip strength and the medicine ball throw, secondborns and thirdborns tended to perform better than firstborns and fourthborns. The sex difference in trends was related to variation in social roles in the cultural context of the Azores (Sobral 1989).

Among a large sample of Belgian adolescent boys, no consistent differences were apparent in the performances of firstborn, intermediate-born, and lastborn boys on a variety of tasks: speed of limb movement, shuttle run, arm strength, vertical jump, leg lifts, flexed-arm hang, and sit-and-reach (Dhont 1978). This large sample of Belgian boys was also categorized in terms of family composition as a proxy for sibling sex status: boys from families with all male children, boys from mixed-sex families, and an only boy in families of all female children. Boys from families with all male children performed better in speed (plate tapping and shuttle run), power (vertical jump), strength (arm pull, leg lifts), and flexibility (sit-and-reach), but the differences were small. Nevertheless, they indicate the need to consider the potential influence of family composition and sibling sex status in studies of performance and physical activity.

Area of Residence

The potential role of area of residence in studies of performance and physical activity is perhaps most apparent in the environmental contrast between inner city and suburban neighborhoods. However, information on the role of area of residence as a factor influencing performance and physical activity is limited. Studies from the 1960s and 1970s indicate negligible differences in the physical fitness of urban and rural children in several European countries (Shephard 1978). Studies of Polish youth 7 to 15 years of age, in contrast, indicate consistent urban-rural differences in tests of motor fitness—vertical jump, medicine ball throw for distance, dash, and agility (Miernik 1965; Pilicz and Sadowska 1973). The differences in motor fitness may reflect the contrasting lifestyles of rural and urban populations in Poland in the 1960s and 1970s because size differences (height and weight) between the samples compared were rather small (Pilicz and Sadowska 1973).

Among Japanese primary school children 4 to 5 years of age, children resident in an island community were more flexible and had better motor coordination than urban children, but the latter performed better in tests of motor ability—standing long jump, ball throw, agility, and dash (Munetaka et al. 1971). Data for Japanese elementary school children and adolescents are variable (Tamura 1975). Rural adolescents of both sexes tend to have higher levels of aerobic power (ml/kg/min) and the urban-rural difference increases with age. On the other hand, corresponding urban-rural contrasts for motor performances vary among prefectures in Japan, but in many instances, urban children showed higher levels of motor ability. The rural-urban difference in endurance was attributed to the

fact that the rural children walked relatively long distances to school and spent more time in physical activity (Tamura 1975). This finding is consistent with the positive association between indicators of physical activity and energy expenditure and measures of cardiovascular endurance (see chapter 22, comparison of habitually active and inactive youth). On the other hand, the proficiency in motor ability among urban children was attributed to better access to school physical education and sport programs.

Urban-rural comparisons of the performance of contemporary American children are not available. A comparison early in the 20th century indicated negligible differences in lung capacity, grip strength, and speed of limb movement between urban and rural children in Missouri (Pyle 1920).

Urban-rural comparisons in developing areas of the world are of limited utility because of the generally marked socioeconomic and nutritional contrasts between communities (Malina 1990, see chapter 23). Nevertheless, results in some studies are variable. For example, rural children in South Africa of low socioeconomic status tend to have lower grip strength compared with urban children of high socioeconomic status, which probably reflects, to some extent, the reduced body size of the rural children. In contrast, comparisons of neuromuscular reaction time and pulse rate before and after exercise show no consistent rural-urban differences (Henneberg and Louw 1998).

The tendency for American minority youth to spend less time in physical activity (discussed in more detail later in the chapter) may reflect limited opportunity for activity associated with area of residence. Many minority families live in the inner city, and opportunities for physical activity and sport may be limited because of inadequate facilities, lack of organized youth sport programs, parental concern for safety of their children, marginal economic resources, or some combination of these and other factors.

Data for Belgian adolescent boys suggest urban-rural variation in sport participation (Renson et al. 1980). Urban boys were more active in sport but with no difference in diversity of sports between urban and rural boys. Similar results were obtained in Belgian adolescent girls. Urban girls were more involved in sports, in part because of parental involvement and differential access to facilities (Taks et al. 1991). Among Taiwan adolescents, estimated energy expenditure in moderate-to-vigorous physical activity was greater in rural youth (Huang and Malina 1996). Thus, area of residence, which is influenced by SES and other factors, needs further examination to identify specific determinants of physical activity or inactivity or of physical fitness or unfitness.

Correlates of Physical Activity

The preceding discussion considers several factors in the social environment that may influence motor development and performance and to a lesser extent physical activity. However, assessment of physical activity is not ordinarily a primary emphasis in these studies. Nevertheless, many factors in the social and physical environments of children and adolescents can influence habits of physical activity and patterns of energy expenditure. Several such factors were considered in chapter 21. Variation in physical activity and energy expenditure associated with race/ethnicity and climate are considered later in this chapter.

Ethnic Variation in Growth and Maturity

Although humans are more genetically similar than dissimilar, populations differ in a variety of genotypic and phenotypic characteristics, including measures of growth and maturity. They also differ in culturally determined habits, attitudes, and behavior patterns as well as in socioeconomic circumstances that can also influence these processes.

The terms ethnic and racial have different meanings, but are related. The term race implies a biologically distinct group, that is, one that has a relatively large percentage of its genes in common by descent. The term ethnic implies a culturally distinct group. Quite frequently, biological and cultural homogeneity overlap or coincide, such as in minorities of color and in linguistic and religious groups who share a common ancestry (Damon 1969). With few exceptions, however, racial background on a global basis has been viewed in terms of area of geographic origin (i.e., European, African, Asian, Amerindian, and Pacific Islands). Within the American culture complex, on the other hand, racial/ethnic background has been historically viewed on a color and surname basis—European Americans (i.e., Whites, non-Hispanic Whites, and Caucasians), African Americans (i.e., Blacks, and non-Hispanic Blacks), Native Americans (i.e., American Indians), Hispanic Americans (i.e., Mexican Americans, Puerto Ricans, Cubans, and Latinos)—and

more recently in terms of geographic origin (i.e., Asian Americans and Pacific Islanders). In Canada, native Canadians are indicated as First Nation (Amerindians), Inuit (Eskimo) and Metis (descendants of French Canadians and Cree Indians). For the sake of convenience, the term ethnic is used in this report, recognizing the complexity of issues related to the concept.

The genetic and cultural heterogeneity of the groups should be recognized. American Whites are derived from virtually all countries of Europe. American Blacks are descended from African slaves, most of whom were imported from West Africa in the 18th century, but have a significant degree of admixture with American Whites. A Hispanic surname is used to classify Hispanic Americans, a heterogeneous group that includes Mexican Americans, Puerto Ricans, Cubans, recent immigrants from Central and South American countries, and Europeans of Spanish ancestry. Mexican Americans, the largest Hispanic group, are largely descendants of admixture between American Indians and Spaniards that began in the 16th century. Thus, although individuals are labeled as belonging to a particular racial/ethnic group, variation is considerable within each of the categories, and many of the labels are arbitrary.

A comprehensive overview of ethnic variation in growth and maturity is beyond the scope of this text. Rather, several comparisons of reasonably well-nourished American and Asiatic children are used as illustrations. Racial/ethnic comparisons in many developing areas of the world are affected by inequities in economic resource distribution and chronic undernutrition. Nevertheless, among preschool children from several ethnic groups, variation in height and weight between social classes within a racial/ethnic group is greater than the variation between racial/ethnic groups (Habicht et al. 1974). Some racial/ethnic variation, however, is apparent among well-nourished children. For example, 2-year-old and 3-year-old Japanese children are, on average, slightly shorter than children of European and African ancestry.

American Children

The literature on ethnic variation in growth and maturation of American children are most readily available for children of African (Black), White (European), and Mexican (Mexican American) ancestry.

Birth Weight   Birth weight is, on average, less in Blacks than in Whites even after controlling for a variety of factors known to influence birth weight. Birth weights of Mexican Americans are similar to Whites (see table 2.5, page 31).

Height and Weight   Data from several national surveys indicate that stature is, on average, slightly greater in Black than in White children even though the majority of Blacks are from lower socioeconomic circumstances than Whites. The magnitude of the differences is generally small. However, the differences are more consistent and greater in girls than boys, but differences in the young adult stature of Blacks and Whites are negligible (Roche 1994). The data for body weight of Black and White children are more variable. White boys tend to be slightly heavier than Black boys at most ages, whereas Black girls tend to be heavier than White girls, especially during the transition into adolescence (Roche, 1994). Mexican American children, on the other hand, tend to be shorter and heavier than Black and White children (Martorell et al. 1989; Ryan and Roche 1990; Ryan et al. 1999).

Ethnic variation in height and weight has implications for obesity. Data from the most recent national health survey (NHANES 1999–2000, see table 3.1, page 51) indicate ethnic variation in the prevalence of risk of overweight and of overweight (obesity) among minor children and adolescents in the United States (see table 25.5). Ethnic variation in obesity among girls 2 to 5 years of age is small but suggests a somewhat higher prevalence among Mexican American boys compared with American White and Black boys 2 to 5 years of age. Among girls 6 to 19 years of age, obesity is more prevalent in American Blacks followed by Mexican Americans and then American Whites, whereas among boys 6 to 19 years of age, obesity is more prevalent in Mexican Americans followed by American Blacks and then American Whites. Moreover, the prevalence of obesity has increased in the past decade, more so in Mexican Americans and American Blacks compared with American Whites (Ogden et al. 2002). Factors that contribute to ethnic variation in the prevalence of obesity in the United States need systematic study.

Information on the growth of Native American (referred to as First Nation in Canada) children is rather limited. Heights are similar, but weights are generally heavier than American White children. Thus, the BMI tends to be high, which is reflected in a high prevalence of obesity in Native

TABLE 25.5   Prevalence (%) and Standard Errors (SE) of the Risk of Overweight and of Overweight (Obesity) in American Children and Adolescents in 1999 to 2000

| | At risk for overweight | | | | Overweight (obese) | | | |
| | Males | | Females | | Males | | Females | |
Age/ethnic group	%	SE	%	SE	%	SE	%	SE
2–5 years								
White	21.4	3.7	19.7	4.1	8.8	3.2	11.5	3.3
Black	12.6	3.1	26.6	6.4	5.9	2.4	11.2	3.8
Mexican American	26.0	4.9	19.5	4.0	13.0	3.9	9.2	2.9
6–11 years								
White	29.4	5.7	22.8	4.7	12.0	3.0	11.6	3.5
Black	34.5	3.6	37.6	3.6	17.1	2.8	22.2	3.3
Mexican American	43.0	4.2	35.1	4.4	27.3	3.1	19.6	3.1
12–19 years								
White	27.4	3.0	25.4	3.3	12.8	2.4	12.4	2.1
Black	35.7	2.8	45.5	3.0	20.7	2.6	26.6	2.7
Mexican American	44.2	3.0	39.6	2.3[a]	27.5	3.0	19.4	2.8

At risk for overweight is defined as a BMI at or higher than age-specific and sex-specific 85th percentiles, and overweight (obese) is defined as a BMI at or higher than age-specific and sex-specific 95th percentiles of the 2000 Centers for Disease Control and Prevention growth charts (see chapter 3).

[a]One "influential observation" was deleted. If it is included, the prevalence is 43.5 with an SE of 4.2 (Ogden et al. 2002).

Adapted from Ogden et al. (2002).

American children and adolescents (Malina 1993; Katzmarzyk and Malina 1999; Eisenmann et al. 2000).

Body Proportions   Variation in body proportions is often viewed in the sitting height/stature ratio. The ratio is consistently lower in Blacks than in Whites from early childhood through late adolescence, and ratios of Mexican American and White children, on average, differ slightly but consistently throughout the age range (see figure 25.3). Thus, for the same height, Black children have relatively shorter trunks or conversely, relatively longer lower extremities than White and Mexican American children. On the other hand, the relative proportion of trunk or lower extremity lengths to height do not differ markedly between Mexican American and White children.

Ethnic variation in the relative contribution of lower extremity length to height is more apparent when estimated leg length is plotted relative to height (see figure 25.4). For the same stature, leg length differs negligibly between White and Mexican American children, whereas Black children have longer lower extremities.

Data for other body dimensions of Mexican American children are limited but are more extensive for American Black and White children. In addition to proportional differences in lower extremity length, Black children have, on average, more slender or narrow hips (bicristal breadth)

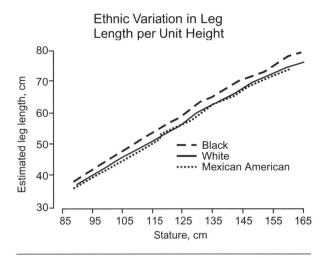

Ethnic Variation in Leg Length per Unit Height

FIGURE 25.4   Mean leg length plotted relative to mean height in Mexican American, American White, and American Black girls.

Data from Martorell et al., 1988.

relative to the shoulders (biacromial breadth) and relatively longer upper extremities than White children (Krogman 1970; Malina 1973a; Roche and Malina 1983).

Body Composition   Because subcutaneous adipose tissue is influenced by a number of factors, including diet, physical activity, and socioeconomic status, ethnic comparisons of absolute fatness may not be relevant. However, ethnic variation exists in the relative distribution of subcutaneous adipose tissue on the extremities and the trunk. Compared with Whites, Black and Mexican American children have proportionally more subcutaneous adipose tissue on the trunk (Mueller 1988; Greaves et al. 1989; Malina et al. 1995). The pattern in Black children reflects, on average, thinner skinfolds on extremity sites but generally similar skinfold thicknesses on trunk sites compared with White children. The pattern in Mexican American children reflects thicker skinfold thicknesses on trunk sites with only small differences in skinfolds on extremity sites compared with White children. Native American youth also have a more centralized distribution of subcutaneous adipose tissue compared with youth of European ancestry (Goran et al. 1995; Katzmarzyk and Malina 1998).

Data dealing with ethnic variation in abdominal visceral and subcutaneous adipose tissue are limited. Some data suggest a higher growth rate in abdominal fat areas at the level of the 4th and 5th lumbar vertebrae in American White compared with American Black children followed for

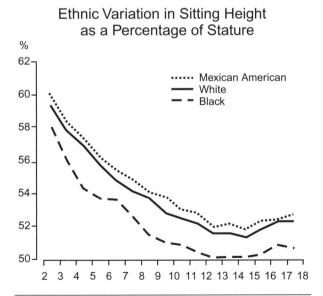

Ethnic Variation in Sitting Height as a Percentage of Stature

FIGURE 25.3   Mean sitting height/stature ratios in Mexican American, American White, and American Black boys.

Data from Martorell et al., 1988.

3 years from about 8 to 11 years of age (Huang et al. 2001). Ethnic variation has also been reported for the amount of adipose tissue partitioned to the visceral depot (Conway et al. 1995; Goran et al. 1997). American Blacks of both sexes have less visceral fat areas than American Whites even when both ethnic groups are matched for age, sex, body mass, body fat, or subcutaneous fat. The same is true in young children, which indicates that the ethnic differential may be apparent relatively early in life. Thus, for the same level of abdominal subcutaneous fat, American Black children 4 to 10 years of age have, on average, less visceral fat, which suggests that they partition fat storage differently compared with American White children (Goran et al. 1997). The mechanisms for this ethnic difference remain unknown but are likely related to the sensitivity of the hypothalamic-pituitary-adrenal axis, levels of androgens and estrogens, growth hormone secretion, and leptin levels, although behavioral and other factors could be involved.

Estimates of body composition based on bioelectrical impedance analysis (BIA, see chapter 5) are available for nationally representative samples of American White, American Black, and Mexican American adolescents 12-20 years of age in the third National Health and Nutrition Examination Survey (NHANES III, see table 3.1) between 1988 and 1994 (Chumlea et al. 2002). BIA provides a measure of resistance which is used with weight and stature to predict total body water (TBW), and then TBW is converted to an estimate of fat-free mass (FFM). Estimated FFM based on BIA is generally less in Mexican American compared to American White and Black adolescents of both sexes, whereas percentage body fat is greater in Mexican American adolescents of both sexes. Differences in estimated FFM based on BIA are small between American White and Black adolescent females, but American White adolescent males have a slightly larger FFM than American Black males.

In contrast, data derived from dual-energy X-ray absorptiometry (DEXA) indicate higher levels of lean tissue mass in American Black compared to American White and Mexican American boys and girls 3 to 18 years of age after statistically adjusting for age, stature and weight among the samples. There are, on the other hand, no differences in lean tissue mass between American White and Mexican American boys and girls (Ellis 1997; Ellis et al. 1997).

The difference between estimates of body composition based on BIA and DEXA probably reflect the respective methods and underlying assumptions. Data using other methods indicate higher body density in American Black compared to American White children, adolescents, and young adults (Boileau et al. 1984; Schutte et al. 1984; Ortiz et al. 1992). The difference in body density reflects ethnic variation in bone mineral content (discussed later in this section) and perhaps in composition of the FFM. Data for adult women matched for age (mean age, 33 years), height, weight, and menstrual status indicate greater density of the FFM and potassium content per unit FFM in American Black compared to American White women (Ortiz et al. 1992). The presently available data highlight the need for further study of ethnic variation in the body composition of children, adolescents, and young adults using the more recently developed multicomponent models (see chapter 5).

Data on estimated muscularity of American Black and White children and adolescents using the newer imaging technologies are lacking. Estimates of muscle mass based on dual photon absorptiometry for adult females matched for age, weight, height, and the BMI suggest that Black women have 10% to 15% more appendicular (extremity) skeletal muscle than White women (Ortiz et al. 1992). The ethnic difference is more apparent in the upper (Blacks 21% greater) than in the lower (Blacks 8% greater) extremities.

Estimated total-body bone mineral content and total-body bone mineral density are greater in American Black children, adolescents, and young adults of both sexes compared with American Whites (Malina 1996). Data for specific bone sites (e.g., distal radius and lumbar vertebrae) also indicate greater bone mineral density in American Black than in American White infants, children, and adolescents (Li et al. 1989; Slaughter et al. 1990; Gilsanz et al. 1991, 1998; McCormick et al. 1991; Rupich et al. 1996). Corresponding data for Hispanic children and adolescents indicate similar lumbar bone mineral density to American Whites but lower bone mineral density compared with American Blacks (McCormick et al. 1991).

Maturation   Ossification centers appear earlier in Blacks than in Whites during infancy and early childhood. At school ages, the skeletal maturity of Black and White boys differs only slightly and inconsistently. For example, skeletal maturity of Black boys is in advance of White boys between 6 and 9 years of age, but skeletal maturity of White boys is slightly in advance of Black boys at most ages during adolescence (see figures 25.5 and 25.6). On the other hand, the skeletal maturity of Black girls is, on average, slightly but consistently advanced compared with White girls in middle childhood and adolescence. The data presented in the two figures are based on the Greulich-Pyle and Tanner-Whitehouse methods of assessing skeletal maturity (see chapter 15), and the observations on ethnic variation are consistent with both methods.

The skeletal maturity data are consistent with age at menarche. Black girls attain menarche, on average, slightly earlier than White girls, 12.5 versus 12.8 years of age in the National Health Examination Survey, 1966–1970 (MacMahon 1973), and 12.1 versus 12.6 years of age in the Third National Health and Nutrition Examination Survey, 1988–1994 (NHANES III, Chumlea et al. 2003). Ages at onset of stages of secondary sex characteristics are also earlier in Black girls and boys (see table 16.3, page 311; Sun et al. 2002).

American Black adolescent females and males attain peak height velocity (PHV) at an earlier age than American White adolescents. Data from

Ethnic Variation in Skeletal Age

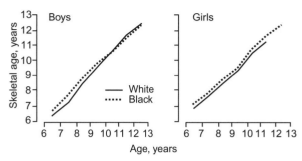

FIGURE 25.6 Mean Tanner-Whitehouse (TW2, 20 bone) skeletal ages for a mixed-longitudinal sample of Philadelphia Black and White children.

Data from Malina, 1970.

the Harvard Six Cities Study (Berkey et al. 1994) indicate the following mean ages at PHV: Black girls 10.8 years, White girls 11.5 years, Black boys 13.3 years, and White boys 13.6 years. Estimated peak height velocities (cm/year), however, are similar in Black and White adolescents: 8.4 and 8.1 cm/year in Black and White girls, respectively, and 9.2 and 9.5 cm/year in Black and White boys, respectively. Comparative data for other samples of North American and European adolescents were summarized in chapter 16 (see table 16.1, page 308).

Maturity data for Mexican American children are limited. The full complement of 28 ossification centers of the hand and wrist appears, on average, later in Mexican American children in the Texas phase of the Ten State Nutrition Survey in the 1960s compared with Black children in Texas and Ohio White children. Sampling variation is a factor in this comparison because areas with nutritional problems were specifically targeted in the Ten State Nutrition Survey.

The estimated age at menarche for Mexican American girls in the Ten State Nutrition Survey is 12.7 years (Malina et al. 1986), which is similar to estimated ages at menarche in Black and White girls from about the same time period in the United States Health Examination Survey, 12.5 and 12.8 years of age, respectively (MacMahon 1973). The estimated median age at menarche for Mexican American girls in NHANES III (1988–1994), 12.3 years, is intermediate between those of American Black and White girls, 12.1 and 12.6 years of age, respectively. The same pattern is generally apparent for median ages at the onset of stages of secondary sex characteristics (see table 16.3, page 311; Sun et al. 2002).

Ethnic Variation in Skeletal Age by Sex

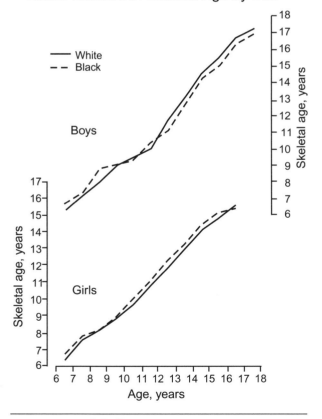

FIGURE 25.5 Mean Greulich-Pyle skeletal ages of American Black and White children in the United States Health Examination Survey (NHES II and III, see table 3.1, page 51).

Data from Roche et al., 1975, 1978.

Asian Children

The growth status of children from a variety of Asiatic countries has been the focus of many health and nutrition surveys. Data for well-nourished children, however, are most extensive for Japanese children (Kimura 1975, 1984; Oiso 1975).

Body Size and Proportions   Children of Asiatic ancestry (e.g., Japanese, Chinese in Hong Kong, and Taiwanese) living in their respective countries as well as outside of Asia (e.g., in the United States, Jamaica, or Brazil) tend to be, on average, shorter and lighter than children of European ancestry and differ in the proportional contribution of the lower extremities and the trunk to stature. This finding is shown in figure 25.7 for stature, sitting height, and estimated leg length of Japanese and American White children. Shorter lower extremities account for the difference in stature between American and Japanese children. Sitting height or trunk length does not differ between children of the two racial groups.

The absolute differences in stature and leg length translate into proportional differences. For the same stature, Japanese children have relatively shorter legs, or conversely, a relative longer trunk, than American White children. However, more recent samples of Japanese children and adolescents are taller than earlier samples and the increase in height over time is largely because of an increase in estimated leg length (see chapter 29). Thus, the proportional differences between American and Japanese youth are reduced.

Body Composition   Directly comparable data on the body composition of Japanese and American children and adolescents are limited. Nevertheless, the body density for pooled samples of Japanese adolescents 11 to 18 years of age grouped by age and sex are generally consistent with those for American adolescents. Moreover, despite differences in body size and proportions, estimates of percentage body fat derived from body density are also reasonably similar in

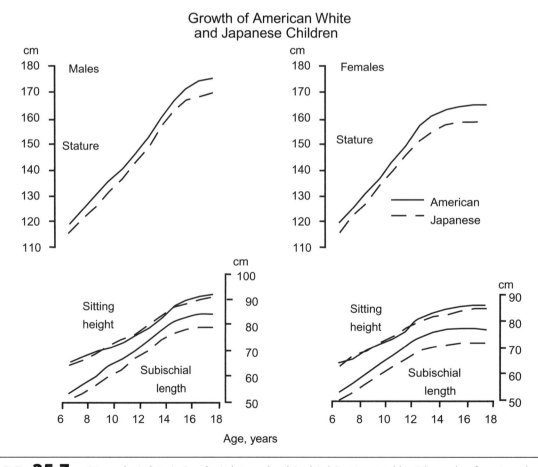

FIGURE 25.7   Mean height, sitting height, and subischial (estimated leg) length of national samples of American White and Japanese children, males on the left and females on the right.

Data from Roche and Malina, 1983, and Kimura, 1984.

Japanese and American adolescents (Tahara et al. 2002, see also chapter 5).

Maturation Although Japanese children and adolescents tend to be, on average, shorter than age and sex peers in the United States and Europe, Japanese youth are somewhat advanced in maturity. On average, age at PHV is earlier in Japanese boys and girls (see table 25.6, compare these means with those in table 16.1, page 308). Menarche also occurs earlier in Japanese girls compared with American White and European girls. Mean ages in three studies are 12.3, 12.4 and 12.5 years (Kato et al. 1992; Ashizawa et al. 1994; Sumiya et al. 2001; compare these means with those in table 16.6, page 314). Data for skeletal maturity are consistent with those for ages at PHV and menarche. Skeletal maturity scores based on the radius, ulna, and short bones in the TW2 method (see chapter 15) for Japanese children are in advance of those for British and Belgian children, especially during adolescence (Murata 1997). Overall, therefore,

TABLE 25.6	Mean Ages at Peak Height Velocity and Peak Height Velocity in Japanese Adolescents From Several Parts of Japan			

Girls		Boys	
Age at PHV (yr)	PHV (cm/yr)	Age at PHV (yr)	PHV (cm/yr)
11.1		12.8	
11.0		12.8	
11.1	8.3	13.1	9.9
11.5	10.2	12.6	11.9
11.1	7.8		
10.7			
10.5		12.4	
10.4		12.2	

Methods of estimating the parameters of the adolescent growth spurt are based on several protocols including graphic, cubic splines, kernel regression, Preece-Baines model I, and the Jolicoeur model (see chapter 16 for a discussion of curve fitting). At times, several estimates of the parameters of the adolescent growth spurt are indicated for the same sample; the parameters are derived from different curve-fitting models. Standard deviations for estimated ages at PHV range from 0.8 to 1.2 cm in girls and 0.8 to 1.4 cm in boys.

Data are from Kato et al. (1992), Suwa et al. (1992), Satake et al. (1993) Ashizawa et al. (1994), Qin et al. (1996), and Ali and Ohtsuki (2000).

Japanese children appear to be advanced in biological maturity compared with American White and European children, particularly in adolescence.

Japanese-American Children in Japan An interesting example of ethnic variation in growth is the offspring of Japanese mothers and American fathers born during the occupation of Japan by United States troops after World War II, primarily between 1946 and 1955 (Suda et al. 1975). Many of these children were raised under relatively good conditions in a private institution, and the majority entered the home before 12 months of age. They were classified as Japanese-White or Japanese-Black (i.e., having a Japanese mother and either an American White or an American Black father). Japanese-Black hybrid boys are slightly but consistently taller than Japanese-White hybrid boys between 6 and 15 years of age. On the other hand, differences between hybrid girls are not consistent. Hybrid girls, on average, have similar statures as Japanese school children during middle childhood, but during adolescence, their statures are more similar to American Black and White girls. Hybrid boys have statures that are virtually identical with Japanese school children between 6 and 15 years of age, and they are consistently shorter than American Black and White boys.

Body proportions show a racially related pattern in the hybrid children. The sitting height/stature ratio of Japanese-White hybrid children is virtually identical to that of Japanese children, but the sitting height/stature ratio of Japanese-Black children is consistently lower, indicating proportionally longer legs. The difference in ratios between Black and White hybrid children of Japanese mothers, however, is of smaller magnitude than that between American Black and White children. Thus, Japanese-Black hybrid children have relatively longer legs than Japanese-White hybrid children, but they still have proportionally shorter legs for their stature compared with American Black and White children.

Ethnic Variation in Motor Development, Performance, and Activity

The study of ethnic variation in motor development, performance, and physical activity has received less attention than corresponding studies of growth and maturation. Nevertheless, interest in ethnic variation in motor competence and physical activity continues. The subsequent discussion focuses primarily on comparisons within the American culture complex.

Motor Development and Performance

Comparisons of the early motor development of American Black and White infants and young children date to the 1930s, and corresponding data for Mexican American infants are few (Malina 1973b, 1988). Black children are generally advanced in motor development during the first 2 years of life as measured on various scales of infant development. The differences are more apparent in infancy than at subsequent ages. Comparisons of mean scores on the motor scale of the Bayley Scales of Infant Development for American Black and White infants are illustrated in figure 25.8. Although small, the differences are consistent across age. Corresponding data for a large sample of Mexican American infants are not available, but the limited evidence indicates negligible differences between Mexican American and White infants in early motor development. After 2 years of age, the data for preschool children are more limited and inconclusive.

Interpretation of ethnic variation in early motor development is difficult, allowing for variation in SES, living conditions, rearing, and cultural expectations. Early motor development

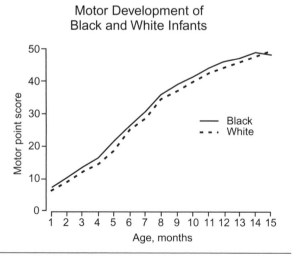

FIGURE 25.8   Mean motor point scores on the Bayley Scales of Infant Development of American Black and White children 1 through 15 months of age.

Data from Bayley, 1965.

is not predictive of later motor achievements in healthy, adequately nourished children. As discussed in chapter 10, scales of infant and early childhood development are used primarily to evaluate the integrity of the developing central nervous system during the first 2 or 3 years, that is, as screening devices to identify children with actual or potential developmental problems. Such problems might be indicative of neurological deficits or potential learning difficulties. Emphasis is on early identification and diagnosis so that therapy or other forms of intervention can be initiated as early as necessary.

Studies of the motor performance of Black, White, and Mexican American school-age children and adolescents also date to the late 1930s and early 1940s. Although demographic patterns, educational programs and opportunities, economic status, health care, and related factors have changed, results of studies conducted from the 1930s through the 1970s are reasonably consistent over time and no reversals, that is, a trend for one racial group to systematically change its position relative to the other over time, are apparent (Malina 1973b, 1988). Mean motor performances of children from the three ethnic groups overlap considerably, but the data are more available for Black and White children. Several trends are apparent in the comparisons. Black children and youth, particularly boys, perform consistently better than White children and youth in running speed (dashes) and the vertical jump, with less consistent results for the standing long jump. In contrast to the trends suggested for running and jumping, comparisons of performances on other tasks (e.g., ball throw for distance, shuttle runs, and static strength) do not show consistent differences between Black and White children.

Performance data for Mexican American children are quite limited. Comparisons indicate small and inconsistent differences between Mexican American and White children and adolescents, and Mexican Americans do not perform as well as Black children in running and jumping tasks (Malina 1988).

Comparative data for muscular strength and physical working capacity or maximal aerobic power indicate few, if any, consistent differences between Black and White children and youth (Rodahl et al. 1961; Maksud et al. 1971; Strong et al. 1978; Pivarnik et al. 1995). Corresponding data on the strength and maximal aerobic power of Mexican American children are not presently available.

Explanations for ethnic variation in motor performance are a different issue. Environmental factors are undoubtedly involved but are not ordinarily controlled or specified. Variation in rearing and parental supervision is mentioned most often as underlying the better performances of Black children and adolescents in some tasks (see discussion of social conditions and performance earlier in this chapter). Comparisons of the motor performances of Black and White children and adolescents have an added dimension in many popular discussions, given the relative numerical dominance of Black athletes in several sports (basketball, football, and track) relative to the proportion of Blacks in the American population. Athletes, however, are a highly select group, and generalizations from highly specialized athletic samples to the general population of a given ethnic group are not warranted. Moreover, they are limited by the scope and nature of available data.

Ethnic comparisons of performance among children and adolescents in several countries would be interesting to consider. Such comparisons are limited by sampling and comparability of test items in adequately nourished children from different countries and by chronic undernutrition in developing areas of the world.

Physical Activity

American Black and Hispanic youth, on average, spend relatively less time in moderate to vigorous physical activity (Centers for Disease Control 1990; Aaron et al. 1993; Heath et al. 1994; Kann et al. 1998; Pratt et al. 1999). In the 1990 Youth Risk Behavior Survey of high school students in grades 9 to 12 (about 14 to 18 years of age), only 43% of Black males reported participation in vigorous physical activity 3 or more days per week compared with 51% of White and 50% of Hispanic males. On the other hand, only 17% of Black and 16% of Hispanic females met the criterion compared with 27% of White females (Heath et al. 1994). Corresponding percentages in the 1997 Youth Behavior Risk Survey are 73%, 67%, and 69% for White, Black, and Hispanic males, respectively, and 58%, 41%, and 50% for White, Black and Hispanic females, respectively (Kann et al. 1998). Similar trends were apparent in several regional surveys using different measures of activity and criteria for vigorous activity (Aaron et al. 1993; Wolf et al. 1993; Myers et al. 1996). In contrast, patterns of participation in vigorous

exercise did not differ among San Diego youth grouped by ethnicity and SES (Sallis et al. 1996). The variation in results may reflect geographic and seasonal differences and perhaps methods of estimating physical activity.

Organized sport is a major form of physical activity and, in turn, energy expenditure for children and adolescents. Data on ethnic variation in sport participation among children are lacking. However, among high school youth, relatively more White males and females report participating in school sports than Hispanic and Black males and females, and relatively more Hispanic students report participating in school sports than Black students (see table 25.7). The Youth Risk Behavior Survey also included participation in nonschool sports. More males than females reported participation in both school and nonschool sports and the ethnic difference between Black and White males was reversed.

TABLE 25.7	Weighted Percentages of Participation in High School Sports and Nonschool Sports: 1997 Youth Risk Behavior Survey		
	High school sports only	**Nonschool sports only**	**Both school and nonschool sports**
Male	23.3	12.8	33.8
White	24.1	12.1	34.6
Black	19.3	14.4	37.3
Hispanic	21.9	15.5	25.0
Female	21.6	8.7	23.1
White	23.9	9.0	25.5
Black	15.2	7.5	17.7
Hispanic	16.7	8.5	15.6

Adapted from Pate et al. (2000).

The determinants of participation in physical activity and sport of children and adolescents of different ethnic backgrounds have not received detailed attention (Sallis et al. 1992). Limited availability of programs, convenience of facility, and neighborhood safety are probably important concerns.

Climate, Growth, and Maturity

Heat, cold, and high altitude may be factors that influence growth and maturity, although partitioning their specific effects from other environmental conditions is often difficult. The major physiological problem for populations in hot climates is the dissipation of excess heat, whereas major physiological problem for populations in cold climates is the preservation of heat. Issues related to thermoregulation in children and adolescents are discussed in chapter 14. In contrast, the major physiological problem for those resident at high altitudes is sufficient arterial oxygenation under conditions of reduced barometric pressure. As altitude increases, barometric pressure decreases and oxygen-transporting capacity from the ambient air to tissues may be impaired.

Heat and Cold

Studies of adaptation to the climatic extremes of heat and cold have focused largely on adults, but trends in the data have implications for developing individuals (Roberts 1973; Katzmarzyk and Leonard 1998). Adults of populations indigenous to hot climates, for example, tend to have generally linear physiques, which maximize surface area over which heat can be dissipated, whereas adults of populations indigenous to cold climates tend to have more stocky, compact physiques, which minimize surface area over which heat can be lost. Thus, populations in hot areas tend to have less weight-for-stature and relatively longer extremities than those in cold areas who have, conversely, more weight-for-stature and relatively shorter extremities.

The trends in the adult data would imply either prolonged growth in tropical areas, given the association between extreme linearity of physique and later maturity, or a shorter growth period in cold areas, given the association between extreme stockiness of physique and earlier maturity. Although these trends are suggestive, data are somewhat contradictory. Mean ages at menarche, for example, show a moderate, negative correlation (–0.5 to –0.6) with mean annual temperature of the habitat (Roberts 1973). The correlations suggest earlier maturity in hot climates and later maturity in cold climates, which is not consistent with the trends suggested by the association between physique and climate.

Correlations between mean annual temperature of the habitat and body weight for 150 samples of children indigenous to the particular habitat are also moderate and negative (–0.5 to –0.7) at several ages during childhood and early adolescence after statistically controlling for height differences among the samples (Roberts 1973). Thus, children in hot climates tend to have lower body weights, whereas those in cold climates tend to have higher body weights after height is controlled, which is consistent with observations on adults. Correlations, of course, do not indicate a cause-and-effect sequence, but simply the relationship between average annual temperature and body weight.

Data on the specific effects of temperature variation on growth in size and proportions, however, are not available. The situation is especially complex, given the overlapping distributions of poor living conditions, marginal or chronically deficient nutritional resources, infectious and parasitic diseases, and tropical and subtropical climates in many parts of the world. For example, how much of the short stature and reduced mass in tropical populations is caused by chronic protein and energy deficiencies and a high infectious/parasitic disease load rather than by temperature per se? Racial/ethnic variation is an additional factor. Black populations in Africa and the United States tend to have more linear physiques and relatively longer extremities than White populations of European ancestry. The physique differences may reflect the effects of natural selection in the earlier habitats of African and European populations over the past few thousand years.

Indicating specific influences of habitat temperature on growth and maturity is difficult. The effects of climate extend beyond temperature and include other components such as relative humidity, precipitation, and topography. Other factors also must be considered, including quality of agricultural land, methods of food production, and availability of suitable conditions for infectious and parasitic disease vectors.

Altitude

In contrast to habitat temperature as a factor that may influence growth and maturity, the effects of residence at high altitudes (3000 m and higher) on growth and maturation have been studied more directly. The major problem at high altitude is reduced barometric pressure, which influences the diffusion of oxygen from the air through the lungs into the blood. Thus the potential for **hypoxia**, a deficiency of oxygen in body tissues, exists. The higher the altitude of residence, the greater the reduction in barometric pressure and, in turn, the potential for hypoxia. Areas of the world where populations have lived at moderate to high altitudes for several thousands of years include Peru and Bolivia in South America (3,200 to 4,800 m), Nepal in Asia (3,400 to 4,100 m) and Ethiopia in Africa (3,000 m).

High altitude areas also tend to have cold temperatures, high aridity and high ultraviolet radiation, and limited agricultural production, and such areas tend to be isolated from major market centers. The potential for nutritional stress is thus rather constant. Cultural variation among the groups living at high altitudes in the diverse geographic areas of the world is an additional factor that may influence growth and maturation.

Evidence from a variety of sources indicates an inverse relationship between altitude and birth weight. Birth weight declines as altitude increases, suggesting that chronic hypoxia depresses infant weight. This trend is apparent in populations of both developed and developing areas of the world and is independent of parity, maternal smoking, and other factors (Haas et al. 1982; Jensen and Moore, 1997), which suggests that chronic hypoxia depresses birth weight.

Reduced birth weight may have implications for subsequent growth of children born and reared at high altitude. Studies of children in Peru, Bolivia, and Nepal generally indicate shorter statures, lighter weights, and later maturity compared with peers of the same age, sex, and ethnic group resident at low altitudes or at sea level (Pawson 1976; Frisancho 1981; Gupta et al. 1989). Possibly, the reduced stature in children resident at high altitudes is partly caused by smaller size at birth because infants born at high altitude often experience intrauterine growth restriction in contrast to preterm birth. On the other hand, children resident at moderately high altitudes in Ethiopia (3,000 m) tend to be slightly taller and heavier and advanced in skeletal maturity compared with children of the same age, sex, and racial ancestry at lower altitudes. Compared with reference data for well-nourished children, children from high-altitude areas are, on average, consistently shorter and lighter and later in maturation. However, variation exists among high altitude populations. Aymara Indian children living at 3,800 to 4,000 m in Bolivia tend to be taller and heavier than Quechua Indian children living at a slightly higher altitude.

The association between altitude and growth and maturity may thus vary among racial/ethnic groups. The favorable growth and maturity status of high-altitude Ethiopian children compared with those resident at lower altitudes can be attributed to better environmental conditions, specifically a very light infectious disease load and the absence of malaria, than at low altitudes. The relatively smaller body size and delayed maturation of Peruvian, Bolivian, and Nepalese children resident at high altitudes perhaps reflects the effects of hypoxia, cold, and chronically marginal-to-poor nutritional circumstances.

High altitude is thus a factor that can affect growth and maturity, but effects observed in certain populations may not be evident in others. As with other factors that influence growth and maturity, hypoxia does not operate in isolation, and partitioning its effects from those of other factors in the environment may be difficult. The variable results probably reflect the interaction of genetic differences among populations, hypoxia, and marginal nutritional conditions in South American and Asian children. Reduced prevalence of infectious diseases is an additional variable in highland Ethiopian children.

Climate, Performance, and Physical Activity

The influence of climate on performance and physical activity of children and adolescents is difficult to specify. In addition to temperature and altitude, relative humidity (hot-dry or hot-wet), seasonal variation in temperature and rainfall, and geographic and topographic variation are important considerations. Changing lifestyles associated with modernization and problems associated with reporting physical activity in different cultures are also important. Most data dealing with climatic influences on performance and activity are based on adults (Shephard 1978; Ulijaszek 2000, 2001). The data are confounded, in part, by degree of acclimatization, variation in mode of subsistence (agricultural, pastoralists, and hunter-gatherers), prior nutritional history, and cultural and perhaps racial/ethnic variation. Additional factors relate to subtle variations in climatic stress within specific ecological settings and different environments (e.g., humid rainforest, woodlands, grasslands, desert, or arctic tundra).

In developed areas of the world with clear seasonal variation in temperatures, children and adolescents tend to be more active in the summer when school is out than during the school year (see chapter 21). In tropical and subtropical zones, cultural practices influence habitual physical activity. Outdoor chores, many of which require physical effort, are routinely done in the early morning and evening hours when the temperatures are relatively cooler, in contrast to the middle of the day when temperatures are hotter.

In Canada (Shephard 1986) and in Finland (Telama et al. 1985), where winters are often harsh and days during winter are short, activity levels during the summer are twice as high as during the winter. For example, parents of 3-year-old and 6-year-old Finnish girls reported 6.7 hours per day of outdoor activities in the summer and only 3.3 hours per day during winter. The respective times for the boys were 7.0 and 3.7 hours per day (Telama et al. 1985).

Chronic undernutrition is a confounding factor in discussions of climate in relation to performance and activity of children and adolescents. Chronic undernutrition is more prevalent in tropical, subtropical, and high-altitude areas. The effects of chronic undernutrition on physical performance and activity in children and adolescents were discussed in chapter 23.

Hypoxia of high altitude is associated with reduced aerobic power but does not apparently affect anaerobic performance (Bedu and Coudert 1998). Activity levels of low SES children resident at high altitude are greater than those of economically better-off children (Kemper and Coudert 1994). In this context, activity levels may be influenced by demands placed on children in different social strata within a specific culture. This finding is illustrated in the after-school activities of urban and rural children of low socioeconomic status in southern Mexico (see table 25.8). Rural children spend a good deal of their after-school free time assisting with household chores. Cooking-related activities in rural girls require cleaning corn, going to the mill, preparing tortilla dough, and making tortillas, whereas in the urban sample chores are largely related to cooking activities within the household. Among rural boys, most are involved with the feeding and care of farm animals, including taking them to and from the pasture. Gathering wood is also an important household activity for boys. As one would expect, urban boys do not have demands related to the care of farm animals. In contrast to household-related activities, urban boys and girls indicate more participation in organized sports and more time viewing television.

Clearly, many factors can influence the physical performance characteristics and physical activity habits of children and adolescents. Better understanding of the determinants of performance and activity of children and adolescents in both developed and developing countries and within the specific cultural contexts of each country is needed.

TABLE 25.8 Household-Related Activities Reported by 4th to 6th Grade Low-Socioeconomic-Status Boys and Girls in Southern Mexico

	Boys				Girls			
	Urban (n = 83)		Rural (n = 77)		Urban (n = 77)		Rural (n = 99)	
	n	%	n	%	n	%	n	%
House cleaning	56	67	32	42	48	62	66	67
Doing dishes	19	23	1		40	52	59	60
Food preparation[a]	2		10	13	8	8	78	79
Cutting wood	1		10	13				
Family business	2		3				12	12
Getting water			9	12			6	6
Animal care[b]			54	70			8	8
Animal feed[c]			53	69			9	9

[a]Cooking also includes activities related to tortilla preparation in rural sample (cleaning corn, going to mill, preparing tortilla dough, making tortillas).

[b]Feeding and taking care of animals, including taking them to pasture.

[c]Cutting and gathering animal feed from pasture.

R.M. Malina and M.E. Peña Reyes (unpublished data).

Summary

Factors associated with the social environments, racial/ethnic background, and climate can influence growth, maturation, performance, and physical activity. These factors are complex and interact with each other. The specific operation of these factors, and undoubtedly others, is difficult to specify and highlights the plastic nature of the processes of growth and maturation. Presently available observations also emphasize the sensitivity of the processes of growth and maturation and of physical performance and activity to conditions in social, cultural, and physical environments of children and adolescents.

Sources and Suggested Readings

Aaron DJ, Kriska AM, Dearwater SR, Anderson RL, Olsen TL, Cauley JA, Laporte RE (1993) The epidemiology of leisure time physical activity in an adolescent population. Medicine and Science in Sports and Exercise 25:847-853.

Ali MA, Uetake T, Ohtsuki F (2000) Secular changes in relative leg length in post-war Japan. American Journal of Human Biology 12:405-416.

Ama PFM, Lagasse P, Bouchard C, Simoneau JA (1990) Anaerobic performances in black and white subjects. Medicine and Science in Sports and Exercise 22:508-511.

Ama PFM, Simoneau JA, Boulay MR, Serresse O, Theriault G, Bouchard C (1986) Skeletal muscle characteristics in sedentary black and caucasian males. Journal of Applied Physiology 61:1758-1761.

Ashcroft MT, Lovell HG (1964) Heights and weights of Jamaican children of various racial origins. Tropical and Geographic Medicine 4:346-353.

Ashizawa K, Kato S, Eto M (1994) Individual adolescent growth of stature, body weight, and chest circumference of girls in Tokyo. Anthropological Science 102:421-446.

Barker DG, Ponthieux NA (1968) Partial relationships between race and fitness with socioeconomic status controlled. Research Quarterly 39:773-775.

Bayley N (1965) Comparisons of mental and motor test scores for ages 1–15 months by sex, birth order, race, geographical location, and education of parents. Child Development 36:379-411.

Bayley N, Jones HE (1937) Environmental correlates of mental and motor development: A cumulative study from infancy to six years. Child Development 8:329-341.

Bedu M, Coudert J (1998) High altitude and anaerobic performance during growth. In E Van Praagh (ed), Pediatric Anaerobic Performance. Champaign, IL: Human Kinetics, pp 337-352.

Berkey CA, Wang X, Dockery DW, Ferris BG (1994) Adolescent height growth of U.S. children. Annals of Human Biology 21:435-442.

Berkey CS, Ware JH, Speizer FE, Ferris BG (1984) Passive smoking and height growth of preadolescent children. International Journal of Epidemiology 13:454-458.

* Bielicki T (1986) Physical growth as a measure of the economic well-being of populations: The twentieth century. In F Falkner, JM Tanner (eds), Human Growth. Volume 3. Methodology, Ecological, Genetic, and Nutritional Effects on Growth. New York: Plenum, pp 283-305.

Bielicki T, Malina RM, Waliszko H (1992) Monitoring the dynamics of social stratification: Statural variation among Polish conscripts in 1976 and 1986. American Journal of Human Biology 4:345-352.

Bielicki T, Szklarska A, Welon Z, Brajczewski C (1997) Nierownosci spoleczne w Polsce w trzydziestoleciu 1965-1995. Wroclaw: Polish Academy of Sciences, Monographs of the Institute of Anthropology, No. 16.

Bielicki T, Waliszko H, Hulanicka B, Kotlarz K (1986) Social-class gradients in menarcheal age in Poland. Annals of Human Biology 13:1-11.

Bielicki T, Welon Z, Waliszko A (1981) Zmiany w rozwoju fizycznym mlodziezy w Polsce w okresie 1955-1977. Wroclaw: Polish Academy of Sciences, Monographs of the Institute of Anthropology, No. 2.

Billewicz WZ, Fellowes H, Thomson AM (1981) Pubertal changes in boys and girls in Newcastle upon Tyne. Annals of Human Biology 8:211-219.

Billewicz WZ, Thomson AM, Fellowes H (1983) A longitudinal study of growth in Newcastle upon Tyne adolescents. Annals of Human Biology 10:125-133.

Blank M (1964) Some maternal influences on infants' rates of sensorimotor development. Journal of the American Academy of Child Psychiatry 3:668-687.

Boileau RA, Lohman TG, Slaughter MH, Ball TE, Going SB, Hendrix MK (1984) Hydration of the fat-free body in children during maturation. Human Biology 56:651-666.

Bronfenbrenner U (1958) Socialization and social class through time and space. In EE Maccoby, TM Newcomb, EL Hartley (eds), Readings in Social Psychology, 3rd edition. New York: Holt, pp 400-425.

* Brumberg JJ (1988) Fasting Girls: The Emergence of Anorexia Nervosa As a Modern Disease. Cambridge: Harvard University Press.

Cameron N, Kgamphe JS, Leschner KF, Farrat PJ (1992) Urban-rural differences in the growth of South African black children. Annals of Human Bioliology 19:23-33.

Centers for Disease Control (1992) Vigorous physical activity among high school students— United States, 1990. Morbidity and Mortality Weekly Report 41:33-35.

Chandler WU (1985) Investing in Children. Washington, DC: Worldwatch Institute.

Chang KSF, Lee MMC, Low WD, Kvan E (1963) Height and weight of southern Chinese children. American Journal of Physical Anthropology 21:497-509.

Chumlea WC, Guo SS, Kuczmarski RJ, Flegal KM, Johnson CL, Heymsfield SB, Lukaski HC, Friedl K, Hubbard VS (2002) Body composition estimates from NHANES III bioelectrical impedance data. International Journal of Obesity and Related Metabolic Disorders 26: 1596-1609.

* Chumlea WC, Schubert CM, Roche AF, Kulin H, Lee PA, Himes JH, Sun SS (2003) Age at menarche and racial comparisons in U.S. girls. Pediatrics 111: 110-113.

Conway JM, Yanovski SZ, Avila NA, Hubbard VS (1995) Visceral adipose tissue differences in black and white women. American Journal of Clinical Nutrition 61:765-771.

* Damon A (1969) Race, ethnic group, and disease. Social Biology 16:69-80.

Dhont J (1978) Somatische ontwikkeling en motorische vaardigheid in samenhang met de gezinssamenstelling qua geslacht, de geboorterang en de socioprofessionele herkomst. Leuven, Belgium: Instituut voor Lichamelijke Opleiding, Katholieke Universiteit te Leuven, Licentiate Thesis.

Douglas JWB (1966) The age of reaching puberty: Some associated factors and some educational implications. In The Scientific Basis of Medicine Annual Reviews, pp 91-105 (as cited by Leistol K [1982] Social conditions and menarcheal age: The importance of early years of life. Annals of Human Biology 9:521-537).

East WB, Hensley LD (1985) The effect of selected sociocultural factors upon the overhand throwing performance of prepubescent children. In JE Clark (ed), Motor Development: Current Selected Research 1, pp 115-127.

Eisenmann JC, Katzmarzyk PT, Arnall DA, Kanuho V, Interpreter C, Malina RM (2000) Growth and overweight of Navajo youth: Secular changes from 1955 to 1997. International Journal of Obesity 24:211-218.

* Ellis BJ, Garber J (2000) Psychosocial antecedents of variation in girls' pubertal timing: Maternal depression, stepfather presence, and marital and family stress. Child Development 71:485-501.

Ellis BJ, McFadyen-Ketchum S, Dodge KA, Pettit GS, Bates JE (1999) Quality of early family relationships and individual differences in the timing of pubertal maturation in girls: Longitudinal test of an evolutionary model. Journal of Personality and Social Psychology 77:387-401.

Ellis KJ (1997) Body composition of a young, multiethnic male population. American Journal of Clinical Nutrition 66: 1323-1331.

Ellis KJ, Abrams SA, Wong WW (1997) Body composition of a young, multiethnic female population. American Journal of Clinical Nutrition 65:724-731.

Erbaugh SJ, Clifton MA (1984) Sibling relationships of preschool-aged children in gross motor environments. Research Quarterly for Exercise and Sport 55:323-331.

Eveleth PB, Tanner JM (1976) Worldwide Variation in Human Growth. Cambridge, UK: Cambridge University Press.

* Eveleth PB, Tanner JM (1990) Worldwide Variation in Human Growth, 2nd edition. Cambridge, UK: Cambridge University Press.

Farmosi I, Nadori L, Bakonyi F (1986) The somatic development and motor performance of 12-year-old children considering factors of sociocultural conditions (order of birth, the number of family and the extent of settlement). International Journal of Physical Education 23:15-19.

Frisancho AR (1981) Ecological interpretation of postnatal growth at high altitude. Seminaire du C.N.R.S., L'Homme et Son Environnement a Haute Altitude. Paris: CNRS, pp 87-93.

Garn SM, Clark DC (1976) Problems in the nutritional assessment of black individuals. American Journal of Public Health 66:262-267.

Garn SM, Clark DC, Trowbridge FL (1973) Tendency toward greater stature in American black children. American Journal of Diseases of Children 126:164-167.

Ge X, Conger RD, Elder GH (1996) Coming of age too early: Pubertal influences on girls' vulnerability to distress. Child Development 67:3386-3400.

Gilsanz V, Roe TF, Mora S, Costin G, Goodman WG (1991) Changes in vertebral bone density between black girls and white girls during childhood and puberty. New England Journal of Medicine 325:1597-1600.

Gilsanz V, Skaggs DL, Kovanlikaya A, Sayre J, Loro ML, Kaufman F, Korenman SG (1998) Differential effect of race on the axial and appendicular skeletons of children. Journal of Clinical Endocrinology and Metabolism 83:1420-1427.

Godin G, Shephard RJ (1986) Psychological factors influencing intentions to exercise of young students from grades 7 to 9. Research Quarterly for Exercise and Sport 57:41-52.

Goran MI, Kaskoun M, Johnson R, Martinez C, Kelly B, Hood V (1995) Energy expenditure and body fat distribution in Mohawk children. Pediatrics 95:89-95.

Goran MI, Nagy TR, Treuth MS, Trowbridge C, Dezenberg C, McGloin A, Gower BA (1997) Visceral fat in white and African American prepubertal children. American Journal of Clinical Nutrition 65:1703-1708.

Gottlieb NH, Chen MS (1985) Sociocultural correlates of childhood sporting activities: Their implications for heart health. Social Science in Medicine 21:533-539.

Graber JA, Brooks-Gunn J, Warren MP (1995) The antecedents of menarcheal age: Heredity, family environment, and stressful life events. Child Development 66:346-359.

Grant MW (1964) Rate of growth in relation to birth rank and family size. British Journal of Preventive and Social Medicine 18:35-42.

Greaves KA, Puhl J, Baranowski T, Gruben D, Seale D (1989) Ethnic differences in anthropometric characteristics of young children and their parents. Human Biology 61: 459-477.

Gupta R, Basu A, Pawson IG, Bharati P, Mukhopadhyay B, Mukhopadhyay S, Roy SK, Majumder PP, Bhattacharya SK, Bhattacharya KK, Das SK (1989) Altitude and human biology: A comparative study of Himalayan, Andean and Ethiopian data. In A Basu, R Gupta (eds), Human Biology of Asian Highland Populations in the Global Context. Calcutta: Indian Anthropological Society, pp 1-80.

Haas JD, Moreno-Black G, Frongillo EA, Pabon J, Pareja G, Ybarnegaray J, Hurtado L (1982) Altitude and infant growth in Bolivia: A longitudinal study. American Journal of Physical Anthropology 59:251-262.

Habicht J-P, Martorell R, Yarbrough C, Malina RM, Klein RE (1974) Height and weight standards for preschool children: How relevant are ethnic differences in growth potential? Lancet 1:611-615.

Hamill PVV, Johnston FE, Lemeshow S (1972) Height and weight of children: Socioeconomic status, United States. Vital and Health Statistics, Series 11, No. 119.

Hamill PVV, Johnston FE, Lemeshow S (1973) Height and weight of youths 12-17 years. Vital and Health Statistics, Series 11, No. 124.

Hamill PVV, Johnston FE, Lemeshow S (1973) Body weight, stature, and sitting height: White and negro youths 12-17 years. Vital and Health Statistics, Series 11, No. 126.

Heath GW, Pratt M, Warren CW, Kahn L (1994) Physical activity patterns in American high school students. Archives of Pediatric and Adolescent Medicine 148:1131-1136.

Henneberg M, Louw GJ (1998) Cross-sectional survey of growth of urban and rural "cape coloured" school children: Anthropometry and functional tests. American Journal of Human Biology 10:73-85.

Herman-Giddens ME, Slora EJ, Wasserman RC, Bourdony CJ, Bhapkar MV, Koch GG, Hasemeier CM (1997) Secondary sexual characteristics and menses in young girls seen in office practice: A study from the pediatric research in office settings network. Pediatrics 99:505-512.

Herman-Giddens ME, Wang L, Koch G (2001) Secondary sexual characteristics in boys: Estimates from the National Health and Nutrition Examination Survey III, 1988-1994. Archives of Pediatrics and Adolescent Medicine 155:1022-1028.

* Hernandez DJ (1994) Children's changing access to resources: A historical perspective. Social Policy Report. Society for Research in Child Development 8, No. 1 (Spring).

Hess RD (1970) Social class and ethnic influences upon socialization. In PH Mussen (ed), Carmichael's Manual of Child Psychology, Volume 2. New York: Wiley, pp 457-557.

Hindley CB, Filliozat AM, Klackenberg G, Nicolet-Meister D, Sand EA (1966) Differences in age of walking in five European longitudinal samples. Human Biology 38:364-379.

Huang TT-K, Johnson MS, Figueroa-Colon R, Dwyer JH, Goran MI (2001) Growth of visceral fat, subcutaneous abdominal fat and total body fat in children. Obesity Research 9: 283-289.

Huang Y-C, Malina RM (1996) Physical activity and correlates of estimated energy expenditure in Taiwanese adolescents 12-14 years of age. Amercan Journal of Human Biology 8:225-236.

Hulanicka B (1999) Acceleration of menarcheal age of girls from dysfunctional families. Journal of Reproductive and Infant Psychology 17:119-132.

Hulanicka B, Brajczewski C, Jedlinska W, Slawinska T, Waliszko A (1990) City-Town-Village: Growth of Children in Poland in 1988. Wroclaw, Poland: Polish Academy of Sciences, Monographs of the Institute of Anthropology 7.

Hulanicka B, Gronkiewicz L, Koniarek J (2001) Effect of familial distress on growth and maturation of girls: A longitudinal study. American Journal of Human Biology 13:771-776.

Hulanicka B, Waliszko A (1991) Deceleration of age at menarche of girls in Poland. Annals of Human Biology 18: 507-513.

Hutinger PW (1959) Differences in speed between American negro and white children in performance of the 35-yard dash. Research Quarterly 30:366-368.

Jackson JJ (1973) Family organization and technology. In KS Miller, RM Dreger (eds), Comparative Studies of Blacks and Whites in the United States. New York: Seminar Press, pp 405-445.

Jensen GM, Moore LG (1997) The effect of high altitude and other risk factors on birthweight: Independent or interactive effects? American Journal of Public Health 87:1003-1007.

Kann L, Kinchen SA, Williams BI, Ross JG, Lowry R, Hill CV, Grunbaum JA, Blumson PS, Collins JL, Kolbe LJ (1998) Youth Behavior Risk Surveillance—United States, 1997. Morbidity and Mortality Weekly Report, Centers for Disease Control 47 (SS-3):1-32.

Kato S, Yamaguchi N, Ashizawa K, Hoshi H (1992) Interrelationship of the age at peak velocity between height, chest girth and weight growth in Japanese. Journal of the Anthropological Society of Nippon 100:433-447 (in Japanese).

Katzmarzyk PT, Leonard WR (1998) Climatic influences on human body size and proportions: Ecological adaptations and secular trends. American Journal of Physical Anthropology 106:483-503.

Katzmarzyk PT, Malina RM (1998) Obesity and relative subcutaneous fat distribution among Canadians of First Nation and European ancestry. International Journal of Obesity 22:1127-1131.

Katzmarzyk PT, Malina RM (1999) Body size and physique among Canadians of First Nation and European ancestry. American Journal of Physical Anthropology 108:161-172.

* Kemper HCG, Coudert J, editors (1994) Physical health and fitness of Bolivian boys. International Journal of Sports Medicine 15 (suppl 2):S71-S114.

Kimura K (1975) Growth studies of the Japanese. In S Watanabe, S Kondo, E Matsunaga (eds), Human Adaptability. Volume 2. Anthropological and Genetic Studies on the Japanese. Tokyo: University of Tokyo Press, pp 15-32.

* Kimura K (1984) Studies on growth and development in Japan. Yearbook of Physical Anthropology 27:179-213.

Knobloch H, Pasamanick B (1958) The relationship of race and socioeconomic status to the development of motor behavior patterns in infancy. Psychiatric Research Reports of the American Psychiatric Association 10:123-133.

Kpedekpo GMK (1970) Heights and weights of children in Ghana. Journal of the Royal Statistical Society, Series A 133:86-93.

Krieger N, Rowley DL, Herman AA, Avery B, Phillips MT (1993) Racism, sexism and social class: Implications for studies of health, disease, and well-being. American Journal of Preventive Medicine 9 (suppl 6):82-122.

Krogman WM (1970) Growth of head, face, trunk, and limbs in Philadelphia white and negro children of elementary and high school age. Monographs of the Society for Research in Child Development 35, serial no. 136.

Kumanyika S (1993a) Ethnicity and obesity development in children. Annals of the New York Academy of Sciences 699:81-92.

Kumanyika S (1993b) Special issues regarding obesity in minority populations. Annals of Internal Medicine 119:650-654.

Laska-Mierzejewska T, Milicer H, Piechaczek H (1982) Age at menarche and its secular trend in urban and rural girls in Poland. Annals of Human Biology 9:227-233.

Lee AM (1980) Child-rearing practices and motor performance of black and white children. Research Quarterly for Exercise and Sport 51:494-500.

Li J-Y, Specker BL, Ho ML, Tsang RC (1989) Bone mineral content in black and white children 1 to 6 years of age: Early appearance of race and sex differences. American Journal of Diseases of Children 143:1346-1349.

Liederman PH, Tulkin SR, Rosenfield A, editors (1977) Culture and Infancy: Variations in the Human Experience. New York: Academic Press.

* Lifshitz F, Moses N (1988) Nutritional dwarfing: Growth, dieting, and fear of obesity. Journal of the American College of Nutrition 7:367-376.

Lin WS, Zhu FC, Chen ACN, Xin WH, Su Z, Li JY, Ye GS (1992a) Physical growth of Chinese school children 7–18 years, in 1985. Annals of Human Biology 19:41-55.

Lin WS, Chen CAN, Su JZX, Zhu FC, Xing WH, Li JY, Ye GS (1992b) The menarcheal age of Chinese girls. Annals of Human Biology 19:503-512.

Lindgren G (1976) Height, weight and menarche in Swedish urban school children in relation to socio-economic status and regional factors. Annals of Human Biology 3:501-528.

Loder RT, Estle DT, Morrison K, Eggleston D, Fish DN, Greenfield ML, Guire KE (1993) Applicability of the Greulich and Pyle skeletal age standards to black and white children of today. American Journal of Diseases of Children 147:1329-1333.

Maccoby EE, Jacklin CN (1974) The Psychology of Sex Differences. Stanford, CA: Stanford University Press.

MacMahon B (1973) Age at menarche. Vital and Health Statistics, Series 11, No. 133.

Macias JA, Tellez FP, Mora Parra JO, Rueda Williamson R, Luna Jaspe H (1978) Estudio seccional de crecimiento y desarrollo de niños y niñas Colombianas de dos clases socioeconomicas de los seis a los veinte años. Archivos Latinoamericanos de Nutricion 28:75-90.

Maksud MG, Coutts KD, Hamilton LH (1971) Oxygen uptake, ventilation, and heart rate: Study in negro children during strenuous exercise. Archives of Enrivonmental Health 23:23-28.

Malina RM (1969) Skeletal maturation rate in North American negro and white children. Nature 223:1075.

Malina RM (1970) Skeletal maturation studied longitudinally over one year in American whites and negroes 6 through 13 years of age. Human Biology 42:377-390.

Malina RM (1973a) Biological substrata. In KS Miller, RM Dreger (eds), Comparative Studies of Blacks and Whites in the United States. New York: Seminar Press, pp 53-123.

Malina RM (1973b) Ethnic and cultural factors in the development of motor abilities and strength in American children. In GL Rarick (ed), Physical Activity: Human Growth and Development. New York: Academic Press, pp 333-363.

Malina RM (1977) Motor development in a cross-cultural perspective. In DM Landers, RW Christina (eds), Psychology of Motor Behavior and Sport. Volume 2. Sport Psychology and Motor Development. Champaign, IL: Human Kinetics, pp 191-208.

* Malina RM (1980) Biosocial correlates of motor development during infancy and early childhood. In LS Greene, FE Johnston (eds), Social and Biological Predictors of Nutritional Status, Physical Growth, and Neurological Development. New York: Academic Press, pp 143-171.

Malina RM (1982) Motor development in the early years. In SG Moore, CR Cooper (eds), The Young Child: Reviews of Research. Volume 3. Washington, DC: National Association for the Education of Young Children, pp 211-229.

Malina RM (1983) Socio-cultural influences on physical activity and performance. Bulletin de la Societe Royale Belge d'Anthropologie et de Prehistoire 94:155-176.

Malina RM (1988) Racial/ethnic variation in the motor development and performance of American children. Canadian Journal of Sport Sciences 13:136-143.

Malina RM (1990) Growth of Latin American children: Socioeconomic, urban-rural and secular comparisons. Revista Brasileira de Ciencia e Movimento 4(3):46-75 (in Portuguese and English).

Malina RM (1993) Ethnic variation in the prevalence of obesity in North American children and youth. Critical Reviews in Food Science and Nutrition 33:389-396.

* Malina RM (1996) Regional body composition: Age, sex, and ethnic variation. In AF Roche, SB Heymsfield, TG Lohman (eds), Human Body Composition. Champaign, IL: Human Kinetics, pp 217-255.

Malina RM, Brown KH, Zavaleta AN (1987) Relative lower extremity length in Mexican American and in American black and white youth. American Journal of Physical Anthropology 72:89-94.

Malina RM, Hamill PVV, Lemeshow S (1974) Body dimensions and proportions, white and negro children 6–11 years. Vital and Health Statistics, Series 11, No. 143.

Malina RM, Himes JH, Stepick CD, Gutierrez Lopez F, Buschang PH (1981) Growth of rural and urban children in the Valley of Oaxaca, Mexico 55:269-280.

Malina RM, Huang Y-C, Brown KH (1995) Subcutaneous adipose tissue distribution in adolescent girls of four ethnic groups. International Journal of Obesity 19:793-797.

Malina RM, Katzmarzyk PT, Bonci CM, Ryan RC, Wellens RE (1997) Family size and age at menarche in athletes. Medicine and Science in Sports and Exercise 29:99-106.

Malina RM, Little BB, Stern MP, Gaskill SP, Hazuda HP (1983) Ethnic and social class differences in selected anthropometric characteristics of Mexican American and Anglo adults: The San Antonio Heart Study. Human Biology 55:867-883.

Malina RM, Martorell R, Mendoza F (1986) Growth status of Mexican American children and youths: Historical trends and contemporary issues. Yearbook of Physical Anthropology 29:45-79.

Malina RM, Pena Reyes ME (2002) Secular change in size and physical fitness in the Valley of Oaxaca, Mexico. Final report, NSF-BCS 9816400. Washington, DC: National Science Foundation.

Malina RM, Roche AF (1983) Manual of Physical Status and Performance in Childhood. Volume 2. Physical Performance. New York: Plenum.

Malina RM, Selby HA, Aronson WL, Buschang PH, Chumlea C (1980) Re-examination of the age at menarche in Oaxaca, Mexico. Annals of Human Biology 7:281-282.

Marques RM, Berquo E, Yunes J, Marcondes E (1974) Crecimiento de criancas Brasileiras: Peso e altura segundo idade e sexo—influencia de fatores socio-economicos. Anais Nestle 84 (suppl II).

Marshall WA (1981) Geographical and ethnic variations in human growth. British Medical Bulletin 37:273-279.

Martorell R, Malina RM, Castillo RO, Mendoza FS, Pawson IG (1988) Body proportions in three ethnic groups: Children and youths 2–17 years in NHANES II and HHANES. Human Biology 60:205-222.

Martorell R, Mendoza F, Castillo R (1989) Genetic and environmental determinants of growth in Mexican Americans. Pediatrics 84:864-871.

McCormick DP, Ponder SW, Fawcett HD, Palmer JL (1991) Spinal bone mineral density in 335 normal and obese children and adolescence: Evidence for ethnic and sex differences. Journal of Bone and Mineral Research 6:507-513.

Meredith HV (1979) Comparative findings on body size of children and youths living at urban centers and in rural areas. Growth 43:95-104.

Meredith HV (1982) Research between 1950 and 1980 on urban-rural differences in body size and growth rate of children and youths. Advances in Child Development and Behavior 17:83-138.

Meredith HV, Knott VB (1962) Illness history and physical growth. American Journal of Diseases of Children 103:146-151.

Miernik Z (1965) Sprawnosc ruchowa chlopcow z miast i ze wsi w wieku 7.5–15.5 lat (Motor fitness of boys 7.5–15.5 years of age from the city and country). Rocznik Naukowy, Wyzsza Szkola Wychowania Fizycznego w Krakowie 4:75-113 (in Polish).

Money J (1977) The syndrome of abuse dwarfism (psychosocial dwarfism or reversible hyposomatotropism). American Journal of Diseases of Children 131:508-513.

Moore DC (1993) Body image and eating behavior in adolescents. Journal of the American College of Nutrition 12:505-510.

Moore LG, Young D, McCullough RE, Droma T, Zamudio S (2001) Tibetan protection from intrauterine growth restriction (IUGR) and reproductive loss at high altitude. American Journal of Human Biology 13:635-644.

Moore S (1977) Mother-child interactions and competence in infants and toddlers. Young Children 32:64-69.

Morrison JA, Guo SS, Specker B, Chumlea WC, Yanovski SZ, Yanovski JA (2001) Assessing the body composition of 6–17 year old Black and White girls in field studies. American Journal of Human Biology 13:249-254.

Mueller WH (1988) Ethnic differences in fat distribution during growth. In C Bouchard, FE Johnston (eds), Fat Distribution during Growth and Later Health Outcomes. New York: Alan R Liss, pp 127-145.

Munetaka H, Matsuura Y, Munetaka H (1971) On the study of the differences in motor ability of children between three different communities: Island, housing development and urban area. Research Journal of Physical Education 16:91-97 (in Japanese).

Murata M (1997) Population-specific reference values for bone age. Acta Paediatrica, 423, (suppl):113-114.

Myers L, Strikmiller PK, Webber LS, Berenson GS (1996) Physical and sedentary activity in school children grades 5–8: The Bogalusa Heart Study. Medicine and Science in Sports and Exercise 28:852-859.

Neligan G, Prudham D (1969) Norms for four standard developmental milestones by sex, social class and place in family. Developmental Medicine and Child Neurology 11:413-422.

* Ogden CL, Flegal KM, Carroll MD, Johnson CL (2002) Prevalence and trends in overweight among US children and adolescents, 1999–2000. Journal of the American Medical Association 288:1728-1732.

Ogden CL, Troiano RP, Briefel RR, Kuczmarski RJ, Flegal KM, Johnson CL (1997) Prevalence of overweight among preschool children in the United States, 1971 through 1994. Pediatrics 99. www.pediatrics.org/cgi/content/full/99/4/e1.

Ohsawa S, Ji CY, Kasai N (1997) Age at menarche and comparison of the growth and performance of pre- and post-menarcheal girls in China. American Journal of Human Biology 9:205-212.

Oiso T (1975) A historical review of nutritional improvement in Japan after World War II. In K Asahina, R Shigiya (eds), Human Adaptability. Volume 4. Physiological Adaptability and Nutritional Status of the Japanese. B. Growth, Work Capacity and Nutrition of Japanese. Tokyo: University of Tokyo Press, pp 171-188.

Ortiz O, Russell M, Daley TL (1992) Differences in skeletal muscle and bone mineral mass between black and white females and their relevance to estimates of body composition. American Journal of Clinical Nutrition 55:8-13.

Pate RR, Trost SG, Levin S, Dowda M (2000) Sports participation and health-related behaviors among US youth. Archives of Pediatric and Adolescent Medicine 154:904-911.

Patton RG (1963) Growth Failure in Maternal Deprivation. Springfield, IL: Charles C Thomas.

* Pawson IG (1976) Growth and development in high altitude populations: A review of Ethiopian, Peruvian and Nepalese studies. Proceedings of the Royal Society of London, B 194:83-98.

Piasecki E, Waliszko A (1975) Zmiennosc wieku menarchy dziewczat wroclawskich w uzaleznieniu od wielkosc rodziny (Variability of age at menarche in Wroclaw girls as conditioned by family size). Materialy i Prace Antropologiczne 89:103-116.

Pilicz S, Sadowska J (1973) Z badan nad rozwojem i sprawnoscia fizyczna mlodziezy szkol podstawowych (Research on development and physical fitness of primary school children). Wychowanie Fizyczne i Sport 1:3-10 (in Polish).

Pivarnik JM, Bray MS, Hergenroeder AC, Hill RB, Wong WW (1995) Ethnicity effects aerobic fitness in U.S. adolescent girls. Medicine and Science in Sports and Exercise 27: 1635-1638.

Pollitzer WS, Anderson JJB (1989) Ethnic and genetic differences in bone mass: A review with a hereditary vs environmental perspective. American Journal of Clinical Nutrition 50:1244-1259.

Ponthieux NA, Barker DG (1965) Relationship between socio-economic status and physical fitness measures. Research Quarterly 36:464-467.

Pratt M, Macera CA, Blanton C (1999) Levels of physical activity and inactivity in children and adults in the United States: Current evidence and research issues. Medicine and Science in Sports and Exercise 31 (suppl):S526-S533.

* Pugliese MT, Lifshitz F, Grad G, Fort P, Marks-Katz M (1983) Fear of obesity: A cause of short stature and delayed puberty. New England Journal of Medicine 309:513-518.

Pyle WH (1920) A manual for the mental and physical examination of school children, revised. The University of Missouri Bulletin 21 (Extension Series 29):13-25.

Qin T, Shohoji T, Sumiya T (1996) Relationship between adult stature and timing of the pubertal growth spurt. American Journal of Human Biology 8:417-426.

Renson R, Beunen G, DeWitte L, Ostyn M, Simons J, VanGerven D (1980) The social spectrum of the physical fitness of 12 to 19 year old boys. In M Ostyn, G Beunen, J Simons (eds), Kinanthropometry II. Baltimore, MD: University Park Press, pp 105-118.

* Roberts DF (1973) Climate and Human Variability. Module in Anthropology No. 34. Reading, MA: Addison-Wesley.

Roberts DF, Danskin MJ, Chinn S (1975) Menarcheal age in Northumberland. Acta Paediatrica Scandinavica 64:845-852.

Roberts DF, Rozner LM, Swan AV (1971) Age at menarche, physique and environment in industrial northeast England. Acta Paediatrica Scandinavica 60:158-164.

Roche AF (1994) Executive summary of the growth chart workshop 1992. Hyattsville, MD: Centers for Disease Control and Prevention, National Center for Health Statistics.

Roche AF (1997) Executive summary of workshop to consider secular trends and possible pooling of data in relation to the revision of the NCHS growth charts. Hyattsville, MD: Centers for Disease Control and Prevention, National Center for Health Statistics.

Roche AF (1999) Postnatal physical growth assessment. Clinical Pediatrics and Endocrinology 8 (suppl):1-12.

Roche AF, Malina RM (1983) Manual of Physical Status and Performance in Childhood. Volume 1. Physical Status. New York: Plenum.

Roche AF, Roberts J, Hamill PVV (1975) Skeletal maturity of children 6–11 years: Racial, geographic area, and socio-economic differentials. Vital and Health Statistics, Series 11, No. 149.

Roche AF, Roberts J, Hamill PVV (1978) Skeletal maturity of youths 12–17 years: Racial, geographic area, and socio-economic differentials. Vital and Health Statistics, Series 11, No. 167.

Rodahl K, Astrand PO, Birkhead NC, Hettinger T, Issekutz B, Jones DM, Weaver R (1961) Physical work capacity: A study of some children and young adults in the United States. Archives of Environmental Health 2:499-510.

Rona R, Wainwright AH, Altman DG, Irwig LM, du V Florey C (1979) Surveillance of growth as a measurement of health in the community. In WW Holland, J Ipsen, J Kostrzewski (eds), Measurement of Levels of Health. Copenhagen: World Health Organization Regional Office for Europe, pp 397-404.

Rueda-Williamson R, Luna-Jaspe H, Macias JA, Tellez FP, Mora Parra JO (1969) Estudio seccional de crecimiento desarrollo y nutricion en 12,138 niños de Bogota, Colombia. I. Tablas de peso y talla de niños Colombianos. Pediatria 10:335-349.

Rupich RC, Specker BL, Lieuw-A-Fa M, Ho M (1996) Gender and race differences in bone mass during infancy. Calcified Tissue International 58:395-397.

Ryan AS, Roche AF, editors (1990) Growth of Mexican-American children: Data from the Hispanic Health and Nutrition Examination Survey (1982–1984). American Journal of Clinical Nutrition 51 (suppl):897S-952S.

Ryan AS, Roche AF, Kuczmarski RJ (1999) Weight, stature, and body mass index data for Mexican Americans from the Third National Health and Nutrition Examination Survey (NHANES III, 1988–1994). American Journal of Human Biology 11:673-686.

Sallis JF, Prochaska JJ, Taylor WC (2000) A review of correlates of physical activity of children and adolescents. Medicine and Science in Sports and Exercise 32:963-975.

Sallis JF, Simons-Morton BG, Stone EJ, Corbin CB, Epstein LH, Faucette N, Iannotti RJ, Killen JD, Klesges RC, Petray CK, Rowland TW, Taylor WC (1992) Determinants of physical activity and interventions in youth. Medicine and Science in Sports and Exercise 24:S248-S257.

Sallis JF, Zakarian JM, Hovel MF, Hofstetter R (1996) Ethnic, socioeconomic and sex differences in physical activity among adolescents. Journal of Clinical Epidemiology 49:125-134.

Satake T, Kikuta F, Ozaki T (1993) Ages at peak velocity and peak velocities of seven body dimensions in Japanese children. Annals of Human Biology 20:67-70.

Schnabl-Dickey EA (1977) Relationships between parents' childrearing attitudes and the jumping and throwing performance of their preschool children. Research Quarterly 48:382-390.

Schutte JE, Townsend EJ, Hugg J, Shoup RF, Malina RM, Blomquist CG (1984) Density of lean body mass is greater in blacks than in whites. Journal of Applied Physiology 56:1647-1649.

Shephard RJ (1978) Human Physiological Work Capacity. Cambridge, UK: Cambridge University Press.

Shephard RJ (1986) Fitness of a Nation: Lessons from the Canada Fitness Survey. Basel: Karger.

Slaughter MH, Lohman TG, Boileau RA, Christ CB, Stillman RJ (1990) Differences in subcomponents of fat-free body in relation to height in black and white children. American Journal of Human Biology 2:209-217.

Sobral F (1989) Estado de Crescimento e Aptidao Fisica na Populacao Escolar dos Acores. Lisboa: Universidade Tecnica de Lisboa.

Spurgeon JH, Meredith HV, Onhuoha GBI, Giese WK (1984) Somatic findings at age 9 years on three ethnic groups of Nigerian urban and rural boys. Growth 48:176-186.

Steinhausen H-C (1994) Anorexia and bulimia nervosa. In M Rutter, E Taylor, L Hersov (eds), Child and Adolescent Psychiatry: Modern Approaches, 3rd edition. Oxford: Blackwell, pp 425-440.

Stinson S (1980) The physical growth of high altitude Bolivian Aymara children. American Journal of Physical Anthropology 52:377-385.

Strong WB, Spencer D, Miller MD, Salehbhai M (1978) The physical working capacity of healthy black children. American Journal of Diseases of Children 132:244-248.

Suda A, Hoshi H, Eto M, Ashizawa K (1975) Longitudinal studies on the Japanese-American hybrids. In S Watanabe, S Kondo, E Matsunaga (ed), Human Adaptability. Volume 2. Anthropological and Genetic Studies on the Japanese. Tokyo: University of Tokyo Press, pp 33-69.

Sumiya T, Nakahara H, Shohoji T (2001) Relationships among biological growth parameters for body weight in Japanese children. Growth, Development and Aging 64:91-112.

* Sun SS, Schubert CM, Chumlea WC, Roche AF, Kulin HE, Lee PA, Himes JH, Ryan AS (2002) National estimates of the timing of sexual maturation and racial differences among U.S. children. Pediatrics 110:911-919.

Surbey MK (1990) Family composition, stress, and the timing of human menarche. In TE Ziegler, FB Bercovitch (eds), Socioendocrinology of Primate Reproduction. New York: Wiley-Liss, pp 11-32.

Sutton-Smith B, Rosenberg BG (1970) The Sibling. New York: Holt, Rinehart, Winston.

Suwa S, Tachibana K, Maesaka H, Tanaka T, Yokoya S (1992) Longitudinal standards for height and height velocity for Japanese children from birth to maturity. Clinical Pediatrics and Endocrinology 1:5-13.

Tahara Y, Moji K, Aoyagi K, Nishizawa S, Yukawa K, Tsunawake N, Muraki S, Mascie-Taylor N (2002) Age-related pattern of body density and body composition in Japanese males and females, 11 to 18 years of age. American Journal of Human Biology 14:327-337.

Taks M, Renson R, Beunen G, Claessens A, Colla M, Lefevre J, Ostyn M, Schueremans C, Simons J, VanGerven D, Vanreusel B (1991) Sociogeographic variation in the physical fitness of a cross-sectional sample of Flemish girls 13 to 18 years of age. American Journal of Human Biology 3:503-513.

Tamura Y (1975) Physical fitness of rural adolescents. In K Asahina, R Shigiya (eds), Human Adaptability. Volume 4. Physiological Adaptability and Nutritional Status of the Japanese. B. Growth, Work Capacity and Nutrition of Japanese. Tokyo: University of Tokyo Press, pp 50-61.

Tanner JM, Hayashi T, Preece MA, Cameron N (1982) Increase in length of leg relative to trunk in Japanese children and adults from 1957 to 1977: Comparison with British and with Japanese Americans. Annals of Human Biology 9:411-423.

Teitelbaum MS, editor (1976) Sex Differences: Social and Biological Perspectives. Garden City, NY: Doubleday.

Telama R, Viikari J, Valimaki I, Siren-Tiusanen H, Akerblom HK, Uhart M, Dahl M, Pesonen E, Lahde PL, Pietikainen M, Suoninen P (1985) Atherosclerosis precursors in Finnish children and adolescents. X. Leisure-time physical activity. Acta Paediatrica Scandinavica 318:169-180.

Troiano RP, Flegal KM (1998) Overweight children and adolescents: Description, epidemiology, and demographics. Pediatrics 101:497-504.

Ulijaszek SJ (2000) Work and energetics. In S Stinson, B Bogin, R Huss-Ashmore, D O'Rourke (eds), Human Biology. New York: Wiley-Liss, pp 345-376.

Ulijaszek SJ (2001) Work and climate in traditional subsistence economies. Journal of Physiological Anthropology and Applied Human Science 20:105-110.

van Wieringen JC, Wafelbakker F, Verbrugge HP, De Haas JH (1971) Growth Diagrams 1965 Netherlands. Groningen: Wolters-Noordhoof Publishing.

Vijaya Raghavan K, Singh D, Swaminathan MC (1971) Heights and weights of well-nourished Indian school children. Indian Journal of Medical Research 59:648-654.

Villanueva M (1979) Adiposidad, muscularidad y linearidad en un grupo de niños Mexicanos de distintos niveles socioeconomicos. Anales de Antropologia 16:407-432.

Villarreal SF, Martorell R, Mendoza F (1989) Sexual maturation of Mexican American adolescents. American Journal of Human Biology 1:87-95.

Waters E, Crandall VJ (1964) Social class and observed maternal behavior from 1940 to 1960. Child Development 35:1021-1032.

Wellens RE (1984) The influence of sociocultural variables and sports participation on the age at menarche of Flemish girls (The Leuven Growth Study of Flemish Girls). Austin: University of Texas at Austin, Master's Thesis.

Widdowson EM (1951) Mental contentment and physical growth. Lancet 260:1316-1318.

Williams JR, Scott RB (1953) Growth and development of negro infants. IV. Motor development and its relationship to child rearing practices in two groups of negro infants. Child Development 24:103-121.

Wolanski N (1993) Culture, economics, demography and genes in motor development of man. In PK Seth, S Seth (eds), New Perspectives in Anthropology. New Delhi: MD Publications Pvt Ltd, pp 83-121.

Wolf AM, Gortmaker SL, Cheung L, Gray HM, Herzog DB, Colditz GA (1993) Activity, inactivity, and obesity: Racial, ethnic, and age differences among school girls. American Journal of Public Health 83:1625-1627.

Wray JD (1971) Population pressures on families: Family size and child spacing. Reports on Population/Family Planning, No. 9. New York: Population Council.

* Zill N, Nord CW (1994) Running in Place: How American Families Are Faring in a Changing Economy and an Individualistic Society. Washington, DC: Child Trends, Inc.

Part VI

Applications

The final section of the book has a more applied focus. Four areas in which the study of growth, maturation, performance, and physical activity has specific applications are delineated. Chapter 26 considers risk factors during growth that have implications for adult diseases. A risk factor is a condition that, when present over an extended period of time, significantly increases the probability of developing a common degenerative disease or increases the probability of premature death. This chapter focuses on biological characteristics that are considered risk factors and on several lifestyle components during childhood and adolescence that may have a bearing on morbidity and mortality in adulthood.

Chapter 27 focuses on several chronic clinical conditions that affect children and adolescents. Relationships between selected pediatric conditions and growth and maturation are initially described, and then the habitual activity and physical performance of afflicted children and adolescents are considered.

The young athlete is the focus of chapter 28. The growth, maturity, body composition, and physiological characteristics of young athletes are first described and then considered in the context of intensive training for sport.

The final chapter of the book discusses secular trends in growth, maturation, and performance. Secular trends refer to change or lack of change over relatively long periods of time. This chapter considers several aspects of research on secular trends in body size and proportions and age at menarche. Corresponding data are quite limited for estimates of body composition. Changes in several measures of physical performance in the context of secular trends are also considered.

RISK FACTORS DURING GROWTH AND ADULT HEALTH

Chapter Outline

Primary and Secondary Prevention

Risk Factors for Common Metabolic Diseases

Current Risk Profile of Children and Adolescents

Blood Lipids and Lipoproteins

Hypertension

Type 2 Diabetes Mellitus

Smoking

Obesity and Abdominal Obesity

Dietary Habits

Inactivity and Sedentarism

Summary

Sources and Suggested Readings

A risk factor is a condition that, when present over an extended period, significantly increases the probability of a common degenerative disease such as, among others, cardiovascular disease, type 2 diabetes mellitus, or osteoporosis, or increases the probability of premature death. These dramatic end points are seldom encountered in childhood and adolescence, but risks, or factors associated with undesirable outcomes, are frequently observed before maturity is reached. Although definitive proof is still lacking, a reasonable assumption is that a healthy lifestyle and a favorable risk profile in adulthood are more likely to be attained if healthy habits, such as regular physical activity and a healthy diet, start during childhood (U.S. Department of Health and Human Services 1996). This chapter focuses on biological characteristics that are considered risk factors and on several lifestyle components during childhood and adolescence that may have a bearing on morbidity and mortality in adulthood. The positive role of enhanced habitual physical activity is highlighted.

Primary and Secondary Prevention

Primary prevention, as commonly defined by health promotion specialists and epidemiologists, is an important consideration. This form of prevention is targeted at the causal factors of a disease or impairment before they are clinically manifested. Primary prevention thus implies a clear understanding of the etiology of the disease or impairment. For example, protecting children from an infectious disease agent through immunization or by removing certain environmental hazards are typical primary prevention efforts.

Secondary prevention attempts to slow the progress of a disease or an impairment that is already present in an individual or to prevent a recurrence of the condition. An example of secondary prevention includes attempts to prevent a second myocardial infarction in a person who has recovered from a first infarction. If reversal of a debilitating condition is not possible, attenuation of its effect is a form of secondary prevention.

In the context of growth and maturation and their relationships with habitual physical activity and physical fitness, primary prevention should be the focus. The goal is to prevent the development of biological and behavioral characteristics during childhood and adolescence that, once established, may lead to negative health consequences in adulthood.

Risk Factors for Common Metabolic Diseases

Several of the more important risk factors for chronic diseases that are usually manifest in adulthood are first identified and are then discussed in more detail in separate sections. Whenever relevant, the effects of enhanced physical activity and physical fitness are emphasized. Given the socioeconomic conditions prevailing in technologically developed nations, emphasis is placed on risk factors for the common metabolic diseases, including atherosclerosis (the hardening

and narrowing of the arteries), hypertension, and type 2 diabetes mellitus.

The natural history of atherosclerosis is depicted in figure 26.1. Only the major features are identified in the evolution of the disease (McGill et al. 1963). Fatty streaks develop and accumulate lipid over time to eventually form fibrous plaques. Subsequently, fibrous plaques enlarge and undergo calcification, hemorrhage, ulceration or rupture, and thrombosis (McGill et al. 2000). Occlusion of a blood vessel by a thrombus causes a disease, and the clinical manifestation depends on the blood vessel affected.

The distribution of atherosclerotic lesions in the aortas of individuals 3 to 36 years of age is shown in figure 26.2. The percentage of the surface area of the aorta covered by fatty streaks was assessed from autopsy samples removed in a standard manner (Berenson et al. 1995b). The figure shows a high degree of interindividual variability in the presence of fatty streaks at any age, beginning in late childhood or early puberty. However, the early stages of the atherosclerosic

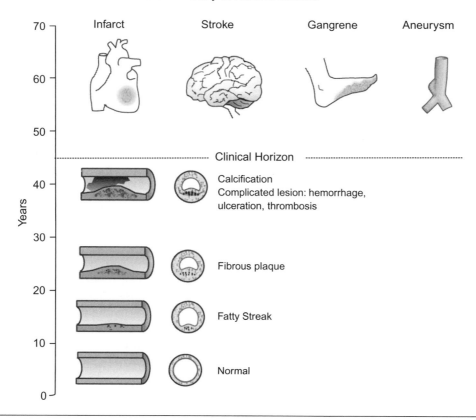

FIGURE 26.1   The natural history of atherosclerosis. See text for explanation.
Adapted from McGill et al., 1963.

Childhood Aortic Lesions

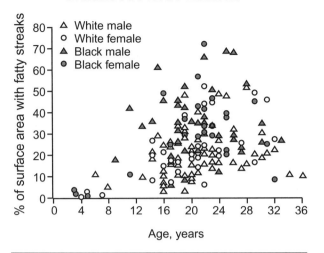

FIGURE 26.2 The distribution of athero-sclerotic lesions in the aortas of children and young adults.

Reprinted, by permission, from G. Berenson et al., 1995, " Rationale to study the early natural history of heart disease," *The American Journal of the Medical Sciences* Suppl 1: S22-S28.

process begin in some individuals during childhood, the degree of involvement increases with age, and the process accelerates during puberty.

Some major risk factors for a first coronary episode or heart attack based on data from 8,000 middle-aged American White men are summarized in table 26.1. The men entered the study at 40 years of age. Values at entry into the study are given for serum cholesterol, systolic and diastolic blood pressures, and the number of packs of cigarettes smoked per day. The data are divided into quintiles based on the distribution of the values in this large sample of men. The **relative risk** of being a victim of a first major coronary episode

over a period of about 20 years is also indicated in the table. The quintile of lowest risk serves as the denominator in calculating the relative risk. Quite clearly, the risk of a coronary episode increases dramatically with higher serum cholesterol, higher blood pressures, and smoking.

High total serum cholesterol levels (hypercholesterolemia), high blood pressure (hypertension), and cigarette smoking taken together at about 40 years of age increase the risk of heart attack in the next 20 years by about six to seven times. This finding is by any standard a serious health concern that must be carefully analyzed for potential precursors during the years of growth and maturation.

Data from the Bogalusa Heart Study (see chapter 1) show that fatty streaks in the aorta and coronary arteries are correlated with important variables of the blood lipid and lipoprotein profile. Figure 26.3 illustrates the relationship between the percentage of the surface area of the respective blood vessels with fatty streaks, and blood lipids and lipoproteins in individuals 6 to 30 years of age. The blood vessels were removed in a standard manner at autopsy, and the lipid and lipoprotein levels were based on assessment when the individuals were alive. The individuals died in accidents (i.e., an unexpected death) and were free from major diseases that would influence health of the blood vessels. Total cholesterol, LDL cholesterol, VLDL cholesterol, and triglycerides are positively correlated with fatty streak lesions, whereas HDL cholesterol is negatively related to fatty streaks (Berenson et al., 1992).

High serum cholesterol, hypertension, and cigarette smoking were the only risk factors considered in the study summarized in table 26.1. The role of risk factors for common metabolic diseases also needs attention. Several studies have

TABLE 26.1	Relative Risk of a First Major Coronary Event Among About 8,000 Men 40 to 64 Years of Age, Based on Major Risk Factors at Entry Into the Study				
Quintile	Serum cholesterol (mg/dl)	Systolic blood pressure (mmHg)	Diastolic blood pressure (mmHg)	Cigarette smoking (pack/day)	Approximate relative risk
I	206	125	78	0.4	1.0
II	222	131	83	0.8	2.0
III	234	135	85	1.2	2.9
IV	246	139	88	1.6	4.2
V	269	151	96	2.0	6.8

The sample is divided into risk quintiles, taking the risk of the lowest quintile as 1.0.

Data from the Pooling Project, adapted from Stamler (1980) and other sources.

Correlation Between Fatty Streaks and Risk Factors

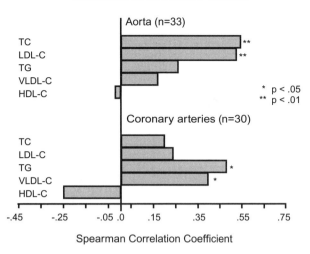

Spearman Correlation Coefficient

FIGURE 26.3 Association between fatty streak involvement and risk factor levels in White male subjects from the Bogalusa Heart Study. A moderate correlation (r = 0.54, p < 0.01) with total cholesterol (TC) and low-density lipoprotein cholesterol (LDL-C) in serum was noted for lesions in the aorta, and an inverse trend was noted for the high-density lipoprotein cholesterol (HDL-C) level. Significant correlations are seen in the coronary vessels with very-low-density lipoprotein cholesterol (VLDL-C) and triglycerides (TG).

Reprinted, by permission, from G. Berenson et al., 1995, " Rationale to study the early natural history of heart disease," *The American Journal of the Medical Sciences* Suppl 1: S22-S28.

addressed this issue, and the list of risk factors that need consideration has been expanded. Table 26.2 summarizes conditions associated with an increasing probability of eventually developing one of the diseases associated with atheroscle-

rosis. Approximate relative risk values are also presented. These values are based on trends emerging from a number of prospective studies (U.S. Department of Health and Human Services 1996). A relative risk represents the probability for a disease in an individual who has the risk factor compared with the probability for a disease assigned to individuals who do not have the risk factor. According to some estimates, for example, individuals who have an abnormal exercise tolerance test have almost a four times greater risk of a coronary episode than those who have a normal exercise tolerance test.

As suggested in table 26.2, individuals with a susceptible genotype are more prone to atherosclerosis than others. Various genotypes fall into this category, and the relative risk, in turn, is quite variable. Information on the relative level of genetic risk for heart disease has begun to accumulate. For instance, in individuals affected by familial hypercholesterolemia, the risk for atherosclerotic disease is extremely high, and homozygotes for an LDL receptor deficiency generally die at an early age. Other mutations have less drastic effects, and some have barely detectable influences or no effect at all.

Obesity and inactivity are characterized by a modest relative risk of about 1.5. The relative risk may increase if inactivity or obesity is more pronounced. The American Heart Association has recognized the importance of these issues and has taken the position that hypercholesterolemia, hypertension, smoking, physical inactivity, and obesity are the five major risk factors for heart disease.

Hypertension is a disease with high prevalence rates in adults of both sexes. Approximately 50 million American adults have elevated blood pressures with values above 140/90 mm/Hg

TABLE 26.2 Approximate Probability of Developing a Disease of Arteriosclerosis When a Condition Defined As a Risk Factor Is Present

Variable	Approximate relative risk
Susceptible genotype	Unknown, but variable with outcome
Abnormal ECG in an exercise stress test	4.0
Age, male, smoking, hypertension, high total plasma cholesterol, high LDL, low HDL	2.5 to 3.0
Hyperglycemia, high plasma triglycerides, high fat intake, abdominal fat	2.0 and higher
Inactivity and sedentarism, overweight and obesity	1.5 to 2.0

The relative risk is defined in relation to that of individuals of similar characteristics who do not have the risk factor, that is, risk =1.0. Approximations based on several prospective studies and other epidemiological evidence. The relative risk values may thus vary among studies.

(The Sixth Report of the Joint National Committee on Prevention, Detection, Evaluation, and Treatment of High Blood Pressure 1997). American Blacks are more affected than American Whites, Mexican Americans, or Native Americans.

The risk factors for hypertension are well known, and several are relevant to the discussion of healthy behaviors during the growing years. These risk factors include a family history of elevated blood pressure; overweight and obesity; a sedentary lifestyle; excessive alcohol intake; high salt consumption; low dietary potassium, calcium, and magnesium intake; and smoking. High blood pressure is also often associated with a high-fat diet. With the exception of a family history and an underlying genetic susceptibility, all other risk factors are rooted in behaviors that can be developed and managed from childhood through adolescence into adulthood. Maintaining a healthy body weight, being physically active, abstinence from smoking and alcohol intake, and adoption of healthy eating habits based on the food pyramid will go a long way towards preventing the early manifestations of elevated blood pressures during childhood and adolescence.

A third metabolic condition of considerable importance is type 2 diabetes mellitus. Almost 7% of adult Americans have this disease. Type 2 diabetes mellitus is a disease that typically evolves progressively. Figure 26.4 shows the major factors involved as an individual progresses from normal glycemia to type 2 diabetes mellitus. It generally begins with a reduced ability of insulin to stimulate the uptake of blood glucose by skeletal muscle and several other tissues. This reduced ability is known as a stage of insulin resistance. Such insulin resistance can normally be compensated for by an increase in insulin production and secretion from the pancreas. Higher insulin levels will normally succeed in maintaining normal blood glucose levels and prevent hyperglycemia. The price, however, is hyperinsulinemia (elevated plasma insulin levels). The pancreas is generally able to cope with the increased demands for insulin over several decades. Unfortunately, if the condition is left untreated in a substantial fraction of individuals, the pancreas becomes exhausted by the high demands for insulin and subsequently

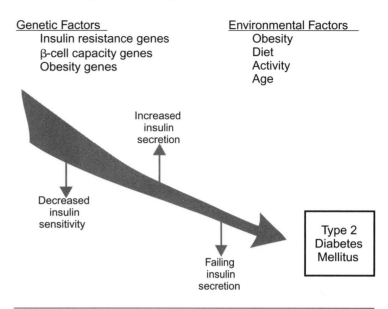

Pathogenesis of Type 2 Diabetes Mellitus

FIGURE 26.4 Pathogenesis of type 2 diabetes mellitus. Genetic and environmental factors can alter the body's response to insulin and glucose and lead to the development of type 2 diabetes mellitus.

Adapted from the Diabetes Research Working Group, 1999.

begins to fail. The result is type 2 diabetes mellitus, which is a difficult condition to manage. When poorly controlled, it is strongly associated with diseases of the large blood vessels, including those of the heart, and also of the small blood vessels, particularly complications in the eyes, kidneys, and nervous system (A Report of the Congressionally Established Diabetes Research Working Group 1999).

Several factors are known to increase the risk of developing type 2 diabetes mellitus. The disease has a strong familial component and genetic predisposition. However, many nongenetic factors influence whether an individual will develop clinical type 2 diabetes mellitus. Overweight or obesity is a major risk factor that can accelerate the manifestation of the disease in an individual who has a genetic predisposition. In contrast, maintaining a normal weight is often sufficient to prevent diabetes, even in the presence of a family history of the disease. Key behavioral factors for the prevention of type 2 diabetes mellitus include a physically active lifestyle and a healthy diet with moderate consumption of fats. Adoption of healthy dietary and exercise habits and maintenance of a normal body weight during childhood and adolescence are highly desirable in the efforts to prevent and reduce the prevalence of type 2 diabetes mellitus. Type 2 diabetes mellitus has assumed particular public health significance. It was previously viewed as a disease that was seen only in adults. It is now often seen in adolescents, a trend that appears to be associated with the increase in obesity in children and adolescents, poor nutritional habits, and a sedentary lifestyle.

Current Risk Profile of Children and Adolescents

The origins of atherosclerosis and other metabolic disease processes can be traced to childhood (Berenson et al. 1998) and perhaps even to fetal life (Barker 1999; see chapter 2). Evidence that primary prevention established during childhood and adolescence can lead subsequently to a decrease in relative risk for these diseases in adult life, however, is primarily circumstantial. Because the issue is of considerable potential significance, the indirect evidence merits careful examination.

One of the lines of evidence that supports the concept of a preventive or healthy lifestyle, or early intervention, is that some children and adolescents already exhibit one or several of the following characteristics (Pinhas-Hamiel et al. 1996; Berenson et al. 1998; Barker 1999):

- High total serum cholesterol
- High serum low-density lipoprotein (LDL) cholesterol
- Low serum high-density lipoprotein (HDL) cholesterol
- High serum triglycerides
- Glucose intolerance
- Insulin resistance
- Hyperinsulinemia
- High blood pressure
- Regular smoking
- Overweight or obesity
- Excess abdominal fat
- High dietary fat intake
- High simple sugar intake
- High dietary salt intake
- Long hours in sedentary activities
- No regular physical activity

These characteristics, when present in adults, are associated with increased morbidity and mortality from cardiovascular diseases and diabetes. These risk conditions, when present for several years, progressively create a degenerative path leading to potentially disastrous health outcomes. However, the period of exposure to such risk conditions that is required to cause degenerative changes varies considerably among individuals and is related in part to family history and the underlying genetic susceptibility.

Several risk factors show age-associated, sex-associated, and maturity-associated variation (Malina 1990). Systolic blood pressure increases from childhood into adolescence, when boys develop slightly higher values than girls. Diastolic blood pressure, on the other hand, shows only a small increase with age. Total cholesterol (TC) and its major fractions, LDL-C and HDL-C, are rather stable during childhood and then decline with the transition into adolescence. The pubertal decline in HDL-C is more marked in boys than in girls. The trends for blood pressures and serum cholesterol suggest changes associated with puberty.

Longitudinal data relating indicators of metabolic fitness to biological maturity are not extensive. Many studies group children by stage of puberty but do not control for variation in chronological age within a specific pubertal stage (see chapter 15). Hence, partitioning the effects of age by itself from changes associated with puberty and their potential interactions may be difficult. In the Fels Longitudinal Study, serum lipids and lipoproteins do not differ between children of the same age who are early (advanced) or late (delayed) in biological maturity. Serum lipids and lipoproteins also do not differ when children are compared relative to the age at peak height velocity or when girls are grouped relative to age at menarche (Siervogel et al. 1989). On the other hand, puberty is associated with a transient decline in insulin sensitivity. Factors underlying pubertal insulin resistance include changes in body mass and increases in adrenal androgens and growth hormone (Bloch et al. 1987; Arslanian and Kalhan 1994).

Hypercholesterolemia, hypertension, obesity, insulin resistance, smoking, physical inactivity, and high fat intake do not exert a major impact on morbidity and mortality during the growing years. Neonatal complications, car accidents, suicide, and cancer are the leading causes of death at this time of life in technologically developed countries. However, given the long incubation time required for these biological and lifestyle characteristics to induce the development of cardiovascular and metabolic diseases, a certain proportion of children and adolescents needs to be targeted for special preventive and even therapeutic procedures

This approach can be justified on several bases. First, some children and adolescents already exhibit levels of serum cholesterol, blood pressure, and body fat, or a regional distribution of body fat, that place them in a higher risk category. About 15% to 20% of children and adolescents probably fall into this category (Raitakari et al. 1994; Bar-Or et al. 1998; Akerblom et al. 1999). Among these children and adolescents, at least 1% are even more at risk for premature heart disease, hypertension, or type 2 diabetes mellitus, and preventive and, if necessary, therapeutic measures should be initiated as early as possible. These children are often at high risk not only because of their individual biological and behavioral profile but also because of a strong familial history for one or more chronic diseases. For example, children of parents with diabetes mellitus have an elevated risk of obesity, of insulin resistance, and of high blood pressure (Berenson et al. 1995a).

Second, some of these biological characteristics have a fairly stable pattern of development from childhood to adolescence and even better tracking from adolescence into adulthood (see table 26.3). This finding implies that if no specific measures are taken to alter the developmental course, a risk condition may become firmly established by late adolescence and exert its detrimental effects into adulthood.

Third, in contrast to metabolic conditions, some of the risk factors are behaviors that are probably amenable to alteration during childhood and adolescence. Unless a risk factor is under close genetic regulation and has little sensitivity to changes in environmental circumstances or lifestyle, favorable modifications can be expected under the influence of preventive and therapeutic measures initiated during childhood and adolescence.

A word of caution, however, is warranted. Tracking of risk factors is quite poor between infancy or early childhood and later years (Roche 1997), with few exceptions that are determined by serious gene deficiencies such as in familial hypercholesterolemia. Primary prevention initiated in the early years will, therefore, be characterized by poor specificity, that is, a high proportion of false positive infants and young children will be incorporated into prevention programs. This outcome is not desirable and may actually result in some

TABLE 26.3 Tracking Coefficients and 95% Confidence Intervals (CI) for Biologic and Lifestyle Coronary Heart Disease Risk Factors From Ages 13 to 27 Years

Risk factor	Tracking coefficient	95% CI
Biologic risk factors		
Total cholesterol (TC)	0.71	0.65–0.78
HDL cholesterol, males	0.51	0.42–0.60
HDL cholesterol, females	0.65	0.54–0.76
TC/HDL ratio	0.71	0.63–0.79
Systolic blood pressure	0.43	0.34–0.53
Diastolic blood pressure	0.34	0.24–0.43
Sum of four skinfolds	0.63	0.56–0.71
Cardiopulmonary fitness	0.31	0.24–0.38
Lifestyle risk factors		
Fat intake	0.42	0.34–0.50
P/S ratio[a]	0.33	0.21–0.44
Carbohydrate intake	0.37	0.28–0.46
Cholesterol intake	0.34	0.26–0.42
Daily physical activity	0.34	0.19–0.49

Data are for 83 males and 98 females in the Amsterdam Growth and Health Study.

[a]P/S ratio = ratio between estimated intakes of polyunsaturated fatty acids and saturated fatty acids.

Adapted from Twisk et al. (1997).

harm, at least psychologically, to the child and family members. Specificity becomes much better at school age and even more during adolescence.

Even though some of the biological and behavioral characteristics underlying risk factors for heart diseases, hypertension, or type 2 diabetes mellitus have been described, the most important of these characteristics are briefly reviewed subsequently in the context of growth and maturation and implications for prevention of common metabolic diseases in adulthood.

Blood Lipids and Lipoproteins

The lipids and lipoproteins of interest in the context of atherosclerosis are typically triglycerides, total serum cholesterol, and low-density and high-density lipoprotein cholesterol. Other characteristics monitored in more advanced clinical settings include blood levels of apolipoprotein B, Lp a, several hemostatic factors, density of low-density particles, and others.

Cholesterol is transported in the blood in a packaged form with protein particles (apolipoproteins) and other substances. The total amount of cholesterol is transported in three main kinds of lipoproteins known as high-density lipoprotein (HDL) cholesterol, low-density lipoprotein (LDL) cholesterol, and very-low-density lipoprotein (VLDL) cholesterol. HDL particles contain more protein and less cholesterol, whereas the opposite is characteristic of LDL particles. LDL is the major carrier of cholesterol at all ages, and its absolute and relative contributions to total cholesterolemia are related to the risk of a coronary episode. The higher the LDL cholesterol or the higher the ratio of LDL cholesterol to total cholesterol (TC), the greater the risk of cardiovascular disease. Hence, it is often labeled as the "bad" cholesterol. On the other hand, high values of HDL cholesterol are associated with a reduction in the probability of having a coronary event. For this reason, it is often called the "good" cholesterol. HDL particles are involved in the reverse transport of cholesterol back to the liver.

Blood lipids and lipoprotein levels are much lower at birth than in adulthood. Interestingly, infant girls tend to have higher levels than infant boys. In the first few days postnatally, serum triglycerides (TG) and total serum cholesterol increase by as much as 50%. Total serum cholesterol and HDL and LDL cholesterol decrease at puberty, followed by a subsequent rise in total and LDL cholesterol into young adulthood.

Of specific interest in the context of risk factors are children and youth who have dyslipidemia, that is, high concentrations of total serum cholesterol, TGs, and LDL cholesterol and low concentrations of HDL cholesterol. How often do such conditions occur in growing individuals? Medians and the 90th or 10th percentiles (depending on which is more relevant) for several blood lipids and lipoproteins are given in tables 26.4 and 26.5 for United States girls and boys, respectively, based on an expert panel report of the National Cholesterol Education Program (1992). Generally similar values are also apparent in other studies in North America (Guo et al. 1994) and Europe (Armstrong et al. 1991; Akerblom et al. 1999).

Although values of lipids and lipoproteins are not necessarily normally distributed, tables 26.4 and 26.5 show that a substantial number of adolescent boys, but not girls, develop high total serum cholesterol, LDL cholesterol, and TGs, and low HDL cholesterol. This trend suggests that a

TABLE 26.4 Serum Lipid Levels in United States Girls

Variable (mg/dl)	Age group (yr)			
	0–4	5–9	10–14	15–19
Total cholesterol				
50th	161	168	163	160
90th	195	201	196	197
LDL cholesterol				
50th	—	101	97	96
90th	—	129	130	133
HDL cholesterol				
50th	—	54	54	53
10th	—	39	41	39
Triglycerides				
50th	61	57	72	70
90th	99	93	117	117

Selected percentiles are based on the 1992 report published by an expert panel on blood cholesterol levels in children and adolescents.

Adapted from the National Cholesterol Education Program (1992).

TABLE 26.5 Serum Lipid Levels in United States Boys

Variable (mg/dl)	Age group (yr)			
	0–4	5–9	10–14	15–19
Total cholesterol				
50th	156	164	160	150
90th	192	197	196	188
LDL cholesterol				
50th	—	93	97	96
90th	—	121	126	127
HDL cholesterol				
50th	—	56	57	47
10th	—	43	41	35
Triglycerides				
50th	53	53	61	71
90th	87	88	105	124

Selected percentiles are based on the 1992 report published by an expert panel on blood cholesterol levels in children and adolescents.

Adapted from the National Cholesterol Education Program (1992).

significant fraction of boys, in contrast to girls, are progressing toward an atherogenic profile during and after sexual maturation. These sex differences are believed to be related, in part, to changes in sex hormones associated with sexual maturity. However, the issue needs further study.

Tracking of the lipid and lipoprotein profile is central to evaluating and promoting primary prevention. If blood lipids and lipoproteins track well over periods of several years, this tracking becomes an important prevention issue because individuals with an atherogenic profile are likely to maintain the same profile or levels of lipids and lipoproteins over several years, if no successful intervention can be implemented. Correlations between initial and final levels of total serum cholesterol over a period of 5 to 6 years, starting in childhood, approach about 0.6. Correlations for serum TGs are lowest (about 0.3 to 0.4) and correlations for LDL cholesterol are highest (about 0.7). More than 40% of children at or above the 90th percentile for total cholesterol and LDL cholesterol remain at these high levels 5 or 6 years after initial observation On the other hand, constancy in ranking for high levels of serum TGs is lower at about 20%. The data show significant tracking over a period of several years. As shown in table 26.3, the correlation for TC over a period of 15 years from adolescence to young adulthood, 13 to 27 years, is about 0.70 for the sexes combined. For HDL cholesterol, correlations over this time span are 0.51 for males and 0.65 for females (Twisk et al. 1997). Thus, tracking for the key features of the lipid profile remains significant even over a 15-year period, which suggests that a significant proportion of children who exhibit an atherogenic profile will retain or maintain this profile from adolescence into adulthood.

For many years, the American Heart Association has advised the public to try to maintain a low total serum cholesterol level, preferably below 200 mg/100 ml (about 5 mmol/L). Although this advice is directed at the adult population, it has significant implications for children and adolescents. Indeed, if a cholesterol level of 200 mg/100 ml or more is a risk factor in adults, its presence during growth should be of concern (National Cholesterol Education Program Expert Panel on Blood Cholesterol Levels in Children and Adolescents 1992). Cholesterolemic values well above 250 mg/100 ml (about 6.2 mmol/L) in children or adolescents should be taken more seriously, as they most likely signify an inherited deficiency.

Although the evidence is less striking, high TGs should also be a cause for concern. Hypertriglyceridemia is associated with genetic abnormalities, obesity, insulin resistance, and hyperinsulinemia. Hypertriglyceridemia is often accompanied by high LDL cholesterol and low HDL cholesterol and is thus with a common feature of an atherogenic blood lipid profile.

Even though heredity is an important factor that determines an individual's lipoprotein profile, any intervention that will effectively reduce total serum cholesterol and LDL cholesterol, or increase HDL cholesterol, is potentially beneficial in terms of prevention. For example, a reduction of total cholesterolemia by 1% has been suggested to be associated with a decrease of at least 2% in the rate of coronary episodes (Stamler 1980).

Some cross-sectional data show that physically active children and adolescents have a better lipoprotein profile (higher HDL-C, lower serum TG, and higher HDL-to-TC ratio) than their sedentary peers. Aerobic exercise programs have generated mixed results for serum lipids, lipoproteins, and TGs in children and adolescents (Despres et al. 1990; Malina 1990; Armstrong and Simons-Morton 1994; Riddoch 1998), although several studies suggest an increase in HDL-C and the HDL-to-TC ratio (Malina 1990; Armstrong and Simons-Morton 1994). Major factors in the comparison of studies are variations in the intensity and duration of the exercise programs and perhaps more important, whether the children had a normal lipid and lipoprotein profile at baseline (i.e., at the start of the programs). Another potential confounder in children and adolescents is growth in body mass. Growth and maturation are associated with positive energy balance as body mass and specific tissues increase. The increase in body mass may possibly influence the response of lipids and lipoproteins to the activity stimulus in children and adolescents. Another possible confounder in training studies during puberty is maturity-associated changes in lipids and lipoproteins.

However, indications are that endurance training can enhance HDL cholesterol concentration and improve the plasma lipoprotein profile in obese subjects (Sasaki et al. 1987; Gutin et al. 1996). To be effective, training must be maintained on a regular basis because the beneficial changes are reversible with cessation of the activity program (Gutin and Humphries 1998). In this context, exercise prescription based on frequently repeated endurance activity sessions as a primary and secondary intervention strategy may be appropriate, along with appropriate dietary recommendations. However, such a program may not be sufficient for children and adolescents with the worst atherogenic profiles, and these individuals should be treated by medication in a lipid clinic.

Hypertension

As defined by a The Joint National Committee of the National Heart, Lung and Blood Institute, hypertension in children and adolescents occurs when the average systolic or diastolic pressure, taken on at least three different occasions, is equal to, or higher than, the 95th percentile for age and sex (see table 26.6). Systolic and diastolic blood pressures were defined in chapter 9. Blood pressure values in children are more variable than in adults. Hence, a child who has high blood pressure on one occasion may have readings, several days or weeks later, that fall in the normal range. Extreme caution should, therefore, be used in the interpretation of occasional or casual blood pressure measurements. The variability of blood pressure measurements in children is related to the biological mechanisms that regulate blood pressure. Some of the regulatory mechanisms act on a very short-term and almost acute basis, whereas others are involved in the long-term control of blood pressures.

Close to 3 million American children and adolescents, ages 6 to 17 years, have hypertension (National High Blood Pressure Education Program Working Group on Hypertension Control in Children and Adolescents 1996). However, the proportion of children and youth with a tendency toward hypertensive values or with intermittent blood pressure values in the hypertensive range may be as high as 15%.

Those with high blood pressure values tend to remain in the high category over a period of several years. In a longitudinal study of blood pressure in 820 children in Muscatine, Iowa, the correlation for measures of systolic and diastolic blood pressure taken 6 years apart were 0.30 and 0.18, respectively (Lauer et al. 1982). The tracking between adolescence and young adulthood is somewhat higher (Palti et al. 1988; Malina 1990; Andersen & Haraldsdottir 1993; Raitakari et al. 1994; Twisk et al. 1997). For example, when Danish adolescents were tested 8 years apart (starting at age 15 to 19 years), correlations were 0.49 and 0.44 for systolic and diastolic pressures, respectively, among the males and 0.54 and 0.38 among the females. Fifty-three percent of the males and 38% of the females stayed in the upper quintile for systolic pressure. Respective values for diastolic pressure were 43% and 36% (Andersen & Haraldsdottir 1993). Similar tracking coefficients were shown for Dutch adolescents

TABLE 26.6 Classification of High Blood Pressure and Hypertension in Children and Adolescents

Age group (yr)	High normal blood pressure 90–94th percentile	Significant hypertension 95–99th percentile	Severe hypertension >99th percentile
< 2	104–111 70–73	112–117 74–81	≥118 ≥82
3–5	108–115 70–75	116–123 76–83	≥124 ≥84
6–9	114–121 74–77	122–129 78–85	≥130 ≥86
10–12	122–125 78–81	126–133 82–89	≥134 ≥90
13–15	130–135 80–85	136–143 86–91	≥144 ≥92
16–18	136–141 84–91	142–149 92–97	≥150 ≥98

All values are in mmHg.
Within each age group, the top line refers to systolic blood pressure and the lower line refers to diastolic blood pressure.
Adapted from the Joint National Committee of the National Heart, Lung and Blood Institute (1993).

(see table 26.3) (Twisk et al. 1997). Hypertension is often associated with overweight and obesity (Williams et al. 1992; McMurray et al. 1995), so a child who is hypertensive and obese is generally more likely to maintain a hypertensive status if the overweight problem persists. High blood pressure also occurs in children and adolescents with insulin resistance, a phenomenon observed with increasing frequency. Tracking of high blood pressure is likely to be more pronounced if the hypertensive individual is and remains obese, performs poorly in a glucose tolerance test or has type 2 diabetes, and is from a family with a history of high blood pressure.

Because hypertension is a dangerous condition, which carries additional risks of cardiovascular disease in adult years, intervention is desirable in children and especially adolescents, who have hypertension or borderline hypertension. Proper referral to a physician is essential in these cases.

Enhanced physical activity induces little or no reduction of blood pressure in children and adolescents who have normal blood pressure at the start of the program. However, endurance activities do help to reduce blood pressure, mostly systolic, in young people with hypertension (Hagberg et al. 1983; Hansen et al. 1991; Alpert & Wilmore 1994), or those at a high risk for hypertension (Ewart et al. 1998). The effect is mild (6 to 10 mmHg), but such a reduction can sometimes make a difference and determine whether the individual will need medication. Regular physical activity can contribute, albeit in a modest manner, to a reduction of blood pressure in some cases. The effect of an endurance training program on blood pressure in children with slightly elevated blood pressure may become beneficial if the program is accompanied by dietary modifications and, in overweight and obese children, by a slower rate of weight gain or by a reduction in body fatness. Dietary changes should include reduction in total calorie intake if the child is overweight or obese, reduction in salt intake, and increased consumption of vegetables, fruits, cereal, and fish because all are related to improved blood pressures.

An excellent example of the effects of a healthy diet on elevated blood pressure is provided in the DASH Study (Dietary Approaches to Stop Hypertension). In a large clinical trial, subjects were fed diets rich in vegetables and fruits, but low in dairy fat products, for 8 weeks (Appel et al. 1997). The systolic and diastolic blood pressures were slightly reduced in normotensive subjects (those with normal blood pressures) but were more reduced in a hypertensive subgroup. In a second intervention study, low dietary sodium was added to the DASH diet (Sacks et al. 2001). The benefits of the diet were more striking on resting blood pressures in both groups of participants (i.e., those who were normotensive or hypertensive at baseline). Moreover, the favorable effects of the diet were generally stronger in American Blacks than in American Whites (Greenland 2001).

Type 2 Diabetes Mellitus

Traditionally considered an "adult onset" disease, type 2 diabetes mellitus, is now seen in growing numbers of children and, in particular, adolescents (Berenson et al. 1995b; Pinhas-Hamiel et al. 1996; Rosenbloom et al. 1999). Its incidence among young people in various countries has increased markedly in the past 2 decades. In the United States and Canada, Native Americans are particularly affected. Mexican Americans and African Americans in the United States are more affected than American Whites (those of European ancestry). A study of Japanese school children noted a more than 30-fold increase in incidence of type 2 diabetes among children between 1976 and 1995 (Kitagawa et al. 1998). In Cincinnati, a 10-fold increase in the incidence of type 2 diabetes occurred between 1982 and 1994 among 1,027 children and adolescents (Pinhas-Hamiel et al. 1996).

This epidemic-like increase has been evolving concurrently with a major increase in the incidence and prevalence of obesity in children and adolescents (see chapter 24). Indeed, type 2 diabetes occurs mostly in overweight and obese individuals (Pinhas-Hamiel et al. 1996). Unlike type 1 diabetes, in which an autoimmune destruction of the β cells of the pancreas leads to a lack of insulin, insulin production in the early phase of type 2 diabetes is adequate. In fact, blood insulin levels in type 2 diabetes are excessive, reflecting the reduced efficacy of insulin to dispose of blood glucose in various body tissues. In type 2 diabetes, the pancreas becomes progressively exhausted as a result of having to maintain elevated levels to compensate for the diminished action of insulin, particularly in skeletal muscle. This insulin resistance, in addition to its strong relationship to obesity, may cluster with dyslipidemia, hyperglycemia, high blood pressure, abnormal platelet aggregation, and altered balance of hemostatic factors (Bergstrom et al. 1996; Gutin and Humphries 1998; Akerblom et al. 1999). The term "metabolic syndrome" has been coined for this cluster of risk factors. Hyperinsulinemia in adults is related in part to abdominal fat, and this relationship has also been documented in 7-year-old to 10-year-old girls (Treuth et al. 1998).

Adolescents with the following characteristics are particularly at risk for type 2 diabetes:

- Female sex in some, but not all, ethnic groups
- Native American or Canadian (Amerindian), Mexican American, and American Black ancestry
- Obesity, especially of the abdominal type
- Recent history of a sharp increase in body weight and body fat
- Family history of type 2 diabetes
- Sedentary lifestyle
- High-fat diet
- Smoking

Changes in glucose metabolism and insulin in response to physical activity programs in children and adolescents have been studied less often than other risk factors (e.g., serum cholesterol and its fractions). Some evidence suggests that glucose tolerance is improved and insulin sensitivity is increased with exposure to an exercise program in prepubertal boys (Boisseau et al. 1997). The beneficial effect of an enhanced physical activity program on insulin sensitivity disappears, however, after cessation of the program. For example, when 7-year-old to 11-year-old obese children were given a 4-month aerobic training program, plasma insulin levels decreased by 10% (compared with an increase of 4% in a control group). However, 4 months after cessation of the program, plasma insulin levels rebounded, increasing by 19% (Ferguson et al. 1999).

Enhanced but sustained physical activity, together with dietary changes, are major factors in the prevention and treatment of type 2 diabetes mellitus (Ivy et al. 1999). Regular physical activity should, therefore, be considered essential for young people who have type 2 diabetes or are at a high risk for it.

Prospective studies have suggested that a high BMI, lack of regular exercise, poor diet, and smoking are associated with an increased risk for type 2 diabetes mellitus (Hu et al. 2001). Studies indicating such associations were recently supported by two randomized controlled trials in which lifestyle intervention programs were implemented in nondiabetic adults who had elevated glucose levels (i.e., they were at risk for diabetes). The first study was conducted in Finland and showed that the risk of diabetes was reduced by 50% in middle-aged subjects who modified their diets and became physically active compared with a control group over a period of 3 years (Tuomilehto et al. 2001). The second study was conducted in the United States and is known as the Diabetes Prevention Program (DPP). The follow-up period was about 3 years, but the study included a much larger sample (3,234 persons) with high blood glucose, which was about six times larger than the Finnish study. The lifestyle intervention involved dietary measures and 150 minutes of physical activity per week. The program reduced the incidence of diabetes in adults by 58%.

Smoking

Approximately one-half of all smokers in the United States start smoking before 18 years of age. This finding is of major importance to public health because smoking is the single most preventable cause of death in the United States (U.S. Department of Health and Human Services 1989). Regular smoking is an established risk factor associated with an increase in morbidity and premature death later in life. This risk is particularly evident for coronary heart disease, a variety of respiratory diseases, and several cancers. Although children and adolescents are apparently well aware of the risks of smoking to their health, almost 40% of them will be smokers by the time they graduate from high school. Data from several surveys in the United States (Centers for Disease Control 1991) and in Canada (Stephens & Craig 1990) indicate that the prevalence of regular smokers increases with age in both sexes during the second decade of life. About 10% of 10-year-old boys and girls in the United States are regular smokers, and the percentage reaches about 40% to 45% in females and 35% in males by 18 to 19 years of age.

Passive smoking, inhalation of tobacco-product smoke because of the habits of others in the nonsmoker's environment, continues to be a cause for concern. Respiratory problems are more frequent among nonsmokers exposed to passive smoke. The severity of morbidity associated with passive smoking depends on the extent of exposure to tobacco smoke.

Family members of the smoking child or adolescent are more likely to be smokers than are relatives who live in a household with a nonsmoking youngster. Adolescents who smoke tend to have friends who are frequent smokers. Finally, children and adolescents who smoke are more likely than nonsmokers to use alcohol and street drugs, even the stronger drugs.

The situation thus poses quite a challenge to those concerned with primary and secondary prevention. The need for education on the risks of habitual smoking in the development of cardiovascular diseases and cancers is clearly indicated. Emphasis on the effects of a "healthy" lifestyle on general health, career, and other outcomes would also be helpful. However, no educational programs have been proven efficacious in preventing or reducing the extent of smoking at a young age.

Several studies have suggested a possible relationship between smoking habits and habitual physical activity. In one study, adolescents who took part in athletic activities had a lower rate of tobacco use than their nonathletic peers (Escobedo and Casperson 1993). In a subsequent analysis (see table 26.7), an inverse relationship was seen between the amount of vigorous activity and the prevalence of regular smoking and of heavy smoking (Escobedo and Casperson 1993). Interestingly, no relationship exists between nonvigorous physical education or community-based activities and the prevalence of smoking. In a 3-year prospective study of 12-year-old to 16-year-old school students, the initiation of tobacco smoking was less frequent among girls who reported a high level of leisure-time physical activity compared with those who reported a medium or low level of activity (Aaron et al. 1995). This relationship was not evident in boys. Data about a relationship between habitual physical activity and the extent of smokeless tobacco use are not consistent. Overall, the presently available data suggest a pattern, albeit inconsistent, where ath-letically inclined children and adolescents smoke less than their less-active peers. However, the data are based only on associations, so a cause-and-effect relationship cannot be established between these behaviors.

Obesity and Abdominal Obesity

Obesity is a risk factor for cardiovascular diseases in general but particularly for type 2 diabetes mellitus (see table 26.2). Obesity often clusters with other risk factors among children and adolescents, as well as in adults (Gutin et al. 1997; Freedman et al. 1999). Based on repeated measurements over a 20-year period in the Bogalusa Heart Study, 58% of 5-year-old to 17-year-old children and adolescents with a BMI $\geq$85th percentile had at least one more risk factor than those with a lower BMI, which suggests clustering of atherosclerosis risk factors around obesity (Freedman et al., 1999).

The risk of an atherosclerotic disease or type 2 diabetes is significantly higher in obese adults with a predominant distribution of fat in the abdominal area (abdominal obesity), compared with obese adults with a predominant fat deposition on the buttocks or the legs (Björntorp 1990). A similar pattern begins to emerge already at a young age, even in the first decade of life (Freedman 1995; Owens et al. 1998). This finding has important implications for primary prevention in children and adolescents. Disease-related symptoms are not manifest until the obese state or the excessive accumulation of adipose tissue in the abdominal area has been present for several years. Presently available information suggests that an "incubation period" of decades is required for the metabolic consequences of obesity and excessive abdominal adiposity to be established and expressed clinically.

TABLE 26.7 Prevalence of Regular and Heavy Smoking in Relation to the Amount of Vigorous Physical Activity

Vigorous physical activity (days/mo)	Regular smoking among ever smokers		Heavy smoking among regular smokers	
	Sample size	Prevalence (%)	Sample size	Prevalence (%)
None	2,249	24	624	42
1–2	2,329	23	687	38
3–5	2,428	23	694	34
6–8	1,290	19	371	26
$\geq$ 9	2,742	15	703	29

Adapted from Escobedo and Casperson (1993).

Excess body weight during infancy and childhood correlates only moderately with obesity later in life. Tracking of body weight, BMI, or adiposity between adolescence and adulthood is better, although a fraction of overweight or obese adolescents will subsequently become normal-weight adults. The converse is also true; a percentage of normal-weight children and adolescents will gain a substantial amount of weight and become obese adults. Identifying the causes of these trends is an important research goal. Information about tracking of regional fat distribution from childhood through adolescence into adulthood is not extensive. About 40% to 50% of the variation among individuals in fat topography is estimated to be associated with genetic differences after controlling for the effects of total-body fat (Bouchard et al. 1997). This finding favors some degree of stability in relative subcutaneous fat distribution over time.

Overall, data from a variety of studies suggest that the relative risk of an obese child becoming an obese adult is about 2.0, whereas the relative risk for an obese adolescent becoming an obese adult may be as high as 5.0, particularly if the parents are obese. A child with two obese parents and an early age of onset of an overweight state has the highest risk of becoming an obese adult (Whitaker et al. 1997). The genes responsible for this strong predisposition have not yet been identified.

The importance of treating childhood and adolescent obesity is also highlighted in the results of several experimental studies. For example, weight loss is generally accompanied by an improvement in the blood lipid and lipoprotein profile and an increase in the sensitivity of peripheral tissues (muscle, adipose, and liver) to the action of insulin. On the other hand, a gain in body weight may result in an increase in total serum cholesterol and LDL cholesterol, an elevation in triglycerides, and a decrease in HDL cholesterol. An increase in body weight is also followed by a progressive deterioration of the response of peripheral tissues to insulin, which leads to an increase in insulin secretion by the pancreas, hyperinsulinemia, and a series of other undesirable metabolic events (Sasaki et al. 1987; Gutin and Owens 1999).

Chronic overfeeding for a few weeks can induce similar metabolic changes even in the

TABLE 26.8	The Effects of 22 Days of Overfeeding on 12 Young Adult Males (Mean Age, 19 Years)	
Variable	**Before overfeeding**	**After overfeeding**
Body weight (kg)	64.7	66.9
Body fat (%)	11.8	13.1
Fasting blood glucose (mg/dl)	86	84
Fasting plasma insulin (m U/ml)	16	19
Serum cholesterol (mg/dl)	146	172
Serum triglycerides (mg/dl)	74	139
LDL-cholesterol (mg/dl)	104	114

Values are group means. Subjects were six pairs of identical twins who were overfed by 1,000 kcal/24 hours for 22 consecutive days.

Adapted from Després et al. (1987).

presence of only slight gains in body weight and body fat. Table 26.8 summarizes the results of an experiment with six pairs of nonobese young adult male monozygotic twins (mean age, 19 years) who were overfed by 1,000 kilocalories for 22 consecutive days. The metabolic profile was altered quite rapidly in the face of the relatively short-term caloric overload.

The influence of regular physical activity on fatness is apparent in several studies of obese children. For example, a daily program of aerobic activity for 2 years resulted in marked decreases in skinfold thicknesses of obese children (Sasaki et al. 1987), and two short-term training programs, one for 10 weeks and the other for 4 months, showed a significant decrease in estimated percentage body fat in obese children 7 to 11 years of age (Gutin et al. 1996, 1997). In obese children 7 to 11 years of age, a 4-month physical activity program (5 days/week, 40 min/session; estimated energy expenditure 226 kcal/session) resulted in minimal change in abdominal visceral adipose tissue but a loss of abdominal subcutaneous adipose tissue. In contrast, obese control subjects who did not participate in the activity program gained in both visceral and subcutaneous abdominal adipose tissue (Gutin and Humphries 1998; Gutin and Owens 1999).

Studies have compared the effects of exercise versus no exercise, of diet plus exercise versus exercise alone, and of different types of exercise prescriptions on fatness and several risk factors in overweight and obese children and adolescents (Bar-Or et al. 1998; Gutin and Humphries 1998;

Epstein and Goldfield 1999). Overall, enhanced physical activity in overweight or obese children and adolescents results in the following changes:

• Decrease in body weight or reduction in weight gain velocity
• Decrease in percentage body fat
• Reduction in abdominal fat
• Lesser gain of visceral fat with age
• Increase in fat-free mass
• Increase in HDL-cholesterol
• Decrease in fasting insulin level
• Decrease in blood pressure if elevated
• Increase in aerobic fitness

The beneficial effects diminish or disappear within weeks after cessation of the activity program (Ferguson et al. 1999). The only way for the youth to continue to enjoy these morphological and metabolic benefits is to maintain an active lifestyle on a regular basis. How much activity is needed to generate and maintain the beneficial effects is currently not fully understood. Exercise programs, preferably with dietary changes, work best if they include behavior modification elements that lead to new lifestyle habits (Epstein et al. 1998; Saelens & Epstein 1998). Ideally, a program should include both the youngster and the parents (Brownell et al. 1983; Epstein 1993). The effects of a program that incorporates recreational, playlike elements seem to last longer than those achieved by structured, regimented activities (Epstein et al. 1990). Likewise, a reduction in sedentary activities through behavior modification techniques (e.g., rewarding a child who reduces the time spent on watching television) yields better results than programs based on prescribed activities (Epstein et al. 1997; Robinson 1999).

The contribution of regular exercise in the treatment and prevention of childhood obesity is often misunderstood. For instance, the view that the total energy expenditure of an exercise bout of the types that can be performed by an obese child is small, is quite common. Based on this rationale, more emphasis should be placed on dietary reduction in energy intake rather than on physical activity when dealing with obese patients and particularly obese children. Indeed, the caloric expenditure of an exercise period is less striking than the negative energy balance caused by a low-calorie diet. For example, a typical 45-minute aerobic session for obese 7-year-old to 12-year-old children will cause an energy expenditure of approximately 200 to 250 kcal (0.8 to 1.0 mJ) (Blaak et al. 1992; Owens et al. 1999). In contrast, a low-calorie diet can easily reduce daily energy intake by 750 to 1,250 kcal (3 to 5 mJ). However, other considerations favor physical activity. First, the metabolic rate remains above resting levels for some time after the cessation of an activity (Poehlman 1989), which increases the total energy expenditure induced by that activity. Second, an exercise regimen has the potential to increase the spontaneous activity of obese children, so the total energy expenditure for the duration of the program could be significantly higher than that expected from the program itself (Blaak et al. 1992). For instance, a single bout of laboratory-based exercise was accompanied by an increase in spontaneous activity and in energy expenditure on the following day (Kriemler et al. 1999). Additionally, whereas a low-calorie diet may induce a reduction in resting metabolic rate, an activity-based program is not accompanied by such a reduction. Hence, the overall energy expenditure of a program that includes exercise is substantially higher than that expected from the energy cost of exercise alone. Moreover, the addition of resistance training to a low-calorie diet has been suggested to help attenuate the loss of fat-free mass that is often observed when a low-calorie diet is the only treatment modality for obesity in adults (Kraemer et al. 1999). Studies with children (Sothern et al. 2000; Treuth et al. 1998) suggest that an activity program that includes resistance training may help preserve, or even increase, fat-free mass (Pikosky et al. 2002).

In light of the preceding, primary and secondary prevention of obesity in children and adolescents should be encouraged. Such programs should begin in childhood. The exercise recommendation should emphasize duration and total energy expenditure and should offer alternative forms and contexts of exercise. The exercise program should be planned so that it can be well tolerated by the obese child or adolescent (e.g., walking or cycling). Dietary recommendations are also essential to successful prevention and treatment programs. Support from family members as well as from peers who may have a similar problem can facilitate the prevention and treatment processes.

Dietary Habits

Nutrition is a key element of a healthy lifestyle and of any program designed to prevent or treat children and adolescents at risk for common metabolic diseases of adulthood. Excess energy intake over time has several long-term health implications that include, among others, chronic positive energy balance, which may lead to overweight and obesity, decrease in glucose tolerance and insulin sensitivity, and elevation of serum cholesterol and triglycerides. On the other hand, a high fat intake is typically associated with large intakes of cholesterol and saturated fats, which increase the risk of an atherogenic profile and insulin resistance.

Leading organizations such as the American Heart Association, the American Academy of Pediatrics, and the National Institutes of Health in the United States have published dietary guidelines for children and adolescents. The major recommendation is that by early childhood five rules should be followed (Baxter 2002):

- Nutritional adequacy should be achieved by eating a wide variety of foods.
- Caloric intake should be adequate to support growth and development and to reach or maintain desirable body weight.
- Total fat should include no more than 30% of total calories and no less than 20% of total calories.
- Saturated fatty acids should comprise less than 10% of total calories.
- Dietary cholesterol should not exceed 300 mg/day.

The recommendations also stipulate that up to 10% total calories should come from polyunsaturated fatty acids, including omega-6 and omega-3 fatty acids (derived mostly from vegetable oils and fish, respectively).

These recommendations are viewed by some as radical and difficult to follow but are considered by others as part of a prudent diet. Such a diet is safe for children and adolescents and will reduce total serum cholesterol, on the average, by as much as 30 to 40 mg per 100 ml and reduce LDL cholesterol proportionally without compromising growth and maturation (Bier et al. 2000).

Individuals differ in their response to dietary alterations (i.e., some respond more favorably than others). Population differences in sensitivity to dietary changes exist (Couch et al. 2000). A limited number of intervention studies has shown that the response of blood lipids and lipoproteins to changes in dietary fat is strongly influenced by the genotype at a few genes (Abbey 1992; Ordovas et al. 1995; Dreon and Krauss 1997).

The United States Department of Agriculture and Department of Health and Human Services have developed the so-called Food Guide Pyramid (see figure 26.5). The Food Guide Pyramid specifies that individuals should consume more grains and cereals, fruits, and vegetables than is currently the case in the American diet. Guidelines designed to translate the principles of the Food Guide Pyramid for children and adolescents have been proposed. These guidelines are summarized in table 26.9. The number of servings for each of the five major food groups is shown for children 2 to 6 years of age, older children, teenage girls, and teenage boys. The Dietary Guidelines for Americans (U.S. Department of Health and Human Services 2000) also emphasize that food choices should reduce the consumption of foods high in salt and that foods should be prepared with as little salt as possible.

Inactivity and Sedentarism

The impact of regular physical activity on growth, maturation, and physical performance in healthy individuals was discussed in chapter 22, and the low activity patterns of children and adolescents with several chronic clinical conditions were discussed in chapter 27. Possible effects of physical activity programs on risk factors are discussed earlier in this chapter. The subsequent discussion focuses on inactivity or sedentarism during childhood and adolescence as a risk factor.

A sedentary lifestyle in adults is recognized as a major, independent risk factor for several chronic diseases (Kannel et al. 1985; Paffenbarger et al. 1991; Powell et al. 1987; Barlow et al. 1995). Less information is available, however, on the role of a sedentary lifestyle in the health of children and youth or on their future health as adults (Després et al. 1990; Kemper et al. 1990; Malina 1990).

Physical inactivity in children is hardly comparable to inactivity or a sedentary lifestyle in adults. Even children who are considered sedentary are generally somewhat active in one way or other. Variation in activity during adolescence is greater than in childhood, mostly because social demands, part-time jobs, and other factors influence the levels of physical activity during adolescence. A growing number of children and adolescents are spending a good number of hours every day in sedentary activities such as

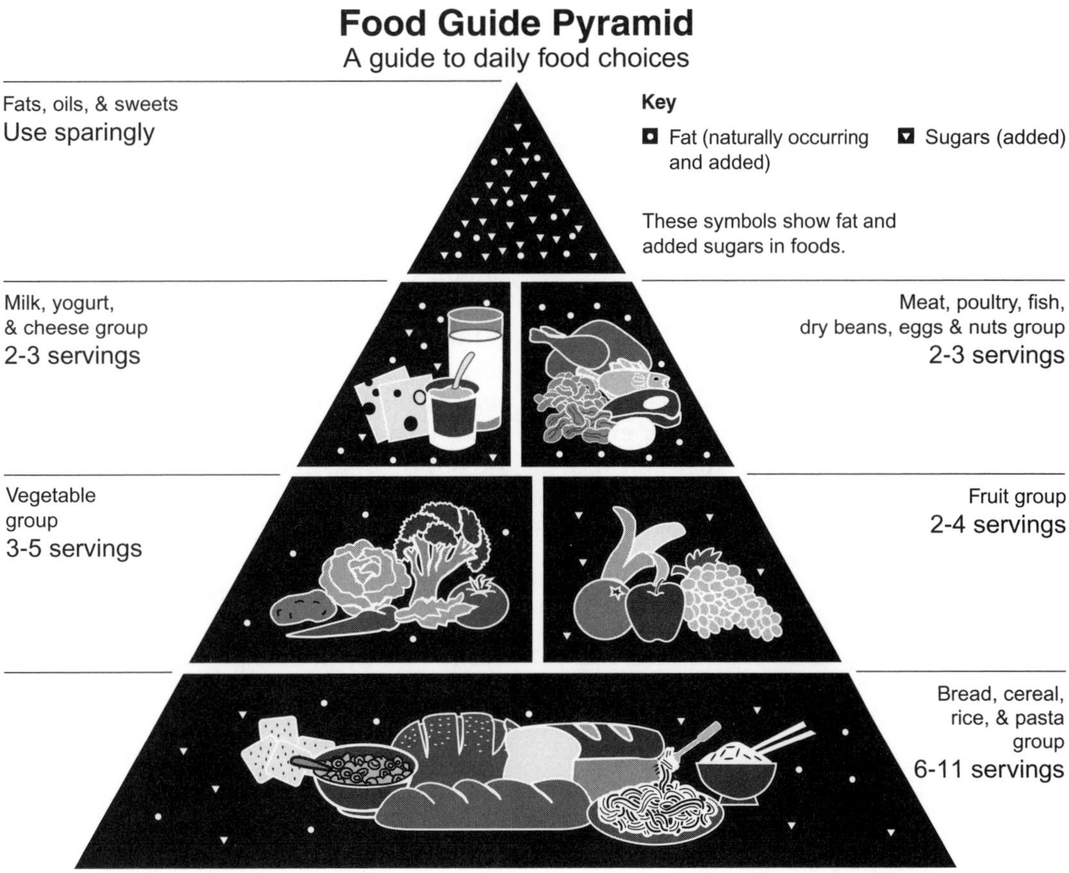

Food Guide Pyramid
A guide to daily food choices

Fats, oils, & sweets
Use sparingly

Key

■ Fat (naturally occurring and added)   ▼ Sugars (added)

These symbols show fat and added sugars in foods.

Milk, yogurt, & cheese group
2-3 servings

Meat, poultry, fish, dry beans, eggs & nuts group
2-3 servings

Vegetable group
3-5 servings

Fruit group
2-4 servings

Bread, cereal, rice, & pasta group
6-11 servings

FIGURE 26.5 The Food Guide Pyramid. The small circles and triangles represent fat and added sugars in foods.

From the U.S. Department of Agriculture, 1996, and the U.S. Department of Health and Human Services, 2000.

TABLE 26.9 Food Servings Needed Each Day

Food group	Children ages 2–6 yrs (about 1,600 cal)	Older children and teenage girls (about 2,200 cal)	Teenage boys (about 2,800 cals)
Grains group			
Bread, cereal, rice and pasta, especially whole grains	6	9	11
Vegetable group	3	4	5
Fruit group	2	3	4
Milk group			
Milk, yogurt, and cheese, preferably fat free or low fat	2 or 3*	2 or 3*	2 or 3*
Meat and beans group			
Meat, poultry, fish, dry beans, eggs, and nuts, preferably lean or low fat	2, for a total of 5 oz	2, for a total of 6 oz	3, for a total of 7 oz

* The number of servings depends on age. Older children and teenagers (ages 9 to 18 years) need three servings daily. Others need two servings daily.

Adapted from US Department of Agriculture, Center for Nutrition Policy and Promotion (1996), The Food Guide Pyramid. Home and Garden Bulletin Number 252.

television viewing, video games, and a variety of computer-based activities (navigating cyberspace). The impact of these trends on the health and well-being of children and adolescents is not understood at this time. However, some data already suggest that these trends play a role in the increase in childhood obesity. The trends may also contribute to the recent surge in the prevalence of type 2 diabetes mellitus in adolescents.

Although data are not entirely consistent among studies, obese children and adolescents are often less active than their leaner peers (see chapter 24). Sedentarism is also more prevalent among adolescents with high blood pressure (Alpert & Wilmore 1994) and dyslipidemia (Armstrong and Simons-Morton 1994). Moreover, on average, a sedentary lifestyle in adolescents is associated with other risk-related behaviors such as smoking, fat intake, and alcohol consumption (Escobedo & Casperson 1993; Kelder et al. 1994).

Studies that have investigated the effects of reg-

ular exercise on healthy children have not shown major changes in risk factors (Malina 1990). The modifications in response to enhanced physical activity observed in adolescents, especially those who are already at risk (e.g., with hypertension, dyslipidemia, or obesity), are somewhat more encouraging. Although the changes resulting from enhanced physical activity are generally small, they may be of considerable significance in terms of prevention and health outcomes in adulthood. However, most studies are short term and rarely include a follow-up component. They are largely focused on demonstrating potentially beneficial effects of regular physical activity but do not generally take a long-term perspective. For example, how much activity is needed to maintain the beneficial changes associated with an enhanced activity program? How do activity programs interact with changes in risk factors associated with normal growth and maturation? These areas need further study in a longitudinal context.

Summary

A risk factor is a condition that, when present over an extended period of time, significantly increases the probability of a common degenerative disease such as, among others, cardiovascular disease, type 2 diabetes mellitus, or osteoporosis or increases the probability of premature death. Factors associated with the development of undesirable outcomes in adulthood are frequently observed in children and adolescents and persist into adulthood. Although definitive proof is still lacking, a lifestyle profile of a healthy diet, including a variety of foods, adequate energy, no more than 30% total fat; regular physical activity, especially in moderate to vigorous physical activity; and an appropriate level of physical fitness, specifically low fatness and high aerobic fitness, is associated with a more favorable metabolic disease risk profile in children and adolescents.

Sources and Suggested Readings

Aaron DJ, Dearwater SR, Anderson RL, Olsen TL, Kriska AM, LaPorte RE (1995) Physical activity and the initiation of high-risk health behaviours in adolescents. Medicine and Science in Sports and Exercise 27:1639-1645.

Abbey M (1992) The influence of apolipoprotein polymorphism on the response to dietary fat and cholesterol. Current Opinions in Lipidology 3:12-16.

Akerblom HK, Viikari J, Raitakari OT, Uhari M. (1999) Cardiovascular risk in Young Finns Study: General outline and recent developments. Annals of Medicine 31 (suppl 1): 45-54.

* Alpert BS, Wilmore JH. (1994). Physical activity and blood pressure in adolescence. Pediatric Exercise Science 6: 361-380.

Andersen LB, Haraldsdottir J (1993) Tracking of cardiovascular disease risk factors including maximal oxygen uptake and physical activity from late teenage to adulthood: An 8-year follow-up study. Journal of Internal Medicine 234: 309-315.

Appel LJ, Moore TJ, Obarzanek E, Vollmer WM, Svetkey LP, Sacks FM, Bray GA, Vogt TM, Cutler JA, Windhauser MM, Lin PH, Karanja N (1997) A clinical trial of the effects of dietary patterns on blood pressure. DASH Collaborative Research Group. New England Journal of Medicine 336: 1117-1124.

* Armstrong N, Simons-Morton B (1994) Physical activity and blood lipids in adolescence. Pediatric Exercise Science 6: 381-405.

Armstrong N, Van Mechelen W (1998) Are young people fit and active? In S Biddle, J Sallis, N Cavill (eds), Young and Active? Young People and Health-Enhancing Physical Activity—Evidence and Implications. London: Health Education Authority, pp 69-97.

Armstrong N, Williams J, Balding J, Gentle P, Kirby B (1991) Cardiopulmonary fitness, physical activity patterns, and selected coronary risk factor variables in 11- to 16-year olds. Pediatric Exercise Science 3:219-228.

Arslanian SA, Kalhan SC (1994) Correlations between fatty acid and glucose metabolism: Potential explanation of insulin resistance of puberty. Diabetes 43:908-914.

Bar-Or O, Baranowski T (1994) Physical activity, adiposity, and obesity among adolescents. Pediatric Exercise Science 6: 348-360.

* Bar-Or O, Foreyt J, Bouchard C, Brownell KD, Dietz WH, Ravussin E, Salbe AD, Schwenger S, St.Jeor S, Torun B (1998) Physical activity, genetic, and nutritional considerations in childhood weight management. Medicine and Science in Sports and Exercise 30:2-10.

Barbeau P, Gutin B, Litaker M, Owens S, Riggs S, Okuyama T (1999) Correlates of individual differences in body composition changes resulting from physical training in obese children. American Journal of clinical Nutrition 69: 705-711.

Barker DJP (1999) Fetal origin of cardiovascular disease. Annals of Medicine 31 (suppl 1): 3-6.

Barlow CE, Kohl HWI, Gibbons LW, Blair SN (1995) Physical fitness, mortality and obesity. International Journal Of Obesity 19:S41-S44.

Baxter SD (2002) Nutrition for healthy children and adolescents ages 2 to 18 years. In CD Berdanier (ed), Handbook of Nutrition and Food. Boca Raton, FL: CRC Press, pp 241-297.

Berenson GS, Radhakrishnamurthy B, Weihang B, Srinivasan SR (1995a) Does adult-onset diabetes mellitus begin in childhood? The Bogalusa Heart Study. American Journal of Medical Sciences 310 (suppl 1):S77-S82.

Berenson GS, Srinivasan SR, Weihand B, Newman III WP, Tracy RE, Wattigney WA (1998). Association between multiple cardiovascular risk factors and atherosclerosis in children and young adults. New England Journal of Medicine 338: 1650-1656.

Berenson GS, Wattigney WA, Tracy RE, Newman WP Srinivasan SR, Webber LS, Dalferes ER, Strong JP (1992) Atherosclerosis of the aorta and coronary arteries and cardiovascular risk factors in persons aged 6 to 30 years and studied at necropsy (the Bogalusa Heart Study). American Journal of Cardiology 70: 851-858.

Berenson GS, Wattigney WA, Weihang BAO, Srinivasan S, Radhakrishnamurthy B (1995b) Rationale to Study the Early Natural History of Heart Disease: The Bogalusa Heart Study. American Journal of the Medical Sciences 310: S22-S28.

Bergstrom E, Hernell O, Persson LA, Vessby B (1996) Insulin resistance syndrome in adolescents. Metabolism 45: 908-914.

Bier DM, Lauer RM, Simell O (2000) Summary (Proceedings of a symposium held in Houston, TX, June 8–9, 1998). American Journal of Clinical Nutrition 72:1410S-1413S.

Björntorp, P (1990) "Portal" adipose tissue as a generator of risk factors for cardiovascular disease and diabetes. Atherosclerosis 10:493-496.

Blaak EE, Westerterp KR, Bar-Or O, Wouters LJM, Saris WHM (1992) Total energy expenditure and spontaneous activity in relation to training in obese boys. American Journal of Clinical Nutrition 55:777-782.

Bloch CA, Clemons P, Sperling MA (1987) Puberty decreases insulin sensitivity. Journal of Pediatrics 110:481-487.

Boisseau N, Rannou F, Delamarche P, Monnier M, Gratas Delamarche A (1997) Peripubertal period decreases insulin sensitivity and glucose utilization during exercise. In N Armstrong, J Welsman (eds), Children and Exercise XIX. London: E & FN Spon, pp 412-417.

Bouchard C, Malina RM, Perusse L (1997) Genetics of Fitness and Physical Performance. Champaign, IL: Human Kinetics.

Brownell KD, Kelman JH, Stunkard AJ (1983) Treatment of obese children with and without their mothers: Changes in weight and blood pressure. Pediatrics 71:515-523.

Centers for Disease Control (1991) Tobacco use among high school students—United States, 1990. Morbidity and Mortality Weekly Reports 40:617-619.

Couch SC, Cross AT, Kida K, Ros E, Plaza I, Shea S, Deckelbaum R (2000) Rapid westernization of children's blood cholesterol in 3 countries: Evidence for nutrient-gene interactions? American Journal of Clinical Nutrition 72: 1266S-1274S.

* Després JP, Bouchard C, Malina RM. (1990). Physical activity and coronary heart disease risk factors during childhood and adolescence. Exercise and Sport Sciences Reviews 18:243-261.

Després JP, Pohelman ET, Tremblay A, Lupien PJ, Moorjani S, Nadeau A, Perusse L, Bouchard C (1987) Genotype-influenced changes in serum HDL cholesterol after short-term overfeeding in man: Association with plasma insulin and triglyceride levels. Metabolism 36:363-368.

Diabetes Research Working Group. (1999) Conquering Diabetes: A strategic plan for the 21st century. Bethesda, MD: National Institutes of Health.

Dreon DM, Krauss RM (1997) Diet-gene interactions in human lipoprotein metabolism. Journal of the American College of Nutrition 16:313-324.

* Epstein LH. (1993). Methodological issues and ten-year outcomes for obese children. Annals of the New York Academy of Sciences 699:237-249.

Epstein LH, Goldfield G (1999) Physical activity in the treatment of childhood overweight and obesity: Current evidence and research issues. Medicine and Science in Sports and Exercise 31:553-559.

Epstein LH, Myers MD, Raynor HA, Saelens BE (1998) Treatment of childhood obesity. Pediatrics 101:554-570.

Epstein LH, Saelens BE, Myers MD, Vito D (1997) Effects of decreasing sedentary behaviors on activity choice in obese children. Health Psychology 16:107-113.

Epstein LH, Valoski A, Wing RR, McCurley J (1990) Ten-year follow-up of behavioral, family-based treatment for obese children. Journal of the American Medical Association 264: 2519-2523.

Escobedo LG, Caspersen CJ (1993) Adolescent tobacco use and physical activity. Journal of the American Medical Association 270:938-939.

Ewart CK, Young DR, Hagberg JM (1998) Effects of school-based aerobic exercise on blood pressure of adolescent girls at risk for hypertension. American Journal of Public Health 88:949-951.

Ferguson MA, Gutin B, Le N-A, Karp W, Litaker M, Humphries M, Okuyama T, Riggs S, Owens S (1999) Effects of exercise training and its cessation on components of the insulin resistance syndrome in obese children. International Journal of Obesity and Related Metabolic Disorders 23: 889-895.

Freedman DS (1995) The importance of body fat distribution in early life. American Journal of Medical Sciences 310: S72-S76.

Freedman DS, Dietz WH, Srinivasan SR, Berenson GS (1999) The relation of overweight to cardiovascular risk factors among children and adolescents: The Bogalusa Heart Study. Pediatrics 103:1175-1182.

Freedman DS, Khan LK, Dietz WH, Srinivasan SR, Berenson GS (2001) Relationship of childhood obesity to coronary heart disease risk factors in adulthood: The Bogalusa Heart Study. Pediatrics 108:712-718.

Gower BA (1999) Syndrome X in children: Influence of ethnicity and visceral fat. American Journal of Human Biology 11:249-257.

Greenland P (2001) Beating high blood pressure with low-sodium DASH. New England Journal of Medicine. 344: 53-55.

* Guo S, Salisbury S, Roche AF, Chumlea WC, Siervogel RM (1994) Cardiovascular disease risk factors and body composition: A review. Nutrition Research 14:1721-1777.

Gutin B, Cucuzzo N, Islam S, Smith C, Stachura ME (1996) Physical Training, lifestyle education and coronary risk factors in obese girls. Medicine and Science in Sports and Exercise 28:19-23.

Gutin B, Humphries, M (1998) Exercise, body composition, and health in children. In DR Lamb, R Murray (eds), Exercise, Nutrition, and Weight Control. Carmel, IN: Cooper, pp 295-347.

Gutin B, Owens S (1999) Role of exercise intervention in improving body fat distribution and risk profile in children. American Journal of Human Biology 11:237-247.

Gutin B, Owens S, Treiber F, Islam S, Karp W, Slavens G (1997) Weight-independent cardiovascular fitness and coronary risk factors. Archives of Pediatrics and Adolescent Medicine 151:462-465.

Hagberg JM, Goldring D, Ehsani AA, Heath GW, Hernandez A, Schechtman K, Holloszy JO (1983) Effects of exercise training on the blood pressure and hemodynamic features of hypertensive adolescents. American Journal of Cardiology 52:763-768.

Hansen HS, Froberg K, Hyldebrandt N, Nielsen JR (1991) A controlled study of eight months of physical training and reduction of blood pressure in children: The Odense Schoolchild Study. British Medical Journal 303:682-685.

Hu FB, Manson JE, Stampfer MJ, Colditz G, Liu S, Solomon CG, Willett WC (2001) Diet, lifestyle and the risk of type 2 diabetes mellitus in women. New England Journal of Medicine 345:790-797.

Ivy JL, Zedric TW, Fogt DL (1999). Prevention and treatment of non-insulin-dependent diabetes mellitus. Exercise and Sport Sciences Reviews 27:1-35.

Joint National Committee of the National Heart, Lung and Blood Institute (1993) The Fifth Report on Detection, Evaluation, and Treatment of High Blood Pressure. Bethesda, MD: National Institutes of Health. NIH Publication 93-1088.

Kannel WB, Wilson P, Blair SN (1985) Epidemiological assessment of the role of physical activity and fitness in development of cardiovascular disease. American Heart Journal 109:876-885.

Kelder SH, Perry CL, Klepp KI, Lytle LL (1994) Longitudinal tracking of adolescent smoking, physical activity, and food choice behaviors. American Journal of Public Health 84:1121-1126.

Kemper HCG, Snel J, Verschurr R, Storm-van Essen L (1990) Tracking of health and risk indicators of cardiovascular disease from teenager to adult: Amsterdam Growth and Health Study. Preventive Medicine 19:642-655.

Kitagawa T, Owada M, Urakami T (1998) Increased incidence of non-insulin dependent diabetes mellitus among Japanese school children correlates with an increased intake of protein and fat. Clinical Pediatrics 37:111-115.

Knowler WC, Barrett-Connor E, Fowler SE, Hamman RF, Lachin JM, Walker EA, Nathan DM (Diabetes Prevention Program Research Group) (2002) Reduction in the incidence of type 2 diabetes with lifestyle intervention or metformin. New England Journal of Medicine 346:393-403.

Kraemer WJ, Volek JS, Clark KL, Gordon SE, Puhl S, Koziris LP, McBride JM, Triplett-McBride NT, Putukian M, Newton RU, Hakinnen K, Bush JA, Sebastianelli WJ (1999) Influence of exercise training on physiological and performance changes with weight loss in men. Medicine and Science in Sports and Exercise 31:1320-1329.

Kriemler S, Hebestreit H, Mikami S, Bar-Or T, Ayub BV, Bar-Or O (1999) Impact of a single exercise bout on energy expenditure and spontaneous physical activity of obese boys. Pediatric Research 46:40-44.

Lagstrom H, Seppanen R, Jokinen E, Niinikoski H, Ronnemaa T, Viikari J, Simell O (1999) Influence of dietary fat on the nutrient intake and growth of children from 1 to 5 years of age: The Special Turku Coronary Risk Factor Intervention Project. American Journal of Clinical Nutrition 69:516-523.

Lauer RM, Burns TL, Mahoney LT, Tipton CM (1982) Blood Pressure in Children. In CV Gisolfi, DR Lamb (eds), Perspectives in Exercise Science and Sports Medicine: Youth, Exercise, and Sport. Carmel, IN: Benchmark Press, pp 431-463.

* Malina RM (1990) Growth, exercise, fitness, and later outcomes. In C Bouchard, RJ Shephard, T Stephens, JR Sutton, BD McPherson (eds), Exercise, Fitness and Health: A Consensus of Current Knowledge. Champaign, IL: Human Kinetics, pp 637-653.

* Malina RM (1995) Cardiovascular health status of Latin American children and youth. In CJR Blimkie, O Bar-Or (eds), New Horizons in Pediatric Exercise Science. Champaign, IL: Human Kinetics, pp 195-220.

McGill HC Jr (1998) Nutrition in early life and cardiovascular disease. Current Opinion in Lipidology 9:23-27.

* McGill HC Jr, Geer JC, Strong JP (1963) Natural history of human atherosclerotic lesions. In M Sandler, GH Bourne (eds), Atheroclerosis and Its Origin. New York: Academic Press, pp 39-65.

McGill HC Jr, McMahan CA, Herderick EE, Malcom GT, Tracy RE, Strong JP (2000) Origin of atherosclerosis in childhood and adolescence. American Journal of Clinical Nutrition 72:1307S-1315S.

McMurray RG, Harrell JS, Levine AA, Gansky SA (1995) Childhood obesity elevates blood pressure and total cholesterol independent of physical activity. International Journal of Obesity 19:881-886.

* National Cholesterol Education Program (1992) Report of the Expert Panel on Blood Cholesterol Levels in Children and Adolescents. Pediatrics 89:525-577.

* National High Blood Pressure Education Program Working Group on Hypertension Control in Children and Adolescents (1996) Update on the 1987 task force report on high blood pressure in children and adolescents: A working group report from the National High Blood Pressure Education Program. Pediatrics 98:649-658.

* National Cholesterol Education Program Expert Panel on Blood Cholesterol Levels in Children and Adolescents (1992) National Cholesterol Education Program: Report of the expert panel on blood cholesterol levels in children and adolescents. Pediatrics 89:525-584.

* National Heart, Lung, and Blood Institute (1997). The Sixth Report of the Joint National Committee on Prevention, Detection, Evaluation, and Treatment of High Blood Pressure. (1997) Bethesda, MD: National Institutes of Health.

Obarzanek E, Hunsberger SA, Van Horn L, Hartmuller VV, Barton BA, Stevens VJ, Kwiterovich PO, Franklin FA, Kimm SY, Lasser NL, Simons-Morton DG, Lauer RM (1997) Safety of a fat-reduced diet: the Dietary Intervention Study in Children (DISC). Pediatrics 100:51-59.

Obarzanek E, Kimm SYS, Barton BA, Van Horn L, Kwiterovich PO, Simons-Morton DG, Hunsberger SA, Lasser NL, Robson AM, Franklin FA, Lauer RM, Stevens VJ, Friedman LA, Dorgan JF, Greenlick MR (2001) Long-term safety and efficacy of a cholesterol-lowering diet in children with elevated low-density lipoprotein cholesterol: Seven-year results of the Dietary Intervention Study in Children (DISC). Pediatrics 107:256-264.

Ordovas JM, Lopez-Miranda J, Mata P, Perez-Jimenez F, Lichtenstein AH, Schaefer EJ (1995) Gene-diet interaction in determining plasma lipid response to dietary intervention. Atherosclerosis 118: S11-S27.

Owens S, Gutin B, Allison J, Riggs S, Ferguson M, Litaker M, Thompson W (1999) Effect of physical training on total and visceral fat in obese children. Medicine and Science in Sports and Exercise 31:143-148.

Owens S, Gutin B, Ferguson M, Allison J, Karp W, Le N-A (1998) Visceral adipose tissue and cardiovascular risk factors in obese children. Journal of Pediatrics 133:41-45.

Paffenbarger RSJR, Jung DL, Leungand RW, Hyde RT (1991) Physical activity and hypertension: An epidemiological view. Annals of Medicine 23:319-327.

Palti H, Gofin R, Adler B, Grafstein O, Belmaker E (1988) Tracking of blood pressure over an eight year period in Jerusalem school children. Journal of Clinical Epidemiology 41: 731-735.

Pikosky M, Faigenbaum A, Westcott W, Rodriguez N (2002) Effects of resistance training on protein utilization in healthy children. Medicine and Science in Sports and Exercise 34: 820-827.

Pinhas-Hamiel O, Dolan LM, Daniels SR, Stanford D, Khoury PR, Zeitler P (1996) Increased incidence of non-insulin-dependent diabetes mellitus among adolescents. Journal of Pediatrics 128:608-615.

Poehlman ET (1989). Exercise and its influence on resting energy metabolism in man. Medicine and Science in Sports and Exercise 21:515-525.

Powell KE, Thompson PD, Caspersen CJ, Kendrick JS (1987) Physical activity and the incidence of coronary heart disease. Annual Reviews of Public Health 8:253-287.

Raitakari OT, Porkka KVK, Taimela S, Telama R, Rasanen L, Viikari SA (1994) Effects of persistent physical activity and inactivity on coronary risk factors in children and young adults: The Cardiovascular Risk in Young Finns Study. American Journal of Epidemiology 140:195-205.

Riddoch C (1998) Relationships between physical activity and physical health in young people. In S Biddle, J Sallis, N Cavill (eds), Young and Active? Young People and Health-Enhancing Physical Activity — Evidence and Implications. London: Health Education Authority, pp 17-48.

Robinson TN (1999) Reducing children's television viewing to prevent obesity: A randomized controlled trial. Journal of the American Medical Association 282:1561-1567.

Roche AF (1997) Tracking in body composition and risk factors for cardiovascular disease from childhood to middle age. In K Froberg, O Lammert, H St. Hansen, CJR Blimkie (eds), Exercise and Fitness—Benefits and Risks. Odense: Odense University Press, pp 79-90.

Roche AF, Wilson ME, Gidding SS, Siervogel RM (1993) Lipids, growth, and development. Metabolism 42 (suppl 1):36-44.

Rosenbloom AL, Young RS, Joe JR, Winter WE (1999) Emerging epidemic of type 2 diabetes in youth. Diabetes Care 22:345-354.

Sacks FM, Svetkey LP, Vollmer WM, Appel LJ, Bray GA, Harsha D, Obarzanek E, Conlin PR, Miller ER 3rd, Simons-Morton DG, Karanja N, Lin PH. (2001) Effects on blood pressure of reduced dietary sodium and the Dietary Approaches to Stop Hypertension (DASH) diet. DASH-Sodium Collaborative Research Group. New England Journal of Medicine. 344:3-10.

Saelens BE, Epstein LH (1998) Behavioral engineering of activity choice in obese children. International Journal of Obesity 22:275-277.

Sasaki J, Shindo M, Tanaka H, Ando M, Arakawa K (1987) A long-term aerobic exercise program decreases the obesity index and increases the high density lipoprotein cholesterol concentrations. International Journal of Obesity 11: 339-345.

Siervogel RM, Baumgartner RN, Roche AF, Chumlea WC, Glueck CJ (1989) Maturity and its relationships to plasma lipid and lipoprotein levels in adolescents: The Fels Longitudinal Study. American Journal of Human Biology 1:217-226.

Sothern M, Loftin JM, Udall JN, Suskind RM, Ewing TL, Tang SC, Blecker U (2000) Safety, feasibility, and efficacy of a resistance training program in preadolescent obese children. American Journal of Medical Sciences 319:370-375.

Stamler J (1980) Can an effective fat-modified diet be safely recommended after weaning for infants and children in general? In RM Lauer, RB Shekelle (eds), Childhood Prevention of Atherosclerosis and Hypertension. New York: Raven Press, pp 387-403.

Stephens T, Craig CL (1990) The well-being of Canadians: Highlights of the 1988 Campbell's Survey. Ottawa: Canadian Fitness and Lifestyle Research Institute.

Treuth MS, Hunter GR, Figueroa-Colon R, Goran MI (1998) Effects of strength training on intra-abdominal adipose tissue in obese prepubertal girls. Medicine and Science in Sports and Exercise 30:1738-1743.

Tuomilehto J, Lindstrom J, Eriksson JG, Valle T, Hamalainen H, Ilanne-Parikka P, Keinanen-Kiukaanniemi S, Laakso M, Louheranta A, Rastas M, Salminen V, Uusitpua M (The Finnish Diabetes Prevention Study Group) (2001) Prevention of type 2 diabetes mellitus by changes in lifestyle among subjects with impaired glucose tolerance. New England Journal of Medicine 344: 1343-1350.

Twisk JWR, Kemper HCG, van Mechelen W, Post GB (1997) Tracking of risk factors for coronary heart disease over a 14-year period: A comparison between lifestyle and biologic risk factors with data from the Amsterdam Growth and Health Study. American Journal of Epidemiology 145: 888-898.

* U.S. Department of Agriculture, Center for Nutrition Policy and Promotion (1996). The Food Guide Pyramid. Home and Garden Bulletin Number 252.

U.S. Department of Health and Human Services (1989) Reducing the Health Consequences of Smoking: 25 Years of Progress. A report of the Surgeon General. Washington, DC: U.S. Department of Health and Human Services, DDHS Publication (CDC) 89-8411.

* U.S. Department of Health and Human Services (1996) Physical Activity and Health. A Report of the Surgeon General. Atlanta, GA: U.S. Department of Health and Human Services, Centers for Disease Control and Prevention, National Center for Chronic Disease Prevention and Health Promotion.

U.S. Department of Health and Human Services (2000) Nutrition and Your Health: Dietary Guidelines for Americans. Washington DC: Department of Agriculture.

Van Lenthe FJ, Kemper HCG, van Mechelen W, Twisk JWR (1996) Longitudinal development and tracking of central patterns of subcutaneous fat in adolescents and adults: the Amsterdam Growth and Health Study. International Journal of Epidemiology 25:1162-1171.

Whitaker RC, Wright JA, Pepe MS, Seidel KD, Dietz WH (1997) Predicting obesity in young adulthood from childhood and parental obesity. New England Journal of Medicine 337:869-873.

Williams DP, Going SB, Lohman TG, Harsha DW, Srinivasan SR, Webber LS, Berenson GS (1992) Body fatness and risk for elevated blood pressure, total cholesterol, and serum lipoprotein ratios in children and adolescents. American Journal of Public Health 82:358-362.

Wolf AM, Gortmaker SL, Cheung L, Gray HM, Herzog DB, Colditz GA (1993) Activity, inactivity, and obesity: Differences related to race, ethnicity, and age among girls. American Journal of Public Health 83:1625-1627.

Although this book focuses on relationships among growth, maturation, physical performance, and physical activity in healthy children and adolescents, relationships in individuals who have a chronic disease or physical disability are also important. Such young people constitute a minority of the school-age population, but this proportion has been on the increase in recent years. This development has resulted mostly from a dramatic increase in the prevalence of obesity and of type 2 (adult onset) diabetes mellitus in children and adolescents. Two other diseases with a growing prevalence are asthma and anorexia nervosa. Survival rates have increased for children who only 2 decades ago would have died in infancy or early childhood because of conditions such as extremely low birth weight or cystic fibrosis.

Ordinary childhood illnesses, such as infections and diarrhea, have little effect on the growth and maturation of adequately nourished children other than a temporary decline in rate of weight gain during severe episodes of illness. However, individuals display a wide range of responses to short-term illnesses. Socioeconomic circumstances are an important factor. Children from better-off socioeconomic conditions generally have more immediate and better access to treatment, whereas those in lower socioeconomic strata may have limited access to health care. In addition, living conditions in the lower socioeconomic strata are probably more amenable to the spread and recurrence of illnesses. Nevertheless, over the long term, ordinary childhood illnesses do not appear to significantly influence the growth and maturation of the adequately nourished child.

Conditions that persist over time, that is, chronic conditions that affect growth, maturation, physical activity, and performance, are relevant to the present discussion. Children and adolescents with these conditions attend school and participate in many of the activities of healthy children. In this context, relationships between selected pediatric conditions and growth and maturation are initially described and then the habitual activity and physical performance of afflicted children and adolescents are considered.

Selected Clinical Conditions That Affect Growth and Maturation

Numerous congenital and other pediatric conditions are accompanied by some aberration in patterns of normal growth and maturation. Discussing all of these is well beyond the scope of this book. Selected examples of such clinical conditions are highlighted in this chapter. They are relatively common and may be encountered within the general child and adolescent population. Table 27.1 lists the conditions in alphabetical order and the direction in which they affect growth or maturity. The ensuing discussion for each condition provides an overview of relevant information. For more details, the interested reader is referred to reviews by Underwood and Van Wyk (1985) and by Boersma and Wit (1997). Obesity that is not secondary to other medical conditions is an increasingly common public health problem and an important clinical condition in the pediatric population. The growth, maturity, physical activity, and performance characteristics of obese children and adolescents are discussed in chapter 24.

Anorexia Nervosa

Anorexia nervosa is an eating disorder characterized by a morbid fear of becoming fat. The prevalence of this eating disorder has been on the rise in recent years, and one possible factor is the increase in societal pressures to the effect that "lean is beautiful" (Brumberg 1988; Lucas et al. 1991). Anorexia nervosa occurs more in girls than in boys, both among athletes and nonathletes. The peak age of occurrence of anorexia is about 14 years, but it can also occur earlier or later (Steinhausen 1994).

The effects of anorexia on growth and maturation emanate both from undernutrition and hormonal alterations. Many patients have normal growth and attain a normal adult height, but others may encounter stunting of growth and delayed skeletal and sexual maturity (Lacey et al. 1979). Whether anorexia nervosa is accompanied by stunting depends on the age of onset and on duration of the anorexic episode before the end of the adolescent growth spurt; those who have had the disorder for more years before puberty are more likely to be stunted. This pattern is similar to that observed in chronic undernutrition through other causes, as discussed in chapter 23.

A state of semistarvation, as in anorexia nervosa, often results in abnormal function of the hypophyseal-pituitary-gonadal axis (see chapter 19). In a prepubertal girl, anorexia is associated with significant delay in skeletal and sexual maturity. Many anorexic patients are in their middle to late teens (ages when healthy girls have already experienced menarche) and are premenarcheal.

TABLE 27.1   Effects of Selected Clinical Conditions in Children and Adolescents on Growth, Maturity, and Adult Height

Condition	Growth	Maturation	Adult height	Comments
Anorexia nervosa	Normal or stunted	Delayed	Normal or short	Effects on height may persist for several years, especially in late childhood and early adolescence
Asthma	Normal or mildly stunted	Delayed	Normal	Effect on height is caused primarily by oral corticosteroid therapy
Cystic fibrosis	Normal or stunted	Delayed	Normal or short	Effect on height depends on severity of nutritional inadequacy
Extremely low birth weight	Short height	No change	Normal (?)	Data are inconsistent because of recent changes in therapy
Type 1 diabetes mellitus	Mild stunting	Delayed	Normal	

Conditions are listed in alphabetical order.

They are classified as having primary amenorrhea. This condition may persist throughout the period of chronic energy deficiency associated with inadequate dietary intake and associated psychological problems. An adolescent who already attained menarche and becomes anorexic will experience the cessation of menstrual cycles, which is labeled secondary amenorrhea. In many patients, secondary amenorrhea develops long before major weight loss occurs, which emphasizes an important role for psychological factors (Vande Wiele 1980). Both conditions may persist for several months after normal nutritional status has been restored.

Asthma

Asthma is characterized by periods of shortness of breath, wheezing and, coughing caused by inflammation of the respiratory airways mucosa and, sometimes, excessive contraction of the bronchial muscles. Such attacks may be triggered by various stimuli, including physical exercise. For unknown reasons, the incidence (occurrence of new cases) and prevalence (proportion of existing cases within a population) of asthma have been on the rise in recent decades. Asthma occurs in as many as 5% to 10% of school-age children, which makes it the second most common chronic pediatric condition after obesity.

Children with asthma are often shorter than their age and sex peers and have delayed puberty (Russell 1994). However, they appear to attain normal adult stature (Van Bever et al. 1999). The mechanisms for these changes in growth and maturity are unclear. One factor traditionally implicated is treatment with corticosteroids (Wolthers et al. 1992), particularly if the medication is taken by mouth, as a pill, and less so if it is inhaled. However, asthma itself, irrespective of treatment, may be accompanied by short stature and delayed puberty (Russell 1994). A relationship also exists between stunting and the severity of asthma.

Cystic Fibrosis

Cystic fibrosis occurs in approximately 0.01% to 0.02% of live births. It is the most prevalent pediatric hereditary disease. It affects several body systems and organs, primarily the lungs, pancreas, and sweat glands. Two to 3 decades ago, most patients died in their teens, usually because of respiratory failure. Since then, improved therapy and nutritional regimens have dramatically increased the survival rate of such patients,

many of whom now reach the fourth decade of life and beyond.

Most children and youth with cystic fibrosis have stunted growth and a delayed adolescent growth spurt and sexual maturity. Boys, for example, may have a 4-year delay in genital maturation. A corresponding delay in sexual maturity of girls is 2 to 3 years. Malabsorption of fats, carbohydrates, and proteins caused by insufficiency of pancreatic exocrine enzymes, is the most likely cause of stunting and delayed puberty. These metabolic abnormalities may also be caused by genetic mutations that add to the complexity of cystic fibrosis (Landon et al. 1987). Another cause for growth impairment is associated with the use of corticosteroids as therapy. A case in point is a study of 149 girls and boys with cystic fibrosis who were treated by prednisone (an oral corticosteroid) or given a placebo for 4 years (Lai et al. 2000). While taking the medication, the boys and girls showed growth retardation compared with the placebo group. On the average, the patients, irrespective of the treatment group, were shorter and lighter than the 50th percentiles of healthy United States children and adolescents.

Type 1 Diabetes Mellitus

Most children and adolescents with type 1 (insulin-dependent) diabetes mellitus have a normal growth pattern. However, some have minor growth retardation. The mechanism for this condition is not clear, as some of these children show a decreased growth velocity even before clinical onset of the disease (Leslie et al. 1991). In contrast, adolescents with non–insulin-dependent (type 2) diabetes mellitus are often tall and obese. The possible mechanism for the tall stature of obese children and adolescents is discussed in chapter 24.

Extremely Low Birth Weight

With the advent of sophisticated neonatal medical treatments, increasing numbers of individuals with very low (less than 1,500 g) and extremely low (less than 1,000 g) birth weight now survive beyond the first years of life, into adolescence and adulthood. For example, a study in Australia has shown that, although survival rate beyond 2 years was 25% in 1979/1980, it increased to over 55% in 1990/1991 (The Victorian Infant Collaborative Group 1997). Despite such impressive improvements, many of the survivors have physical and psychosocial deficiencies. These include high prevalence of cerebral palsy, reduced lung functions, impaired vision and hearing, deficient fine motor skills, low cognitive skills, and behavioral aberrations (Hebestreit et al. 2000). As mentioned in chapter 2, prematurity and low birth weight are often accompanied by reduced body length, at least in the first years of life (Ross et al. 1990; Kitchen et al. 1992). A catch-up in growth usually occurs during the school-age years, such that adult height is often within the normal range. Maturity does not seem to be affected in adolescents with extremely low birth weight, but data are not extensive.

Physical Activity of Children and Adolescents With Chronic Conditions

Children and adolescents with a chronic disease or a disability are often less active than their healthy age and sex peers (Longmuir & Bar-Or 1994). Figure 27.1 is a composite graph depicting changes with age in the activity level of 987 children and adolescents who had a chronic illness or a physical disability. They are a representative sample of children and youth in Ontario, Canada, who are afflicted by these conditions. The overall pattern—a reduction in activity level in the second decade of life and a lower level in females than in males, particularly during late adolescence—is similar to that in the general population (see chapter 21). However, the extent of activity of this sample was lower than in the general Canadian population (Canada Fitness Survey 1983), particularly at moderate and intense levels of activity.

Several reasons for hypoactivity, a level of activity that is lower than in the general population, are apparent in children and adolescents with a chronic clinical condition. For some individuals, it is the disease or disability itself that limits them from being fully active. For example, a child with severe muscle weakness will not be able to run or to jump. More often, however, the cause for a sedentary lifestyle is psychosocial rather than physical, and it is only indirectly related to the disease process itself. In some cases (e.g., epilepsy), parents are overprotective, feeling that physical activity may be dangerous to the child. In other conditions (e.g., asthma or diabetes), the child may develop a fear of being active because of prior experience in which activity caused abnormal responses, such as an asthma attack or hypoglycemia. Some young people (e.g., the

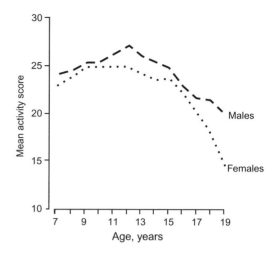

Physical Activity in Chronic Clinical Conditions

FIGURE 27.1 Habitual physical activity of 987 Canadian children and adolescents with a chronic disease or a physical disability. The activity score was based on a questionnaire.

Adapted, by permission, from P.E. Longmuir and O. Bar-Or, 1994, "Physical activity of children and adolescents with a disability: Methodology and effects of age and gender," Pediatric Exercise Science 6(2):168-177.

obese or those with a scoliosis or short stature) may be socially isolated by their peers because of their appearance or inability to perform well in sports and other physical activities. Sometimes, adults (parents, teachers, and physicians) will not permit a young person to participate in sports because of ignorance regarding possible effects of exertion. Finally, hypoactivity itself may be the cause for further hypoactivity because a sedentary lifestyle is usually accompanied by a reduction in fitness and performance capacity, which makes physical activity on a regular basis even harder for the child.

The following discussion briefly reviews the activity patterns of children and adolescents with selected chronic diseases or illnesses. Some of the conditions listed in table 27.1 are included as examples. For details regarding activity behavior in other clinical conditions see Bar-Or (1983), Goldberg (1995), and Rowland (1990).

Anorexia Nervosa

Although chronic undernutrition is associated with reduced levels of energy expenditure (see chapter 23), activity levels in patients with anorexia nervosa tend to be high and at times are excessive, even though they show marked reductions in body weight. In the early stages of the disease, many patients adopt very high levels of physical activity. In the majority of patients, excessive activity predates the time when anorexia nervosa is diagnosed (Davis et al. 1994). This pattern is depicted in figure 27.2. "Premorbid" activity levels are good predictors of the extent of excessive activity that subsequently accompanies the disease (Davis et al. 1997).

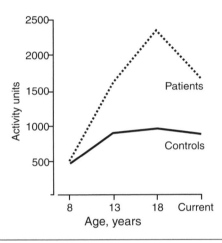

High Activity Level Predates Anorexia Nervosa

FIGURE 27.2 Excessive physical activity precedes the appearance of anorexia nervosa. Retrospective information was obtained from young adult women (n = 45), in whom anorexia nervosa was diagnosed at about 16 to 20 years of age. They were compared with 51 healthy control subjects. Units for activity are based on the amount, frequency, and intensity of the reported activities.

Reprinted from Davis et al. 1994.

Enhanced activity is a means of expending metabolic energy, and in many patients, it is used as part of a strategy of inducing negative energy balance and weight loss (Chalmers et al. 1985; Davis et al. 1994; Eisler et al. 1990). Daily activities of individuals with anorexia nervosa commonly include 1 to 2 hours of jogging, as many as several hundred push-ups and jumping jacks, running up and down several hundreds of stairs, and constantly moving in the chair while doing homework or watching TV. These young people commonly choose activities that do not require the participation of others and deliberately isolate themselves from peers or family members.

In advanced stages of the disease, when the state of undernutrition and muscle wasting has progressed, individuals with anorexia nervosa may become less active than their healthy peers (Bouten et al. 1996). Muscle wasting indicates major changes in body composition. For example, among 10 anorectic females 13 to 22 years of age (Forbes et al. 1984) and five anorectic males and 10 anorectic females 12 to 17 years of age (Fohlin 1977), estimated fat-free mass (estimated with ^{40}K, see chapter 5) was less than expected for age, height, and body weight. Such patients often complain of a "low energy level" and a progressive inability to perform physical activities. This inability may add to their frustration, but they are simply incapable of performing the planned activity regimen. After nutritional rehabilitation, such patients can resume a higher activity pattern.

Asthma

Children and adolescents with asthma vary markedly in levels of physical activity. Whereas some are as active as their peers and may participate in high-level competitive sports, others opt for a sedentary lifestyle. The main reason for avoiding exertion is exercise-induced asthma, which is manifested by coughing and shortness of breath during or, more commonly, several minutes after a bout of exercise. Exercise-induced asthma is triggered by cooling or drying of the airways resulting from the high ventilation during exercise (Bar-Or et al. 1977; McFadden 1987). This airway distress, in turn, causes an inflammatory response of the respiratory mucosa and excessive contraction of the bronchial muscles. The end result is narrowing of the airways and an increase in airway resistance to air flow. In most cases, exercise-induced asthma lasts only several minutes and then resolves spontaneously. Some patients, however, need medication to resume normal breathing. Proper medications are available that, when taken just before an exercise bout, can prevent the occurrence of exercise-induced asthma. Individuals who suffer from exercise-induced asthma, to the extent that they curtail their activities, should be highly encouraged to take a proper medication so that they can exercise without symptoms. For example, children and adolescents who suffer from exercise-induced asthma should be allowed to bring their "asthma puffer" to school so that they can use it just before a physical education class.

The objective evidence for exercise-induced asthma is a drop in pulmonary functions, primarily those that reflect airway resistance. Figure 27.3 illustrates the typical changes that occur in forced-expiratory volume in the first second ($FEV_{1.0}$) after an 8-minute bout of exercise. For more details about exercise-induced asthma, see Orenstein (1996).

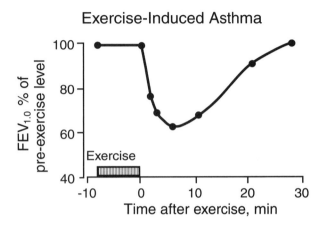

FIGURE 27.3 A typical exercise-induced asthma response to an 8-minute exercise task of moderate intensity. $FEV_{1.0}$ is the forced expiratory volume in the first second. A slight increase in $FEV_{1.0}$ is often seen immediately after exercise, followed by a decrease during the next several minutes. The figure displays a spontaneous recovery, which started approximately 5 minutes after the cessation of exercise.

Cerebral Palsy

Cerebral palsy is the most common pediatric neuromuscular disease, affecting 0.2% of live births. It results from an insult to the brain (e.g., lack of oxygen) that occurs before, during, or soon after birth. Cerebral palsy has several clinical manifestations, but increased muscle tone (spasticity) and deficient neuromuscular coordination are present in almost all patients. The condition may affect primarily the lower limbs (diplegia), the limbs on one side of the body (hemiplegia), or all four limbs (tetraplegia).

Compared with other youngsters who have a chronic disease or a disability, children and adolescents with cerebral palsy are among the least active. Their perceived physical fitness is likewise among the lowest. The main perceived barrier for being physically active is "having the disease." In a large-scale survey, 82% of 6-year-old to 20-year-old participants with cerebral palsy reported this barrier as the main reason for their sedentary lifestyle. This percentage is very high compared with that reported, for example, by individuals with cystic fibrosis (30%) or head injury (48%) (Longmuir and Bar-Or 2000).

Objective measurement of total daily energy expenditure confirms the considerably low activity level of children with cerebral palsy. The ratio of total energy expenditure/sleeping energy expenditure provides information about the energy that is expended above the resting level, mostly by physical activity. By use of the doubly labeled water technique to measure total energy expenditure under free-living conditions and a respiration chamber to determine the sleeping metabolic rate, one can determine this ratio (see chapter 21). This approach was used in a study of 7-year-old to 9-year-old Dutch children with spastic cerebral palsy and a control group of healthy children (Van Den Berg-Emons et al. 1995). The ratio of total energy expenditure to sleeping energy expenditure was higher in healthy children compared with cerebral palsy patients (1.83 and 1.56, respectively). In a study of American adolescents with cerebral palsy, those who were bound to a wheelchair had a 30% lower ratio of total energy to resting energy expenditure than healthy control subjects (Bandini et al. 1991). Interestingly, the ratio in adolescent patients who were ambulatory (i.e., those who were able to walk as part of their daily activities) was similar to that of healthy control subjects.

Cystic Fibrosis

Children with cystic fibrosis, unless they have a very severe form of the disease, are usually as active as their healthy peers. Based on an activity log (Bouchard et al. 1983), 7-year-old to 15-year-old patients with mild-to-moderate severity of cystic fibrosis were rated as having "moderate" to "high" activity levels but not "sedentary" or "athletic" levels (Hanning et al. 1993). Based on 24-hour heart rate monitoring, the ratio of estimated total energy expenditure to resting energy expenditure was similar in 8-year-old to 24-year-old cystic fibrosis patients and healthy control subjects (Spicher et al. 1991).

With progression of disease severity during adolescence, activity level is gradually curtailed. This curtailment is both because of objective physiologic reasons (a reduction in aerobic performance and in muscle power, see section on fitness and performance) and because of mood changes that result from the perceived inevitability of early death. Some children and adolescents with cystic fibrosis respond to exercise with O_2 desaturation in the arterial blood, and physicians usually recommend that if the saturation level is 85% or lower, such patients be exempt from high-intensity exertion.

Based on doubly labeled water analysis, children with cystic fibrosis often have an above normal total energy expenditure (Shepherd et al. 1988; Tomezsko et al. 1994). This finding reflects a high resting metabolic rate (Vaisman et al. 1987; Tomezsko et al. 1994) and does not connote a high physical activity level. This excessive energy expenditure, combined with deficient intestinal absorption, is likely the cause of an undernourished state in many patients. The cause of a high resting metabolic rate is not clear. It may reflect a high metabolic cost of ventilation (Vaisman et al. 1987; Amin et al. 1994), although some patients have a high resting metabolic rate even before they display clinical manifestation of lung disease. Other possible causes include an aberration at the mitochondrial level (Buchdahl et al. 1988) and a high relative fat-free mass (Bronstein et al. 1995).

Type 1 Diabetes Mellitus

Activity behavior of patients with type 1 diabetes is important to the metabolic control of the disease. Fluctuations in activity may cause uncontrollable changes in blood glucose concentrations, unless a concurrent adjustment is made in carbohydrate consumption or the dose of injected insulin. Clinical experience and limited research suggest that children and adolescents with type 1 diabetes mellitus vary considerably in activity behaviors. Whereas some are as active as their healthy peers and participate in high-level competitive activities, others have a sedentary lifestyle. Level of habitual activity appears to decrease with age. Among 136 Swedish children with type 1 diabetes, those in elementary school (7 to 14 years of age) attended physical education classes as regularly as did their healthy peers, but those in high school were less active than the control subjects (Sterky 1963). In another Swedish study, 50% of type 1 diabetes patients reported that they were active daily, but the study did not provide a comparison with healthy control children (Ludvigsson et al. 1980).

The main reason for the reluctance of many patients to be active is the fear of disrupting the control of blood glucose. Specifically, prolonged exercise (more than 30 minutes) often induces hypoglycemia or dangerously low blood glucose levels (McNiven et al. 1995; Riddell et al. 1999). To prevent such occurrences, patients prefer to follow a sedentary lifestyle in which energy expenditure is fairly constant from day to day. Recent studies have shown that a drink of carbohydrates (e.g., glucose or sucrose) just before and periodically during exercise can ameliorate, or even prevent, the hypoglycemic response in type 1 diabetes patients (Riddell et al. 1999). Another possible reason for the reluctance of adolescents with type 1 diabetes to be active is that they perceive exercise intensities as harder, when compared with healthy peers (Riddell et al. 2000).

Extremely Low Birth Weight

Very little information is available on the activity patterns of children of very low or extremely low birth weight. Based on recall questionnaires given to the parents of 5-year-old to 7-year-old year old girls and boys who were of extremely low birth weight and with no overt manifestations of a neuromuscular disability, the children were as active as children who were of normal birth weight (Keller et al. 1998). If low birth weight is accompanied by a neuromuscular disability, such as cerebral palsy, the child will likely be hypoactive.

Fitness and Performance of Children and Adolescents With Chronic Conditions

As a group, children and adolescents with a chronic disease or a physical disability have below average physical fitness and performance capacities (Bar-Or 1983, 1986; Rowland 1990; Goldberg 1995). This finding often results from a low physical activity level, but it sometimes reflects a corresponding pathophysiology, which may affect a specific fitness component (Bar-Or 1986). Table 27.2 is a summary of several of the latter conditions.

Anorexia Nervosa

Research on physical fitness of patients with anorexia has focused on aerobic performance. Maximal aerobic power is often lower than in the general population. For example, maximal aerobic power is reduced by about 40% to 45%

TABLE 27.2 Effects of Pediatric Diseases and Physical Disabilities on Indicators of Physical Fitness and Performance

Condition	Component	Process	Comments
Anorexia nervosa	Aerobic, anaerobic, strength	Undernutrition; reduced muscle mass; low iron stores	Changes seldom occur when undernourished state is mild
Asthma	Aerobic	Resistance to air flow	Only in severe asthma
Cerebral palsy	Aerobic, anaerobic, strength, flexibility	Spasticity; reduced muscle mass and range of motion; high antagonist cocontraction	Oxygen transport system is not directly affected; cocontraction increases energy cost of movement
Cystic fibrosis	Aerobic, anaerobic	Reduced lung function; oxygen desaturation; undernutrition	Fitness is often normal in the first years
Type 1 diabetes mellitus	Aerobic	Low capillary-to- muscle fiber ratio; hypoglycemia during prolonged exercise	Most children and adolescents have normal fitness levels
Extremely low birth weight	Aerobic, anaerobic, motor coordination	Reduced lung functions; impaired neuromuscular function	Immaturity of the lungs, insult to the brain and central nervous system and neonatal care may play a role

Conditions are listed in alphabetical order.

in adolescent anorectic patients (10 girls and 5 boys), and the reduction is greater than that associated with changes in body weight and estimated body composition (Davies et al. 1978). Severe undernutrition associated with anorexia is characterized by lower performance (the more severe the undernutriton, the lower the performance [Lands et al. 1992]). Note that some studies of anorectic patients use submaximal heart rate to predict maximal $\dot{V}O_2$, so a word of caution is warranted. Resting heart rate in patients with advanced anorexia nervosa is often very low (30 to 35 beats/min, and even lower). Likewise, their submaximal heart rate is low, which may yield a false conclusion that their aerobic fitness is high. However, such patients also have a rather low maximal heart rate (e.g., 165 to 175 instead of 195 to 200 beats/min [Nudel et al. 1984]), so prediction based on submaximal heart rate is likely to overestimate the real maximal aerobic power.

Will nutritional rehabilitation restore aerobic fitness in patients with anorexia? Evidence suggests that improvement in aerobic performance lags behind an increase in body weight and muscle mass that results from enhanced feeding of young women with anorexia nervosa (Waller et al. 1996). Electrical stimulation of the adductor pollicis (a muscle of the thumb) in young adult anorectic patients is associated with reduced power, increased fatigability, and slower relaxation rates (Russell et al. 1983). With the exception of power, the indicators of muscle function appear to be restored to normal after 8 weeks of refeeding. These observations suggest possibly altered muscle function in anorectic patients.

Asthma

Most children and adolescents with asthma have normal levels of physical fitness (Bevegard et al. 1971; Graff-Lonnevig 1978; Orenstein 1996). In fact, with currently available medications, patients with asthma can reach elite levels in sports, including Olympic medals and world championships (Fitch et al. 1976). The main reason for reduced fitness of patients with asthma is a sedentary lifestyle. However, when asthma is severe, aerobic fitness may be low because of increased airways resistance and deficient lung functions. Other components of fitness, such as muscle strength, anaerobic performance, and running speed, are within the normal range (Day et al. 1973; Counil et al. 1995). The somewhat short stature of some children with severe asthma does not seem to interfere with their fitness.

Cerebral Palsy

Most motor functions are deficient in patients with cerebral palsy, as are muscular strength and aerobic and anaerobic performances. For example, maximal O_2 uptake is typically around 20 to 30 ml/kg body weight/min compared with 40 to 50 ml/kgmin in healthy children and youth (Bar-Or et al. 1976; Hoofwijk et al. 1995). Such low aerobic power does not reflect cardiopulmonary deficiency. Rather, it reflects weak and uncoordinated skeletal muscles that cannot generate a high metabolic or cardiopulmonary drive.

In performing submaximal aerobic tasks, children and adolescents with cerebral palsy expend exceptionally high metabolic energy. For example, at any given walking speed, $\dot{V}O_2$ is 50% to 100% higher in cerebral palsy patients than in age-matched control subjects (Unnithan et al. 1996). As a result, these patients use a much higher percentage of their $\dot{V}O_2$max when performing a certain task, which explains the early fatigability. The high energy cost of locomotion can be explained by mechanical wastefulness during the gait cycle (Unnithan et al. 2000) and by poor synchronization between antagonist muscle groups, for example, the knee extensors do not relax sufficiently while the knee flexors contract (Unnithan et al. 1996).

Muscle strength and anaerobic performance are markedly deficient in patients with cerebral palsy (Parker et al. 1992; Van Den Berg-Emons 1996). Total mechanical work during the 30-second Wingate Anaerobic Test is considerably lower in patients with cerebral palsy than in healthy peers (see figure 27.4). Regardless of the anatomic distribution of the spastic muscles, the patients scored well below minus two standard deviations of the reference group (Parker et al. 1992). A subsequent study has shown that the low anaerobic performance of cerebral palsy patients is correlated with limitations in daily gross motor tasks (Parker et al. 1993).

Despite the low aerobic fitness of children and adolescents with cerebral palsy, the correlation between the ability of these patients to perform daily tasks (e.g., walking) and $\dot{V}O_2$max is low (Bar-Or 1996). The main fitness components that limit their performance appear to be the high energy cost of locomotion and reduced muscular strength, anaerobic power, and endurance.

Cystic Fibrosis

Because of its deleterious effect on the lungs, cystic fibrosis is accompanied by impaired aero-

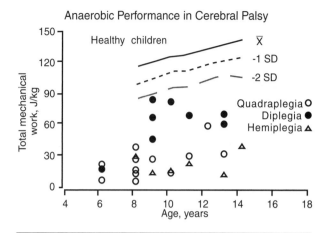

FIGURE 27.4 Anaerobic performance of children and adolescents with spastic cerebral palsy. Total mechanical work, using the Wingate Anaerobic Test, was determined in 29 male patients. Reference data are displayed for healthy boys who were tested in the same laboratory.

Reprinted from Parker et al. 1992.

bic performance (Cerny et al. 1982; Nixon et al. 1992; Inbar et al. 1993). Muscular performance may also be affected because of chronic undernutrition, specifically of protein and energy, that occurs in some patients (Hanning et al. 1993; Boas et al. 1996). The extent of deficiency in aerobic performance is strongly related to the severity of the disease, mostly the status of the lungs (Hjeltnes et al. 1984) but also nutritional status (Gulmans et al. 1997).

Type 1 Diabetes Mellitus

Individuals with type 1 diabetes can reach elite levels of performance in various sports, including world championships and Olympic medals. However, numerous studies have shown that children and adolescents with type 1 diabetes often have deficient aerobic fitness, whether assessed by maximal O_2 uptake or by maximal aerobic power (Poortmans et al. 1986; Baraldi et al. 1992; Barkai et al. 1996). This deficiency occurs primarily in those who are under poor metabolic control (Poortmans et al. 1986). Although the reasons for such low aerobic fitness are not clear, several possible mechanisms have been proposed. These mechanisms include low levels of habitual physical activity (Sterky 1963), impaired control of blood flow to the exercising muscles (Ewald et al. 1985), deficiency in gas exchange in the lungs (Baraldi et al. 1992), impaired carbohydrate utilization (Riddell et al. 2000), and excessively high ratings of perceived exertion during submaximal exercise (Riddell et al. 2000).

Extremely Low Birth Weight

Some, but not all, studies show that the aerobic performance of children and adolescents with extremely low and very low birth weight is deficient (Bader et al. 1987; Baraldi et al. 1991; Pianosi et al. 2000). This finding is particularly true for the prematurely born child who suffered a lung complication called bronchopulmonary dysplasia during the first months of life. Indeed, survivors of this condition often have impaired pulmonary diffusion capacity at rest and during exercise (Santuz et al. 1995; Mitchell et al. 1998).

Anaerobic muscle performance is often limited in children of extremely low birth weight, even among those who show no overt manifestations of a neuromuscular disability (Falk et al. 1997; Keller et al. 2000). Such a deficiency may occur as late as during adolescence (Small et al. 1995). One possible reason for the deficient anaerobic power is low muscle strength (Ericson et al. 1998). However, it may also result from reduced motor coordination while pedaling against "zero" resistance in performing an anaerobic test (see figure 27.5). Reduced motor coordination in low-birth-weight children may explain the high energy cost of locomotion (Baraldi et al. 1991), slow reaction time (Keller et al. 2000), uncoordinated generation of forces during a vertical jump (Falk et al. 1997), and low scores in a total-body coordination test (Keller et al. 2000). An unanswered question is whether systematic training and practice would help children of extremely low birth weight to catch up to age and sex peers of normal birth weight.

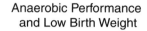

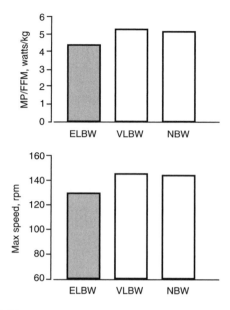

FIGURE 27.5 Anaerobic performance and low birth weight. Children ages 5 to 7 years of age performed the Wingate Anaerobic Test. They comprised three groups: extremely low birth weight (ELBW, 500 to 999 g, n = 14), very low birth weight (VLBW, 1,000 to 1,499 grams, n = 20) and normal birth weight (NBW, >2,500 g, n = 24). The top panel displays mean power per unit fat-free mass. The bottom panel displays maximal pedaling speed against "zero" resistance.

Reproduced with permission from Keller et al. (2000).

Summary

Many chronic medical conditions affect growth and maturation per se and influence levels of fitness and habitual physical activity. Several selected clinical conditions reviewed in this chapter (diabetes, asthma, and disordered eating) are being seen in increasing numbers among school-age children and adolescents and have implications for their ability to participate in physical education and sport. Children with other conditions, specifically cystic fibrosis and extremely low birth weight, now survive at a higher rate than in the past. Children and adolescents with these clinical conditions are often less physically active and are often impaired in physical fitness and performance compared with healthy age and sex peers.

Sources and Suggested Readings

Amin N, Dozor AJ (1994) Effects of administration of aerosolized recombinant human deoxyribonuclease on resting energy expenditure in patients with cystic fibrosis. Pediatric Pulmonology 18:150-154.

Bader D, Ramos AD, Lew CD, Platzker AC, Stabile MW, Keens TG (1987) Childhood sequelae of infant lung disease: exercise and pulmonary function abnormalities after bronchopulmonary dysplasia. Journal of Pediatrics 110: 693-699.

Bandini LG, Schoeller DA, Fukugawa NK, Wykes LJ, Dietz WH (1991) Body composition and energy expenditure in adolescents with cerebral palsy or myelodysplasia. Pediatric Research 29:70-77.

Baraldi E, Monciotti C, Filippone M, Santuz P, Magagnin G, Zanconato S, Zacchello F (1992) Gas exchange during exercise in diabetic children. Pediatric Pulmonology, Supplement 13:155-160.

Baraldi E, Zanconato S, Zorzi C, Santuz P, Benini F, Zacchello F (1991) Exercise performance in very low birth weight children at the age 7-12 years. European Journal of Pediatrics 1:713-716.

Barkai L, Peja M, Vamosi I (1996) Physical working capacity in diabetic children and adolescents with and without cardiovascular autonomic function. Diabetes Medicine 13:254-258.

* Bar-Or O (1983) Pediatric sports medicine for the practitioner. From physiologic principles to clinical applications. New York: Springer-Verlag.

Bar-Or O (1986) Pathophysiologic factors which limit the exercise capacity of the sick child. Medicine and Science in Sports and Exercise 18:276-282.

Bar-Or O (1996) Role of exercise in the assessment and management of neuromuscular disease in children. Medicine and Science in Sports and Exercise 28:421-427.

Bar-Or O, Inbar O, Spira R (1976) Physiological effects of a sports rehabilitation program on cerebral palsied and post-poliomyelitic adolescents. Medicine and Science in Sports 8:157-161.

Bar-Or O, Neuman I, Dotan R (1977) Effects of dry and humid climates on exercise-induced asthma in children and pre-adolescents. Journal of Allergy and Clinical Immunology 69:163-168.

Bevegard S, Eriksson BO, Graff-Lonnevig V, Kraepelien S, Saltin B (1971) Circulatory and respiratory dimensions and functional capacity in boys aged 8 to 13 years with bronchial asthma. Acta Paediatrica Scandinavica, Supplement 217:86-89.

Boas SR, Joswiak ML, Nixon APA, Fulton JA, Orenstein DM (1996) Factors limiting anaerobic performance in adolescent males with cystic fibrosis. Medicine and Science in Sports and Exercise 28:291-298.

* Boersma B, Maarten Wit J (1997) Catch-up growth. Endocrine Reviews 18:646-661.

Bouchard C, Tremblay A, Lebanc C, Lortie G, Savard R, Thériault GA (1983) A method to assess energy expenditure in children and adults. American Journal of Clinical Nutrition 37:461-467.

Bouten CV, Van Marekn Lichtenbelt WD, Westerterp KR (1996) Body mass index and daily physical activity in anorexia nervosa. Medicine and Science in Sports and Exercise 28: 967-973.

Bronstein MN, Davies PSW, Hambidge KM, Accurso FJ (1995) Normal energy expenditure in the infant with presymptomatic cystic fibrosis. Journal of Pediatrics 126:28-33.

Brumberg JJ (1988) Fasting Girls: The Emergence of Anorexia Nervosa as a Modern Disease. Cambridge, MA: Harvard University Press.

Buchdahl RM, Cox M, Fulleylove C (1988). Increased resting energy expenditure in cystic fibrosis. Journal of Applied Physiology 64:1810-1816.

Canada Fitness Survey (1983) Canadian Youth and Physical Activity. Ottawa: Fitness Canada.

Carpenter WH, Poehlman ET, O'Connell M, Goran MI (1995) Influence of body composition and resting metabolic rate on variation in total energy expenditure: a meta analysis. American Journal of Clinical Nutrition 61:4-10.

Cerny FJ, Pullano TP, Cropp GJA (1982) Cardiorespiratory adaptations to exercise in cystic fibrosis. American Review of Respiratory Diseases 126:217-220.

Chalmers J, Catalan J, Day A, Fairburn C (1985) Anorexia nervosa presenting as morbid exercising. Lancet 1:286-287.

Counil F-P, Varray A, Karila C, Hayot M, Voisin M, Prefaut C (1995) Wingate test performance in children with asthma: Aerobic or anaerobic limitation? Medicine and Science in Sports and Exercise 29:430-435.

Davies CTM, von Dobeln W, Fohlin L, Freyschuss U, Thoren C (1978) Total body potassium fat free weight and maximal aerobic power in children with anorexia nervosa. Acta Paediatrica Scandinavica 67:229-234.

Davis C, Katzman DK, Kaptein S, Kirsh C, Brewer H, Kalmbach K, Olmsted MP, Woodside DB, Kaplan AS (1997) The prevalence of high-level exercise in the eating disorders: Etiological implications. Comprehensive Psychiatry 38: 321-326.

Davis C, Kennedy SH, Ravelski E, Dionne M (1994) The role of physical activity in the development and maintenance of eating disorders. Psychological Medicine 24:957-967.

Day G, Mearns MB (1973) Bronchial lability in cystic fibrosis. Archives of Disease in Childhood 48:355-359.

Eisler Ile Grange D (1990) Excessive exercise and anorexia nervosa. International Journal of Eating Disorders 9: 377-386.

Ericson A, Kallen B (1998) Very low birthweight boys at the age of 19. Archives of Disease in Childhood, Fetal and Neonatal Edition 78:F171-F174.

Ewald U, Tuvemo T (1985) Reduced vascular reactivity in diabetic children and its relation to diabetic control. Acta Paediatrica Scandinavica 74:77-84.

Falk B, Dotan R, Liebermann DG, Regev R, Dolphin ST, Bar-Or O (1997) Birth weight and physical ability in 5-8 year old healthy children born prematurely. Medicine and Science in Sports and Exercise 29:1124-1130.

Fitch KD, Godfrey S (1976) Asthma and athletic performance. Journal of the American Medical Association 236:152-157.

Fohlin L (1977) Body composition, cardiovascular and renal function in adolescent patients with anorexia nervosa. Acta Paediatrica Scandinavica, Supplement 268:1-20.

Forbes GB, Kreipe RE, Lipinski BA, Hodgman CH (1984) Body composition changes during recovery from anorexia nervosa: Comparison of two dietary regimes. American Journal of Clinical Nutrition 40:1137-1145.

* Goldberg B (1995) Sports and Exercise for Children with Chronic Health Conditions. Champaign, IL: Human Kinetics.

Graff-Lonnevig V (1978) Cardio-respiratory function, aerobic capacity and effect of physical activity in asthmatic boys. Medical thesis. Stockholm: Karolinska Institute.

Gulmans VAM, De Meer K, Brackel HJL, Helders PJM (1997) Maximal work capacity in relation to nutritional status in children with cystic fibrosis. European Respiratory Journal 10:2014-2017.

Hanning RM, Blimkie CJR, Bar-Or O, Lands LC, Moss LA, Wilson WM (1993) Relationships among nutritional status, skeletal and respiratory muscle function in cystic fibrosis: Does early dietary supplementation make a difference? American Journal of Clinical Nutrition 57:580-587.

Hebestreit H, Bar-Or O (2001). Exercise and the child born prematurely. Sports Medicine, 31:591-599.

Hjeltnes N, Stanghelle JK, Skyberg D (1984) Pulmonary function and oxygen uptake during exercise in 16 year old boys with cystic fibrosis. Acta Paediatrica Scandinavica 73:548-553.

Hoofwijk M, Unnithan VB, Bar-Or O (1995) Maximal treadmill walking test for children with cerebral palsy. Pediatric Exercise Science 7:305-313.

Horswill CA, Zipf WB, Kien CL, Kahle EB (1997) Insulin's contribution to growth in children and the potential of exercise to mediate insulin action. Pediatric Exercise Science 9:18-32.

Inbar O, Dlin RA, Sheinberg A, Scheinowitz M (1993) Response to progressive exercise in patients with cystic fibrosis and asthma. Medicine, Exercise, Nutrition and Health 2:55-61.

Kaplan AS, Zemel BS, Stallings VA (1996) Differences in resting energy expenditure in prepubertal Black children and White children. Journal of Pediatrics 129:643-647.

Keller H, Ayub BV, Saigal S, Bar-Or O (1998) Neuromotor ability

in 5- to 7-year-old children with very low or extremely low birthweight. Developmental Medicine and Child Neurology 40:661-666.

Keller H, Bar-Or O, Kriemler S, Ayub BV, Saigal S (2000) Anaerobic performance in 5- to 7-yr-old children of low birthweight. Medicine and Science in Sports and Exercise 32:278-283.

Kitchen WH, Dozle LW, Ford GW, Callanan C (1992) Very low birthweight and growth to age 8 years. American Journal of Diseases of Children 146:40-45.

Lacey JH, Crisp AH, Hart F, Kirkwood BA (1979) Weight and skeletal maturation – A study of radiological and chronological age in an anorexia nervosa population. Postgraduate Medical Journal 55:381-385.

Lai H-C, Fitzsimmons SC, Allen DB, Kosorok MR, Rosenstein BJ, Campbell PW, Farrell PM (2000) Risk of persistent growth impairment after alternate-day prednisone treatment in children with cystic fibrosis. New England Journal of Medicine 342:851-859.

Landon C, Rosenfeld RG (1987) Short stature and pubertal delay in cystic fibrosis. Pediatrician 14:253-260.

Lands L, Pavilanis A, Charge A, Coates AL (1992) Cardiopulmonary response to exercise in anorexia nervosa. Pediatric Pulmonology 13:101-107.

Leslie RDG, Lo S, Millward BA, Honour J, Pyke DA (1991) Decreased growth velocity before IDDM onset. Diabetes 40:211-216.

Longmuir PE, Bar-Or O (1994) Physical activity of children and adolescents with a disability: Methodology and effects of age and gender. Pediatric Exercise Science 6:168-177.

Longmuir PE, Bar-Or O (2000) Factors influencing the physical activity levels of youths with physical and sensory disabilities. Adapted Physical Activity Quarterly 17:40-53.

Lucas AR, Beard CM, O'Fallon WM, Kurland LT (1991) 50-year trends in the incidence of anorexia nervosa in Rochester, Minn.: A population-based study. American Journal of Psychiatry 148:917-922.

Ludvigsson J, Larsson Y, Svensson PG (1980) Attitudes towards physical exercise in juvenile diabetics. Acta Paediatrica Scandanavia 283:106-111.

McFadden ER (1987) Exercise-induced asthma: Assessment of current etiologic concepts. Chest 91:151S-157S.

McNiven MY, Bar-Or O, Riddell M (1995) The reliability and repeatability of the blood glucose response to prolonged exercise in adolescent males with insulin-dependent diabetes mellitus. Diabetes Care 18:326-32.

Mitchell SH, Teague WG (1998) Reduced gas transfer at rest and during exercise in school-age survivors of bronchopulmonary dysplasia. American Journal of Respiratory Critical Care Medicine 157:1406-1412.

Nixon PA, Orenstein DM, Kelsey SF, Doershuk CF (1992) The prognostic value of exercise testing in patients with cystic fibrosis. New England Journal of Medicine 327:1785-1788.

Nudel DB, Gootman N, Nussbaum MP, Shenker JR (1984) Altered exercise performance and abnormal sympathetic responses to exercise in patients with anorexia nervosa. Journal of Pediatrics 105:34-37.

Orenstein DM (1996) Asthma and Sports. In O Bar-Or (Ed): The Child and Adolescent Athlete. Oxford: Blackwell, pp 433-454.

Parker DF, Carriere L, Hebestreit H, Bar-Or O (1992) Anaerobic endurance and peak muscle power in children with spastic cerebral palsy. American Journal of Diseases of Chidren 146: 1069-1073.

Parker DF, Carriere L, Hebestreit H, Salsberg A, Bar-Or O (1993) Muscle performance and gross motor function in children with spastic cerebral palsy. Developmental Medicine and Child Neurology 35:17-23.

Pianosi PT, Fisk M (2000) Cardiopulmonary exercise performance in prematurely born children. Pediatric Research 47:653-658.

Poortmans JR, Saerens PH, Edelman R, Vertongen F, Dorchy H (1986) Influence of the degree of metabolic control on physical fitness in Type 1 diabetic adolescents. International Journal of Sports Medicine 7:232-235.

Riddell MC, Bar-Or O, Ayub BV, Calvert RE, Heigenhauser JF (1999) Glucose ingestion matched with total carbohydrate utilization attenuates hypoglycemia during exercise in adolescents with IDDM. International Journal of Sports Nutrition 9:24-34.

Riddell MC, Bar-Or O, Gerstein HC, Heigenhauser GJF (2000) Perceived exertion with glucose ingestion in adolescent males with IDDM. Medicine and Science in Sports and Exercise 32:167-173.

Riddell MC, Bar-Or O, Hollidge-Horvat M, Schwarcz HP, Heigenhauser GJ (2000) Glucose ingestion and substrate utilization during exercise in boys with IDDM. Journal of Applied Physiology 88:1239-1246.

Ross G, Lipper EG, Auld PAM (1990) Growth achievement of very low birth weight premature children at school age. Journal of Pediatrics 117:307-309.

* Rowland TW (1990) Exercise and Children's Health. Champaign, IL: Human Kinetics.

Russell D McR, Prendergast PJ, Darby PL, Garfinkel PE, Whitwell J, Jeejeebhoy KN (1983) A comparison between muscle function and body composition in anorexia nervosa: The effect of refeeding. American Journal of Clinical Nutrition 38:229-237.

* Russell G (1994) Childhood asthma and growth - a review of the literature. Respiratory Medicine 88 (Supplement A):31-37.

Salbe AD, Fontville AM, Harper IT, Ravussin E (1997) Low levels of physical activity in 5-year-old children. Journal of Pediatrics 131:423-429.

Santuz P, Baraldi E, Zarmella P, Filippone M, Zacchello F (1995) Factors limiting exercise performance in long-term survivors of bronchopulmonary dysplasia. American Journal of Respiratory and Critical Care Medicine 152:1284-1289.

Shepherd RW, Holt TL, Vasques-Velasquez L, Coward WA, Prentice A, Lucas A (1988) Increased energy expenditure in young children with cystic fibrosis. Lancet 1:1300-1303.

Small E, Van Mil E, Bar-Or O, Saigal S (1995) Muscle performance and habitual physical activity of 11- to 16-year-old females born at extremely low birthweight (500-1000g). Pediatric Exercise Science 7:112-110.

Spicher V, Roulet M, Schutz Y (1991) Assessment of total energy expenditure in free-living patients with cystic fibrosis. Journal of Pediatrics 118:865-872.

* Steinhausen H-C (1994) Anorexia and bulimia nervosa. In M Rutter, E Taylor, L Hersov (eds): Child and Adolescent Psychiatry: Modern Approaches, 3rd editition. Oxford: Blackwell, pp 425-440.

Sterky G (1963) Physical work capacity in diabetic school children. Acta Paediatrica Scandinavica 52:1-10.

Tomezsko JL, Stallings VA, Kawchak A, Goin JE, Diamond G, Scanlin TF (1994) Energy expenditure and genotype of children with cystic fibrosis. Pediatric Research 35:451-460.

* Underwood LE, Van Wyk, JJ (1985) Normal and Aberrant Growth. In JD Wilson, DW Foster (eds): Textbook of Endocrinology. Philadelphia: Saunders, pp 155-205.

Unnithan VB, Dowling JJ, Frost G, Bar-Or O (1996) Role of cocontraction in the O_2 cost of walking in children with cerebral palsy. Medicine and Science in Sports and Exercise 28:1498-1504.

Unnithan VB, Dowling JJ, Frost G, Bar-Or O (2000) Role of mechanical power estimates in the O_2 cost of walking in children with cerebral palsy. Medicine and Science in Sports and Exercise 31:1703-1708.

Vaisman N, Pencharz PB, Corey M, Canny GI, Hahn E (1987) Energy expenditure of patients with cystic fibrosis. Journal of Pediatrics 111:496-500.

Van Bever HP, Desager KN, Lijssens N, Weyler JJ, Du Caju MVL (1999) Does treatment of asthmatic children with inhaled corticosteroids affect their adult height? Pediatric Pulmonology 27:369-375.

Van Den Berg-Emons HJG, Saris WHM, de Barbanson DC, Westerterp KR, Huson A, van Baak MA (1995) Daily physical activity of school children with spastic diplegia and of healthy controls. Journal of Pediatrics 127:578-584.

Van Den Berg-Emons HJG (1996) Physical training of school children with spastic cerebral palsy. Doctoral thesis. Maastricht: Krips Repo Meppel.

Vande Wiele RL (1980) Anorexia nervosa and the hypothalamus. In DT Krieger, JC Hughes (eds): Neuroendocrinology. Sunderland, MA: Sinauer Associations, pp 205-211.

Victorian Infant Collaborative Study Group (1997) Improved outcome into the 1990s for infants weighing 500-999 grams at birth. Archives of Disease in Childhood 77: F91-F94.

Waller EG, Wade AJ, Treasure J, Ward A, Leonard T, Powell-Tuck J (1996) Physical measures of recovery from anorexia nervosa during hospitalised re-feeding. European Journal of Clinical Nutrition 50:165-170.

Wolthers O, Pedersen S (1992) A controlled study of linear growth in asthmatic children during treatment with inhaled glucocorticosteroids. Pediatrics 89:839-842.

Chapter Outline

Sport is perhaps the most visible form of physical activity and is also an important source of physical activity for many children and adolescents. Participation in sport at the community level is a feature of daily living for many children and adolescents the world over. The number of adolescents competing in sports at national and international levels is increasing, and significant numbers of children and adolescents of both sexes begin systematic training and specialization in a sport at relatively young ages. A related factor is the process of identification and selection of talented individuals, which often begins in childhood for many sports.

The success of youth in sports and the selection of talented individuals at young ages give rise to a number of concerns. These concerns include the potential influence of intensive training on growth and maturation, among other concerns related to social and psychological development. Growth and maturation of children and adolescents who excel in sport deserve careful consideration. Such consideration is the focus of this chapter. After briefly discussing who is an athlete and the selective nature of such samples, the growth, maturity, body composition, and physiological characteristics of young athletes are considered. The currently available data are then evaluated in the context of training: Are the demands of intensive training for a sport sufficient to influence the growth and maturation of young athletes? Discussion of the influence of intensive training for sport on social and psychological development is beyond the scope of this chapter. The reader is referred to Malina and Clark (2003) and Coelho e Silva and Malina (2003) for more detailed considerations of a variety of issues related to youth sports, including competitive anxiety, burnout, cross-cultural comparisons, and social aspects of training for sport among children and adolescents.

Participation in Youth Sports

More than one-half of North American children have their first experiences in organized sport by 8 to 9 years of age. Participation rates increase during childhood but subsequently decline during the transition into adolescence—after about 12 to 13 years of age. The decline in participation after 12 to 13 years of age parallels declining rates of participation in physical activities in general (see chapter 21). This age period includes adolescence and puberty with their multiple physical, physiological, psychological, and social demands on youth.

Organized sport implies the presence of a coach and regular practices and competitions during the course of a season. Estimates of the number of participants in the United States for the mid-1990s suggest that approximately 22 million youth 5 to 17 years of age participate in sport programs sponsored by community organizations, such as Kiwanis, Police Athletic League, American Youth Soccer Organizations, Little League Baseball, and Pop Warner Football. About 2.4 million youth participate in club sports that are generally fee-based as in gymnastics, figure skating, swimming, and, more increasingly in soccer. An additional 14.5 million youth are estimated to be involved in municipal recreational sports programs, which emphasize participation for everyone, whereas only a small number, about 450,000, participate in intramural sports programs in middle and high schools. Expressed as percentages of the United States population 5 to 17 years of age in 1995 (about 48.4 million), 45%, 5%, 30%, and 0.1% participate in agency, club, recreation, and intramural sports, respectively (Carnegie Corporation of New York 1996).

Historical statistics for participation in youth sports are difficult to estimate because of the lack of specific and uniform information by age, sex, and sport. The assumption that the number of participants in youth sports has increased over time is reasonable. A relevant question, however, is how has the number of participants in organized sports changed relative to the general increase in the youth population? This change can be estimated within the more restricted age range of high school students, about 14 to 18 years of age. High schools in the United States have an extensive program of interschool competition in a variety of sports. The estimated number of participants in high school sports from 1971 to 2000 is illustrated in figure 28.1. Although the number of students enrolled in high school declined from the late 1970s to 1990, the number of athletes was rather stable after a slight decrease, 3.3 to 3.5 million males and 1.7 to 1.9 million females. Since 1990, numbers of high school students and athletes increased, but the increase in athletes was somewhat less in males (3.4 to 3.9 million) than in females (1.9 to 2.7 million). The larger increase in females reflected implementation of Title IX legislation and increased interest in sports for girls.

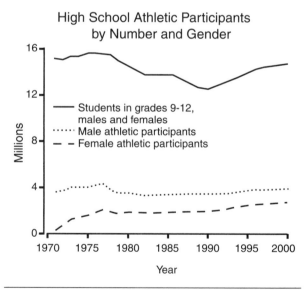

FIGURE 28.1 Participants in high school sports by sex and number of high school students in grades 9 through 12 in the United States from 1971 to 2000.

Data from the National Federation of State High School Associations, 2001, and the National Center for Education Statistics, 2000.

As a percentage of total students in grades 9 to 12, the number of male athletes was, with few exceptions, rather stable between 24% and 26% from 1971 to 2000 (see figure 28.2). The percentage of female athletes increased from 2% in 1971 to 10% in 1975 and then more gradually from 12% in 1978 to 18% in 1999 to 2000. As a percentage of the number of male athletes the number of female athletes increased from 8% in 1971 to 53% in 1980 and then more gradually to 69% in 1999 to 2000.

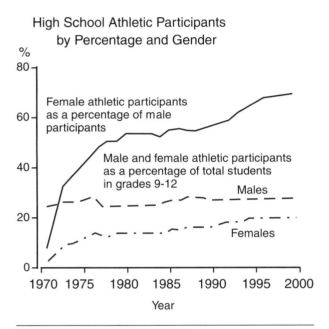

FIGURE **28.2**   Participants in high school sports as a percentage of total students in grades 9 to 12, and the number of female high school athletes as a percentage of the number of male high school male athletes from 1971 to 2000.

Data from the National Federation of State High School Associations, 2001, and the National Center for Education Statistics, 2000.

The numbers are estimates, and some youth participate in more than one sport or type of program. Reported participation in high school sports in the Youth Risk Behavior Survey (YRBS) includes participation in both school and nonschool sports (see table 25.7, page 573). More males than females reported participation in both school and nonschool sports. Participation in both school and nonschool sports is an issue for parents, schools, and sport organizations, largely in terms of the time demands as well as increas-

ing demands and pressures from nonschool sport organizations for year-round participation in a single sport.

Corresponding estimates for other countries are not available. Intramural and to a lesser extent interschool sports competition are offered in some countries, but highly developed interscholastic sports programs as in the United States are not available. Most sports are organized in the context of specific clubs, independent of the schools. The structure of youth sport programs also varies among countries (De Knop et al. 1996), which makes estimation of participation rates difficult. Nevertheless, significant numbers of children and adolescents are involved in organized sport throughout the world.

The distribution of participants has the shape of a pyramid with a wide base. Numbers of participants decrease as sport becomes more demanding and specialized and as interests of children and early adolescents change. Sport has many participants at the novice levels, but as the level of skill and competition increases, sport becomes more exclusive or selective. The number of successful participants, in turn, becomes progressively smaller.

The term "athlete" is often used for participants at higher levels of competition. Those at the highest levels of competition are often labeled as "elite." Careful definitions are needed for samples of children and adolescents involved in sport when describing and comparing their growth and maturity status. A sample of participants in a local league may be quite different from the league "all stars," who are specially selected for skill and performance during the season. The local "all stars," in turn, are not as elite as a team selected to represent the region, state, or nation.

Selection and Exclusion in Sport

The distribution of youth sport participants is related to the selectivity and exclusivity of sport. Although participation in organized sport is extensive, a major limiting factor is the availability of local resources, in particular human resources in the form of qualified adults to coach and supervise programs. The majority of coaches at this level are volunteers, who have little or no experience in teaching and principles of training. Club sports, such as swimming, gymnastics, and figure skating, and in some areas ice hockey and soccer (European football), require parental financial support, so economic considerations may limit access for many children and youth. Increased selectivity and time demands as sports become more rigorous and increased levels of competition are other constraints on organized sport participation with increasing age, especially during the transition into and during adolescence. Ballet, with its selective criteria, is often considered as a sport with gymnastics and figure skating for young girls.

Community-based programs emphasize mass participation; age, parental support, and willingness to participate are the primary criteria. On the other hand, some programs emphasize the elite and have as their objective the identification and subsequent training of young athletes with potential for success in regional, national, and international competitions—high performance or elite sports (Hartley 1987; Malina 1993, 1996). The selection/exclusion process begins early and is systematic. It begins at about 5 years of age in some sports (e.g., gymnastics); criteria and timing of evaluation vary for other sports, including ballet. Identifying and selecting the potentially talented athlete at an early age is the first step in a relatively long-term process. The perfection of talent requires long hours of systematic and often repetitive training, dietary regulation and perhaps manipulation in some sports, special schooling or preferential treatment, and, in many cases, separation from family.

Economic resources are often a limiting factor in securing access to sport programs, facilities, expert coaches, and related requisites for success. On the other hand, potential exploitation of youngsters, especially those from minority and impoverished backgrounds, is a factor in some sports, especially in interscholastic basketball and American football in many United States communities and youth soccer in many countries. High school athletes in the United States are often the objects of rigorous and competitive selective recruiting practices by collegiate and university level athletic coaches and in some cases by professional sport organizations. Youth soccer players in many countries are often signed at young ages (i.e., owned by the clubs). Thus, an adolescent who becomes an intercollegiate or national level athlete has been the product of selective practices beginning in childhood or early adolescence.

Who Is the Young Athlete?

Youth sports have many participants and many levels of competition. In studies of young athletes, the level of skill or competition must be specified. As noted, comparisons of the growth and maturity status of sport participants at the local level may provide a different picture than comparisons of elite athletes of the same age at national or international levels. Many youth participate in a sports program for a year or several years and then move on to other activities as interests change, as skill demands become greater with higher levels of competition, and as competitive sport becomes more selective and exclusive. Hence, the meaning of the term young athlete needs to be specified.

Young athletes are usually defined in terms of success on agency or school teams (especially baseball, basketball, football, ice hockey, and track), in selected athletic club and age group competitions (especially figure skating, gymnastics, swimming, and tennis), and in national and international selections and competitions (e.g., under 12 years of age regional selection or under 16 years of age national selection in soccer). The majority of studies considered in this chapter include children and adolescents who can be classified as select, elite, junior national, or national caliber. International caliber athletes are often included in some sports.

Elite young athletes are a select group. Selection is related primarily to the skill requirements of a particular sport. Size and physique are additional factors in some sports. Larger size, for example, is an advantage in American football, basketball, and swimming but may be a limiting factor in sports such as gymnastics, figure skating, and diving. Size, physique, and performance are related in part to the timing and tempo of biological maturation (see chapters 16 and 17), so maturity status may be a selective factor. Coaches of female gymnasts and figure skaters, for example, are especially concerned about the transition into puberty and may perceive puberty as a factor that limits performances of young athletes in these sports.

Skill and physical characteristics may give a child an initial advantage in some sports. More importantly, perhaps, they probably assist the young athlete to secure the expert coaching that is necessary to refine skills to the level required for success at higher levels of competition.

The growth and maturity of young athletes must be viewed on a sport-specific basis. Within each sport, two approximate age periods merit special attention: first, about 9 through 14 years of age, when maturity-associated variation in size is especially marked, and second, about 15 through 17 years of age, when the catch-up of late-maturing individuals reduces maturity-associated variation in size and performance. These contrasts lead to several important questions. What are the characteristics of successful athletes in childhood and in early and late adolescence? Characteristics of a sample of young athletes at preadolescent or early-adolescent ages may be different from those in later adolescence. Is maturity-associated variation in size and performance as significant in late adolescence as it is in early adolescence? Indeed, many youngsters drop out of sport as the level of competition becomes more difficult and specialization is required. How does selective retention and elimination of young athletes within a sport influence the trends in the data for growth and maturation?

A variety of factors are involved in successful athletic performance during childhood and adolescence, and comparisons of the characteristics of young athletes have limitations. Growth and maturity status are important, but they are not the only determinants of successful performance. They are part of a complex matrix of biocultural characteristics related to the demands of specific sports.

The subsequent discussion of the growth and maturity of young athletes is based largely on two reviews, which contain the references for specific studies (Malina 1994, 1998a). Consideration is first given to the stature and weight of young athletes in several sports, followed by a summary of information on maturity status. The physique, body composition, and physiological characteristics of young athletes in several sports are then summarized.

Stature and Weight of Young Athletes

Data are more readily available for male athletes in team sports, with the exception of swimming. Data for female athletes in team sports during childhood and early adolescence are limited, but more data are available for individual sports, particularly swimming and gymnastics. This discrepancy will likely change as opportunities for girls to participate in a variety of sports increase.

Trends suggested in the average heights and weights of young athletes in several sports relative to age-specific and sex-specific percentiles of the United States reference data (see chapter 3) are summarized in table 28.1 for males and females.

TABLE 28.1 Heights and Weights of Child and Adolescent Athletes Relative to Percentiles (P) of United States Reference Data

Sport	Males		Females	
	Stature	**Weight**	**Stature**	**Weight**
Basketball	P50->P90	P50->P90	P75->P90	P50–P75
Volleyball			P75	P50–P75
Soccer	P50±	P50±	P50	P50
Ice hockey	P50±	P50		
Distance runs	P50±	≤P50	≥P50	<P50
Sprints	≥P50	≥P50	≥P50	≤P50
Swimming	P50–P90	>P50–P75	P50–P90	P50–P75
Diving	<P50	≤P50	≤P50	P50
Gymnastics	≤P10–P25	≤P10–P25	≤P10–<P50	P10–<P50
Tennis	P50±	≥P50	>P50	P50±
Figure skating	P10–P25	P10–P25	P10–<P50	P10–<P50
Alpine skiing	P50±	P50±	P50±	P50±
Rowing[a]	≥P50	≥P50	≥P50	≤P50
Ballet	<P50	P10–P50	≤P50	P10–<P50

[a]Includes canoeing.

Adapted from Malina (1994, 1998a), which contains the references for individual studies. Additional data are from Klika and Malina (1999) and Vadocz (1999).

Many samples of athletes in different sports have heights that fluctuate above and below the reference median. This fluctuation is indicated in the tables as ±P50, which refers to the 50th percentile. Average heights and weights of the athletes in a sport that are consistently above the median are indicated as >P50, and average body sizes consistently below the median are indicated as <P50. In some cases, the mean heights and weights of a sample of athletes vary about a specific percentile on the charts (e.g., P10 or P75).

Athletes of both sexes in most sports have, on average, statures that equal or exceed the reference medians. In some sports, variation is by position (e.g., basketball and soccer). Gymnastics is the only sport that consistently presents a profile of short stature in both sexes. Figure skaters of both sexes also present shorter statures, on average, but data are not as extensive as for gymnasts. Variation also exists among figure skaters by discipline—free skating, dancing, and pairs. Pair skaters tend to be shorter and lighter than free skaters and dancers. Female ballet dancers tend to have shorter statures during childhood and early adolescence but catch up to nondancers in late adolescence.

Body weights present a similar pattern. Young athletes in most sports tend to have body weights that, on average, equal or exceed the reference medians. Gymnasts, figure skaters, and ballet dancers of both sexes consistently show lighter weights. Gymnasts and figure skaters, however, have appropriate weight-for-height, whereas ballet dancers have low weight-for-height. A similar trend in indicated in female distance runners.

Data for sports other than those listed in table 28.1 are limited by the sport. For example, wrestling and weight lifting are organized by competitive weight categories, which influences height and weight data for young athletes in these sports. Data for several other sports are variable and less available (Malina 1994).

Maturity Status and Progress of Young Athletes

A summary of trends in maturity status of young athletes based on skeletal maturity (specifically skeletal age) and secondary sex characteristics (menarche is discussed in a separate section) is presented in table 28.2. Maturity differences are most apparent during the transition into ado-

lescence and the adolescent growth spurt and reflect individuality in timing and tempo. With few exceptions, male athletes in many sports tend to be average ("on time") or advanced in biological maturity status. Other than gymnasts, who show later skeletal maturity, few later-maturing boys are successful in sport during early adolescence. However, later-maturing boys are often successful in some sports in later adolescence, 16 to 18 years of age (e.g., track and basketball), which emphasizes the catch-up in growth and skeletal maturity and the reduced significance of maturity-associated variation in body size on the performances of boys in late adolescence.

The pubertal progress of boys active in sport suggests no differences in tempo of maturation compared with nonathletic boys. Mean intervals for progression from one stage to the next or across two stages are similar to those for nonactive youth (Malina 1997) and are well within the range of normal variation observed in several European longitudinal studies (see chapter 16). The data suggest earlier timing, but a similar tempo of sexual maturation in athletes compared with boys not active in sport.

The pubertal progress of girls active in sport (Malina 1997) is also similar to nonactive girls. The issue of slower and altered pubertal progression in female ballet dancers is discussed later. On average, the interval between ages at PHV and menarche for girls active in sport and nonactive girls does not differ and is similar to those for several samples of nonathletic girls, mean intervals of 1.2 to 1.5 years of age (Geithner et al. 1998).

Limited data for age at PHV are summarized in table 28.3. The data for male athletes are generally consistent with the data for SA, that is, ages at PHV tend to be average or early in male athletes. Exceptions are gymnasts, who experience a later age at PHV. Velocities of growth in height during the interval of PHV for boys active in sport do not differ from velocities for nonactive boys and are within the range of means for boys in longitudinal studies discussed in chapters 16 and 25.

Longitudinal data for girls active in sport are very limited. The two samples in table 28.3 indicate ages at PHV and peak height velocities that approximate the means for the general population. In contrast, age at PHV for gymnasts is later than average. The growth and maturity of gymnasts are discussed in more detail later in the chapter.

TABLE 28.2	Trends in Maturity Status Based on Skeletal Age and Secondary Sex Characteristics (Excluding Menarche) in Child and Adolescent Athletes		
Males	**Childhood (<11.0 yr)**	**Adolescence (11.0–15.9 yr)**	**Late adolescence (>16.0 yr)**
Baseball	*	Advanced	No difference
Football	*	Advanced	No difference
Basketball	No difference	Average/advanced	No difference
Soccer	Average	Average	Advanced
Ice hockey	Average	Average/advanced	Advanced
Distance runs	*	Slightly later/average	No difference
Track & field	*	Advanced	No difference
Swimming	Average/advanced	Advanced	*
Gymnastics	Average	Later	*
Females	**Childhood (<10.0 yr)**	**Adolescence (10.0–14.9 yr)**	**Late adolescence (>15.0 yr)**
Basketball	*	*	Average
Volleyball	*	*	Average
Distance runs	*	Slightly later/average	Slightly later/average
Track and field	*	Average	Average
Swimming	Average/advanced	Average/advanced	Average
Gymnastics	Average	Later/average	Later
Ballet	*	Later/average	Later

*Satisfactory data are not available.

These are trends suggested in a review of data from a variety of studies of young athletes. Characterizing maturity status in late adolescence is influenced by the early attainment of maturity in early-maturing individuals, who are excluded from estimates of statistical parameters for skeletal age, and catch-up of average and later maturing individuals, that is, all youth eventually reach skeletal and sexual maturity. The upper limit in the Tanner-Whitehouse assessment method is 16.0 years of age (maturity) for girls. Indicated ages and ranges are approximate.

Adapted from Malina (1994, 1998a).

Age at Menarche in Athletes

Most discussions of the maturation of female athletes focus on the age at menarche. Later average ages at menarche are often reported in athletes in many, but not all, sports. Confusion about later ages at menarche in athletes is related to a rather narrow clinical definition of "delayed" menarche and to the different methods for estimating age at menarche for a sample. "Delayed" menarche is often defined clinically as an age at menarche of 14 years or older (Constantini and Warren 1994; Warren 1995). Presumably, 14 years means that menarche is attained after the 14th birthday (>14.0 years). This definition is a narrow view of normal human variation in ages at menarche reported in samples of adequately nourished healthy girls

worldwide (see chapter 16; see also Eveleth and Tanner 1976, 1990). Assuming a mean age at menarche of 13.0 years with a standard deviation of 1.0 year (see table 16.6), about two-thirds of girls attain menarche between 12.0 and 14.0 years, and about 95% of girls reach this milestone between 11.0 and 15.0 years of age.

Ages at menarche can be estimated with three methods: prospective, status quo, or retrospective (see chapter 15). **Prospective** or **longitudinal** studies for girls regularly training in a sport are limited to small, select samples and provide an estimate of age at menarche for individual adolescents. Athletes who drop out of elite programs, however, are ordinarily not included, so mean ages in such studies are biased toward the athletes who persist in the sport. **Status quo** data for young athletes provide an estimate for the sample, which does not apply to individual

TABLE
28.3

Estimated Mean Ages at Peak Height Velocity and Peak Height Velocities (± Standard Deviations) in European and Japanese Adolescent Athletes in Several Sports

Activity status/sport	n	Age at PHV (yr)	PHV (cm/yr)	Method[a]
Males in Europe				
Soccer	32	14.2±0.9	9.5±1.5	G, P
Soccer	8	14.2±0.9		G
Basketball and athletics	8	14.1±0.9	10.1±1.2	G
Cycling	6	12.9±0.4		G
Rowing	11	13.5±0.5		G
Ice Hockey	16	14.5±1.0		G
Ice Hockey	11	12.8±0.5	9.3±3.0	G
Gymnasts	14	15.0±0.8	7.5±1.1	P
	11	14.9±0.8	7.4±0.8	KR
Several sports[b]	25	13.6±0.9	9.7±1.1	PB
Several sports[c]	21	13.1±1.0	9.3±1.2	KR
Range of means for nonathletes[d]		13.8–14.4	8.2–10.3	
Males in Japan				
Basketball and track	15	11.6±0.9		W
Distance runs	4	12.6		G
Baseball	126	13.1±1.0	9.3±1.2	PB
Basketball	39	12.8±1.1	9.0±1.1	PB
Soccer	83	13.7±1.1	8.8±1.1	PB
Volleyball	53	13.2±0.8	9.3±1.0	PB
Range of means for nonathletes[e]		12.2–13.1	9.9–11.9	
Females in Europe				
Gymnasts	9	13.1±0.8	5.6±0.5	P
	6	13.1±0.7	5.8±0.5	KR
Several sports[b]	13	12.3±0.8	7.8±0.6	PB
Several sports[c]	23	12.0±0.8	8.0±1.3	KR
Range of means for nonathletes[d]		11.4–12.2	7.1–9.0	

[a]Methods for estimating ages at PHV and peak velocities: G = graphic interpolation, P = polynomials, PB = Preece-Baines model I, KR = kernel regression, W = wavelet interpolation. Some of the variation among estimated ages at PHV and peak velocities reflects differences among methods and the precision of graphic interpolation.

[b]Several individual and team sports.

[c]Largely in track and rowing, several participated in swimming.

[d]Range of mean ages at PHV and peak velocities reported in European longitudinal studies (see table 16.1), based on a variety of methods. Among male nonathletes, 25 of the 26 estimated ages at PHV were between 13.8 and 14.2 years, and among female nonathletes, 24 of the 25 estimated ages at PHV were between 11.6 and 12.2 years.

[e]Range of mean ages at PHV and peak velocities in several Japanese longitudinal studies. Age at PHV occurs earlier, on average, in Japanese than in European adolescents (see tables 16.1 and 25.6).

Adapted from Malina (1998a), which contains the references for individual studies. Data for a combined sample of Japanese basketball (n = 6) and track (n = 9) athletes (Fujii 1998), for Japanese junior high interscholastic athletes (Nariyama et al. 2001), and for gymnasts (Ziemilska 1981) were added. The data for individual gymnasts reported by Ziemilska were fitted with polynomials for 14 males and 9 females and with kernel regression for 11 males and 6 females (Malina 1999). One-half of a year (0.5) was added to the mean age reported for the combined sample of Japanese basketball and track athletes because exact ages were not used in calculating ages at PHV; rather, whole years were used (6.0, 7.0, etc.), which probably underestimates the age by 0.5 year (Fujii, personal communication).

athletes. Given the age range needed to derive an estimate of menarche with the status quo method (i.e., about 9 to 17 years of age), athletes at the younger ages likely may not be as elite as those at the older ages. The chronologically older athletes have already persisted in the sport for several years, whereas others have dropped out or have been eliminated. In contrast to estimates based on the prospective and status quo methods, the majority of data for athletes (and most discussions of menarche in athletes) are based on the **retrospective** method, which has the potential for error of recall.

Information on the age at menarche in adolescent athletes (i.e., those 9 to 17 years of age) is quite limited. Presently available data derived from prospective and status quo studies of adolescent athletes are illustrated in figure 28.3. Average ages at menarche in North American and European girls vary between 12.5 and 13.5 years (see table 16.6). As noted previously, about 95% of girls attain menarche between 11.0 and 15.0 years of age. This range is marked in the figure; the figure also includes the range within which menarche may normally occur in a population, 9 to 17 years of age. Most samples of adolescent athletes have average ages at menarche within the range of normal variation, but mean ages for samples of adolescent gymnasts, ballet dancers, figure skaters, and divers tend to be older than those for athletes in other sports, which have mean ages at menarche that approximate 13 years.

Sample sizes in studies of adolescent athletes are generally small. Further, studies in which the athletes are followed from prepuberty through puberty are limited to small, select samples so that a potentially confounding factor is selective exclusion or drop out. For example, do sports like gymnastics and figure skating, and the arts like ballet select late-maturing girls, or do earlier-maturing girls selectively drop out of gymnastics, figure skating, and ballet?

Ages at menarche for late adolescent and adult athletes based on the retrospective method are more extensive than for adolescent athletes. The distribution of recalled ages at menarche in a sample of 370 university athletes in seven sports (swimming, diving, tennis, golf, volleyball, basketball, and track and field) and 314 nonathlete students at the same university is shown in figure 28.4. The overlap between athletes and nonathletes is considerable. The range of reported ages at menarche in the university athletes is 9.2 to 17.7 years, and early and late maturers are found

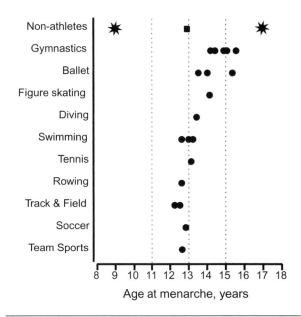

FIGURE 28.3 Mean/median ages at menarche in samples of adolescent athletes based on the prospective and status quo methods. Drawn from data reported in Malina (1994, 1998a) that contain the references for individual studies, with the addition of data for competitive figure skaters (Vadocz et al. 2002). Assuming a mean age at menarche of 13.0±1.0 years for nonathletes, about 95% of girls will attain menarche between 11.0 and 15.0 years of age. These ages are indicated by dashed lines in the figure; the range within which menarche may normally occur in a population, 9 to 17 years of age, is also indicated with asterisks.

Data from Malina, 1994, 1988b, and Vadocz et al., 2002.

in all seven sports (Malina et al. 1997). The range of ages in athletes completely overlaps that for nonathletes, 9.1 to 17.4 years. The distribution for athletes is simply shifted to the right, or later ages, by about 1 year or so. Note, both early-maturing and late-maturing athletes and nonathletes are common, but later-maturing athletes are more common than nonathletes.

Mean recalled ages at menarche for late adolescent and adult athletes in a variety of sports are summarized in figure 28.5. The majority of mean ages are above 13.0 years, but variation by sport and within sports is apparent. Prospective and status quo data for gymnasts and ballet dancers and status quo data for Junior Olympic divers and soccer players (see figure 28.3) are generally

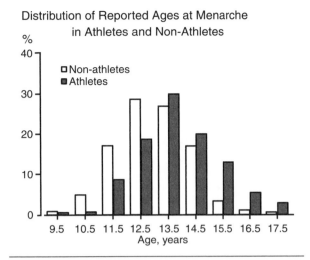

FIGURE 28.4 Distribution of recalled ages at menarche in university athletes from seven sports (swimming, diving, tennis, golf, basketball, volleyball, and track and field) and nonathlete students enrolled at the same university.

Drawn from unpublished data of R.M. Malina.

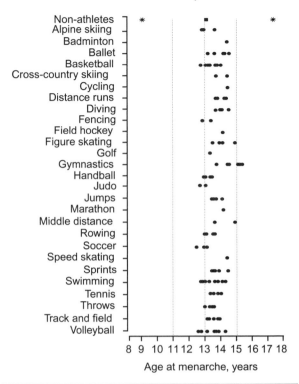

FIGURE 28.5 Mean ages at menarche in samples of late adolescent and adult athletes in a variety of sports based on the retrospective method. Data and original references are in Malina (1983, 1996, 1998a, and unpublished data for university athletes), with the addition of data for competitive figure skaters (Vadocz et al. 2002). Assuming a mean age at menarche of 13.0±1.0 years for nonathletes, about 95% of girls will attain menarche between 11.0 and 15.0 years of age. These ages are indicated by dashed lines in the figure; the range of reported ages at menarche in a large sample of university students who were nonathletes, 9.2 to 17.2 years of age (see figure 28.4), is also indicated with asterisks.

consistent with the retrospective data. The limited prospective and status quo data for tennis players, rowers, and track athletes and more available data for age group swimmers indicate earlier mean ages at menarche compared with retrospective estimates for each sport, respectively. In other words, late adolescent and young adult athletes (retrospective data) in these sports tend to attain menarche later than those involved in the respective sports during the circumpubertal years (prospective and status quo data). The differences probably represent the interaction among several factors, including the longer growth period associated with later maturity (many late maturers do not attain adult body size until the late teens or perhaps early 20s), selective success of late-maturing girls, selective drop out of early-maturing girls, and probably others.

Variation in mean ages at menarche within a sport is especially evident in swimmers. Status quo data for age group swimmers and retrospective data for young swimmers, Olympic swimmers, and national level swimmers from several countries collected in the 1950s to 1970s indicate mean ages at menarche that approximate the mean of the general population (about 13.0 years), and no differences between younger and older swimmers (Malina 1983). However, university level swimmers from elite programs in the United States between 1985 and 1994 have mean recalled ages at menarche of 14.3 and 14.4

years. This trend reflects, in part, increased opportunities for adolescent girls in swimming. In the 1950s to 1970s, female swimmers commonly retired by 16 to 17 years of age. With the advent of Title IX legislation, many universities added or improved their swim programs so that more opportunities were available. Also, later-maturing age group swimmers, catching up to their peers in size and strength in late adolescence, probably experienced more success in swimming and persisted in the sport. A related factor may be change in the size and physique of female swimmers. University level female swimmers between 1985 and 1994 are taller and more linear, a physique characteristic of later-maturing girls, than university swimmers in the mid-1970s. The more recent swimmers are also significantly more androgynous in physique, specifically in the proportion of the shoulders (biacromial breadth) to the hips (bicristal breadth). More recent samples of swimmers have shoulder–hip proportions that are more similar to those of males than to nonathlete females (Malina and Merrett 1995).

Physique of Young Athletes

Physique is an important selective factor in some sports. Mean somatotypes of young male and female Junior Olympic divers and several samples of young adult national and international level divers are shown as an example in table 28.4. Although some variation is associated with sampling and expected changes with growth and maturation, mean somatotypes of Junior Olympic divers are quite similar to and fall within the ranges of mean somatotypes of national and international caliber divers. The data suggest that a model exists that is characteristic of successful performance for divers from young ages onward. Corresponding data for gymnasts, soccer play-

ers, and young athletes in other sports suggest a similar pattern (Carter 1988; Carter and Brallier 1988; Carter and Heath 1990). Thus, young athletes in a given sport tend to have somatotypes that are similar to those of adult athletes in the same sport. This tendency emphasizes a potentially important role for physique in the selection or exclusion process.

Body Composition of Young Athletes

Estimates of the relative fatness of young athletes in several sports are plotted relative to data for nonathletes in figure 28.6. The age trends for nonathletes are based on those described in the discussion of body composition changes during growth (see chapter 5). With one exception, the estimates for young athletes are from the literature, and the constants used to derive relative fatness from density are not adjusted for age-associated and sex-associated variation in the composition of the FFM during growth, which was done for the estimates of relative fatness in nonathletes. Hence, estimates of relative fatness in the younger athletes may be slightly higher than the actual composition, whereas those for late-adolescent athletes are probably correct.

Allowing for variation among samples and methodology, athletes have less relative fatness than nonathletes of the same age and sex. Male athletes and nonathletes both show a decline in relative fatness during adolescence, but athletes have less relative fatness at most ages. Female athletes also have less relative fatness than nonathletes, especially during adolescence, and differences between female athletes and nonathletes appear to be greater than corresponding differences between male athletes and nonathletes. Relative fatness, on the average, shows little variation with age during adolescence in female athletes, whereas it increases with age in nonathletes. Allowing for the sports represented in the available data, variation in relative fatness appears to occur more among female athletes 13 to 18 years of age than among male athletes 14 to 18 years of age.

Measurements of skinfold thicknesses of young athletes are generally consistent with the trends for estimates of relative fatness. Despite some variation among skinfold sites, athletes of both sexes generally have thinner skinfolds. Evidence from samples of primarily young adult athletes indicates no trends towards variation in subcutaneous fat distribution among athletes in several sports.

TABLE 28.4	Heath-Carter Anthropometric Somatotypes in Junior Olympic Divers 11 to 18 Years of Age and Several Samples of Young Adult National and International Level Divers					
Age group	**Male divers**			**Female divers**		
	Endo	**Meso**	**Ecto**	**Endo**	**Meso**	**Ecto**
11	2.1	4.9	3.2	2.8	4.1	3.6
12	2.5	4.9	3.3	2.5	4.0	3.6
13	2.7	5.3	2.9	2.7	4.1	3.3
14	2.2	5.0	3.3	3.0	4.2	2.9
15	1.9	5.1	3.1	3.1	4.2	2.6
16	2.0	5.2	2.8	3.2	4.3	2.5
17	2.3	5.6	2.5	3.3	4.6	2.1
18	1.9	5.6	2.4	3.5	4.8	2.0
Adult	1.9	6.1	1.8	3.3	3.7	2.3
Adult	1.5	5.6	2.6	2.7	4.3	2.5
Adult	1.9	5.4	2.7	2.9	4.1	2.9

Adapted from Geithner and Malina (1993).

Percentage Fat in Young Athletes

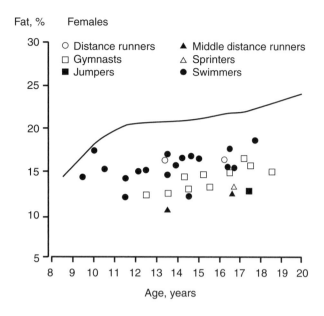

Percentage Fat in Young Athletes

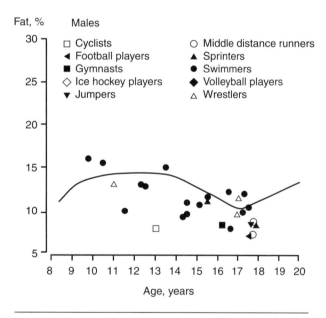

FIGURE 28.6 Densitometric estimates of relative fatness in samples of young athletes in several sports compared with age trends in nonathletes—females (top), males (bottom). Mean values and specific references for athletes are reported in Malina et al. (1982b) and Boileau et al. (1985, 1989), and those for nonathletes (solid line) are from chapter 5. Unpublished means (J Pivarnik and RM Malina) for U.S. junior and senior national female gymnasts based on DEXA are also included. Scales for percentage body fat are the same for boys and girls to facilitate comparison.

Motor Performance Characteristics of Young Athletes

How do young athletes compare with nonathletes in motor performance? A priori, athletes might be assumed to perform better, given the premium placed on skill and practice and on sport-related motor skills. However, data comparing the performances of athletes and nonathletes on standard tasks are quite limited.

Comparisons of athletes in three sports—diving (Geithner et al.1999), downhill skiing (Klika and Malina 1999), and distance running (Eisenmann and Malina 2003)—with nonathletes can be made for one commonly used test, the vertical jump. Divers consistently exceed the values for nonathletes at all ages, and downhill (alpine) skiers approximate the values for nonathletes. Distance runners are near nonathletes until about 13 years of age and then lag behind. The trends for athletes in these three sports may reflect the specific training demands of the respective sports. Diving places a premium on vertical jumping ability, whereas the other sports do not. Downhill skiing places more emphasis on side-to-side jumping, whereas distance running often focuses on endurance training to the neglect of explosive power. In contrast to the vertical jump, the young athletes have greater flexibility of the hamstrings/lower back (sit and reach) than nonathletes. This trend probably reflects the emphasis on stretching as a preliminary to more specific training activities in a sport.

The limited data emphasize the need for further comparative research with young athletes. They also emphasize the specificity of training. Training programs focus on the specific skills or demands of a sport. Other basic skills are perhaps taken for granted or neglected. Early specialization and exclusive training in a specific sport may be an additional contributing factor.

Sex differences in motor performance for the general population of children and adolescents have been summarized in chapter 11. A question of interest is the following: What is the magnitude of sex differences in the performances of elite young athletes within the same sport? Such data are not extensive, but suggest several interesting contrasts. Comparative data for elite female and male athletes in three sports—diving (Geithner et al. 1999), downhill (alpine) skiing (Klika and Malina 1999), and distance running (Eisenmann and Malina 2003)—suggest the following. Sex differences in the performances of elite young athletes in the same sport on tests of agility, power, and muscular endurance are not apparent or are rather minor before 12 to 13 of age (i.e., until the male adolescent growth spurt). The male growth spurts in muscle mass, specifically upper body musculature, and in strength and power contribute to the sex difference in strength and power at this time. In contrast, female athletes in these three sports are more flexible than male athletes at all ages and have less intense adolescent growth spurts in strength and power.

Physiological Characteristics of Young Athletes

Maximal aerobic power per unit body mass (ml/kg/min) for young athletes in several sports is shown in figure 28.7. The data are limited to cross-sectional, mixed-longitudinal, and longitudinal observations of young athletes in several sports, with more data available for males than for females. Compared with trends in $\dot{V}O_2$max per unit body mass in the general population of nonathletic children and adolescents, young athletes in running, swimming, soccer, cycling, and ice hockey have greater levels of aerobic power per unit body mass. Female swimmers and distance runners have a $\dot{V}O_2$max that is especially higher than nonathletic females but quite similar to nonathletic males. The differences between young male athletes and nonathletes increases with age from the transition into adolescence through late adolescence.

Because maximal aerobic power is related to body size and body size and maturity status varies among young athletes in many sports, the differences in $\dot{V}O_2$max per unit body mass (ml/kg/min) between athletes and nonathletes are more significant. Absolute and relative maximal aerobic power are greater in young athletes who train regularly in endurance sports such as swimming, running, and cycling. The same is also true for soccer and ice hockey, which also have a major aerobic component. This greater aerobic power is in keeping with the aerobic demands of these sports and the effects of regular aerobic training in contrast to limited aerobic training in such sports as baseball and American football. The differences between athletes and nonathletes in $\dot{V}O_2$max become progressively greater during adolescence, especially in males.

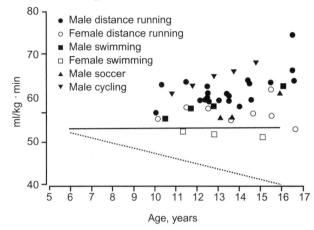

FIGURE 28.7 Maximal aerobic power per unit body mass (ml/kg/min) in young athletes in several sports. Data for the athletes are plotted relative to the estimated age trend for nonathlete males (solid line) and females (dashed line) reported by Krahenbuhl et al. (1985). Cross-sectional data are from means reported in Rowland (1996), which includes references for specific studies. Longitudinal and mixed-longitudinal data are from Daniels and Oldrige (1971), Daniels et al. (1978), Elovainio and Sunberg (1983), Paterson et al. (1987), Baxter-Jones et al. (1993), and Eisenmann et al. (2001).

Comparisons of the aerobic power of young male and female athletes in the same sports indicate a relatively similar pattern of sex differences. Among young distance runners, sex differences in absolute $\dot{V}O_2$max (L/min) are small in late childhood and the transition into early adolescence (about 4% to 8%) but increase during adolescence so that the sex difference is more than 20% between 15 to 17 years of age. When $\dot{V}O_2$max of the young runners is expressed per unit body weight, a similar pattern is apparent (Eisenmann et al. 2001).

Young athletes who train in endurance sports tend to have larger heart volumes. This condition is shown for young swimmers in figure 28.8. Absolute heart volume differs slightly at the beginning of training and reflects the larger size of swimmers because heart volume is related to body size (see chapter 9). Heart volume per unit body weight is greater in the swimmers at the start of training and becomes even greater after 1 year of regular swim training (lower part of the figure). The greater heart volume of the young athletes is a function of increases in the left ventricular diameter and wall thickness as measured

Heart Volumes of Swimmers and Non-athletes

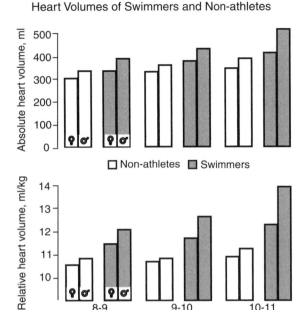

☐ Non-athletes ■ Swimmers

FIGURE 28.8   Absolute (top) and relative (bottom) heart volumes in young swimmers and nonathletes of both sexes followed longitudinally over 1 year.

Reprinted, by permission, from Hollmann et al., Longitudinal study of the aerobic capacity and the heart size in children during an 1-year high performance training. In *Human Growth: A multidisciplinary review*, edited by A. Demirjian (London: Taylor and Francis), 235-242.

by echocardiography (Hollmann 1986). Young swimmers also have lower resting heart rates, or training bradycardia. In other words, young endurance athletes show the characteristics of "athlete's heart," which have been described for adult endurance athletes. The observations for children are limited largely to young swimmers and runners, with little data for other sports (see Rowland 2003).

In addition to greater maximal aerobic power and larger heart volumes, young athletes who train regularly in endurance sports have increased blood volume, total blood hemoglobin, and lung volumes. The differences between athletes and nonathletes relate to the effects of regular training over several years, although some of the variation may reflect differences in body size.

The significant role for regular training in the maintenance of physiological parameters is demonstrated in a follow-up study of 30 elite teenage swimmers as young adults in their early 20s (Erickson et al. 1971). While regularly training for competitive swimming, the girls had very large maximal aerobic power, heart and lung volumes, and total-blood hemoglobin in terms of both absolute values for age and relative values for body size. However, 5 years after regular training stopped, $\dot{V}O_2$max (ml/kg/min) and total-blood hemoglobin declined by about 29% and 13%, respectively. The $\dot{V}O_2$max per unit mass of the formerly active swimmers declined to the level of untrained young adult women. In contrast, heart and lung volumes did not change appreciably with the cessation of training.

The functional advantages of young athletes compared with the general population are thus related to training. Moreover, regular training is necessary for the maintenance of some functional parameters (aerobic power and total hemoglobin) but perhaps not for others (heart and lung volumes), although the detraining period was only 5 years.

Does Training for Sport Influence the Growth and Maturity of Young Athletes?

The role of regular physical activity as a factor that may influence growth and maturation was discussed earlier (see chapter 22). Regular physical activity is not the same as regular training. Training refers to systematic, specialized practice for a specific sport or sport discipline for most of the year or over several years. The measurement, quantification, and specification of training programs in specific sports need attention as does the overall training environment, including quality of coaching, coach–athlete relationships, dietary control and manipulation, parental involvement, and related psychosocial factors.

Intensive training for sport during childhood and adolescence has come under scrutiny in the past decade or so, especially in the context of potentially negative influences, although the data on which some of the conclusions are based can be questioned. For example, based on few case studies that appear to be youth with constitutional delay in growth and maturation, Laron and Klinger (1989, p. 3) asked "What are the mechanisms of slowed growth and delayed or suppressed puberty induced by intensive physical activity?" Theintz et al. (1993) concluded that intensive gymnastics training stunts the adolescent growth spurt, specifically in leg length, and thus affects the stature of girls, although the longitudinal observations spanned only about 2 years.

Many authors have suggested that regular training in gymnastics, swimming, track, ballet, and speed skating before menarche causes the later sexual maturity commonly observed in these athletes (Frisch et al. 1981; Casey et al. 1986; Hamilton et al. 1988; Lindholm et al. 1994; see also Malina 1983, 1998a, 1998b). The American Medical Association and the American Dietetic Association (1991, p. 4) suggest that:

> "Some fitness programs may be detrimental to adolescents if they mandate prolonged, strenuous exercise and/or very low body fat to maximize their competitive edge. . . These regimens may delay sexual maturation, decrease bone growth and ultimate height. . ."

Only on the basis of longitudinal studies of children and adolescents regularly training for sport can such generalizations and others be evaluated. What specific longitudinal data underlie these generalizations? How should the growth and maturity data for young athletes in a variety of sports be interpreted in the context of the preceding generalizations?

As noted in chapter 22, positive changes attributed to regular training are often in the same direction as those that accompany normal growth and maturity, so partitioning specific effects of training is difficult. Suggested negative influences on growth and maturation are often attributed to training without considering other factors that are known to influence these processes. An obvious factor is selection; elite young athletes in many sports are rigorously selected for specific features related to morphology and maturity. Selective drop out by some athletes and exclusion ("cutting") of others by coaches are related factors. Do those who cease participation in a sport differ from those who persist in a sport?

Allowing for these caveats, a critical discussion of training as a factor that may influence the growth and maturation of young athletes follows. The discussion should be viewed in the context of the trends in the growth and maturity of young athletes summarized earlier and expected changes in size and body composition that accompany normal growth and maturation. Special consideration is given to girls in artistic gymnastics and ballet because these highly selective sports receive considerable attention in the medical and popular literature.

Growth in Stature

Longitudinal data for young athletes that span childhood and adolescence are extremely limited. Available short-term and, to a lesser extent, long-term longitudinal data indicate mean statures for young athletes that maintain their position relative to reference values over time, which suggests that height is not influenced by regular training for sport. Estimated growth rates for male and female athletes in several of sports—volleyball, diving, distance running, track, basketball, rowing, cycling, and ice hockey—are within the ranges expected for nonathletes (Malina 1994, 1998a). In the context of these observations, and allowing for selective criteria in some sports, regular participation in sport and training for sport has no apparent effect on attained stature and rate of growth in stature.

Adolescent Growth Spurt

Age at PHV does not appear to be affected by regular training for sport. The data are limited largely to boys, with only few observations for girls (see table 28.3). The observations for male athletes are consistent with the data for skeletal age, that is, ages at PHV tend to occur early or close to the average in male athletes. The limited data for female athletes in a few sports indicate ages at PHV that approximate the average. With the exception of artistic gymnastics, longitudinal data for female athletes in ballet, figure skating, and diving, sports in which later-maturing girls tend to excel during adolescence, are insufficient to estimate ages at PHV. The limited data for gymnasts suggest a later age at PHV and a smaller or less intense peak velocity compared with nonathletes (data for gymnasts are discussed in more detail later in the chapter). Samples of ballet dancers show shorter statures during early adolescence but late adolescent statures that do not differ from nondancers, which indicate later attainment of adult stature. This growth pattern is characteristic of late-maturing girls.

Skeletal Maturation

In boys active in sport, skeletal age (SA) and chronological age (CA) show similar gains before the adolescent growth spurt, but SA progresses faster than CA during the growth spurt and puberty in boys, reflecting the advanced maturity status of male athletes during puberty. In a corresponding sample of girls actively training in sport, SA and CA progress at the same pace from late childhood through the adolescent growth spurt and puberty (Malina and Bielicki 1996). Although young athletes in several sports, including gymnasts of both sexes, differ in skeletal maturity, short-term longitudinal observations indicate similar gains in both SA and CA (Malina 1994). The data imply no effect of training for sport on skeletal maturity as assessed in hand-wrist X-rays.

Sexual Maturation of Males

The effects of training for sport on the sexual maturation of boys has not generally been considered. This omission may not be surprising, because early and average maturity are characteristic of the majority of young male athletes. Male gymnasts tend to be late maturing, but their maturity status is not discussed in the context of the demands of regular training as it is for female gymnasts. Further, males do not have an outcome variable of puberty equivalent to menarche.

Wrestling is the primary sport among males that periodically receives attention because it places emphasis on weight regulation. The emphasis on weight control, however, is usually short term and includes repeated periods of weight loss and weight gain during the course of a season. Longitudinal observations over a season indicate no significant effects of training and competition on the maturity and hormonal profiles of adolescent wrestlers (Roemmich and Sinning 1997a, 1997b). Hormonal data for adolescent male athletes in other sports indicate gonadotrophic hormone and testosterone responses to acute or chronic exercise that vary with pubertal status and that are equivocal (Malina 1991).

It has been proposed that males are ". . .better prepared physically for metabolic demands during the development of reproductive maturity. . ." (Warren 1983, p. 370). This proposition presumably includes the demands associated with rigorous physical activity and training. In the context of Warren's (1983) suggestion, other investigators have proposed that ". . .the significant gains in strength and muscle mass which are possible in prepubertal boys undergoing resistance training could accelerate pubertal onset" (Cumming et al. 1996, pp. 56-57). Presently available data are not consistent with this proposition. Longitudinal studies of males indicate no effect of regular training for sport on the timing and tempo of indicators of somatic, skeletal, and sexual maturity. Further, prepubertal boys respond to strength training without or with minimal associated muscular hypertrophy, and when hypertrophy occurs in adolescent boys, it is a late response during the training regimen (see chapter 22).

Menarche

The later ages at menarche in adolescent and young adult athletes are commonly attributed to regular training before menarche. The correlation between years of training before menarche and age at menarche is used to infer that training before menarche "delays" this maturational event. This inference is erroneous and misleading. Assume that two girls begin training at 6 years of age; one is early maturing and attains menarche at 11.0 years of age, whereas the other is a late maturing and reaches menarche at 16.0 years of age. A priori a correlation will occur between the two events; the early maturer will have 5 years of training before menarche, whereas the late maturer will have 10 years of training before menarche. Correlation does not imply a cause-and-effect sequence; confounding factors or covariates may also be present.

Intensity of training is not ordinarily considered or quantified in studies of menarche, and the distinction between initial participation in a sport and systematic, formal training is not made. Athletes who take up systematic training after menarche are excluded in discussions of an assumed training effect. Moreover, not all athletes experience menarche late (figure 28.4).

In adequately nourished individuals, age at menarche is a heritable characteristic (see chapter 18). A familial tendency is also evident for later maturation in athletes (see table 28.5). Mother-daughter and sister-sister correlations for samples of athletes are similar to those for the general population. Menarche is also influenced by several socially or bioculturally mediated variables (see chapter 25). In addition, sport-specific selective factors must be considered as a part of the biocultural matrix of factors that may influence the age at menarche in adolescent athletes.

The number of children in the family, for example, is associated with menarche in both nonathletes and athletes. Girls from larger families tend to attain menarche later than girls from smaller families (see chapter 25). The estimated magnitude

TABLE 28.5 Familial Correlations for Age at Menarche in Athletes		
Mother-daughter	Ballet	0.32
	Athletes in seven sports	0.25
	Figure skaters	0.45
Sister-sister	Swimmers	0.37
	Athletes in seven sports	0.44

Data for ballet are from Brooks-Gunn and Warren (1988), for figure skating are from Vadocz et al. (2002), and for swimming are from Stager et al. (1988), and the data for athletes in seven sports (swimming, diving, tennis, golf, basketball, volleyball, and track and field) are from Malina et al. (1994). Corresponding mother-daughter interclass correlations for samples of nonathletes range from 0.15 to 0.40; corresponding sister-sister intraclass correlations for samples of nonathletes range from 0.25 to 0.30. Assuming no dominance, the expected correlation between first-degree relatives is 0.50 (Malina et al., 1994).

of the family size effect in high school, university, and Olympic level athletes in several sports (see table 28.6) overlaps that in samples of nonathletes (see table 25.3, page 557). Some data suggest that athletes tend to be from larger families than nonathletes (Malina et al. 1982a, 1997). Aspects of the home environment and familial relationships are also implicated in the timing of menarche (see chapter 25) and should to be considered in interpretations of data from athletes. Similar attention should be paid to the training environments of young athletes, which are regulated primarily by adults, in many cases adult males.

TABLE 28.6 Estimated Effects of Family Size (Number of Children in the Family) on the Age at Menarche in Samples of Athletes	
	Estimated years per additional sibling in the family
High school varsity	0.15
Olympic (Montreal games)	0.22
University	
White	0.22
Black	0.20

The reported values are partial regression coefficients controlling for birth order. See table 25.3 for corresponding estimates for samples of nonathletes.
Adapted from Malina et al. (1997).

Dietary concerns are additional but important factors among adolescent athletes, specifically in sports that emphasize weight control. Factors that interact with marginal caloric status and altered eating habits merit closer attention in evaluating the growth and sexual maturity of young athletes. Such factors may include the psychological and emotional stress associated with maintaining body weight when the natural course of growth is to gain; year-round training, often before school in the morning and after school in the late afternoon; frequent competitions; altered social relationships with peers and parents; and perhaps overbearing and demanding coaches.

The mechanisms that link this complex of factors to menarche are not known. The interactions operate along the hypothalamic-pituitary-ovarian axis (see chapter 19). Puberty is primarily a brain-driven event, and the brain and central nervous system are the filters through which environmental factors and stresses are processed. Given the complexity of factors involved, they must be considered before attributing causality to training before or during puberty as the factor that determines the timing of this maturational event in presumably healthy adolescent athletes.

Body Weight and Composition

Regular training influences body mass and specific components of body composition. Male athletes and nonathletes show a decline in relative fatness during adolescence, but athletes have less fatness. Relative fatness does not increase as much with age during adolescence in female athletes as it does in nonathletes. Thus, the difference between female athletes and nonathletes is greater than the corresponding trend in males (see figure 28.6).

Training is associated with a decrease in fatness in both sexes and occasionally with an increase in fat-free mass, although data for child and adolescent athletes that span a season or several seasons are very limited. Observations on 15 university level swimmers (19.1±1.3 years of age) over a season indicate a reduction in body mass, fat mass, and relative fatness and an increase in fat-free mass during the first part of the season when training is more intense (see table 28.7). This part of the season included both swim training (10 practices per week, 4,572 to 7,772 m per session) and weight training (three times per week, high repetition–low resistance). Changes in estimated body composition during the second half of the

	Interval			
	October– December		**December– March**	
Measurement	**Mean**	**SD**	**Mean**	**SD**
Weight (kg)	−1.3	1.8	0.8	1.2
Fat mass (kg)	−2.4	1.2	0.8	1.5
Relative fatness (%)	−3.8	1.9	1.2	2.0
Fat-free mass (kg)	1.1	1.8	0.0	1.1

TABLE 28.7 Changes in Estimated Body Composition of University Level Female Swimmers During the Course of a Season

Adapted from Meleski et al. (1985).

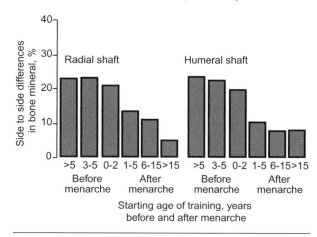

FIGURE 28.9 Bone mineral content of the dominant and nondominant arms of adult tennis and squash players relative to the onset of systematic training—humerus (right), radius (left).

Data from Kannus et al., 1995.

season were relatively small. Training during the second half of the season was reduced in quantity (six sessions per week) and distances swum were gradually reduced (1,372 to 4,572 m) and weight training was reduced as the swimmers tapered in preparation for the national championships in the spring of the year. The data suggest that the training program in the second half of the season maintained the body composition changes experienced during the more intense program in the first part of the season (Meleski and Malina 1985).

Changes in fatness depend on continued training (or caloric restriction, which often occurs in sports such as gymnastics and ballet for girls and wrestling for boys) for maintenance. When training is significantly reduced, fatness tends to accumulate, and when training resumes again, fatness tends to decline (Parizkova 1977).

Skeletal Tissue

Regular training for sport is associated with increased bone mineral content in young athletes from late childhood through young adulthood. The data are derived largely from female athletes in gymnastics, figure skating, ballet, swimming, and running (Grimston et al. 1993; Slemenda and Johnston 1993; Taaffe et al. 1995; Young et al. 1994; Cassell et al. 1996). The long-term effect of early sport training on skeletal tissue is especially apparent in the dominant compared with the nondominant arms of racket sport athletes (see figure 28.9). The difference in the mineral content of the humerus and radius of the dominant and nondominant arms of female tennis and squash players who began formal training 3 or

more years before menarche is greater than that in athletes who began training near the time of menarche or after menarche (Kannus et al. 1995). This study and others of extreme unilateral activity in athletes indicate rather localized increases in bone mineralization.

The integrity of skeletal tissue in some female athletes, which is in part related to later sexual maturity, is cause for concern. Later sexual maturity is presumably associated with reduced total estrogen exposure and, in turn, potentially less bone mineral content and mass. As noted previously, adolescent female athletes in several sports have greater bone mineral, specifically at the skeletal sites at which mechanical strains occur. Enhanced bone mineral accretion associated with training for sport may offset the potential effect of reduced estrogen exposure associated with later maturity.

In contrast to the positive influence of training on bone mineralization, excessive training associated with altered menstrual function (cessation of regular menstrual cycles) in some, but not all, postmenarcheal athletes is associated with loss of bone mineral (Drinkwater et al. 1984; Okano et al. 1995). High levels of training in endurance sports are associated with demineralization of bones in some very active female athletes. The decrease in bone mineral is apparently related to altered menstrual function with excessive training and, in turn, to an estrogen deficit or to a more androgenic hormone profile. Although these observations are seemingly in contrast to studies that show increases in bone mineralization in physically active individuals, a point may exist up to which training has a beneficial effect on the mineralization process and beyond which training has an opposite effect in sexually mature adolescents and young adults. Demineralization of bones occurs in only some athletes, which emphasizes the role of individual differences in response to training.

Restrictive diets or disordered eating contribute to the demineralization of bones in some female athletes. The interaction of disordered eating and an energy-deficient diet, cessation of regular menstrual cycles, and osteoporosis in high-performance athletes is called the "female athlete triad." It is of concern for some, but not all, adolescent athletes, and it may impact the accretion of skeletal mineral during adolescence. Several years are often required after menarche for normal menstrual cycles to be established (see chapter 19), so application of the triad concept to adolescent athletes requires caution. More importantly, perhaps, can adolescent athletes at risk for the triad be identified in the context of what is known about normal variation in menstrual cycles for the years immediately after menarche?

Skeletal Muscle and Adipose Tissues

Specific information on the biochemical and metabolic properties of skeletal muscle and adipose tissues of young athletes is not available. Data for short-term training studies, which were not done on young athletes, were summarized in chapter 22. The distribution of muscle fiber types in youth does not change as a result of training, but the metabolic potential of skeletal muscle (succinate dehydrogenase and phosphofructokinase) can be influenced by regular training. Changes in response to short-term programs are generally not permanent and depend on regular training for their maintenance. How much training is needed to maintain the beneficial changes?

Information on the effects of regular training on adipose tissue cellularity and metabolism in young athletes is lacking. The decrease in fatness associated with training in adults is attributable solely to a reduction in estimated adipocyte size. Trained adults also have increased ability to mobilize and oxidize fat.

Gymnastics and Ballet: Special Cases?

Short stature and late maturity characterize gymnasts of both sexes, and average stature and late maturity characterize female ballet dancers. The growth and maturity characteristics of the former and the late maturity of the latter are often attributed to intensive training (Ziemilska 1981; Hamilton et al. 1988; Thientz et al. 1993; Lindholm et al. 1994; Tofler et al. 1996).

The data for female gymnasts and ballet dancers need to be considered in the context of extremely selective physical and aesthetic criteria of both sports. In addition to skill and coordination, the sport of artistic gymnastics selects for short stature, a somewhat more muscular and slender physique, and late maturation (Bajin 1987; Hartley 1987). Gymnastics coaches commonly ask for photos of a potential gymnast's mother when she was an adolescent (Press 1992). Ballet has rigid selection criteria that place an emphasis on thinness and linearity of physique (Hamilton 1986), both of which are associated with later maturity.

Diet is a confounding factor in both sports. The diets of elite young female gymnasts are routinely closely monitored (Ryan 1995) and perhaps manipulated. Young East German female gymnasts, for example, were kept on a dietary regimen ". . . intended to maintain the optimal body weight [for performance], that is, a slightly negative energy balance, and thus [had] a limited energy depot over a long period" (Jahreis et al. 1991, p. 98). Over time, this regimen is probably chronic undernutrition. Significant numbers of young ballerinas have persistent problems with disordered eating (Hamilton et al. 1988). Estimated energy intakes of child (Davies et al. 1997) and adolescent (Lindholm et al. 1995; Zonderland et al. 1997) gymnasts and young adult dancers (Hamilton et al. 1988; Dahlstrom et al. 1990) are less than estimated energy needs. Other factors that may interact with marginal caloric status and altered eating habits need attention when evaluating the growth and maturity status of young athletes in these sports.

Gymnasts

An editorial on artistic gymnastics for girls cautioned: "Training more than 18 hours per week before and during puberty may alter the growth rate and prevent the full attainment of full adult height" (Toffler et al. 1996, p. 281). Longitudinal data for female gymnasts that span late childhood and adolescence are extremely limited, so this caution needs careful consideration. Nine Polish gymnasts followed for 6 years beginning at 10 to 12 years of age show a mean age at PHV of 13.1±1.0 years and a mean PHV of 5.6±0.5 cm/year (calculated from data reported by Ziemilska 1981; see Malina 1999). These estimates compare closely with a maximum increment of 5.5±0.3 cm/year at a chronological age of 13.0 years and a skeletal age of 12.5 years in Swiss gymnasts followed for periods of only 2.0 to 3.7 years (Thientz et al. 1993). The estimated maximum increments are slightly lower than means for samples of nonathletic adolescent girls but are within the lower end of the range of normal variation (see table 16.2, page 310).

Koziel (1997) considered the adolescent growth spurt of early-maturing, average-maturing and late-maturing Polish boys in the Wroclaw Growth Study with, respectively, tall, medium, and short midparent statures. A similar analysis was done for girls, providing characteristics of the adolescent growth spurt of 18 late-maturing girls with short parents (menarche >13.7 years, midparent stature <162.5 cm) (Koziel, personal communication; see Malina 1999).

The estimated age at PHV and PHV of Polish female gymnasts (13.1±1.0 years and 5.6±0.5 cm/year) are similar to corresponding estimates for late-maturing Polish girls with short parents (12.9±0.6 years and 7.2±1.0 cm/year). Allowing for methodological differences in estimating parameters of the adolescent growth spurt, Polish gymnasts (13.1±1.0 years of age) and late-maturing Polish girls with short parents (12.9±0.6 years of age) compare quite closely in age at PHV. In contrast, estimated PHV is slightly less in the gymnasts (5.6±0.5 cm/year) compared with late-maturing girls with short parents (7.2±1.0 cm/year) but within the range of normal variation (Malina 1999).

The pattern of growth and maturation of female gymnasts is also similar to that for short, normal slow-maturing girls from several United States longitudinal studies. These girls have statures at or below the 10th percentiles of reference data and an SA at least one standard deviation less than CA (Khamis and Roche 1995). The mean age at PHV for short, normal slow-maturing girls is 12.4±1.0 years, with an estimated PHV of 6.8 cm/year. The mean midparent stature for parents of the short, normal slow-maturing American girls is 167.3 cm, which compares favorably with mean midparent

statures for parents of gymnasts: nationally select Dutch, 167.8 cm (Peltenburg et al. 1984); Swiss, 166.6 cm (Thientz et al. 1989); and Polish, 166.4 cm (Ziemilska 1981). The stature deficit in short, normal, slow-maturing children is apparent by 2 years of age. Select Dutch gymnasts have statures that are about one standard deviation score below average by 2 years of age, long before they were nationally selected (figure 28.10).

Early Heights of Gymnasts, Swimmers, and Schoolgirls

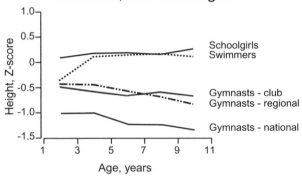

FIGURE 28.10 Standard scores (z-scores) for length/height of Dutch gymnasts at three different levels of selection. Corresponding standard scores for age-group swimmers and nonathletes (school girls) are included for comparison.

Adapted, by permission, from A.L. Peltenburg et al., 1984, "A retrospective growth study of female gymnasts and girl swimmers," *International Journal of Sports Medicine* 5: 262-267.

Young male gymnasts, who also present short stature and later maturity, do not receive attention in clinical and popular discussions. Data for 16 male Polish gymnasts followed for 6 years beginning at 10 to 13 years of age show an estimated mean age at PHV of 14.9±1.1 years and a PHV of 7.8±1.4 cm/year (calculated from data reported by Ziemilska 1981; see Malina 1999). These estimates are, respectively, slightly later and lower than those for nonathletes (see table 16.2, page 310) but are virtually identical to those for 18 late-maturing boys with short parents from the Wroclaw Growth Study in Poland, 14.7±0.7 years and 7.9 cm/year, respectively (Koziel 1997). Longitudinal observations on elite East German male gymnasts from 12 to 14 years of age indicate similar gains in SA and CA, leading the authors to conclude that the slow growth and later maturity are ". . . more a sequelae of selecting than caused by the influence of sports activities" (Keller and Frohner 1989, p. 18).

As in the case of female gymnasts, the pattern of growth and maturity of male gymnasts is similar to that of short, normal slow-maturing boys (Khamis and Roche 1995). The mean age at PHV for short, normal slow-maturing boys is 13.5±0.9 years, with an estimated PHV of 7.8 cm/year. The mean midparent stature for parents of the short, normal slow-maturing boys, 165.4 cm, compares favorably with the mean midparent stature for parents of the male Polish gymnasts, 163.9±1.7 cm (Ziemilska 1981).

Differential drop out must be considered when evaluating the growth of young gymnasts. Not all young gymnasts persist in the sport. How do the size and maturity of those who drop out compare with the size and maturity of those who persist in the sport? In two longitudinal series of elite Polish (Ziemilska 1981) and Swiss (Tonz et al. 1990) female gymnasts, those who discontinued participation in the sport were taller and heavier age for age and advanced in biological maturity compared with those who persisted in the sport. In other words, those who persisted in the sport were later maturing than those who dropped out. The same trend was also evident in Polish male gymnasts. One might speculate as whether the decision to discontinue participation is related to individual perceptions of size and maturity relative to the demands of the sport, coaches, and judges.

Thus, female and male gymnasts as a group have adolescent growth spurts that are similar in timing to other short, normal slow-maturing girls and boys with short parents, although variation exists in estimated PHVs. Allowing for the limited data and the variety of factors that need to be considered, intensive training cannot be easily implicated as the factor influencing the adolescent growth spurts of young female and male gymnasts. Further, in the context of human variation and individual differences in responses to training (see chapter 22), why would one expect all children and adolescents to respond to training in the same way? Perhaps identifying those children and adolescents who might be at more risk for potentially negative consequences of intensive training is more important. This task, however, has not been performed by the sports medicine community.

Gymnasts of both sexes are also described as having relatively short legs for their stature (Buckler and Brodie 1977) or as having been selected for short limbs (Jahreis et al. 1991). Investigators

have suggested that the growth rate of leg length is stunted in highly trained gymnasts (Jahreis et al. 1991; Theintz et al. 1993), leading to disproportionately short legs and short stature. However, cross-sectional data for several samples of male and female gymnasts, including three from international competitions, indicate relative leg lengths (sitting height expressed as a percentage of standing height) that are similar to reference values for European and American children and adolescents. Although gymnasts are absolutely shorter, they have similar proportional relationships of the legs and trunk relative to nonathletes. This finding is shown in figure 28.11 for two cross-sectional samples of female gymnasts, one participants at an international competition and the other United States junior and senior national level gymnasts. On average, the sitting height as a percentage of stature in gymnasts is virtually identical with reference values for nonathletes.

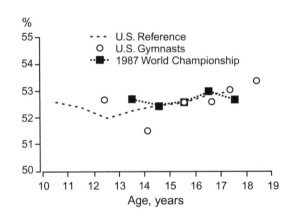

FIGURE 28.11 Sitting height as a percentage of stature (%) in two cross-sectional samples of female gymnasts, participants in an international competition (Claessens et al. 1992) and United States junior and senior national level gymnasts (RM Malina, unpublished data), with corresponding reference values for United States youth (Roche and Malina 1983).

Data from Roche and Malina, 1983.

Ballet Dancers

The growth pattern of female ballet dancers is consistent with that observed in late-maturing girls, that is, shorter statures during early adolescence and eventual catch up with reference data and later attainment of adult stature (see chapter 17). SA lags behind CA and sexual maturity is later. Variation is apparent in reported ages at menarche among ballet dancers: 14.3 to 15.6 years in prospective and status quo studies (see figure 28.3) and 13.0 to 14.8 years in retrospective studies (see figure 28.5). The correlation between age at menarche of ballet dancers (13.3±1.3 years) and their mothers (12.7±1.5 years) is 0.32 (Brooks-Gunn and Warren 1988), which is similar to correlations observed for athletes in several sports (see table 28.5). The difference in ages at menarche between ballet dancers and their mothers is similar to corresponding differences among athletes in other sports. The later maturity may thus be in part familial.

Disharmony in breast and pubic hair development has been suggested among elite ballet dancers. Although pubic hair progresses normally, ". . . the progression from a breast stage 3 to a stage 4 or 5 in the dancers (is) very variable. . ." (Warren 1980, p. 1153). These observations should be viewed in the context of the extremely linear physiques of elite ballet dancers. Weight-for-height of this sample of elite dancers decreased during puberty and did not stabilize until after 17 years of age (Warren 1980). Fat is a major component of body weight in pubertal girls, and extreme linearity is associated with leanness. The criteria for the assessment of breast stages are in part dependent on physique and fatness, specifically B4 (see figure 15.3). The areolar mound that characterizes B4 does not occur in all girls and also may be relatively slight in some girls (Tanner 1962). Given the decline in weight-for-height during puberty in elite ballet dancers, as well as the observation that significant numbers of young ballerinas have persistent problems with disordered eating related to concerns for body weight, the slow and variable maturation of the breasts may be related to low weight gain, low levels of fatness, and energy deficient dietary intakes during puberty rather than to the intensity of ballet training.

Overview

Child and adolescent athletes grow in a manner similar to nonathletes. Much of the variation in body size is associated with selective or exclusionary criteria of some sports and with variation in rate of biological maturation. In other words, the experience of athletic training and competition does not appear to accelerate or decelerate the growth and maturity of young athletes. Regular training has no apparent effects on stature, body proportions, and biological maturity. By inference, the size, physique, and maturity characteristics of children, athletes and nonathletes, are probably associated with the genotypic characteristics of the individual. On the other hand, training is a significant factor affecting body composition, performance, and physiological parameters. This finding would imply that some of the variation between athletes and nonathletes represents an interaction between individual characteristics and selective considerations for sports participation. Several aspects of the selection process have been indicated in the chapter.

The unique growth and maturity characteristics of young athletes are evident in many instances during childhood. For example, young Dutch female swimmers and gymnasts, who were studied in early adolescence, already differed in stature and weight as early as 2 years of age (see figure 28.11). Age-group swimmers were taller and heavier, whereas gymnasts were shorter and lighter than the Dutch reference since 2 years of age. In addition, midparent heights and weights were also greater for parents of the swimmers than for parents of the gymnasts (Peltenburg et al. 1984). The same is true for athletes, 9 to 13 years of age, systematically training in swimming, tennis, gymnastics, and team handball in select Danish sport clubs at the national level (Damsgaard et al. 2000). At 2 to 4 years of age, standard deviation scores for height in swimmers, tennis players, and team handball players were positive, indicating taller stature, whereas corresponding scores for gymnasts of both sexes were negative, indicating shorter statures. Among samples of select French adolescent basketball players, 15 males and 17 females, mean standard deviation scores for height in boys by 2 years of age and in girls by 3 years of age were three standard deviation units above the population mean and remained above this level throughout childhood and adolescence (Filliard et al. 1996). Thus, selection for body size is an important factor in sports such as gymnastics, swimming, and basketball (and probably others), and this factor must be considered in making inferences about potential effects of training on growth and maturation in comparisons of young athletes.

Similar trends are apparent for biological maturity. Differences between SA and CA for two small samples of Czech boys, one that chose to train for sport whereas the other did not, are shown in figure 28.12. Both groups had no specific sports training before 11 years of age. Those who chose (or perhaps were selected) to train regularly in track and basketball and persisted in training between 11 and 18 years of age were consistently advanced in skeletal maturity, whereas those who chose not to train were consistently later in skeletal maturity. Maturity-related factors and the size differences associated with variation in maturity status are thus important components of the selection process for sport among youth.

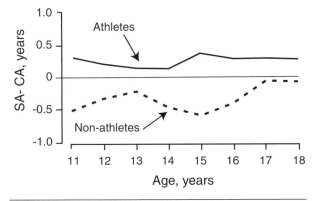

FIGURE 28.12 Differences between skeletal age (SA) and chronological age (CA) expressed as SA minus CA in young athletes and nonathletes followed longitudinally from 11 to 18 years of age.

Data from Ulbrich, 1971.

The presently available data emphasize individual characteristics in the sport selection process at relatively young ages. These characteristics include skill, body size, maturity, and functional parameters, among others. Given the association among maturity status, body size, and many functional parameters (see chapter 17), the greater maximal aerobic power, heart volume, and lung volume of young athletes may be in part a function of maturity-associated variation in body size. Functional variables are influenced by regular training, whereas body size and maturity are not. Hence, the greater functional capacities of trained young athletes may be larger than would be predicted on the basis of their body size or maturity status.

Allowing for variation in methodology and sampling in studies of young athletes, regular training for sport during childhood and during puberty and the adolescent growth spurt does not apparently influence size attained, growth rate, and the timing and tempo of somatic, sexual, and skeletal maturity in presumably healthy girls and boys. The data emphasize a primary role for constitutional factors in the selection and sorting processes of competitive sport. More longitudinal data on the growth, maturation, and performance of young athletes are obviously necessary to evaluate the importance of selective factors as well as potential effects of training.

From another perspective and recognizing for the wide range of individual differences in normal growth and maturation and in responsiveness to training, why would all children and adolescents be expected to respond to training in a similar manner? Rather, can we identify the young athlete who might be at risk for potentially compromised growth and maturation in the context of sport training? If so, how can the sport environment be modified to eliminate or reduce the risk?

Summary

Child and adolescent athletes grow in a manner similar to nonathletes. Much of the variation in body size among young athletes compared with nonathletes is associated with selective or exclusionary criteria of specific sports and with variation in the rate of biological maturation. The experience of regular athletic training and competition beginning at relatively young ages does not appear to accelerate or decelerate growth in height and skeletal, sexual, and somatic maturation. On the other hand, systematic training for sport is a significant factor affecting body composition, performance, and physiological parameters of young athletes.

Sources and Suggested Readings

American Medical Association/American Dietetic Association (1991) Targets for Adolescent Health: Nutrition and Physical Fitness. Chicago: American Medical Association.

Astrand P-O, Engstrom L, Eriksson BO, Karlberg P, Nylander I, Saltin B, Thoren C (1963) Girl swimmers. Acta Paediatrica Scandinavica, Supplement 147:1-75.

Bajin B (1987) Talent identification program for Canadian female gymnasts. In Petiot B, Salmela JH, Hoshizaki TB, eds. World Identification for Gymnastic Talent. Montreal: Sports Psyche Editions, pp 34-44.

Baxter-Jones ADG, Goldstein H, Helms P (1993) The development of aerobic power in young athletes. Journal of Applied Physiology 75:1160-1167.

Baxter-Jones ADG, Helms P, Baines-Preece J, Preece M (1994) Menarche in intensively trained gymnasts, swimmers and tennis players. Annals of Human Biology 21:407-415.

Beunen G, Malina RM (1996) Growth and biological maturation: Relevance to athletic performance. In O Bar-Or (ed), The Child and Adolescent Athlete. Oxford: Blackwell Science, pp 3-24.

Beunen GP, Malina RM, Thomis M (1999) Physical growth and maturation of female gymnasts. In FE Johnston, B Zemel, PB Eveleth (eds), Human Growth in Context. London: Smith-Gordon, pp 281-289.

Boileau RA, Horswill CA, Slaughter MH (1989) Body composition in the young athlete. In WJ Klish, N Kretchmer (eds), Body Composition Measurements in Infants and Children. Columbus, OH: Ross Laboratories, pp 104-110.

Boileau RA, Lohman TG, Slaughter MH. (1985) Exercise and body composition of children and youth. Scandinavian Journal of Sports Science 7:17-27.

Bompa TO (1985) Talent Identification. Ottawa: Coaching Association of Canada.

Brooks-Gunn J, Warren MP (1988) Mother-daughter differences in menarcheal age in adolescent girls attending national dance company schools and non-dancers. Annals of Human Biology 15:35-43.

Buckler JMH, Brodie DA (1977) Growth and maturity characteristics of schoolboy gymnasts. Annals of Human Biology 4:455-463.

Carnegie Corporation of New York (1996) The Role of Sports in Youth Development. New York: Carnegie Corporation of New York, pp 1-157.

* Carter JEL (1988) Somatotypes of children in sports. In RM Malina (ed), Young Athletes: Biological, Psychological, and Educational Perspectives. Champaign, IL: Human Kinetics, pp 153-165.

Carter JEL, Brallier RM (1988) Physiques of specially selected young female gymnasts. In RM Malina (ed), Young Athletes: Biological, Psychological, and Educational Perspectives. Champaign, IL: Human Kinetics, pp 167-175.

Carter JEL, Heath BH (1990) Somatotyping—Development and Applications. Cambridge, UK: Cambridge University Press.

Casey MJ, Jones EC, Foster C, Pollock ML (1986) Effect of the onset and intensity of training on menarchal age and menstrual irregularity among elite speedskaters. In DM Landers (ed), Sport and Elite Performers. Champaign, IL: Human Kinetics, pp 33-44.

Cassell C, Benedict M, Specker B (1996) Bone mineral density in elite 7- to 9-yr-old female gymnasts and swimmers. Medicine and Science in Sports and Exercise 28: 1243-1246.

Claessens AL, Malina RM, Lefevre J, Beunen B, Stijnen V, Maes H, Veer FM (1992) Growth and menarcheal status of elite female gymnasts. Medicine and Science in Sports and Exercise 24:755-763.

Clapp JF, Little KD (1995) The interaction between regular exercise and selected aspects of women's health. American Journal of Obstetrics and Gynecology 173:2-9.

* Coelho e Silva MJ, Malina RM, editors (2003) Biosocial approaches to youth sports. Coimbra, Portugal: Centro de Estudes de Desporto Infanto-Juvenil, Faculdade de Ciencias de Desporto e Educacao Fisica, Universidade de Coimbra.

Constantini NW, Warren MP (1994) Physical activity, fitness, and reproductive health in women: Clinical observations. In Bouchard C, Shephard RJ, Stephens T (eds), Physical Activity, Fitness, and Health. Champaign, IL: Human Kinetics, pp 955-966.

Cumming DC, Wheeler GD, Harber VJ (1996) Physical activity, nutrition, and reproduction. Annals of the New York Academy of Sciences 709:55-74.

Dahlstrom M, Jansson E, Nordevang E, Kaijser L (1990) Discrepancy between estimated energy intake and requirement in female dancers. Clinical Physiology 10:11-25.

Damsgaard R, Bencke J, Matthiesen G, Petersen JH, Muller J (2000). Is prepubertal growth adversely affected by sport? Medicine and Science in Sports and Exercise 32: 1698-1703.

Daniels J, Oldridge N (1971) Changes in oxygen consumption of young boys during growth and running training. Medicine and Science in Sports 3:161-165.

Daniels J, Oldrige N, Nagel F, White B (1978) Differences and changes in VO_2 among young runners 10 to 18 years of age. Medicine and Science in Sports 10:200-203.

Davies PSW, Feng J-Y, Crisp JA, Day JME, Laidlaw A (1997) Total energy expenditure and physical activity in young Chinese gymnasts. Pediatric Exercise Science 9:243-252.

De Knop P, Engstrom LM, Skirstad B, Weiss MR, editors (1996) Worldwide Trends in Youth Sport. Champaign, IL: Human Kinetics.

Drinkwater BL, Nilson K, Chesnut CH, Bremner WJ, Shainholtz S, Southworth MB (1984) Bone mineral content of amenorrheic and eumenorrheic athletes. New England Journal of Medicine 311:277-281.

Eisenmann JC, Malina RM (2003) Age- and sex-associated variation in neuromuscular capacities of adolescent distance runners. Journal of Sport Sciences 21:551-557.

Eisenmann JC, Pivarnik JM, and Malina RM (2001) Scaling peak $\dot{V}O_2$ to body mass in young male and female distance runners. Journal of Applied Physiology 90:2172-2180.

Elovainio R, Sundberg S (1983) A five-year follow-up study on cardiorespiratory function in adolescent elite endurance runners. Acta Paediatrica Scandinavica 72:351-356.

Engstrom I, Eriksson BO, Karlberg P, Saltin B, Thoren C (1971) Preliminary report on the development of lung volumes in young girl swimmers. Acta Paediatrica Scandinavica, Supplement 217:73-76.

Erickson BO, Engstrom I, Karlberg P, Saltin B, Thoren C (1971) A physiological analysis of former girl swimmers. Acta Paediatrica Scandinavica, Supplement 217:68-72.

Eveleth PB, Tanner JM (1976) Worldwide Variation in Human Growth. Cambridge, UK: Cambridge University Press.

Eveleth PB, Tanner JM (1990) Worldwide Variation in Human Growth, 2nd edition. Cambridge, UK: Cambridge University Press.

Filliard JR, Pineau JC, Szczesny S (1996) Croissance des sujets de tres grandes tailles: Application a un echantillon de jeunes basketteurs (Growth of very tall subjects: Application to a group of basketball players). Cahiers d'Anthropologie er Biometrie Humaine 14:567-579.

Frisch RE, Gotz-Welbergen AB, McArthur JW, Albright T, Witschi J, Bullen B, Birnholz J, Reed RB, Hermann H (1981) Delayed menarche and amenorrhea of college athletes in relation to age of onset of training. Journal of the American Medical Association 246:1559-1563.

Frisch RE, Wyshak G, Vincent L (1980) Delayed menarche and amenorrhea in ballet dancers. New England Journal of Medicine 303:17-19.

Fujii K (1998) An investigation regarding sequence of age at MPV in physique growth of male athletes: Studies of Growth and Development, Japanese Society of Physical Education 26:26-32 (in Japanese).

Geithner CA, Malina RM (1993) Somatotypes of Junior Olympic divers. In RM Malina, JL Gabriel (eds), U.S. Diving 1993 Sport Science Seminar Proceedings. Indianapolis, IN: U.S. Diving, pp 36-40.

Geithner CA, O'Brien RO, Gabriel JL, Malina RM (1999) Sex differences in the motor performances of elite young divers. Medicine and Science in Sports and Exercise 31 (suppl): S170 (abstract).

Geithner CA, Woynarowska B, Malina RM (1998) The adolescent spurt and sexual maturation in girls active and not active in sport. Annals of Human Biology 25:415-423.

Grimston SK, Willows ND, Hanley DA (1993) Mechanical loading regime and its relationship to bone mineral density in children. Medicine and Science in Sports and Exercise 25:1203-1210.

Hamilton LJ, Brooks-Gunn J, Warren MP, Hamilton GW (1988) The role of selectivity in the pathogenesis of eating problems in ballet dancers. Medicine and Science in Sports and Exercise 20:560-565.

Hamilton WG (1986) Physical prerequisites for ballet dancers: Selectivity that can enhance (or nullify) a career. Journal of Musculoskeletal Medicine 3:61-66.

Hartley G (1987) A comparative view of talent selection for sport in two socialist states—the USSR and the GDR—with particular reference to gymnastics. In The Growing Child in Competitive Sport. Leeds: The National Coaching Foundation, pp 50-56.

Hollmann W, Rost R, Gerhardus G, Liesen H (1986) Longitudinal study of the aerobic capacity and the heart size in children during a 1-year high performance training. In A Demirjian (ed), Human Growth: A Multidisciplinary Review. London: Taylor and Francis, pp 235-242.

Jahreis G, Kauf E, Frohner G, Schmidt HE (1991) Influence of intensive exercise on insulin-like growth factor I, thyroid and steroid hormones in female gymnasts. Growth Regulation 1:95-99.

Kannus P, Haapasalo H, Sankelo M, Sievanen H, Pasanen M, Heinonen A, Oja P, Vuori I (1995) Effect of starting age of physical activity on bone mass in the dominant arm of tennis and squash players. Annals of Internal Medicine 123:27-31.

Kannus P, Sievanen H, Vuori I (1996) Physical loading, exercise, and bone. Bone 18:1S-3S.

Keller E, Frohner G (1989) Growth and development of boys with intensive training in gymnastics during puberty. In Z Laron, AD Rogol (eds), Hormones and Sport. New York: Raven, pp 11-20.

Khamis HJ, Roche AF (1995) Growth outcome of "normal" short children who are retarded in skeletal maturation. Journal of Pediatric Endocrinology and Metabolism 8: 85-96.

Klika RJ, Malina RM (1999) Sex differences in motor performance in elite young alpine skiers. Medicine and Science in Sports and Exercise 31 (suppl):S319 (abstract).

Koziel SM (1997) Combined effects of the tempo of maturation and midparent height on the shape of individual growth curves. American Journal of Human Biology 9:555-563.

Krahenbuhl GS, Skinner JS, Kohrt WM (1985) Developmental aspects of maximal aerobic power in children. Exercise and Sport Sciences Reviews 13:503-538.

Laron Z, Klinger B (1989) Does intensive sport endanger normal growth and development. In Z Laron, AD Rogol (eds), Hormones and Sport. New York: Raven, pp 1-9.

Lindholm C, Hagenfeldt K, Hagman U (1995) A nutrition study in juvenile elite gymnasts. Acta Paediatrica 84: 273-277.

Lindholm C, Hagenfeldt K, Ringertz B-M (1994) Pubertal development in elite juvenile gymnasts. Acta Obstetrica et Gynecologica Scandinavica 73:269-273.

* Loucks AB, Vaitukaitis J, Cameron JL, Rogol AD, Skrinar G, Warren MP, Kendrick J, Limacher MC (1992) The reproductive system and exercise in women. Medicine and Science in Sports and Exercise 24:S288-S293.

* Malina RM (1983) Menarche in athletes: A synthesis and hypothesis. Annals of Human Biology 10:1-24.

Malina RM (1991) Darwinian fitness, physical fitness and physical activity. In CGN Mascie-Taylor, GW Lasker (eds), Applications of Biological Anthropology to Human Affairs. Cambridge, UK: Cambridge University Press, pp 143-184.

Malina RM (1993) Youth sports: Readiness, selection and trainability. In W Duquet, JAP Day (eds), Kinanthropometry IV. London: E & FN Spon, pp 285-301.

Malina RM (1994) Physical growth and biological maturation of young athletes. Exercise and Sports Sciences Reviews 22:389-433.

Malina RM (1995) Physical activity and fitness of children and youth: Questions and implications. Medicine, Exercise, Nutrition, and Health 4:123-135.

Malina RM (1996) The young athlete: Biological growth and maturation in a biocultural context. In FL Smoll, RE Smith (eds), Children and Youth in Sport: A Biopsychosocial Perspective. Dubuque, IA: Brown and Benchmark, pp 161-186.

Malina RM (1997) Prospective and retrospective longitudinal studies of the growth, maturation, and fitness of Polish youth active in sport. International Journal of Sports Medicine 18 (suppl 3): S139-S154.

* Malina RM (1998a) Growth and maturation of young athletes: Is training for sport a factor? In KM Chang, L Micheli (eds), Sports and Children. Hong Kong: Williams and Wilkins, pp 133-161.

Malina RM (1998b) Physical activity, sport, social status and Darwinian fitness. In SS Strickland and PS Shetty (eds), Human Biology and Social Inequality. Cambridge, UK: Cambridge University Press, pp 165-192.

Malina RM (1999) Growth and maturation of elite female gymnasts: Is training a factor? In FE Johnston, B Zemel, PB Eveleth (eds), Human Growth in Context. London: Smith-Gordon, pp 291-301.

Malina RM (2001) Growth and maturity status of young artistic gymnasts: Status, progress, and issues. In M Lenoir, R Philippaerts (eds), Science in Artistic Gymnastics. Ghent, Belgium: Publicatiefonds Voor Lichamelijke Opvoeding, pp 21-38.

Malina RM (2003) Growth and Maturity Status of Young Soccer (Football) Players. In T Reilly, M Williams (eds), Science and Soccer, 2nd edition. London: Routledge, pp. 287-306.

Malina RM, Bielicki T (1996) Retrospective longitudinal growth study of boys and girls active in sport. Acta Paediatrica 85:570-576.

Malina RM, Bouchard C, Shoup RF, Lariviere G. (1982a). Age, family size and birth order in Montreal Olympic athletes. In JEL Carter (ed), Physical Structure of Olympic Athletes: Part I. The Montreal Olympic Games Anthropological Project. Basel: Karger, pp 13-24.

* Malina RM, Clark MA, editors (2003) Youth Sports: Perspectives in a New Century. Monterey, CA: Coaches Choice.

Malina RM, Katzmarzyk PT, Bonci CM, Ryan RC, Wellens RE (1997) Family size and age at menarche in athletes. Medicine and Science in Sports and Exercise 29:99-106.

Malina RM, Meleski BW, Shoup RF (1982b) Anthropometric, body composition, and maturity characteristics of selected school-age athletes. Pediatric Clinics of North America 29: 1305-1323.

Malina RM, Merrett DMS (1995) Androgyny of physique of women athletes: Comparisons by sport and over time. In R Hauspie, G Lindgren, F Falkner (eds), Essays on Auxology. Welwyn Garden City, Hertfordshire: Castlemead Publications, pp 355-363.

Malina RM, Peña Reyes ME, Eisenmann JC, Horta L, Rodrigues J, Miller R (2000) Height, mass and skeletal maturity of elite Portuguese soccer players 11–16 years. Journal of Sports Sciences 18:685-693.

Malina RM, Ryan RC, Bonci CM (1994) Age at menarche in athletes and their mothers and sisters. Annals of Human Biology 21:417-422.

Meleski BW, Malina RM (1985) Changes in body composition and physique of elite university level swimmers during a competitive season. Journal of Sports Sciences 3:33-40.

Meleski BW, Shoup RF, Malina RM (1982) Size, physique, and body composition of competitive female swimmers 11 through 20 years of age. Human Biology 54:609-625.

Nariyama K, Hauspie RC, Mino T (2001) Longitudinal growth study of male Japanese junior high school athletes. American Journal of Human Biology 13:356-364.

National Center for Education Statistics (2000) Encyclopedia of ED Stats. Chapter 1. All Levels of Education. www.nces.ed.gov.

National Federation of State High School Associations (2001) 1999–2000 Athletics Participation Summary. www.nfsh.org/part_survey99-00.htm.

Okano H, Mizunuma H, Soda M-Y, Matsui H, Aoki I, Honjo S-I, Ibuki Y (1995) Effects of exercise and amenorrhea on bone mineral density in teenage runners. Endocrinology Journal 42:271-276.

Parizkova J (1977) Body Fat and Physical Fitness. The Hague: Martinus Nijhoff.

Paterson DH, McLellan TM, Stella S, Cunningham DA (1987) Longitudinal study of ventilation threshold and maximal O_2 uptake in athletic boys. Journal of Applied Physiology 62:2051-2057.

Peltenburg AL, Erich WBM, Zonderland ML, Bernink MJE, van den Brande JL, Huisveld IA (1984) A retrospective growth study of female gymnasts and girl swimmers. International Journal of Sports Medicine 5:262-267.

Press A (1992) Old too soon, wise too late? Newsweek 10: 22-24.

Robinson TL, Snow-Harter C, Taaffe DR, Gillis D, Shaw J, Marcus R (1995) Gymnasts exhibit higher bone mass than runners despite similar prevalence of amenorrhea and oligomenorrhea. Journal of Bone and Mineral Research 10:26-35.

Roche AF, Malina RM (1983) Manual of Physical Status and Performance in Childhood. Volume 1. Physical Status. New York: Plenum.

Roemmich JN, Sinning WE (1997a) Weight loss and wrestling training: Effects on nutrition, growth, maturation, body composition, and strength. Journal of Applied Physiology 82:1751-1759.

Roemmich JN, Sinning WE (1997b) Weight loss and wrestling training: Effects on growth-related hormones. Journal of Applied Physiology 82:1760-1764.

Rost R, Hollmann W (1983) Athlete's heart: A review of its historical assessment and new aspects. International Journal of Sports Medicine 4:147-165.

Rowland TW (1996) Developmental Exercise Physiology. Champaign, IL: Human Kinetics.

Rowland TW (2003) Cardiac characteristics of the child endurance athlete. In RM Malina, MA Clark (eds), Youth Sports: Perspectives for a New Century. Monterey, CA: Coaches Choice, pp 53-68.

Rowland TW, Delaney BC, Siconolfi SF (1987) "Athlete's heart" in prepubertal children. Pediatrics 79:800-804.

Ryan J (1995) Little Girls in Pretty Boxes: The Making and Breaking of Elite Gymnasts and Figure Skaters. New York: Warner Books.

Slemenda CW, Johnston CC (1993) High intensity activities in young women: Site specific bone mass effects among female figure skaters. Bone and Mineral 20:125-132.

Stager JM, Hatler LK (1988) Menarche in athletes: The influence of genetics and prepubertal training. Medicine and Science in Sports and Exercise 20:369-373.

Sundgot-Borgen J, Larsen S (1993) Preoccupation with weight and menstrual function in female elite athletes. Scandinavian Journal of Medicine and Science in Sports 3:156-163.

Taaffe DR, Snow-Harter C, Connolly DC, Robinson TR, Brown MD, Marcus R (1995) Differential effects of swimming versus weight-bearing activity on bone mineral status of eumenorrheic athletes. Journal of Bone and Mineral Research 10:586-593.

Tanner JM (1962) Growth at Adolescence, 2nd edition. Oxford: Blackwell.

Theintz GE, Howald H, Allemann Y, Sizonenko PC (1989) Growth and pubertal development of young female gymnasts and swimmers: A correlation with parental data. International Journal of Sports Medicine 10:87-91.

Theintz GE, Howald H, Weiss U, Sizonenko PC (1993) Evidence for a reduction of growth potential in adolescent female gymnasts. Journal of Pediatrics 122:306-313.

Tofler IR, Stryer BK, Micheli LJ, Herman LR (1996) Physical and emotional problems of elite female gymnasts. New England Journal of Medicine 335:281-283.

Tönz O, Stronski SM, Gmeiner CYK (1990) Wachstum und Pubertät bei 7- bis 16-jährigen Kunstturneirinnen: eine prospektive Studie. Schweirische Medizinische Wochenschrift 120:10-20.

Ulbrich J (1971) Individual variants of physical fitness in boys from the age of 11 up to maturity and their selection for sports activities. Medicina dello Sport 24:118-136.

Vadocz EA (1999) A psychobiological profile of adolescent competitive figure skaters. East Lansing, MI: Michigan State University, Doctoral Dissertation.

Vadocz EA, Siegel SR, Malina RM (2002) Age at menarche in competitive figures skaters: Variation by level and discipline. Journal of Sports Sciences 20:93-100.

Warren MP (1980) The effects of exercise on pubertal progression and reproductive function in girls. Journal of Clinical Endocrinology and Metabolism 51:1150-1157.

Warren MP (1983) Effects of undernutrition on reproductive function in the human. Endocrine Reviews 4:363-377.

Warren MP (1995) Amenorrhea in ballet dancers. Eleventh International Jerusalem Symposium on Sports Injuries. Tel Aviv: Israel Society of Sports Medicine, p 18 (abstract).

Young N, Formica C, Szmukler G, Seeman E (1994) Bone density at weight-bearing and nonweight-bearing sites in ballet dancers: The effects of exercise, hypogonadism, and body weight. Journal of Clinical Endocrinology and Metabolism 78:449-454.

Ziemilska A (1981) Wplyw intensywnego treningu gimnastycznego na rozwoj somatyczny i dojrzewanie dzieci (Effect of intensive gymnastics training on somatic growth and maturation of children). Warsaw: Akademia Wychowania Fizycznego.

Zonderland ML, Claessens AL, Lefevre J, Philippaerts R, Thomis M (1997) Delayed growth and decreased energy intake in female gymnasts. In N Armstrong, B Kirby, J Welsman (eds), Children and Exercise XIX. London: E & FN Spon, pp 533-536.

Chapter

29

SECULAR TRENDS IN GROWTH, MATURATION, AND PERFORMANCE

Chapter Outline

Definitions

Sources of Secular Trend Data

Limitations and Assumptions of Secular Comparisons

Secular Trends in Body Size
United States
Europe
Japan

Secular Trends in Body Proportions

Secular Trends in Indicators of Maturity
Age at Menarche

Age at Peak Height Velocity
Other Secondary Sex Characteristics

Secular Trends in Performance
Strength
Motor Performance
Aerobic Power
Is There an Optimal Size for Performance?

Secular Trends in Developing Countries

Factors Underlying Secular Trends

Summary

Sources and Suggested Readings

The attainment of larger size and acceleration of maturation over several generations are collectively labeled as the secular trend. In this context, the secular trend actually includes several trends—increases in height and weight during childhood and adolescence, reductions in the age at menarche and ages at attaining other indicators of biological maturity, and increases in adult stature—that have occurred over several generations in Europe and Japan and in areas of the world largely inhabited by populations of European ancestry (United States, Canada, and Australia). The time at which secular changes are evident in different populations varies in part because of the limited availability of satisfactory data for earlier samples in some populations and because of differential rates of improvement in health and nutritional circumstances that underlie improvements in growth and maturity status.

Secular trends are complex phenomena that reflect the remarkable sensitivity, or plasticity, of the processes of growth and maturation to the environmental conditions under which children and adolescents are reared.

Strength and performance are, in part, related to body size and maturity status. Hence, the increased size and advanced maturity that characterize the secular trend have implications for physical performance.

This chapter considers several aspects of research on secular trends in body size and proportions and age at menarche. Data are quite limited for estimates of body composition, and inferences are generally made based on changes in the relationship of weight-for-height and more recently the BMI. Changes in several measures of physical performance in the context of secular trends are also considered.

Definitions

Secular trends can be positive, negative, or absent. The observation that children today are, on average, taller and heavier and mature earlier than children of several generations ago indicate a **positive secular trend**. On the other hand, in some parts of the developing world, children and adults are shorter than those of a generation or two ago, or girls are attaining menarche later, indicating a **negative secular trend**. Lack of change in size or age at menarche over several generations indicates the **absence of a secular trend**, which reflects different situations. The population in question may have attained, or is near, its genetic potential for height and timing of maturity, so further changes may not be possible. Further changes, however, are possible in body weight, which is more susceptible to environmental influences, especially chronically excessive energy intake and physical inactivity. On the other hand, the population in question may be living under environmental conditions that have not sufficiently improved over time to result in a positive secular trend in body size and timing of maturation. Alternatively, environmental conditions may be such that they cannot support a positive secular trend but are not sufficiently impoverished to induce a negative trend over time, as is the case in populations in some developing countries.

Secular trends are not universal, and they are reversible. If health and nutritional conditions in a society deteriorate, they are ordinarily reflected in the form of shorter heights, lighter weights and later maturation of children and adolescents, and, ultimately, shorter adult heights. Conversely, if the poor conditions improve, they are reflected in increased heights and earlier maturation. The reversibility of secular trends is especially evident during conditions of war. The positive secular trend in the heights of children and adolescents have been temporarily stopped and even reversed in some countries during the conditions of war. This negative change occurred during World Wars I and II in Europe (van Wieringen 1986) and during World War II in Japan (Takaishi 1995; Ali and Ohtsuki 2000). When conditions improved after the wars, positive secular changes in height resumed. More recent examples of the reversibility of secular trends are apparent in the slightly later ages at menarche during the period of social and political change after the collapse of the Soviet dominated communist system in

Poland in the 1980s (Hulanicka et al. 1993) and during the war conditions that characterized the political breakup of the former Yugoslavia in the 1990s (Prebeg and Bralic 2000).

Sources of Secular Trend Data

Data for observations of secular changes in body size and maturation are derived primarily from two sources: height and weight records of children, adolescents, and young adults (most often university students and military conscripts), and reports on ages at menarche in girls and women. The available data span approximately 100 to 150 years and in some instances almost 200 years. Secular change information for measures of muscular strength and performance are much less extensive. They are largely limited to measures of grip strength, running, and jumping. The period over which secular comparisons of strength and performance can be made is generally not as extensive as that for size and maturity.

Limitations and Assumptions in Secular Comparisons

Comparisons of data across several generations, or for that matter across two contemporary groups, have certain underlying limitations and assumptions (Roche 1979). The first concern is sampling. Are corresponding population samples being compared? For example, to compare children attending the same school over a 40- or 50-year period may be misleading as the size, socioeconomic, and perhaps ethnic/racial composition of the community and, in turn, the school may have changed over this time.

A second assumption deals with measurement. Did the authors use the same measurement techniques so that the reported data are comparable? Was height measured to the nearest centimeter, to the last completed centimeter, or to the nearest millimeter? The measurement of body weight is somewhat more problematic. In early surveys, scales were not calibrated or checked for error, and some early surveys did not include body weight because of the lack of an accurate portable scale. Clothing is also an issue. Was nude body weight measured, or were the subjects wearing "ordinary indoor clothing?" How does weight of clothing vary with season of the year? How has the weight of clothing changed over time? Other related factors in the measurement process (e.g., diurnal and seasonal variation) may also influence the interpretation of secular changes in height and weight (see chapter 3, see also Krogman 1948).

A third problem in secular comparisons is reported age or age categories. Ideally, exact ages, verified by birth certificates, should be used. However, this information is not always available, especially in earlier studies. Interpretation of reported ages also needs caution. For example, does 13 years of age refer to the 13th year of life (i.e., 12.0 to 12.99 years) or to the year after the 13th birthday (13.0 to 13.99 years)? A reevaluation of reported ages and age criteria in early Norwegian data for age at menarche has resulted in a lower estimated average age at menarche in the 19th century from slightly above 17 years of age to about 16 years of age (Brundtland and Walloe 1976) and has altered somewhat the view of secular change in this maturity indicator.

Secular comparisons are ordinarily made by age groups, so the method of grouping children is important. As noted in chapter 1, children are routinely grouped into yearly age categories. However, are they grouped so that the whole year is the midpoint of the age category (6.50 to 7.49 with a mean of about 7.0 years), or are they grouped by age at the last birthday so that the midyear is the midpoint of the age category (7.00 to 7.99 with a mean of about 7.5 years)? Both groups would be called 7 years of age; yet, they differ in mean age by about one-half of a year. Longitudinal studies may present an additional problem for secular comparisons. Children are often measured within a narrow time period just before or just after their birthdays (e.g., 7.0± 2 weeks). Such data for 7-year-old children have a reduced range of variability.

Most of the information on secular change in the tempo of maturation is based on the age at menarche. In addition to the method of reporting ages, accuracy of recall is an important factor. Limitations of the retrospective method were discussed earlier. Although retrospective data are influenced by error of recall, most teenagers and women can recall this landmark within a range of 3 months (see chapter 15). Repeated surveys of populations utilizing the status quo method are limited to the past two generations.

The reliability of strength and performance data must be considered in evaluating secular changes in performance. Static strength tests usually yield reliable results. However, different dynamometers are used for strength testing, calibration of the instruments may or may not have been considered, and the type of instrument may not be reported. The most commonly reported performance data are for grip strength. The reliability of motor performance tests can be variable, depending on the task. Tasks requiring an all-out effort as in the standing long jump generally give reliable results. Attention to the details of motor testing (techniques and conditions and number of trials) is needed in making secular comparisons. The more commonly used tests are runs and jumps, but distances vary in the former (e.g., 30 versus 50 meters) and technique varies in the latter (standing versus running long jump). Issues related to motivation or opportunity for practice obviously cannot be controlled.

Secular Trends in Body Size

Positive secular trends in height and weight have occurred in all socioeconomic groups in Europe, Japan, and the United States since the early part of the 19th century through the 1960s. More recent changes from the 1960s through the 1990s are variable among countries (Tanner 1966, 1968, 1992; Meredith 1963, 1976; Roche 1979; van Wieringen 1986; Takaishi 1995; Hauspie et al. 1997; Bodzsar and Susanne 1998). Similar trends have occurred in Canada and Australia, although data are less extensive.

United States

Estimated secular trends in the height and weight of North American boys from approximately 1880 to 1960 are illustrated in figures 29.1 and 29.2, respectively. Secular changes in birth weight and length have been small. This finding may be expected in terms of the size constraints of the female pelvis. A marked secular increase in birth size without a concomitant increase in pelvic dimensions of women would be biologically inefficient. Although increases in birth size are small, secular increases in height and weight are apparent by the end of the first year and become progressively larger until 12 to 13 years of age in girls and 14 to 15 years of age in boys. From puberty until young adulthood (early to mid-20s), there is a progressive reduction in the magnitude of the secular increase in height more so than for body weight. The largest secular differences in height and weight are apparent during the pubertal years, which reflect not only secular change in body size but also the secular trend towards earlier maturation. As noted in chapter 17, early-maturing children and adolescents are taller and heavier age for age than those who mature later. Thus, comparisons of 15-year-old boys in the 1960s with those in the 1880s are, to some extent, misleading in the sense that more recent adolescents are maturationally advanced compared with those of three or four generations ago. Corresponding data for North American girls, although not as extensive, indicate similar trends (Meredith 1976).

Heights of North American Boys 1880-1960

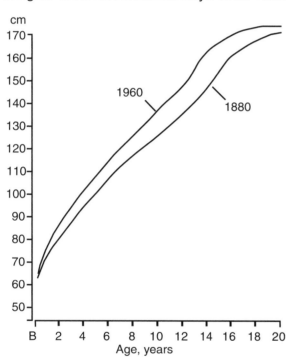

FIGURE 29.1 Schematic curves for mean heights of North American boys from 1880 to 1960.

Adapted from *Advances in child development and behavior*, H.V. Meredith, pp. 69-114, Copyright © 1963, with permission from Elsevier.

The secular increase in body size appears early in life and becomes greater through puberty. In contrast to this notion, which is supported by the majority of data (Roche 1979), some investigators have suggested that accelerated growth only during infancy and childhood is responsible for

Weights of North American Boys 1880-1960

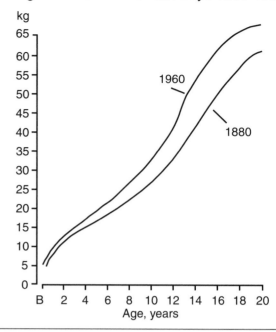

FIGURE 29.2 Schematic curves for mean weights of North American boys from 1880 to 1960.

Adapted from *Advances in child development and behavior*, H.V. Meredith, pp. 69-114, Copyright © 1963, with permission from Elsevier.

the secular increase in height (Boyne et al. 1957; Lenz and Ort 1959; Brundtland et al. 1980). Data for infants 3.0 to 4.9 months of age indicate no secular differences from 1963 to 1994 (Roche and Guo 2001). This issue needs further study.

Some evidence indicates that the secular trend may have stopped as early as 1918 in children from the upper social strata in the United States (Roche 1979). Two major longitudinal studies in the United States (Fels Research Institute in Ohio and Child Research Council in Colorado) show negligible changes in statures of children who were born before and after about 1940 (Garn and French 1967; Maresh 1972). However, longitudinal analysis of generational changes within families of the Fels Research Institute indicates that a secular increase in stature continues (Bock and Sykes 1989). The seemingly discrepant observations illustrate an important problem in studying secular trends. Given the more or less constantly changing demographic composition of the United States population, valid cross-sectional analysis of secular changes may be difficult. Further, participants in longitudinal studies may not be representative of the general population.

Age-specific median heights of representative samples of United States boys and girls 6 through 17 years of age in four national surveys between 1963 and 1994 (see table 3.1, page 51) are shown in figures 29.3 and 29.4, respectively. Data for the most recent survey (NHANES III 1988–1994), indicate, on average, slightly greater statures at some ages during childhood and adolescence. Some of the differences are 2 cm or more, but all are not statistically significant (Troiano and Flegal 1998). Overall, data from the four national surveys of American children from the 1960s through 1994 indicate relatively small changes in height (Roche 1995; Troiano and Flegal 1998; Roche and Guo 2001). Although comparisons show a very slight increase in stature at the 5th and 10th percentiles, the data suggest that the trend towards increased height has apparently ceased, on average, in the United States in the mid-1960s.

Height of U.S. Boys in Four National Surveys Between 1963 and 1994

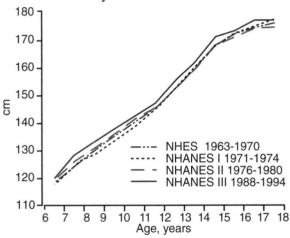
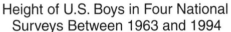

FIGURE 29.3   Median heights of United States boys in four national surveys between 1963 and 1994.

Drawn from data reported by Hamill et al. (1970 1973, 1977), Najjar and Rowland (1987), and SS Sun (unpublished).

The earlier national surveys of children and adolescents in the United States, NHES II and III (1963–1970), NHANES I (1971–1974), and NHANES II (1976–1980), included adequate numbers of children and adolescents of Black (African American) and White (European American) ancestry. The most recent survey, NHANES III, oversampled African Americans and Mexican Americans compared with their numbers in the

Height of U.S. Girls in Four National Surveys Between 1963 and 1994

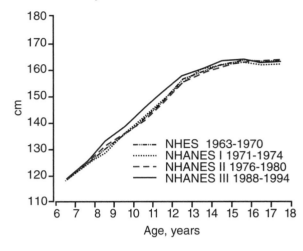

FIGURE 29.4   Median heights of United States girls in four national surveys between 1963 and 1994.

Drawn from data reported by Hamill et al. (1970, 1973, 1977), Najjar and Rowland (1987), and SS Sun (unpublished).

total population of the United States in 1990. There is no consistent evidence of differences in secular increases in stature between American Black and White children in earlier comparisons (Meredith 1963, 1976), but the data from NHANES III indicate greater statures among Black youth. The differences are apparently related to greater values in the taller statures (right tail of the distribution) rather than to an overall shift in the distribution (Troiano and Flegal 1998).

Data from the Hispanic Health and Nutrition Examination Survey (HHANES 1982–1984) indicate that Mexican American children and adolescents tend to be, on average, taller than earlier samples of Mexican Americans in various localities in the southwestern United States (Malina et al. 1986). In contrast, Mexican American children and adolescents in NHANES III (1988–1994) do not systematically differ in stature from those in HHANES (Ryan et al. 1999).

Age-specific median weights of United States boys and girls 6 through 17 years of age in the four national surveys between 1963 and 1994 are shown in figures 29.5 and 29.6, respectively. Median body weights have not changed appreciably in the nationally representative samples of American children and adolescents from 1963 to 1980. However, in contrast to the small secular changes in heights of American children and adolescents from NHANES II to NHANES III, body weights have increased considerably between 1976 and 1980 and between 1988 and 1994. As a result, body weights of children 6 years of age and older in NHANES III were not used in the derivation of the new growth charts (Kuczmarski et al. 2000; see also chapter 3). This decision was made because the gain in body weight from NHANES II to NHANES III was not viewed as desirable from a public health perspective (Roche 1999).

Weight of U.S. Boys in Four National Surveys Between 1963 and 1994

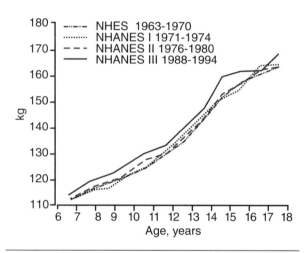

FIGURE 29.5   Median weights of United States boys in four national surveys between 1963 and 1994.

Drawn from data reported by Hamill et al. (1970, 1973, 1977), Najjar and Rowland (1987), and SS Sun (unpublished).

The marked secular gain in body weight and the negligible gain in height from the 1970s through the 1990s has resulted in greater weight-for-height and, in turn, an increase in the prevalence of overweight in American children and adolescents (see table 29.1). Overweight (obesity) was defined as a BMI at or higher than age-specific and sex-specific 95th percentiles of the new United States growth charts (Ogden et al. 2002; see chapter 3). The prevalence of overweight was stable in national samples of American children and adolescents from the 1960s through the late 1970s. Subsequently, the prevalence has approximately doubled between 1976 and 1980 and between 1988 and 1994 and has continued to increase to 1999 and 2000. Moreover, the recent secular increase in the prevalence

Weight of U.S. Girls in Four National Surveys Between 1963 and 1994

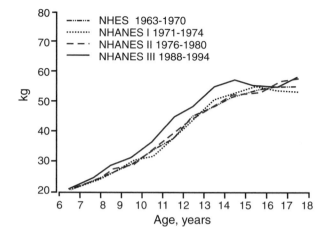

FIGURE 29.6   Median weights of United States girls in four national surveys between 1963 and 1994.

Drawn from data reported by Hamill et al. (1970, 1973, 1977), Najjar and Rowland (1987), and SS Sun (unpublished).

is greater in Mexican Americans and American Blacks compared with American Whites (Ogden et al. 2002).

The health implications of this recent trend are considerable. Overweight tends to track from childhood into adulthood, that is, individuals overweight as children and adolescents are more likely to be overweight when they are adults. Overweight or obesity in adulthood has important public health implications for several diseases, especially heart disease and type 2 diabetes mellitus. The secular trend in the prevalence of overweight among children and adolescents is consistent with data for adults across the same time span, indicating a national epidemic of obesity in the United States (Flegal et al. 1998, 2002). Similar trends are also evident in Canada and several European countries (see chapter 24).

Europe

Secular trends in the body size of children and adolescents in several European countries extend further back in time than those in the United States (e.g., 1830 to 1980 for Belgium) (Hauspie et al. 1997), 1860 to 1994 for the Netherlands (Burgmeijer and van Wieringen 1998), and 1880 to 1995 for Jena, Germany (Jaeger 1998). Some data for marine recruits 13 to 16 years of age in the United Kingdom cover the period 1769 to 1869,

Age group/ survey years	Males %	Males SE	Females %	Females SE
2–5 Years				
1971–1974	5.0	0.9	4.9	0.8
1976–1980	4.7	0.6	5.3	1.0
1988–1994	6.1	0.8	8.2	1.1
1999–2000	9.9	2.2	11.0	2.5
6–11 Years				
1963–1965	4.0	0.4	4.5	0.6
1971–1974	4.3	0.8	3.6	0.6
1976–1980	6.6	0.8	6.4	1.0
1988–1994	11.6	1.3	11.0	1.4
1999–2000	16.0	2.3	14.5	2.5
12–19 Years				
1966–1970	4.5	0.4	4.7	0.3
1971–1974	6.1	0.8	6.2	0.8
1976–1980	4.8	0.5	5.3	0.8
1988–1994	11.3	1.3	9.7	1.1
1999–2000	15.5	1.6	15.5	1.6

TABLE 29.1 Prevalence (%) and Standard Errors (SE) of Overweight in American Children and Adolescents 2-19 years of Age in National Surveys Between the 1960s and 1999 to 2000

Overweight is defined as a BMI-for-age and sex at or above the 95th percentile of the 2000 Centers for Disease Control and Prevention growth charts (see chapter 3).

Adapted from Ogden et al. (2002)

Heights of nationwide samples of Dutch boys and girls from the 1860s to 1993 to 1994 are illustrated in figure 29.7. The data are presented as standard deviation scores or z-scores, which were calculated relative to the Dutch national survey of 1980. Negative scores indicate heights below the 1980 data, whereas positive scores indicate heights above the 1980 data. Two broad age groups are represented, one approximating childhood (6 to 10 years of age in girls and 6 to 12 years of age in boys) and the other adolescence (>10 years of age in girls and >12 years of age in boys). The heights of Dutch children have increased considerably over this span of about 135 years, with the major gain occurring between the 1860s and 1950s and a slower gain from the 1950s to 1980. The more recent data suggest that the secular trend continues in the Netherlands, albeit

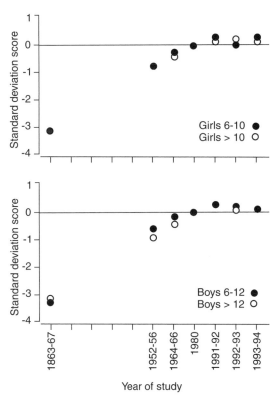

FIGURE 29.7 Secular change in heights of Dutch children from the 1860s through 1994: girls, top; boys, bottom. The data are expressed as standard deviation scores with the 1980 nationwide survey as the reference of comparison (standard deviation score = 0). Data are based on nationwide samples.

Data from Burgmeijer and van Wieringen, 1998.

and data for Norwegian conscripts span 1760 to the 1960s (Tanner 1981; Chamla and Gloor 1986). Data for children, adolescents, and young adults (military conscripts and university students) in other European countries span more variable time periods (Bodzsar and Susanne 1998).

The earliest data indicate that the secular trend towards taller stature began in the early part of the 19th century and continued through most of the 20th century. The positive secular trend was interrupted in some countries by the conditions of World Wars I (1914 to 1918) and II (1939 to 1945), but as conditions improved after the respective wars, growth in height also improved to its secular trajectory before the wars.

at a slower pace. Over the entire time period, the extent of the secular gain in height is about four standard deviations, or about 20 to 30 cm in children and about 30 cm in adolescents (Burgmeijer and van Wieringen 1998).

Considerable data for young adult males are available because of mandatory military conscription in many European countries during the 20th century. Changes in mean heights of conscripts in several western European countries between 1880 and 1980 are shown in table 29.2. On average, young adult height has increased in all countries, but the magnitude of the increase varies considerably, 3.7 cm in Portugal to 15.1 cm in the Netherlands. The north-south gradient in adult height in Europe should also be noted. Young adult males in northern countries tend to be tallest, and heights decrease from north to south.

TABLE 29.2	Average Heights (cm) of Military Conscripts (Young Adult Males)		
Country	1880	1980	Difference
Netherlands	165.2	180.3	15.1
Denmark	167.7	179.8	12.1
Switzerland	163.5	175.5	12.0
Germany (West)	166.5	178.0	11.5
Sweden	168.6	179.1	10.5
Norway	169.3	179.5	10.2
Belgium	165.5	175.3	9.8
Italy	162.8	172.2	9.4
France	165.4	173.8	8.4
Spain	163.7	171.3	7.6
Portugal	163.4	167.1	3.7

Adapted from Chamla (1983).

Perhaps the most complete current conscript data are available for Poland, where four nationally representative samples of 19-year-old males are available between 1965 and 1995 (Bielicki et al. 1997). On the average, height has increased by 6.4 cm over the 30-year interval (see figure 29.8, top), but the estimated rate of secular change has declined gradually: 1965 to 1976, 2.4 cm/decade; 1976 to 1986, 2.1 cm/decade; and 1986 to 1995, 1.8 cm/decade. The data for Polish conscripts show clear social stratification, that is, those from families of better social and educational

circumstances are taller than those from families of lesser means. Nevertheless, the secular trend occurred at about the same estimated rate in all social groups (see figure 29.8, bottom). Similar results are evident in a comparison of the heights of British adults born between the turn of the century (about 1900) and 1958; they attained adulthood, respectively, about the 1920s and the 1980s. Young adult men and women classified as better off (nonmanual working class background) and unskilled (manual working class background) showed similar secular gains in height, although the better-off men and women were, on average, consistently taller by about 2.0 cm and 1.6 cm, respectively (Kuh et al. 1991).

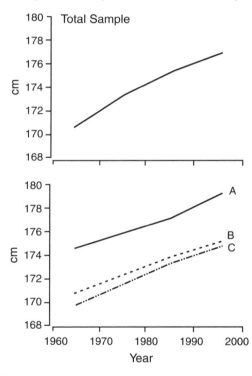

Heights of 19-yr old Polish Conscripts

FIGURE 29.8 Secular change in the heights of Polish conscripts 19 years of age from 1965 through 1995: top, total sample in four surveys; bottom, sample stratified by social background: A = conscripts from largest cities with both parents having a college education, B = conscripts from small towns with their fathers being semiskilled workers and both parents having an elementary education, and C = conscripts from rural areas with their fathers being peasants and both parents having an elementary education.

Data from Bielicki et al., 1997.

Information on body weight for European samples is less extensive. However, increasing data indicate secular change in the BMI, but results for children and adolescents vary among countries (Sorenson and Price 1990; Cernerud 1993; Hulens et al. 2001). Secular changes in mean or median values tend to be rather small; however, they are more apparent at the higher percentiles (e.g., 75th, 85th, or 95th percentiles). Among Belgian males 12 to 18 years of age, for example, no changes occurred in the median BMI between surveys in 1969 to 1974 and 1990 to 1993. However, increases in the 85th percentile over the 20-year interval ranged from 0.5 to 1.3 kg/m^2, and those in the 95th percentile ranged from 0.9 to 1.9 kg/m^2. Corresponding data for Belgian females 12 to 18 years of age indicate a small increase in the median BMI between surveys in 1979 to 1980 and 1990 to 1993, but the increases in the 85th and 95th percentiles of the BMI over this relatively short interval were greater than corresponding increases in boys over a 20-year interval. Increases in the 85th percentile ranged from 1.0 to 2.2 kg/m^2, and those in the 95th percentile ranged from 1.1 to 2.7 kg/m^2 (Hulens et al. 2001). The results thus indicate an increase in the prevalence of overweight/obesity without corresponding increases in the median BMI over the last 2 decades.

Japan

Japan has a history of annual surveys of the heights and weights of school children, the School Health Surveys conducted by the Ministry of Education. The surveys have been conducted every year since 1900 with the exception of the years of World War II (Takaishi 1995). The children are measured at a specific time of the school year, so the data are comparable from year to year. The available height and weight data provide a valuable resource to examine secular change in Japan in successive cross-sectional samples of school children.

Mean heights of Japanese children at selected ages from 1900 through 1990 are illustrated in figure 29.9. Secular changes in height before World War II (1940 to 1945) are rather small, but during the war and immediately after the war, the growth status of Japanese school children deteriorated (negative secular trend). Conditions of the war years appear to have affected the growth status of adolescents (10 to 12 years of age in girls and 12 to 14 years of age in boys)

of both sexes more than younger children and older adolescents. After the war years, heights of Japanese children show a major secular increase in all age groups, but the slope of the increase is greater in adolescents than in younger children and older adolescents. The rapid secular increase after the war years probably reflected improved health and living conditions. The data for Japanese children suggest that the secular trend has slowed in the 1980s and 1990s, with further small gains expected to the year 2000 (Takaishi 1994a, 1994b). Data for the 2000 School Health Survey are not available at present.

Secular changes in the weights of Japanese school children have not been systematically analyzed in a manner similar to analyses of height.

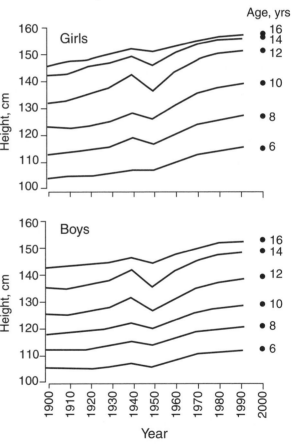

FIGURE 29.9 Secular change in the heights of Japanese children and adolescents 6 to 16 years of age from 1900 through 1990: top, girls; bottom, boys. The points for 2000 are projections.

Data from Takaishi, 1994a and 1995.

Overweight and obesity in many Japanese studies is viewed as relative weight, which is the individual's body weight divided by the standard weight at each age. Obesity is defined as a relative weight greater than 120%, that is, the individual's weight is 20% more than expected for the individual's age. Some data for Japan indicate a negligible change in the prevalence of obese children 6 to 11 years of age from 1979 to about 1985 (6% to 7%), after which the prevalence of obesity in children 6 to 11 years of age increased (about 12% in boys and 9% in girls in 1990). Among youth 12 to 14 years of age, the prevalence of obesity increased in the late 1980s in boys (from 6% in 1985 to about 9% in 1990) but not in girls (about 8% from 1979 to 1990) (Shira et al. 1990; Saito et al. 1990). In a survey of young adults 18 to 19 years of age, the prevalence of obesity (BMI >27.2 kg/m² in males and >24.5 kg/m² in females) was about 5% (Yanai et al. 1997).

Secular Trends in Body Proportions

Although the suggestion has been made that secular increases in stature and other body dimensions are proportional (Tanner 1962), evidence indicates a tendency towards a larger secular increase in absolute and relative leg length. For example, in an analysis of secular change in urban American Black children between 1890 and 1968, Moore (1970) noted minor differences in sitting height but a secular increase in estimated leg length. The differences, however, were not large and were not entirely consistent across the age groups compared. Himes (1979) compared the sitting height and standing height of Milwaukee children in 1880 with a national sample of children in the 1960s and noted that American White children in the 1960s tended to have slightly longer legs relative to stature. The differences were most apparent during adolescence when more recent children had slightly smaller sitting heights per unit stature, which would imply relatively longer legs.

Corresponding observations have been reported for Japanese children. Tanner et al. (1982) mathematically fitted growth curves to the statures, sitting heights, and estimated leg lengths of large cross-sectional samples of Japanese children measured in 1957 and 1977 (see table 29.3). The significant gain in stature over the 20-year period was almost entirely the result of an increase in leg

length. Ali et al. (2000) have extended these observations in an analysis of the relative leg length of Japanese children between 1949 and 1997. Although recent samples of Japanese children have relatively longer legs than earlier samples, changes in the relative leg length of recent samples of Japanese boys and girls are small compared with those observed before the 1970s.

TABLE 29.3 Differences in Estimated Young Adult Height, Sitting Height, and Estimated Leg Length Between Japanese Children Surveyed in 1957 and 1977

	Stature	Sitting height	Leg length
Males	4.3	0.5	3.8
Females	2.7	−0.1	2.8

Secular change: Differences between 1957 and 1977 (cm)

Leg length was estimated as stature minus sitting height.
Adapted from Tanner et al. (1982).

Thus, a significant portion of the secular increase in standing height appears to be accounted for by leg length. The data are limited primarily to Japanese samples, so the issue needs further study in different samples.

Secular Trends in Indicators of Maturity

Stature differences between children of different generations reflect, in part, maturity-associated variation. Children in Europe, North America, and Japan also experienced an accelerated rate of maturation, which is best illustrated in the decline in the age at menarche.

Age at Menarche

The mean age at menarche in European populations has declined by about 0.3 year/decade between 1880 and 1960 (Tanner 1968). Estimates of mean ages at menarche in the mid-19th century varied between 16 and 17 years, although the reliability of the early data has been questioned. Reanalysis of the method of reporting age at menarche in Norwegian data has led to the conclusion that age at menarche was rather stable from 1820 to about 1910 to 1920, 16 years of age in the lower social strata and 14 years of age in the higher social strata. Subsequently, age at menarche declined to about 13.3 years of age in the early 1950s and has been at this level through the mid-1980s (Brundtland and Walloe 1976; Leistol and Rosenberg 1995). An analysis of data for Danish women indicates a continuous decline in age at menarche from the 1930s (about 14.3 years) through the 1980s (13.2 years) (Olesen et al. 2000).

Mean ages at menarche in the United States have declined from about 14.7 years in the 1870s to about 14.0 years at the turn of the century to 12.8 years in the 1950s (Wyshak and Frisch 1982). The estimated age at menarche in a nationally representative sample of American girls in the 1960s (NHES II/III, 1963 to 1970) was also 12.8 years in the total sample, but ethnic-specific estimates were 12.8 years in White girls and 12.5 years in Black girls (MacMahon 1973). The median age at menarche in the most recent national sample, NHANES III 1988 to 1994, is 12.4 years for the total sample. Ethnic-specific median ages are 12.6 in White girls, 12.1 in Black girls, and 12.3 in Mexican American girls (Chumlea et al. 2003). As noted earlier, NHANES III oversampled American Blacks and Mexican Americans, which may influence the estimate for the total sample. Nevertheless, the data suggest a secular decline of about 0.2 to 0.4 years in the median age at menarche in national samples of American girls as a group and in each ethnic group over the past 25 to 30 years.

Corresponding data for Japan based on cohort studies of girls born between 1878 to 1887 and 1985, a span of about 103 years, are shown in figure 29.10. The earliest cohort would have attained menarche around the turn of the century (1900), and the most recent sample would have attained menarche in the late 1990s. The trend suggests a gradual decline from a mean age at menarche a bit over 16.0 years in girls born near the end of the 19th and the beginning of the 20th century to about 15.0 years in girls born around 1930. Mean ages at menarche for girls born in the early 1930s are variable and show little change. These girls would have attained menarche during the hardship years of World War II. Subsequently, mean ages at menarche decline more sharply from about 15.0 to about 13.0 years among those born after World War II (1945) through the early 1950s. Age at menarche, on average, has since

declined more gradually in girls born in the late 1950s through the 1960s and 1970s to about 12.3 to 12.5 years. Data for the most recent samples of girls born in 1980 and 1985 indicate a mean age at menarche of 12.2 years (Moriyama et al. 1980; Tsuzaki et al. 1989; Noda and Nishiyama 2000). The data for Japanese girls thus suggest a slowing or cessation of the secular trend towards earlier menarche.

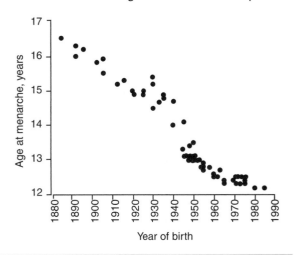

Secular Trend in Age at Menarche in Japan

FIGURE 29.10   Secular trend in the age at menarche of cohorts of Japanese girls born between 1878 to 1887 and 1985. The earliest sample of girls would have attained menarche in the 1890s, and the most recent sample would have attained menarche in the late 1990s.

Data from Noda and Nishiyama, 2000.

The trend towards an earlier age at menarche has slowed or stopped in several other countries. The secular trend to an earlier age at menarche began to cease in several prospective samples of American White girls at about 12.8 years in the 1940s and 1950s, and the median age at menarche was the same in a national sample of American White girls in the 1960s. Changes since the 1960s have been small though the mid-1990s, about 0.2 year in American White girls and about 0.4 year in American Black girls. In the two national surveys of Dutch girls in 1965 and 1985, the median age at menarche declined by only 0.1 year, 13.4 and 13.3 years, respectively (Roede and van Wieringen 1985). The secular decline in the age at menarche has also halted or slowed between the 1950s and 1970s in several European populations (college samples in the United Kingdom and girls in Oslo, London, Gorlitz [former German Democratic Republic], Szeged [Hungary], Zagreb [Croatia], and Brussels [Belgium]) but continues in others (see Danker-Hopfe 1986; Bodzsar and Susanne 1998). Of course, variation occurs within specific countries, and some areas of countries in Eastern Europe have shown a reversal of the trend towards earlier menarche associated with political, social, and economic changes that accompanied the collapse of the Soviet/Communist Bloc.

These recent trends for Eastern Europe are clearly apparent in the data for Poland. Data for Polish girls surveyed between 1955 and 1988 illustrate both social gradients and secular changes in age at menarche in large samples of girls from cities, towns, and villages (see table 29.4). The cities include Warsaw, the national capital, and two others with populations over 600,000. The towns are local administrative centers with a population of about 10,000. The villages are rural communities with smaller populations. In Poland, this division among cities, towns, and rural areas reflects, to a large extent, educational and economic stratification and corresponding variation in the distribution of resources. Mean ages at menarche are earliest in girls from cities, followed by girls from towns and then those from villages in each of the four surveys. Mean ages at menarche have declined from 1955 through 1978 in girls from the three areas. The secular decline was a bit more marked in urban girls from 1955 to 1966 (0.51 year) than in girls from towns and villages (0.36 and 0.33 year, respectively). Between 1966 and 1978, however, the secular decline was more marked in girls from towns and villages (0.43 and 0.48 year, respectively) than in urban girls (0.06 year). Subsequently, mean ages at menarche increased from 1978 to 1988, more so in girls from towns (0.25 year) and least among girls from villages (0.06 year). Similar trends are also evident in more local studies throughout Poland (Laska-Mierzejewska and Luczak 1993; Hulanicka et al. 1994). The recent increase in ages at menarche (negative secular change) was probably related to political, social, and economic changes associated with the collapse of the Soviet/Communist Bloc countries (Bielicki 1999; Bielicki and Hulanicka 1998). Given the agricultural base of villages, better access to nutritional resources likely alleviated the impact of these changes in rural girls in contrast to those in the towns and cities. The data also indicate greater sensitivity of menarche to

TABLE 29.4	Secular Changes in Mean Age at Menarche in Poland: Variation by Area of Residence		
Year of survey	Cities	Towns	Villages
1955	13.41	13.94	14.28
1966	12.90	13.58	13.95
1978	12.84	13.15	13.47
1988	12.96	13.40	13.53

The cities included the capital Warsaw and the two largest cities with a population greater than 600,000. The towns included four administrative centers with a population of about 10,000. The villages were smaller, rural communities within the administrative districts.
Adapted from Bielicki and Hulanicka (1998).

environmental constraints near the time of occurrence of this maturity milestone. This possibility is suggested by the observation that heights of girls and boys in the cities, towns, and villages increased, on average, by about 1 to 2 cm between 1978 and 1988 (Hulanicka et al. 1990).

Some data for university students in the United Kingdom (Dann and Roberts 1973, 1984) also suggest a recent reversal of the trend (i.e., a slight upward trend in age at menarche) based on retrospective data. In the British data, for example, young adults entering university in 1981 had a mean age at menarche of 12.9 years compared with 12.7 years for those entering in 1972 (Dann and Roberts 1984). The slight upward trend was not related to variation in region of origin, number of siblings, birth order, father's occupation, stature, weight, or the ponderal index. Interpretation of this shift is not clear at present. Corresponding observations based on retrospective data for university students in the United States indicate stable mean ages at menarche since the early 1970s: 12.9±1.2 (1970 to 1976), 13.0±1.3 (1982), and 12.9±1.3 (1987 to 1994) years (Malina unpublished data).

A question of interest is whether the secular decline in age at menarche occurs in the total population or in specific parts of the distribution. This question is presented by the data in figure 29.11 for Belgian girls of Flemish ancestry (Wellens et al. 1990). The figure shows mean ages at menarche and the 10th and 90th percentiles. The mean age at menarche appears to have been fairly stable at about 14.3 years among girls born between 1915 and 1934, with the exception of the cohort born between 1925 and 1929. The latter cohort, of course, would have spent their infancy and early childhood in the worldwide economic depression and would have attained menarche near or during World War II. The mean age at menarche then declined to 13.6 and 13.2 years in girls born just before and during World War II, between 1935 to 1939 and 1940 to 1944, respectively. Other than a slight rise in the mean age at menarche to 13.3 years among those born after World War II (1945 to 1949), mean ages at menarche derived from surveys of Belgian girls born between 1943 and 1971 are fairly stable between 13.0 and 13.2 years. Thus, the decline in the average age at menarche in Flemish girls appears to have occurred after World War II (i.e., girls born before and during the war), and that the trend has stopped since the early to middle 1950s. The same trend is also apparent for the 10th percentiles of the distributions of menarcheal ages. The age at which 10% of Flemish girls attain menarche has been fairly stable since the 1950s, varying between 11.5 and 11.8 years. On the other hand, the 90th percentiles of the distributions of menarcheal ages are more variable during this time, fluctuating between 14.0 to 15.1 years. This finding suggests that the secular decline in the age at menarche in Belgium is associated, to a large extent, with a reduction in the number of girls who mature late.

Age at Peak Height Velocity

Longitudinal data are required to estimate the age at peak height velocity (PHV) for individuals, and such data that span a significant period of time are lacking. Data for age at PHV summarized in table 16.1 (page 308) are derived from studies that span approximately 50 years in European samples. In the European longitudinal studies, 25 of the 26 estimated ages at PHV for males are between 13.8 and 14.2 years, and 24 of the 25 estimated ages at PHV for females are between 11.6 and 12.2 years. Data for American White adolescents are less extensive. They are derived from five longitudinal studies that span about 75 years. Estimated ages at PHV among girls range from 11.3 to 11.9 years and among boys range from 13.3 to 14.1 years. Allowing for the different methods used to estimate age at PHV and the uniqueness of longitudinal samples (they are usually small and may not be representative of the population), the data suggest no clear evidence for a secular change in this maturity indicator over the past two generations or so in the major longitudinal studies.

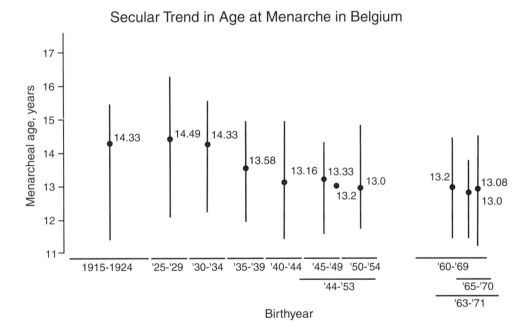

Secular Trend in Age at Menarche in Belgium

FIGURE 29.11 Secular change in mean ages at menarche and the 10th and 90th percentiles in Belgian girls of Flemish ancestry grouped by year of birth.

Adapted, by permission, from R. Wellens et al., 1990, "Age at menarche in Flemish girls: Current status and secular changes in the 20th century," *Annals of Human Biology* 17: 145-152.

In contrast to data for Europe and the United States, the annual School Health Surveys conducted in Japan include a longitudinal component. Because the surveys were carried out annually and because population mobility in Japan is not great, the data likely include a longitudinal component. These data have been used to identify birth year cohorts, and ages at maximum growth in height during adolescence have been estimated for different birth cohorts over time (Ali and Ohtsuki 2000). Age at maximum growth was estimated as a **maximum increment age** (MIA), that is, the age at which the maximum increment occurs during the adolescent growth spurt, which is similar to but not identical with the age at PHV. The estimates show a gradual decline in MIA in both sexes from the turn of the century until the onset of World War II (positive trend). During the war and years after the war, MIA increases (negative trend) but then continues to decline through the 1990s (positive trend). The decline in estimated MIA has slowed between 1960 and 1990, suggesting that the trend towards earlier maturation in Japan may be nearing its end. As noted earlier, PHV occurs somewhat earlier, on average, in Japanese compared with European and American adolescents (see table 25.6, page 571).

Similar analyses have been done with school survey data from the Peoples Republic of China and Taiwan, Republic of China. The trends indicate a secular decline in estimated ages at maximum growth in height during adolescence from the 1964 to 1988 in Taiwan (Huang and Malina 1995) and from the 1950s to 1985 in the Peoples Republic of China (Ohsawa and Ji 1993; Ji et al. 1995).

Other Secondary Sex Characteristics

Secular data dealing with breast, genital, and pubic hair development are not widely available. The data are confounded in part by variation in assessing stages of each characteristic (interobserver and intraobserver variability in assessments is rarely reported, self-assessment), lack of standardization of criteria, and variation in methods of estimating ages at attaining each stage or on being in a stage (see chapter 15). Comparison of data for American girls and boys in two national surveys, a survey in a pediatric-based research network and two local studies between 1969 and 1974 and the mid-1990s indicates no clear evidence for earlier onset of puberty and

for ages at attaining later stages of secondary sex characteristics (Lee et al. 2001). This finding is generally consistent with the menarche data for American girls discussed earlier.

Secular Trends in Performance

Relationships among size, physique, body composition, maturity, and physical performance have been discussed in earlier chapters. Given the established associations, secular changes in size and maturity have implications for performance.

Strength

Secular comparisons of muscular strength must be tempered with care because of variation in type and calibration of dynamometer used. Data for Belgian children between the 1830s and 1971, American children between 1899 and 1964, and Japanese children between 1923 and 1969 indicate secular increases in height and grip strength. Although some variation is present when mean grip strength is plotted relative to mean height, the secular gain in strength is generally proportional to the change in height. The data for American children indicate a similar trend for gains in strength and body weight, that is, secular gains in strength are proportional to gains in body weight (Malina 1978).

The Japanese data also include a measure of back strength in samples measured in 1929 and 1969. Over the 40-year interval, the more recent sample was systematically taller. However, back strength did not differ between girls in 1929 and 1969 and was greater in the more recent sample of boys only in later adolescence. When plotted relative to height, the more recent sample of Japanese children and adolescents had less back strength for height compared with the earlier sample (Ikai and Fukunaga 1975). Note, however, that back strength is a more difficult measure to obtain than grip strength and may be influenced by variation in technique. Motivation is an additional problem in obtaining maximal efforts on strength tests.

Body size and strength of 13-year-old California adolescents in 1934 to 1935 and in 1958 to 1959 are compared in table 29.5. The data are unique in that the more recent sample was enrolled in the same school as the initial sample, which was part of the California adolescent studies (see chapter

1, see also Espenschade 1940; Jones 1949). Both samples were given the same strength and motor performance tests. Although the general socioeconomic status (higher income) and racial composition (more non-White children) of the community changed over the 24-year period, the general make-up of the earlier and more recent samples was reasonably similar (Jones 1960). Data for non-White children were deleted for comparison because the initial sample was entirely White (Espenschade and Meleney 1961). Allowing for these caveats, the more recent sample of 13-year-old boys and girls is taller and heavier. The more recent sample of boys is also stronger in grip strength and pull strength, whereas no difference is seen in push strength. The differences in strength are related to body size. When mean strength scores are ex-pressed per unit mean height or mean weight, the results are virtually identical except for push strength. Among girls, on the other hand, only pull strength is greater in the more recent sample. Grip strength shows only a slight difference, whereas push strength is less in the more recent girls. Strength per unit height is reasonably similar in the two samples, but strength per unit weight is less in the more recent girls with the exception of pull strength.

A more recent comparison of the strength of Danish children over a 25-year period between 1956 and 1981 indicates consistently lower strength scores in the more recent sample (see table 29.6). The data are presented for children of the same height (150 cm) in 1956 and 1981. Hence, for the same body size, Danish boys and girls in 1981 are not as strong as their peers in 1956.

TABLE 29.5 Body Size and Strength of 13-Year-Old California Boys and Girls

	Boys (spring)			Girls (fall)		
	1935 Mean	1959 Mean	Difference	1934 Mean	1958 Mean	Difference
Height (cm)	158.0	163.6	5.6	156.2	158.5	2.3
Weight (kg)	46.3	51.0	4.7	47.7	50.4	2.7
Grip (kg)	33.4	35.6	2.2	27.7	27.4	−0.3
Push (kg)	30.5	30.7	0.2	28.8	26.2	−2.6
Pull (kg)	25.7	28.7	3.0	19.2	21.5	2.3

Adapted from Espenschade and Meleney (1961).

TABLE 29.6 Strength of Different Muscle Groups (kg) Calculated for a Stature of 150 cm in Danish Children

Strength test (kg)	Boys			Girls		
	1956	1981	% Change	1956	1981	% Change
Back	48.3	45.4	−6	41.6	36.5	−12
Abdominal	35.2	35.9	2	30.1	26.8	−11
Hand grip	26.7	23.3	−13	24.8	23.7	−5
Arm pull, horizontal	26.2	24.4	−7	22.2	21.5	−3
Arm push, horizontal	18.9	16.5	−12	16.7	14.6	−13
Arm pull, down	28.5	26.3	−7	26.0	25.1	−3
Leg extension, one leg	147.0	126.5	−14	135.4	117.2	−13
Leg extenstion, both legs	260.4	236.7	−9	241.8	205.3	−15

Adapted from Heeboll-Nielsen (1982). Minus signs indicate a relative decrease in strength over time.

Motor Performance

Motor performance is somewhat more difficult to evaluate over time, as tests and conditions of testing are variable. One of the few test items that is reasonably consistent in test batteries over time and whose testing protocol is generally described in a standard manner is the standing long jump. Mean performances of American boys and girls 11 to 15 years of age on the standing long jump between the mid-1920s and the mid-1980s are summarized in figure 29.12. The data for the mid-1920s are for school children from New York City, New Jersey, Philadelphia, Chicago, Ohio, and California (Bliss 1927). The data for 1958 through 1985 are from national surveys of the physical fitness of school children in the United States (Hunsicker and Reiff 1966, 1977;

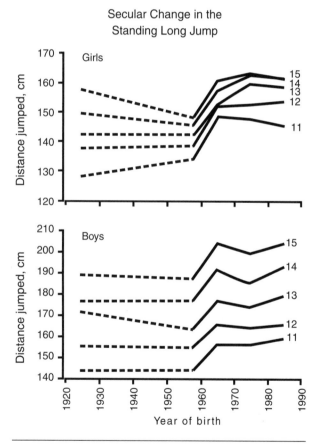

Secular Change in the Standing Long Jump

FIGURE 29.12   Secular change in the standing long jump performance of American youth 11 to 15 years of age from the mid-1920s to 1958, and 1958 through 1985: girls, top; boys, bottom.

Drawn from the data of Bliss (1927) for the mid-1920s and the data of Hunsicker and Reiff (1966, 1977) and Reiff et al. (1986) for 1958 to 1985.

Reiff et al. 1986). The data indicate little evidence of secular improvement in jumping performance between the mid-1920s and 1958, but from 1958 to 1965, performance improved in all ages groups. Since 1965, jumping performance of American children has changed little. The major improvement in performance from 1958 to 1965 reflected national emphasis on the physical fitness of American youth and fitness testing in schools. As a result, many school physical education programs routinely permitted children to practice the fitness tests, including the standing long jump. Hence, the improvement in performance from 1958 to 1965 reflects in part practice or test effects. After 1965, this national emphasis on the performance aspects of physical fitness declined (Malina 1991).

Heights and weights of the early and more recent samples of American youth are not available to evaluate the relationship between secular changes in size and performance between the 1920s and 1960s. However, secular data for Czechoslovak boys 11 to 15 years of age over approximately the same interval, 1923 and 1969 to 1970, provide insights into the relationship between secular changes in size and jumping performance. The boys showed significant secular gains in height, weight, and standing long jump performance over this interval of about 50 years (Malina 1978). Mean jumping performances of the boys are plotted relative to their mean heights and weights at each age from 11 to 15 years in figure 29.13. Apparently, the secular improvement in performance is largely a function of the secular increase in body size. More recent data from the former Czechoslovakia indicate a continued secular increase in height, weight, and standing long jump performance from 1966 to 1987 in 11-year-old to 15-year-old children (Mekota 1990). Given the manner of reporting, however, relating the secular increments in jumping performance and body size between 1966 and 1987 was not possible.

Secular data for other performance tasks are more variable. Among Japanese children measured (height) and tested in 1929 (standing long jump), 1935 (100-meter dash for boys) and 1939 (50-meter dash for girls) and in 1969 (same tests), only body size showed positive secular changes. Boys and girls in 1969 did not perform in the standing long jump as well as their predecessors in 1929, and virtually no differences were seen in performances on the dashes between 1935/ 1939 and 1969 (Ikai and Fukunaga 1975; see also

Jumping Performance

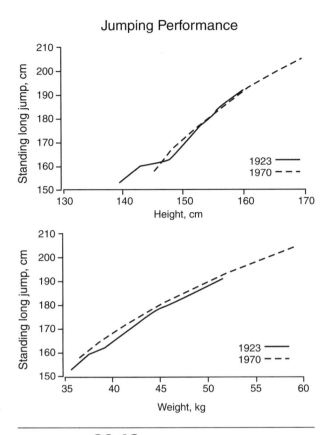

FIGURE 29.13 Standing long jump performance relative to height (top) and weight (bottom) of Czechoslovak boys 11to 15 years of age in 1923 and 1970.

Data from Roubal and Roubal, 1925, and Jurinova, 1974.

Malina 1978). Thus, relative to height, Japanese boys and girls in 1929 to 1939 performed better on these two motor tasks than Japanese boys and girls in 1969. Conversely, the more recent samples did not perform as well for their body size.

Data for children in southwestern Poland (upper Silesia) include height and several performance items measured in surveys at 10-year intervals between 1965 and 1995 (Raczek 2002). Height increased systematically from one survey to the other. The same was not true for performance tasks. With the data for 1965 as the reference, performances in strength and endurance tasks declined in each 10-year survey so that values for the 1995 survey were lowest compared with 1965. Declines in strength and endurance were most marked after 12 to 14 years of age in both sexes. On the other hand, running speed did not change appreciably between 1965 and 1985 but was especially poorer in 1995. In contrast, agility did not change appreciably among the four sur-

veys. The results for Polish children thus indicate negative secular changes in several performance tasks, whereas height showed positive secular changes over the same interval.

Aerobic Power

Data for maximal aerobic power ($\dot{V}O_2$max) of American boys span the period from the late 1930s to 2000, whereas those for American girls are available only from the 1960s. The data are limited because most studies are based on rather small sample sizes that are often combined across several age categories. Overweight children are not likely to be included in studies requiring maximal exercise tests such as required to derive $\dot{V}O_2$max. Data are derived from both the treadmill and cycle ergometer protocols. The available data for the cycle were adjusted to account for differences in estimates between the treadmill and cycle ergometer (see chapter 12). Allowing for these limitations, the data provide some insights into secular changes in maximal aerobic power (Eisenmann and Malina, 2002). The regression line for absolute aerobic power ($\dot{V}O_2$max [L/min]) in boys 6 to 12 years of age is flat over time from the late 1930s to 2000, but the corresponding regression lines for older boys 13 to 18 years of age suggest an increase over time, although data for older boys are not as extensive as for young boys. The regression line for $\dot{V}O_2$max (L/min) is stable from the 1970s in girls 6 to 11 years of age and from the 1960s in girls 12 to 14 years of age. However, among older girls 15 to 18 years of age, the regression line for $\dot{V}O_2$max (L/min) is curvilinear, suggesting an increase from the early 1960s to the late 1970s and then a decline into the late 1990s.

When $\dot{V}O_2$max is expressed per unit body weight (ml/kg/min), thus accommodating secular change in body mass, the regression lines indicate fairly stable levels of relative aerobic power between 1938 and the present in boys 6 to 12 and 16 to 18 years of age. Although the trend is rather stable over time in 13-year-old to 15-year-old boys, values for relative aerobic power are more variable, perhaps reflecting variation in the timing and intensity of the adolescent growth spurt. The corresponding trends for relative aerobic power in girls are similar to those for absolute values. The regression lines are rather stable in girls 6 to 11 and 12 to 14 years of age, and indicate a curvilinear trend in girls 15 to 18 years of age.

Allowing for secular increases in body weight, the data for absolute $\dot{V}O_2max$ suggest positive secular trends in the aerobic power of American boys since the late 1930s and a lack of change in girls 6 to 14 years of age since the 1960s. The available data for older adolescent girls 15 to 18 years of age suggest an increase in relative aerobic power from the early 1960s to the late 1970s and then a decline. However, relative $\dot{V}O_2max$ in late adolescent girls in the 1990s is similar to that for girls in the early 1960s. The trend in late adolescent girls should be interpreted with caution. As noted earlier, sampling variation is an important consideration in aerobic testing and secular trend research. If the earliest data for the 1960s are not considered, the trend for late adolescent girls indicates rather stable levels of maximal aerobic power until the recent decline.

Is There an Optimal Size for Performance?

Evidence suggests that secular improvements in several performance tasks are, to a large extent, proportional to secular gains in body size. Two questions of interest regarding secular change and performance can be raised. First, does an optimal body size at which the best levels of performance are attained by children and adolescents exist? Second, if an optimal size exists, has this size changed over time?

Welon (1979) addressed this question in boys 10 to 18 years of age using height, weight, and three motor tests requiring power and speed: 60-meter dash, a high jump, and a ball throw for distance. Optimal size was defined as the height and weight at which best performances were attained. Age for age from 10 to 18 years, the heights and weights at which best performances were attained were taller and heavier than the average heights and weights for each age group. The optimal heights and weights were rather similar for the run and jump; however, they were larger for the distance throw, especially between 10 and 14 years of age, which emphasizes the role of absolute body size in performance of this task. At the older ages, optimal heights did not differ much among the three performance tasks, whereas the optimal weight for throwing was slightly greater. The results thus suggest the hypothesis that some heights and weights are optimal for the performances of adolescent boys in running, jumping, and throwing tasks.

Welon et al. (1981) subsequently considered the stability of optimal sizes for performance

over time in Polish adolescent boys 17 years of age in 1951, 1966, and 1978 (see figure 29.14). The optimal size for performance in three power tasks (high jump, long jump, and ball throw) increased in the same magnitude as the secular increase in mean height and weight from 1951 to 1966. From 1966 to 1978, however, the optimal size for performance remained stable, whereas mean height and weight continued to increase. These observations would seem to suggest that optimal sizes for performance in these power tasks are more related to functional requirements of the tasks without regard to body size. In contrast to the observations for 17-year-old males, the increase in optimal size for performance in the same tasks in 14-year-old boys from 1951 to 1966 was considerably greater than the secular increase in mean height and weight (Welon 1979). Unfortunately, more recent data for 14-year-old boys were not available.

The differences in secular gains in the optimal size for performance and in mean body size in 14-year-old and 17-year-old males from 1951 to 1966 may reflect maturity-associated variation during male adolescence. At 14 years of age, the optimal size may represent early-maturing boys, who are larger in size and tend to be better performers than their age peers. However, at 17 years of age,

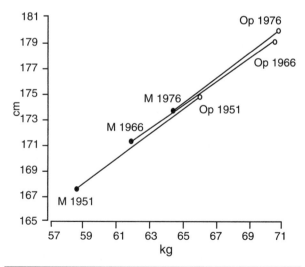

Secular Change in Body Size and Optimal Size for Performance

FIGURE 29.14   Changes in mean (M) stature and weight, and in optimal (Op) stature and weight for motor performance in 17-year-old Polish boys in 1951, 1966, and 1978.

Data from Welon, 1979, and Welon et al., 1981.

the size and performance differences, especially in power, between early-maturing, average-maturing, and late-maturing boys are reduced (see chapter 17).

The observations of Welon and colleagues (Welon 1979; Welon et al. 1981) permit a functional interpretation of secular changes in body size. However, they need to be extended to other samples, including girls.

Secular Trends in Developing Countries

Data on long-term secular trends in developing areas of the world are not as extensive compared with the relative wealth of information for Europe, the United States, and Japan. In contrast to developed countries, the available data for developing countries are variable. Within the same countries, positive secular trends are present in some segments of society but at the same time are absent or negative in other segments of society.

Secular increases in stature and reductions in age at menarche are most often limited to children from better-off socioeconomic circumstances in developing countries, although trends vary among countries. Short-term observations on high socioeconomic status children of Guatemalan, European, and mixed Guatemalan-European ancestry indicate no secular differences in stature and skeletal maturation in two cohorts, one born between 1945 and 1955 and the other born between 1956 and 1965 (Bogin and MacVean 1982). These results are consistent with similar data for other samples of well-off children in whom the secular trend has apparently stopped. In Mexico, on the other hand, public school children in Mexico City in the 1920s are consistently shorter and lighter than well-off children in the 1970s (Ramos Galvan 1978). More recent samples of Mexican school children from Sonora, Veracruz, and Mexico City in the 1990s are as tall as the well-off children of the 1970s, indicating a reduction of social class variation in the country, but tend to be heavier (Siegel 1999; Pena Reyes et al. 2002).

Evidence from Venezuela (Farid-Coupal et al. 1981; Lopez de Blanco et al. 1988; Lopez Contreras-Blanco et al. 1988), Chile (Rona 1975), Argentina (Lejarraga 1986), Peru (Gonzales et al. 1982, 1984), and Brazil (Castilho and Lahr 2001) indicates positive secular changes in height and age at menarche across social classes. More comprehensive data for Venezuela indicate secular increases in height in all social classes and in both urban and rural children between 1948 and 1983 (Lopez de Blanco et al. 1988) and a continued secular increase in children of Carabobo between 1978 and 1987 (Lopez Contreras-Blanco et al. 1988). Secular increases in stature in Venezuela are accompanied by corresponding secular declines in the age at menarche. Across all social classes, mean age at menarche declined from about 14.4 years in the mid-1930s to about 12.7 years in 1969, followed by a decline to about 12.5 years in 1981. Among girls in high social strata, mean age at menarche declined from about 14.5 years in the mid-1930s to 12.6 years in 1957, followed by a decline to 12.3 years in 1981. The secular decline in the age at menarche was considerably less in urban girls from the lowest social strata and in rural girls between 1940 and about 1980 (Lopez de Blanco et al. 1988).

Secular trends towards larger size and earlier maturation are not universal. Little or no secular increase in childhood and adult stature has occurred in some populations of developing or underdeveloped areas of Asia, Africa, and Latin America (Tobias 1985; Malina 1990). For example, no secular change occurred over about 2 decades in the 1960s and 1970s in nonagrarian, semiurban indigenous children living in Guatemala (Bogin and MacVean 1984). Rural indigenous Amerindian (Zapotec) school children in a rural community in Oaxaca in southern Mexico showed no change in height and weight between 1968 and 1978 (Malina et al. 1980). However, a major secular increase in height and weight has since occurred between 1978 and 2000 (Malina and Peña Reyes 2002). Age at menarche has also declined, on average, in girls from this rural community, 14.7 years in 1978 (Malina et al. 1983) to about 13.0 years in 2001 to 2002 (Malina, unpublished).

Populations in parts of Africa, India, and South America have experienced a negative secular trend (i.e., reduction in stature). Between 1920 and 1960, for example, the adult male population of Chile experienced a decline in height of about 5.5 cm. Over the same interval, military conscripts in Chile experienced a decline of about 1.5 cm (Kenntner 1968). The difference between the general population and recruits is probably related to selection criteria for the military. On the other hand, age at menarche in Chilean girls has declined (i.e., a positive secular trend) by more than 1 year from the 1930s to 1970 (Rona 1975). As noted earlier, size and maturity may react independently to environmental stresses. Nevertheless, these divergent trends in Chile need further examination.

In addition to an absence of secular trends, Tobias (1985) has described negative trends in adult statures of several African populations in the 20th century, and Ganguly (1979) has described similar negative trends in adult stature in a survey of 60 Indian population groups. In the survey of adult heights in India, 43 out of 60 population groups showed a decrease in stature since the late 19th century or early 20th century. The intervals between surveys of the same populations varied from 29 to 68 years (about one to two generations). Overall, the data suggest a gradual decrease in adult height in India of about 1.0 cm from the 1880s through the 1960s.

In contrast to long-term trends, other more acute factors may be involved in short-term observations in developing countries. For example, a reversal in age at menarche in Bangladesh was attributed to severe undernutrition associated with war, postwar inflation of prices, floods, and famine between 1971 and 1976 (Alauddin Chowdhury et al. 1977). This reversal is similar to the reversals described earlier in the chapter for girls in Poland and the former Yugoslavia in association, respectively, with the transition from a Communist regime to a western-style republic and with war conditions in the 1990s.

Factors Underlying Secular Trends

Many reasons have been postulated for the secular trends towards larger body size and earlier maturity (Meredith 1963, 1976; Tanner 1966, 1968, 1981, 1992; Malina 1979; Bielicki 1986; van Wieringen 1986). Nevertheless, the underlying causes are not known with certainty. A reasonable assumption is that many interrelated factors are involved, including the elimination of growth-inhibiting factors. Improved environmental quality and nutritional circumstances are most often offered as the major contributors to larger body size and earlier maturity.

Improved conditions of public health as reflected in the marked reduction in infant and childhood mortality and morbidity during the 19th and 20th centuries are primary contributors to the observed positive secular trends (Malina 1979). More recently, the suggestion has been made that reduction in the transmission of microbes associated with infections (i.e., pathogenic microorganisms), particularly during infancy and early childhood, is the critical factor underlying the secular trend in height (Beard and Blaser 2002). Indeed, many epidemic and endemic diseases were eliminated or their incidence was greatly reduced as conditions conducive to the maintenance and spread of disease in a population were brought into check. For example, the reduction in waterborne and foodborne diseases was facilitated by safer water and food supplies. As socioeconomic circumstances improved, crowded living conditions and, in turn, the risk for transmitting infections were also reduced. Most infectious and parasitic diseases take their tolls in infancy and childhood. With a reduced incidence of such diseases during infancy and early childhood, a larger proportion of these children not only survive but also probably experience fewer insults that have the potential to drain their energy and nutrient reserves. As a result, more children are likely to approximate their genetic potentials for growth and maturation.

Improved nutrition associated with beneficial changes in public health is another primary contributor to positive secular changes. A regularly available food supply in conjunction with reduced infectious and parasitic disease loads probably worked synergistically in contributing to positive secular trends. A major factor was a regularly available supply of energy and associated nutrients to support growth, maturation, and physical activity. With a reduced infectious disease load, energy and nutrients that would be diverted to ward off infection would then be available to support the cellular processes of growth and maturation. A regular supply of energy would also be essential to support physical activity, especially in the context of work. Energy consumed as food eventually is converted to work output that contributes to the growth of the economy and, in turn, to the economic well-being of families in the form of regular jobs and income. Presumably, these favorable economic circumstances were translated into improved living conditions and associated health and nutritional benefits for growing and maturing infants, children, and adolescents.

Genetic changes in the population have also been suggested as contributory to positive secular trends in size and maturity. However, secular trends have occurred too rapidly to be accounted for by genetic changes in populations. Genetic changes such as population admixture or increased outbreeding have occurred with increased migration and interclass mobility, but changes in height associated with increased heterozygosity are rather small in the context of the major height changes that characterize secular trends.

The improved health and nutritional conditions that have contributed to positive secular trends in growth and maturation have not occurred or have not been sufficiently adequate in developing countries, or in regions of these countries, to support secular trends in growth and maturation. For example, the persistence of traditional agricultural practices, relatively poor farmland, and limited economic resources for the improvement of agriculture is characteristic of many rural areas in developing countries (Malina et al. 1983). Lifestyles are also changing in some rural areas, resulting in a shift from subsistence farming to cash crops in parts of Latin America or to a "depastoralized" lifestyle in some parts of Africa (Tobias 1985). Crowded living conditions, especially in rapidly growing urban slums, inadequate or marginal nutrition, disease, and associated social stresses persist in many developing countries (see chapters 23 and 25). These conditions have similarities to those that were persistent in Europe in the 18th and 19th centuries, during which little or no secular increase in adult height occurred. Conditions, however, subsequently improved as evidence for positive secular changes were apparent in the second half of the 19th century.

Summary

Secular trends collectively refer to the attainment of larger size and acceleration of maturation over several generations, although changes over shorter intervals are also included. The trends are complex phenomena that reflect the remarkable plasticity of the processes of growth and maturation to the environmental conditions under which children and adolescents are reared. Increases in height and weight during childhood and adolescence, reductions in the age at menarche and ages at attaining other indicators of biological maturity, and increases in adult stature have occurred over several generations in Europe and Japan and in areas of the world largely inhabited by populations of European ancestry (United States, Canada, and Australia). Corresponding trends have occurred to a lesser extent, or have not occurred, in many developing countries. Secular trends in height have stopped in many developed countries, but weight has continued to increase, resulting in a secular increase in overweight/obesity. Secular improvements have occurred in several measures of strength and performance during the last century, and the gains are generally proportional to the size increases. However, some more recent comparisons over shorter time intervals suggest that contemporary children are not as strong as earlier children and that changes in several performance tasks have been minimal.

Sources and Suggested Readings

Alauddin Chowdhury AKM, Huffman SL, Curlin GT (1977) Malnutrition, menarche, and marriage in rural Bangladesh. Social Biology 24:316-325.

Ali MA, Ohtsuki F (2000) Estimation of maximum increment age in height and weight during adolescence and the effect of World War II. American Journal of Human Biology 12:363-370.

Ali MA, Uetake T, Ohtsuki F (2000) Secular changes in relative leg length in post-war Japan. American Journal of Human Biology 12:405-416.

* Beard AS, Blaser MJ (2002) The ecology of height: The effect of microbial transmission on human height. Perspectives in Biology and Medicine 45:475-498.

* Bielicki T (1986) Physical growth as a measure of the economic well-being of populations: The twentieth century. In F Falkner, JM Tanner (eds), Human Growth. Volume 3. Methodology, Ecological, Genetic, and Nutritional Effects of Growth. New York: Plenum, pp 283-305.

* Bielicki T (1999) Secular trends in growth: Human biologists' contribution to the study of social change. In FE Johnston, B Zemel, PB Eveleth (eds), Human Growth in Context. London: Smith-Gordon, pp 303-311.

Bielicki T, Hulanicka B (1998) Secular trend in stature and age at menarche in Poland. In EB Bodzsar, C Susanne (eds), Secular Growth Changes in Europe. Budapest: Eotvos Lorand University Press, pp 263-279.

Bielicki T, Szklarska A, Welon Z, Brajczewski C (1997) Niewrownosci spoleczne w Polsce: Antropologiczne Badania Poborowych w Trzydziestoleciu 1965–1995. Wroclaw, Poland: Polish Academy of Sciences, Institute of Anthropology, Monographs of the Institute of Anthropogy 16 (in Polish).

Bliss JG (1927) A study of progression based on age, sex, and individual differences in strength and skill. American Physical Education Review 32:11-21, 85-89.

Bock RG, Sykes RC (1989) Evidence for continuing secular increase in height within families in the United States. American Journal of Human Biology 1:143-148.

* Bodzsar EB, Susanne C, editors (1998) Secular Growth Changes in Europe. Budapest: Eotvos University Press.

Bogin B, MacVean RB (1982) Ethnic and secular influences on the size and maturity of seven year old children living in Guatemala City. American Journal of Physical Anthropology 59:393-398.

Bogin B, MacVean RB (1984) Growth status of non-agrarian, semi-urban living Indians in Guatemala. Human Biology 56:527-538.

Boyne AW, Aitken FC, Leitch I (1957) Secular change in height and weight of British children, including analysis of measurements of English children in primary schools, 1911-1953. Nutrition Abstracts and Reviews 27:1-18.

Brudevoll JE, Leistol K, Walloe L (1979) Menarcheal age in Oslo during the last 140 years. Annals of Human Biology 6:407-416.

Brundtland GH, Leistol K, Walloe L (1980) Height, weight and menarcheal age of Oslo schoolchildren during the last 60 years. Annals of Human Biology 7:307-322.

Brundtland GH, Walloe L (1976) Menarcheal age in Norway in the 19th century: A re-evaluation of the historical sources. Annals of Human Biology 3:363-374.

Budiansky S (2002) Creatures of our own making. Science 298:80-81, 84-86.

Burgmeijer RJF, van Wieringen JC (1998) Secular changes of growth in the Netherlands. In EB Bodzsar, C Susanne (eds), Secular Growth Changes in Europe. Budapest: Eotvos Lorand University Press, pp 233-262.

Cameron N (1979) The growth of London schoolchildren 1904-1966: An analysis of secular trend and intra-county variation. Annals of Human Biology 6:505-525.

Castilho LV, Lahr MM (2001) Secular trends in growth among urban Brazilian children of European descent. Annals of Human Biology 28:564-574.

Cernerud L (1993) Height and body mass index of seven-year-old Stockholm schoolchildren from 1940 to 1990. Acta Paediatrica 82:304-305.

Chamla M-C (1983) L'evolution de la stature en Europe occidentale entre 1960 et 1980. Hypothese sur les facteurs responsables. Compte Rendu de l'Académie des Sciences de Paris 296 (ser. III):217-220.

Chamla M-C, Gloor P-A (1986) Variations diachroniques depuis trois siecles. Donnees et facteurs responsables.

In D Ferembach, C Susanne, M-C Chamla (eds), L'Homme son Evolution sa Diversite. Paris: Editions du CNRS, pp, 463-490.

Chinn S, Rona RJ, Price CE (1989) The secular trend in height in primary school children in England and Scotland 1972–1979 and 1979–1986. Annals of Human Biology 16:387-395.

Chumlea WC, Schubert CM, Roche AF, Kulin H, Lee PA, Himes JH, Sun SS (2003) Age at menarche and racial comparisons in U.S. girls. Pediatrics 111:110-113.

* Danker-Hopfe H (1986) Menarcheal age in Europe. Yearbook of Physical Anthropology 29:81-112.

Dann TC, Roberts DF (1973) End of the trend? A 12-year study of age at menarche. British Medical Journal 4:265-267.

Dann TC, Roberts DF (1984) Menarcheal age in University of Warwick students. Journal of Biosocial Science 16:511-519.

Eisenmann JC, Malina RM (2002) Secular change in peak oxygen consumption among United States youth in the 20th century. American Journal of Human Biology 14:699-706.

Espenschade A (1940) Motor performance in adolescence, including the study of relationships with measures of physical growth and maturity. Monographs of the Society for Research in Child Development 5, serial no. 24.

Espenschade A, Meleney HE (1961) Motor performance of adolescent boys and girls of today in comparison with those of 24 years ago. Research Quarterly 32:186-189.

Eveleth PB, Tanner JM (1976) Worldwide Variation in Human Growth. Cambridge, UK: Cambridge University Press.

Eveleth PB, Tanner JM (1990) Worldwide Variation in Human Growth, 2nd edition. Cambridge, UK: Cambridge University Press.

Farid-Coupal N, Lopez-Contreras M, Mendez Castellano H (1981) The age at menarche in Carabobo, Venezuela with a note on the secular trend. Annals of Human Biology 8:283-288.

Flegal KM, Carroll MD, Kuczmarski RJ, Johnson CL (1998) Overweight and obesity in the United States: Prevalence and trends, 1960–1994. International Journal of Obesity 22:39-47.

Flegal KM, Carroll MD, Ogden CL, Johnson CL (2002) Prevalence and trends in obesity among US adults, 1999–2000. Journal of the American Medical Association 288:1723-1727.

Ganguly P (1979) Progressive decline in stature in India: Study of 60 population groups. In WA Stini (ed), Physiological and Morphological Adaptation and Evolution. The Hague: Mouton, pp 315-337.

Garn SM, French Y (1967) Magnitude of Secular Trend in Fels Population. Yellow Springs, OH: Fels Research Institute (now Lifespan Health Research Center, Department of Community Health, Wright State University, Kettering, OH).

Gonzales G, Crespo-Retes I, Guerra-Garcia R (1982) Secular change in growth of native children and adolescents at high altitude. I. Puno, Peru (3800 meters). American Journal of Physical Anthropology 58:191-195.

Gonzales GF, Valera J, Rodriguez L, Vega A, Guerra-Garcia R (1984) Secular change in growth of native children and adolescents at high altitude Huancayo, Peru (3280 meters). American Journal of Physical Anthropology 64:47-51.

Gurri FD, Pereira GB, Moran EF (2001) Well-being changes in response to 30 years of regional integration in Mayan populations from Yucatan, Mexico. American Journal of Human Biology 13:590-602.

Hamill PVV, Drizd TA, Johnson CL, Reed RB, Roche AF (1977) NCHS growth curves for children birth–18 years, United States. Vital and Health Statistics, Series 11, No. 165 (U.S. Department of Health, Education, and Welfare, DHEW Publication No. (PHS) 78-1650).

Hamill PVV, Johnston FE, Grams W (1970) Height and weight of children, United States. Vital and Health Statistics, Series 11, No. 104 (U.S. Department of Health, Education, and Welfare, Public Health Service Publication No. 1000-Series 11-Number 104).

Hamill PVV, Johnston FE, Lemeshow S (1973) Height and weight of youths 12–17 years, United States. Vital and Health Statistics, Series 11, No. 124 (U.S. Department of Health, Education, and Welfare, DHEW Publication No. (HSM) 73-1606).

Hauspie RC, Vercauteren M, Susanne C (1997) Secular changes in growth and maturation: An update. Acta Paediatrica 423 (suppl):20-27.

Heeboll-Nielsen K (1982) Muscle strength of boys and girls, 1981 compared to 1956. Scandinavian Journal of Sports Sciences 4:37-43.

Herman-Giddens ME, Slora EJ, Wasserman RC, Bourdony CJ, Bhapkar MV, Koch GG, Hasemeier CM (1997) Secondary sexual characteristics and menses in young girls seen in office practice: A study from the pediatric research in office settings network. Pediatrics 99:505-512.

Himes JH (1979) Secular changes in body proportions and composition. Monographs of the Society for Research in Child Development 44, serial no. 179, pp 28-58.

Huang Y-C, Malina RM (1995) Secular changes in the stature and weight of Taiwanese children, 1964–1988. American Journal of Human Biology 7:485-496.

Hulanicka B, Brajczewski C, Jedlinska W, Slawinska T, Waliszko A (1990) City-Town-Village: Growth of Children in Poland in 1988. Wroclaw, Poland: Polish Academy of Sciences, Institute of Anthropology, Monographs of the Institute of Anthropogy 7.

Hulanicka B, Kolassa E, Waliszko A (1993) Age at menarche of girls as an indicator of the socio-political changes in Poland. Bulletin de la Societe Royale Belge d'Anthropologie et de Prehistoire 104:133-141.

Hulanicka B, Kolassa E, Waliszko A (1994) Dziewczeta a Gornego Slaska. Wroclaw, Poland: Polish Academy of Sciences, Institute of Anthropology, Monographs of the Institute of Anthropogy 11 (in Polish).

Hulens M, Beunen G, Claessens A, Lefevre J, Thomis M, Philippaerts R, Borms J, Vrijens J, Lysens R, Vansant G (2001) Trends in BMI among Belgian children, adolescents and adults from 1969 to 1996. International Journal of Obesity 25:395-399.

Hunsicker PA, Reiff GG (1966) A survey and comparison of youth fitness 1958–1965. Journal of Health, Physical Education and Recreation 37:23-25 (Jan).

Hunsicker PA, Reiff GG (1977) Youth fitness report: 1958–1965–1975. Journal of Physical Education and Recreation 48:31-33 (Jan).

Ikai M, Fukunaga T (1975) Imbalance between growth and physical fitness. In K Asahina, R Shigaya (eds), Physiological Adaptability and Nutritional Status of the Japanese. B. Growth, Work Capacity and Nutrition of Japanese. Tokyo: University of Tokyo Press, pp 26-30.

Jaeger U (1998) Secular trend in Germany. In EB Bodzsar, C Susanne (eds), Secular Growth Changes in Europe. Budapest: Eotvos Lorand University Press, pp 135-159.

Ji C-Y, Ohsawa S, Kasai N (1995) Secular changes in the stature, weight, and age at maximum growth increments of urban Chinese girls from the 1950s to 1985. American Journal of Human Biology 7:474-484.

Jones HE (1949) Motor Performance and Growth. Berkeley: University of California Press.

Jones MC (1960) A comparison of changes in the attitudes and interests of ninth-grade students over two decades. Journal of Educational Psychology 51:175-186.

Jurinova I (1974) Akcelerace motorickych projevu. A. Akceleraci motoriky. In Cesky Ustredni Vybor (ed), Vyvojova Akcelerace a Jeji Dusledky v Telesne Vychove a Sportu. Prague: CSTV, pp 103-114 (in Czech).

Katzmarzyk PT (2002) The Canadian obesity epidemic: An historical perspective. Obesity Research 10:666-674.

Kenntner G (1968) Absolute Unterschiede in der durchschnittlichen Korpergrosse und Veranderungen der durchschnittlichen Korpergrosse der Chilenen. Zeitschrift fur Morphologie und Anthropologie 60:32-52.

Kondo S, Eto M (1975) Physical growth studies on Japanese-American children in comparison with native Japanese. In SM Horvath, S Kondo, H Matsui, H Yoshimura (eds), Comparative Studies on Human Adaptability of Japanese, Caucasians and Japanese Americans. Tokyo: University of Tokyo Press, pp 13-45.

Krogman WM (1948) A handbook of the measurement and interpretation of height and weight in the growing child. Monographs of the Society for Research in Child Development 13, serial no. 48 (published in 1950).

Kuczmarski RJ, Ogden CL, Grummer-Strawn LM, Flegal KM, Guo SS, Wei R, Mei Z, Curtin LR, Roche AF, Johnson CL (2000) CDC Growth Charts: United States. Advance Data from Vital and Health Statistics, No. 314. Hyattsville, MD: National Center for Health Statistics.

Kuh DL, Power C, Rodgers B (1991) Secular trends in social class and sex differences in adult height. International Journal of Epidemiology 20:1001-1009.

Laska-Mierzejewska T, Luczak E (1993) Biologiczne mierniki sytuacji spoleczno ekonomicznej ludnosci wiejskiej w Polsce w latach 1967, 1977, 1987. Wroclaw, Poland: Polish Academy of Sciences, Monographs of the Institute of Anthropology 10.

Lee PA, Guo SS, Kulin HE (2001) Age of puberty: Data from the United States of America. Acta Pathologica, Microbiologica et Immunologica Scandinavica 109:S156-S163.

Leistol K, Rosenberg M (1995) Height, weight and menarcheal age of schoolgirls in Oslo: An update. Annals of Human Biology 22:199-205.

Lejarraga H (1986) Peso y talla de 15,214 adolescentes de todo el pais. Tendencia secular. Archivos Argentinas de Pediatria 84:219-235.

Lenz W, Ort BW (1959) Das Wachstum von Hamburger Schulern in den Jahren 1877 und 1957. Medizinische 47: 2265-2271.

Lopez Contreras-Blanco M, Landaeta-Jimenez MI, Méndez Castellano H (1988) Secular trend in height and weight, Carabobo, Venezuela, 1978–1987. Fifth International Auxology Conference, Exeter University, United Kingdom.

Lopez de Blanco M, Landaeta de Jimenez M, Mendez Castellano H (1988) Como esperamos y queremos que sea en su desarrollo el Venezolano del ano 2000. In Fundacion Cavendes (ed), La Nutricion Ante la Crisis. Carracas, Venezuela: Ediciones Fundacion Cavendes, pp 235-274.

MacMahon B (1973) Age at menarche. Vital and Health Statistics, Series 11, No. 133.

* Malina RM (1978) Secular changes in growth, maturation, and physical performance. Exercise and Sport Sciences Reviews 6:203-255 (published in 1979).

* Malina RM (1979) Secular changes in size and maturity: Causes and effects. Monographs for Research in Child Development 44, serial no. 179, pp 59-102.

Malina RM (1990) Research on secular trends in auxology. Anthropologischer Anzeiger 48:209-227.

Malina RM (1991) Fitness and performance: Adult health and the culture of youth. In RJ Park, HM Eckert (eds), New Possibilities, New Paradigms? American Academy of Physical Education Papers No 24. Champaign, IL: Human Kinetics, pp 30-38.

* Malina RM, Martorell R, Mendoza F (1986) Growth status of Mexican American children and youths: Historical trends and contemporary issues. Yearbook of Physical Anthropology 29:45-79.

Malina RM, Peña Reyes ME (2002) Secular change in size and physical fitness in the Valley of Oaxaca, Mexico. Final report, NSF-BCS 9816400. Washington, DC: National Science Foundation.

Malina RM, Selby HA, Buschang PH, Aronson WL (1980) Growth status of schoolchildren in a rural Zapotec community in the Valley of Oaxaca, Mexico, in 1968 and 1978. Annals of Human Biology 7:367-374.

Malina RM, Selby HA, Buschang PH, Aronson WL, Wilkinson RG (1983) Adult stature and age at menarche in Zapotec-speaking communities in the Valley of Oaxaca, Mexico, in a secular perspective. American Journal of Physical Anthropology 60:437-449.

Malina RM, Zavaleta AN (1980) Secular trend in the stature and weight of Mexican American children in Texas between 1930 and 1970. American Journal of Physical Anthropology 52:453-461.

Malina RM, Zavaleta AN, Little BB (1987) Secular changes in the stature and weight of Mexican American school children in Brownsville, Texas, between 1928 and 1983. Human Biology 59:509-522.

Maresh M (1972) A forty-five year investigation for secular changes in physical maturation. American Journal of Physical Anthropology 36:103-109.

McCullough JM (1982) Secular trend for stature in adult male Yucatec Maya to 1968. American Journal of Physical Anthropology 58:221-225.

Mekota K (1990) Secular trend in physical fitness in Czechoslovak school population. In Proceedings of IV Congress of Sports Pedagogues of Yugoslovia and I International Symposium: Sport of the Young. Ljubljana-Bled, Yugoslavia: Faculty of Physical Culture, University of Ljubljana, pp 321-323.

Meredith HV (1963) Change in stature and body weight of North American boys during the last 80 years. In LP Lipsitt, CC Spiker (eds), Advances in Child Development and Behavior. New York: Academic Press, pp 69-114.

Meredith HV (1976) Findings from Asia, Australia, Europe, and North America on secular change in mean height of children, youths, and young adults. American Journal of Physical Anthropology 44:315-325.

Mokdad AH, Bowman BA, Ford ES, Vinicor F, Marks JS, Koplan JP (2001) The continuing epidemics of obesity and diabetes in the United States. Journal of the American Medical Association 286:1195-1200.

Moore WM (1970) The secular trend in physical growth of urban North American negro schoolchildren. Monographs of the Society for Research in Child Development 35, serial no. 140, pp 62-73.

Moriyama M, Kashiwazaki H, Suzuki T (1980) A secular trend in age at menarche in Japan. Minzoku Eisei 46:22-32.

Najjar MF, Rowland M (1987) Anthropometric reference data and prevalence of overweight, United States, 1976–1980. Vital and Health Statistics, Series 11, No. 238 (U.S. Department of Health and Human Services, DHHS Publication No. (PHS) 87-1688).

Noda T, Nishiyama M (2000) A trend of age at menarche and predictive factors in the Meiji, Taisyo, and Syowa eras (women born from 1883 to 1986). Dokkyo Journal of Medical Sciences 27:189-202 (in Japanese).

Ogden CL, Flegal KM, Carroll MD, Johnson CL (2002) Prevalence and trends in overweight among US children and adolescents, 1999–2000. Journal of the American Medical Association 288:1728-1732.

Ohsawa S, Ji C-Y (1993) Studies on the secular growth trend of Chinese children and youth: The advanced adolescent growth of Chinese urban boys. Japanese Journal of School Health 35:342-351 (in Japanese).

Olesen AW, Jeune B, Boldsen JL (2000) A continuous decline in menarcheal age in Denmark. Annals of Human Biology 27:377-386.

Peña Reyes ME, Cardena Barahona EE, Cahuich MB, Barragan A, Malina RM (2002) Growth status of children 6–12 years from two different geographic regions of Mexico. Annals of Human Biology 29:11-25.

Prebeg A, Bralic I (2000) Changes in menarcheal age in girls exposed to war conditions. American Journal of Human Biology 12:503-508.

Raczek J (2002) Entwicklungsveranderungen der motorischen Leistungsfahigkeit der Schuljugend in drei Jahrehnten (1965–1995). Sportwissenschaft 32:201-216.

Ramos Galvan R (1978) Analisis de dos estudios de peso y talla hechos con 50 años de diferencia en niños de la ciudad de Mexico. Boletin Medico del Hospital Infantil 35:441-463.

Reiff GG, Dixon WR, Jacoby D, Ye GX, Spain CG, Hunsicker PA (1986) The President's Council on Physical Fitness and Sports 1985 National School Population Fitness Survey. Ann Arbor, MI: University of Michigan.

Richter J (1982) Hat die Sexualakzeleration ihren Hohepunkt uberschritten? Anthropos 22:333-339.

Richter J (1989) Ergebnisse langfristiger Entwicklungs-beobachtungen bei Madchen. Sonder. Sozialpadiatrie Praxis Klinisch 11:650-657.

* Roche AF (1979) Secular trends in stature, weight, and maturation. Monographs of the Society for Research in Child Development 44, serial no. 179, pp 3-27.

* Roche AF (1995) Executive summary of workshop to consider secular trends and possible pooling of data in relation to the revision of the NCHS growth charts. Washington, DC: U.S. Department of Health and Human Services, Centers for Disease Control and Prevention, National Center for Health Statistics (6-0689[3/97]).

Roche AF (1999) Postnatal physical growth assessment. Clinical Pediatrics and Endocrinology 8 (suppl 12):1-12.

Roche AF, Guo SS (2001) The new growth charts. Pediatric Basics 94:2-13.

Roede MJ, van Wieringen JC (1985) Growth diagrams 1980: Netherlands third nation-wide survey. Tijdschrift voor Sociale Gezondheidszorg 63 (suppl) 1-34.

Rona R (1975) Secular trend of pubertal development in Chile. Journal of Human Evolution 4:251-257.

Roubal E, Roubal J (1925) Telesna vyspelost stredoskolskych zaku podle mereni z r. 1923. Anthropologie 3:45 (as cited by Teply Z [1967] K soucasne urovni a ontogenetickemu vyvoji telesne zdatnosti a vykonnosti mladeze. Prague: Olympia, pp 11-28) (in Czech).

Ryan AS, Roche AF, Kuczmarski RJ (1999) Weight, stature, and body mass index data for Mexican Americans from the Third National Health and Nutrition Examination Survey (NHANES III, 1988-1994). American Journal of Human Biology 11:673-686.

Saito Y, Shinomiya M, Shirai K, Ishikawa Y, Yoshida S, Ohara R, Sawai A, Takahashi K, Wagai M, Umezono T, Hon-Iden T (1990) Plasma lipid profiles of Japanese obese children in the last ten years. In Y Oomura, S Tarui, S Inoue and T Shimazu (eds), Progress in Obesity Research 1990. London: John Libbey, pp 295-297.

Shirai K, Shinomiya M, Saito Y, Umezono T, Takahashi K, Yoshida S (1990) Incidence of childhood obesity over the last 10 years in Japan. Diabetes Research and Clinical Practice 10:565-570.

Siegel SR (1999) Patterns of sport participation and physical activity in urban Mexican youth. East Lansing, MI: Michigan State University, Doctoral Dissertation .

Sorensen TIA, Price RA (1990) Secular trends in body mass index among Danish young men. International Journal of Obesity 14:411-419.

Takaishi M (1994a) Estimations for body height and body weight of Japanese children and youth at the end of the 20th century. In O Eiben (ed), Auxology '94: Children and Youth at the End of the 20th Century (Human Biologia Budapestinensis 25). Budapest: Eotvos Lorand University Press, pp 267-275.

Takaishi M (1994b) Secular changes in growth of Japanese children. Journal of Pediatric Endocrinology 7:163-173.

Takaishi M (1995) Growth standards for Japanese children—an overview with special reference to secular change in growth. In R Hauspie, G Lindgren, F Falkner (eds), Essays on Auxology. Welwyn Garden City, Hertfordshire, UK: Castlemead Publications, pp 302-311.

Tanner JM (1962) Growth at Adolescence, 2nd edition. Oxford: Blackwell Scientific Publications.

Tanner JM (1966) The secular trend towards earlier physical maturation. Tidjschrift voor Sociale Geneeskunde 44: 524-539.

Tanner JM (1968) Earlier maturation in man. Scientific American 218:21-27 (Jan).

* Tanner JM (1981) A History of the Study of Human Growth. Cambridge, UK: Cambridge University Press.

Tanner JM (1988) Human growth and constitution. In GA Harrison, JM Tanner, DR Pilbeam, PT Baker, Human Biology: An Introduction to Human Evolution, Variation, Growth, and Adaptability, 3rd edition. New York: Oxford University Press, pp 337-435.

* Tanner JM (1992) Growth as a measure of the nutritional and hygienic status of a population. Hormone Research 3 (suppl 1):106-115.

Tanner JM, Hayashi T, Preece MA, Cameron N (1982) Increase in length of leg relative to trunk in Japanese children and adults from 1957 to 1977: Comparison with British and Japanese Americans. Annals of Human Biology 9: 411-423.

Tobias PV (1985) The negative secular trend. Journal of Human Evolution 14:347-356.

Troiano RP, Flegal KM (1998) Overweight children and adolescents: Description, epidemiology, and demographics. Pediatrics 101:497-504.

Tsuzaki S, Matsuo N, Ogata T, Osano M (1989) Lack of linkage between height and weight and age at menarche during the secular shift in growth of Japanese children. Annals of Human Biology 16:429-436.

* van Wieringen JC (1986) Secular growth changes. In F Falkner, JM Tanner (eds), Human Growth. Volume 3. Methodology, Ecological, Genetic, and Nutritional Effects of Growth. New York: Plenum, pp 307-331.

Wellens R, Malina RM, Beunen G, Lefevre J (1990) Age at menarche in Flemish girls: Current status and secular changes in the 20th century. Annals of Human Biology 17:145-152.

Welon Z (1979) The relationship of secular increase in size to physical ability. Studies in Physical Anthropology 5:13-20.

Welon Z, Sekita B, Slawinska T (1981) Secular increase in body size and physical ability. Studies in Physical Anthropology 7:13-18.

Wyshak G, Frisch RE (1982) Evidence for a secular trend in age of menarche. New England Journal of Medicine 306:1033-1035.

Yanai M, Kon A, Kumasaka K, Kawano K (1997) Body mass index variations by age and sex, and prevalence of overweight in Japanese adults. International Journal of Obesity 21: 484-488.

Appendix

A

CONVERSION TABLES

TABLE A.1 Conversion Factors for Commonly Encountered Variables in Exercise Physiology

Variable	From	To	Multiply by
Distance	centimeter (cm)	inch (in)	0.394
	meter (m)	foot (ft)	3.281
	kilometer (km)	mile (mi)	0.622
Weight (mass)	gram (g)	ounce (oz)	0.035
	kilogram (kg)	pound (lb)	2.21
Volume	liter (L)	quart (qt)	1.06
	liter (L)	pint (pt)	2.12
Force	Newton (N)	kilogram (kg)	0.102
	Newton (N)	pound (lb)	0.225
Work (energy)	kilocalorie (kcal)	kiloJoule (kJ)	4.18
	kilocalorie (kcal)	kilogram meter (kgm)	426.9
Power	kilogram meter per min (kgm/min)	Watt (W)	0.163
	kilocalorie per minute (kcal/min)	Watt (W)	69.8
Temperature	Celsius (°C)	Fahrenheit (°F)	°F = (°C x 1.8) + 32

TABLE A.2 — Conversion Table for Biochemical Variables

Variable	From	To	Multiply by
Calcium	mmol/L	mg/dl	4.008
Cholesterol	mmol/L	mg/dl	38.6
Corticosterone	pmol/L	ng/dl	0.347
Cortisol	nmol/L	μg/dl	0.0363
Creatinine (urine)	μmol/L	mg/24 h	0.1131
Dehydroepiandrosterone			
Sulfate (DHAS)	nmol/L	μg/dl	0.0368
Epinephrine	pmol/L	pg/ml	0.1831
Estradiol	pmol/L	ng/dl	0.0272
Folic acid	pmol/L	ng/dl	0.0441
Glycogen			
Glucose	mmol/L	mg/dl	1.80
IGF-I	nmol/L	ng/ml	7.6490
Insulin	pmol/L	μU/ml	0.1394
Low-density lipoprotein (LDL)	mmol/L	mg/dl	38.6
Norepinephrine	pmol/L	pg/ml	0.1692
Parathyroid hormone	pmol/L	pg/ml	9.500
Progesterone	pmol/L	ng/dl	0.0315
Testosterone	pmol/L	ng/dl	0.0288
Testosterone, free	pmol/L	pg/ml	0.2884
Thyroxine (T-4)	mmol/L	μg/dl	0.0777
Triiodothyronine (T-3)	pmol/L	ng/dl	0.0651

SUGGESTIONS FOR INDIVIDUAL AND GROUP ACTIVITIES

The first edition of *Growth, Maturation, and Physical Activity* was structured in part for a class that included one 2-hour laboratory session per week. These sessions incorporated many of the methods for the study of growth and maturation in a series of exercises related to anthropometry, assessment of growth status, estimation of physique and body composition, and assessment of skeletal age. The necessary equipment, materials, and facilities for a formal laboratory were available, including a teaching assistant. However, all departments do not have the necessary equipment and materials, and many professors do not have extensive experience with the variety of techniques used to assess growth, maturity, and physical activity.

In designing activities to complement the revision of *Growth, Maturation, and Physical Activity*, the authors decided on a series of suggested activities designed for individual or class involvement. Many are based on the availability of Web sites that include an abundance of materials and data related to growth, maturation, and physical activity of children and adolescents. If equipment and facilities are available, many of the activities can be modified to include direct measurement of body dimensions and skinfolds on members of the class. Otherwise, the suggested activities involve actual data for children and adolescents. The suggested activities follow the five sections of the text.

PART I   **Introduction**

ACTIVITY
I.1   **Prenatal Development**

Chapter 2 is not intended as a basic primer of human embryology. Nevertheless, it is important to have a grasp of changes that occur early in pregnancy as tissues, organs, and systems are differentiating. The following Web site from the University of North Carolina provides an opportunity to observe embryonic changes:

> www.med.unc.edu/embryo_images: Embryo Images—Normal and Abnormal Mammalian Development

Early in embryonic development, distinguishing between humans and other mammals is difficult. This Web site is based on mouse embryos, and each image provides an estimate of the human equivalent, that is, a mouse embryo at 8 days is similar to a human embryo at approximately 23 days of gestation.

The site provides images on the development of overall body form, body cavities and limb formation, the nervous system, the cardiovascular system, the head and face, the ears and eyes, the digestive and respiratory systems, and the urogenital system. Begin with overall body form and trace the emergence of morphology through the embryonic period. Then, select a system of interest and follow its development. For example, the cardiovascular system is central to the discussion in chapter 9 on the heart, and the formation of limbs is important to understanding bone (chapter 6) and skeletal muscle (chapter 7).

The Virtual Human Embryo project at Louisiana State University, Baton Rouge, is creating an atlas of changes during the first two months of pregnancy:

> http://virtualhumanembryo.lsuhsc.edu

The project is ongoing and is based on computer processed images from the Carnegie Collection of human embryos which have been systematically studied and described over the last 115 years.

PART II   Postnatal Growth

ACTIVITY II.1   Growth Charts and Assessment of Growth Status

The study of growth is comparative. The growth status of individuals and groups is often compared with reference values for a large sample of healthy children free from overt disease. Chapter 3 discussed reference data and described the new charts prepared for use in the United States. These charts are available as the Web site of the Centers for Disease Control and Prevention:

www.cdc.gov/growthcharts/

Read the background materials and the interactive training modules. Then, access the tables of percentiles for height and weight for boys and girls 2 to 19 years of age. Plot the medians (50th percentile) for boys and girls on a graph with age as the horizontal (X) axis and height/weight as the vertical (Y) axis. This graph will illustrate growth in body size and the emergence of sex differences during the adolescent growth spurt.

Some of you were likely measured by your parents on a regular basis. These measurements are usually recorded in "baby books." Ask your parents for this information. Convert the inches and pounds to the metric system (see the table of conversion factors in the appendix) as follows:

$$\text{inches} \times 2.54 = \text{centimeters}$$
$$\text{pounds} \div 2.21 = \text{kilograms}$$

After you convert the values, plot them on the growth charts for infancy and early childhood (birth to 3 years of age) and childhood through adolescence (2 to 19 years of age). This plot will provide you with some idea of your own course of growth. Also, plot your current height and weight on the chart to indicate current status.

ACTIVITY II.2   Growth Rate and Velocity Curves

The heights (cm) of a girl and a boy from childhood through adolescence are given in table B.1. Assume that they were measured on their birthdays (e.g., 2 = 2.0, 3 = 3.0, and 4 = 4.0). Estimate the growth rates or velocities for each youngster. This estimate is done by subtracting the older age from the immediately younger age (e.g., for the boy, height at 4 years minus height at 3 years is 8.9 cm, height at 5 years minus height at 4 years is 5.1 cm, and so on.) The differences are estimated velocities of growth (i.e., 8.9 cm/yr and 5.1 cm/yr). Derive the velocities for the entire growth period in these two individuals. Prepare a table of the velocities and then plot them on a graph, with age as the X axis and height velocity as the Y axis. The ages should be plotted at the midpoint of the age interval (e.g., at 3.5 for the interval between 3 and 4 and at 4.5 for the interval between 4 and 5). The graph will yield velocity curves for the boy and the girl, respectively. Compare sex differences in the velocity curve for height, and compare these curves with the typical velocity curves in figure 3.11.

If you have your own height data that spans childhood and adolescence, including the exact age at which you were measured, or the data of any of your siblings, estimate the velocities and plot the respective curves. If a sufficient number of students in the class have their own data, compare the velocity curves, especially around the time of adolescence. This comparison will illustrate individual differences in the timing and magnitude of the adolescent growth spurt (this is discussed in detail in chapter 16).

TABLE B.1	Heights of a Boy and a Girl	
Age	Boy	Girl
3	101.6	94.6
4	110.5	104.1
5	115.6	110.5
6	123.2	119.4
7	129.2	125.7
8	135.6	127.0
9	141.6	133.3
10	148.0	138.4
11	152.4	144.8
12	158.7	151.8
13	163.8	158.7
14	168.3	165.7
15	173.1	167.6
16	181.3	168.9
17	187.0	170.2
18	191.8	170.2
19	192.7	170.2

ACTIVITY II.3   Somatotype and Body Composition

The following website, "Somatotype and Somatotyping," provides more detailed information on the history of the concept, methods of assessment, somatotype date, and links to other sites:

www.somatotype.org

The site is compiled by J.E. Lindsay Carter and Monte Goulding. A somatotype calculation program, "Somatotype Calculation and Analysis," is available for trial puchase.

Anthropometric dimensions for six 10-year-old children, three boys and three girls, are presented in the table B.2. Using the algorithms for the estimation of somatotype presented in chapter 4, derive the somatotypes of the six children. Note that the skinfolds are measured in millimeters but must be converted to centimeters (mm/10) for correcting the limb circumferences in the derivation of mesomorphy. Compare the estimates for each of the children to the mean values reported in tables 4.1 and 4.2. What is the dominant component of each child? Is the somatotype balanced?

Using the triceps and medial calf skinfolds, estimate the relative fatness of each child with the following equations:

Males: % Fat = 0.735 Sum Skf (mm) + 1.0

Females: % Fat = 0.610 Sum Skf (mm) + 5.0

These equations are based on American children 6 to 18 years of age (Cooper Institute for Aerobics Research 1994, 1999). The more recent edition of the Fitnessgram has a table that converts the sum of the two skinfolds to an estimated percent fat (% Fat). After you calculate % Fat, derive fat mass (FM) and fat-free mass (FFM) for each child and FFM per unit height. The procedures are indicated in chapter 5. Then, compare the status of these six children to the trends illustrated in figures 5.2 through 5.4. You can also compare them to the recommended "healthy zone" for fatness in the Fitnessgram (Cooper Institute for Aerobics Research 1999).

> Cooper Institute for Aerobics Research (1994) The Prudential Fitnessgram Test Administration Manual. Dallas: Cooper Institute for Aerobics Research.
>
> Cooper Institute for Aerobics Research (1999) Fitnessgram Test Administration Manual, 2nd edition. Champaign, IL: Human Kinetics.

The composition of the body is dependent on the contributions of specific tissues. Skeletal (bone), adipose, and skeletal muscle tissues are major contributors to variation in body composition. Considerable progress has been made in understanding the structure, composition, and function of these tissues. A good deal of this information is available on recently developed Web sites, which should be checked for recent developments.

Skeletal Muscle Tissue
The following Web site from the Muscle Physiology Laboratory of the University of California, San Diego, provides a tutorial on skeletal muscle structure, function, and metabolism:

> www.muscle.ucsd/musintro/jump.shtml.

Adipose Tissue
Various types of adipose cells are illustrated at the following Web site:

> http://www.udel.edu/Biology/Wags/histopage/colorpage/ca/ca.htm.

Materials on variety of topics related to adipose tissue are indicated on the following Web site:

> http://www.health.xq23.com/diet_and_nutrition/Adipose_tissue.html.

Skeletal Tissue
The Web site for the Skeletal Gene Database of the National Institutes of Health provides information on about 200 genes involved in the normal and abnormal formation of cartilage and bone in both mice and humans.

> www.sgd.nia.nih.gov.

TABLE B.2 Anthropometric Dimensions of Six 10-Year-Old Children

Age (yr)	HT (cm)	WT (kg)	BIEP (cm)	BICO (cm)	ACFX (cm)	CC (cm)	TRI (mm)	SUB (mm)	SUPR (mm)	CALF (mm)
B10.9	137.1	38.0	5.8	8.3	22.8	26.6	11.0	10.0	15.0	12.0
B10.5	130.9	28.0	5.0	8.1	18.3	26.3	6.0	4.0	6.0	7.0
B10.4	149.0	58.0	6.1	10.3	27.5	34.8	14.0	16.0	18.0	16.0
G10.6	139.7	40.5	5.5	8.4	23.5	30.6	11.0	11.0	13.0	9.0
G10.2	125.7	25.5	4.7	7.3	18.6	24.6	7.0	10.0	11.0	8.0
G10.8	133.0	39.0	6.1	8.8	24.0	30.4	12.0	13.0	13.0	14.0

B = boy, G = girl, HT = height, WT = weight, BIEP = biepicondylar breadth, BICO = bicondylar breadth, ACFX = arm circumference flexed, CC = calf circumference, TRI = triceps skinfold, SUB = subscapular skinfold, SUPR = suprailiac skinfold, CALF = medial calf skinfold.

PART III   **Functional Development**

ACTIVITY
III.1   Movement Behaviors of Preschool Children

Most colleges and universities are reasonably close to day care centers, preschools, kindergartens, and primary grades (1 to 3). Make arrangements to spend an hour or so observing the movement behaviors of children during free play. The class should develop a checklist of specific movements and activities to observe and record. Each student should select one child and record the child's activities during a 15-minute or 30-minute observation period, for example, types of movements (run, jump, or climb), context of movements (alone or with others, with or without an object, or on specific equipment), and level of proficiency of movement patterns (beginner/immature, intermediate, or mature). A stopwatch is very useful to document time spent in different activities. At the conclusion of the observation period, the class should break into groups and compile the observations in the context of the items noted previously.

An alternative would be to have more than one person monitor the same child. This method will permit an estimate of interobserver reliability, that is, the degree to which different observers agree or disagree in their observations of the same child, and of interobserver reliability objectivity (Are they seeing the same thing?).

The following papers describe protocols for observing the activities of young children:

> Klesges RC, Coates TJ, Klesges LM, Holzer B, Gustavson J, Barnes J (1984) The FATS: An observational system for assessing physical activity in children and associated parent behavior. Behavioral Assessment 6:333-345.
>
> McKenzie TL, Sallis JF, Patterson TL, Elder JP, Berry CC, Rupp JW, Atkins CJ, Buono MJ, Nader PR (1991) BEACHES: An observational system for assessing children's eating and physical activity behaviors and associated events. Journal of Applied Behavior Analysis 24:141-151.

ACTIVITY
III.2   Motor Performance

Most schools regularly assess the physical fitness of students, especially in grades 4 through 6. These assessments include measures of performance-related fitness (e.g., dashes, jumps, and agility runs) and health-related fitness (distance runs, flexibility, sit-ups, and body fatness; see chapters 11 and 22). Professors can contact a local school and volunteer the class to assist in physical fitness testing. This arrangement would require discussion and practice in class on specific test protocols. Several protocols are summarized in the following manuals:

American Alliance for Health, Physical Education, Recreation and Dance (1984) Technical Manual, Health Related Physical Fitness. Reston, VA: AAHPERD.

American Association for Health, Physical Education, and Recreation (1976) Youth Fitness Test Manual, revised edition. Reston, VA: AAHPER.

Cooper Institute for Aerobics Research (1994) The Prudential Fitnessgram Test Administration Manual. Dallas: Cooper Institute for Aerobics Research.

Cooper Institute for Aerobics Research (1999) Fitnessgram Test Administration Manual, 2nd edition. Champaign, IL: Human Kinetics.

Council of Europe, Committee for the Development of Sport (1988) EUROFIT: European Test of Physical Fitness. Rome: Edigrag Editoriale Grafica for the Council of Europe, Committee for the Development of Sport.

Upon completion of the testing, arrange with the classroom teacher to have access to the records of the children, including the chronological age of each child. Working in small groups, the class can then reduce the data and compare the performance/fitness of the school children to the appropriate reference values.

PART IV **Biological Maturation**

ACTIVITY

IV.1   Skeletal Age

If hand-wrist radiographs are available, the skeletal anatomy of the bones of the hand and wrist can be reviewed and skeletal age can be estimated. If a medical school is on campus, hand-wrist films might be available from departments of pediatric radiology and endocrinology. These units should also have the Greulich-Pyle and Tanner-Whitehouse manuals (see chapter 15 for the references). Given the availability of the films and manuals, have the students assess the skeletal maturity of one or several children. In our experience, novices work better in groups of 2 or 3 so that the criteria can be discussed as they are applied to specific bones on a hand-wrist film.

Skeletal maturity is ordinarily expressed as skeletal age (SA), which is, in turn, related to chronological age (CA). Methods of expressing the relationship between SA and CA are summarized in chapter 15. The SAs (based on the Tanner-Whitehouse 2 method) and CAs of a sample of 11-year-old children are summarized in the table B.3. Calculate the difference between SA and CA and then classify the children as early-maturing (advanced), average-maturing (on time), or late-maturing (delayed). Recommended cutoff points for classification are indicated in chapter 15. This activity will provide insights about the normal range of variation expected within a sample of children of the same chronological age.

| **TABLE B.3** | Chronological Ages (CA) and Skeletal Ages (SA) of a Sample of 11-Year-Old Boys and Girls |

Boys				Girls			
CA (yr)	**SA (yr)**	**SA minus CA**	**Classification**	**CA (yr)**	**SA (yr)**	**SA minus CA**	**Classification**
11.6	10.4			11.4	12.6		
11.5	10.5			11.6	12.0		
11.8	13.6			11.7	12.9		
11.4	11.9			11.3	12.5		
11.5	11.9			11.3	12.3		
11.6	10.6			11.8	12.6		
11.7	12.0			11.5	11.1		
11.5	9.9			11.7	11.4		
11.1	10.7			11.1	10.9		
11.5	10.3			11.3	10.3		
11.6	14.3			11.5	12.3		
11.5	11.1			11.4	12.4		
11.5	12.6			11.9	13.3		
11.7	9.9			11.9	12.9		
11.5	11.6			11.6	10.8		

Classification of maturity status: advanced (early), average (on time), delayed (late).

ACTIVITY

IV.2   Menarche and Peak Height Velocity (PHV)

Age at menarche is the commonly used marker of sexual maturity status in adolescents and young adults. Three methods for estimated age at menarche were discussed in chapter 15. The retrospective method can be used with young women in the class. Each of the women should try to recall the age at which they attained menarche to the nearest month. To narrow the time of the year, use such prompts as the school year (beginning, exam periods, spring break), holidays (Thanksgiving, Christmas, , Easter), and season of the year (summer, fall, winter, spring). The young women in the class might also consider interviewing their mothers and sisters as to when each attained menarche. These data can then be summarized for the class and compared with estimates summarized in chapter 15. Ages at menarche in samples of athletes are summarized in chapter 28. Mother-daughter and sister-sister similarities can also be used to evaluate familial trends, which are summarized in chapter 18.

No marker of maturity status corresponding to menarche exists for boys. To estimate the time of adolescence in boys, the young men in the class should try to recall when they experienced most of their growth during the adolescent growth spurt. Some boys will gain 10 to 12 cm (about 4 to 5 inches) within a very short period of time, and parents and relatives often comment on this. Using prompts, especially season of the year and the school year, try to recall the approximate age at which you went through maximum growth during adolescence (PHV). This exercise might provide an approximation of the age at peak height velocity, which can be compared with values summarized in chapter 15.

If parents recorded your height a on a regular basis, you can use these values to derive velocities, and by plotting this data on a graph relative to age, you should be able to estimate when your reached the maximum rate of growth (peak height velocity) during the adolescent growth spurt. As an example, check the velocities curves of the boy and girl plotted earlier in the semester (see section II.2), and try to estimate the age at PHV.

PART V   Influencing Factors

ACTIVITY V.1   Genetic Regulation

Genetic inheritance plays a major role in influencing individual and population variability in growth and maturation. Although many advances have been made in identifying genes involved in the regulation of the processes of growth and maturation, application of this information to understanding genetic effects in normal children and adolescents is still relatively limited. Studies utilizing identical (monozygotic [MZ]) and fraternal (dizygotic [DZ]) twins have provided insights into the genetic contribution to variation in growth and maturation.

TABLE B.4   Heights (cm) of Monozygotic (MZ) and Dizygotic (DZ) Twin Pairs

Age	MZ Girls		DZ Girls		MZ Boys		DZ Boys	
	A	B	A	B	A	B	A	B
8.0	124.1	127.0	131.5	129.3				
8.5	127.2	128.9	135.6	132.4	144.0	143.4	124.0	124.8
9.0	130.2	131.3	138.9	135.4	147.0	146.8	126.3	126.7
9.5	133.3	133.8	141.8	138.4	149.6	149.6	129.1	128.9
10.0	136.3	136.7	145.7	141.1	152.0	152.2	131.9	131.6
10.5	139.1	139.8	150.9	144.1	154.6	154.6	134.5	134.8
11.0	142.0	142.7	154.9	148.2	157.6	157.6	136.6	138.1
11.5	144.8	145.8	157.9	152.5	160.1	160.8	140.2	141.4
12.0	148.1	149.3	160.5	156.0	162.4	163.7	143.1	144.3
12.5	152.0	153.0	162.1	159.0	165.5	166.7	144.9	146.7
13.0	155.1	155.7	163.3	161.5	168.6	169.8	146.4	148.7
13.5	157.5	157.5	164.3	163.4	171.0	172.8	149.2	149.8
14.0	159.0	159.0	164.9	164.5	173.5	175.8	153.1	151.2
14.5	160.0	159.3	165.4	165.1	176.6	179.3	156.4	154.4
15.0	160.4	159.8	165.7	165.4	180.5	183.2	159.3	159.4
15.5	160.7	160.0	166.0	165.6	184.9	187.0	162.0	163.9
16.0	160.9	160.2	166.1	165.6	188.5	190.0	164.1	167.5
16.5	161.0	160.2	166.1	165.7	190.7	192.0	165.6	169.2
17.0	161.0	160.2	166.1	165.7	192.0	193.4	166.5	170.1
17.5					192.6	193.8	167.2	170.6
18.0					192.9	193.8	167.5	171.0

A refers to one twin and B refers to the other twin within each pair.

The data are from the Wroclaw Twin Study (Poland) and were provided through the courtesy of Professor Tadeusz Bielicki, Director, Institute of Anthropology, Polish Academy of Sciences, Wroclaw, Poland.

The growth records for height for pairs of female MZ and DZ twins and pairs of male MZ and DZ twins are indicated on table B.4. Select the female or the male MZ and DZ twins and do the following:

1. In separate graphs for each twin pair, plot the distance curves for the height of each twin.
2. Calculate the semiannual velocities (see II.2). Multiply each semiannual velocity by 2 to estimate the annual velocity. On separate graphs for each twin pair, plot the annual velocities at the midpoint of each interval to derive velocity curves.
3. By careful interpolation, estimate to the nearest 10th of a year (0.1) the age at take-off of the adolescent growth spurt and the age at peak height velocity, and also estimate to the nearest millimeter the magnitude of peak height velocity (cm/yr) for each twin.
4. Prepare a summary statement on the pattern of growth in height and the adolescent growth spurt in MZ and DZ twins. Compare the estimates with those of your classmates.
5. Another option is to plot the heights of each twin pair on the Centers for Disease Control and Prevention growth charts (www.cdc.gov/growthcharts/). Check the percentile position of each twin on the charts. As a rule, youngsters tend to maintain the same position on the charts, with some deviation during adolescence. The variation during adolescence is the result of individual differences in the timing and tempo of the adolescent growth spurt.

ACTIVITY
V.2 Hormonal Regulation

Some of our earliest insights into the influence of different hormones on growth and maturation were based on the growth characteristics of children with specific hormone deficiencies. Growth hormone (GH) deficiency has received considerable attention, given its association with short height and the present availability of synthetic GH. Table B.5 presents the chronological age (CA), skeletal age (SA), and heights of two children with growth hormone deficiency who were eventually treated with GH.

1. Compare the SA and CA of both children, and note the extreme lateness or delay of skeletal maturity.
2. Using the Centers for Disease Control and Prevention growth charts (www.cdc.gov/growthcharts/), plot the growth status of each child first by CA and then by SA. To plot height by SA, simply use SA instead of CA on the X axis of the graph. Make sure that you have the appropriate growth chart for boys and girls.
3. When you plot the heights by SA, you will note that the child's height is more appropriate for biological age than it is for chronological age.
4. Given the growth curve for height plotted by CA, can you detect when GH treatment may have started?
5. Estimate the growth velocity for height. Do not forget to adjust the data to an annual interval, because the measurements were taken at relatively short intervals.

This adjustment is common in clinical growth studies. You should be able to detect the acceleration of growth velocity with the onset of treatment. This accelerated rate persists for a time and then becomes gradually less.

6. Compare the response of the boy and the girl to the GH treatment.

TABLE B.5	Chronological Age (CA), Skeletal Age (SA), and Height (Ht) of Two Children With Growth Hormone Deficiency				
	Boy			**Girl**	
CA (yr)	**SA (yr)**	**Ht (cm)**	**CA (yr)**	**SA (yr)**	**Ht (cm)**
4.3	2.1	82.7	9.5	4.2	93.0
4.7	2.2	84.0	10.0	4.2	94.5
5.0	2.5	87.2	10.5	4.9	94.4
5.5	3.2	93.6	11.0	5.1	95.7
6.0	4.4	97.3	11.5	5.1	96.2
6.4	4.5	100.0	11.7	5.5	96.0
6.8	4.6	102.2	12.2	5.9	102.8
7.1	5.8	103.8	12.4	7.0	105.9
7.3	6.1	104.8	12.7	7.4	109.3
7.6	6.2	106.5	12.9	7.8	111.2
7.8	6.2	107.6	13.2	7.8	113.7
8.1	6.4	108.9	13.5	8.1	116.2
8.3	6.4	110.5	13.7	8.1	117.9
8.5	6.8	110.6	13.9	8.3	119.9
8.8	7.0	110.7	14.2	8.5	122.5
9.1	7.8	112.5	14.4	8.5	125.0
9.3	7.8	113.7	14.7	8.7	126.8
9.6	8.4	115.4	14.9	8.7	128.0
9.9	8.4	117.2	15.2	8.9	129.9
10.3	8.4	119.8	15.4	9.7	132.3
10.6	8.7	120.9	15.7	10.3	134.3
10.9	8.9	122.3	15.9	10.4	135.8
11.3	8.9	124.4	16.2	10.4	137.5
11.8	9.8	126.3	16.4	10.4	138.5
12.6	10.6	129.2	16.7	10.4	140.7
13.8	11.8	133.1	16.9	10.6	141.9
14.8	12.3	137.2	17.2	10.9	142.8
15.8	13.1	141.5	17.5	10.9	143.1
16.8	13.9	146.4	17.7	11.5	144.0
17.8	14.0	150.4	17.9	11.7	144.6
18.3	14.6	152.4	18.2	11.7	146.5

The data are extracted from Tanner JM, Whitehouse RH (1982) Atlas of Children's Growth. Normal Variation and Growth Disorders. New York: Academic Press.

ACTIVITY
V.3   Energy and Nutrition

Estimating the intake of energy and nutrients from food and drink consumed during the course of a day and over time provides some indication of whether individuals are meeting their daily needs. Keep a record (diary) of the specific foods and drinks, as well as portions of foods and sizes of drinks consumed during a 24-hour period. Try to be as accurate as possible in recording foods consumed at breakfast, lunch, and dinner, as well as between meals. Do not overlook soft drinks and other beverages.

With this record of items consumed and portions or sizes in hand, convert each item to its energy and nutrient equivalents. Focus on the major nutrients—proteins, carbohydrates (sugars and complex carbohydrates), fats, calcium, and iron. Many food items have "nutrition facts" printed on the labels, which give the calorie (energy) and nutrient content per serving. Most dietetics textbooks have tables of food composition.

The following Web site of the United States Department of Agriculture includes information on the nutritive value of specific foods:

www.nal.usda.gov/fnic/foodcomp/Data/HG72/hg72_2002.pdf.

The URL is for a PDF file of a 103-page publication (Nutritive Value of Foods) giving the type of food, the serving size or weight (g), and calorie content and the amounts of water (%), protein (g), fat (total, saturated, monounsaturated and polyunsaturated) cholesterol, carbohydrate, fiber, calcium, iron potassium, sodium, vitamin A, thiamine, riboflavin, niacin, and ascorbic acid.

Once each food or drink item is reduced to its energy and nutrient content, tally the total number of calories, protein, carbohydrates (sugars and complex carbohydrates), fats, calcium, and iron consumed in 24 hours. Tables in chapter 20 indicate the recommended intakes for young adults. For example, the recommended daily calorie intake for young adults 19 to 24 years of age is 2,200 kcal for women and 2,900 kcal for men. Compare your intakes with the recommended values. The Institute of Medicine of the National Academy of Sciences (www.nap.edu) has many items dealing with reference energy and nutrient intakes, and these can be read on-line.

The Web site of the dietitians of Canada (www.dietitians.ca) provides additional information. Look under "Eat Well Live Well" and then "Your Nutrition Profile." The information will allow the students to compare their own intake with the current Canadian recommendations.

ACTIVITY
V.4   Physical Activity and Energy Expenditure

As is evident from chapter 21, the assessment of physical activity and energy expenditure is not an easy task. Nevertheless, the class should access the protocol used in the Quebec Family Study:

Bouchard C, Tremblay A, Leblanc C, Lortie G, Savard R, Theriault GA (1983) A method to assess energy expenditure in children and adults. American Journal of Clinical Nutrition 37:461-467.

This diary method requires you to keep a record of all of your activities during a 24-hour period. For convenience, the day is partitioned into 96 15-minute segments. Note your activity in each segment of the day. Do this for 1 weekday and 1 weekend day (activity levels often differ substantially between week and weekend days). A table in the report helps you convert the activities to estimated energy expenditure. Sum the expenditures for the 24-hour period to estimate your daily energy expenditure. The following two references provide updated estimates of the energy costs of different physical activities:

Ainsworth BE, Haskell WL, Leon AS, Jacobs DR, Montoye HJ, Sallis JF, Paffenbarger RS (1993) Compendium of physical activities: Classification of energy costs of human physical activities. Medicine and Science in Sports and Exercise 25:71-80.

Ainsworth BE, Haskell WL, Whitt MC, Irwin ML, Swartz AM, Strath SJ, O'Brien WL, Bassett DR, Schmitz KH, Emplaincourt PO, Jocobs DR, Leon AS (2000) Compendium of physical activities: An update of activity codes and MET intensities. Medicine and Science in Sports and Exercise 32 (suppl):S498-S516.

The concept of metabolic energy equivalent (MET) is discussed in chapter 21.

Compare the estimated energy expenditure for a weekday and weekend day. Then, compare your estimated energy expenditure to your estimated daily energy intake. Hopefully, one approximately equals the other, and you are in energy balance. If intake exceeds expenditure over a long term, you are likely to gain weight, the major portion of which is adipose tissue.

To examine the current trends in physical activity and inactivity in the United States, access the Centers for Disease Control and Prevention Website: www.cdc.gov. Search the health topics under physical activity and health. Check also CDC data and statistics, and select the Youth Risk Behavior Surveillance System and look for the earlier surveys (1990 to 1999). The surveys include information about physical activity, physical education, television viewing, and participation on sport teams among high school youth in the United States, as well as information on a variety of health-related behaviors.

ACTIVITY

V.5   Undernutrition

Undernutrition, specifically among preschool children, continues as a worldwide epidemic. Needless to say, estimates vary among countries and in the face of international problems such as political instability and war. For example, the price of coffee on the world market is currently quite low, and as a result, incomes of coffee bean pickers have been drastically reduced. This loss of income, in turn, has been associated with an increase in child undernutrition in some coffee-growing areas of the world. Other examples related to ongoing political and military crises in many parts of the world, which affect the nutritional status and health of young children. Follow the daily newspapers to catch a glimpse of crisis areas around the world.

Meanwhile, the World Health Organization (WHO) maintains a Global Database on Child Growth and Nutrition. This database can be accessed at the WHO Web site: www.who.int/health_topics/nutrition. Access the database and select an area of the world or several specific countries to document the current nutritional status of children younger than 5 years of age. The criteria for different types of undernutrition were described in chapter 23. All are based on age, height, and weight, and they are routinely expressed as z-scores or standard deviation scores:

z-score = (observed value − median value of reference population) ÷ standard deviation of the reference population

Another valuable resource on the nutritional and health status of children and adolescents is the Web site of the United Nations International Children's Emergency Fund: www.unicef.org. Check information and resources. This site will permit you access to the UNICEF report on the State of the World's Children. The report contains important information for specific countries and regions on social and economic indicators that affect the health and nutritional status of children. Select a country and compare the information in the WHO Global Database with the information in the UNICEF report on the State of the World's Children.

ACTIVITY V.6   Obesity

Obesity is at epidemic proportions in children, adolescents, and adults in the United States and is increasing in many other countries. Moreover, in many developing countries, undernutrition persists among the poor while obesity is increasing in the more affluent segment of the population. To examine the current epidemic of obesity in the United States, access the Centers for Disease Control and Prevention Web site:

http://www.cdc.gov/nccdphp/dnpa/obesity/index.htm.

Search the health topics for overweight and obesity and for physical activity and health.

The National Heart, Lung, and Blood Institute's Obesity Education Initiative in cooperation with the National Institute of Diabetes and Digestive and Kidney Diseases has many references and educational materials at the following Web site:

http://www.nhlbi.nih.gov/guidelines/obesity/e_txtbk/intro/intro.htm

The body mass index (BMI [kg/m^2]) is the indicator that is used worldwide to monitor the prevalence of obesity. Cutoff points for underweight, normal weight, overweight, and obesity in adults are summarized in table 24.4 (see also the www.cdc.gov, overweight and obesity). Calculate your BMI. Then, collate the BMIs of students in the class and examine the distributions. Use measured height and weight. Although reported heights and weights are often used, individuals tend to overestimate height and underestimate weight.

Calculate the BMI for the six children whose heights and weights are indicated in table B.2. Compare the BMIs to the recommended cutoff points for overweight and obesity summarized in chapter 24, table 24.4. Also, compare the BMIs of the six children with the recommended "healthy zone" of the Fitnessgram described earlier in the section on physique and body composition (section II.3).

INDEX

ABOUT THE AUTHORS

Oded Bar-Or, Robert M. Malina, and Claude Bouchard

Robert M. Malina, PhD, FACSM, earned a doctoral degree in physical education from the University of Wisconsin at Madison and a doctoral degree in anthropology from the University of Pennsylvania at Philadelphia. He earned honorary degrees from the Catholic University of Leuven in Belgium and the Academy of Physical Education, Jagiellonian University in Krakow, Poland. He was a professor of kinesiology and anthropology at the University of Texas at Austin from 1967 to 1995 and then moved to a similar position in kinesiology and anthropology at Michigan State University. Dr. Malina retired from Michigan State University in the summer of 2002. He currently is a research professor at Tarleton State University at Stephenville, Texas, and a research associate at the Center for Latin American and Caribbean Studies at Michigan State University.

Professor Malina served as editor in chief of the American Journal of Human Biology (1990-2002), editor of the Yearbook of Physical Anthropology (1980-1986), and section editor for growth and development for Exercise and Sport Sciences Reviews (1981-1999) and Research Quarterly for Exercise and Sport (1981-1993). He also serves on the editorial boards of 13 journals in the sport sciences and biological anthropology.

His primary area of interest is the biological growth and maturation of children and adolescents with a focus on performance, youth sports and young athletes, and the potential influences of physical activity and training for sport. He has also worked extensively with the anthropometric correlates of physique and body composition in female athletes at the university level. Related areas of interest are the role of physical activity in the well being of children, adolescents, and young adults and the influence of chronic undernutrition on the growth, performance, and physical activity of Latin American youth.

Claude Bouchard, PhD, FACSM, is the executive director of the Pennington Biomedical Research Center and the George A. Bray chair in nutrition. He holds a BPed from Laval University, an MSc in exercise physiology from the University of Oregon at Eugene, and a PhD in population genetics from the University of Texas at Austin. His research deals with the genetics of adaptation to exercise and to nutritional interventions as well as the genetics of obesity and its comorbidities. He has authored or coauthored several books and more than 800 scientific papers. He received the Honor Award from the Canadian Association of Sport Sciences in 1988 and 2002, a Citation Award from the American College of Sports Medicine in 1992, the Benjamin Delessert Award in nutrition in France in 1993, the Willendorf Award from the International Association for the Study of Obesity in 1994, the Sandoz Award from the Canadian Atherosclerosis Society in 1996, the Albert Creff Award in Nutrition from the National Academy of Medicine of France in 1997, the TOPS award from the North American Association for the Study of Obesity in 1998, the W. Henry Sebrell Award from the Weight Watchers Foundation in 1999, and of an honorary doctoral degree in science from the Katholieke Universiteit Leuven in 1998. He has been a foreign member of the Royal Academy of Medicine of Belgium since 1996 and was the Leon Mow visiting professor at the International Diabetes Institute in Melbourne in 1998. In 2001, he became a member of the Order of Canada as well as professor emeritus of the faculty of medicine at Laval University. Dr. Bouchard is a former president of the North American Associa-tion for the Study of Obesity and the president of the International Association for the Study of Obesity (2002-2006). Prior to coming to Penning-ton, he held the Donald B. Brown research chair on obesity at Laval University.

Oded Bar-Or, MD, FACSM, is professor of pediatrics and founder and director of the Chil-dren's Exercise and Nutrition Centre at McMas-ter University in Hamilton, Ontario, Canada. His 35-year research and clinical career has focused on the effects of physical activity and inactivity on the health, well-being, and performance of healthy children and those with disease. His work has been widely published. During his career, he served as president of the Canadian Association of Sports Sciences, vice president of the Ameri-can College of Sports Medicine, and president of the International Council for Physical Fitness Research. In 2000, the University of Blaise Pascal in France awarded him an honorary doctorate degree. He also received the Honor Award of the North American Society for Pediatric Medicine in 1998 and the Citation Award of the ACSM in 1997.